A complete checklist of the
Birds of the World

Richard Howard
Alick Moore

A complete checklist of the
Birds of the World

With a Foreword by
Leslie Brown

Revised by Alick Moore

Macmillan London

First published 1980 by Oxford University Press

This revised edition published in paperback 1984 by
PAPERMAC
a division of Macmillan Publishers Limited
4 Little Essex Street London WC2R 3LF
and Basingstoke

Associated companies in Auckland, Dallas, Delhi, Dublin,
Hong Kong, Johannesburg, Lagos, Manzini, Melbourne, Nairobi,
New York, Singapore, Tokyo, Washington and Zaria

ISBN 0 333 36229 2

Printed in Hong Kong

Contents

Foreword

A great many people enjoy making lists of birds they have seen, very often once only, on some distant journey, with very little likelihood of being able to see and watch the same bird again. Certainly, knowing what a bird is and where it occurs is the first step towards the wider interest that may stem from merely ticking a bird off on a list — twitching, as the vulgar parlance has it. If a bird does not occur where it ought to then one may question why, and that leads to further thoughts of the why and wherefore.

Most available lists cover a district, a country, a region or a continent, perhaps an ocean. Here is one that covers the whole world, down to subspecies level. As the authors remark, the need for an authoritative world list has been in the minds of professional ornithologists and amateurs for many years, and this need has never yet been adequately satisfied for amateurs. There is, and long has been, an official world list for the professionals, the Peters' list, compiled long ago and revised since by many different authorities. It is, however, a multi-volume work, not all of it up to date, and it is not the sort of thing that a traveller can carry around in his or her luggage. Wisely, the authors of the present list have based theirs largely on the Peters' list, incorporating various new ideas, and thereby avoid making confusion worse confounded by riding their own hobby-horse. There have been several other world lists prepared in recent times but at least one of these departs radically from any generally accepted systematic order and they all pursue a somewhat differing approach which may appeal to the author but not always to others.

The authors have made a great effort to supply what is wanted in this present list. Having helped to prepare a checklist myself I know only too well how difficult it is, and how much unexpected work arises from trying to reconcile differing approaches and conflicting ideas resulting in varying treatment of families, genera, species, and subspecies. The present list is based on the sequence of families proposed by Ernst Mayr, often called the father of modern systematics, and it builds on the Peters' list. It should meet with the general approval of many taxonomists and professional ornithologists while its contents are not too difficult or academic for an ordinary birdwatcher to understand. Thorough cross-referencing to other authorities will enable anyone interested to dig deeper among other sources of information.

The fact that there is as yet no absolute agreement on the order in which species, genera, even families should be placed is really a reflection of the fact that we are dealing with some 8500 species of highly mobile living beings, themselves still in the process of evolution. Many, too, are still very little-known and a few new species are discovered almost every year — there have been three in Ethiopia alone in the last two decades. Research in museums and in the field is constantly throwing up new ideas and facts that may suggest different or fresh relationships. Thus it is really asking too much, at our present state of knowledge, to say that the last 'i' has been dotted and the last 't' crossed, and that such a bird is without doubt thus and thus now and forever more. One has only to think of the common and widespread Little Grebe which is given a different generic name in three standard reference books that I own. The authors of this list have done their best to crystallize what is known now of species and their relationships with one another and within families; and they have adopted a geographical approach to subspecies more useful for the ordinary ornithologist than argument about whether such a sub-species is or is not valid, or even should be considered a good species (some probably should). They have consulted widely with experts all over the world, or on particular groups and they have, above all, wisely eschewed that counsel of despair, listing in alphabetical order – quite seriously advocated by some eminent authorities only about a decade ago – which absolutely obscures the relationships of one species to another.

I have never myself been much of a lister. I have on the whole concentrated on deeper study of a few families or species which have taken my fancy. However, I know that most birdwatchers are interested in seeing and identifying as many birds as they can, and association with some such people has often shown me how ignorant I am. I have very little sympathy with those who tick a bird off on a list and thereafter forget it. They've seen it, it's number so and so, and that's that. Every bird seen and clearly identified should be unforgettable and one should record where and when one saw it. If one has never seen it, and recorded the fact, one can have no idea about its habits except at second hand. Possession of a handy, compact list will help those going to a new area to be aware of what they might see, or have heard of. For those interested in particular families or groups it pinpoints objects and areas of study, and can save much valuable hard won time and money.

I will certainly look forward to using this list as it is meant to be used, as a handy reference tool for recording species seen, and where and when. It will be scribbled over, as it should be, and I shall undoubtedly use it to draw up that long-deferred life list of my own – simply because I have never previously had all the species available in one volume. It will be interesting to see if I am even approximately right about my own guess of the number of species I think I have seen, and probably humbling too. Many of us think we know more about birds than we do and the hard fact on the printed page can bring us up short with a jerk. Have I or have I not *seen* a Prothonotary Warbler? Yes, I have, and I can tell you where, too, but I wouldn't be certain that I could infallibly recognize it again!

Leslie Brown
Karen, Kenya 1980

Introduction

The late Professor David Lack once presented a proposal for an 'official' authoritative list of the orders, families, subfamilies, genera, and species of the birds of the world and, of course, in an agreed order. This was an idea likely to be accepted much more readily by amateur ornithologists than by professional taxonomists and thus it did not ever get a start. During the past four years, however, no fewer than five checklists of the world's birds have been published, four in the United States and one in Britain. A comparison of these lists reveals some of the difficulties, disagreements, and varying opinions and points of view that arise in compiling such a list. It also reveals the need for a more accurate and authoritative world list for the use of both amateur and professional ornithologists.

This list was started in 1972 and very quickly we perceived the need to go to subspecific level to do justice to the correct status of a species, and to cover adequately the geographical distribution. How often in lists of European birds do we see both *Corvus corone* and *Corvus cornix* included, not because the author really believes they are separate species, but to be able to document a large black and grey bird which would otherwise be described and pictured as all black? Therefore, we attempt now to list all the birds of the world, including their generally recognized subspecies, that are definitely not extinct, in the best accepted order, and following those whom we believe to be the best available authorities.

Order of families

At once we run into a major dispute involving the most eminent ornithologists. We have opted for the order described by Ernst Mayr, partly because we believe this to be the easiest to comprehend and partly owing to the fact that the authority to which we refer most, the JL Peters' *Checklist of the Birds of the World,* also follows Mayr in what has become known as the Basel sequence.

Order of genera and species

These again generally bear most reference to Peters' *Checklists*, but where that list has been updated and revised, then the more recent version has been used.

Subspecies

These are listed in common geographical order which is to say generally from north-west to south-east, though there are naturally many places where the order of subspecies is arguable and doubtless readily acceptable if changed.

Inevitably the question now arises of what is a valid or recognised subspecies, and we then become involved in another area of contention, but we have tried to select the most generally accepted subspecies and certainly have attempted to include those erected during most recent years. Of course, it is recognized that clinal variations of size or plumage colour make the arbitrary selection of subspecies very difficult, but once again we have tried to follow authorities in these matters.

Other taxonomic divisions have, as far as possible, and for the sake of simplicity, been avoided. The suborder is only used where the relevant authority followed deems it necessary, and subfamilies are adhered to according to the Basel sequence. Many authors subscribe to tribes, and though in compiling this list we have disagreed with this taxonomic refinement, we have found it necessary on a few occasions. Much work has been done on the existence of subgenera and superspecies, groups of species sufficiently similar to be grouped together away from near-relatives, yet not sufficiently dissimilar from those near-relatives to be placed within another genus. Additionally, there are subspecies closer to one another in groups to be classed separately from other subspecies within the same species. There is without question validity for recognizing these subdivisions, but their use does very much complicate a simple and clear list.

References

For each family or large subfamily we have given a list of the references used in the compilation of that family. At the head of each list of references is the name of the book or journal publication used as the principal authority and after this follow the books and articles used to update and refine the family.

Geographical distribution

The names of countries are as up to date as we can make them; many have changed since we started the list and no doubt many more will change within a short time of publication. In the interests of clarity and general knowledge we have deliberately disregarded some more recent changes. We refer, for instance, to New Guinea rather than differentiating between Papua New Guinea and West Irian. We still refer to Celebes instead of Sulawesi, and Borneo is still the whole island, but Malaya we call Malaysia without the distinction of being Malaysia West.

Where the migration of a bird takes it well outside its breeding area, the migration area is indicated by »

North, south, east, and west etc. are abbreviated to N, S, E, and W throughout and central becomes C so that south-central would be SC. Island(s) is abbreviated to I(s). a ? indicates that a bird's distribution is uncertain.

English names

We have given every species an English name, but this is a hazardous task and wide open to argument. There is no doubt that many English names could and should be improved, and in particular shortened and clarified. Generally, when a bird becomes well known its English name becomes more reasonable. There must be some better English name for *Hemispingus superciliaris* than Superciliaried Hemispingus, and the translation of guttulatus as 'guttulated' is not helpful.

Extinct birds

Where a bird is known to be extinct it is omitted from the list. Where some doubt still exists, and the bird is possibly or even probably extinct, it is included and marked by **e?**

General references

Several reference books of a general nature have been used throughout the compilation of the list, and in writing this introduction.

J.L. Peters & successors 1931–72 *Checklist of the Birds of the World* vols. I–VII, IX, X, XII–XV. (Harvard University Press & Mus. Comp. Zool., Cambridge. Mass.)

Mayr & Zimmer 1943 'Species described 1938–41' *Auk* 60

Mayr & Amadon 1951 *'Classification of Recent Birds' Amer. Mus. Novit.* 1964

Verhuyen 1951 'New Classification of Non-passerine Birds' *Bull. instr. r. Sci. Bolg.* 37

Mayr & Greenway 1956 *Breviora Mus. Comp. Zool.* 58

Mayr 1957 'Species described 1941–55' *Journ. f. Orn.* 98

Stresemann 1959 'Status of Avian Systematics' *Auk* 76

Greenway 1967 *Extinct and Vanishing Birds of the World* (Dover, New York)

Austin 1967 *Auk* 84

Mayr 1969 *Principles of Systematic Zoology* (Amer. Mus. Nat. Hist., New York)

Mayr & Short 1970 'Species Taxa of North American Birds' *Publ. Nuttall Orn. Cl.* 9

Mayr 1971 'Species described 1956–65' *Journ. f. Orn.* 112

Voous 1973 'List of Recent Holarctic Bird Species, Non-passerines' *Ibis* 115

Lack 1975 *Evolution illustrated by Waterfowl* (Blackwell, Oxford)

Morony, Bock & Farrand 1975 *Reference List of the Birds of the World* (Amer. Mus. Nat. Hist., New York)

Gruson 1975 *Checklist of the Birds of the World* (Collins, London)

Zoological Record (London)

Acknowledgements

The authors would like to express their appreciation of the help given by Dr. Amadon, Michael Everett, and Dr. D. W. Snow and would also like to thank Howard Brokaw, Trevor Gunton, and Dr. C. M. Perrins for their comments and encouragement.

Note to revised edition

Due to lack of space, it has not been possible to include in this revision additions to the list of references which concern additions and emendations to the text.

/

Arrangement of orders and families

Class **AVES**

Order **Struthioniformes**

1 STRUTHIONIDAE	OSTRICHES

Order **Rheiiformes**

2 RHEIDAE	RHEAS

Order **Casuariiformes**

3 CASUARIIDAE	CASSOWARIES
4 DROMAIIDAE	EMUS

Order **Apterygiformes**

5 APTERYGIDAE	KIWIS

Order **Tinamiformes**

6 TINAMIDAE	TINAMOUS

Order **Sphenisciformes**

7 SPHENISCIDAE	PENGUINS

Order **Gaviiformes**

8 GAVIIDAE	DIVERS

Order **Podicipediformes**

9 PODICIPEDIDAE	GREBES

Order **Procellariiformes**

10 DIOMEDEIDAE	ALBATROSSES
11 PROCELLARIIDAE	PETRELS, SHEARWATERS
12 HYDROBATIDAE	STORM PETRELS
13 PELECANOIDIDAE	DIVING PETRELS

Order **Pelecaniformes**

14 PHAETHONTIDAE	TROPIC BIRDS
15 PELECANIDAE	PELICANS
16 SULIDAE	GANNETS, BOOBIES
17 PHALACROCORACIDAE	CORMORANTS
18 ANHINGIDAE	ANHINGAS
19 FREGATIDAE	FRIGATE BIRDS

Order **Ciconiiformes**

20 ARDEIDAE	HERONS, BITTERNS
21 BALAENICIPITIDAE	WHALE HEADED STORK
22 SCOPIDAE	HAMMERKOP
23 CICONIIDAE	STORKS
24 THRESKIORNITHIDAE	IBISES, SPOONBILLS
25 PHAENICOPTERIDAE	FLAMINGOS

Order **Anseriformes**

26	ANHIMIDAE	SCREAMERS
27	ANATIDAE	DUCKS, GEESE, SWANS

Order **Falconiformes**

28	CATHARTIDAE	NEW WORLD VULTURES
29	PANDIONIDAE	OSPREYS
30	ACCIPITRIDAE	HAWKS, EAGLES
31	SAGITTARIIDAE	SECRETARY BIRD
32	FALCONIDAE	FALCONS, CARACARAS

Order **Galliformes**

33	MEGAPODIIDAE	MEGAPODES
34	CRACIDAE	CURASSOWS, GUANS
35	PHASIANIDAE	PHEASANTS, GROUSE
36	OPISTHOCOMIDAE	HOATZIN

Order **Gruiformes**

37	MESITORNITHIDAE	MESITES
38	TURNICIDAE	BUTTON QUAILS
39	PEDIONOMIDAE	PLAINS WANDERER
40	GRUIDAE	CRANES
41	ARAMIDAE	LIMPKIN
42	PSOPHIIDAE	TRUMPETERS
43	RALLIDAE	RAILS, COOTS
44	HELIORNITHIDAE	SUNGREBES
45	RHYNOCHETIDAE	KAGU
46	EURYPYGIDAE	SUNBITTERNS
47	CARIAMIDAE	SERIEMAS
48	OTIDIDAE	BUSTARDS

Order **Charadriiformes**

49	JACANIDAE	JACANAS
50	ROSTRATULIDAE	PAINTED SNIPE
51	DROMADIDAE	CRAB-PLOVER
52	HAEMATOPODIDAE	OYSTER-CATCHERS
53	IBIDORHYNCHIDAE	IBIS-BILL
54	RECURVIROSTRIDAE	AVOCETS, STILTS
55	BURHINIDAE	STONE CURLEWS
56	GLAREOLIDAE	COURSERS, PRATINCOLES
57	CHARADRIIDAE	PLOVERS
58	SCOLOPACIDAE	SANDPIPERS, SNIPE
59	THINOCORIDAE	SEED SNIPE
60	CHIONIDIDAE	SHEATHBILLS
61	STERCORARIIDAE	SKUAS
62	LARIDAE	GULLS, TERNS
63	RYNCHOPIDAE	SKIMMERS
64	ALCIDAE	AUKS

Order **Columbiformes**

65	PTEROCLIDIDAE	SANDGROUSE
66	COLUMBIDAE	DOVES, PIGEONS

Order **Psittaciformes**

67	LORIIDAE	LORIES
68	CACATUIDAE	COCKATOOS
69	PSITTACIDAE	PARROTS

Order **Cuculiformes**

70	MUSOPHAGIDAE	TURACOS
71	CUCULIDAE	CUCKOOS

Order **Strigiformes**

72	TYTONIDAE	BARN OWLS
73	STRIGIDAE	OWLS

Order **Caprimulgiformes**

74	STEATORNITHIDAE	OILBIRD
75	PODARGIDAE	FROGMOUTHS
76	NYCTIBIIDAE	POTOOS
77	AEGOTHELIDAE	OWLET-NIGHTJARS
78	CAPRIMULGIDAE	NIGHTJARS

Order **Apodiformes**

79	APODIDAE	SWIFTS
80	HEMIPROCNIDAE	TREE SWIFTS
81	TROCHILIDAE	HUMMING BIRDS

Order **Coliiformes**

82	COLIIDAE	MOUSEBIRDS

Order **Trogoniformes**

83	TROGONIDAE	TROGONS

Order **Coraciiformes**

84	ALCEDINIDAE	KINGFISHERS
85	TODIDAE	TODIES
86	MOMOTIDAE	MOTMOTS
87	MEROPIDAE	BEE EATERS
88	CORACIIDAE	ROLLERS
89	BRACHYPTERACIIDAE	GROUND ROLLERS
90	LEPTOSOMATIDAE	COUROLS
91	UPUPIDAE	HOOPOES
92	PHOENICULIDAE	WOOD HOOPOES
93	BUCEROTIDAE	HORNBILLS

Order **Piciformes**

94	GALBULIDAE	JACAMARS
95	BUCCONIDAE	PUFFBIRDS
96	CAPITONIDAE	BARBETS
97	INDICATORIDAE	HONEYGUIDES
98	RAMPHASTIDAE	TOUCANS
99	PICIDAE	WOODPECKERS

Order **Passeriformes**

100	EURYLAIMIDAE	BROADBILLS
101	DENDROCOLAPTIDAE	WOODCREEPERS
102	FURNARIIDAE	OVENBIRDS
103	FORMICARIIDAE	ANTBIRDS
104	CONOPOPHAGIDAE	GNATEATERS
105	RHINOCRYPTIDAE	TAPACULOS
106	COTINGIDAE	COTINGAS
107	PIPRIDAE	MANAKINS

108	TYRANNIDAE	TYRANT FLYCATCHERS
109	OXYRUNCIDAE	SHARPBILL
110	PHYTOTOMIDAE	PLANTCUTTERS
111	PITTIDAE	PITTAS
112	XENICIDAE	NEW ZEALAND WRENS
113	PHiLEPITTIDAE	ASITIES
114	MENURIDAE	LYREBIRDS
115	ATRICHORNITHIDAE	SCRUB BIRDS
116	ALAUDIDAE	LARKS
117	HIRUNDINIDAE	SWALLOWS, MARTINS
118	MOTACILLIDAE	WAGTAILS, PIPITS
119	CAMPEPHAGIDAE	CUCKOO SHRIKES
120	PYCNONOTIDAE	BULBULS
121	IRENIDAE	LEAFBIRDS, IORAS
122	LANIIDAE	SHRIKES
123	VANGIDAE	VANGA SHRIKES
124	BOMBYCILLIDAE	WAXWINGS
125	DULIDAE	PALM CHAT
126	CINCLIDAE	DIPPERS
127	TROGLODYTIDAE	WRENS
128	MIMIDAE	MOCKING BIRDS, THRASHERS
129	PRUNELLIDAE	ACCENTORS
130–142	MUSCICAPIDAE	THRUSHES, WARBLERS ETC.
143	AEGITHALIDAE	LONGTAILED TITS
144	REMIZIDAE	PENDULINE TITS
145	PARIDAE	TITS, CHICKADEES
146	SITTIDAE	NUTHATCHES
147	CERTHIIDAE	TREE CREEPERS
148	RHABDORNITHIDAE	PHILIPPINE CREEPERS
149	CLIMACTERIDAE	AUSTRALIAN CREEPERS
150	DICAEIDAE	FLOWERPECKERS
151	NECTARINIIDAE	SUNBIRDS
152	ZOSTEROPIDAE	WHITE EYES
153	MELIPHAGIDAE	HONEYEATERS
154–158	EMBERIZIDAE	BUNTINGS, TANAGERS
159	PARULIDAE	NEW WORLD WARBLERS
160	DREPANIDIDAE	HAWAIIAN HONEYCREEPERS
161	VIREONIDAE	VIREOS
162	ICTERIDAE	NEW WORLD BLACKBIRDS
163	FRINGILLIDAE	FINCHES
164	ESTRILDIDAE	WAXBILLS
165	PLOCEIDAE	WEAVERS, SPARROWS
166	STURNIDAE	STARLINGS
167	ORIOLIDAE	ORIOLES
168	DICRURIDAE	DRONGOS
169	CALLAEIDAE	WATTLEBIRDS
170	GRALLINIDAE	MAGPIE LARKS
171	ARTAMIDAE	WOOD SWALLOWS
172	CRACTICIDAE	BUTCHER BIRDS
173	PTILONORHYNCHIDAE	BOWER BIRDS
174	PARADISAEIDAE	BIRDS OF PARADISE
175	CORVIDAE	CROWS, JAYS

References

Family **STRUTHIONIDAE**

J.L. Peters, 1931, *Checklist of the Birds of the World* I (Harvard University Press, Cambridge, Mass.)

C. Vaurie, 1965, *Birds of the Palaearctic Fauna* II (Witherby, London)
C.M.N. White, 1965, *Revised Checklist of African Non-passerine Birds* (Govt. Printer, Lusaka)

Family **RHEIDAE**

J.L. Peters, 1931, *Checklist of the Birds of the World* I

R. Meyer de Schauensee, 1966, *The Species of Birds of South America* (Acad. Nat. Sci., Philadelphia)
E.R. Blake, 1977, *Manual of Neotropical Birds* I (Chicago University Press, Chicago)

Family **CASUARIIDAE**

J.L. Peters, 1931, *Checklist of the Birds of the World* I

E. Mayr, 1940, *Amer. Mus. Novit.* 1056
A.L. Rand & E.T. Gilliard, 1967, *Handbook of New Guinea Birds* (Weidenfeld & Nicholson, London)

Family **DROMAIIDAE**

J.L. Peters, 1931, *Checklist of the Birds of the World* I

1965, *Bull. Zool. Nomencl.* 22
H.T. Condon, 1975, *Checklist of the Birds of Australia* Pt. I (R.A.O.U., Melbourne)

Family **APTERYGIDAE**

J.L. Peters, 1931, *Checklist of the Birds of the World* I

O.S.N.Z. 1970, *Annotated Checklist of the Birds of New Zealand* (Reed, Wellington)

Family **TINAMIDAE**

J.L. Peters, 1931, *Checklist of the Birds of the World* I

E.R. Blake, 1977, *Manual of Neotropical Birds* I (Chicago University Press, Chicago)
C.E. Hellmayr & Conover, 1942, *Field Mus. Nat. Hist. Zool.* Ser. 13.1
A. Wetmore, 1951, *Proc. Biol. Soc. Wash.* 68
E. Eisenmann, 1955, 'The Species of Middle American Birds', *Trans. Lin. Soc. N.Y.* 7
C.C. Olrog, 1959, *Neotropica* 5
M. Koepcke, 1962, *Journ. f. Orn.* 103
W.H. Phelps and Phelps, 1963, *Boll. Soc. Venez. Cienc. Nat.* 12.19.24
R. Meyer de Schauensee, 1964, *Birds of Colombia* (Livingston, Narberth, Pennsylvania)
R. Meyer de Schauensee, 1966, *The Species of Birds of South America* (Acad. Nat. Sci., Philadelphia)
J.R. Jehl, 1971, *Trans. San Diego Soc. Nat. Hist.* 16

Family **SPHENISCIDAE**

J.L. Peters, 1931, *Checklist of the Birds of the World* I

G.M. Mathews & T. Iredale, 1921, *Austr. Av. Rec.* 4
N.W. Cayley, 1925, *Emu* 25
R.C. Murphy, 1947, *Auk* 64

V. Serventy & Whittell, 1952, *Emu* 52
W.R.B. Oliver, 1953, *Emu* 53
W.B. Alexander, 1963, *Birds of the Ocean* 2nd edn. (Putnam, New York)
R.A. Falla *et al*, 1966, *Field Guide to the Birds of New Zealand* (Collins, London)
R.A. Falla *et al*, 1970, *Notornis* 17
O.S.N.Z., 1970, *Annotated Checklist of the Birds of New Zealand* (Reed, Wellington)
B. Stonehouse, 1970, *Ibis* 112
B. Stonehouse, 1971, *Ibis* 113
H.T. Condon, 1975, *Checklist of the Birds of Australia* Pt. I (R.A.O.U., Melbourne)

Family **GAVIIDAE**

J.L. Peters, 1931, *Checklist of the Birds of the World* I

1956, *ICZN; Opinion* 401
C. Vaurie, 1965, *Birds of the Palaearctic Fauna* II (Witherby, London)

Family **PODICIPEDIDAE**

J.L. Peters, 1931, *Checklist of the Birds of the World* I

J. Delacour, 1932, *Ois. Rev. Fr. Orn.* 2.6
E. Mayr, 1943, *Emu* 43
E. Mayr, 1945, *Emu* 44
1956, *ICZN; Opinion* 401
K.E.L. Simmons, 1962, *Bull. B.O.C.* 82
R.W. Storer, 1963, *Proc. 13th Int. Orn. Cong.* 126
C. Vaurie, 1965, *Birds of the Palaearctic Fauna* II (Witherby, London)
K.H. Voous & Payne, 1965, *Ardea* 53
R. Meyer de Schauensee, 1966, *The Species of Birds of South America* (Acad. Nat. Sci., Philadelphia)
K.E.L. Simmons, 1968, *British Birds* 61
1972, *Bull. Zool. Nomencl.* 29
L. Rumboll, 1974, *Comm. Mus. Arg. Cienc. Nat. Bernardino Rivadavia* 4 (5) 33
H.T. Condon, 1975, *Checklist of the Birds of Australia* Pt. I (R.A.O.U., Melbourne)
D.R. Wells & Lord Medway, 1976, *Bull. B.O.C.* 96

Family **DIOMEDEIDAE**

J.L. Peters, 1931, *Checklist of the Birds of the World* I
W.B. Alexander, 1963, *Birds of the Ocean* 2nd edn. (Putnam, New York)

R.C. Murphy, 1930, *Amer. Mus. Novit.* 419
W.H. Bierman & K.H. Voous, 1950, *Ardea* 37
A.M. Bailey & J.H. Sorensen, 1962, *Proc. Denver Mus. Nat. Hist.* 10
W.B. Alexander *et al*, 1965, *Ibis* 107
P.A. Clancey, 1965, *Ostrich* 36
O.S.N.Z., 1970, *Annotated Checklist of the Birds of New Zealand* (Reed, Wellington)
V. Serventy *et al*, 1971, *Handbook of Australian Seabirds* (Sydney)
G.E. Watson *et al*, 1971, *Birds of the Antarctic and Subantarctic* (Amer. Geog. Soc., New York)
H.T. Condon, 1975, *Checklist of the Birds of Australia* Pt. I (R.A.O.U., Melbourne)
S. Cramp, *et al*, 1977, *Handbook of the Birds of Europe, the Middle East, and North Africa* I (Oxford University Press, Oxford)

Family **PROCELLARIIDAE**

J.L. Peters, 1931, *Checklist of the Birds of the World* I
W.B. Alexander, 1963, *Birds of the Ocean* 2nd edn. (Putnam, New York)
H.T. Condon, 1975, *Checklist of the Birds of Australia* Pt. I (R.A.O.U., Melbourne)

R.A. Falla, 1942, *Emu* 42
K.H. Voous, 1949, *Ardea* 37

R.C. Murphy, 1951, *Amer. Mus. Novit.* 1512
R.C. Murphy & Pennoyer, 1952, *Amer. Mus. Novit.* 1580
H.T. Condon, 1955, *Emu* 55
C. Jouanin, 1955, *L'Oiseau* 25
W.W.A. Phillips & Sims, 1958, *Journ. Bombay Nat. Hist. Soc.* 55
J. Warham, 1962, *Auk* 79
Bartle, 1963, *Notornis,* 15
C. Jouanin, 1963, *Bull. Mus. Nat. Hist. Paris* 35(2)
W.R.P. Bourne, 1964, *Notornis* 11
W.B. Alexander, *et al,* 1965, *Ibis* 107
R.C. Murphy, 1965, *Amer. Mus. Novit.* 1586
W.R.P. Bourne & J. Warham, 1966, *Ardea* 54
C. Jouanin & Gill, 1967, *L'Oiseau* 37
I.A. Strange, 1968, *Ibis* 110
M.J. Imber & Crockett, 1970, *Notornis* 17
O.S.N.Z., 1970, *Annotated Checklist of the Birds of New Zealand* (Reed, Wellington)
W.R.P. Bourne, 1971, *Sea Swallow* 21
G.E. Watson, *et al,* 1971, *Birds of the Antarctic and Subantarctic* (Amer. Geog. Soc., New York)
S. Cramp, *et al,* 1977, *Handbook of the Birds of Europe, the Middle East, and North Africa* I
  (Oxford University Press, Oxford)

Family **HYDROBATIDAE**

J.L. Peters, 1931, *Checklist of the Birds of the World* I
W.B. Alexander, 1963, *Birds of the Ocean* 2nd edn. (Putnam, New York)

G.M. Mathews, 1933, *Novit Zool.* 39
R.C. Murphy & S. Irving, 1951, *Amer. Mus. Novit.* 1506
O.L. Austin, 1952, *Bull. Mus. Comp. Zool.* 107
R.C. Murphy & J.P. Snyder, 1952, *Amer. Mus. Novit.* 1596
W.B. Alexander, *et al,* 1965, *Ibis* 107
C. Vaurie, 1965, *Birds of the Palaearctic Fauna* II (Witherby, London)
G.E. Watson, *et al,* 1971, *Birds of the Antarctic and Subantarctic (Amer. Geog. Soc., New York)*
H.T. Condon, 1975, *Checklist of the Birds of Australia* Pt. 1 (R.A.O.U., Melbourne)

Family **PELECANOIDIDAE**

J.L. Peters, 1931, *Checklist of the Birds of the World* I

W.B. Alexander, 1963, *Birds of the Ocean* 2nd edn. (Putnam, New York)
W.R.P. Bourne, 1968, *Bull. B.O.C.* 88

Family **PHAETHONTIDAE**

J.L. Peters, 1931, *Checklist of the Birds of the World* I

W.B. Alexander, 1963, *Birds of the Ocean* 2nd edn. (Putnam, New York)

Family **PELECANIDAE**

J.L. Peters, 1931, *Checklist of the Birds of the World* I

W.B. Alexander, 1963, *Birds of the Ocean* 2nd edn. (Putnam, New York)

Family **SULIDAE**

J.L. Peters, 1931, *Checklist of the Birds of the World* I

W.B. Alexander, 1963, *Birds of the Ocean* 2nd edn. (Putnam, New York)

Family **PHALACROCORACIDAE**

J.L. Peters, 1931, *Checklist of the Birds of the World* I

W.B. Alexander, 1963, *Birds of the Ocean* 2nd edn. (Putnam, New York)
P.A. Clancey, 1965–6, *Durban Mus. Novit.* 7
G.F. van Tets, 1965, *Orn. Monogr.* 2
J.G. Williams, 1966, *Bull. B.O.C. 86*
J-F, Voisin, 1973, *Notornis* 20(3)
H.T. Condon, 1975, *Checklist of the Birds of Australia* Pt. I (R.A.O.U., Melbourne)

Family **ANHINGIDAE**

J.L. Peters, 1931, *Checklist of the Birds of the World* I

E. Mayr & Short, 1970, *Publ. Nuttall Orn. Cl. 9*

Family **FREGATIDAE**

J.L. Peters, 1931, *Checklist of the Birds of the World* I

W.B. Alexander, 1963, *Birds of the Ocean* 2nd edn. (Putnam, New York)

Family **ARDEIDAE**

J. Hancock & H. Elliott, 1978, *Herons of the World* (London Editions)
W.J. Bock, 1956, *Amer. Mus. Novit.* 1779
J.L. Peters, 1931, *Checklist of the Birds of the World* I

K.C. Parkes, 1955, *Ann. Carnegie Mus.* 33
C.W. Mackworth Praed & C.H.B. Grant, 1962, *African Handbook of Birds* Ser. 1—3 (Longmans, London)
R.A. Falla, 1963, *Notornis* 10
P.S. Humphrey & K.C. Parkes, 1963, *Proc. 13th Inst. Orn. Cong.* 84
E. Eisenmann, 1965, *Hornero* 10
R. Meyer de Schauensee, 1966, *The Species of Birds of South America* (Acad. Nat. Sci., Philadelphia)
O.S.N.Z., 1970, *Annotated Checklist of Birds of New Zealand* (Reed, Wellington)
C.W. Benson, R.K. Brooke, & M.P.S. Irwin, 1971, *Bull. B.O.C.* 91
K. Curry-Lindahl, 1971, *Ostrich* Suppl. 9
R.K. Murton, 1972, *Biol. Conserv.* 4(2)
R.W. Dickerman, 1973, *Bull. B.O.C.* 93
R.B. Payne, 1974, *Bull. B.O.C.* 94
H.T. Condon, 1975, *Checklist of the Birds of Australia* Pt. I (R.A.O.U., Melbourne)
M.P.S. Irwin, 1975, *Bonn. Zool. Beitr.* 26
R.B. Payne & C.J. Risley, 1976, *Univ. Mich. Mus. Zool. Misc. Publ.* 150
D.R. Wells & Lord Medway, 1976, *Bull. B.O.C.* 96
S. Cramp, *et al*, 1977, *Handbook of the Birds of Europe, The Middle East, and North Africa* 1 (Oxford University Press, Oxford)

Family **BALAENICIPITIDAE**

J.L. Peters, 1931, *Checklist of the Birds of the World* I

C.M.N. White, 1965, *Revised Checklist of African Non-passerine Birds* (Govt. Printer, Lusaka)

Family **SCOPIDAE**

J.L. Peters, 1931, *Checklist of the Birds of the World* I

A.L. Rand, 1936, *Bull. Amer. Mus. Nat. Hist.* 72
C.M.N. White, 1965, *Revised Checklist of African Non-passerine Birds* (Govt. Printer, Lusaka)

Family **CICONIIDAE**

M.P. Kahl, 1972, *Journ. Zool.* 167

J.L. Peters, 1931, *Checklist of the Birds of the World* I
M.P. Kahl, 1971, *Living Birds* 10
M.P. Kahl & Schüz, 1972, *Vogelwarte* 26

Family THRESKIORNITHIDAE

J.L. Peters, 1931, *Checklist of the Birds of the World* I

D. Amadon & Woolfenden, 1953, *Amer. Mus. Novit.* 1564
D. Holyoak, 1970, *Bull. B.O.C.* 90

Family PHOENICOPTERIDAE

J.L. Peters, 1931, *Checklist of the Birds of the World* I

R. Meyer de Schauensee, 1966, *The Species of Birds of South America* (Acad. Nat. Sci., Philadelphia)
C.G. Sibley, *et al*, 1969, *Condor* 71
C.G. Sibley & J.E. Ahlqvist, 1972, *Bull. Peabody Mus. Nat. Hist.* 39
J. Kear & N. Duplaix-Hall, 1975, *Flamingoes* (Berkhampstead)

Family ANHIMIDAE

J.L. Peters, 1931, *Checklist of the Birds of the World* I

R. Meyer de Schauensee, 1966, *The Species of Birds of South America* (Acad. Nat. Sci., Philadelphia)

Family ANATIDAE

P.A. Johnsgard, 1965, *Handbook of Waterfowl Behaviour*, (Cornell, New York)
J. Delacour, 1954, *Waterfowl of the World* 1–4 (Country Life, London)

J.L. Peters, 1931, *Checklist of the Birds of the World* I
E. Mayr, 1940, *Amer. Mus. Novit.* 1056
J. Delacour & Mayr, 1945, *Wilson Bull.* 57
H. Friedmann, 1947, *Condor,* 49
R.E. Stewart & J.W. Aldrich, 1956, *Proc. Biol. Soc. Wash.* 69
P. Scott, 1957, *Coloured Key to the Wildfowl of the World,* (Wildfowl Trust, Slimbridge)
S.D. Ripley, 1964, *Bull. Peabody Mus. Nat. Hist.* 19
H.J. Frith, 1967, *Waterfowl of Australia* (A.H. & A.W. Reed, Sydney)
H.T. Condon, 1975, *Checklist of the Birds of Australia* Pt. I (R.A.O.U., Melbourne)
S. Cramp, *et al.* 1977, *Handbook of the Birds of Europe, the Middle east, and North Africa* 1 (Oxford University Press, Oxford)

Family CATHARTIDAE

L. Brown & D. Amadon, 1968, *Eagles, Hawks and Falcons of the World* (Country Life, London)

Family PANDIONIDAE

L. Brown & D. Amadon, 1968, *Eagles, Hawks and Falcons of the World* (Country Life, London)

Family ACCIPITRIDAE

L. Brown & D. Amadon, 1968, *Eagles, Hawks and Falcons of the World* (Country Life, London)

J.L. Peters, 1931, *Checklist of the Birds of the World* I

A.C.V. van Bemmell, 1948, *Treubia* 19
C.E. Hellmayr, 1949, *Catalogue of Birds of the Americas* 1.4
D. Amadon, 1953, *Ibis* 492
C. Vaurie, 1965, *Birds of the Palaearctic Fauna* II (Witherby, London)
C.M.N. White, 1965, *Revised Checklist of African Non-passerine Birds* (Govt. Printer, Lusaka)
A.L. Rand & E.T. Gilliard, 1967, *Handbook of New Guinea Birds* (Weidenfeld & Nicholson, London)
M. Desfayes, 1973, *Bull. B.O.C.* 94
K.C. Parkes, 1973, *Nemouria* 11
H.T. Condon, 1975, *Checklist of the Birds of Australia* Pt. I (R.A.O.U., Melbourne)

Family **SAGITTARIIDAE**

L. Brown & D. Amadon, 1968, *Eagles, Hawks and Falcons of the World* (Country Life, London)

Family **FALCONIDAE**

L. Brown & D. Amadon, 1968, *Eagles, Hawks and Falcons of the World* (Country Life, London)

J.L. Peters, 1931, *Checklist of the Birds of the World* I
C.W. Mackworth-Praed & C.H.B. Grant, 1933, *Bull. B.O.C.* 54
H.T. Condon, 1950, *Emu* 50
D. Amadon, 1964, *Amer. Mus. Novit.* 2166
C. Vaurie, 1965, *Birds of the Palaearctic Fauna* II (Witherby, London)
C.M.N. White, 1965, *Revised Checklist of African Non-passerine Birds* (Govt. Printer, Lusaka)
A.L. Rand & E.T. Gilliard, 1967, *Handbook of New Guinea Birds* (Weidenfeld & Nicholson, London)
P. Schwartz, 1972, *Condor* 74

Family **MEGAPODIIDAE**

J.L. Peters, 1934, *Checklist of the Birds of the World* II (Harvard University Press, Cambridge, Mass.)

E. Mayr, 1938, *Amer. Mus. Novit.* 1006
D. Amadon, 1942, *Amer. Mus. Novit.* 1175
H.J. Frith, 1956, *Ibis* 98
A.L. Rand & E.T. Gilliard, 1967, *Handbook of New Guinea Birds* (Weidenfeld & Nicholson, London)

Family **CRACIDAE**

J. Delacour & D. Amadon, 1973, *Curassows and Related Birds* (Amer. Mus. Nat. Hist., New York)

J.L. Peters, 1934, *Checklist of the Birds of the World* II
C. Vaurie, 1964–5, *Amer. Mus. Novit.* 2197, 2222, 2232, 2237
Vuilleumier, 1965, *Bull. Mus. Comp Zool.* 134
C. Vaurie, 1966, *Amer. Mus. Novit.* 2251
C. Vaurie, 1967, *Amer. Mus. Novit.* 2296, 2299, 2305, 2307
C. Vaurie, 1968, *Bull. Amer. Mus. Nat. Hist.* 138
E.R. Blake, 1977, *Manual of Neotropical Birds* I (Chicago University Press, Chicago)

Family **PHASIANIDAE**

P.A. Johnsgard, 1973, *Grouse and Quails of North America* (Nebraska University Press, Lincoln)
J. Delacour, 1977, *Pheasants of the World* 2nd edn. (Spur, Hindhead)

J.L. Peters, 1934, *Checklist of the Birds of the World* II
M. Hachisuka, 1941, *Zoologica* 26
A. Dugand, 1943, *Caldasia* 2
F. Ludlow, 1944, *Ibis* 86
R. Meyer de Schauensee, 1946, *Proc. Acad. Nat. Sci. Phil.* 91
C.W. Mackworth-Praed & C.H.B. Grant, 1951, *Ibis* 92
C.M.N. White, 1952, *Ibis* 94
C.M.N. White, 1958, *Bull. B.O.C.* 78
S.D. Ripley, 1961, *Synopsis of the Birds of India and Pakistan* (Nat. Hist. Soc, Bombay)
G.E. Watson, 1962, *Ibis* 104
B.P. Hall, 1963, *Bull. Brit. Mus. Nat. Hist.* 10(2)
A. Wetmore, 1963, *Smiths. Misc. Coll.* 145(6)
C. Vaurie, 1965, *Birds of the Palaearctic Fauna* II (Witherby, London)
C.M.N. White, 1965, *Revised Checklist of African Non-passerine Birds* (Govt. Printer, Lusaka)
R. Meyer de Schauensee, 1966, *The Species of Birds of South America* (Acad. Nat. Sci., Philadelphia)
Short, 1967, *Amer. Mus. Novit.* 2289
J. Farrand Jr. & S.L. Olsen, 1973, *Bull. B.O.C.* 93(2)
A.M. Rea, 1973, *Condor* 75(3)
G.W.H. Davison, 1974, *Bull. B.O.C.* 94(4)
D.G. Roles, 1976, *Rare Pheasants of the World* (Spur Publications, Liss, Hampshire)

Family **OPISTHOCOMIDAE**

J.L. Peters, 1934, *Checklist of the Birds of the World* II

C.G. Sibley & J.E. Ahlqvist, 1973, *Auk 90*

Family **MESITORNITHIDAE**

J.L. Peters, 1934, *Checklist of the Birds of the World* II

A.L. Rand, 1936, *Bull. Amer. Mus. Nat. Hist.* 72

Family **TURNICIDAE**

J.L. Peters, 1934, *Checklist of the Birds of the World* II

E. Hartert, 1928, *Novit. Zool.* 34
E. Mayr, 1938, *Amer. Mus. Novit.* 1007
E. Mayr, 1944, *Bull. Amer. Mus. Nat. Hist.* 83
J.D. Macdonald, 1971, *Sunbird* 2
H.T. Condon, 1975, *Checklist of the Birds of Australia* Pt. I (R.A.O.U., Melbourne)

Family **PEDIONOMIDAE**

J.L. Peters, 1934, *Checklist of the Birds of the World* II

W.J. Bock & McEvey, 1969, *Proc. R. Soc. Victoria* 82(2)

Family **GRUIDAE**

J.L. Peters, 1934, *Checklist of the Birds of the World* II

T.H. Cheng, 1955, *Distributional List of Chinese Birds* Pt. I (Acad. Sin., Peking)
C. Vaurie, 1965, *Birds of the Palaearctic Fauna* II (Witherby, London)
J.W. Aldrich, 1972, *Proc. Biol. Soc. Wash.* 85
L. Walkinshaw, 1973, *Cranes of the World* (Winchester, New York)

Family **ARAMIDAE**

A.O.U., 1957, *Checklist of North American Birds* (A.O.U., Baltimore)

J.L. Peters, 1934, *Checklist of the Birds of the World* II

J. Bond, 1971, *Birds of the West Indies* (Collins, London)

Family **PSOPHIIDAE**

J.L. Peters, 1934, *Checklist of the Birds of the World* II

R. Meyer de Schauensee, 1966, *The Species of Birds of South America* (Acad. Nat. Sci., Philadelphia)

Family **RALLIDAE**

S.D. Ripley, 1977, *Rails of the World* (Feheley, Toronto)

E. Mayr, 1933, *Amer. Mus. Novit.* 590
H.B. Conover, 1934, *Auk* 51(3)
J.L. Peters, 1934, *Checklist of the Birds of the World* II
C.E. Hellmayr & Conover, 1942, *Field Mus. Nat. Hist.* 12–13
J.T. Zimmer & W.H. Phelps, 1944, *Amer. Mus. Novit.* 1270
E. Mayr, 1950, *Amer. Mus. Novit.* 1417(3)
A.M. Lysaght, 1953, *Bull. B.O.C.* 73
W.W.A. Phillips & R.W. Sims, 1958, *Bull. B.O.C.* 78
K.C. Parkes & D. Amadon, 1959, *Wilson Bull.* 71(4)
F.B. Gill, 1964, *Condor* 66
R. Meyer de Schauensee, 1966, *The Species of Birds of South America* (Acad. Nat. Sci., Philadelphia)
A.L. Rand & E.T. Gilliard, 1967, *Handbook of New Guinea Birds* (Weidenfeld & Nicholson, London)
H.T. Hendrickson, 1969, *Ibis* 111
L.B. Keith, C.W. Benson, & M.P.S. Irwin, 1970, *Bull. Amer. Mus. Nat. Hist.* 143
O.S.N.Z., 1970, *Annotated Checklist of Birds of New Zealand* (Reed, Wellington)
S.L. Olsen, 1973, *Wilson Bull.* 85
G.M. Storr, 1973, 'List of Queensland Birds' *Spec. Publs. W. Aust. Mus.* 5
H.T. Condon, 1975, *Checklist of the Birds of Australia* Pt. I (R.A.O.U., Melbourne)
S.L. Olson, 1975, *Emu* 75

Family **HELIORNITHIDAE**

J.L. Peters, 1934, *Checklist of the Birds of the World* II

C.M.N. White, 1965, *Revised Checklist of African Non-passerine Birds* (Govt. Printer, Lusaka)
R. Meyer de Schauensee, 1966, *The Species of Birds of South America* (Acad. Nat. Sci., Philadelphia)

Family **RHYNOCHETIDAE**

J.L. Peters, 1934, *Checklist of the Birds of the World* II

E. Mayr, 1945, *Birds of the Southwest Pacific* (Macmillan, New York)

Family **EURYPYGIDAE**

J.L. Peters, 1934, *Checklist of the Birds of the World* II

R. Meyer de Schauensee, 1966, *The Species of Birds of South America* (Acad. Nat. Sci., Philadelphia)

Family **CARIAMIDAE**

J.L. Peters, 1934, *Checklist of the Birds of the World* II

R. Meyer de Schauensee, 1966, *The Species of Birds of South America* (Acad. Nat. Sci., Philadelphia)

Family **OTIDAE**

J.L. Peters, 1934, *Checklist of the Birds of the World* II

A. Roberts, 1937, *Ostrich* 8
J. Vincent, 1949, *Ostrich* 20
S.D. Ripley, 1961, *Synopsis of the Birds of India and Pakistan* (Nat. Hist. Soc., Bombay)
C.M. N. White, 1965, *Revised Checklist of African Non-passerine Birds* (Govt. Printer, Lusaka)

Family **JACANIDAE**

J.L. Peters, 1934, *Checklist of the Birds of the World* II

A. Wetmore, 1965, *Smiths. Misc. Coll.* 150(1)
J.R. Jehl, 1968, *Mem. San Diego Soc. Nat. Hist.* 3

Family **ROSTRATULIDAE**

J.L. Peters, 1934, *Checklist of the Birds of the World* II

C. Vaurie, 1965, *Birds of the Palaearctic Fauna* II (Witherby, London)
R. Meyer de Schauensee, 1966, *The Species of Birds of South America* (Acad. Nat. Sci., Philadelphia)

Family **DROMADIDAE**

J.L. Peters, 1934, *Checklist of the Birds of the World* II

C.M.N. White, 1965, *Revised Checklist of African Non-passerine Birds* (Govt. Printer, Lusaka)

Family **HAEMATOPODIDAE**

J.L. Peters, 1934, *Checklist of the Birds of the World* II

J.R. Jehl, 1968, *Mem. San Diego Soc. Nat. Hist.* 3
E. Mayr & Short, 1970, *Publ. Nuttall Orn. Cl.* 9
O.S.N.Z., 1970, *Annotated Checklist of the Birds of New Zealand* (Reed, Wellington)
H.T. Condon, 1975, *Checklist of the Birds of Australia* Pt. I (R.A.O.U., Melbourne)

Family **IBIDORHYNCHIDAE**

J.L. Peters, 1934, *Checklist of the Birds of the World* II

S.D. Ripley, 1961, *Synopsis of the Birds of India and Pakistan* (Nat. Hist. Soc., Bombay)

Family **RECURVIROSTRIDAE**

J.L. Peters, 1934, *Checklist of the Birds of the World* II

S.D. Ripley, 1961, *Synopsis of the Birds of India and Pakistan* (Nat. Hist. Soc., Bombay)
R. Meyer de Schauensee, 1966, *The Species of Birds of South America* (Acad. Nat. Sci., Philadelphia)
E. Mayr & Short, 1970, *Publ. Nuttall Orn. Cl.* 9
H.T. Condon, 1975, *Checklist of the Birds of Australia* Pt. 2 (R.A.O.U., Melbourne)

Family **BURHINIDAE**

J.L. Peters, 1934, *Checklist of the Birds of the World* II

C. Vaurie, 1965, *Birds of the Palaearctic Fauna* II (Witherby, London)
C.M.N. White, 1965, *Revised Checklist of African Non-passerine Birds* (Govt. Printer, Lusaka)
R. Meyer de Schauensee, 1966, *The Species of Birds of South America* (Acad. Nat. Sci., Philadelphia)

Family **GLAREOLIDAE**

J.L. Peters, 1934, *Checklist of the Birds of the World* II

W.J. Bock, 1959, *Bull. Mus. Comp. Zool.* 118(2)
C.M.N. White, 1965, *Revised Checklist of African Non-passerine Birds* (Govt. Printer, Lusaka)
J.R. Jehl, 1968, *Mem. San Diego Soc. Nat. Hist.* 3

Family **CHARADRIIDAE**

W.J. Bock, 1958, *Bull. Mus. Comp. Zool. Harvard* 118(2)
J.L. Peters, 1934, *Checklist of the Birds of the World* II

W. Serle, 1956, *Bull. B.O.C.* 76
A.O.U., 1957, *Checklist of North American Birds* (A.O.U., Baltimore)
J. Warham, 1960, *Emu* 60
C. Vaurie, 1964, *Amer. Mus. Novit.* 2177
C. Vaurie, 1964, *Bull. Amer. Mus. Nat. Hist.* 127
C. Vaurie, 1965, *Birds of the Palaearctic Fauna* II (Witherby, London)
C.M.N. White, 1965, *Revised Checklist of African Non-passerine Birds* (Govt. Printer, Lusaka)
G.F. van Tets *et al*, 1967, *Emu* 67
J.R. Jehl, 1968, *Mem. San Diego Soc. Nat.Hist.* 3
E. Mayr & Short, 1970, *Publ. Nuttall Orn. Cl.* 9
R.L. Zusi & J.R. Jehl, 1970, *Auk* 87
H.E. Wolters, 1974, *Bonn. Zool. Beitr.* 25(4)
H.T. Condon, 1975, *Checklist of the Birds of Australia* Pt. I (R.A.O.U., Melbourne)

Family **SCOLOPACIDAE**

J.R. Jehl, 1968, *Mem. San Diego Soc. Nat. Hist.* 3
J.L. Peters, 1934, *Checklist of the Birds of the World* II

1956, *Bull. Zool. Nomencl. Dir.* 39
A.O.U., 1957, *Checklist of North American Birds* (A.O.U., Baltimore)
C. Vaurie, 1965, *Birds of the Palaearctic Fauna* II (Witherby, London)
R.L. Zusi & J.R. Jehl, 1970, *Auk* 87
H.T. Condon, 1975, *Checklist of the Birds of Australia* Pt. I (R.A.O.U., Melbourne)

Family **THINOCORIDAE**

J.L. Peters, 1934, *Checklist of the Birds of the World* II

R. Meyer de Schauensee, 1966, *The Species of Birds of South America* (Acad. Nat. Sci., Philadelphia)

Family **CHIONIDIDAE**

J.L. Peters, 1934, *Checklist of the Birds of the World* II

Family **STERCORARIIDAE**

W.B. Alexander, 1963, *Birds of the Ocean* 2nd edn. (Putnam, New York)
J.L. Peters, 1937, *Checklist of the Birds of the World*

Family **LARIDAE**

W.B. Alexander, 1963, *Birds of the Ocean* 2nd edn. (Putnam, New York)
J.L. Peters, 1934, *Checklist of the Birds of the World* II

M. Moynihan, 1959, *Amer. Mus. Novit.* 1928
C. Vaurie, 1965, *Birds of the Palaearctic Fauna* II (Witherby, London)
E. Mayr & Short, 1970, *Publ. Nuttall Orn. Cl.* 9

F. Goethe, 1973, *Stuttgarter Beitr. Naturk.* 261
Schnell, 1970, *Syst. Zool.* 19
D.R. Wells & Lord Medway, 1976, **Bull. B.O.C.** 96

Family **RYNCHOPIDAE**

W.B. Alexander, 1963, *Birds of the Ocean* 2nd edn. (Putnam, New York)
J.L. Peters, 1934, *Checklist of the Birds of the World* II

A.O.U., 1957, *Checklist of North American Birds* (A.O.U., Baltimore)
S.D. Ripley, 1961, *Synopsis of the Birds of India and Pakistan* (Nat. Hist. Soc., Bombay)
C. Vaurie, 1965, *Birds of the Palaearctic Fauna* II (Witherby, London)

Family **ALCIDAE**

W.B. Alexander, 1963, *Birds of the Ocean* 2nd edn. (Putnam, New York)
J.L. Peters, 1934, *Checklist of the Birds of the World* II

A.O.U., 1957, *Checklist of North American Birds* (A.O.U., Baltimore)
C. Vaurie, 1965, *Birds of the Palaearctic Fauna* II (Witherby, London)

Family **PTEROCLIDIDAE**

J.L. Peters, 1937, *Checklist of the Birds of the World* III (Harvard University Press, Cambridge, Mass.)

C.W. Benson, 1947, *Bull. B.O.C.* 67
C.M.N. White, 1965, *Revised Checklist of African Non-passerine Birds* (Govt. Printer, Lusaka)
M. Maclean, 1967, *Journ. f. Orn.* 108

Family **COLUMBIDAE**

D. Goodwin, 1970, *Pigeons and Doves of the World* (Brit. Mus. Nat. Hist., London)
J.L. Peters, 1937, *Checklist of the Birds of the World* III

C.W. Benson, 1943, *Bull. B.O.C.* 63
E. Mayr, 1945, *Birds of the Southwest Pacific* (Macmillan, New York)
W.E.C. Todd, 1947, *Proc. Biol. Soc. Wash.* 60
A.J. van Rossem, 1947, *Proc. Biol. Soc. Wash.* 60
E. Mayr, 1951, *Emu* 51
D. Amadon, 1953, *Bull. Amer. Mus. Nat. Hist.* 100
A.J. Cain, 1954, *Bull. Brit. Mus. Nat. Hist. Zool.* 2
S.D. Ripley, 1961, *Synopsis of the Birds of India and Pakistan* (Nat. Hist. Soc., Bombay)
C. Vaurie, 1965, *Birds of the Palaearctic Fauna* II (Witherby, London)
C.M.N. White, 1965, *Revised Checklist of African Non-passerine Birds* (Govt. Printer, Lusaka)
A.L. Rand & E.T. Gilliard, 1967, *Handbook of New Guinea Birds* (Weidenfeld & Nicholson, London)
D. Goodwin, 1969, *Bull. B.O.C.* 89
T.H. Cheng, *et al,* 1973, *Acta. Zool. Sin.* 19(8)
D. Holyoak, 1974, *Bull. B.O.C.* 94
H.T. Condon, 1975, *Checklist of the Birds of Australia* Pt. I (R.A.O.U., Melbourne)
P.A. Clancey, 1976, *Bull. B.O.C.* 96
M.D. Bruce, 1976, *Bull. B.O.C.* 96

Family **LORIIDAE**

J.M. Forshaw, 1973, *Parrots of the World* (Lansdowne, Melbourne)

J.L. Peters, 1937, *Checklist of the Birds of the World* III
E. Mayr & Condon, 1968, *Bull. Zool. Nom.* 25
A.W. Diamond, 1972, *Publ. Nuttall Orn. Cl.* 12
H.T. Condon, 1975, *Checklist of the Birds of Australia* Pt. I (R.A.O.U., Melbourne)

Family **CACATUIDAE**

J.M. Forshaw, 1973, *Parrots of the World* (Lansdowne, Melbourne)

J.L. Peters, 1937, *Checklist of the Birds of the World* III
H.M. Whittell, 1950, *West Aust. Nat.* 2
E. Mayr, Keast, & Serventy, 1964, *Bull. Zool. Nom.* 21(5)
J.M. Forshaw, 1968, *Emu* 67
H.T. Condon, 1975, *Checklist of the Birds of Australia* Pt. I (R.A.O.U., Melbourne)

Family **PSITTACIDAE**

J.M. Forshaw, 1973, *Parrots of the World* (Lansdowne, Melbourne)

J.L. Peters, 1937, *Checklist of the Birds of the World* III
H.T. Condon, 1941, *Rec. S. Aust. Mus.* 7
A.J. Cain, 1955, *Ibis* 97
C.M.N. White, 1965, *Revised Checklist of African Non-passerine Birds* (Govt. Printer, Lusaka)
R. Meyer de Schauensee, 1966, *The Species of Birds of South America* (Acad. Nat. Sci., Philadelphia)
J.M. Forshaw, 1966, *Mem. Qd. Mus.* 14
J.M. Forshaw, 1967, *Mem. Qd. Mus.* 15
A.L. Rand & E.T. Gilliard, 1967, *Handbook of New Guinea Birds* (Weidenfeld & Nicholson, London)
E. Mayr & Condon, 1968, *Bull. Zool. Nom.* 25
D. Holyoak, 1970, *Emu* 70
A.W. Diamond, 1972, *Publ. Nuttall Orn. Cl.* 12
D. Holyoak, 1973, *Emu* 73
G.M. Storr, 1973, *Spec. Publs. W.Aust. Mus.* 5
H.T. Condon, 1975, *Checklist of the Birds of Australia* Pt. I (R.A.O.U., Melbourne)
K.C. Parkes, 1976, *Bull. B.O.C.* 96

Family **MUSOPHAGINAE**

R.E. Moreau, 1958, *Ibis* 100(1 and 2)

C.M.N. White, 1965, *Revised Checklist of African Non-passerine Birds* (Govt. Printer, Lusaka)
C.W. Benson, *et al,* 1971, *Birds of Zambia* (Collins, London)

Family **CUCULIDAE**

J.L. Peters, 1940, *Checklist of the Birds of the World* IV (Harvard University Press, Cambridge, Mass.)

A.L. Rand, 1936, *Bull. Amer. Mus. Nat. Hist.* 72
W.W.A. Phillips, 1949, *Bull. B.O.C.* 69
A.J. Berger, 1955, *U.S. Nat. Mus. Bull.* 103
E. Stresemann, 1961, *Journ. f. Orn.* 102
C. Vaurie, 1965, *Birds of the Palaearctic Fauna* II (Witherby, London)
C.M.N. White, 1965, *Revised Checklist of African Non-passerine Birds* (Govt. Printer, Lusaka)
R. Meyer de Schauensee, 1966, *The Species of Birds of South America* (Acad. Nat. Sci., Philadelphia)
A.L. Rand & E.T. Gilliard, 1967, *Handbook of New Guinea Birds* (Weidenfeld & Nicholson, London)
C.W. Mackworth-Praed & C.H.B. Grant, 1970, *African Handbook of Birds* III (Longmans, London)
J.E. DuPont, 1971, *Philippine Birds* (Mus. Nat. Hist., Greenville, Del.)
H.T. Condon, 1975, *Checklist of the Birds of Australia* Pt. 1 (R.A.O.U., Melbourne)
Becking, 1975, *Ibis* 117
R. Woodell, 1976, *Bull. B.O.C.* 96

Family **TYTONIDAE**

J.L. Peters, 1940, *Checklist of the Birds of the World* IV

H. Schouteden, 1952, *Rev. Zool. Bot. Afr.* 46
W.H. Marshall, 1966, *Nat. Hist. Bull. Siam Soc.* 21
Sparks & Soper, 1970, *Owls* (David & Charles, Newton Abbott)
A.W. Diamond, 1972, *Publ. Nuttall Orn. Cl.* 12

Family **STRIGIDAE**

J.L. Peters, 1940, *Checklist of the Birds of the World* IV

R.T. Moore, 1947, *Proc. Biol. Soc. Wash.* 60
W.E.C. Todd, 1947, *Proc. Biol. Soc. Wash.* 60
W.N. Koelz, 1950, *Amer. Mus. Novit.* 1452
C. Vaurie, 1960–3, *Amer. Mus. Novit.* 2000, 2015, 2021, 2132
Marshall, 1966, *Nat. Hist. Bull, Siam Soc.* 21
S.D. Ripley, 1966, *Ibis* 108(1)
J. Sparks & T. Soper, 1970, *Owls* (David & Charles, Newton Abbott)
A.A. Soares, 1973, *Archives Mus. Bocage* 2 Ser. 3(2, 5)
J.P. O'Neill & G.R. Graves, 1977, *Auk* 94

Family **STEATORNITHIDAE**

J.L. Peters, 1940, *Checklist of the Birds of the World* IV

R. Meyer de Schauensee, 1966, *The Species of Birds of South America* (Acad. Nat. Sci., Philadelphia)
R. ffrench, 1973, *Guide to the Birds of Trinidad and Tobago* (Livingston, Wynnewood)

Family **PODARGIDAE**

J.L. Peters, 1940, *Checklist of the Birds of the World* IV

H.T. Condon, 1975, *Checklist of the Birds of Australia* Pt. I (R.A.O.U., Melbourne)

Family **NYCTIBIIDAE**

J.L. Peters, 1940, *Checklist of the Birds of the World* IV

R. Meyer de Schauensee, 1966, *The Species of Birds of South America* (Acad. Nat. Sci., Philadelphia)

Family **AEGOTHELIDAE**

J.L. Peters, 1940, *Checklist of the Birds of the World* IV

G.C.A. Junge, 1953, *Zool. Verh.* 20
A.L. Rand & E.T. Gilliard, 1967, *Handbook of New Guinea Birds* (Weidenfeld & Nicholson, London)
A.W. Diamond, 1972, *Publ. Nuttall Orn. Cl.* 12
H.T. Condon, 1975, *Checklist of the Birds of Australia* Pt. I (R.A.O.U., Melbourne)

Family **CAPRIMULGIDAE**

J.L. Peters, 1940, *Checklist of the Birds of the World* IV

E. Mayr, 1941, 'List of New Guinea Birds', *Amer. Mus. Nat. Hist.* 82
C. Vaurie, 1960, *Amer. Mus. Novit.* 1985
A.H. Davis, 1962, *Tex. Journ. Sci.* 14(1)
C.M.N. White, 1965, *Revised Checklist of African Non-passerine Birds* (Govt. Printer, Lusaka)
R. Meyer de Schauensee, 1966, *The Species of Birds of South America* (Acad. Nat. Sci., Philadelphia)
J. Bond, 1971, *Birds of the West Indies* (Collins, London)

Family **APODIDAE**

R.K. Brooke, 1970, *Durban Mus. Novit.* 8

C.M.N. White, *1965, Revised Checklist of African Non-passerine Birds* (Govt. Printer, Lusaka)

R. Meyer de Schauensee, 1966, *The Species of Birds of South America* (Acad. Nat. Sci., Philadelphia)

H.G. Deignan, 1955, *Bull. B.O.C.* 75
D. Lack, 1955, *Ibis* 98
D. Lack, 1956, *Auk* 73
D. Lack, 1956, *Bull. B.O.C.* 76
D. Lack, 1957, *Auk* 74
R.W. Sims, 1961, *Ibis* 103
H.G. Deignan, 1962, *Bull. B.O.C.* 82
E. Eisenmann & Lehmann, 1962, *Amer. Mus. Novit.* 2117
B.P. Hall & R.E. Moreau, 1962, *Bull. Brit. Mus. Nat. Hist. Zool.* 8
Orr, 1963, *Proc. 13th Int. Orn. Cong.* 126
Lord Medway, 1966, *Proc. Linn. Soc. London* 177(2)
C.W. Benson, 1967, *Bull. B.O.C.* 87
P. Somadikarta, 1967, *Proc. U.S. Nat. Mus.* 124
de Roo, 1968, *Rev. Zool. Bot. Afr.* 77
R.K. Brooke, 1971, *Ostrich Suppl.* 8
C.T. Collins, 1972, *Contr. Sci. L.A. County Mus.* 229(4)
A.W. Diamond, 1972, *Publ. Nuttall Orn. Cl.* 12
Behle, 1973, *Auk* 90
W.H. Phelps. 1973, *Bol. Soc. Venez. Cienc. Nat.* 30.124
D. Holyoak, 1974, *Bull. B.O.C.* 94(4) 146
D. Holyoak & Thibault, 1978, *Bull. B.O.C.* 98

Family **HEMIPROCNIDAE**

J.L. Peters, 1940, *Checklist of the Birds of the World* IV

R.K. Brooke, 1969, *Bull. B.O.C.* 89(6)

Family **TROCHILIDAE**

J.L. Peters, 1945, *Checklist of the Birds of the World* V (Harvard University Press, Cambridge, Mass.)

A. Wetmore, 1947, *Smiths. Misc. Coll.* 106
H. Friedman, Griscom, & Moore, 1950, *Pacific Coast Avifauna* 29(1)
E. Eisenmann, 1955, 'The Species of Middle American Birds', *Trans. Lin. Soc. N.Y.* 7
W.H. Phelps, 1956, *Proc. Biol. Soc. Wash.* 69
W.H. Phelps & Phelps, 1963, *Bol. Soc. Venez. Cienc. Nat.* 24
A. Wetmore, 1963, *Smiths. Misc. Coll.* 145
R. Meyer de Schauensee, 1964, *Birds of Colombia* (Livingston, Narbeth, Penn.)
Rowley & Orr, 1964, *Condor* 66(2)
J. Berlioz, 1965, *L'Oiseau* 35(1)
R. Meyer de Schauensee, 1966, *The Species of Birds of South America* (Acad. Nat. Sci., Philadelphia)
R. Meyer de Schauensee, 1967, *Not. Nat.* 402
Grantsau, 1968, *Pap. Avuls Zool.* 22(7)
Grantsau, 1969, *Pap. Avuls Zool.* 22(23)
J. Bond, 1971, *Birds of the West Indies* (Collins, London)
Ruschi, 1972, *Bol. Mus. Biol. Mello Leitao* 35
R. ffrench, 1973, *Guide to the Birds of Trinidad and Tobago* (Livingston, Wynnewood)
Ruschi, 1973, *Bol. Mus. Biol. Mello Leitao* 36
J. Berlioz, 1974, *L'Oiseau* 44(4)
J.S. Weske & J.W. Terborgh, 1977, *Condor* 79

R. Meyer de Schauensee & W.H. Phelps, 1978, *Birds of Venezuela* (Princeton University Press, Princeton)

Family **COLIIDAE**

J.L. Peters, 1945, *Checklist of the Birds of the World* V (Harvard University Press, Cambridge, Mass.)

C.M.N. White, 1965, *Revised Checklist of African Non-passerine Birds* (Govt. Printer, Lusaka)

Family **TROGONIDAE**

J.L. Peters, 1945, *Checklist of the Birds of the World* V

C.M.N. White, 1965, *Revised Checklist of African Non-passerine Birds* (Govt. Printer, Lusaka)
R. Meyer de Schauensee, 1966, *The Species of Birds of South America* (Acad. Nat. Sci., Philadelphia)

Family **ALCEDINIDAE**

J.L. Peters, 1945, *Checklist of the Birds of the World* V

C.M.N. White, 1965, *Revised Checklist of African Non-passerine Birds* (Govt. Printer, Lusaka)
A.L. Rand & E.T. Gilliard, 1967, *Handbook of New Guinea Birds* (Weidenfeld & Nicholson, London)
C.W. Benson, 1974, *L'Oiseau* 44(2)
D. Holyoak, 1974, *Bull. B.O.C.* 94(4) 147
H.T. Condon, 1975, *Checklist of the Birds of Australia* Pt. I (R.A.O.U., Melbourne)

Family **TODIDAE**

J.L. Peters, 1945, *Checklist of the Birds of the World* V

J. Bond, 1971, *Birds of the West Indies* (Collins, London)

Family **MOMOTIDAE**

J.L. Peters, 1945, *Checklist of the Birds of the World* V

A. Wetmore, 1947, *Smiths. Misc. Coll.* 106.16
A. Wetmore, 1968, *Smiths. Misc. Coll.* 150. 2

Family **MEROPIDAE**

C. Fry, 1969, *Ibis* 111
J.L. Peters, 1945, *Checklist of the Birds of the World* V

C.H.B. Grant & C.W. Mackworth-Praed, 1937, *Bull. B.O.C.* 57
H.G. Deignan, 1955, *Bull. B.O.C.* 75
C.M.N. White, 1965, *Revised Checklist of African Non-passerine Birds* (Govt. Printer, Lusaka)

Family **CORACIIDAE**

J.L. Peters, 1945, *Checklist of the Birds of the World* V

A.L. Rand, 1936, *Bull. Amer. Mus. Nat. Hist.* 72
C.M.N. White, 1965, *Revised Checklist of African Non-passerine Birds* (Govt. Printer, Lusaka)
J. Cracraft, 1971, *Auk* 88

Family **BRACHYPTERACIIDAE**

J.L. Peters, 1945, *Checklist of the Birds of the World* V

A.L. Rand, 1936, *Bull. Amer. Mus. Nat. Hist.* 72
J. Cracraft, 1971, *Auk* 88

Family **LEPTOSOMATIDAE**

J.L. Peters, 1945, *Checklist of the Birds of the World* V

A.L. Rand, 1936, *Bull. Amer. Mus. Nat. Hist.* 72

Family **UPUPIDAE**

J.L. Peters, 1945, *Checklist of the Birds of the World* V

C.M.N. White, 1965, *Revised Checklist of African Non-passerine Birds* (Govt. Printer, Lusaka)

Family **PHOENICULIDAE**

J.L. Peters, 1945, *Checklist of the Birds of the World* V

J.D. Macdonald, 1947, *Bull. B.O.C.* 67
W. Serle, 1949, *Bull. B.O.C.* 69
C.M.N. White, 1965, *Revised Checklist of African Non-passerine Birds* (Govt. Printer, Lusaka)

Family **BUCEROTIDAE**

J.L. Peters, 1945, *Checklist of the Birds of the World* V

C.H.B. Grant, 1957, *Bull. B.O.C.* 67
K. Sanft, 1960, *Das Tierreich* 76.1
S.D. Ripley, 1961, *Synopsis of the Birds of India and Pakistan* (Nat. Hist. Soc., Bombay)
C.M.N. White, 1965, *Revised Checklist of African Non-passerine Birds* (Govt. Printer, Lusaka)
J.E. DuPont, 1971, Philippine Birds (Mus. Nat. Hist., Greenville, Del.)

Family **GALBULIDAE**

J.L. Peters, 1948, *Checklist of the Birds of the World* VI (Harvard University Press, Cambridge, Mass.)

W.E.C. Todd, 1943, *Ann. Carnegie Mus.* 30
R. Meyer de Schauensee, 1966, *The Species of Birds of South America* (Acad. Nat. Sci., Philadelphia)
J. Haffer, 1974, *Publ. Nuttall Orn. Cl.* 14

Family **BUCCONIDAE**

J.L. Peters, 1948, *Checklist of the Birds of the World* VI

W.H. Phelps, 1955, *Proc. Biol. Soc. Wash.* 60
R. Meyer de Schauensee, 1966, *The Species of Birds of South America* (Acad. Nat. Sci., Philadelphia)

Family **CAPITONIDAE**

J.L. Peters, 1948, *Checklist of the Birds of the World* VI

W. Serle, 1949, *Bull. B.O.C.* 69
M.A. Traylor, 1951, *Auk* 68
Mukheriee, 1952, *Bull. B.O.C.* 72
S.D. Ripley, 1953, *Ibis* 95
C.W. Benson, 1956, *Bull. B.O.C.* 76
P.A. Clancey, 1956, *Durban Mus. Novit.* 4. 15
H.G. Deignan, 1956, *Proc. Biol. Soc. Wash.* 59
S.D. Ripley, 1961, *Synopsis of the Birds of India and Pakistan* (Nat. Hist. Soc., Bombay)
C.W. Benson & M.P.S. Irwin, 1965, *Bull. B.O.C.* 85(1)
C.M.N. White, 1965, *Revised Checklist of African Non-passerine Birds* (Govt. Printer, Lusaka)

R. Meyer de Schauensee, 1966, *The Species of Birds of South America* (Acad. Nat. Sci., Philadelphia)
Wickler, 1973, *Journ. f. Orn.* 114. 123
C. Erard, 1976, *Bull. B.O.C.* 96

Family INDICATORIDAE

J.L. Peters, 1948, *Checklist of the Birds of the World* VI

J.P. Chapin, 1958, *Bull. B.O.C.* 78
B.P. Hall, 1958, *Bull. B.O.C.* 78
J.P. Chapin, 1962, *Ibis* 104
C.M.N. White, 1965, *Revised Checklist of African Non-passerine Birds* (Govt. Printer, Lusaka)

Family RAMPHASTIDAE

J. Haffer, 1974, *Publ. Nuttall Orn. Cl.* 14

R. Meyer de Schauensee, 1945, *Proc. Acad. Nat. Sci. Phil.* 97
J.L. Peters, 1948, *Checklist of the Birds of the World* VI
R. Meyer de Schauensee, 1966, *The Species of Birds of South America* (Acad. Nat. Sci., Philadelphia)
R. Meyer de Schauensee & Phelps, 1978, *Birds of Venezuela* (Princeton University Press, Princeton)

Family PICIDAE

J.J. Morony Jr., W.J. Bock, & J. Farrand Jr., 1975, *Reference List of the Birds of the World* (Amer. Mus. Nat. Hist., New York)

J.L. Peters, 1948, *Checklist of the Birds of the World* VI
R. Meinertzhagen, 1949, *Bull. B.O.C.* 69
T.H. Cheng, 1955, *Distributional List of Chinese Birds* Pt. I (Acad. Sin., Peking)
T.H. Cheng, 1956, *Act. Sinica* 8.2
K.C. Parkes, 1960, *Bull. B.O.C.* 80
B.E. Smythies, 1960, *Birds of Borneo* (Oliver & Boyd, Edinburgh)
S.D. Ripley, 1961, *Synopsis of the Birds of India and Pakistan* (Nat. Hist. Soc., Bombay)
C. Vaurie, 1965, *Birds of the Palaearctic Fauna* II (Witherby, London)
C.M.N. White, 1965, *Revised Checklist of African Non-passerine Birds* (Govt. Printer, Lusaka)
R. Meyer de Schauensee, 1966, *The Species of Birds of South America* (Acad. Nat. Sci., Philadelphia)
K.E. Stager, 1968, *Contr. Sci. L.A. County Mus.* 153.1
J.E. DuPont, 1971, *Philippine Birds* (Mus. Nat. Hist., Greenville, Del.)
L.L. Short, 1971, *Bull. Amer. Mus. Nat. Hist.* 145
W.R. Goodge, 1972, *Auk* 89
L.L. Short, 1972, *Amer. Mus. Novit.* 2487
L.L. Short, 1972, *Bull. Amer. Mus. Nat. Hist.* 149
L.L. Short, 1973, *Wilson Bull.* 85(4)
O.H. Garrido, 1973, *Poeyana* 119
W.H. Phelps, 1973, *Bol. Soc. Venez. Cienc. Nat.* 30.124
G.F. Mees, 1974, *Zool. Meded. Leiden* 48(7)
R. Meyer de Schauensee & W.H. Phelps, 1978, *Birds of Venezuela* (Princeton University Press, Princeton)

Family EURYLAIMIDAE

J.L. Peters, 1951, Checklist of the Birds of the World VII (Harvard University Press, Cambridge, Mass.)

T.H. Cheng, 1958, *Distributional List of Chinese Birds* II (Acad. Sin., Peking)

B.E. Smythies, 1960, *Birds of Borneo (Oliver & Boyd, Edinburgh)*
S.D. Ripley, 1961, *A Synopsis of the Birds of India and Pakistan* (Nat. Hist. Soc., Bombay)
C.M.N. White, 1961, *Revised Checklist of African Broadbills etc.*(Govt. Printer, Lusaka)
P.A. Clancey, 1970, *Bull. B.O.C.* 90
B.P. Hall & R.E. Moreau, 1970, *An Atlas of Speciation in African Passerine Birds* (Brit. Mus. Nat. Hist., London)
S.L. Olsen, 1971, *Ibis* 113

Family **DENDROCOLAPTIDAE**

J.L. Peters, 1951, *Checklist of the Birds of the World* VII

E. Eisenmann, 1955, *Trans. Lin. Soc. N.Y.* 7
J.T. Zimmer & W.H. Phelps, 1955, *Amer. Mus. Novit.* 1709
W.H. Phelps & W.H. Phelps, 1963, *Bol. Soc. Venez. Cienc. Nat.* 24
R. Meyer de Schauensee, 1964, *Birds of Colombia* (Livingston, Narberth, Pennsylvania)
L.C. Binford, 1965, *Occ. Pap. Mus. Zool. La. St. Univ.* 30
R. Meyer de Schauensee, 1966, *The Species of Birds of South America* (Acad. Nat. Sci., Philadelphia)
A. Wetmore, 1970, *Proc. Biol. Soc. Wash.* 82
E.R. Blake, 1972, *Birds of Mexico* (Chicago University Press, Chicago)
A. Feduccia, 1973, *Orn. Monog.* 13
G.F. Mees, 1974, *Zool. Meded. Leiden* 48(7)
O. Pinto, 1974, *Pap. Avuls. S. Paulo* 27(14)
R. Meyer de Schauensee & W.H. Phelps, 1978, *Birds of Venezuela* (Princeton University Press, Princeton)

Family **FURNARIIDAE**

C. Vaurie, 1971, *Classification of the Ovenbirds* (Witherby, London)

J.L. Peters, 1951, *Checklist of the Birds of the World* VII
M. Koepcke, 1953, *Beitr. Neotrop. Fauna* 1
E. Eisenmann, 1955, *Trans. Lin. Soc. N.Y.* 7
W.H. Phelps & Phelps, 1963, *Bol. Soc. Venez. Cienc. Nat.* 24
R. Meyer de Schauensee, 1964, *Birds of Colombia* (Livingston, Narberth, Penn.)
M. Koepcke, 1965, *Beitr. Neotrop. Fauna* 4
R. Meyer de Schauensee, 1966, *The Species of Birds of South America* (Acad. Nat. Sci., Philadelphia)
H. Sick, 1969, *Beitr. Neotrop. Fauna* 4
E.R. Blake, 1971, *Auk* 88
E. Mayr, 1971, *Journ. f. Orn.* 112
C. Vaurie, 1971, *Ibis* 113
C.C. Olrog, 1972, *Neotropica* 18
C. Vaurie, Weske, & Terborgh, 1972, *Bull. B.O.C.* 92
A. Feduccia, 1973, *Orn. Monog.* 13
W.H. Phelps, 1973, *Bol. Soc. Venez. Cienc. Nat.* 30.124
J.P. O'Neill & T.A. Parker III, 1976, *Bull. B.O.C.* 96
R. Meyer de Schauensee & W.H. Phelps, 1978, *Birds of Venezuela* (Princeton University Press, Princeton)

Family **FORMICARIIDAE**

J.L. Peters, 1951, *Checklist of the Birds of the World* VII

E. Eisenmann, 1955, *Trans. Lin. Soc. N.Y.* 7.128
W.H. Phelps & Phelps, 1963, *Bol. Soc. Venez. Cienc. Nat.* 24
R. Meyer de Schauensee, 1964, *Birds of Colombia* (Livingston, Narbeth, Penn.)
R. Meyer de Schauensee, 1966, *The Species of Birds of South America* (Acad. Nat. Sci., Philadelphia)
G.H. Lowery & O'Neill, 1969, *Auk* 86

E.R. Blake, 1972, *Birds of Mexico* (Chicago University Press, Chicago)
R. ffrench, 1973, *Guide to the Birds of Trinidad and Tobago* (Livingston, Wynnewood)
G.F. Mees, 1974, *Bull. B.O.C.* 59
R. Meyer de Schauensee & W.H. Phelps, 1978, *Birds of Venezuela* (Princeton University Press, Princeton)

Family **CONOPOPHAGIDAE**

J.L. Peters, 1951, *Checklist of the Birds of the World* VII

W.H. Phelps & Phelps, 1963, *Bol. Soc. Venez. Cienc. Nat.* 24
R. Meyer de Schauensee, 1964, *Birds of Colombia* (Livingston, Narberth, Penn.)
R. Meyer de Schauensee, 1966, *The Species of Birds of South America* (Acad. Nat. Sci., Philadelphia)
M.A. Heimerdinger & P.L. Ames, 1967, *Postilla* 105
P.L. Ames, *et al,* 1968, *Postilla* 114

Family **RHINOCRYPTIDAE**

J.L. Peters, 1951, *Checklist of the Birds of the World* VII

W.H. Phelps & Phelps, 1963, *Bol. Soc. Venez. Cienc. Nat.* 24
R. Meyer de Schauensee, 1964, *Birds of Colombia* (Livingston, Narberth, Penn.)
R. Meyer de Schauensee, 1966, *The Species of Birds of South America* (Acad. Nat. Sci., Philadelphia)
A. Wetmore, 1972, *Smiths. Misc. Coll.* 150
A. Wetmore, 1972, *Birds of Panama* III (Smiths. Inst., Washington)

Family **COTINGIDAE**

D.W. Snow, 1973, *Breviora* 409

J.T. Zimmer, 1936, *Amer. Mus. Novit.* 893/4
W.H. Phelps & E.T. Gilliard, 1941, *Amer. Mus. Novit.* 1153
C.E. Hellmayr & Conover, 1942, *Catalogue of Birds of the Americas* (Chicago University Press, Chicago)
W.H. Phelps & Phelps, 1949, *Proc. Biol. Soc. Wash.* 62
R. Meyer de Schauensee, 1950, *Not. Nat.* 221
N. Gyldenstolpe, 1951, *Ark. Zool.* (2)2
R. Meyer de Schauensee, 1953, *Proc. Acad. Nat. Sci. Phil.* 105
W.H. Phelps & Phelps, 1953, *Proc. Biol. Soc. Wash.* 66
E. Eisenmann, 1955, *Trans. Lin. Soc. N.Y.* 7
W.H. Phelps & Phelps, 1955, *Proc. Biol. Soc. Wash.* 68
W.H. Phelps & Phelps, 1963, *Bol. Soc. Venez. Cienc. Nat.* 24
R. Meyer de Schauensee, 1964, *Birds of Colombia* (Livingston, Narberth, Penn.)
R. Meyer de Schauensee, 1966, *The Species of Birds of South America (Acad. Nat. Sci., Philadelphia)*
A.R. Phillips, 1966, *Bull. B.O.C.* 86
E.R. Blake, 1972, *Birds of Mexico* (Chicago University Press, Chicago)
R. ffrench, 1973, *Guide to the Birds of Trinidad and Tobago* (Livingston, Wynnewood)
A. Wetmore, 1973, *Birds of Panama* III (Smiths. Inst., Washington)
J.J. Morony Jr., W.J. Bock, & J. Farrand Jr., 1975, *Reference Book of Birds of the World* (Amer. Mus. Nat. Hist., New York)
R. Meyer de Schauensee & Phelps, 1978, *Birds of Venezuela* (Princeton University Press, Princeton)

Family **PIPRIDAE**

D.W. Snow, 1975, *Bull. B.O.C.* 95

C.B. Cory, C.E. Hellmayr, *et al,* 1927, *Catalogue of Birds of the Americas* (Chicago University Press, Chicago)

E. Eisenmann, 1955, *Trans. Lin. Soc. N.Y.* 7
W.H. Phelps & Phelps, 1963, *Bol. Soc. Venez. Cienc. Nat.* 24
R. Meyer de Schauensee, 1964, *Birds of Colombia* (Livingston, Narberth, Penn.)
Novaes, 1964, *Bol. Mus. Paraense Emilio Goeldi (Zool.)* 47
R. Meyer de Schauensee, 1966, *The Species of Birds of South America* (Acad. Nat. Sci., Philadelphia)
R. ffrench, 1973, *Guide to the Birds of Trinidad and Tobago* (Livingston, Wynnewood)
R. Meyer de Schauensee & W.H. Phelps, 1978, *Birds of Venezuela* (Princeton University Press, Princeton)

Family **TYRANNIDAE/OXYRUNCIDAE**

C.B. Cory, C.E. Hellmayr, *et al*, 1927, *Catalogue of Birds of the Americas* (Chicago University Press, Chicago)

R. Meyer de Schauensee, 1966, *Species of Birds of South America* (Acad. Nat. Sci., Philadelphia)

W.P. Brodkorb, 1943, *Occ. Pap. Mus. Zool. Mich.* 478
W.P. Brodkorb, 1950, *Auk* 67
W.E.C. Todd, 1952, *Ann. Carnegie Mus.* 32
J.T. Zimmer, 1953, *Amer. Mus. Novit.* 1605
W. Meise, 1954, *Auk* 71
E. Eisenmann, 1955, *Trans. Lin. Soc. N.Y.* 7:128
J.T. Zimmer, 1955, *Amer. Mus. Novit.* 1749
J.T. Zimmer & W.H. Phelps, 1955, *Amer. Mus. Novit.* 1709
A.O.U., 1957, *Checklist of the Birds of North America* (A.O.U., Baltimore)
W.E. Lanyon, 1963, *Amer. Mus. Novit.* 2129
W.H. Phelps & Phelps, 1963, *Bol. Soc. Venez. Cienc. Nat.* 24
R. Meyer de Schauensee, 1964, *Birds of Colombia* (Livingston, Narberth, Penn.)
L.C. Binford, 1965, *Occ. Pap. Mus. Zool. La. St. Univ.* 30
A.H. Howell, 1965, *Auk* 82
Olivares, 1965, *Caldasia* 9
C.C. Olrog & Contino, 1966, *Neotropica* 12
A.R. Phillips, 1966, *Bull. B.O.C.* 86
W.E. Lanyon, 1967, *Bull. Amer. Mus. Nat. Hist.* 136
L.L. Short, 1969, *Auk* 86
E. Mayr & Short, 1970, 'Species Taxa of N. American Birds', *Publ. Nuttall Orn. Cl.* 9
J. Bond, 1971, *Birds of the West Indies* (Collins, London)
E. Eisenmann & W.H. Phelps, 1971, *Ornitologia* XXIX
E. Eisenmann & W.H. Phelps, 1971, *Bol. Soc. Venez. Cienc. Nat.* 29
Palerm, 1971, *Bol. Soc. Zool. Uruguay* 1
F. Vuilleumier, 1971, *Bull. Mus. Comp. Zool. Harv.* 141
E.R. Blake, 1972, *Birds of Mexico* (Chicago University Press, Chicago)
A. Wetmore, 1972, *Birds of Panama* III (Smiths. Inst., Washington)
E. Eisenmann & W.H. Phelps, 1973, *Bol. Soc. Venez. Cienc. Nat.* 29.119
E. Eisenmann, 1973, *Auk* 90
O.H. Garrido, 1973, *Poeyana* 119
R. ffrench, 1973, *Guide to the Birds of Trinidad and Tobago* (Livingston, Wynnewood)
D.W. Snow, 1973, *Breviora* 409
J.P. O'Neill & T.A. Parker III, 1976, *Bull. B.O.C.* 96
R. Meyer de Schauensee & W.H. Phelps, 1978, *Birds of Venezuela* (Princeton University Press, Princeton)
G.F. Mees, 1974, *Zool. Meded. Leiden* 48(7)

Family **PHYTOTOMIDAE**

C.B. Cory, C.E. Hellmayr, *et al*, 1927, *Catalogue of Birds of the Americas* (Chicago University Press, Chicago)

R. Meyer de Schauensee, 1966, *The Species of Birds of South America* (Acad. Nat. Sci., Philadelphia)

Family **PITTIDAE**

J.J. Morony Jr., W.J. Bock, & J. Farrand Jr., 1975, *Reference List of the Birds of the World* (Amer. Mus. Nat. Hist., New York)

B.B. Rensch, 1929, *Journ. f. Orn.* Erg. III
B.B. Rensch, 1931, *Mitt. Zool. Mus. Berl.* 17
E. Stresemann, 1939–41, 'Die Vögel von Celebes', *J. f. Orn.* 87. 88. 89
S.D. Ripley, 1941, *Occ. Pap. N.H.S. Boston* 8
H.M. Whittell, 1943, *Emu* 43
H.G. Deignan, 1945, *Smiths. Inst. Bull.* 186
E. Mayr, 1945, *Birds of the Southwest Pacific* (Macmillan, New York)
J. Delacour, 1947, *Birds of Malaysia* (Hamilton, New York)
A.C.V. van Bemmell, 1948, *Treubia* 19
B.E. Smythies, 1953, *Birds of Burma* (Oliver & Boyd, Edinburgh)
E. Mayr, 1955, *Amer. Mus. Novit.* 1707
T.H. Cheng, 1958, *Distributional List of Chinese Birds* Pt. II (Acad. Sin., Peking)
J. Delacour & Jabouille, 1960, *L'Oiseau* 10
B.E. Smythies, 1960, *Birds of Borneo* (Oliver & Boyd, Edinburgh)
S.D. Ripley, 1961, *Synopsis of the Birds of India and Pakistan* (Nat. Hist. Soc., Bombay)
C.M.N. White, 1961, *Revised Checklist of African Broadbills etc.* (Govt. Printer, Lusaka)
S.D. Ripley & Rabor, 1962, 'New Birds from Culion Is. and Palawan', *Postilla* 73
A.L. Rand & E.T. Gilliard, 1967, *Handbook of New Guinea Birds* (Weidenfeld & Nicholson, London)
V. Serventy, 1968, *Bull. B.O.C.* 88
B.P. Hall & R.E. Moreau, 1970, *Atlas of Speciation in African Passerine Birds* (Brit. Mus. Nat. Hist., London)
J.E. DuPont, 1971, *Philippine Birds* (Mus. Nat. Hist., Greenville, Del.)
K.C. Parkes, 1971, *Bull. B.O.C.* 91
R. Schodde, 1975, *Interim List of Australian Songbirds, Passerines* (R.A.O.U., Melbourne)
B. King, 1978, *Bull. B.O.C.* 98

Family **XENICIDAE**

O.S.N.Z., 1970, *Annotated Checklist of the Birds of New Zealand* (Reed, Wellington)

R.A. Falla, Sibson, & Turbot, 1966, *Field Guide to the Birds of New Zealand* (Collins, London)

Family **PHILEPITTIDAE**

A.L. Rand, 1936, *Bull. Amer. Mus. Nat. Hist.* 72

D. Amadon, 1951, *L'Oiseau* 21
A.L. Thomson, 1964, *New Dictionary of Birds* (McGraw-Hill, New York)

Family **MENURIDAE**

R. Schodde, 1975, *Interim List of Australian Songbirds, Passerines* (R.A.O.U., Melbourne)

J.D. Macdonald, 1973, *Birds of Australia* (Witherby, London)
P. Slater, 1975, *Field Guide to Australian Birds, Passerines* (S.A.P., Edinburgh)

Family **ATRICHORNITHIDAE**

R. Schodde, 1975, *Interim List of Australian Songbirds, Passerines* (R.A.O.U., Melbourne)

J.D. Macdonald, 1973, *Birds of Australia* (Witherby, London)
P. Slater, 1975, *Field Guide to Australian Birds, Passerines* (S.A.P., Edinburgh)

Family **ALAUDIDAE**

J.L. Peters, 1960, *Checklist of the Birds of the World* IX (Harvard University Press, Cambridge, Mass.)

C.W. Mackworth-Praed & C.H.B. Grant, 1933–70, *African Handbook of Birds* Ser. 1–3 (Longmans, London)

C.W. Mackworth-Praed & C.H.B. Grant, 1939, *Bull. B.O.C.* 59

A.O.U., 1957, *Checklist of North American Birds* (A.O.U., Baltimore)

T.H. Cheng, 1958, *Distributional List of Chinese Birds* Pr. II (Acad. Sin., Peking)

C. Vaurie, 1959, *Birds of the Palaearctic Fauna* I (Witherby, London)

C.M.N. White, 1960, *Bull. B.O.C.* 80

S.D. Ripley, 1961, *Synopsis of the Birds of India and Pakistan* (Nat. Hist. Soc., Bombay)

C.M.N. White, 1961, *Revised Checklist of African Broadbills etc.* (Govt. Printer, Lusaka)

C.W. Benson & M.P.S. Irwin, 1965, *Arnoldia* 37

A.A. Da Rosa Pinto, 1965, *Mem. Inst. Invest. Cient. Mozambique* 5

Winterbottom 1965 *L'Oiseau* 35

C. W. Benson 1966 *Bull. B.O.C.* 86

P. A. Clancey 1966 *Durban Mus. Novit.* 7

R. Meyer De Schauensee 1966 *The Species of Birds of South America* (Acad. Nat. Sci., Philadelphia)

R. D. Etchecopar & Hüe 1964 *Les Oiseaux du Nord de l'Afrique* (Boubée, Paris)

L. S. Stepanyan 1967 *Acta. Orn.* 10(4)

H. Kumerloeve 1969 *Journ. Orn. Leipzig* 110

B. P. Hall & R. E. Moreau 1970 *Atlas of Speciation in African Passerine Birds* (Brit. Mus. Nat. Hist., London)

H. Kumerloeve 1970 *Beitr. Vogelk.* 16

G. Rudebeck 1970 *Ornis. Scand.* 1

E. R. Blake 1972 *Birds of Mexico* (Chicago University Press, Chicago)

P. A. Clancey 1972 *Durban Mus. Novit.* 9

A. R. Phillips 1972 *Bull. B.O.C.* 90

J. M. Winterbottom 1972 *Ostrich* 43

C. Erard & G. Jarry 1973 *Bull. B.O.C.* 93

C. Erard & R. De Naurois 1973 *Bull. B.O.C.* 93

Family **HIRUNDINIDAE**

J. L. Peters 1960 *Checklist of the Birds of the World* IX

C.W. Mackworth-Praed & C.H.B. Grant 1933–70 *African Handbook of Birds* Ser. 1–3 (Longmans, London)

C. M. N. White 1937 *Bull. B.O.C.* 57

E. Mayr & Bond 1943 *Ibis* 85

E. Eisenmann 1955 *Trans. Lin. Soc. N.Y.* 7.

A.O.U. 1957 *Checklist of North American Birds* (A.O.U., Baltimore)

C. Vaurie, 1959, *Birds of the Palaearctic Fauna* I (Witherby, London)

S.D. Ripley, 1960, *Postilla* 43

S.D. Ripley, 1961, *Synopsis of the Birds of India and Pakistan* (Nat. Hist. Soc., Bombay)

C.M.N. White, 1961, *Revised Checklist of African Broadbills etc.* (Govt. Printer, Lusaka)

P.A. Clancey & Irwin, 1966, *Durban Mus. Novit.* 8

R. Meyer de Schauensee, 1966, *The Species of Birds of South America* (Acad. Nat. Sci., Philadelphia)

E.T. Gilliard & Lecroy, 1967, *Bull. Amer. Mus. Nat. Hist.* 135

K. Thonglongya, 1968, *Thai. Mus. Sci. Pap. Fauna* 1

P.A. Clancey, 1969, *Durban Mus. Novit.* 8

J. Bond, 1971, *Birds of the West Indies* (Collins, London)

K.C. Parkes, 1971, *Nemouria* 4

H.E. Wolters, 1971, *Bonn. Zool. Beitr.* 22

R.K. Brooke, 1972, *Bull. B.O.C.* 92

R.K. Brooke, 1974, *Durban Mus. Novitates* 10(a)

L.S. Stepanyan, 1974, *Zool. Zh.* 53.8

R. Schodde, 1975, *Interim List of Australian Songbirds, Passerines* (R.A.O.U., Melbourne)

Family **MOTACILLIDAE**

J.L. Peters, 1960, *Checklist of the Birds of the World* IX

B.E. Smythies, 1953, *Birds of Burma* (Oliver & Boyd, Edinburgh)
T.H. Cheng, 1958, *Distributional List of Chinese Birds* II (Acad. Sin., Peking)
C. Vaurie, 1959, *Birds of the Palaearctic Fauna* I (Witherby, London)
B.P. Hall, 1961, *Bull. Amer. Mus. Nat. Hist.* 7(5)
C.M.N. White, 1961, *Revised Checklist of African Broadbills etc.* (Govt. Printer, Lusaka)
R. Meyer de Schauensee, 1966, *The Species of Birds of South America* (Acad. Nat. Sci., Philadelphia)
B.P. Hall & R.E. Moreau, 1970, *Atlas of Speciation in African Passerine Birds* (Brit. Mus. Nat. Hist., London)
O.S.N.Z., 1970, *Annotated Checklist of the Birds of New Zealand* (Reed, Wellington)

Family **CAMPEPHAGIDAE**

J.L. Peters, Mayr, & Deignan, 1960, in J.L. Peters *Checklist of the Birds of the World* IX

B. Rensch, 1929, *Journ. f. Orn. Erg.* III
E. Mayr, 1940, *Emu* 40
S.D. Ripley, 1941, *Auk* 58
E. Mayr, 1945, *Birds of the Southwest Pacific* (Macmillan, New York)
A.C.V. van Bemmell, 1948, *Treubia* 19
K.H. Voous & van Marle, 1949, *Bijdr. Dierk* 28
E. Mayr, 1955, *Amer. Mus. Novit.* 1707
A.J. Keast, 1958, *Aust. Journ. Zool.* 6
S.D. Ripley, 1961, *Synopsis of the Birds of India and Pakistan* (Nat. Hist. Soc., Bombay)
I.C.J. Galbraith & E.H. Galbraith, 1962, *Bull. Brit. Mus. Nat. Hist.* 9
C.M.N. White, 1962, *Revised Checklist of African Shrikes etc.* (Govt. Printer, Lusaka)
F. Salamonsen, 1964, *Noona Dan Pap.* 9
E.T. Gilliard & Lecroy, 1967, *Bull. Amer. Mus. Nat. Hist.* 135(4)
A.L. Rand & E.T. Gilliard, 1967, *Handbook of New Guinea Birds* (Weidenfeld & Nicholson, London)
A.W. Diamond, 1969, *Amer. Mus. Novit.* 2362
I.C.J. Galbraith, 1969, *Emu* 69
K.C. Parkes, 1971, *Nemouria* 4
J.E. DuPont, 1972, *Nemouria* 7
K.C. Parkes, 1974, *Annals Carn. Mus.* 45.3
R. Schodde, 1975, *Interim Checklist of Australian Songbirds, Passerines* (R.A.O.U., Melbourne)

Family **PYCNONOTIDAE**

A.L. Rand & Deignan, 1960, in J.L. Peters *Checklist of the Birds of the World* IX

C.W. Mackworth-Praed & C.H.B. Grant, 1933–70, *African Handbook of Birds*, Ser. 1–3 (Longmans, London)
A.L. Rand, 1958, *Fieldiana* 35
C.M.N. White, 1962, *Revised Checklist of African Shrikes etc.* (Govt. Printer, Lusaka)
H.G. Deignan, 1963, *Checklist of the Birds of Thailand* (Smiths. Inst., Washington)
A. Hoogerwerf, 1965, *Bull. B.O.C.* 85
De Roo, 1967, *Rev. Zool. Bot. Afr.* 75
P.A. Clancey, 1969, *Durban Mus. Novit.* 8
A. Prigogine, 1969, *Rev. Zool. Bot. Afr.* 79
A.L. Rand & Rabor, 1969, *Fieldiana, Zool.* 51
B.P. Hall & R.E. Moreau, 1970, *Atlas of Speciation in African Passerine Birds* (Brit. Mus. Nat. Hist., London)
P.R. Colston, 1972, *Ibis* 114(1)
A. Prigogine, 1972, *Bull. B.O.C.* 92(5)

Family **IRENIDAE**

J. Delacour, 1960, in J.L. Peters *Checklist of the Birds of the World* IX

Marien, 1952, *Amer. Mus. Novit.* 1589
B.P. Hall, 1957, *Ibis* 74
S.D. Ripley, 1961, *Synopsis of the Birds of India and Pakistan* (Nat. Hist. Soc., Bombay)
Prescott, 1970, *Bull. B.O.C.* 90
J.E. Dupont, 1972, *Philippine Birds* (Mus. Nat. Hist., Greenville, Del.)

Family **LANIIDAE**

A.L. Rand, 1960, in J.L. Peters *Checklist of the Birds of the World* IX

E. Mayr, 1943, *Ibis* 57
C. Vaurie, 1959, *Birds of the Palaearctic Fauna* I (Witherby, London)
S.D. Ripley, 1961, *Synopsis of the Birds of India and Pakistan* (Nat. Hist. Soc., Bombay)
C.M.N. White, 1962, *Revised Checklist of African Shrikes etc.* (Govt. Printer, Lusaka)
P.A. Clancey, 1965, *Arnoldia* 23
A.A. Da Rosa Pinto, 1965, *Mem. Inst. Invest. Cient. Mozambique* 5
P.A. Clancey, 1969, *Durban Mus. Novit.* 8
P.A. Clancey, 1970, *Durban Mus. Novit.* 9
B.P. Hall & R.E. Moreau, 1970, *Atlas of Speciation in African Passerine Birds* (Brit. Mus. Nat. Hist., London)
C.W. Benson, *et al,* 1971, *Birds of Zambia* (Collins, London)
G.D. Field, 1979, *Bull. B.O.C.* 99.2

Family **VANGIDAE**

A.L. Rand, 1960, in J.L. Peters *Checklist of the Birds of the World* IX

A.L. Rand, 1936, *Bull. Amer. Mus. Nat. Hist.* 72

Family **BOMBYCILLIDAE**

J.C. Greenway, 1960, in J.L. Peters *Checklist of the Birds of the World* IX

O.L. Austin & N. Kuroda, 1953, *Bull. Mus. Comp. Zool.* 109(4)
R. Meinertzhagen, 1954, *Birds of Arabia* (Oliver & Boyd, Edinburgh)
A.O.U., 1957, *Checklist of the Birds of North America* (A.O.U., Baltimore)
C. Vaurie, 1959, *Birds of the Palaearctic Fauna* I (Witherby, London)
E.R. Blake, 1972, *Birds of Mexico* (Chicago University Press, Chicago)
A.R. Phillips, 1966, *Bull. B.O.C.* 86

Family **DULIDAE**

J.C. Greenway, 1960, in J.L. Peters *Checklist of the Birds of the World* IX

J. Bond, 1971, *Birds of the West Indies* (Collins, London)

Family **CINCLIDAE**

J.C. Greenway, 1960, in J.L. Peters *Checklist of the Birds of the World* IX

C. Vaurie, 1955, *Amer. Mus. Novit.* 1751
J.C. Greenway & C. Vaurie, 1958, *Mus. Comp. Zool.* 89
C. Vaurie, 1959, *Birds of the Palaearctic Fauna* I (Witherby, London)
R. Meyer de Schauensee, 1966, *The Species of Birds of South America* (Acad. Nat. Sci., Philadelphia)
A.R. Phillips, 1966, *Bull. B.O.C.* 86

Family **TROGLODYTIDAE**

R.A. Paynter & C. Vaurie, 1960, in J.L. Peters *Checklist of the Birds of the World* IX

W.H. Phelps & Phelps, 1963, *Bol. Soc. Venez. Cienc. Nat.* 24
R. Meyer de Schauensee, 1964, *Birds of Columbia* (Livingstone, Narberth, Penn.)
P. Slud, 1964, *Bull. Amer. Mus. Nat. Hist.* 128
R. Meyer de Schauensee, 1966, *The Species of Birds of South America* (Acad. Nat. Sci., Philadelphia)
A.R. Phillips, 1966, *Bull. B.O.C.* 86
E.R. Blake, 1972, *Birds of Mexico* (Chicago University Press, Chicago)
L. Irby Davies, 1972, *Field Guide to the Birds of Mexico and Central America* (Texas University, Austin)
R.S. Crossin & C.A. Ely, 1973, *Condor* 75(2)
R.W. Dickermann, 1973, *Condor* 75(3)
H.M. Stevenson, 1973, *Auk* 90
A. Wetmore, 1973, *Birds of Panama* III (Smiths. Inst., Washington)
R.W. Dickermann, 1975, *Amer. Mus. Novit.* 2569
R. Meyer de Schauensee & W.H. Phelps, 1978, *Birds of Venezuela* (Princeton University Press, Princeton)

Family **MIMIDAE**

J. Davis & A.H. Miller, 1960, in J.L. Peters *Checklist of the Birds of the World* IX

A.R. Phillips, 1964, *Revta. Soc. Mex. Hist. Nat.* 25
R. Meyer de Schauensee, 1966, *The Species of Birds of South America* (Acad. Nat. Sci., Philadelphia)
J. Bond, 1971, *Birds of the West Indies* (Collins, London)
E.R. Blake, 1972, *Birds of Mexico* (Chicago University Press, Chicago)
L. Irby Davis, 1972, *Field Guide to the Birds of Mexico and Central America* (Texas University, Austin)

Family **PRUNELLIDAE**

S.D. Ripley, 1964, in J.L. Peters *Checklist of the Birds of the World* X (Harvard, University Press, Cambridge, Mass.)

C. Vaurie, 1959, *Birds of the Palaearctic Fauna* I (Witherby, London)
H.G. Deignan, 1964, *Bull. B.O.C.* 84
Mauersberger, 1971, *Journ. f. Orn.* 112

Subfamily TURDINAE

S.D. Ripley, 1964, in J.L. Peters *Checklist of the Birds of the World* X (Mus. Comp. Zool.,
Cambridge, Mass.)

E. Stresemann, 1940, *Journ. f. Orn.* 88
J. Dorst, 1950, *Ois. Rev. Fr. Orn.* 20
J.P. Chapin, 1953, *Bull. Amer. Mus. Nat. Hist.* 75A
G.P. Dementiev & Gladkov (eds.), 1954, *Birds of the Soviet Union* (Moscow)
R. Meinertzhagen, 1954, *Birds of Arabia* (Oliver & Boyd, Edinburgh)
C. Vaurie, 1955, *Amer. Mus. Novit.* 1731
J.T. Zimmer & W.H. Phelps, 1955, *Amer. Mus. Novit.* 1709
S.D. Ripley, 1958, *Postilla* 37
C. Vaurie, 1959, *Birds of the Palaearctic Fauna* I (Witherby, London)
B.P. Hall, 1961, *Bull. B.O.C.* 81
C.M.N. White, 1961, *Bull. B.O.C.* 81
I.C.J. Galbraith & E.H. Galbraith, 1962, *Bull. Brit. Mus. Nat. Hist.* 9
S.D. Ripley, 1962, *Postilla* 63

C.M.N. White, 1962, *Revised Checklist of African Shrikes etc.* (Govt. Printer, Lusaka)
A.H. Howell, 1965, *Auk* 82
N. Kuroda, 1965, *Misc. Rep. Yamashina Inst. Orn. Zool.* 4
Phillips & Rook, 1965, *Condor* 67
L.S. Stepanyan, 1965, *Trudy Zool. Mus. Moscow* 9
P.A. Clancey, 1966, *Durban Mus. Novit.* 7
R. Meyer de Schauensee, 1966, *The Species of Birds of South America* (Acad. Nat. Sci., Philadelphia)
A.R. Phillips, 1966, *Bull. B.O.C.* 86
S.D. Ripley & Heinrich, 1966, *Postilla* 95
E.T. Gilliard & Lecroy, 1967, *Bull. Amer. Mus. Nat. Hist.* 135(4)
C.G. Sibley, 1968, *Postilla* 125
P.A. Clancey, 1969, *Durban Mus. Novit.* 8
P.A. Clancey & Lawson, 1969, *Bull. B.O.C.* 89
A.R. Phillips, 1969, *Auk* 86
A. Prigogine, 1969, *Rev. Zool. Bot. Afr.* 79
A. Berlioz & W. Roche, 1970, *Monitore Zool. Ital.* Suppl. 3.12
B.R. Hall & R.E. Moreau, 1970, *Atlas of Speciation in African Passerine Birds* (Brit. Mus. Nat. Hist., London)
T. Farkas, 1971, *Ostrich* 42(9)
H.E. Wolters, 1971, *Bonn. Zoo. Beitr.* 22
P.A. Clancey, 1972, *Durban Mus. Novit.* 9
T. Farkas, 1972, *Ostrich* 43
T. Farkas, 1973, *Bull. B.O.C.* 93
Olrog, 1973, *Acta. Zool. Lilloana* 30
J.D. Webster, 1973, *Auk* 90
P.A. Clancey, 1974, *Durban Mus. Novit.* 10
P.A. Clancey, 1974, *Arnoldia* 6(28)
M.P.S. Irwin & P.A. Clancey, 1974, *Arnoldia* 6(34)
Harrison, 1977, *Bull. B.O.C.* 97
A. Prigogine, 1977, *Bull. B.O.C.* 97
Orenstein, 1979, *Ibis,* 121

Subfamily ORTHONYCHINAE

H.G. Deignan, 1964, in J.L. Peters *Checklist of the Birds of the World* X

H.T. Condon, 1962, *Rec. South Austr. Mus.* 14
A.L. Rand & E.T. Gilliard, 1967, *Handbook of New Guinea Birds* (Weidenfeld & Nicholson, London)
J.D. Macdonald, 1968, *Emu* 68
A.W. Diamond, 1969, *Amer. Mus. Novit.* 2362
J. Ford, 1971, *Emu* 71
J. Ford & Parker, 1973, *Emu* 73
J. Ford, 1974, *Emu* 74
R. Schodde, 1975, *Interim List of Australian Songbirds, Passerines* (R.A.O.U., Melbourne)
J. Ford, 1977, *Proc. 16th Int. Orn Cong.*

Subfamily TIMALIINAE

H.G. Deignan, 1964, in J.L. Peters *Checklist of the Birds of the World* X

J.P. Chapin, 1953, *Bull. Amer. Mus. Nat. Hist.* 75A
B.E. Smythies, 1953, *The Birds of Burma* (Oliver & Boyd, Edinburgh)
T.H. Cheng, 1958, *Distributional List of Chinese Birds* Pt. II (Acad. Sin., Peking)
C. Vaurie, 1959, *Birds of the Palaearctic Fauna* I (Witherby, London)
H.G. Deignan, 1960, *Emu* 60
B.E. Smythies, 1960, *The Birds of Borneo* (Oliver & Boyd, Edinburgh)
S.D. Ripley, 1961, *Synopsis of the Birds of India and Pakistan* (Nat. Hist. Soc., Bombay)
C.M.N. White, 1962, *Revised Checklist of African Shrikes etc.* (Govt. Printer, Lusaka)
R.B. Cowles, 1964, *Emu* 64

A. Prigogine, 1964, *Rev. Zool. Bot. Afr.* 70
C. Vaurie, 1965, *L'Oiseau* 34
A. Hoogerwerf, 1966, *Misc. Rep. Yamashina Inst. Orn.* 4
S.D. Ripley & Heinrich 1966, *Postilla* 95
S. Ali & S.D. Ripley, 1971, *Birds of India and Pakistan* VI (Oxford University Press, Oxford)
J.E. DuPont, 1971, *Philippine Birds* (Mus. Nat. Hist., Greenville, Del.)
J.E. DuPont, 1971, *Nemouria* 3
J. Ford, 1971, *Emu* 71
J.E. Dupont & Rabor, 1973, *Nemouria* 9
P.A. Clancey, 1974, *Durban Mus. Novit.* X.2
T.H. Cheng, 1974, *Acta. Zool. Sin.* 20(1)
D.R. Wells & Lord Medway, 1976, *Bull. B.O.C.* 96
C.F. Mann, *et al*, 1978, *Bull. B.O.C.* 98

Subfamily PANURINAE

H.G. Deignan, 1964, in J.L. Peters *Checklist of the Birds of the World* X

C. Vaurie, 1954, *Amer. Mus. Novit.* 1669
T.H. Cheng, 1958, *Distributional List of Chinese Birds* Pt. II (Acad. Sin., Peking)
C. Vaurie, 1959, *Birds of the Palaearctic Fauna* I (Witherby, London)
T.H. Cheng, 1973, *Acta. Zool. Sin.* 19(1)

Subfamily PICATHARTINAE

H.G. Deignan, 1964, in J.L. Peters *Checklist of the Birds of the World* X

C.M.N. White, 1960, *Revised Checklist of African Muscicapidae etc.* (Govt. Printer, Lusaka)

Subfamily POLIOPTILINAE

R.A. Paynter, 1964, in J.L. Peters *Checklist of the Birds of the World* X

W.H. Phelps & Phelps, 1950, *Bol. Soc. Venez. Cienc. Nat.* 12
R. Meyer de Schauensee, 1951, *Caldasia* 5
E.R. Blake, 1953, *Birds of Mexico* (Chicago University Press, Chicago)
A.L. Rand & Traylor, 1953, *Auk* 70
E. Eisenmann, 1955, 'The Species of Middle American Birds', *Trans. Lin. Soc. N.Y.* 7
A.H. Miller, *et al*, 1957, 'Pacific Coast Avifauna', *Cooper Orn. Soc.* 33
R. Meyer de Schauensee, 1966, *A Guide to the Birds of South America* (Livingston, Wynnewood, Pennsylvania)
K.C. Parkes, 1979, *Bull. B.O.C.* 99(2)

Subfamily SYLVIINAE

J.J. Morony Jr., W.J. Bock, & J. Farrand Jr., 1975, *Reference List of the Birds of the World* (Amer. Mus. Nat. Hist., New York)

C. Vaurie, 1959, *Birds of the Palaearctic Fauna* Pt. I (Witherby, London)

B. Rensch, 1929, *Journ. f. Orn.* Erg. III
H. Lynes, 1930, *Ibis* 12(6)
G.M. Mathews, 1930, *Syst. Avium Austr.* Pt. II (B.O.U., London)
A.L. Rand, 1936, *Bull. Amer. Mus. Nat. Hist.* 72
C.B. Ticehurst, 1938, *The Genus Phylloscopus* (Brit. Mus. Nat. Hist., London)
H.F. Witherby, *et al*, 1938, *Handbook of British Birds* II
E. Stresemann, 1939–41, *Journ. f. Orn.* 87(3). 88(1). 88(3). 89(1)
S.D. Ripley, 1941, *Occ. Pap. N.H.S. Boston* 8
E. Mayr, 1944, *Bull. Amer. Mus. Nat. Hist.* 83(2)
E. Mayr, 1945, *Birds of the Southwest Pacific* (Macmillan, New York)
J. Delacour, 1947, *Birds of Malaysia* (Macmillan, New York)

E. Mayr, 1948, *Emu* 47
A.C.V. van Bemmell, 1948, *Treubia* 19(2)
E. Stresemann & J. Arnold, 1949, *Journ. Bombay Nat. Hist. Soc.* 48
J. Baker, 1951, *Univ. Kan. Pub. Mus. Nat. Hist.* 3(1)
J. Delacour, 1952, *Ibis* 94
H. Schouteden, 1952, *Rev. Zool. Bot. Afr.* XLVI
B.E. Smythies, 1953, *Birds of Burma* (Oliver & Boyd, Edinburgh)
G.P. Dementiev & Gladkov (eds.), 1954, *Birds of the Soviet Union* (Moscow)
C.W. Mackworth-Praed & C.H.B. Grant, 1955–73, *African Handbook of Birds* Ser. 1–3 (Longmans, London)
E. Mayr, 1955, *Amer. Mus. Novit.* 1707
C. Vaurie, 1956, *Ibis* 99
T.H. Cheng, 1958, *Distributional List of Chinese Birds* Pt. II (Acad. Sin., Peking)
C.W. Benson, 1960, *Ibis* 103 b
E.T. Gilliard, 1960, *Amer. Mus. Novit.* 2008
G.C. Munro, 1960, *Birds of Hawaii* (Bridgeway Press, Rutland, Vermont)
B.E. Smythies, 1960, *Birds of Borneo* (Oliver & Boyd, Edinburgh)
C.M.N. White, 1960, 'Checklist of Ethiopian Musc. (Sylv.) 1 + 2', *Occ. Pap. Nat. Mus. Sci. Rhodesia*
A.J. Keast, 1961, *Bull. Amer. Mus. Nat. Hist.* 123(8)
S.D. Ripley, 1961, *Synopsis of the Birds of India and Pakistan* (Nat. Hist. Soc., Bombay)
I.C.J. Galbraith & E.H. Galbraith, 1962, *Bull. Brit. Mus. Nat. Hist.* 9
H.G. Deignan, 1963, *Bull. U.S. Nat. Mus.* 226
E. Mayr, 1963, *Emu* 63
A.R. Phillips, 1964, *Revta. Soc. Mex. Hist. Nat.* 25
P.A. Clancey, 1965, *Durban Mus. Novit.* VII
F. Salomonsen, 1965, *Vidensk. Meddr. dansk naturh Foren* 128
C.W. Benson & M.P.S. Irwin, 1966, *Arnoldia* (2)27
M.P.S. Irwin, 1966, *Bull. Brit. Orn. Cl.* 86
M.P.S. Irwin, 1966, *Durban Mus. Novit.* VIII
S.D. Ripley & Heinrich, 1966, *Postilla* 95/96
E.T. Gilliard & Lecroy, 1967, *Bull. Amer. Mus. Nat. Hist.* 135(4)
A.L. Rand & E.T. Gilliard, 1967, *Handbook of New Guinea Birds* (Weidenfeld & Nicholson, London)
G.M. Storr, 1967, *Spec. Publs. West Aust. Mus.* 4
C.W. Benson & Penny, 1968, *Bull. B.O.C.* 88
Phillips, 1968, *Journ. Bombay Nat. Hist. Soc.* 65
P.A. Clancey, 1969, *Bull. B.O.C.* 89
P.A. Clancey, 1970, *Durban Mus. Novit.* VIII
de Roo, 1970, *Rev. Zool. Bot. Afr.* 82
B.P. Hall & R.E. Moreau, 1970, *Atlas of Speciation in African Passerine Birds* (Brit. Mus. Nat. Hist., London)
O.S.N.Z., 1970, *Annotated Checklist of the Birds of New Zealand* (Reed, Wellington)
K.C. Parkes, 1970, *Bull. B.O.C.* 90
L.S. Stepanyan, 1970, *Biol. Nauki* 1970 (11)
P.A. Clancey, 1971, *Durban Mus. Novit.* IX
J.E. DuPont, 1971, *Philippine Birds* (Mus. Nat. Hist., Greenville, Del.)
K.C. Parkes, 1971, *Nemouria* 4
A.W. Diamond, 1972, *Publ. Nuttall Orn. Cl.* 12
L.S. Stepanyan, 1972, *Zool. Zhurn.* 51(12)
C. Chappuis & C. Erard, 1973, *Bull. B.O.C.* 93
P.A. Clancey, 1973, *Durban Mus. Novit.* X(i)
B.A. Kazakov, 1973, *Zoologicheskij Zh.* 52(4)
P.A. Clancey, 1973, *Arnoldia* 6
A. Prigogine, 1973, *Rev. Zool. Bot. Afr.* 87(3)
P.A. Clancey, 1974, *Durban Mus. Novit.* IX(ii)
P.A. Clancey, 1974, *Durban Mus. Novit.* X(VII)
C. Erard, 1974, *Bull. B.O.C.* 94(1)
C. Erard, 1974, *Bonn Zool. Beitr.* 25(1–3)
Ford & Parker, 1974, *Emu* 74
C.H. Fry, K. Williamson & I.J. Ferguson Lees, 1974, *Ibis* 116(3)
L.G. Grimes, 1974, *Bull. B.O.C.* 94(3)

B.A. Kazokov, 1974, *Vestriik Zool.* 1974(2)
Kinsky, 1975, *Bull. B.O.C.* 95
C. Erard, 1978, *Bull. B.O.C. 98*
D.T. Holyoak & J-C Thibault, 1978, *Bull. B.O.C.* 98
D.B. Hanmer, 1979, *Bull. B.O.C.* 99

Subfamily MALURINAE

J.J. Morony Jr., W.J. Bock, & J. Farrand Jr., 1975, *Reference List of the Birds of the World* (Amer. Mus. Nat. Hist., New York)

R. Schodde, 1975, *Interim List of Australian Songbirds, Passerines* (R.A.O.U., Melbourne)

G.M. Mathews, 1930, *Syst. Avium Aust.* Pt. II (B.O.U., London)
W. Meise, 1931, *Novit. Zool.* 36
G. Mack, 1934, *Mem. Natn. Mus. Vict.* 8
G. Mack, 1936, *Mem. Natn. Mus. Vict.* 10
E. Mayr, 1937, *Amer. Mus. Novit.* 904
E. Mayr & Serventy, 1938, *Emu* 38
H.T. Condon, 1951, *S. Aust. Orn.* 20
A.J. Keast, 1957, *Proc. R. Zool. Soc. N.S.W.* 1955–6
A.J. Keast, 1957, *Aust. Journ. Zool.* 6
A.J. Keast, 1961, *Bull. Mus. Comp. Zool.* 123(8)
G.F. Mees, 1961, *Journ. Proc. R. Soc. West Aust.* 44
A.H. Miller, 1964, *Auk* 81(2)
J. Ford, 1966, *Emu* 66
J.C. Greenway, 1966, *Amer. Mus. Novit.* 2258
A.L. Rand & E.T. Gilliard, 1967, *Handbook of New Guinea Birds* (Weidenfeld & Nicholson, London)
N.J. Favaloro & McEvey, 1968, *Mem. Natn. Mus. Vict.* 28
H.T. Condon, 1969, *Mem. Qd. Mus.* 15
A.W. Diamond, 1969, *Amer. Mus. Novit.* 2362
J. Ford, 1969, *Emu* 68
J. Ford, 1970, *Emu* 70
E.T. Gilliard & Lecroy, 1970, *Amer. Mus. Novit.* 2420
A.R. McGill, 1970, *Australian Warblers* (B.O.C., Melbourne)
O.S.N.Z. 1970, *Annotated Checklist of the Birds of New Zealand* (Reed, Wellington)
A.W. Diamond, 1972, *Publ. Nuttall Orn. Cl.* 12
C.J.O. Harrison, 1972, *Bull. Brit. Mus. Nat. Hist. (Zool.)* 21
S. Parker, 1972, *Emu* 72
J. Ford & Parker, 1974, *Emu* 74

Subfamily MUSCICAPINAE/PLATYSTEIRINAE

C. Vaurie, 1953, *Bull. Amer. Mus. Nat. Hist.* 100(4)

J.J. Morony Jr., W.J. Bock, & J. Farrand Jr., 1975, *Reference List of the Birds of the World* (Amer. Mus. Nat. Hist., New York)

B. Rensch, 1929, *Journ. f. Orn. Erg.* II
A.L. Rand, 1936, *Bull. Amer. Mus. Nat. Hist.* 72
E. Stresemann, 1939–41, *Journ. f. Orn.* 87. 88. 89
J. Delacour & Jabouille, 1941, *L'Oiseau* 11
E. Mayr, 1941, *Amer. Mus. Novit.* 1133
E. Mayr, 1944, *Bull. Amer. Mus. Nat. Hist.* 83(2)
E. Mayr, 1945, *Birds of the Southwest Pacific* (Macmillan, New York)
H.G. Deignan, 1947, *Auk* 64
J. Delacour, 1947, *Birds of Malaya* (Macmillan, New York)
A.C.V. van Bemmell, 1948, *Treubia* 19
C.A. Fleming, 1950, *R.S.N.Z.* 78

J. Baker, 1951, *Univ. Kan. Pub. Mus. Nat. Hist.* 3
C. Vaurie, 1952, *Amer. Mus. Novit.* 1570
B.E. Smythies, 1953, *Birds of Burma* (Oliver & Boyd, Edinburgh)
G.P. Dementiev & Gladkov, 1954, *Birds of the Soviet Union* (Moscow)
C.W. Mackworth-Praed & C.H.B. Grant, 1955–70, *African Handbook of Birds* Ser. 1–3 (Longmans, London)
P.A. Clancey, 1957, *Ibis* 99
H.G. Deignan, 1957, *Ibis* 99
C. Vaurie, 1957, *Ibis* 99
A.J. Keast, 1958, *Rec. Aust. Mus.* XXIV/8
G.M. Storr, 1958, *Emu* 58
C. Vaurie, 1959, *Birds of the Palaearctic Fauna* I (Witherby, London)
B.E. Smythies, 1960, *Birds of Borneo* (Oliver & Boyd, Edinburgh)
S.D. Ripley, 1961, *Synopsis of the Birds of India and Pakistan* (Nat. Hist. Soc., Bombay)
I.C.J. Galbraith & E.H. Galbraith, 1962, *Bull. Brit. Mus. Nat. Hist.* 9
S.D. Ripley & Rabor, 1962, *Postilla* 1973
H.G. Deignan, 1963, *Bull. U.S. Nat. Mus.* 226
P.A. Clancey, 1966, *Ostrich* 37
W.J. Lawson, 1966, *Bull. B.O.C.* 86
E.T. Gilliard & Lecroy, 1967, *Bull. Amer. Mus. Nat. Hist.* 135(4)
A.L. Rand & E.T. Gilliard, 1967, *Handbook of New Guinea Birds* (Weidenfeld & Nicholson, London)
S.D. Ripley & Marshall, 1967, *Proc. Biol. Soc. Wash.* 80
H.R. Officer, 1969, *Australian Flycatchers* (B.O.C., Melbourne)
D. Amadon & J.E. Dupont, 1970, *Occ. Pap. Delaware Mus. N.H.* 1
A.D. Forbes-Watson, 1970, *Bull. B.O.C.* 90
B.P. Hall & R.E. Moreau, 1970, *Atlas of Speciation in African Passerine Birds* (Brit. Mus. Nat. Hist., London)
M.A. Traylor, 1970, *Bull. B.O.C.* 90
M.A. Traylor, 1970, *Ibis* 112
J.E. DuPont, 1971, *Nemouria* 3
J.E. DuPont, 1971, *Philippine Birds* (Mus. Nat. Hist., Greenville, Del.)
J. Ford, 1971, *Emu* 71
K.C. Parkes, 1971, *Nemouria* 4
P. Bruner, 1972, *Birds of French Polynesia* (Pac. Sci. Inf. Ctr., B.P. Bishop Mus., Hawaii)
A.W. Diamond, 1972, *Publ. Nuttall Orn. Cl.* 12
K.C. Parkes, 1973, *Emu* 73
R. Schodde, 1975, *Interim List of Australian Songbirds, Passerines* (R.A.O.U., Melbourne)
P.A. Clancey, 1976, *Bull. B.O.C.* 96

Subfamily MONARCHINAE/RHIPIDURINAE

J.J. Morony Jr., W.J. Bock, & J. Farrand Jr., 1975, *Reference List of the Birds of the World* (Amer. Mus. Nat. Hist., New York)

G.M. Mathews, 1930, *Syst. Avium Aust.* Pt. II (B.O.U., London)
J. Delacour & Jabouille, 1941, *L'Oiseau* 11
E. Mayr & Moynihan, 1946, *Amer. Mus. Novit.* 1321
C.G. Sibley, 1946, *Condor* 46
A.C.V. van Bemmell, 1948, *Treubia* 19
C. Vaurie, 1951, *Bull. B.O.C.* 71
E. Mayr, 1955, *Amer. Mus. Novit.* 1707
A.J. Cain & I.C.J. Galbraith, 1956, *Ibis* 98
A.J. Keast, 1958, *Rec. Aust. Mus.* XXIV/8
K.C. Parkes, 1958, *Amer. Mus. Novit.* 1891
F. Salomonsen, 1964, *Noona Dan Papers* 9
G.F. Mees, 1965, *Zool.* 31
A.W. Diamond, 1967, *Amer. Mus. Novit.* 2284
A.L. Rand & E.T. Gilliard, 1967, *Handbook of New Guinea Birds* (Weidenfeld & Nicholson, London)

R. Schodde & Hitchcock, 1968, *Div. Wildlife Res. Tech. Pap.* 13
A.L. Rand & Rabor, 1969, *Fieldiana Zool.* 51
A.L. Rand, 1970, *Nat. Hist. Bull. Siam Soc.* 23
J.R. Ford, 1971, *Emu* 71
A.W. Diamond, 1972, *Publ. Nuttall Orn. Cl.* 12
G.F. Mees, 1973, *Zool. Meded* 46 (12)
R. Schodde, 1975, *Interim List of Australian Songbirds, Passerines* (R.A.O.U., Melbourne)

Subfamily PACHYCEPHALINAE

E, Mayr, 1967, J.L. Peters *Checklist of the Birds of the World* XII (Mus. Comp. Zool., Cambridge, Mass.)

B. Rensch, 1929, *Journ. f. Orn.* Erg. II
E. Mayr, 1941, 'List of New Guinea Birds', *Amer. Mus. Nat. Hist.* 82
A.L. Rand, 1941, *Amer. Mus. Novit.* 1102
P.J. Oliver, 1945, *Emu* 45
E. Mayr, 1953, *Emu* 53
E. Mayr, 1954, *Amer. Mus. Novit.* 1653
E. Mayr & E.T. Gilliard, 1954, *Bull. Amer. Mus. Nat. Hist.* 103
E. Mayr, 1955, *Amer. Mus. Novit.* 1707
I.C.J. Galbraith, 1956, *Bull. Brit. Mus. Nat. Hist.* 4/4
J.C. Greenway, 1966, *Amer. Mus. Novit.* 2258
K.C. Parkes, 1966, *Bull. B.O.C.* 86
Galbraith, 1967, *Emu* 66
A.L. Rand & E.T. Gilliard, 1967, *Handbook of New Guinea Birds* (Weidenfeld & Nicholson, London)
J. Ford, 1971, *Emu* 71
A.W. Diamond, 1972, *Publ. Nuttall Orn. Cl.* 12
R. Schodde, 1975, *Interim List of Australian Songbirds, Passerines* (R.A.O.U., Melbourne)

Family **CERTHIIDAE**

J.C. Greenway, 1967, in J.L. Peters *Checklist of the Birds of the World* XII

C. Vaurie, 1950, *Amer. Mus. Novit.,* 1472
C. Vaurie, 1959, *Birds of the Palaearctic Fauna* I (Witherby, London)
S.D. Ripley, 1961, *Synopsis of the Birds of India and Pakistan* (Nat. Hist. Soc., Bombay)
C.M.N. White, 1963, *Revised Checklist of African Flycatchers etc.* (Govt. Printer, Lusaka)
A.R. Phillips, 1966, *Bull. B.O.C.* 86
E.R. Blake, 1972, *Birds of Mexico* (Chicago University Press, Chicago)
P.A. Clancey, 1975, *Durban Mus. Novit.* X

Family **RHABDORNITHIDAE**

J.C. Greenway, 1967, in J.L. Peters *Checklist of the Birds of the World* XII

J. Delacour & Mayr, 1946, *Birds of the Philippines* (Macmillan, New York)
J.E. DuPont, 1971, *Philippine Birds* (Mus. Nat. Hist., Greenville, Del.)
K.C. Parkes, 1973, *Nemouria* 11

Family **CLIMACTERIDAE**

J.C. Greenway, 1967, in J.L. Peters *Checklist of the Birds of the World* XII

A.J. Keast, 1957, *Aust. Journ. Zool.* 5
A.J. Keast, 1961, *Bull. Mus. Comp. Zool Harvard* 123
J.D. Macdonald, 1966, *Emu* 66
Harrison, 1970, *Emu,* 70
J. Ford, 1971, *Emu* 71
R. Schodde, 1975, *Interim List of Australian Songbirds, Passerines* (R.A.O.U., Melbourne)

Family **SITTIDAE**

J.C. Greenway, 1967, in J.L. Peters *Checklist of the Birds of the World* XII

E. Mayr, 1950, *Emu* 49
C. Vaurie, 1957, *Amer. Mus. Novit.* 1854
S.D. Ripley, 1959, *Postilla* 42
Löhrl, 1960, *Journ. f. Orn.* 101
A.L. Rand, 1960, *Fieldiana Zool.* 35
J.D. Macdonald, 1969, *Emu* 69
J. Ford & Parker, 1974, *Emu* 74
R. Schodde, 1975, *Interim List of Australian Songbirds, Passerines* (R.A.O.U., Melbourne)
Vieilliard, 1976, *Alauda* 44

Family **AEGITHALIDAE**

D.W. Snow, 1967, in J.L. Peters *Checklist of the Birds of the World* XII

C. Vaurie, 1957, *Amer. Mus. Novit.* 1853
C. Vaurie, 1959, *Birds of the Palaearctic Fauna* I (Witherby, London)
E.R. Blake, 1972, *Birds of Mexico* (Chicago University Press, Chicago)
E. Eisenmann, *et al*, 1973, *Auk* 90

Family **REMIZIDAE**

D.W. Snow, 1967, in J.L. Peters *Checklist of the Birds of the World* XII

C. Vaurie, 1957, *Amer. Mus. Novit.* 1853
C. Vaurie, 1959, *Birds of the Palaearctic Fauna* I (Witherby, London)
C.M.N. White, 1963, *Revised Checklist of African Flycatchers etc.* (Govt. Printer, Lusaka)

Family **PARIDAE**

D.W. Snow, 1967 in J.L. Peters *Checklist of the Birds of the World* XII

C. Vaurie, 1956, *Amer. Mus. Novit.* 1833
C. Vaurie & Snow, 1957, *Amer. Mus. Novit.* 1852
K.C. Parkes, 1958, *Proc. Biol. Soc. Wash.* 71
C. Vaurie, 1959, *Birds of the Palaearctic Fauna* I (Witherby, London)
C.M.N. White, 1963, *Revised Checklist of African Flycatchers etc.* (Govt. Printer, Lusaka)
P.A. Clancey, 1964, *Durban Mus. Novit.* 7
Kniprath, 1967, *Journ. f. Orn.* 108
B.P. Hall & R.E. Moreau, 1970, *Atlas of Speciation in African Passerine Birds* (Brit. Mus. Nat. Hist., London)
Martens, 1971, *Journ. f. Orn.* 112
K.C. Parkes, 1971, *Nemouria* 4
E.R. Blake, 1972, *Birds of Mexico* (Chicago University Press, Chicago)
P.A. Clancey, 1972, *Durban Mus. Novit.* 9
L.S. Stepanyan, 1974, *By. Mosk. Ob. Isp. Priv.* 99(6)

Family **DICAEIDAE**

F. Salomonsen, 1967, in J.L. Peters *Checklist of the Birds of the World* XII

B. Rensch, 1931, *Mitt. Zool. Mus. Berlin* 17
K.A. Hindwood & Mayr, 1946, *Emu* 46
E. Mayr & Amadon, 1947, *Amer. Mus. Novit.* 1360
F. Salomonsen, 1960, *Amer. Mus. Novit.* 1960, 1990/1, 2016
F. Salomonsen, 1961, *Amer. Mus. Novit.* 2057, 2067, 2068
G.F. Mees, 1965, *Emu* 65
C.J.O. Harrison & S.A. Parker, 1966, *Bull. B.O.C.* 86
S.D. Ripley & Rabor, 1966, *Proc. Biol. Soc. Wash.* 79

E.T. Gilliard & Lecroy, 1967, *Bull. Amer. Mus. Nat. Hist.* 135(4)
A.L. Rand & E.T. Gilliard, 1967, *Handbook of New Guinea Birds* (Weidenfeld & Nicholson, London)
J.D. Macdonald, 1969, *Emu* 69
A.L. Rand & Rabor, 1969, *Fieldiana Zool.* 51
J.E. DuPont, 1971, *Philippine Birds* (Mus. Nat. Hist., Greenville, Del.)
K.C. Parkes, 1971, *Nemouria* 4
R. Schodde, 1975, *Interim List of Australian Songbirds, Passerines* (R.A.O.U., Melbourne)

Family **NECTARINIIDAE**

A. L. Rand, 1967, in J.L. Peters *Checklist of the Birds of the World* XII

J. Delacour, 1944, *Zoologica (N.Y.)* 39
C.W. Mackworth-Praed & C.H.B. Grant, 1955–70, *African Handbook of Birds* Ser. 1–3 (Longmans, London)
H.G. Deignan, 1961, *Bull. U.S. Nat. Mus.* 221
S.D. Ripley, 1961, *Synopsis of the Birds of India and Pakistan* (Nat. Hist. Soc., Bombay)
C.M.N. White, 1963, *Revised Checklist of African Flycatchers etc.* (Govt. Printer, Lusaka)
G.F. Mees, 1966, *Zool. Meded* 41
E.T. Gilliard & Lecroy, 1967, *Bull. Amer. Mus. Nat. Hist.* 135(4)
A.L. Rand & E.T. Gilliard, 1967, *A Handbook of New Guinea Birds* (Weidenfeld & Nicholson, London)
P.A. Clancey, 1970, *Durban Mus. Novit.* VIII, IX
B.P. Hall & R.E. Moreau, 1970, *Atlas of Speciation in African Passerine Birds* (Brit. Mus. Nat. Hist., London)
J.E. DuPont, 1971, *Nemouria* 3
K.C. Parkes, 1971, *Nemouria* 4
P.A. Clancey, 1973, *Durban Mus. Novit.* X
P.A. Clancey, 1975, *Durban Mus. Novit.* XI

Family **ZOSTEROPIDAE**

E. Mayr & R.E. Moreau, 1967, in J.L. Peters *Checklist of the Birds of the World* XII

E. Mayr, 1945, *Birds of the Southwest Pacific* (Macmillan, New York)
J. Delacour & Mayr, 1946, *Birds of the Philippines* (Macmillan, New York)
R.E. Moreau, 1953, *Bull. B.O.C.* 73
G.F. Mees, 1957, *Zool. Verh. Rijksmus. Nat. Hist. Leiden* 35
R.E. Moreau, 1957, *Bull. Brit. Mus. Nat. Hist. (Zool.)*
T.H. Cheng, 1958, *Distributional List of Chinese Birds* Pt. II (Acad. Sin., Peking)
T. Mishima, 1959, *Tori* 15
G.F. Mees, 1961, *Zool. Verh. Rijksmus. Nat. Hist. Leiden* 50
S.D. Ripley, 1961, *Synopsis of the Birds of India and Pakistan* (Nat. Hist. Soc., Bombay)
C.M.N. White, 1963, *Revised Checklist of African Flycatchers etc.* (Govt. Printer, Lusaka)
E. Mayr, 1965, *Breviora Mus. Comp. Zool. Harvard* 228
P.A. Clancey, 1966, *Durban Mus. Novit.* VII
R.W. Storer & Gill, 1966, *Occ. Pap. Mus. Zool. Univ. Michigan* 648
A.L. Rand & E.T. Gilliard, 1967, *Handbook of New Guinea Birds* (Weidenfeld & Nicholson, London)
G.F. Mees, 1969, *Zool. Verh. Rijksmus. Nat. Hist. Leiden* 102
J.E. DuPont, 1971, *Nemouria* 3
K.C. Parkes, 1971, *Nemouria* 4
G.M. Storr, 1973, *List of Queensland Birds* (Spec. Publs. W. Aust. Mus.)

Family **MELIPHAGIDAE**

F. Salomonsen, 1967, in J.L. Peters *Checklist of the Birds of the World* XII

E. Mayr, 1944, *Bull. Amer. Mus. Nat. Hist.* 83
E. Mayr & E.T. Gilliard, 1954, *Bull. Amer. Mus. Nat. Hist.* 103

E. Mayr, 1955, *Amer. Mus. Novit.* 1707
E.T. Gilliard, 1959, *Amer. Mus. Novit.* 1959
D.L. Serventy & H.M. Whittell, 1962, *Birds of Western Australia* 3rd edn. (Lamb Publs., Perth)
H.R. Officer, 1964, *Australian Honeyeaters* (R.A.O.U., Melbourne)
D.M. Skead, 1964, *Ostrich* 35
F. Salomonsen, 1966, *Breviora Mus. Comp. Zool. Harvard* 254
A.W. Diamond, 1967, *Amer. Mus. Novit.* 2284
A.L. Rand & E.T. Gilliard, 1967, *Handbook of New Guinea Birds* (Weidenfeld & Nicholson, London)
A.W. Diamond, 1969, *Amer. Mus. Novit.* 2362
A.L. Rand & Rabor, 1969, *Fieldiana Zool.* 51
A.W. Diamond, 1971, *Condor* 73
J. Ford, 1971, *Emu* 71
S. Parker, 1971, *Emu* 71
S. Parker, 1971, *Sunbird* 2
A.W. Diamond, 1972, *Publ. Nuttall Orn. Cl.* 12
F.H.J. Crome, 1973, *Emu* 73
R. Schodde, 1975, *Interim List of Australian Songbirds, Passerines* (R.A.O.U., Melbourne)

Subfamily EMBERIZINAE/CARDINALINAE

R.A. Paynter, 1970, in J.L. Peters *Checklist of the Birds of the World* XIII (Mus. Comp. Zool., Cambridge, Mass.)

D. Lack, 1947, *Darwin's Finches* (Cambridge University Press)
R. Meyer de Schauensee, 1952, *Proc. Acad. Nat. Sci., Phil.* 104
K.C. Parkes, 1954, *Condor* 56
A.L. Rand, 1955, *Fieldiana Zool. (Chicago)* 37
R.W. Storer, 1955, *Condor* 57
C. Vaurie, 1956, *Amer. Mus. Novit.* 1795
M. Koepcke, 1957, *Scientia* 4
T.H. Cheng, 1958, *Distributional List of Chinese Birds* Pt. II (Acad. Sin., Peking)
C. Vaurie, 1959, *Birds of the Palaearctic Fauna* I (Witherby, London)
J.D. Webster, 1959, *Condor* 61
D.M. Skead, et al, 1960, *Canaries, Seedeaters and Buntings of South* Africa (S.A. Bird Book Fund, Johannesburg)
K.H. Voous, 1960, *Atlas of European Birds* (Nelson, London)
S.D. Ripley, 1961, *Synopsis of the Birds of India and Pakistan* (Nat. Hist. Soc., Bombay)
W.H. Phelps & Phelps, 1963, *Bol. Soc. Venez. Cienc. Nat.* 24
C.M.N. White, 1963, *Revised Checklist of African Flycatchers etc.* (Govt. Printer, Lusaka)
P.A. Clancey, 1964, *Bull. B.O.C.* 84
R. Meyer de Schauensee, 1964, *Birds of Colombia* (Livingston, Narberth, Penn.)
R.A. Paynter, 1964, *Condor* 66
A.R. Phillips, J. Marshall, & G. Monson, 1964, *Birds of Arizona* (University of Arizona, Tucson)
P.A. Clancey, 1965, *Ostrich* 36
W.E. Godfrey, 1965, *Auk* 82
P.A. Clancey, 1966, *Durban Mus. Novit.* VII
R. Meyer de Schauensee, 1966, *The Species of Birds of South America* (Acad. Nat. Sci., Philadelphia)
R.W. Dickerman & Phillips, 1967, *Condor* 69
R.A. Paynter, 1967, *Breviora Mus. Comp. Zool. Harvard* 278
J.C. Bent, et al, 1968, *Bull. Amer. Mus. Nat. Hist.* 237
L.L. Short, 1969, *Wilson Bull.* 81
R. Meyer de Schauensee, 1970, *Notulae Naturae* 428
E.R. Blake, 1972, *Birds of Mexico* (Chicago University Press, Chicago)
Johnson & Brush, 1972, *Syst. Zool.* 21
Martins, 1972, *Bonn. Zool. Beitr.* 23
B. Matousek, 1972, *Annotationes Zool. bot. Bratislava* 82
B. Matousek, 1973, *Zbornik slov. narod. Mus.* 17(1)
K.C. Parkes, 1974, *Wilson Bull.* 86(3)

L.L. Short, 1974, *Bull. Amer. Mus. Nat. Hist.* 154
P.R. Colston, 1978, *Bull. B.O.C.* 98

Subfamily THRAUPINAE/CATAMBLYRHNCHINAE/TERSINAE

R.W. Storer, 1970, in J.L. Peters *Checklist of the Birds of the World* XIII

J.T. Zimmer, 1942, *Amer. Mus. Novit.* 1193
J.T. Zimmer, 1943, *Amer. Mus. Novit.* 1225
J.T. Zimmer, 1944, *Amer. Mus. Novit.* 1262
J. Bond, 1947, *Auk* 64
J.T. Zimmer, 1947, *Amer. Mus. Novit.* 1367
E. Eisenmann, 1955, *Trans. Lin. Soc. N.Y.* 7
J. Bond, 1956, *Checklist of Birds of the West Indies* 4th edn. (Acad. Nat. Sci., Philadelphia)
E. Eisenmann, 1957, *Condor* 59
Novaes, 1959, *Bol. Mus. Goeldi* 22
W.H. Phelps & Phelps, 1964, *Bol. Soc. Venez. Cienc. Nat.* 24
R. Meyer de Schauensee, 1964, *Birds of Colombia* (Livingston, Narberth, Penn.)
R. Meyer de Schauensee, 1966, *The Species of Birds of South America* (Acad. Nat. Sci., Philadelphia)
A.R. Phillips, 1966, *Bull. B.O.C.* 86
A.W. Johnson, 1967, *Birds of Chile* 2
E. Mayr & Phelps, 1967, *Bull. Amer. Mus. Nat. Hist.* 136
F. Haverschmidt, 1968, *List of the Birds of Surinam* (Oliver & Boyd, Edinburgh)
K.C. Parkes, 1969, *Bull. B.O.C.* 89
K.C. Parkes, 1969, *Auk* 86
R.W. Storer, 1969, *Living Bird* 8
E.R. Blake & Hocking, 1974, *Wilson Bull.* 86(4)
J.S. Weske, 1974, *Wilson Bull.* 86(2)
J.S. Weske & J.W. Terborgh, 1974, *Wilson Bull.* 86(2)
K.C. Parkes, 1977, *Bull. B.O.C.* 97
R. Meyer de Schauensee & W.H. Phelps, 1978, *Birds of Venezuela* (Princeton University Press, Princeton)

Family **PARULIDAE**

G.H. Lowery & B.L. Monroe, 1968, in J.L. Peters *Checklist of the Birds of the World* XIV (Mus. Comp. Zool., Cambridge, Mass.)

R. Meyer de Schauensee, 1946, *Notulae Naturae* 167
J.T. Zimmer, 1949, *Amer. Mus. Novit.* 1428
J.C. Bent, 1953, *Bull. U.S. Nat. Mus.* 203
A.O.U., 1957, *Checklist of North American Birds* (A.O.U., Baltimore)
L. Griscom & A. Sprunt Jr. (eds.), 1957, *Warblers of North America* (Devin-Adair, New York)
J. Bond, 1961, *Birds of the West Indies* (Collins, London)
K.C. Parkes, 1961, *Wilson Bull.* 73
J.D. Webster, 1961, *Auk* 78
E. Eisenmann, 1962, *Auk* 79
George, 1962, *Amer. Mus. Novit.* 2103
A.F. Skutch, 1962, *Condor* 64
J.D. Webster, 1962, *Wilson Bull.* 74
W.H. Phelps & Phelps, 1963, *Bol. Soc. Venez. Cienc. Nat.* 24
R. Meyer de Schauensee, 1964, *Birds of Colombia* (Livingston, Narberth, Penn.)
R. Meyer de Schauensee, 1966, *The Species of Birds of South America* (Acad. Nat. Sci., Philadelphia)
J. Bond, 1967, *Checklist of Birds of the West Indies* Suppl. 12 (Acad. Nat. Sci., Philadelphia)
R.W. Storer, 1967, in J.L. Peters *Checklist of the Birds of the World* XIII
Orr & J.D. Webster, 1968, *Proc. Biol. Soc. Wash.* 81
C.G. Sibley, 1968, *Postilla* 125
R.W. Dickerman, 1970, *Condor* 72

E.R. Blake, 1972, *Birds of Mexico* (Chicago University Press, Chicago)
A.W. Johnson & W.R. Millie, 1972, *Supplement to The Birds of Chile* p. 6. Platt Est. Graf., Buenos Aires
C.B. Kepler & K.C. Parkes, 1972, *Auk* 89
S.L. Olsen, 1975, *Bull. B.O.C.* 95
R. Meyer de Schauensee & W.H. Phelps, 1978, *Birds of Venezuela* (Princeton University Press, Princeton)

Family **DREPANIDIDAE**

G.C. Munro, 1944, *Birds of Hawaii*

G.C. Munro, 1945, *Elepaio (Journ. Honolulu Audubon Soc.)* 5
D. Amadon, 1950, *Bull. Amer. Mus. Nat. Hist.* 95
J.C. Greenway, 1968, in J.L. Peters *Checklist of the Birds of the World* XIV
T.L.C. Casey & J.D. Jacobi, 1974, *Occ. Pap. Bernice P. Bishop Mus.* 24
W.J. Bock, 1977, *Ibis* 120

Family **VIREONIDAE**

E.R. Blake, 1968, in J.L. Peters *Checklist of the Birds of the World* XIV

J. Bond, 1953, *Notulae Naturae* 255
A.F. Skutch, 1960, *Pacific Coast Avifauna* 34
J. Bond, 1961, *Caribbean Journ. Sci.* 1
T.H. Hamilton, 1962, *Wilson Bull.* 70
W.H. Phelps & Phelps, 1963, *Bol. Soc. Venez. Cienc. Nat.* 24
R. Meyer de Schauensee, 1964, *Birds of Colombia* (Livingston, Narberth, Penn.)
R. Meyer de Schauensee, 1966, *The Species of Birds of South America* (Acad. Nat. Sci., Philadelphia)
O.H. Garrido, 1971, *Poeyana* 81
E.R. Blake, 1972, *Birds of Mexico* (Chicago University Press, Chicago)
O.H. Garrido, 1973, *Poeyana* 119
G.F. Mees, 1974, *Zool. Meded. Leiden* 48(7)

Family **ICTERIDAE**

E.R. Blake, 1968, in J.L. Peters *Checklist of he Birds of the World* XIV

E. Eisenmann, 1955, 'The Species of Middle American Birds , *Trans. Lin. Soc., N.Y.* 7
J.C. Bent, 1958, *Bull. U.S. Nat. Mus.* 211
W.H. Phelps & Phelps, 1963, *Bol. Soc. Venez. Cienc. Nat.* 24
R. Meyer de Schauensee, 1964, *Birds of Colombia* (Livingston, Narberth, Penn.)
K.C. Parkes & Blake, 1965, *Fieldiana Zool. (Chicago)* 44
R. Meyer de Schauensee, 1966, *The Species of Birds of South America* (Acad. Nat. Sci., Philadelphia)
L.L. Short, 1968, Amer. Mus. Novit. 2349
L.L. Short, 1969, *Occ. Pap. Mus. Zool. La. State Univ.* 36
R.W. Dickerman & Phillips, 1970, *Condor* 72
O.H. Garrido, 1970, *Poeyana* 68
Markham, 1971, *Ann. Inst. Patagonia* 2
R.W. Dickerman, 1974, *Amer. Mus. Novit.* 2538

Family **FRINGILLIDAE**

E. Mayr, 1968, in J.L. Peters *Checklist of the Birds of the World* XIV

K.H. Voous, 1949, *Condor* 51
C. Vaurie, 1956, *Amer. Mus. Novit.* 1775, 1786, 1788
T.H. Cheng, 1958, *Distributional List of Chinese Birds* Pt. II Passeriformes (Acad. Sin., Peking)
J. Nicolai, 1959, *Zool. Jahrb. Abt. Syst.* 87
C. Vaurie, 1959, *Birds of the Palaearctic Fauna* I Passeriformes (Witherby, London)

D.M. Skead, *et al*, 1960, *Canaries, Seedeaters & Buntings of South Africa* (S.A. Bird Book Fund, Johannesburg)
S.D. Ripley & Rabor, 1961, *Postilla* 50
S.D. Ripley, 1961, *Synopsis of the Birds of India and Pakistan* (Nat. Hist. Soc., Bombay)
B.P. Hall & R.E. Moreau, 1962, *Bull. Brit. Mus. Nat. Hist. Zool.* 8
D. Amadon, 1965, *Ibis* 107
P.A. Clancey, 1966, *Durban Mus. Novit.* VII
R. Meyer de Schauensee, 1966, *The Species of Birds of South America* (Acad. Nat. Sci., Philadelphia)
Ackermann, 1967, *Journ. f. Orn.* 108
H.E. Wolters, 1967, *Bonn. Zool. Beitr.* 18
T.R. Howell, R.A. Paynter, & A.L. Rand, 1968, in J.L. Peters *Checklist of the Birds of the World* XII
A.L. Rand, 1968, *Fieldiana Zool. (Chicago)* 50
B.P. Hall & R.E. Moreau, 1970, *Atlas of Speciation in African Passerine Birds* (Brit. Mus. Nat. Hist., London)
E.R. Blake, 1972, *Birds of Mexico* (Chicago University Press, Chicago)
M.A. Traylor, 1972, *Bull. B.O.C.* 90
A.G. Knox, 1976, *Bull. B.O.C.* 96
K.H. Voous, 1977, *Ibis* 119
J.S. Ash, 1979, *Ibis* 121

Family **ESTRILDIDAE**

E. Mayr, R.A. Paynter, & M.A. Traylor, 1968, in J.L. Peters *Checklist of the Birds of the World* XIV

S.D. Ripley, 1961, *Synopsis of the Birds of India and Pakistan* (Nat. Hist. Soc., Bombay)
C.M.N. White, 1963, Revised Checklist of African Flycatchers etc. (Govt. Printer, Lusaka)
K. Immelman, 1965, *Australian Finches* (Angus & Robertson, Sydney)
H.E. Wolters, 1966, *Ostrich* Suppl. 6
A.L. Rand & E.T. Gilliard, 1967, *Handbook of New Guinea Birds* (Weidenfeld & Nicholson, London)
Zisweiler, 1967, *Zool. Jahrb. Abt. Syst.* 94
E. Mayr, 1968, *Breviora Mus. Comp. Zool. Harvard* 287
P.A. Clancey, 1969, *Durban Mus. Novit.* VIII
Hald Mortensen, 1970, *Dansk Orn. Foren. Tids. skr.* 64
B.P. Hall & R.E. Moreau, 1970, *Atlas of Speciation in African Passerine Birds* (Brit. Mus. Nat. Hist., London)
P.A. Clancey, 1971, *Durban Mus. Novit.* IX
J.E. DuPont, 1972, *Wilson Bull.* 84
H.E. Wolters, 1972, *Bonn. Zool. Beitr.* 23
Zisweiler, Guttinger, & Bregulla, 1972, *Bonn. Zool. Monogr.* 12
P.A. Clancey, 1974, *Arnoldia* 6(28)

Family **PLOCEIDAE**

M.A. Traylor, J.C. Greenway, & R.E. Moreau, 1962/8, in J.L. Peters *Checklist of the Birds of the World* XIV, XV

A.L. Rand, 1936, *Bull. Amer. Mus. Nat. Hist.* 72
T.H. Cheng, 1958, *Distributional List of Chinese Birds* Pt. II (Acad. Sin., Peking)
C. Vaurie, 1959, *Birds of the Palaearctic Fauna* I. Passeriformes (Witherby, London)
R.E. Moreau, 1960, *Ibis* 102
S.D. Ripley, 1961, *Synopsis of the Birds of India and Pakistan* (Nat. Hist. Soc., Bombay)
C.M.N. White, 1963, *Revised Checklist of African Flycatchers etc.* (Govt. Printer, Lusaka)
J. Nicolai, 1967, *Journ. f. Orn.* 108
R.B. Payne, 1968, *Bull. B.O.C.* 88
P.A. Clancey, 1970, *Durban Mus. Novit.* VIII
B.P. Hall & R.E. Moreau, 1970, *Atlas of Speciation in African Passerine Birds* (Brit. Mus. Nat. Hist., London)

P.A. Clancey, 1972, *Durban Mus. Novit.* IX
J. Nicolai, 1972, *Journ. f. Orn.* 113
J.C. Benson, *et al.* 1973, *Birds of Zambia* (Collins, London)
R.B. Payne, 1973, *Ornithological Monograms* 11 (A.O.U.)
P.A. Clancey, 1974, *Durban Mus. Novit.* X
H.E. Wolters, 1974, *Bonn. Zool. Beitr.* 25(4)

Family **STURNIDAE**

D. Amadon, 1962, in J.L. Peters *Checklist of the Birds of the World* XV (Mus. Comp. Zool. Cambridge, Mass.)

S.B. Wilson, 1907, *Ibis* 3
E. Mayr, 1945, *Birds of the Southwest Pacific* (Macmillan, New York)
J. Delacour, 1974, *Birds of Malaysia* (Hamilton, New York)
B.E. Smythies, 1953, *Birds of Burma* (Oliver & Boyd, Edinburgh)
D. Amadon, 1956, *Amer. Mus. Novit.* 1803
T.H. Cheng, 1958, *Distributional List of Chinese Birds* Pt. II (Acad. Sin., Peking)
C. Vaurie, 1959, *Birds of the Palaearctic Fauna* I. Passerines (Witherby, London)
S.D. Ripley, 1961, *Synopsis of the Birds of India and Pakistan* (Nat. Hist. Soc., Bombay)
C.M.N. White, 1962, *Revised Checklist of African Shrikes etc.* (Govt. Printer, Lusaka)
A.L. Rand & E.T. Gilliard, 1967, *Handbook of New Guinea Birds* (Weidenfeld & Nicholson, London)
J.E. DuPont, 1971, *Philippine Birds* (Mus. Nat. Hist., Greenville, Del.)
P.A. Clancey, 1973, *Durban Mus. Novit.* IX
Brooke, 1976, *Bull. B.O.C.* 96
P.A. Clancey, 1976, *Bull. B.O.C.* 96

Family **ORIOLIDAE**

J.C. Greenway, 1962, in J.L. Peters *Checklist of the Birds of the World* XV

A.J. Keast, 1956, *Proc. R. Soc. N.S.W.* 1954/5
T.H. Cheng, 1958, *Distributional List of Chinese Birds* Pt. II (Acad. Sin., Peking)
S.D. Ripley, 1961, *Synopsis of the Birds of India and Pakistan* (Nat. Hist. Soc., Bombay)
H.G. Deignan, 1963, *Checklist of the Birds of Thailand* (Smiths. Inst., Washington)
A.L. Rand & E.T. Gilliard, 1967, *Handbook of New Guinea Birds* (Weidenfeld & Nicholson, London)
W.J. Lawson, 1969, *Bull. B.O.C.* 89
Wolters & Clancey, 1969, *Bull. B.O.C.* 89
B.P. Hall & R.E. Moreau, 1970, *Atlas of Speciation in African Passerine Birds* (Brit. Mus. Nat. Hist., London)
K.C. Parkes, 1971, *Nemouria* 4
J. Ford, 1975, *Emu* 75

Family **DICRURIDAE**

C. Vaurie, 1962, in J.L. Peters *Checklist of the Birds of the World* XV

C. Vaurie, 1958, *Amer. Mus. Novit.* 1869

Family **CALLAEIDAE**

D. Amadon, 1962, in J.L. Peters *Checklist of the Birds of the World* XV

O.S.N.Z., 1970, *Annotated Checklist of the Birds of New Zealand* (Reed, Wellington)

Family **GRALLINIDAE**

E. Mayr, 1962, in J.L. Peters *Checklist of the Birds of the World* XV

D. Amadon, 1950, *Emu* 50

A.L. Rand & E.T. Gilliard, 1967, *Handbook of New Guinea Birds* (Weidenfeld & Nicholson, London)
R. Schodde, 1975, *Interim List of Australian Songbirds, Passerines* (R.A.O.U., Melbourne)

Family **ARTAMIDAE**

E. Mayr, 1962, in J.L. Peters *Checklist of the Birds of the World* XV

T.H. Cheng, 1958, *Distributional List of Chinese Birds* Pt. II (Acad. Sin., Peking)
A.J. Keast, 1958, *Emu* 58
A.L. Rand & E.T. Gilliard, 1967, *Handbook of New Guinea Birds* (Weidenfeld & Nicholson, London)
R. Schodde, 1975, *Interim List of Australian Songbirds, Passerines* (R.A.O.U., Melbourne)

Family **CRACTICIDAE**

D. Amadon, 1962, in J.L. Peters *Checklist of the Birds of the World* XV

D. Amadon, 1951, *Amer. Mus. Novit.* 1504
A.L. Rand & E.T. Gilliard, 1967, *Handbook of New Guinea Birds* (Weidenfeld & Nicholson, London)
O.S.N.Z., 1970, *Annotated Checklist of the Birds of New Zealand* (Reed, Wellington)
G.M. Storr, 1973, *Spec. Publs. West. Aust. Mus.* 5
R. Schodde, 1975, *Interim List of Australian Songbirds, Passerines* (R.A.O.U., Melbourne)

Family **PTILINORHYNCHIDAE**

W.J. Cooper & J.M. Forshaw, 1977, *Birds of Paradise and Bowerbirds* (Collins, London)

E. Mayr & Jennings, 1952, *Amer. Mus. Novit.* 1602
A.J. Marshall, 1954, *Bowerbirds: their Displays and Breeding Cycles* (Oxford University Press)
E. Mayr, 1962, in J.L. Peters *Checklist of the Birds of the World* XV
W.J. Bock, 1963, *Condor* 65
A.L. Rand & E.T. Gilliard, 1967, *Handbook of New Guinea Birds* (Weidenfeld & Nicholson, London)
E.T. Gilliard, 1969, *Birds of Paradise and Bowerbirds* (Weidenfeld & Nicholson, London)
R. Schodde & McKean, 1973, *Emu* 73

Family **PARADISAEIDAE**

W.J. Cooper & J.M. Forshaw, 1977, *Birds of Paradise and Bowerbirds* (Collins, London)

E. Mayr, 1962, in J.L. Peters *Checklist of the Birds of the World* XV
W.J. Bock, 1963, *Condor* 65
A.L. Rand & E.T. Gilliard, 1967, *Handbook of New Guinea Birds* (Weidenfeld & Nicholson, London)
A.W. Diamond, 1969, *Amer. Mus. Novit.* 2362
E.T. Gilliard, 1969, *Birds of Paradise and Bowerbirds* (Weidenfeld & Nicholson, London)
A.W. Diamond, 1972, *Publ. Nuttall Orn. Cl.* 12
R. Schodde & McKean, 1972, *Emu* 72
R. Schodde & McKean, 1973, *Emu* 73

Family **CORVIDAE**

C. Vaurie & Blake, 1962, in J.L. Peters *Checklist of the Birds of the World* XV
D. Goodwin, 1976, *Crows of the World* (Brit. Mus. Nat. Hist., London)

E. Mayr, 1944, *Bull. Amer. Mus. Nat. Hist.* 83

E. Mayr, 1945, *Birds of the Southwest Pacific* (Macmillan, New York)
J. Dorst, 1947, *Ois. Rev. Fr. Orn.* 17
G.P. Dementiev & Gladkov, 1954, *Birds of the Soviet Union* (Moscow)
C. Vaurie, 1954, *Amer. Mus. Novit.* 1668
L.I. Davis, 1958, *Wilson Bull.* 70
R.K. Selander & D.R. Giller, 1959, *Condor* 61
C. Vaurie, 1959, *Birds of the Palaearctic Fauna* I. Passerines (Witherby, London)
S.D. Ripley, 1961, *Synopsis of the Birds of India and Pakistan* (Nat. Hist. Soc., Bombay)
C.M.N. White, 1963, *Revised Checklist of African Shrikes etc.* (Govt. Printer, Lusaka)
R. Meyer de Schauensee, 1966, *The Species of Birds of South America* (Acad. Nat. Sci., Philadelphia)
E.T. Gilliard & Lecroy, 1967, *Bull. Amer. Mus. Nat. Hist.* 135
I. Rowley, 1967, *Emu* 67
J.W. Hardy, 1969, *Condor* 71
I. Rowley, 1970, *CSIRO Wildlife Res.* 15
J. Bond, 1971, *Birds of the West Indies* (Collins, London)
E.R. Blake, 1972, *Birds of Mexico* (Chicago University Press, Chicago)
A. Keve, 1973, *Zool. Abh. St. Mus. Tierk. Dresden* 32(12)
R. Schodde, 1975, *Interim List of Australian Songbirds, Passerines* (R.A.O.U., Melbourne)

CHECKLIST

Struthioniformes

1 STRUTHIONIDAE (OSTRICHES)

STRUTHIO
Struthio camelus (Ostrich)
  S. c. camelus
    N Africa, Sudan
  S. c. syriacus
    Syrian & Arabian deserts
  S. c. molybdophanes
    Somalia, NE Kenya
  S. c. massaicus
    E Kenya, E Tanzania
  S. c. australis
    Southern Africa

Rheiformes

2 RHEIDAE (RHEAS)

RHEA
Rhea americana (Greater Rhea)
  R. a. americana
    N & E Brazil
  R. a. intermedia
    S Brazil, Uruguay
  R. a. nobilis
    E Paraguay
  R. a. araneipes
    E Bolivia, SE Brazil
  R. a. albescens
    N Argentina

PTEROCNEMIA
Pterocnemia pennata (Lesser Rhea)
  P. p. garleppi
    SE Peru, Bolivia, NW Argentina
  P. p. tarapacensis
    N Chile
  P. p. pennata
    S Argentina

Casuariiformes

3 CASUARIIDAE (CASSOWARIES)

CASUARIUS
Casuarius casuarius (Double-wattled Cassowary)
  C. c. casuarius
    Ceram I

  C. c. bicarunculatus
    Aru Is, NW New Guinea
  C. c. tricarunculatus
    Geelvink Bay, New Guinea
  C. c. lateralis
    N New Guinea
  C. c. sclaterii
    S New Guinea
  C. c. aruensis
    Wokan I
  C. c. violicollis
    Trangan I
  C. c. johnsonii
    N Queensland
Casuarius bennetti (Dwarf Cassowary)
  C. b. papuanus
    NW New Guinea
  C. b. goodfellowi
    Japen I
  C. b. claudii
    NC New Guinea
  C. b. hecki
    NE New Guinea
  C. b. picticollis
    SE New Guinea
  C. b. bennetti
    New Britain
  C. b. shawmayeri
    Krätke Mts (New Britain)
Casuarius unappendiculatus (One-wattled Cassowary)
  C. u. rothschildi
    W New Guinea
  C. u. philipi
    Sepik river, New Guinea
  C. u. unappendiculatus
    Salawati I, Misol I
  C. u. occipitalis
    Japen I
  C. u. rufotinctus
    N New Guinea
  C. u. aurantiacus
    NE New Guinea

4 DROMAIIDAE (EMUS)

DROMAIUS
Dromaius novaehollandiae (Emu)
  D. n. woodwardi
    NW & Western Australia, Northern Territory
  D. n. rothschildi
    SW Australia

D. n. novaehollandiae
     C & S Queensland to Victoria, S Australia

Apterygiformes

5 APTERYGIDAE (KIWIS)

APTERYX
Apteryx australis (Brown Kiwi)
 A. a. mantelli
   S North I (New Zealand)
 A. a. novaezelandiae
   N North I (New Zealand)
 A. a. australis
   South I (New Zealand)
 A. a. lawryi
   Stewart I
Apteryx owenii (Little Spotted Kiwi)
 A. o. iredalei
   North I (New Zealand)
 A. o. owenii
   South I (New Zealand)
Apteryx haastii (Great Spotted Kiwi)
   W South I (New Zealand)

Tinamiformes

6 TINAMIDAE (TINAMOUS)

TINAMUS
Tinamus tao (Grey Tinamou)
 T. t. septentrionalis
   Colombia, Venezuela, Guyana
 T. t. larensis
   C Colombia, Venezuela
 T. t. tao
   N & C Brazil
 T. t. kleei
   N Bolivia, E Peru
Tinamus solitarius (Solitary Tinamou)
 T. s. pernambucensis
   E Brazil
 T. s. solitarius
   C Brazil, Paraguay
Tinamus osgoodi (Black Tinamou)
 T. o. hershkovitzi
   S Columbia
 T. o. osgoodi
   Peru
Tinamus major (Great Tinamou)
 T. m. robustus
   EC Guatemala to N Nicaragua
 T. m. percautus
   S Mexico, Guatemala
 T. m. fuscipennis
   E Nicaragua to Panama
 T. m. brunneiventris
   C Panama

T. m. castaneiceps
   SW Costa Rica, W Panama
T. m. saturatus
   E Panama, N Colombia
T. m. latifrons
   W Colombia, W Ecuador
T. m. zuliensis
   E Colombia, W Venezuela
T. m. major
   the Guianas, N Brazil
T. m. olivascens
   E Brazil
T. m. peruvianus
   E Colombia, E Ecuador, E Peru
T. m. serratus
   S Venezuela, W Brazil
Tinamus guttatus (White-throated Tinamou)
   E Ecuador & N Bolivia to E Brazil

NOTHOCERCUS
Nothocercus bonapartei (Highland Tinamou)
 N. b. frantzii
   Costa Rica, W Panama
 N. b. intercedens
   W Colombia
 N. b. discrepans
   Colombia
 N. b. bonapartei
   E Colombia, W Venezuela
 N. b. plumbeiceps
   E Ecuador
Nothocercus julius (Tawny-breasted Tinamou)
   W Venezuela & Colombia to S Peru
Nothocercus nigrocapillus (Hooded Tinamou)
 N. n. cadwaladeri
   N Peru
 N. n. nigrocapillus
   C Bolivia

CRYPTURELLUS
Crypturellus cinereus (Cinereous Tinamou)
   the Guianas to E Peru
Crypturellus berlepschi (Berlepsch's Tinamou)
   NW Colombia, N Ecuador
Crypturellus soui (Little Tinamou)
 C. s. meserythrus
   S Mexico to Honduras
 C. s. modestus
   Nicaragua to W Panama
 C. s. capnodes
   NW Panama
 C. s. poliocephalus
   W Panama

C. s. panamensis
Pearl Is (Panama)
C. s. caucae
W Colombia
C. s. harterti
NW Colombia, W Ecuador
C. s. mustelinus
NE Colombia
C. s. caquetae
SE Colombia
C. s. nigriceps
E Ecuador
C. s. soui
E Colombia, Venezuela, the Guianas,
N Brazil
C. s. andrei
Trinidad
C. s. albigularis
E Brazil
C. s. inconspicuus
C Bolivia
Crypturellus ptaritepui (Tepui Tinamou)
SE Venezuela
Crypturellus obsoletus (Brown Tinamou)
C. o. cerviniventris
Venezuela
C. o. castaneus
E Colombia, E Ecuador, N Peru
C. o. ochraceiventris
C Peru
C. o. punensis
S Peru, W Bolivia
C. o. griseiventris
Santarem, Brazil
C. o. obsoletus
S Brazil, Paraguay, NE Argentina
C. o. traylori
E Peru
C. o. hypochracea
SW Brazil
**Crypturellus undulatus (Undulated
Tinamou)**
C. u. manapiare
S Venezuela
C. u. simplex
S Guyana
C. u. adspersus
N Brazil
C. u. yapura
E Ecuador, E Peru, W Brazil
C. u. vermiculatus
E Brazil
C. u. undulatus
E Bolivia, SW Brazil, Paraguay
**Crypturellus transfasciatus (Pale-browed
Tinamou)**
W Ecuador, W Peru

**Crypturellus strigulosus (Brazilian
Tinamou)**
Brazil
**Crypturellus duidae (Grey-legged
Tinamou)**
SE Venezuela
**Crypturellus erythropus (Red-footed
Tinamou)**
C. e. colombianus
NC Colombia
C.e. saltuarius
NC Colombia
C. e. idoneus
NE Colombia, W Venezuela
C. e. cursitans
N Colombia, NW Venezuela
C. e. spencei
N Venezuela
C. e. margaritae
Margarita I
C. e. erythropus
E Venezuela, Guyana, Surinam, N Brazil
**Crypturellus noctivagus (Yellow-legged
Tinamou)**
C. n. zabele
NE Brazil
C. n. noctivagus
SE Brazil
**Crypturellus atrocapillus (Black-capped
Tinamou)**
C. a. atrocapillus
SE Peru
C. a. garleppi
N Bolivia
**Crypturellus cinnamomeus (Thicket
Tinamou)**
C. c. occidentalis
W coast of Mexico
C. c. mexicanus
NE Mexico
C. c. sallaei
S Mexico
C. c. goldmani
SE Mexico, N Belize
C. c. soconuscensis
C Chiapas
C. c. cinnamomeus
El Salvador to Nicaragua
C. c. vicinior
Chiapas to C Honduras
C. c. delattrei
Nicaragua
C. c. praepes
NW Costa Rica
**Crypturellus boucardi (Slaty-breasted
Tinamou)**
C. b. boucardi
S Mexico to N Nicaragua

C. b. costaricensis
E Honduras to Costa Rica
Crypturellus kerriae (Choco Tinamou)
Colombia
Crypturellus variegatus (Variegated Tinamou)
Amazonia, E Brazil
Crypturellus brevirostris (Rusty Tinamou)
E Peru, W Brazil, French Guiana
Crypturellus bartletti (Bartlett's Tinamou)
E Peru
Crypturellus parvirostris (Small-billed Tinamou)
SE Peru to S Brazil & NE Argentina
Crypturellus casiquiare (Barred Tinamou)
E Colombia, S Venezuela
Crypturellus tataupa (Tataupa Tinamou)
C. t. inops
NW Peru
C. t. peruviana
WC Peru
C. t. lepidotus
NE Brazil
C. t. tataupa
S Brazil, E Bolivia, Paraguay

RHYNCHOTUS
Rhynchotus rufescens (Red-winged Tinamou)
R. r. catingae
C Brazil
R. r. rufescens
E Bolivia to NE Brazil and Uruguay
R. r. pallescens
N Argentina
R. r. maculicollis
W & S Bolivia to W Argentina

NOTHOPROCTA
Nothoprocta taczanowskii (Taczanowski's Tinamou)
C & S Peru
Nothoprocta kalinowskii (Kalinowski's Tinamou)
℮ Peru
Nothoprocta ornata (Ornate Tinamou)
N. o. branickii
C Peru
N. o. ornata
SE Peru, Bolivia
N. o. rostrata
W Argentina
Nothoprocta perdicaria (Chilian Tinamou)
N. p. perdicaria
N & C Chile
N. p. sanborni
W Argentina, S Chile

Nothoprocta cinerascens (Brushland Tinamou)
N. c. cinerascens
W Argentina
N. c. parvimaculata
La Rioja (Argentina)
Nothoprocta pentlandii (Andean Tinamou)
N. p. ambigua
S Ecuador
N. p. oustaleti
S Ecuador, NW Peru
N. p. niethammeri
central coast of Peru
N. p. fulvescens
SE Peru
N. p. pentlandii
Bolivia to NW Argentina
N. p. doeringi
C Argentina
N. p. mendozae
WC Argentina
Nothoprocta curvirostris (Curve-billed Tinamou)
N. c. curvirostris
C Ecuador
N. c. peruviana
C Peru

NOTHURA
Nothura boraquira (White-bellied Nothura)
NE Brazil, E Bolivia, Paraguay
Nothura minor (Lesser Nothura)
S Brazil
Nothura darwinii (Darwin's Nothura)
N. d. peruviana
S Peru
N. d. agassizii
SE Peru, W Bolivia
N. d. boliviana
W Bolivia
N. d. salvadorii
W Argentina
N. d. darwinii
SC Argentina
Nothura maculosa (Spotted Nothura)
N. m. cearensis
S Ceara, Brazil
N. m. major
E Brazil
N. m. paludivaga
C Paraguay, NC Argentina
N. m. maculosa
SE Brazil, E Paraguay, Uruguay
NE Argentina
N. m. pallida
NW Argentina
N. m. annectens
E Argentina

N. m. submontana
  SW Argentina
N. m. nigroguttata
  S Argentina
N. m. chacoensis
  Paraguay, N Argentina

TAONISCUS
Taoniscus nanus (Dwarf Tinamou)
  Paraguay, SW Brazil

EUDROMIA
Eudromia elegans (Elegant Crested-Tinamou)
  E. e. intermedia
    NW Argentina
  E. e. magnistriata
    NW Argentina
  E. e. riojana
    NW Argentina
  E. e. albida
    W Argentina
  E. e. elegans
    C Argentina
  E. e. multiguttata
    EC Argentina
  E. e. devia
    SW Argentina
  E. e. patagonica
    S Chile, S Argentina

Eudromia formosa (Quebracho Crested-Tinamou)
  N Argentina

TINAMOTIS
Tinamotis pentlandii (Puna Tinamou)
  C Peru, W Argentina, N Chile
Tinamotis ingoufi (Patagonian Tinamou)
  S Chile, S Argentina

Sphenisciformes

7 SPHENISCIDAE (PENGUINS)

APTENODYTES
Aptenodytes patagonica (King Penguin)
  A. p. patagonica
    Staten I, S Georgia I, Falkland Is
  A. p. halli
    Macquarie I, Kerguelen I, Crozet Is, Marion I
Aptenodytes forsteri (Emperor Penguin)
  Antarctica

PYGOSCELIS
Pygoscelis papua (Gentoo Penguin)
  P. p. papua
    Falkland Is, S Georgia I
  P. p. taeniata
    Macquarie I, Heard I, Kerguelen I, Marion I

P. p. ellsworthi
  S Orkney Is, Deception I, S Shetlands Is
Pygoscelis adeliae (Adelie Penguin)
  Antarctica, S Orkney Is, S Shetland Is
Pygoscelis antarctica (Bearded Penguin)
  Antarctic Ocean, S Atlantic

EUDYPTES
Eudyptes pachyrhynchus (Victoria Penguin)
  E. p. pachyrhynchus
    New Zealand, Stewart I
  E. p. atratus
    Snares I
Eudyptes robustus (Snares I. Penguin)
  Snares I
Eudyptes sclateri (Big-crested Penguin)
  Auckland Is, Antipodes Is
Eudyptes crestatus (Rockhopper Penguin)
  E. c. crestatus
    Tierra del Fuego, Falkland Is
  E. c. filholi
    Kerguelen I & islands S of New Zealand
  E. c. moseleyi
    Tristan da Cunha I, St Paul I, Amsterdam I,
Eudyptes schlegeli (Royal Penguin)
  Macquarie I.
Eudyptes chrysolophus (Macaroni Penguin)
  S Georgia I, Kerguelen I, Falkland Is
    S Orkney Is, S Shetland Is

MEGADYPTES
Megadyptes antipodes (Yellow-eyed Penguin)
  South I, New Zealand & southern islands

EUDYPTULA
Eudyptula minor (Little Penguin)
  E. m. novaehollandiae
    Tasmania, S Australian islands
  E. m. minor
    New Zealand, Stewart I
  E. m. chathamensis
    Indian Ocean Is, Chatham I
  E. m. variabilis
    Wellington, New Zealand
Eudyptula albosignata (White-flippered Penguin)
  E South I, New Zealand

SPHENISCUS
Spheniscus demersus (Jackass Penguin)
  coast of S Africa and islands
Spheniscus humboldti (Humboldt Penguin)
  W coast of S America & islands
Spheniscus magellanicus (Magellanic Penguin)
  S South America & islands
Spheniscus mendiculus (Galapagos Penguin)
  Galapagos Is

Gaviiformes

8 GAVIIDAE (DIVERS)

GAVIA
Gavia stellata (Red-throated Diver)
Holarctic, Circumpolar » S Europe
S China, Florida
Gavia arctica (Black-throated Diver)
G. a. arctica
N Europe, N Russia
G. a. suschkini
W Siberia to EC Asia
G. a. viridigularis
NE Siberia to W Alaska
Gavia pacifica (Pacific Diver)
Arctic of N America, Alaska » W North
America
Gavia immer (Great Northern Diver)
G. i. immer
N North America, N Europe » N Mexico
Florida, North Sea
G. i. elasson
W Canada, N Dakota
Gavia adamsii (White-billed Diver)
Arctic, E Siberia, N North America
» Norway, S Alaska

Podicipediformes

9 PODICIPEDIDAE (GREBES)

TACHYBAPTUS
Tachybaptus ruficollis (Little Grebe)
T. r. ruficollis
Europe to Urals, NW Africa
T. r. iraquensis
Iraq, SW Iran
T. r. capensis
Caucasus to Burma, Ghana to Ethiopia
& Cape Province
T. r. poggei
E China, Hainan I, Malaysia
T. r. kunikyonis
C Riukiu Is
T. r. philippensis
Taiwan, Borneo, Philippine Is
T. r. cotabato
Mindanao I
T. r. javanicus
Java
T. r. vulcanorum
Bali I to Timor I
T. r. tricolor
Celebes to Solomon Is.

Tachybaptus novaehollandiae (Australian Dabchick)
New Guinea, Australia, New Caledonia
Tachybaptus pelzelni (Madagascar Little Grebe)
Madagascar
Tachybaptus rufolavatus (Delacour's Little Grebe)
Madagascar

PODILYMBUS
Podilymbus podiceps (Pied-billed Grebe)
P. p. podiceps
Canada & USA » Panama & Cuba
P. p. antillarum
Gtr & Lssr Antilles
P. p. antarcticus
Colombia & Venezuela to S Argentina
Podilymbus gigas (Atitlan Grebe)
Lake Atitlan, Guatemala

ROLLANDIA
Rollandia rolland (White-tufted Grebe)
R. r. morresoni
C Peru
R. r. chilensis
S Brazil & S Peru to Tierra del Fuego
R. r. rolland
Falkland Is
Rollandia micropterum (Short-winged Grebe)
Lake Titicaca, Bolivia

PODICEPS
Podiceps major (Great Grebe)
Amazonia to S Chile
Podiceps poliocephalus (Hoary-headed Grebe)
Australia, Tasmania
Podiceps rufopectus (New Zealand Dabchick)
New Zealand
Podiceps dominicus (Least Grebe)
P. d. brachypterus
S Texas to Panama
P. d. bangsi
S Baja California
P. d. dominicus
Gtr Antilles, S. Mexico to Argentina
P. d. speciosus
Columbia
Podiceps grisegena (Red-necked Grebe)
P. g. grisegena
Holarctic, Scandinavia to Siberia» N. Africa
and Iran
P. g. holbollii
N America, NE Asia » China, Japan,
S USA

Podiceps cristatus (Great Crested Grebe)
P. c. cristatus
    Europe to China, India, N Africa
P. c. infuscatus
    Senegal to Ethiopia & Cape Province
P. c. australis
    S Australia, Tasmania, South I, New
    Zealand
Podiceps auritus (Slavonian Grebe)
    N America, N Europe, N Asia
    » Mediterranean, E China, S USA
Podiceps nigricollis (Black-necked Grebe)
P. n. nigricollis
    Europe, Russia
P. n. gurneyi
    S Angola to Ethiopia & Cape Province
P. n. californicus
    W Canada, W USA » Guatemala
P. n. andinus
    C Colombia
Podiceps occipitalis (Silvery Grebe)
P. o. juninensis
    Peru, Bolivia
P. o. occipitalis
    NW Argentina to Tierra del Fuego
Podiceps taczanowskii (Puna Grebe)
    Lake Junin, Peru
Podiceps gallardoi (Hooded Grebe)
    NW Argentina

AECHMOPHORUS
Aechmophorus occidentalis (Western Grebe)
    W Canada, NW USA » SW USA
    & C Mexico

Procellariiformes

10 DIOMEDEIDAE (ALBATROSSES)

DIOMEDEA
Diomedea exulans (Wandering Albatross)
D. e. exulans
    Southern Ocean, South Georgia I
D. e. dabbenena
    Tristan da Cunha, Gough I
D. e. chionoptera
    S Indian Ocean, Macquarie I
Diomedea epomophora (Royal Albatross)
D. e. sanfordi
    South I, New Zealand, Chatham I
D. e. epomophora
    Auckland I to S Australia, S South America
Diomedea irrorata (Waved Albatross)
    Peru, Galapagos Is
Diomedea albatrus (Short-tailed Albatross)
    N Pacific, Riukiu Is, Bonin Is

Diomedea nigripes (Black-footed Albatross)
    N Pacific, Hawaii Is, Marshall Is
Diomedea immutabilis (Laysan Albatross)
    NW Hawaii Is
Diomedea melanophris (Black-browed Albatross)
D. m. impavida
    islands S of New Zealand
D. m. melanophris
    S South America
Diomedea bulleri (Buller's Albatross)
    South Pacific, Snares I
Diomedea cauta (Shy Albatross)
D. c. cauta
    Bass Strait, Albatross I
D. c. eremita
    Chatham I
D. c. salvini
    S South America, Snares I, Bounty I
Diomedea chlororhynchos (Yellow-nosed Albatross)
    Tristan da Cunha, Gough I
Diomedea chrysostoma (Grey-headed Albatross)
    S Georgia, Marion I, Crozet Is, Kerguelen I

PHOEBETRIA
Phoebetria fusca (Sooty Albatross)
    Tristan da Cunha, Gough I, St Paul I
Phoebetria palpebrata (Light-mantled Sooty Albatross)
P. p. palpebrata
    South Georgia I
P. p. huttoni
    Kerguelen I, Crozet Is, Heard I, Antipodes
    Is, Macquarie I

11 PROCELLARIIDAE (PETRELS, SHEARWATERS)

MACRONECTES
Macronectes giganteus (Giant Petrel)
    Southern Ocean
Macronectes halli (Hall's Giant Petrel)
    Southern Ocean (N of *M. giganteus*)?

FULMARUS
Fulmarus glacialis (Fulmar)
F. g. glacialis
    Greenland, Br Isles, Iceland, Norway
F. g. rodgersii
    NE Asian Is, Bering Sea
F. g. minor
    N Greenland
Fulmarus glacialoides (Southern Fulmar)
    Antarctic, New Zealand

THALASSOICA
Thalassoica antarctica (Antarctic Petrel)
Antarctic

DAPTION
Daption capense (Pintado Petrel)
D. c. capense
Antarctica, S Georgia I
D. c. australe
Snares I, Antipodes Is, Bounty I

PAGODROMA
Pagodroma nivea (Snow Petrel)
P. n nivea
Antarctica, S Georgia I, S Orkney Is
P. n. major
Adelie Land

PTERODROMA
Pterodroma macroptera (Great-winged Petrel)
P. m. macroptera
Tristan da Cunha, Crozet Is, Marion I, Kerguelen I
P. m. gouldi
SW Australia, North I, New Zealand
Pterodroma aterrima (Mascarene Black Petrel)
Reunion I
Pterodroma lessonii (White-headed Petrel)
Auckland I, Kerguelen I, Antipodes Is, Macquarie I,
Pterodroma hasitata (Black-capped Petrel)
Dominica, Caribbean Sea
Pterodroma cahow (Cahow)
Bermuda I
Pterodroma incerta (Schlegel's Petrel)
Tristan da Cunha, S Atlantic
Pterodroma rostrata (Tahiti Petrel)
P. r. rostrata
Marquesas Is, Society Is
P. r. trouessarti
New Caledonia
P. r. becki
Solomon Is
Pterodroma alba (Phoenix Petrel)
Christmas I, Phoenix I, Tonga I, Marquesas Is
Pterodroma inexpectata (Peale's Petrel)
New Zealand, Chatham I
Pterodroma solandri (Solander's Petrel)
Lord Howe I, Austral I
Pterodroma brevirostris (Kerguelen Petrel)
Gough I, Kerguelen I, Marion I
Pterodroma ultima (Murphy's Petrel)
S Pacific, Tuamotu I, Austral I
Pterodroma neglecta (Kermadec Petrel)
P. n. neglecta
Lord Howe I, Kermadec I, Tuamotu I, Austral I

P. n. juana
Juan Fernandez Is
Pterodroma magentae (Chatham Island Taiko)
Chatham I
Pterodroma arminjoniana (Trinidade Petrel)
P. a. arminjoniana
Mauritius I, S Trinidad I (Brazil)
P. a. heraldica
Tonga I, Marquesas Is, Tuamotu I
P. a. paschae
Easter I
Pterodroma mollis (Soft-plumaged Petrel)
P. m. mollis
Tristan da Cunha, Gough I, St Paul I, Kerguelen I
P. m. feae
Cape Verde Is
P. m. madeira
Madeira I
Pterodroma baraui (Barau's Petrel)
Reunion I
Pterodroma phaeopygia (Hawaiian Petrel)
P. p. phaeopygia
Galapagos Is
P. p. sandwichensis
Hawaiian Is
Pterodroma externa (White-necked Petrel)
P. e. cervicalis
Kermadec Is
P. e. externa
Masafuera I, Juan Fernandez Is
P. e. tristani
Tristan da Cunha
Pterodroma cookii (Cook's Petrel)
P. c. cookii
Little Barrier I, New Zealand
P. c. orientalis
W South America
P. c. defilippiana
Juan Fernandez Is
Pterodroma leucoptera (White-winged Petrel)
P. l. leucoptera
Pt Stephens (NS Wales)
P. l. masafuerae
Masafuera I
Pterodroma brevipes (Collared Petrel)
New Caledonia, New Hebrides, Fiji Is
Pterodroma hypoleuca (Bonin Petrel)
Bonin Is, W Hawaiian Is
Pterodroma nigripennis (Black-winged Petrel)
Lord Howe I, Kermadec Is
Pterodroma axillaris (Chatham Island Petrel)
Chatham I

Pterodroma longirostris (Stejneger's Petrel)
Masafuera I
Pterodroma pycrofti (Pycroft's Petrel)
New Zealand
Pterodroma macgillivrayi (Macgillivray's Petrel)
Fiji Is.

HALOBAENA
Halobaena caerulea (Blue Petrel)
Kerguelen I, Crozet Is, Falkland Is

PACHYPTILA
Pachyptila vittata (Broad-billed Prion)
P. v. vittata
Tristan da Cunha, S Georgia I, Chatham I, SW New Zealand
P. v. macgillivrayi
Amsterdam I, St Pauls I
Pachyptila salvini (Salvin's Prion)
Marion I
Pachyptila desolata (Dove Prion)
P. d. desolata
Kerguelen I
P. d. peringueyi
S Africa
P. d. alexanderi
SW Australia
P. d. macquariensis
Macquarie I
P. d. alter
Auckland I, Heard I
P. d. banksi
S Georgia I, S Orkney Is
Pachyptila belcheri (Slender-billed Prion)
Kerguelen I, Falkland Is
Pachyptila turtur (Fairy Prion)
SE Australia, New Zealand, Falkland Is
Pachyptila crassirostris (Thick-billed Prion)
P. c. eatoni
Kerguelen I, Heard I, Antipodes Is
P. c. crassirostris
Bounty I
P. c. pyramidalis
Chatham I

BULWERIA
Bulweria bulwerii (Bulwer's Petrel)
Pacific & Atlantic Oceans
Bulweria fallax (Jouanin's Petrel)
Indian Ocean

PROCELLARIA
Procellaria cinerea (Brown Petrel)
Tristan de Cunha, Gough I, Kerguelen I, Macquarie I

Procellaria aequinoctialis (White-chinned Petrel)
P. a. aequinoctialis
S Georgia I, Falkland Is, Crozet Is, Kerguelen I
P. a. conspicillata
Inaccessible I, Tristan da Cunha
P. a. steadi
Auckland I, Antipodes Is, Campbell I, Macquarie I
Procellaria parkinsoni (Black Petrel)
New Zealand
Procellaria westlandica (Westland Petrel)
South I, New Zealand

CALONECTRIS
Calonectris leucomelas (White-faced Shearwater)
NW Pacific Ocean
Calonectris diomedea (Cory's Shearwater)
C. d. diomedea
Mediterranean Islands
C. d. borealis
Portugal, Canary Is, Madeira I, Azores Is
C. d. edwardsi
Cape Verde Is
C. d. flavirostris
W Indian Ocean, Kerguelen I

PUFFINUS
Puffinus creatopus (Pink-footed Shearwater)
E Pacific, Juan Fernandez Is
Puffinus carneipes (Pale-footed Shearwater)
P. c. carneipes
SW Australia
P. c. hullianus
Lord Howe I, New Zealand
Puffinus gravis (Greater Shearwater)
Tristan da Cunha, Gough I, Falkland Is
Puffinus pacificus (Wedge-tailed Shearwater)
P. p. chlororhynchus
W Australian islands
P. p. pacificus
Kermadec I
P. p. cuneatus
Bonin Is, Hawaiian Is
P. p. royanus
E Australian islands
Puffinus bulleri (Grey-backed Shearwater)
islands off New Zealand
Puffinus griseus (Sooty Shearwater)
South I, New Zealand to Chile, Falkland Is
Puffinus tenuirostris (Short-tailed Shearwater
SE Australia, Tasmania

***Puffinus heinrothi* (Heinroth's Shearwater)**
New Britain
***Puffinus nativitatis* (Christmas Island Shearwater)**
Hawaii Is, Christmas I, Tuamotu I
***Puffinus puffinus* (Manx Shearwater)**
P. p. puffinus
E North Atlantic
P. p. yelkouan
E Mediterranean
P. p. mauretanicus
W Mediterranean
P. p. newelli
Hawaii
***Puffinus gavia* (Fluttering Shearwater)**
islands off New Zealand
***Puffinus huttoni* (Hutton's Shearwater)**
South I, New Zealand
***Puffinus opisthomelas* (Black-vented Shearwater)**
W North America
***Puffinus auricularis* (Townsend's Shearwater**
W Mexico
***Puffinus assimilis* (Little Shearwater)**
P. a. baroli
Azores Is, Madeira I, Canary Is
P. a. boydi
Cape Verde Is
P. a. elegans
Tristan da Cunha, Gough I
P. a. tunneyi
islands off SW Australia
P. a. assimilis
Lord Howe I, Norfolk I
P. a. haurakiensis
New Zealand
P. a. munda
Chatham I
P. a. kermadecensis
Kermadec Is
***Puffinus lherminieri* (Audubon's Shearwater)**
P. l. bailloni
Mauritius I, Reunion I, Seychelles
P. l. bannermani
Bonin Is
P. l. nugax
New Hebrides
P. l. dichrous
Palau Is, Phoenix I, Christmas Is
P. l. polynesiae
Samoa Is, Society Is, Marquesas Is, Tuamotu I
P. l. subalaris
Galapagos Is
P. l. lherminieri
West Indies, Bahama Is, Bermuda I
P. l. persicus
NW India, Iran

P. l. loyemilleri
Costa Rica to Guyana

12 HYDROBATIDAE (STORM-PETRELS)

OCEANITES
***Oceanites oceanicus* (Wilson's Petrel)**
O. o. oceanicus
N Antarctic Is
O. o. exasperatus
S Antarctic Is
***Oceanites gracilis* (Elliot's Storm Petrel)**
O. g. gracilis
W South America
O. g. galapagoensis
Galapagos Is
GARRODIA
***Garrodia nereis* (Grey-backed Storm Petrel)**
S Georgia I, Falkland Is, Kerguelen I, Chatham I
PELAGODROMA
***Pelagodroma marina* (White-faced Storm Petrel)**
P. m. hypoleuca
Madeira I, Canary Is, Cape Verde Is
P. m. marina
Tristan da Cunha
P. m. dulciae
W & S Australia
P. m. maoriana
New Zealand, Auckland I, Chatham I
P. m. albiclunis
Kermadec Is
FREGETTA
***Fregetta grallaria* (White-bellied Storm Petrel)**
F. g. royana
Lord Howe I
F. g. titan
Austral I
F. g. grallaria
Juan Fernandez Is
***Fregetta tropica* (Black-bellied Storm Petrel)**
F. t. tropica
Tristan da Cunha
F. t. melanogaster
Kerguelen I, Crozet Is
F. t. lineata
Samoa Is
NESOFREGETTA
***Nesofregetta fuliginosa* (White-throated Storm Petrel)**
N. f. fuliginosa
Christmas I, Marquesas Is, Fiji Is, New Hebrides
N. f. moestissima
Samoa Is

HYDROBATES
Hydrobates pelagicus (British Storm Petrel)
E North Atlantic, Mediterranean

HALOCYPTENA
Halocyptena microsoma (Least Storm Petrel)
W Mexico to Ecuador

OCEANODROMA
Oceanodroma tethys (Galapagos Storm Petrel)
O. t. tethys
Galapagos Is
O. t. kelsalli
coast of Peru
Oceanodroma castro (Madeiran Storm Petrel)
O. c. cryptoleucura
North Pacific, Hawaiian Is
O. c. bangsi
South Pacific, Cocos Is, Galapagos Is
O. c. castro
E Atlantic islands, St Helena I
Oceanodroma leucorhoa (Leach's Storm Petrel)
O. l. leucorhoa
N Pacific & N Atlantic coasts
O. l. beali
SE Alaska to California
O. l. kaedingi
Guadelupe I (Baja California)
Oceanodroma markhami (Sooty Storm Petrel)
O. m. markhami
W South America
O. m. owstoni
Hawaiian Is
Oceanodroma matsudairae (Matsudaira's Storm Petrel)
Volcano I
Oceanodroma tristrami (Tristram's Storm Petrel)
Japan, Laysan I, Midway I
Oceanodroma monorhis (Swinhoe's Storm Petrel)
O. m. monorhis
E North Pacific, Taiwan, Japan
O. m. socorroensis
W North Pacific, Baja California
Oceanodroma homochroa (Ashy Storm Petrel)
California, Santa Barbara I
Oceanodroma hornbyi (Ringed Storm Petrel)
W South America
Oceanodroma furcata (Fork-tailed Storm Petrel)
N Pacific Ocean

Oceanodroma melania (Black Storm Petrel)
E Pacific, Baja California

13 PELECANOIDIDAE (DIVING PETRELS)

PELECANOIDES
Pelecanoides garnoti (Peruvian Diving Petrel)
coasts of Peru & Chile
Pelecanoides magellani (Magellan Diving Petrel)
S Chile, Cape Horn
Pelecanoides georgicus (Georgian Diving Petrel)
P. g. georgicus
South Georgia I
P. g. novus
Macquarie I
Pelecanoides urinatrix (Common Diving Petrel)
P. u. berard
Falkland Is
P. u. coppingeri
S Chile
P. u. dacunhae
Tristan da Cunha
P. u. elizabethae
Gough I
P. u. urinatrix
SE Australia, Tasmania, New Zealand
P. u. chathamensis
Chatham I, Antipodes Is, Snares I
P. u. exsul
Crozet Is, Marion I, Heard I, Kerguelen I, Auckland I

Pelecaniformes

14 PHAETHONTIDAE (TROPIC BIRDS)

PHAETHON
Phaethon aethereus (Red-billed Tropic Bird)
P. a. limatus
Tower I, Galapagos Is
P. a. mesonauta
Daphne I, Lesser Antilles to Cape Verde Is
P. a. aethereus
Fernando Noronha I, St Helena I, Ascension I
P. a. indicus
Persian Gulf, Gulf of Aden
Phaethon rubricauda (Red-tailed Tropic Bird)
P. r. rubricauda
Mauritius I, Aldabra I

P. r. westralis
Christmas I, Cocos Keeling Is,
NW Australia
P. r. roseotincta
Lord Howe I, Norfolk I, Kermadec Is
P. r. melanorhynchus
Society Is, Palmerston I
P. r. rothschildi
Bonin Is, Hawaiian Is
Phaethon lepturus (White-tailed Tropic Bird)
P. l. catesbyi
West Indies, Bahama Is, Bermuda I
P. l. ascensionis
Fernando Noronha I, Ascension I,
Gulf of Guinea
P. l. lepturus
Mascarene Is, Seychelles, Andaman Is
P. l. fulvus
Christmas I (Java)
P. l. dorotheae
SW Pacific islands

15 PELECANIDAE (PELICANS)

PELECANUS
Pelecanus onocrotalus (Eastern White Pelican)
S Europe, Africa, C Asia
Pelecanus roseus (White Pelican)
China, Persian Gulf
Pelecanus rufescens (Pink-backed Pelican)
C & S Africa
Pelecanus philippensis (Grey Pelican)
S Asia, Iran to Philippine Is
Pelecanus crispus (Dalmatian Pelican)
SE Europe to China
Pelecanus conspicillatus (Australian Pelican)
Australia, Tenimber Is, New Guinea
Pelecanus erythrorhynchos (American White Pelican)
North & C America, W Indies
Pelecanus occidentalis (Brown Pelican)
P. o. occidentalis
West Indies
P. o. carolinensis
coasts of S Carolina to Venezuela
P.o. californicus
coast of California, W Mexico
P. o. murphyi
coasts of W Columbia & Ecuador
P. o. urinator
Galapagos Is
P. o. thagus
coasts of Peru & Chile

16 SULIDAE (GANNETS, BOOBIES)

MORUS
Morus bassanus (Northern Gannet)
E Canada, Iceland, Br Isles
Morus capensis (Cape Gannet)
Southern Africa
Morus serrator (Australian Gannet)
M. s. serrator
S Australian coast, Tasmania, Bass Str
M. s. rex
North I, New Zealand

SULA
Sula nebouxii (Blue-footed Booby)
S. n. nebouxii
California to Peru
S. n. excisa
Galapagos Is
Sula variegata (Peruvian Booby)
coasts of Peru & Chile
Sula abbotti (Abbott's Booby)
Tropical Indian Ocean
Sula dactylatra (Blue-faced Booby)
S. d. dactylatra
Caribbean, Bahama Is, Acension I
S. d. melanops
W Indian Ocean, Seychelles Is
S. d. californica
W Mexico Islands
S. d. granti
Galapagos Is
S. d. bedouti
Christmas I (Java), Lesser Sunda Is
S. d. personata
N Australian & Pacific Is
Sula sula (Red-footed Booby)
S. s. sula
Caribbean Is & South Trinidad I,
(Brazil)
S. s. rubripes
Indian Ocean & Pacific islands
S. s. websteri
Galapagos Is
Sula leucogaster (Brown Booby)
S. l. leucogaster
Caribbean & Atlantic Is
S. l. brewsteri
coast of California & W Mexico
S. l. etesiaca
C American & Colombian islands
S. l. plotus
Indian & W Pacific Ocean Islands & Java
to N Australia
S. l. nesiotes
Clipperton I

17 PHALACROCORACIDAE (CORMORANTS)

PHALACROCORAX

Phalacrocorax auritus (Double-crested Cormorant)
P. a. cincinatus
Alaska to Oregon
P. a. albociliatus
California to W Mexico
P. a. auritus
C & E Canada, E USA
P. a. floridanus
S USA to Bahama Is & Honduras
Phalacrocorax olivaceus (Olivaceous Cormorant)
P. o. mexicanus
S USA to Nicaragua & Cuba
P. o. olivaceus
Panama to Patagonia
P. o. choncho
Sonora (NW Mexico)
P. o. hornensis
Tierra del Fuego
Phalacrocorax sulcirostris (Little Black Cormorant)
P. s. territori
Malaysia to New Guinea & N Australia
P. s. sulcirostris
E & S Australia, Tasmania
P. s. purpuragula
New Zealand
Phalacrocorax carbo (Common Cormorant)
P. c. carbo
E Canada to Br Isles
P. c. maroccanus
N Africa
P. c. lugubris
NE Africa
P. c. sinensis
C Europe to India & China
P. c. hanedae
Japan
P. c. novaehollandiae
Australia & Tasmania
P. c. steadi
New Zealand, Chatham I
Phalacrocorax lucidus (White-breasted Cormorant)
Cape Verde Is, Senegal to E & S Africa
Phalacrocorax fuscicollis (Indian Cormorant)
India, Sri Lanka, Burma
Phalacrocorax capensis (Cape Cormorant)
coasts of South Africa
Phalacrocorax nigrogularis (Socotra Cormorant)
S Red Sea, Persian Gulf

Phalacrocorax neglectus (Bank Cormorant)
coasts of South Africa
Phalacrocorax capillatus (Japanese Cormorant)
NE Asia to China, Japan
Phalacrocorax penicillatus (Brandt's Cormorant)
S Alaska to NW Mexico
Phalacrocorax aristotelis (Shag)
P. a. aristotelis
Iceland & Lapland to Portugal
P. a. desmaresti
C Mediterranean
P. a. riggenbachi
coast of Morocco
Phalacrocorax pelagicus (Pelagic Cormorant)
P. p. pelagicus
N Pacific islands
P. p. resplendens
British Columbia to Mexico
Phalacrocorax urile (Red-faced Cormorant)
Bering Sea to Taiwan
Phalacrocorax magellanicus (Magellan Cormorant)
Tierra del Fuego, Falkland Is
Phalacrocorax bougainvillei (Guanay Cormorant)
coasts of Peru & Chile
Phalacrocorax featherstoni (Chatham Cormorant)
Chatham I
Phalacrocorax varius (Pied Cormorant)
Australia, Tasmania, New Zealand
Phalacrocorax fuscescens (Black-faced Cormorant)
S Australia, Tasmania
Phalacrocorax carunculatus (Rough-faced Cormorant)
P. c. carunculatus
South I, New Zealand
P. c. chalconotus
Stewart I
P. c. onslowi
Chatham I
Phalacrocorax campbelli (Campbell Is Cormorant)
P. c. campbelli
Campbell I
P. c. colensoi
Auckland I
P. c. ranfurlyi
Bounty I
Phalacrocorax verrucosus (Kerguelen Cormorant)
Kerguelen I, Marion I

Phalacrocorax gaimardi (Red-legged Cormorant)
P. g. gaimardi
    Coast of Peru & Chile
P. g. cirriger
    Coast of S Argentina
Phalacrocorax punctatus (Spotted Cormorant)
P. p. punctatus
    New Zealand
P. p. oliveri
    Stewart I
Phalacrocorax atriceps (Blue-eyed Cormorant)
P. a. atriceps
    S South America
P. a. nivalis
    Heard I
P. a. gaini
    Antarctica
Phalacrocorax georgianus (South Georgia Cormorant)
    South Georgia I
Phalacrocorax albiventer (King Cormorant)
P. a. albiventer
    Patagonia, Falkland Is
P. a. melanogenis
    Crozet Is
P. a. purpurascens
    Macquarie I

HALIETOR
Haliëtor melanoleucos (Little Pied Cormorant)
H. m. melvillensis
    Malaysia to N Australia
H. m. melanoleucos
    S Australia, Tasmania
H. m. brevirostris
    New Zealand
H. m. brevicauda
    Rennell I
Haliëtor africanus (Reed Cormorant)
H. a. africanus
    Senegal to Egypt & Cape Province
H. a. pictilis
    Madagascar
H. a. coronatus
    Namibia
Haliëtor niger (Javanese Cormorant)
    India to Java and Borneo
Haliëtor pygmeus (Pigmy Cormorant)
    C Europe, N Africa to C Asia

NANNOPTERUM
Nannopterum harrisi (Flightless Cormorant)
    Galapagos Is

18 ANHINGIDAE (ANHINGAS)

ANHINGA
Anhinga rufa (African Darter)
A. r. rufa
    Senegal to Cape Province
A. r. vulsini
    Madagascar
A. r. chantrei
    Tigris & Euphrates rivers
A. r. papua
    New Guinea
Anhinga melanogaster (Indian Darter)
    India to Philippine Is & Celebes
Anhinga novaehollandiae (Australian Darter)
    New Guinea, Australia
Anhinga anhinga (American Darter)
A. a. anhinga
    Brazil, Argentina
A. e. leucogaster
    SE USA to Colombia

19 FREGATIDAE (FRIGATE BIRDS)

FREGATA
Fregata aquila (Ascension Frigate Bird)
    Ascension I
Fregata andrewsi (Christmas I Frigate Bird)
    E Indian Ocean, Christmas I
Fregata magnificens (Magnificent Frigate Bird)
F. m. magnificens
    Galapagos Is
F. m. rothschildi
    SE USA, C America, W Indies
F. m. lowei
    Cape Verde Is
Fregata minor (Great Frigate Bird)
F. m. aldabrensis
    Seychelles, Aldabra I
F. m. minor
    Christmas I, Cocos Keeling Is
F. m. peninsulae
    Raine I (Queensland)
F. m. palmerstoni
    C & S Pacific
F. m. strumosa
    Hawaiian Is
F. m. ridgwayi
    Galapagos Is
F. m. nicolli
    S Trinidad I (Brazil)
Fregata ariel (Lesser Frigate Bird)
F. a. iredalei
    W Indian Ocean, Aldebra I
F. a. ariel
    Philippine Is to N Australia, S Pacific
F. a. trinitatis
    S Trinidad I (Brazil)

Ciconiiformes

20 ARDEIDAE (HERONS, BITTERNS)

BOTAURINAE

BOTAURUS

Botaurus stellaris (Eurasian Bittern)
  B. s. stellaris
    Europe to E Asia » N & C Africa
  B. s. capensis
    C Botswana to Natal & Cape Province
Botaurus poiciloptilus (Australian Bittern)
    Australia, Tasmania, New Zealand
Botaurus lentiginosus (American Bittern)
    Canada to SW & NE USA » C America
Botaurus pinnatus (Pinnated Bittern)
  B. p. pinnatus
    Colombia to SE Brazil
  B.p. caribaeus
    SE Mexico, Belize

IXOBRYCHUS

Ixobrychus exilis (Least Bittern)
  I. e. exilis
    North America to W Indies » Brazil
  I. e. pullus
    S Sonora
  I. e. bogotensis
    C Colombia
  I. e. erythromelas
    Trinidad, the Guianas to Paraguay
  I. e. limoncochae
    E Ecuador
  I. e. peruvianus
    coast of Peru
Ixobrychus minutus (Little Bittern)
  I. m. minutus
    C & S Europe to C Asia and NW India
    » Africa
  I. m. payesii
    Senegal to Aden » Cape Province
  I. m. podiceps
    Madagascar
  I. m. dubius
    E & SW Australia
  I. m. novaezelandiae
    New Zealand
Ixobrychus sinensis (Chinese Little Bittern)
    Manchuria, Japan » India, Sunda Is,
    Philippine Is
Ixobrychus involucris (Stripe-backed Bittern)
    S. Brazil to Patagonia
Ixobrychus eurhythmus (Schrenk's Little Bittern)
    E Asia » Malaysia, Sunda Is, Philippine Is

Ixobrychus cinnamomeus (Cinnamon Bittern)
    India to China, Phil Is & Celebes
Ixobrychus sturmii (Dwarf Bittern)
    Senegal to Sudan & Cape Province
Ixobrychus flavicollis (Black Bittern)
  I. f. flavicollis
    C China to India, Malaysia, Celebes
  I. f. australis
    Timor I
  I. f. nesophilus
    New Britain, New Ireland
  I. f. woodfordi
    Solomon Is
  I. f. gouldi
    Moluccas, New Guinea, Australia
  I. f. pallidior
    Rennell I

ARDEINAE

TIGRIORNITHINI

ZONERODIUS
Zonerodius heliosylus (Forest Bittern)
    New Guinea, Aru Is
TIGRIORNIS
Tigriornis leucolophus (African Tiger Bittern)
    Sierra Leone to SW & NE Zaire
TIGRISOMA
Tigrisoma lineatum (Rufescent Tiger Heron)
  T. l. lineatum
    Honduras to NW South America
  T. l. marmoratum
    Brazil, Paraguay, N. Argentina
Tigrisoma fasciatum (Fasciated Tiger Heron)
  T. f. fasciatum
    SE Brazil
  T. f. salmoni
    Colombia, Ecuador
  T. f. bolivianum
    Bolivia, N Argentina
  T. f. pallescens
    NW Argentina
Tigrisoma mexicanum (Bare-throated Tiger Heron)
  T. m. fremitus
    S Sonora
  T. m. mexicanum
    W Mexico to E Panama, NW Colombia
ZEBRILUS
Zebrilus undulatus (Zigzag Heron)
    the Guianas to C Brazil

GORSACHIUS
Gorsachius goisagi (Japanese Night Heron)
  E China, Japan, Philippine Is
Gorsachius melanolophus (Tiger Bittern)
  G. m. melanolophus
    S India, S China to Sumatra, Java
  G. m. minor
    Nicobar Is
  G. m. kutteri
    Philippine Is
  G. m. rufolineatus
    Palawan I
Gorsachius magnificus (Magnificent Night Heron)
  SE China, Hainan I
Gorsachius leuconotus (White-backed Night Heron)
  Senegal to Sudan & Natal

NYCTICORAX
Nycticorax nycticorax (Black-crowned Night Heron)
  N. n. nycticorax
    Holland to Japan, Sudan Is, Africa
  N. n. hoactli
    SE Canada to Argentina, Hawaii Is
  N. n. obscurus
    S Peru to Tierra del Fuego
  N. n. falklandicus
    Falkland Is
Nycticorax caledonicus (Rufous Night Heron)
  N. c. manillensis
    Philippine Is, N Borneo
  N. c. minahassae
    Celebes
  N. c. pelewensis
    Palau Is
  N. c. mandibularis
    Solomon Is
  N. c. caledonicus
    New Caledonia
  N. c. hilli
    Moluccas, New Guinea, Australia
  N. c. cancrivorus
    Bismarck Archipelago
Nycticorax violaceus (Yellow-crowned Night Heron)
  N. v. violaceus
    EC USA, ECentral America, W Indies
  N. v. bancrofti
    W Baja California
  N. v. gravirostris
    Socorro I.

N. v. caliginis
  Colombia
N. v. cayennensis
  S Colombia to Peru & S Brazil
N. v. pauper
  Galapagos Is

COCHLEARIINI

COCHLEARIUS
Cochlearius cochlearius (Boat-billed Heron)
  C. c. zeledoni
    W Mexico
  C. c. phillipsi
    S Mexico, Belize
  C. c. ridgwayi
    Guatemala, Honduras
  C. c. panamensis
    S Costa Rica, Panama
  C. c. cochlearius
    Trinidad, N & C South America

PILHERODIUS
Pilherodius pileatus (Capped Heron)
  E Panama to E Peru & S Brazil

ARDEINI

ARDEOLA
Ardeola ralloides (Squacco Heron)
  S Europe to Iran & Africa
Ardeola idae (Madagascar Squacco Heron)
  E Africa, Madagascar
Ardeola grayii (Indian Pond Heron)
  A. g. grayii
    Iran to India, Burma, Sri Lanka
  A. g. phillipsi
    S Maldive Is
Ardeola bacchus (Chinese Pond Heron)
  China to Malaysia & Borneo
Ardeola speciosa (Javanese Pond Heron)
  Borneo Celebes, Sumatra, Java
Ardeola rufiventris (Rufous-bellied Heron)
  S Angola to Tanzania & Cape Province

BUBULCUS
Bubulcus ibis (Cattle Egret)
  B. i. ibis
    Spain to Iran, N & C Africa, E North
      America, C & N South America
  B. i. coromandus
    India to S Japan, Philippine Is, Moluccas
  B. i. seychellarum
    Seychelle

SYRIGMA
Syrigma sibilator (Whistling Heron)
  S. s. fostersmithi
    NW Venezuela, NE Colombia
  S. s. sibilator
    S Brazil, Paraguay, Uruguay

Butorides striatus (Striated (Green) Heron)
  B. s. anthonyi
    SW USA, W Mexico
  B. s. frazari
    S Baja California
  B. s. virescens
    E North America » Panama
  B. s. bahamensis
    Bahama Is
  B. s. maculatus
    W Indies, EC America
  B. s. margaritophilus
    Pearl Is (Panama)
  B. s. curacensis
    Curaçao I
  B. s. patens
    C Panama
  B. s. striatus
    E Panama to S Brazil
  B. s. robinsoni
    Margarita I
  B. s. sundevalli
    Galapagos Is
  B. s. cyanurus
    Paraguay, Uruguay, N Argentina
  B. s. fuscicollis
    Bolivia
  B. s. brevipes
    Somalia, Red Sea Coast
  B. s. atricapillus
    Senegal to Sudan & Cape Province
  B. s. rutenbergi
    Madagascar, Réunion I
  B. s. rhizophorae
    Comoro Is
  B. s. degens
    Seychelle
  B. s. crawfordi
    Assumption I, Aldabra I
  B. s. albolimbatus
    Diego Garcia I
  B. s. didii
    C & N Maldive Is
  B. s. albidulus
    S Maldive Is
  B. s. chloriceps
    India, Sri Lanka
  B. s. spodiogaster
    Andaman Is, Nicobar Is, W Sumatran
      islands
  B. s. amurensis
    NE Asia » Philippine Is, Sunda Is
  B. s. abbotti
    Malaysia
  B. s. connectens
    China
  B. s. banggaiensis
    Banggai I, Peleng I

  B. s. actophilus
    S China, N Indochina » Indonesia
  B. s. javanicus
    E India to Philippine Is & Sunda Is
  B. s. moluccarum
    S Moluccas
  B. s. solomonensis
    Solomon Is
  B. s. papuensis
    NW New Guinea
  B. s. macrorhynchus
    S New Guinea E Australia
  B. s. stagnatilis
    N & NW Australia
  B. s. patruelis
    Tahiti I
  B. s. rogersi
    WC Australia

EGRETTA
Egretta picata (Pied Heron)
    Celebes to New Guinea, N Australia
Egretta ardesiaca (Black Heron)
    Senegal to Sudan & Natal
Egretta vinaceigula (Red-throated Heron)
    Transvaal
Egretta caerulea (Little Blue Heron)
    S USA to C South America
Egrette tricolor (Louisiana Heron)
  E. t. ruficollis
    SE USA to NW South America
  E. t. tricolor
    French Guiana, Surinam, NE Brazil
  E. t. rufimentum
    Trinidad.
Egretta rufescens (Reddish Egret)
  E. r. rufescens
    S USA, Mexico, Cuba, Jamaica,
      Hispaniola
  E. r. colorata
    Yucatan peninsula
  E. r. dickeyi
    San Luis I
Egretta sacra (Eastern Reef Heron)
  E. s. sacra
    SE Asia to Australia, New Zealand
  E. s. albolineata
    New Caledonia
Egretta eulophotes (Swinhoe's Egret)
    S & C China, Taiwan, Celebes
Egretta thula (Snowy Egret)
  E. t. brewsteri
    W USA
  E. t. thula
    SE USA to N Chile, N Argentina
Egretta gularis (Western Reef Heron)
  E. g. gularis
    Senegal to Gabon

E. g. asha
Red Sea to W Indian coast
E. g. dimorpha
Madagascar, Aldabra I
Egretta garzetta (Little Egret)
E. g. garzetta
S Europe to Japan & Africa
E. g. nigripes
Sunda Is, Philippine Is to New Guinea,
Australia
Egretta intermedia (Intermediate Egret)
E. i. brachyrhyncha
Sudan to Cape Province
E. i. intermedia
S India to Japan & Gtr Sunda Is
E. i. plumifera
S Moluccas, New Guinea, Australia
Egretta alba (Great Egret)
E. a. alba
SE Europe, N Asia » N Africa, India
S China
E. a. modestus
India to Japan & Australia
E. a. maorianus
South I, New Zealand
E. a. melanorhynchos
Senegal to Sudan & Cape Province
E. a. egretta
S USA to Patagonia

ARDEA
Ardea purpurea (Purple Heron)
A. p. purpurea
S Europe to Iran, Africa
A. p. bournei
Cape Verde Is
A. p. madagascariensis
Madagascar
A. p. manilensis
India, China, Gtr Sunda Is
Ardea novaehollandiae (White-faced Heron)
A. n. novaehollandiae
Lombok I to Timor I, Australia, New
Zealand
A. n. parryi
NW Australia
Ardea pacifica (White-necked Heron)
Australia, Tasmania
Ardea cinerea (Grey Heron)
A. c. cinerea
Europe to W China, Africa
A. c. monicae
Banc d'Arguin Is, Mauretania
A. c. rectirostris
E Siberia, Japan, Taiwan, E China
A. c. firasa
Madagascar, Aldebra I, Comoro Is

A. c. altirostris
Java, Sumatra
Ardea herodias (Great Blue Heron)
A. h. fannini
W Canada
A. h. hyperonca
W USA
A. h. treganzai
WC USA, NW Mexico
A. h. herodias
NE North America » C America
A. h. wardi
SE USA
A. h. sanctilucae
Baja California
A. h. lessonii
Panama
A. h. cognata
Galapagos Is
A. h. occidentalis
SE USA, Cuba, Jamaica
Ardea cocoi (Cocoi Heron)
South America
Ardea melanocephala (Black-headed Heron)
Gambia to Sudan & Cape Province
Ardea humbloti (Madagascar Heron)
E Madagascar, Aldabra I
Ardea goliath (Goliath Heron)
Senegal to Sudan & Cape Province
Ardea imperialis (Great White-bellied Heron)
Sikkim to C Burma
Ardea sumatrana (Dusky-grey Heron)
Burma, Malaysia to Philippine Is, New
Guinea, N Australia

AGAMIA
Agamia agami (Chestnut-bellied Heron)
E Mexico to Peru & Brazil

21 BALAENICIPITIDAE (WHALE-HEADED STORK)

BALAENICEPS
Balaeniceps rex (Whale-headed Stork)
Sudan to Zambia

22 SCOPIDAE (HAMMERKOP)

SCOPUS
Scopus umbretta (Hammerkop)
S. u. umbretta
Senegal to Nigeria
S. u. minor
coast from Sierra Leone to Nigeria
S. u. bannermanni
Cameroun to Aden & Cape Province

23 CICONIIDAE (STORKS)

MYCTERIINI

MYCTERIA
Mycteria americana (American Wood Ibis)
SE USA to C South America
Mycteria cinerea (Milky Stork)
Malaysia, Sumatra, Java
Mycteria ibis (Yellow-billed Stork)
Senegal to Sudan & Cape Province
Mycteria leucocephala (Painted Stork)
India to SW China, Indochina

ANASTOMUS
Anastomus oscitans (Asian Open-bill Stork)
India to Indochina
Anastomus lamelligerus (African Open-bill Stork)
A. l. lamelligerus
Senegal to Sudan & Rhodesia
A. l. madagascariensis
Madagascar

CICONIINI

CICONIA
Ciconia nigra (Black Stork)
Europe to N China » Africa, India
Ciconia abdimii (Abdim's Stork)
Ethiopia to Angola & Transvaal
Ciconia episcopus (Woolly-necked Stork)
C. e. microscelis
Senegal to Sudan & Cape Province
C. e. episcopus
India, Sri Lanka, Burma
C. e. neglecta
Malaysia to Philippine Is, Sunda Is
C. e. stormi
Borneo
Ciconia maguari (Maguari Stork)
the Guianas to Chile & S Argentina
Ciconia ciconia (White Stork)
C. c. ciconia
Europe, N Africa » S Africa
C. c. asiatica
C Asia » India
C. c. boyciana
NE Asia, Japan

LEPTOPTILINI

EPHIPPIORHYNCHUS
Ephippiorhynchus asiaticus (Black-necked Stork)
E. a. asiaticus
India to Malaysia & Indochina
E. a. australis
New Guinea, N & E Australia

Ephippiorhynchus senegalensis (Saddle-bill Stork)
Senegal to Sudan & Transvaal

JABIRU
Jabiru mycteria (Jabiru)
S Mexico to C Argentina

LEPTOPTILOS
Leptoptilos javanicus (Lesser Adjutant Stork)
C India to S China, Gtr Sunda Is
Leptoptilos dubius (Greater Adjutant Stork)
India to Indochina, Gtr Sunda Is
Leptoptilos crumeniferus (Marabou Stork)
Senegal to Sudan & Transvaal

24 THRESKIORNITHIDAE (IBISES, SPOONBILLS)

THRESKIORNITHINAE

THRESKIORNIS
Threskiornis aethiopicus (Sacred Ibis)
T. a. aethiopicus
Africa, Saudi Arabia
T. a. abbotti
Aldabra I
T. a. bernieri
Madagascar
Threskiornis melanocephalus (Oriental Ibis)
India to China, Japan
Threskiornis molucca (Australian White Ibis)
T. m. molucca
W Papuan Is, Kei Is, New Guinea
T. m. strictipennis
Australia

CARPHIBIS
Carphibis spinicollis (Straw-necked Ibis)
Australia, Tasmania

PSEUDIBIS
Pseudibis papillosa (Black Ibis)
N India
Pseudibis davisoni (Davison's Ibis)
E Burma to S Indochina

THAUMATIBIS
Thaumatibis gigantea (Giant Ibis)
S Thailand, S Indochina

GERONTICUS
Geronticus eremita (Hermit Ibis) (Waldrapp)
N Africa, Ethiopia
Geronticus calvus (Bald Ibis)
S Africa

NIPPONIA
Nipponia nippon (Japanese Crested Ibis)
  NE Asia, Japan

LAMPRIBIS
Lampribis olivacea (Olive Ibis)
  L. o. olivacea
  Sierra Leone, Liberia
  L. o. cupreipennis
  S Cameroun to W Zaire
  L. o. rothschildi
  Principé I **e?**
  L. o. bocagei
  Sao Thomé I
  L. o. akleyorum
  Kenya
Lampribis rara (Spot-breasted Ibis)
  Liberia to E Zaire & Angola

HAGEDASHIA
Hagedashia hagedash (Hadada Ibis)
  H. h. brevirostris
  Gambia to Zaire ·
  H. h. nilotica
  Ethiopia to Uganda
  H. h. erlangeri
  Somalia to Malawi
  H. h. hagedash
  Southern Africa

BOSTRYCHIA
Bostrychia carunculata (Wattled Ibis)
  Ethiopia

HARPIPRION
Harpiprion caerulescens (Plumbeous Ibis)
  C Brazil to N Argentina

THERISTICUS
Theristicus caudatus (Buff-necked Ibis)
  T. c. caudatus
  E Panama to French Guiana
  T. c. hyperorious
  C South America
Theristicus melanopis (Black-faced Ibis)
  T. m. melanopis
  S Chile, S Argentina
  T. m. branickii
  Ecuador, Peru, N Bolivia

CERCIBIS
Cercibis oxycerca (Sharp-tailed Ibis)
  SE Colombia to Surinam, N Brazil

MESEMBRINIBIS
Mesembrinibis cayennensis (Green Ibis)
  Panama to NE Argentina

PHIMOSUS
Phimosus infuscatus (Bare-faced Ibis)
  P. i. berlepschi
  N South America
  P. i. nudifrons
  C & S Brazil

P. i. infuscatus
  Paraguay, Uruguay, NE Argentina

EUDOCIMUS
Eudocimus albus (White Ibis)
  S USA to N South America
Eudocimus ruber (Scarlet Ibis)
  N South America, Trinidad

PLEGADIS
Plegadis falcinellus (Glossy Ibis)
  P. f. falcinellus
  S Europe, Asia, Africa, Central America
  P. f. peregrinus
  Philippine Is, Celebes, Java to Australia
Plegadis chihi (White-faced Ibis)
  NW USA to SC South America
Plegadis ridgwayi (Puna Ibis)
  Peru, Bolivia

LOPHOTIBIS
Lophotibis cristata (Crested Wood Ibis)
  L. c. cristata
  E Madagascar
  L. c. urschi
  W Madagascar

PLATALEINAE

PLATALEA
Platalea leucorodia (White Spoonbill)
  P. l. leucorodia
  Holland, S Europe to Asia Minor » Africa
  P. l. major
  C Asia to Japan, Egypt, India, Taiwan
  P. l. balsaci
  Mauretania
  P. l. archeri
  Red Sea coasts, Somalia
Platalea minor (Black-faced Spoonbill)
  S Japan to S China, Taiwan
Platalea alba (African Spoonbill)
  Gambia to Sudan, Cape Province
Platalea regia (Royal Spoonbill)
  Australia to New Guinea, Celebes, New
    Zealand

PLATIBIS
Platibis flavipes (Yellow-billed Spoonbill)
  Australia

AJAIA
Ajaia ajaja (Roseate Spoonbill)
  S USA to C Argentina & C Chile

25 PHOENICOPTERIDAE (FLAMINGOS)

PHOENICOPTERUS
Phoenicopterus ruber (Greater Flamingo)
  P. r. ruber
  Atlantic, Central & South America,
    W Indies

P. r. roseus
  S Europe, C Asia, NW India, S Africa
Phoenicopterus chilensis (Chilian Flamingo)
  Peru, Uruguay to Tierra del Fuego

Phoeniconaias minor (Lesser Flamingo)
  S & E Africa, NW India, Madagascar

Phoenicoparrus andinus (Andean Flamingo)
  Chile & NW Argentina
Phoenicoparrus jamesi (James' Flamingo)
  S Peru, N Chile, NW Argentina

Anseriformes

26 ANHIMIDAE (SCREAMERS)

Anhima cornuta (Horned Screamer)
  N South America

Chauna torquata (Crested Screamer)
  Paraguay, S Brazil, N & E Argentina
Chauna chavaria (Northern Screamer)
  N Colombia, N Venezuela

27 ANATIDAE (DUCKS, GEESE, SWANS)

ANSERANATINAE

Anseranas semipalmata (Magpie Goose)
  S New Guinea, N Australia

ANSERINAE

DENDROCYGNINI

Dendrocygna guttata (Spotted Whistling Duck)
  Mindanao I to Celebes & New Guinea
Dendrocygna eytoni (Plumed Whistling Duck)
  Australia, Tasmania
Dendrocygna bicolor (Fulvous Whistling Duck)
  D. b. helva
    S USA, N Mexico
  D. b. bicolor
    N South America, E Africa, India
Dendrocygna arcuata (Wandering Whistling Duck)
  D. a. arcuata
    Sumatra to Philippine Is, Timor I,
    Moluccas
  D. a. australis
    Australia, New Guinea

D. a. pygmaea
  New Britain, Fiji Is
Dendrocygna javanica (Indian Whistling Duck)
  India to Java & Indochina
Dendrocygna viduata (White-faced Whistling Duck)
  S America, C Africa
Dendrocygna arborea (Black-billed Whistling Duck)
  West Indies
Dendrocygna autumnalis (Red-billed Whistling Duck)
  D. a. autumnalis
    SE Texas to Panama
  D. a. discolor
    E Panama to Ecuador & N Argentina

ANSERINI

Cygnus olor (Mute Swan)
  Europe to C Asia » N Africa, India
Cygnus atratus (Black Swan)
  Australia, Tasmania
Cygnus melanocoryphus (Black-necked Swan)
  S South America, Falkland Is
Cygnus cygnus (Whooper Swan)
  C. c. cygnus
    N Europe, N Asia » C Europe, C Asia,
    China
  C. c. islandicus
    S Greenland, Iceland
  C. c. buccinator
    N Canada, N USA » USA
Cygnus columbianus (Whistling Swan)
  C. c. columbianus
    N Canada » coasts of USA
  C. c. bewickii
    N Russia, N Siberia » N Europe, C Asia
  C. c. jankowskii
    NE Asia » China, Japan

Coscoroba coscoroba (Coscoroba Swan)
  S South America

Anser cygnoides (Swan Goose)
  NC Asia & Siberia » China
Anser fabalis (Bean Goose)
  A. f. fabalis
    Lapland to Ural Mts » W & E Europe
  A. f. johanseni
    W Siberia
  A. f. middendorffi
    E Siberia » E China & Japan
  A. f. rossicus
    N Russia, NW Siberia » WC Europe,
    C Asia

A. f. serrirostris
N Siberia » China, Japan
A. f. brachyrhynchus
Greenland, Iceland, Spitzbergen »
W Europe
Anser albifrons (White-fronted Goose)
A. a. albifrons
N Europe, N Asia » W Europe, S Russia,
India, China
A. a. frontalis
E Siberia, N Canada » W USA, China,
Japan
A. a. flavirostris
NW Greenland » British Isles
A. a. gambelli
NW Canada » C California
A. a. elgasi
Alaska
**Anser erythropus (Lesser White-fronted
Goose)**
N Russia, N Asia » SE Europe & China
Anser anser (Greylag Goose)
A. a. anser
N Europe, N Asia » NW Africa
A. a. rubrirostris
C & E Asia » NW India, China
Anser indicus (Bar-headed Goose)
C Asia » N India, N Burma
Anser caerulescens (Snow Goose)
A. c. caerulescens
N Canada » S USA
A. c. atlanticus
N Greenland » NE USA
Anser rossi (Ross's Goose)
N Canada » N California
Anser canagicus (Emperor Goose)
NE Siberia, NW Alaska » Aleutian Is

BRANTA
Branta sandvicensis (Hawaiian Goose)
Hawaii
Branta canadensis (Canada Goose)
B. c. leucopareia
Aleutian Is » Japan & W USA
B. c. minima
W Alaska » W USA
B. c. occidentalis
Gulf of Alaska
B. c. fulva
S Alaska, W British Colombia
B. c. taverneri
N Canada » SW USA, Mexico
B. c. parvipes
Interior Canada » SC USA
B. c. moffitti
SW Canada » NW USA
B. c. hutchinsii
NC Canada » Texas, Mexico

B. c. interior
C & E Canada » E USA
B. c. canadensis
(Introduced Europe, New Zealand)
E Canada » E USA
Branta leucopsis (Barnacle Goose)
NE Greenland, Spitzbergen to W Europe
Branta bernicla (Brent Goose)
B. b. bernicla
N Europe, NW Asia » W Europe
B. b. hrota
E Canada, Greenland » NE USA,
NW Europe
B. b. nigricans
NE Canada » New Jersey
B. b. orientalis
E Siberia, W Canada » E Asia, W USA
Branta ruficollis (Red-breasted Goose)
N Siberia » S Russia

CEREOPSIS
**Cereopsis novaehollandiae (Cereopsis
Goose)**
Islands off S Australia

STICTONETTINI

STICTONETTA
Stictonetta naevosa (Freckled Duck)
Southern Australia, Tasmania

ANATINAE
TADORNINI

CYANOCHEN
**Cyanochen cyanopterus (Blue-winged
Goose)**
Ethiopia

CHLOEPHAGA
Chloephaga melanoptera (Andean Goose)
Peru to Tierra del Fuego
Chloephaga picta (Magellan Goose)
C. p. picta
S Chile, S Argentina
C. p. leucoptera
Falkland Is
Chloephaga hybrida (Kelp Goose)
C. h. hybrida
S Chile
C. h. malvinarum
Falkland Is
**Chloephaga poliocephala (Ashy-headed
Goose)**
S Chile, Argentina
**Chloephaga rubidiceps (Ruddy-headed
Goose)**
Tierra del Fuego, Falkland Is

NEOCHEN
Neochen jubatus (Orinoco Goose)
Orinoco & Amazon basins

ALOPOCHEN
Alopochen aegyptiacus (Eygptian Goose)
Africa (Introduced UK)

TADORNA
Tadorna ferruginea (Ruddy Shelduck)
SE Europe & C Asia » India & S China
Tadorna cana (South African Shelduck)
Transvaal, Cape Province
Tadorna variegata (Paradise Shelduck)
New Zealand
Tadorna tadornoides (Australian Shelduck)
Southern Australia, Tasmania
Tadorna tadorna (Common Shelduck)
W Europe to E Asia » N Africa, India,
S China
Tadorna radjah (Radjah Shelduck)
T. r. radjah
S Moluccas, Aru Is, New Guinea
T. r. rufitergum
N & E Australia

TACHYERINI

TACHYERES
**Tachyeres patachonicus (Flying Steamer
Duck)**
S South America
**Tachyeres pteneres (Flightless Steamer
Duck)**
S South America
**Tachyeres brachypterus (Falkland Is
Flightless Steamer Duck)**
Falkland Is
**Tachyeres leucocephalus (White-headed
Flightless Steamer Duck)**
S Argentina

CAIRININI

PLECTROPTERUS
**Plectropterus gambensis (Spur-winged
Goose)**
P. g. gambensis
Gambia to Sudan & Rhodesia
P. g. niger
Southern Africa

CAIRINA
Cairina moschata (Muscovy Duck)
Mexico to Peru & Uruguay
**Cairina scutulata (White-winged Wood
Duck)**
Assam & Thailand to Sumatra & Java

SARKIDIORNIS
Sarkidiornis melanotos (Comb Duck)
S. m. melanotos
Africa, India, SE China
S. m. sylvatica
Colombia
S. m. carunculatus
Venezuela to N Argentina

PTERONETTA
Pteronetta hartlaubii (Hartlaub's Duck)

P. h. hartlaubii
Liberia to E Zaire
P. h. albifrons
EC Africa

NETTAPUS
Nettapus pulchellus (Green Pygmy Goose)
S Moluccas, S New Guinea, N Australia
**Nettapus coromandelianus (Cotton Pygmy
Goose)**
N. c. coromandelianus
India to S China & NW Indonesia
N. c. albipennis
NE Australia
Nettapus auritus (African Pygmy Goose)
Gambia to Kenya & Cape Province

CALLONETTA
Callonetta leucophrys (Ringed Teal)
C South America

AIX
Aix sponsa (Wood Duck)
S Canada, USA, Cuba
Aix galericulata (Mandarin)
NE Asia, E China, Japan

CHENONETTA
Chenonetta jubata (Maned Goose)
Australia, Tasmania

AMAZONETTA
Amazonetta brasiliensis (Brazilian Teal)
A. b. brasiliensis
Venezuela to N Argentina
A. b. ipecutiri
C & S Argentina

ANATINI

HYMENOLAIMUS
**Hymenolaimus malacorhynchus (Moun-
tain Duck)**
New Zealand

MERGANETTA
Merganetta armata (Torrent Duck)
M. a. colombiana
W Venezuela, Colombia, Ecuador
M. a. leucogenis
C & S Ecuador, Peru
M. a. turneri
S Peru
M. a. garleppi
Bolivia
M. a. berlepschi
NW Argentina
M. a. armata
C Chile, W Argentina
M. a. fraenata
SC Chile

ANAS
Anas waigiuensis (Salvadori's Duck)
New Guinea, Waigeu I

Anas sparsa (African Black Duck)
  A. s. maclatchyi
    Cameroun, Gabon
  A. s. leucostigma
    Sudan & Ethiopia to Tanzania
  A. s. sparsa
    Angola, Malawi to Cape Province
Anas penelope (European Wigeon)
    N Europe, N Asia » N Africa, India, Japan
Anas americana (American Wigeon)
    W Canada, USA » Costa Rica, W Indies
Anas sibilatrix (Chiloe Wigeon)
    S South America
Anas falcata (Falcated Teal)
    NE Asia » E & S China
Anas strepera (Gadwall)
    Europe, Asia, W North America » N Africa,
    India, China, Mexico
Anas formosa (Baikal Teal)
    NE Asia » China, Japan
Anas crecca (Green-winged Teal)
  A. c. crecca
    Europe, Asia » N Africa, India, China
  A. c. nimia
    Aleutian Is
  A. c. carolinensis
    N Canada » S USA, Central America,
    W Indies
Anas flavirostris (Chilean Teal)
  A. f. flavirostris
    C Chile, NW Argentina to Tierra del Fuego
  A. f. andium
    C & S Colombia, Ecuador
  A. f. altipetens
    W Venezuela, E Colombia
  A. f. oxyptera
    N Peru to N Chile, Argentina
Anas capensis (Cape Teal)
    S Ethiopia to Botswana, Cape Province
Anas gibberifrons (Grey Teal)
  A. g. gibberifrons
    Java to Celebes, Timor I, Wetar I
  A. g. remissa
    Rennell I
  A. g. gracilis
    New Guinea, Australia, New Zealand
  A. g. albogularis
    Andaman Is, Cocos Is
Anas bernieri (Madagascar Teal)
    W Madagascar
Anas castanea (Chestnut-breasted Teal)
    Southern Australia, Tasmania
Anas aucklandica (New Zealand Teal)
  A. a. aucklandica
    Auckland I
  A. a. nesiotis
    Campbell I
  A. a. chlorotis
    New Zealand

Anas platyrhynchos (Mallard)
  A. p. platyrhynchos
    Europe, Asia, N America » N Africa, India,
    Mexico
  A. p. conboschas
    Greenland
  A. p. wyvilliana
    Hawaiian Is
  A. p. laysanensis
    Laysan I
  A. p. fulvigula
    SE USA
  A. p. diazi
    N & C Mexico
  A. p. maculosa
    Mexico
Anas rubripes (North American Black Duck)
    NE North America to SE USA
Anas melleri (Meller's Duck)
    E Madagascar
Anas undulata (African Yellow-bill)
  A. u. ruppelli
    Ethiopia, Sudan
  A. u. undulata
    Angola to Uganda, Cape Province
Anas poecilorhyncha (Spotbill Duck)
  A. p. poecilorhyncha
    India, Sri Lanka
  A. p. haringtoni
    Burma, SW China
  A. p. zonorhyncha
    NE Asia, China
  A. p. pelewensis
    Palau Is, Solomon Is, Fiji Is, N New Guinea
  A. p. percna
    Sunda Is, Celebes
  A. p. superciliosa
    S New Guinea, Australia, Tasmania, New
    Zealand
Anas luzonica (Philippine Duck)
    Philippine Is
Anas specularis (Bronze-winged Duck)
    S Chile, S Argentina
Anas specularioides (Crested Duck)
  A. s. alticola
    C Peru, Bolivia, N Chile
  A. s. specularioides
    C & S Chile, WC Argentina
Anas acuta (Pintail)
  A. a. acuta
    N Europe, Asia, N America » Africa, China,
    Central America
  A. a. eatoni
    Kerguelen I
  A. a. drygalskii
    Crozet Is
Anas georgica (Georgian Teal)
  A. g. niceforoi
    EC Colombia

A. g. spinicauda
  S Colombia to Tierra del Fuego
A. g. georgica
  South Georgia I
Anas bahamensis (Bahama Pintail)
A. b. bahamensis
  Bahama Is, Gtr Antilles, N South
  America
A. b. rubrirostris
  S Brazil to C Peru
A. b. galapagensis
  Galapagos Is
Anas erythrorhyncha (Red-billed Pintail)
  S & E Africa
Anas versicolor (Versicolor Teal)
A. v. versicolor
  Bolivia to C Chile, C Argentina
A. v. fretensis
  S Chile, S Argentina
A. v. puna
  Highlands of C Peru to N Chile
Anas punctata (Hottentot Teal)
  Uganda to Cape Province, Madagascar
Anas querquedula (Garganey)
  W Europe to Japan » Africa, India,
  Indonesia
Anas discors (Blue-winged Teal)
A. d. discors
  S Canada, C USA » Central America &
  N South America
A. d. orphna
  SE Canada, E USA » W Indies, South
  America
Anas cyanoptera (Cinnamon Teal)
A. c. septentrionalium
  W North America to N South America
A. c. tropica
  Lowlands of Colombia
A. c. borreroi
  Highlands of Colombia
A. c. orinomus
  Peru, Bolivia, N Chile
A. c. cyanoptera
  S Brazil to Tierra del Fuego
Anas platalea (Argentine Shoveller)
  Peru, S Brazil to Tierra del Fuego
Anas smithi (Cape Shoveller)
  Angola, Transvaal to Cape Province
Anas rhynchotis (Australian Shoveller)
A. r. rhynchotis
  Australia, Tasmania
A. r. variegata
  New Zealand
Anas clypeata (Common Shoveller)
  Europe, Asia, N America » E Africa, India,
  China, Mexico

MALACORHYNCHUS
**Malacorhynchus membranaceus
  (Pink-eared Duck)**
  Australia, Tasmania **e?**

MARMARONETTA
**Marmaronetta angustirostris (Marbled
  Teal)**
  S Spain to NW India

AYTHYINI

RHODONESSA
**Rhodonessa caryophyllacea (Pink-headed
  Duck)**
  NE & E India **e?**

NETTA
Netta rufina (Red-crested Pochard)
  E Europe, C Asia » N Africa, India
Netta erythrophthalma (Southern Pochard)
N. e. brunnea
  Angola to Ethiopia & Cape Province
N. e. erythrophthalma
  W South America
Netta peposaca (Rosybill)
  C Chile, N & C Argentina, Paraguay

AYTHYA
Aythya valisineria (Canvasback)
  WC Canada, WC USA » S USA, Mexico
Aythya ferina (European Pochard)
  W Europe to C Asia » N Africa, India,
  S China
Aythya americana (Redhead)
  W Canada, W USA » NW Mexico
Aythya collaris (Ring-necked Duck)
  W Canada, NW USA » S USA,
  Central America, W Indies
**Aythya australis (Australian White-eyed
  Duck)**
A. a. australis
  Australia, Tasmania, New Zealand
A. a. extima
  New Hebrides
A. a. papuana
  W New Guinea
Aythya baeri (Baer's Pochard)
  NE Asia » China, Burma, Japan
Aythya nyroca (Ferruginous Duck)
  S & E Europe to C Asia » NE Africa, Iran,
  Burma
Aythya innotata (Madagascar Pochard)
  N & E Madagascar
**Aythya novaeseelandiae (New Zealand
  Scaup)**
  New Zealand, Auckland I
Aythya fuligula (Tufted Duck)
  Europe, Asia » India, S China, Philippine Is
Aythya marila (Greater Scaup)

A. m. marila
 N Europe, Asia » W & S Europe,
 NW India
A. m. mariloides
 Bering Is » China, Korea, Japan
A. m. nearctica
 N & W Canada » W & E USA, W Indies
Aythya affinis (Lesser Scaup)
 W & C Canada, W USA » S USA, Panama,
 W Indies

MERGINI

SOMATERIA
Somateria mollissima (Eider)
 S. m. v-nigra
 Alaska, NE Asia » Aleutian Is
 S. m. borealis
 N Canada, W Greenland » Maine
 S. m. dresseri
 NE Canada » Newfoundland
 S. m. mollissima
 Iceland to Novaya Zemlya » NW Europe
 S. m. sedentaria
 Hudson Bay
 S. m. faroeensis
 Faroe Is
Somateria spectabilis (King Eider)
 N Europe, N Asia, N Canada
Somateria fischeri (Spectacled Eider)
 NE Siberia, Alaska » Aleutian Is

POLYSTICTA
Polysticta stelleri (Steller's Eider)
 NE Siberia, Alaska » Aleutian Is

HISTRIONICUS
Histrionicus histrionicus (Harlequin Duck)
 H. h. histrionicus
 Iceland, Greenland, N Labrador
 H. h. pacificus
 E Siberia, Alaska, W USA to Japan,
 California

CLANGULA
Clangula hyemalis (Long-tailed Duck)
 N Europe, Asia, N America » W Europe,
 Japan, S USA

MELANITTA
Melanitta nigra (Common Scoter)
 M. n. nigra
 N Europe, N Asia, » W Europe to Black Sea
 M. n. americana
 NE Asia, W Alaska » China, Gt Lakes,
 California
Melanitta perspicillata (Surf Scoter)
 N Canada, NE Siberia to coasts of USA
Melanitta fusca (Velvet Scoter)
 M. f. fusca
 N Europe, NW Asia to W Europe, SW Asia
 M. f. stejnegeri
 C & E Asia » China & Japan

M. f. dixoni
 W Alaska » W USA
M. f. deglandi
 NW Canada, NW USA to Gt Lakes, E USA

BUCEPHALA
Bucephala albeola (Bufflehead)
 N & W Canada » USA
Bucephala islandica (Barrow's Goldeneye)
 SC Alaska to Iceland » coasts of USA
Bucephala clangula (Goldeneye)
 B. c. clangula
 N Europe, N Asia » S Europe, India, Japan
 B. c. americana
 Canada » California, S Carolina

MERGUS
Mergus cucullatus (Hooded Merganser)
 SC Canada to SE USA » S USA
Mergus albellus (Smew)
 N Europe, N Asia » N India, China, Japan
**Mergus octosetaceus (Brazilian
Merganser)**
 S Brazil, E Paraguay, NE Argentina
Mergus serrator (Red-breasted Merganser)
 M. s. serrator
 N Europe, Asia, N America » China,
 Mexico
 M. s. schioleri
 Greenland
Mergus squamatus (Chinese Merganser)
 NE Asia » China
Mergus merganser (Goosander)
 M. m. merganser
 Iceland to NE Asia » Mediterranean &
 China
 M. m. orientalis
 C Asia to Himalayas » Assam & Japan
 M. m. americanus
 Canada, W USA » E & S USA

OXYURINI

HETERONETTA
**Heteronetta atricapilla (Black-headed
Duck)**
 C Chile, Paraguay, N & C Argentina

OXYURA
Oxyura dominica (Masked Duck)
 Gtr Antilles, N & C South America
Oxyura jamaicensis (Ruddy Duck)
 O. j. rubida
 W Canada, W USA » Mexico, E & S USA
 O. j. jamaicensis
 W Indies
 O. j. andina
 Colombia
 O. j. ferruginea
 Peru, Bolivia
Oxyura leucocephala (White-headed Duck)
 Mediterranean to C Asia to Egypt, N India

Oxyura maccoa (Maccoa Duck)
S Ethiopia to Cape Province
Oxyura vittata (Argentine Lake Duck)
N Chile, S Brazil to Tierra del Fuego
Oxyura australis (Australian Blue-billed Duck)
S Australia, Tasmania

BIZIURA
Biziura lobata (Musk Duck)
S Australia, Tasmania

THALASSORNIS
Thalassornis leuconotos (White-backed Duck)
T. l. leuconotos
E Cameroun, to S Ethiopia & Cape Province
T. l. insularis
Madagascar

Falconiformes

Cathartae

28 CATHARTIDAE (NEW WORLD VULTURES)

CATHARTES
Cathartes aura (Turkey Vulture)
C. a. aura
S Canada to Costa Rica & Cuba
C. a. septentrionalis
E North America
C. a. ruficollis
Panama to N Argentina, Trinidad
C. a. jota
Colombia to Patagonia, Falkland Is
Cathartes burrovianus (Lesser Yellow-headed Vulture)
E Mexico to N Argentina
Cathartes melambrotus (Greater Yellow-headed Vulture)
C South America

CORAGYPS
Coragyps atratus (American Black Vulture)
C. a. atratus
W & S USA, N Mexico
C. a. brasiliensis
C Mexico to Peru & Brazil
C. a. foetens
Ecuador to C Chile & Patagonia

SARCORHAMPHUS
Sarcorhamphus papa (King Vulture)
C Mexico to N Argentina, Trinidad

GYMNOGYPS
Gymnogyps californianus (Californian Condor)
S California

VULTUR
Vultur gryphus (Andean Condor)
Andes from W Venezuela to Tierra del Fuego

Accipitres

29 PANDIONIDAE (OSPREY)
PANDION

Pandion haliaetus (Osprey)
P. h. haliaetus
Europe, Asia » S Africa, India, Sunda Is
P. h. carolinensis
N America » C South America
P. h. ridgwayi
Bahama Is, E Belize
P. h. melvillensis
Philippine Is to Sumatra & C Australia
P. h. microhaliaetus
New Caledonia, N Australia
P. h. cristatus
S Australia, Tasmania

30 ACCIPITRIDAE (HAWKS, EAGLES)

AVICEDA
Aviceda cuculoides (African Cuckoo Falcon)
A. c. cuculoides
Gambia to N Zaire
A. c. verreauxi
Angola to Uganda & Cape Province
A. c. batesi
Guinea to Cameroun
A. c. emini
NE Zaire
Aviceda madagascariensis (Madagascar Cuckoo Falcon)
Madagascar
Aviceda jerdoni (Jerdon's Baza)
A. j. jerdoni
E Himalayas, N India
A. j. ceylonensis
S India, Sri Lanka
A. j. borneensis
Borneo
A. j. magnirostris
Philippine Is
A. j. celebensis
Celebes, Banggai I, Sula Is
Aviceda subcristata (Crested Baza)
A. s. timorlaonsis
Lombok I to Timor I & Babar I
A. s. rufa
Obi Is, N Moluccas
A. s. stresemanni
Buru I
A. s. reinwardtii
Ceram I, Ambon I

A. s. pallida
Kei Is
A. s. obscura
Biak I
A. s. waigeuensis
Waigeu I
A. s. stenozona
W New Guinea, Aru Is, Misol I
A. s. megala
E New Guinea, Fergusson I, Goodenough I
A. s. bismarckii
New Britain, New Ireland, New Hanover
A. s. coultasi
Admiralty Is, Manus I
A. s. gurneyi
San Cristobal I, Ugi I, Santa Anna I,
Malaita I, Guadaicanal I
A. s. robusta
Choiseul I, Ysabel I
A. s. proxima
Bougainville I, Shortland I
A.s. njikena
NW Australia
A. s. subcristata
NE & E Australia
Aviceda leuphotes (Black Baza)
A. l. leuphotes
Himalayas to SW India
A. l. burmana
Burma, Malaysia & Indochina
A. l. sayama
Nepal, S China » Indo China
A. l. wolfi
Szechwan
A. l. andamanica
Andaman Is

LEPTODON
Leptodon cayanensis (Grey-headed Kite)
EC Mexico to N Argentina, Trinidad

CHONDROHIERAX
Chondrohierax uncinatus (Hook-billed Kite)
C. u. uncinatus
S Mexico to N Argentina, Trinidad
C. u. aquilonis
Mexico
C. u. mirus
Grenada
C. u. wilsonii
E Cuba

HENICOPERNIS
Henicopernis longicauda (Long-tailed Honey Buzzard)
H. l. longicauda
New Guinea
H. l. minimus
islands off W New Guinea

H. l. fraterculus
Japen I
Henicopernis infuscata (Black Honey Buzzard)
New Britain

PERNIS
Pernis apivorus (Honey Buzzard)
Europe, N Asia » Africa
Pernis ptilorhynchus (Oriental Honey Buzzard)
P. p. orientalis
E Siberia » Burma, China
P. p. ruficollis
India, Burma, SW China
P. p. torquatus
Malaysia, Thailand, Sumatra, Borneo
P. p. ptilorynchus
Java
P. p. palawanensis
Palawan I
P. p. philippensis
Philippine Is
Pernis celebensis (Barred Honey Buzzard)
P. c. celebensis
Celebes
P. c. steerei
Philippine Is

ELANOIDES
Elanoides forficatus (Swallow-tailed Kite)
E. f. forficatus
S USA, N Mexico
E. f. yetapa
S Mexico to N Argentina

MACHAERHAMPHUS
Machaerhamphus alcinus (Bat Hawk)
M. a. alcinus
Malaysia, Sumatra, Borneo
M. a. papuanus
SE New Guinea
M. a. anderssoni
Gambia to Somalia & Natal

GAMPSONYX
Gampsonyx swainsonii (Pearl Kite)
G. s. leonae
W Nicaragua, N South America
G. s. swainsonii
C Brazil to N Argentina
G. s. magnus
S Ecuador, N Peru

ELANUS
Elanus leucurus (White-tailed Kite)
E. l. majusculus
S USA & E Mexico
E. l. leucurus
N South America to C Chile
Elanus caeruleus (Black-shouldered Kite)

E. c. caeruleus
Africa, S Asia
E. c. sumatranus
Sumatra
E. c. hypoleucus
Java to Philippine Is & Celebes
E. c. wahgiensis
E & C New Guinea
Elanus notatus (Australian Black-shouldered Kite)
Australia
Elanus scriptus (Letter-winged Kite)
C Australia

CHELICTINIA
Chelictinia riocourii (African Swallow-tailed Kite)
Senegal to Somalia & N Kenya

ROSTRHAMUS
Rostrhamus sociabilis (Everglade Kite)
R. s. plumbeus
Florida
R. s. levis
Cuba, Isle of Pines
R. s. major
E Mexico, Guatemala
R. s. sociabilis
Nicaragua to Argentina
Rostrhamus hamatus (Slender-billed Kite)
E Panama to Peru & E Brazil

HARPAGUS
Harpagus bidentatus (Double-toothed Kite)
H. b. fasciatus
S Mexico to W Colombia & Ecuador
H. b. bidentatus
E Bolivia to E Colombia & E Brazil
Harpagus diodon (Rufous-thighed Kite)
the Guianas to Paraguay & N Argentina

ICTINIA
Ictinia plumbea (Plumbeous Kite)
EC Mexico to Paraguay & N Argentina
Ictinia misisippiensis (Mississippi Kite)
S USA to C South America

LOPHOICTINIA
Lophoictinia isura (Square-tailed Kite)
Australia

HAMIROSTRA
Hamirostra melanosternon (Black-breasted Buzzard Kite)
N & C Australia

MILVUS
Milvus migrans (Black Kite)
M. m. migrans
Europe, Middle East, W Asia
M. m. tenebrosus
Cape Verde Is, Madeira

M. m. arabicus
Egypt
M. m. aegyptius
N Africa, Somalia, S Yemen
M. m. parasitus
Senegal to Sudan & Cape Province
M. m. lineatus
C & E Asia, Japan to Himalayas
M. m. govinda
India to Indochina & Malaysia
M. m. formosanus
Hainan I, Taiwan
M. m. affinis
Lombok I to Timor I, Celebes, New Guinea, Australia
Milvus milvus (Red Kite)
M. m. milvus
Europe, Asia Minor, NW Africa, Canary Is
M. m. fasciicauda
Cape Verde Is

HALIASTUR
Haliastur sphenurus (Whistling Hawk)
E New Guinea, New Caledonia, Australia
Haliastur indus (Brahminy Kite)
H. i. indus
India, Sri Lanka to S China, Indochina
H. i. intermedius
Malaysia, Philippine Is, Borneo, Indonesia
H. i. girrenera
Australia, New Guinea, Bismarck Archipelago
H. i. flavirostris
Solomon Is

HALIAEETUS
Haliaeetus leucogaster (White-bellied Sea Eagle)
India to China & Australia
Haliaeetus sanfordi (Sanford's Sea Eagle)
Solomon Is
Haliaeetus vocifer (African Fish Eagle)
Senegal to Ethiopia & Cape Province
Haliaeetus vociferoides (Madagascar Fish Eagle)
Madagascar
Haliaeetus leucoryphus (Pallas' Sea Eagle)
C Asia to Iraq, N India & Burma
Haliaeetus leucocephalus (American Bald Eagle)
H. l. alascensis
Alaska, W Canada
H. i. leucocephalus
C & S USA
Haliaeetus albicilla (White-tailed Sea Eagle)
H. a. albicilla
Europe, N Asia, Japan to India, China
H. a. groenlandicus
Greenland

Haliaeetus pelagicus (Steller's Sea Eagle)
  H. p. pelagicus
    NE Asia, N China, Japan
  H. p. niger
    Korea

ICHTHYOPHAGA
Ichthyophaga nana (Lesser Fishing Eagle)
  I. n. plumbea
    Himalayas to N Vietnam, Hainan I
  I. n. nana
    Thailand to Malaysia, Sumatra to Celebes
Ichthyophaga ichthyaetus (Grey-headed Fishing Eagle)
  India to Borneo & Philippine Is

GYPOHIERAX
Gypohierax angolensis (Palm-nut Vulture)
  Senegal to Kenya & Cape Province

NEOPHRON
Neophron percnopterus (Egyptian Vulture)
  N. p. percnopterus
    S Europe, Middle East, Africa
  N. p. ginginianus
    Himalayas to S India

GYPAETUS
Gypaetus barbatus (Lammergeier)
  G. b. aureus
    S Europe, Middle East, C Asia
  G. b. haemachalanus
    E Asia
  G. b. barbatus
    NW Africa to.Egypt
  G. b. meridionalis
    Yemen, Ethiopia to S Africa

NECROSYRTES
Necrosyrtes monachus (Hooded Vulture)
  N. m. monachus
    Senegal to Sudan
  N. m. pileatus-
    E Sudan & Angola to CapeProvince

GYPS
Gyps bengalensis (Indian White-backed Vulture)
  India to Indochina
Gyps africanus (African White-backed Vulture)
  Senegal to Sudan & Transvaal
Gyps indicus (Indian Griffon)
  G. i. indicus
    N & S India to Indochina
  G. i. nudiceps
    NE India
Gyps rüeppellii (Rüppell's Griffon)
  G. r. rüepellii
    Egypt, Senegal to Uganda, Tanzania
  G. r. erlangeri
    Ethiopia, Somalia

Gyps himalayensis (Himalayan Griffon)
  C Asia to N India
Gyps fulvus (Griffon Vulture)
  G. f. fulvus
    S Europe, N Africa to C. Asia
  G. f. fulvescens
    Afghanistan, NW India
Gyps coprotheres (Cape Vulture)
  SW Rhodesia, South Africa

TORGOS
Torgos tracheliotus (Lappet-faced Vulture)
  T. t. tracheliotus
    NW Sahara to Ethiopia & Cape Province
  T. t. negevensis
    S Neger Desert

AEGYPIUS
Aegypius monachus (European Black Vulture)
  Spain to C Asia » N Africa, India & China
Aegypius occipitalis (White-headed Vulture)
  Senegal to Sudan & Cape Province

SARCOGYPS
Sarcogyps calvus (Asiatic King Vulture)
  India to Laos & SW China

CIRCAETUS
Circaetus gallicus (Short-toed Eagle)
  C. g. gallicus
    S Europe, N Africa to India & China
  C. g. heptneri
    E Asia
  C. g. beaudouini
    Senegal to Sudan & W Kenya
  C. g. pectoralis
    E & S Africa
Circaetus cinereus (Brown Harrier Eagle)
  Senegal to Ethiopia & Cape Province
Circaetus fasciolatus (Southern Banded Snake Eagle)
  E Kenya to Natal
Circaetus cinerascens (Smaller Banded Snake Eagle)
  Guinea to Ethiopia & Tanzania

TERATHOPIUS
Terathopius ecaudatus (Bateleur)
  Senegal to Iraq & Cape Province

SPILORNIS
Spilornis holospilus (Philippine Serpent Eagle)
  Philippine Is
Spilornis rufipectus (Celebes Serpent Eagle)
  S. r. rufipectus
    Celebes
  S. r. sulaensis
    Sula Is
Spilornis cheela (Crested Serpent Eagle)
  S. c. cheela
    N India

S. c. melanotis
S India
S. c. spilogaster
Sri Lanka
S. c. burmanicus
Burma to C & S Indochina
S. c. ricketti
SE China, N Indochina
S. c. malayensis
S Burma, Malaysia, N Sumatra
S. c. davisoni
Andaman Is
S. c. rutherfordi
Hainan I
S. c. hoya
Taiwan
S. c. perplexus
S Riukiu Is
S. c. pallidus
Borneo
S. c. kinabaluensis
Borneo
S. c. natunensis
Bunguran I, Billiton I
S. c. sipora
Mentawei Is, Sipora I
S. c. batu
Batu I, S Sumatra
S. c. asturinus
Nias I
S. c. abbottii
Simalur I
S. c. bido
Java, Bali I
S. c. baweanus
Bawean I
S. c. palawanensis
Palawan I, Balabac I, Calamian I
S. c. minimus
C Nicobar Is
Spilornis klossi (Nicobar Serpent Eagle)
Gt Nicobar I
Spilornis elgini (Andaman Serpent Eagle)
Andaman Is

DRYOTRIORCHIS
Dryotriorchis spectabilis (Congo Serpent Eagle)
D. s. spectabilis
Liberia to N Cameroun
D. s. batesi
S Cameroun & Gabon to C Zaire

EUTRIORCHIS
Eutriorchis astur (Madagascar Serpent Eagle)
Madagascar

POLYBOROIDES
Polyboroides typus (African Harrier Hawk)

P. t. typus
Sudan to Angola & Cape Province
P. t. pectoralis
Gambia to Gabon & W Zaire
Polyboroides radiatus (Madagascar Harrier Hawk)
Madagascar

GERANOSPIZA
Geranospiza caerulescens (Crane Hawk)
G. c. livens
NW Mexico
G. c. nigra
Mexico to C Panama
G. c. balzarensis
E Panama to NW Peru
G. c. caerulescens
E Ecuador & Colombia to the Guianas, N Brazil
G. c. gracilis
NE Brazil
G. c. flexipes
S Brazil & Bolivia to N Argentina

CIRCUS
Circus assimilis (Spotted Harrier)
Celebes, Timor I & W N & E Australia
Circus aeruginosus (Marsh Harrier)
C. a. aeruginosus
Europe, Israel, C Asia
C. a. harterti
Morocco & Algeria
C. a. spilonotus
E Asia to Japan, Philippine Is & Borneo
C. a. macrosceles
Madagascar, Comoro Is
C. a. maillardi
Reunion I
C. a. spilothorax
W New Guinea
C. a. approximans
New Caledonia, Fiji Is, Tonga, New Hebrides
C. a. gouldi
SE New Guinea, E & S Australia, New Zealand
Circus ranivorus (African Marsh Harrier)
Angola & Kenya to Cape Province
Circus maurus (Black Harrier)
Natal & Cape Province
Circus cyaneus (Hen Harrier)
C. c. cyaneus
Europe, Asia, N Africa
C. c. hudsonius
North & Central America
Circus cinereus (Cinereous Harrier)
W & S South America, Falkland Is
Circus macrourus (Pallid Harrier)
E Europe & C Asia to Africa & India

Circus pygargus (Montagu's Harrier)
W Europe & EC Asia to Africa, China
Circus melanoleucus (Pied Harrier)
E Siberia to India & Indochina
Circus buffoni (Long-winged Harrier)
Colombia, Trinidad, the Guianas to
C Argentina

MELIERAX

Melierax metabates (Dark Chanting
Goshawk)
M. m. metabates
Senegal to Ethiopia
M. m. theresae
SW Morocco
M. m. neumanni
Mali to N Sudan
M. m. ignoscens
Yemen
M. m. mechowi
Angola & N Namibia to Kenya & Rhodesia
Melierax canorus (Pale Chanting Goshawk)
M. c. poliopterus
Somalia to Tanzania
M. c. canorus
South Africa
Melierax gabar (Gabar Goshawk)
Senegal to Yemen & Cape Province

ACCIPITER

Accipiter doriae (Doria's Goshawk)
New Guinea
Accipiter radiatus (Red Goshawk)
NC Australia
Accipiter gentilis (Northern Goshawk)
A. g. gentilis
Europe, SW Asia, Morocco
A. g. buteoides
N Scandinavia, N Russia
A. g. albidus
NE Siberia
A. g. arrigonii
Corsica, Sardinia
A. g. schvedowi
SE Russia to W China
A. g. fujiyamae
Japan
A. g. atricapillus
North America
A. g. laingi
British Columbian islands
A. g. apache
SW USA, NW Mexico
Accipiter henstii (Henst's Goshawk)
Madagascar
Accipiter melanoleucus (Great Sparrow
Hawk)

A. m. melanoleucus
Central African Republic & Ethiopia to
Cape Province
A. m. temminckii
Ghana to Gabon, Cape Verde Is
Accipiter meyerianus (Meyer's Goshawk)
Moluccas, New Britain, Solomon Is
Accipiter buergersi (Bürger's Sparrow
Hawk)
E New Guinea
Accipiter ovampensis (Ovampo Sparrow
Hawk)
Ghana & Ethiopia to E Transvaal
Accipiter madagascariensis (Madagascar
Sparrow Hawk)
Madagascar
Accipiter gularis (Japanese Lesser Sparrow
Hawk)
NE Asia, Japan to S China & Philippine Is
Accipiter virgatus (Besra Sparrow Hawk)
A. v. affinis
W Himalayas to W & S China, Indochina
A. v. besra
S India, Sri Lanka, Andaman Is
A. v. confusus
Philippine Is
A. v. quegga
Leyte I
A. v. rufotibialis
N Borneo
A. v. vanbemmeli
Sumatra
A. v. virgatus
Java
Accipiter nanus (Celebes Little Sparrow
Hawk)
Celebes
Accipiter rhodogaster (Vinous-breasted
Sparrow Hawk)
A. r. rhodogaster
Celebes
A. r. butonensis
Muna I, Buton I
A. r. sulaensis
Peling I, Sula Is
Accipiter erythrauchen (Moluccan
Sparrow Hawk)
A. e. erythrauchen
Batjan I, Halmahera I, Morotai I, Obi Is
A. e. ceramensis
Ceram I, Buru I
Accipiter cirrhocephalus (Collared
Sparrow Hawk)
A. c. papuanus
New Guinea, Aru Is, Waigeu I, Japen I
A. c. rosselianus
Louisiades Archipelago, Rossel I

A. c. quaesitandus
Cape York Peninsular, & N Australia
A. c. cirrhocephalus
S Australia, Tasmania
Accipiter brachyurus (New Britain Sparrow Hawk)
New Britain
Accipiter nisus (European Sparrow Hawk)
A. n. nisus
Europe to C Russia & Iran
A. n. punicus
Morocco, Algeria, Tunisia
A. n. granti
Madeira, Canary Is
A. n. wolterstorffi
Corsica, Sardinia
A. n. nisosimilis
N Iran to Manchuria & Japan
A. n. melaschistos
Himalayas to W China
Accipiter rufiventris (Rufous-breasted Sparrow Hawk)
A. r. rufiventris
C Zaire to Kenya & Cape Province
A. r. perspicillaris
Ethiopia
Accipiter striatus (Sharp-shinned Hawk)
A. s. perobscurus
Queen Charlotte Is (British Columbia)
A. s. velox
Canada, USA
A. s. suttoni
N Mexico
A. s. madrensis.
SW Mexico
A. s. chionogaster
S Mexico, Guatemala to Nicaragua
A. s. fringilloides
Cuba
A. s. striatus
Hispaniola
A. s. venator
Puerto Rico
A. s. ventralis
W Venezuela & Colombia to W Bolivia
A. s. erythronemius
E Bolivia & S Brazil to Uruguay, N Argentina
Accipiter erythropus (Red-thighed Sparrow Hawk)
A. e. erythropus
Gambia to Togo
A. e. zenkeri
Cameroun to S Angola & Uganda
Accipiter minullus (African Little Sparrow Hawk)
Ethiopia to Angola & Cape Province

Accipiter castanilus (Chestnut-bellied Sparrow Hawk) 81
A. c. castanilus
Nigeria to W Zaire
A. c. beniensis
E Zaire
Accipiter tachiro (African Goshawk)
A. t. macroscelides
Sierra Leone to W Cameroun
A. t. lopezi
Fernando Po I
A. t. toussenelii
Cameroun, Gabon, N & W Zaire
A. t. canescens
E Zaire
A. t. unduliventer
E & S Ethiopia
A. t. croizati
SW Ethiopia
A. t. sparsimfasciatus
Uganda & S Zaire to Somalia & Tanzania
A. t. tachiro
S Angola & Mozambique to Cape Province
Accipiter trivirgatus (Crested Goshawk)
A. t. peninsulae
SW India
A. t. layardi
Sri Lanka
A. t. indicus
NE India to S China, Malaysia
A. t. trivirgatus
Sumatra
A. t. niasensis
Nias I
A. t. javanicus
Java
A. t. microstictus
Borneo
A. t. palawanus
Palawan I, Calamian Is
A. t. castroi
Polillo Is
A. t. extimus
Negros I, Samar I, Leyte I, Mindanao I
Accipiter griseiceps (Celebes Crested Goshawk)
Celebes, Muna I, Buton I
Accipiter trinotatus (Spot-tailed Accipiter)
Celebes, Muna I, Buton I
Accipiter luteoschistaceus (Blue and Grey Sparrow Hawk)
New Britain
Accipiter fasciatus (Australian Goshawk)
A. f. natalis
Christmas I
A. f. wallacei
Lombok I to Wetar I, Damar I, Moa I

A. f. tjendanae
Sumba I
A. f. stresemanni
Djampea I, Tukangbesi Is
A. f. savu
Savu I
A. f. hellmayri
Alor I, Samao I, Timor I
A. f. buruensis
Buru I
A. f. dogwa
S New Guinea
A. f. polycryptus
E New Guinea
A. f. vigilax
New Caledonia, New Hebrides
A. f. didimus
N coast of Australia
A. f. fasciatus
Rennell I, Australia, Tasmania
***Accipiter henicogrammus* (Gray's Goshawk)**
Batjan I, Halmahera I, Morotai I
***Accipiter novaehollandiae* (White Goshawk)**
A. n. misoriensis
Biak I
A. n. hiogaster
Ceram I, Ambon I
A. n. albiventris
Kei Is
A. n. pallidiceps
Buru I
A. n. matthiae
South Matthias Is
A. n. manusi
Admiralty Is
A. n. lavongai
New Hanover
A. n. rubianae
New Georgia, Rendova I, Vellalavella I
A. n. rufoschistaceus
Ysabel I, Choiseul I
A. n. bougainvillei
Faure I, Bougainville I
A. n. malaitae
Malaita I
A. n. pulchellus
Guadalcanal I
A. n. sylvestris
Sumbawa I, Flores I, Pantar I, Alor I
A. n. dampieri
Rook I
A. n. lihirensis
Lihir Is, Tanga I
A. n. misulae
Louisiade Archipelago

A. n. leucosomus
New Guinea & islands
A. n. polionotus
Babar I, Damar I, Timorlaut I, Banda Is
A. n. pallidimas
D'Entrecasteaux Archipelago
A. n. novaehollandiae
N & E Australia, Tasmania
***Accipiter griseogularis* (Grey-throated Goshawk)**
A. g. mortyi
Morotai I
A. g. griseogularis
C Moluccas
A. g. obiensis
Obi Is
***Accipiter melanochlamys* (Black-mantled Accipiter)**
New Guinea
***Accipiter imitator* (Imitator Sparrow Hawk)**
Choiseul I, Ysabel I
***Accipiter albogularis* (Pied Goshawk)**
A. a. woodfordi
Bougainville I, Guadalcanal I, Malaita I, Choiseul I
A. a. gilvus
New Georgia I, Rendova I, Vellalavella I
A. a. albogularis
San Cristobal I, Ugi I, Santa Anna I
A. a. eichorni
Feni I
A. a. sharpei
Vanikoro I, Utupua I
***Accipiter haplochrous* (New Caledonia Sparrow Hawk)**
New Caledonia
***Accipiter rufitorques* (Fiji Goshawk)**
Fiji Is
***Accipiter poliocephalus* (New Guinea Grey-headed Goshawk)**
New Guinea & islands
***Accipiter princeps* (New Britain Grey-headed Goshawk)**
New Britain
***Accipiter soloensis* (Grey Frog Hawk)**
S & NE China to Indonesia
***Accipiter brevipes* (Levant Sparrow Hawk)**
Balkans to S Russia & Egypt
***Accipiter badius* (Shikra)**
A. b. sphenurus
Gambia to Ethiopia & Tanzania
A. b. polyzonoides
S Tanzania & S Zaire to Cape Province
A. b. cenchroides
Transcaucasia, N Iran to Tien Shan
A. b. dussumieri
Himalayas, N India
A. b. badius
S India, Sri Lanka

A. b. polyopsis
Assam to Taiwan & Indochina
Accipiter butleri (Nicobar Shikra)
A. b. butleri
Car Nicobar Is
A. b. obsoletus
S Nicobar Is
Accipiter francesii (France's Sparrow Hawk)
A. f. francesii
Madagascar
A. f. griveaudi
Gd Comoro I
A. f. pusillus
Anjouan I
A. f. brutus
Mayotte I
Accipiter collaris (American Collared Sparrow Hawk)
W Venezuela, E & S Colombia, Ecuador
Accipiter superciliosus (Tiny Sparrow Hawk)
A. s. fontanieri
SE Nicaragua to W Colombia, Ecuador
A. s. superciliosus
E Peru to Venezuela, the Guianas & N Argentina
Accipiter gundlachii (Gundlach's Hawk)
Cuba e?
Accipiter cooperii (Cooper's Hawk)
S Canada to N Central America
Accipiter bicolor (Bicoloured Sparrow Hawk)
A. b. bicolor
S Mexico to E Bolivia
A. b. fidens
SW Mexico
A. b. pileatus
S Brazil
A. b. guttifer
S Bolivia, Paraguay, N Argentina
A. b. chilensis
Andes of Chile, Argentina to Tierra del Fuego
Accipiter poliogaster (Grey-bellied Goshawk)
N & C South America
Accipiter amadoni (African Long-tailed Hawk)
Ghana to C Zaire

BUTASTUR
Butastur rufipennis (Grasshopper Buzzard-Eagle)
Senegal to Ethiopia & Tanzania
Butastur liventer (Rufous-winged Buzzard-Eagle)
S Burma to Java & Sula I

India, Burma
Butastur indicus (Grey-faced Buzzard-Eagle)
NE Asia, Japan, Philippine Is
KAUPIFALCO
Kaupifalco monogrammicus (Lizard Buzzard)
K. m. monogrammicus
Senegal to Ethiopia & Kenya
K. m. meridionalis
Angola to Tanzania & Natal

LEUCOPTERNIS
Leucopternis schistacea (Slate-coloured Hawk)
Amazonia
Leucopternis plumbea (Plumbeous Hawk)
E Panama to NW Peru
Leucopternis princeps (Prince's Hawk)
Costa Rica to N Ecuador
Leucopternis melanops (Black-faced Hawk)
N Amazonia
Leucopternis kuhli (White-browed Hawk)
S Amazonia
Leucopternis lacernulata (White-necked Hawk)
E & S Brazil
Leucopternis semiplumbea (Semi-plumbeous Hawk)
Honduras to NW Ecuador
Leucopternis albicollis (White Hawk)
L. a. ghiesbreghti
S Mexico to Nicaragua
L. a. costaricensis
Honduras to NW Colombia
L. a. williaminae
NW Colombia to W Venezuela
L. a. albicollis
Trinidad, C Venezuela & the Guianas to S Brazil
Leucopternis occidentalis (Grey-backed Hawk)
W Ecuador
Leucopternis polionota (Mantled Hawk)
E & S Brazil to N Argentina

BUTEOGALLUS
Buteogallus anthracinus (Common Black Hawk)
B. a. anthracinus
SW USA to NW Guyana, St Vincent I
B. a. utilensis
Bay I, Honduras
B. a. gundlachii
Cuba, Isle of Pines
Buteogallus subtilis (Mangrove Black Hawk)
Coast from S Mexico to NW Peru

Buteogallus aequinoctialis (Rufous Crab Hawk)
Venezuela to SE Brazil
Buteogallus urubitinga (Great Black Hawk)
B. u. ridgwayi
N Mexico to Panama
B. u. urubitinga
N & C South America, Trinidad
Buteogallus meridionalis (Savannah Hawk)
E Panama to C Argentina

HARPYHALIAETUS
Harpyhaliaetus solitarius (Black Solitary Eagle)
NW Mexico to Venezuela & Peru
Harpyhaliaetus coronatus (Crowned Solitary Eagle)
S Brazil to E Bolivia & C Argentina

BUSARELLUS
Busarellus nigricollis (Fishing Buzzard)
B. n. nigricollis
Mexico to N Argentina
B. n. leucocephalus
Paraguay, NC Argentina

GERANOAETUS
Geranoaetus melanoleucus (Grey Eagle-Buzzard)
G. m. australis
Venezuela, W South America, Tierra del Fuego
G. m. melanoleucus
S Brazil, Uruguay, Paraguay, N Argentina

PARABUTEO
Parabuteo unicinctus (Harris's Hawk)
P. u. harrisi
S Texas to N Peru
P. u. superior
SE California, W Mexico
P. u. unicinctus
South America

ASTURINA
Asturina nitida (Grey Hawk)
A. n. plagiata
S USA to NW Costa Rica
A. n. costaricensis
SW Costa Rica to W Ecuador
A. n. nitida
Trinidad, N Amazonia
A. n. pallida
S Brazil, E Bolivia to NC Argentina

BUTEO
Buteo magnirostris (Large-billed Hawk)
B. m. griseocauda
Mexico to W Panama
B. m. conspectus
SE Mexico, N Belize

B. m. gracilis
Cozumel I, Holbox I
B. m. sinushonduri
Bonacca I, Ruatan I, (Honduras)
B. m. petulans
SW Costa Rica, SW Panama
B. m. alius
Pearl Is (Panama)
B. m. magnirostris
South America (N of R Amazon)
B. m. occiduus
E Peru, W Brazil
B. m. saturatus
Bolivia to W Argentina
B. m. nattereri
NE Brazil
B. m. magniplumis
S Brazil, NW Argentina
B. m. pucherani
E Argentina, Paraguay
Buteo leucorrhous (Rufous-thighed Hawk)
Venezuela to Bolivia & NE Argentina
Buteo ridgwayi (Ridgway's Hawk)
Hispaniola
Buteo lineatus (Red-shouldered Hawk)
B. l. lineatus
E North America
B. l. alleni
Florida to E Texas
B. l. extimus
S Florida & Keys
B. l. texanus
SC Texas to C Mexico
B. l. elegans
S Oregon to Baja California
Buteo platypterus (Broad-winged Hawk)
B. p. platypterus
SE Canada, E USA to Peru & Brazil
B. p. cubanensis
Cuba
B. p. brunnescens
Puerto Rico
B. p. insulicola
Antigua I
B. p. rivierei
Dominica I, Martinique I, St Lucia I
B. p. antillarum
Barbados I, St Vincent I, Grenada I, Tobago I
Buteo brachyurus (Short-tailed Hawk)
B. b., fuliginosus
S Florida to Panama
B. b. brachyurus
South America (below 7000ft)
B. b. albigula
Andes from Colombia to C Chile
Buteo swainsonii (Swainson's Hawk)
W Canada & W USA & C Argentina

Buteo galapagoensis (Galapagos Hawk)
Galapagos Is
Buteo albicaudatus (White-tailed Hawk)
B. a. hypospodius
Texas to N Colombia, W Venezuela
B. a. colonus
E Colombia to Surinam
B. a. albicaudatus
S Brazil to C Argentina
Buteo polyosoma (Red-backed Buzzard)
B. p. polyosoma
NW Colombia to Tierra del Fuego,
Falkland Is
B. p. exsul
Masafuera I
Buteo poecilochrous (Gurney's Buzzard)
SW Colombia to N Chile
Buteo albonotatus (Zone-tailed Hawk)
SW USA to N South America
Buteo solitarius (Hawaiian Hawk)
Hawaii Is
Buteo ventralis (Red-tailed Buzzard)
S Chile, S Argentina
Buteo jamaicensis (Red-tailed Hawk)
B. j. borealis
E North America to N Mexico
B. j. calurus
W North America » Central America
B. j. harlani
N British Columbia, N Alberta » S USA
B. j. alascensis
SE Alaska
B. j. kriderii
SC Canada, NC USA » S USA
B. j. fuertesi
SW USA, NW Mexico
B. j. umbrinus
S Florida, Bahama Is
B. j. hadropus
N to SC Mexico
B. j. socorroensis
Socorro I
B. j. fumosus
Tres Marias Is
B. j. solitudinis
Cuba, Isle of Pines
B. j. jamaicensis
Jamaica, Hispaniola, Puerto Rico
B. j. kiemsiesi
S Mexico to Nicaragua
B. J. costaricensis
Costa Rica, W Panama
Buteo buteo (Common Buzzard)
B. b. buteo
W & S Europe, Atlantic islands
B. b. vulpinus
N & E Europe, C Asia, E & S Africa

B. b. menetriesi
Caucasus & Elburz Mts
B. b. japonicus
Transbaikalia & Tibet to Japan, Indochina
B. b. toyoshimae
Bonin Is, Izu Is
Buteo oreophilus (African Mountain Buzzard)
B. o. oreophilus
S Ethiopia to C Tanzania
B. o. trizonatus
S Natal, E Cape Province
Buteo brachypterus (Madagascar Buzzard)
Madagascar
Buteo lagopus (Rough-legged Buzzard)
B. l. lagopus
Europe, C Asia
B. l. menzbieri
NE Asia
B. l. kamchatkensis
Kamchatka, N Kurile Is
B. l. sanctijohannis
Canada, N USA
Buteo rufinus (Long-legged Buzzard)
B. r. rufinus
C Europe to C Asia
B. r. cirtensis
Morocco to Egypt
Buteo hemilasius (Upland Buzzard)
C & E Asia
Buteo regalis (Ferruginous Hawk)
SW Canada, WC USA
Buteo auguralis (African Red-tailed Buzzard)
Sierra Leone to Ethiopia & Angola
Buteo rufofuscus (Augur Buzzard)
B. r. archeri
Somalia
B. r. augur
S Ethiopia to Angola & Mozambique
B. r. rufofuscus
Namibia, South Africa

MORPHNUS
Morphnus guianensis (Guiana Crested Eagle)
Honduras to N Paraguay & Argentina
HARPIA
Harpia harpyja (Harpy Eagle)
S Mexico to E Bolivia & N Argentina
HARPYOPSIS
Harpyopsis novaeguineae (New Guinea Harpy Eagle)
New Guinea
PITHECOPHAGA
Pithecophaga jefferyi (Philippine Eagle)
Luzon I, Mindanao I

Ictinaetus malayensis (Indian Black Eagle)
   I. m. perniger
      India, Sri Lanka
   I. m. malayensis
      Burma to S China & Moluccas

AQUILA

Aquila pomarina (Lesser Spotted Eagle)
   A. p. pomarina
      C & E Europe, Caucasus, Transcaucasia
   A. p. hastata
      India, N Burma
Aquila clanga (Greater Spotted Eagle)
      E Europe to E Asia, & NE Africa to S China
Aquila rapax (Tawny Eagle)
   A. r. orientalis
      E Europe, C Asia to C Africa
   A. r. nipalensis
      EC Asia & India
   A. r. vindhiana
      Baluchistan, India, N Burma
   A. r. belisarius
      Morocco to Nigeria & Ethiopia
   A. r. rapax
      SC & South Africa
Aquila heliaca (Imperial Eagle)
   A. h. adalberti
      Spain
   A. h. heliaca
      Greece to C Siberia » NE Africa, India
Aquila wahlbergi (Wahlberg's Eagle)
      Gambia to Ethiopia to N Cape Province
Aquila gurneyi (Gurney's Eagle)
      N Moluccas, New Guinea
Aquila chrysaetos (Golden Eagle)
   A. c. chrysaetos
      Scotland, Alps, N Europe, W Asia
   A. c. daphanea
      Russian Turkestan to SW China
   A. c. japonica
      Korea, C Japan
   A. c. canadensis
      NE Siberia, N Mongolia, Canada, W USA
   A. c. homeyeri
      Spain, N Africa
Aquila audax (Wedge-tailed Eagle)
   A. a. audax
      S New Guinea, Australia
   A. a. fleayi
      Tasmania
Aquila verreauxii (Verreaux's Eagle)
      Ethiopia, Sudan to Cape Province

HIERAAETUS

Hieraaetus fasciatus (Bonelli's Eagle)
   H. f. fasciatus
      S Europe, N Africa to India & China

   H. f. spilogaster
      Gambia to Ethiopia & Cape Province
   H. f. renschii
      Lesser Sunda Is
Hieraaetus pennatus (Booted Eagle)
   H. p. pennatus
      S Europe to N Africa & Caucasus
   H. p. harterti
      SW & C Asia
Hieraaetus morphnoides (Little Eagle)
   H. m. morphnoides
      Australia
   H. m. weiskei
      New Guinea
Hieraaetus dubius (Ayres' Hawk Eagle)
      Nigeria to Ethiopia & Cape Province
Hieraaetus kienerii (Chestnut-bellied Hawk Eagle)
   H. k. kienerii
      S Himalayas, W India, Sri Lanka
   H. k. formosus
      Burma to Philippine Is, Celebes & Java

SPIZASTUR

Spizastur melanoleucus (Black & White Hawk Eagle)
      E & S Mexico to Paraguay & NE Argentina

LOPHOAETUS

Lophaetus occipitalis (Long-crested Eagle)
      Senegal to Ethiopia & Cape Province

SPIZAETUS

Spizaetus africanus (Cassin's Hawk Eagle)
      Togo to C Zaire & Uganda
Spizaetus cirrhatus (Crested Hawk Eagle)
   S. c. cirrhatus
      India
   S. c. ceylanensis
      Sri Lanka
   S. c. limnaetus
      NE India to Mindanao, Borneo & Java
   S. c. andamanensis
      Andaman Is
   S. c. vanheurni
      Simalur I
   S. c. floris
      Sumbawa I, Flores I
Spizaetus nipalensis (Mountain Hawk Eagle)
   S. n. nipalensis
      W India, Himalayas to SE China
   S. n. kelaarti
      Sri Lanka
   S. n. orientalis
      Japan
Spizaetus bartelsi (Java Hawk Eagle)
      W Java

Spizaetus lanceolatus (**Celebes Hawk Eagle**)
  Sula I & Celebes
Spizaetus philippensis (**Philippine Hawk Eagle**)
  Philippine Is, Palawan
Spizaetus alboniger (**Blyth's Hawk Eagle**)
  S Burma to Sumatra & Borneo
Spizaetus nanus (**Wallace's Hawk Eagle**)
  S. n. nanus
    Malaysia, Borneo, Sumatra
  S. n. stresemanni
    Nias I
Spizaetus tyrannus (**Black Hawk Eagle**)
  S. t. serus
    C Mexico to E Peru
  S. t. tyrannus
    E & S Brazil
Spizaetus ornatus (**Ornate Hawk Eagle**)
  S. o. vicarius
    Mexico to Colombia, W Ecuador
  S. o. ornatus
    C Colombia to Guianas & N Argentina

STEPHANOAETUS
Stephanoaetus coronatus (Crowned Eagle)
  Guinea to Ethiopia and Cape Province

OROAETUS
Oroaetus isidori (Isidor's Eagle)
  W Venezuela to Bolivia & NW Argentina

POLEMAETUS
Polemaetus bellicosus (Martial Eagle)
  Senegal to Somalia & Cape Province

31 SAGITTARIIDAE (SECRETARY BIRD)

SAGITTARIUS
Sagittarius serpentarius (Secretary Bird)
  Senegal to Somalia & Cape Province

32 FALCONIDAE (FALCONS, CARACARAS)

DAPTRIUS
Daptrius ater (Yellow-throated Caracara)
  Amazonia
Daptrius americanus (Red-throated Caracara)
  S Mexico to C Peru & S Brazil, Bolivia

PHALCOBOENUS
Phalcoboenus carunculatus (Carunculated Caracara)
  Andes of Ecuador & SW Colombia
Phalcoboenus megalopterus (Mountain Caracara)
  Andes of Peru to N Chile

Phalcoboenus albogularis (**White-throated Caracara**)
  S Chile, S Argentina
Phalcoboenus australis (**Forster's Caracara**)
  Falkland Is, Cape Horn islands

POLYBORUS
Polyborus plancus (Common Caracara)
  P. p. auduboni
    S USA to W Panama, Cuba
  P. p. pallidus
    Tres Marias Is
  P. p. cheriway
    E Panama & South America
    (N of R Amazon)
  P. p. plancus
    S South America, Falkland Is

MILVAGO
Milvago chimango (Chimango)
  M. c. chimango
    Paraguay & Uruguay to S Argentina
  M. c. temucoensis
    S Chile, Tierra del Fuego
Milvago chimachima (Yellow-headed Caracara)
  Panama to E Bolivia & N Argentina

HERPETOTHERES
Herpetotheres cachinnans (Laughing Falcon)
  H. c. cachinnans
    NW Mexico to N Argentina
  H. c. fulvescens
    W Panama to N Peru

MICRASTUR
Micrastur ruficollis (Barred Forest Falcon)
  M. r. guerilla
    Mexico to Nicaragua
  M. r. interstes
    Costa Rica to W Colombia & Ecuador
  M. r. zonothorax
    N Venezuela, E Colombia
  M. r. pelzelni
    W Brazil, E Peru
  M. r. ruficollis
    E Brazil, Paraguay, N Argentina
  M. r. olrogi
    NW Argentina
Micrastur gilvicollis (Lined Forest Falcon)
  S Venezuela, Guianas, Amazonia
Micrastur plumbeus (Sclater's Forest Falcon)
  W Colombia, NW Ecuador
Micrastur mirandollei (Slaty-backed Forest Falcon)
  E Costa Rica to E Peru & SE Brazil

Micrastur semitorquatus **(Collared Forest Falcon)**
M. s. naso
Mexico to NW Peru
M. s. semitorquatus
E Colombia & N Peru to Brazil &
N Argentina
Micrastur buckleyi **(Traylor's Forest Falcon)**
E Ecuador, NE Peru

SPIZIAPTERYX
Spiziapteryx circumcinctus **(Spot-winged Falconet)**
N & W Argentina

POLIHIERAX
Polihierax semitorquatus **(African Pigmy Falcon)**
P. s. castanotus
E Zaire & Ethiopia to C Tanzania
P. s. semitorquatus
S Angola, Namibia, Botswana, W South
Africa
Polihierax insignis **(Fieldens Falconet)**
P. i. insignis
N Burma
P. i. cinereiceps
S Burma, Thailand, N Indochina
P. i. harmandi
S Laos, S Vietnam

MICROHIERAX
Microhierax caerulescens **(Red-legged Falconet)**
M. c. caerulescens
Himalayas, N India
M. c. burmanicus
Burma to Indochina
Microhierax fringillarius **(Black-legged Falconet)**
S Burma to Bali I & Sumatra
Microhierax latifrons **(Bornean Falconet)**
NW Borneo
Microhierax erythrogonys **(Philippine Falconet)**
Philippine Is
Microhierax melanoleucus **(Pied Falconet)**
Assam, SE China, N Indochina

FALCO
Falco naumanni **(Lesser Kestrel)**
S Europe to China » S Africa
Falco rupicoloides **(Greater Kestrel)**
F. r. fieldi
Somalia, N Kenya
F. r. arthuri
C & S Kenya, N Tanzania
F. r. rupicoloides
S Tanzania & Angola to S Transvaal

Falco alopex **(Fox Kestrel)**
Ghana to Sudan & W Kenya
Falco sparverius **(American Kestrel)**
F. s. sparverius
Alaska & Canada to S Mexico
F. s. paulus
SE USA .
F. s. peninsularis
Baja California, NW Mexico
F. s. tropicalis
S Mexico, Guatemala, N Honduras
F. s. nicaraguensis
NW Honduras, Nicaragua
F. s. sparveroides
S Bahama Is, Cuba
F. s. dominicensis
Hispaniola
F. s. caribearum
Puerto Rico, Virgin Is, Lesser Antilles
F. s. brevipennis
Netherlands West Indies
F. s. isabellinus
the Guianas, E Venezuela, N Brazil
F. s. ochraceus
E Colombia, NW Venezuela
F. s. aequatorialis
NW Colombia, N Ecuador
F. s. peruvianus
SW Ecuador, Peru, N Chile
F. s. cinnamominus
SE Peru to Paraguay & Tierra del Fuego
F. s. fernandensis
Mastierra I, Juan Fernandez Is
F. s. cearae
S Brazil
Falco tinnunculus **(Common Kestrel)**
F. t. tinnunculus
Europe to NE Asia, » C Africa & India
F. t. canariensis
Madeira, W Canary Is
F. t. dacotiae
Lanzarote, E Canary Is
F. t. neglectus
N Cape Verde Is
F. t. alexanderi
S Cape Verde Is
F. t. rupicolaeformis
Egypt, S Yemen
F. t. archeri
Socotra I, Somalia, NE Kenya
F. t. rufescens
Guinea & N Angola to Ethiopia & Tanzania
F. t. rupicolus
C Angola & S Tanzania to Cape Province
F. t. interstinctus
Himalayas to Japan & Philippine Is
F. t. objurgatus
S India

Falco newtoni (Madagascar Kestrel)
F. n. newtoni
  Madagascar
F. n. aldabranus
  Aldabra I, Anjouan I
Falco punctatus (Mauritius Kestrel)
  Mauritius
Falco araea (Seychelles Kestrel)
  Seychelles
Falco moluccensis (Moluccan Kestrel)
F. m. moluccensis
  Ambon I, Ceram I, Buru I
F. m. bernsteini
  N Moluccas
F. m. timorensis
  Timor I, Tenimber Is
F. m. microbalia
  Lombok I to Alor I, Celebes, Solombo
  Besar I
F. m. renschii
  Sumba I
F. m. javensis
  Java, Bali I, Kangean I
Falco cenchroides (Australian Kestrel)
F. c. baru
  C New Guinea
F. c. cenchroides
  Australia, Tasmania
Falco ardosiaceus (Grey Kestrel)
  Senegal to Ethiopia & S Tanzania
Falco dickinsoni (Dickinson's Kestrel)
  Angola to Tanzania & Natal
Falco zoniventris (Madagascar Banded Kestrel)
  Madagascar
Falco vespertinus (Red-footed Falcon)
F. v. vespertinus
  C Europe to C Asia » W & SW Africa
F. v. amurensis
  E Siberia, N China » E & S Asia
Falco chicquera (Red-headed Falcon)
F. c. chicquera
  Pakistan, India
F. c. ruficollis
  Gambia to Ethiopia » Zambia
F. c. horsbrughi
  Rhodesia, South Africa
Falco columbarius (Merlin)
F. c. subaesalon
  Iceland to Britain & Belgium
F. c. aesalon
  Europe to N Russia & W Siberia
F. c. insignis
  E Siberia to Japan, Indochina, India
F. c. pallidus
  Transcaucasia to SC Asia
F. c. lymani
  E Altai, Tien Shan to W China

F. c. columbarius
  Alaska to Newfoundland & N South
  America
F. c. suckleyi
  W British Columbia to N California
F. c. richardsoni
  SW C Canada to WC USA ·
Falco berigora (Brown Hawk)
F. b. novaeguineae
  New Guinea, Dampier I
F. b. berigora
  humid parts of Australia
F. b. centralis
  dry interior of Australia
F. b. tasmanica
  Tasmania
Falco novaezeelandiae (New Zealand Falcon)
  New Zealand
Falco subbuteo (European Hobby)
F. s. subbuteo
  Europe to Japan » Africa & India
F. s. streichi
  C & S China, Laos
Falco cuvierii (African Hobby)
  Ghana to Ethiopia & Cape Province
Falco severus (Oriental Hobby)
F. s. severus
  E Himalayas to Philippine Is & N Borneo
F. s. papuanus
  Celebes to New Guinea & Solomon Is
Falco longipennis (Australian Hobby)
F. l. murchisonianus
  dry Northern Australia
F. l. longipennis
  SE & SW Australia, Tasmania
Falco eleonorae (Eleonora's Falcon)
  Canary Is, Mediterranean Is »
    Madagascar
Falco concolor (Sooty Falcon)
  NE Africa » Madagascar
Falco rufigularis (Bat Falcon)
F. r. petrophilus
  W Mexico
F. r. rufigularis
  C Mexico, all E South America to
  N Argentina
Falco femoralis (Aplomado Falcon)
F. f. septentrionalis
  SW USA & Mexico
F. f. pichinchae
  Andes from Colombia to Chile
F. f. femoralis
  Central & South America
Falco hypoleucos (Grey Falcon)
  C N & Western Australia
Falco subniger (Black Falcon)
  Australia

***Falco biarmicus* (Lanner Falcon)**
F. b. feldeggi
SE Europe, Asia minor
F. b. erlangeri
NW Africa
F. b. tanypterus
NE Africa, Arabia, Iraq
F. b. abyssinicus
Ghana to N Zaire, Uganda, Ethiopia
F. b. biarmicus
E Zaire & Kenya to Angola & Cape
Province
***Falco mexicanus* (Prairie Falcon)**
SW Canada, W USA, NW Mexico
***Falco jugger* (Laggar Falcon)**
Baluchistan, Himalayas, N & C India
***Falco cherrug* (Saker Falcon)**
F. c. cyanopus
C Europe, W Russia
F. c. cherrug
C Asia, NW Mongolia to N Africa, N India
F. c. milvipes
SC Asia
F. c. altaicus
mountains of C Asia
***Falco rusticolus* (Gyrfalcon)**
Arctic Europe, Asia, N America
***Falco deiroleucus* (Orange-breasted
Falcon)**
Central America to N Argentina
***Falco fasciinucha* (Taita Falcon)**
S Ethiopia to Zambia & Malawi
***Falco kreyenborgi* (Kleinschmidt's Falcon)**
S Chile, Tierra del Fuego
***Falco peregrinus* (Peregrine Falcon)**
F. p. pealei
coast of W Canada, W USA
F. p. anatum
N Central & South America
F. p. cassini
S Chile, Tierra del Fuego, Falkland Is
F. p. peregrinus
Europe to N Russia & Caucasus
F. p. calidus
N Russia, N Siberia to Southern Africa
& New Guinea
F. p. japonensis
E Siberia, Japan, Taiwan
F. p. brookei
Mediterranean, Asia Minor
F. p. pelegrinoides
North Africa, N Sudan
F. p. babylonicus
Iraq to Mongolia, N India
F. p. peregrinator
India, Sri Lanka to S China
F. p. minor
Ghana to Ethiopia » Cape Province

F. p. submelanogenys
SW Australia
F. p. macropus
Australia (except SW)
F. p. madens
Cape Verde Is
F. p. radama
Madagascar, Comoro Is
F. p. furuitii
Volcano I
F. p. ernesti
Indonesia, Philippine Is, New Guinea
F. p. nesiotes
New Hebrides, Loyalty Is, New Caledonia

Galliformes

33 MEGAPODIIDAE (MEGAPODES)

MEGAPODIUS
***Megapodius freycinet* (Common Scrub
Hen)**
M. f. nicobariensis
N Nicobar Is
M. f. abbotti
Gt & Little Nicobar Is
M. f. pusillus
Philippine Is
M. f. tabon
Mindanao I
M. f. cumingii
Palawan I, Balabac I
M. f. sanghirensis
Sanghir Is, Talaut Is
M. f. gilbertii
Celebes
M. f. bernsteinii
Sula Is
M. f. perrufus
Peling I
M. f. tenimberensis
Tenimber Is
M. f. aruensis
Aru Is
M. f. affinis
N New Guinea
M. f. duperryii
W & S New Guinea
M. f. reinwardt
Lesser Sunda Is
M. f. buruensis
Buru I
M. f. forstenii
S Moluccas
M. f. macgillivrayi
Louisiade & D'Entrecasteaux Archipelago
M. f. tumulus
Melville I, Northern Territory

M. f. yorki
N Queensland
M. f. eremita
Admiralty Is, Bismarck Archipelago
M. f. brenchleyi
Solomon Is
M. f. freycinet
N Moluccas, W Papuan Is
M. f. geelvinkianus
Biak I, Numfor I, Meosnum I, Japen I
M. f. castanonotus
N & C Queensland
M. f. layardi
Banks I, N New Hebrides
Megapodius laperouse (Marianas Scrub Hen)
M. l. senex
Palau Is
M. l. laperouse
Mariana Is
Megapodius pritchardii (Polynesian Scrub Hen)
Friendly Is

EULIPOA
Eulipoa wallacei (Moluccas Scrub Hen)
Moluccas, Misol I

LEIPOA
Leipoa ocellata (Mallee Fowl)
Southern Australia

ALECTURA
Alectura lathami (Brush Turkey)
A. l. purpureicollis
N Queensland
A. l. lathami
C & S Queensland, N South Wales

TALEGALLA
Talegalla cuvieri (Red-billed Brush Turkey)
NW New Guinea, Salawati I, Misol I
Talegalla fuscirostris (Black-billed Brush Turkey)
T. f. fuscirostris
S & E New Guinea
T. f. occidentis
Aru Is, SW New Guinea
Talegalla jobiensis (Brown-collared Brush Turkey)
T. j. jobiensis
Japen I, N New Guinea
T. j. longicaudus
SE New Guinea

AEPYPODIUS
Aepypodius arfakianus (Wattled Brush Turkey)
A. a. arfakianus
NW New Guinea

A. a. misoliensis
Misol I
Aepypodius bruijnii (Bruijn's Brush Turkey)
Waigeu I

MACROCEPHALON
Macrocephalon maleo (Maleo Fowl)
Celebes

34 CRACIDAE (CURASSOWS, GUANS)

ORTALIS
Ortalis vetula (Plain Chachalaca)
O. v. mccallii
S Texas, SE Mexico
O. v. vetula
E Mexico to C Nicaragua
O. v. pallidiventris
N Yucatan
O. v. deschauenseei
Utila I (Honduras)
Ortalis cinereiceps (Grey-headed Chachalaca)
SE Honduras to NW Colombia
Ortalis garrula (Chestnut-winged Chachalaca)
O. g. mira
Panama
O. g. chocoensis
NW Colombia
O. g. garrula
N Colombia
Ortalis ruficauda (Rufous-vented Chachalaca)
O. r. ruficrissa
. N Colombia, NW Venezuela
O. r. lamprophonia
Guajira peninsula
O. r. baliolus
Lake Maracaibo
O. r. ruficauda
Venezuela, Tobago I, Lesser Antilles Is
Ortalis erythroptera (Rufous-headed Chachalaca)
W Ecuador, NW Peru
Ortalis poliocephala (West Mexican Chachalaca)
O. p. wagleri
NW Mexico
O. p. lajuelae
C Mexico
O. p. poliocephala
W Mexico
Ortalis canicollis (Chaco Chachalaca)
O. c. canicollis
E Bolivia, W Paraguay, N Argentina
O. c. pantanalensis
SW Brazil

Ortalis leucogastra (White-bellied Chachalaca)
SE Mexico to NW Nicaragua
Ortalis motmot (Variable Chachalaca)
O. m. motmot
S Venezuela, the Guianas, N Brazil
O. m. ruficeps
NC Brazil
O. m. superciliaris
NE Brazil
O. m. araucuan
E Brazil
O. m. squamata
SE Brazil
O. m. caucae
N Colombia
O. m. colombiana
SC Colombia, NW Upper Amazonia
O. m. guttata
W Upper Amazonia
O. m. subaffinis
NE & E Bolivia, W Brazil

PENELOPE
Penelope argyrotis (Band-tailed Guan)
P. a. mesaeus
W Venezuela, N Colombia
P. a. albicauda
W Venezuela, NE Colombia
P. a. colombiana
Santa Marta Mts
P. a. argyrotis
NW Colombia, N Venezuela
P. a. olivaceiceps
N Venezuela
Penelope barbata (Bearded Guan)
S Ecuador, NW Peru
Penelope montagnii (Andean Guan)
P. m. montagnii
N & C Colombia
P. m. atrogularis
S Colombia, WC Ecuador
P. m. brookei
S Colombia, EC Ecuador
P. m. plumosa
C Peru
P. m. sclateri
C Bolivia, NW Argentina
Penelope ortoni (Orton's Guan)
W Colombia, W Ecuador
Penelope marail (Marail Guan)
P. m. jacupeba
SE Venezuela, N Brazil
P. m. marail
E Venezuela, the Guianas
Penelope superciliaris (Rusty-margined Guan)
P. s. superciliaris
NC & E Brazil

P. s. jacupemba
C & S Brazil
P. s. major
S Brazil, E Paraguay, NE Argentina
Penelope dabbenei (Red-faced Guan)
S Bolivia, NW Argentina
Penelope obscura (Dusky-legged Guan)
P. o. bronzina
E Brazil
P. o. obscura
S Brazil, E Paraguay, Uruguay,
NE Argentina
P. o. bridgesi
C Bolivia, NW Argentina
Penelope jacquaçu (Spix's Guan)
P. j. granti
E Venezuela, Guyana
P. j. orienticola
NW Brazil, SE Venezuela
P. j. jacquaçu
Upper Amazonia
P. j. speciosa
C & E Bolivia
Penelope albipennis (White-winged Guan)
NW Peru
Penelope perspicax (Cauca Guan)
W & C Colombia
Penelope purpurascens (Crested Guan)
P. p. purpurascens
NE & NW Mexico to Honduras, Nicaragua
P. p. aequatorialis
S Honduras to NW Colombia
P. p. brunnescens
N Colombia, E Venezuela
Penelope jacucaca (White-browed Guan)
NE Brazil
Penelope ochrogaster (Chestnut-bellied Guan)
SC Brazil
Penelope pileata (White-crested Guan)
NC Brazil

ABURRIA
Aburria pipile (Common Piping Guan)
A. p. pipile
Trinidad
A. p. cumanensis
the Guianas to C Colombia & NW Peru,
W Brazil
A. p. grayi
E Bolivia, NE Paraguay, SW Brazil
A. p. nattereri
S & W Amazonia
A. p. cujubi
NC Brazil
Aburria jacutinga (Black-fronted Piping Guan)
SE Brazil, SE Paraguay
Aburria aburri (Wattled Guan)
N Colombia, E Venezuela to SC Peru

CHAMAEPETES
Chamaepetes unicolor (Black Guan)
Costa Rica, Panama
Chamaepetes goudotii (Sickle-winged Guan)
C. g. goudotii
C & W Colombia
C. g. sanctaemarthae
Santa Marta Mts
C. g. fagani
SW Colombia, W Ecuador
C. g. tschudii
EC Ecuador, N Peru
C. g. rufiventris
EC Peru

PENELOPINA
Penelopina nigra (Highland Guan)
S Mexico to N Nicaragua

OREOPHASIS
Oreophasis derbianus (Horned Guan)
SE Mexico, SW Guatemala

NOTHOCRAX
Nothocrax urumutum (Nocturnal Curassow)
Upper Amazonia

CRAX
Crax tomentosa (Crestless Curassow)
SE Colombia to Guyana, NW Brazil
Crax salvini (Salvin's Curassow)
SW Colombia, E Ecuador, NE Peru
Crax mitu (Razor-billed Curassow)
C. m. tuberosa
S Amazonia
C. m. mitu
E Brazil **e?**
Crax pauxi (Northern Helmeted Curassow)
C. p. pauxi
NC to W Venezuela
C. p. gilliardi
Venezuela-Colombia border
Crax unicornis (Southern Helmeted Curassow)
C. u. unicornis
NE Bolivia
C. u. koepckeae
E Peru
Crax rubra (Great Curassow)
C. r. rubra
E Mexico to W Colombia & W Ecuador
C. r. griscomi
Cozumel I
Crax alberti (Blue-bellied Curassow)
N Colombia
Crax daubentoni (Yellow-knobbed Curassow)
N Venezuela

Crax alector (Black Curassow)
E Colombia to the Guianas, N Brazil
Crax globulosa (Wattled Curassow)
W Upper Amazonia
Crax fasciolata (Bare-faced Curassow)
C. f. fasciolata
C & SW Brazil, Paraguay
C. f. pinima
NE Brazil
C. f. grayi
E Bolivia
Crax blumenbachii (Red-billed Curassow)
SE Brazil

35 PHASIANIDAE (PHEASANTS, GROUSE)

MELEAGRIDINAE

MELEAGRIS
Meleagris gallopavo (Common Turkey)
M. g. silvestris
SE USA
M. g. osceola
S Florida
M. g. intermedia
N Texas to NE Mexico
M. g. onusta
NW Mexico
M. g. mexicana
NC Mexico
M. g. merriami
SW USA, NW Mexico
M. g. gallopavo
WC Mexico

AGRIOCHARIS
Agriocharis ocellata (Ocellated Turkey)
SE Mexico, Belize, Guatemala

TETRAONINAE

DENDRAGAPUS
Dendragapus falcipennis (Siberian Spruce Grouse)
NE Asia, Sakhalin
Dendragapus canadensis (Spruce Grouse)
D. c. osgoodi
Alaska
D. c. atratus
S Alaska
D. c. canadensis
C Alberta to Labrador
D. c. torridus
Nova Scotia
D. c. canace
SE Canada, N & NE USA
Dendragapus obscurus (Dusky Grouse)
D. o. sitkensis
SE Alaska

D. o. fuliginosus
S Yukon to NW California

D. o. sierrae
Oregon to NC California

D. o. howardi
C California

D. o. richardsonii
N British Columbia to SE Idaho

D. o. pallidus
SE British Columbia to NE Oregon

D. o. obscurus
Utah to New Mexico

LAGOPUS

Lagopus lagopus (Willow/Red Grouse)

L. l. scoticus
Scotland, Wales, N England

L. l. hibernicus
Outer Hebrides, Ireland

L. l. lagopus
Circumpolar, N Europe, N Asia, N Canada

L. l. birulai
N Siberian islands

L. l. leucopterus
islands N of N America

L. l. rossicus
European Russia

L. l. maior
SE Russia

L. l. brevirostris
S Siberia

L. l. kozlowae
C Asia, N Mongolia

L. l. alexandrae
S & SE Alaska islands, NW British
Columbia

L. l. alleni
Newfoundland

Lagopus mutus (Rock Ptarmigan)

L. m. hyperboreus
Spitzbergen, Franz Josef Land

L. m. mutus
N Scandinavia, N Russia

L. m. millaisi
Scotland

L. m. helveticus
Alps

L. m. pyrenaicus
Pyrenees

L. m. komensis
N Ural Mts

L. m. pleskei
N Siberia

L. m. macrorhynchus
Tarbagatai

L. m. nadezdae
Altai, C Asia

L. m. transbaicalicus
SE Siberia

L. m. ridgwayi
Commander Is

L. m. kurilensis
N & C Kurile Is

L. m. japonicus
Honshu I, Japan

L. m. evermanni
Attu I (Aleutian Is)

L. m. townsendi
Kiska I (Aleutian Is)

L. m. sanfordi
Tanaga I (Aleutian Is)

L. m. chamberlaini
Adak I (Aleutian Is)

L. m. atkhensis
Atka I (Aleutian Is)

L. m. nelsoni
Unimak I, Unalaska I, to S Alaska

L. m. gabrielsoni
C Alaska

L. m. dixoni
Glacier Bay islands

L. m. rupestris
N North America

L. m. saturatus
W Greenland

L. m. welchi
Newfoundland

L. m. reinhardi
SW Greenland

L. m. captus
E Greenland

L. m. islandorum
Iceland

Lagopus leucurus (White-tailed Ptarmigan)

L. l. peninsularis
C Alaska, Yukon

L. l. leucurus
N British Columbia to Vancouver I

L. l. rainierensis
Mt Rainier, C & S Washington

L. l. saxatilis
Vancouver I

L. l. altipetens
Rocky Mts from Montana to New Mexico

TETRAO

Tetrao mlokosiewiczi (Georgian Black Grouse)
Caucasus

Tetrao tetrix (Black Grouse)

T. t. britannicus
Scotland, N England

T. t. tetrix
Scandinavia & France to N Siberia

T. t. viridanus
SE Russia, SW Siberia

T. t. tschusii
S Siberia
T. t. baikalensis
N Mongolia, W Manchuria
T. t. mongolicus
C Tien Shan, W Altai
T. t. ussuriensis
N Manchuria, NE Korea
Tetrao parvirostris (Siberian Capercaillie)
T. p. turensis
NC Siberia
T. p. janensis
NE Siberia
T. p. parvirostris
E Siberia, Sakhalin
T. p. macrurus
C Asia, N Mongolia
T. p. kamschaticus
Kamchatka
Tetrao urogallus (Capercaillie)
T. u. aquitanicus
Pyrenees & N Spain
T. u. urogallus
Scandinavia, Scotland
T. u. major
C Europe, W Russia
T. u. lugens
Finland, NW Russia
T. u. pleskei
N Russia
T. u. volgensis
C Russia
T. u. uralensis
C Ural Mts
T. u. grisescens
S Ural Mts
T. u. kureikensis
Lower Yenisei valley
T. u. taczanowskii
C Siberia, NW Mongolia

BONASA
Bonasa sewerzowi (Severtzov's Hazel Grouse)
B. s. sewerzowi
Kansu
B. s. secunda
W Szechwan
Bonasa bonasia (Hazel Grouse)
B. b. bonasia
Scandinavia to Ural Mts
B. b. griseonota
N Sweden
B. b. rupestris
C Germany to Alps & Bulgaria
B. p. horicei
E Carpathians
B. b. volgensis
C Poland to C Russia

B. b. sibiricus
C Siberia, N Mongolia
B. b. kolymensis
E Siberia
B. b. amurensis
Korea, S Amur, N Manchuria
B. b. vicinitas
Sakhalin, Hokkaido
Bonasa umbellus (Ruffed Grouse)
B. u. yukonensis
Alaska, NW Canada
B. u. umbelloides
S British Columbia to Manitoba
& N Colorado
B. u. castaneus
Olympic Mt, Washington
B. u. affinis
British Columbia, Oregon
B. u. obscura
N Ontario
B. u. sabini
coast of British Columbia to California
B. u. brunnescens
Vancouver I
B. u. togata
NC & NE USA
B. u. medianus
Minnesota
B. u. phaios
Idaho
B. u. incanus
Utah
B. u. monticola
W Virginia
B. u. umbellus
EC USA
B. u. thayeri
Nova Scotia

CENTROCERCUS
Centrocercus urophasianus (Sage Hen)
S British Columbia to E California
& Nebraska
TYMPANUCHUS
Tympanuchus phasianellus (Sharp-tailed Grouse)
T. p. kennicottii
NW Canada
T. p. phasianellus
EC Canada
T. p. columbianus
British Columbia to N California & Utah
T. p. jamesi
EC Colorado
T. p. campestris
C Canada to Wisconsin
Tympanuchus cupido (Prairie Chicken)
T. c. pinnatus
SC Canada to NE Texas

T. c. attwateri
    coast of Texas & SW Louisiana
T. c. pallidicinctus
    Kansas to New Mexico
(*T.c. cupido* — extinct)

ODONTOPHORINAE

DENDRORTYX

Dendrortyx barbatus (Bearded Wood Partridge)
    Vera Cruz (Mexico)
Dendrortyx macroura (Long-tailed Wood Partridge)
D. m. macroura
    Vera Cruz (Mexico)
D. m. griseipectus
    Morales (Mexico)
D. m. diversus
    NW Jalisco
D. m. striatus
    Michoacan & Colima (Mexico),
    Guerrero (Mexico)
D. m. oaxacae
    E Oaxaca (Mexico)
Dendrortyx leucophrys (Buffy-crowned Wood Partridge)
D. l. leucophrys
    SE Mexico, Guatemala
D. l. nicaraguae
    Honduras, Nicaragua
D. l. hypospodius
    Costa Rica

OREORTYX

Oreortyx picta (Mountain Quail)
O. p. palmeri
    coast from SW Washington to California
O. p. picta
    Columbia river to California
O. p. russelli
    California
O. p. confinis
    Baja California

CALLIPEPLA

Callipepla squamata (Scaled Quail)
C. s. pallida
    SW USA, NW Mexico
C. s. squamata
    NC & C Mexico
C. s. castanogastris
    S Texas, NE Mexico
C. s. hargravei
    New Mexico

LOPHORTYX

Lophortyx californica (California Quail)
L. c. brunnescens
    coast from SW Oregon to C California

L. c. canfieldae
    EC California
L. c. decolorata
    Baja California
L. c. californica
    E Oregon to Baja California
L. c. catalinensis
    Santa Catalina I (Los Coronados Is)
L. c. achrustera
    S Baja California
Lophortyx gambelii (Gambel's Quail)
L. g. gambelii
    SW USA, NW Mexico
L. g. sana
    W Colorado
L. g. friedmann
    coast of NW Mexico
L. g. fulvipectus
    SW Sonora
L. g. pembertoni
    Tiburon I
Lophortyx douglasii (Elegant Quail)
L. d. bensoni
    Sonora
L. d. douglasii
    Sinaloa, Jalisco
L. d. languens
    C Chihuahua
L. d. impedita
    Nayarit
L. d. teres
    NW Jalisco

PHILORTYX

Philortyx fasciatus (Banded Quail)
    Colima, Guerrero, Puebla (SW Mexico)

COLINUS

Colinus virginianus (Bobwhite)
C. v. virginianus
    C & E USA
C. v. floridanus
    Florida, Bahama Is
C. v. cubanensis
    Cuba
C. v. ridgwayi
    N & SC Sonora
C. v. texanus
    NE Mexico
C. v. maculatus
    C Mexico
C. v. aridus
    NC Mexico
C. v. graysoni
    WC Mexico
C. v. nigripectus
    SC Mexico
C. v. pectoralis
    C Vera Cruz

C. v. godmani
  E Vera Cruz
C. v. minor
  NE Chiapas
C. v. insignis
  NW Guatemala, W Chiapas
C. v. salvini
  S Chiapas
C. v. coyolcos
  S Mexico
C. v. thayeri
  NE Oaxaca
C. v. atriceps
  W Oaxaca
C. v. nelsoni
  C Chiapas
Colinus nigrogularis (Black-throated Bobwhite)
C. n. caboti
  Campeche (Mexico)
C. n. persiccus
  N Yucatan
C. n. nigrogularis
  Yucatan
C. n. segoviensis
  Guatemala, Honduras
Colinus leucopogon (White-faced Bobwhite)
C. l. incanus
  Guatemala
C. l. hypoleucus
  W Guatemala, W El Salvador
C. l. leucopogon
  El Salvador
C. l. leylandi
  Honduras
C. l. sclateri
  W Honduras, W Nicaragua
C. l. dickeyi
  SW Nicaragua, W Costa Rica
Colinus cristatus (Crested Bobwhite) ı
C. c. panamensis
  W Panama
C. c. decoratus
  N Colombia
C. c. bogotensis
  C Colombia
C. c. badius
  C Colombia
C. c. leucotis
  S Colombia
C. c. parvicristatus
  EC Colombia
C. c. littoralis
  NE Colombia
C. c. cristatus
  E Colombia, W Venezuela, Aruba I, Curaçao
C. c. horvathi
  Venezuela

C. c. sonnini
  E Venezuela, the Guianas, N Brazil
C. c. mocquerysi
  NE Venezuela, Margarita I
C. c. mariae
  W Panama
C. c. continentis
  NW Venezuela
C. c. barnesi
  NC Venezuela

ODONTOPHORUS
Odontophorus gujanensis (Marbled Wood Quail)
O. g. castigatus
  SW Costa Rica, NW Panama
O. g. marmoratus
  N Colombia, E Panama
O. g. polionotus
  NW Venezuela
O. g. gujanensis
  E Venezuela, the Guianas
O. g. medius
  Mt Duida (S Venezuela)
O. g. buckleyi
  SE Colombia, E Ecuador, W Brazil
O. g. rufogularis
  NE Peru
O. g. pachyrhynchus
  E Peru
O. g. simonsi
  NW Bolivia
Odontophorus capueira (Spot-winged Wood Quail)
  E Brazil, Paraguay
Odontophorus erythrops (Rufous-fronted Wood Quail)
O. e. verecundus
  Honduras
O. e. melanotis
  Nicaragua, N & E Costa Rica
O. e. coloratus
  W Panama
O. e. erythrops
  W Ecuador
O. e. parambae
  W Colombia, NW Ecuador
Odontophorus atrifrons (Black-fronted Wood Quail)
O. a. atrifrons
  Santa Marta Mts (Colombia)
O. a. variegatus
  E Colombia
O. a. navai
  W Venezuela
Odontophorus melanonotus (Black-backed Wood Quail)
  W Ecuador

Odontophorus hyperythrus (Chestnut Wood Quail)
　Andes of Colombia
Odontophorus speciosus (Rufous-breasted Wood Quail)
O. s. söderströmi
　C Ecuador
O. s. speciosus
　E Ecuador, E Peru
O. s. loricatus
　C Bolivia
Odontophorus strophium (Gorgeted Wood Quail)
　C Colombia
Odontophorus dialeucos (Black-crowned Wood Quail)
　Panama
Odontophorus colombianus (Venezuela Wood Quail)
　N Venezuela
Odontophorus leucolaemus (White-throated Wood Quail)
　N Costa Rica, W Panama
Odontophorus balliviani (Stripe-faced Wood Quail)
　Peru, Bolivia
Odontophorus stellatus (Starred Wood Quail)
　E Ecuador, E Peru
Odontophorus guttatus (Spotted Wood Quail)
　S Mexico to W Panama

DACTYLORTYX
Dactylortyx thoracicus (Singing Quail)
D. t. thoracicus
　E coast of Mexico
D. t. sharpei
　Yucatan peninsula
D. t. devius
　W Mexico
D. t. lineolatus
　S Mexico
D. t. chiapensis
　W Guatemala, C Chiapas
D. t. fuscus
　E Chiapas to S Honduras
D. t. salvadoranus
　C El Salvador
D. t. taylori
　N El Salvador, S Honduras
D. t. colophonus
　W Guatamela
D. t. rufescens
　Honduras
D. t. conoveri
　EC Honduras

CYRTONYX
Cyrtonyx montezumae (Montezuma's Quail)
C. m. mearnsi
　S USA, NW Mexico
C. m. montezumae
　N & C Mexico
C. m. merriami
　Mt Orizaba (Vera Cruz, Mexico)
Cyrtonyx sallei (Salle's Quail)
　SW Mexico
Cyrtonyx ocellatus (Ocellated Quail)
C. o. ocellatus
　SW Mexico, W Guatemala
C. o. differens
　W Honduras, N Nicaragua

RHYNCHORTYX
Rhynchortyx cinctus (Tawny-faced Quail)
R. c. pudibundus
　N Honduras
R. c. cinctus
　Nicaragua to SE Panama
R. c. hypopius
　NE Panama
R. c. australis
　W Colombia, NW Ecuador

PHASIANINAE

LERWA
Lerwa lerwa (Snow Partridge)
　Afghanistan, Himalayas, W China

AMMOPERDIX
Ammoperdix griseogularis (See See Partridge)
A. g. peraticus
　W Afghanistan
A. g. griseogularis
　S Russia, Iran to NW India
Ammoperdix heyi (Sand Partridge)
A. h. heyi
　River Jordan to Sinai
A. h. nicolli
　N Egypt
A. h. cholmleyi
　River Nile to Red Sea
A. h. intermedia
　S Arabia

TETRAOGALLUS
Tetraogallus caucasicus (Caucasian Snowcock)
　Caucasus
Tetraogallus caspius (Caspian Snowcock)
T. c. caspius
　Taurus Mts to N Iran
T. c. semenowtianschanskii
　Zagros Mts (Iran)
Tetraogallus tibetanus (Tibetan Snowcock)
T. t. tibetanus
　Pamir Mts (W Tibet)

T. t. tschimenensis
N Tibet
T. t. centralis
NE & C Tibet
T. t. przewalskii
E Tibet, W Kansu
T. t. henrici
W China
T. t. aquilonifer
S Tibet, Sikkim
Tetraogallus altaicus (Altai Snowcock)
T. a. altaicus
Altai Mts, Sajan Mts
T. a. orientalis
NW Mongolia
Tetraogallus himalayensis (Himalayan Snowcock)
T. h. sewerzowi
SE Turkestan
T. h. himalayensis
W Himalayas, E Afghanistan
T. h. bendi
NW Afghanistan
T. h. grombczewskii
W Kwenlun Mts
T. h. koslowi
Humboldt & S Kokonor Mts

TETRAOPHASIS
Tetraophasis obscurus (Verreaux's Monal Partridge)
NE Tibet, W China
Tetraophasis szechenyii (Szechenyi's Monal Partridge)
E Tibet, SW China

ALECTORIS
Alectoris graeca (Rock Partridge)
A. g. saxatilis
Alps
A. g. graeca
SE Europe
A. g. scotti
Crete
A. g. sinaica
Syria to Sinai
A. g. daghestanica
N Caucasus
A. g. caucasica
S Caucasus
A. g. werae
SW Iran
A. g. koroviakovi
E & S Iran
A. g. shestoperovi
S Transcaspia
A. g. subpallida
Kyzylkum Mts

A. g. falki
W & C Tien Shan Mts
A. g. dzungarica
Tarbagatai Mts
A. g. fallax
E Tien Shan Mts
A. g. pallida
S Chinese Turkestan
A. g. pallescens
N India
A. g. obscurata
W Tannu Ola Mts
Alectoris chukar (Chukar Partridge)
A. c. kleini
E Greece
A. c. cypriotes
Cyclades, Asia Minor
A. c. kurdestanica
S Kurdistan
A. c. chukar
Himalayas
A. c. potanini
W Mongolia
A. c. pubescens
S Manchuria, N China
Alectoris magna (Przewalski's Rock Partridge)
E Tibet, W Kansu
Alectoris philbyi (Philby's Rock Partridge)
SW Arabia
Alectoris barbara (Barbary Partridge)
A. b. barbara
N Morocco, N Algeria, N Tunisia
A. b. theresae
S Morocco
A. b. koenigi
Canary Is
A. b. spatzi
S Algeria, S Tunisia
A. b. barbata
Libya
Alectoris rufa (Red-legged Partridge)
A. r. rufa
SC Europe
A. r. hispanica
NW Spain & N Portugal
A. r. intercedens
S Spain
A. r. corsa
Corsica
A. r. australis
Gran Canaria I
Alectoris melanocephala (Arabian Chukar)
A. m. melanocephala
SW Arabia

100   *A. m. guichardi*
        E Hadhramaut

ANUROPHASIS
**Anurophasis monorthonyx (Snow
Mountain Quail)**
        Oranje Mts (New Guinea)

FRANCOLINUS
Francolinus francolinus (Black Partridge)
    F. f. francolinus
        Cyprus to Caucasia & N Iran
    F. f. billypaynei
        Syria
    F. f. arabistanicus
        S Iraq, W Iran
    F. f. bogdanovi
        S Iran
    F. f. henrici
        Pakistan
    F. f. asiae
        N India
    F. f. melanonotus
        E Himalayas, Assam
Francolinus pictus (Painted Partridge)
    F. p. pallidus
        NC India
    F. p. pictus
        S India
    F. p. watsoni
        Sri Lanka
**Francolinus pintadeanus (Chinese
Francolin)**
    F. p. phayrei
        NE India to S China, Indochina
    F. p. pintadeanus
        SE China
Francolinus afer (Bare-throated Francolin)
    F. a. nyanzae
        Uganda, W Kenya, W Tanzania
    F. a. harterti
        Rwanda, Burundi
    F. a. cranchii
        N Angola, N Zambia, W Tanzania
    F. a. leucoparaeus
        E Kenya, N Tanzania
    F. a. böhmi
        W Tanzania
    F. a. itigi
        C Tanzania
    F. a. intercedens
        SE Zaire, S Tanzania, N Zambia
    F. a. castaneiventer
        E Cape Province
    F. a. loangwae
        NE Zambia
    F. a. benguellensis
        W Angola

F. a. punctulatus
        C Angola
F. a. afer
        S Angola
F. a. cunenensis
        S Angola, N Namibia
F. a. humboldtii
        S Malawi, W Mozambique
F. a. swynnertoni
        Rhodesia, S Mozambique
F. a. lehmanni
        E Transvaal
F. a. krebsi
        SE Cape Province, S Natal
F. a. notatus
        S Cape Province
**Francolinus swainsonii (Swainson's
Francolin)**
    F. s. gilli
        N Namibia, N Botswana, W Zambia
    F. s. damarensis
        Waterburg, Namibia
    F. s. chobiensis
        NE Botswana, Rhodesia, W Mozambique
    F. s. swainsonii
        S Botswana, Transvaal, S Mozambique
Francolinus rufopictus (Painted Francolin)
        SE Lake Victoria
**Francolinus leucoscepus (Yellow-necked
Francolin)**
    F. l. leucoscepus
        E Ethiopia, N Somalia
    F. l. muhamedbenabdullah
        S Somalia, N Kenya
    F. l. infuscatus
        NE Uganda, S Ethiopia to N Tanzania
Francolinus erckelii (Erckel's Francolin)
    F. e. erckelii
        Ethiopia
    F. e. pentoni
        NE Sudan
**Francolinus ochropectus (Pale-bellied
Francolin)**
        Somalia
**Francolinus castaneicollis (Chestnut-
naped Francolin)**
    F. c. ogoensis
        Somalia
    F. c. castaneicollis
        E Ethiopia
    F. c. bottegi
        S Ethiopia
    F. c. kaffanus
        W Ethiopia
    F. c. gofanus
        SW Ethiopia
    F. c. atrifrons
        S Ethiopia

Francolinus jacksoni (Jackson's Francolin)
F. j. jacksoni
Higher Aberdare Mts
F. j. pollenorum
Mt Kenya
F. j. gurae
Lower Aberdare Mts
Francolinus nobilis (Handsome Francolin)
F. n. nobilis
E Zaire, SW Uganda
F. n. chapini
Ruwenzori Mts (E Zaire)
Francolinus camerunensis (Cameroun Mountain Francolin)
Cameroun Mts
Francolinus swierstrai (Swierstra's Francolin)
S Angola
Francolinus ahantensis (Ahanta Francolin)
F. a. hopkinsoni
Gambia, Guinea
F. a. ahantensis
Guinea to Nigeria
Francolinus squamatus (Scaly Francolin)
F. s. squamatus
S Nigeria to N Zaire
F. s. schuetti
Angola to Ethiopia, W Kenya
F. s. zappeyi
Uganda, W Kenya
F. s. tetraoninus
W Ethiopia
F. s. maranensis
S Kenya
F. s. usambarae
Usambara Mts (Tanzania)
F. s. uzungwensis
Uzungwe Mts (Tanzania)
F. s. doni
Vipya plateau (W Malawi)
Francolinus griseostriatus (Grey-striped Francolin)
N Angola
Francolinus bicalcaratus (Double-spurred Francolin)
F. b. ayesha
W Morocco
F. b. bicalcaratus
Senegal to Niger & N Nigeria
F. b. thornei
Sierra Leone to Benin
F. b. adamauae
N Nigeria, Cameroun
F. b. ogilvie-granti
Cameroun

Francolinus icterorhynchus (Yellow-billed Francolin)
F. i. icterorhynchus
Central African Republic to SW Sudan
F. i. dybowskii
NE Zaire, W Uganda
F. i. ugandensis
C Uganda
Francolinus clappertoni (Clapperton's Francolin)
F. c. clappertoni
Mali to W Sudan
F. c. heuglini
SW Sudan
F. c. cavei
SE Sudan
F. c. gedgii
Mt Elgon
F. c. sharpii
E Ethiopia
F. c. testis
Ethiopia
F. c. nigrosquamatus
Ethiopia
Francolinus hildebrandti (Hildebrandt's Francolin)
F. h. helleri
N Kenya
F. h. altumi
W Kenya
F. h. hildebrandti
E Kenya to NE Zambia & W Malawi
F. h. fischeri
C Tanzania
F. h. grotei
SE Tanzania
F. h. johnstoni
S Tanzania, E Zambia, S Malawi, Mozambique
Francolinus natalensis (Natal Francolin)
F. n. neavei
NE Zambia, W Mozambique
F. n. natalensis
S Zambia to Natal
Francolinus hartlaubi (Hartlaub's Francolin)
F. h. hartlaubi
Angola
F. h. bradfieldi
N Namibia
F. h. crypticus
Onguato area, C Namibia
Francolinus harwoodi (Harwood's Francolin)
S Ethiopia
Francolinus adspersus (Red-billed Francolin)
S Angola, Namibia, Botswana
Francolinus capensis (Cape Francolin)
Cape Province

Francolinus sephaena (Crested Francolin)
F. s. somaliensis
Somalia
F. s. grantii
Ethiopia to C Tanzania
F. s. rovuma
E Tanzania & E Mozambique
F. s. sephaena
E Rhodesia to Mozambique & N Natal
F. s. zambesiae
Namibia to S Malawi
Francolinus streptophorus (Ring-necked Francolin)
Cameroun, W Kenya, NW Tanzania
Francolinus psilolaemus (Montane Francolin)
C Ethiopia
Francolinus shelleyi (Shelley's Francolin)
F. s. elgonensis
Kenya
F. s. theresae
Mt Kenya
F. s. shelleyi
Uganda to Natal
F. s. trothae
W Tanzania
F. s. whytei
SE Zaire, Zambia, N Malawi
Francolinus africanus (Greywing Francolin)
F. a. gutteralis
N Ethiopia
F. a. eritreae
NE Ethiopia
F. a. lorti
Somalia
F. a. ellenbecki
C Ethiopia
F. a. archeri
SC Ethiopia
F. a. triedmanni
S Ethiopia
F. a. uluensis
C Kenya
F. a. macarthuri
SE Kenya
F. a. africanus
South Africa
Francolinus levalliantoides (Archer's Greywing Francolin)
F. l. jugularis
S Angola
F. l. cunenensis
S Angola, N Namibia
F. l. pallidior
Etosha Pan, N Namibia
F. l. wattii

C Namibia
F. l. kalaharica
C Botswana
F. l. langi
NE Botswana
F. l. levalliantoides
E Botswana, Orange Free State
F. l. ludwigi
SW Transvaal
F. l. gariepensis
S Transvaal, N Orange Free State
Francolinus levaillantii (Red-winged Francolin)
F. l. kikuyuensis
Uganda, Kenya
F. l. crawshayi
N Malawi
F. l. benguellensis
S Angola
F. l. clayi
W Zambia
F. l. levaillantii
Transvaal, Natal, NE Cape Province
Francolinus finschi (Finsch's Francolin)
SW Zaire, Angola
Francolinus coqui (Coqui Francolin)
F. c. buckleyi
Ghana to S Nigeria
F. c. spinetorum
Mali to Nigeria
F. c. maharao
S Ethiopia
F. c. angolensis
Gabon to Angola & Zambia
F. c. ruahdae
S Uganda
F. c. hubbardi
W Kenya
F. c. thikae
C Kenya
F. c. coqui
Kenya to Botswana & Natal
F. c. kasaicus
C Zaire
F. c. vernayi
Botswana
F. c. hoeschianus
N Namibia
Francolinus albogularis (White-throated Francolin)
F. a. albogularis
Senegal, Gambia
F. a. buckleyi
Ghana to Cameroun
F. a. dewittei
SE Zaire
F. a. meinertzhageni
E Angola, NW Zambia

Francolinus schlegelii **(Schlegel's Francolin)**
S Central African Republic to SW Sudan
Francolinus lathami **(Latham's Francolin)**
F. l. lathami
Sierra Leone to Gabon & NW Zaire
F. l. schubotzi
NE Zaire to SW Sudan & Uganda
Francolinus nahani **(Nahan's Forest Francolin)**
NE Zaire, Uganda
Francolinus pondicerianus **(Indian Grey Francolin)**
F. p. mecranensis
S Iran to Pakistan
F. p. interpositus
N India
F. p. pondicerianus
S India
F. p. ceylonensis
Sri Lanka
Francolinus gularis **(Swamp Partridge)**
NE India, Assam

PERDIX
Perdix perdix **(Grey Partridge)**
P. p. perdix
British Isles, W & C Europe
P. p. armoricana
NW France
P. p. sphagnetorum
NE Holland, NW Germany
P. p. hispaniensis
Pyrenees, N Spain
P. p. italica
Italy
P. p. lucida
NE Europe
P. p. robusta
NW Russia
P. p. arenicola
WC Russia
P. p. furvescens
SW Russia, N Iran
P. p. canescens
Transcaucasia to NW Iran
Perdix dauuricae **(Daurian Partridge)**
P. d. dauuricae
EC Asia, Mongolia, N China
P. d. castaneothorax
S Manchuria
P. d. turcomana
E Turkestan, E Tien Shan
P. d. przewalskii
E Nanshans, NW China
P. d. suschkini
C Amur, Ussuriland
Perdix hodgsoniae **(Tibetan Partridge)**

P. h. koslowi
W Nanshans, S Kokonor Mts
P. h. sifanica
E Nanshans, SE Tibet, W China
P. h. caraganae
E Ladak, W Himalayas
P. h. hodgsoniae
Tibet, E Himalayas, Assam

RHIZOTHERA
Rhizothera longirostris **(Long-billed Wood Partridge)**
R. l. longirostris
Malaysia, Sumatra, W Borneo
R. l. dulitensis
N Borneo

MARGAROPERDIX
Margaroperdix madagarensis **(Madagascar Partridge)**
Madagascar

MELANOPERDIX
Melanoperdix nigra **(Black Wood Partridge)**
M. n. nigra
Malaysia, Sumatra
M. n. borneensis
Borneo

COTURNIX
Coturnix coturnix **(Common Quail)**
C. c. coturnix
Europe, W Asia to C Africa & India
C. c. ussuriensis
NE Asia, Mongolia
C. c. conturbans
Azores
C. c. confisa
Madeira, Canary Is
C. c. inopinata
Cape Verde Is
C. c. africana
Southern Africa, Madagascar
Coturnix japonica **(Japanese Quail)**
Sakhalin, Japan to Indochina
Coturnix coromandelica **(Black-breasted Quail)**
India, Sri Lanka, Burma
Coturnix delegorguei **(Harlequin Quail)**
C. d. delegorguei
Senegal to Ethiopia & S Africa
C. d. histrionica
Sao Thomé I
C. d. arabica
S Arabia
Coturnix pectoralis **(Pectoral Quail)**
Australia, Tasmania

SYNOICUS
Synoicus ypsilophorus **(Brown Quail)**

S. y. raaltenii
Flores I, Timor I
S. y. pallidior
Sumba I, Savu I
S. y. saturatior
N New Guinea
S. y. lamonti
C New Guinea
S. y. dogwa
S New Guinea
S. y. mafulu
SE New Guinea
S. y. castaneus
Lesser Sunda Is
S. y. plumbeus
SE New Guinea
S. y. cervinus
NW Australia
S. y. queenslandicus
N Queensland
S. y. australis
SW Australia & S Queensland to Victoria
S. y. ypsilophorus
SE Australia, Tasmania

EXCALFACTORIA
Excalfactoria adansonii (Blue Quail)
Ethiopia to Sierra Leone & E Cape Province
Excalfactoria chinensis (Indian Blue Quail)
E. c. chinensis
India to Malaysia, S China & Indochina
E. c. trinkutensis
Nicobar Is
E. c. palmeri
Sumatra, Java
E. c. lineata
Philippine Is, Borneo, Celebes
E. c. lineatula
Lombok I, Sumba I, Flores I, Timor I
E. c. lepida
Bismarck Archipelago
E. c. papuensis
SE New Guinea
E. c. australis
Queensland to Victoria
E. c. colletti
Northern Territory

PERDICULA
Perdicula asiatica (Jungle Bush Quail)
Himalayas, N & C India
Perdicula argoondah (Rock Bush Quail)
SE India
Perdicula erythrorhyncha (Painted Bush Quail)
P. e. erythrorhyncha
SW India
P. e. blewitti
C India

Perdicula manipurensis (Manipur Bush Quail)
P. m. inglisi
N Assam
P. m. manipurensis
S Assam

ARBOROPHILA
Arborophila torqueola (Common Hill Partridge)
A. t. millardi
NW India
A. t. torqueola
N & E India, S Tibet
A. t. batemani
N Burma
A. t. griseata
W N Vietnam
Arborophila rufogularis (Rufous-throated Hill Partridge)
A. r. rufogularis
N India
A. r. intermedia
Assam to NW Burma
A. r. tickelli
S Burma to SW Laos
A. r. euroa
S China, N Laos
A. r. guttata
C Vietnam
A. r. annamensis
S Vietnam
Arborophila atrogularis (White-cheeked Hill Partridge)
Assam, N Burma
Arborophila crudigularis (White-throated Hill Partridge)
Taiwan
Arborophila mandellii (Red-breasted Hill Partridge)
Sikkim to E Assam
Arborophila brunneopectus (Brown-breasted Hill Partridge)
A. b. brunneopectus
E Assam & S Yunnan to S Thailand
A. b. henrici
N & C Vietnam
A. b. albigula
S Vietnam
Arborophila rufipectus (Boulton's Hill Partridge)
W Szechwan
Arborophila gingica (Rickett's Hill Partridge)
SE China
Arborophila davidi (David's Tree Partridge)
S Vietnam

**Arborophila cambodiana (Chestnut-
headed Tree Partridge)**
A. c. cambodiana
  Cambodia
A. c. diversa
  SE Thailand
**Arborophila orientalis (Sumatran Hill
Partridge)**
A. o. campbelli
  Malaysia
A. c. rolli
  NW Sumatra
A. o. sumatrana
  C Sumatra
A. o. orientalis
  E Java
**Arborophila javanica (Chestnut-bellied
Tree Partridge)**
A. j. javanica
  W Java
A. j. bartelsi
  C Java
A. j. lawuana
  C Java
**Arborophila rubrirostris (Red-billed
Tree Partridge)**
  Sumatra
**Arborophila hyperythra (Red-breasted
Tree Partridge)**
  NW Borneo
Arborophila ardens (Hainan Hill Partridge)
  Hainan I

TROPICOPERDIX
**Tropicoperdix charltonii (Chestnut-
breasted Tree Partridge)**
T. c. charltonii
  S Thailand, Malaysia
T. c. atjehensis
  N Sumatra
T. c. tonkinensis
  N Vietnam
T. c. graydoni
  Borneo
**Tropicoperdix chloropus (Green-legged
Hill Partridge)**
T. c. chloropus
  N Burma to W & S Thailand
T. c. olivacea
  Laos, Cambodia
T. c. cognacqi
  S Vietnam
**Tropicoperdix merlini (Annamese Hill
Partridge)**
T. m. merlini
  C Vietnam
T. m. vivida
  EC Vietnam

CALOPERDIX
**Caloperdix oculea (Ferruginous Wood
Partridge)**
C. o. oculea
  S Thailand, Malaysia
C. o. sumatrana
  Sumatra
C. o. borneensis
  Borneo

HAEMATORTYX
**Haematortyx sanguiniceps (Crimson-
headed Wood Partridge)**
  N Borneo

ROLLULUS
**Rollulus roulroul (Crested Wood
Partridge)**
  S Thailand, Malaysia, Sumatra, Borneo

PTILOPACHUS
Ptilopachus petrosus (Stone Partridge)
P. p. petrosus
  Gambia to Cameroun
P. p. saturatior
  NC Cameroun
P. p. brehmi
  Lake Chad to Sudan
P. p. major
  N Ethiopia
P. p. florentiae
  S Sudan to NE Zaire, Uganda & Kenya

BAMBUSICOLA
Bambusicola fytchii (Bamboo Partridge)
B. f. fytchii
  W China, Burma, N Vietnam
B. f. hopkinsoni
  Assam, S Burma
**Bambusicola thoracica (Chinese Bamboo
Partridge)**
B. t. thoracica
  China
B. t. sonorivox
  Taiwan

GALLOPERDIX
Galloperdix spadicea (Red Spurfowl)
G. s. spadicea
  W Nepal to SE India
G. s. caurina
  Rajputana
G. s. stewarti
  C & S Travancore
Galloperdix lunulata (Painted Spurfowl)
  India
**Galloperdix bicalcarata (Ceylon
Spurfowl)**
  Sri Lanka

Ophrysia superciliosa (Himalayan Mountain Quail)
NW Himalayas

ITHAGINIS
Ithaginis cruentus (Blood Pheasant)
I. c. cruentus
Nepal, Sikkim, W Bhutan
I. c. affinis
Sikkim
I. c. tibetanus
E Bhutan, SE Tibet
I. c. kuseri
E Assam to Yunnan
I. c. holoptilus
Yunnan
I. c. rocki
W Yunnan
I. c. clarkei
W Yunnan
I. c. annae
NW Szechwan
I. c. beicki
N Kansu
I. c. marionae
NE Burma
I. c. geoffroyi
SE Tibet to W Szechwan
I. c. berezowskii
S Kansu, N Szechwan
I. c. sinensis
Shensi
I. c. michaëlis
W Kansu

TRAGOPAN
Tragopan melanocephalus (Western Tragopan)
NW Himalayas
Tragopan satyra (Satyr Tragopan)
C & E Himalayas
Tragopan blythii (Blyth's Tragopan)
T. b. molesworthi
SE Tibet
T. b. blythii
Assam, NW Burma
Tragopan temminckii (Temminck's Tragopan)
SE Tibet, W China, N Vietnam
Tragopan caboti (Cabot's Tragopan)
SE China

PUCRASIA
Pucrasia macrolopha (Koklass Pheasant)
P. m. castanea
Afghanistan, N Pakistan
P. m. biddulphi
N Kashmir, Ladakh

P. m. macrolopha
W Himalayas
P. m. bethelae
Punjab
P. m. nipalensis
W Nepal
P. m. meyeri
SE Tibet, W Yunnan
P. m. ruficollis
Kansu, W Shansi
P. m. xanthospila
SE Mongolia
P. m. joretiana
W Anhwei
P. m. darwini
Hupeh & E China

LOPHOPHORUS
Lophophorus impeyanus (Himalayan Monal Pheasant)
Himalayas
Lophophorus sclateri (Sclater's Monal Pheasant)
L. s. sclateri
E Assam, N Burma, W Yunnan
L. s. orientalis
Myitkyina, Burma
Lophophorus lhuysii (Chinese Monal Pheasant)
W & NW Szechwan

GALLUS
Gallus gallus (Red Junglefowl)
G. g. murghi
Kashmir to Assam & C India
G. g. gallus
S Indochina, Thailand, Sumatra
G. g. spadiceus
SW Yunnan, N Indochina, Burma, Malaysia
G. g. jabouillei
N Vietnam
G. g. bankiva
Java
Gallus lafayettei (Ceylon Jungle-fowl)
Sri Lanka
Gallus sonneratii (Grey Jungle-fowl)
W & S India
Gallus varius (Green Junglefowl)
Java to Sumba & Flores

LOPHURA
Lophura leucomelana (Kalij Pheasant)
L. l. hamiltonii
W Himalayas
L. l. moffitti
C Bhutan
L. l. leucomelana
Nepal

L. l. melanotus
E Nepal
L. l. lathami
E Bhutan, Assam, W Burma
L. l. williamsi
N Burma
L. l. oatesi
S Burma
L. l. lineatus
E Burma, Thailand
L. l. crawfurdi
S & W Thailand
Lophura nycthemera (Silver Pheasant)
L. n. occidentalis
NW Yunnan, NE Burma
L. n. rufipes
SW Yunnan, N Burma
L. n. jonesi
SW Yunnan, C Thailand, C Burma
L n. ripponi
S Burma
L. n. beaulieui
SE Yunnan, N Indochina
L. n. omeiensis
Szechwan
L. n. fokiensis
NW Fokien
L. n. nycthemera
S China, NE Vietnam
L. n. berliozi
WC Indochina
L. n. beli
C Vietnam
L. n. annamensis
S Vietnam
L. n. lewisi
Cambodia
L. n. engelbachi
S Laos
L. n. whiteheadi
Hainan I
Lophura imperialis (Imperial Pheasant)
NC Indochina
Lophura edwardsi (Edwards' Pheasant)
C Vietnam
Lophura swinhoii (Swinhoe's Pheasant)
Taiwan
Lophura inornata (Salvadori's Pheasant)
L. i. hoogewerfi
N Sumatra
L. i. inornata
W Sumatra
Lophura erythrophthalma (Crestless Fireback Pheasant)
L. e. erythrophthalma
S Malaysia, NE Sumatra
L. e. pyronota
N Borneo

Lophura ignita (Crested Fireback Pheasant) 107
L. i. rufa
S Thailand, Malaysia, N & C Sumatra
L. i. macartneyi
SE Sumatra
L. i. nobilis
N Borneo
L. i. ignita
S Borneo
Lophura diardi (Siamese Fireback Pheasant)
Burma, Thailand, C & S Indochina
Lophura bulweri (Bulwer's Pheasant)
Borneo

CROSSOPTILON
Crossoptilon crossoptilon (White Eared-Pheasant)
C. c. dolani
S Kokonor
C. c. crossoptilon
C Szechwan, NW Yunnan
C. c. lichiangense
NW Yunnan
C. c. drouynii
SE Tibet
C. c. harmani
SE Tibet
Crossoptilon mantchuricum (Brown Eared-Pheasant)
NE China
Crossoptilon auritum (Blue Eared-Pheasant)
W China

CATREUS
Catreus wallichii (Cheer Pheasant)
Himalayas

SYRMATICUS
Syrmaticus ellioti (Elliot's Pheasant)
SE China
Syrmaticus humiae (Mrs Hume's Pheasant)
S. h. humiae
N Burma
S. h. burmanicus
SW Yunnan, NE Burma
Syrmaticus mikado (Mikado Pheasant)
Taiwan
Syrmaticus soemmerringi (Copper Pheasant)
S. s. scintillans
Honshu I
S. s. subrufus
W Honshu I
S. s. intermedius
SW Honshu I, Shikoku I
S. s. soemmerringi
N & C Kyushu I

S. s. ijimae
SE Kyushu I
Syrmaticus reevesii (Reeves' Pheasant)
N & C China

PHASIANUS
Phasianus colchicus (Ring-necked Pheasant)
P. c. septentrionalis
N Caucasus, W Caspian Sea
P. c. colchicus
Transcaucasia, E & SE Black Sea
P. c. talischensis
SW & S Caspian Sea
P. c. persicus
SW Transcaspia
P. c. principalis
S Turkestan, N Afghanistan
P. c. chrysomelas
Russian Turkestan
P. c. zarudnyi
Russian Turkestan
P. c. bianchii
Pamir, Hindukush Mts
P. c. zerafschanicus
Samarkand
P. c. bergii
Aral Sea
P. c. turcestanicus
Russian Turkestan
P. c. mongolicus
NE Russian Turkestan, S Dzungaria
P. c. shawii
Chinese Turkestan
P. c. tarimensis
E Chinese Turkestan
P. c. vlangalii
E Zaidam
P. c. satscheuensis
W Kansu
P. c. edzinensis
C Gobi
P. c. sohokotensis
Soho-khoto Oasis
P. c. alaschanicus
C Alaschan Mts
P. c. hagenbecki
W Mongolia
P. c. pallasi
SE Siberia, C Manchuria
P. c. karpowi
S Manchuria, Korea
P. c. kiangsuensis
SE Mongolia, N Shansi, N Shensi
P. c. strauchi
Kansu, C & S Shensi, NE Szechwan
P. c. süehschanensis
NW Szechwan

P. c. elegans
SW Szechwan to N Burma
P. c. rothschildi
SE Yunnan, N Vietnam
P. c. decollatus
WC China
P. c. torquatus
E China
P. c. takatsukasae
NE Vietnam
P. c. formosanus
Taiwan
Phasianus versicolor (Japanese Pheasant)
P. v. robustipes
Sado I, NW Honshu
P. v. versicolor
Kyushu, E & S Honshu, Shikoku
P. v. tanensis
S peninsulas & islands off Honshu

CHRYSOLOPHUS
Chrysolophus pictus (Golden Pheasant)
C China
Chrysolophus amherstiae (Lady Amherst's Pheasant)
SE Tibet, SW China, N Burma

POLYPLECTRON
Polyplectron chalcurum (Sumatran Peacock-Pheasant)
P. c. scutulatum
N Sumatra
P. c. chalcurum
S Sumatra
Polyplectron inopinatum (Rothschild's Peacock-Pheasant)
C Malaysia
Polyplectron germaini (Germain's Peacock-Pheasant)
S Vietnam
Polyplectron bicalcaratum (Burmese Peacock-Pheasant)
P. b. bakeri
Sikkim to E Assam
P. b. bicalcaratum
C & S Burma to Laos
P. b. bailyi
N Thailand
P. b. ghigii
N Vietnam
P. b. katsumatae
Hainan I
Polyplectron malacense (Malay Peacock-Pheasant)
P. m. malacense
SW Thailand, Malaysia, Sumatra
P. m. schleiermacheri
Borneo

Polyplectron emphanum (Palawan Peacock-Pheasant)
Palawan I

RHEINARTIA
Rheinartia ocellata (Rheinard's Pheasant)
R. o. ocellata
C Vietnam
R. o. nigrescens
C Malaysia

ARGUSIANUS
Argusianus argus (Great Argus Pheasant)
A. a. grayi
C Borneo
A. a. argus
SW Thailand, Malaysia, Sumatra

PAVO
Pavo cristatus (Common Peafowl)
India, Sri Lanka
Pavo muticus (Green Peafowl)
P. m. spicifer
SE Assam, W Burma
P. m. imperator
E Burma, Thailand, Indochina
P. m. muticus
Java, Malaysia

AFROPAVO
Afropavo congensis (Congo Peafowl)
Ituri Forest, EC Zaire

NUMIDINAE
PHASIDUS
Phasidus niger (Black Guineafowl)
S Cameroun to C Zaire

AGELASTES
Agelastes meleagrides (White-breasted Guineafowl)
Liberia, Ghana

NUMIDA
Numida meleagris (Helmet Guineafowl)
N. m. sabyi
W Morocco
N. m. galeata
Senegal to Air & Cameroun
N. m. bannermanni
Cape Verde Is
N. m. marchei
Gabon, Central African Republic
N. m. strasseni
E Cameroun, N Central African Republic
N. m. meleagris
Chad, Sudan, N Ethiopia, SW Arabia
N. m. somaliensis
SE Ethiopia, Somalia, N Kenya
N. m. major
NE Zaire, S Ethiopia, NW Kenya, N Uganda

N. m. toruensis
E Zaire, W Uganda
N. m. intermedia
SW Uganda
N. m. mitrata
S Kenya to Rhodesia, Madagascar
N. m. macroceras
W Kenya
N. m. reichenowi
SW Kenya, NW Tanzania
N. m. uhehensis
SC Tanzania
N. m. callewaerte
N Angola to SC Zaire
N. m. marungensis
S Zaire, Zambia
N. m. maxima
S Angola
N. m. rikwae
SW Tanzania
N. m. papillosa
S Angola
N. m. damarensis
N Namibia
N. m. transvaalensis
W Transvaal
N. m. coronata
E Transvaal, Natal, E Cape Province

GUTTERA
Guttera plumifera (Plumed Guineafowl)
G. p. plumifera
Cameroun, Gabon, N Angola
G. p. schubotzi
N Zaire
Guttera edouardi (Crested Guineafowl)
G. e. verreauxi
Guinea to Togo
G. e. sclateri
W Cameroun
G. e. schoutedeni
S Zaire
G. e. chapini
S Angola
G. e. sethsmithi
E Zaire, NW Tanzania
G. e. suahelica
C Tanzania
G. e. barbata
SW Tanzania, W Mozambique
G. e. kathleenae
W Zambia
G. e. edouardi
S Malawi, E Transvaal, Natal
Guttera pucherani (Kenya Crested Guineafowl)
SE Somalia, E Kenya, NE Tanzania, Zanzibar

ACRYLLIUM
Acryllium vulturinum (Vulturine Guineafowl)
E Uganda, S Somalia, E Kenya, NE Tanzania

36 OPISTHOCOMIDAE (HOATZIN)

OPISTHOCOMUS
Opisthocomus hoazin (Hoatzin)
Northern Amazonian forest

Gruiformes

37 MESITORNITHIDAE (MESITES)

MESITORNIS
Mesitornis variegata (White-breasted Mesite)
E Madagascar
Mesitornis unicolor (Brown Mesite)
E Madagascar

MONIAS
Monias benschi (Bensch's Monia)
SW Madagascar

38 TURNICIDAE (BUTTON QUAILS)

TURNIX
Turnix sylvatica (Little Button Quail)
T. s. sylvatica
S Iberia, NW Africa
T. s. lepurana
Senegal to Sudan & Cape Province
T. s. dussumier
India, Burma
T. s. mikado
Thailand, S China, N Indochina, Taiwan
T. s. davidi
S Indochina
T. s. bartelsorum
Java
T. s. whiteheadi
Luzon I
T. s. celestinoi
Bohol I
T. s. nigrorum
Negros I, Umod I
T. s. masaaki
Mindanao I
T. s. suluensis
Sulu Is
T. s. kinneari
Peling I
T. s. beccarii
Celebes, Tukang Besi Is
T. s. maculosa
Lesser Sunda Is, Kei Is
T. s. everetti

Sumba I.
T. s. saturata
New Britain, Duke of York I
T. s. furva
New Guinea
T. s. giluwensis
C New Guinea
T. s. savuensis
Savu Is
T. s. sumbana
Sumba I
T. s. floresiana
Flores I
T. s. horsbrughi
S New Guinea, Sudest I
T. s. salamonis
Guadalcanal I, Bismarck Archipelago
T. s. pseutes
NW Australia
Turnix worcesteri (Worcester's Button Quail)
Luzon I
Turnix nana (Natal Button Quail)
T. n. nana
Ghana to Uganda & SE Cape Province
T. n. luciana
C Kenya
Turnix hottentotta (Hottentot Button Quail)
SW Cape Province
Turnix tanki (Yellow-legged Button Quail)
T. t. tanki
India, Nicobar & Andaman Is
T. t. blanfordii
Manchuria to Burma, S China, Indochina
Turnix suscitator (Bustard Quail)
T. s. plumbipes
Nepal to N Burma
T. s. bengalensis
NE India
T. s. taigoor
India
T. s. leggei
Sri Lanka
T. s. blakistoni
S China, N Indochina
T. s. rostrata
Taiwan
T. s. pallescens
SC Burma
T. s. thai
C Thailand
T. s. interrumpens
S Burma, S Thailand
T. s. atrogularis
Malaysia, N Sumatra

T. s. machetes
C Sumatra
T. s. suscitator
SE Sumatra, Java, Bali I
T. s. kuiperi
Billiton I
T. s. okinavensis
Okinawa I
T. s. fasciata
Palawan I, N & W Philippine Is
T. s. nigrescens
Negros I, Cebu I
T. s. rufilata
Celebes
T. s. powelli
Lesser Sunda islands
Turnix nigricollis (Madagascar Button Quail)
Madagascar
Turnix ocellata (Spotted Button Quail)
Luzon I
Turnix melanogaster (Black-breasted Button Quail)
Queensland, New South Wales
Turnix varia (Painted Button Quail)
T. v. scintillans
Houtman (Abrolhos) Is
T. v. varia
Australia
T. v. novaecaledoniae
New Caledonia
Turnix castanota (Chestnut-backed Button Quail)
T. c. castanota
NW Australia, Northern Territory, Melville I
T. c. olivii
N Queensland
Turnix pyrrhothorax (Red-chested Button Quail)
N, E & SE Australia
Turnix velox (Little Quail)
Australia

ORTYXELOS
Ortyxelos meiffrenii (Quail Plover)
Senegal to C Sudan, N Kenya

39 PEDIONOMIDAE (PLAINS WANDERER)

PEDIONOMUS
Pedionomus torquatus (Plains Wanderer)
New South Wales, Victoria, South
Australia

40 GRUIDAE (CRANES)

GRUINAE

GRUS
Grus grus (Common Crane)

G. g. grus
N & E Europe, W Russia » NE Africa
G. g. lilfordi
C & E Asia, China, N India
Grus nigricollis (Black-necked Crane)
C Asia to Assam, S China
Grus monacha (Hooded Crane)
SE Siberia, N China, Japan
Grus canadensis (Sandhill Crane)
G. c. canadensis
E Siberia, NW Canada to NW USA
G. c. tabida
SW Canada, W USA, N Mexico
G. c. pratensis
SE USA
G. c. pulla
Gulf Coast, S USA
G. c. nesiotes
Isle of Pines, W Cuba
Grus japonensis (Manchurian Crane)
Manchuria » E China
Grus americana (Whooping Crane)
N Sasketchewan » SE Texas
Grus vipio (Japanese White-necked Crane)
NW Mongolia » E China
Grus antigone (Sarus Crane)
G. a. antigone
N India
G. a. sharpii
E Assam, Burma to S Indochina
Grus rubicunda (Brolga)
S New Guinea, N, E & S Australia
Grus leucogeranus (Great White Crane)
SE Russia, Siberia » NW India & China

BUGERANUS
Bugeranus carunculatus (Wattled Crane)
Somalia to Angola & South Africa

ANTHROPOIDES
Anthropoides virgo (Demoiselle Crane)
SE Europe, NE Africa to C Asia & China
Anthropoides paradisea (Stanley Crane)
Southern Africa

BALEARICINAE

BALEARICA
Balearica pavonina (Crowned Crane)
B. p. pavonina
Senegal to Chad & N Zaire
B. p. ceciliae
Sudan, Ethiopia
B. p. gibbericeps
E Zaire, Uganda, Kenya, N Tanzania
Balearica regulorum (South African Crowned Crane)
Southern Africa

41 ARAMIDAE (LIMPKIN)

ARAMUS
Aramus guarauna (Limpkin)
  A. g. pictus
    SE USA, Cuba, Jamaica
  A. g. elucus
    Hispaniola, Puerto Rico
  A. g. dolosus
    S Mexico to Panama
  A. g. guarauna
    N South America to Paraguay &
    Argentina

42 PSOPHIIDAE (TRUMPETERS)

PSOPHIA
Psophia crepitans (Common Trumpeter)
  P. c. crepitans
    S Venezuela, the Guianas, NE Brazil
  P. c. napensis
    N Upper Amazonia
**Psophia leucoptera (White-winged
Trumpeter)**
  P. l. leucoptera
    E Peru, N Bolivia, W Brazil
  P. l. ochroptera
    NW Brazil
**Psophia viridis (Green-winged
Trumpeter)**
  P. v. viridis
    N Brazil
  P. v. dextralis
    NC Brazil
  P. v. interjecta
    C Brazil
  P. v. obscura
    NE Brazil

43 RALLIDAE (RAILS, COOTS)

HIMANTORNIS
Himantornis haematopus (Nkulengu Rail)
  H. h. haematopus
    Liberia to S Cameroun
  H. h. petiti
    Gabon to N Angola
  H. h. whitesidei
    C Zaire

CANIRALLUS
Canirallus oculeus (Grey-throated Rail)
  C. o. oculeus
    Liberia to Nigeria
  C. o. batesi
    S Cameroun to C Zaire
**Canirallus kioloides (Madagascar Grey-
throated Rail)**
  C. k. berliozi
    NW Madagascar

  C. k. kioloides
    E Madagascar
Canirallus cuvieri (White-throated Rail)
  C. c. cuvieri
    Madagascar, Mauritius I
  C. c. aldabranus
    Aldabra I

EULABEORNIS
**Eulabeornis castaneoventris (Chestnut-
bellied Rail)**
  E. c. sharpei
    Aru Is
  E. c. castaneoventris
    coast of N & NE Australia
**Eulabeornis plumbeiventris (Bare-eyed
Rail)**
  E. p. plumbeiventris
    N Moluccas, New Ireland, N New Guinea
  E. p. hoeveni
    S New Guinea, Aru Is
Eulabeornis rosenbergii (Bald-faced Rail)
    N & C Celebes
**Eulabeornis calopterus (Red-winged
Wood Rail)**
    E Ecuador, E Peru
**Eulabeornis saracura (Slaty-breasted
Wood Rail)**
    SE Brazil, Paraguay
Eulabeornis ypecaha (Giant Wood Rail)
    E Brazil to C Argentina
Eulabeornis wolfi (Brown Wood Rail)
    Colombia to SW Ecuador
Eulabeornis mangle (Little Wood Rail)
    E Brazil
**Eulabeornis cajaneus (Grey-necked Wood
Rail)**
  E. c. mexicanus
    S Mexico
  E. c. vanrossemi
    Guatemala, El Salvador
  E. c. albiventris
    Yucatan to Belize
  E. c. pacificus
    Honduras, Nicaragua
  E. c. plumbeicollis
    NE Costa Rica
  E. c. cajaneus
    Costa Rica to Paraguay & N Argentina
  E. c. latens
    San Miguel I, Pearl Is (Panama)
  E. c. morrisoni
    Pearl Is (Panama)
**Eulabeornis axillaris (Rufous-necked
Wood Rail)**
    S Mexico to Guyana & Ecuador
Eulabeornis concolor (Uniform Crake)
  E. c. guatemalensis
    S Mexico to Ecuador

E. c. castaneus
  NE South America
  (*E. c. concolor* — *extinct*)

RALLUS
Rallus plateni (Platen's Celebes Rail)
  Celebes
Rallus wallacii (Wallace's Rail)
  Halmahera I
Rallus insignis (New Britain Rail)
  New Britain
Rallus lafresnayanus (New Caledonian Wood Rail)
  New Caledonia **e?**
Rallus sylvestris (Lord Howe Wood Rail)
  Lord Howe I
Rallus poecilopterus (Barred Wing Rail)
  R. p. poecilopterus
    Taveuni I, Viti Levu I **e?**
  R. p. woodfordi
    Guadalcanal I
  R. p. immaculatus
    Ysabel I
  R. p. tertius
    Bougainville I
Rallus sanguinolentus (Plumbeous Rail)
  R. s. simonsi
    NW Peru, N Chile
  R. s. tschudii
    C Peru
  R. s. zelebori
    Rio de Janeiro, Brazil
  R. s. sanguinolentus
    S Brazil, W Argentina
  R. s. landbecki
    C Chile
  R. s. luridus
    Tierra del Fuego
Rallus nigricans (Blackish Rail)
  R. n. nigricans
    E Ecuador to E Brazil and E Argentina
  R. n. caucae
    Cauca valley, Colombia
Rallus maculatus (Spotted Rail)
  R. m. insolitus
    S Mexico to Costa Rica
  R. m. maculatus
    Venezuela to C Argentina, Trinidad, Cuba
Rallus philippensis (Banded Rail)
  R. p. philippensis
    Celebes, Mindoro I, Luzon I, Batan I
  R. p. xerophilus
    Banda Sea islands
  R. p. wilkinsoni
    S Flores I
  R. p. andrewsi
    Cocos Keeling Is

R. p. admiralitatis
  Admiralty Is
R. p. praedo
  Skoki I
R. p. lesouefi
  New Hanover
R. p. meyeri
  Witu I, New Britain
R. p. anchoretae
  Anchorite I
R. p. pelewensis
  Palau Is
R. p. christophori
  E Solomon Is
R. p. randi
  Mt Wilhelmina (New Guinea)
R. p. lacustris
  Sentani Lake (W New Guinea)
R. p. reductus
  NE New Guinea
R. p. wahgiensis
  SE New Guinea
R. p. yorki
  W & S New Guinea, N Queensland
R. p. australis
  E & S Australia, Tasmania
R. p. mellori
  Sandy Hooks I, SW Australia
R. p. assimilis
  New Zealand
R. p. norfolkensis
  Norfolk I
R. p. swindellsi
  New Caledonia
R. p. sethsmithi
  New Hebrides, Fiji Is
R. p. goodsoni
  Samoa Is
R. p. ecaudatus
  Tonga
Rallus striatus (Blue-breasted Banded Rail)
  R. s. gularis
    Java
  R. s. albiventer
    India, Burma, N Malaysia
  R. s. obscurior
    Andman Is, Nicobar Is
  R. s. jouyi
    SE China
  R. s. taiwanus
    Taiwan
  R. s. striatus
    Borneo, Celebes, Philippine Is
  R. s. paratermus
    Samar I

***Rallus torquatus* (Barred Rail)**
  R. t. torquatus
    Philippine Is
  R. t. celebensis
    Celebes
  R. t. sulcirostris
    Peling I, Sula Is
  R. t. kuehni
    Tukang Besi Is
  R. t. limarius
    Salawati I, NW New Guinea
***Rallus owstoni* (Guam Rail)**
    Guam I
***Rallus pectoralis* (Slate-breasted Rail)**
  R. p. exsul
    Flores I
  R. p. mayri
    NW New Guinea
  R. p. insulsus
    Hertzog Mts (New Guinea)
  R. p. captus
    Mt Hagen (New Guinea)
  R. p. alberti
    S C New Guinea
  R. p. pectoralis
    SW, S & E Australia
  R. p. brachipus
    Tasmania
  R. p. muelleri
    Adams I, S New Zealand
  R. p. mirificus
    Luzon I
***Rallus caerulescens* (Kaffir Rail)**
    N Angola to Ethiopia & Cape Province
***Rallus madagascariensis* (Madagascar Rail)**
    E Madagascar
***Rallus aquaticus* (Water Rail)**
  R. a. aquaticus
    W Europe to W Siberia, NW Africa
  R. a. hibernans
    Iceland
  R. a. korejewi
    Turkey to NW India
  R. a. indicus
    Siberia to Japan, N India & China
***Rallus semiplumbeous* (Bogota Rail)**
    Colombia, Ecuador, Peru
***Rallus longirostris* (Clapper Rail)**
  R. l. obsoletus
    N California
  R. l. levipes
    S California
  R. l. yumanensis
    SW USA, N Mexico
  R. l. beldingi
    S Mexico to N Colombia

  R. l. tenuirostris
    SC Mexico
  R. l. pallidus
    Yucatan
  R. l. grossi
    Quintana Roo
  R. l. belizensis
    Belize
  R. l. elegans
    C & E USA
  R. l. crepitans
    E Coast USA, Connecticut to N Carolina
  R. l. waynei
    S Carolina to Florida
  R. l. saturatus
    coast of Texas, Alabama
  R. l. scotti
    W Florida
  R. l. insularum
    Florida Keys
  R. l. coryi
    Bahama Is
  R. l. ramsdeni
    Cuba
  R. l. leucophaeus
    Isle of Pines
  R. l. caribaeus
    Cuba, Jamaica, Hispaniola, Puerto Rico, Antigua I
  R. l. margaritae
    N Venezuela
  R. l. phelpsi
    Colombia, Venezuela
  R. l. pelodramus
    Trinidad
  R. l. longirostris
    Coast of the Guianas
  R. l. crassirostris
    Coast of Brazil
  R. l. cypereti
    W Ecuador, N Peru
***Rallus wetmorei* (Plain-flanked Rail)**
    N Venezuela
***Rallus limicola* (Virginia Rail)**
  R. l. limicola
    USA, N Mexico
  R. l. friedmanni
    C Mexico
  R. l. aequatorialis
    Colombia, Ecuador, Peru
  R. l. antarcticus
    C & S Chile, S Argentina

ATLANTISIA
***Atlantisia rogersi* (Inaccessible Island Rail)**
    Inaccessible I

GALLIRALLUS
Gallirallus australis (Weka Rail)
  G. a. greyi
    North I, New Zealand
  G. a. australis
    N & W South I, New Zealand
  G. a. hectori
    E South I, New Zealand
  G. a. scotti
    Stewart I

ROUGETIUS
Rougetius rougetii (Rouget's Rail)
  N Ethiopia

CYANOLIMNAS
Cyanolimnas cerverai (Zapata Rail)
  S Cuba

RALLINA
Rallina rubra (New Guinea Chestnut Rail)
  R. r. rubra
    NW New Guinea
  R. r. telefolminensis
    WC New Guinea
  R. r. klossi
    C & SW New Guinea
Rallina leucospila (White-striped Chestnut Rail)
  NW & W New Guinea
Rallina forbesi (Forbes' Chestnut Rail)
  R. f. forbesi
    SE New Guinea
  R. f. dryas
    Huon peninsula, New Guinea
  R. f. steini
    C New Guinea
Rallina mayri (Mayr's Chestnut Rail)
  R. m. mayri
    Cyclops Mts (New Guinea)
  R. m. carmichaeli
    NE New Guinea
Rallina castaneiceps (Chestnut-headed Crake)
  R. c. coccineipes
    SW Colombia, NE Ecuador
  R. c. castaneiceps
    E Ecuador, N Peru
Rallina tricolor (Red-necked Crake)
  R. t. tricolor
    N Queensland, New Guinea & islands
  R. t. victa
    Damar I, Tenimber Is, St Matthias I
  R. t. convicta
    New Hanover, New Ireland
Rallina canningi (Andaman Banded Crake)
  Andaman Is
Rallina fasciata (Red-legged Crake)
  S Burma to Philippine Is, Moluccas, Java
Rallina eurizonoides (Banded Crake)

  R. e. amauroptera
    India » Sri Lanka
  R. e. telmatophila
    Burma to Indochina & Java
  R. e. sepiaria
    Riukiu Is
  R. e. formosana
    Taiwan
  R. e. eurizonoides
    Philippine Is
  R. e. minahasa
    Celebes, Sula Is
Rallina paykullii (Band-bellied Crake)
  NE Asia, China » Borneo, Java

COTURNICOPS
Coturnicops rufa (Red-chested Crake)
  C. r. bonapartii
    Sierra Leone to Gabon
  C. r. elizabethae
    NE Zaire, Uganda, N Kenya
  C. r. rufa
    Angola, South Africa
Coturnicops pulchra (White-spotted Crake)
  C. p. pulchra
    Sierra Leone to NW Cameroun
  C. p. zenkeri
    S Cameroun
  C. p. batesi
    S Cameroun
  C. p. centralis
    SE Cameroun to N Kenya, N Angola
Coturnicops lugens (African Chestnut-headed Crake)
  C. l. lugens
    Angola to NE Zaire, Tanzania
  C. l. lynesi
    NE Zambia
Coturnicops boehmi (Streaky-breasted Crake)
  Guinea to N Kenya & Malawi
Coturnicops elegans (Buff-spotted Crake)
  C. e. reichenovi
    Liberia to Angola & Uganda
  C. e. elegans
    Somalia to E Cape Province
Coturnicops affinis (Chestnut-tailed Crake)
  C. a. antonii
    Sudan to Zambia & Malawi
  C. a. affinis
    Rhodesia to Natal, E Cape Province
Coturnicops insularis (Madagascar Crake)
  Madagascar
Coturnicops watersi (Waters' Crake)
  Madagascar
Coturnicops ayresi (White-winged Crake)
  Ethiopia & E South Africa
Coturnicops schomburgkii (Ocellated Crake)

116
C. s. schomburgkii
   Venezuela, Guyana, French Guiana
C. s. chapmani
   S Brazil
Coturnicops notata (Darwins Rail)
   Guyana, Uruguay to S Argentina
Coturnicops noveboracensis (Yellow Rail)
C. n. noveboracensis
   E Canada to SW USA
C. n. goldmani
   Lerma, Mexico
C. n. exquisitus
   Siberia to Japan, China

LATERALLUS
Laterallus fasciatus (Black-banded Crake)
   SE Colombia, NE Peru, NW Brazil
Laterallus levraudi (Rusty-flanked Crake)
   N Venezuela
Laterallus ruber (Ruddy Crake)
   C Mexico to N Nicaragua
Laterallus viridis (Russet-crowned Crake)
L. v. brunnescens
   C Colombia
L. v. viridis
   E Peru, the Guianas, Brazil
Laterallus exilis (Grey-breasted Crake)
   Peru to the Guianas, Trinidad
Laterallus spilonotus (Galapagos Rail)
   Galapagos Is
Laterallus melanophaius (Rufous-sided Crake)
L. m. oenops
   E Colombia, E Ecuador
L. m. melanophaius
   Guyana to C Argentina
Laterallus albigularis (White-throated Crake)
L. a. cinereiceps
   Nicaragua to W Panama
L. a. albigularis
   SW Costa Rica to W Ecuador
L. a. cerdaleus
   E Colombia
Laterallus leucopyrrhus (Red & White Crake)
   S Brazil, Paraguay, Uruguay
Laterallus jamaicensis (Black Rail)
L. j. jamaicensis
   C & E USA, Jamaica, Cuba
L. j. coturniculus
   S California
L. j. murivagans
   W Peru
L. j. salinasi
   C Chile
Laterallus xenopterus (Rufous-faced Crake)
   Paraguay

CREX
Crex crex (Corncrake)
   Europe, N Africa to C Asia
PORZANA
Porzana egregia (African Crake)
   Gambia to E Ethiopia & Natal
Porzana flavirostra (Black Crake)
   Senegal to Sudan & Cape Province
Porzana olivieri (Olivier's Rail)
   W Madagascar
Porzana flaviventer (Yellow-breasted Crake)
P. f. gossii
   Cuba, Jamaica
P.f. hendersoni
   Hispaniola, Puerto Rico
P. f. woodi
   El Salvador
P. f. bangsi
   NC Colombia
P. f. flaviventer
   SW Colombia to French Guiana
Porzana cinerea (White-browed Rail)
P. c. cinerea
   Malaysia, Sumatra to Sumbawa I,
   Moluccas
P. c. ocularis
   Philippine Is, Celebes
P. c. micronesiae
   Guam I, Yap I, Truk I
P. c. leucophrys
   Bismarck Archipelago, New Guinea,
   N Australia
P. c. meeki
   St Matthias I
P. c. tannensis
   New Caledonia, New Hebrides, Fiji Is,
   Samoa Is
Porzana spiloptera (Dot-winged Crake)
   Uruguay, NE Argentina
Porzana albicollis (White-throated Crake)
P. a. olivacea
   N Colombia, the Guianas, Venezuela
P. a. albicollis
   E Brazil, E Bolivia, Paraguay,
   NW Argentina
Porzana marginalis (Striped Crake)
   Irregular distribution throughout Africa
Porzana erythrops (Paint-billed Crake)
P. e. olivascens
   Venezuela, the Guianas to NW Argentina
P. e. erythrops
   Peru, Brazil, N Argentina
Porzana columbiana (Colombian Crake)
P. c. ripleyi
   S Panama, NW Colombia
P. c. columbiana
   N Colombia, NW Ecuador

Porzana tabuensis (Sooty Crake)
P. t. tabuensis
  Fiji Is, New Caledonia, Samoa Is, Tonga,
    Marquesas Is
P. t. edwardi
  EC New Guinea
P. t. richardsoni
  C New Guinea
P. t. plumbea
  Chatham I, S Australia, Tasmania
Porzana atra (Henderson Island Crake)
  Henderson I
Porzana parva (Little Crake)
  E & S Europe to W India
Porzana pusilla (Baillon's Crake)
P. p. intermedia
  W Europe to Iran & N Africa
P. p. pusilla
  C Asia to India & China
P. p. obscura
  Uganda to Angola & Cape Province,
    Madagascar
P. p. mira
  Borneo, Malaysia, Sumatra
P. p. mayri
  New Guinea
P. p. palustris
  Australia, Tasmania
P. p. affinis
  New Zealand
Porzana fluminea (Australian Spotted Crake)
  SW to E Australia, Tasmania
Porzana porzana (Spotted Crake)
  W Europe, N Africa to C Asia, India
Porzana carolina (Sora Rail)
  Canada to Venezuela, Peru, W Indies
Porzana fusca (Ruddy-breasted Crake)
P. f. fusca
  N India to Philippine Is, Celebes, Flores I
P. f. erythrothorax
  Japan, China
P. f. phaeopyga
  Riukiu Is
P. f. zeylonica
  SW India, Sri Lanka

AMAURORNIS
Amaurornis olivaceus (Rufous-tailed Moorhen)
A. o. moluccanus
  N & E New Guinea, Moluccas
A. o. olivaceus
  Philippine Is
A. o. nigrifrons
  Bismarck Archipelago, Solomon Is
A. o. ultimus
  Gower I

A. o. ruficrissus   117
  SE New Guinea, Northern Territory,
    N Queensland
Amaurornis isabellinus (Celebes Water Hen)
  N & SE Celebes
Amaurornis ineptus (New Guinea Flightless Rail)
A. e. ineptus
  N Coast & SW Coast, New Guinea
A. e. pallidus
  S New Guinea
Amaurornis akool (Brown Crake)
A. a. akool
  N India
A. a. coccineipes
  SE China, NE Indochina
Amaurornis bicolor (Elwes' Crake)
  Nepal to W China, N Indochina
Amaurornis phoenicurus (White-breasted Water Hen)
A. p. phoenicurus
  Philippine Is, Indochina to S India, Sri
    Lanka
A. p. insularis
  Andaman Is, Nicobar Is
A. p. leucomelanus
  Celebes, Lesser Sunda Is

GALLICREX
Gallicrex cinerea (Water Cock)
  India to Japan, Philippine Is, Celebes

GALLINULA
Gallinula ventralis (Black-tailed Native Hen)
  Australia
Gallinula m. mortierii (Tasmanian Native Hen)
  Tasmania (other sub spp extinct)
Gallinula silvestris (San Cristobal Mountain Rail)
  San Cristobal I
Gallinula pacifica (Samoan Wood Rail)
  Samoa e?
Gallinula nesiotis comeri (Gough Is Coot)
  Gough Is
  (G. n. nesiotis—extinct)
Gallinula tenebrosa (Dusky Moorhen)
G. t. frontata
  SE Borneo, Celebes, S Moluccas, S New
    Guinea
G. t. neumanni
  N New Guinea
G. t. tenebrosa
  Australia
Gallinula chloropus (Moorhen)
G. c. correiana
  Azores Is
G. c. chloropus
  Europe, N Africa, Mid East, Russia

G. c. indica
India to Japan, Taiwan, Malaysia
G. c. pyrrhorrhoa
Madagascar, Reunion I, Mauritius I
G. c. orientalis
Africa (S of Sahara) & S Malaysia to
Philippine Is
G. c. guami
Mariana Is
G. c. sandvicensis
Hawaii Is
G. c. cachinnans
USA, Bermuda I, Galapagos Is
G. c. cerceris
Gtr & Lesser Antilles
G. c. pauxilla
N & W Colombia, W Ecuador, NW Peru
G. c. garmani
Peru, Bolivia, N Chile, NW Argentina
G. c. galeata
the Guianas, Uruguay, N Argentina,
Trinidad
Gallinula angulata (Lesser Moorhen)
Senegal to Sudan, Cape Province
Gallinula melanops (Spot-flanked
Gallinule)
G. m. bogotensis
C Colombia
G. m. melanops
E Brazil to Paraguay, N Argentina
G. m. crassirostris
C Chile
Gallinula flavirostris (Azure Gallinule)
the Guianas, N & C Brazil, Paraguay
Gallinula alleni (Allen's Gallinule)
Senegal to Sudan, Cape Province
Gallinula martinica (Purple Gallinule)
SE USA to Argentina, W Indies

PORPHYRIO
Porphyrio porphyrio (Purple Swamphen)
P. p. porphyrio
SW Europe, NW Africa
P. p. madagascariensis
E & S Africa, Madagascar
P. p. seistanicus
E Turkey, E Iran
P. p. poliocephalus
Iraq to Thailand, Andaman Is, Nicobar Is
P. p. viridis
Burma, Malaysia, S China, Indochina
P. p. indicus
Sumatra to Bali I, Borneo, Celebes
P. p. melanopterus
Timor I, Moluccas, New Guinea
P. p. bellus
SW Australia
P. p. chathamensis
Chatham I

P. p. melanotus
S New Guinea, E Australia
P. p. pulverulentus
Philippine Is
P. p. pelewensis
Palau Is
P. p. samoensis
Western Pacific Islands
Porphyrio mantelli (Takahe)
P. m. mantelli
North Island, New Zealand
P. m. hochstetteri
SE South Island, New Zealand

FULICA
Fulica armillata (Red-gartered Coot)
Paraguay & S Brazil to Cape Horn
Fulica leucoptera (White-winged Coot)
Bolivia & S Brazil to Cape Horn
Fulica rufifrons (Red-fronted Coot)
N Chile & Uruguay to S Argentina
Fulica gigantea (Giant Coot)
Peru, Bolivia, N Chile
Fulica cornuta (Horned Coot)
Bolivia, N Chile, NW Argentina
Fulica caribaea (Caribbean Coot)
W Indies, Trinidad, NE Venezuela
Fulica americana (American Coot)
F. a. alai
Hawaii Is
F. a. americana
Canada to Nicaragua, West Indies
F. a. colombiana
C Colombia to N Ecuador
Fulica ardesiaca (Andean Coot)
F. a. ardesiaca
C Peru to N Chile
F. a. atrura
S Colombia, Ecuador, NW Peru
Fulica atra (Common Coot)
F. a. atra
Europe to SE Asia, N Africa
F. a. lugubris
Java
F. a. novaeguineae
NW & C New Guinea
F. a. australis
Buru I, Australia, Tasmania
Fulica cristata (Red-knobbed Coot)
S Spain, Ethiopia to Cape Province
Madagascar

44 HELIORNITHIDAE (SUNGREBES)

PODICA
Podica senegalensis (Peters' Finfoot)
P. s. senegalensis
Senegal to N Zaire
P. s. camerunensis
Cameroun, Gabon to C Zaire
P. s. albipectus
W Angola

P. s. petersii
N Kenya to Cape Province

HELIOPAIS
Heliopais personata (Masked Finfoot)
NE India to Malaysia, Sumatra

HELIORNIS
Heliornis fulica (American Finfoot)
S Mexico to Paraguay & NE Argentina

45 RHYNOCHETIDAE (KAGU)

RHYNOCHETOS
Rhynochetos jubatus (Kagu)
New Caledonia

46 EURYPYGIDAE (SUN BITTERNS)

EURYPYGA
Eurypyga helias (Sun-Bittern)
E. h. major
Guatemala to Colombia, E Ecuador
E. h. meridionalis
SC Peru
E. h. helias
Upper Amazonia, the Guianas, N Brazil

47 CARIAMIDAE (SERIEMAS)

CARIAMA
Cariama cristata (Red-legged Seriema)
C Brazil to NW Argentina & Paraguay

CHUNGA
Chunga burmeisteri (Black-legged Seriema)
NW Argentina

48 OTIDAE (BUSTARDS)

TETRAX
Tetrax tetrax (Little Bustard)
T. t. tetrax
NW France to NW Africa
T. t. orientalis
E Europe to C Asia

OTIS
Otis tarda (Great Bustard)
O. t. tarda
C & S Europe, W Asia
O. t. korejewi
Turkestan, C Tien Shan
O. t. dybowskii
Altai & Amur to China

NEOTIS
Neotis cafra (Barrow's Bustard)
N. c. denhami
Guinea & Mauretania to Ethiopia
N. c. jacksoni
Angola, S Zaire to Kenya & Malawi

N. c. cafra
Botswana, E South Africa
N. c. mackenziei
SW Zaire, Zambia
Neotis ludwigii (Ludgwig's Bustard)
Namibia, W South Africa
Neotis burchellii (Burchell's Bustard)
E Sudan
Neotis nuba (Nubian Bustard)
Niger to N Sudan
Neotis heuglinii (Heuglin's Bustard)
Somalia

CHORIOTIS
Choriotis arabs (Arabian Bustard)
C. a. lynesi
NW Morocco
C. a. stieberi
E Gambia, Ivory Coast to Sudan
C. a. butleri
S Sudan
C. a. arabs
S Arabia, E Sudan, Somalia
Choriotis kori (Kori Bustard)
C. k. struthiunculus
Ethiopia to Uganda & C Tanzania
C. k. kori
Rhodesia, Transvaal
Choriotis nigriceps (Great Indian Bustard)
C India
Choriotis australis (Australian Bustard)
S New Guinea, Australia

CHLAMYDOTIS
Chlamydotis undulata (Houbara Bustard)
C. u. fuertaventurae
Canary Is
C. u. undulata
N Sahara to Nile valley
C. u. macqueenii
Syria to C Asia, N India

LOPHOTIS
Lophotis savilei (Lynes' Bustard)
Senegal to S Sudan
Lophotis ruficrista (Crested Bustard)
L. r. hilgerti
N & C Somalia
L. r. gindiana
S Somalia, NE Kenya
L. r. ochrofacies
Namibia
L. r. ruficrista
Southern Africa

AFROTIS
Afrotis atra (Little Black Bustard)
A. a. etoschae
NW Namibia
A. a. mababiensis
Lake Ngami area
A. a. afraoides
Transvaal to N Cape Province

A. a. atra
S Cape Province
A. a. kalaharica
Kalahari Desert
A. a. damarensis
N & C Namibia, Botswana

EUPODOTIS
Eupodotis vigorsii (Black-throated Bustard)
  E. v. scolopacea
  S Botswana, W Cape Province
  E. v. vigorsii
  Transvaal, C Cape Province
  E. v. orangensis
  W Cape Province
  E. v. harei
  E Namibia
  E. v. barlowi
  C Namibia
  E. v. karrooensis
  W Cape Province
Eupodotis rueppellii (Rüppell's Bustard)
  E. r. picturata
  NW Namibia
  E. r. rueppellii
  NE Namibia
  E. r. fitzsimmonsi
  S Namibia
Eupodotis humilis (Little Brown Bustard)
  N Somalia
Eupodotis senegalensis (White-bellied Bustard)
  E. s. senegalensis
  Senegal to Nile valley
  E. s. barrowii
  Botswana, Transvaal, Cape Province
  E. s. somaliensis
  Ethiopia to W Kenya
  E. s. canicollis
  E Kenya, E Tanzania
Eupodotis caerulescens (Blue Bustard)
  S Africa

LISSOTIS
Lissotis melanogaster (Black-bellied Bustard)
  L. m. melanogaster
  Senegal to Ethiopia, Angola, Zambia
  L. m. notophila
  SE Africa
Lissotis hartlaubii (Hartlaub's Bustard)
  E Sudan to Uganda & C Tanzania

HOUBAROPSIS
Houbaropsis bengalensis (Bengal Florican)
  H. b. bengalensis
  Himalayas, N India
  H. b. blandini
  Cambodia

SYPHEOTIDES
Sypheotides indica (Lesser Florican)
India

Charadriiformes

49 JACANIDAE (JACANAS)

MICROPARRA
Microparra capensis (Smaller Jacana)
  Sudan to Natal & Cape Province
ACTOPHILORNIS
Actophilornis africana (African Jacana)
  Senegal to Sudan & Cape Province
Actophilornis albinucha (Madagascar Jacana)
  Madagascar
IREDIPARRA
Irediparra gallinacea (Comb-crested Jacana)
  I. g. gallinacea
  S Borneo, Mindanao I to Moluccas & Timor
  I. g. novaeguinae
  Misol I, Aru Is, N & C New Guinea
  I. g. novaehollandiae
  S New Guinea, N & E Australia
HYDROPHASIANUS
Hydrophasianus chirurgus (Pheasant-tailed Jacana)
  India to Philippine Is, Taiwan & Java
METOPIDIUS
Metopidius indicus (Bronze-winged Jacana)
  India to Cambodia, Java, Sumatra
JACANA
Jacana spinosa (Northern Jacana)
  J. s. gymnostoma
  S Mexico
  J. s. violacea
  Cuba, Jamaica, Hispaniola
  J. s. spinosa
  Guatemala to W Panama
Jacana jacana (Wattled Jacana)
  J. j. hypomelaena
  E Panama, N Colombia
  J. j. melanopygia
  W Colombia, W Venezuela
  J. j. intermedia
  N Venezuela
  J. j. jacana
  Trinidad, the Guianas to E Bolivia & N Argentina
  J. j. scapularis
  W Ecuador
  J. j. peruviana
  E Peru

50 ROSTRATULIDAE (PAINTED SNIPES)

ROSTRATULA
Rostratula benghalensis (Painted Snipe)
  R. b. benghalensis
    Africa, S Asia to Java & Philippine Is
  R. b. australis
    Australia & Tasmania

NYCTICRYPHES
Nycticryphes semicollaris (South American Painted Snipe)
  C Chile to N Argentina & Uruguay

51 DROMADIDAE (CRAB PLOVER)

DROMAS
Dromas ardeola (Crab Plover)
  E Africa, Indian Ocean, Andaman Is

52 HAEMATOPODIDAE (OYSTER-CATCHERS)

HAEMATOPUS
Haematopus ostralegus (Oystercatcher)
  H. o. palliatus
    E Coast N & Central America, West Indies
  H. o. pratti
    Bahama Is
  H. o. galapagensis
    Galapagos Is
  H. o. pitanay
    W coast of South America
  H. o. durnfordi
    E coast of South America
  H. o. malacophaga
    Iceland, Faroe Is
  H. o. occidentalis
    British Isles
  H. o. ostralegus
    Europe, Asia Minor, N Africa
  H. o. longipes
    Russia, Siberia
  H. o. osculans
    NE Asia, China, Japan
  H. o. meade-waldoi
    E Canary Is
  H. o. longirostris
    Aru Is, S New Guinea, Australia
  H. o. finschi
    South I, New Zealand
Haematopus bachmani (American Black Oystercatcher)
  H. b. bachmani
    Aleutian Is to N Baja California
  H. b. frazeri
    S Baja California, W Mexico

Haematopus moquini (African Black Oystercatcher)
  Gabon to Natal
Haematopus unicolor (New Zealand Sooty Oystercatcher)
  H. u. unicolor
    New Zealand
  H. u. chathamensis
    Chatham I
Haematopus leucopodus (Magellanic Oystercatcher)
  South America, Falkland Is
Haematopus ater (Blackish Oystercatcher)
  South America, Falkland Is
Haematopus fuliginosus (Sooty Oyster-catcher)
  H. f. fuliginosus
    coast of Australia
  H. f. ophthalmicus
    coast of N Australia

53 IBIDORHYNCHIDAE (IBIS BILL)

IBIDORHYNCHA
Ibidorhyncha struthersii (Ibis Bill)
  C Asia, Himalayas, N India

54 RECURVIROSTRIDAE (AVOCETS, STILTS)

HIMANTOPUS
Himantopus himantopus (Black-winged Stilt)
  S Europe to China, India, C Africa
Himantopus leucocephalus (Australian Stilt)
  Philippine Is to Java & Australia
Himantopus melanurus (Black-tailed Stilt)
  Peru to C Argentina, C Chile
Himantopus mexicanus (Black-necked Stilt)
  USA to N South America, West Indies
Himantopus ceylonensis (Sri Lanka Stilt)
  Sri Lanka
Himantopus knudseni (Hawaiian Stilt)
  Hawaii
Himantopus novaezelandiae (New Zealand Stilt)
  New Zealand
Himantopus meridionalis (South African Stilt)
  South Africa

CLADORHYNCHUS
Cladorhynchus leucocephalus (Banded Stilt)
  Australia

RECURVIROSTRA
Recurvirostra avosetta (Avocet)
Europe to China, India, S Africa
Recurvirostra americana (American Avocet)
W USA to Guatemala
Recurvirostra novaehollandiae (Red-necked Avocet)
Australia, Tasmania
Recurvirostra andina (Andean Avocet)
S Peru to N Chile, NW Argentina '

55 BURHINIDAE (STONE-CURLEWS)

BURHINUS
Burhinus oedicnemus (Stone-Curlew)
B. o. distinctus
W Canary Is
B. o. insularum
E Canary Is
B. o. jordansi
Balearic Is
B. o. oedicnemus
Europe, SW Asia to N & E Africa
B. o. theresae
W Morocco
B. o. saharae
N Africa to Israel
B. o. astutus
Afghanistan, Pakistan
B. o. indicus
India, Sri Lanka to S Indochina
Burhinus senegalensis (Senegal Stone-Curlew)
B. s. senegalensis
Senegal to Central African Republic & Angola
B. s. inornatus
Egypt to N Uganda, Ethiopia
Burhinus vermiculatus (Water Dikkop)
B. v. buttikoferi
Liberia to N Zaire
B. v. vermiculatus
Kenya to Cape Province
Burhinus capensis (Cape Dikkop)
B. c. maculosus
Senegal to Niger, N Nigeria
B. c. affinis
Sudan, Ethiopia, Uganda, Somalia
B. c. ehrenbergi
Dahlak Is
B. c. dodsoni
S Arabia, N Somalia
B. c. capensis
Angola to Kenya & Cape Province
B. c. damarensis
Namibia
Burhinus bistriatus (Double-striped Stone-Curlew)

B. b. bistriatus
S Mexico to W Costa Rica
B. b. vocifer
N Colombia to Guyana & N Brazil
B. b. pediacus
N Colombia
B. b. dominicensis
Hispaniola
Burhinus superciliaris (Peruvian Stone-Curlew)
Ecuador to S Peru
Burhinus magnirostris (Australian Stone-Curlew)
B. m. rufescens
NW Australia, Northern Territory
B. m. ramsayi
N Queensland
B. m. magnirostris
S Queensland to SW Australia, Tasmania

ESACUS
Esacus recurvirostris (Great Stone Plover)
India, Burma, Sri Lanka
Esacus magnirostris (Great Australian Stone Plover)
Malaysia to New Guinea & Australia

56 GLAREOLIDAE (COURSERS, PRATINCOLES)

CURSORIINAE

PLUVIANUS
Pluvianus aegyptius (Egyptian Plover)
P. a. aegyptius
Senegal to N Zaire & Egypt
P. a. angolae
N Angola, W Zaire

CURSORIUS
Cursorius cursor (Cream-coloured Courser)
C. c. bogolubovi
N & E Iran
C. c. cursor
N Africa to NW India
C. c. bannermani
Canary Is, W Morocco
C. c. exsul
Cape Verde Is
C. c. dahlakensis
Dahlak Is
C. c. somalensis
N Somalia
C. c. littoralis
S Somalia, Kenya
C. c. meruensis
C Kenya
C. c. theresae
NW Cape Province

C. c. rufus
  Botswana, Transvaal, Cape Province
Cursorius coromandelicus (Indian Courser)
  India, N Sri Lanka
Cursorius temminckii (Temminck's Courser)
  C. t. temminckii
    Senegal to Ethiopia & Cape Province
  C. t. damarensis
    Namibia

Rhinoptilus africanus (Two-banded Courser)
  R. a. raffertyi
    C Ethiopia
  R. a. hartingi
    Somalia
  R. a. gracilis
    C Kenya, N Tanzania
  R. a. illustris
    C Tanzania
  R. a. bisignatus
    Angola
  R. a. sharpei
    Namibia
  R. a. africanus
    S Namibia, W Cape Province
  R. a. granti
    Transvaal, C Cape Province
Rhinoptilus cinctus (Heuglin's Courser)
  R. c. cinctus
    Sudan, Somalia to N Tanzania
  R. c. emini
    islands in Lake Victoria
  R. c. seebohmi
    S Angola, Namibia to Rhodesia
Rhinoptilus chalcopterus (Bronze-winged Courser)
  R. c. chalcopterus
    Senegal to Sudan & Kenya
  R. c. albofasciatus
    Angola & Tanzania to Cape Province
Rhinoptilus bitorquatus (Jerdon's Courser)
  C India **e?**

GLAREOLINAE
STILTIA
Stiltia isabella (Australian Pratincole)
  Australia to Borneo, Java, New Guinea
GLAREOLA
Glareola pratincola (Pratincole)
  G. p. pratincola
    Mediterranean to NW India & N Africa
  G. p. boweni
    Senegal to Chad & Gabon
  G. p. limbata
    Sudan, Ethiopia, Somalia, S Arabia

G. p. erlangeri
  S Somalia, N Kenya
G. p. fulleborni
  E Zaire, C Kenya to Cape Province
Glareola maldivarus (Large Indian Pratincole)
  C & E Asia to Indochina, Malaysia
Glareola nordmanni (Black-winged Pratincole)
  SE Europe, C Asia, Africa
Glareola ocularis (Madagascar Pratincole)
  E Africa, Madagascar
Glareola nuchalis (White-collared Pratincole)
  G. n. liberiae
    Sierra Leone to W Cameroun
  G. n. nuchalis
    Chad to Ethiopia & Mozambique
Glareola cinerea (Cream-coloured Pratincole)
  G. c. cinerea
    Ghana to C Zaire
  G. c. colorata
    Upper Niger river
Glareola lactea (Small Indian Pratincole)
  India, Sri Lanka to S Indochina

57 CHARADRIIDAE (PLOVERS)

VANELLUS
Vanellus vanellus (Lapwing)
  W Europe to China & Japan
Vanellus crassirostris (Long-toed Lapwing)
  V. c. crassirostris
    Sudan, Uganda
  V. c. hybrida
    Kenya to Malawi
  V. c. leucoptera
    Mozambique, N Natal
Vanellus spinosus (Spur-winged Plover)
  Middle East, C & E Africa
Vanellus duvaucelii (River Lapwing)
  N India to Indochina
Vanellus tectus (Blackhead Plover)
  V. t. tectus
    Senegal to Ethiopia
  V. t. latifrons
    S Somalia to E Kenya
Vanellus malabaricus (Yellow-wattled Lapwing)
  India, Sri Lanka
Vanellus albiceps (White-crowned Wattled Plover)
  Liberia to Sudan & Rhodesia
Vanellus lugubris (Senegal Plover)
  Sierra Leone to Uganda & Natal
Vanellus melanopterus (Black-winged Plover)
  V. m. minor
    Kenya to Cape Province

V. m. melanopterus
S Arabia, Ethiopia
Vanellus coronatus (Crowned Plover)
V. c. demissus
Somalia
V. c. coronatus
Ethiopia to Angola & Cape Province
Vanellus senegallus (Senegal Wattled Plover)
V. s. senegallus
Senegal to Sudan & Uganda
V. s. major
W Ethiopia
V. s. lateralis
E Zaire, Uganda to Angola & Natal
Vanellus melanocephalus (Spot-breasted Plover)
N Ethiopia
Vanellus superciliosus (Brown-chested Wattled Plover)
Benin to Uganda & Kenya
Vanellus gregarius (Sociable Plover)
C Asia to NE Africa, N India
Vanellus leucurus (White-tailed Plover)
W & C Asia, NE Africa, NW India
Vanellus cayanus (Cayenne Plover)
S Venezuela, the Guianas, Upper Amazonia
Vanellus chilensis (Chilian Lapwing)
V. c. cayennensis
Colombia, Venezuela, the Guianas, N Brazil
V. c. lampronotus
S Brazil to C Argentina, Uruguay
V. c. chilensis
C Chile, SW Argentina
V. c. fretensis
S Chile, S Argentina
Vanellus resplendens (Andean Lapwing)
Ecuador to N Chile, NW Argentina
Vanellus cinereus (Grey-headed Lapwing)
China, Japan, Indochina
Vanellus indicus (Red-wattled Lapwing)
V. i. aigneri
Middle East to Pakistan
V. i. indicus
India, Sri Lanka
V. i. atronuchalis
Burma, Malaysia, Indochina
Vanellus macropterus (Javanese Wattled Lapwing)
Java
Vanellus tricolor (Banded Plover)
S Australia, Tasmania
Vanellus miles (Masked Plover)
V. m. miles
S Moluccas, Kei Is, S New Guinea, N Australia
V. m. novaehollandiae
E Australia

ANITIBYX
Anitibyx armatus (Blacksmith Plover)
S Angola to Kenya & Natal

PLUVIALIS
Pluvialis apricaria (Golden Plover)
P. a. apricaria
N Europe & N Asia » Mediterranean, N India
P. a. oreophilos
N & W British Isles, Denmark, Germany
Pluvialis dominica (American Golden Plover)
P. d. fulva
N Siberia, NE Asia, Alaska, » SE Asia & Australia
P. d. dominica
N Canada » C South America
Pluvialis squatarola (Grey Plover)
Circumpolar » Africa, Australia & South America
Pluvialis obscura (New Zealand Dotterel)
New Zealand

CHARADRIUS
Charadrius hiaticula (Ringed Plover)
C. h. psammodroma
NE Canada, Greenland, Iceland
C. h. hiaticula
British Isles, Sweden to Mediterranean
C. h. tundrae
N Europe, N Asia » Iran, E Africa
Charadrius semipalmatus (Semi-palmated Plover)
N Canada » C & South America
Charadrius placidus (Long-billed Ring Plover)
NE Asia » China, Burma, Indochina
Charadrius dubius (Little Ringed Plover)
C. d. curonicus
Europe, N Asia » S Africa, India, China
C. d. jerdoni
India » Indochina & Lssr Sunda Is
C. d. papuanus
New Ireland, New Guinea
C. d. dubius
S Japan, S China, Philippine Is
Charadrius wilsonia (Wilson's Plover)
C. w. wilsonia
S & SE USA, E Central America
C. w. rufinucha
Bahama Is, Gtr Antilles, N Lesser Antilles
C. w. beldingi
Baja California to Peru
C. w. cinnamominus
Colombia to French Guiana, Arubu I, Trinidad

Charadrius vociferus (Killdeer Plover)
  C. v. vociferus
    W Canada, USA » West Indies, N South
    America
  C. v. ternominatus
    Gtr Antilles
  C. v. peruvianus
    W Peru
Charadrius melodus (Piping Plover)
  S Canada, E USA, N Mexico
Charadrius thoracicus (Black-banded Sand
Plover)
  Madagascar
Charadrius pecuarius (Kittlitz's Sand
Plover)
  C. p. allenbyi
    Nile valley
  C. p. pecuarius
    Senegal to Sudan & Cape Province,
    Madagascar
Charadrius sanctaehelenae (St Helena
Sand Plover)
  St Helena I
Charadrius tricollaris (Three-banded
Plover)
  C. t. forbesi
    Guinea to S Zaire
  C. t. tricollaris
    Sudan to Angola & Cape Province
  C. t. bifrontatus
    Madagascar
Charadrius alexandrinus (Kentish Plover)
  C. a. alexandrinus
    W Europe to C Asia » Africa, China
  C. a. spatzi
    W African coast
  C. a. dealbatus
    S Japan » Indochina & S Thailand
  C. a. seebohmi
    Sri Lanka
  C. a. javanicus
    Java
  C. a. hesperius
    Liberia to Central African Republic
Charadrius marginatus (White-fronted
Sand Plover)
  C. m. pons
    S Somalia
  C. m. tenellus
    E Africa to Natal, Madagascar
  C. m. marginatus
    Angola to Cape Province
Charadrius occidentalis (Snowy Plover)
  C. c. nivosus
    W USA, W Mexico
  C. c. tenuirostris
    C & SE USA, Cuba, Hispaniola, Puerto
    Rico
  C. c. occidentalis
    Peru to Chile

Charadrius ruficapillus (Red-capped
Dotterel)
  S New Guinea, Australia, Tasmania
Charadrius peronii (Malaysian Sand
Plover)
  Philippine Is, Celebes, Java, Borneo
Charadrius venustus (Chestnut-banded
Sand Plover)
  C. v. pallidus
    Angola to S Cape Province
  C. v. venustus
    S Kenya, Tanzania
Charadrius collaris (Collared Plover)
  S Mexico to N Argentina, Trinidad
Charadrius bicinctus (Double-banded
Plover)
  C. b. bicinctus
    Australia, Tasmania, New Zealand
  C. b. exilis
    Auckland Is
Charadrius falklandicus (Two-banded
Plover)
  S South America, Falkland Is
Charadrius mongolus (Mongolian Plover)
  C. m. atrifrons
    C Asia » India, Malaysia, E Africa
  C. m. mongolus
    E Siberia, Japan » Australia
  C. m. stegmani
    Bering Is
Charadrius leschenaultii (Great Sand
Plover)
  E Asia & Red Sea » S Africa, Australia
Charadrius asiaticus (Caspian Plover)
  SE Russia & Iran » India, E & S Africa
Charadrius veredus (Eastern Sand Plover)
  N China » Celebes & Australia
Charadrius modestus (Rufous-chested
Dotterel)
  S Chile, Argentina, Falkland Is
Charadrius montanus (Mountain Plover)
  W USA to C Mexico
Charadrius melanops (Black-fronted
Plover)
  Australia, Tasmania
Charadrius cinctus (Red-kneed Dotterel)
  Australia
Charadrius rubricollis (Hooded Plover)
  S Australia, Tasmania
Charadrius novaeseelandiae (Long-billed
Plover)
  Chatham I

ANARHYNCHUS
Anarhynchus frontalis (Wry-bill)
  New Zealand

PHEGORNIS
Phegornis mitchellii (Mitchell's Plover)
  Peru to N Chile, W Argentina

PELTOHYAS
Pelt'ohyas australis (Australian Courser)
  SW Australia to Victoria & New South
  Wales

EUDROMIAS
Eudromias morinellus (Dotterel)
  N Europe & N Asia » Med & Iran
**Eudromias ruficollis (Tawny-throated
Dotterel)**
  E. r. pallidus
  N Peru
  E. r. ruficollis
  Peru & E Argentina to Tierra del Fuego

PLUVIANELLUS
Pluvianellus socialis (Magellanic Plover)
  Straits of Magellan

58 SCOLOPACIDAE (SANDPIPERS, SNIPE)

TRINGINAE

LIMOSA
Limosa limosa (Black-tailed Godwit)
  L. l. limosa
  Europe, W Asia » N Africa & India
  L. l. melanuroides
  NE Asia » China, N Australia
Limosa haemastica (Hudsonian Godwit)
  NW Canada » S South America
Limosa lapponica (Bar-tailed Godwit)
  L. l. lapponica
  N Europe, N Asia » tropical Africa, N India
  L. l. baueri
  NE Asia, NW Canada » Australia, Pacific
  islands
Limosa fedoa (Marbled Godwit)
  WC Canada » S USA & Peru

NUMENIUS
Numenius minutus (Little Curlew)
  C & E Siberia » Moluccas, Australia
Numenius borealis (Eskimo Curlew)
  N Canada » S South America **e?**
Numenius phaeopus (Whimbrel)
  N. p. phaeopus
  N Europe, N Asia» Africa, NW India
  N. p. variegatus
  E Siberia » Australia, Pacific Is
  N. p. hudsonicus
  N Canada » N South America
**Numenius tahitiensis (Bristle-thighed
Curlew)**
  W Alaska » Hawaii, Society Is
**Numenius tenuirostris (Slender-billed
Curlew)**
  SW Siberia to E Europe » Iran
Numenius arquata (Curlew)
  N. a. arquata
  N Europe & Russia » Africa & NW India

N. a. orientalis
  C Asia » E Africa, India, Indochina
**Numenius madagascariensis (Far Eastern
Curlew)**
  E Siberia » China & Australia
**Numenius americanus (Long-billed
Curlew)**
  N. a. occidentalis
  WC Canada to N Mexico
  N. a. americanus
  WC USA to Guatemala

BARTRAMIA
Bartramia longicauda (Upland Sandpiper)
  W & S Canada, NC USA » C South
  America

TRINGA
Tringa erythropus (Spotted Redshank)
  N Europe, N Russia » Africa & China
Tringa totanus (Redshank)
  T. t. robusta
  Iceland to W Europe, » W Africa
  T. t. britannica
  British Isles to W Europe
  T. t. totanus
  N Europe & W Siberia » Africa & W Asia
  T. t. eurhinus
  C & E Asia » India, China, Celebes
Tringa stagnatilis (Marsh Sandpiper)
  SE Europe to Mongolia » Africa, Australia
Tringa nebularia (Greenshank)
  N Palaearctic » Africa, India to
  New Zealand
Tringa guttifer (Spotted Greenshank)
  E Siberia » India, Malaysia
Tringa melanoleuca (Greater Yellowlegs)
  N Canada » C & South America
Tringa flavipes (Lesser Yellowlegs)
  N Canada » South America
Tringa ochropus (Green Sandpiper)
  N Palaearctic » C Africa to Philippine Is
Tringa solitaria (Solitary Sandpiper)
  T. s. cinnamonea
  NW Canada » C South America
  T. s. solitaria
  C Canada » West Indies & N South
  America
Tringa glareola (Wood Sandpiper)
  N Palaearctic » Africa, SE Asia, Australia

CATOPTROPHORUS
Catoptrophorus semipalmatus (Willet)
  C. s. inornatus
  S Canada, W USA » Peru
  C. s. semipalmatus
  E Canada, E USA, Cuba, Puerto Rico

XENUS
Xenus cinereus (Terek Sandpiper)
  NE Europe, W Siberia » E Africa, India
  to Australia

ACTITIS
Actitis hypoleucos (Common Sandpiper)
Palaearctic » Africa, NE Asia to Australia
Actitis macularia (Spotted Sandpiper)
North America » West Indies, C South
America

HETEROSCELUS
Heteroscelus brevipes (Grey-rumped Sandpiper)
E Siberia » China, Australia
Heteroscelus incanus (Wandering Tattler)
NW Canada » W USA, Pacific islands

PROSOBONIA
Prosobonia cancellata (Tuamotu Sandpiper)
Tuamotu Is

ARENARIINAE

ARENARIA
Arenaria interpres (Turnstone)
A. i. interpres
N Palaearctic » Africa, SE Asia, Australia,
South America
A. i. morinella
N Canada » SE USA, West Indies,
E South America
Arenaria melanocephala (Black Turnstone)
Alaska to W USA

PHALAROPODINAE

PHALAROPUS
Phalaropus tricolor (Wilson's Phalarope)
SW Canada, W USA » S South America
Phalaropus lobatus (Red-necked Phalarope)
N America, N Palaearctic » Southern coasts
Phalaropus fulicarius (Grey Phalarope)
N Holarctic » coasts of Africa & Chile

SCOLOPACINAE

SCOLOPAX
Scolopax rusticola (Woodcock)
Palaearctic » India, S China
Scolopax mira (Amami Woodcock)
Amami-Oshima (Riukiu Is)
Scolopax saturata (East Indian Woodcock)
S. s. saturata
Sumatra, Java
S. s. rosenbergii
New Guinea
Scolopax celebensis (Celebes Woodcock)
S. c. heinrichi
N Celebes
S. c. celebensis
C Celebes
Scolopax rochussenii (Obi Woodcock)
Obi I

Scolopax minor (American Woodcock)   127
S Canada, SE USA, Gulf coast

GALLINAGONINAE

COENOCORYPHA
Coenocorypha aucklandica (Sub-Antarctic Snipe)
C. a. pusilla
Mangare I
C. a. iredalei
Jack Lees I
C. a. huegeli
Snares I
C. a. meinertzhagenae
Antipodes Is
C. a. aucklandica
Auckland Is

GALLINAGO
Gallinago solitaria (Solitary Snipe)
G. s. solitaria
C Asia, Himalayas, N Burma
G. s. japonica
E Asia, Japan, E China
Gallinago hardwickii (Japanese Snipe)
Kurile Is, Japan, Australia
Gallinago nemoricola (Wood Snipe)
Himalayas, Burma, S India
Gallinago stenura (Pintail Snipe)
NE Asia » India, S China & Timor I
Gallinago megala (Swinhoe's Snipe)
EC Asia » Burma, Borneo, Australia
Gallinago nigripennis (African Snipe)
G. n. nigripennis
Ethiopia to Namibia & Cape Province
G. n. angolensis
Angola, Zambia, Botswana
Gallinago macrodactyla (Madagascar Snipe)
Madagascar, Mauritius
Gallinago media (Great Snipe)
N Europe, W Asia » E Africa
Gallinago gallinago (Common Snipe)
G. g. faroeensis
Iceland, Faroe Is
G. g. gallinago
N Palaearctic » E Africa, India, China
G. g. delicata
N Canada » SW USA, Central America
West Indies
Gallinago paraguaiae (Paraguayan Snipe)
G. p. paraguaiae
Colombia to Uruguay
G. p. magellanica
S South America, Tierra del Fuego
G. p. andina
Peru, N Chile
G. p. innotata
N Chile

Gallinago nobilis (Noble Snipe)
  C & E Colombia, N Ecuador
Gallinago undulata (Giant Snipe)
  G. u. undulata
  Guyana, French Guiana, Surinam
  G. u. gigantea
  Brazil, Paraguay, N & E Argentina
Gallinago stricklandii (Strickland's Snipe)
  S Chile, Falkland Is
Gallinago jamesoni (Jameson's Snipe)
  N Colombia to Bolivia
Gallinago imperialis (Banded Snipe)
  C Colombia

LYMNOCRYPTES
Lymnocryptes minima (Jack Snipe)
  N Europe, W Asia » N Africa, Iran, India

LIMNODROMUS
Limnodromus griseus (Short-billed Dowitcher)
  L. g. caurinus
  Alaska, W USA » Peru
  L. g. griseus
  NE Canada » E Caribbean
Limnodromus scolopaceus (Long-billed Dowitcher)
  NW Canada, » S USA to Ecuador, Cuba, Jamaica
Limnodromus semipalmatus (Semi-palmated Snipe)
  W Siberia, Mongolia » China, Japan, Indochina

CALIDRIDINAE

APHRIZA
Aphriza virgata (Surf-bird)
  SC Alaska, W coast to S Chile

CALIDRIS
Calidris canutus (Knot)
  C. c. canutus
  Spitzbergen, Taimyr Peninsula » Africa
  C. c. rogersi
  Siberian islands, E Asia» Australia
  C. c. rufus
  Greenland, N Canada » S South America
Calidris tenuirostris (Great Knot)
  NE Siberia » China, India & Australia
Calidris alba (Sanderling)
  N Holarctic » South America, India & Australia
Calidris pusilla (Semipalmated Sandpiper)
  N Canada » South America, West Indies
Calidris mauri (Western Sandpiper)
  NW Canada » W South America, Trinidad
Calidris ruficollis (Rufous-necked Stint)
  NE Siberia, Alaska » China, Australia

Calidris minuta (Little Stint)
  N Europe » S Africa, W India
Calidris temminckii (Temminck's Stint)
  N Europe, N Asia » NE Africa to China
Calidris subminuta (Long-toed Stint)
  E Siberia » India, China, Philippine Is
Calidris minutilla (Least Sandpiper)
  N North America » S USA & N South America
Calidris fuscicollis (White-rumped Sandpiper)
  N Canada » S South America
Calidris bairdii (Baird's Sandpiper)
  E Siberia & N Canada » S South America
Calidris melanotos (Pectoral Sandpiper)
  E Siberia & N Canada » SC South America
Calidris acuminata (Sharp-tailed Sandpiper)
  NE Asia » Australia, Pacific Is
Calidris maritima (Purple Sandpiper)
  Arctic America & Europe » NE USA, W Europe
Calidris ptilocnemis (Rock Sandpiper)
  C. p. couesi
  NE Siberia, Alaska, W Canada
  C. p. ptilocnemis
  Bering Sea, SE Alaska
  C. p. quarta
  Commander Is
  C. p. kurilensis
  Kurile Is
Calidris alpina (Dunlin)
  C. a. arctica
  E Greenland
  C. a. alpina
  N Europe, NW Asia » NE Africa, SW Asia
  C. a. schinzii
  British Isles, Holland
  C. a. centralis
  N Siberia, Mongolia » India
  C. a. pacifica
  NE Asia, NW Canada » E China, W USA & SE USA
Calidris ferruginea (Curlew Sandpiper)
  N Asia to Europe, » Africa, India & Australia

EURYNORHYNCHUS
Eurynorhynchus pygmeus (Spoon-billed Sandpiper)
  NE Asia » S China

LIMICOLA
Limicola falcinellus (Broad-billed Sandpiper)
  L. f. falcinellus
  N Europe, N Russia » Middle East, W India

L. f. sibirica
   NE Siberia » E India & Australia

MICROPALAMA
Micropalama himantopus (Stilt Sandpiper)
   N Canada » C South America & West Indies

TRYNGITES
Tryngites subruficollis (Buff-breasted Sandpiper)
   N Canada » SC South America

PHILOMACHUS
Philomachus pugnax (Ruff)
   N Europe & Asia » Africa, India, Burma

59 THINOCORIDAE (SEED SNIPE)

ATTAGIS
Attagis gayi (Rufous-bellied Seedsnipe)
   A. g. latreillii
      Ecuador
   A. g. simonsi
      Peru, N Bolivia
   A. g. gayi
      Chile, Argentina
Attagis malouinus (White-bellied Seedsnipe)
   A. m. cheeputi
      C Argentina
   A. m. malouinus
      Tierra del Fuego

THINOCORUS
Thinocorus orbignyianus (Grey-breasted Seedsnipe)
   T. o. ingae
      S Peru, W Bolivia
   T. o. orbignyianus
      C & S Chile, S Argentina
Thinocorus rumicivorus (Least Seedsnipe)
   T. r. pallidus
      SW Ecuador
   T. r. cuneicauda
      W Peru, N Chile
   T. r. bolivianus
      SW Bolivia
   T. r. rumicivorus
      C Chile, C Argentina, Uruguay
   T. r. patagonicus
      S Argentina

60 CHIONIDIDAE (SHEATHBILLS)

CHIONIS
Chionis alba (Snowy Sheathbill)
   S Georgia, S Orkneys, Falkland Is
Chionis minor (Black-faced Sheathbill)
   C. m. marionensis
      Prince Edward I, Marion I

C. m. crozettensis
   Crozet I, Possession I
C. m. minor
   Kerguelen I
C. m. nasicornis
   Heard I

61 STERCORARIIDAE (SKUAS)

CATHARACTA
Catharacta skua (Great Skua)
   C. s. skua
      NW Europe to E Canada & SW Europe
   C. s. antarctica
      Falkland Is, Tristan da Cunha
   C. s. clarkei
      S Georgia, S Orkney Is, S Shetland Is
   C. s. lonnbergi
      South I New Zealand to S Australia
   C. s. intercedens
      Kerguelen I to S Africa
Catharacta chilensis (Chilean Skua)
   S Chile to W USA & E Argentina
Catharacta maccormicki (McCormick's Skua)
   Ross Sea, Weddell Sea, S Shetland Is to New Zealand

STERCORARIUS
Stercorarius pomarinus (Pomarine Skua)
   N Holarctic » Peru, S Africa, India, N Australia
Stercorarius parasiticus (Arctic Skua)
   N Holarctic » S South America, S Africa, India, Australia
Stercorarius longicaudus (Long-tailed Skua)
   N Holarctic » W Africa, S South America, Mediterranean & Japan

62 LARIDAE (GULLS, TERNS)

LARINAE

GABIANUS
Gabianus pacificus (Pacific Gull)
   S coast Australia, Tasmania
Gabianus scoresbii (Magellan Gull)
   S coast America, Falkland Is

PAGOPHILA
Pagophila alba (Ivory Gull)
   Circumpolar to N Europe, N Asia, N America

LARUS
Larus fuliginosus (Dusky Gull)
   Galapagos Is
Larus modestus (Grey Gull)
   coast of Peru & Chile
Larus heermanni (Heermann's Gull)
   W USA, W Mexico

Larus leucophthalmus (White-eyed Gull)
S Red Sea, Somali coast
Larus hemprichii (Sooty Gull)
S Red Sea, Iran & E Africa coast
Larus belcheri (Band-tailed Gull)
L. b. belcheri
coast of Peru
L. b. atlanticus
coast of Argentina
Larus crassirostris (Japanese Gull)
coasts of Japan Sea, China Sea
Larus audouinii (Audouin's Gull)
Mediterranean Is
Larus delawarensis (Ring-billed Gull)
Canada & USA coasts to S Mexico, Cuba
Larus canus (Common Gull)
L. c. canus
NW Europe to Mediterranean
L. c. brachyrhynchus
Alaska, W Canada, W USA
Larus kamtschatschensis (Eastern
Common Gull)
E Siberia to China, Japan
Larus argentatus (Herring Gull)
L. a. smithsonianus
Canada to W Mexico
L. a. argentatus
NW Europe, Mediterranean
L. a. lusitanius
Portugal
L. a. omissus
White Sea islands
L. a. birulae
Arctic Ocean islands
L. a. heuglini
N Siberia to Persian Gulf
L. a. vegae
NE Siberia to China, Japan
L. a. atlantis
Azores, Madeira, Canary Is
L. a. michahelles
W & C Mediterranean
L. a. cachinnans
S Russia, SC Asia, N Red Sea
Larus thayeri (Thayer's Gull)
Arctic Canada, W USA
Larus fuscus (Lesser Black-backed
Gull)
L. f. fuscus
Scandinavia to W & E Africa
L. f. graellsii
British Isles to W Mediterranean &
W Africa
Larus californicus (California Gull)
W USA, W Mexico
Larus occidentalis (Western Gull)
L. o. occidentalis
W USA
L. o. wymani
S California, Baja California

L. o. livens
Gulf of California islands
Larus dominicanus (Southern Black-
backed Gull)
S South America, S Africa, New Zealand
Larus schistisagus (Slaty-backed Gull)
NE Asia to Alaska & Japan
Larus marinus (Great Black-backed Gull)
N Atlantic to Cuba, Azores, Mediterranean
Larus glaucescens (Glaucous-winged Gull)
NE Asia & Alaska to W USA & China
Larus hyperboreus (Glaucous Gull)
Circumpolar to W Europe, China, USA
Larus glaucoides (Iceland Gull)
NE Canada, Greenland, N Siberia, Baltic
Larus ichthyaetus (Great Black-headed
Gull)
S Russia, Mongolia to Red Sea, India
Larus atricilla (Laughing Gull)
Maine to Brazil & W Central America
Larus brunnicephalus (Indian Black-
headed Gull)
C & S Asia
Larus cirrocephalus (Grey-headed Gull)
L. c. cirrocephalus
EC South America
L. c. poiocephalus
Ethiopia to Malawi, S Madagascar
Larus serranus (Andean Gull)
coast of Peru & Andean Lakes
Larus pipixcan (Franklin's Gull)
S Canada, NC USA to W South America
Larus novaehollandiae (Silver Gull)
L. n. forsteri
New Caledonia, N Australia
L. n. novaehollandiae
S Australia, Tasmania
L. n. scopulinus
New Zealand, Chatham I
L. n. hartlaubii
W Cape Province
Larus melanocephalus (Mediterranean
Gull)
SE Europe, C & W Asia
Larus relictus (Relict Gull)
C Asia
Larus bulleri (Buller's Gull)
New Zealand
Larus maculipennis (Brown-hooded Gull)
S South America, Falkland Is
Larus ridibundus (Black-headed Gull)
Europe, Asia to N Africa, India, Phillipine I
Larus genei (Slender-billed Gull)
Mediterranean, Black Sea, Asia
Minor
Larus philadelphia (Bonaparte's Gull)
W Canada, W & E USA

Larus minutus (Little Gull)
N Europe, Siberia to Mediterranean, Black
Sea
Larus saundersi (Saunders' Gull)
Mongolia, N China, Japan
RHODOSTETHIA
Rhodostethia rosea (Ross's Gull)
N Siberia, Alaska, Greenland
RISSA
Rissa tridactyla (Kittiwake)
R. t. tridactyla
NE Canada, NW Europe to Azores, USA,
W Africa
R. t. pollicaris
Bering Sea & islands, Japan, W USA
Rissa brevirostris (Red-legged Kittiwake)
Pribilov Is, Commander Is
CREAGRUS
Creagrus furcatus (Swallow-tailed Gull)
Galapagos Is
XEMA
Xema sabini (Sabine's Gull)
Arctic Regions » W Africa and W Americas

STERNINAE

CHLIDONIAS
Chlidonias hybrida (Whiskered Tern)
C. h. hybrida
S Europe, SW Asia » E & W Africa
C. h. swinhoei
S China, Taiwan, Indochina
C. h. indica
Iran to India
C. h. sclateri
Kenya to Cape Province, Madagascar
C. h. javanica
Sri Lanka, Malaysia, Java, Celebes
C. h. fluviatilis
Moluccas, New Guinea, Australia
**Chlidonias leucoptera (White-winged Black
Tern)**
S E Europe, C Asia » S Africa, India, China,
Australia
Chlidonias nigra (Black Tern)
C. n. nigra
Europe, W Asia » SC Africa
C. n. surinamensis
Canada, N USA » South America
PHAETUSA
Phaetusa simplex (Large-billed Tern)
P. s. simplex
N & E South America
P. s. chloropoda
SC & S South America
GELOCHELIDON
Gelochelidon nilotica (Gull-billed Tern)
G. n. nilotica
Europe, C Asia » N & E Africa & India

G. n. addenda
S China
G. n. macrotarsa
Australia
G. n. aranea
E USA, Cuba, Gulf Coast
G. n. vanrossemi
S California, W Mexico to Ecuador
G. n. grönvoldi
Mexiana I, SE Brazil
HYDROPROGNE
Hydroprogne caspia (Caspian Tern)
H. c. caspia
N America, Europe, Africa, C & S Asia
H. c. strenua
W & S Australia, New Zealand
STERNA
Sterna aurantia (Indian River Tern)
Iran, India, Malaysia
**Sterna hirundinacea (South American
Tern)**
Peru, N Brazil to Tierra del Fuego
Sterna hirundo (Common Tern)
S. h. hirundo
N America, Europe, W Asia, » South America,
W Africa
S. h. tibetana
Turkestan, Tibet » India & Malaysia
S. h. minussensis
C Asia, N Mongolia
S. h. longipennis
NE Asia » Japan, China, New Guinea
Sterna paradisaea (Arctic Tern)
Arctic regions » Chile, S Africa &
Antarctica
Sterna vittata (Swallow-tailed Tern)
S. v. vittata
Ascension I, St Helena I, Gough I,
Kerguelen I
S. v. tristanensis
Tristan da Cunha
S. v. georgiae
S Georgia, S Orkneys
S. v. gaini
S Shetlands
S. v. bethunei
Sub-Antarctic islands of New Zealand
Sterna trudeaui (Snowy-crowned Tern)
S Indian Ocean islands
Sterna forsteri (Forster's Tern)
W Canada, USA, N Central America
Sterna trudeaui (Trudeau's Tern)
S South America
Sterna dougallii (Roseate Tern)
S. d. dougallii
E & W North Atlantic coasts » Brazil,
Azores, S Africa
S. d. korustes
Sri Lanka, Andaman Is

S. d. arideensis
Seychelles, Mascarane Is
S. d. bangsi
Riukiu Is, Philippine Is, Kei Is,
Solomon Is
S. d. gracilis
Moluccas, N & W coasts of Australia
Sterna striata (White-fronted Tern)
S. s. striata
New Zealand
S. s. incerta
Tasmania to SE Australia
S. s. aucklandorna
Auckland Is, Chatham I, Snares I
Sterna repressa (White-cheeked Tern)
S Red Sea to Kenya & Persian Gulf
Sterna sumatrana (Black-naped Tern)
S. s. sumatrana
E Indian & Pacific Ocean islands,
N Australia
S. s. mathewsi
W Indian Ocean islands
Sterna melanogaster (Black-bellied Tern)
India, Burma, S Indochina
Sterna aleutica (Aleutian Tern)
Bering Sea to Japan
Sterna lunata (Spectacled Tern)
Moluccas & Fiji to Hawaiian Is
Sterna anaethetus (Bridled Tern)
S. a. anaethetus
Taiwan to Japan and Australia
S. a. fuligula
S Red Sea to E Africa & W India
S. a. antarctica
Seychelles, Mauritius, Maldive Is
S. a. rogersi
N Western Australia
S. a. novaehollandiae
Queensland
S. a. nelsoni
W coast of Mexico & Central America
S. a. melanoptera
West Indies
Sterna fuscata (Sooty Tern)
S. f. fuscata
West Indies, W African islands
S. f. crissalis
W Mexican islands, Galapagos Is
S. f. oahuensis
Hawaii, Bonin Is
S. f. kermadeci
Kermadec Is
S. f. serrata
Australia, New Guinea, N Caledonia
S. f. somaliensis
Mait I, Gulf of Aden
S. f. nubilosa
Indian Ocean & China Sea islands,
Riukiu Is

Sterna nereis (Fairy Tern)
S. n. horni
Western Australia
S. n. nereis
S Australia, Victoria, Tasmania
S. n. davisae
New Zealand
S. n. exsul
New Caledonia
Sterna albistriata (Black-fronted Tern)
New Zealand
Sterna superciliaris (Amazon Tern)
E South America
Sterna balaenarum (Damara Tern)
SW Africa
Sterna lorata (Chilean Tern)
W South America
Sterna albifrons (Little Tern)
S. a. albifrons
Europe, W Asia » N Africa, NW India
S. a. guineae
Ghana to Gabon
S. a. innominata
Persian Gulf islands
S. a. pusilla
N India, Burma, Java, Sumatra
S. a. sinensis
Japan & Indochina » Philippine Is & New
Guinea
S. a. placens
Australia
S. a. antillarum
E USA » West Indies & NE Brazil
S. a. mexicana
Sonora, Sinaloa
S. a. browni
W American coast from California to Peru
Sterna saundersii (Black-shafted Tern)
S Red Sea, Somalia to NW India

THALASSEUS
Thalasseus bergii (Crested Tern)
T. b. bergii
Southern Africa coast, Madagascar
T. b. thalassinus
Seychelles, Aldabra I, Rodriguez I
T. b. velox
NE Africa to Sri Lanka, Red Sea
T. b. cristatus
Malaysia to Riukiu Is & E Australia
T. b. gwendolenae
W & NW Australia
Thalasseus maximus (Royal Tern)
T. m. maximus
California to Peru, Florida to Argentina,
West Indies
T. m. albidorsalis
coast of W Africa

Thalasseus bengalensis (Lesser Crested Tern)
T. b. par
  N & E Africa, Madagascar
T. b. bengalensis
  Persian Gulf to Singapore » Celebes
T. b. torresii
  Aru Is, N Australia
Thalasseus bernsteini (Chinese Crested Tern)
  E China, Philippine Is
Thalasseus elegans (Elegant Tern)
  California to Chile
Thalasseus sandvicensis (Sandwich Tern)
T. s. sandvicensis
  W & S Europe » Africa, NW India
T. s. acuflavidus
  Florida, Gulf Coast » Brazil, West Indies
T. s. eurygnatha
  E South America, Trinidad

Larosterna inca (Inca Tern)
  coast of Peru & Chile

Procelsterna cerulea (Blue-grey Noddy)
P. c. saxatilis
  W Hawaiian Is, Marcus I
P. c. cerulea
  Christmas I, Marquesas Is
P. c. nebouxi
  Phoenix I, Ellis Is, Samoa Is
P. c. teretirostris
  Tuamotu I, Society Is
P. c. albivitta
  Kermadec Is, Friendly Is, Norfolk I
P. c. skottsbergii
  Easter I
P. c. imitatrix
  St Ambrose I (Chile)

Anoüs stolidus (Common Noddy)
A. s. stolidus
  Caribbean & Tropical Atlantic islands
A. s. plumbeigularis
  S Red Sea
A. s. pileatus
  Seychelles to Hawaian Is & N Australia
A. s. ridgwayi
  islands of W Mexico & W Central America
A. s. galapagensis
  Galapagos Is
Anoüs tenuirostris (Lesser Noddy)
A. t. tenuirostris
  Seychelles, Madagascar, Mascarene Is
A. t. melanops
  Houtman Abrolhos Is (W Australia)

Anoüs minutus (White-capped Noddy)
A. m. minutus
  islands from Tuamotu to New Guinea
A. m. worcesteri
  Cavilli I (Sulu Sea)
A. m. marcusi
  Marcus I & Wake I to Caroline Is
A. m. melanogenys
  Hawaiian Is
A. m. diamesus
  Clipperton I, Cocos I
A. m. americanus
  islands off Belize, Central America
A. m. atlanticus
  Tropical South Atlantic islands

Gygis alba (White Tern)
G. a. alba
  South Atlantic Ocean islands
G. a. monte
  Seychelles, Madagascar, Mascarene Is
G. a. royana
  Norfolk I, Kermadec Is
G. a. candida
  S W Pacific Ocean islands
G. a. rothschildi
  Laysan I
G. a. leucopes
  Henderson I
G. a. microrhyncha
  Marquesas Is
G. a. pacifica
  S Pacific Ocean islands

63 RYNCHOPIDAE (SKIMMERS)

Rynchops niger (Black Skimmer)
R. n. niger
  New Jersey to Gulf Coast & N Brazil
R. n. cinerascens
  N & E South America
R. n. intercedens
  E & S South America
Rynchops flavirostris (African Skimmer)
  Senegal to Sudan & Transvaal
Rynchops albicollis (Indian Skimmer)
  India, Burma, Indochina

64 ALCIDAE (AUKS)

Alle alle (Little Auk)
A. a. alle
  N Atlantic Ocean » New Jersey &
    W Europe
A. a. polaris
  Franz Josef Land, Barents Sea

ALCA
Alca torda (Razorbill)
A. t. pica
NE Canada, NE USA
A. t. islandica
Iceland, Faroe Is, British Isles
A. t. torda
Baltic Sea islands

URIA
Uria lomvia (Brunnich's Guillemot)
U. l. lomvia
Arctic Sea & N Atlantic Ocean
U. l. arra
Bering Sea, N Pacific ocean
Uria aalge (Common Guillemot)
U. a. aalge
Labrador to Orkneys & Norway
U. a. hyperborea
Bear I
U. a. spiloptera
Faroe Is
U. a. albionis
British Isles to Portugal
U. a. intermedia
Islands in Baltic Sea
U. a. inornata
Bering Sea, N Pacific ocean
U. a. californica
California

CEPPHUS
Cepphus grylle (Black Guillemot)
C. g. mandtii
Arctic Sea, Spitzbergen to N Greenland
C. g. arcticus
N Labrador, S Greenland
C. g. grylle
North Atlantic, Baltic & White Sea
Cepphus columba (Pigeon Guillemot)
C. c. columba
Bering Sea, N Pacific Ocean
C. c. snowi
Kurile Is, N Hokkaido I
Cepphus carbo (Spectacled Guillemot)
Kurile Is, Okhotsk Sea to N Japan

BRACHYRAMPHUS
Brachyramphus marmoratus (Marbled Murrelet)
B. m. perdix
Kamchatka to Kurile Is, Hokkaido I
B. m. marmoratus
Alaska to California
Brachyramphus brevirostris (Kittlitz's Murrelet)
Bering Sea, N Pacific ocean
Brachyramphus hypoleucus (Xantus' Murrelet)
California & islands

Brachyramphus craveri (Craveri's Murrelet)
Gulf of California, Raza I

SYNTHLIBORAMPHUS
Synthliboramphus antiquus (Ancient Murrelet)
Bering Sea, N Pacific ocean
Synthliboramphus wumizusume (Crested Murrelet)
coast of Japan

PTYCHORAMPHUS
Ptychoramphus aleuticus (Cassin's Auklet)
Aleutian Is to S California

CYCLORRHYNCHUS
Cyclorrhynchus psittacula (Parakeet Auklet)
Bering Sea, N Pacific ocean

AETHIA
Aethia cristatella (Crested Auklet)
Bering Sea, N Pacific ocean
Aethia pusilla (Least Auklet)
Bering Sea, N Pacific ocean
Aethia pygmaea (Whiskered Auklet)
Kurile Is, Aleutian Is to N Japan

CERORHINCA
Cerorhinca monocerata (Rhinoceros Auklet)
Aleutian Is, & N Pacific coasts

FRATERCULA
Fratercula arctica (Atlantic Puffin)
F. a. naumanni
Greenland to Novaya Zemlya
F. a. arctica
NE Canada to N Norway
F. a. grabae
Faroe Is, British Isles, S Norway
Fratercula corniculata (Horned Puffin)
Bering Sea, N Pacific ocean

LUNDA
Lunda cirrhata (Tufted Puffin)
Bering Sea, N Pacific Ocean & coasts

Columbiformes

65 PTEROCLIDIDAE (SANDGROUSE)

SYRRHAPTES
Syrrhaptes tibetanus (Tibetan Sandgrouse)
C Asia, India
Syrrhaptes paradoxus (Pallas' Sandgrouse)
C Asia, N China » NE China

PTEROCLES
Pterocles alchata (Pintailed Sandgrouse)
P. a. alchata
S Spain, S France

P. a. caudacutus
N Africa, Israel to C Asia & India
**Pterocles namaqua (Namaqua
Sandgrouse)**
Namibia to Transvaal & W Cape Province
**Pterocles exustus (Chestnut-bellied
Sandgrouse)**
P. e. exustus
Senegal to Ethiopia
P. e. floweri
Egypt
P. e. ellioti
NE Africa to Kenya
P. e. olivascens
Kenya
P. e. erlangeri
SW Saudi Arabia
P. e. hindustan
Iraq, India
Pterocles senegallus (Spotted Sandgrouse)
NE Africa, Middle East, India
**Pterocles orientalis (Black-bellied
Sandgrouse)**
P. o. aragonica
Spain, Canary Is, Morocco
P. o. orientalis
N Africa, Middle East, India
P. o. arenarius
S Russia, N Afghanistan
**Pterocles coronatus (Crowned
Sandgrouse)**
P. c. coronatus
Algeria & Niger to Egypt
P. c. vastitas
Sinai
P. c. saturatus
E Saudi Arabia
P. c. atratus
Iraq to India
P. c. ladas
Sind
**Pterocles gutturalis (Yellow-throated
Sandgrouse)**
P. g. saturatior
N Ethiopia to N Tanzania
P. g. tanganjicae
Tanzania
P. g. gutturalis
Zambia to Mozambique & Transvaal
**Pterocles burchelli (Variegated
Sandgrouse)**
P. b. makarikari
Namibia, N Botswana
P. b. burchelli
E Botswana, W Transvaal
**Pterocles personatus (Madagascar
Sandgrouse)**
W Madagascar

**Pterocles decoratus (Black-faced
Sandgrouse)**
P. d. ellenbecki
S Somalia, N Kenya
P. d. decoratus
S Kenya
P. d. katharinae
N Tanzania
P. d. loveridgei
C Tanzania
**Pterocles lichtensteinii (Lichtenstein's
Sandgrouse)**
P. l. targius
S Algeria, Niger
P. l. lichtensteinii
Ethiopia, N Sudan, Egypt
P. l. ingramsi
S Saudi Arabia
P. l. sukensis
Kenya
P. l. arabicus
E Saudi Arabia to Afghanistan &
Pakistan
**Pterocles bicinctus (Double-banded
Sandgrouse)**
P. b. ansorgei
S Angola
P. b. elizabethae
W Namibia
P. b. bicinctus
C & E Namibia to SW Zambia
P. b. usheri
E Zambia, S Malawi
P. b. multicolor
S Zambia, Rhodesia, Mozambique,
Transvaal
Pterocles indicus (Painted Sandgrouse)
India
**Pterocles quadricinctus (Four-banded
Sandgrouse)**
P. q. quadricinctus
Senegal & Gambia to N Nigeria
P. q. lowei
Chad to Sudan, Uganda, NW Kenya

66 COLUMBIDAE (DOVES, PIGEONS)

COLUMBA
Columba livia (Feral Rock Dove)
C. l. livia
W Europe, NW Africa
C. l. atlantis
Cape Verde Is, Madeira, Azores
C. l. canariensis
Canary Is
C. l. gymnocyclus
Senegal, Ghana

C. l. targia
Air to Darfur
C. l. lividior
Mali
C. l. butleri
NE Sudan
C. l. daklae
Dakla & Kharga Oases, Libya
C. l. schimperi
Nile valley
C. l. palestinae
Israel, Sinai, W Arabia
C. l. gaddi
Asia Minor, Iraq
C. l. neglecta
Turkestan, Pakistan
C. l. intermedia
S India, Sri Lanka
C. l. nigricans
Mongolia, N China
Columba rupestris (Eastern Rock Pigeon)
C. r. turkestanica
C Asia, Himalayas
C. r. rupestris
N China, Manchuria
Columba leuconota (Snow Pigeon)
C. l. leuconota
Himalayas, W China
C. l. gradaria
C China
Columba guinea (Speckled Pigeon)
C. g. guinea
Senegal to Ethiopia, Tanzania
C. g. phaeonota
S Africa
C. g. bradfieldi
C Namibia
Columba albitorques (White-collared Pigeon)
C & E Ethiopia
Columba oenas (Stock Dove)
C. o. oenas
Europe, N Africa, Asia Minor
C. o. hyrcana
N Iran
C. o. yarkandensis
E Turkestan, Tien Shan
Columba eversmanni (Yellow-eyed Stock Dove)
Turkestan to NW India
Columba oliviae (Somali Stock Dove)
Somalia
Columba palumbus (Wood Pigeon)
C. p. palumbus
Europe, W Russia
C. p. madarensis
Madeira

C. p. azorica
Azores
C. p. excelsa
N Africa
C. p. iranica
Iran
C. p. casiotis
N India
Columba trocaz (Trocaz Pigeon)
Madeira
Columba bollii (Boll's Pigeon)
Canary Is
Columba unicincta (African Wood Pigeon)
Liberia to Zaire, Uganda
Columba junoniae (Laurel Pigeon)
Palma, Gonera (Canary Is)
Columba arquatrix (Olive Pigeon)
Ethiopia & Angola to E South Africa
Columba sjöstedi (Cameroun Olive Pigeon)
SE Nigeria, Cameroun
Columba thomensis (Sao Thomé Olive Pigeon)
Sao Thomé I
Columba pollenii (Comoro Olive Pigeon)
Comoro Is
Columba hodgsonii (Speckled Wood Pigeon)
Himalayas, Burma, W China
Columba albinucha (White-naped Pigeon)
E Zaire, W Uganda
Columba pulchricollis (Ashy Wood Pigeon)
Tibet, N Burma, N Thailand
Columba elphinstonii (Nilgiri Wood Pigeon)
SW India
Columba torringtoni (Sri Lanka Wood Pigeon)
Sri Lanka
Columba punicea (Purple Wood Pigeon)
NE India to N Malaysia, Vietnam
Columba argentina (Silver Pigeon)
islands W of Sumatra & N of Borneo
Columba palumboides (Andaman Wood Pigeon)
Andaman Is, Nicobar Is
Columba janthina (Black Wood Pigeon)
C. j. janthina
S Japanese Is, N Riukiu Is
C. j. stejnegeri
S Riukiu Is
C. j. nitens
Bonin Is, Volcano I
Columba vitiensis (White-throated Pigeon)
C. v. halmaheira
Moluccas, New Guinea, Solomon Is
C. v. leopoldi
New Hebrides

C. v. hypoenochroa
New Caledonia
C. v. griseogularis
Philippine Is, N Bornean Is
C. v. anthracinus
Palawan
C. v. mendeni
Sula Is
C. v. metallica
Lesser Sunda Is
C. v. vitiensis
Fiji Is
C. v. castaneiceps
Samoa
Columba leucomela (White-headed Pigeon)
E Australia
Columba jouyi (Silver-banded Black Pigeon)
Okinawa I **e?**
Columba pallidiceps (Yellow-legged Pigeon)
Solomon Is, Bismarck Arch
Columba leucocephala (White-crowned Pigeon)
West Indies, S Florida
Columba squamosa (Red-necked Pigeon)
Gtr, Lesser & Dutch Antilles
Columba speciosa (Scaled Pigeon)
S Mexico to Brazil & Paraguay
Columba picazuro (Picazuro Pigeon)
C. p. marginalis
NE Brazil
C. p. picazuro
E Brazil to NE Argentina
Columba corensis (Bare-eyed Pigeon)
N Colombia, N Venezuela, Dutch Antilles
Columba maculosa (Spotted Pigeon)
C. m. albipennis
S Peru, W Bolivia
C. m. maculosa
N Argentina, Uruguay, Paraguay
Columba fasciata (Band tailed Pigeon)
C. f. fasciata
W North America
C. f. monilis
N Baja California
C. f. vioscae
S Baja California
C. f. letonai
Honduras, El Salvador
C. f. parva
N Nicaragua
C. f. crissalis
Costa Rica, W Panama
C. f. albilinea
N & W Colombia to E Bolivia

C. f. roraimae
Mt Duida, Mt Roraima (Venezuela)
Columba araucana (Chilean Pigeon)
C & S Chile
Columba caribaea (Jamaican Band-tailed Pigeon)
Jamaica
Columba cayennensis (Rufous Pigeon)
C. c. pallidicrissa
S Mexico to Colombia
C. c. cayennensis
Venezuela, the Guianas, N Brazil
C. c. sylvestris
E Peru to N Argentina
C. c. occidentalis
W Colombia
C. c. tamboensis
SW Colombia
Columba flavirostris (Red-billed Pigeon)
C. f. flavirostris
Texas, E & S Mexico to El Salvador
C. f. madrensis
Tres Marias Is
C. f. restricta
W Mexico
C. f. minima
W Costa Rica
Columba oenops (Salvin's Pigeon)
N Peru
Columba inornata (Plain Pigeon)
C. i. inornata
Cuba, Hispaniola, Isle of Pines
C. i. exigua
Jamaica
C. i. wetmorei
Puerto Rico
Columba plumbea (Plumbeous Pigeon)
C. p. bogotensis
Colombia to N Peru
C. p. chapmani
W Ecuador
C. p. pallescens
SE Ecuador to E Brazil
C. p. baeri
C Brazil
C. p. wallacei
Lower Amazon, the Guianas
C. p. plumbea
SE Brazil, Paraguay
Columba subvinacea (Ruddy Pigeon)
C. s. subvinacea
Costa Rica, W Panama
C. s. berlepschi
E Panama to S Ecuador
C. s. ruberrima
NW Colombia
C. s. peninsularis
N Venezuela

C. s. zuliae
W Venezuela
C. s. purpureotincta
E Colombia, E Venezuela, the Guianas
C. s. anolaimae
SC Colombia
C. s. ogilvie-granti
SE Colombia
Columba nigrirostris (Short-billed Pigeon)
SE Mexico to E Panama
Columba goodsoni (Goodson's Pigeon)
W Colombia, W Ecuador
Columba delegorguei (Delegorgue's Pigeon)
C. d. sharpei
S Sudan, Kenya, Tanzania
C. d. delegorguei
Natal
Columba iriditorques (Bronze-naped Pigeon)
Sierra Leone to Angola, E Zaire
Columba malherbii (Sao Thomé Bronze-naped Pigeon)
Sao Thomé I, Principé I, Annobon I
Columba mayeri (Pink Pigeon)
Mauritius I

STREPTOPELIA
Streptopelia turtur (Turtle Dove)
S. t. turtur
Europe, Asia Minor, Azores Is
S. t. arenicola
N Africa, SW Asia
S. t. hoggara
S Sahara
S. t. isabellina
E Libya, N Egypt
Streptopelia lugens (Dusky Turtle Dove)
S. l. bishaensis
SW Arabia
S. l. lugens
Ethiopia, Somalia
S. l. funebrea
Uganda to Tanzania, Malawi
Streptopelia hypopyrrha (Pink-bellied Turtle Dove)
E Nigeria, Cameroun
Streptopelia orientalis (Eastern Turtle Dove)
S. o. meena
W Himalayas
S. o. erythrocephala
S India
S. o. agricola
Burma, NE India
S. o. orientalis
Siberia, China, Japan
S. o. stimpsoni
Riukiu Is

S. o. orii
Taiwan
Streptopelia bitorquata (Javanese Collared Dove)
S. b. dusumieri
Philippine Is, N Borneo
S. b. bitorquata
Java to Timor I
Streptopelia decaocto (Collared Dove)
S. d. decaocto
Europe to W China
S. d. stoliczkae
Chinese Turkestan
S. d. xanthocyclus
Burma to E China
Streptopelia roseogrisea(African Collared Dove)
S. r. bornuensis
Mali, N Nigeria, Chad
S. r. roseogrisea
Sudan, W Ethiopia
S. r. arabica
E Ethiopia, Somalia, Arabia
Streptopelia reichenowi (White-winged Collared Dove)
S Somalia, NE Kenya
Streptopelia decipiens (Mourning Collared Dove)
S. d. decipiens
E Chad, Sudan, Ethiopia
S. d. shelleyi
Senegal to N Nigeria
S. d. logonensis
E Cameroun, N Zaire
S. d. ambigua
Angola, S Zaire, W Zambia
S. d. perspicillata
Somalia to Malawi, Mozambique
Streptopelia semitorquata (Red-eyed Dove)
S. s. semitorquata
Angola to Ethiopia & N Mozambique
S. s. minor
S Somalia, E Kenya, NE Tanzania
S. s. australis
S Mozambique, Rhodesia, South Africa
Streptopelia capicola (Ring-necked Dove)
S. c. hilgerti
N Somalia
S. c. electa
S Ethiopia
S. c. somalica
S Ethiopia, S Somalia, E Kenya
S. c. anceps
S Kenya, C Tanzania
S. c. tropica
Uganda, W Tanzania to Mozambique

S. c. dryas
E Zaire
S. c. bailunduensis
Angola
S. c. ongouati
Namibia
S. c. damarensis
C & W South Africa
S. c. capicola
Transvaal, Natal, Cape Province
Streptopelia vinacea (Vinaceous Dove)
S. v. vinacea
Senegal to Sudan
S. v. grotei
Chad, N Cameroun
S. v. savannae
Sierra Leone to N Zaire
Streptopelia tranquebarica (Red-collared Dove)
S. t. humilis
N Tibet to Indochina & N Philippine Is
S. t. murmensis
E Nepal, Sikkim, NE India
S. t. tranquebarica
India
Streptopelia picturata (Madagascar Turtle Dove)
S. p. picturata
Madagascar
S. p. coppingeri
Glorioso Is
S. p. comorensis
Anjouan I (Comoro)
S. p. aldabrana
Aldabra I
S. p. assumptionis
Assumption I
S. p. saturata
Amirante I
S. p. rostrata
Seychelles
S. p. chuni
Diego Garcia I
Streptopelia chinensis (Spotted Dove)
S. c. ceylonensis
Sri Lanka
S. c. suratensis
India
S. c. forresti
NE Burma, NW Yunnan
S. c. chinensis
E China
S. c. formosa
Taiwan
S. c. hainana
Hainan I
S. c. vacillans
SE Yunnan

S. c. tigrina
Burma to Palawan, Borneo & Sumatra
Streptopelia senegalensis (Laughing Dove)
S. s. phoenicophila
Morocco, Algeria, Tunisia
S. s. daklae
Dakhla Oasis, Libya
S. s. aegyptiaca
Nile valley, Egypt
S. s. senegalensis
Senegal to Ethiopia & Cape Province
S. s. thomé
Sao Thomé I
S. s. sokotrae
Socotra I
S. s. cambayensis
Iran, India
S. s. ermanni
Afghanistan, Turkestan

APLOPELIA
Aplopelia larvata (Lemon Dove)
A. l. bronzina
Ethiopia
A. l. larvata
SE Sudan to Cape Province
A. l. jacksoni
E Zaire, Uganda, W Tanzania
A. l. plumbescens
S Cameroun
A. l. samaliyae
Angola, NW Zambia
A. l. inornata
Cameroun Mt, E Nigeria
A. l. poensis
Fernando Po
A. l. principalis
Principé I
A. l. simplex
Sao Thomé I
A. l. hypoleuca
Annobon I

MACROPYGIA
Macropygia unchall (Bar tailed Cuckoo Dove)
M. u. tusalia
Himalayas, W China, N Burma
M. u. minor
SE China, N Indochina, Hainan I
M. u. unchall
Malaysia, Sumatra, Java, Lombok I
Macropygia amboinensis (Pink-breasted Cuckoo Dove)
M. a. sanghirensis
Sanghir Is, Talaut Is
M. a. albicapilla
Celebes
M. a. sedecima
Sula Is

M. a. batchianensis
N Moluccas
M. a. amboinensis
S Moluccas
M. a. keyensis
Kei Is
M. a. doreya
NW New Guinea, W Papuan Is
M. a. maforensis
Numfor I
M. a. griseinucha
Meos Num I
M. a. kerstingi
N New Guinea, Japen I
M. a. meeki
Vulcan I
M. a. cinereiceps
D'Entrecasteaux Arch
M. a. cunctata
Louisiade Archipelago
M. a. carteretia
Bismarck Archipelago
M. a. hüskeri
New Hanover
Macropygia phasianella (Large Brown Cuckoo Dove)
M. p. septentrionalis
Botel Tobago I, Batan I
M. p. phaea
Calayan I
M. p. tenuirostris
Philippine Is, Palawan, Sulu Arch
M. p. borneensis
N Borneo
M. p. hypopercna
Simalur I
M. p. modiglianii
Nias I
M. p. elassa
Mentawi I
M. p. cinnamomea
Enggano I
M. p. emiliana
Sumatra to Flores I
M. p. megala
Kangean I
M. p. robinsoni
N Australia
M. p. phasianella
S Queensland, New South Wales
Macropygia magna (Large Cuckoo Dove)
M. m. macassariensis
S Celebes, Saleyer I
M. m. longa
Djampea I
M. m. magna
Timor I, Alor I, Wetar I

M. m. timorlaoënsis
Tenimber Is
Macropygia rufipennis (Andaman Cuckoo Dove)
M. r. rufipennis
Andaman Is, Nicobar Is
M. r. tiwarii
Gt Nicobar I
Macropygia nigrirostris (Lesser Bar-tailed Cuckoo Dove)
New Guinea & NE Islands
Macropygia mackinlayi (Mackinlay's Cuckoo Dove)
M. m. mackinlayi
Santa Cruz, Banks I, N Hebrides
M. m. arossi
Solomon Is
M. m. krakari
Karkar I
M. m. goodsoni
St Matthias Is, NE New Guinea
Macropygia ruficeps (Little Cuckoo Dove)
M. r. assimilis
S Burma, NW Thailand
M. r. malayana
Malaysia
M. r. engelbachi
N Indochina
M. r. nana
Borneo
M. r. sumatrana
Sumatra
M. r. simalurensis
Simalur I
M. r. ruficeps
Java, Bali I
M. r. orientalis
Sumbawa I, Flores I, Timor I

REINWARDTOENA
Reinwardtoena reinwardtsi (Reinwardt's Long-tailed Pigeon)
R. r. reinwardtsi
Moluccas
R. r. griseotincta
New Guinea, W New Guinea Is
R. r. brevis
Biak I
Reinwardtoena browni (Brown's Long-tailed Pigeon)
New Britain, Duke of York I
Reinwardtoena crassirostris (Crested Long-tailed Pigeon)
Solomon Is

TURACOENA
Turacoena manadensis (White-faced Pigeon)
T. m. manadensis
Celebes

T. m. sulaënsis
Peling I, Sula Is
Turacoena modesta (Timor Black Pigeon)
Timor I, Wetar I

TURTUR
Turtur chalcospilos (Emerald-spotted Wood Dove)
T. c. chalcospilos
Somalia to Angola & Cape Province
T. c. volkmanni
Namibia
Turtur abyssinicus (Black-billed Wood Dove)
Senegal to N Ethiopia
Turtur afer (Blue-spotted Wood Dove)
Senegal to Ethiopia & Transvaal
Turtur tympanistria (Tambourine Dove)
T. t. fraseri
Sierra Leone to Ethiopia & Tanzania
T. t. tympanistria
E Rhodesia, Natal, E Cape Province
Turtur brehmeri (Blue-headed Wood Dove
T. b. infelix
Sierra Leone to Cameroun Mt
T. b. brehmeri
S Cameroun, Gabon, Zaire

OENA
Oena capensis (Namaqua Dove)
O. c. capensis
Senegal to Arabia & Cape Province
O. c. aliena
Madagascar

CHALCOPHAPS
Chalcophaps indica (Emerald Dove)
C. i. indica
India to the Philippine Is, Moluccas, Gtr Sunda Is
C. i. robinsoni
Sri Lanka
C. i. maxima
Andaman Is
C. i. natalis
Christmas I
C. i. formosanus
Taiwan
C. i. yamashinae
Riukiu Is
C. i salimali
Kerala (S India)
C. i. minima
Numfor I, Biak I, Meos Num I
C. i. timorensis
Lesser Sunda Is
C. i. chrysochlora
New Guinea & islands, E Australia

C. i. sandwichensis
Santa Cruz Is, New Hebrides, New Caledonia
C. i. longirostris
Northern Territory, (Australia)
C. i. melvillensis
Melville I
Chalcophaps stephani (Brown-backed Emerald Dove)
C. s. wallacei
Celebes
C. s. stephani
New Guinea & surrounding islands
C. s. mortoni
Solomon Is

HENICOPHAPS
Henicophaps albifrons (Black Bronzewing)
H. a. albifrons
New Guinea, Waigeu I, Misol I, Japen I
H. a. schlegeli
Aru Is
Henicophaps foersteri (New Britain Bronzewing)
New Britain

PHAPS
Phaps chalcoptera (Common Bronzewing)
P. c. murchisoni
mid Western & SW Australia
P. c. consobrina
N Australia
P. c. chalcoptera
S Queensland to Tasmania, S Australia
Phaps elegans (Brush Bronzewing)
P. e. neglecta
Southern Australia
P. e. elegans
Tasmania
Phaps histrionica (Flock Pigeon)
P. h. alisteri
NW Australia
P. h. histrionica
W Queensland, W New South Wales

OCYPHAPS
Ocyphaps lophotes (Crested Pigeon)
O. l. whitlocki
WC Australia
O. l. lophotes
C & EC Australia

PETROPHASSA
Petrophassa plumifera (White-bellied Plumed Pigeon)
P. p. plumifera
N Western Australia to NW Queensland
P. p. mungi
Derby District N Western Australia

P. p. proxima
· Upper Fitzroy river, N Western Australia
P. p. leucogaster
N South Australia, S Northern Territory
Petrophassa ferruginea (Red-Plumed Pigeon)
NW Australia
Petrophassa scripta (Partridge Bronzewing)
P. s. peninsulae
N Queensland
P. s. scripta
C Queensland, C New South Wales
Petrophassa smithii (Bare-eyed Partridge Bronzewing)
N & NW Australia
Petrophassa rufipennis (Chestnut-quilled Rock Pigeon)
N Territory (Australia)
Petrophassa albipennis (White-quilled Rock Pigeon)
P. a. albipennis
N Western Australia
P. a. boothi
N Northern Territory

GEOPELIA
Geopelia cuneata (Diamond Dove)
N & C Australia
Geopelia striata (Zebra Dove)
G. s. striata
S Burma to Philippine Is, Borneo, Lombok I
G. s. papua
S New Guinea
G. s. maugeus
Sumbawa I to Timor I
G. s. audacis
Tenimber Is, Kei Is
G. s. placida
N Australia
G. s. tranquilla
C Australia
G. s. clelandi
mid Western Australia
Geopelia humeralis (Bar-shouldered Dove)
G. h. gregalis
S New Guinea
G. h. humeralis
N & NE Australia

LEUCOSARCIA
Leucosarcia melanoleuca (Wonga Pigeon)
Queensland to Victoria

ZENAIDA
Zenaida macroura (Mourning Dove)
Z. m. marginella
W North America & Central America

Z. m. carolinensis
E North America, Bahama Is
Z. m. macroura
Cuba, Isle of Pines, Hispaniola
Z. m. tresmariae
Tres Marias Is
Z. m. clarionensis
Clarion I
Z. m. graysoni
Socorro I (Revillagigedo Is)
Zenaida auriculata (Eared Dove)
Z. a. caucae
W Colombia
Z. a. vulcania
C Colombia
Z. a. hypoleuca
W Ecuador, W Peru
Z. a. auriculata
Chile, W Argentina
Z. a. chrysauchenia
Bolivia to Uruguay & S Argentina
Z. a. noronha
NE Brazil
Z. a. marajoensis
River Amazon Estuary
Z. a. stenura
Grenada I, Trinidad, NE South America
Z. a. penthera
E Colombia, NW Venezuela
Z. a. antioquiae
NC Colombia
Z. a. vinaceorufa
Curaçao I, Aruba I, Bonaire I
Zenaida aurita (Zenaida Dove)
Z. a. salvadorii
Yucatan coast & islands
Z. a. zenaida
Bahama Is, Gtr Antilles, Virgin Is
Z. a. aurita
Lesser Antilles
Zenaida galapagoensis(Galapagos Dove)
Z. g. galapagoensis
Galapagos Is
Z. g. exsul
Culpepper I, Wenman I
Zenaida asiatica (White-winged Dove)
Z. a. mearnsi
SW USA, W Mexico, Tres Marias Is
Z. a. asiatica
S USA, E Mexico, Gtr Antilles Is
Z. a. australis
W Costa Rica
Z. a. meloda
SW Ecuador to N Chile

COLUMBINA
Columbina passerina (Scaly-breasted Ground Dove)

C. p. passerina
SE Coast of USA
C. p. bahamensis
Bahama Is, Bermuda I
C. p. insularis
Gtr Antilles, Cayman Is
C. p. jamaicensis
Jamaica
C. p. navassae
Navassa I
C. p. exigua
Gt Inagua I, Mona I
C. p. portoricensis
Puerto Rico, Virgin Is
C. p. nigrirostris
St Croix I, N Lesser Antilles
C. p. trochila
Martinique I
C. p. antillarum
S Lesser Antilles
C. p. pallescens
S USA to Guatemala & Belize
C. p. socorroensis
Socorro I
C. p. neglecta
Honduras to Costa Rica
C. p. albivitta
N Colombia, N Venezuela, Dutch Antilles
C. p. parvula
NC Colombia
C. p. nana
W Colombia
C. p. quitensis
C Ecuador
C. p. griseola
S Venezuela, the Guianas, N Brazil
C. p. tortugensis
Los Hermanos I, La Tortuga I
Columbina minuta (Plain-breasted Ground Dove)
C. m. interrupta
SE Mexico, Guatemala, Belize
C. m. elaeodes
SW Costa Rica, WC Columbia
C. m. minuta
Venezuela, the Guianas, Peru, Brazil, Paraguay
Columbina buckleyi (Ecuadorean Ground Dove)
NW Ecuador, NW Peru
Columbina talpacoti (Ruddy Ground Dove)
C. t. eluta
W Mexico
C. t. rufipennis
SE Mexico to N Colombia, N Venezuela, Trinidad

C. t. caucae
Cauca valley, Colombia
C. t. talpacoti
C & E South America from the Guianas to C Argentina
Columbina picui (Picui Dove)
C. p. strepitans
NE Brazil
C. p. picui
Bolivia & S Brazil to C Chile & Argentina
Columbina cruziana (Gold-billed Ground Dove)
N Ecuador to NW Chile
Columbina cyanopis (Blue-eyed Ground Dove)
C Brazil

CLARAVIS
Claravis pretiosa (Blue Ground Dove)
SE Mexico to Paraguay & N Argentina
Claravis godefrida (Purple-barred Ground Dove)
SE Brazil, E Paraguay
Claravis mondetoura (Purple-breasted Ground Dove)
SE Mexico to Venezuela & E Peru

METRIOPELIA
Metriopelia ceciliae (Barefaced Ground Dove)
M. c. ceciliae
W Peru
M. c. obsoleta
E Peru
M. c. gymnops
S Peru, Bolivia, N Chile
Metriopelia morenoi (Moreno's Barefaced Ground Dove)
NW Argentina
Metriopelia melanoptera (Black-winged Ground Dove)
M. m. saturatior
S Colombia, Ecuador
M. m. melanoptera
Peru to Chile or W Argentina
Metriopelia aymara (Bronze-winged Ground Dove)
S Peru to Chile, W Argentina

SCARDAFELLA
Scardafella inca (Inca Dove)
Arizona to N Costa Rica
Scardafella squammata (Scaly Dove)
S. s. ridgwayi
coast of Colombia & Venezuela, Trinidad
S. s. squammata
E & S Brazil

UROPELIA
Uropelia campestris (Mauve-spotted Ground Dove)
E Bolivia, C Brazil

LEPTOTILA
Leptotila verreauxi (White-fronted Dove)
L. v. capitalis
Tres Marias Is
L. v. angelica
N & C Mexico
L. v. fulviventris
S Mexico, E Guatemala, Belize
L. v. bangsi
W Guatemala to W Nicaragua
L. v. nuttingi
Ometepe I (Lake Nicaragua)
L. v. verreauxi
SW Nicaragua to N Venezuela,
Dutch Antilles
L. v. insularis
Trinidad
L. v. tobagensis
Tobago I
L. v. decolor
W Colombia, W Ecuador, N Peru
L. v. brasiliensis
the Guianas, N Brazil
L. v. approximans
E Brazil
L. v. decipiens
E Peru, E Bolivia, W Brazil
L. v. chalcauchenia
S Bolivia, Uruguay, N Argentina
Leptotila megalura (White-faced Dove)
L. m. megalura
N & C Bolivia
L. m. saturata
S Bolivia, NW Argentina
Leptotila rufaxilla (Grey-fronted Dove)
L. r. pallida
W Colombia, SW Ecuador
L. r. pallidipectus
E Colombia
L. r. dubusi
E Ecuador to E Venezuela
L. r. rufaxilla
E Venezuela, French Guiana
L. r. hellmayri
N Venezuela, Trinidad
L. r. bahiae
E Brazil
L. r. reichenbachii
C Brazil to Paraguay & Uruguay
Leptotila plumbeiceps (Grey-headed Dove)
L. p. plumbeiceps
SE Mexico to W Costa Rica
L. p. notius
W Panama

L. p. malae
Mala peninsula, W Panama
L. p. battyi
Coiba I
Leptotila pallida (Pallid Dove)
W Colombia, SW Ecuador
Leptotila wellsi (Grenada Dove)
Grenada I
Leptotila jamaicensis (White-bellied Dove)
L. j. gaumeri
N Yucatan peninsula & islands
L. j. collaris
Gd Cayman I
L. j. jamaicensis
Jamaica
L. j. neoxena
St Andrews I
Leptotila cassini (Cassin's Dove)
L. c. cerviniventris
E Guatemala to Panama
L. c. rufinucha
SW Costa Rica, W Panama
L. c. cassini
E Panama, N Colombia
Leptotila ochraceiventris (Buff-bellied Dove)
SW Ecuador
Leptotila conoveri (Conover's Dove)
C Colombia

GEOTRYGON
Geotrygon lawrencii (Lawrence's Quail Dove)
G. l. carrikeri
Vera Cruz, Mexico
G. l. lentipes
NW Costa Rica
G. l. lawrencii
E Costa Rica, W Panama
Geotrygon costaricensis (Costa Rican Quail Dove)
Costa Rica, W Panama
Geotrygon goldmani (Goldman's Quail Dove)
G. g. goldmani
E Darien (E Panama)
G. g. oreas
Quebrada (E Panama)
Geotrygon saphirina (Purple Quail Dove)
G. s. purpurata
W Colombia, W Ecuador
G. s. saphirina
E Ecuador
G. s. rothschildi
Marcapata valley, Peru
Geotrygon caniceps (Grey-faced Quail Dove)

G. c. caniceps
Cuba
G. c. leucometopius
Hispaniola
Geotrygon versicolor (Crested Quail Dove)
Jamaica
Geotrygon veraguensis (Veragua Quail Dove)
E Costa Rica to NW Ecuador
Geotrygon linearis (White-faced Quail Dove)
G. l. albifacies
SE Mexico, NE Guatemala
G. l. rubida
Guerrero, Mexico
G. l. anthonyi
S Mexico, W Guatemala
G. l. silvestris
El Salvador, Honduras, N Nicaragua
G. l. chiriquensis
Costa Rica, W Panama
G. l. infusca
Santa Marta, Colombia
G. l. linearis
E Colombia, W Venezuela
G. l. trinitatis
NE Venezuela, Trinidad
Geotrygon frenata (Pink-faced Quail Dove)
G. f. bourcieri
Colombia, Ecuador
G. f. subgrisea
SW Ecuador
G. f. frenata
Peru, Bolivia
Geotrygon chrysia (Key West Quail Dove)
Bahama Is, Cuba, Hispaniola
Geotrygon mystacea (Bridled Quail Dove)
Virgin Is, Lesser Antilles
Geotrygon violacea (Violaceous Quail Dove)
G. v. albiventer
Nicaragua to N Colombia
G. v. violacea
Surinam to Paraguay
Geotrygon montana (Ruddy Quail Dove)
G. m. martinica
Lesser Antilles Is
G. m. montana
Mexico to N Argentina, Gtr Antilles, Trinidad

STARNOENAS
Starnoenas cyanocephala (Blue-headed Quail Dove)
Cuba, Isle of Pines

CALOENAS
Caloenas nicobarica (Nicobar Pigeon)

C. n. nicobarica
Nicobar Is to Luzon I, New Guinea, Solomon Is
C. n. pelewensis
Palau Is

GALLICOLUMBA
Gallicolumba luzonica (Luzon Bleeding Heart)
Luzon I, Polillo Is
Gallicolumba criniger (Bartlett's Bleeding Heart)
Mindanao, Leyte I, Samar I, Basilan I
Gallicolumba platenae (Mindoro Bleeding Heart)
Mindoro I
Gallicolumba keayi (Negros Bleeding Heart)
Negros I
Gallicolumba menagei (Tawitawi Bleeding Heart)
Tawitawi Is
Gallicolumba rufigula (Golden Heart)
G. r. helviventris
Aru Is
G. r. rufigula
W New Guinea
G. r. septentrionalis
N New Guinea
G. r. alaris
S New Guinea
G. r. orientalis
SE New Guinea
Gallicolumba tristigmata (Celebes Quail Dove)
G. t. tristigmata
N Celebes
G. t. auripectus
C & SE Celebes
G. t. bimaculata
S Celebes
Gallicolumba jobiensis (White-breasted Ground Pigeon)
G. j. jobiensis
New Guinea, Bismarck Archipelago
G. j. chalconota
Vella Lavella I, Guadalcanal (Solomon Is)
Gallicolumba kubaryi (Truk Is Ground Dove)
E Caroline Is
Gallicolumba erythroptera (Society Is Ground Dove)
Society Is, Tuamotu Is
Gallicolumba xanthonura (White-throated Dove)
Mariana Is, Yap I
Gallicolumba stairi (Friendly Quail Dove)
Fiji, Tonga, Samoan Is

Gallicolumba sanctaecrucis (Santa Cruz
Ground Dove)
Santa Cruz Is
Gallicolumba salamonis (Thick-billied
Ground Dove)
San Cristobal I, Ramos I
Gallicolumba rubescens (Marquesas
Ground Dove)
Marquesas Is
Gallicolumba beccarii (Grey-breasted
Quail Dove)
G. b. eichhorni
St Matthias Is
G. b. admiralitatis
Admiralty Is
G. b. johannae
Bismarck Archipelago, Dampier I
G. b. beccarii
New Guinea
G. b. intermedia
W Solomon Is
G. b. solomonensis
Rennell I, E Solomon Is
Gallicolumba canifrons (Palau Ground
Dove)
Palau Is
Gallicolumba hoedtii (Wetar Is Ground
Dove)
Wetar I

TRUGON
Trugon terrestris (Thick-billed Ground
Pigeon)
T. t. terrestris
NW New Guinea, Salawati I
T. t. mayri
N New Guinea
T. t. leucopareia
S New Guinea

MICROGOURA
Microgoura meeki (Solomon Is Ground
Pigeon)
Choiseul I **e?**

OTIDIPHAPS
Otidiphaps nobilis (Pheasant Pigeon)
O. n. nobilis
W New Guinea
O. n. cervicalis
E & SE New Guinea
O. n. insularis
Fergusson I
O. n. aruensis
Aru Is

GOURA
Goura cristata (Blue Crowned Pigeon)
G. c. cristata
NW New Guinea
G. c. minor
W Papuan islands

Goura scheepmakeri (Maroon-breasted
Crowned Pigeon)
G. s. sclaterii
S New Guinea
G. s. wadai
S New Guinea
G. s. scheepmakeri
SE New Guinea
Goura victoria (Victoria Crowned Pigeon)
G. v. victoria
Japen I, Biak I
G. v. beccarii
N New Guinea

DIDUNCULUS
Didunculus strigirostris (Tooth-billed
Pigeon)
Upolu I, Savaii (Samoa)

PHAPITRERON
Phapitreron leucotis (Lesser Brown Fruit
Dove)
P. l. leucotis
Catanduanes I, Luzon I, Mindoro I
P. l. nigrorum
Tablas I, Masbate I, Panay I, Negros I,
Cebu I
P. l. albifrons
Bohol I, Samar I, Siquijor I
P. l. brevirostris
Leyte I, Mindanao I
P. l. occipitalis
Basilan I, Sulu Is
Phapitreron amethystina (Greater Brown
Fruit Dove)
P. a. amethystina
Luzon I, Samar I, Leyte I, Bohol I, Mindanao
P. a. maculipectus
Negros I
P. a. frontalis
Cebu I
P. a. brunneiceps
Basilan I
P. a. cinereiceps
Tawitawi Is

TRERON
Treron fulvicollis (Cinnamon-headed Green
Pigeon)
T. f. fulvicollis
Malaysia, Sumatra, S Borneo
T. f. oberholseri
Natuna Is
T. f. melopogenys
Nias I
T. f. baramensis
N Borneo & islands
Treron olax (Little Green Pigeon)
Malaysia, Sumatra, Borneo, Java

***Treron vernans* (Pink-necked Green Pigeon)**
- *T. v. griseicapilla*
  Malaysia, S Indochina, W Java, N Borneo
- *T. v. parva*
  NE Sumatra
- *T. v. miza*
  Simalur I
- *T. v. mesochloa*
  Nias I, Siberut I, Enggano I, Pagi I
- *T. v. adina*
  Natuna Is, Anamba Is
- *T. v. purpurea*
  S Borneo, Java to Sumbawa I
- *T. v. vernans*
  Philippine Is, Palawan I
- *T. v. zalepta*
  Celebes

***Treron bicincta* (Orange-breasted Green Pigeon)**
- *T. b. bicincta*
  India to Indochina & Malaysia
- *T. b. leggei*
  Sri Lanka
- *T. b. domvilii*
  Hainan I
- *T. b. javana*
  Java

***Treron pompadora* (Pompadour Green Pigeon)**
- *T. p. pompadora*
  Sri Lanka
- *T. p. affinis*
  W India
- *T. p. phayrei*
  E India to Thailand & S Indochina
- *T. p. chloroptera*
  Andaman Is, Nicobar Is
- *T. p. axillaris*
  Philippine Is
- *T. p. everetti*
  Sulu Archipelago
- *T. p. pallidior*
  Djampea I, Kalao I
- *T. p. ada*
  Madu I, Kalao Tua I
- *T. p. aromatica*
  Buru I

***Treron curvirostra* (Thick-billed Green Pigeon)**
- *T. c. nipalensis*
  W Nepal to Thailand & Indochina
- *T. c. curvirostris*
  Malaysia, Sumatra
- *T. c. harterti*
  NE Sumatra
- *T. c. hainana*
  Hainan I
- *T. c. erimacra*
  Philippine Is
- *T. c. nasica*
  Borneo
- *T. c. haliploa*
  Simalur I
- *T. c. pega*
  Nias I
- *T. c. smicra*
  Sipora I, Siberut I, Batu I
- *T. c. hypothapsina*
  Enggano I

***Treron griseicauda* (Grey-faced Thick-billed Green Pigeon)**
- *T. g. sanghirensis*
  Sanghir Is
- *T. g. griseicauda*
  Celebes
- *T. g. goodsoni*
  Tukang Besi Is
- *T. g. pulverulenta*
  S Sumatra, Java, Bali
- *T. g. vordermani*
  Kangean I

***Treron teysmanni* (Sumba Is Green Pigeon)**
  Sumba I

***Treron floris* (Flores Green Pigeon)**
  Lesser Sunda Is from Lombok I to Alor I

***Treron psittacea* (Timor Green Pigeon)**
  Timor I, Samau I

***Treron capellei* (Large Green Pigeon)**
- *T. c. magnirostris*
  Malaysia, N Sumatra, Borneo
- *T. c. capellei*
  S Sumatra, Java

***Treron phoenicoptera* (Yellow-legged Green Pigeon)**
- *T. p. phoenicoptera*
  N India
- *T. p. chlorigaster*
  S India
- *T. p. phillipsi*
  Sri Lanka
- *T. p. viridifrons*
  Burma, W Thailand
- *T. p. annamensis*
  E Thailand, Indochina

***Treron waalia* (Yellow-bellied Green Pigeon)**
  Senegal to S Arabia

***Treron australis* (Madagascar Green Pigeon)**
- *T. a. australis*
  E Madagascar
- *T. a. xenia*
  W Madagascar
- *T. a. griveaudi*
  Moheli I (Comoro Is)

***Treron calva* (African Green Pigeon)**
- *T. c. nudirostris*
  Senegal to Guinea
- *T. c. sharpei*
  Sierra Leone to N Cameroun

T. c. calva
Gabon, N Angola, W Zaire
T. c. poensis
Fernando Po
T. c. virescens
Principé I
T. c. uellensis
N Zaire, Uganda
T. c. brevicera
SW Ethiopia, E Kenya
T. c. salvadorii
Lake Kivu area, NE Zaire
T. c. gibberifrons
S Zaire, W Kenya
T. c. wakefieldii
E Kenya, NE Tanzania
T. c. orientalis
S Tanzania, Mozambique
T. c. schalowi
Zambia, S Zaire
T. c. chobiensis
NW Zambia
T. c. ansorgei
S Angola
T. c. damarensis
N Namibia
T. c. vylderi
NE Namibia
T. c. granti
E Kenya to N Malawi
T. c. delalandii
Mozambique to Natal
Treron pembaensis (Pemba I Green Pigeon)
Pemba I
Treron sanctithomae (Sao Thomé Green Pigeon)
Sao Thomé I
Treron apicauda (Pin-tailed Green Pigeon)
T. a. apicauda
Himalayas, W Burma
T. a. laotinus
N Indochina
T.a.lowei
S Vietnam
Treron oxyura (Yellow-bellied Pin-tailed Green Pigeon)
Sumatra, W Java
Treron seimundi (White-bellied Pin-tailed Green Pigeon)
T. s. seimundi
S Thailand, Malaysia
T. s. modestus
C Vietnam
Treron sphenura (Wedge-tailed Green Pigeon)
T. s. sphenura
Kashmir to Burma

T. s. yunnanensis
SW China, N Vietnam
T. s. annamensis
C Vietnam
T. s. oblitus
Hainan I
T. s. robinsoni
Malaysia
T. s. etorques
Sumatra
T. s. korthalsi
Sumatra, Java, Lombok I
Treron sieboldii (White-bellied Wedge-tailed Green Pigeon)
T. s. fopingenis
Shensi
T. s. sieboldii
Japan
T. s. sororius
Taiwan
T. s. murielae
N & C Vietnam
Treron formosae (Formosan Green Pigeon)
T. f. permagna
N Riukiu Is
T. f. medioximus
S Riukiu Is
T. f. formosae
Taiwan, Botel Tobago I
T. f. australis
Batan I, Calayan I, Camiguin I (Phil Is)

PTILINOPUS

Ptilinopus cincta (Black-backed Fruit Dove)
P. c. albocincta
Bali I to Flores I
P. c. everetti
Pantar I, Alor I
P. c. cincta
Timor I, Wetar I, Roma I
P. c. lettiensis
Letti I, Moa I, Luang I, Sermatta I
P. c. ottonis
Damar I, Babar I
Ptilinopus alligator (Black-banded Pigeon)
N Territory (Australia)
Ptilinopus dohertyi (Red-naped Fruit Dove)
Sumba I
Ptilinopus porphyrea (Pink-necked Fruit Dove)
Sumatra, Java, Bali
Ptilinopus marchei (Marche's Fruit Dove)
Luzon I,Polillo Is
Ptilinopus merrilli (Merrill's Fruit Dove)
P. m. faustinoi
Mt Tabuan (N Luzon I)
P. m. merrilli
E & S Luzon I, Polillo Is

Ptilinopus occipitalis (Yellow-breasted Fruit Dove)
   Philippine Is
Ptilinopus fischeri (Fischer's Fruit Dove)
   P. f. fischeri
   N Celebes
   P. f. centralis
   C & SE Celebes
   P. f. meridionalis
   S Celebes
Ptilinopus jambu (Jambu Fruit Dove)
   Malaysia, Sumatra, Borneo
Ptilinopus subgularis (Dark-chinned Fruit Dove)
   P. s. epia
   Celebes
   P. s. subgularis
   Peling I, Banggai I
   P. s. mangoliensis
   Sula Mangoli I
Ptilinopus leclancheri (Black-chinned Fruit Dove)
   P. l. leclancheri
   Philippine Is
   P. l. gironieri
   Palawan I
Ptilinopus formosus (Scarlet-breasted Fruit Dove)
   N Moluccas
Ptilinopus magnificus (Magnificent Fruit Dove)
   P. m. puella
   NW New Guinea & islands
   P. m. interposita
   WC & SW New Guinea
   P. m. septentrionalis
   N & NE New Guinea, Japen I, Dampier I
   P. m. poliura
   SE New Guinea
   P. m. assimilis
   N Queensland
   P. m. keri
   Bellenden Ker, Queensland
   P. m. magnificus
   S Queensland to Victoria
Ptilinopus perlatus (Pink-spotted Fruit Dove)
   P. p. perlatus
   NW New Guinea & islands
   P. p. plumbeicollis
   NE New Guinea
   P. p. zonurus
   SE New Guinea, Aru Is, Fergusson I
Ptilinopus ornatus (Ornate Fruit Dove)
   P. o. ornatus
   NW New Guinea
   P. o. gestroi
   C & E New Guinea

   P. o. kaporensis
   SW New Guinea
Ptilinopus tannensis (Silver-shouldered Fruit Dove)
   New Hebrides, Banks Is
Ptilinopus aurantiifrons (Orange-fronted Fruit Dove)
   New Guinea & NW islands
Ptilinopus wallacii (Wallace's Fruit Dove)
   Babar I, Kei I, Aru Is, SW New Guinea
Ptilinopus superbus (Superb Fruit Dove)
   P. s. temminckii
   Celebes, Sulu Arch
   P. s. superbus
   Moluccas to Solomon Is, NE Australia
Ptilinopus perousii (Many-coloured Fruit Dove)
   P. p. perousii
   Samoan Is
   P. p. mariae
   Tonga, Fiji Is
Ptilinopus porphyraceus (Purple-capped Fruit Dove)
   P. p. fasciatus
   Samoan Is
   P. p. graeffei
   Uvea I
   P. p. ponapensis
   Caroline Is
   P. p. porphyraceus
   Tonga, Fiji Is
Ptilinopus pelewensis (Palau Fruit Dove)
   Palau Is
Ptilinopus rarotongensis (Rarotongan Fruit Dove)
   P. r. rarotongensis
   Rarotonga I
   P. r. goodwini
   Cook Is
Ptilinopus roseicapilla (Marianas Fruit Dove)
   Mariana Is
Ptilinopus regina (Pink-capped Fruit Dove)
   P. r. roseipileum
   Wetar I, Roma I, Kissar I, Moa I
   P. r. xanthogaster
   Banda Is, Kei Is, Damar I, Babar I
   P. r. flavicollis
   Flores I, Samoa Is, Timor I
   P. r. ewingii
   Northern Territory, Melville I
   P. r. regina
   Cape York to New South Wales
Ptilinopus richardsii (Silver-capped Fruit Dove)
   P. r. richardsii
   E Solomon Is

P. r. cyanopterus
Rennell I
Ptilinopus purpuratus (Grey-green Fruit Dove)
P. p. chrysogaster
W Society Is
P. p. frater
Moorea I
P. p. purpuratus
Tahiti
P. p. chalcurus
Mahatea I
P. p. coralensis
Tuamotu Is
Ptilinopus greyii (Grey's Fruit Dove)
Santa Cruz Is, New Hebrides, New Caledonia
Ptilinopus huttoni (Rapa I Fruit Dove)
Rapa I
Ptilinopus dupetithouarsii (White-capped Fruit Dove)
P. d. viridior
N Marquesas Is
P. d. dupetithouarsii
S Marquesas Is
Ptilinopus mercierii (Red-moustached Fruit Dove)
P. m. mercierii
Nukuhiva I
P. m. tristrami
Hivaoa I
Ptilinopus insularis (Henderson I Fruit Dove)
Henderson I (Pitcairn Is)
Ptilinopus coronulatus (Lilac-capped Fruit Dove)
P. c. trigeminus
NW New Guinea, Salawati I
P. c. geminus
N New Guinea, Japen I
P. c. quadrigeminus
N New Guinea, Vulcan I
P. c. huonensis
SE New Guinea
P. c. coronulatus
S New Guinea, Aru Is
Ptilinopus pulchellus (Crimson-capped Fruit Dove)
P. p. pulchellus
New Guinea & western Islands
P. p. decorus
N New Guinea
Ptilinopus monacha (Blue-capped Fruit Dove)
N Moluccas
Ptilinopus rivoli (White-bibbed Fruit Dove)
P. r. buruanus
Buru I

P. r. prasinorrhous
Moluccas, Kei Is, W Papuan Is
P. r. rivoli
Bismarck Archipelago
P. r. strophium
Louisiade Archipelago, Egum Atoll
P. r. miquelii
Japen I, Meos Num I
P. r. bellus
New Guinea, Admiralty Is
Ptilinopus solomonensis (Yellow-bibbed Fruit Dove)
P. s. johannis
St Matthias Is, New Hanover
P. s. meyeri
New Britain, Rook I
P. s. neumanni
Nissan I
P. s. bistictus
Bougainville I
P. s. vulcanorum
C Solomon Is
P. s. ocularis
Guadalcanal I
P. s. ambiguus
Malaita I
P. s. solomonensis
San Cristobal I, Ugi I
P. s. speciosus
Numfor I, Biak I
Ptilinopus viridis (Red-bibbed Fruit Dove)
P. v. viridis
S Moluccas
P. v. vicinus
Trobriand Is, D'Entrecasteaux Archipelago
P. v. lewisii
W Solomon Is
P. v. geelvinkiana
islands of Geelvink Bay
P. v. pseudogeelvinkiana
Meos Num I
P. v. pectoralis
W Papuan Is, NW New Guinea
P. v. salvadorii
N New Guinea
Ptilinopus eugeniae (White-headed Fruit Dove)
San Cristobal I, Ugi I
Ptilinopus iozonus (Orange-bellied Fruit Dove)
P. i. humeralis
W Papuan Is, NW New Guinea
P. i. jobiensis
Japen I, Vulcan I, N New Guinea
P. i. pseudohumeralis
C New Guinea
P. i. finschii
SE New Guinea

P. i. iozonus
  Aru Is
Ptilinopus insolitus (Knob-billed Fruit Dove)
P. i. insolitus
  New Ireland, New Britain, Lihir Is
P. i. inferior
  St Matthias Is
Ptilinopus hyogastra (Grey-headed Fruit Dove)
  Halmahera I, Batjan I
Ptilinopus granulifrons (Carunculated Fruit Dove)
  Obi Major I
Ptilinopus melanospila (Black-naped Fruit Dove)
P. m. bangueyensis
  Philippine Is, N Bornean Is
P. m. talautensis
  Talaut Is
P. m. xanthorrhoa
  Sangir Is
P. m. melanospila
  Celebes, Togian I
P. m. aurescentior
  Tukang Besi Is
P. m. pelingensis
  Peling I, Banggai I
P. m. chrysorrhoa
  Sula Is, Ceram I
P. m. margaretha
  Kalaotoa I, Madu I
P. m. massoptera
  Pulo Mata Siri I
P. m. melanauchen
  Java, Bali to Alor I, Kangean I
Ptilinopus naina (Dwarf Fruit Dove)
P. n. minimus
  W Papuan Is
P. n. naina
  S New Guinea
Ptilinopus arcanus (Ripley's Fruit Dove)
  NC Negros I
Ptilinopus victor (Orange Dove)
  Fiji Is
Ptilinopus luteovirens (Golden Dove)
  Fiji Is
Ptilinopus layardi (Yellow-headed Dove)
  Kandavu I (Fiji Is)

DREPANOPTILA
Drepanoptila holosericea (Cloven-feathered Dove)
  New Caledonia I

ALECTROENAS
Alectroenas madagascariensis (Madagascar Blue Pigeon)
  Madagascar

Alectroenas sganzini (Comoro Blue Pigeon)
A. s. minor
  Aldabra I
A. s. sganzini
  Comoro Is
Alectroenas pulcherrima (Seychelles Blue Pigeon)
  Seychelles

DUCULA
Ducula poliocephala (Philippine Zone-tailed Pigeon)
  Philippine Is
Ducula forsteni (Green & White Zone-tailed Pigeon)
  Celebes
Ducula mindorensis (Mindoro Zone-tailed Pigeon)
  Mindoro I
Ducula radiata (Grey-headed Zone-tailed Pigeon)
  Celebes
Ducula carola (Grey-necked Fruit Pigeon)
D. c. carola
  Luzon I, Mindoro I
D. c. nigrorum
  Negros I
D. c. mindanensis
  Mindanao I
Ducula aenea (Green Imperial Pigeon)
D. a. pusilla
  S India, Sri Lanka
D. a. sylvatica
  N India, Thailand, Indochina
D. a. nicobarica
  Nicobar Is
D. a. aenea
  Malaysia, Borneo, Sumatra to Alor I
D. a. mista
  Simalur I
D. a. babiensis
  Pulo Babi I
D. a. consobrina
  Nias I
D. a. vicina
  Mentawi Is
D. a. palawanensis
  S Philippine Is
D. a. chalybura
  N Philippine Is
D. a. paulina
  Celebes, Talaut Is
D. a. sulana
  Sula Is
D. a. aneothorax
  Engano I
D. a. intercedus
  Banggai I, Peleng I

Ducula perspicillata **(White-eyed Imperial Pigeon)**
D. p. perspicillata
N Moluccas
D. p. neglecta
S Moluccas
Ducula concinna **(Blue-tailed Imperial Pigeon)**
D. c. intermedia
Talaut Is
D. c. concinna
Islands E of Celebes
D. c. aru
Aru Is
D. c. separata
Tenimber Is, Kei Is
Ducula pacifica **(Pacific Pigeon)**
D. p. tarrali
N New Guinea Is, New Hebrides
D. p. pacifica
Ellis Is, Tonga I
D. p. intensitincta
Fiji Is
D. p. microcera
Samoa Is
D. p. sejuncta
Bismarck Archipelago
Ducula oceanica **(Micronesian Pigeon)**
D. o. monacha
Yap I, Palau Is
D. o. tereokai
Truk I
D. o. townsendi
Ponapé I
D. o. oceanica
Kusaie I, Marshall Is
D. o. ratakensis
Arno I, Wotje I (Marshall Is)
Ducula aurorae **(Society Is Pigeon)**
Society Is
Ducula galeata **(Marquesas Pigeon)**
Nukuhiva I
Ducula rubricera **(Red-knobbed Pigeon)**
D. r. rubricera
Bismarck Archipelago, Lihir Is
D. r. rufigula
Solomon Is
Ducula myristicivora **(Black-knobbed Pigeon)**
D. m. myristicivora
W Papuan Is
D. m. geelvinkiana
Meos Num I, Numfor I, Biak I
Ducula rufigaster **(Rufous-bellied Fruit Pigeon)**
D. r. rufigaster
W Papuan Is, W New Guinea
D. r. pallida
S New Guinea

D. r. uropygialis
N New Guinea
Ducula basilica **(Moluccan Rufous-bellied Fruit Pigeon)**
D. b. basilica
N Moluccas
D. b. obiensis
Obi I
Ducula finschii **(Finsch's Rufous-bellied Fruit Pigeon)**
Bismarck Archipelago
Ducula chalconota **(Mountain Rufous-bellied Fruit Pigeon)**
D. c. chalconota
NW New Guinea
D. c. smaragdina
New Guinea
Ducula pistrinaria **(Island Imperial Pigeon)**
D. p. rhodinolaema
Admiralty Is, New Hanover
D. p. vanwyckii
Bismarck Archipelago
D. p. postrema
Islands off SE New Guinea
D. p. pistrinaria
Solomon Is, Lihir Is
Ducula rosacea **(Pink-headed Imperial Pigeon)**
D. r. rosacea
Lesser Sunda Is from Duizend I to Sudest I
D. r. zamydra
Arends I, Colombo Besar I (Java Sea)
Ducula whartoni **(Christmas I Imperial Pigeon)**
Christmas I
Ducula pickeringii **(Grey Imperial Pigeon)**
D. p. pickeringii
N Bornean Is, Sulu Archipelago, Talaut Is
D. p. langhornei
Bolod I, Loran I
D. p. palmasensis
Palmas I
Ducula latrans **(Peale's Pigeon)**
Fiji Is
Ducula brenchleyi **(Chestnut-bellied Pigeon)**
Solomon Is
Ducula bakeri **(Baker's Pigeon)**
New Hebrides
Ducula goliath **(New Caledonian Pigeon)**
New Caledonia
Ducula pinon **(Pinon Imperial Pigeon)**
D. p. pinon
W Papuan Is, SW New Guinea
D. p. rubiensis
C & S New Guinea
D. p. jobiensis
N New Guinea, Japen I, Dampier I

D. p. salvadorii
  D'Entrecasteaux & Louisiade Archi-
    pelago
Ducula melanochroa (Black Imperial
Pigeon)
  Bismarck Archipelago
Ducula mullerii (Black-collared Fruit
Pigeon)
D. m. aurantia
  N New Guinea
D. m. mullerii
  S New Guinea, Aru Is
Ducula zoeae (Banded Imperial Pigeon)
  New Guinea & SW & SE islands
Ducula badia (Mountain Imperial Pigeon)
D. b. insignis
  Himalayas
D. b. cuprea
  SW India
D. b. griseicapilla
  Burma, Thailand, Indochina
D. b. obscurata
  SE Thailand
D. b. badia
  Malaysia, Sumatra, Borneo
D. b. capistrata
  W Java
Ducula lacernulata (Dark-backed Imperial
Pigeon)
D. l. lacernulata
  W & C Java
D. l. williami
  E Java, Bali I
D. l. sasakensis
  Lombok I, Flores I
Ducula cineracea (Timor Imperial Pigeon)
D. c. cineracea
  Timor I
D. c. schistacea
  Wetar I
Ducula bicolor (Pied Imperial Pigeon)
D. b. bicolor
  Andaman Is to Philippine Is & Lesser
    Sunda Is
D. b. melanura
  Moluccas
Ducula luctuosa (Celebes Pied Imperial
Pigeon)
  Celebes, Sula Is
Ducula spilorrhoa (Australian Pied Imperial
Pigeon)
D. s. subflavescens
  Bismarck Archipelago, Admiralty Is
D. s. spilorrhoa
  Aru Is, W New Guinea & islands
D. s. tarara
  S New Guinea

D. s. melvillensis
  SE New Guinea, N & NE Australia, Lord
    Howe I

LOPHOLAIMUS
Lopholaimus antarcticus (Top-knot
Pigeon)
  N Queensland to Victoria

HEMIPHAGA
Hemiphaga novaeseelandiae (New Zealand
Pigeon)
H. n. novaeseelandiae
  New Zealand
H. n. chathamensis
  Chatham I

CRYPTOPHAPS
Cryptophaps poecilorrhoa (Celebes Dusky
Pigeon)
  N & SE Celebes

GYMNOPHAPS
Gymnophaps albertisii (Bare-eyed
Mountain Pigeon)
G. a. exsul
  Batjan I (Moluccas)
G. a. albertisii
  New Guinea, Bismarck Archipelago
Gymnophaps mada (Long-tailed Mountain
Pigeon)
G. m. mada
  Buru I
G. m. stalkeri
  Ceram I
Gymnophaps solomonensis (Pale
Mountain Pigeon)
  Solomon Is

Psittaciformes

67 LORIIDAE (LORIES)

CHALCOPSITTA
Chalcopsitta atra (Black Lory)
C. a. bernsteini
  Misol I
C. a. atra
  Batanta I, Salawati I, NW New Guinea
C. a. insignis
  Amberpon, NW New Guinea
C. a. spectabilis
  NW New Guinea
Chalcopsitta duivenbodei (Duyvenbode's
Lory)
C. d. duivenbodei
  coast of NW New Guinea
C. d. syringanuchalis
  coast of NE New Guinea

Chalcopsitta sintillata (Yellow-streaked Lory)
  C. s. rubrifrons
    Aru Is
  C. s. sintillata
    S New Guinea
  C. s. chloroptera
    SE New Guinea
Chalcopsitta cardinalis (Cardinal Lory)
  Islands NW of New Ireland, Solomon Is

EOS
Eos cyanogenia (Black-winged Lory)
  Islands in Geelvink Bay
Eos squamata (Violet-necked Lory)
  E. s. obiensis
    Obi I
  E. s. atrocaerulea
    Maju I
  E. s. riciniata
    N Moluccas
  E. s. squamata
    W Papuan islands
Eos reticulata (Blue-streaked Lory)
  Tenimber Is, Kei Is, Damar I
Eos histrio (Red and Blue Lory)
  E. h. histrio
    Gt Sangi I, Siao I
  E. h. talautensis
    Talaut Is
  E.h. challengeri
    Nenusa I
Eos bornea (Red Lory)
  E. b. bornea
    Ambon I, Saparua I
  E.b. cyanonothus
    Buru I
  E.b. rothschildi
    Ceram I
  E. b. bernsteini
    Kei Is
Eos semilarvata (Blue-eared Lory)
  C Ceram I

PSEUDEOS
Pseudeos fuscata (Dusky Lory)
  Salawati I, Japen I, New Guinea

TRICHOGLOSSUS
Trichoglossus ornatus (Ornate Lory)
  Celebes
Trichoglossus haematodus (Rainbow Lory)
  T. h. mitchellii
    Bali I, Lombok I
  T. h. forsteni
    Sumbawa I
  T. h. djampeanus
    Djampea I
  T. h. stresemanni
    Kalaotua I

  T. h. fortis
    Sumba I
  T. h. weberi
    Flores I
  T. h. capistratus
    Timor I
  T. h. flavotectus
    Wetar I, Roma I
  T. h. haematodus
    S Moluccas, W New Guinea
  T. h. rosenbergii
    Biak I
  T. h. intermedius
    N New Guinea
  T. h. micropteryx
    E New Guinea
  T. h. caeruleiceps
    S New Guinea
  T. h. nigrogularis
    E Kei Is, Aru Is
  T. h. brooki
    Trangan I (Aru Is)
  T. h. massena
    New Hebrides, Bismarck Archipelago,
    Solomon Is
  T. h. flavicans
    New Hanover, Admiralty Is
  T. h. nesophilus
    Ninigo I
  T. h. deplanchii
    New Caledonia, Loyalty Is
  T. h. moluccanus
    E Australia, Tasmania
  T. h. rubritorquis
    N Australia
Trichoglossus rubiginosus (Ponapé Lory)
  Ponapé I
Trichoglossus johnstoniae (Johnstone's Lorikeet)
  T. j. johnstoniae
    C & SE Mindanao
  T. j. pistra
    W Mindanao
Trichoglossus flavoviridis (Yellow and Green Lorikeet)
  T. f. meyeri
    Celebes
  T. f. flavoviridis
    Sula Is
Trichoglossus chlorolepidotus (Scaly-breasted Lorikeet)
  NE Australia
Trichoglossus euteles (Perfect Lorikeet)
  Timor I, Lomblen I to Babar I
Trichoglossus versicolor (Varied Lorikeet)
  N Australia
Trichoglossus iris (Iris Lorikeet)
  T. i. iris
    W Timor I

T. i. rubripileum
E Timor I
T. i. wetterensis
Wetar I
Trichoglossus goldiei (Goldie's Lorikeet)
C New Guinea

Lorius hypoinochrous (Purple-bellied Lory)
L. h. devittatus
Bismark Archipelago, SE New Guinea & islands
L. h. hypoinochrous
Misima I, Tagula I
L. h. rosselianus
Rossel I
Lorius lory (Black-capped Lory)
L. l. lory
NW New Guinea & islands
L. l. erythrothorax
C New Guinea
L. l. somu
S New Guinea
L. l. salvadorii
NE New Guinea
L. l. viridicrissalis
N New Guinea
L. l. jobiensis
Japen I, Meos Num I
L. l. cyanuchen
Biak I
Lorius albidinuchus (White-naped Lory)
New Ireland
Lorius amabilis (Stresemann's Lory)
New Britain
Lorius chlorocercus (Yellow-bibbed Lory)
E Solomon islands
Lorius domicellus (Purple-naped Lory)
Ceram I, Ambon I
Lorius tibialis (Blue-thighed Lory)
unknown
Lorius garrulus (Chattering Lory)
L. g. garrulus
Halmahera I, Weda I
L. g. flavopalliatus
Batjan I, Obi I
L. g. morotaianus
Morotai I

Phigys solitarius (Collared Lory)
Fiji Is

Vini australis (Blue-crowned Lory)
Samoa Is, Tonga I, Lau Archipelago
Vini kuhlii (Kuhl's Lory)
Rimitara I, Tubuai I
Vini stepheni (Stephen's Lory)
Henderson I

Vini peruviana (Tahitian Lory)
Cook Is, Society Is
Vini ultramarina (Ultramarine Lory)
Marquesas Is

Glossopsitta concinna (Musk Lorikeet)
E & SE Australia, Tasmania
Glossopsitta pusilla (Little Lorikeet)
E & SE Australia, Tasmania
Glossopsitta porphyrocephala (Purple-crowned Lorikeet)
SW & SE Australia

Charmosyna palmarum (Palm Lorikeet)
New Hebrides, Banks Is
Charmosyna rubrigularis (Red-chinned Lorikeet)
C. r. rubrigularis
New Britain, New Ireland
C. r. krakari
Karkar I
Charmosyna meeki (Meek's Lorikeet)
Solomon Is
Charmosyna toxopei (Blue-fronted Lorikeet)
Buru I
Charmosyna multistriata (Striated Lorikeet)
WC New Guinea
Charmosyna wilhelminae (Wilhelmina's Lorikeet)
C New Guinea
Charmosyna rubronotata (Red-spotted Lorikeet)
C. r. rubronotata
Salawati I, NW New Guinea
C. r. kordoana
Biak I
Charmosyna placentis (Red-flanked Lorikeet)
C. p. intensior
N Moluccas
C. p. placentis
S Moluccas, Kei Is, Aru Is, S New Guinea
C. p. ornata
NW New Guinea & islands
C. p. subplacens
E New Guinea
C. p. pallidior
Bismarck Archipelago, W Solomon Is
Charmosyna diadema (New Caledonian Lorikeet)
New Caledonia e?
Charmosyna amabilis (Red-throated Lorikeet)
Viti Levu I, Ovalau I, Taviuni I

***Charmosyna margarethae* (Duchess Lorikeet)**
Solomon Is
***Charmosyna pulchella* (Fairy Lorikeet)**
C. p. pulchella
NW, C & SE New Guinea
C. p. rothschildi
NC New Guinea
C. p. bella
SE New Guinea
***Charmosyna josefinae* (Josephine's Lory)**
C. j. josefinae
NW New Guinea
C. j. sepikiana
Sepik Mtn area, New Guinea
C. j. cyclopum
Cyclops Mtns, New Guinea
***Charmosyna papou* (Papuan Lory)**
C. p. papou
NW New Guinea
C. p. stellae
SE New Guinea
C. p. goliathina
C New Guinea
C. p. wahnesi
Huon peninsula, New Guinea

OREOPSITTACUS
***Oreopsittacus arfaki* (Whiskered Lorikeet)**
O. a. arfaki
NW New Guinea
O. a. major
C New Guinea
O. a. grandis
SE New Guinea

NEOPSITTACUS
***Neopsittacus musschenbroekii* (Musschenbroek's Lorikeet)**
N. m. musschenbroekii
NW New Guinea
N. m. medius
W New Guinea
N. m. major
SE New Guinea
***Neopsittacus pullicauda* (Emerald Lorikeet)**
N. p. alpinus
W New Guinea
N. p. socialis
EC New Guinea
N. p. pullicauda
SE New Guinea

68 CACATUIDAE (COCKATOOS)

CACATUINAE

PROBOSCIGER
***Probosciger aterrimus* (Palm Cockatoo)**
P. a. goliath
W Papuan Is, NW to SE New Guinea

P. a. stenolophus
Japen I, N New Guinea
P. a. aterrimus
Aru Is, Misol I, S New Guinea, Cape York, Queensland

CALYPTORHYNCHUS
***Calyptorhynchus funereus* (Black Cockatoo)**
C. f. baudinii
SW Australia
C. f. tenuirostris
SW Australia
C. f. funereus
E Australia
C. f. xanthonotus
SE Australia, Tasmania
***Calyptorhynchus magnificus* (Red-tailed Cockatoo)**
C. m. naso
SW Australia
C. m. samueli
SW Queensland, W New South Wales
C. m. macrorhynchus
N Australia
C. m. magnificus
Queensland to S New South Wales, W Victoria
***Calyptorhynchus lathami* (Glossy Cockatoo)**
C Queensland to E Victoria, Kangaroo I

CALLOCEPHALON
***Callocephalon fimbriatum* (Gang-gang Cockatoo)**
SE Australia, N Tasmania

EOLOPHUS
***Eolophus roseicapillus* (Galah)**
E. r. kuhli
NW Australia
E. r. assimilis
Western Australia
E. r. roseicapillus
NC & E Australia

CACATUA
***Cacatua leadbeateri* (Major Mitchell's Cockatoo)**
C. l. mollis
mid-Western Australia
C. l. leadbeateri
interior of Australia
***Cacatua sulphurea* (Lesser Sulphur-crested Cockatoo)**
C. s. sulphurea
Celebes, Buton I
C. s. djampeana
Alor I to Madu I, Tukangbesi Is
C. s. abbotti
Solombo Besar I

C. s. occidentalis
Lombok I, Sumbawa I, Flores I
C. s. parvula
Timor I, Samao I
C. s. citrinocristata
Sumba I
Cacatua galerita (Sulphur-crested Cockatoo)
C. g. eleonora
Aru Is
C. g. triton
New Guinea & N & E islands
C. g. fitzroyi
N Australia to W Queensland
C. g. galerita
E & SE Australia
Cacatua ophthalmica (Blue-eyed Cockatoo)
New Britain, New Ireland
Cacatua moluccensis (Salmon-crested Cockatoo)
S Moluccas
Cacatua alba (White Cockatoo)
N & C Moluccas
Cacatua haematuropygia (Red-vented Cockatoo)
Philippine Is, Palawan I
Cacatua goffini (Goffin's Cockatoo)
Tenimber Is
Cacatua sanguinea (Little Corella)
C. s. normantoni
S New Guinea, NW Queensland
C. s. sanguinea
W, NW & EC Australia
Cacatua tenuirostris (Long-billed Corella)
C. t. pastinator
SW Australia
C. t. tenuirostris
SE Australia
Cacatua ducorps (Ducorp's Cockatoo)
E Solomon Is

NYMPHICINAE

NYMPHICUS
Nymphicus hollandicus (Cockatiel)
Australia (mainly interior)

69 PSITTACIDAE (PARROTS)

NESTORINAE

NESTOR
Nestor notabilis (Kea)
C South I, New Zealand
Nestor meridionalis (Kaka)
New Zealand

MICROPSITTA
Micropsitta pusio (Buff-faced Pygmy Parrot)
M. p. beccarii
N New Guinea
M. p. pusio
SE New Guinea, Bismarck Archipelago
M. p. harterti
Fergusson I
M. p. stresemanni
Misima I, Tagula I
Micropsitta keiensis (Yellow-capped Pygmy Parrot)
M. k. keiensis
Kei Is, Aru Is
M. k. chloroxantha
W Papuan islands, NW New Guinea
M. k. viridipectus
S New Guinea
Micropsitta geelvinkiana (Geelvink Pygmy Parrot)
M. g. geelvinkiana
Numfor I
M. g. misoriensis
Biak I
Micropsitta meeki (Meek's Pygmy Parrot)
M. m. meeki
Admiralty Is
M. m. proxima
St Matthias Is, Squally I
Micropsitta finschii (Finsch's Pygmy Parrot)
M. f. viridifrons
New Hanover, New Ireland, Lihir Is
M. f. finschii
Ugi I, San Cristobal I, Rennell I
M. f. aolae
Guadalcanal I, Malaita I, Russell I
M. f. tristami
Vella Lavella I, Kulambangra I, Rendova I
M. f. nanina
Bougainville I, Choiseul I, Ysabel I
Micropsitta bruijnii (Red-breasted Pygmy Parrot)
M. b. pileata
Buru I, Ceram I
M. b. bruijnii
New Guinea
M. b. necopinata
New Britain, New Ireland
M. b. rosea
Bougainville I, Guadalcanal I, Kulambangra I

OPOPSITTA

Opopsitta gulielmitertii (Orange-breasted Fig Parrot)
  O. g. gulielmitertii
    Salawati I, NW New Guinea
  O. g. nigrifrons
    N New Guinea
  O. g. ramuensis
    Ramu R, N New Guinea
  O. g. amabilis
    NE New Guinea
  O. g. suavissima
    SE New Guinea
  O. g. fuscifrons
    S New Guinea
  O. g. melanogenia
    Aru Is

Opopsitta diophthalma (Double-eyed Fig Parrot)
  O. d. diophthalma
    W New Guinea & islands
  O. d. coccineifrons
    E & NE New Guinea
  O. d. aruensis
    Aru Is, S New Guinea
  O. d. virago
    Goodenough I, Fergusson I
  O. d. inseparabilis
    Tagula I
  O. d. marshalli
    Cape York Peninsula
  O. d. macleayana
    coast of N Queensland
  O. d. coxeni
    coast of N New South Wales

PSITTACULIROSTRIS

Psittaculirostris desmarestii (Desmarest's Fig Parrot)
  P. d. blythii
    Misol I
  P. d. occidentalis
    Salawati I, Batanta I, NW New Guinea
  P. d. desmarestii
    NW New Guinea
  P. d. intermedia
    Onin peninsula, NW New Guinea
  P. d. godmani
    S New Guinea
  P. d. cervicalis
    SE New Guinea

Psittaculirostris edwardsii (Edwards' Fig Parrot)
  NE New Guinea

Psittaculirostris salvadorii (Salvadori's Fig Parrot)
  NW New Guinea

BOLBOPSITTACUS

Bolbopsittacus lunulatus (Guaiabero)
  B. l. lunulatus
    Luzon I
  B. l. intermedius
    Leyte I
  B. l. callainipictus
    Samar I
  B. l. mindanensis
    Mindanao I, Panaon I

PSITTINUS

Psittinus cyanurus (Blue-rumped Parrot)
  P. c. cyanurus
    SW Thailand, Malaysia, Sumatra, Borneo
  P. c. pontius
    Siberut I, Sipora I, Mentawei Is
  P. c. abbotti
    Simalur I, Siumat I

PSITTACELLA

Psittacella brehmii (Brehm's Parrot)
  P. b. brehmii
    NW New Guinea
  P. b. intermixta
    WC New Guinea
  P. b. harterti
    E New Guinea
  P. b. pallida
    S & SE New Guinea

Psittacella picta (Painted Parrot)
  P. p. picta
    SE New Guinea
  P. p. excelsa
    C New Guinea
  P. p. lorentzi
    WC New Guinea

Psittacella modesta (Modest Parrot)
  P. m. modesta
    NW New Guinea
  P. m. collaris
    WC New Guinea
  P. m. subcollaris
    C New Guinea

Psittacella madaraszi (Maderasz's Parrot)
  P. m. major
    WC New Guinea
  P. m. hallstromi
    C New Guinea
  P. m. huonensis
    E New Guinea
  P. m. maderaszi
    SE New Guinea

GEOFFROYUS

Geoffroyus geoffroyi (Red-cheeked Parrot)
  G. g. floresianus
    Lombok I, Sumbawa I, Flores I, Sumba I
  G. g. geoffroyi
    Timor I, Wetar I

G. g. cyanicollis
  N Moluccas
G. g. obiensis
  C Moluccas
G.g. rhodops
  S Moluccas
G. g. explorator
  Goram I
G. g. keyensis
  Kei Is
G. g. timorlaoensis
  Tenimber Is
G. g. aruensis
  Aru Is, S New Guinea, NE Queensland
G. g. orientalis
  NE New Guinea
G. g. sudestiensis
  Misima I, Tagula I
G. g. cyanicarpus
  Rossel I
G. g. minor
  N New Guinea
G. g. jobiensis
  Japen I, Meos Num I
G. g. mysoriensis
  Biak I, Numfor I
G. g. pucherani
  W Papuan islands, NW New Guinea
Geoffroyus simplex (Blue-collared Parrot)
G. s. simplex
  NW New Guinea
G. s. buergersi
  C & SE New Guinea
Geoffroyus heteroclitus (Singing Parrot)
G. h. heteroclitus
  Lihir Is, New Ireland, New Britain,
  Solomon Is
G. h. hyacinthinus
  Rennell I

PRIONITURUS
Prioniturus luconensis (Green Racket-tailed Parrot)
  Luzon I, Marinduque I
Prioniturus discurus (Blue-crowned Racket-tailed Parrot)
P. d. discurus
  Mindanao I, Basilan I, Luzon I
P. d. whiteheadi
  Negros I, Bohol I, Samar I, Leyte I,
  Masbate I, Cebu I
P. d. nesophilus
  Catanduanes I, Sibuyan I, Tablas I
P. d. mindorensis
  Mindoro I
P. d. platenae
  Palawan I, Balabac I
Prioniturus montanus (Mountain Racket-tailed Parrot)

P. m. montanus
  Luzon I
P. m. verticalis
  Sulu Archipelago
P. m. waterstradti
  Mindanao I
P. m. malindangensis
  Mt Malindang, Mindanao I
Prioniturus flavicans (Red-spotted Racket-tailed Parrot)
  N Celebes
Prioniturus platurus (Golden-mantled Racket-tailed Parrot)
P. p. platurus
  Celebes, Togian I, Peleng I, Banggai I
P. p. talautensis
  Talaut Is
P. p. sinerubris
  Taliabu I
Prioniturus mada (Buru Racket-tailed Parrot)
  Buru I

TANYGNATHUS
Tanygnathus megalorhynchos (Great-billed Parrot)
T. m. megalorhynchos
  Talaut Is, Sanghir Is, N & C Moluccas
T. m. affinis
  S Moluccas
T. m. subaffinis
  Tenimber Is
T. m. hellmayri
  W Timor I, Semao I
T. m. viridipennis
  Kalaotua I, Madu I
T. m. djampeae
  Djampea I, Kalao I
T. m. floris
  Flores I
T. m. sumbensis
  Sumba I
Tanygnathus lucionensis (Blue-naped Parrot)
T. l. lucionensis
  Luzon I, Mindoro I
T. l. hybridus
  Polillo Is
T. l. talautensis
  C & S Philippine Is, Palawan I, Sulu
  Archipelago
Tanygnathus sumatranus (Müller's Parrot)
T. s. duponti
  Luzon I
T. s. freeri
  Polillo Is
T. s. everetti
  Panay I, Samar I, Leyte I, Negros I,
  Mindanao I

T. s. burbidgii
Sulu Archipelago
T. s. sangirensis
Sanghir Is, Talaut Is
T. s. incognitus
Banggai I, Peleng I
T. s. sumatranus
Celebes, Muna I, Buton I
Tanygnathus heterurus (Rufous-tailed Parrot)
Celebes?
Tanygnathus gramineus (Blacklored Parrot)
Buru I

ECLECTUS
Eclectus roratus (Eclectus Parrot)
E. r. vosmaeri
N & C Moluccas
E. r. roratus
S Moluccas
E. r. westermani
not known
E. r. cornelia
Sumba I
E. r. riedeli
Tenimber Is
E. r. polychloros
Kei Is, New Guinea & islands
E. r. biaki
Biak I
E. r. aruensis
Aru Is
E. r. macgillivrayi
NE Queensland
E. r. solomonensis
Admiralty Is, Bismarck Archipelago,
Solomon Is

PSITTRICHAS
Psittrichas fulgidus (Pesquet's Parrot)
Mts of New Guinea

PROSOPEIA
Prosopeia tabuensis (Red Shining Parrot)
P. t. atrogularis
Vanua Levu I, Kio I
P. t. koroensis
Koro I
P. t. taviunensis
Taviuni I, Ngamea I
P. t. tabuensis
Ngau I, Eua I
P. t. splendens
Kandavu I
Prosopeia personata (Masked Shining Parrot)
Viti Levu I

ALISTERUS
Alisterus scapularis (Australian King Parrot)

A. s. minor
NE Queensland
A. s. scapularis
Eastern Australia
Alisterus chloropterus (Green-winged King Parrot)
A. c. moszkowskii
N New Guinea
A. c. callopterus
C New Guinea
A. c. chloropterus
E New Guinea
Alisterus amboinensis (Amboina King Parrot)
A. a. amboinensis
Ambon I, Ceram I
A. a. sulaensis
Sula Is
A. a. versicolor
Peleng I
A. a. buruensis
Buru I
A. a. hypophonius
Halmahera I
A. a. dorsalis
NW New Guinea & islands

APROSMICTUS
Aprosmictus erythropterus (Red-winged Parrot)
A. e. papua
S New Guinea
A. e. coccineopterus
N Australia
A. e. erythropterus
interior Eastern Australia
Aprosmictus jonquillaceus (Timor Red-winged Parrot)
A. j. jonquillaceus
Timor I
A. j. wetterensis
Wetar I

POLYTELIS
Polytelis swainsonii (Superb Parrot)
interior New South Wales, N Victoria
Polytelis anthopeplus (Regent Parrot)
P. a. anthopeplus
NW Victoria
P. a. westralis
SW Australia
Polytelis alexandrae (Princess Parrot)
interior C & Western Australia

PURPUREICEPHALUS
Purpureicephalus spurius (Red-capped Parrot)
SW Australia

BARNARDIUS
Barnardius barnardi (Mallee Ringneck Parrot)
B. b. macgillivrayi
NW Queensland, E Northern Territory
B. b. whitei
Flinders Range, South Australia
B. b. barnardi
interior of SE Australia
Barnardius zonarius (Port Lincoln Parrot)
B. z. occidentalis
NW Western Australia
B. z. semitorquatus
SW Western Australia
B.z. dundasi
SW Australia
B. z. myrtae
C Australia
B. z. zonarius
S Australia

PLATYCERCUS
Platycercus caledonicus (Green Rosella)
Tasmania, Bass Strait
Platycercus elegans (Crimson Rosella)
P. e. nigrescens
NE Queensland
P. e. elegans
SE Queensland to SE South Australia
P. e. melanoptera
Kangaroo I
P. e. fleurieuensis
Fleurieu Peninsula, S Australia
Platycercus flaveolus (Yellow Rosella)
interior of SE Australia
Platycercus adelaidae (Adelaide Rosella)
S South Australia
Platycercus eximius (Eastern Rosella)
P. e. cecilae
SE Queensland, NE New South Wales
P. e. eximius
SE Australia
P. e. diemenensis
Tasmania
Platycercus adscitus (Pale-headed Rosella)
P. a. adscitus
N Queensland
P. a. mackaiensis
NE Queensland
P. a. amathusiae
NE Queensland
P. a. palliceps
C Queensland to N New South Wales
Platycercus venustus (Northern Rosella)
NW & N Australia
Platycercus icterotis (Western Rosella)
P. i. icterotis
coast of SW Australia

P. i. xanthogenys
interior of SW Australia

PSEPHOTUS
Psephotus haematonotus (Red-rumped Parrot)
P. h. caeruleus
Innamincka, South Australia
P. h. haematonotus
interior of SE Australia
Psephotus varius (Mulga Parrot)
P. v. varius
interior of S Australia
P. v. orientalis
SW New South Wales, W Victoria
Psephotus haematogaster (Blue Bonnet)
P. h. narethae
SE Western Australia
P. h. pallescens
Lake Eyre Basin
P. h. haematorrhous
S Queensland, N New South Wales
P. h. haematogaster
W & S New South Wales, NW Victoria, SE South Australia
Psephotus chrysopterygius (Golden-shouldered Parrot)
P. c. chrysopterygius
S Cape York Peninsula
P. c. dissimilis
NE Northern Territory
Psephotus pulcherrimus (Paradise Parrot)
C & S Queensland, N New South Wales

CYANORAMPHUS
Cyanoramphus unicolor (Antipodes Green Parakeet)
Antipodes Is
Cyanoramphus novaezelandiae (Red-fronted Parakeet)
C. n. novaezelandiae
New Zealand, Auckland I
C. n. cyanurus
Kermadec Is
C. n. chathamensis
Chatham I
C. n. hochstetteri
Antipodes Is
C. n. cookii
Norfolk I
C. n. saissetti
New Caledonia
Cyanoramphus auriceps (Yellow-fronted Parakeet)
C. a. auriceps
New Zealand, Stewart I, Auckland I
C. a. forbesi
Chatham I

Cyanoramphus malherbi (Orange-fronted Parakeet)
South I, New Zealand
Cyanoramphus cornutus (Horned Parakeet)
C. c. cornutus
New Caledonia
C. c. uvaeensis
Ouvea I

NEOPHEMA
Neophema bourkii (Bourke's Parrot)
interior of C & S Australia
Neophema chrysostoma (Blue-winged Parrot)
SE Australia, Tasmania
Neophema elegans (Elegant Parrot)
SW & SE Australia
Neophema petrophila (Rock Parrot)
N. p. petrophila
coast of W Australia
N. p. zietzi
coast of S Australia
Neophema chrysogaster (Orange-bellied Parrot)
Tasmania, coast of W Victoria
Neophema pulchella (Turquoise Parrot)
SE Queensland to N Victoria
Neophema splendida (Scarlet-chested Parrot)
interior of S Australia

LATHAMUS
Lathamus discolor (Swift Parrot)
SE Australia, Tasmania

MELOPSITTACUS
Melopsittacus undulatus (Budgerigar)
Australia

PEZOPORUS
Pezoporus wallicus (Ground Parrot)
P. w. flaviventris
coast of SW Australia
P. w. wallicus
SE Australia, W Tasmania

GEOPSITTACUS
Geopsittacus occidentalis (Night Parrot)
interior of Australia

CORACOPSIS
Coracopsis vasa (Vasa Parrot)
C. v. drouhardi
W Madagascar
C. v. vasa
E Madagascar
C. v. comorensis
Great Comoro I, Moheli I, Anjouan I
Coracopsis nigra (Black Parrot)
C. n. libs
W Madagascar

C. n. nigra
E Madagascar
C. n. sibilans
Great Comoro I, Anjouan I
C. n. barklyi
Praslin I

PSITTACUS
Psittacus erithacus (Grey Parrot)
P. e. timneh
S Guinea to Ivory Coast
P. e. erithacus
SE Ivory Coast to W Kenya & N Angola
P. e. princeps
Principé I, Fernando Po I

POICEPHALUS
Poicephalus robustus (Cape Parrot)
P. r. fuscicollis
Gambia to N Ghana & Togo
P. r. suahelicus
Angola to S Zaire, Tanzania & Mozambique
P. r. robustus
E Cape Province to N Natal
Poicephalus gulielmi (Jardine's Parrot)
P. g. fantiensis
Liberia to Cameroun
P. g. gulielmi
S Cameroun to N Angola
P. g. permistus
C Kenya
P. g. massaicus
S Kenya, N Tanzania
Poicephalus cryptoxanthus (Brown-headed Parrot)
P. c. tanganyikae
C. Tanzania
P. c. zanzibaricus
Zanzibar I, Pemba I
P. c. cryptoxanthus
Natal to SE Kenya
Poicephalus crassus (Niam-Niam Parrot)
E Cameroun to SW Sudan
Poicephalus senegalus (Senegal Parrot)
P. s. senegalus
Senegal to Guinea, S Mali
P. s. versteri
Ivory Coast, Ghana to Nigeria
P. s. mesotypus
E & NE Nigeria, SW Chad, N Cameroun
Poicephalus rufiventris (Red-bellied Parrot)
P. r. rufiventris
C Ethiopia to NE Tanzania
P. r. pallidus
Somalia, E Ethiopia
Poicephalus meyeri (Meyer's Parrot)
P. m. meyeri
S Chad, NE Cameroun to W Ethiopia

P. m. saturatus
  Uganda, Kenya, W Tanzania
P. m. matschiei
  SE Kenya to Zambia, Malawi
P. m. transvaalensis
  N Mozambique, Transvaal
P. m. reichenowi
  N & C Angola, SW Zaire
P. m. damarensis
  S Angola, SW Africa
Poicephalus rueppellii (Rüppell's Parrot)
  S Angola, N Namibia
Poicephalus flavifrons (Yellow-faced Parrot)
P. f. flavifrons
  N & C Ethiopia
P. f. aurantiiceps
  SW Ethiopia

AGAPORNIS
Agapornis cana (Grey-headed Lovebird)
A. c. cana
  coast of Madagascar
A. c. ablectanea
  SW Madagascar
Agapornis pullaria (Red-faced Lovebird)
A. p. guineensis
  Guinea to N Zaire
A. p. pullaria
  S Ethiopia & S Sudan to NW Tanzania
A. p. ugandae
  SW Ethiopia to NW Tanzania
Agapornis taranta (Black-winged Lovebird)
  Ethiopia
Agapornis swinderniana (Black-collared Lovebird)
A. s. swinderniana
  Liberia
A. s. zenkeri
  Cameroun, Gabon to C Zaire
A. s. emini
  E Zaire, W Uganda
Agapornis roseicollis (Peach-faced Lovebird)
A. r. roseicollis
  Namibia, NW Cape Province
A. r. catumbella
  S Angola
Agapornis fischeri (Fischer's Lovebird)
  S Kenya, N Tanzania
Agapornis personata (Masked Lovebird)
  NE Tanzania
Agapornis lilianae (Nyasa Lovebird)
  NW Mozambique to E Zambia
Agapornis nigrigenis (Black-cheeked Lovebird)
  SW Zambia

LORICULUS
Loriculus vernalis (Vernal Hanging Parrot)
  SW India to S Vietnam
Loriculus beryllinus (Ceylon Hanging Parrot)
  Sri Lanka
Loriculus philippensis (Philippine Hanging Parrot)
L. p. philippensis
  Luzon I, Marinduque I
L. p. mindorensis
  Mindoro I
L. p. bournsi
  Tablas I, Romblon I, Sibuyan I
L. p. panayensis
  Ticao I, Masbate I, Panay I
L. p. regulus
  Guimaras I, Negros I
L. p. chrysonotus
  Cebu I
L. p. worcesteri
  Samar I, Leyte I, Bohol I
L. p. siquijorensis
  Siquijor I
L. p. apicalis
  Mindanao I
L. p. dohertyi
  Basilan I
L. p. bonapartei
  Jolo I, Bongas I, Tawitawi Is
Loriculus galgulus (Blue-crowned Hanging Parrot)
  Malaysia, Borneo, Sumatra
Loriculus stigmatus (Celebes Hanging Parrot)
L. s. stigmatus
  Celebes
L. s. quadricolor
  Togian I
L. s. croconotus
  Butung I, Muna I
Loriculus amabilis (Moluccan Hanging Parrot)
L. a. amabilis
  Halmahera I, Batjan I
L. a. catamene
  Gt Sangi I
L. a. sclateri
  Sula Is
L. a. ruber
  Peling I, Banggai I
Loriculus exilis (Green Hanging Parrot)
  N & SE Celebes
Loriculus flosculus (Wallace's Hanging Parrot)
  Flores I

164 ***Loriculus pusillus* (Yellow-throated Hanging Parrot)**
Java, Bali I
***Loriculus aurantiifrons* (Orange-fronted Hanging Parrot)**
L. a. aurantiifrons
Misol I
L. a. batavorum
Waigeu I, W Papuan Is, NW New Guinea
L. a. meeki
New Guinea, Fergusson I, Goodenough I
L. a. tener
Bismarck Archipelago

PSITTACULA
***Psittacula eupatria* (Alexandrine Parakeet)**
P. e. eupatria
Sri Lanka, S India
P. e. nipalensis
E Afghanistan to Assam
P. e. magnirostris
Andaman Is
P. e. avensis
E Assam, Burma
P. e. siamensis
N & W Thailand, Indochina
***Psittacula krameri* (Rose-ringed Parakeet)**
P. k. krameri
Senegal to S Sudan
P. k. parvirostris
Sudan to NW Somalia
P. k. borealis
W Pakistan, N India to C Burma
P. k. manillensis
S India, Sri Lanka
***Psittacula echo* (Mauritius Parakeet)**
Mauritius
***Psittacula himalayana* (Slatyheaded Parakeet)**
P. h. himalayana
E Afghanistan to N Assam
P. h. finschii
S Assam to SW China, N Indochina
***Psittacula cyanocephala* (Plum-headed Parakeet)**
India, Sri Lanka
***Psittacula roseata* (Blossom-headed Parakeet)**
P. r. roseata
N Assam, N Burma
P. r. juneae
S Assam, S Burma to Indochina
***Psittacula intermedia* (Intermediate Parrot)**
N India
***Psittacula columboides* (Malabar Parakeet)**
SW India

***Psittacula calthorpae* (Emerald-collared Parakeet)**
Sri Lanka
***Psittacula derbiana* (Derbyan Parakeet)**
NE Assam, SE Tibet
***Psittacula alexandri* (Moustached Parakeet)**
P. a. alexandri
Java, Bali I
P. a. fasciata
N India to S China, Indochina
P. a. abbotti
Andaman Is
P. a. cala
Simalur I
P. a. major
Lasia I, Babi I
P. a. perionca
Nias I
P. a. dammermani
Karimon Java I
P. a. kangeanensis
Kangean I
***Psittacula caniceps* (Blyth's Parakeet)**
Nicobar Is
***Psittacula longicauda* (Long-tailed Parakeet)**
P. l. tytleri
Andaman Is
P. l. nicobarica
Nicobar Is
P. l. longicauda
Malaysia, Borneo, Sumatra
P. l. defontainei
Natuna Is, Riau Archipelago
P. l. modesta
Enggano I

ANODORHYNCHUS
***Anodorhynchus hyacinthinus* (Hyacinth Macaw)**
SC Brazil
***Anodorhynchus glaucus* (Glaucous Macaw)**
Paraguay, NE Argentina
***Anodorhynchus leari* (Indigo Macaw)**
NE Brazil

CYANOPSITTA
***Cyanopsitta spixii* (Spix's Macaw)**
EC Brazil

ARA
***Ara ararauna* (Blue and Yellow Macaw)**
E Panama to Paraguay & S Brazil
***Ara caninde* (Wagler's Macaw)**
Bolivia, Paraguay, N Argentina
***Ara militaris* (Military Macaw)**

A. m. mexicana
  N & C Mexico
A. m. militaris
  W Colombia, NE Ecuador, N Peru
A. m. boliviana
  Bolivia, NW Argentina
Ara ambigua (Buffon's Macaw)
A. a. ambigua
  Nicaragua to W Colombia
A. a. guayaquilensis
  W Ecuador
Ara macao (Scarlet Macaw)
  SC Mexico to Bolivia & C Brazil
Ara chloroptera (Green-winged Macaw)
  E Panama & N Argentina
Ara rubrogenys (Red-fronted Macaw)
  Bolivia
Ara auricollis (Yellow-collared Macaw)
  S Brazil, NW Argentina
Ara severa (Chestnut-fronted Macaw)
A. s. castaneifrons
  E Panama to N Bolivia, C Brazil
A. s. severa
  E Venezuela, the Guianas, NW Brazil
Ara manilata (Red-bellied Macaw)
  S Colombia to N & C Brazil
Ara maracana (Illiger's Macaw)
  E Brazil, NE Argentina
Ara couloni (Blue-headed Macaw)
  E Peru
Ara nobilis (Red-shouldered Macaw)
A. n. nobilis
  the Guianas, E Venezuela, NE Brazil
A. n. cumanensis
  C Brazil
A. n. longipennis
  S Brazil
ARATINGA
Aratinga acuticaudata (Blue-crowned Conure)
A. a. haemorrhous
  E Colombia, N Venezuela to C & SW Brazil
A. a. neoxena
  Margarita I
A. a. acuticaudata
  E Bolivia to N Argentina & Uruguay
A. a. neumanni
  C Bolivia
Aratinga guarouba (Golden Conure)
  NE Brazil
Aratinga holochlora (Green Conure)
A. h. brewsteri
  NW Mexico
A. h. strenua
  W Mexico to NW Nicaragua
A. h. holochlora
  E & S Mexico

A. h. rubritorquis
  E Guatemala, N Nicaragua
A. h. brevipes
  Socorro I
Aratinga finschi (Finsch's Conure)
  S Nicaragua to W Panama
Aratinga wagleri (Red-fronted Conure)
A. w. wagleri
  NW Venezuela, Colombia
A. w. transilis
  N Venezuela, E Colombia
A. w. frontata
  W Ecuador, W Peru
A. w. minor
  C & S Peru
Aratinga mitrata (Mitred Conure)
A. m. mitrata
  C Peru to NW Argentina
A. m. alticola
  C Peru
Aratinga erythrogenys (Red-masked Conure)
  W Ecuador, NW Peru
Aratinga leucophthalmus (White-eyed Conure)
A. l. leucophthalmus
  the Guianas to Paraguay, Uruguay
A. l. callogenys
  E Ecuador, NE Peru, NW Brazil
A. l. propinquus
  SE Brazil, NE Argentina
A. l. nicefori
  S Colombia
Aratinga chloroptera (Hispaniolan Conure)
  Hispaniola
Aratinga euops (Cuban Conure)
  Cuba
Aratinga auricapilla (Golden-capped Conure)
A. a. auricapilla
  NE Brazil
A. a. aurifrons
  SE Brazil
Aratinga jandaya (Jandaya Conure)
  NE Brazil
Aratinga solstitialis (Sun Conure)
  the Guianas, NE Brazil
Aratinga weddellii (Dusky-headed Conure)
  W Amazonia
Aratinga nana (Olive-throated Conure)
A. n. nana
  Jamaica
A. n. astec
  E Mexico to SE Costa Rica
A. n. vicinalis
  NE Mexico
Aratinga canicularis (Orange-fronted Conure)

166

A. c. eburnirostrum
  SW Mexico
A. c. clarae
  WC & SW Mexico
A. c. canicularis
  SW Mexico to W Costa Rica
Aratinga pertinax (Brown-throated Conure)
A. p. ocularis
  W Panama
A. p. pertinax
  Curaçao I
A. p. xanthogenia
  Bonaire I
A. p. arubensis
  Aruba I
A. p. aeruginosa
  N Colombia, NW Venezuela
A. p. griseipecta
  NE Colombia
A. p. lehmanni
  E Colombia
A. p. tortugensis
  Tortuga I
A. p. margaritensis
  Margarita I, Los Frailes I
A. p. venezuelae
  Venezuela
A. p. chrysophrys
  SE Venezuela, S Guyana, NE Brazil
A. p. surinama
  NE Venezuela, French Guiana, Surinam
A. p. chrysogenys
  NW Brazil
A. p. paraensis
  NC Brazil
Aratinga cactorum (Cactus Conure)
A. c. caixana
  NE Brazil
A. c. cactorum
  NE Brazil (South of A. c. caixana)
Aratinga aurea (Peach-fronted Conure)
A. a. aurea
  C & S Brazil, E Bolivia
A. a. major
  S Bolivia, NW Argentina

NANDAYUS
Nandayus nenday (Nanday Conure)
  SE Bolivia, Paraguay, N Argentina

LEPTOSITTACA
Leptosittaca branickii (Golden-plumed Conure)
  Colombia, Ecuador, Peru

OGNORHYNCHUS
Ognorhynchus icterotis (Yellow-eared Conure)
  S Colombia, N Ecuador

RHYNCHOPSITTA
Rhynchopsitta pachyrhyncha (Thick-billed Parrot)
R. p. pachyrhyncha
  NW & C Mexico
R. p. terrisi
  Nuevo Leon, Mexico

CYANOLISEUS
Cyanoliseus patagonus (Patagonian Conure)
C. p. byroni
  C Chile
C. p. andinus
  NW Argentina
C. p. patagonus
  C & S Argentina

PYRRHURA
Pyrrhura cruentata (Blue-throated Conure)
  E Brazil
Pyrrhura devillei (Blaze-winged Conure)
  E Bolivia, SW Brazil
Pyrrhura frontalis (Maroon-bellied Conure)
P. f. frontalis
  SE Brazil
P. f. kriegi
  S & SE Brazil
P. f. chiripepe
  Paraguay, Uruguay, N Argentina
Pyrrhura perlata (Pearly Conure)
P. p. lepida
  NE Brazil
P. p. coerulescens
  NE Brazil
P. p. anerythra
  C Brazil
P. p. perlata
  unknown
Pyrrhura rhodogaster (Crimson-bellied Conure)
  C Brazil
Pyrrhura molinae (Green-cheeked Conure)
P. m. molinae
  E Bolivia
P. m. phoenicura
  NE Bolivia, SW Brazil
P. m. sordida
  S Brazil
P. m. restricta
  Chiquitos, Bolivia
P. m. australis
  S Bolivia, NW Argentina
P. m. hypoxantha
  SW Brazil
Pyrrhura leucotis (White-eared Conure)
P. l. emma
  N Venezuela

P. l. auricularis
NE Venezuela
P.l. pfrimeri
NE Brazil
P. l. griseipectus
NE Brazil
P. l. leucotis
E & SE Brazil
Pyrrhura picta (Painted Conure)
P. p. subandina
NW Colombia
P. p. caeruleiceps
N Colombia
P. p. roseifrons
NW Brazil
P. p. picta
E Venezuela, the Guianas, N Brazil
P. p. amazonum
N Brazil
P. p. pantchenkoi
NW Venezuela
P. p. microtera
NC Brazil
P. p. lucianii
E Peru, Bolivia, W Brazil
Pyrrhura viridicata (Santa Marta Conure)
N Colombia
**Pyrrhura egregia (Fiery-shouldered
Conure)**
P. e. egregia
W Guyana, SE Venezuela
P. e. obscura
Roraima, N Brazil
Pyrrhura melanura (Maroon-tailed Conure)
P. m. pacifica
SW Colombia
P.m. melanura
NE Peru, NW Brazil, S Venezuela
P. m. souancei
S Colombia, E Ecuador, N Peru
P. m. berlepschi
E Peru
P. m. chapmani
.S Colombia
Pyrrhura rupicola (Black-capped Conure)
P. r. rupicola
C Peru
P. r. sandiae
SE Peru, W Brazil, N Bolivia
Pyrrhura albipectus (White-necked Conure)
SE Ecuador
**Pyrrhura calliptera (Brown-breasted
Conure)**
C Colombia
Pyrrhura hoematotis (Red-eared Conure)
P. h. immarginata
N Venezuela

P. h. hoematotis
NC Venezuela
**Pyrrhura rhodocephala (Rose-crowned
Conure)**
W Venezuela
Pyrrhura hoffmanni (Hoffman's Conure)
P. h. hoffmanni
S Costa Rica
P. h. gaudens
W Panama

ENICOGNATHUS
**Enicognathus ferrugineus (Austral
Conure)**
E. f. minor
S Chile, SW Argentina
E. f. ferrugineus
S Chile, S Argentina, Tierra del Fuego
**Enicognathus leptorhynchus (Slender-
billed Conure)**
C Chile

MYIOPSITTA
Myiopsitta monachus (Monk Parakeet)
M. m. luchsi
C Bolivia
M. m. cotorra
SE Bolivia, S Brazil, N Argentina
M. m. calita
W Argentina
M. m. monachus
SE Brazil, Uruguay, NE Argentina

BOLBORHYNCHUS
Bolborhynchus aymara (Sierra Parakeet)
E Andes from C Bolivia to NW Argentina
**Bolborhynchus aurifrons (Mountain
Parakeet)**
B. a. robertsi
NW Peru
B. a. aurifrons
coast of W Andes of C Peru
B. a. margaritae
S Peru to N Chile & NW Argentina
B. a. rubrirostris
WC Argentina, C Chile
Bolborhynchus lineola (Barred Parakeet)
B. l. lineola
S Mexico to W Panama
B. l. tigrinus
NW Venezuela to SW Colombia, C Peru
**Bolborhynchus orbygnesius (Andean
Parakeet)**
Peru & N Bolivia
**Bolborhynchus ferrugineifrons (Rufous-
fronted Parakeet)**
WC Colombia

Forpus cyanopygius (Mexican Parrotlet)
F. c. insularis
Tres Marias Is
F. c. pallidus
SE Sonora, NW Mexico
F. c. cyanopygius
NW Mexico
Forpus passerinus (Green-rumped Parrotlet)
F. p. cyanophanes
N Colombia
F. p. viridissimus
Trinidad, N Venezuela
F. p. passerinus
the Guianas
F. p. cyanochlorus
N Brazil
F. p. deliciosus
NC & E Brazil
Forpus xanthopterygius (Blue-winged Parrotlet)
F. x. spengeli
NW Colombia
F. x. crassirostris
SE Colombia, NE Peru, NW Brazil
F. x. olallae
NW Brazil
F. x. flavissimus
NE Brazil
F. x. flavescens
SE & E Peru, E Bolivia
F. x. xanthopterygius
C & EC Brazil to Paraguay & NE Argentina
Forpus conspicillatus (Spectacled Parrotlet)
F. c. conspicillatus
E Panama, N & C Colombia
F. c. metae
C Colombia to W Venezuela
F. c. caucae
SW Colombia
Forpus sclateri (Sclater's Parrotlet)
F. s. eidos
S Venezuela & the Guianas, N Brazil, E Colombia
F. s. sclateri
N & W Brazil to S Colombia, E Peru & N Bolivia
Forpus coelestis (Pacific Parrotlet)
W Ecuador, NW Peru
Forpus xanthops (Yellow-faced Parrotlet)
NE Peru

BROTOGERIS
Brotogeris tirica (Plain Parakeet)
E & SE Brazil
Brotogeris versicolorus (Canary-winged Parakeet)

B. v. versicolurus
E Ecuador to S French Guiana & N Brazil
B. v. chiriri
N Bolivia, N Argentina to E & S Brazil
B. v. behni
C & S Bolivia, NW Argentina
Brotogeris pyrrhopterus (Grey-cheeked Parakeet)
W Ecuador, NW Peru
Brotogeris jugularis (Orange-chinned Parakeet)
B. j. jugularis
SW Mexico to N Colombia & NW Venezuela
B. j. exsul
SE Colombia, W Venezuela
Brotogeris cyanoptera (Cobalt-winged Parakeet)
B. c. cyanoptera
W Upper Amazonia
B. c. gustavi
N Peru
B. c. beniensis
N Bolivia
Brotogeris chrysopterus (Golden-winged Parakeet)
B. c. chrysopterus
E Venezuela, N Brazil, the Guianas
B. c. tuipara
N & NE Brazil
B. c. chrysosema
Madeira River, N Brazil
B. c. solimoensis
Upper Amazon River, N Brazil
B. c. tenuifrons
NW Brazil
Brotogeris sanctithomae (Tui Parakeet)
B. s. sanctithomae
C & W Brazil, SE Colombia, NE Peru
B. s. takatsukasae
NE Brazil

NANNOPSITTACA
Nannopsittaca panychlora (Tepui Parrotlet)
E Venezuela, W Guyana

TOUIT
Touit batavica (Seven-coloured Parrotlet)
N Venezuela, the Guianas, Trinidad
Touit huetii (Scarlet-shouldered Parrotlet)
C Colombia, N Venezuela, NE Brazil, E Ecuador
Touit dilectissima (Red-winged Parrotlet)
T. d. costaricensis
SE Costa Rica, W Panama
T. d. dilectissima
E Panama, N & W Colombia, NW Ecuador
Touit purpurata (Sapphire-rumped Parrotlet)

T. p. purpurata
S Venezuela, the Guianas, NE Brazil
T. p. viridiceps
SE Colombia, NW & NC Brazil
Touit melanonota (Brown-backed Parrrotlet)
SE Brazil
Touit surda (Golden-tailed Parrotlet)
T. s. ruficauda
Recife, E Brazil
T. s. surda
SE Brazil
Touit stictoptera (Spot-winged Parrotlet)
SW Colombia, W Ecuador

PIONITES
Pionites melanocephala (Black-headed Caique)
P. m. pallida
S Colombia to NE Peru
P. m. melanocephala
E & S Venezuela, the Guianas, N Brazil
Pionites leucogaster (White-bellied Caique)
P. l. leucogaster
N Brazil
P. l. xanthurus
NW Brazil
P. l. xanthomeria
W Brazil, E Ecuador

PIONOPSITTA
Pionopsitta pileata (Pileated Parrot)
SE Brazil, E Paraguay, NE Argentina
Pionopsitta haematotis (Brown-hooded Parrot)
P. h. haematotis
S Mexico to W Panama
P. h. coccinicollaris
E Panama, NW Colombia
Pionopsitta pulchra (Rose-faced Parrot)
W Colombia, W Ecuador
Pionopsitta barrabandi (Barraband's Parrot)
P. b. barrabandi
N Upper Amazonia
P. b. aurantiigena
W Upper Amazonia
Pionopsitta pyrilia (Saffron-headed Parrot)
E Panama, N Colombia
Pionopsitta caica (Caica Parrot)
E Venezuela, the Guianas, NE Brazil

GYPOPSITTA
Gypopsitta vulturina (Vulturine Parrot)
Guyana, NE Brazil

HAPALOPSITTACA
Hapalopsittaca melanotis (Black-winged Parrot)

H. m. peruviana
C Peru
H. m. melanotis
WC Bolivia
Hapalopsittaca amazonina (Rusty-faced Parrot)
H. a. amazonina
C Colombia to NW Venezuela
H. a. theresae
NW Venezuela
H. a. fuertesi
C Colombia
H. a. pyrrhops
W Ecuador

GRAYDIDASCALUS
Graydidascalus brachyurus (Short-tailed Parrot)
E Ecuador to NE Brazil

PIONUS
Pionus menstruus (Blue-headed Parrot)
P. m. rubrigularis
S Costa Rica to W Ecuador
P. m. menstruus
the Guianas, Upper Amazonia, E Peru
P. m. reichenowi
NE Brazil
Pionus sordidus (Red-billed Parrot)
P. s. ponsi
N Colombia, NW Venezuela
P. s. sordidus
NW Venezuela
P. s. saturatus
N Colombia
P. s. antelius
NE Venezuela
P. s. corallinus
C Colombia to N Bolivia
P. s. mindoensis
W Ecuador
Pionus maximiliani (Scaly-headed Parrot)
P. m. maximiliani
NE Brazil
P. m. melanoblepharus
C Brazil, E Paraguay, NE Argentina
P. m. siy
S Brazil, E Bolivia, Paraguay
P. m. lacerus
NW Argentina
Pionus tumultuosus (Plum-crowned Parrot)
Andes of E Peru & Bolivia
Pionus seniloides (White-headed Parrot)
NW Venezuela to SW Ecuador
Pionus senilis (White-capped Parrot)
E Mexico to W Panama
Pionus chalcopterus (Bronze-winged Parrot)
P. c. chalcopterus
NW Venezuela, NE & C Colombia

P. c. cyanescens
SW Colombia, W Ecuador, NW Peru
Pionus fuscus (Dusky Parrot)
NE Colombia, S Venezuela, the Guianas,
NE Brazil

AMAZONA
Amazona collaria (Yellow-billed Amazon)
Jamaica
Amazona leucocephala (Cuban Amazon)
A. l. palmarum
W Cuba, Isle of Pines
A. l. leucocephala
C & E Cuba
A. l. bahamensis
Bahama Is
A. l. caymanensis
Gd Cayman I
A. l. hesterna
Little Cayman I, Cayman Brac I
Amazona ventralis (Hispaniolan Amazon)
Hispaniola
**Amazona albifrons (White-fronted
Amazon)**
A. a. saltuensis
NW Mexico
A. a. albifrons
WC Mexico to SW Guatemala
A. a. nana
SE Mexico to NW Costa Rica
**Amazona xantholora (Yellow-lored
Amazon)**
Yucatan, SE Mexico & Belize
Amazona agilis (Black-billed Amazon)
Jamaica
Amazona vittata (Puerto Rican Amazon)
Puerto Rico
Amazona tucumana (Tucuman Amazon)
SE Bolivia, N Argentina
Amazona pretrei (Red-spectacled Amazon)
SE Brazil, N Uruguay, NE Argentina
**Amazona viridigenalis (Green-cheeked
Amazon)**
NE Mexico
Amazona finschi (Lilac-crowned Amazon)
A. f. woodi
NW Mexico
A. f. finschi
WC & SW Mexico
Amazona autumnalis (Red-lored Amazon)
A. a. autumnalis
E Mexico to N Nicaragua
A. a. salvini
SE Nicaragua to W Colombia
A. a. lilacina
W Ecuador
A. a. diadema
NW Brazil
Amazona brasiliensis (Red-tailed Amazon)
SE Brazil
**Amazona dufresniana (Blue-cheeked
Amazon)**

A. d. dufresniana
SE Venezuela, the Guianas
A. d. rhodocorytha
E Brazil
Amazona festiva (Festive Amazon)
A. f. bodini
C Venezuela, NW Guyana
A. f. festiva
E Ecuador, NE Peru to C Brazil
Amazona xanthops (Yellow-faced Amazon)
E & C Brazil
**Amazona barbadensis (Yellow-shouldered
Amazon)**
A. b. barbadensis
coast of Venezuela, Aruba I
A. b. rothschildi
Bonaire I, Margarita I
Amazona aestiva (Blue-fronted Amazon)
A. a. aestiva
E Brazil
A. a. xanthopteryx
N & E Bolivia, Paraguay, N Argentina
**Amazona ochrocephala (Yellow-crowned
Amazon)**
A. o. oratrix
SW & S Mexico
A. o. tresmariae
Tres Marias Is
A. o. auropalliata
S Mexico to NW Costa Rica
A. o. parvipes
E Honduras, NE Nicaragua
A. o. belizensis
Belize
A. o. panamensis
W Panama, N Colombia, Pearl Is
A. o. nattereri
S Colombia to E Peru, W Brazil
A. o. xantholaema
Marajo I (N Brazil)
A. o. ochrocephala
W Colombia to Surinam, N Brazil,
Trinidad
**Amazona amazonica (Orange-winged
Amazon)**
A. a. amazonica
Colombia to N Bolivia & C & E Brazil
A. a. tobagensis
Trinidad, Tobago I
**Amazona mercenaria (Scaly-naped
Amazon)**
A. m. canipalliata
NW Venezuela, Colombia, C Ecuador
A. m. mercenaria
N Peru to N Bolivia
Amazona farinosa (Mealy Amazon)
A. f. guatemalae
S Mexico to Honduras

A. f. virenticeps
Nicaragua to W Panama
A. f. inornata
E Panama to NW Ecuador & W Venezuela
A. f. chapmani
SE Colombia to NE Bolivia
A. f. farinosa
S Venezuela, the Guianas, C & E Brazil,
N Bolivia
Amazona vinacea (Vinaceous Amazon)
SE Brazil, NE Argentina
Amazona versicolor (St Lucia Amazon)
St Lucia I
Amazona arausiaca (Red-necked Amazon)
Dominica I
Amazona guildingii (St Vincent Amazon)
St Vincent I
Amazona imperialis (Imperial Amazon)
Dominica I

DEROPTYUS
**Deroptyus accipitrinus (Hawk-headed
Parrot)**
D. a. accipitrinus
the Guianas, S Venezuela, N Brazil,
NE Peru
D. a. fuscifrons
C & NE Brazil

TRICLARIA
**Triclaria malachitacea (Purple-bellied
Parrot)**
SE Brazil

STRIGOPINAE

STRIGOPS
Strigops habroptilus (Kakapo)
S South I, New Zealand

Cuculiformes

70 MUSOPHAGIDAE (TURACOS)

CORYTHAEOLA
Corythaeola cristata (Great Blue Turaco)
Portuguese Guinea to N Angola &
W Kenya

CRINIFER
Crinifer piscator (Grey Plantain-eater)
Senegal to N Zaire
**Crinifer zonurus (Eastern Grey Plantain-
eater)**
N Zaire, Ethiopia, NW Tanzania

CORYTHAIXOIDES
Corythaixoides concolor (Go-away Bird)
C. c. pallidiceps
Cabinda to C Namibia

C. c. concolor   171
S Zaire & Tanzania to S Africa
**Corythaixoides personata (Bare-faced
Go-away Bird)**
C. p. personata
Ethiopia
C. p. leopoldi
E Zaire, Kenya to Zambia, Malawi
**Corythaixoides leucogaster (White-bellied
Go-away Bird)**
Ethiopia to E Tanzania

MUSOPHAGA
Musophaga violacea (Violet Turaco)
Gambia to Nigeria
Musophaga rossae (Lady Ross's Turaco)
N Cameroun to Sudan, N Angola, Zambia

TAURACO
Tauraco corythaix (Knysna Turaco)
T. c. buffoni
Gambia to Sierra Leone
T. c. persa
Ivory Coast to N Angola
T. c. zenkeri
S Cameroun, N Gabon
T. c. schuetii
N Zaire
T. c. emini
NE Zaire, Uganda, SW Sudan
T. c. fischeri
Juba River & SE Kenya
T. c. schalowi
SW Kenya (isolate), C Angola, S Zaire
to Malawi
T. c. chalcolophus
NC Tanzania
T. c. zanzibaricus
Zanzibar I
T. c. livingstonii
E Tanzania to N Natal & SE Zaire (isolate)
T. c. phoebus
E Transvaal
T. c. corythaix
Natal, SE Cape Province
**Tauraco erythrolophus (Red-crested
Turaco)**
SW Zaire, Angola
**Tauraco bannermani (Bannerman's
Turaco)**
N Cameroun
Tauraco macrorhynchus (Crested Turaco)
T. m. macrorhynchus
Sierra Leone to Ivory Coast
T. m. verreauxi
S Nigeria to W Zaire
Tauraco hartlaubi (Hartlaub's Turaco)
Kenya, N Tanzania
Tauraco leucotis (White-cheeked Turaco)

T. l. leucotis
Ethiopia
T. l. donaldsoni
E Ethiopia, W Somalia
Tauraco ruspolii (Prince Ruspoli's Turaco)
S Ethiopia
Tauraco leucolophus (White-crested Turaco)
Central African Republic to S Sudan
Tauraco porphyreolophus (Violet-crested Turaco)
T. p. chlorochlamys
S Kenya to Mozambique
T. p. porphyreolophus
Rhodesia, E Transvaal, Natal
Tauraco johnstoni (Ruwenzori Turaco)
T. j. johnstoni
Ruwenzori Mtns
T. j. kivuensis
Kivu area, E Zaire
T. j. bredoi
Mt Kabobo

71 CUCULIDAE (CUCKOOS)

CUCULINAE

CLAMATOR
Clamator glandarius (Great Spotted Cuckoo)
Spain to Iran, NE & S Africa
Clamator coromandus (Red-winged Crested Cuckoo)
Himalayas to S China, Java, Borneo
Clamator jacobinus (Black & White Cuckoo)
C. j. serratus
Sengal to S Africa, N India, Burma
C. j. jacobinus
S India, Sri Lanka
Clamator levaillanti (Levaillant's Cuckoo)
Senegal to Somalia & S Africa

PACHYCOCCYX
Pachycoccyx audeberti (Thick-billed Cuckoo)
P. a. validus
Guinea to S Sudan, S Zaire, NE Tanzania
P. a. canescens
Angola to Malawi & N Cape Province
P. a. audeberti
Madagascar

CUCULUS
Cuculus crassirostris (Celebes Hawk Cuckoo)
N & C Celebes
Cuculus sparverioides (Large Hawk Cuckoo)
C. s. sparverioides
Himalayas, SE Asia, to Philippine Is & Celebes

C. s. bocki
Malaysia, Sumatra, Borneo
Cuculus varius (Common Hawk Cuckoo)
C. v. varius
India (except NW)
C. v. ciceliae
Sri Lanka
Cuculus vagans (Small Hawk Cuckoo)
Malaysia, Thailand, Java, Borneo
Cuculus fugax (Fugitive Hawk Cuckoo)
C. f. hyperythrus
NE Asia, China, Indochina
C. f. nisicolor
E Himalayas to Malaysia, Sumatra
C. f. pectoralis
Luzon I, Cebu I, Mindoro I
C. f. fugax
Malaysia, Sumatra, Java, Borneo
Cuculus solitarius (Red-chested Cuckoo)
Guinea to Ethiopia & Cape Province
Cuculus cafer (Black Cuckoo)
C. c. cafer
Gambia to Ethiopia & South Africa
C. c. gabonensis
Nigeria to N Zaire, Uganda
Cuculus micropterus (Short-winged Cuckoo)
C. m. micropterus
India to E Asia & E Asian islands
C. m. ognevi
NE Asia
C. m. concretus
Sumatra, Java, Borneo
Cuculus canorus (European Cuckoo)
C. c. canorus
Europe & W Siberia » E & S Africa
C. c. bangsi
Iberia, N Africa
C. c. kleinschmidti
Corsica, Sardinia
C. c. johanseni
C Asia
C. c. telephonus
NE Asia & Japan » India & New Guinea
C. c. fallax
C & S China
C. c. bakeri
NW China, Burma, Indochina
C. c. subtelephonus
Transcaspia to W Chinese Turkestan
C. c. gularis
Gambia to Sudan & N South Africa
Cuculus saturatus (Oriental Cuckoo)
C. s. horsfieldi
C & E Asia » SE Asia
C. s. lepidus
Malaysia & Sumatra to Timor I

C. s. saturatus
S Himalayas to S China
Cuculus poliocephalus (Little Cuckoo)
C. p. rochii
Madagascar
C. p. poliocephalus
Himalayas to India, C China, Japan
C. p. insulindae
Borneo
Cuculus pallidus (Pallid Cuckoo)
C. p. occidentalis
W Australia, Northern Territory
C. p. pallidus
E & S Australia, Tasmania

CERCOCOCCYX
**Cercococcyx mechowi (Dusky Long-
tailed Cuckoo)**
Sierra Leone to N Uganda & N Angola
**Cercococcyx olivinus (Olive Long-tailed
Cuckoo)**
Ghana, Cameroun to N Angola
**Cercococcyx montanus (Mountain Long-
tailed Cuckoo)**
C. m. montanus
Ruwenzori-Mtns
C. m. patulus
N Tanzania

PENTHOCERYX
**Penthoceryx sonneratii (Banded Bay
Cuckoo)**
P. s. sonneratii
India, Burma, Thailand, S Indochina
P. s. waiti
Sri Lanka
P. s. malayanus
N & C Malaysia
P. s. fasciolatus
S Malaysia, Sumatra, Borneo, Philippine Is
P. s. musicus
Java

CACOMANTIS
Cacomantis merulinus (Plaintive Cuckoo)
C. m. passerinus
W Himalayas, India, Sri Lanka
C. m. querulus
E Himalayas to S China, Indochina
C. m. threnodes
Malaysia, Sumatra, Borneo
C. m. subpallidus
Nias I
C. m. lanceolatus
Java
C. m. merulinus
Philippine Is
C. m. celebensis
Celebes

Cacomantis variolosus (Brush Cuckoo)   173
C. v. sepulcralis
Malaysia, Borneo, Sumatra to Flores I,
Philippine Is
C. v. everetti
Basilan I, Sulu Archipelago
C. v. virescens
Celebes, Tukangbesi Is
C. v. oblitus
N Moluccas
C. v. aeruginosus
Buru I
C. v. stresemanni
Ceram I, Ambon I
C. v. infaustus
W Papuan Is, N & C New Guinea
C. v. chivae
Biak I
C. v. obscuratus
Numfor I
C. v. fortior
Goodenough I, Fergusson I
C. v. oreophilus
S New Guinea
C. v. blandus
Admiralty Is
C. v. websteri
New Hanover
C. v. macrocercus
New Britain, New Ireland
C. v. addendus
Kulambangra I, Malaita I, Rubiana I
C. v. variolosus
N & E Australia » Moluccas, New Guinea
**Cacomantis castaneiventris (Chestnut-
breasted Cuckoo)**
C. c. arfakianus
W Papuan Is, NW New Guinea
C. c. weiskei
C & E New Guinea
C. c. castaneiventris
Cape York Peninsula
**Cacomantis heinrichi (Heinrich's Brush
Cuckoo)**
Halmahera I, Batjan I
**Cacomantis pyrrhophanus (Fan-tailed
Cuckoo)**
C. p. prionurus
E & S Australia, Tasmania
C. p. excitus
New Guinea
C. p. meeki
Solomon Is
C. p. schistaceigularis
New Hebrides
C. p. pyrrhophanus
New Caledonia, Loyalty Is
C. p. simus
Fiji Is

Rhamphomantis megarhynchus (Little Long-billed Cuckoo)
R. m. sanfordi
Waigeu I
R. m. megarhynchus
NW & N New Guinea, Aru Is

MISOCALIUS
Misocalius osculans (Black-eared Cuckoo)
Interior of Australia

CHRYSOCOCCYX
Chrysococcyx cupreus (African Emerald Cuckoo)
C. c. cupreus
Gambia to S Ethiopia
C. c. intermedius
Cameroun to S Zaire, N Kenya
C. c. sharpei
S Angola to Zambia & Cape Province
Chrysococcyx flavigularis (Yellow-throated Green Cuckoo)
Sierra Leone to N & C Zaire
Chrysococcyx klaas (Klaas' Cuckoo)
C. k. klaas
Senegal to Ethiopia & Cape Province
C. k. arabicus
S Arabia
Chrysococcyx caprius (Didric Cuckoo)
Senegal to Ethiopia & Cape Province

CHALCITES
Chalcites maculatus (Emerald Cuckoo)
Himalayas to China, SE Asia
Chalcites xanthorhynchus (Violet Cuckoo)
C. x. xanthorhynchus
NE India to SE Asia, Borneo & Java
C. x. limborgi
S Burma
C. x. bangueyensis
Banguey I
C. x. amethystinus
Philippine Is
Chalcites basalis (Horsfield's Bronze Cuckoo)
S Australia » Gtr Sunda Is
Chalcites lucidus (Golden-Bronze Cuckoo)
C. l. plagosus
S Australia to Lesser Sunda Is & New Guinea
C. l. lucidus
New Zealand to Solomon Is
C. l. layardi
New Caledonia, Loyalty Is
C. l. aeneus
New Hebrides, Banks Is
C. l. harterti
Rennell I, Bellona I

Chalcites malayanus (Malay Emerald Cuckoo)
C. m. malayanus
Malaysia, Sumatra, Philippine Is
C. m. albifrons
Java
C. m. aheneus
Borneo
C. m. jungei
C & S Celebes
C. m. rufomerus
Lesser Sunda Is
C. m. salvadorii
Babar I
C. m. misoriensis
Biak I
C. m. poecilurus
W Papuan Is, New Guinea
C. m. russatus
Cape York Peninsula
C. m. minutillus
Melville I, N Australia
Chalcites crassirostris (Moluccan Bronze Cuckoo)
Moluccas, Kei Is, New Guinea
Chalcites ruficollis (Reddish-throated Bronze Cuckoo)
NW New Guinea
Chalcites meyeri (Meyer's Bronze Cuckoo)
NW New Guinea

CALIECHTHRUS
Caliechthrus leucolophus (White-crowned Koel)
Salawati I, New Guinea

SURNICULUS
Surniculus lugubris (Drongo-Cuckoo)
S. l. dicruroïdes
N & C India to S China, Indochina
S. l. stewarti
SW India, Sri Lanka
S. l. barussarum
Malaysia, Sumatra, Borneo
S. l. minimus
Palawan I, Balabac I
S. l. lugubris
Java, Bali I
S. l. velutinus
Philippine Is
S. l. musschenbroeki
Celebes

MICRODYNAMIS
Microdynamis parva (Black-capped Cuckoo)
M. p. parva
SW & E New Guinea
M. p. grisescens
N New Guinea

EUDYNAMYS
Eudynamys scolopacea (Koel)
  E. s. scolopacea
    India, Sri Lanka, Nicobar Is
  E. s. chinensis
    W & S China, Indochina
  E. s. harterti
    Hainan I
  E. s. simalurensis
    Simalur I, Babi I
  E. s. malayana
    Assam to Thailand, Malaysia, Sumatra to
    Flores I
  E. s. paraguena
    Palawan I, Busuanga I
  E. s. dolosa
    Andaman Is
  E. s. mindanensis
    Philippine Is, Sangir Is, Talaut Is
  E. s. frater
    Calayan I, Fuga I
  E. s. melanorhyncha
    Celebes, Togian I, Peling I
  E. s. facialis
    Sula Is
  E. s. everetti
    Sumba I to Timor I & Roma I, Kei Is
  E. s. corvina
    N Moluccas
  E. s. orientalis
    S Moluccas
  E. s. salvadorii
    Bismarck Archipelago
  E. s. alberti
    Solomon Is
  E. s. rufiventer
    W Papuan Is, & N & C New Guinea
  E. s. minima
    S New Guinea
Eudynamys cyanocephala (Australian Koel)
  E. s. subcyanocephala
    NW Australia, W Queensland
  E. s. cyanocephala
    N Queensland, N New South Wales

URODYNAMIS
Urodynamis taitensis (Long-tailed Koel)
  New Zealand & SW Pacific Is

SCYTHROPS
Scythrops novaehollandiae (Channel-billed Cuckoo)
  Flores I to E Australia

PHAENICOPHAEINAE

COCCYZUS
Coccyzus pumilus (Dwarf Cuckoo)
  W Venezuela, E Colombia

Coccyzus cinereus (Ash-coloured Cuckoo)
  Paraguay, S Brazil to C Argentina
Coccyzus erythrophthalmus (Black-billed Cuckoo)
  S Canada » NW South America
Coccyzus americanus (Yellow-billed Cuckoo)
  C. a. americanus
    C & E USA » N South America
  C. a. occidentalis
    SW Canada » W Mexico
Coccyzus euleri (Pearly-breasted Cuckoo)
  NE South America
Coccyzus minor (Mangrove Cuckoo)
  C. m. palloris
    coast of W Mexico to E Panama, Tres
    Marias Is
  C. m. continentalis
    coast of E Mexico to Panama
  C. m. cozumelae
    Cozumel I
  C. m. maynardi
    S Florida, Bahama Is
  C. m. caymanensis
    Cayman Is
  C. m. nesiotes
    Jamaica
  C. m. teres
    Greater Antilles
  C. m. rileyi
    Barbuda I, Antigua I
  C. m. dominicae
    Montserrat I, Guadeloupe I, Dominica I
  C. m. vincentis
    Martinique I, St Lucia I, St Vincent I
  C. m. grenadensis
    Grenada I, Bequia I
  C. m. abbotti
    Old Providence I, St Andrews I
  C. m. minor
    N South America
  C. m. ferrugineus
    Cocos I (E Pacific)
Coccyzus melacoryphus (Dark-billed Cuckoo)
  South America, Galapagos Is
Coccyzus lansbergi (Grey-capped Cuckoo)
  Colombia, Venezuela, W Ecuador

PIAYA
Piaya rufigularis (Rufous-breasted Cuckoo)
  Hispaniola
Piaya pluvialis (Chestnut-bellied Cuckoo)
  Jamaica
Piaya cayana (Squirrel Cuckoo)
  P. c. extima
    NW Mexico

P. c. mexicana
W Mexico
P. c. stirtoni
W coast of Guatemala to NW Costa Rica
P. c. thermophila
E Mexico to Panama
P. c. mesura
E Colombia, E Ecuador
P. c. nigricrissa
W Colombia, W Ecuador, NW & EC Peru
P. c. mehleri
NE Colombia, N Venezuela
P. c. circe
W Venezuela
P. c. insulana
Trinidad
P. c. cayana
E & S Venezuela, the Guianas, N Brazil
P. c. boliviana
EC Peru to N Bolivia
P. c. obscura
C Brazil
P. c. hellmayri
C & E Brazil
P. c. pallescens
E Brazil
P. c. cearae
Ceara, Brazil
P. c. cabanisi
SC Brazil
P. c. macroura
SE Brazil, NE Argentina, Paraguay,
Uruguay
P. c. mogenseni
S Bolivia, NW Argentina
Piaya melanogaster (Black-bellied Cuckoo)
P. m. melanogaster
N & C Amazonia
P. m. ochracea
SE Colombia, S Peru
Piaya minuta (Little Cuckoo)
P. m. panamensis
E Panama
P. m. gracilis
W Colombia, W Ecuador
P. m. minuta
N & W Amazonia
P. m. chaparensis
N Bolivia

SAUROTHERA
Saurothera merlini (Great Lizard Cuckoo)
S. m. bahamensis
New Providence I, Eleuthera I
S. m. andria
Andros I
S. m. merlini
Cuba

S. m. decolor
Isle of Pines
Saurothera vetula (Jamaican Lizard Cuckoo)
S. v. vetula
Jamaica
S. v. petersi
Gonave I
S. v. longirostris
Hispaniola, Tortuga I
S. v. saonae
Saona I
S. v. vieilloti
Puerto Rico

CEUTHMOCHARES
Ceuthmochares aereus (Yellow-bill)
C. a. flavirostris
Senegal to W Nigeria
C. a. aereus
Nigeria to N Angola
C. a. intermedius
N Zaire & Uganda to W Tanzania
C. a. australis
Kenya to Malawi & Natal

RHOPODYTES
Rhopodytes diardi (Lesser Green-billed Malcoha)
R. d. diardi
S Malaysia, Sumatra
R. d. borneensis
Borneo
Rhopodytes sumatranus (Rufous-bellied Malcoha)
R. s. sumatranus
S Burma, Malaysia, Sumatra
R. s. minor
Borneo
Rhopodytes tristis (Greater Green-billed Malcoha)
R. t. tristis
W Himalayas to N Burma
R. t. saliens
Burma, N Indochina, S China
R. t. longicaudatus
S Burma, Malaysia, S Indochina
R. t. hainanus
Hainan I
R. t. elongatus
Sumatra
R. t. kangeangensis
Kangean I
Rhopodytes viridirostris (Small Green-billed Malcoha)
S India, Sri Lanka

TACCOCUA
Taccocua leschenaultii (Sirkeer Cuckoo)

T. l. sirkee
  NW India
T. l. infuscata
  W Himalayas
T. l. affinis
  NE India
T. l. leschenaultii
  S India

RHINORTHA
Rhinortha chlorophaea (Raffles' Malcoha)
R. c. chlorophaea
  S Burma, Malaysia, Sumatra
R. c. fuscigularis
  N Borneo & islands
R. c. mayri
  S Borneo

ZANCLOSTOMUS
Zanclostomus javanicus (Red-billed Malcoha)
Z. j. pallidus
  S Burma, Malaysia, Sumatra, Borneo
Z. j. factus
  Tanahmasa I
Z. j. javanicus
  Java
Z. j. natunensis
  Natuna Is

RHAMPHOCOCCYX
Rhamphococcyx calyorhynchus (Celebes Malcoha)
R. c. calyorhynchus
  N Celebes, Togian I
R. c. centralis
  C Celebes
R. c. meridionalis
  S Celebes
R. c. rufiloris
  Buton I
Rhamphococcyx curvirostris (Chestnut-breasted Malcoha)
R. c. erythrognathus
  S Burma, Malaysia, Sumatra
R. c. oeneicaudus
  Islands off SW Sumatra
R. c. curvirostris
  W & C Java
R. c. deningeri
  E Java, Bali I
R. c. borneensis
  Borneo, Natuna Is
R. c. harringtoni
  Palawan I, Balabac I

PHAENICOPHAEUS
Phaenicophaeus pyrrhocephalus (Red-faced Malcoha)
  S India, Sri Lanka

DASYLOPHUS
Dasylophus superciliosus (Rough-crested Cuckoo)
  N Philippine Is

LEPIDOGRAMMUS
Lepidogrammus cumingi (Scale-feathered Cuckoo)
  Luzon I, Marinduque I

CROTOPHAGINAE

CROTOPHAGA
Crotophaga major (Greater Ani)
  E Panama to N Argentina, Trinidad
Crotophaga ani (Smooth-billed Ani)
  Bahama Is, Antilles, N South America
Crotophaga sulcirostris (Groove-billed Ani)
C. s. pallidula
  S Baja California
C. s. sulcirostris
  Mexico to C South America, Curaçao I, Trinidad

GUIRA
Guira guira (Guira Cuckoo)
  S & E Brazil, N Argentina, Uruguay

NEOMORPHINAE

TAPERA
Tapera naevia (Striped Cuckoo)
T. n. excellens
  SE Mexico to Panama
T. n. naevia
  N South America, Trinidad
T. n. chochi
  S Brazil, N Argentina

MOROCOCCYX
Morococcyx erythropygus (Lesser Ground Cuckoo)
M. e. dilutus
  W Mexico
M. e. simulans
  Guerrero, Mexico
M. e. mexicanus
  SW & S Mexico
M. e. erythropygus
  S Mexico to N Costa Rica
M. e. macrourus
  Guatemala

DROMOCOCCYX
Dromococcyx phasianellus (Pheasant Cuckoo)
D. p. rufigularis
  SE Mexico to Colombia
D. p. phasianellus
  C & S Brazil, Paraguay, Bolivia

***Dromococcyx pavoninus* (Pavonine Cuckoo)**
  D. p. perijanus
    NW Venezuela
  D. p. pavoninus
    N South America, intermittently

GEOCOCCYX
Geococcyx californina (Road-runner)
  S USA to CS Mexico
Geococcyx velox (Lesser Road-runner)
  G. v. melanchima
    W Mexico
  G. v. velox
    EC Mexico
  G. v. affinis
    El Salvador, W Guatemala
  G. v. pallidus
    Yucatan, E Guatemala
  G. v. longisignum
    Honduras, N Nicaragua

NEOMORPHUS
Neomorphus geoffroyi (Rufous-vented Ground Cuckoo)
  N. g. salvini
    Nicaragua to W Colombia
  N. g. aequatorialis
    E Ecuador
  N. g. australis
    S Peru, NW Bolivia
  N. g. geoffroyi
    C & S Brazil
  N. g. dulcis
    E Brazil
Neomorphus squamiger (Scaled Ground Cuckoo)
  N. s. squamiger
    EC Brazil
  N. s. iungens
    C Brazil
Neomorphus radiolosus (Banded Ground Cuckoo)
  NW Ecuador
Neomorphus rufipennis (Rufous-winged Ground Cuckoo)
  N. r. rufipennis
    NE Venezuela
  N. r. nigrogularis
    S Venezuela, Guyana, N Brazil
Neomorphus pucheranii (Red-billed Ground Cuckoo)
  N. p. pucheranii
    W Brazil, E Ecuador, NE Peru
  N. p. lepidophanes
    E Peru, SW Brazil

CARPOCOCCYX
Carpococcyx radiceus (Ground Cuckoo)
  C. r. radiceus
    Borneo

  C. r. viridis
    Sumatra
Carpococcyx renauldi (Coral-billed Ground Cuckoo)
  SE Thailand, Indochina

COUINAE

COUA
Coua gigas (Giant Madagascar Coucal)
  W & S Madagascar
Coua coquereli (Coquerel's Madagascar Coucal)
  W Madagascar
Coua serriana (Rufous-breasted Madagascar Coucal)
  NE Madagascar
Coua reynaudii (Red-footed Madagascar Coucal)
  NW & E Madagascar
Coua cursor (Running Coucal)
  SW Madagascar
Coua ruficeps (Red-capped Madagascar Coucal)
  C. r. ruficeps
    NW Madagascar
  C. r. olivaceiceps
    SW Madagascar
Coua cristata (Crested Madagascar Coucal)
  C. c. dumonti
    W Madagascar
  C. c. cristata
    N & E Madagascar
  C. c. pyropyga
    SW Madagascar
  C. c. maxima
    SE Madagascar
Coua verreauxi (Southern Crested Madagascar Coucal)
  SW Madagascar
Coua caerulea (Blue Madagascar Coucal)
  NW & E Madagascar

CENTROPODINAE

CENTROPUS
Centropus milo (Buff-headed Coucal)
  C. m. albidiventris
    Vella Lavella I, Kulambangra I, Gizo I, Rendova I
  C. m. milo
    Florida I, Guadalcanal I
Centropus goliath (Large Coucal)
  N Moluccas
Centropus violaceus (Violet Coucal)
  New Ireland, New Britain
Centropus menbecki (Greater Coucal)
  C. m. menbecki
    W Papuan islands, New Guinea
  C. m. jobiensis
    Japen I

C. m. aruensis
  Aru Is
Centropus ateralbus (New Britain Coucal)
  New Britain, New Ireland
Centropus chalybeus (Biak Island Coucal)
  Biak I, Numfor I
Centropus phasianius (Pheasant Coucal)
  C. p. propinquus
    N New Guinea
  C. p. nigricans
    SE New Guinea
  C. p. obscuratus
    Goodenough I, Fergusson I, E New Guinea
  C. p. thierfelderi
    S New Guinea
  C. p. phasianius
    NE Australia
  C. p. macrourus
    N & mid Western Australia
Centropus spilopterus (Moluccan Coucal)
  Kei Is
Centropus bernsteini (Bernstein's Coucal)
  C. b. manam
    Vulcan I
  C. b. bernsteini
    W New Guinea
Centropus chlororhynchus (Ceylon Coucal)
  SW Sri Lanka
Centropus rectunguis (Short-toed Coucal)
  Malaysia, Sumatra, Borneo
Centropus steerii (Steere's Coucal)
  Mindoro I
Centropus sinensis (Common Crow-Pheasant)
  C. s. parroti
    C & S India, Sri Lanka
  C. s. sinensis
    N India to S China
  C. s. intermedius
    Burma, S Thailand, Indochina, Hainan I
  C. s. eurycercus
    Malaysia, Sumatra, Borneo, Palawan I
  C. s. bubutus
    Java, Bali I
  C. s. anonymous
    C Philippine Is
  C. s. kangeanensis
    Kangean I
  C. s. andamanensis
    Cocos I, Andaman Is
Centropus nigrorufus (Sunda Coucal)
  Sumatra, Java
Centropus viridis (Philippine Coucal)
  C. v. viridis
    Philippine Is
  C. v. carpenteri
    Batan I

C. v. mindorensis
  Mindoro I, Semirara I
Centropus toulou (Black Coucal)
  C. t. toulou
    Madagascar
  C. t. insularis
    Aldabra I
  C. t. assumptionis
    Assumption I **e?**
Centropus bengalensis (Lesser Coucal)
  C. b. bengalensis
    India, Burma to Indochina
  C. b. lignator
    SE China, Taiwan
  C. b. javanensis
    Malaysia, Sumatra, Java, Borneo,
    Philippine Is
  C. b. sarasinorum
    Celebes, Lesser Sunda Is
  C. b. medius
    Moluccas
Centropus grillii (Black-chested Coucal
  C. g. grillii
    Guinea to Kenya & Malawi
  C. g. caeruleiceps
    S Ethiopia
  C. g. wahlbergi
    Natal
**Centropus epomidis (Rufous-bellied
Coucal)**
    Ghana, S Nigeria
**Centropus leucogaster (Black-throated
Coucal)**
  C. l. leucogaster
    Sierra Leone to Nigeria
  C. l. efulenensis
    W Cameroun, Gabon
  C. l. neumanni
    N Zaire
Centropus anselli (Gabon Coucal)
    S Cameroun to Angola, S Zaire
**Centropus monachus (Blue-headed
Coucal)**
  C. m. occidentalis
    Ghana to NE Zaire
  C. m. angolensis
    N Angola
  C. m. fischeri
    Sudan, Uganda, N Kenya
  C. m. monachus
    Ethiopia, Kenya
  C. m. songweensis
    S Tanzania, N Malawi
  C. m. cupreicaudus
    S Angola to S Tanzania, Namibia
Centropus senegalensis (Senegal Coucal)
  C. s. aegyptius
    Egypt

C. s. senegalensis
Senegal to Sudan, Angola, Tanzania
C. s. incertus
NW Kenya
C. s. flecki
Botswana, Rhodesia, Transvaal
Centropus superciliosus (White-browed Coucal)
C. s. loandae
Angola to Uganda & Malawi
C. s. superciliosus
Sudan to Somalia & Tanzania
C. s. sokotrae
Socotra I
C. s. burchellii
S Tanzania to Cape Province
Centropus melanops (Black-faced Coucal)
C. m. melanops
Leyte I, Bohol I, Mindanao I, Basilan I
C. m. banken
Samar I
Centropus celebensis (Celebes Coucal)
C. c. celebensis
N Celebes
C. c. rufescens
C & S Celebes
Centropus unirufus (Rufous Coucal)
C. u. unirufus
Luzon I
C. u. polillensis
Polillo Is

Strigiformes

72 TYTONIDAE (BARN OWLS)

TYTONINAE

TYTO
Tyto soumagnei (Madagascar Grass Owl)
Madagascar
Tyto alba (Barn Owl)
T. a. schmitzi
Madeira
T. a. gracilirostris
E Canary Is
T. a. alba
W Europe
T. a. ernesti
Corsica, Sardinia
· T. a. guttata
C Europe
T. a. detorta
Cape Verde Is
T. a. affinis
Gambia to Sudan & Cape Province
T. a. poensis
Fernando Po I

T. a. thomensis
Sao Thomé I
T. a. erlangeri
Arabia to Syria & Iraq
T. a. hypermetra
Comoro Is, Madagascar
T. a. stertens
India, N Burma, Sri Lanka
T. a. javanica
Burma to Indochina, Java to Timor I
T. a. deroepstorffi
S Andaman Is
T. a. sumbaensis
Sumba I
T. a. everetti
Savu Is
T. a. kuehni
Kisar I
T. a. bellonae
Bellona I
T. a. meeki
SE New Guinea, Vulcan I, Dampier I
T. a. delicatula
Australia, Solomon Is
T. a. crassirostris
Boang I
T. a. interposita
Santa Cruz I, Banks Is, New Hebrides
T. a. lulu
New Caledonia, Fiji Is, Tonga I, Samoa Is
T. a. pratincola
C & NE USA to E Nicaragua
T. a. guatemalae
W Guatemala to Panama
T. a bondi
Honduras
T. a. niveicauda
I de Pinhos
T. a. lucayana
Bahama Is
T. a. furcata
Cuba, Cayman Is, Jamaica
T. a. bargei
Curaçao I
T. a. subandeana
Colombia, Ecuador
T. a. contempta
W Colombia to Venezuela & Peru
T. a. hellmayri
the Guianas, N Brazil
T. a. tuidara
C Brazil to Chile, Argentina
T. a. glaucops
Tortuga I, Hispaniola
T. a. nigrescens
Dominica I
T. a. insularis
S Lesser Antilles
T. a. punctatissima
Galapagos Is

Tyto *rosenbergii* (Celebes Barn Owl)
Celebes
Tyto *nigrobrunnea* (Sula Is Barn Owl)
Sula Is
Tyto *inexspectata* (Minahassa Barn Owl)
N Celebes
Tyto *novaehollandiae* (Masked Owl)
  T. n. sorocula
    Tenimber Is
  T. n. cayelii
    Buru I
  T. n. manusi
    Manus I
  T. n. kimberli
    S New Guinea, N Australia
  T. n. novaehollandiae
    SE Australia
  T. n. perplexa
    SW Australia
  T. n. castanops
    Tasmania
Tyto *aurantia* (New Britain Barn Owl)
New Britain
Tyto *tenebricosa* (Sooty Owl)
  T. t. arfaki
    New Guinea, Japen I
  T. t. tenebricosa
    E & S Australia
Tyto *capensis* (Grass Owl)
  T. c. cameroonensis
    Cameroun
  T. c. liberatus
    Kenya
  T. c. damarensis
    S Angola, N Namibia
  T. c. capensis
    SE Zaire to Cape Province
Tyto *longimembris* (Eastern Grass Owl)
  T. l. longimembris
    India, possibly to Indochina
  T. l. melli
    Kwangsi, Kwangtung
  T. l. chinensis
    Fukien
  T. l. amauronota
    Philippine Is
  T. l. walleri
    N & E Australia, Celebes? Fiji?
  T. l. papuensis
    SE New Guinea

PHODILINAE

PHODILUS
Phodilus *badius* (Bay Owl)
  P. b. saturatus
    Nepal to Indochina
  P. b. parvus
    Billiton I

  P. b. badius
    C Burma to Malaysia, Sumatra, Java,
    Borneo
  P. b. assimilis
    Sri Lanka
  P. b. arixuthus
    Bunguran I
Phodilus *prigoginei* (Tanzanian Bay Owl)
  E Zaire, NW Tanzania

73 STRIGIDAE (OWLS)

BUBONINAE

OTUS
Otus *sagittatus* (White-fronted Scops Owl)
  S Burma, Thailand, Malaysia
Otus *rufescens* (Rufous Scops Owl)
  O. r. malayensis
    Malaysia
  O. r. rufescens
    Sumatra, Java, Borneo
  O. r. burbidgei
    Jolo I
Otus *icterorhynchus* (Sandy Scops Owl)
  O. i. icterorhynchus
    Ghana
  O. i. holerythrus
    S Cameroun to N Zaire
Otus *ireneae* (Sokoke Scops Owl)
  SE Kenya
Otus *spilocephalus* (Spotted Scops Owl)
  O. s. huttoni
    W Himalayas
  O. s. spilocephalus
    E Himalayas to Burma
  O. s. latouchei
    SE China, N Indochina
  O. s. hambroecki
    Taiwan
  O. s. siamensis
    Thailand, S Indochina
  O. s. vulpes
    Malaysia
  O. s. stresemanni
    Sumatra
  O. s. angelinae
    Java
  O. s. luciae
    Borneo
Otus *balli* (Andaman Scops Owl)
  Andaman Is
Otus *alfredi* (Flores Scops Owl)
  Flores I
Otus *brucei* (Striated Scops Owl)
  Middle East to Pakistan
Otus *scops* (Scops Owl)
  O. s. scops
    W Europe to Russia & C Africa

O. s. cycladum
  Cyclades Is, Crete
O. s. cyprius
  Cyprus
O. s. turanicus
  Transcaspia, N Iran
O. s. pulchellus
  Caucasus, Russia to C Asia & NW India
O. s. stictonotus
  Manchuria to China, Taiwan
O. s. japonicus
  N Japan
O. s. modestus
  Assam to S China, Indochina
O. s. malayanus
  Malaysia
O. s. sunia
  Himalayas, N India
O. s. rufipennis
  C & S India
O. s. leggei
  Sri Lanka
O. s. interpositus
  Borodino Is
O. s. elegans
  Riukiu Is (?)
O. s. botelensis
  Botel Tobago I
O. s. calayensis
  Calayan I
O. s. longicornis
  Luzon I
O. s. mindorensis
  Mindoro I
O. s. romblonis
  Banton I, Romblon I
O. s. cuyensis
  Cuyo I
O. s. mantananensis
  Mantanani I
Otus umbra (Mentaur Scops Owl)
O. u. umbra
  Simalur I
O. u. enganensis
  Enggano I
Otus senegalensis (African Scops Owl)
O. s. senegalensis
  Senegal to Sudan
O. s. pygmea
  S Sudan, NW Ethiopia
O. s. caecus
  C & S Ethiopia, Somalia, N Kenya
O. s. socotranus
  Socotra I
O. s. pamelae
  Saudi Arabia
O. s. ugandae
  W Uganda, N & NE Zaire

O. s. feae
  Annobon I
O. s. graueri
  E Kenya, Tanzania
O. s. hendersonii
  Angola, SW Zaire
O. s. pusillus
  Mozambique, E Malawi, E Rhodesia
O. s. intermedius
  Namibia to S Mozambique & N Natal
O. s. latipennis
  Cape Province
Otus flammeolus (Flammulated Owl)
O. f. flammeolus
  SW Canada to W Mexico
O. f. rarus
  Guatemala
Otus brookii (Rajah's Scops Owl)
O. b. brookii
  Java, Borneo
O. b. solokensis
  Sumatra
Otus rutilus (Madagascar Scops Owl)
O. r. pembaensis
  Pemba I
O. r. capnodes
  Anjouan I **e?**
O. r. rutilus
  Madagascar
Otus manadensis (Celebes Scops Owl)
O. m. sibutuensis
  Sibutu I
O. m. steerei
  Tumindao I
O. m. manadensis
  Celebes
O. m. mendeni
  Peling I
O. m. siaoënsis
  Siao I
O. m. sulaensis
  Sula Mangoli I
O. m. kalidupae
  Kalidupa I
O. m. morotensis
  Morotai I, Ternate I
O. m. leucospilus
  Halmahera I, Batjan I
O. m. bouruensis
  Buru I
O. m. magicus
  Ceram I, Ambon I
O. m. albiventris
  Lombok I, Sumbawa I, Flores I, Lomblen I
O. m. tempestatis
  Wetar I
Otus beccarii (Biak I Scops Owl)
  Biak I

Otus silvicola (Lesser Sunda Scops Owl)
  Flores I, Sumbawa I
Otus whiteheadi (Whitehead's Scops Owl)
  Luzon I
Otus insularis (Bare-legged Scops Owl)
  Mahé I **e?**
Otus bakkamoena (Collared Scops Owl)
  O. b. ussuriensis
    S Manchuria to Korea, Sakhalin I
  O. b. semitorques
    Kurile Is, Japan, Quelpart I
  O. b. pryeri
    Hachijo I, Okinawa I
  O. b. aurorae
    N China
  O. b. erythrocampe
    S China, N Vietnam
  O. b. glabripes
    Taiwan
  O. b. umbratilis
    Hainan I
  O. b. lettia
    E Himalayas to Burma, N Thailand
  O. b. manipurensis
    Manipur, Assam
  O. b. plumipes
    NW Himalayas
  O. b. deserticolor
    SE Saudi Arabia, S Iran, Pakistan
  O. b. gangeticus
    NW & NC India
  O. b. marathae
    C India
  O. b. bakkamoena
    S India, Sri Lanka
  O. b. condorensis
    Pulo Condor I
  O. b. kangeana
    Kangean I
  O. b. cnephaeus
    Malaysia
  O. b. hypnodes
    Singapore, Sumatra
  O. b. lempiji
    Java, Bali, Borneo
  O. b. mentawi
    Siberut I, Sipora I, Pagi Is
  O. b. fuliginosus
    Palawan I
  O. b. boholensis
    Bohol I
  O. b. everetti
    Samar I, Mindanao I, Basilan I
Otus asio (Screech Owl)
  O. a. kennicotti
    SE Alaska to W Washington
  O. a. brewsteri
    S Washington to NW California

O. a. bendirei
  W California
O. a. macfarlanei
  S British Columbia to Idaho
O. a. inyoensis
  E California to N Utah
O. a. maxwelliae
  E Montana to C Colorado
O. a. aikeni
  C Colorado to N Mexico
O. a. swenki
  SC Canada to Oklahoma
O. a. naevius
  EC Canada to Georgia
O. a. asio
  E Virginia to Kansas
O. a. floridanus
  Florida & Gulf Coast
O. a. hasbroucki
  C Oklahoma to N Texas
O. a. mychophilus
  NC Utah, N Arizona
O. a. mccallii
  S Texas, NE Mexico
O. a. cineraceus
  C Arizona to NW Texas
O. a. cardonensis
  W Baja California
O. a. yumanensis
  SW Arizona
O. a. clazus
  S California
O. a. quercinus
  SW California
O. a. xantusi
  S Baja California
O. a. vinaceus
  NE Sinaloa
O. a. sinaloensis
  SE Sonora, NW Sinaloa
Otus trichopsis (Whiskered Owl)
  O. t. aspersus
    SE Arizona, NW Mexico
  O. t. pinosus
    E Mexico
  O. t. trichopsis
    W & S Mexico
  O. t. guerrerensis
    S W Mexico
  O. t. mesamericanus
    Guatemala, El Salvador
  O. t. pumilus
    Honduras
Otus barbarus (Bearded Screech Owl)
  N Guatemala
Otus guatemalae (Vermiculated Screech Owl)

O. g. tomlini
NW Mexico
O. g. hastatus
W Mexico
O. g. cassini
N Vera Cruz
O. g. fuscus
C Vera Cruz
O. g. thompsoni
Yucatan, Campeche
O. g. guatemalae
SE Vera Cruz, Guatemala, Honduras
U. g. dacrysistactus
N Nicaragua
O. g. vermiculatus
Costa Rica, Panama
O. g. napensis
E Ecuador
O. g. roraimae
SE Venezuela, S Guyana

Otus roboratus (West Peruvian Screech Owl)
NW Peru

Otus cooperi (Pacific Screech Owl)
O. c. chiapensis
S Mexico
O. c. cooperi
El Salvador, NW Costa Rica

Otus choliba (Tropical Screech Owl)
O. c. luctisonus
Costa Rica to NW Colombia
O. c. margaritae
N Colombia, N Venezuela, Margarita I
O. c. crucigerus
Upper Amazonia, C Brazil
O. c. alticola
C Colombia
O. c. duidae
SE Venezuela
O. c. decussatus
SC & E Brazil
O. c. choliba
S Brazil, Paraguay, N Argentina, Uruguay
O. c. wetmorei
SE Bolivia, W Paraguay, NW Argentina

Otus atricapillus (Long-tufted Screech Owl)
C & SE Brazil

Otus ingens (Rufescent Screech Owl)
O. i. colombianus
C Colombia
O. i. ingens
Ecuador
O. i. venezuelanus
W Venezuela

Otus watsonii (Tawny-bellied Screech Owl)
O. w. watsonii
Northern & Upper Amazonia
O. w. usta
C Brazil to N Argentina

Otus nudipes (Puerto Rico Screech Owl)
O. n. nudipes
Puerto Rico
O. n. newtoni
St Thomas I, St John I, St Croix I

Otus clarkii (Bare-legged Screech Owl)
Costa Rica, Panama

Otus albogularis (White-throated Screech Owl)
O. a. albogularis
Colombia, N Ecuador
O. a. obscurus
NW Venezuela
O. a. meridensis
W Venezuela
O. a. aequatorialis
E Ecuador

Otus marshalli (Cloud-forest Screech Owl)
SE Peru

Otus minimus (Least Screech Owl)
W Bolivia

Otus leucotis (White-faced Scops Owl)
O. l. leucotis
Senegal to Ethiopia & Kenya
O. l. margarethae
Sudan
O. l. granti
S Zaire & Tanzania to Cape Province

Otus hartlaubi (Sao Thomé Scops Owl)
Sao Thomé I

PYRROGLAUX
Pyrroglaux podargina (Palau Scops Owl)
Palau Is

MIMIZUKU
Mimizuku gurneyi (Giant Scops Owl)
Marinduque I, Mindanao I

JUBULA
Jubula lettii (Akun Scops Owl)
Liberia to N Zaire

LOPHOSTRIX
Lophostrix cristata (Crested Owl)
L. c. stricklandi
S Mexico to W Colombia
L. c. wedeli
E Panama
L. c. cristata
the Guianas, N & W Brazil

BUBO
Bubo virginianus (Great Horned Owl)
B. v. algistus
W Alaska
B. v. lagophonus
C Alaska to NE Oregon & Idaho
B. v. saturatus
SW Alaska to California
B. v. pacificus
S Oregon, California

B. v. wapacuthu
W & C Canada
B. v. occidentalis
WC Canada to WC USA
B. v. pallescens
SW USA to NC Mexico
B. v. heterocnemis
E Canada
B. v. virginianus
SE Canada, EC USA
B. v. elachistus
S Baja California
B. v. mayensis
C Mexico to W Panama
B. v. elutus
E Colombia
B. v. colombianus
C Colombia
B. v. nigrescens
W Ecuador
B. v. scotinus
E Venezuela
B. v. deserti
E Brazil
B. v. nacurutu
Peru & NW Brazil to Tierra del Fuego

Bubo bubo (Eagle Owl)
B. b. bubo
Scandinavia, W Europe to W Russia
B. b. hispanus
Iberian peninsula
B. b. interpositus
SW Russia to Syria
B. b. ruthenus
SE Russia
B. b. sibiricus
WC & C Asia
B. b. yenisseensis
C & EC Siberia
B. b. dauricus
N Mongolia
B. b. jakutensis
NE Siberia
B. b. ussuriensis
Lower Amur, Ussuriland
B. b. inexpectatus
Manchuria, N China
B. b. tenuipes
Korea, S Kurile Is, Hokkaido I
B. b. borissowi
Sakhalin I
B. b. turcomanus
Turkestan
B. b. zaissanensis
SC Asia
B. b. nikolskii
Iran, Iraq

B. b. tibetanus
C Tibet to NW China
B. b. kiautschensis
C & E China
B. b. jarlandi
SE Yunnan
B. b. swinhoei
SE China
B. b. hemachalana
W Tien Shan, W Himalayas
B. b. bengalensis
N & C India
B. b. ascalaphus
semi desert of N Africa
B. b. desertorum
desert of N Africa
Bubo capensis (Cape Eagle Owl)
B. c. dillonii
Ethiopia
B. c. mackinderi
Kenya, Tanzania
B. c. capensis
Natal, Cape Province
Bubo africanus (Spotted Eagle Owl)
B. a. cinerascens
French Guinea to Somalia
B. a. africanus
Uganda & Kenya to Angola
B. a. milesi
S Saudi Arabia
Bubo poensis (Nduk Eagle Owl)
B. p. poensis
Ghana to N Zaire
B. p. vosseleri
N Tanzania
Bubo nipalensis (Forest Eagle Owl)
B. n. nipalensis
Himalayas to C Burma, India
B. n. blighi
Sri Lanka
Bubo sumatrana (Malay Eagle Owl)
B. s. sumatrana
S Burma, Malaysia, Sumatra
B. s. strepitans
Java, Bali, Borneo
Bubo shelleyi (Banded Eagle Owl)
Liberia to S Cameroun
Bubo lacteus (Verreaux's Eagle Owl)
Senegal to Ethiopia to Cape Province
Bubo coromandus (Dusky Eagle Owl)
B. c. coromandus
N & C India
B. c. klossii
S Burma, Malaysia
Bubo leucostictus (Akun Eagle Owl)
Sierra Leone to Zaire

Pseudoptynx philippensis (Philippine Horned Owl)
P. p. philippensis
Luzon I, Cebu I
P. p. mindanensis
Mindanao I

KETUPA
Ketupa blakistoni (Blakiston's Fish Owl)
K. b. piscivorus
W Manchuria
K. b. doerriesi
NE Asia
K. b. karafutonis
Sakhalin I
K. b. blakistoni
Hokkaido I
Ketupa zeylonensis (Brown Fish Owl)
K. z. semenowi
Israel to NW India
K. z. leschenault
India, Burma, Thailand
K. z. zeylonensis
Sri Lanka
K. z. orientalis
NE Burma to SE China, Indochina
Ketupa flavipes (Tawny Fish Owl)
Himalayas to W China, Indochina
Ketupa ketupu (Malay Fish Owl)
K. k. ketupu
Malaysia, Sumatra, Java, Borneo
K. k. aagaardi
S Assam to S Thailand & Vietnam
K. k. pageli
NE Borneo
K. k. minor
Nias I

SCOTOPELIA
Scotopelia peli (Pel's Fishing Owl)
Senegal to Ethiopia & Cape Province
Scotopelia ussheri (Rufous Fishing Owl)
Sierra Leone to Ghana
Scotopelia bouvieri (Vermiculated Fishing Owl)
S Cameroun, Congo, N Angola

PULSATRIX
Pulsatrix perspicillata (Spectacled Owl)
P. p. saturata
S Mexico to W Panama
P. p. chapmani
E Costa Rica to W Ecuador
P. p. perspicillata
N South America
P. p. trinitatis
Trinidad
P. p. pulsatrix
E Brazil, Paraguay

P. p. boliviana
S Bolivia, N Argentina
Pulsatrix koeniswaldiana (Tawny-browed Owl)
S Brazil, NE Argentina
Pulsatrix melanota (Band-bellied Owl)
P. m. melanota
E Ecuador, E Peru
P. m. philoscia
Bolivia

NYCTEA
Nyctea scandiaca (Snowy Owl)
N Asia, N Canada, Holarctic Region

SURNIA
Surnia ulula (Hawk Owl)
S. u. ulula
N Europe, N Asia
S. u. tianschanica
Tien Shan
S. u. caparoch
W & C Canada, N USA

GLAUCIDIUM
Glaucidium passerinum (Eurasian Pygmy Owl)
G. p. passerinum
N Europe, W Asia
G. p. orientale
E Siberia, Manchuria
Glaucidium gnoma (Northern Pygmy Owl)
G. g. grinnelli
SE Alaska to N California
G. g. swarthi
Vancouver I
G. g. californicum
C British Columbia to S California
G. g. pinicola
WC USA
G. g. hoskinsii
Baja California
G. g. gnoma
N & C Mexico
G. g. cobanense
Guatemala
Glaucidium siju (Cuban Pygmy Owl)
G. s. siju
Cuba
G. s. vittatum
Isle of Pines
Glaucidium minutissimum (Least Pygmy Owl)
G. m. oberholseri
C & S Sinaloa
G. m. palmarum
W Mexico
G. m. griseiceps
E Guatemala, Belize, E Honduras

G. m. rarum
Costa Rica, Panama
G. m. minutissimum
Guyana, Surinam, Brazil
G. m. griscomi
SW Morelos, NE Guerrero
G. m. occultum
E Oaxaca, Chiapas
G. m. sanchezi
S San Luis Potosi
Glaucidium jardinii (Jardine's Pygmy Owl)
G. j. jardinii
Colombia, Ecuador, Peru, Venezuela
G. j. costaricanum
Costa Rica, Panama
Glaucidium brasilianum (Ferruginous Pygmy Owl)
G. b. cactorum
S Arizona, W Mexico
G. b. ridgwayi
S Texas to C Panama
G. b. medianum
N Colombia
G. b. phaloenoides
N Venezuela, Trinidad
G. b. olivaceum
Mt Augun-tepui (Venezuela)
G. b. margaritae
Margarita I
G. b. duidae
Mt Duida (Venezuela)
G. b. ucayalae
SE Colombia to Peru
G. b. brasilianum
W & S Amazonia, NE Argentina
G. b. pallens
E Bolivia, W Paraguay, NW Argentina
G. b. tucumanum
W Argentina
G. b. nanum
S Chile, S Argentina
Glaucidium perlatum (Pearl-spotted Owlet)
G. p. perlatum
Senegal to Cameroun
G. p. kilimense
E & NE Africa
G. p. licua
Southern Africa
Glaucidium tephronotum (Red-chested Owlet)
G. t. tephronotum
Ghana
G. t. pycrafti
S Cameroun
G. t. medje
N Zaire

G. t. lukolelae
C Zaire
G. t. kivuense
E Zaire
G. t. elgonense
Mt Elgon (Kenya)
Glaucidium capense (Barred Owlet)
G. c. castaneum
E Zaire
G. c. scheffleri
SE Kenya, NE Tanzania
G. c. ngamiense
S Zaire, NE Angola
G. c. robertsi
W Tanzania, W Mozambique
G. c. capense
Angola, Southern Africa
Glaucidium brodiei (Collared Pygmy Owl)
G. b. brodiei
Himalayas to N Indochina & Malaysia
G. b. pardalotum
Taiwan
G. b. peritum
Sumatra
G. b. borneense
Borneo
Glaucidium radiatum (Jungle Owlet)
G. r. radiatum
India, Sri Lanka
G. r. malabaricum
SW India
Glaucidium cuculoides (Cuckoo Owl)
G. c. castanonotum
Sri Lanka
G. c. cuculoides
W Himalayas
G. c. rufescens
NE India, N Burma
G. c. brügeli
S Burma, S Thailand
G. c. austerum
NE Assam
G. c. delacouri
N Indochina
G. c. deignani
SE Thailand, S Indochina
G. c. whitelyi
W, C & SE China, NE Vietnam
G. c. persimile
Hainan I
G. c. castanopterum
Java, Bali
Glaucidium sjostedti (Sjostedt's Barred Owlet)
Cameroun to C Zaire

XENOGLAUX
Xenoglaux loweryi (Long-whiskered Owlet)
    N Peru

MICRATHENE
Micrathene whitneyi (Elf Owl)
    M. w. whitneyi
        SW USA, NW Mexico
    M. w. idonea
        Texas, C Mexico
    M. w. sanfordi
        Baja California
    M. w. graysoni
        Socorro I

UROGLAUX
Uroglaux dimorpha (Papuan Hawk Owl)
    New Guinea, Japen I

NINOX
Ninox rufa (Rufous Owl)
    N. r. humeralis
        New Guinea, Waigeu I
    N. r. aruensis
        Aru Is
    N. r. rufa
        N Australia
    N. r. queenslandica
        E Queensland
Ninox strenua (Powerful Owl)
    New South Wales, Victoria
Ninox connivens (Barking Owl)
    N. c. rufostrigata
        N Moluccas
    N. c. assimilis
        E New Guinea, Vulcan I, Dampier I
    N. c. occidentalis
        NW Australia, N Territory
    N. c. peninsularis
        Cape York Peninsula
    N. c. enigma
        C North Queensland
    N. c. addenda
        SW Australia
    N. c. connivens
        S & E Australia
Ninox novaeseelandiae (Boobook Owl)
    N. n. rudolfi
        Sumba I
    N. n. plesseni
        Alor I
    N. n. fusca
        Timor I
    N. n. cinnamomina
        Babar I
    N. n. remigialis
        Kei Is
    N. n. pusilla
        S New Guinea

    N. n. ocellata
        N Australia, Melville I
    N. n. marmorata
        S & SW Australia
    N. n. lurida
        NE Queensland
    N. n. boobook
        E Australia
    N. n. leucopsis
        Tasmania
    N. n. albaria
        Lord Howe I
    N. n. undulata
        Norfolk I
    N. n. venatica
        North I, New Zealand
    N. n. novaeseelandiae
        South I, New Zealand
Ninox scutulata (Brown Hawk Owl)
    N. s. ussuriensis
        NE Asia
    N. s. scutulata
        Japan, E China to Lesser Sunda Is
    N. s. burmanica
        S Assam to Malaysia & Indochina
    N. s. lugubris
        N & C India
    N. s. hirsuta
        S India, Sri Lanka
    N. s. obscura
        Andaman Is, Nicobar Is
    N. s. malaccensis
        S Malaysia, Sumatra, Bangka I
    N. s. javanensis
        W Java
    N. s. borneensis
        Borneo, N Natuna Is
    N. s. randi
        Philippine Is
Ninox affinis (Andaman Brown Hawk Owl)
    N. a. affinis
        Andaman Is
    N. a. isolata
        Nicobar Is
    N. a. rexpimenti
        Gt Nicobar I
Ninox superciliaris (White-browed Owl)
    W Madagascar
Ninox philippensis (Philippine Hawk Owl)
    N. p. philippensis
        Luzon I, Marinduque I, Leyte I
    N. p. proxima
        Ticao I, Masbate I
    N. p. centralis
        Panay I, Guimaras I, Negros I, Siquijor I
Ninox spilonota (Spotted Hawk Owl)
    Mindoro I, Tablas I, Sibuyan I
Ninox spilocephala (Tweeddale's Hawk Owl)

N. s. mindorensis
Mindoro I
N. s. spilocephala
Mindanao I, Basilan I
N. s. reyi
Jolo I, Bongao I
N. s. everetti
Siasi I
Ninox perversa (Ochre-bellied Hawk Owl)
Celebes
Ninox squamipila (Indonesian Hawk Owl)
N. s. hypogramma
N Moluccas
N. s. hantu
Buru I
N. s. squamipila
Ceram I
N. s. forbesi
Tenimber Is
N. s. natalis
Christmas I
Ninox theomacha (Brown Owl)
N. t. hoedtii
Waigeu I, Misol I
N. t. goldii
D'Entrecasteaux Archipelago
N. t. theomacha
New Guinea
N. t. rosseliana
Louisiade Archipelago
Ninox punctulata (Speckled Hawk Owl)
Celebes
Ninox meeki (Admiralty Is Hawk Owl)
Admiralty Is
Ninox solomonis (New Ireland Hawk Owl)
N. s. superior
New Hanover
N. s. solomonis
New Britain, New Ireland
Ninox odiosa (New Britain Hawk Owl)
New Britain
Ninox jacquinoti (Solomon Is Hawk Owl)
N. j. eichhorni
Bougainville I, Choiseul I
N. j. mono
Mono I
N. j. jacquinoti
Ysabel I, St George I
N. j. floridae
Florida I
N. j. granti
Guadalcanal I
N. j. malaitae
Malaita I
N. j. roseoaxillaris
San Cristobal I

Gymnoglaux lawrencii (Bare-legged Owl)
G. l. exsul
W Cuba, Isle of Pines
G. l. lawrencii
C & E Cuba

SCELOGLAUX
Sceloglaux albifacies (White-faced Owl)
South I, New Zealand

ATHENE
Athene noctua (Little Owl)
A. n. vidalii
W Europe
A. n. noctua
C Europe
A. n. sarda
Sardinia
A. n. indigena
N Iran, Greece, S Russia
A. n. glaux
N Africa
A. n. saharae
S Morocco to N Saudi Arabia
A. n. solitudinis
C Sahara
A. n. lilith
Syria, Israel
A. n. bactriana
Transcaspia to Pakistan
A. n. orientalis
NE Russian & Chinese Turkestan
A. n. ludlowi
Tibet
A. n. impasta
Kokonor, W Kansu
A. n. plumipes
EC Asia
A. n. spilogastra
E Sudan, NE Ethiopia
A. n. somaliensis
E Ethiopia, Somalia
Athene brama (Spotted Little Owl)
A. b. albida
Iran
A. b. indica
N & C India
A. b. brama
S India
A. b. pulchra
Burma to SW Indochina
Athene blewitti (Forest Spotted Owlet)
C India

SPEOTYTO
Speotyto cunicularia (Burrowing Owl)
S. c. hypugaea
SW Canada to W Mexico

S. c. rostrata
Clarion I
S. c. floridana
C & S Florida, Bahama Is
S. c. troglodytes
Hispaniola, Gonave I
S. c. arubensis
Aruba I
S. c. brachyptera
Margarita I, N Venezuela
S. c. minor
S Guyana, S Surinam, NE Brazil
S. c. carrikeri
E Colombia
S. c. tolimae
W Colombia
S. c. pichinchae
W Ecuador
S. c. punensis
SW Ecuador, NW Peru
S. c. intermedia
W Peru
S. c. apurensis
NC Venezuela
S. c. juninensis
C Peru, W Bolivia
S. c. boliviana
Bolivia
S. c. nanodes
SW Peru
S. c. grallaria
E & S Brazil
S. c. cunicularia
S Bolivia & S Brazil to Tierra del Fuego
S. c. partridgei
Corrientes, Argentina

CICCABA
Ciccaba virgata (Mottled Owl)
C. v. tamaulipensis
S Tamaulipas
C. v. squamulata
W Mexico
C. v. centralis
S Mexico to W Panama
C. v. virgata
E Panama to Venezuela & Ecuador, Trinidad
C. v. macconnelli
the Guianas
C. v. superciliaris
NC & NE Brazil
C. v. minuscula
W Colombia
C. v. borelliana
S Brazil, Paraguay, NE Argentina
Ciccaba nigrolineata (Black & White Owl)
S Mexico to W Ecuador
Ciccaba huhula (Black-banded Owl)
the Guianas to C & S Brazil
Ciccaba albitarsus (Rufous-banded Owl)

C. a. albitarsus
Colombia, Ecuador, Venezuela
C. a. tertia
Bolivia
Ciccaba woodfordii (African Wood Owl)
C. w. umbrina
Ethiopia
C. w. nigricantior
Kenya, Tanzania
C. w. nuchalis
Sierra Leone to N Angola
C. w. bohndorffi
Central African Republic to Sudan
& S Zaire
C. w. woodfordii
Zambia & Malawi to Cape Province

STRIGINAE

STRIX
Strix butleri (Hume's Tawny Owl)
SW Asia
Strix seloputo (Spotted Wood Owl)
S. s. seloputo
S Burma to S Indochina, Malaysia, Java
S. s. baweana
Bawean I
S. s. wiepkeni
Palawan I
Strix ocellata (Mottled Wood Owl)
S. o. ocellata
Himalayas, N India
S. o. grandis
W India
S. o. grisescens
NC India
Strix leptogrammica (Brown Wood Owl)
S. l. newarensis
Himalayas, N Burma, N Thailand
S. l. indranee
S India
S. l. connectens
C India
S. l. ochrogenys
Sri Lanka
S. l. maingayi
S Burma, S Thailand, Malaysia
S. l. ticehursti
SE China, N Indochina
S. l. laotiana
S Indochina
S. l. caligata
Taiwan, Hainan I
S. l. myrtha
Sumatra
S. l. nyctiphasma
Banjak I
S. l. niasensis
Nias I

S. l. chaseni
Billiton I
S. l. bartelsi
W & C Java
S. l. vaga
N Borneo
S. l. leptogrammica
S & C Borneo
Strix aluco (Tawny Owl)
S. a. sylvatica
Britain, W Europe
S. a. mauritanica
N Africa, Syria, Israel
S. a. aluco
Scandinavia, C & E Europe
S. a. volhyniae
SW Russia
S. a. siberiae
E Russia, W Siberia
S. a. willkonskii
Caucasus
S. a. obscurata
S Russia, N Iran
S. a. sanctinicolae
Iraq, W & SW Iran
S. a. härmsi
Russian Turkestan
S. a. biddulphi
Pakistan, NW India
S. a. nivicola
Himalayas, S & W China
S. a. yamadae
S Taiwan
S. a. ma
NE China, Korea
Strix occidentalis (Spotted Owl)
S. o. caurina
S British Colombia to N California
S. o. occidentalis
S California
S. o. lucida
SW USA to C Mexico
Strix varia (Barred Owl)
S. v. varia
S Canada, EC USA
S. v. georgica
S & SE USA
S. v. helveola
SC Texas
S. v. sartorii
N & C Mexico
S. v. fulvescens
S Mexico, W Guatemala, Honduras
Strix hylophila (Rusty Barred Owl)
Brazil, Paraguay, N Argentina
Strix rufipes (Rufous-legged Owl)
S. r. chacoensis
Paraguay, N Argentina

S. r. sanborn
Chiloe I
S. r. rufipes
S Chile, S Argentina
Strix uralensis (Ural Owl)
S. u. liturata
N Scandinavia to C Russia
S. u. uralensis
E Russia to W Siberia
S. u. yenisseensis
C Siberia
S. u. daurica
Lake Baikal to W Amurland
S. u. nikolskii
Sea of Okhotsk to E Amurland
S. u. tatibanai
Sakhalin I
S. u. coreensis
SE Manchuria, Korea, Hokkaido I
S. u. hondoensis
N Honshu I
S. u. momiyamae
C. Honshu I
S. u. fuscescens
S Honshu I, Kyushu I
Strix davidi (David's Wood Owl)
W Szechwan
Strix nebulosa (Great Grey Owl)
S. n. nebulosa
N North America
S. n. lapponica
N Europe, N Asia, Sakhalin I
S. n. elisabethae
N Mongolia

RHINOPTYNX
Rhinoptynx clamator (Striped Owl)
R. c. clamator
SE Mexico to C South America
R. c. oberi
Tobago I
R. c. midas
S Brazil, Paraguay, Uruguay, N Argentina

ASIO
Asio otus (Long-eared Owl)
A. o. otus
Europe, Asia, NW Africa
A. o. canariensis
Canary Is
A. o. tuftsi
Canada
A. o. wilsonianus
S Canada, W & C USA
Asio stygius (Stygian Owl)
A. s. lambi
NW Mexico
A. s. robustus
E Mexico, Guatemala, Nicaragua

A. s. siguapa
Cuba, Isle of Pines
A. s. noctipetens
Hispaniola, Gonave I
A. s. stygius
C & S Brazil
A. s. barberoi
Paraguay, N Argentina
Asio abyssinicus (Abyssinian Long-eared Owl)
A. a. abyssinicus
Ethiopia
A. a. graueri
E Zaire, Mt Kenya
Asio madagascariensis (Madagascar Long-eared Owl)
Madagascar
Asio flammeus (Short-eared Owl)
A. f. flammeus
Europe, N Asia, N Africa, North America
A. f. bogotensis
Colombia, Ecuador
A. f. pallidicaudus
Venezuela
A. f. suinda
S Peru, S Brazil to Tierra del Fuego
A. f. sanfordi
Falkland Is
A. f. sandwichensis
Hawaiian Is
A. f. ponapensis
Ponapé I
A. f. domingensis
Hispaniola
A. f. portoricensis
Puerto Rico
A. f. galapagoensis
Galapagos Is
Asio capensis (African Marsh Owl)
A. c. tingitanus
NW Africa, Senegal to Cameroun
A. c. capensis
Ethiopia to Angola & Cape Province
A. c. hova
Madagascar

PSEUDOSCOPS
Pseudoscops grammicus (Jamaican Owl)
Jamaica

NESASIO
Nesasio solomonensis (Fearful Owl)
Bougainville I, Choiseul I, Ysabel I

AEGOLIUS
Aegolius funereus (Tengmalm's Owl)
A. f. funereus
N & C Europe, W Siberia
A. f. caucasicus
N Caucasus

A. f. sibiricus
NC & NE Asia
A. f. pallens
Tien Shan, Tarbagatai
A. f. jakutorum
C Siberia
A. f. beickianus
N Kansu
A. f. magnus
NE Siberia
A. f. richardsoni
N Canada to N USA
Aegolius acadicus (Saw-whet Owl)
A. a. acadicus
Canada, W USA, N Mexico
A. a. brooksi
Queen Charlotte Is
Aegolius ridgwayi (Unspotted Saw-whet Owl)
A. r. tacanensis
S Mexico
A. r. rostratus
Guatemala
A. r. ridgwayi
Costa Rica
Aegolius harrisii (Buff-fronted Owl)
A. h. harrisii
Colombia, Ecuador, Venezuela
A. h. iheringi
SE Brazil, Paraguay, N Argentina

Caprimulgiformes

74 STEATORNITHDAE (OILBIRD)

STEATORNIS
Steatornis caripensis (Oilbird)
Peru, Ecuador to the Guianas, Trinidad

75 PODARGIDAE (FROGMOUTHS)

PODARGUS
Podargus strigoides (Tawny Frogmouth)
P. s. phalaenoides
NW Australia, Northern Territory,
Melville I
P. s. lilae
Groote Eylandt I
P. s. gouldi
W Cape York Peninsula
P. s. cornwalli
E Queensland
P. s. brachypterus
NW Victoria, C Australia
P. s. strigoides
SE Queensland, New South Wales
P. s. victoriae
S New South Wales, E South Australia
P. s. cuvieri
Tasmania

Podargus papuensis (Papuan Frogmouth)
New Guinea & Is, Cape York Peninsula
Podargus ocellatus (Marbled Frogmouth)
P. o. ocellatus
New Guinea & islands
P. o. marmoratus
Cape York Peninsula
P. o. intermedius
Triobriand Is, Fergusson I, Goodenough I
P. o. meeki
Tagula I
P. o. inexpectatus
Solomon Is

BATRACHOSTOMUS
Batrachostomus auritus (Large Frogmouth)
Malaysia, Sumatra, Borneo
Batrachostomus harterti (Dulit Frogmouth)
C Borneo
Batrachostomus septimus (Philippine Frogmouth)
B. s. microrhynchus
N Luzon I
B. s. menagei
Panay I, Negros I
B. s. septimus
Mindanao I, Basilan I
Batrachostomus stellatus (Gould's Frogmouth)
Malaysia, Sumatra, Borneo
Batrachostomus moniliger (Ceylon Frogmouth)
SW India, Sri Lanka
Batrachostomus hodgsoni (Hodgson's Frogmouth)
B. h. hodgsoni
Sikkim to Assam & N Burma
B. h. indochinae
C Burma to Indochina
Batrachostomus poliolophus (Pale-headed Frogmouth)
Sumatra
Batrachostomus mixtus (Sharpe's Frogmouth)
Borneo
Batrachostomus javensis (Javan Frogmouth)
B. j. continentalis
S Burma, SE Thailand
B. j. javensis
W & C Java
B. j. cornutus
Sumatra, Bangka I, Billiton I, Borneo
B. j. chaseni
Palawan I, Banguey I
Batrachostomus affinis (Blyth's Frogmouth)
Malaysia, Sumatra, Borneo

76   NYCTIBIIDAE (POTOOS)   193

NYCTIBIUS
Nyctibius grandis (Great Potoo)
Panama to Peru & S Brazil
Nyctibius aethereus (Long-tailed Potoo)
N. a. chocoensis
W Colombia
N. a. longicaudatus
E Ecuador, E Peru to Guyana
N. a. aethereus
SE Brazil, Paraguay
Nyctibius griseus (Common Potoo)
N. g. mexicanus
S Mexico to Honduras
N. g. costaricensis
Nicaragua to W Panama
N. g. panamensis
C Panama to Peru
N. g. cornutus
C & S Brazil, Paraguay, N Argentina
N. g. griseus
N Brazil, the Guianas, Trinidad
N. g. jamaicensis
Jamaica
N. g. abbotti
Hispaniola, Gonave I
Nyctibius leucopterus (White-winged Potoo)
N. l. maculosus
E Colombia, E Ecuador
N. l. leucopterus
E Brazil
Nyctibius bracteatus (Rufous Potoo)
Guyana, S Colombia, E Ecuador, E Peru

77   AEGOTHELIDAE (OWLET-NIGHTJARS)

AEGOTHELES
Aegotheles crinifrons (Halmahera Owlet-Nightjar)
Halmahera I, Batjan I
Aegotheles insignis (Large Owlet-Nightjar)
A. i. insignis
NW & N New Guinea
A. i. tatei
S New Guinea
A. i. pulcher
SE New Guinea
Aegotheles cristatus (Owlet-Nightjar)
A. c. major
S New Guinea
A. c. leucogaster
N Australia
A. c. cristatus
C & S Australia
A. c. tasmanicus
Tasmania

***Aegotheles savesi* (New Caledonian Owlet-Nightjar)**
New Caledonia
***Aegotheles bennettii* (Barred Owlet-Nightjar)**
A. b. affinis
NW New Guinea
A. b. wiedenfeldi
N New Guinea
A. b. terborghi
EC New Guinea
A. b. bennettii
SE New Guinea
A. b. plumiferus
Fergusson I, Goodenough I
***Aegotheles wallacii* (Wallace's Owlet-Nightjar)**
A. w. wallacii
W New Guinea, Aru Is
A. w. gigas
WC New Guinea
A. w. manni
SW New Guinea
***Aegotheles albertisi* (Mountain Owlet-Nightjar)**
A. a. albertisi
NW New Guinea
A. a. wondiwoi
C New Guinea
A. a. salvadorii
C & S New Guinea
***Aegotheles archboldi* (Eastern Mountain Owlet-Nightjar)**
EC New Guinea

78 CAPRIMULGIDAE (NIGHTJARS)

CHORDEILINAE

LUROCALIS
***Lurocalis semitorquatus* (Semi-collared Nighthawk)**
L. s. stonei
Nicaragua
L. s. noctivagus
Panama
L. s. semitorquatus
N Colombia to the Guianas, N Brazil
L. s. schaeferi
NC Venezuela
L. s. nattereri
C & S Brazil
L. s. rufiventris
W Venezuela, E Colombia to Peru

CHORDEILES
***Chordeiles pusillus* (Least Nighthawk)**
C. p. septentrionalis
NW Brazil, E Venezuela, Guyana
C. p. pusillus
CE & S Brazil

C. p. esmeraldae
Venezuela
***Chordeiles rupestris* (Sand-coloured Nighthawk)**
C. r. xyostictus
C Colombia
C. r. rupestris
Upper Amazonia
***Chordeiles acutipennis* (Lesser Nighthawk)**
C. a. texensis
SW USA » C America
C. a. inferior
Baja California
C. a. micromeris
S Mexico, Guatemala
C. a. acutipennis
N South America
C. a. aequatorialis
W Ecuador
C. a. exilis
W Peru
C. a. crissalis
C Colombia
***Chordeiles minor* (Common Nighthawk)**
C. m. minor
Canada, C & E USA » C South America
C. m. hesperis
SW Canada, W USA » C South America
C. m. sennetti
NW USA » C South America
C. m. howelli
WC USA » C South America
C. m. henryi
SW USA » C South America
C. m. aserriensis
SE Texas » C South America
C. m. chapmani
SE USA » C South America
C. m. panamensis
Panama
C. m. vicinus
Bahama Is
C. m. gundlachii
Cuba, Jamaica, Puerto Rico

NYCTIPROGNE
***Nyctiprogne leucopyga* (Band-tailed Nighthawk)**
N. l. exigua
E Colombia, Venezuela
N. l. pallida
WC Venezuela
N. l. majuscula
C Brazil
N. l. leucopyga
E Venezuela, the Guianas, E & S Brazil
N. l. latifascia
C Venezuela

PODAGER
Podager nacunda (Nacunda Nighthawk)
  P. n. minor
    N & NE South America
  P. n. nacunda
    E Peru & C Brazil to Patagonia

CAPRIMULGINAE

EUROSTOPODUS
Eurostopodus guttatus (Spotted Nightjar)
  E. g. insulanus
    Babar I
  E. g. harterti
    NW Australia
  E. g. gilberti
    Groote Eylandt I
  E. g. guttatus
    E Australia, Aru Is
Eurostopodus mystacalis (White-throated Nightjar)
  E. m. mystacalis
    E Australia, New Guinea
  E. m. nigripennis
    Solomon Is
  E. m. exul
    New Caledonia
Eurostopodus diabolicus (Devilish Nightjar)
  N Celebes
Eurostopodus papuensis (Papuan Nightjar)
  E. p. papuensis
    Salawati I, W New Guinea
  E. p. astrolabae
    E New Guinea
Eurostopodus archboldi (Archbold's Nightjar)
  New Guinea
Eurostopodus temminckii (Malaysian Eared Nightjar)
  Malaysia, Sumatra, Borneo
Eurostopodus macrotis (Great Eared Nightjar)
  E. m. cerviniceps
    Assam to N Malaysia, W China, Indochina
  E. m. bourdilloni
    S India
  E. m. macrotis
    Luzon I, Mindoro I, Mindanao I
  E. m. jacobsoni
    Simalur I
  E. m. macropterus
    Celebes

VELES
Veles binotatus (Brown Nightjar)
  Ghana to E Cameroun

NYCTIDROMUS
Nyctidromus albicollis (Pauraque)
  N. a. insularis
    Tres Marias Is
  N. a. merrilli
    S Texas, E Mexico
  N. a. yucatanensis
    NW Mexico to Guatemala
  N. a. albicollis
    W Guatemala to Peru & E Brazil
  N. a. gilvus
    N Colombia
  N. a. derbyanus
    C & S Brazil, Paraguay

PHALAENOPTILUS
Phalaenoptilus nuttallii (Poorwill)
  P. n. nuttallii
    W & WC USA » C Mexico
  P. n. californicus
    W California
  P. n. hueyi
    SE California, SW Arizona
  P. n. dickeyi
    S Baja California
  P. n. centralis
    C Mexico

SIPHONORHIS
Siphonorhis brewsteri (Least Pauraque)
  Hispaniola, Gonave I

OTOPHANES
Otophanes mcleodii (Eared Poorwill)
  O. m. mcleodii
    Chihuahua, Jalisco
  O. m. rayi
    Guerrero
Otophanes yucatanicus (Yucatan Poorwill)
  SE Mexico, N Guatemala

NYCTIPHRYNUS
Nyctiphrynus ocellatus (Ocellated Poorwill)
  N. o. lautus
    NE Nicaragua
  N. o. rosenbergi
    W Colombia, NW Ecuador
  N. o. ocellatus
    E Ecuador, C Brazil to NE Argentina

CAPRIMULGUS
Caprimulgus carolinensis (Chuck Will's Widow)
  EC & S USA » Central America
Caprimulgus rufus (Rufous Nightjar)
  C. r. minimus
    Panama to Venezuela
  C. r. otiosus
    St Lucia I
  C. r. rufus
    the Guianas, NE Brazil

C. r. noctivigulus
C Colombia
C. r. rutilus
S Brazil, Paraguay
Caprimulgus cubanensis (Greater Antillean Nightjar)
C. c. cubanensis
Cuba, Isle of Pines
C. c. ekmani
Hispaniola
Caprimulgus sericocaudatus (Silky-tailed Nightjar)
C. s. sericocaudatus
Peru
C. s. mengeli
Upper Amazonia
Caprimulgus salvini (Tawny-collared Nightjar)
E Mexico
Caprimulgus badius (Yucatan Tawny-collared Nightjar)
Yucatan, Belize
Caprimulgus ridgwayi (Ridgway's Whippoorwill)
C. r. ridgwayi
W Mexico
C. r. troglodytes
Guatemala, Honduras
Caprimulgus vociferus (Whippoorwill)
C. v. vociferus
S Canada, E USA » Honduras
C. v. arizonae
SW USA, N Mexico
C. v. setosus
E Mexico
C. v. oaxacae
SC Mexico
C. v. chiapensis
S Mexico, Guatemala
C. v. vermiculatus
Honduras, El Salvador
C. v. noctitherus
Puerto Rico e?
Caprimulgus saturatus (Dusky Nightjar)
Costa Rica, W Panama
Caprimulgus longirostris (Band-winged Nightjar)
C. l. ruficervix
Colombia, Venezuela, Ecuador
C. l. roraimae
Mt Duida, Mt Roraima (Venezuela)
C. l. decussatus
W Peru
C. l. atripunctatus
Peru, Bolivia, N Chile
C. l. bifasciatus
C Chile
C. l. longirostris
Argentina

Caprimulgus cayennensis (White-tailed Nightjar)
C. c. albicauda
Costa Rica to N Colombia
C. c. apertus
W Colombia
C. c. insularis
Curaçao I, Bonaire I, Margarita I, N Venezuela
C. c. leopetes
Trinidad, Tobago I
C. c. cayennensis
E Colombia, S Venezuela, The Guianas, N Brazil
Caprimulgus candicans (White-winged Nightjar)
C Brazil, Paraguay
Caprimulgus maculicaudus (Spot-tailed Nightjar)
N & W Amazonia
Caprimulgus parvulus (Little Nightjar)
C. p. anthonyi
W Ecuador
C. p. heterurus
N Colombia
C. p. parvulus
E Peru to E Brazil & C Argentina
Caprimulgus maculosus (Cayenne Nightjar)
French Guiana
Caprimulgus nigrescens (Blackish Nightjar)
W & N Amazonia
Caprimulgus whitelyi (Roraiman Nightjar)
Mt Roraima (Venezuela)
Caprimulgus hirundinaceus (Pygmy Nightjar)
C. h. cearae
E Brazil
C. h. hirundinaceus
E Brazil
Caprimulgus ruficollis (Red-necked Nightjar)
C. r. ruficollis
Portugal, S Spain, Morocco
C. r. desertorum
Algeria, Tunisia » S Sahara
Caprimulgus indicus (Jungle Nightjar)
C. i. hazarae
Himalayas, Burma, Malaysia
C. i. indicus
India
C. i. kelaarti
Sri Lanka
C. i. jotaka
NE Asia, N China, Japan » Java, Borneo
C. i. phalaena
Palau Is
Caprimulgus europaeus (European Nightjar)

C. e. europaeus
N Europe, Russia, » C & S Africa
C. e. meridionalis
S Europe, N Africa, Caucasus » W Africa
C. e. sarudnyi
W Siberia, C Asia
C. e. unwini
SW Asia, Iran, Afghan » E Africa, NW India
C. e. plumipes
E Turkestan » SW Africa
Caprimulgus mahrattensis **(Sykes' Nightjar)**
Afghanistan to NW India
Caprimulgus centralasicus **(Vaurie's Nightjar)**
W China
Caprimulgus nubicus **(Nubian Nightjar)**
C. n. tamaricis
Dead Sea to Aden
C. n. nubicus
N Sudan
C. n. torridus
Somalia to N Tanzania
C. n. jonesi
Socotra I
Caprimulgus aegyptius **(Egyptian Nightjar)**
C. a. aegyptius
S Russia, Iran » Egypt & Sudan
C. a. saharae
N Sahara
Caprimulgus eximius **(Golden Nightjar)**
C. e. simplicior
N Niger, N Chad
C. e. eximius
W & N Sudan
Caprimulgus madagascariensis
(Madagascar Nightjar)
C. m. aldabrensis
Aldabra I
C. m. madagascariensis
Madagascar
Caprimulgus macrurus **(Long-tailed Nightjar)**
C. m. albonotatus
N & NE India
C. m. atripennis
S India
C. m. aequabilis
Sri Lanka
C. m. ambiguus
Burma, Thailand, S Indochina
C. m. bimaculatus
Malaysia, Sumatra
C. m. andamanicus
Andaman Is
C. m. macrurus
Java, Borneo, Palawan I
C. m. hainanus
Hainan I

C. m. manillensis
Philippine Is
C. m. delacouri
Mindanao I
C. m. jungei
Sula Is
C. m. celebensis
Celebes, Wetar I
C. m. oberholseri
Lombok I, Sumbawa I, Djampea I, Saleyer I
C. m. mesophanis
S Moluccas
C. m. kuehni
Babar I, Tenimber Is, Kei Is
C. m. schillmölleri
Halmahera I, W Papuan Is
C. m. yorki
New Britain, Aru Is, New Guinea, N Australia
C. m. meeki
Tagula I
Caprimulgus pectoralis **(African Dusky Nightjar)**
C. p. nigriscapularis
Guinea to E Zaire, Uganda
C. p. fervidus
Angola to Tanzania & Natal
C. p. pectoralis
Namibia, S Natal, Cape Province
Caprimulgus rufigena **(Rufous-cheeked Nightjar)**
C. r. fraenatus
Ethiopia to S Kenya
C. r. quanzae
Angola
C. r. rufigena
Southern Africa » W Africa
Caprimulgus donaldsoni **(Donaldson Smith's Nightjar)**
W Somalia & Kenya
Caprimulgus poliocephalus **(Abyssinian Nightjar)**
C. p. poliocephalus
Ethiopia to N Tanzania
C. p. ruwenzorii
E Zaire, Rwanda
C. p. guttifer
C Tanzania
C. p. koesteri
W Angola
Caprimulgus asiaticus **(Indian Nightjar)**
C. a. asiaticus
India to S Indochina
C. a. eidos
Sri Lanka
C. a. siamensis
N Thailand
Caprimulgus natalensis **(African White-tailed Nightjar)**

C. n. accrae
Liberia to W Cameroun
C. n. chadensis
Chad to Sudan, N Zaire
C. n. gabonensis
Gabon to C Zaire
C. n. carpi
Caprivi Strip, Namibia
C. n. fulviventris
Angola
C. n. mpusa
Zambia
C. n. natalensis
Natal
Caprimulgus inornatus (Plain Nightjar)
C. i. vinaceabrunneus
S Niger, N Nigeria
C. i. inornatus
Niger & Nigeria to Tanzania & Yemen
C. i. malbranti
Ennedi Mts
Caprimulgus stellatus (Star-spotted Nightjar)
C. s. stellatus
W Ethiopia, Somalia & Kenya
C. s. simplex
S Ethiopia
Caprimulgus ludovicianus (Ludovic's Nightjar)
SW Ethiopia
Caprimulgus monticolus (Franklin's Nightjar)
C. m. monticolus
India
C. m. burmanicus
E Himalayas to Thailand
C. m. amoyensis
SE China
C. m. stictomus
Indochina, Taiwan
Caprimulgus affinis (Allied Nightjar)
C. a. affinis
Sumatra, Borneo, Java
C. a. kasuidori
Savu I, Sumba I
C. a. griseatus
Luzon I, Mindoro I, Negros I, Cebu I
C. a. mindanensis
Mindanao I
C. a. propinquus
C & S Celebes
C. a. undulatus
Lesser Sunda Is
C. a. timorensis
Timor I
Caprimulgus tristigma (Freckled Nightjar)
C. t. sharpei
Senegal to S Sudan

C. t. tristigma
E Sudan & Ethiopia to S Kenya
C. t. lentiginosus
Angola to Tanzania & Transvaal
Caprimulgus concretus (Bonaparte's Nightjar)
Sumatra, Borneo, Billiton I
Caprimulgus pulchellus (Salvadori's Nightjar)
C. p. pulchellus
Sumatra
C. p. bartelsi
Java
Caprimulgus enarratus (Collared Nightjar)
NW & E Madagascar
Caprimulgus batesi (Bates' Nightjar)
S Cameroun to C Zaire

SCOTORNIS
Scotornis fossii (Gabon Nightjar)
Cameroun to Zaire & Mozambique
Scotornis climacurus (Long-tailed Nightjar)
S. c. clarus
Ethiopia to C Tanzania
S. c. climacurus
Senegal to Sudan
S. c. nigricans
W Sudan
S. c. leoninus
Sierra Leone
S. c. sclateri
Nigeria to C Zaire

MACRODIPTERYX
Macrodipteryx longipennis (Standard-winged Nightjar)
Senegal to Ethiopia

SEMEIOPHORUS
Semeiophorus vexillarius (Pennant-winged Nightjar)
Angola to Transvaal » Nigeria & Uganda

HYDROPSALIS
Hydropsalis climacocerca (Ladder-tailed Nightjar)
H. c. schomburgki
E Venezuela, Guyana, Surinam
H. c. climacocerca
Upper Amazonia
H. c. pallidior
C Brazil
H. c. intercedens
C Brazil
H. c. canescens
C Brazil
Hydropsalis brasiliana (Scissor-tailed Nightjar)
H. b. brasiliana
C & E Brazil

H. b. furcifera
  E Bolivia, S Brazil, Uruguay

UROPSALIS
Uropsalis segmentata (Swallow-tailed Nightjar)
  U. s. segmentata
    Colombia, Ecuador, Peru, Bolivia
  U. s. kalinowskii
    C Peru
Uropsalis lyra (Lyre-tailed Nightjar)
  U. l. lyra
    Colombia, Ecuador, Venezuela
  U. l. peruana
    Peru

MACROPSALIS
Macropsalis creagra (Long-trained Nightjar)
  SE Brazil

ELEOTHREPTUS
Eleothreptus anomalus (Sickle-winged Nightjar)
  Paraguay, N Argentina, SE Brazil

Apodiformes

79 APODIDAE (SWIFTS)

CYPSELOIDINAE

CYPSELOIDES
Cypseloides fumigatus (Sooty Swift)
  E Panama to S Brazil
Cypseloides cherriei (Spot-fronted Swift)
  Costa Rica
Cypseloides cryptus (White-chinned Swift)
  Costa Rica, Guyana, Peru
Cypseloides lemosi (White-chested Swift)
  Cauca (Colombia)
Cypseloides major (Great Swift)
  S Bolivia, NW Argentina
Cypseloides phelpsi (Tepui Swift)
  S Venezuela
Cypseloides rutilus (Chestnut-collared Swift)
  C. r. griseifrons
    W Mexico
  C. r. brunnitorques
    SE Mexico to Peru
  C. r. rutilus
    the Guianas, Trinidad

NEPHOECETES
Nephoecetes niger (Black Swift)
  N. n. borealis
    SE Alaska to SW USA » Mexico
  N. n. costaricensis
    Honduras to Costa Rica

N. n. niger
  West Indies, Trinidad

AERORNIS
Aerornis senex (Great Dusky Swift)
  S Brazil, Paraguay, NE Argentina

STREPTOPROCNE
Streptoprocne zonaris (White-collared Swift)
  S. z. mexicana
    S Mexico, Belize to El Salvador
  S. z. pallidifrons
    Greater Antilles
  S. z. albicincta
    Honduras to NW & C South America
  S. z. altissima
    Colombia, Ecuador
  S. z. zonaris
    S Brazil, Bolivia, W Argentina
Streptoprocne biscutatus (Biscutate Swift)
  E Brazil
Streptoprocne semicollaris (White-naped Swift)
  C Mexico

APODINAE

COLLOCALIINI

COLLOCALIA
Collocalia gigas (Giant Swiftlet)
  Malaysia, Sumatra, Java
Collocalia spodiopygia (White-rumped Swiftlet)
  C. s. sororum
    C S & SE Celebes
  C. s. infuscata
    N Moluccas
  C. s. ceramensis
    S Moluccas
  C. s. eichhorni
    Bismarck Archipelago
  C. s. reichenowi
    Guadalcanal I
  C. s. terraereginae
    N Queensland
  C. s. leucopygia
    Loyalty Is, New Hebrides, New Caledonia
  C. s. assimilis
    Fiji Is
  C. s. townsendi
    Tonga I
  C. s. spodiopygia
    Samoa Is
Collocalia francica (Grey-rumped Swiftlet)
  C. f. francica
    Mauritius, Réunion I
  C. f. inexpectata
    Andaman Is, Nicobar Is

C. f. germani
Malaysia, Indochina, N Borneo
C. f. amechana
Anamba Is
C. f. amelis
Luzon I, Cebu I, Mindanao I
C. f. perplexa
E Bornean islands
C. f. bartelsi
Java, Kangean I
C. f. dammermanni
Lesser Sunda Is, Bali I to Flores I
C. f. micans
Sumba I, Savu I, Timor I
C. f. pelewensis
Palau Is
C. f. bartschi
Guam I
Collocalia elaphra (Seychelles Cave Swiftlet)
Seychelles
Collocalia unicolor (Indian Edible-nest Swiftlet)
SW India, Sri Lanka
Collocalia vanikorensis (Uniform Swiftlet)
C. v. aenigma
C & SE Celebes
C. v. heinrichi
S Celebes
C. v. moluccarum
Moluccas, Kei Is
C. v. coultasi
Admiralty Is
C. v. lihirensis
St Matthias Is, Lihir Is
C. v. waigeuensis
Waigeo I
C. v. steini
Numfor I
C. v. granti
S & E New Guinea, Fergusson I
C. v. tagulae
Louisiade Archipelago, Tagula I, Misima I
C. v. yorki
Cape York Peninsula
C. v. vanikorensis
Solomon Is, Santa Cruz I, New Hebrides, New Caledonia
Collocalia inquieta (Carolines Swiftlet)
C. i. rukensis
Caroline Is, Truk I, Yap I
C. i. ponapensis
Ponapé I
C. i. inquieta
Kusaie I
Collocalia salangana (Mossy Swiftlet)
C. s. salangana
India, China, Indochina

C. s. natunae
N Borneo, Natuna Is
Collocalia hirundinacea (Mountain Swiftlet)
C. h. baru
Japen I
C. h. hirundinacea
New Guinea, Dampier I, Goodenough I
C. h. excelsa
Snowy Mts, New Guinea
Collocalia leucophaea(Tahitian Swiftlet)
Society Is
Collocalia ocista (Marquesan Swiftlet)
Marquesas Is
Collocalia sawtelli (Cook Is Swiftlet)
Cook Is
Collocalia brevirostris (Himalayan Swiftlet)
C. b. innominata
C & W China to Malaysia, N Vietnam
C. b. rogersi
NW Thailand, N Laos
C. b. brevirostris
Himalayas, N Burma, SE Tibet
Collocalia whiteheadi (Whitehead's Swiftlet)
C. w. tsubame
Palawan I
C. w. whiteheadi
Philippine Is, New Guinea
C. w. origenis
Mindanao I
C. w. apoensis
Mt Apo (Mindanao I)
Collocalia nuditarsus (Schrader Mountain Swiftlet)
NC New Guinea
Collocalia papuensis (Idenburg River Swiftlet)
New Guinea
Collocalia orientalis (Guadalcanal Swiftlet)
Guadalcanal I
Collocalia fuciphaga (Thunberg's Swiftlet)
Java
Collocalia maxima (Lowe's Swiftlet)
C. m. maxima
Malaysia, Anamba Is
C. m. lowi
Sumatra, Nias I, Labuan I, N & W Borneo
C. m. tichelmani
SE Borneo
C. m. palawanensis
Palawan I
C. m. vulcanorum
Java
Collocalia esculenta (White-bellied Swiftlet)

C. e. affinis
Andaman Is, Nicobar Is
C. e. elachyptera
S Thailand, Mergui Archipelago
C. e. cyanoptila
Malaysia, E Sumatra, Billiton I, Borneo
C. e. oberholseri
W Sumatra, Nias I, Mentawi Is
C. e. linchi
SE Sumatra, Java to Lombok I, Kangean I
C. e. natalis
Christmas I
C. e. dodgei
N Borneo
C. e. isonota
Luzon I, Mindoro I, Mindanao I
C. e. bagobo
Mt Apo (Mindanao I)
C. e. sumbawae
Sumbawa I, Flores I, Sumba I
C. e. minuta
Tanahdjampea I, Kalao I
C. e. neglecta
Alor I to Damar I, Timor I
C. e. esculenta
Celebes, Moluccas, New Guinea
C. e. erwini
S New Guinea
C. e. stresemanni
Admiralty Is, Bismarck Archipelago
C. e. becki
N & C Solomon Is
C. e. makirensis
San Cristobal I
C. e. desiderata
Rennell I
C. e. uropygialis
New Caledonia, New Hebrides
Collocalia marginata (Philippine Swiftlet)
C. m. marginata
Luzon I, Mindoro I, Masbate I, Cebu I,
Bohol I, Palawan I
C. m. septentrionalis
Babuyan I, Calayan I, Camiguin I (North)
Collocalia troglodytes (Pygmy Swiftlet)
Philippine Is, Palawan I

SCHOUTEDENAPUS
Schoutedenapus myioptilus (Scarce Swift)
S. m. poensis
Fernando Po I
S. m. myioptilus
Kenya to Malawi
S. m. chapini
E Zaire
**Schoutedenapus schoutedeni
(Schouteden's Swift)**
E Zaire

CHAETURINI

MEARNSIA
**Mearnsia picina (Philippine Spinetailed
Swift)**
Leyte I, Cebu I, Mindanao I
**Mearnsia novaeguineae (New Guinea
Spinetailed Swift)**
M. n. bürgersi
New Guinea
M. n. novaeguineae
S New Guinea

ZOONAVENA
**Zoonavena grandidieri (Madagascar
Spinetailed Swift)**
Madagascar
**Zoonavena thomensis (Sao Thomé
Spinetailed Swift)**
Sao Thomé I
**Zoonavena sylvatica (Indian White-
rumped Spinetailed Swift)**
India, Burma

TELACANTHURA
**Telacanthura ussheri (Mottle-throated
Spinetailed Swift)**
T. u. ussheri
Senegal to N Nigeria
T. u. sharpei
S Cameroun to E Zaire
T. u. stictilaema
SW Kenya to S Malawi
T. u. marwitzi
C Tanzania
T. u. benguellensis
Angola
**Telacanthura melanopygia (Ituri Mottle-
throated Spinetailed Swift)**
N Zaire

RAPHIDURA
**Raphidura leucopygialis (White-rumped
Spinetailed Swift)**
S Burma to Sumatra, Java, Borneo
**Raphidura sabini (Sabine's Spinetailed
Swift)**
Sierra Leone to NE Zaire

NEAFRAPUS
**Neafrapus cassini (Cassin's Spinetailed
Swift)**
S Cameroun to N Zaire
**Neafrapus boehmi (Boehm's Spinetailed
Swift)**
W Angola to Mozambique & Tanzania

HIRUNDAPUS
**Hirundapus caudacuta (White-throated
Spinetailed Swift)**
H. c. caudacuta
NE Asia, Japan » E China, Australia

H. c. nudipes
Himalayas » Java
H. c. bourreti
Indochina
H. c. formosanus
Taiwan
Hirundapus cochinchinensis (White-vented Spinetailed Swift)
H. c. rupchandi
Nepal
H. c. cochinchinensis
E Himalayas to Indochina, Malaysia, Java, Sumatra
Hirundapus gigantea (Brown Spinetailed Swift)
H. g. indicus
E India to Indochina, Andaman Is
H. g. gigantea
Malaysia, Sumatra, Java, Borneo, Palawan I
H. g. dubius
Luzon, Mindoro I, Negros I, Mindanao I
H. g. ernsti
W Java
Hirundapus celebensis (Celebes Spinetailed Swift)
N Celebes

CHAETURA
Chaetura spinicauda (Band-rumped Swift)
C. s. fumosa
W Costa Rica, Panama, N Colombia
C. s. aetherodroma
Panama
C. s. latirostris
Amacuro (Venezuela)
C. s. spinicauda
E Venezuela, the Guianas, N Brazil
C. s. aethalea
C Brazil
Chaetura martinica (Lesser Antillian Swift)
Lesser Antilles
Chaetura cinereiventris (Grey-rumped Swift)
C. c. phaeopygos
E Nicaragua to Panama
C. c. lawrencei
Grenada I, Trinidad, Tobago I
C. c. schistacea
E Colombia, W Venezuela
C. c. guianensis
Guyana, E Venezuela
C. c. occidentalis
W Colombia, W Ecuador
C. c. sclateri
Upper Amazonia
C. c. egregia
Bolivia

C. c. cinereiventris
E Brazil
Chaetura pelagica (Chimney Swift)
S Canada to S USA » C South America
Chaetura vauxi (Vaux's Swift)
C. v. vauxi
SW Canada to SW USA » Central America
C. v. tamaulipensis
E Mexico
C. v. richmondi
S Mexico to Costa Rica
C. v. ochropygia
E Panama
C. v. gaumeri
Yucatan peninsula, Cozumel I
C. v. aphanes
N Venezuela
Chaetura chapmani (Chapman's Swift)
C. c. chapmani
French Guiana, Trinidad
C. c. viridipennis
C Brazil
Chaetura andrei (Ashy-tailed Swift)
C. a. andrei
C Venezuela
C. a. meridionalis
C South America » Colombia
Chaetura brachyura (Short-tailed Swift)
C. b. praevelox
Grenada I, St Vincent I
C. b. brachyura
Upper Amazonia, the Guianas, S Brazil
C. b. ocypetes
Peru
C. b. cinereocauda
E Brazil
APODINI

AERONAUTES
Aeronautes saxatilis (White-throated Swift)
A. s. saxatilis
SW Canada to SW USA » Mexico
A. s. nigrior
Guatemala, El Salvador
Aeronautes montivagus (White-tipped Swift)
A. m. montivagus
N Venezuela, Peru, Bolivia
A. m. tatei
Mt Duida (Venezuela)
Aeronautes andecolus (Andean Swift)
A. a. parvulus
W Peru, N Chile
A. a. peruvianus
SE Peru
A. a. andecolus
Bolivia, W Argentina

TACHORNIS
Tachornis phoenicobia (Antillean Palm Swift)
T. p. iradii
Cuba, Isle of Pines
T. p. phoenicobia
Hispaniola, Jamaica
Tachornis furcata (Pygmy Swift)
T. f. furcata
NE Colombia, NW Venezuela
T. f. nigrodorsalis
W Venezuela
Tachornis squamata (Fork-tailed Palm Swift)
T. s. semota
E Peru, S Venezuela
T. s. squamata
Trinidad, the Guianas, C & E Brazil

PANYPTILA
Panyptila sanctihieronymi (Great Swallow-tailed Swift)
W Guatemala
Panyptila cayennensis (Lesser Swallow-tailed Swift)
P. c. veraecrucis
E Mexico
P. c. cayennensis
SE Nicaragua to N South America

CYPSIURUS
Cypsiurus batasiensis (Asian Palm Swift)
C. b. batasiensis
India, Sri Lanka
C. b. infumatus
Burma to Indochina, Malaysia, Sumatra, Java, Borneo
C. b. pallidior
Philippine Is
Cypsiurus parvus (African Palm Swift)
C. p. parvus
Senegal to N Ethiopia
C. p. brachypterus
Sierra Leone to Angola & S Zaire
C. p. myochrous
S Ethiopia to S Malawi
C. p. gracilis
Madagascar

APUS
Apus melba (Alpine Swift)
A. m. melba
S Europe to Himalayas » N Africa
A. m. tuneti
N Africa, Israel to Iran
A. m. archeri
Somalia
A. m. maximus
Mt Ruwenzori (Zaire)
A. m. africanus
E & S Africa

A. m. marjoriae
Namibia
A. m. willsi
Madagascar
A. m. bakeri
S India, Sri Lanka
Apus aequatorialis (Mottled Swift)
A. a. aequatorialis
Ethiopia to Angola & Malawi
A. a. reichenowi
S Kenya
A. a. furensis
W Sudan
A. a. bamendae
E Cameroun
A. a. schubotzi
Mt Ruwenzori (Zaire)
A. a. lowei
Sierra Leone
Apus alexandri (Alexander's Swift)
Cape Verde Is
Apus barbatus (African Black Swift)
A. b. barbatus
S Malawi to Cape Province
A. b. hollidayi
Zambia
A. b. balstoni
Madagascar
A. b. mayottensis
Mayotte I
A. b. sladeniae
Fernando Po I, S Cameroun
A. b. roehli
Kivu area (E Zaire)
A. b. granvillei
Sierra Leone
Apus berliozi (Berlioz' Swift)
A. b. berliozi
Socotra I
A. b. bensoni
N Kenya
Apus bradfieldi (Bradfield's Swift)
Namibia
Apus niansae (Nyanza Swift)
A. n. niansae
N Ethiopia to Malawi
A. n. somalicus
Somalia
Apus pallidus (Pallid Swift)
A. p. brehmorum
Madeira I, Canary Is, SW Europe, C Sahara
A. p. illyricus
Yugoslavia, Cyprus
A. p. pallidus
Egypt, Israel, to Iran & Pakistan
Apus apus (Common Swift)
A. a. apus
W Europe to C Asia » Africa

A. a. pekinensis
Middle East to N China » India
& E & S Africa
A. a. unicolor
Madeira I, W Canary Is
Apus acuticauda (Dark-backed Swift)
Nepal, Assam
Apus pacificus (Northern White-rumped Swift)
A. p. pacificus
NE Asia, China, Japan » SE Asia, Australia
A. p. leuconyx
Himalayas, N India
A. p. cooki
C Burma, Malaysia to S China, N Indochina
A. p. kanoi
Taiwan
Apus affinis (House Swift)
A. a. bannermani
Sao Thomé I, Principé I, Fernando Po I
A. a. abessynicus
Gambia to Somalia & Cape Province
A. a. galilejensis
N Africa, Middle East, Iran
A. a. theresae
NW Cape Province
A. a. affinis
India
A. a. singalensis
S India, Sri Lanka
A. a. nipalensis
Nepal to N Assam
A. a. subfurcatus
S China, Burma to Philippine Is, Borneo,
Java, Sumatra
Apus horus (Horus Swift)
Ethiopia to Rhodesia
Apus caffer (White-rumped Swift)
A. c. streubelii
N Sudan & Ethiopia to S Kenya
A. c. ansorgei
S Zaire, N Angola
A. c. caffer
South Africa
Apus batesi (Bates' Black Swift)
Cameroun to NE Zaire

80 HEMIPROCNIDAE (TREE SWIFTS)

HEMIPROCNE
Hemiprocne coronata (Indian Crested Swift)
India to Indochina
Hemiprocne coronata (Indian Crested Tree Swift)
H. l. harterti
S Burma, Malaysia, Sumatra, Borneo
H. l. perlonga
Simalur I

H. l. ocyptera
Nias I
H. l. thoa
Batu I, Pagi Is, Enggano I
H. l. longipennis
Java, Bali I
H. l. wallacii
Celebes, Sula Is
Hemiprocne mystacea (Whiskered Tree Swift)
H. m. confirmata
Moluccas, Aru Is
H. m. mystacea
W Papuan islands & New Guinea
H. m. aëroplanes
Bismarck Archipelago
H. m. woodfordiana
Solomon Is
Hemiprocne comata (Lesser Tree Swift)
H. c. comata
Malaysia, Sumatra, Borneo
H. c. stresemanni
Pagi Is
H. c. major
Philippine Is
H. c. nakamurai
Mindanao I, Basilan I

81 TROCHILIDAE (HUMMINGBIRDS)

DORYFERA
Doryfera johannae (Blue-fronted Lancebill)
D. j. johannae
SE Colombia, E Ecuador, NE Peru
D. j. guianensis
SE Venezuela, S Guyana
Doryfera ludoviciae (Green-fronted Lancebill)
D. l. veraguensis
Costa Rica, W Panama
D. l. ludoviciae
C Colombia, W Venezuela, C Peru
D. l. rectirostris
C Ecuador
D. l. grisea
NW Bolivia

ANDRODON
Androdon aequatorialis (Tooth-billed Hummingbird)
E Panama, W Colombia, W Ecuador
RAMPHODON
Ramphodon naevius (Saw-billed Hermit)
SE Brazil
GLAUCIS
Glaucis dohrnii (Hook-billed Hermit)
E Brazil
Glaucis aenea (Bronzy Hermit)
Nicaragua to NW Ecuador

Glaucis hirsuta (Rufous-breasted Hermit)
G. h. affinis
E Panama to W Venezuela & NE Peru
G. h. insularum
Grenada I, Trinidad, Tobago I
G. h. hirsuta
N & E Venezuela, the Guianas, N Brazil,
Bolivia

THRENETES
Threnetes niger (Sooty Barbthroat)
French Guiana
Threnetes grzimeki (Black Barbthroat)
Brazil
Threnetes leucurus (Pale-tailed Barbthroat)
T. l. loehkeni
N Brazil
T. l. cervinicauda
E Colombia, E Ecuador, NE Peru
T. l. rufigastra
E Peru
T. l. leucurus
the Guianas, S Venezuela, N & C Brazil
T. l. medianus
NE Brazil
Threnetes ruckeri (Band-tailed Barbthroat)
T. r. ventosus
Nicaragua to W Panama
T. r. darienensis
E Panama, N Colombia
T. r. ruckeri
W Colombia, W Ecuador
T. r. venezuelensis
W Venezuela

PHAETHORNIS
Phaethornis yaruqui (White-whiskered Hermit)
P. y. sanctijohannis
W Colombia
P. y. yaruqui
W Ecuador
Phaethornis guy (Green Hermit)
P. g. coruscus
Costa Rica, Panama, W Colombia
P. g. apicalis
C Colombia, E Ecuador, E Peru
P. g. guy
NE Venezuela, Trinidad
P. g. emiliae
WC Colombia
Phaethornis syrmatophorus (Tawny-bellied Hermit)
P. s. syrmatophorus
W Colombia, W Ecuador
P. s. columbianus
E Colombia, E Ecuador
P. s. huallagae
NE Peru

Phaethornis superciliosus (Long-tailed Hermit)
P. s. mexicanus
SW Mexico
P. s. veraecrucis
SE Mexico
P. s. longirostris
S Mexico to N Honduras
P. s. cephalus
S Honduras to W Panama
P. s. cassinii
E Panama, NW Colombia
P. s. moorei
E Colombia, E Ecuador, E Peru
P. s. baroni
W Ecuador
P. s. bolivianus
Bolivia
P. s. susurrus
N Colombia
P. s. saturatior
E Venezuela, NW Brazil
P. s. superciliosus
the Guianas, NE Brazil
P. s. muelleri
N Brazil
P. s. insignis
N Brazil
P. s. ochraceiventris
W Brazil
Phaethornis malaris (Great-billed Hermit)
P. m. ucayalii
Rio Ucayali (Peru)
P. m. insolitus
Venezuela
P. m. malaris
French Guiana
Phaethornis margarettae (Klabin Farm Long-tailed Hermit)
Brazil
Phaethornis eurynome (Scale-throated Hermit)
SE Brazil, Paraguay, NE Argentina
Phaethornis nigrirostris (Black-billed Hermit)
Brazil
Phaethornis hispidus (White-bearded Hermit)
Upper Amazonia
Phaethornis anthophilus (Pale-bellied Hermit)
P. a. hyalinus
Pearl Is (Panama)
P. a. anthophilus
N Colombia, W Venezuela
P. a. fuliginosus
S Colombia
Phaethornis koepckeae (Koepcke's Hermit)
Peru

Phaethornis bourcieri **(Straight-billed Hermit)**
P. b. whitelyi
SE Colombia, S Venezuela, the Guianas
P. b. bourcieri
E Ecuador, NE Peru, W Brazil

Phaethornis philippii **(Needle-billed Hermit)**
W Brazil

Phaethornis squalidus **(Dusky-throated Hermit)**
P. s. rupurumii
E Venezuela, Guyana, NW Brazil
P. s. maranhaoensis
EC Brazil
P. s. amazonicus
C Brazil
P. s. squalidus
SE Brazil

Phaethornis augusti **(Sooty-capped Hermit)**
P. a. augusti
E Colombia, N Venezuela
P. a. vicarius
EC Colombia
P. a. incanescens
SE Venezuela, S Guyana

Phaethornis pretrei **(Planalto Hermit)**
E Bolivia to SE Brazil

Phaethornis subochraceus **(Buff-bellied Hermit)**
NE Bolivia

Phaethornis nattereri **(Cinnamon-throated Hermit)**
C & E Brazil

Phaethornis gounellei **(Broad-tipped Hermit)**
C & E Brazil

Phaethornis ruber **(Reddish Hermit)**
P. r. episcopus
E & S Venezuela, Guyana
P. r. ruber
Surinam, French Guiana, N & C Brazil
P. r. nigricinctus
E Ecuador, W Brazil, NE Peru, E Bolivia
P. r. longipennis
EC Peru

Phaethornis stuarti **(White-browed Hermit)**
Bolivia

Phaethornis griseogularis **(Grey-chinned Hermit)**
P. g. griseogularis
Colombia, Ecuador, E Peru
P. g. zonura
N Peru
P. g. porcullae
W Peru

Phaethornis longuemareus **(Little Hermit)**
P. l. adolphi
SE Mexico
P. l. saturatus
Guatemala to C Panama
P. l. subrufescens
E Panama, W Colombia, W Ecuador
P. l. nelsoni
NW Colombia
P. l. striigularis
N & C Colombia
P. l. atrimentalis
E Ecuador, E Peru
P. l. ignobilis
San Esteban to Santa Lucia, Venezuela
P. l. imatacae
Bolivar (Venezuela)
P. l. longuemareus
French Guiana, Surinam, Trinidad
P. l. aethopyga
C Brazil

Phaethornis idaliae **(Minute Hermit)**
SE Brazil

EUTOXERES
Eutoxeres aquila **(White-tipped Sicklebill)**
E. a. salvini
E & SW Costa Rica, W Panama
E. a. munda
E Panama, W Colombia
E. a. aquila
E Colombia, E Ecuador
E. a. heterura
SW Colombia, W Ecuador

Eutoxeres condamini **(Buff-tailed Sicklebill)**
E. c. condamini
SE Colombia, E Ecuador
E. c. gracilis
E Peru

PHAEOCHROA
Phaeochroa cuvierii **(Scaly-breasted Hummingbird)**
P. c. roberti
E Guatemala to E Nicaragua
P. c. maculicauda
Costa Rica, W Panama
P. c. saturatior
Coiba Is, (Panama)
P. c. cuvierii
E Panama
P. c. berlepschi
N Colombia

CAMPYLOPTERUS
Campylopterus curvipennis **(Wedge-tailed Sabrewing)**
C. c. curvipennis
SE Mexico

C. c. yucatanensis
  Yucatan peninsula
C. c. excellens
  S Vera Cruz (Mexico)
C. c. pampa
  E Guatemala
Campylopterus largipennis (Grey-breasted Sabrewing)
C. l. largipennis
  E Venezuela, the Guianas, NW Brazil
C. l. obscurus
  NE Brazil
C. l. aequatorialis
  Northern Upper Amazonia
Campylopterus rufus (Rufous Sabrewing)
  S Mexico, W Guatemala, El Salvador
Campylopterus hyperythrus (Rufous-breasted Sabrewing)
  S Guyana, SE Venezuela
Campylopterus duidae (Buff-breasted Sabrewing)
C. d. duidae
  Mt Duida (Venezuela)
C. d. guayquinimae
  S Venezuela
Campylopterus hemileucurus (Violet Sabrewing)
C. h. hemileucurus
  S Mexico to Nicaragua
C. h. mellitus
  Costa Rica, W Panama
Campylopterus ensipennis (White-tailed Sabrewing)
  · NE Venezuela, Trinidad, Tobago I
Campylopterus falcatus (Lazuline Sabrewing)
  E Ecuador, Colombia, W Venezuela
Campylopterus phainopeplus (Santa Marta Sabrewing)
  N Colombia
Campylopterus villaviscensio (Napo Sabrewing)
  E Ecuador

EUPETOMENA
Eupetomena macroura (Swallow-tailed Hummingbird)
E. m. macroura
  the Guianas, Brazil, Paraguay
E. m. simoni
  NE Brazil
E. m. hirundo
  E Peru, NE Bolivia
E. m. boliviana
  Beni (Bolivia)

FLORISUGA
Florisuga mellivora (White-necked Jacobin)

F. m. mellivora
  C America, N South America, Trinidad
F. m. flabellifera
  Tobago I

MELANOTROCHILUS
Melanotrochilus fuscus (Black Jacobin)
  E Brazil

COLIBRI
Colibri delphinae (Brown Violetear)
  Guatemala to Panama, N & W South America
Colibri thalassinus (Green Violetear)
C. t. thalassinus
  C Mexico to Guatemala
C. t. minor
  Honduras
C. t. cabanidis
  Costa Rica, W Panama
C. t. cyanotus
  Venezuela, Colombia to Peru
C. t. crissalis
  Bolivia
Colibri coruscans (Sparkling Violetear)
C. c. coruscans
  Venezuela, Colombia to NW Argentina
C. c. germanus
  SE Venezuela, S Guyana
C. c. rostratus
  S Venezuela
Colibri serrirostris (White-vented Violetear)
  E Bolivia, S Brazil, N Argentina

ANTHRACOTHORAX
Anthracothorax viridigula (Green-throated Mango)
  NE Venezuela, the Guianas, NE Brazil
Anthracothorax prevostii (Green-breasted Mango)
A. p. prevostii
  C Mexico to Guatemala & Belize
A. p. gracilirostris
  El Salvador to Costa Rica
A. p. hendersoni
  Old Providence I
A. p. pinchoti
  St Andrews I
A. p. viridicordatus
  NW Venezuela
Anthracothorax nigricollis (Black-throated Mango)
A. n. nigricollis
  E Panama tropical South America
A. n. iridescens
  W Colombia, W Ecuador
Anthracothorax veraguensis (Veraguan Mango)
  W Panama

Anthracothorax dominicus (Antillean Mango)
A. d. dominicus
Hispaniola
A. d. aurulentus
Puerto Rico, St Thomas I
Anthracothorax viridis (Green Mango)
Puerto Rico
Anthracothorax mango (Jamaican Mango)
Jamaica

AVOCETTULA
Avocettula recurvirostris (Fiery-throated Awlbill)
Guyana, French Guiana, NE Brazil,
E Ecuador

EULAMPIS
Eulampis jugularis (Purple-throated Carib)
Lesser Antilles Is

SERICOTES
Sericotes holosericeus (Green-throated Carib)
S. h. holosericeus
E Puerto Rico, Virgin Is, Lesser Antilles
S. h. chlorolaemus
Grenada I

CHRYSOLAMPIS
Chrysolampis mosquitus (Ruby-Topaz Hummingbird)
N & E South America

ORTHORHYNCUS
Orthorhyncus cristatus (Antillean Crested Hummingbird)
O. c. exilis
Virgin Is & Lesser Antilles to St Lucia I
O. c. ornatus
St Vincent I
O. c. cristatus
Barbados I
O. c. emigrans
Union I to Grenada I

KLAIS
Klais guimeti (Violet-headed Hummingbird)
K. g. guimeti
Nicaragua to W Venezuela & E Ecuador
K. g. pallidiventris
E Peru, C Bolivia

ABEILLIA
Abeillia abeillei (Emerald-chinned Hummingbird)
A. a. abeillei
SE Mexico to N Honduras
A. a. aurea
S Honduras, N Nicaragua

STEPHANOXIS
Stephanoxis lalandi (Black-breasted Plovercrest)

S. l. lalandi
SE Brazil
S. l. loddigesii
S Brazil, Paraguay, NE Argentina

LOPHORNIS
Lophornis ornata (Tufted Coquette)
E Venezuela, the Guianas, Trinidad
Lophornis gouldii (Dot-eared Coquette)
N & C Brazil
Lophornis magnifica (Frilled Coquette)
C & S Brazil
Lophornis delattrei (Rufous-crested Coquette)
L. d. brachylopha
SW Mexico
L. d. lessoni
W Costa Rica, Panama, C Colombia
L. d. delattrei
NE & C Peru, Bolivia
Lophornis stictolopha (Spangled Coquette)
W Venezuela, E Colombia, E Ecuador
Lophornis chalybea (Festive Coquette)
L. c. verreauxii
C Colombia to C Bolivia
L. c. klagesi
E Venezuela
L. c. chalybea
SE Brazil
Lophornis pavonina (Peacock Coquette)
L. p. punctigula
Venezuela
L. p. pavonina
SE Venezuela, S Guyana
L. p. duidae
Mt Duida (Venezuela)
Lophornis insignibarbis(Bearded Coquette)
Colombia

PAPHOSIA
Paphosia helenae (Black-crested Coquette)
C Mexico to E Costa Rica
Paphosia adorabilis (White-crested Coquette)
SW Costa Rica

POPELAIRIA
Popelairia popelairii (Wire-crested Thorntail)
E Colombia, E Ecuador, NE Peru
Popelairia langsdorffi (Black-bellied Thorntail)
P. l. melanosternon
E Ecuador, E Peru, W Brazil
P. l. langsdorffi
E Brazil
Popelairia letitiae (Coppery Thorntail)
Bolivia
Popelairia conversii (Green Thorntail)
Costa Rica to W Ecuador

DISCOSURA
Discosura longicauda (Racquet-tailed Coquette)
  E Venezuela, Guyana, French Guiana, E Brazil

CHLORESTES
Chlorestes notatus (Blue-chinned Sapphire)
  C. n. obsoletus
    SE Colombia
  C. n. notatus
    Ecuador & W Brazil to Trinidad & Surinam
  C. n. cyanogenys
    C & E Brazil

CHLOROSTILBON
Chlorostilbon mellisugus (Blue-tailed Emerald)
  C. m. mellisugus
    Surinam, French Guiana, NE Brazil
  C. m. subfurcatus
    E & S Venezuela, Guyana, NW Brazil
  C. m. duidae
    S Venezuela
  C. m. phoeopygus
    Upper Amazonia
  C. m. peruanus
    Peru, E Bolivia
Chlorostilbon vitticeps (Simon's Emerald)
  E Ecuador
Chlorostilbon aureoventris (Glittering-bellied Emerald)
  C. a. pucherani
    E Brazil
  C. a. aureoventris
    Bolivia, Paraguay, W Argentina
  C. a. berlepschi
    Uruguay, E Argentina
Chlorostilbon canivetii (Fork-tailed Emerald)
  C. c. auriceps
    C & W Mexico
  C. c. canivetii
    SE Mexico, Belize, N Guatemala
  C. c. forficatus
    Holbox I, Cozumel I
  C. c. osberti
    C & W Guatemala, El Salvador, Honduras
  C. c. salvini
    W Nicaragua, W Costa Rica
  C. c. assimilis
    SW Costa Rica, SW Panama, Pearl Is (Panama)
  C. c. caribaeus
    Netherlands Antilles, Trinidad, NE Venezuela
  C. c. nitens
    N Colombia, NW Venezuela

C. c. nanus
    C Venezuela
Chlorostilbon ricordii (Cuban Emerald)
  C. r. bracei
    Bahama Is
  C. r. ricordii
    Cuba, Isle of Pines
Chlorostilbon swainsonii (Hispaniolan Emerald)
    Hispaniola, Gonave I
Chlorostilbon maugaeus (Puerto Rican Emerald)
    Puerto Rico
Chlorostilbon gibsoni (Red-billed Emerald)
  C. g. gibsoni
    C Colombia
  C. g. chrysogaster
    N Colombia
  C. g. pumilus
    W Colombia, W Ecuador
  C. g. melanorhynchus
    SC Colombia, NE Ecuador
Chlorostilbon russatus (Coppery Emerald)
    N Colombia, NW Venezuela
Chlorostilbon stenura (Narrow-tailed Emerald)
  C. s. stenura
    Colombia, Venezuela
  C. s. ignota
    N Venezuela
Chlorostilbon alice (Green-tailed Emerald)
    N Venezuela
Chlorostilbon poortmani (Short-tailed Emerald)
  C. p. poortmani
    Colombia, NW Venezuela
  C. p. euchloris
    Colombia

CYNANTHUS
Cynanthus sordidus (Dusky Hummingbird)
    W & S Mexico
Cynanthus latirostris (Broad-billed Hummingbird)
  C. l. magicus
    SW USA, NW Mexico
  C. l. latirostris
    EC Mexico
  C. l. propinquus
    C Mexico
  C. l. toroi
    W Mexico
  C. l. doubledayi
    W Mexico (S of *C. l. toroi*)
  C. l. lawrencei
    Tres Marias Is
  C. l. nitida
    SW Mexico

CYANOPHAIA
Cyanophaia bicolor (Blue-headed Hummingbird)
Guadelupe I, Dominica I, Martinique I

THALURANIA
Thalurania furcata (Fork-tailed Woodnymph)
T. f. ridgwayi
W Jalisco (Mexico)
T. f. townsendi
E Guatemala to SE Honduras
T. f. venusta
Nicaragua to W Panama
T. f. subtropicalis
E Panama, W Colombia
T. f. fannyi
W Colombia
T. f. colombica
N Colombia, W Venezuela
T. f. viridipectus
SC Colombia
T. f. verticeps
S Colombia, N Ecuador
T. f. hypochlora
W Ecuador
T. f. nigrofasciata
S Colombia, Ecuador, NW Brazil
T. f. taczanowskii
NE Peru
T. f. jelskii
E Peru
T. f. boliviana
NE Bolivia
T. f. simoni
W Brazil
T. f. rostrifera
W Venezuela
T. f. orenocensis
E Venezuela
T. f. fissilis
E Venezuela
T. f. refulgens
NE Venezuela
T. f. furcata
the Guianas, NE Brazil
T. f. furcatoides
NE Brazil
T. f. balzani
W Brazil, E Bolivia
T. f. baeri
NE C Brazil to SE Bolivia
T. f. eriphile
E & SE Brazil, Paraguay
Thalurania watertonii (Long-tailed Woodnymph)
Guyana, E Brazil
Thalurania glaucopis (Violet-capped Woodnymph)
E & S Brazil, Uruguay, Paraguay

Thalurania lerchi (Lerch's Woodnymph)
NC Colombia

NEOLESBIA
Neolesbia nehrkorni (Blue-tailed Sylph)
C Colombia

PANTERPE
Panterpe insignis (Fiery-throated Hummingbird)
Costa Rica, W Panama

DAMOPHILA
Damophila julie (Violet-bellied Hummingbird)
D. j. panamensis
Panama
D. j. julie
N Colombia
D. j. feliciana
W Ecuador

LEPIDOPYGA
Lepidopyga coeruleogularis (Sapphire-throated Hummingbird)
L. c. coeruleogularis
W Panama
L. c. confinis
NE Panama, NW Colombia
L. c. coelina
NE Colombia
Lepidopyga lilliae (Sapphire-bellied Hummingbird)
N Colombia
Lepidopyga goudoti (Shining Green Hummingbird)
L. g. goudoti
NC Colombia
L. g. zuliae
NW Venezuela
L. g. luminosa
N Colombia
L. g. phaeochroa
N Venezuela

HYLOCHARIS
Hylocharis xantusii (Black-fronted Hummingbird)
S Baja (California)
Hylocharis leucotis (White-eared Hummingbird)
H. l. borealis
SE Arizona, N Mexico
H. l. leucotis
C & S Mexico, Guatemala
H. l. pygmaea
El Salvador, Honduras, Nicaragua
Hylocharis eliciae (Blue-throated Goldentail)
S Mexico to W Panama

***Hylocharis sapphirina* (Rufous-throated Sapphire)**
E Venezuela and the Guianas to N Argentina
***Hylocharis cyanus* (White-chinned Sapphire)**
H. c. viridiventris
N Colombia to the Guianas, N Brazil
H. c. cyanus
E Brazil
H. c. rostrata
E Peru, NE Bolivia, W Brazil
H. c. conversa
Bolivia
***Hylocharis pyropygia* (Flame-rumped Sapphire)**
NE Brazil
***Hylocharis chrysura* (Gilded Hummingbird)**
E Bolivia, S Brazil, Uruguay, N Argentina
***Hylocharis grayi* (Blue-headed Sapphire)**
H. g. grayi
C Colombia to N Ecuador
H. g. humboldtii
W Colombia to NW Ecuador

CHRYSURONIA
***Chrysuronia oenone* (Golden-tailed Sapphire)**
C. o. oenone
N & E Venezuela, C Ecuador
C. o. longirostris
C Colombia
C. o. azurea
Ecuador
C. o. intermedia
Upper Amazon River
C. o. josephinae
E Peru, NE Bolivia

GOLDMANIA
***Goldmania violiceps* (Violet-capped Hummingbird)**
E Panama

GOETHALSIA
***Goethalsia bella* (Pirre Hummingbird)**
E Panama

TROCHILUS
***Trochilus polytmus* (Streamertail)**
T. p. polytmus
Jamaica
T. p. scitulus
NE Jamaica

LEUCOCHLORIS
***Leucochloris albicollis* (White-throated Hummingbird)**
SE Brazil, Paraguay, N Argentina

***Polytmus guainumbi* (White-tailed Goldenthroat)**
P. g. doctus
Colombia
P. g. guainumbi
Venezuela, the Guianas, Trinidad
P. g. thaumantias
E & C Brazil, Paraguay, Bolivia
***Polytmus milleri* (Tepui Goldenthroat)**
SE Venezuela
***Polytmus theresiae* (Green-tailed Goldenthroat)**
P. t. theresiae
the Guianas, N Brazil
P. t. leucorrhous
N Peru, NW Brazil

LEUCIPPUS
***Leucippus fallax* (Buffy Hummingbird)**
L. f. cervina
NE Colombia, NW Venezuela
L. f. richmondi
N Venezuela, Margarita I
L. f. fallax
N Venezuela
***Leucippus baeri* (Tumbes Hummingbird)**
W Peru
***Leucippus taczanowskii* (Spot-throated Hummingbird)**
L. t. fractus
N Peru
L. t. taczanowskii
C Peru
***Leucippus chlorocercus* (Olive-spotted Hummingbird)**
E Peru

TAPHROSPILUS
***Taphrospilus hypostictus* (Many-spotted Hummingbird)**
T. h. hypostictus
E Ecuador
T. h. peruvianus
E Peru, N Bolivia

AMAZILIA
***Amazilia chionogaster* (White-bellied Hummingbird)**
A. c. chionogaster
N & C Peru
A. c. hypoleucus
Bolivia, NW Argentina
***Amazilia viridicauda* (Green and White Hummingbird)**
Peru
***Amazilia candida* (White-bellied Emerald)**
A. c. genini
EC Mexico
A. c. candida
SE Mexico to Nicaragua

A. c. pacifica
W Guatemala

Amazilia chionopectus (White-chested Emerald)
A. c. chionopectus
E Venezuela to Surinam, Trinidad
A. c. whitelyi
Guyana
A. c. orienticola
French Guiana

Amazilia versicolor (Versicoloured Emerald)
A. v. millerii
E Colombia, Venezuela, W Brazil
A. v. hollandi
E Venezuela
A. v. nitidifrons
NE Brazil
A. v. versicolor
E Bolivia, Paraguay

Amazilia luciae (Honduras Emerald)
Honduras

Amazilia fimbriata (Glittering-throated Emerald)
A. f. elegantissima
N Venezuela
A. f. obscuricauda
Venezuela
A. f. maculicauda
E Venezuela to Surinam
A. f. fimbriata
French Guiana, E Brazil
A. f. apicalis
E Colombia, W Venezuela
A. f. fluviatilis
S Colombia, E Ecuador
A. f. laeta
NE Peru, W Brazil
A. f. alia
C Brazil
A. f. nigricauda
Bolivia to E Brazil
A. f. tephrocephala
SE Brazil

Amazilia distans (Tachira Emerald)
W Venezuela

Amazilia lactea (Sapphire-spangled Emerald)
A. l. bartletti
E & SE Peru, N Bolivia
A. l. zimmeri
SE Venezuela
A. l. lactea
E Brazil

Amazilia amabilis (Blue-chested Hummingbird)
A. a costaricensis
E Nicaragua to C Panama

A. a. decora
SW Costa Rica, W Panama
A. a. amabilis
E Panama, W Colombia, W Ecuador

Amazilia rosenbergi (Purple-chested Hummingbird)
W Colombia, NW Ecuador

Amazilia boucardi (Mangrove Hummingbird)
W Costa Rica

Amazilia franciae (Andean Emerald)
A. f. franciae
C Colombia
A. f. viridiceps
SW Colombia, W Ecuador
A. f. cyanocollis
N Peru
A. f. veneta
Colombia?

Amazilia leucogaster (Plain-bellied Emerald)
A. l. leucogaster
the Guianas, N Brazil
A. l. bahiae
E Brazil

Amazilia cyanocephala (Red-billed Azurecrown)
A. c. cyanocephala
SE Mexico, NW Guatemala
A. c. guatemalensis
Guatemala to N Nicaragua

Amazilia microrhyncha (Small-billed Azurecrown)
Honduras?

Amazilia cyanifrons (Indigo-capped Hummingbird)
A. c. alfaroana
Costa Rica
A. c. cyanifrons
N Colombia

Amazilia beryllina (Berylline Hummingbird)
A. b. viola
N & W Mexico
A. b. beryllina
E & C Mexico
A. b. lichtensteinei
S Mexico
A. b. devillei
S Mexico to Belize, El Salvador

Amazilia cyanura (Blue-tailed Hummingbird)
A. c. guatemalae
S Mexico, Guatemala
A. c. cyanura
El Salvador to W Nicaragua

Amazilia saucerrottei (Steely-vented Hummingbird)

A. s. hoffmanni
W & S Nicaragua, Costa Rica
A. s. saucerrottei
C Colombia
A. s. australis
S Colombia
A. s. warscewiczi
N & E Colombia
A. s. braccata
W Venezuela
Amazilia tobaci (Copper-rumped Hummingbird)
A. t. feliciae
N Venezuela
A. t. monticola
NW Venezuela
A. t. caudata
NE Venezuela
A. t. caurensis
E & SE Venezuela
A. t. aliciae
NE Venezuela, Margarita I
A. t. erythronotos
Trinidad
A. t. tobaci
Tobago I
Amazilia virdigaster (Green-bellied Hummingbird)
A. v. viridigaster
E Colombia, W Venezuela
A. v. duidae
Mt Duida (Venezuela
A. v. cupreicauda
S Venezuela, S Guyana
Amazilia edward (Snowy-breasted Hummingbird)
A. e. niveoventer
SW Costa Rica, W Panama
A. e. edward
C Panama
A. e. margaritarum
Pearl Is (Panama)
A. e. crosbyi
SE Panama
Amazilia rutila (Cinnamon Hummingbird)
A. r. diluta
NW Mexico
A. r. rutila
W & S Mexico to W Costa Rica
A. r. corallirostris
SW Mexico to El Salvador
A. r. graysoni
Maria Madre I
Amazilia yucatanensis (Buff-bellied Hummingbird)
A. y. chalconota
S Texas, NE Mexico

A. y. cerviniventris
S Mexico
A. y. yucatanensis
SE Mexico, N Guatemala, Belize
Amazilia tzacatl (Rufous-tailed Hummingbird)
A. t. tzacatl
E Mexico to W Venezuela
A. t. jucunda
SW Colombia, W Ecuador
Amazilia castaneiventris (Chestnut-bellied Hummingbird)
NC Colombia
Amazilia amazilia (Amazilia Hummingbird)
A. a. dumerilii
W Ecuador, NW Peru
A. a. alticola
S Ecuador, N Peru
A. a. amazilia
W Peru
A. a. caeruleigularis
W Peru
A. a. leucophoea
E & S Peru
Amazilia viridifrons (Green-fronted Hummingbird)
SW & S Mexico
Amazilia violiceps (Violet-crowned Hummingbird)
A. v. ellioti
W Mexico
A. v. violiceps
SC Mexico

EUPHERUSA
Eupherusa poliocerca (White-tailed Hummingbird)
SW Mexico
Eupherusa eximia (Stripe-tailed Hummingbird)
E. e. nelsoni
SE Mexico
E. e. eximia
S Mexico to N Nicaragua
E. e. egregia
Costa Rica, W Panama
Eupherusa cyanophrys (Black-fronted Hummingbird)
Oaxaca (Mexico)
Eupherusa nigriventris (Black-bellied Hummingbird)
E Costa Rica

ELVIRA
Elvira chionura (White-tailed Emerald)
SW Costa Rica
Elvira cupreiceps (Coppery-headed Emerald)
E Costa Rica

MICROCHERA

Microchera albocoronata (Snowcap)
M. a. parvirostris
E Nicaragua, E Costa Rica
M. a. albocoronata
NW Panama

CHALYBURA
Chalybura buffonii (White-veined Plumeleteer)
C. b. micans
E Panama, NW Colombia
C. b. buffonii
NC Colombia, W Venezuela
C. b. aeneicauda
NE Colombia, N Venezuela
C. b. caeruleogaster
E Colombia
C. b. intermedia
SW Ecuador
Chalybura urochrysia (Bronze-tailed Plumeleteer)
C. u. melanorrhoa
E Nicaragua, E Costa Rica
C. u. isaurae
NW Panama
C. u. incognita
E Panama
C. u. urochrysia
W Colombia, NW Ecuador

APHANTOCHROA
Aphantochroa cirrochloris (Sombre Hummingbird)
C & E Brazil

LAMPORNIS
Lampornis clemenciae (Blue-throated Hummingbird)
L. c. bessophilus
SW USA, NW Mexico
L. c. clemenciae
S USA, N & C Mexico
Lampornis amethystinus (Amethyst-throated Hummingbird)
L. a. amethystinus
E Mexico
L. a. brevirostris
W Mexico
L. a. margaritae
SW Mexico
L. a. salvini
S Mexico, C Guatemala
L. a. nobilis
Honduras
Lampornis viridipallens (Green-throated Mountain Gem)
L. v. ovandensis
S Mexico
L. v. viridipallens
S Mexico, Guatemala

L. v. nubivagus
El Salvador, W Honduras
L. v. connectens
El Salvador
L. v. sybillae
C Honduras, N Nicaragua
Lampornis hemileucus (White-bellied Mountain Gem)
NE Costa Rica
Lampornis castaneoventris (White-throated Mountain Gem)
L. c. pectoralis
W Nicaragua, NW Costa Rica
L. c. calolaema
N & C Costa Rica, W Panama
L. c. castaneoventris
W Panama
Lampornis cinereicauda (Grey-tailed Mountain Gem)
SW Costa Rica

LAMPROLAIMA
Lamprolaima rhami (Garnet-throated Hummingbird)
L. r. rhami
S Mexico
L. r. saturatior
Honduras & N El Salvador

ADELOMYIA
Adelomyia melanogenys (Speckled Hummingbird)
A. m. cervina
W & C Colombia
A. m. connectens
Colombia
A. m. melanogenys
E Colombia, W Venezuela
A. m. aeneosticta
C & N Venezuela
A. m. maculata
C Ecuador, N Peru
A. m. chlorospila
SE Peru
A. m. inornata
Bolivia, NW Argentina

ANTHOCEPHALA
Anthocephala floriceps (Blossomcrown)
A. f. berlepschi
C Colombia
A. f. floriceps
N Colombia

UROSTICTE
Urosticte benjamini (Whitetip)
U. b. rostrata
W Colombia
U. b. benjamini
W Ecuador, SW Colombia
U. b. ruficrissa
E Ecuador

U. b. intermedia
NE Peru

PHLOGOPHILUS
Phlogophilus hemileucurus (Ecuadorean Piedtail)
E Ecuador
Phlogophilus harterti (Peruvian Piedtail)
S Peru

CLYTOLAEMA
Clytolaema rubricauda (Brazilian Ruby)
SE Brazil

POLYPLANCTA
Polyplancta aurescens (Gould's Jewelfront)
E Ecuador, E Peru, S Venezuela, N Brazil

HELIODOXA
Heliodoxa rubinoides (Fawn-breasted Brilliant)
H. r. rubinoides
E Colombia
H. r. aequatorialis
W Colombia, W Ecuador
H. r. cervinigularis
E Ecuador, E Peru
Heliodoxa leadbeateri (Violet-fronted Brilliant)
H. l. leadbeateri
Upper Amazonia
H. l. sagitta
SC Colombia
H. l. parvula
W Venezuela
Heliodoxa jacula (Green-crowned Brilliant)
H. j. henryi
Costa Rica, W Panama
H. j. jacula
E Panama, E Colombia
H. j. jamesoni
W Ecuador
Heliodoxa xanthogonys (Velvet-browed Brilliant)
SE Venezuela, S Guyana
Heliodoxa schreibersii (Black-throated Brilliant)
H. s. schreibersii
E Ecuador, NE Peru, NW Brazil
H. s. whitelyana
E Peru
Heliodoxa gularis (Pink-throated Brilliant)
E Ecuador, NE Peru
Heliodoxa branickii (Rufous-webbed Brilliant)
C Peru
Heliodoxa imperatrix (Empress Brilliant)
W Ecuador

Eugenes fulgens (Rivoli's Hummingbird)
E. f. fulgens
SW USA, N & C Mexico
E. f. viridiceps
S Mexico to Nicaragua
E. f. spectabilis
Costa Rica, W Panama

HYLONYMPHA
Hylonympha macrocerca (Scissor-tailed Hummingbird)
Venezuela

STERNOCLYTA
Sternoclyta cyanopectus (Violet-chested Hummingbird)
NW Venezuela

TOPAZA
Topaza pella (Crimson Topaz)
T. p. pella
N Brazil, S Venezuela, Guyana, Surinam
T. p. smaragdula
French Guiana
T. p. microrhyncha
NE Brazil
T. p. pamprepta
E Ecuador
Topaza pyra (Fiery Topaz)
SE Colombia, E Ecuador, W Brazil

OREOTROCHILUS
Oreotrochilus melanogaster (Black-breasted Hillstar)
C Peru
Oreotrochilus estella (Andean Hillstar)
O. e. jamesonii
N Ecuador
O. e. söderströmi
Mt Quillotoa (Ecuador)
O. e. chimborazo
Mt Chimborazo (Ecuador)
O. e. stolzmanni
N Peru
O. e. estella
S Peru to N Chile & NW Argentina
O. e. boliviana
C Bolivia
Oreotrochilus leucopleurus (White-sided Hillstar)
S Bolivia, Chile, W Argentina
Oreotrochilus adela (Wedgetailed Hillstar)
C Bolivia

UROCHROA
Urochroa bougueri (White-tailed Hillstar)
U. b. bougueri
SW Colombia, NW Ecuador
U. b. eulcura
SW Colombia
U. b. leucura
E Ecuador

PATAGONA
Patagona gigas (Giant Hummingbird)
P. g. peruviana
Ecuador to N Chile, NW Argentina
P. g. gigas
C Chile, W Argentina

AGLAEACTIS
Aglaeactis cupripennis (Shining Sunbeam)
A. c. cupripennis
Colombia, N & C Ecuador
A. c. parvulus
S Ecuador, N Peru
A. c. ruficauda
C Peru
A. c. caumatonotus
SC Peru
**Aglaeactis aliciae (Purple-backed
Sunbeam)**
N Peru
**Aglaeactis castelnaudii (White-tufted
Sunbeam)**
C Peru
**Aglaeactis pamela (Black-hooded
Sunbeam)**
Bolivia

LAFRESNAYA
**Lafresnaya lafresnayi (Mountain
Velvetbreast)**
L. l. liriope
N Colombia, W Venezuela
L. l. lafresnayi
C Colombia
L. l. greenewalti
W Venezuela
L. l. saül
W Colombia, Ecuador, N Peru
L. l. rectirostris
C Peru

PTEROPHANES
**Pterophanes cyanopterus (Great Sapphire-
wing)**
P. c. cyanopterus
Colombia, Ecuador
P. c. caeruleus
S Colombia
P. c. peruvianus
Peru, N Bolivia

COELIGENA
Coeligena coeligena (Bronzy Inca)
C. c. ferruginea
W Colombia
C. c. columbiana
C Colombia to C Ecuador & W Venezuela
C. c. zuloagae
NW Venezuela
C. c. boliviana
C Peru, C Bolivia

C. c. coeligena
N Venezuela
C. c. zuliana
W Venezuela, NE Colombia
Coeligena wilsoni (Brown Inca)
SW Colombia, W Ecuador
Coeligena prunellei (Black Inca)
E Colombia
Coeligena torquata (Collared Inca)
C. t. torquata
Colombia, E Ecuador
C. t. fuligidigula
W Ecuador
C. t. margaretae
N Peru
C. t. insectivora
NC Peru
C. t. omissa
S Peru
C. t. conradii
NE Colombia, NW Venezuela
C. t. inca
S Peru, N Bolivia
**Coeligena phalerata (White-tailed
Starfrontlet)**
N Colombia
**Coeligena bonapartei (Golden-bellied
Starfrontlet)**
C. b. consita
NE Colombia, NW Venezuela
C. b. bonapartei
E Colombia
C. b. eos
NW Venezuela
Coeligena orina (Dusky Starfrontlet)
Colombia
**Coeligena helianthea (Blue-throated
Starfrontlet)**
C. h. tamae
NE Colombia
C. h. helianthea
E Colombia
**Coeligena lutetiae (Buff-winged
Starfrontlet)**
C Colombia, Ecuador
**Coeligena violifer (Violet-throated
Starfrontlet)**
C. v. dichroura
N & C Peru
C. v. osculans
S Peru
C. v. violifer
NW Bolivia
Coeligena iris (Rainbow Starfrontlet)
C. i. iris
S Ecuador
C. i. aurora
S Ecuador, N Peru

C. i. fulgidiceps
N Peru
C. i. flagrans
N Peru
C. i. hypocrita
N Peru
C. i. eva
N Peru
C. i. hesperus
SC Ecuador

ENSIFERA
Ensifera ensifera (Sword-billed Humming-bird)
Venezuela, Colombia to N Bolivia

SEPHANOIDES
Sephanoides sephaniodes (Green-Backed Firecrown)
Chile, SW Argentina
Sephanoides fernandensis (Fernandez Firecrown)
S. f. fernandensis
Masatierra I
S. f. leyboldi
Masafuera I

BOISSONNEAUA
Boissonneaua flavescens (Buff-tailed Coronet)
B. f. flavescens
Colombia, W Venezuela
B. f. tinochlora
W Ecuador
Boissonneaua matthewsii (Chestnut-breasted Coronet)
Ecuador, Peru
Boissonneaua jardini (Velvet-Purple Coronet)
W Colombia, W Ecuador

HELIANGELUS
Heliangelus mavors (Orange-throated Sunangel)
NE Colombia, W Venezuela
Heliangelus spencei (Merida Sunangel)
W Venezuela
Heliangelus amethysticollis (Amethyst-throated Sunangel)
H. a. clarisse
N Colombia, W Venezuela
H. a. violiceps
NE Colombia
H. a. viridiscutatus
NE Colombia
H. a. laticlavus
S Ecuador to C Peru
H. a. amethysticollis
S Peru, Bolivia

Heliangelus strophianus (Gorgeted Sunangel)
W Ecuador
Heliangelus regalis (Royal Sunangel)
N Peru
Heliangelus exortis (Tourmaline Sunangel)
Colombia, E Ecuador
Heliangelus viola (Purple-throated Sunangel)
W Ecuador, NW Peru
Heliangelus micraster (Little Sunangel)
H. m. micraster
S Ecuador
H. m. cutervensis
N Peru
Heliangelus squamigularis (Olive-throated Sunangel)
Colombia

ERIOCNEMIS
Eriocnemis nigrivestris (Black-breasted Puffleg)
NW Ecuador
Eriocnemis söderströmi (Söderström's Puffleg)
Ecuador
Eriocnemis vestitus (Glowing Puffleg)
E. v. vestitus
E Colombia, W Venezuela
E. v. paramillo
NW Colombia
E. v. smaragdinipectus
SC Colombia, E Ecuador
Eriocnemis godini (Turquoise-throated Puffleg)
Ecuador
Eriocnemis cupreoventris (Coppery-bellied Puffleg)
E Colombia, W Venezuela
Eriocnemis luciani (Sapphire-vented Puffleg)
E. l. luciani
W Ecuador
E. l. catharina
N Peru
E. l. sapphiropygia
C Peru
Eriocnemis isaacsonii (Isaacson's Puffleg)
Colombia
Eriocnemis mosquera (Golden-breasted Puffleg)
Colombia, N Ecuador
Eriocnemis glaucopoides (Blue-capped Puffleg)
Bolivia, N Argentina
Eriocnemis mirabilis (Colourful Puffleg)
N Peru
Eriocnemis alinae (Emerald-bellied Puffleg)
E. a. alinae
Colombia, N Ecuador

E. a. dybowskii
N & C Peru

Eriocnemis derbyi (Black-thighed Puffleg)
E. d. longirostris
NC Colombia
E. d. derbyi
S Colombia, N Ecuador

HAPLOPHAEDIA
Haplophaedia aureliae (Greenish Puffleg)
H. a. caucensis
E Panama, W Colombia
H. a. aureliae
C & E Colombia
H. a. russata
E Ecuador
H. a. affinis
N Peru
H. a. assimilis
SE Peru
Haplophaedia lugens (Hoary Puffleg)
WC Colombia, C Ecuador

OCREATUS
Ocreatus underwoodii (Booted Racquet-tail)
O. u. polystictus
N Venezuela
O. u. underwoodii
Colombia, W Venezuela
O. u. ambiguus
S Colombia
O. u. discifer
W Venezuela
O. u. melanantherus
W Ecuador
O. u. peruanus
E Ecuador, NE Peru
O. u. annae
C Peru
O. u. addae
Bolivia

LESBIA
Lesbia victoriae (Black-tailed Trainbearer)
L. v. victoriae
S & E Colombia.
L. v. eucharis
Colombia
L. v. aequatorialis
W Ecuador
L. v. juliae
N & C Peru
L. v. berlepschi
SW Peru
Lesbia nuna (Green-tailed Trainbearer)
L. n. gouldii
Colombia, W Venezuela
L. n. gracilis
Ecuador
L. n. pallidiventris

N Peru
L. n. chlorura
C Peru
L. n. nuna
SW Peru
L. n. boliviana
N Bolivia

SAPPHO
Sappho sparganura (Red-tailed Comet)
S. s. sparganura
N & C Bolivia
S. s. sappho
S Bolivia, N & W Argentina

POLYONYMUS
Polyonymus caroli (Bronze-tailed Comet)
Peru

ZODALIA
Zodalia glyceria (Purple-tailed Comet)
Colombia, Ecuador

RAMPHOMICRON
Ramphomicron microrhynchum (Purple-backed Thornbill)
R. m. andicolum
W Venezuela
R. m. microrhynchum
Colombia, Ecuador
R. m. albiventre
Peru
Ramphomicron dorsale (Black-backed Thornbill)
N Colombia

METALLURA
Metallura phoebe (Black Metaltail)
Peru, Bolivia, N Chile
Metallura theresiae (Coppery Metaltail)
N Peru
Metallura purpureicauda (Purple-tailed Thornbill)
Ecuador
Metallura aeneocauda (Scaled Metaltail)
M. a. aeneocauda
S Peru, Bolivia
M. a. malagae
Bolivia
Metallura baroni (Violet-throated Metaltail)
SW Ecuador
Metallura eupogon (Fire-throated Metaltail)
N & C Peru
Metallura odomae (Neblina Metaltail)
N Peru
Metallura williami (Viridian Metaltail)
M. w. williami
C Colombia
M. w. primolina
NE Ecuador

M. w. atrigularis
S Ecuador
Metallura tyrianthina (Tyrian Metaltail)
M. t. chloropogon
N Venezuela
M. t. oreopola
W Venezuela
M. t. districta
N Colombia
M. t. tyrianthina
Colombia, E & S Ecuador
M. t. quitensis
NW Ecuador
M. t. septentrionalis
N Peru
M. t. peruviana
C Peru
M. t. smaragdinicollis
S Peru, Bolivia
Metallura iracunda (Perija Metaltail)
E Colombia, W Venezuela

CHALCOSTIGMA
Chalcostigma ruficeps (Rufous-capped Thornbill)
C. r. aureofastigata
S Ecuador
C. r. ruficeps
Peru, N Bolivia
Chalcostigma olivaceum (Olivaceous Thornbill)
C. o. olivaceum
N & C Peru, Bolivia
C. o. pallens
WC Peru
Chalcostigma stanleyi (Blue-mantled Thornbill)
C. s. stanleyi
Ecuador
C. s. versigularis
C Peru
C. s. vulcani
SE Peru, Bolivia
Chalcostigma heteropogon (Bronze-tailed Thornbill)
E Colombia, W Venezuela
Chalcostigma herrani (Rainbow-bearded Thornbill)
C. h. tolimae
W Colombia
C. h. herrani
S Colombia, N Ecuador

OXYPOGON
Oxypogon guerinii (Bearded Helmetcrest)
O. g. stübelii
C Colombia
O. g. guerinii
E Colombia

O. g. cyanolaemus
N Colombia
O. g. lindenii
W Venezuela

OPISTHOPRORA
Opisthoprora euryptera (Mountain Avocetbill)
S Colombia, NE Ecuador

TAPHROLESBIA
Taphrolesbia griseiventris (Grey-bellied Comet)
Peru

AGLAIOCERCUS
Aglaiocercus kingi (Long-tailed Sylph)
A. k. berlepschi
Venezuela
A. k. margarethae
Venezuela
A. k. kingi
E Colombia
A. k. mocoa
C Colombia to N Peru
A. k. smaragdinus
C Peru, N Bolivia
A. k. emmae
NC Colombia
A. k. caudata
Colombia, W Venezuela
Aglaiocercus coelestis (Violet-tailed Sylph)
A. c. coelestis
W Colombia, NW Ecuador
A. c. pseudocoelestis
SW Colombia
A. c. aethereus
SW Ecuador

OREONYMPHA
Oreonympha nobilis (Bearded Mountaineer)
O. n. albolimbata
WC Peru
O. n. nobilis
S Peru

AUGASTES
Augastes scutatus (Hyacinth Visor-bearer)
Brazil
Augastes lumachellus (Hooded Visor-bearer)
E Brazil
SCHISTES
Schistes geoffroyi (Wedge-billed Hummingbird)
S. g. albogularis
WC Colombia, W Ecuador
S. g. geoffroyi
N Venezuela, E Colombia to E Peru

HELIOTHRYX
Heliothryx barroti (Purple-crowned Fairy)
Guatemala to W Ecuador
Heliothryx aurita (Black-eared Fairy)
H. a. aurita
N Colombia to the Guianas, N Brazil
H. a. major
W Ecuador
H. a. phainolaema
NE Brazil
H. a. auriculata
E Peru, Bolivia, C & S Brazil

HELIACTIN
Heliactin cornuta (Horned Sungem)
C & E Brazil

LODDIGESIA
Loddigesia mirabilis (Marvellous Spatuletail)
N Peru

HELIOMASTER
Heliomaster constantii (Plain-capped Starthroat)
H. c. surdus
NW Mexico
H. c. pinicola
W Mexico
H. c. leocadiae
W Mexico, W Guatemala
H. c. constantii
El Salvador to Costa Rica
Heliomaster longirostris (Long-billed Starthroat)
H. l. pallidiceps
S Mexico to Nicaragua
H. l. longirostris
E Costa Rica to N & NW South America
H. l. stuartae
Colombia
H. l. albicrissa
W Ecuador, NW Peru
Heliomaster squamosus (Stripe-breasted Starthroat)
EC Brazil
Heliomaster furcifer (Blue-tufted Starthroat)
C Brazil to Bolivia & N Argentina

RHODOPIS
Rhodopis vesper (Oasis Hummingbird)
R. v. tertia
N Peru
R. v. koepckeae
Peru
R. v. vesper
SW Peru, N Chile
R. v. atacamensis
N Chile

THAUMASTURA
Thaumastura cora (Peruvian Sheartail)
W Peru

PHILODICE
Philodice evelynae (Bahama Woodstar)
P. e. evelynae
Bahama Is
P. e. lyrura
Gt Inagua I
P. e. salita
Caicos Is
Philodice bryantae (Magenta-throated Woodstar)
Costa Rica, W Panama
Philodice mitchellii (Purple-throated Woodstar)
W Colombia, W Ecuador

DORICHA
Doricha enicura (Slender Sheartail)
S Mexico, Guatemala, El Salvador
Doricha eliza (Mexican Sheartail)
SE Mexico, Holbox I

TILMATURA
Tilmatura dupontii (Dupont's Hummingbird)
S Mexico to N Nicaragua

MICROSTILBON
Microstilbon burmeisteri (Slender-tailed Woodstar)
C & S Bolivia, N Argentina

CALOTHORAX
Calothorax lucifer (Lucifer Hummingbird)
SW USA to SC Mexico
Calothorax pulcher (Beautiful Hummingbird)
S Mexico

ARCHILOCHUS
Archilochus colubris (Ruby-throated Hummingbird)
S Canada, E USA to Panama
Archilochus alexandri (Black-chinned Hummingbird)
SW Canada, W USA to W Mexico

CALLIPHLOX
Calliphlox amethystina (Amethyst Woodstar)
Ecuador & Bolivia to the Guianas, NE Argentina

MELLISUGA
Mellisuga minima (Vervain Hummingbird)
M. m. minima
Jamaica
M. m. vieilloti
Gonave I, Hispaniola

Calypte anna (Anna's Hummingbird)
C California, NW Baja, California
Calypte costae (Costa's Hummingbird)
SW USA, NW Mexico
Calypte helenae (Bee Hummingbird)
Cuba, Isle of Pines

STELLULA
Stellula calliope (Calliope Hummingbird)
S. c. calliope
W USA to SC Mexico
S. c. lowei
Guerrero, (Mexico)

ATTHIS
Atthis heloisa (Bumblebee Hummingbird)
A. h. margarethae
NW Mexico
A. h. heloisa
C & S Mexico

Atthis ellioti (Wine-throated Hummingbird)
A. e. ellioti
S Mexico, Guatemala
A. e. selasphoroides
Honduras

MYRTIS
Myrtis fanny (Purple-collared Woodstar)
Ecuador, W Peru

EULIDIA
Eulidia yarrellii (Chilean Woodstar)
N Chile

MYRMIA
Myrmia micrura (Short-tailed Woodstar)
W Ecuador, W Peru

ACESTRURA
Acestrura mulsant (White-bellied Woodstar)
Colombia

Acestrura bombus (Little Woodstar)
Ecuador, N Peru
Acestrura heliodor (Gorgeted Woodstar)
A. h. astreans
N Colombia
A. h. heliodor
W Ecuador to W Venezuela
A. h. cleavesi
NE Ecuador
A. h. meridae
Venezuela
Acestrura berlepschi (Esmeralda's Woodstar)
W Ecuador
Acestrura harterti (Hartert's Woodstar)
Ecuador

Chaetocercus jourdanii (Rufous-shafted Woodstar)
C. j. andinus
W Venezuela, NE Colombia
C. j. jourdanii
NE Venezuela, Trinidad
C. j. rosae
E Colombia, N & W Venezuela

SELASPHORUS
Selasphorus playcercus (Broad-tailed Hummingbird)
S. p. platycercus
W USA to WC Mexico
S. p. guatemalae
W Guatemala
Selasphorus rufus (Rufous Hummingbird)
SE Alaska to WC Mexico
Selasphorus sasin (Allen's Hummingbird)
S. s. sasin
SW California, NW Mexico
S. s. sedentarius
Santa Barbara I (California)
Selasphorus flammula (Rose-throated Hummingbird)
Costa Rica
Selasphorus torridus (Heliotrope-throated Hummingbird)
Costa Rica, W Panama
Selasphorus simoni (Cerise-throated Hummingbird)
Costa Rica
Selasphorus ardens (Glow-throated Hummingbird)
W Panama
Selasphorus scintilla (Scintillant Hummingbird)
Costa Rica, W Panama

Coliiformes

82 COLIIDAE (MOUSEBIRDS)

COLIUS
Colius striatus (Speckled Mousebird)
C. s. nigricollis
N Nigeria to W Zaire
C. s. leucophthalmus
S Sudan, NE Zaire
C. s. leucotis
W Sudan, Ethiopia
C. s. hilgerti
E Ethiopia, Somalia
C. s. erlangeri
W Ethiopia

C. s. jebelensis
SW Sudan, NE Zaire
C. s. ugandensis
Uganda, NW Tanzania
C. s. kikuyensis
W & C Kenya
C. s. marangu
N Tanzania
C. s. cinerascens
NW Tanzania
C. s. affinis
S Somalia, E Kenya, E Tanzania
C. s. berlepschi
S Tanzania, Malawi, NW Mozambique
C. s. kivuensis
Kivu (Rwanda)
C. s. congicus
S Zaire
C. s. lungae
W Zambia
C. s. rhodesiae
E Rhodesia
C. s. minor
Mozambique to E Cape Province
C. s. striatus
S Cape Province
Colius castanotus (Red-backed Mousebird)
Angola
Colius colius (White-backed Mousebird)
W South Africa
Colius leucocephalus (White-headed Mousebird)
C. l. turneri
N & NE Kenya
C. l. leucocephalus
SE Kenya to NE Tanzania
Colius indicus (Red-faced Mousebird)
C. i. lualabae
S Zaire
C. i. angolensis
S Angola
C. i. lacteifrons
S Angola, N Namibia
C. i. pallidus
S Tanzania, N Malawi
C. i. transvaalensis
Rhodesia, Transvaal, Natal
C. i. indicus
Cape Province
Colius macrourus (Blue-naped Mousebird)
C. m. macrourus
Senegal to Somalia
C. m. laeneni
Niger to Aïr Mountains
C. m. pulcher
W Uganda, S Ethiopia to N Tanzania

C.m. griseogularis
Sudan to E Zaire

Trogoniformes

83 TROGONIDAE (TROGONS)

PHAROMACHRUS
Pharomachrus mocinno (Resplendent Quetzal)
P. m. mocinno
S Mexico to N Nicaragua
P. m. costaricensis
Costa Rica to W Panama
Pharomachrus antisianus (Crested Quetzal)
W Venezuela, Colombia to Brazil
Pharomachrus fulgidus (White-tipped Quetzal)
P. f. festatus
N Colombia
P. f. fulgidus
NE & NC Venezuela
Pharomachrus auriceps (Golden-headed Trogon)
Venezuela, Colombia to N Bolivia
Pharomachrus pavoninus (Pavonine Quetzal)
P. p. hargitti
E Colombia, W Venezuela
P. p. heliactin
W Ecuador
P. p. pavoninus
Upper Amazonia
P. p. viridiceps
NE Brazil

EUPTILOTIS
Euptilotis neoxenus (Eared Trogon)
C Mexico

PRIOTELUS
Priotelus temnurus (Cuban Trogon)
P. t. temnurus
Cuba
P. t. vescus
Isle of Pines

TEMNOTROGON
Temnotrogon roseigaster (Hispaniolan Trogon)
Hispaniola

TROGON
Trogon massena (Slaty-tailed Trogon)
T. m. massena
S Mexico to Nicaragua
T. m. hoffmanni
Costa Rica, Panama

T. m. australis
W Colombia
Trogon clathratus (Lattice-tailed Trogon)
E Costa Rica, W Panama
Trogon melanurus (Black-tailed Trogon)
T. m. macroura
E Panama, N Colombia
T. m. mesurus
W Ecuador, NW Peru
T. m. eumorphus
Peru
T. m. occidentalis
Brazil
T. m. melanurus
Colombia to Bolivia & N Brazil
Trogon comptus (Blue-tailed Trogon)
Colombia
Trogon viridis (White-tailed Trogon)
T. v. bairdii
SW Costa Rica, W Panama
T. v. chionurus
E Panama, W Colombia, W Ecuador
T. v. viridis
Colombia to Peru, Brazil & Trinidad
T. v. melanopterus
SE Brazil
Trogon citreolus (Citreoline Trogon)
T. c. citreolus
W Mexico
T. c. sumichrasti
S Mexico
T. c. melanocephala
E Mexico to NE Costa Rica
T. c. illaetabilis
W Costa Rica
Trogon mexicanus (Mountain Trogon)
T. m. clarus
NW Mexico
T. m. mexicanus
C Mexico to W Guatemala
T. m. lutescens
Honduras
Trogon elegans (Coppery-tailed Trogon)
T. e. canescens
S Arizona, NW Mexico
T. e. ambiguus
S Texas, E & C Mexico
T. e. elegans
Guatemala
T. e. lubricus
Nicaragua, Costa Rica
T. e. goldmani
Tres Marias Is
Trogon collaris (Collared Trogon)
T. c. puella
C Mexico to W Panama
T. c. extimus
E Panama

T. c. virginalis
W Colombia, W Ecuador, NW Peru
T. c. subtropicalis
C Colombia
T. c. exoptatus
N Venezuela
T. c. collaris
Colombia to Bolivia, Trinidad, S Brazil
T. c. castaneus
SE Colombia, NW Brazil
Trogon aurantiiventris (Orange-bellied Trogon)
T. a. underwoodi
NW Costa Rica
T. a. aurantiiventris
C Costa Rica to W Panama
T. a. flavidior
E Panama
Trogon personatus (Masked Trogon)
T. p. sanctaemartae
N Colombia
T. p. ptaritepui
Venezuela
T. p. personatus
W Venezuela, E Colombia, E Peru
T. p. assimilis
W Ecuador
T. p. temperatus
C Colombia, Ecuador
T. p. submontanus
Bolivia
T. p. duidae
Mt Duida (Venezuela)
T. p. roraimae
SE Venezuela, S Guyana
Trogon rufus (Black-throated Trogon)
T. r. tenellus
SE Honduras to NW Colombia
T. r. cupreicauda
W Colombia, W Ecuador
T. r. rufus
E Venezuela, the Guianas, N Brazil
T. r. sulphureus
E Peru, W Brazil
T. r. amazonicus
NE Brazil
T. r. chrysochloros
S Brazil, Paraguay, NE Argentina
Trogon surrucura (Surucua Trogon)
T. s. aurantius
E Brazil
T. s. surrucura
S Brazil, Paraguay, Uruguay, N Argentina
Trogon curucui (Blue-crowned Trogon)
T. c. bolivianus
S Colombia to Bolivia, W Brazil
T. c. peruvianus
SC Colombia

T. c. curucui
 E Brazil
T. c. behni
 E Bolivia, S Brazil, Paraguay, N Argentina
Trogon violaceus (Violaceous Trogon)
T. v. braccatus
 C Mexico to Nicaragua
T. v. concinnus
 Costa Rica to W Ecuador
T. v. caligatus
 N Colombia, W Venezuela
T. v. violaceus
 Venezuela, the Guianas, N Brazil, Trinidad
T. v. ramonianus
 Upper Amazonia
T. v. crissalis
 E Brazil

APALODERMA
Apaloderma narina (Narina's Trogon)
A. n. constantia
 Liberia to Ghana
A. n. brachyurum
 S Cameroun to Uganda, Zaire
A. n. narina
 Sudan & Ethiopia to Cape Province
A. n. littoralis
 E Kenya, E Tanzania, Zanzibar I
Apaloderma aequatoriale (Bare-cheeked Trogon)
 Cameroun to S Zaire

HETEROTROGON
Heterotrogon vittatus (Bartailed Trogon)
H. v. camerunensis
 Cameroun, Angola, Zaire
H. v. vittatus
 Kenya, Tanzania

HARPACTES
Harpactes reinwardtii (Reinwardt's Blue-tailed Trogon)
H. r. mackloti
 Sumatra
H. r. reinwardtii
 Java
Harpactes fasciatus (Malabar Trogon)
H. f. malabaricus
 W & S India
H. f. fasciatus
 Sri Lanka
H. f. parvus
 Sri Lanka
Harpactes kasumba (Red-naped Trogon)
H. k. kasumba
 Malaysia, Sumatra
H. k. impavidus
 Borneo

Harpactes diardii (Diard's Trogon)
H. d. sumatranus
 Malaysia, Sumatra
H. d. diardii
 Borneo, Bangka I
Harpactes ardens (Philippine Trogon)
H. a. ardens
 Philippine Is
H. a. luzoniensis
 Luzon, Bataan I
Harpactes whiteheadi (Whitehead's Trogon)
 Mt Kinabalu (N Borneo)
Harpactes orrhophaeus (Cinnamon-rumped Trogon)
H. o. orrhophaeus
 Malaysia, Sumatra
H. o. vidua
 NW Borneo
Harpactes duvaucelii (Scarlet-rumped Trogon)
 S Burma, Malaysia, Sumatra
Harpactes oreskios (Orange-breasted Trogon)
H. o. stellae
 S Burma, S Indochina
H. o. uniformis
 S Burma, Malaysia, Sumatra
H. o. oreskios
 Java
H. o. dulitensis
 NW Borneo
H. o. nias
 Nias I
Harpactes erythrocephalus (Red-headed Trogon)
H. e. erythrocephalus
 Himalayas, Burma, NW Thailand
H. e. helenae
 W Yunnan, N Burma
H. e. yamakanensis
 SE China
H. e. rosa
 SC China
H. e. intermedius
 N Laos, N Vietnam
H. e. annamensis
 NE Thailand, S Indochina
H. e. klossi
 W Cambodia
H. e. chaseni
 Malaysia
H. e. hainanus
 Hainan I
H. e. flagrans
 Sumatra
Harpactes wardi (Ward's Trogon)
 N Burma, NE Vietnam

Coraciiformes

84 ALCEDINIDAE (KINGFISHERS)

CERYLINAE

CERYLE

Ceryle lugubris (Greater Pied Kingfisher)
  C. l. guttulata
  Himalayas, China, Burma, Thailand
  C. l. pallida
  Hokkaido I
  C. l. lugubris
  Japan, Korea
Ceryle maxima (Giant Kingfisher)
  C. m. maxima
  Senegal to Nigeria, Ethiopia to Cape
  Province
  C. m. gigantea
  S Nigeria to Zaire, Tanzania
Ceryle torquata (Ringed Kingfisher)
  C. t. torquata
  Mexico to N Argentina, Peru
  C. t. stictipennis
  Guadeloupe I, Dominica I
  C. t. stellata
  Chile, Argentina
Ceryle alcyon (Belted Kingfisher)
  C. a. caurina
  Alaska to W Mexico
  C. a. alcyon
  C & E Canada to N South America
  & West Indies
Ceryle rudis (Lesser Pied Kingfisher)
  C. r. rudis
  Asia Minor, Iran, Africa
  C. r. leucomelanura
  Pakistan to Burma, Indochina
  C. r. travancoreensis
  SW India
  C. r. insignis
  SE China, Hainan I

CHLOROCERYLE

Chloroceryle amazona (Amazon Kingfisher)
  C. a. mexicana
  S Mexico to E Panama
  C. a. amazona
  N South America
Chloroceryle americana (Green Kingfisher)
  C. a. hachisukai
  W Texas, NW Mexico
  C. a. septentrionalis
  SE Texas, E Mexico, Guatemala
  C. a. isthmica
  Honduras to N Colombia, Pearl Is
  (Panama)

C. a. americana
  N South America (East of Andes)
C. a. hellmayri
  W Colombia
C. a. ecuadorensis
  W Ecuador
C. a. cabanisii
  W Peru
C. a. croteta
  Trinidad, Tobago I
C. a. mathewsii
  C & SC South America
Chloroceryle inda (Green and Rufous Kingfisher)
  C. i. inda
  Panama & tropical South America
  C. i. chocoensis
  W Colombia, W Ecuador
Chloroceryle aenea (Pygmy Kingfisher)
  C. a. stictoptera
  S Mexico to Nicaragua
  C. a. aenea
  Costa Rica, Panama, N South America,
  Trinidad

ALCEDININAE

ALCEDO

Alcedo hercules (Blyth's Kingfisher)
  E Himalayas to N Vietnam
Alcedo atthis (Common Kingfisher)
  A. a. ispida
  Europe
  A. a. atthis
  Mediterranean, Syria, Arabia
  A. a. bengalensis
  N India to Philippine Is & Gtr Sunda Is
  A. a. taprobana
  S India, Sri Lanka
  A. a. japonica
  Sakhalin I, Japan, Taiwan
  A. a. floresiana
  Bali to Timor I
  A. a. hispidoides
  Celebes to Bismarck Archipelago
  & NE New Guinea
  A. a. salomonensis
  Solomon Is
Alcedo semitorquata (Half-collared Kingfisher)
  Ethiopia to Angola & Cape Province
Alcedo meninting (Blue-eared Kingfisher)
  A. m. coltarti
  Sikkim to S Burma & Laos
  A. m. laubmanni
  E India
  A. m. phillipsi
  SW India, Sri Lanka

226

A. m. scintillans
S Burma, S Thailand
`A. m. rufigaster
Andaman Is
A. m. verreauxii
Malaysia, Sumatra, Borneo
A. m. proxima
Pagi Is
A. m. subviridis
Banjak Is, Nias I
A. m. callima
Batu Is
A. m. meninting
Java to Lombok I & Sula Is
**Alcedo quadribrachys (Shining-blue
Kingfisher)**
A. q. quadribrachys
Gambia to N Nigeria
A. q. guentheri
S Nigeria to Uganda, S Zaire & Angola
Alcedo euryzona (Broad-zoned Kingfisher)
A. e. peninsulae
Malaysia, Sumatra
A. e. euryzona
Java, Borneo
**Alcedo coerulescens (Small
Blue Kingfisher)**
Java to Sumbawa I
Alcedo cristata (Malachite Kingfisher)
A. c. cristata
Senegal to Ethiopia & Cape Province
A. c. robertsi
Botswana
A. c. johannae
Comoro Is
A. c. vintsioides
Madagascar
**Alcedo leucogaster (White-bellied
Kingfisher)**
A. l. leucogaster
S Nigeria to N Angola, Fernando Po I
A. l. bowdleri
Guinea to Ghana
A. l. thomensis
Sao Tomé I
A. l. nais
Principé I
A. l. leopoldi
WC Zaire

MYIOCEYX
**Myioceyx lecontei (African Dwarf
Kingfisher)**
M. l. lecontei
Sierra Leone to Angola & E Zaire
M. l. ugandae
W Uganda

ISPIDINA
Ispidina picta (African Pygmy Kingfisher)
I. p. picta
Senegal to Angola, Kenya & Ethiopia
I. p. jubaensis
S Somalia
I. p. natalensis
S Zaire & Tanzania to Natal
**Ispidina madagascariensis (Madagascar
Pygmy Kingfisher**
I. m. madagascariensis
Madagascar
I. m. diluta
Sakaraha, Madagascar

CEYX
Ceyx cyanopectus (Dwarf River Kingfisher)
C. c. cyanopectus
Luzon I, Mindoro I, Masbate I,
Ticao I
C. c. nigrirostris
Panay I, Negros I, Cebu I
Ceyx argentatus (Silvery Kingfisher)
C. a. argentatus
Panay I, Negros I, Cebu I, Mindanao I
C. a. flumenicolus
Samar I, Leyte I
**Ceyx goodfellowi (Goodfellow's
Kingfisher)**
C. g. goodfellowi
Mindanao I
C. g. virgicapitus
Tawitawi Is
Ceyx lepidus (Dwarf Kingfisher)
C. l. margarethae
S Philippine Is
C. l. wallacii
Sula Is
C. l. lepidus
Moluccas
C. l. cajeli
Buru I
C. l. solitarius
New Guinea & islands, Aru Is
C. l. dispar
Admiralty Is
C. l. mulcatus
New Hanover, New Ireland
C. l. sacerdotis
New Britain, Rook I
C. l. pallidus
Bougainville I, Buka I
C. l. collectoris
Choiseul I, Vella Lavella I, New Georgia I,
Rendova I
C. l. meeki
Choiseul I, Ysabel I
C. l. malaitae
Malaita I

C. l. nigromaxilla
Guadalcanal I
C. l. gentianus
San Cristobal I
Ceyx azureus (Azure Kingfisher)
C. a. affinis
N Moluccas
C. a. yamdenae
Tenimber Is
C. a. wallaceanus
Aru Is
C. a. lessonii
W Papuan Is, New Guinea lowlands
C. a. ochrogaster
N New Guinea & Geelvinck Bay Is
C. a. ruficollaris
Northern Australia
C. a. mixtus
NE Queensland

C. a. azureus
E & S Australia, Tasmania
Ceyx websteri (Bismarck Pygmy Kingfisher)
Bismarck Archipelago
Ceyx pusillus (Mangrove Kingfisher)
C. p. halmaherae
Halmahera I, Obi I
C. p. pusillus
W Papuan Is, New Guinea, Kei Is
C. p, laetior
N New Guinea
C. p. ramsayi
N Territory (Australia)
C. p. halli
N Queensland
C. p. masauji
Bismarck Archipelago
C. p. bougainvillei
Bougainville I, Choiseul I, Ysabel I
C. p. richardsi
Vella Lavella I, Kolambangaa I,
New Georgia I
C. p. aolae
Guadalcanal I
Ceyx erithacus (Three-toed Kingfisher)
C. e. erithacus
India to SE China, Indochina, Sumatra
C. e. macrocarus
Andaman Is, Nicobar Is
C. e. motleyi
N Bornean Is, Borneo
C. e. captus
Nias I
C. e. vargasi
Mindoro I

Ceyx rufidorsum (Malay Forest Kingfisher)
C. r. rufidorsum
Malaysia to W Philippine Is, Borneo &
Flores I
C. r. jungei
Batu Is, Simalur I
Ceyx melanurus (Philippine Forest Kingfisher)
C. m. melanurus
Luzon I
C. m. samarensis
Samar I, Leyte I
C. m. mindanensis
Mindanao I, Basilan I
Ceyx fallax (Celebes Pygmy Kingfisher)
C. f. sangirensis
Sanghir Is
C. f. fallax
Celebes

DACELONINAE

PELARGOPSIS
Pelargopsis amauroptera (Brown-winged Kingfisher)
NE India to Malaysia
Pelargopsis capensis (Stork-billed Kingfisher)
P. c. capensis
Nepal, India, Sri Lanka
P. c. burmanica
Burma to Indochina & N Malaysia
P. c. intermedia
Nicobar Is
P. c. malaccensis
S Malaysia
P. c. cyanopteryx
Sumatra, Bangka I, Billiton I
P. c. simalurensis
Simalur I
P. c. sodalis
Banjak Is
P. c. nesoeca
Nias I, Batu Is
P. c. isoptera
Pagi Is, Siberut I, Sipora I
P. c. fraseri
Java
P. c. floresiana
Bali I to Flores I
P. c. javana
Borneo
P. c. gouldi
N & W Philippine Is
P. c. smithi
SE Luzon, Masbate I, Panay I, Negros I
P. c. gigantea
S Philippine Is

Pelargopsis melanorhyncha (Black-bellied Kingfisher)
P. m. melanorhyncha
N, NC & SE Celebes
P. m. dicrorhyncha
Peleng I, Banggai Is
P. m. eutreptorhyncha
Sula Is

LACEDO
Lacedo pulchella (Banded Kingfisher)
L. p. amabilis
S Burma, Thailand, S Vietnam
L. p. deignani
S Thailand
L. p. pulchella
Malaysia, Sumatra, Java
L. p. melanops
Borneo, Bangka I

DACELO
Dacelo novaeguineae (Laughing Kookaburra)
D. n. minor
N Queensland
D. n. novaeguineae
Australia, Tasmania
Dacelo leachii (Blue-winged Kookaburra)
D. l. superflua
S New Guinea
D. l. intermedia
SE New Guinea
D. l. cliftoni
NW Australia
D. l. kempi
N Queensland
D. l. cervina
Melville I, N Northern Territory
D. l. leachii
C Northern Territory, S Queensland
Dacelo tyro (Aru Giant Kingfisher)
D. t. archboldi
S New Guinea
D. t. tyro
Aru Is
Dacelo gaudichaud (Rufous-bellied Giant Kingfisher)
New Guinea, New Guinea Is, Aru Is

CLYTOCEYX
Clytoceyx rex (Shovel-billed Kingfisher)
C. r. rex
E New Guinea
C. r. imperator
C New Guinea

MELIDORA
Melidora macrorrhina (Hook-billed Kingfisher)
M. m. waigiuensis
Waigeu I

M. m. macrorrhina
Misoöl I, Batanta I, New Guinea
M. m. jobiensis
Japen I, N New Guinea

CITTURA
Cittura cyanotis (Celebes Blue-eared Kingfisher)
C. c. sanghirensis
Sanghir Is
C. c. cyanotis
N Celebes
C. c. modesta
E & SE Celebes

HALCYON
Halcyon coromanda (Ruddy Kingfisher)
H. c. major
Korea, Japan to S China & Celebes
H. c. coromanda
Nepal to Malaysia & Indochina
H. c. mizorhina
Andaman & Nicobar Is
H. c. minor
S Malaysia, Borneo, Sumatra, Java
H. c. bangsi
Riukiu Is, Taiwan, N & W Philippine Is
H. c. ochrothorectis
S Philippine Is
H. c. pelingensis
Celebes, Peling Is
H. c. rufa
Sula Is
Halcyon badia (Chocolate-backed Kingfisher)
H. b. lopezi
Fernando Po I
H. b. badia
Liberia to Gabon & E Zaire
H. b. budongensis
W & C Uganda
Halcyon smyrnensis (White-Breasted Kingfisher)
H. s. smyrnensis
Asia Minor to S Yemen & India
H. s. fusca
W India, Sri Lanka
H. s. saturatior
Andaman Is
H. s. perpulchra
Burma, Malaysia to Indochina
H. s. fokiensis
S & E China, Taiwan
H. s. gularis
Philippine Is
Halcyon pileata (Black-capped Kingfisher)
India to China, Philippine Is, Celebes
Halcyon cyanoventris (Java Kingfisher)
Java, Bali I

Halcyon leucocephala (Grey-headed
   Kingfisher)
H. l. acteon
   Cape Verde Is
H. l. leucocephala
   Senegal to N Zaire & Ethiopia
H. l. semicaerulea
   Yemen & S Yemen
H. l. centralis
   Kenya, N Tanzania
H. l. hyacinthina
   E Kenya to Mozambique
H. l. pallidiventris
   S Zaire to Namibia & Rhodesia
Halcyon senegalensis (Woodland
   Kingfisher)
H. s. fuscopilea
   Sierra Leone to Angola & S Zaire
H. s. senegalensis
   Senegal to Ethiopia & Kenya
H. s. cyanoleuca
   S Angola to Malawi & Transvaal
Halcyon senegaloides (African Mangrove
   Kingfisher)
H. s. ranivora
   coast of E Africa
H. s. senegaloides
   coast of SE Africa
Halcyon malimbica (Blue-breasted
   Kingfisher)
H. m. fortis
   Senegal
H. m. torquata
   Gambia, Guinea
H. m. forbesi
   Sierra Leone to S Cameroun
H. m. dryas
   Principé I
H. m. malimbica
   S Cameroun to Angola & Zaire
H. m. prenticei
   Sudan, E Zaire, Uganda
Halcyon albiventris (Brown-hooded
   Kingfisher)
H. a. erlangeri
   S Somalia, NE Kenya
H. a. orientalis
   S Gabon & Angola to N Kenya &
      Mozambique
H. a. albiventris
   Rhodesia to E Cape Province
H. a. vociferans
   NE South Africa
Halcyon chelicuti (Striped Kingfisher)
H. c. eremogiton
   S Niger to E Sudan

H. c. chelicuti   229
   Senegal to Ethiopia & Zambia
H. c. damarensis
   S Angola to Transvaal & Mozambique
Halycon nigrocyanea (Blue-black
   Kingfisher)
H. n. nigrocyanea
   W New Guinea
H. n. quadricolour
   Japen I, N New Guinea
H. n. stictolaema
   S New Guinea
Halcyon winchelli (Winchell's Kingfisher)
H. w. nigrorum
   Negros I
H. w. winchelli
   S Philippine Is
Halcyon diops (Moluccan Kingfisher)
   N Moluccas
Halcyon lazuli (South Moluccan Kingfisher)
   S Moluccas
Halcyon macleayii (Forest Kingfisher)
H. m. elizabeth
   E New Guinea
H. m. insularis
   Aru Is   '
H. m. macleayii
   N & E Australia to New Guinea
H. m. incincta
   E Queensland » E New Guinea
Halcyon albonotata (White-backed
   Kingfisher)
   New Britain
Halcyon leucopygia (Ultramarine Kingfisher)
   Solomon Is
Halcyon farquhari (Chestnut-bellied
   Kingfisher)
   C New Hebrides
Halcyon pyrrhopygia (Red-backed
   Kingfisher)
   dry areas of Australia
Halcyon torotoro (Lesser Yellow-billed
   Kingfisher)
H. t. torotoro
   W Papuan Is & W New Guinea
H. t. tentelare
   Aru Is
H. t. pseustes
   S New Guinea
H. t. brevirostris
   S New Guinea
H. t. meeki
   SE New Guinea
H. t. flavirostris
   N Queensland
H. t. ochracea
   D'Entrecasteaux Archipelago

Halcyon megarhyncha (Mountain Yellow-billed Kingfisher)
H. m. wellsi
C New Guinea
H. m. sellamontis
E New Guinea
H. m. megarhyncha
SE New Guinea
Halcyon australasia (Timor Kingfisher)
H. a. australasia
Lombok I, Sumba I, Timor I, Wetar I
H. a. tringorum
Roma I
H. a. dammeriana
Damar I, Babar I
H. a. interposita
Leti I, Moa I
H. a. odites
Timorlaut
Halcyon sancta (Sacred Kingfisher)
H. s. sancta
Australia to Sumatra, Borneo, Philippine Is
H. s. vagans
New Zealand, Kermadec Is
H. s. norfolkiensis
Norfolk I
H. s. adamsi
Lord Howe I
H. s. canacorum
New Caledonia I
H. s. macmillani
Loyalty Is
Halcyon cinnamomina (Micronesian Kingfisher)
H. c. pelewensis
Palau Is
H. c. reichenbachii
Ponapé I
H. c. cinnamomina
Guam I
Halcyon funebris (Sombre Kingfisher)
Halmahera I, Ternate I
Halcyon chloris (White-collared Kingfisher)
H. c. abyssinica
Red Sea
H. c. kalbaensis
E Arabia
H. c. vidali
W India
H. c. davisoni
Andaman Is
H. c. occipitalis
Nicobar Is
H. c. humii
Burma, Malaysia, NE Sumatra
H. c. armstrongi
S Thailand, S Vietnam
H. c. chloroptera
W Sumatran Is

H. c. azela
Enggano I
H. c. palmeri
Java, Bali I
H. c. laubmanniana
Borneo & Bornean Is, S Sumatra
H. c. collaris
Philippine Is
H. c. enigma
Talaut I
H. c. chloris
Celebes to NW New Guinea, E Lesser Sunda Is
H. c. sordida
SE New Guinea, Louisiade Archipelago
H. c. colona
SE New Guinea, Louisiade Arch
H. c. teraokai
Palau Is
H. c. owstoni
Ascuncion I, Pagan I, Alamagan Is (Mariana Is)
H. c. albicilla
Saipan I, Tinan I (Mariana Is)
H. c. orii
Rota I
H. c. matthiae
St Matthias Is
H. c. stresemanni
.French I, Rook I
H. c. nusae
Bismarck Archipelago
H. c. novaehiberniae
SW New Ireland
H. c. bennetti
Nissan I
H. c. tristrami
New Britain
H. c. alberti
N & C Solomon Is
H. c. mala
Malaita I
H. c. pavuvu
Pavuvu I
H. c. solomonis
Ugi I, San Cristobal I, St Anna I
H. c. amoena
Rennell I
H. c. brachyura
Reef I
H. c. vicina
Duff I
H. c. ornata
Santa Cruz Is, Tinakula I
H. c. utupuae
Utupua I
H. c. melanodera
Vanikoro I

H. c. torresiana
Torres I
H. c. santoensis
Espiritu Santo I, Banks Is
H. c. erromangae
Erromanga I
H. c. tannensis
Tanna I
H. c. juliae
Aneitum I, Efate I
H. c. vitiensis
Viti Levu I, Vanua Levu I, Taviuni I
H. c. eximia
Kandavu I, Ono I, Vanua Kula I
H. c. marina
Lau Archipelago
H. c. sacra
Tonga I
H. c. regina
Futuna I
H. c. pealei
Tutuila I, Samoa
H. c. manuae
Ofu I, Olosinga I, Tau I

Halcyon saurophaga (White-headed Kingfisher)
H. s. saurophaga
N Moluccas to Solomon Is
H. s. anachoreta
Hermit I, Ninigo I
H. s. admiralitatis
Admiralty Is

Halcyon recurvirostris (Flat-billed Kingfisher)
Samoa

Halcyon venerata (Tahitian Kingfisher)
H. v. venerata
Tahiti I
H. v. youngi
Moorea I

Halcyon tuta (Borabora Kingfisher)
H. t. tuta
Borabora I
H. t. atiu
Atiu I (Cook Is)
H. t. mauke
Mauke I (Cook Is)

Halcyon ruficollaris (Mangaia Kingfisher)
Mangaia I (Cook Is)

Halcyon gambieri (Tuamotu Kingfisher)
H. g. gambieri
Mangareva I
H. g. gertrudae
Niau I

Halcyon godeffroyi (Marquesas Kingfisher)
Marquesas Is

Halcyon bougainvillei (Moustached Kingfisher)
H. b. bougainvillei
Bougainville I
H. b. excelsa
Guadalcanal I

Halcyon concreta (Chestnut-collared Kingfisher)
H. c. concreta
S Burma, Malaysia, Sumatra, Bangka I
H. c. peristephes
S Thailand
H. c. borneana
Borneo

Halcyon lindsayi (Spotted Wood Kingfisher)
H. l. lindsayi
Luzon I
H. l. moseleyi
Negros I
H. l. hombroni
Mindanao I
H. l. burtoni
Mindanao I

Halcyon fulgida (Glittering Kingfisher)
H. f. fulgida
Lombok I, Sumbawa I
H. f. gracilirostris
Flores I

Halcyon monacha (Lonely Kingfisher)
H. m. monacha
N Celebes
H. m. intermedia
NC Celebes
H. m. capucina
E, S & SE Celebes

Halcyon princeps (Princely Kingfisher)
H. p. princeps
NE Celebes
H. p. erythrorhamphus
NW & C Celebes
H. p. regalis
SE Celebes

TANYSIPTERA

Tanysiptera hydrocharis (Aru Paradise Kingfisher)
S New Guinea, Aru Is

Tanysiptera galatea (Common Paradise Kingfisher)
T. g. emiliae
Rau I, Moluccas
T. g. doris
Morotai I
T. g. margarethae
Halmahera I, Batjan I
T. g. sabrina
Kayoa I, Moluccas
T. g. obiensis
Obi I, Oblilatu I

T. g. actis
Buru I
T. g. nais
S Moluccas Is
T. g. galatea
NW New Guinea & W Papuan Is
T. g. meyeri
N New Guinea
T. g. minor
S & SE New Guinea
T. g. vulcani
Vulcan I
T. g. rosseliana
Rossel I
Tanysiptera riedelii (Biak Paradise Kingfisher)
Biak I
Tanysiptera carolinae (Numfor Paradise Kingfisher)
Numfor I
Tanysiptera ellioti (Kofiau Paradise Kingfisher)
Kofiau I
Tanysiptera nympha (Pink-breasted Paradise Kingfisher)
New Guinea
Tanysiptera danae (Brown-backed Paradise Kingfisher)
SE New Guinea
Tanysiptera sylvia (White-tailed Kingfisher)
T. s. leucura
Rook I
T. s. nigriceps
New Britain, Duke of York I
T. s. salvadoriana
SE New Guinea
T. s. sylvia
N Queensland to S New Guinea

85 TODIDAE (TODIES)

TODUS
Todus multicolor (Cuban Tody)
Cuba, Isle of Pines
Todus angustirostris (Narrow-billed Tody)
Hispaniola
Todus todus (Jamaican Tody)
Jamaica
Todus mexicanus (Puerto Rican Tody)
Puerto Rico
Todus subulatus (Broad-billed Tody)
Hispaniola, Gonave I

86 MOMOTIDAE (MOTMOTS)

HYLOMANES
Hylomanes momotula (Tody-Motmot)
H. m. chiapensis
(Pacific) S Mexico

H. m. momotula
(Carribean) S Mexico to Honduras
H. m. obscurus
NW Costa Rica to NW Colombia

ASPATHA
Aspatha gularis (Blue-throated Motmot)
S Mexico to Honduras, El Salvador

ELECTRON
Electron platyrhynchum (Broad-billed Motmot)
E. p. minor
E Honduras to C Colombia
E. p. platyrhynchum
W Colombia, W Ecuador
E. p. pyrrholaemum
E Colombia, E Ecuador, Peru, N Bolivia
E. p. orienticola
W Brazil
E. p. chlorophrys
SW & C Brazil
E. p. colombianum
Colombia
Electron carinatum (Keel-billed Motmot)
S Mexico to NW Costa Rica

EUMOMOTA
Eumomota superciliosa (Turquoise-browed Motmot)
E. s. bipartita
S Mexico, W Guatemala
E. s. superciliosa
SE Mexico
E. s. vanrossemi
C Guatemala
E. s. sylvestris
E Guatemala
E. s. apiaster
El Salvador, W Honduras, NW Nicaragua
E. s. euroaustris
N Honduras
E. s. australis
NW Costa Rica

BARYPHTHENGUS
Baryphthengus ruficapillus (Rufous-capped Motmot)
B. r. semirufus
Panama to W Ecuador
B. r. costaricensis
E Nicaragua, E Costa Rica
B. r. ruficapillus
S & E Brazil, Paraguay, NE Argentina
Baryphthengus martii (Rufous Motmot) Motmot)
Upper Amazonia

Momotus mexicanus (Russet-crowned Motmot)
M. m. vanrossemi
  NW Mexico
M. m. mexicanus
  NC & C Mexico
M. m. saturatus
  SW Mexico
M. m. castaneiceps
  C Guatemala
Momotus momota (Blue-crowned Motmot)
M. m. coeruliceps
  NE & C Mexico
M. m. goldmani
  SE Mexico, N Guatemala
M. m. exiguus
  S Mexico
M. m. lessonii
  S Mexico to W Panama
M. m. conexus
  S Panama, NW Colombia
M. m. reconditus
  E Panama, N Colombia
M. m. spatha
  Colombia
M. m. olivaresi
  Colombia
M. m. subrufescens
  N Colombia, N Venezuela
M. m. osgoodi
  W Venezuela
M. m. bahamensis
  Trinidad, Tobago I
M. m. aequatorialis
  WC Colombia, E Ecuador
M. m. chlorolaemus
  E Peru
M. m. microstephanus
  SE Colombia, E Ecuador, NW Brazil
M. m. momota
  E Venezuela, the Guianas, N Brazil
M. m. argenticinctus
  W Ecuador, NW Peru
M. m. ignobilis
  E Peru, W Brazil
M. m. nattereri
  NE Bolivia
M. m. simplex
  W Brazil
M. m. cametensis
  NC Brazil
M. m. parensis
  NE Brazil
M. m. pilcomajensis
  S Bolivia, S Brazil, NW Argentina

87 MEROPIDAE (BEE EATERS) 233

Nyctyornis amicta (Red-bearded Bee Eater)
  Malaysia, Sumatra, Borneo
Nyctyornis athertoni (Blue-bearded Bee Eater)
N. a. athertoni
  SW India & S Himalayas to Indochina
N. a. brevicaudata
  Hainan I
MEROPOGON
Meropogon forsteni (Celebes Bearded Bee Eater)
  Celebes
MEROPS
Merops gularis (Black Bee Eater)
M. g. gularis
  Sierra Leone to Niger river
M. g. australis
  Cameroun to Uganda & Angola
Merops muelleri (Blue-headed Bee Eater)
M. m. mentalis
  Sierra Leone to Cameroun
M. m. muelleri
  S Cameroun to E Zaire
M. m. yalensis
  Uganda, W Kenya
Merops bulocki (Red-throated Bee Eater)
M. b. bulocki
  Senegal to Central African Republic
M. b. frenatus
  E Sudan to N Zaire & N Uganda
Merops bullockoides (White-fronted Bee Eater)
  Gabon to Angola, Kenya & Natal
Merops pusillus (Little Bee Eater)
M. p. pusillus
  Senegal to N Zaire
M. p. ocularis
  Sudan, W Ethiopia
M. p. cyanostictus
  Ethiopia & Somalia to Tanzania
M. p. meridionalis
  S Zaire & Tanzania to Namibia & Natal
Merops variegatus (Blue-breasted Bee Eater)
M. v. loringi
  Cameroun to Uganda
M. v. variegatus
  Gabon to Zaire & Angola
M. v. bangweoloensis
  S Zaire & Zambia
M. v. lafresnayii
  Ethiopia
Merops oreobates (Cinnamon-chested Bee Eater)
  S Sudan, E Zaire, N Tanzania

Merops hirundineus (Swallow-tailed Bee Eater)
  M. h. chrysolaimus
    Senegal to Ghana & Central African Republic
  M. h. heuglini
    N Zaire, Uganda to Tanzania
  M. h. hirundineus
    SE Kenya to Angola & Natal
Merops breweri (Black-headed Bee Eater)
  Cameroun, Gabon, W Zaire
Merops revoilii (Somali Bee Eater)
  SE Ethiopia, Somalia, NE Kenya
Merops albicollis (White-throated Bee Eater)
  Senegal to Ethiopia & Tanzania
Merops orientalis (Little Green Bee Eater)
  M. o. viridissimus
    Senegal to Aïr & N Ethiopia
  M. o. cleopatra
    Nile valley, Egypt
  M. o. cyanophrys
    W Saudi Arabia
  M. o. muscatensis
    Oman
  M. o. najdanus
    C Saudi Arabia
  M. o. beludschicus
    SE Iran to NW India
  M. o. orientalis
    India
  M. o. ceylonicus
    Sri Lanka
  M. o. birmanus
    Assam, Burma, W China, Indochina
Merops boehmi (Boehm's Bee Eater)
  Tanzania, E Zambia, Malawi
Merops viridis (Chestnut-headed Bee Eater)
  M. v. viridis
    SE China to Sumatra, Java, Borneo
  M. v. americanus
    Philippine Is
Merops superciliosus (Blue-cheeked Bee Eater)
  M. s. persicus
    Israel to C Asia » NW India & Africa
  M. s. chrysocercus
    N Africa to W Africa
  M. s. superciliosus
    Madagascar to S, C & E Africa
Merops philippinus (Blue-tailed Bee Eater)
  M. p. philippinus
    India to SE China, Borneo & Lesser Sunda Is
  M. p. celebensis
    S Celebes

  M. p. salvadorii
    E New Guinea, New Britain
Merops ornatus (Australian Bee Eater)
  Australia to Lesser Sunda Is
Merops apiaster (European Bee Eater)
  S Europe & C Asia » N India & Africa
Merops leschenaulti (Bay-headed Bee Eater)
  M. l. leschenaulti
    W India to Malaysia & Indochina
  M. l. quinticolor
    Java, Bali I
  M. l. andamanensis
    S Andaman Is
Merops malimbicus (Rosy Bee Eater)
  Ghana to N & W Zaire
Merops nubicus (Carmine Bee Eater)
  M. n. nubicus
    Senegal to Zaire & Ethiopia
  M. n. nubicoides
    Angola to Natal » S Zaire & Tanzania

88 CORACIIDAE (ROLLERS)

CORACIAS
Coracias garrulus (Common Roller)
  C. g. garrulus
    S Europe & C Asia » Africa & India
  C. g. semenowi
    Transcaspia to NW India
Coracias abyssinica (Abyssinian Roller)
  Senegal to S Yemen & Kenya
Coracias caudata (Lilac-breasted Roller)
  C. c. lorti
    S Ethiopia, Somalia, N Kenya
  C. c. caudata
    Uganda to Angola & N & E South Africa
Coracias spatulata (Racquet-tailed Roller)
  Angola to Tanzania & Mozambique
Coracias naevia (Rufous-crowned Roller)
  C. n. naevia
    Senegal to Ethiopia & N Tanzania
  C. n. mosambica
    Angola & S Zaire to E Cape Province
Coracias benghalensis (Indian Roller)
  C. b. benghalensis
    E Saudi Arabia to NE India
  C. b. indica
    S India, Sri Lanka
  C. b. affinis
    Bhutan to Malaysia & Indochina
Coracias temminckii (Celebes Roller)
  Celebes
Coracias cyanogaster (Blue-bellied Roller)
  Senegal to N Zaire & Sudan

EURYSTOMUS
Eurystomus glaucurus (Broad-billed Roller)
　E. g. afer
　　Senegal to NE Zaire & E Ethiopia
　E. g. aethiopicus
　　Sudan, W Ethiopia
　E. g. rufobuccalis
　　C & S Uganda
　E. g. suahelicus
　　Somalia to C Zaire & NE Zambia
　E. g. pulcherrimus
　　Angola to Mozambique & Natal
　E. g. glaucurus
　　Madagascar to C Africa
Eurystomus gularis (Blue-throated Roller)
　E. g. gularis
　　Senegal to Mali & Togo
　E. g. neglectus
　　Cameroun to Angola & E Zaire
Eurystomus orientalis (Eastern Broad-billed Roller)
　E. o. abundus
　　N Himalayas to Korea, Indochina, Malaysia
　E. o. deignani
　　N Thailand to Sumatra, Java, Borneo
　E. o. orientalis
　　S Himalayas to Sumatra & N Celebes
　E. o. gigas
　　S Andaman Is
　E. o. oberholseri
　　Simalur I
　E. o. latouchei
　　NE China
　E. o. connectens
　　S Celebes, Lombok I to Damar I
　E. o. azureus
　　N Moluccas
　E. o. waigiouensis
　　New Guinea & islands
　E. o. pacificus
　　Australia to New Guinea & Kei Is
　E. o. crassirostris
　　Bismarck Archipelago
　E. o. solomonensis
　　Feni I, Solomon Is

89 BRACHYPTERACIIDAE (GROUND ROLLERS)

BRACHYPTERACIAS
Brachypteracias leptosomus (Short-legged Ground Roller)
　NE Madagascar
Brachypteracias squamigera (Scaly Ground Roller)
　NE Madagascar

ATELORNIS 235
Atelornis pittoides (Pitta-like Ground Roller)
　Madagascar
Atelornis crossleyi (Crossley's Ground Roller)
　NE Madagascar

URATELORNIS
Uratelornis chimaera (Long-tailed Ground Roller)
　SW Madagascar

90 LEPTOSOMATIDAE (COUROLS)

LEPTOSOMUS
Leptosomus discolor (Courol)
　L. d. gracilis
　　Gd Comoro I
　L. d. intermedius
　　Anjouan I
　L. d. discolor
　　Mayotte I, Madagascar

91 UPUPIDAE (HOOPOES)

UPUPA
Upupa epops (Hoopoe)
　U. e. epops
　　Europe & W Asia to W & C Africa & India
　U. e. major
　　Egypt
　U. e. senegalensis
　　Senegal to Ethiopia & NE Tanzania
　U. e. orientalis
　　NW India
　U. e. ceylonensis
　　C & S India, Sri Lanka
　U. e. saturata
　　E Siberia to N & E China
　U. e. longirostris
　　Assam to Indochina, Malaysia, Sumatra
　U. e. marginata
　　Madagascar
　U. e. africana
　　S Zaire to Uganda, Kenya & Cape Province
　U. e. waibeli
　　Cameroun to N Kenya

92 PHOENICULIDAE (WOOD HOOPOES)

PHOENICULUS
Phoeniculus purpureus (Green Wood Hoopoe)
　P. p. senegalensis
　　Senegal to Ghana
　P. p. guineensis
　　Mali to N Ivory Coast & Central African Republic

P. p. niloticus
N Sudan to E Zaire
P. p. abyssinicus
N Ethiopia
P. p. somaliensis
Somalia
P. p. neglectus
S Ethiopia
P. p. marwitzi
E Uganda, E Zaire to Natal, Zanzibar
P. p. angolensis
Angola
P. p. purpureus
C & SW South Africa
Phoeniculus damarensis (Violet Wood Hoopoe)
N & C Namibia
Phoeniculus granti (Grant's Wood Hoopoe)
S Ethiopia, W Kenya
Phoeniculus bollei (White-headed Wood Hoopoe)
P. b. bollei
Ghana to Cameroun
P. b. jacksoni
E Zaire, W Kenya
P. b. okuensis
S Cameroun
Phoeniculus castaneiceps (Forest Wood Hoopoe)
P. c. castaneiceps
Ghana, SW Nigeria
P. c. brunneiceps
S Cameroun, N Zaire
P. c. adolfifriederici
E Zaire, Uganda, W Kenya
Phoeniculus aterrimus (Black Wood Hoopoe)
P. a. aterrimus
Senegal to N Zaire, S Sahara
P. a. emini
S Sudan, NE Zaire
P. a. notatus
N Ethiopia
P. a. anchietae
SW Zaire, N Angola

RHINOPOMASTUS
Rhinopomastus minor (Abyssinian Scimitar-bill)
R. m. minor
Ethiopia to C Somalia
R. m. somalicus
S Somalia, E Kenya
R. m. cabanisi
Uganda, N Kenya
R. m. extimus
S Kenya to C Tanzania

Rhinopomastus cyanomelas (Scimitar-bill)
R. c. schalowi
N Kenya to E Zaire, NE Transvaal & Mozambique
R. c. cyanomelas
Angola to Namibia, Botswana & Natal

93 BUCEROTIDAE (HORNBILLS)

TOCKUS
Tockus birostris (Indian Grey Hornbill)
N & C India
Tockus fasciatus (Pied Hornbill)
T. f. semifasciatus
Senegal to Ghana
T. f. fasciatus
Cameroun to SW Sudan, Zaire, Angola
Tockus alboterminatus (Crowned Hornbill)
T. a. geloensis
Ethiopia to Zambia & Malawi
T. a. stegmanni
Uganda to E Zaire, W Kenya, W Tanzania
T. a. alboterminatus
Mozambique to Angola » Somalia
T. a. australis
E South Africa
Tockus bradfieldi (Bradfield's Hornbill)
T. b. bradfieldi
S Angola, N Namibia
T. b. williaminae
Botswana, W Rhodesia
Tockus pallidirostris (Pale-billed Hornbill)
T. p. pallidirostris
Angola to SW Tanzania
T. p. neumanni
S Kenya, E Tanzania, Malawi
Tockus nasutus (African Grey Hornbill)
T. n. nasutus
Senegal to Ethiopia & N Kenya
T. n. forskalii
NE Ethiopia, W & S Saudi Arabia
T. n. epirhinus
S Kenya to Angola, Botswana & Natal
T. n. dorsalis
S Angola, Namibia
Tockus hemprichii (Hemprich's Hornbill)
T. h. hemprichii
Ethiopia, Somalia
T. h. exsul
NW Kenya
Tockus monteiri (Monteiro's Hornbill)
S Angola, N Namibia
Tockus griseus (Malabar Grey Hornbill)
T. g. griseus
W India
T. g. gingalensis
Sri Lanka

Tockus hartlaubi (Black Dwarf Hornbill)
 T. h. hartlaubi
  Guinea to S Cameroun
 T. h. granti
  WC to NE Zaire
Tockus camurus (Red-billed Dwarf Hornbill)
 T. c. pulchrirostris
  Liberia to S Nigeria
 T. c. camurus
  Cameroun & Gabon to NE Zaire
Tockus erythrorhynchus (Red-billed Hornbill)
 T. e. erythrorhynchus
  Senegal to Somalia & Tanzania
 T. e. rufirostris
  Angola to Malawi & Transvaal
 T. e. damarensis
  N Namibia
Tockus flavirostris (Yellow-billed Hornbill)
 T. f. flavirostris
  Ethiopia & W Somalia to S Kenya
 T. f. somaliensis
  E Somalia
 T. f. elegans
  Angola
 T. f. leucomelas
  Namibia to Mozambique & Natal
Tockus deckeni (Von der Decken's Hornbill)
 C Ethiopia to C Tanzania
Tockus jacksoni (Jackson's Hornbill)
 C Ethiopia to C Tanzania

BERENICORNIS
Berenicornis comatus (Long-crested Hornbill)
 S Vietnam, Malaysia, Sumatra, Borneo
Berenicornis albocristatus (African White-crested Hornbill)
 B. a. albocristatus
  Sierra Leone to Ivory Coast
 B. a. macrourus
  Ghana & Togo
 B. a. cassini
  W Nigeria to Gabon & Uganda

PTILOLAEMUS
Ptilolaemus tickelli (Tickell's Hornbill)
 P. t. austeni
  S Assam
 P. t. tickelli
  S Burma
 P. t. indochinensis
  Indochina

ANORRHINUS
Anorrhinus galeritus (Bushy-crested Hornbill)
 A. g. carinatus
  S Burma, S Thailand, Malaysia

 A. g. galeritus
  Sumatra, N Borneo
 A. g. minor
  S Borneo

PENELOPIDES
Penelopides panini (Rufous-tailed Hornbill)
 P. p. manilloe
  Luzon I, Marinduque I
 P. p. subnigra
  Polillo Is
 P. p. mindorensis
  Mindoro I
 P. p. ticaensis
  Ticao I
 P. p. panini
  Masbate I, Panay I, Negros I
 P. p. samarensis
  Samar I, Leyte I, Bohol I
 P. p. affinis
  Dinagat I, Mindanao I
 P. p. basilanica
  Basilan I
Penelopides exarhatus (Temminck's Hornbill)
 P. e. exarhatus
  N Celebes
 P. e. sanfordi
  C, SE & S Celebes

ACEROS
Aceros nipalensis (Rufous-necked Hornbill)
 Nepal to N Indochina
Aceros corrugatus (Wrinkled Hornbill)
 A. c. corrugatus
  Malaysia, Borneo
 A. c. megistus
  Sumatra, Batu Is
Aceros leucocephalus (White-headed Hornbill)
 A. l. waldeni
  Panay I, Guimaras I, Negros I
 A. l. leucocephalus
  Mindanao I, Camiguin (South I)
Aceros cassidix (Celebes Hornbill)
 Celebes
Aceros undulatus (Wreathed Hornbill)
 A. u. ticehursti
  S Assam to Indochina & N Malaysia
 A. u. undulatus
  S Malaysia, Sumatra, Java, Bali I, Borneo
Aceros plicatus (Blyth's Hornbill)
 A. p. subruficollis
  S Burma, S Thailand, Malaysia, Sumatra, Borneo
 A. p. plicatus
  S Moluccas
 A. p. ruficollis
  N Moluccas, W & N New Guinea & Is

A. p. jungei
E New Guinea, Fergusson I, Goodenough I
A. p. dampieri
Bismarck Archipelago
A. p. harterti
Buka I, Bougainville I, Shortland I
A. p. mendanae
Choiseul I, Ysabel I, Guadalcanal I, Malaita I
Aceros everetti (Everett's Hornbill)
Sumba I
Aceros narcondami (Narcondam Hornbill)
Narcondam I

ANTHRACOCEROS
Anthracoceros malayanus (Black Hornbill)
S Malaysia, Sumatra, Borneo
Anthracoceros malabaricus (Indian Pied Hornbill)
A. m. malabaricus
S Himalayas, N Burma
A. m. leucogaster
Burma to Malaysia, Indochina, SE China
Anthracoceros coronatus (Malabar Pied Hornbill)
A. c. coronatus
S India, Sri Lanka
A. c. convexus
Malaysia, Sumatra, Java, Borneo
Anthracoceros montani (Sulu Hornbill)
Jolo I, Tawitawi Is
Anthracoceros marchei (Palawan Hornbill)
Calamian I, Palawan I, Balabac I

BYCANISTES
Bycanistes bucinator (Trumpeter Hornbill)
B. b. fistulator
Senegal to W Nigeria
B. b. sharpii
SE Nigeria to C Zaire & N Angola
B. b. duboisi
Cameroun to W Uganda
B. b. bucinator
Angola to N Kenya & E Cape Province
Bycanistes cylindricus (Brown-cheeked Hornbill)
B. c. cylindricus
Sierra Leone to Benin
B. c. albotibialis
Nigeria & Cameroun to Uganda
Bycanistes subcylindricus (Black and White Casqued Hornbill)
B. s. subcylindricus
Ghana to S Nigeria
B. s. subquadratus
Kenya & E Zaire to Cameroun » Angola
Bycanistes brevis (Silvery-cheeked Hornbill)
B. b. brevis
S Kenya to Malawi & Rhodesia

B. b. omissus
Ethiopia to C Kenya
CERATOGYMNA
Ceratogymna atrata (Black-casqued Hornbill)
Liberia to Sudan & Angola
Ceratogymna elata (Yellow-casqued Hornbill)
Guinea to W Cameroun

BUCEROS
Buceros rhinoceros (Rhinoceros Hornbill)
B. r. rhinoceros
Malaysia
B. r. sumatranus
Sumatra, Billiton I
B. r. silvestris
Java
B. r. borneoensis
Borneo
Buceros bicornis (Great Indian Hornbill)
B. b. bicornis
W India, Himalayas to Indochina, Malaysia
B. b. cavatus
SW India
Buceros hydrocorax (Rufous Hornbill)
B. h. hydrocorax
Luzon I, Marinduque I
B. h. semigaleatus
Samar I, Leyte I, Bohol I
B. h. mindanensis
Mindanao I
B. h. basilanicus
Basilan I

RHINOPLAX
Rhinoplax vigil (Helmeted Hornbill)
Malaysia, Sumatra, Borneo

BUCORVUS
Bucorvus abyssinicus (Abyssinian Ground Hornbill)
Gambia to C Kenya
Bucorvus leadbeateri (Southern Ground Hornbill)
N Angola to Kenya & E Cape Province

Piciformes

94 GALBULIDAE (JACAMARS)

GALBALCYRHYNCHUS
Galbalcyrhynchus leucotis (White-eared Jacamar)
N Upper Amazonia
Galbalcyrhynchus purusianus (Purus Jacamar)
E & S Peru, W Brazil, N Bolivia

Brachygalba albogularis (White-throated Jacamar)
E Peru
Brachygalba lugubris (Black-billed Jacamar)
B. l. fulviventris
E Colombia
B. l. caquetae
SE Colombia to E Peru
B. l. lugubris
E & S Venezuela, the Guianas, N Brazil
B. l. obscuriceps
S Venezuela, NW Brazil
B. l. naumbergi
NE Brazil
B. l. melanosterna
E Bolivia, C & SW Brazil
B. l. phaeonota
C Brazil
Brachygalba goeringi (Pale-headed Jacamar)
E Colombia, N Venezuela
Brachygalba salmoni (Dusky-backed Jacamar)
E Panama, NW Colombia

JACAMARALCYON
Jacamaralcyon tridactyla (Three-toed Jacamar)
SE Brazil

GALBULA
Galbula albirostris (Yellow-billed Jacamar)
G. a. chalcocephala
S Colombia, Ecuador, NW Peru, W Brazil
G. a. albirostris
E Venezuela, the Guianas, N Brazil
Galbula cyanicollis (Blue-necked Jacamar)
C Brazil
Galbula galbula (Green-tailed Jacamar)
E & S Venezuela, the Guianas, N & C Brazil
Galbula ruficauda (Rufous-tailed Jacamar)
G. r. melanogenis
S Mexico to W Ecuador
G. r. ruficauda
C Colombia, Venezuela, the Guianas, N Brazil
G. r. pallens
N Colombia
G. r. brevirostris
NW Venezuela
G. r. rufoviridis
S Brazil, N Bolivia, Paraguay, N Argentina
G. r. heterogyna
E Bolivia, SW Brazil
Galbula tombacea (White-chinned Jacamar)
G. t. tombacea
S Colombia, Ecuador, Peru, W Brazil

G. t. mentalis
C & WC Brazil
Galbula cyanescens (Bluish-fronted Jacamar)
W Brazil, E Peru
Galbula pastazae (Coppery-chested Jacamar)
W Brazil, E Ecuador
Galbula leucogastra (Bronzy Jacamar)
G. l. chalcothorax
W Brazil, E Ecuador, E Peru
G. l. leucogastra
S Venezuela, the Guianas, W Brazil
G. l. viridissima
C Brazil
Galbula dea (Paradise Jacamar)
G. d. dea
Venezuela, the Guianas, N Brazil
G. d. amazonum
N Bolivia, SW Brazil
G. d. brunneiceps
E Colombia, E Peru, W Brazil
G. d. phainopepla
WC Brazil

JACAMEROPS
Jacamerops aurea (Great Jacamar)
J. a. penardi
Costa Rica to W Colombia
J. a. aurea
E Colombia, the Guianas, Venezuela
J. a. ridgwayi
NE & C Brazil
J. a. isidori
E Ecuador, E Peru, N Bolivia, W Brazil

95 BUCCONIDAE (PUFFBIRDS)

NOTHARCHUS
Notharchus macrorhynchos (White-necked Puffbird)
N. m. cryptoleucus
El Salvador, NW Nicaragua
N. m. hyperrhynchus
S Mexico to NW South America
N. m. macrorhynchos
the Guianas, N Brazil
N. m. paraensis
E Brazil
N. m. swainsoni
SE Brazil, E Paraguay, NE Argentina
Notharchus pectoralis (Black-breasted Puffbird)
E Panama to NW Ecuador
Notharchus ordii (Brown-banded Puffbird)
S Venezuela, NW Brazil
Notharchus tectus (Pied Puffbird)
N. t. subtectus
E Panama to C Colombia & SW Ecuador

N. t. picatus
E Ecuador, E Peru
N. t. tectus
S Venezuela, the Guianas, N Brazil

BUCCO
Bucco macrodactylus (Chestnut-capped Puffbird)
B. m. macrodactylus
N & W Amazonia
B. m. caurensis
S Venezuela
Bucco tamatia (Spotted Puffbird)
B. t. pulmentum
S Colombia, E Ecuador, E Peru, W Brazil
B. t. tamatia
E Colombia, Venezuela, the Guianas,
N Brazil
B. t. inexpectatus
NC Brazil
B. t. punctuliger
C Brazil
B. t. hypneleus
EC Brazil
B. t. interior
SW Brazil
Bucco noanamae (Sooty-capped Puffbird)
W Colombia
Bucco capensis (Collared Puffbird)
B. c. dugandi
SE Colombia, Ecuador, C Peru
B. c. capensis
the Guianas, Brazil, E Peru

NYSTALUS
Nystalus radiatus (Barred Puffbird)
W Panama to W Ecuador
Nystalus chacuru (White-eared Puffbird)
N. c. uncirostris
E Peru, E Bolivia
N. c. chacuru
S Brazil, Paraguay, NE Argentina
Nystalus striolatus (Striolated Puffbird)
N. s. striolatus
W Amazonia
N. s. torridus
S Brazil
Nystalus maculatus (Spot-backed Puffbird)
N. m. maculatus
E Brazil
N. m. parvirostris
C Brazil
N. m. pallidigula
SW Brazil
N. m. striatipectus
E & S Bolivia, N Argentina

HYPNELUS
Hypnelus ruficollis (Russet-throated Puffbird)
H. r. ruficollis
N Colombia, W Venezuela
H. r. decolor
NE Colombia, NW Venezuela
H. r. striaticollis
NW Venezuela
H. r. coloratus
W Venezuela
H. r. bicinctus
N Venezuela
H. r. stoicus
Margarita I

MALACOPTILA
Malacoptila striata (Crescent-chested Puffbird)
M. s. minor
E Brazil
M. s. striata
SE Brazil
Malacoptila fusca (White-chested Puffbird)
M. f. fusca
N & NW Amazonia
M. f. venezuelae
S Venezuela
Malacoptila semicincta (Semicollared Puffbird)
S Peru, N Bolivia, W Brazil
Malacoptila fulvogularis (Black-streaked Puffbird)
M. f. substriata
Colombia
M. f. huilae
N Colombia
M. f. fulvogularis
E Ecuador to Bolivia
Malacoptila rufa (Rufous-necked Puffbird)
M. r. rufa
E Ecuador, E Peru, W Brazil
M. r. brunnescens
C Brazil
Malacoptila panamensis (White-whiskered Puffbird)
M. p. inornata
S Mexico to N Nicaragua
M. p. fuliginosa
SE Nicaragua to W Panama
M. p. panamensis
SW Costa Rica to W Colombia
M. p. poliopis
SW Colombia, W Ecuador
M. p. magdalenae
N Colombia
Malacoptila mystacalis (Moustached Puffbird)
Colombia, NW Venezuela

MICROMONACHA
Micromonacha lanceolata (Lanceolated Monklet)
M. l. austinsmithi
E Costa Rica, W Panama
M. l. lanceolata
W Colombia, E Ecuador, E Peru, W Brazil

NONNULA
Nonnula rubecula (Rusty-breasted Nunlet)
N. r. duidae
S Venezuela
N. r. interfluvialis
S Venezuela, N Brazil
N. r. cineracea
W Brazil, NE Peru
N. r. simplex
NE Brazil
N. r. rubecula
SE Brazil, Paraguay, NE Argentina
Nonnula sclateri (Fulvous-chinned Nunlet)
W Brazil
Nonnula brunnea (Brown Nunlet)
S Colombia, E Ecuador, E Peru
Nonnula ruficapilla (Grey-cheeked Nunlet)
N. r. frontalis
E Panama, N Colombia
N. r. pallescens
NE Colombia
N. r. rufipectus
NE Peru
N. r. ruficapilla
E Peru, W Brazil
N. r. nattereri
SW Brazil
Nonnula amaurocephala (Chestnut-headed Nunlet)
W Brazil

HAPALOPTILA
Hapaloptila castanea (White-faced Nunbird)
W Colombia, W Ecuador

MONASA
Monasa atra (Black Nunbird)
S Venezuela, the Guianas, N Brazil
Monasa nigrifrons (Black-fronted Nunbird)
M. n. nigrifrons
W & NW Amazonia
M. n. canescens
E Bolivia
Monasa morphoeus (White-fronted Nunbird)
M. m. grandior
Nicaragua to NW Panama
M. m. fidelis
E Panama
M. m. pallescens
E Panama, NW Colombia

M. m. sclateri
N Colombia
M. m. peruana
SE Colombia, E Peru, NW Brazil
M. m. morphoeus
S & E Brazil
M. m. boliviana
NE Bolivia
Monasa flavirostris (Yellow-billed Nunbird)
E Colombia, E Ecuador, E Peru, W Brazil

CHELIDOPTERA
Chelidoptera tenebrosa (Swallow-wing Puffbird)
C. t. tenebrosa
NE & NC South America
C. t. brasiliensis
E & SE Brazil
C. t. pallida
W Venezuela

96 CAPITONIDAE (BARBETS)

CAPITO
Capito aurovirens (Scarlet-crowned Barbet)
Upper Amazonia
Capito maculicoronatus (Spot-crowned Barbet)
C. m. maculicoronatus
W Panama
C. m. pirrensis
E Panama (Pacific), NW Colombia
C. m. melas
E Panama (Caribbean)
C. m. rubrilateralis
W Colombia
Capito squamatus (Orange-fronted Barbet)
SW Colombia, W Ecuador
Capito hypoleucus (White-mantled Barbet)
N Colombia
Capito dayi (Black-girdled Barbet)
W Brazil
Capito quinticolòr (Five-coloured Barbet)
W Colombia
Capito niger (Black-spotted Barbet)
C. n. niger
the Guianas, NE Brazil
C. n. punctatus
E Colombia to E Peru
C. n. intermedius
WC Venezuela
C. n. aurantiicinctus
S Venezuela
C. n. auratus
NW Peru
C. n. orosae
NW Peru, NW Brazil

C. n. amazonicus
NW Brazil
C. n. transilens
NW Brazil
C. n. nitidior
NW Brazil
C. n. hypochondriacus
NC Brazil
C. n. novaolindae
NW Brazil
C. n. arimae
NW Brazil
C. n. insperatus
SE Peru, N Bolivia, W Brazil
C. n. bolivianus
W Bolivia
C. n. brunneipectus
NC Brazil

EUBUCCO
Eubucco richardsoni (Lemon-throated Barbet)
E. r. richardsoni
SE Colombia, E Ecuador, E Peru
E. r. nigriceps
NW Peru
E. r. aurantiicollis
E Peru, W Brazil
E. r. coccineus
C Peru
Eubucco bourcierii (Red-headed Barbet)
E. b. salvini
Costa Rica, W Panama
E. b. anomalus
E Panama
E. b. occidentalis
W Colombia
E. b. bourcierii
C & E Colombia
E. b. aequatorialis
W Ecuador
E. b. orientalis
E Ecuador
Eubucco tucinkae (Scarlet-hooded Barbet)
SE Peru
Eubucco versicolor (Versicoloured Barbet)
E. v. steerii
N Peru
E. v. glaucogularis
C Peru
E. v. versicolor
S Peru, NW Bolivia

SEMNORNIS
Semnornis frantzii (Prong-billed Barbet)
Costa Rica, W Panama
Semnornis ramphastinus (Toucan Barbet)
S. r. caucae
W Colombia

S. r. ramphastinus
C Ecuador

PSILOPOGON
Psilopogon pyrolophus (Fire-tufted Barbet)
Malaysia, Sumatra

MEGALAIMA
Megalaima virens (Great Barbet)
M. v. marshallorum
NW Himalayas
M. v. magnifica
Assam, N Burma
M. v. clamator
C Burma
M. v. virens
E & S China to S Burma, Thailand,
N Indochina
Megalaima lagrandieri (Red-vented Barbet)
M. l. rothschildi
N Laos, N Vietnam
M. l. lagrandieri
S Laos, S Vietnam
Megalaima zeylanica (Oriental Green Barbet)
M. z. kangrae
W Himalayas
M. z. inornata
W India
M. z. caniceps
C & E India
M. z. zeylanica
S India, Sri Lanka
Megalaima lineata (Lineated Barbet)
M. l. hodgsoni
W Himalayas to Malaysia & Indochina
M. l. lineata
Java, Bali I
Megalaima viridis (Small Green Barbet)
S India
Megalaima faiostricta (Green-eared Barbet)
M. f. praetermissa
S China, N Vietnam
M. f. faiostricta
Thailand, Laos, S Vietnam
Megalaima corvina (Brown-throated Barbet)
Java
Megalaima chrysopogon (Gold-whiskered Barbet)
M. c. laeta
S Thailand, Malaysia
M. c. chrysopogon
Sumatra
M. c. chrysopsis
Borneo

Megalaima rafflesii (Many-coloured Barbet)
M. r. malayensis
  S Burma, Malaysia
M. r. rafflesii
  Sumatra, Bangka I
M. r. billitonis
  Billiton I, Mendanau I
M. r. borneensis
  Borneo

Megalaima mystacophanos (Gaudy Barbet)
M. m. mystacophanos
  S Burma, Malaysia, Sumatra
M. m. humii
  Borneo
M. m. ampala
  Batu Is

Megalaima javensis (Black-banded Barbet)
Java

Megalaima flavifrons (Yellow-fronted Barbet)
Sri Lanka

Megalaima franklinii (Golden-throated Barbet)
M. f. franklinii
  E Himalayas to S China & N Vietnam
M. f. ramsayi
  S Burma, N & W Thailand
M. f. auricularis
  S Laos, S Vietnam
M. f. trangensis
  S Thailand
M. f. minor
  Malaysia

Megalaima oorti (Muller's Barbet)
M. o. oorti
  Malaysia, Sumatra
M. o. annamensis
  S Indochina
M. o. nuchalis
  Taiwan
M. o. faber
  Hainan I
M. o. sini
  SE China

Megalaima asiatica (Blue-throated Barbet)
M. a. asiatica
  N India, Assam, N & C Burma
M. a. rubescens
  S Assam, NW Burma
M. a. davisoni
  S Burma to S China, N Indochina
M. a. chersonesus
  S Thailand
M. a. monticola
  N Borneo

Megalaima incognita (Hume's Blue-throated Barbet) 243
M. i. incognita
  S Burma
M. i. elbeli
  S Thailand
M. i. euroa
  S Thailand, Indochina

Megalaima henricii (Yellow-crowned Barbet)
M. h. henricii
  S Thailand, Malaysia, Sumatra
M. h. brachyrhyncha
  Borneo

Megalaima armillaris (Blue-crowned Barbet)
M. a. armillaris
  W & C Java
M. a. baliensis
  E Java, Bali I

Megalaima pulcherrima (Golden-naped Barbet)
NW Borneo

Megalaima australis (Blue-eared Barbet)
M. a. cyanotis
  Himalayas to Indochina
M. a. stuarti
  S Burma, S Thailand
M. a. duvaucelii
  Malaysia, Sumatra, Borneo
M. a. gigantorhinus
  Nias I
M. a. tanamassae
  Batu Is
M. a. australis
  Java
M. a. herbereri
  Bali I

Megalaima eximia (Black-throated Barbet)
M. e. eximia
  N Borneo
M. e. cyanea
  NE Borneo

Megalaima rubricapilla (Crimson-throated Barbet)
M. r. malabarica
  SW India
M. r. rubricapilla
  Sri Lanka

Megalaima haemacephala (Crimson-breasted Barbet)
M. h. indica
  NW India to Malaysia & Indonesia
M. h. delica
  Sumatra
M. h. rosea
  Java, Bali I

M. h. haemacephala
Luzon I, Mindoro I, Samar I, Leyte I
Mindanao I
M. h. intermedia
Tablas I, Romblon I, Masbate I, Negros I,
Cebu I

CALORHAMPHUS
Calorhamphus fuliginosus (Brown Barbet)
C. f. hayii
S Burma, Malaysia, Sumatra
C. f. fuliginosus
Borneo (except North)
C. f. tertius
N Borneo

GYMNOBUCCO
Gymnobucco calvus (Naked-faced Barbet)
G. c. calvus
Sierra Leone to S Nigeria
G. c. major
S Cameroun, Gabon
G. c. congicus
SW Zaire, N Angola
G. c. vernayi
S Angola
Gymnobucco peli (Bristle-nosed Barbet)
Ghana to Gabon
Gymnobucco sladeni (Sladen's Barbet)
N & E Zaire
Gymnobucco bonapartei (Grey-throated Barbet)
G. b. bonapartei
W Cameroun to E Zaire
G. b. intermedius
S Sudan, Uganda to NW Tanzania
G. b. cinereiceps
W Kenya

SMILORHIS
Smilorhis leucotis (White-eared Barbet)
S. l. kenyae
C & S Kenya
S. l. kilimensis
S Kenya, N Tanzania
S. l. leucogrammicus
Tanzania
S. l. leucotis
Malawi to Natal

CRYPTOLYBIA
Cryptolybia olivacea (Green Barbet)
C. o. olivacea
E Kenya, Tanzania
C. o. howelli
Morogoro, E Tanzania
C. o. woodwardi
N Natal
C. o. rungweensis
SW Tanzania, N Malawi
C. o. belcheri
Malawi, N Mozambique

STACTOLAEMA
Stactolaema anchietae (Yellow-headed Barbet)
S. a. rex
Angola
S. a. anchietae
Angola, S Zaire
S. a. katangae
S Zaire, N Zambia
Stactolaema whytii (Whyte's Barbet)
S. w. stresemanni
S Tanzania
S. w. whytii
S Malawi
S. w. terminatum
Iringa (E Tanzania)
S. w. sowerbyi
S Malawi, Rhodesia
S. w. buttoni
N Zambia
S. w. irwini
E Rhodesia
S. w. eurorum
S Tanzania
S. w. angoniensis
W Malawi, NE Zambia

POGONIULUS
Pogoniulus duchaillui (Yellow-spotted Barbet)
P. d. duchaillui
Sierra Leone & Gabon to Uganda
P. d. gabriellae
W Zaire
P. d. bannermani
W Cameroun
Pogoniulus scolopaceus (Speckled Tinkerbird)
P. s. scolopaceus
Sierra Leone & E Nigeria
P. s. stellatus
Fernando Po I
P. s. flavisquamatus
Cameroun to NE & S Zaire
P. s. aloysii
Uganda, W Kenya
P. s. flavior
N Angola
Pogoniulus leucomystax (Moustached Green Tinkerbird)
P. l. leucomystax
W Kenya to W Malawi
P. l. chyulu
WC Kenya
Pogoniulus simplex (Green Tinkerbird)
S Kenya, Tanzania to S Malawi
Pogoniulus coryphaeus (Western Green Tinkerbird)
P. c. coryphaeus
N & W Cameroun

P. c. hildamariae
E Zaire, W Uganda
P. c. angolensis
W Angola
Pogoniulus pusillus (Red-fronted Tinkerbird)
P. p. uropygialis
Ethiopia, N Somalia
P. p. affinis
Kenya, S Somalia, N Tanzania
P. p. eupterus
SE Uganda, SW Kenya, NW Tanzania
P. p. pusillus
SE South Africa
Pogoniulus chrysoconus (Yellow-fronted Tinkerbird)
P. c. chrysoconus
Senegal to EC Nigeria
P. c. schubotzi
Niger, Chad, W Sudan
P. c. centralis
N & NE Zaire, Uganda
P. c. zedlitzi
E Sudan
P. c. schoanus
Ethiopia
P. c. xanthostictus
C & S Ethiopia
P. c. rhodesiae
E Zaire to NE Rhodesia & N Malawi
P. c. extoni
S Angola & Namibia to SE Malawi
& N Transvaal
P. c. mayri
S Zaire to NE Angola
Pogoniulus bilineatus (Golden-rumped Tinkerbird)
P. b. sharpei
Gambia to S Nigeria
P. b. leucolaima
Cameroun to Uganda & N Angola
P. b. poensis
Fernando Po I
P. b. mfumbiri
S Uganda, E Zaire, Rwanda
P. b. urungensis
SE Zaire, SW Tanzania, NE Zambia
P. b. jacksoni
W Kenya
P. b. alius
C Kenya
P. b. fischeri
E Kenya, Tanzania, Zanzibar I
P. b. conciliator
EC Tanzania
P. b. bilineatus
Malawi, Mozambique, E South Africa

Pogoniulus makawai (Black-chinned Tinkerbird)
NW Zambia
Pogoniulus subsulphureus (Yellow-throated Tinkerbird)
P. s. chrysopygus
Guinea to Ghana
P. s. flavimentum
S Nigeria to Uganda & SW Zaire
P. s. subsulphureus
Fernando Po I
Pogoniulus atroflavus (Red-rumped Tinkerbird)
Guinea to NE Zaire

TRICHOLAEMA
Tricholaema lacrymosum (Spotted-flanked Barbet)
T. l. lacrymosum
N Uganda & S Ethiopia to C Tanzania
T. l. narokense
SW Kenya
T. l. radcliffei
E Zaire, Rwanda, W Tanzania
T. l. ruahae
C Tanzania
Tricholaema leucomelan (Pied Barbet)
T. l. namaqua
W Cape Province
T. l. nkatiense
N Botswana
T. l. centrale
Transvaal
T. l. zuluense
E Rhodesia, E Transvaal, N Natal
T. l. leucomelan
Orange Free State, S Cape Province
T. l. affine
Natal
Tricholaema diadematum (Red-fronted Barbet)
T. d. diadematum
S Sudan, Ethiopia, N Somalia
T. d. mustum
NE Uganda to C Kenya
T. d. massaicum
S Kenya, N Tanzania
T. d. frontatum
Angola, S Zaire, N Zambia, Malawi
Tricholaema melanocephalum (African Black-throated Barbet)
T. m. melanocephalum
N Ethiopia, NW Somalia
T. m. stigmatothorax
S Ethiopia, S Somalia to C Tanzania
T. m. blandi
C & E Somalia, SE Ethiopia

Tricholaema flavibuccale (Yellow-cheeked Barbet)
C Tanzania
Tricholaema hirsutum (Hairy-breasted Barbet)
T. h. hirsutum
Sierra Leone to Togo
T. h. hybridum
S Nigeria
T. h. flavipunctatum
Cameroun, Gabon, Cabinda
T. h. chapini
SE Cameroun to N & C Zaire
T. h. angolense
S Zaire, N Angola
T. h. ansorgii
E Zaire, Uganda

LYBIUS
Lybius undatus (Banded Barbet)
L. u. thiogaster
N Ethiopia
L. u. undatus
C Ethiopia
L. u. leucogenys
W & SW Ethiopia
L. u. squamatus
E Ethiopia
Lybius vieilloti (Vieillot's Barbet)
L. v. buchanani
S Sahara
L. v. rubescens
Senegal to N Cameroun
L. v. vieilloti
Ethiopia, S Sudan, N Zaire
Lybius torquatus (Black collared Barbet)
L. t. albigularis
S Tanzania
L. t. zombae
S Malawi
L. t. pumilio
E Zaire, Burundi
L. t. irroratus
E Kenya, NE Tanzania
L. t. congicus
SE Zaire, N Angola, N Zambia,
SW Tanzania
L. t. vivacens
Mozambique
L. t. bocagei
SW Angola
L. t. torquatus
S Angola, Rhodesia, South Africa
Lybius guifsobalito (Black-billed Barbet)
L. g. guifsobalito
Ethiopia, E Sudan
L. g. ugandae
S Sudan, NE Zaire, Uganda
Lybius rubrifacies (Red-faced Barbet)
S Uganda, NW Tanzania

Lybius chaplini (Chaplin's Barbet)
S Zambia
Lybius leucocephalus (White-headed Barbet)
L. l. leucocephalus
S Sudan, Uganda, NE Zaire
L. l. adamauae
N Nigeria to N Zaire
L. l. usukumae
NW Tanzania
L. l. albicauda
S Kenya, N Tanzania
L. l. senex
C Kenya
L. l. leucogaster
SW Angola
Lybius minor (Black-backed Barbet)
L. m. minor
SW Zaire, NW Angola
L. m. intercedens
C & S Zaire, N Angola
L. m. macclounii
C & SE Zaire, Zambia, N Malawi
Lybius melanopterus (Brown-breasted Barbet)
S Somalia to Malawi, Mozambique
Lybius bidentatus (Double-toothed Barbet)
L. b. bidentatus
Guinea to S Nigeria
L. b. friedmanni
S Cameroun to N Angola
L. b. aequatorialis
N Zaire, W Kenya, NW Tanzania
L. b. aethiops
SW Sudan, S Ethiopia
Lybius dubius (Bearded Barbet)
Senegal to S Chad
Lybius rolleti (Black-breasted Barbet)
Central African Republic to
W & SW Sudan
TRACHYPHONUS
Trachyphonus purpuratus (Yellow-billed Barbet)
T. p. goffinii
Sierra Leone to Ghana
T. p. togoensis
Togo, SW Nigeria
T. p. purpuratus
Cameroun to N Zaire & N Angola
T. p. elgonensis
NE Zaire & Uganda
Trachyphonus vaillantii (Levaillant's Barbet)
T. v. suahelicus
N Angola to Tanzania
T. v. nobilis
Botswana

T. v. vaillantii
Southern Africa
Trachyphonus erythrocephalus (Red and Yellow Barbet)
T. e. gallarum
SC Ethiopia
T. e. shelleyi
E Ethiopia, N Somalia
T. e. jacksoni
S Ethiopia, N & C Kenya
T. e. versicolor
N Uganda, W Kenya
T. e. erythrocephalus
S Kenya, N Tanzania
Trachyphonus darnaudii (d'Arnaud's Barbet)
T. d. darnaudii
E Sudan, W Ethiopia, N Uganda, W Kenya
T. d. zedlitzi
WC Kenya
T. d. böhmi
S Somalia, E Kenya, NE Tanzania
T. d. emini
C & SW Tanzania
Trachyphonus usambiro (Usambiro Barbet)
C Kenya to NW Tanzania
Trachyphonus margaritatus (Yellow-breasted Barbet)
T. m. kingi
NE Sudan
T. m. berberensis
N Sudan
T. m. margaritatus
Niger & N Nigeria to W Ethiopia
T. m. somalicus
C Ethiopia, N Somalia

97 INDICATORIDAE (HONEYGUIDES)

PRODOTISCUS
Prodotiscus insignis (Cassin's Honeybird)
P. i. flavodorsalis
Sierra Leone to Togo
P. i. insignis
S Cameroun & W Zaire to Uganda
P. i. ellenbecki
S Ethiopia to C Tanzania
P. i. zambesiae
SE Zaire, N Angola to Rhodesia & Mozambique
P. i. lathburyi
C Angola
Prodotiscus regulus (Wahlberg's Honeybird)
P. r. camerunensis
Cameroun
P. r. regulus
Ethiopia to N Angola and Natal

Melignomon zenkeri (Zenker's Honeyguide)
S Cameroun to Uganda

INDICATOR
Indicator maculatus (Spotted Honeyguide)
I. m. maculatus
Gambia to Ghana
I. m. stictithorax
Cameroun to NE Zaire
Indicator variegatus (Scaly-throated Honeyguide)
I. v. jubaensis
S Somalia to N Tanzania
I. v. pseudonymus
Mozambique
I. v. variegatus
S Ethiopia to Cape Province
Indicator indicator (Black-throated Honeyguide)
Senegal to Ethiopia & Cape Province
Indicator minor (Lesser Honeyguide)
I. m. senegalensis
Senegal
I. m. alexanderi
N Ghana, N Nigeria to W Sudan
I. m. riggenbachi
W Cameroun to N Zaire
I. m. diadematus
E Sudan, Ethiopia, Somalia
I. m. erlangeri
S Somalia, E Kenya
I. m. teitensis
Uganda, Kenya to Malawi
I. m. valens
Zambia
I. m. minor
N Angola to Natal & Cape Province
I. m. albigularis
Transvaal
I. m. damarensis
Namibia
I. m. ussheri
Ghana
I. m. conirostris
N Nigeria to W Uganda
I. m. pallidus
S Nigeria
Indicator exilis (Least Honeyguide)
I. e. poensis
Fernando Po I
I. e. exilis
S Nigeria to E Zaire
I. e. pachyrhynchus
Sudan, Uganda to W Tanzania
I. e. angolensis
N Angola
I. e. cerophagus
Zambia

Indicator willcocksi (Willcocks'
Honeyguide)
   I. w. ansorgei
     Guinea
   I. w. willcocksi
     Ghana
   I. w hutsoni
     Nigeria, N Cameroun
Indicator meliphilus (Eastern Least
Honeyguide)
   Kenya to Malawi, Rhodesia
Indicator pumilio (Pygmy Honeyguide)
   E Zaire, Rwanda
Indicator xanthonotus (Indian Honeyguide)
   I. x. xanthonotus
     W Himalayas to E Assam
   I. x. fulvus
     Naga Hills (E Assam)
Indicator archipelagus (Malay
Honeyguide)
   Malaysia, Sumatra, Borneo

MELICHNEUTES
Melichneutes robustus (Lyre-tailed
Honeyguide)
   Cameroun to C Zaire

98 RAMPHASTIDAE (TOUCANS)

AULACORHYNCHUS
Aulacorhynchus prasinus (Emerald
Toucanet)
   A. p. wagleri
     SW Mexico
   A. p. prasinus
     SE Mexico
   A. p. stenorhabdus
     S Mexico, W Guatemala, El Salvador
   A. p. virescens
     N Guatemala, Belize to N Nicaragua
   A. p. volcanius
     E El Salvador
   A. p. maxillaris
     Costa Rica, W Panama
   A. p. caeruleogularis
     EC Panama
   A. p. cognatus
     E Panama
   A. p. griseigularis
     NW Colombia
   A. p. phaeolaemus
     W Colombia
   A. p. lautus
     N Colombia
   A. p. albivitta
     E Colombia, E Ecuador, W Venezuela
   A. p. cyanolaemus
     SE Ecuador, N Peru

   A. p. dimidiatus
     N Peru
   A. p. atrogularis
     E Peru
Aulacorhynchus sulcatus (Groove-billed
Toucanet)
   A. s. sulcatus
     N Venezuela
   A. s. erythrognathus
     NE Venezuela
   A. s. calorhynchus
     N Colombia, NW Venezuela
Aulacorhynchus derbianus (Chestnut-
tipped Toucanet)
   A. d. derbianus
     E Ecuador, E Peru, NE Bolivia
   A. d. nigrirostris
     C Peru
   A. d. duidae
     S Venezuela
   A. d. whitelianus
     S Venezuela, S Guyana
   A. d. osgoodi
     S Guyana
Aulacorhynchus haematopygus (Crimson-
rumped Toucanet)
   A. h. sexnotatus
     SW Colombia, W Ecuador
   A. h. haematopygus
     N Colombia, W Venezuela
Aulacorhynchus huallagae (Yellow-
browed Toucanet)
   NC Peru
Aulacorhynchus coeruleicinctis (Blue-
banded Toucanet)
   S Peru, N Bolivia

PTEROGLOSSUS
Pteroglossus viridis (Green Aracari)
   P. v. humboldti
     SE Colombia to N Bolivia, W Brazil
   P. v. didymus
     ?
   P. v. viridis
     E Venezuela, the Guianas, N Brazil
Pteroglossus inscriptus (Lettered Aracari)
   C & S Brazil
Pteroglossus bitorquatus (Red-necked
Aracari)
   P. b. sturmii
     WC Brazil
   P. b. reichenowi
     NC Brazil
   P. b. bitorquatus
     NE Brazil
Pteroglossus flavirostris (Ivory-billed
Aracari)
   P. f. flavirostris
     N Upper Amazonia

P. f. azara
NW Brazil
P. f. mariae
NE Peru, W Brazil, N Bolivia
**Pteroglossus aracari (Black-necked
Aracari)**
P. a. roraimae
S & E Venezuela, Guyana, Surinam
P. a. atricollis
French Guiana, N Brazil
P. a. aracari
C & E Brazil
P. a. vergens
S & SE Brazil
**Pteroglossus castanotis (Chestnut-eared
Aracari)**
P. c. castanotis
E Colombia, E Ecuador, E Peru, NW Brazil
P. c. australis
E Bolivia, W Brazil, NE Argentina
**Pteroglossus pluricinctus (Many-banded
Aracari)**
E Peru & E Colombia to E Venezuela
Pteroglossus torquatus (Collared Aracari)
P. t. torquatus
S Mexico to W Panama
P. t. erythrozonus
SE Mexico, N Guatemala, Belize
P. t. frantzii
Costa Rica, W Panama
P. t. nuchalis
N Colombia, N Venezuela
P. t. pectoralis
NW Venezuela
P. t. sanguineus
W Colombia, NW Ecuador
P. t. erythropygius
W Ecuador
**Pteroglossus beauharnaesii (Curl-crested
Aracari)**
E Peru, N Bolivia, W Brazil

**Selenidera maculirostris (Spot-billed
Toucanet)**
S. m. hellmayri
NC Brazil
S. m. maculirostris
SE Brazil
Selenidera gouldii (Gould's Toucanet)
NE Brazil
**Selenidera reinwardtii (Golden-collared
Toucanet)**
S. r. reinwardtii
S Colombia, E Ecuador, NE Peru
S. r. langsdorffii
E Peru, W Brazil

**Selenidera nattereri (Tawny-tufted
Toucanet)**   249
E Venezuela, NW Brazil
Selenidera culik (Guianan Toucanet)
the Guianas, N Brazil
**Selenidera spectabilis (Yellow-eared
Toucanet)**
Honduras to Panama, NC & NW Colombia

BAILLONIUS
Baillonius bailloni (Saffron Toucanet)
SE Brazil

ANDIGENA
**Andigena hypoglauca (Grey-breasted
Mountain Toucan)**
A. h. hypoglauca
C Colombia
A. h. lateralis
E Ecuador, E Peru
**Andigena laminirostris (Plate-billed
Mountain Toucan)**
SW Colombia, W Ecuador
**Andigena cucullata (Hooded Mountain
Toucan)**
S Peru, W Bolivia
**Andigena nigrirostris (Black-billed
Mountain Toucan)**
A. n. occidentalis
W Colombia
A. n. spilorhynchus
S Colombia, NE Ecuador
A. n. nigrirostris
E Colombia

RAMPHASTOS
**Ramphastos dicolorus (Red-breasted
Toucan)**
SE Brazil, Paraguay, NE Argentina
**Ramphastos vitellinus (Channel-billed
Toucan)**
R. v. culminatus
Upper Amazonia
R. v. citreolaemus
C Colombia
R. v. vitellinus
Trinidad, Venezuela, the Guianas, N Brazil
R. v. ariel
C & S Brazil
R. v. pintoi
SE Brazil
R. v. theresae
NE Brazil
Ramphastos brevis (Choco Toucan)
E Panama, W Colombia, W Ecuador
**Ramphastos sulfuratus (Keel-billed
Toucan)**
R. s. sulfuratus
S Mexico, N Guatemala, Belize

R. s. brevicarinatus
  SE Guatemala to N Colombia,
  NW Venezuela
Ramphastos toco (Toco Toucan)
  R. t. toco
    the Guianas, N & E Brazil
  R. t. albogularis
    E & S Brazil, Paraguay, Bolivia,
    N Argentina
Ramphastos tucanus (Cuvier's Toucan)
  R. t. tucanus
    SE Venezuela, the Guianas, N Brazil
  R. t. cuvieri
    Upper Amazonia
  R. t. oblitus
    NC Brazil
  R. t. inca
    E Bolivia
Ramphastos ambiguus (Black-mandibled Toucan)
  R. a. swainsonii
    SE Honduras to W Ecuador
  R. a. ambiguus
    N Upper Amazonia
  R. a. abbreviatus
    W Venezuela, NE Colombia

99 PICIDAE (WOODPECKERS)

JYNGINAE

JYNX
Jynx torquilla (Wryneck)
  J. t. torquilla
    Europe, W Asia
  J. t. tschusii
    Italy, Sardinia, Corsica
  J. t. mauretanica
    N Algeria
  J. t. chinensis
    C & SE Asia, India
  J. t. japonica
    Sakhalin I, Japan
Jynx ruficollis (Red-breasted Wryneck)
  J. r. thorbeckei
    C Cameroun
  J. r. rougeoti
    Gabon
  J. r. pulchricollis
    W Zaire to SW Sudan, W Uganda
  J. r. aequatorialis
    Ethiopia
  J. r. cosensi
    Kenya, Tanzania
  J. r. ruficollis
    Southern Africa

PICUMNINAE

PICUMNUS
Picumnus cinnamomeus (Chestnut Piculet)
  P. c. cinnamomeus
    N Colombia, NW Venezuela
  P. c. perijanus
    NW Venezuela
  P. c. venezuelensis
    W Venezuela
Picumnus rufiventris (Rufous-breasted Piculet)
  P. r. rufiventris
    E Ecuador, NE Peru, W Brazil
  P. r. grandis
    C Peru, N Bolivia
Picumnus fulvescens (Tawny Piculet)
    NE Brazil
Picumnus fuscus (Rusty-necked Piculet)
    S Brazil
Picumnus castelnau (Plain-breasted Piculet)
    E Ecuador, NE Peru
Picumnus spilogaster (White-bellied Piculet)
  P. s. leucogaster
    C Venezuela, N Brazil
  P. s. orinocensis
    E Venezuela
  P. s. spilogaster
    Guyana
Picumnus minutissimus (Arrowhead Piculet)
  P. m. minutissimus
    Surinam, French Guiana
  P. m. pallidus
    NE Brazil
  P. m. guttifer
    C Brazil
  P. m. corumbanus
    SW Brazil
  P. m. albosquamatus
    Bolivia
Picumnus squamulatus (Scaled Piculet)
  P. s. squamulatus
    N & E Colombia
  P. s. röhli
    N Venezuela
  P. s. obsoletus
    NE Venezuela
Picumnus limae (Ochraceous Piculet)
    E Brazil
Picumnus olivaceus (Olivaceous Piculet)
  P. o. dimotus
    Honduras, Nicaragua
  P. o. flavotinctus
    Costa Rica, W Panama

P. o. olivaceus
E Panama, N Colombia
P. o. antioquensis
N Colombia
P. o. eisenmanni
NE Colombia, NW Venezuela
P. o. tachirensis
C Colombia, NE Venezuela
P. o. harterti
SW Colombia, W Ecuador
Picumnus granadensis (Greyish Piculet)
NC Colombia
Picumnus nebulosus (Mottled Piculet)
S Brazil
Picumnus nigropunctatus (Black-dotted Piculet)
NE Venezuela
Picumnus exilis (Golden-spangled Piculet)
P. e. salvini
?
P. e. clarus
EC Venezuela
P. e. undulatus
SE Venezuela, S Guyana, N Brazil
P. e. buffoni
Surinam, French Guiana, NE Brazil
P. e. pernambucensis
E Brazil
P. e. alegriae
NE Brazil
P. e. exilis
E Brazil
Picumnus borbae (Bar-breasted Piculet)
P. b. juruanus
E Peru, W Brazil
P. b. borbae
C Brazil
Picumnus aurifrons (Gold-fronted Piculet)
P. a. lafresnayei
S Colombia, E Ecuador, N Peru
P. a. taczanowskii
NE Peru
P. a. punctifrons
C Peru
P. a. flavifrons
E Peru, W Brazil
P. a. purusianus
W Brazil
P. a. pusillus
W Brazil
P. a. wallacei
WC Brazil
P. a. aurifrons
C Brazil
P. a. transfasciatus
EC Brazil

Picumnus temminckii (Ochre-collared Piculet) 251
SE Brazil, Paraguay, NE Argentina
Picumnus cirratus (White-barred Piculet)
P. c. confusus
Guyana
P. c. macconnelli
N Brazil
P. c. cirratus
SE Brazil
P. c. pilcomayensis
SW Brazil, Paraguay, N Argentina
P. c. tucumanus
N Argentina
P. c. thamnophiloides
S Bolivia, NW Argentina
Picumnus dorbygnianus (Ocellated Piculet)
P. d. jelskii
C Peru
P. d. dorbygnianus
N & C Bolivia
Picumnus sclateri (Ecuadorean Piculet)
P. s. parvistriatus
W Ecuador
P. s. sclateri
SW Ecuador, NW Peru
Picumnus subtilis (Fine-barred Piculet)
Cuzco (SE Peru)
Picumnus steindachneri (Speckle-chested Piculet)
NE Peru
Picumnus varzeae (Varzea Piculet)
central Amazon Is
Picumnus pygmaeus (Spotted Piculet)
P. p. pygmaeus
NE Brazil
P. p. distinctus
NE Brazil
Picumnus asterias (Blackish Piculet)
Brazil
Picumnus pumilus (Orinoco Piculet)
Colombia?
Picumnus innominatus (Speckled Piculet)
P. i. simlaensis
NW Himalayas
P. i. innominatus
Assam, E Himalayas
P. i. avunculorum
S India
P. i. malayorum
E India to Indochina, Sumatra, Borneo
P. i. chinensis
W & S China

SASIA
Sasia africana (African Piculet)
Nigeria to C Zaire

Sasia ochracea (White-browed Rufous Piculet)
  S. o. ochracea
    Himalayas
  S. o. kinneari
    S China, N Vietnam
  S. o. querulivox
    NE India, NW Burma
  S. o. reichenowi
    Burma, Thailand, Indochina
  S. o. hasbroucki
    S Burma
Sasia abnormis (Rufous Piculet)
  S. a. abnormis
    S Burma, Malaysia, Sumatra, Java, Borneo
  S. a. magnirostris
    Nias I

NESOCTITES
Nesoctites micromegas (Antillean Piculet)
  N. m. micromegas
    Hispaniola
  N. m. abbotti
    Gonave I

PICINAE

MELANERPES
Melanerpes candidus (White Woodpecker)
  N & E Brazil to C Argentina
Melanerpes lewis (Lewis's Woodpecker)
  W Canada to NW Mexico
Melanerpes herminieri (Guadeloupe Woodpecker)
  Guadeloupe I
Melanerpes portoricensis (Puerto Rican Woodpecker)
  Puerto Rico
Melanerpes erythrocephalus (Red-headed Woodpecker)
  M. e. caurinus
    WC USA
  M. e. erythrocephalus
    SC Canada, E USA
Melanerpes formicivorus (Acorn Woodpecker)
  M. f. bairdi
    coast of SW USA
  M. f. martirensis
    W Baja California
  M. f. angustifrons
    S Baja California
  M. f. formicivorus
    SW USA, NW Mexico
  M. f. lineatus
    S Mexico to N Nicaragua
  M. f. albeolus
    coast of Belize
  M. f. striatipectus
    Costa Rica, W Panama

  M. f. flavigula
    Colombia
Melanerpes cruentatus (Yellow-tufted Woodpecker)
  M. c. extensus
    Upper Amazonia
  M. c. cruentatus
    E Venezuela, the Guianas, NE Brazil
Melanerpes flavifrons (Yellow-fronted Woodpecker)
  M. f. flavifrons
    SC Brazil
  M. f. rubriventris
    SE Brazil, Paraguay, NE Argentina
Melanerpes chrysauchen (Golden-naped Woodpecker)
  M. c. chrysauchen
    SW Costa Rica, W Panama
  M. c. pulcher
    N Colombia
Melanerpes pucherani (Black-cheeked Woodpecker)
  M. p. perileucus
    S Mexico to N Honduras
  M. p. pucherani
    SE Honduras to C Colombia & W Ecuador
Melanerpes cactorum (White-fronted Woodpecker)
  S Peru to C Argentina
Melanerpes chrysogenys (Golden-cheeked Woodpecker)
  M. c. chrysogenys
    NW Mexico
  M. c. flavinuchus
    SW Mexico
  M. c. morelensis
    Morelos (C Mexico)
Melanerpes striatus (Hispaniolan Woodpecker)
  Hispaniola
Melanerpes hypopolius (Grey-breasted Woodpecker)
  M. h. albescens
    California, S Nevada to S Sonora
  M. h. cardonensis
    C Baja California
  M. h. brewsteri
    S Baja California
  M. h. fuscescens
    NW Mexico
  M. h. tiburonensis
    Tiburon I
  M. h. sulfuriventer
    W Mexico
  M. h. hypopolius
    C & SW Mexico

Melanerpes radiolatus (Jamaican Woodpecker)
Jamaica
Melanerpes rubricapillus (Red-crowned Woodpecker)
M. r. rubricomus
N Yucatan
M. r. pygmaeus
Cozumel I
M. r. tysoni
Bonacca I
M. r. costaricensis
SW Costa Rica
M. r. rubricapillus
Panama, N Colombia, W Venezuela
M. r. seductus
Pearl Is (Panama)
M. r. paraguanae
NW Venezuela
M. r. terricolor
N Venezuela, Margarita I, Trinidad, Tobago I
Melanerpes hoffmannii (Hoffmann's Woodpecker)
Nicaragua, W Costa Rica
Melanerpes uropygialis (Gila Woodpecker)
S Arizona, New Mexico, N Sonora
Melanerpes aurifrons (Golden-fronted Woodpecker)
M. a. polygrammus
SW Mexico
M. a. frontalis
S Mexico, NW Guatemala
M. a. aurifrons
Texas to SC Mexico
M. a. incanescens
Big Bend (W Texas)
M. a. grateloupensis
E Mexico
M. a. veraecrucis
S Mexico, N Guatemala
M. a. dubius
SE Mexico, Belize
M. a. leei
Mecos, Cozumel I
M. a. santacruzi
S Chiapas to N Nicaragua
M. a. pauper
E Honduras
M. a. insulans
Utilla I
M. a. canescens
Ruatan I, Barburat I
Melanerpes carolinus (Red-bellied Woodpecker)
M. c. zebra
C & S USA

M. c. carolinus
E USA
M. c. perplexus
S Florida
Melanerpes superciliaris (West Indian Red-bellied Woodpecker)
M. s. bahamensis
Gt Bahama I
M. s. nyeanus
Watling's I
M. s. blakei
Abaco I
M. s. superciliaris
Cuba
M. s. sanfelipensis
Cuba
M. s. murceus
Isle of Pines
M. s. caymanensis
Gd Cayman I

SPHYRAPICUS
Sphyrapicus varius (Yellow-bellied Sapsucker)
S Canada, E USA to C America
Sphyrapicus nuchalis (Red-naped Sapsucker)
W Canada, W USA, W Mexico
Sphyrapicus ruber (Red-breasted Sapsucker)
S. r. ruber
SE Alaska to W Oregon
S. r. daggetti
S Oregon to SC California
Sphyrapicus thyroideus (Williamson's Sapsucker)
S. t. thyroideus
S British Columbia to S California
S. t. nataliae
SE British Columbia, WC USA, C Mexico

XIPHIDIOPICUS
Xiphidiopicus percussus (Cuban Green Woodpecker)
X. p. percussus
Cuba
X. p. insulae-pinorum
Isle of Pines

CAMPETHERA
Campethera nubica (Nubian Woodpecker)
C. n. nubica
Sudan, Ethiopia to SC Tanzania
C. n. pallida
coast of S Somalia, Kenya, Tanzania
Campethera bennettii (Bennett's Woodpecker)
C. b. uniamwesica
N Angola to C Tanzania

C. b. scriptoricauda
C Tanzania to N Mozambique

C. b. vincenti
Malawi

C. b. bennettii
Rhodesia, Transvaal, Natal

C. b. capricorni
S Angola, N Namibia

Campethera punctuligera (Fine-spotted Woodpecker)

C. p. punctuligera
Senegal to Niger & Central African Republic

C. p. batesi
E Cameroun

C. p. balia
S Chad, S Sudan, N Zaire

Campethera abingoni (Golden-tailed Woodpecker)

C. a. chrysura
Senegal to N Zaire & S Sudan

C. a. tessmanni
E Cameroun

C. a. annectens
Gabon to N Angola, E Zaire, Malawi

C. a. kavirondensis
SW Kenya to SC Tanzania

C. a. mombassica
coast from S Somalia to NE Tanzania

C. a. suahelica
C Tanzania

C. a. abingoni
Malawi, Mozambique to E Transvaal & Natal

C. a. smithii
W Rhodesia, W Transvaal, Botswana

C. a. anderssoni
Namibia

Campethera notata (Knysna Woodpecker)
S Natal, S & E Cape Province

Campethera cailliautii (Little Spotted Woodpecker)

C. c. togoensis
Ghana to S Nigeria

C. c. permista
Cameroun to E Zaire & N Angola

C. c. kaffensis
SW Ethiopia

C. c. nyansae
Rwanda, NW Tanzania

C. c. cailliautii
coast of Kenya, N Tanzania

C. c. fülleborni
S Zaire to Zambia & Mozambique

Campethera maculosa (Western Golden-backed Woodpecker)
Guinea to Ghana

Campethera tullbergi (Tullberg's Woodpecker)

C. t. tullbergi
Cameroun

C. t. bansoensis
Banso Mountains

C. t. wellsi
Oku district, Cameroun

C. t. taeniolaema
W Kenya, W Uganda, E Zaire

C. t. barakae
SE Zaire

C. t. hausburgi
E & C Kenya

Campethera nivosa (Buff-spotted Woodpecker)

C. n. nivosa
Guinea to Ghana

C. n. poensis
Fernando Po I

C. n. efulenensis
Cameroun to N Angola

C. n. herberti
N Zaire to Uganda

C. n. yalensis
W Kenya

Campethera caroli (Brown-eared Woodpecker)

C. c. arizela
Liberia

C. c. caroli
Guinea to C Zaire & Angola

C. c. budongoensis
Uganda & W Kenya

GEOCOLAPTES

Geocolaptes olivaceus (Ground Woodpecker)

G. o. theresae
NW Cape Province

G. o. olivaceus
S Cape Province to S Transvaal & Natal

G. o. prometheus
Natal, E Cape Province

DENDROPICOS

Dendropicos elachus (Little Grey Woodpecker)
Senegal to W Sudan

Dendropicos abyssinicus (Golden-backed Woodpecker)
Ethiopia

Dendropicos poecilolaemus (Uganda Spotted Woodpecker)
N Cameroun to Uganda, Kenya

Dendropicos fuscescens (Cardinal Woodpecker)

D. f. cosensi
Senegal

D. f. lafresnayei
Gambia to Nigeria
D. f. camerunensis
W Cameroun to N Zaire
D. f. sharpei
Gabon to C Zaire
D. f. loandae
N Angola, S Zaire
D. f. camacupae
W Angola to SE Zaire & Malawi
D. f. stresemanni
N Namibia
D. f. harei
S Namibia, W Botswana
D. f. capriviensis
SW Zambia, N Botswana
D. f. transvaalensis
NE Transvaal, S Rhodesia
D. f. orangensis
S Transvaal, Orange Free State
D. f. intermedius
SE Transvaal, W Natal
D. f. fuscescens
S & E Cape Province
D. f. natalensis
E Transvaal, N Natal
D. f. noomei
NE Natal, S Mozambique
D. f. hartlaubii
coast from N Kenya to S Mozambique
D. f. massaicus
C Kenya to C Tanzania
D. f. chyulu
SC Kenya
D. f. lepidus
W Ethiopia, Uganda, W Kenya, E Zaire
D. f. hemprichii
Ethiopia, Somalia
***Dendropicos gabonensis* (Gabon
Woodpecker)**
D. g. lugubris
Guinea to Ghana
D. g. reichenowi
NW Cameroun
D. g. gabonensis
Cameroun & Gabon to NE & C Zaire
***Dendropicos stierlingi* (Stierling's
Woodpecker)**
S Tanzania, N Mozambique
***Dendropicos namaquus* (Bearded
Woodpecker)**
D. n. schoënsis
W Sudan, S Ethiopia, N Kenya
D. n. saturatus
Central African Republic
D. n. decipiens
SW Uganda & N Kenya to C Tanzania

D. n. namaquus
N Angola to Malawi & Cape Province
D. n. coalescens
E Cape Province to S Mozambique
***Dendropicos xantholophus* (Yellow-
crested Woodpecker)**
Cameroun to S Angola & W Kenya
***Dendropicos pyrrhogaster* (Fire-bellied
Woodpecker)**
Sierra Leone to SE Nigeria
***Dendropicos elliotii* (Elliot's Woodpecker)**
D. e. schultzei
Fernando Po I
D. e. johnstoni
Cameroun Mt
D. e. sordidatus
Oku district, W Cameroun
D. e. elliotii
Cameroun to N Angola & W Kenya
D. e. kupeensis
Mt. Kupé (Cameroun)
D. e. gabela
NW Angola
***Dendropicos goertae* (Grey Woodpecker)**
D. g. königi
Mali to N Sudan
D. g. goertae
Senegal to N Nigeria
D. g. agmen
Gambia to S Sudan
D. g. centralis
Cameroun to NW Kenya, NE Zaire
D. g. oreites
C Cameroun
D. g. abessinicus
E Sudan, N & C Ethiopia
D. g. spodocephalus
S Ethiopia
D. g. rhodeogaster
C Kenya, N Tanzania
***Dendropicos griseocephalus* (African
Grey-headed Woodpecker)**
D. g. ruwenzori
E Zaire, Rwanda, NW Tanzania
D. g. persimilis
W Angola to N Malawi
D. g. kilimensis
N Tanzania
D. g. griseocephalus
N Transvaal to Natal & Cape Province

PICOIDES
***Picoides temminckii* (Celebean Pied
Woodpecker)**
Celebes, Togian Is
***Picoides moluccensis* (Brown-capped Pied
Woodpecker)**
P. m. nanus
N & C India

P. m. cinereigula
SW India
P. m. hardwickii
SE India
P. m. gymnophthalmus
Sri Lanka
P. m. moluccensis
Malaysia, Sumatra, Java, Borneo
P. m. grandis
Lombok I, Sumbawa I, Flores I, Lomblen I
P. m. excelsior
Alor I

Picoides maculatus (Philippine Pygmy Woodpecker)
P. m. validirostris
Luzon, Catanduanes I, Mindoro I
P. m. menagei
Sibuyan I
P. m. maculatus
Panay I, Cebu I, Negros I
P. m. leytensis
Samar I, Leyte I, Bohol I
P. m. fulvifasciatus
Mindanao I, Basilan I
P. m. apo
Mt Apo (Mindanao I)
P. m. ramsayi
Jolo I, Tawitawi Is, Bongao I
P. m. siasiensis
Siasi I

Picoides obsoletus (Brown-backed Woodpecker)
P. o. obsoletus
Gambia to NE Zaire
P. o. heuglini
N Sudan, NE Ethiopia
P. o. nigricans
S Ethiopia, N Uganda
P. o. ingens
W Kenya
P. o. crateri
N Tanzania

Picoides kizuki (Japanese Pygmy Woodpecker)
P. k. wilderi
NE Hopeh (NE China)
P. k. permutatus
NE Asia
P. k. acutirostris
E Korea
P. k. kurilensis
Kurile Is
P. k. shikokuensis
S Honshu I, Shikoku I
P. k. kizuki
Kyushu I
P. k. matsudairai
Takushima I

P. k. seebohmi
Sakhalin I, Hokkaido I
P. k. nippon
N & C Honshu I, Korea
P. k. kotataki
Oki Is, Tsushima I
P. k. amamii
N Riukiu Is
P. k. nigrescens
C Riukiu Is
P. k. orii
S Riukiu Is

Picoides canicapillus (Grey-headed Pygmy Woodpecker)
P. c. doerriesi
NE Asia
P. c. scintilliceps
N & E China
P. c. nagamichii
S & W China
P. c. kaleënsis
Taiwan
P. c. swinhoei
Hainan I
P. c. omissus
SE Sikang, Szechwan, NW Yunnan
P. c. obscurus
SE Yunnan
P. c. tonkinensis
N Indochina
P. c. semicoronatus
Bhutan, Sikkim, E Assam
P. c. mitchellii
Nepal
P. c. canicapillus
Burma, Thailand, S Vietnam
P. c. delacouri
E Thailand
P. c. auritus
Malaysia
P. c. volzi
NW Sumatra
P. c. aurantiiventris
N & E Borneo

Picoides minor (Lesser Spotted Woodpecker)
P. m. comminutus
C & S England
P. m. hortorum
NC Europe
P. m. jordansi
C Europe
P. m. wagneri
Romania
P. m. hispaniae
Spain
P. m. ledouci
N Algeria, N Tunisia

P. m. buturlini
SE France, Switzerland, Italy
P. m. serbicus
Yugoslavia, Greece
P. m. danfordi
Asia Minor
P. m. colchicus
Caucasus
P. m. quadrifasciatus
S Caucasus
P. m. hyrcanus
N Iran
P. m. morgani
SW Iran
P. m. minor
Scandinavia, N & C Russia
P. m. mongolicus
W Siberia, NW Mongolia
P. m. kamtschatkensis
E Siberia, Altai
P. m. immaculatus
Anadyr, Kamchatka
P. m. amurensis
N & C Manchuria, Sakhalin I, Hokkaido I
P. m. nojidoensis
NE Korea
**Picoides macei (Fulvous-breasted
Woodpecker)**
P. m. westermanni
W Himalayas
P. m. macei
E Himalayas, N Burma
P. m. longipennis
C & S Burma to S Vietnam
P. m. andamanensis
Andaman Is
P. m. montis
W Java
P. m. analis
Sumatra, E Java, Bali I
**Picoides atratus (Stripe-breasted
Woodpecker)**
Burma, N Thailand, Laos
**Picoides auriceps (Brown-fronted Pied
Woodpecker)**
NW Himalayas
**Picoides mahrattensis (Yellow-crowned
Woodpecker)**
P. m. pallescens
NW India
P. m. aurocristatus
N India
P. m. mahrattensis
S & SW India
P. m. koelzi
SE Madras, Sri Lanka
P. m. blanfordi
Burma

Picoides dorae (Arabian Woodpecker) 257
C Arabia
**Picoides hyperythrus (Rufous-bellied Pied
Woodpecker)**
P. h. marshalli
NW Himalayas, W Tibet
P. h. hyperythrus
E Himalayas to N Thailand
P. h. subrufinus
C Manchuria to C China
P. h. annamensis
S Laos, S Vietnam
**Picoides cathpharius (Lesser Pied
Woodpecker)**
P. c. cathpharius
E Himalayas
P. c. pyrrothorax
S Assam
P. c. tenebrosus
W Yunnan, C Burma to N Indochina
P. c. pernyii
W China
P. c. innixus
C Hupeh
**Picoides darjellensis (Darjeeling Pied
Woodpecker)**
P. d. darjellensis
Nepal to N Burma, N Vietnam
P. d. desmursi
W China
**Picoides leucotos (White-backed
Woodpecker)**
P. l. leucotos
Scandinavia, E Europe, N Russia
P. l. lilfordi
Greece, Asia Minor
P. l. uralensis
S Urals, W Siberia
P. l. voznesenskii
E Siberia, Kamchatka
P. l. saghalinensis
Sakhalin I
P. l. ussuriensis
Amurland, N Manchuria, NE Korea
P. l. sinicus
NE China, Korea
P. l. tangi
W China
P. l. quelpartensis
Quelpart I
P. l. subcirrus
S Kurile Is, Hokkaido I
P. l. stejnegeri
N & C Honshu I
P. l. namiyei
SW Honshu I, Shikoku I, Kyushu I
P. l. takahashii
Dagelet Is

P. l. fohkiensis
SE China
P. l. owstoni
N Riukiu Is
P. l. insularis
Taiwan
Picoides medius (Middle Spotted Woodpecker)
P. m. medius
S Sweden, C Europe
P. m. lilianae
NW Spain
P. m. splendidior
SE Europe
P. m. anatoliae
Asia Minor
P. m. caucasicus
N Caucasia
P. m. laubmanni
Transcaucasia, N Iran
P. m. sancti-johannis
SW Iran
Picoides himalayensis (Himalayan Pied Woodpecker)
P. h. albescens
W Himalayas
P. h. himalayensis
C Himalayas
Picoides assimilis (Sind Pied Woodpecker)
SE Iran to W Punjab
Picoides syriacus (Syrian Woodpecker)
P. s. balcanicus
E Yugoslavia, Bulgaria, Romania
P. s. syriacus
Asia Minor, Israel, W Iran
P. s. transcaucasicus
Transcaucasia
P. s. milleri
SE Iran
Picoides leucopterus (White-winged Pied Woodpecker)
P. l. albipennis
S & E Transcaspia
P. l. jaxartensis
S Kazakhstan
P. l. leptorhynchus
Turkestan
P. l. korejevi
SE Kazakhstan
P. l. leucopterus
N Sinkiang
Picoides major (Great Spotted Woodpecker)
P. m. major
Scandinavia, N Russia
P. m. pinetorum
C & S Europe

P. m. anglicus
England & Scotland
P. m. italiae
S France, Switzerland, Italy
P. m. alpestris
S Switzerland
P. m. parroti
Corsica
P. m. harterti
Sardinia
P. m. hispanus
Portugal, S Spain
P. m. canariensis
Tenerife I
P. m. thanneri
Gran Canaria I
P. m. mauritanus
N Morocco
P. m. lynesi
C Morocco
P. m. numidus
Algeria, Tunisia
P. m. candidus
Romania, Bulgaria, S Russia
P. m. tenuirostris
Caucasus, Transcaucasia
P. m. paphlagoniae
N Turkey
P. m. poelzami
N Iran
P. m. brevirostris
Siberia, S Altai, N Mongolia
P. m. tianshanicus
Tien Shan
P. m. kamtschaticus
Kamchatka
P. m. tscherskii
Ussuriland, Sakhalin I
P. m. japonicus
S Kurile Is, Hokkaido I, NE Korea
P. m. hondoensis
N & C Hoshu I, S Korea
P. m. cabanisi
S Manchuria, NE China
P. m. mandarinus
S & SE China, N Indochina
P. m. biecki
W China
P. m. stresemanni
SW China, N Burma
P. m. hainanus
Hainan I
Picoides mixtus (Checkered Woodpecker)
P. m. cancellatus
SE Brazil
P. m. mixtus
E Paraguay, Uruguay, E Argentina

P. m. malleator
  W Paraguay, SE Bolivia, N & W Argentina
P. m. berlepschi
  W & S Argentina
Picoides lignarius (Striped Woodpecker)
  Bolivia, Chile, W & S Argentina
**Picoides scalaris (Ladder-backed
Woodpecker)**
P. s. cactophilus
  SW USA, NW Mexico
P. s. eremicus
  N Baja California
P. s. lucasanus
  S Baja California
P. s. graysoni
  Tres Marias Is
P. s. sinaloensis
  S Sonora, Sinaloa
P. s. centrophilus
  W Mexico
P. s. azelus
  SW Mexico
P. s. symplectus
  SC USA to E Mexico
P. s. giraudi
  C & E Mexico
P. s. scalaris
  NE Vera Cruz
P. s. ridgwayi
  SE Vera Cruz
P. s. parvus
  N Yucatan, Cozumel I
P. s. percus
  S Mexico
P. s. leucoptilurus
  Belize
Picoides nuttallii (Nuttall's Woodpecker)
  W California, NW Baja California
Picoides pubescens (Downy Woodpecker)
P. p. glacialis
  E Alaska
P. p. gairdnerii
  S British Columbia to N California
P. p. turati
  SW Oregon, W California
P. p. leucurus
  WC USA
P. p. nelsoni
  W & C Canada
P. p. microleucus
  Newfoundland, Anticosti I
P. p. medianus
  S Canada to EC USA
P. p. pubescens
  SE USA

Picoides borealis (Red-cockaded 259
Woodpecker)
P. b. borealis
  SC & SE USA
P. b. hylonomus
  C & S Florida
**Picoides stricklandi (Brown-backed
Woodpecker)**
P. s. arizonae
  Arizona, NW Mexico
P. s. fraterculus
  W Mexico
P. s. aztecus
  C Mexico
P. s. stricklandi
  E Mexico
Picoides villosus (Hairy Woodpecker)
P. v. septentrionalis
  SC Alaska, S Canada
P. v. terraenovae
  Newfoundland
P. v. villosus
  SE Canada, NC & E USA
P. v. audubonii
  SE USA
P. v. piger
  Grand Bahama I, Mores I, Abaco I
P. v. maynardi
  New Providence I, Andros I
P. v. picoideus
  Queen Charlotte Is
P. v. sitkensis
  SE Alaska, N British Columbia
P. v. harrisi
  S British Columbia to N California
P. v. hyloscopus
  W California
P. v. scrippsae
  N Baja California
P. v. orius
  SC Washington to NW Nevada
P. v. monticola
  WC USA
P. v. leucothorectis
  E California to W Texas
P. v. icastus
  SE Arizona, NW Mexico
P. v. intermedius
  E Mexico
P. v. jardinii
  S Mexico
P. v. sanctorum
  Chiapas, Guatemala
P. v. parvulus
  El Salvador, N & W Honduras
P. v. fumeus
  S Honduras, N Nicaragua

P. v. extimus
Costa Rica, W Panama

Picoides albolarvatus (White-headed Woodpecker)
P. a. albolarvatus
W USA
P. a. gravirostris
S California

Picoides tridactylus (Three-toed Woodpecker)
P. t. tridactylus
Scandinavia to NE Asia
P. t. alpinus
Alps to Romania
P. t. crissoleucus
N Siberia, N Mongolia
P. t. tianschanicus
Tien Shan, N Sikang
P. t. albidior
Kamchatka
P. t. sakhalinensis
Sakhalin I
P. t. inouyei
EC Hokkaido I
P. t. funebris
W.China
P. t. fasciatus
N Alaska, W Canada, NW USA
P. t. dorsalis
N Montana to New Mexico
P. t. bacatus
C & E Canada, NE USA

Picoides arcticus (Black-backed Woodpecker)
Canada, W & N USA

VENILIORNIS
Veniliornis callonotus (Scarlet-backed Woodpecker)
V. c. callonotus
W Ecuador
V. c. major
SW Ecuador, N Peru

Veniliornis dignus (Yellow-fronted Woodpecker)
V. d. dignus
W Colombia
V. d. abdominalis
SW Venezuela
V. d. baezae
E Ecuador
V. d. valdizani
C Peru

Veniliornis nigriceps (Bar-bellied Woodpecker)
V. n. equifasciatus
WC Colombia, N Ecuador
V. n. pectoralis
C Peru

V. n. nigriceps
W Bolivia

Veniliornis fumigatus (Smoky-brown Woodpecker)
V. f. oleagineus
E Mexico
V. f. sanguinolentus
C & S Mexico to W Panama
V. f. exsul
N Colombia
V. f. reichenbachi
N Venezuela
V. f. tectricialis
NE Venezuela
V. f. fumigatus
Upper Amazonia
V. f. obscuratus
NW Peru

Veniliornis passerinus (Little Woodpecker)
V. p. fidelis
E Colombia, W Venezuela
V. p. modestus
NE Venezuela
V. p. diversus
N Brazil
V. p. agilis
E Ecuador to N Bolivia, W Brazil
V. p. insignis
WC Brazil
V. p. tapajozensis
C Brazil
V. p. saturatus
W French Guiana
V. p. passerinus
the Guianas, NE Brazil
V. p. taenionotus
E Brazil
V. p. transfluvialis
EC Brazil
V. p. olivinus
S Bolivia, S Brazil, Paraguay,
N Argentina

Veniliornis frontalis (Dot-fronted Woodpecker)
NW Argentina

Veniliornis spilogaster (White-spotted Woodpecker)
S Brazil, Paraguay, NE Argentina

Veniliornis sanguineus (Blood-coloured Woodpecker)
the Guianas

Veniliornis maculifrons (Yellow-eared Woodpecker)
SE Brazil

Veniliornis affinis (Red-stained Woodpecker)
V. a. chocoensis
W Colombia

V. a. orenocensis
E Colombia, E Venezuela, N Brazil
V. a. hilaris
E Ecuador, E Peru, N Bolivia, W Brazil
V. a. ruficeps
C & E Brazil
V. a. affinis
E Brazil
Veniliornis cassini (Golden-collared Woodpecker)
V. c. caquetanus
S Colombia
V. c. cassini
Venezuela, the Guianas, N Brazil
Veniliornis kirkii (Red-rumped Woodpecker)
V. k. neglectus
SW Costa Rica, Panama
V. k. cecilii
E Panama, W Colombia, W Ecuador
V. k. continentalis
N & W Venezuela
V. k. monticola
Mt Roraima (S Venezuela)
V. k. kirkii
Trinidad, Tobago I

PICULUS
Piculus leucolaemus (White-throated Woodpecker)
P. l. allophyeus
Honduras
P. l. simplex
Nicaragua to W Panama
P. l. callopterus
E Panama
P. l. litae
W Colombia, NW Ecuador
P. l. leucolaemus
E Colombia to Bolivia, W Brazil
Piculus flavigula (Yellow-throated Woodpecker)
P. f. flavigula
Northern Amazonia
P. f. magnus
SE Colombia, NW Brazil
P. f. erythropis
E & SE Brazil
Piculus chrysochloros (Golden-green Woodpecker)
P. c. aurosus
Panama
P. c. xanthochlorus
NE Colombia, NW Venezuela
P. c. capistratus
C Colombia to Guyana, NW Brazil
P. c. guianensis
French Guiana

P. c. laemostictus
W Brazil
P. c. hypochryseus
W Brazil, N Bolivia
P. c. paraensis
NE Brazil
P. c. polyzonus
SE Brazil
P. c. chrysochlorus
C & S Brazil, Bolivia, N Argentina
Piculus aurulentus (White-browed Woodpecker)
SE Brazil, N Argentina
Piculus rubiginosus (Golden-olive Woodpecker)
P. r. aeruginosus
NE Mexico
P. r. yucatanensis
C & S Mexico to Nicaragua
P. r. differens
W Guatemala
P. r. maximus
E & C Guatemala
P. r. uropygialis
Costa Rica, W Panama
P. r. alleni
N Colombia
P. r. buenavistae
E Colombia, E Ecuador
P. r. meridensis
W Venezuela
P. r. rubiginosus
N Venezuela
P. r. deltanus
NE Venezuela
P. r. paraquensis
E Venezuela
P. r. guianae
SE Venezuela, S Guyana
P. r. viridissimus
S Venezuela
P. r. nigriceps
S Guyana
P. r. trinitatis
Trinidad
P. r. tobagensis
Tobago I
P. r. fortirostris
Nassau Gebergte (Surinam)
P. r. poliocephalus
Brownsberg (Surinam)
P. r. gularis
C Colombia
P. r. pacificus
SW Colombia
P. r. michaelis
C Colombia

P. r. palmitae
NC Colombia
P. r. rubripileus
SW Colombia, NW Peru
P. r. coloratus
NC Peru
P. r. chrysogaster
C Peru
P. r. canipileus
N Bolivia
P. r. tucumanus
C Bolivia to NW Argentina
Piculus auricularis (Grey-crowned Woodpecker)
P. a. sonoriensis
NW Mexico
P. a. auricularis
W Mexico
Piculus rivolii (Crimson-mantled Woodpecker)
P. r. quindiuna
NC Colombia
P. r. rivolii
W Venezuela, EC Colombia
P. r. meridae
W Venezuela
P. r. brevirostris
SW Colombia to C Peru
P. r. atriceps
SE Peru, Bolivia

COLAPTES
Colaptes atricollis (Black-necked Woodpecker)
C. a. atricollis
W Peru
C. a. peruvianus
E Peru
Colaptes punctigula (Spot-breasted Woodpecker)
C. p. lutescens
E Panama
C. p. ujhelyii
N Colombia
C. p. striatigularis
WC Colombia
C. p. punctipectus
E Colombia, Venezuela
C. p. notatus
? Colombia
C. p. zuliae
NW Venezuela
C. p. speciosus
Upper Amazonia
C. p. punctigula
Surinam, French Guiana
C. p. rubidipectus
NE Brazil

C. p. guttatus
NC Brazil
Colaptes melanochloros (Green-barred Woodpecker)
C. m. mariae
Marajo I
C. m. flavilumbis
E Brazil
C. m. nattereri
E Bolivia, S Brazil
C. m. melanochloros
C Brazil
C. m. cristatus
E Paraguay, Uruguay, NE Argentina
C. m. melanolaimus
Bolivia, W Argentina
C. m. nigroviridis
S Bolivia, Paraguay
C. m. perplexus
E Argentina
C. m. patagonicus
W Argentina
Colaptes auratus (Common Flicker)
C. a. cafer
S Alaska to N California
C. a. collaris
SE British Colombia to NW Mexico
C. a. sedentarius
Santa Cruz Is
C. a. martirensis
W Baja California
C. a. nanus
NE Mexico
C. a. mexicanus
C Mexico
C. a. mexicanoïdes
S Mexico, Guatemala
C. a. pinicolus
El Salvador, Honduras, N Nicaragua
C. a. borealis
Canada, C USA
C. a. luteus
S Canada, WC & S USA
C. a. auratus
SE USA
C. a. chrysocaulosus
Cuba
C. a. gundlachi
Gd Cayman I
C. a. mearnsi
SE California, NW Baja California
C. a. tenebrosus
NW Mexico
C. a. brunnescens
C Baja California
C. a. chrysoïdes
S Baja California

Colaptes fernandinae (Fernandina's Flicker)
  Cuba
Colaptes pitius (Chilean Flicker)
  C. p. pitius
    C & S Chile
  C. p. cachinnans
    S Argentina
Colaptes rupicola (Andean Flicker)
  C. r. cinereicapilla
    N Peru
  C. r. puna
    C & S Peru
  C. r. rupicola
    Bolivia, N Chile, NW Argentina
Colaptes campestris (Campo Flicker)
  C. c. chrysosternus
    NE Brazil
  C. c. campestris
    E Bolivia, C & SE Brazil
  C. c. campestroïdes
    S Brazil, Paraguay, Uruguay,
      N & C Argentina

CELEUS
Celeus loricatus (Cinnamon Woodpecker)
  C. l. diversus
    SE Costa Rica, W Panama
  C. l. mentalis
    E Panama, NW Colombia
  C. l. innotatus
    N Colombia
  C. l. degener
    NC Colombia
  C. l. loricatus
    W Colombia, W Ecuador
Celeus undatus (Waved Woodpecker)
  C. u. amarcurensis
    NE Venezuela
  C. u. undatus
    the Guianas, N Brazil
  C. u. multifasciatus
    NE Brazil
Celeus grammicus (Scale-breasted Woodpecker)
  C. g. verreauxii
    SE Colombia, E Ecuador
  C. g. grammicus
    S Venezuela, NE Peru, W Brazil
  C. g. undulatus
    SC Venezuela
  C. g. subcervinus
    NC Brazil
  C. g. latifasciatus
    SE Peru, NE Bolivia
Celeus brachyurus (Rufous Woodpecker)
  C. b. humei
    NW Himalayas
  C. b. phaioceps
    E Himalayas, NE India

C. b. jerdonii
  W India, Sri Lanka
C. b. kanarae
  W India
C. b. annamensis
  Laos, Cambodia, S Vietnam
C. b. fokiensis
  SE China, N Vietnam
C. b. holroydi
  Hainan I
C. b. squamigularis
  Malaysia
C. b. badius
  Sumatra, Bangka I, Billiton I
C. b. celaenephis
  Nias I
C. b. brachyurus
  Java
C. b. badiosus
  Borneo, N Natuna Is
Celeus castaneus (Chestnut-coloured Woodpecker)
  SE Mexico to C Panama
Celeus elegans (Chestnut Woodpecker)
  C. e. hellmayri
    E Venezuela, Guyana, Surinam
  C. e. deltanus
    NE Venezuela
  C. e. leotaudi
    Trinidad
  C. e. approximans
    NE Brazil, S Guyana
  C. e. elegans
    NE Brazil, French Guiana
  C. e. citreopygius
    SE Colombia, E Ecuador, Peru
  C. e. jumana
    E Colombia, S Venezuela, N Brazil
  C. e. saturatus
    N Bolivia
Celeus lugubris (Pale-crested Woodpecker)
  Bolivia
Celeus flavescens (Blond-crested Woodpecker)
  C. f. ochraceus
    E Brazil
  C. f. intercedens
    NE Brazil
  C. f. flavescens
    SE Brazil, E Paraguay
  C. f. roosevelti
    SE Bolivia, SW Brazil
  C. f. kerri
    W Paraguay, N Argentina

***Celeus flavus* (Cream-coloured Woodpecker)**
C. f. semicinnamomeus
N Venezuela
C. f. flavus
C Colombia to the Guianas, N Brazil
C. f. peruvianus
W Brazil, E Peru
C. f. inornatus
C Brazil
C. f. tectricialis
NE Brazil
C. f. subflavus
E Brazil
***Celeus spectabilis* (Rufous-headed Woodpecker)**
C. s. spectabilis
E Ecuador
C. s. obrieni
Piauhy, (Brazil)
C. s. exsul
C Bolivia
***Celeus torquatus* (Ringed Woodpecker)**
C. t. torquatus
E Venezuela, the Guianas, N Brazil
C. t. occidentalis
E Peru, W Brazil
C. t. angustus
C Brazil
C. t. tinnunculus
E Brazil

DRYOCOPUS
***Dryocopus galeatus* (Helmeted Woodpecker)**
S Brazil, Paraguay, NE Argentina
***Dryocopus schulzi* (Black-bodied Woodpecker)**
N Argentina
***Dryocopus lineatus* (Lineated Woodpecker)**
D. l. obsoletus
NW Mexico
D. l. scapularis
W Mexico
D. l. petersi
NE Mexico
D. l. similis
S Mexico to NW Costa Rica
D. l. mesorhynchus
E & S Costa Rica, W Panama
D. l. nuperus
E Panama, N & W Colombia
D. l. lineatus
Trinidad, N & W Amazonia
D. l. fuscipennis
W Ecuador, NW Peru
D. l. improcerus
E Brazil

D. l. erythrops
SE & S Brazil
D. l. fulcitus
N Argentina
***Dryocopus pileatus* (Pileated Woodpecker)**
D. p. picinus
SW Canada, W USA
D. p. abieticola
C & E Canada, NE USA
D. p. pileatus
C & E USA
D. p. floridanus
SE USA
***Dryocopus javensis* (White-bellied Black Woodpecker)**
D. j. hodgei
Andaman Is
D. j. hodgsonii
W India
D. j. richardsi
C & S Korea
D. j. forresti
SE Sikang, W Yunnan, N Vietnam
D. j. feddeni
Burma, N Thailand, S Indochina
D. j. javensis
Malaysia, Sumatra, Java, Borneo
D. j. parvus
Simalur I
D. j. buttikoferi
Nias I
D. j. hargitti
Palawan I
D. j. confusus
Luzon I
D. j. mindorensis
Mindoro I
D. j. philippensis
Masbate I, Panay I, Negros I
D. j. pectoralis
Leyte I
D. j. samarensis
Samar I, Bohol I
D. j. multilunatus
Mindanao I, Basilan I
D. j. suluënsis
Sulu Archipelago
***Dryocopus martius* (Black Woodpecker)**
D. m. pinetorum
C & S Europe to N Iran
D. m. martius
Scandinavia to NE Asia, Japan
D. m. khamensis
W China

Campephilus guatemalensis (Pale-bellied Woodpecker)
  C. g. regius
    E & C Mexico
  C. g. dorsofasciatus
    NW Mexico
  C. g. nelsoni
    W Mexico
  C. g. guatemalensis
    S Mexico to W Panama

Campephilus melanoleucos (Crimson-crested Woodpecker)
  C. m. malherbii
    E Panama to W Venezuela
  C. m. melanoleucos
    N & W Amazonia
  C. m. albirostris
    S Brazil, Paraguay, NW Argentina
  C. m. cearae
    NE Brazil

Campephilus gayaquilensis (Guayaquil Woodpecker)
  W Ecuador, NW Peru

Campephilus pollens (Powerful Woodpecker)
  C. p. pollens
    Colombia, Ecuador
  C. p. peruvianus
    E Peru

Campephilus haematogaster (Crimson-bellied Woodpecker)
  C. h. splendens
    Panama to NW Ecuador
  C. h. haematogaster
    N Colombia to S Peru

Campephilus robustus (Robust Woodpecker)
  SE Brazil, Paraguay, NE Argentina

Campephilus rubricollis (Red-necked Woodpecker)
  C. r. rubricollis
    C Colombia to the Guianas, N Brazil
  C. r. trachelopyrus
    E Peru, N Bolivia, W Brazil
  C. r. olallae
    W Bolivia to C & E Brazil

Campephilus leucopogon (Cream-backed Woodpecker)
  Bolivia to Uruguay & NE Argentina

Campephilus magellanicus (Magellanic Woodpecker)
  S South America

Campephilus principalis (Ivory-billed Woodpecker)
  C. p. principalis
    N Louisiana

  C. p. bairdii
    Cuba

Campephilus imperialis (Imperial Woodpecker)
  NW & W Mexico

PICUS

Picus miniaceus (Banded Red Woodpecker)
  P. m. perlutus
    S Burma, SW Thailand
  P. m. malaccensis
    Malaysia, Sumatra, NW Borneo
  P. m. niasensis
    Nias I
  P. m. miniaceus
    W & C Java
  P. m. dayak
    Borneo

Picus puniceus (Crimson-winged Woodpecker)
  P. p. continentis
    S Burma, Malaysia
  P. p. observandus
    Sumatra, Borneo
  P. p. soligae
    Nias I
  P. p. puniceus
    Java

Picus chlorolophus (Lesser Yellow-naped Woodpecker)
  P. c. simlae
    NW Himalayas
  P. c. chlorolophus
    E Himalayas, N India, N Burma
  P. c. chlorigaster
    C & S India
  P. c. wellsi
    Sri Lanka
  P. c. chlorolophoides
    S Burma, N Thailand
  P. c. citrinocristatus
    SE China, N Indochina
  P. c. longipennis
    Hainan I
  P. c. laotianus
    NE Thailand, N Laos
  P. c. annamensis
    S Indochina
  P. c. krempfi
    S Vietnam
  P. c. rodgeri
    NW Malaysia
  P. c. vanheysti
    Sumatra

Picus mentalis (Checker-throated Woodpecker)
  P. m. humii
    S Burma, Malaysia, Sumatra, W Borneo

P. m. mentalis
Java
P. m. saba
S & E Borneo
Picus flavinucha (Greater Yellow-naped Woodpecker)
P. f. flavinucha
E Himalayas, Nepal to N Assam
P. f. archon
NE Thailand, N Vietnam
P. f. kumaonensis
W Himalayas
P. f. marianae
S Assam
P. f. styani
SE China, NE Vietnam, Hainan I
P. f. lylei
NW & SW Thailand
P. f. pierrei
C, E & SE Thailand, S Indochina
P. f. ricketti
C Fukien
P. f. mystacalis
N Sumatra
P. f. korinchi
S Sumatra
Picus vittatus (Laced Green Woodpecker)
P. v. viridanus
Burma, SW Thailand
P. v. weberi
S Thailand, N Malaysia
P. v. eisenhoferi
E Burma, N Indochina
P. v. eurous
SE Thailand, W Cambodia
P. v. connectens
Langkawi Is
P. v. vittatus
S Malaysia, Sumatra, W Java
P. v. limitans
E Java, Bali I, Kangean I
Picus xanthopygaeus (Little Scaly-bellied Green Woodpecker)
Himalayas, India to Indochina
Picus squamatus (Scaly-bellied Green Woodpecker)
P. s. flavirostris
Caspian Sea to Afghanistan
P. s. squamatus
W & C Himalayas
Picus awokera (Japanese Green Woodpecker)
P. a. awokera
Honshu I
P. a. horii
Shikoku I, Kyushu I
P. a. takatsukasae
Tanegashima I, Yakushima I

Picus canus (Grey-headed Green Woodpecker)
P. c. canus
Norway to Alps & E Europe
P. c. perspicuus
Bulgaria, SE Yugoslavia
P. c. biedermanni
Altai, C Asia, N Mongolia
P. c. jessoensis
Manchuria, Korea, Hokkaido I
P. c. zimmermanni
NE China
P. c. kogo
W China
P. c. setschuanus
SW China
P. c. brunneatus
Szechwan
P. c. guerini
E China
P. c. sobrinus
SE China, N Vietnam
P. c. tancolo
Taiwan, Hainan I
P. c. sordidior
NW Yunnan
P. c. sanguiniceps
NW Himalayas
P. c. gyldenstolpei
E Nepal, Assam, N Burma
P. c. hessei
S Burma, Thailand, Indochina
P. c. robinsoni
Malaysia
P. c. dedemi
Sumatra
Picus erythropygius (Red-rumped Green Woodpecker)
P. e. nigrigenis
Burma, S Thailand
P. e. erythropygius
SE Thailand, S Indochina
Picus rabieri (Red-collared Woodpecker)
Indochina
Picus viridis (Green Woodpecker)
P. v. pluvius
England, Wales
P. v. viridis
Scandinavia, W Russia
P. v. frondium
C Europe
P. v. pronus
S Switzerland, Italy
P. v. dofleini
SE Europe
P. v. romaniae
Romania

P. v. sharpei
Iberia
P. v. saundersi
Caucasus
P. v. karelini
N Turkey, N Iran
P. v. innominatus
W & SW Iran
P. v. bampurensis
Baluchistan
Picus vaillantii (Algerian Green Woodpecker)
Morocco to Tunisia

DINOPIUM
Dinopium rafflesii (Olive-backed Three-toed Woodpecker)
D. r. peninsulare
S Burma, S Thailand, Malaysia
D. r. rafflesii
Sumatra, Bangka I
D. r. dulitense
Borneo
Dinopium shorii (Himalayan Three-toed Woodpecker)
Himalayas, N Burma
Dinopium javanense (Golden-backed Three-toed Woodpecker)
D. j. malabaricum
SW India
D. j. intermedium
NE India to Indochina
D. j. javanense
Malaysia, Sumatra, W & C Java
D. j. exsul
E Java, Bali I
D. j. borneonense
Borneo
D. j. raveni
NE Borneo
D. j. everetti
SW Philippine Is
Donopium benghalense (Lesser Golden-backed Woodpecker)
D. b. benghalense
E & C India
D. b. dilutum
Baluchistan, Pakistan
D. b. puncticolle
S India
D. b. tehminae
W India
D. b. jaffnense
N Sri Lanka
D. b. erithronothon
S Sri Lanka

CHRYSOCOLAPTES
Chrysocolaptes lucidus (Crimson-backed Woodpecker)
C. l. sultaneus
NW Himalayas
C. l. guttacristatus
E India, Burma, Thailand, S Indochina
C. l. chersonesus
S India, S Malaysia, Sumatra, Java
C. l. stricklandi
Sri Lanka
C. l. strictus
E Java, Bali I, Kangean I
C. l. andrewsi
Sebattick Is, Borneo
C. l. erythrocephalus
Palawan I, Balabac I
C. l. haematribon
N Luzon, Marinduque I
C. l. grandis
Polillo Is
C. l. ramosi
S Luzon
C. l. xanthocephalus
Masbate I, Panay I, Negros I
C. l. rufopunctatus
Samar I, Leyte I, Bohol I
C. l. lucidus
Mindanao I
C. l. maculiceps
Basilan I
Chrysocolaptes festivus (Black-backed Woodpecker)
C. f. festivus
C & S India
C. f. tantus
Sri Lanka

GECINULUS
Gecinulus grantia (Pale-headed Woodpecker)
G. g. grantia
Nepal to E Assam, N Burma
G. g. indochinensis
N & C Indochina
G. g. poilanei
SE Indochina
G. g. viridanus
S China
Gecinulus viridis (Bamboo Woodpecker)
G. v. viridis
C Burma to E Thailand
G. v. robinsoni
SE Thailand, Malaysia

SAPHEOPIPO
Sapheopipo noguchii (Pryer's Woodpecker)
Okinawa I

BLYTHIPICUS

Blythipicus rubiginosus (Lesser Bay Woodpecker)
B. r. parvus
Sumatra, Borneo
B. r. rubiginosus
S Burma, S Thailand, Malaysia
Blythipicus pyrrhotis (Bay Woodpecker)
B. p. pyrrhotis
NE Himalayas, NE India to Indochina
B. p. cameroni
Malaysia
B. p. annamensis
S Indochina
B. p. sinensis
SE China
B. p. hainanus
Hainan I

REINWARDTIPICUS
Reinwardtipicus validus (Orange-backed Woodpecker)
R. v. xanthopygius
Malaysia, Sumatra, Borneo
R. v. validus
W & C Java

MEIGLYPTES
Meiglyptes tristis (Fulvous-rumped Barred Woodpecker)
M. t. grammithorax
S Burma, S Thailand, Malaysia
M. t. micropterus
Sumatra, Borneo
M. t. microterus
Nias I
M. t. tristis
Java
Meiglyptes jugularis (Black and Buff Woodpecker)
Burma to S Indochina
Meiglyptes tukki (Buff-necked Barred Woodpecker)
M. t. tukki
Malaysia, Sumatra, Borneo
M. t. azaleus
N Natuna Is
M. t. pulonis
Banggai I
M. t. percnerpes
S Borneo
M. t. calceuticus
Banjak Is
M. t. infuscatus
Nias I
M. t. batu
Batu Is

HEMICIRCUS
Hemicircus concretus (Malaysian Grey-breasted Woodpecker)
H. c. sordidus
S Burma, S Thailand, Malaysia
H. c. coccometopus
Sumatra, Borneo
H. c. concretus
W & C Java
Hemicircus canente (Heart-spotted Woodpecker)
H. c. canente
NE India to S Indochina
H. c. cordatus
W India

MULLERIPICUS
Mulleripicus fulvus (Fulvous Woodpecker)
M. f. fulvus
N Celebes, Togian Is
M. f. wallacei
C & S Celebes
Mulleripicus funebris (Sooty Woodpecker)
M. f. funebris
Luzon I, Marinduque I
M. f. fuliginosus
Samar I, Leyte I, Mindanao I
Mulleripicus pulverulentus (Great Slaty Woodpecker)
M. p. harterti
N India to C & S Indochina
M. p. pulverulentus
Malaysia, Sumatra, Java, Borneo, Palawan I

Passeriformes

100 EURYLAIMIDAE (BROADBILLS)

EURYLAIMINAE
SMITHORNIS
Smithornis capensis (African Broadbill)
S. c. delacouri
Liberia, Ghana, Ivory Coast
S. c. camerunensis
S Cameroun, Gabon
S. c. albigularis
N Angola, S Zaire
S. c. medianus
E Zaire, Uganda, Kenya
S. c. capensis
S Kenya, Tanzania, Zambia, Rhodesia, Malaysia, Mozambique, Natal

Smithornis rufolateralis (Red-sided Broadbill)
S. r. rufolateralis
  West Africa, Cameroun, Central African Republic
S. r. budongoensis
  NE Zaire, W Uganda
Smithornis sharpei (Grey-headed Broadbill)
S. s. sharpei
  Fernando Po I
S. s. zenkeri
  Cameroun
S. s. eurylaemus
  E Zaire

PSEUDOCALYPTOMENA
Pseudocalyptomena graueri (Grauer's Broadbill)
  E Zaire

CORYDON
Corydon sumatranus (Dusky Broadbill)
C. s. laoensis
  S Burma, Thailand Laos, N Vietnam
C. s. morator
  S Thailand
C. s. pallescens
  Malaysia
C. s. ardescens
  SE Thailand
C. s. sumatranus
  Sumatra
C. s. brunnescens
  N Borneo, N Natuna Is
C. s. orientalis
  S Borneo

CYMBIRHYNCHUS
Cymbirhynchus macrorhynchos (Black and Red Broadbill)
C. m. affinis
  SE Burma
C. m. siamensis
  S Burma, S Thailand, Cambodia, S Vietnam
C. m. malaccensis
  S Malaysia
C. m. lemniscatus
  Sumatra, Bangka I, Billiton I
C. m. tenebrosus
  SE Sumatra
C. m. macrorhynchos
  Borneo

EURYLAIMUS
Eurylaimus javanicus (Banded Broadbill)
E. j. pallidus
  S Burma, Malaysia, Thailand, Laos, S Vietnam
E. j. harterti
  Sumatra

E. j. javanicus
  Java
E. j. billitonis
  Billiton I
E. j. brookei
  Borneo
Eurylaimus ochromalus (Black and Yellow Broadbill)
E. o. ochromalus
  S Burma, Malaysia, Sumatra
E. o. mecistus
  Banjak Is
E. o. kalamantan
  Borneo
Eurylaimus steerii (Wattled Broadbill)
E. s. samarensis
  Samar I, Leyte I, Philippine Is
E. s. steerii
  Mindanao I, Basilan I
E. s. mayri
  Mindanao I

SERILOPHUS
Serilophus lunatus (Silver-breasted Broadbill)
S. l. rubropygius
  Nepal, N Burma
S. l. atrestus
  E Burma, E Thailand, N Laos, N Vietnam
S. l. polionotus
  Hainan I
S. l. impavidus
  S Laos
S. l. lunatus
  S Burma
S. l. intrepidus
  NW Thailand
S. l. stolidus
  S Burma, S Thailand
S. l. rothschildi
  Malaysia
S. l. moderatus
  N Sumatra
S. l. intensus
  S Sumatra

PSARISOMUS
Psarisomus dalhousiae (Long-tailed Broadbill)
P. d. dalhousiae
  Himalayas, Burma, N & W Thailand, Laos, N Vietnam
P. d. cyanicauda
  SE Thailand
P. d. divinus
  Cambodia, S Vietnam
P. d. psittacinus
  Malaysia, Sumatra
P. d. borneensis
  mountains of NW Borneo

CALYPTÓMENA

Calyptomena viridis (Lesser Green Broadbill)
C. v. continentis
S Burma, S Thailand, Malaysia
C. v. viridis
Nias I, N Natuna Is, Sumatra, Borneo
C. v. siberu
Siberut I, S Pagi Is

Calyptomena hosii (Magnificent Green Broadbill)
mountains of N Borneo

Calyptomena whiteheadi (Black-throated Green Broadbill)
Mt Kinabalu (N Borneo)

101 DENDROCOLAPTIDAE (WOOD-CREEPERS)

DENDROCINCLA

Dendrocincla tyrannina (Tyrannine Woodcreeper)
D. t. tyrannina
Colombia
D. t. hellmayri
E Colombia, W Venezuela

Dendrocincla macrorhyncha (Large Tyrannine Woodcreeper)
E Ecuador

Dendrocincla fuliginosa (Plain-brown Woodcreeper)
D. f. ridgwayi
E C America, W Colombia, W Ecuador
D. f. lafresnayei
N & E Colombia, NW Venezuela
D. f. meruloides
coast of N Venezuela, Trinidad
D. f. deltana
delta of R Orinoco
D. f. barinensis
C Venezuela
D. f. phaeochroa
S Colombia, E Ecuador, E Peru
D. f. neglecta
W Brazil
D. f. atrirostris
NE Bolivia, SW Brazil
D. f. fuliginosa
E Venezuela, the Guianas, N Brazil
D. f. rufoolivacea
EC Brazil
D. f. taunayi
NE Brazil
D. f. turdina
· E & S Brazil, E Paraguay, NE Argentina
D. f. brumaii
C Brazil

Dendrocincla anabatina (Tawny-winged Woodcreeper)
D. a. anabatina
S Mexico to Costa Rica
D. a. typhla
SE Mexico

Dendrocincla merula (White-chinned Woodcreeper)
D. m. bartletti
S Venezuela, W Brazil, NE Paraguay
D. m. merula
the Guianas, N Brazil
D. m. obidensis
Brazil
D. m. remota
EC Bolivia
D. m. olivascens
Brazil
D. m. castanoptera
C Brazil
D. m. badia
C Brazil

Dendrocincla homochroa (Ruddy Woodcreeper)
D. h. homochroa
S Mexico to Honduras
D. h. acedesta
SW Nicaragua, W Costa Rica
D. h. ruficeps
Panama, W Venezuela
D. h. meridionalis
NE Colombia

DECONYCHURA

Deconychura longicauda (Long-tailed Woodcreeper)
D. l. typica
SW Costa Rica, W Panama
D. l. darienensis
E Panama
D. l. minor
N Colombia
D. l. longicauda
the Guianas, N Brazil
D. l. connectens
NW Amazonia
D. l. pallida
SE Peru, N Bolivia, W Brazil
D. l. zimmeri
Pará, Brazil

Deconychura stictolaema (Spot-throated Woodcreeper)
D. s. clarior
French Guiana, NE Brazil
D. s. secunda
E Ecuador, NE Peru, W Brazil,
S Venezuela
D. s. stictolaema
C Brazil

SITTASOMUS
Sittasomus griseicapillus (Olivaceous Woodcreeper)
S. g. jaliscensis
SW Mexico
S. g. sylvioides
SE Mexico to Costa Rica
S. g. gracileus
E Mexico
S. g. levis
W Panama, N Colombia
S. g. veraguensis
E Panama
S. g. aequatorialis
W Ecuador, NW Peru
S. g. perijanus
NW Venezuela
S. g. tachiranus
W Venezuela
S. g. griseus
coast of N Venezuela, Tobago I
S. g. enochrus
Colombia
S. g. amazonus
SE Colombia, S Venezuela, E Ecuador, W Brazil
S. g. axillaris
E Venezuela, N Brazil
S. g. viridis
N & E Bolivia
S. g. viridior
E Bolivia
S. g. transitivus
C Brazil
S. g. griseicapillus
S Bolivia, W Brazil, W Paraguay, NW Argentina
S. g. reiseri
NE Brazil
S. g. olivaceus
E Brazil
S. g. sylviellus
SE Brazil, NE Argentina

GLYPHORHYNCHUS
Glyphorhynchus spirurus (Wedge-billed Woodcreeper)
G. s. pectoralis
S Mexico to Nicaragua
G. s. sublestus
Costa Rica to W Ecuador, W Venezuela
G. s. subrufescens
W Colombia
G. s. integratus
NE Colombia
G. s. rufigularis
E Colombia, S Venezuela, N Ecuador
G. s. amacurensis
NE Venezuela
G. s. coronobscurus
S Venezuela
G. s. spirurus
E Venezuela, the Guianas, N Brazil
G. s. pallidulus
Panama
G. s. castelnaudii
E Ecuador, N Peru
G. s. albigularis
SE Peru, N Bolivia
G. s. inornatus
C Brazil
G. s. cuneatus
EC Brazil
G. s. paraensis
Belem (Brazil)

DRYMORNIS
Drymornis bridgesii (Scimitar-billed Woodhewer)
Paraguay, Uruguay, Argentina

NASICA
Nasica longirostris (Long-billed Woodcreeper)
W Amazonia to French Guiana

DENDREXETASTES
Dendrexetastes rufigula (Cinnamon-throated Woodcreeper)
D. r. devillei
W Amazonia
D. r. rufigula
the Guianas, N Brazil
D. r. moniliger
W Brazil
D. r. paraensis
NE Brazil

HYLEXETASTES
Hylexetastes perrotii (Red-billed Woodcreeper)
H. p. perrotii
E Venezuela, Guyana, French Guiana, N Brazil
H. p. uniformis
N Brazil
Hylexetastes stresemanni (Bar-bellied Woodcreeper)
H. s. insignis
NW Brazil
H. s. stresemanni
NW Brazil
H. s. undulatus
E Peru, W Brazil

XIPHOCOLAPTES
Xiphocolaptes promeropirhynchus (Strong-billed Woodcreeper)
X. p. omiltemensis
SW Mexico
X. p. sclateri
S Mexico

X. p. emigrans
S Mexico to N Nicaragua
X. p. costaricensis
Costa Rica
X. p. panamensis
S Panama
X. p. rostratus
N Colombia
X. p. sanctaemartae
N Colombia, W Venezuela
X. p. virgatus
C Colombia
X. p. macarenae
WC Colombia
X. p. promeropirhynchus
EC Colombia, W Venezuela
X. p. procerus
N Venezuela
X. p. tenebrosus
E Venezuela
X. p. neblinae
S Venezuela
X. p. ignotus
W Ecuador
X. p. crassirostris
SW Ecuador, NW Peru
X. p. compressirostris
N Peru
X. p. phaeopygus
E Peru
X. p. solivagus
E Peru
X. p. lineatuscephalus
SE Peru, N & W Bolivia
X. p. orenocensis
Venezuela, E Ecuador, E Peru, W Brazil
X. p. berlepschi
E Peru, W Brazil
X. p. paraensis
C Brazil
X. p. obsoletus
N & E Bolivia
Xiphocolaptes albicollis (White-throated Woodcreeper)
X. a. bahiae
NE Brazil
X. a. albicollis
SE Brazil, E Paraguay, NE Argentina
Xiphocolaptes villanovae (Vila Nova Woodcreeper)
E Brazil
Xiphocolaptes falcirostris (Moustached Woodcreeper)
NE Brazil
Xiphocolaptes franciscanus (Snethlage's Woodcreeper)
C Brazil

Xiphocolaptes major (Great Rufous Woodcreeper)
X. m. remoratus
C Brazil
X. m. castaneus
S Brazil, E & S Bolivia, NW Argentina
X. m. major
Paraguay, N Argentina

DENDROCOLAPTES

Dendrocolaptes certhia (Barred Woodcreeper)
D. c. sanctithomae
S Mexico to Nicaragua
D. c. scheffleri
Oaxaca (Mexico)
D. c. nigrirostris
Costa Rica, Panama
D. c. hesperius
SW Costa Rica
D. c. colombianus
W Colombia, NW Ecuador
D. c. hyleorus
NE Colombia
D. c. radiolatus
SE Colombia, E Ecuador, NE Peru, NW Brazil
D. c. punctipectus
NW Venezuela
D. c. certhia
S Venezuela, the Guianas, N Brazil
D. c. juruanus
E Peru, E Bolivia, W Brazil
D. c. polyzonus
N Bolivia
D. c. ridgwayi
N Brazil
D. c. medius
NE Brazil
Dendrocolaptes concolor (Concolor Woodcreeper)
N Brazil
Dendrocolaptes hoffmannsi (Hoffmann's Woodcreeper)
C Brazil
Dendrocolaptes picumnus (Black-banded Woodcreeper)
D. p. puncticollis
Guatemala, Honduras
D. p. costaricensis
Costa Rica, W Panama
D. p. veraguensis
S Panama
D. p. multistrigatus
E Colombia, W Venezuela
D. p. seilerni
N Colombia, N Venezuela
D. p. picumnus
E Venezuela, the Guianas, N Brazil

D. p. validus
  W Amazonia
D. p. transfasciatus
  C Brazil
D. p. olivaceus
  C Bolivia
D. p. pallescens
  S Brazil, S Bolivia, Paraguay
D. p. extimus
  E Paraguay
D. p. casaresi
  NW Argentina
Dendrocolaptes platyrostris (Planalto Woodcreeper)
D. p. intermedius
  NE Brazil, N Paraguay
D. p. platyrostris
  SE Brazil, Paraguay, N Argentina

XIPHORHYNCHUS
Xiphorhynchus picus (Straight-billed Woodcreeper)
X. p. extimus
  S Panama
X. p. dugandi
  N Colombia
X. p. picirostris
  NW Colombia, W Venezuela
X. p. saturatior
  E Colombia, W Venezuela
X. p. borreroi
  SW Colombia
X. p. choicus
  N Venezuela
X. p. paraguanae
  NW Venezuela
X. p. longirostris
  Margarita I
X. p. altirostris
  Trinidad
X. p. phalera
  S Venezuela
X. p. deltans
  NE Venezuela
X. p. picus
  E Colombia to the Guianas, N Brazil
X. p. duidae
  S Venezuela, NW Brazil
X. p. peruvianus
  E Peru, W Brazil, N Bolivia
X. p. kienerii
  W Brazil
X. p. rufescens
  C Brazil
X. p. bahiae
  NE Brazil
Xiphorhynchus necopinus (Zimmer's Woodcreeper)
  C & NE Brazil

Xiphorhynchus obsoletus (Striped Woodcreeper)
X. o. palliatus
  W Amazonia, Bolivia
X. o. notatus
  E Colombia, SW Venezuela, NW Brazil
X. o. obsoletus
  E Venezuela to French Guiana, N Brazil
X. o. caicarae
  NE Venezuela
Xiphorhynchus ocellatus (Ocellated Woodcreeper)
X. o. napensis
  SE Colombia, E Ecuador, NE Peru
X. o. lineatocapillus
  E Venezuela
X. o. ocellatus
  E Colombia, S Venezuela, NE Peru, NW Brazil
X. o. perplexus
  NE Peru, W Brazil
X. o. chunchotambo
  E Peru
X. o. brevirostris
  SE Peru, NE Bolivia
Xiphorhynchus spixii (Spix's Woodcreeper)
X. s. buenavistae
  W Colombia
X. s. insignis
  EC Peru
X. s. juruanus
  SE Peru, NE Bolivia, W Brazil
X. s. spixii
  S Brazil
Xiphorhynchus elegans (Elegant Woodcreeper)
X. e. ornatus
  SE Colombia, E Ecuador, NE Peru, W Brazil.
X. e. elegans
  S Brazil
Xiphorhynchus pardalotus (Chestnut-rumped Woodcreeper)
X. p. caurensis
  SE Venezuela, W Guyana
X. p. pardalotus
  the Guianas, N Brazil
Xiphorhynchus guttatus (Buff-throated Woodcreeper)
X. g. confinis
  E Guatemala, N Honduras
X. g. costaricensis
  SW Honduras to W Panama
X. g. marginatus
  E Panama
X. g. nanus
  E Panama, N Colombia, W Venezuela

X. g. rosenbergi
W Colombia
X. g. demonstratus
E Colombia, NW Venezuela
X. g. susurrans
NE Venezuela, Trinidad, Tobago I
X. g. jardinei
NE Venezuela
X. g. margaritae
Margarita I
X. g. polystictus
E Colombia to the Guianas, N Brazil
X. g. connectens
N Brazil
X. g. guttatoides
W Amazonia
X. g. vicinalis
S Brazil
X. g. dorbignyanus
NE Bolivia, SW Brazil
X. g. guttatus
coast of E Brazil
Xiphorhynchus eytoni (Dusky-billed Woodcreeper)
E & S Brazil
Xiphorhynchus flavigaster (Ivory-billed Woodcreeper)
X. f. tardus
NW Mexico
X. f. mentalis
W Mexico
X. f. flavigaster
SW Mexico
X. f. saltuarius
NE Mexico
X. f. yucatanensis
Yucatan peninsula, Meco I
X. f. ascensor
S Mexico
X. f. eburneirostris
SE Mexico to NW Costa Rica
X. f. ultimus
NW Costa Rica
Xiphorhynchus striatigularis (Stripe-throated Woodcreeper)
NE Mexico
Xiphorhynchus lachrymosus (Black-striped Woodcreeper)
X. l. lachrymosus
E Nicaragua to W Ecuador
X. l. alarum
N Colombia
Xiphorhynchus erythropygius (Spotted Woodcreeper)
X. e. erythropygius
S Mexico
X. e. parvus
S Mexico to N Nicaragua

X. e. punctigula
S Nicaragua to W Panama
X. e. insolitus
E Panama, NW Colombia
X. e. aequatorialis
W Colombia, W Ecuador
Xiphorhynchus triangularis (Olive-backed Woodcreeper)
X. t. triangularis
Colombia, W Venezuela, E Ecuador,
N Peru
X. t. hylodromus
N Venezuela
X. t. intermedius
C & S Peru
X. t. bangsi
Bolivia

LEPIDOCOLAPTES
Lepidocolaptes leucogaster (White-striped Woodcreeper)
L. l. umbrosus
NW Mexico
L. l. leucogaster
C & S Mexico
Lepidocolaptes souleyetii (Streak-headed Woodcreeper)
L. s. guerrerensis
W Mexico
L. s. insignis
SE Mexico to N Honduras
L. s. compressus
S Mexico to W Panama
L. s. lineaticeps
E Panama, N Colombia, W Venezuela
L. s. littoralis
N Colombia to Guyana, Trinidad, N Brazil
L. s. uaireni
SE Venezuela
L. s. esmeraldae
SW Colombia, W Ecuador
L. s. souleyetii
SW Ecuador, NW Peru
Lepidocolaptes angustirostris (Narrow-billed Woodcreeper)
L. a. griseiceps
Sipaliwini (Surinam)
L. a. coronatus
N Brazil
L. a. bahiae
NE Brazil
L. a. bivittatus
E Bolivia, C & E Brazil
L. a. hellmayri
WC Bolivia
L. a. certhiolus
C Bolivia to Paraguay, NW Argentina
L. a. dabbenei
SW Paraguay, N Argentina

L. a. angustirostris
E Paraguay, SW Brazil, N Argentina
L. a. praedatus
W Uruguay, E & S Argentina
Lepidocolaptes affinis (Spot-crowned Woodcreeper)
L. a. lignicida
NE Mexico
L. a. affinis
S Mexico to N Nicaragua
L. a. neglectus
Costa Rica, W Panama
L. a. sanctaemartae
N Colombia
L. a. sneiderni
W Colombia
L. a. lacrymiger
E Colombia, W Venezuela
L. a. lafresnayi
N Venezuela
L. a. aequatorialis
SW Colombia, Ecuador
L. a. frigidus
SW Colombia
L. a. warscewiczi
N & C Peru
L. a. carabayae
SE Peru
L. a. bolivianus
Bolivia
Lepidocolaptes squamatus (Scaled Woodcreeper)
L. s. wagleri
NE Brazil
L. s. squamatus
E Brazil
L. s. falcinellus
SE Brazil, Paraguay
Lepidocolaptes fuscus (Lesser Woodcreeper)
L. f. atlanticus
E Brazil
L. f. brevirostris
NE Brazil
L. f. tenuirostris
E Brazil
L. f. fuscus
SE Brazil, E Paraguay, NE Argentina
Lepidocolaptes albolineatus (Lineated Woodcreeper)
L. a. albolineatus
E Venezuela, the Guianas, N Brazil
L. a. duidae
S Venezuela, NW Brazil
L. a. fuscicapillus
SW Amazonia
L. a. madeirae
C Brazil

L. a. layardi
C Brazil

CAMPYLORHAMPHUS
Campylorhamphus pucheranii (Greater Scythebill)
S Colombia, E Ecuador
Campylorhamphus trochilirostris (Red-billed Scythebill)
C. t. brevipennis
E Panama, W Colombia
C. t. venezuelensis
N Colombia, N Venezuela
C. t. thoracicus
SW Colombia, W Ecuador
C. t. zarumillanus
NW Peru
C. t. napensis
E Ecuador, E Peru
C. t. notabilis
W Brazil
C. t. snethlageae
C Brazil
C. t. devius
N Bolivia
C. t. lafresnayanus
E Bolivia, N Paraguay
C. t. major
NE Brazil
C. t. omissus
NE Brazil
C. t. trochilirostris
NE Brazil
C. t. hellmayri
N Argentina
Campylorhamphus falcularius (Black-billed Scythebill)
SE Brazil, Paraguay, NE Argentina
Campylorhamphus pusillus (Brown-billed Scythebill)
C. p. borealis
Costa Rica, W Panama
C. p. olivaceus
C Panama
C. p. tachirensis
NE Colombia
C. p. pusillus
Colombia, W Ecuador
Campylorhamphus procurvoides (Curve-billed Scythebill)
C. p. sanus
E Colombia, Venezuela, W Guyana, N Brazil
C. p. procurvoides
French Guiana, N Brazil
C. p. probatus
C Brazil
C. p. multistriatus
C Brazil

FURNARIINAE

GEOSITTA

Geositta poeciloptera (Campo Miner)
   Brazil

Geositta cunicularia (Common Miner)
   G. c. juninensis
      C Peru
   G. c. titicacae
      S Peru to N Chile, NW Argentina
   G. c. georgei
      Peru
   G. c. frobeni
      S Peru
   G. c. deserticolor
      SW Peru, N Chile
   G. c. fissirostris
      C Chile
   G. c. hellmayri
      W Argentina
   G. c. cunicularia
      S Brazil, Uruguay, Argentina

Geositta maritima (Greyish Miner)
   Peru, N Chile

Geositta peruviana (Coastal Miner)
   G. p. paytae
      N Peru
   G. p. peruviana
      C Peru
   G. p. rostrata
      SC Peru

Geositta punensis (Puna Miner)
   Bolivia, Peru, Chile, N Argentina

Geositta saxicolina (Dark-winged Miner)
   C Peru

Geositta isabellina (Creamy-rumped Miner)
   C Chile, W Argentina

Geositta antarctica (Short-billed Miner)
   S Chile, S Argentina

Geositta rufipennis (Rufous-banded Miner)
   G. r. fasciata
      W Bolivia, C Chile, W Argentina
   G. r. hellmayri
      N Chile
   G. r. rufipennis
      W Argentina
   G. r. giaii
      Bariloche, Argentina
   G. r. ottowi
      Cordoba, Argentina

Geositta crassirostris (Thick-billed Miner)
   central coast of Peru

Geositta excelsior (Stout-billed Miner)
   G. e. colombiana
      C Colombia
   G. e. excelsior
      SW Colombia, Ecuador

   G. e. aricomae
      N Peru

Geositta tenuirostris (Slender-billed Miner)
   S Peru, W Bolivia, NW Argentina

UPUCERTHIA

Upucerthia certhioides (Chaco Earthcreeper)
   U. c. harterti
      S Bolivia
   U. c. luscinia
      W Argentina
   U. c. estebani
      S Paraguay, N Argentina
   U. c. certhioides
      N & C Argentina

Upucerthia ruficauda (Straight-billed Earthcreeper)
   U. r. montana
      S Peru
   U. r. ruficauda
      W Bolivia, N Chile, NW Argentina

Upucerthia andaecola (Rock Earthcreeper)
   W Bolivia, NW Argentina

Upucerthia albigula (White-throated Earthcreeper
   S Peru, N Chile

Upucerthia serrana (Striated Earthcreeper)
   U. s. serrana
      N Peru
   U. s. huancavelicae
      SW Peru

Upucerthia dumetaria (Scale-throated Earthcreeper)
   U. d. hypoleuca
      SW Bolivia, N Chile, W Argentina
   U. d. hallinani
      N Chile, NW Argentina
   U. d. saturatior
      C Chile
   U. d. dumetaria
      Tierra del Fuego, C & S Argentina

Upucerthia validirostris (Buff-breasted Earthcreeper)
   U. v. saturata
      W Peru
   U. v. pallida
      S Peru, Bolivia, N Chile, NW Argentina
   U. v. validirostris
      W Argentina

Upucerthia jelskii (Plain-breasted Earthcreeper)
   C Peru

CINCLODES

Cinclodes fuscus (Bar-winged Cinclodes)
   C. f. heterurus
      W Venezuela

C. f. oreobates
N Colombia
C. f. paramo
SW Colombia
C. f. albidiventris
Ecuador
C. f. longipennis
N Peru
C. f. rivularis
C & S Peru
C. f. albiventris
S Peru, Bolivia, N Chile, NW Argentina
C. f. fuscus
S Brazil, Uruguay, S Chile, S Argentina
Cinclodes olrogi (Olrog's Cinclodes)
C Argentina
**Cinclodes comechingonus
(Comechingones Cinclodes)**
C Argentina
**Cinclodes pabsti (Long-tailed
Cinclodes)**
S Brazil
**Cinclodes atacamensis (White-winged
Cinclodes)**
C. a. atacamensis
S Peru, W Bolivia, N Chile, N Argentina
C. a. schocolatinus
C Argentina
**Cinclodes palliatus (White-bellied
Cinclodes)**
C Peru
**Cinclodes oustaleti (Grey-flanked
Cinclodes)**
C. o. oustaleti
S Chile
C. o. hornensis
Cape Horn Is, Tierra del Fuego
C. o. baeckstroemii
Juan Fernandez I
**Cinclodes patagonicus (Dark-bellied
Cinclodes)**
C. p. chilensis
C Chile, W Argentina
C. p. patagonicus
S Chile, S Argentina
**Cinclodes nigrofumosus (Seaside
Cinclodes)**
coast of N Chile
**Cinclodes taczanowskii (Taczanowski's
Cinclodes)**
central coast of Peru
Cinclodes antarcticus (Blackish Cinclodes)
C. a. maculirostris
Cape Horn Is
C. a. antarcticus
Falkland Is
CHILIA
Chilia melanura (Crag Chilia)
C. m. atacamae
N Chile

C. m. melanura
C Chile
FURNARIUS
Furnarius minor (Lesser Hornero)
NE Peru, W Brazil
Furnarius figulus (White-banded Hornero)
F. f. pileatus
C Brazil
F. f. figulus
E Brazil
Furnarius tricolor (Tricolour Hornero)
E Peru, W Brazil, N Bolivia
Furnarius leucopus (Pale-legged Hornero)
F. l. longirostris
N Colombia, NW Venezuela
F. l. endoecus
C Colombia, W Venezuela
F. l. leucopus
Guyana, N Brazil
F. l. cinnamomeus
SW Ecuador, NW Peru
F. l. assimilis
E & S Brazil, SE Bolivia
F. l. torridus
NE Peru, W Brazil
Furnarius rufus (Rufous Hornero)
F. r. albogularis
SE Brazil
F. r. commersoni
Bolivia, W Brazil
F. r. schuhmacheri
S Bolivia
F. r. paraguayae
Paraguay, N Argentina
F. r. rufus
S Brazil, Uruguay, C & E Argentina
Furnarius cristatus (Crested Hornero)
Paraguay, N Argentina

SYNALLAXINAE

SYLVIORTHORHYNCHUS

**Sylviorthorhynchus desmursii (Des Murs'
Wiretail)**
S Chile, W Argentina

APHRASTURA
**Aphrastura spinicauda (Thorn-tailed
Rayadito)**
A. s. spinicauda
Tierra del Fuego, S Chile, W Argentina
A. s. bullocki
Moncha I, (Chile)
A. s. fulva
Chiloé I, (Chile)
**Aphrastura masafuerae (Masafuera
Rayadito)**
Mas Afuera Is

Leptasthenura fuliginiceps (Brown-capped Tit-Spinetail)
L. f. fuliginiceps
W Bolivia
L. f. paranensis
W Argentina
Leptasthenura yanacensis (Tawny Tit-Spinetail)
W Peru, W Bolivia
Leptasthenura platensis (Tufted Tit-Spinetail)
S Brazil, Uruguay, Argentina
Leptasthenura aegithaloides (Plain-mantled Tit-Spinetail)
L. a. grisescens
S Peru, N Chile
L. a. berlepschi
S Peru, Bolivia, N Chile, W Argentina
L. a. aegithaloides
C Chile
L. a. pallida
W & S Argentina
Leptasthenura setaria (Araucaria Tit-Spinetail)
S Brazil
Leptasthenura striata (Streaked Tit-Spinetail)
L. s. superciliaris
C Peru
L. s. albigularis
W Peru
L. s. striata
SW Peru, N Chile
Leptasthenura striolata (Striolated Tit-Spinetail)
SE Brazil
Leptasthenura pileata (Rusty-crowned Tit-Spinetail)
L. p. latistriata
W Peru
L. p. cajabambae
C Peru
L. p. pileata
central coast of Peru
L. p. xenothorax
S Peru
Leptasthenura andicola (Andean Tit-Spinetail)
L. a. certhia
W Venezuela
L. a. extima
N Colombia
L. a. exterior
E Colombia
L. a. andicola
C Colombia, Ecuador

L. a. peruviana
C Peru, N Bolivia

Schizoeaca fuliginosa (White-chinned Spinetail)
S. f. fumigata
Colombia
S. f. coryi
Venezuela
S. f. fuliginosa
W Venezuela, E Colombia, N Ecuador
S. f. griseomurina
S Ecuador
S. f. peruviana
N Peru
S. f. avacuchensis
Ayacucho (Peru)
S. f. vilcabambae
Cuzco (Peru)
S. f. plengei
C Peru
S. f. palpebralis
C Peru
S. f. helleri
SE Peru
S. f. harterti
N Bolivia
Schizoeaca moreirae (Itatiaya Spinetail)
Rio de Janeiro

Schoeniophylax phryganophila (Chotoy Spinetail)
S. p. phryganophila
E Bolivia, S Brazil, N Argentina
S. p. petersi
E Brazil

Synallaxis ruficapilla (Rufous-capped Spinetail)
SE Brazil to N Argentina
Synallaxis superciliosa (Buff-browed Spinetail)
S. s. samaipatae
S Bolivia
S. s. superciliosa
NW Argentina
Synallaxis frontalis (Sooty-fronted Spinetail)
S. f. poliophrys
French Guiana
S. f. fuscipennis
Bolivia, NW Argentina
S. f. frontalis
Brazil, Paraguay, Uruguay, N Argentina

Synallaxis azarae (Azara's Spinetail)
S. a. media
  W Colombia, N Ecuador
S. a. ochracea
  S Ecuador, NW Peru
S. a. fruticicola
  N Peru
S. a. infumata
  NC Peru
S. a. urubambae
  SE Peru
S. a. carabayae
  SE Peru, N Bolivia
S. a. azarae
  N Bolivia
Synallaxis elegantior (Elegant Spinetail)
  E Colombia, W Venezuela
Synallaxis albigularis (Dark-breasted Spinetail)
S. a. rodolphei
  S Colombia
S. a. albigularis
  S Colombia, E Ecuador, E Peru
Synallaxis albescens (Pale-breasted Spinetail)
S. a. latitabunda
  SW Costa Rica
S. a. hypoleuca
  S Panama, NW Colombia
S. a. insignis
  C Colombia
S. a. occipitalis
  E Colombia, NW Venezuela
S. a. littoralis
  coast of N Colombia
S. a. perpallida
  NE Colombia, NW Venezuela
S. a. nesiotis
  N Colombia, N Venezuela, Margarita I
S. a. trinitatis
  E Venezuela, Trinidad
S. a. josephinae
  S Venezuela, Guyana, Surinam, N Brazil
S. a. inaequalis
  French Guiana
S. a. griseonota
  C Brazil
S. a. albescens
  E Brazil, Paraguay, NE Argentina
S. a. australis
  E Bolivia, W Paraguay, NW Argentina
Synallaxis spixi (Chicli Spinetail)
  S Brazil to N Argentina
Synallaxis hypospodia (Cinereous-breasted Spinetail)
  E Peru, N Bolivia, W Brazil
Synallaxis infuscata (Plain Spinetail)
  E Brazil

Synallaxis brachyura (Sooty Spinetail)   279
S. b. nigrofumosa
  E Honduras to Panama
S. b. chapmani
  SW Costa Rica to W Ecuador
S. b. caucae
  C Colombia
S. b. brachyura
  E Colombia
S. b. jaraguana
  N Brazil
Synallaxis courseni (Apurimac Spinetail)
  Apurimac, Peru
Synallaxis moesta (Dusky Spinetail)
S. m. moesta
  E Colombia
S. m. obscura
  SE Colombia
S. m. brunneicaudalis
  E Ecuador, NE Peru
S. m. yavii
  Venezuela
S. m. obscurior
  French Guiana
S. m. cabanisi
  Peru
S. m. fulviventris
  Bolivia
Synallaxis macconnelli (McConnell's Spinetail)
  Mt Roraima (Venezuela)
Synallaxis subpudica (Silvery-throated Spinetail)
  E Colombia, Ecuador
Synallaxis tithys (Blackish-headed Spinetail)
  SW Ecuador, NW Peru
Synallaxis cinerascens (Grey-bellied Spinetail)
  SE Brazil, Paraguay, NE Argentina
Synallaxis maranonica (Maranon Spinetail)
  N Peru
Synallaxis propinqua (White-bellied Spinetail)
  N & W Amazonia
Synallaxis hellmayri (Reiser's Spinetail)
  NE Brazil
Synallaxis gujanensis (Plain-crowned Spinetail)
S. g. colombiana
  E Colombia
S. g. gujanensis
  Venezuela, the Guianas, N Brazil
S. g. huallagae
  NE Peru
S. g. canipileus
  SE Peru

S. g. inornata
W Bolivia, W & C Brazil
S. g. certhiola
N Bolivia
S. g. simoni
C Brazil
Synallaxis albilora (Ochre-breasted Spinetail)
SE Brazil, N Paraguay
Synallaxis rutilans (Ruddy Spinetail)
S. r. caquetensis
SE Colombia, E Ecuador, NE Peru
S. r. confinis
NW Brazil
S. r. dissors
E Colombia to the Guianas, N Brazil
S. r. amazonica
E Peru, N Bolivia, W & C Brazil
S. r. rutilans
C & S Brazil
S. r. omissa
EC Brazil
S. r. tertia
NE Bolivia, SW Brazil
Synallaxis cherriei (Chestnut-throated Spinetail)
S. c. napoensis
E Ecuador, N Peru
S. c. cherriei
S Brazil
Synallaxis unirufa (Rufous Spinetail)
S. u. unirufa
N Colombia, E Ecuador
S. u. munotztebari
NE Colombia
S. u. meridana
E Colombia, W Venezuela
S. u. ochrogaster
Peru
Synallaxis castanea (Black-throated Spinetail)
N Venezuela
Synallaxis fuscorufa (Santa Marta Spinetail)
N Colombia
Synallaxis zimmeri (Russet-bellied Spinetail)
C Peru
Synallaxis erythrothorax (Rufous-breasted Spinetail)
S. e. furtiva
SE Mexico
S. e. erythrothorax
SE Mexico to NW Honduras
S. e. pacifica
S Mexico to El Salvador

Synallaxis cinnamomea (Stripe-breasted Spinetail)
S. c. carri
Trinidad
S. c. terrestris
Tobago I
S. c. cinnamomea
E Colombia, NW Venezuela
S. c. aveledoi
W Venezuela
S. c. bolivari
N Venezuela
S. c. striatipectus
NE Venezuela
S. c. pariae
Paria peninsula (Venezuela)
Synallaxis stictothorax (Necklaced Spinetail)
S. s. stictothorax
NW Ecuador, Puna Is
S. s. maculata
NW Peru
S. c. chinchipensis
N Peru
Synallaxis candei (White-whiskered Spinetail)
S. c. candei
N Colombia, W Venezuela
S. c. atrigularis
NC Colombia
S. c. venezuelensis
NE Colombia, NW Venezuela
Synallaxis kollari (Hoary-throated Spinetail)
N Brazil
Synallaxis scutatus (Ochre-cheeked Spinetail)
S. s. scutatus
E & C Brazil
S. s. whitei
E Bolivia, S Brazil, NW Argentina
Synallaxis gularis (Lafresnaye's White-browed Spinetail)
S. g. gularis
Colombia, N Ecuador, W Venezuela
S. g. brunneidorsalis
NE Colombia
S. g. cinereiventris
W Venezuela
S. g. rufiventris
C Peru
CERTHIAXIS
Certhiaxis erythrops (Red-faced Spinetail)
C. e. rufigenis
Costa Rica
C. e. griseigularis
W Colombia

C. e. erythrops
  W Ecuador
Certhiaxis demissa (Tepui Spinetail)
  S Venezuela
Certhiaxis antisiensis (Fraser's Spinetail)
  C. a. antisiensis
    S Ecuador
  C. a. palamblae
    N Peru
  C. a. furcata
    N Peru
Certhiaxis pallida (Pallid Spinetail)
  SE Brazil
Certhiaxis curtata (Ash-browed Spinetail)
  C. c. curtata
    E Colombia
  C. c. cisandina
    C Colombia, E Ecuador, N Peru
  C. c. debilis
    C Peru
Certhiaxis obsoleta (Olive Spinetail)
  SE Brazil, E Paraguay, N Argentina
Certhiaxis hellmayri (Streak-capped Spinetail)
  N Colombia
Certhiaxis subcristata (Crested Spinetail)
  C. s. fuscivertex
    NE Colombia
  C. s. subcristata
    E Colombia, N Venezuela
Certhiaxis pyrrhophia (Stripe-crowned Spinetail)
  C. p. rufipennis
    C Bolivia
  C. p. striaticeps
    E Bolivia
  C. p. pyrrhophia
    S Bolivia to Uruguay, N Argentina
Certhiaxis marcapatae (Marcapata Spinetail)
  Cuzco (SE Peru)
Certhiaxis albiceps (Light-crowned Spinetail)
  C. a. albiceps
    La Paz (Bolivia)
  C. a. discolor
    Cochabamba (Bolivia)
Certhiaxis semicinerea (Grey-headed Spinetail)
  C. s. semicinerea
    Ceara (Brazil), Baia (Brazil)
  C. s. goyana
    Goiaz, N Brazil
Certhiaxis albicapilla (Creamy-chested Spinetail)
  C. a. albicapilla
    C Peru

C. a. albigula
  SE Peru
Certhiaxis vulpina (Rusty-backed Spinetail)
  C. v. apurensis
    SW Venezuela
  C. v. alopecias
    E Colombia, W Venezuela, N Brazil
  C. v. vulpecula
    NE Peru, W Brazil, NE Bolivia
  C. v. vulpina
    W & C Brazil
  C. v. foxi
    W Bolivia
  C. v. reiseri
    NE Brazil
Certhiaxis muelleri (Scaled Spinetail)
  N Brazil
Certhiaxis gutturata (Speckled Spinetail)
  C. g. peruviana
    S Colombia to N Bolivia
  C. g. hyposticta
    S Venezuela to Surinam, N Brazil
  C. g. gutturata
    S Venezuela to French Guiana, N Brazil
Certhiaxis sulphurifera (Sulphur-throated Spinetail)
  E Argentina, Uruguay
Certhiaxis cinnamomea (Yellow-throated Spinetail)
  C. c. fuscifrons
    N Colombia
  C. c. marabina
    NW Venezuela
  C. c. valenciana
    Venezuela
  C. c. orenocensis
    Orinoco valley (Venezuela)
  C. c. cinnamomea
    Trinidad, NE Venezuela, the Guianas, NE Brazil
  C. c. pallida
    N Brazil
  C. c. cearensis
    E Brazil
  C. c. russeola
    W Bolivia, S Brazil, Paraguay, NW Argentina
Certhiaxis mustelina (Red and White Spinetail)
  NE Peru

THRIPOPHAGA
Thripophaga pyrrholeuca (Lesser Canastero)
  T. p. affinis
    S Bolivia, W Argentina
  T. p. pyrrholeuca
    Paraguay, NW Argentina

T. p. sordida
Chile, W Argentina

T. p. flavogularis
E & S Argentina

Thripophaga baeri (Short-billed Canastero)

T. b. chacoensis
NW Paraguay

T. b. baeri
S Brazil, NE & C Argentina

Thripophaga pudibunda (Canyon Canastero)

T. p. neglecta
W Peru

T. p. pudibunda
SC Peru

Thripophaga ottonis (Rusty-fronted Canastero)
SE Peru

Thripophaga heterura (Iquico Canastero)
Bolivia

Thripophaga modesta (Cordillera Canastero)

T. m. cactorum
Peru

T. m. lachayensis
central coast of Peru

T. m. monticola
W Peru

T. m. proxima
C & S Peru

T. m. modesta
S Peru to N Chile, W Argentina

T. m. rostrata
N Bolivia

T. m. australis
Chile, C Argentina

Thripophaga dorbignyi (Creamy-breasted Canastero)

T. d. huancavelicae
C Peru

T. d. usheri
SC Peru

T. d. arequipae
S Peru, N Chile, W Bolivia

T. d. consobrina
NW Bolivia

T. d. dorbignyi
E Bolivia, NW Argentina

Thripophaga berlepschi (Berlepsch's Canastero)
N Bolivia

Thripophaga steinbachi (Chestnut Canastero)
W Argentina

Thripophaga humicola (Dusky-tailed Canastero)

T. h. humicola
N & C Chile

T. h. polysticta
S Chile

Thripophaga patagonica (Patagonian Canastero)
S Argentina

Thripophaga humilis (Streak-throated Canastero)

T. h. cajamarcae
W Peru

T. h. humilis
C Peru

T. h. robusta
SE Peru, W Bolivia

Thripophaga anthoides (Austral Canastero)
S Chile, S Argentina

Thripophaga wyatti (Streak-backed Canastero)

T. w. wyatti
NC Colombia

T. w. sanctaemartae
N Colombia

T. w. mucuchiesi
NW Venezuela

T. w. perijanus
W Venezuela

T. w. aequatorialis
C Ecuador

T. w. azuay
S Ecuador

T. w. graminicola
Peru

T. w. cuchacanchae
Bolivia

T. w. lilloi
NW Argentina

Thripophaga punensis (Puna Canastero)
SE Peru, W Bolivia

Thripophaga sclateri (Cordoba Canastero)
C Argentina

Thripophaga urubambensis (Line-fronted Canastero)

T. u. huallagae
N Peru

T. u. urubambensis
SE Peru, N Bolivia

Thripophaga virgata (Junin Canastero)
C Peru

Thripophaga maculicauda (Scribble-tailed Canastero)
Peru, Bolivia, NW Argentina

Thripophaga flammulata (Many-striped Canastero)

T. f. multostriata
E Colombia

T. f. quindiana
C Colombia

T. f. flammulata
S Colombia, Ecuador

T. f. pallida
NE Peru
T. f. taczanowskii
NC Peru
Thripophaga cherriei (Orinoco Softtail)
Venezuela
Thripophaga macroura (Striated Softtail)
E Brazil
Thripophaga hudsoni (Hudson's Canastero)
Uruguay, NE Argentina
Thripophaga hypochondriacus (Great Spinetail)
N Peru

PHACELLODOMUS
Phacellodomus rufifrons (Rufous-fronted Thornbird)
P. r. inornatus
N Venezuela
P. r. peruvianus
N Peru
P. r. specularis
NE Brazil
P. r. rufifrons
E Brazil
P. r. fargoi
S Brazil, Paraguay
P. r. sincipitalis
Bolivia, W Argentina
Phacellodomus sibilatrix (Little Thornbird)
Paraguay, Argentina
Phacellodomus striaticeps (Streak-fronted Thornbird)
P. s. griseipectus
SE Peru
P. s. striaticeps
Bolivia, N Argentina
Phacellodomus erythrophthalmus (Red-eyed Thornbird)
P. e. erythrophthalmus
coast of E Brazil
P. e. ferrugineigula
SE Brazil
Phacellodomus striaticollis (Freckle-breasted Thornbird)
P. s. maculipectus
E Bolivia, NW Argentina
P. s. striaticollis
SE Brazil, Uruguay, E Argentina
Phacellodomus dorsalis (Chestnut-backed Thornbird)
N Peru
Phacellodomus ruber (Greater Thornbird)
Bolivia, C Brazil to Argentina
Phacellodomus fusciceps (Plain Softtail)
P. f. dimorpha
Ecuador, E Peru

P. f. obidensis
N Brazil
P. f. fusciceps
Bolivia
Phacellodomus berlepschi (Russet-mantled Softtail)
N Peru
Phacellodomus dendrocolaptoides (Canebrake Groundcreeper)
SE Brazil, Paraguay, NE Argentina

SPARTONOICA
Spartonoica maluroides (Bay-capped Wren Spinetail)
S Brazil, Uruguay, Argentina

PHLEOCRYPTES
Phleocryptes melanops (Wren-like Rushbird)
P. m. brunnescens
S Peru
P. m. juninensis
C Peru
P. m. schoenobaenus
S Peru, W Bolivia, NW Argentina
P. m. loaensis
N Chile
P. m. melanops
S Brazil to C Chile, C Argentina

LIMNORNIS
Limnornis curvirostris (Curve-billed Reedhaunter)
S Brazil, E Argentina
Limnornis rectirostris (Straight-billed Reedhaunter)
SE Uruguay, NE Argentina

ANUMBIUS
Anumbius annumbi (Firewood Gatherer)
SE Brazil to N Argentina

CORYPHISTERA
Coryphistera alaudina (Lark-like Brushrunner)
C. a. campicola
E Bolivia, W Paraguay
C. a. alaudina
S Bolivia, NW Argentina

EREMOBIUS
Eremobius phoenicurus (Band-tailed Earthcreeper)
W & S Argentina

SIPTORNIS
Siptornis striaticollis (Spectacled Prickletail)
Colombia, E Ecuador

METOPOTHRIX
Metopothrix aurantiacus (Orange-fronted Plushcrown)
W Amazonia

XENERPESTES
Xenerpestes minlosi (Double-banded Greytail)
X. m. minlosi
E Panama, Colombia
X. m. umbraticus
W Colombia
Xenerpestes singularis (Equatorial Greytail)
C Ecuador

PHILYDORINAE

MARGARORNIS
Margarornis adustus (Roraima Barbtail)
M. a. obscurodorsalis
SE Venezuela
M. a. duidae
Mt Duida (S Venezuela)
M. a. adustus
E Venezuela, W Guyana
Margarornis guttuligera (Rusty-winged Barbtail)
M. g. guttuligera
Colombia, Ecuador, Peru
M. g. venezuelana
NW Venezuela
Margarornis brunnescens (Spotted Barbtail)
M. b. brunneicauda
Costa Rica, W Panama
M. b. distinctus
C Panama
M. b. mnionophilus
Panama
M. b. albescens
E Panama
M. b. coloratus
N Colombia
M. b. brunnescens
Venezuela, Colombia, Ecuador, N Peru
M. b. stictonotus
SE Peru, W Bolivia
M. b. rostratus
N Venezuela
Margarornis tatei (White-throated Barbtail)
M. t. tatei
NE Venezuela
M. t. pariae
NE Venezuela
Margarornis rubiginosus (Ruddy Treerunner)
M. r. rubiginosus
Costa Rica, W Panama
M. r. boultoni
C Panama

Margarornis stellatus (Fulvous-dotted Tree Runner)
W Colombia, NW Ecuador
Margarornis bellulus (Beautiful Tree Runner)
E Panama
Margarornis squamiger (Pearled Tree Runner)
M. s. perlatus
Venezuela, Colombia, Ecuador, N Peru
M. s. peruvianus
C Peru
M. s. squamiger
SE Peru, W Bolivia

LOCHMIAS
Lochmias nematura (Sharp-tailed Streamcreeper)
L. n. nelsoni
E Panama
L. n. sororia
Venezuela, Colombia, E Ecuador, NE Peru
L. n. chimantae
SE Venezuela
L. n. castanonota
E Venezuela
L. n. obscurata
Peru, Bolivia
L. n. nematura
Brazil, Paraguay, Uruguay, NE Argentina

PSEUDOSEISURA
Pseudoseisura cristata (Rufous Cachalote)
P. c. cristata
E Brazil
P. c. unirufa
E Bolivia, S Brazil
Pseudoseisura lophotes (Brown Cachalote)
Paraguay, Uruguay, N Argentina
Pseudoseisura gutturalis (White-throated Cachalote)
W Argentina

PSEUDOCOLAPTES
Pseudocolaptes lawrencii (Buffy Tuftedcheek)
P. l. lawrencii
Costa Rica, W Panama
P. l. panamensis
C Panama
P. l. johnsoni
W Colombia, W Ecuador
Pseudocolaptes boissonneautii (Streaked Tuftedcheek)
P. b. striaticeps
N Venezuela
P. b. meridae
W Venezuela
P. b. boissonneautii
C Colombia, NW Ecuador

P. b. oberholseri
S Colombia
P. b. orientalis
S Ecuador
P. b. intermedius
NW Peru
P. b. pallidus
NW Peru
P. b. medianus
N Peru
P. b. auritus
C Peru
P. b. carabayae
SE Peru, W Bolivia

BERLEPSCHIA
Berlepschia rikeri (Point-tailed Palmcreeper)
S Venezuela, Guyana, N Brazil

PHILYDOR
Philydor strigilatus (Chestnut-winged Hookbill)
P. s. strigilatus
NW Amazonia
P. s. cognitus
NC Brazil
Philydor subulatus (Striped Woodhaunter)
P. s. nicaraguae
E Nicaragua
P. s. virgatus
Costa Rica, W Panama
P. s. assimilis
E Panama, W Colombia, W Ecuador
P. s. cordobae
NW Colombia
P. s. lemae
SE Venezuela
P. s. subulatus
N & W Amazonia
Philydor guttulatus (Guttulated Foliage-gleaner)
P. g. guttulatus
N Venezuela
P. g. pallidus
NE Venezuela
P. g. mirandae
C Brazil
Philydor subalaris (Striped-bellied Foliage-gleaner)
P. s. lineata
Costa Rica, W Panama
P. s. tacarcunae
E Panama
P. s. subalaris
W Colombia, W Ecuador
P. s. striolatus
N Colombia, W Venezuela

P. s. mentalis
E Ecuador
P. s. colligatus
NW Peru
P. s. ruficrissus
C Peru
Philydor rufosuperciliatus (Buff-browed Foliage-gleaner)
P. r. similis
N Peru
P. r. cabanisi
W Peru, W Bolivia
P. r. oleagineus
SE Bolivia, NW Argentina
P. r. rufosuperciliatus
SE Brazil
P. r. acritus
S Brazil, Paraguay, Uruguay, N Argentina
Philydor striaticollis (Montane Foliage-gleaner)
P. s. striaticollis
Colombia, Venezuela
P. s. anxius
N Colombia
P. s. perijanus
NW Venezuela
P. s. venezuelanus
N Venezuela
P. s. montanus
E Ecuador, C Peru
P. s. yungae
SE Peru, NW Bolivia
Philydor amaurotis (White-browed Foliage-gleaner)
SE Brazil
Philydor variegaticeps (Scaly-throated Foliage-gleaner)
P. v. variegaticeps
S Mexico to W Panama
P. v. temporalis
W Colombia, Ecuador
Philydor ruficaudatus (Rufous-tailed Foliage-gleaner)
P. e. ruficaudatus
N & W Amazonia
P. e. flavipectus
S Venezuela, N Brazil
Philydor erythrocercus (Rufous-rumped Foliage-gleaner)
P. e. fuscipennis
W Panama
P. e. subfulvus
SE Colombia, E Ecuador, N Peru
P. e. ochrogaster
C & SE Peru, Bolivia
P. e. lyra
E Peru, NE Bolivia, S Brazil

P. e. suboles
W Brazil
P. e. erythrocercus
Guyana, French Guiana, N Brazil
Philydor erythropterus (Chestnut-winged Foliage-gleaner)
P. e. erythropterus
W Amazonia
P. e. diluvialis
NC Brazil
Philydor lichtensteini (Lichtenstein's Foliage-gleaner)
SE Brazil, Paraguay, NE Argentina
Philydor erythronotus (Rufous-backed Foliage-gleaner)
E Panama to NW Ecuador
Philydor atricapillus (Black-capped Foliage-gleaner)
SE Brazil, E Paraguay, NE Argentina
Philydor rufus (Buff-fronted Foliage-gleaner)
P. r. panerythrus
Costa Rica to E Colombia
P. r. riveti
W Colombia, NW Ecuador
P. r. colombianus
N Venezuela
P. r. cuchiverus
Venezuela
P. r. bolivianus
E Peru, Bolivia
P. r. chapadensis
S Brazil
P. r. rufus
C & S Brazil, E Paraguay, NE Argentina
Philydor pyrrhodes (Cinnamon-rumped Foliage-gleaner)
N & C South America
Philydor dimidiatus (Russet-mantled Foliage-gleaner)
P. d. dimidiatus
SC Brazil
P. d. baeri
S & SE Brazil, N Paraguay
Philydor fuscus (White-collared Foliage-gleaner)
SE Brazil
Philydor ucayalae (Recurvebill)
P. u. ucayalae
Peru
P. u. striatus
N Bolivia

CICHLOCOLAPTES
Cichlocolaptes leucophrus (Pale-browed Treehunter)
SE Brazil

THRIPADECTES
Thripadectes ignobilis (Uniform Treehunter)
W Colombia, NW Ecuador
Thripadectes rufobrunneus (Streak-breasted Treehunter)
Costa Rica, W Panama
Thripadectes melanorhynchus (Black-billed Treehunter)
T. m. melanorhynchus
E Ecuador, E Peru
T. m. striaticeps
Colombia
Thripadectes holostictus (Striped Treehunter)
T. h. striatidorsus
SW Colombia, W Ecuador
T. h. holostictus
Colombia, E Ecuador, N Peru
T. h. moderatus
E Peru, N Bolivia
Thripadectes virgaticeps (Streak-capped Treehunter)
T. v. sclateri
W Colombia
T. v. magdelenae
N Colombia
T. v. virgaticeps
NW Ecuador
T. v. sumaco
E Ecuador
T. v. klagesi
N Venezuela
T. v. tachirensis
NW Venezuela
Thripadectes scrutator (Buff-throated Treehunter)
C Peru
Thripadectus flammulatus (Flammulated Treehunter)
T. f. flammulatus
Colombia, Ecuador
T. f. bricenoi
Venezuela

AUTOMOLUS
Automolus ruficollis (Rufous-necked Foliage-gleaner)
A. r. celicae
SW Ecuador
A. r. ruficollis
NW Peru
Automolus ochrolaemus (Buff-throated Foliage-gleaner)
A. o. cervinigularis
S Mexico to Nicaragua
A. o. amusos
SE Guatemala to Honduras

A. o. hypophaeus
E Nicaragua to NW Panama
A. o. exsertus
SW Costa Rica, W Panama
A. o. pallidigularis
E Panama, Colombia, NW Ecuador
A. o. turdinus
N & W Amazonia
A. o. ochrolaemus
E Peru, N Bolivia, W Brazil
A. o. auricularis
NE Bolivia, W Brazil
Automolus infuscatus (Olive-backed Foliage-gleaner)
A. i. infuscatus
SE Colombia, E Ecuador, E Peru
A. i. badius
S Venezuela, E Colombia, NW Brazil
A. i. cervicalis
E Venezuela, Guyana, Surinam, N Brazil
A. i. perusianus
W Brazil
A. i. paraensis
C Brazil
Automolus dorsalis (Crested Foliage-gleaner)
SE Colombia, E Ecuador, Peru
Automolus leucophthalmus (White-eyed Foliage-gleaner)
A. l. lammi
E Brazil
A. l. leucophthalmus
EC Brazil
A. l. sulphurascens
S Brazil, NE Paraguay, NE Argentina
Automolus melanopezus (Brown-rumped Foliage-gleaner)
SE Colombia, E Ecuador, W Brazil
Automolus albigularis (White-throated Foliage-gleaner)
A. a. paraquensis
S Venezuela
A. a. duidae
Mt Duida (S Venezuela)
A. a. albigularis
SE Venezuela
A. a. roraimae
Mt Roraima (SE Venezuela)
Automolus rubiginosus (Ruddy Foliage-gleaner)
A. r. guerrerensis
SW Mexico
A. r. rubiginosus
E Mexico
A. r. veraepacis
N Guatemala
A. r. umbrinus
S Mexico to N Nicaragua

A. r. fumosus
W Panama
A. r. saturatus
E Panama, NW Colombia
A. r. sasaimae
N Colombia
A. r. nigricauda
W Colombia, W Ecuador
A. r. rufipectus
N Colombia
A. r. cinnamomeigula
E Colombia
A. r. caquetae
SE Colombia
A. r. venezuelanus
S Venezuela
A. r. obscurus
French Guiana
A. r. brunnescens
E Ecuador, NE Peru
A. r. moderatus
N Peru
A. r. watkinsi
SE Peru, N Bolivia
Automolus rufipileatus (Chestnut-crowned Foliage-gleaner)
A. r. consobrinus
N & W Amazonia
A. r. rufipileatus
C Brazil
Automolus rectirostris (Chestnut-capped Foliage-gleaner)
C Brazil
Automolus erythrocephalus (Henna-hooded Foliage-gleaner)
A. e. erythrocephalus
SW Ecuador, N Peru
A. e. palamblae
W Peru

SCLERURUS
Sclerurus mexicanus (Tawny-throated Leafscraper)
S. m. mexicanus
SE Mexico to Honduras
S. m. pullus
Costa Rica to W Panama
S. m. andinus
E Panama, Colombia, to Guyana
S. m. obscurior
W Colombia, W Ecuador
S. m. peruvianus
W Amazonia
S. m. macconnelli
N Brazil, Guyana, French Guiana
S. m. bahiae
E Brazil

Sclerurus rufigularis (Short-billed
Leafscraper)
  S. r. fulvigularis
    E & S Venezuela to French Guiana,
    N Brazil
  S. r. brunnescens
    N Brazil
  S. r. furfurosus
    C Brazil
  S. r. rufigularis
    N Bolivia, SW Brazil
Sclerurus albigularis (Grey-throated
Leafscraper)
  S. a. canigularis
    Costa Rica, W Panama
  S. a. propinquus
    N Colombia
  S. a. albigularis
    E Colombia, Venezuela, Trinidad, Tobago I
  S. a. kunanensis
    Venezuela
  S. a. zamorae
    SE Ecuador, N Peru
  S. a. albicollis
    N Bolivia
Sclerurus caudacutus (Black-tailed
Leafscraper)
  S. c. caudacutus
    Guyana, French Guiana
  S. c. insignis
    S Venezuela, N Brazil
  S. c. brunneus
    W Amazonia
  S. c. olivascens
    Peru, Bolivia
  S. c. pallidus
    N Brazil
  S. c. umbretta
    coast of E Brazil
Sclerurus scansor (Rufous-breasted
Leafscraper)
  S. s. cearensis
    NE Brazil
  S. s. scansor
    C & E Brazil, Paraguay, NE Argentina
Sclerurus guatemalensis (Guatemala
Leafscraper)
  S. g. guatemalensis
    S Mexico to Panama
  S. g. salvini
    W Colombia, W Ecuador
  S. g. ennosiphyllus
    C Colombia

XENOPS

Xenops contaminatus (Sharp-billed
Treehunter)
  SE Brazil, Paraguay, NE Argentina

Xenops milleri (Rufous-tailed Xenops)
  N Amazonia
Xenops tenuirostris (Slender-billed
Xenops)
  X. t. acutirostris
    SE Colombia, S Venezuela, E Ecuador,
    NE Peru
  X. t. hellmayri
    French Guiana, Surinam
  X. t. tenuirostris
    S Venezuela, E Peru, N Bolivia,
    N & W Brazil
Xenops minutus (Plain Xenops)
  X. m. mexicanus
    S Mexico to Honduras
  X. m. ridgwayi
    Nicaragua to W Panama
  X. m. littoralis
    E Panama to W Ecuador
  X. m. neglectus
    N Colombia, N Venezuela
  X. m. remoratus
    E Colombia, Venezuela, N Brazil
  X. m. ruficaudus
    E Colombia, Venezuela, the Guianas,
    N Brazil
  X. m. olivaceus
    NE Colombia
  X. m. obsoletus
    E Ecuador, E Peru, N Bolivia, W Brazil
  X. m. genibarbis
    N Brazil
  X. m. minutus
    E & SE Brazil, E Paraguay
Xenops rutilans (Streaked Xenops)
  X. r. septentrionalis
    Costa Rica, W Panama
  X. r. heterurus
    E Panama to NE Ecuador, Venezuela
  X. r. incomptus
    Darien (Panama)
  X. r. perijanus
    NE Colombia
  X. r. phelpsi
    N Colombia
  X. r. guayae
    W Ecuador, NW Peru
  X. r. peruvianus
    E Ecuador, E Peru
  X. r. purusianus
    C Brazil
  X. r. connectens
    E Bolivia, NW Argentina
  X. r. chapadensis
    SW Brazil, N Bolivia
  X. r. rutilans
    SE Brazil, Paraguay, NE Argentina

MEGAXENOPS
Megaxenops parnaguae (Reiser's Recurvebill)
NE Brazil

PYGARRHICHAS
Pygarrhichas albogularis (White-throated Treerunner)
S Chile, SW Argentina, Tierra del Fuego

103 FORMICARIIDAE (ANTBIRDS)

CYMBILAIMUS
Cymbilaimus lineatus (Fasciated Antshrike)
C. l. fasciatus
Nicaragua to NW Ecuador
C. l. intermedius
Upper Amazonia
C. l. lineatus
SE Venezuela, the Guianas, NE Brazil
C. l. sanctaemariae
NE Bolivia

HYPOEDALEUS
Hypoedaleus guttatus (Spot-backed Antshrike)
H. g. leucogaster
E Brazil
H. g. guttatus
S Brazil, Paraguay, NE Argentina

BATARA
Batara cinerea (Giant Antshrike)
B. c. excubitor
E Bolivia
B. c. argentina
S Bolivia, NW Argentina
B. c. cinerea
SE Brazil, NE Argentina

MACKENZIAENA
Mackenziaena leachii (Large-tailed Antshrike)
SE Brazil, NE Argentina
Mackenziaena severa (Tufted Antshrike)
SE Brazil, NE Argentina

FREDERICKENA
Frederickena viridis (Black-throated Antshrike)
E Venezuela, Guyana
Frederickena unduligera (Undulated Antshrike)
F. u. fulva
SE Colombia, E Ecuador
F. u. diversa
E & SE Peru
F. u. unduligera
NW Brazil
F. u. pallida
Brazil

TARABA
Taraba major (Great Antshrike)
T. m. melanocrissa
SE Mexico to W Panama
T. m. obscura
SW Costa Rica to NW Colombia
T. m. transandeana
SW Colombia, W Ecuador, NW Peru
T. m. granadensis
E Colombia, Venezuela
T. m. semifasciata
E Colombia to the Guianas, N & E Brazil
T. m. duidae
SE Venezuela
T. m. melanura
Upper Amazonia
T. m. borbae
C Brazil
T. m. stagura
E & NE Brazil
T. m. major
E Bolivia, S Brazil, Paraguay, N Argentina

SAKESPHORUS
Sakesphorus canadensis (Black-crested Antshrike)
S. c. pulchellus
N Colombia, W Venezuela
S. c. paraguanae
NE Colombia, NW Venezuela
S. c. intermedius
S Venezuela, N Brazil
S. c. fumosus
S Venezuela
S. c. trinitatis
NE Venezuela, Guyana, Trinidad
S. c. canadensis
Surinam, French Guiana
S. c. loretoyacuensis
SE Colombia, NW Brazil
Sakesphorus cristatus (Silvery-cheeked Antshrike)
E Brazil
Sakesphorus bernardi (White-naped Antshrike)
S. b. bernardi
W Ecuador
S. b. piurae
SW Ecuador, N Peru
S. b. cajamarcae
W Peru
S. b. shumbae
N Peru
Sakesphorus melanonotus (Black-backed Antshrike)
NE Colombia, W Venezuela
Sakesphorus melanothorax (Black-throated Antshrike)
French Guiana

Sakesphorus luctuosus (Glossy Antshrike)
S. l. luctuosus
NE Brazil
S. l. araguayae
C Brazil

BIATAS
Biatas nigropectus (White-bearded Antshrike)
SE Brazil

THAMNOPHILUS
Thamnophilus doliatus (Barred Antshrike)
T. d. intermedius
E Mexico to E Costa Rica
T. d. yucatanensis
S Mexico, N Guatemala
T. d. pacificus
W Honduras to W Costa Rica
T. d. nigricristatus
E Panama, N Colombia
T. d. albicans
N Colombia
T. d. zarumae
SW Ecuador, NW Peru
T. d. palamblae
NW Peru
T. d. nigrescens
NE Colombia, NW Venezuela
T. d. tobagensis
Tobago I
T. d. nesiotes
Isla del Rey
T. d. fraterculus
E Colombia, N Venezuela, Trinidad
T. d. doliatus
E Venezuela, the Guianas, N Brazil
T. d. subradiatus
E Peru, W Brazil
T. d. signatus
NE Bolivia, SW Brazil
T. d. difficilis
E Brazil
T. d. capistratus
E Brazil
T. d. radiatus
E Bolivia, S Brazil, N Argentina
T. d. cadwaladeri
S Bolivia
Thamnophilus multistriatus (Bar-crested Antshrike)
T. m. brachyurus
W Colombia
T. m. selvae
W Colombia
T. m. multistriatus
C Colombia
T. m. oecotonophilus
NE Colombia

Thamnophilus palliatus (Lined Antshrike)
T. p. tenuepunctatus
E Colombia
T. p. tenuifasciatus
SE Colombia, E Ecuador
T. p. berlepschi
SE Ecuador, N Peru
T. p. similis
C Peru
T. p. puncticeps
SE Peru, Bolivia, W Brazil
T. p. palliatus
C & E Brazil
Thamnophilus bridgesi (Black-hooded Antshrike)
SW Costa Rica, W Panama
Thamnophilus nigriceps (Black Antshrike)
T. n. nigriceps
E Panama, NW Colombia
T. n. magdalenae
N Colombia
Thamnophilus praecox (Cocha Antshrike)
S Ecuador
Thamnophilus nigrocinereus (Blackish-grey Antshrike)
T. n. cinereoniger
Colombia, Venezuela, NW Brazil
T. n. kulczynskii
French Guiana
T. n. nigrocinereus
NE Brazil
T. n. tschudii
W Brazil
T. n. huberi
N Brazil
Thamnophilus cryptoleucus (Castelnau's Antshrike)
NE Peru, W Brazil
Thamnophilus aethiops (White-shouldered Antshrike)
T. a. aethiops
E Ecuador, NE Peru
T. a. wetmorei
SE Colombia
T. a. polionotus
S & E Venezuela, NW Brazil
T. a. kapouni
E & SE Peru, N Bolivia, W Brazil
T. a. juruanus
W Brazil
T. a. injunctus
NE Brazil
T. a. punctuliger
C Brazil
T. a. atriceps
C Brazil
T. a. incertus
NE Brazil

Thamnophilus unicolor (Uniform
Antshrike)
T. u. unicolor
W Ecuador
T. u. grandior
Colombia, E Ecuador, N Peru
T. u. caudatus
N Peru
Thamnophilus schistaceus (Black-capped
Antshrike)
T. s. capitalis
Upper Amazonia
T. s. dubius
S Ecuador, N Peru
T. s. schistaceus
SE Peru, N Bolivia, W Brazil
T. s. heterogynus
W Brazil
T. s. inornatus
C Brazil
Thamnophilus murinus (Mouse-coloured
Antshrike)
T. m. murinus
E Ecuador, E Colombia to Surinam
T. m. cayennensis
French Guiana, N Brazil
T. m. canipennis
NE Peru, W Brazil
Thamnophilus aroyae (Upland Antshrike)
SE Peru, NW Bolivia
Thamnophilus punctatus (Slaty Antshrike)
T. p. atrinucha
Honduras to Ecuador & Venezuela
T. p. gorgonae
Gorgona I
T. p. subcinereus
N Colombia, NW Venezuela
T. p. interpositus
E Colombia
T. p. punctatus
E Venezuela, the Guianas, N Brazil
T. p. leucogaster
N Peru
T. p. saturatus
C Brazil
T. p. zimmeri
C Brazil
T. p. stictocephalus
C Brazil
T. p. sticturus
Bolivia, S Brazil
T. p. pelzelni
C & E Brazil
T. p. ambiguus
coastal SE Brazil

Thamnophilus amazonicus (Amazonian   291
Antshrike)
T. a. cinereiceps
Venezuela, Colombia
T. a. huallagae
Peru
T. a. amazonicus
S Colombia to N Bolivia
T. a. obscurus
C Brazil
T. a. paraensis
E Venezuela, the Guianas, N Brazil
Thamnophilus insignis (Streak-backed
Antshrike)
T. i. insignis
S Venezuela
T. i. nigrofrontalis
S Venezuela
Thamnophilus caerulescens (Variable
Antshrike)
T. c. subandinus
N Peru
T. c. melanochrous
C & S Peru
T. c. aspersiventer
N Bolivia
T. c. connectens
E Bolivia
T. c. dinellii
C & S Bolivia, NW Argentina
T. c. paraguayensis
S Brazil, N Paraguay
T. c. gilvigaster
SE Brazil, NE Argentina
T. c. caerulescens
S Brazil, E Paraguay, NE Argentina
T. c. albonotatus
EC Brazil
T. c. ochraceiventer
SC Brazil
T. c. pernambucensis
E Brazil
T. c. cearensis
E Brazil
Thamnophilus torquatus (Rufous-winged
Antshrike)
Brazil
Thamnophilus ruficapillus (Rufous-capped
Antshrike)
T. r. jaczewskii
N Peru
T. r. marcapatae
SE Peru
T. r. subfasciatus
W Bolivia
T. r. cochabambae
W Bolivia, NW Argentina

T. r. ruficapillus
S & E Brazil, NE Argentina

PYGIPTILA
Pygiptila stellaris (Spot-winged Antshrike)
P. s. maculipennis
SE Colombia to NE Peru
P. s. occipitalis
S Colombia to the Guianas, N Brazil
P. s. purusiana
W Brazil
P. s. stellaris
C Brazil

MEGASTICTUS
Megastictus margaritatus (Pearly Antshrike)
N Upper Amazonia

NEOCTANTES
Neoctantes niger (Black Bushbird)
E Ecuador, N Peru, W Brazil

CLYTOCTANTES
Clytoctantes alixii (Recurvebill Bushbird)
Colombia

XENORNIS
Xenornis setifrons (Speckle-breasted Antshrike)
E Panama, NW Colombia

THAMNISTES
Thamnistes anabatinus (Russet Antshrike)
T. a. anabatinus
SE Mexico to Honduras
T. a. saturatus
Nicaragua to W Panama
T. a. coronatus
C & E Panama
T. a. intermedius
W Colombia, W Ecuador
T. a. gularis
C Colombia
T. a. aequatorialis
SE Colombia, E Ecuador
T. a. rufescens
C & SE Peru, N Bolivia

DYSITHAMNUS
Dysithamnus stictothorax (Spot-breasted Antvireo)
SE Brazil
Dysithamnus mentalis (Plain Antvireo)
D. m. septentrionalis
S Mexico to W Panama
D. m. suffusus
E Panama, NW Colombia
D. m. extremus
C Colombia
D. m. semicinereus
NE Colombia

D. m. viridis
NE Colombia, NW Venezuela
D. m. cumbreanus
N Venezuela
D. m. andrei
E Venezuela, Trinidad
D. m. oberi
Tobago
D. m. ptaritepui
S Venezuela
D. m. spodionotus
S & E Venezuela
D. m. aequatorialis
W Ecuador, NW Peru
D. m. napensis
E Ecuador
D. m. tambillanus
N Peru
D. m. olivaceus
C Peru
D. m. tavarae
SE Peru, Bolivia
D. m. emiliae
E Brazil
D. m. affinis
C Brazil
D. m. mentalis
S & SE Brazil, E Paraguay, NE Argentina
Dysithamnus striaticeps (Streak-crowned Antvireo)
E Nicaragua, E Costa Rica
Dysithamnus puncticeps (Spot-crowned Antvireo)
D. p. puncticeps
E Costa Rica, Panama, N Colombia
D. p. intensus
S Panama, W Colombia
D. p. flemmingi
SW Colombia, W Ecuador
Dysithamnus xanthopterus (Rufous-backed Antvireo)
SE Brazil
Dysithamnus ardesiacus (Grey-throated Antvireo)
D. a. ardesiacus
SE Colombia, E Ecuador, N & C Peru
D. a. obidensis
S Venezuela, the Guinas, N Brazil

THAMNOMANES
Thamnomanes saturninus (Saturnine Antshrike)
T. s. huallagae
E Peru, W Brazil
T. s. saturninus
WC Brazil

Thamnomanes occidentalis (Chapman's Antshrike)
T. o. occidentalis
S Colombia
T. o. punctitectus
S Ecuador
Thamnomanes plumbeus (Plumbeous Antshrike)
T. p. tucuyensis
NW Venezuela
T. p. leucostictus
E Colombia, E Ecuador
T. p. plumbeus
SE Brazil
Thamnomanes caesius (Cinereous Antshrike)
T. c. glaucus
N & W Amazonia
T. c. intermedius
C Peru
T. c. persimilis
C Brazil
T. c. hoffmannsi
SC Brazil
T.-c. caesius
E Brazil
Thamnomanes schistogynus (Bluish-slate Antshrike)
SE Peru, W Brazil

MYRMOTHERULA
Myrmotherula brachyura (Pygmy Antwren)
M. b. ignota
C & E Panama, NW Colombia
M. b. brachyura
N & W Amazonia
Myrmotherula obscura (Short-billed Antwren)
SE Colombia, NE Peru, W Brazil
Myrmotherula sclateri (Sclater's Antwren)
C Brazil
Myrmotherula klagesi (Klages' Antwren)
NE Brazil
Myrmotherula surinamensis (Streaked Antwren)
M. s. pacifica
E Panama to E Ecuador
M. s. surinamensis
S Venezuela, the Guianas, N Brazil
M. s. multostriata
W Amazonia
Myrmotherula ambigua (Yellow-throated Antwren)
E Colombia, S Venezuela, NW Brazil
Myrmotherula cherriei (Cherrie's Antwren)
E Colombia, W Venezuela, N Brazil

Myrmotherula guttata (Rufous-bellied Antwren)
N Amazonia
Myrmotherula longicuada (Stripe-chested Antwren)
M. l. söderströmi
E Ecuador
M. l. pseudoaustralis
E Ecuador, N Peru
M. l. longicauda
E Peru
M. l. australis
SE Peru, N Bolivia
Myrmotherula hauxwelli (Plain-throated Antwren)
M. h. suffusa
SE Colombia, E Ecuador, NE Peru
M. h. hauxwelli
E Peru, W Brazil
M. h. clarior
C Brazil
M. h. hellmayri
NE Brazil
Myrmotherula gularis (Star-throated Antwren)
SE Brazil
Myrmotherula gutturalis (Brown-bellied Antwren)
the Guianas, Venezuela, N Brazil
Myrmotherula fulviventris (Checker-throated Antwren)
M. f. costaricensis
S Honduras to W Panama
M. f. fulviventris
E Panama to W Ecuador
M. f. salmoni
C Colombia
Myrmotherula leucophthalma (White-eyed Antwren)
M. l. dissita
SE Peru, N Bolivia
M. l. leucophthalma
WC Brazil
M. l. phaeonota
NC Brazil
M. l. sordida
NE Brazil
Myrmotherula haematonota (Stipple-throated Antwren)
M. h. pyrrhonota
SE Colombia, S Venezuela, NW Brazil
M. h. spodionota
E Ecuador
M. h. haematonota
NE Peru
M. h. sororia
N & C Peru

M. h. amazonica
W Brazil

Myrmotherula ornata (Ornate Antwren)
M. o. ornata
E Colombia
M. o. saturata
SE Colombia, E Ecuador, NE Peru
M. o. atrogularis
N & C Peru
M. o. meridionalis
SE Peru, N Bolivia
M. o. hoffmannsi
C Brazil

Myrmotherula erythrura (Rufous-tailed Antwren)
M. e. erythrura
NW Amazonia
M. e. septentrionalis
E Peru, W Brazil

Myrmotherula erythronotos (Black-hooded Antwren)
SE Brazil

Myrmotherula axillaris (White-flanked Antwren)
M. a. albigula
Central America, W Colombia, Ecuador
M. a. melaena
NW Amazonia
M. a. heterozyga
E Peru, W Brazil
M. a. axillaris
Trinidad, Venezuela, the Guianas, N Brazil
M. a. fresnayana
SE Peru, Bolivia
M. a. luctuosa
E Brazil

Myrmotherula schisticolor (Slaty Antwren)
M. s. schisticolor
Mexico to W Ecuador
M. s. sanctaemartae
N Colombia, N Venezuela
M. s. interior
E Colombia, E Ecuador, N Peru

Myrmotherula sunensis (Rio Suno Antwren)
M. s. sunensis
E Ecuador, NE Peru
M. s. yessupi
W Peru

Myrmotherula longipennis (Long-winged Antwren)
M. l. longipennis
N & W Amazonia
M. l. zimmeri
E Ecuador, NE Peru
M. l. garbei
NE Peru, W Brazil

M. l. transitiva
WC Brazil
M. l. ochrogyna
C Brazil
M. l. paraensis
EC Brazil

Myrmotherula minor (Salvadori's Antwren)
NE Peru, W Brazil

Myrmotherula iheringi (Ihering's Antwren)
M. i. heteroptera
SC Brazil
M. i. iheringi
C Brazil

Myrmotherula grisea (Ashy Antwren)
W Bolivia

Myrmotherula unicolor (Unicoloured Antwren)
SE Brazil

Myrmotherula behni (Plain-winged Antwren)
M. b. behni
E Colombia
M. b. yavii
S Venezuela
M. b. inornata
SE Venezuela, Guyana
M. b. camanii
S Venezuela

Myrmotherula urosticta (Band-tailed Antwren)
SE Brazil

Myrmotherula menetriesii (Menetries' Antwren)
M. m. pallida
NW & W Amazonia
M. m. cinereiventris
E Venezuela, the Guianas, N Brazil
M. m. menetriesii
E Peru, N Bolivia, W Brazil
M. m. berlepschi
WC Brazil
M. m. omissa
NE Brazil

Myrmotherula assimilis (White-backed Antwren)
NE Peru, W Brazil

DICHROZONA
Dichrozona cincta (Banded Antcatcher)
D. c. cincta
E Colombia, S Venezuela, NW Brazil
D. c. stellata
E Ecuador, W Brazil
D. c. zononota
C Brazil, N Bolivia

MYRMORCHILUS
Myrmorchilus strigilatus (Stripe-backed Antbird)
M. s. strigilatus
E Brazil
M. s. suspicax
S Bolivia, S Brazil, W Paraguay, N Argentina

HERPSILOCHMUS
Herpsilochmus pileatus (Black-capped Antwren)
H. p. pileatus
E Brazil
H. p. atricapillus
C & S Brazil, Bolivia, Paraguay, N Argentina
H. p. motacilloides
C Peru
Herpsilochmus sticturus (Spot-tailed Antwren)
H. s. dugandi
Colombia
H. s. sticturus
S Venezuela, the Guianas, N Brazil
Herpsilochmus stictocephalus (Todd's Antwren)
E Venezuela, the Guianas
Herpsilochmus dorsimaculatus (Spot-backed Antwren)
S Venezuela, NW Brazil
Herpsilochmus roraimae (Roraiman Antwren)
SE Venezuela, SW Guyana
Herpsilochmus pectoralis (Pectoral Antwren)
E Brazil
Herpsilochmus longirostris (Large-billed Antwren)
SC Brazil
Herpsilochmus axillaris (Yellow-breasted Antwren)
H. a. senex
SW Colombia
H. a. aequatorialis
E Ecuador
H. a. puncticeps
N Peru
H. a. axillaris
S Peru
Herpsilochmus rufimarginatus (Rufous-winged Antwren)
H. r. exiguus
E Panama
H. r. frater
N & W Amazonia
H. r. scapularis
E Brazil

H. r. rufimarginatus
SE Brazil, E Paraguay, NE Argentina

MICRORHOPIAS
Microrhopias quixensis (Dot-winged Antwren)
M. q. boucardi
S Mexico to SW Honduras
M. q. virgata
Nicaragua to W Panama
M. q. consobrina
E Panama to W Ecuador
M. q. quixensis
E Ecuador, NE Peru
M. q. intercedens
N Peru
M. q. nigriventris
C Peru
M. q. albicauda
SE Peru
M. q. microsticta
French Guiana
M. q. bicolor
N Bolivia, C Brazil
M. q. emiliae
C Brazil

FORMICIVORA
Formicivora iheringi (Narrow-billed Antwren)
E Brazil
Formicivora grisea (White-fringed Antwren)
F. g. alticincta
Pearl Is (Panama)
F. g. hondae
N Colombia
F. g. fumosa
E Colombia, W Venezuela
F. g. intermedia
NE Colombia, NW Venezuela, Margarita I
F. g. tobagensis
Tobago I
F. g. orenocensis
S Venezuela
F. g. rufiventris
E Colombia, S Venezuela
F. g. grisea
the Guianas, NE Brazil
F. g. deluzae
SE Brazil
Formicivora serrana (Serra Antwren)
SE Brazil
Formicivora melanogaster (Black-bellied Antwren)
F. m. melanogaster
E Bolivia, W & C Brazil
F. m. bahiae
E Brazil

Formicivora rufa (Rusty-backed Antwren)
  F. r. urubambae
    E Peru
  F. r. chapmani
    E Brazil
  F. r. rufa
    E Bolivia, E Paraguay, C & S Brazil

DRYMOPHILA
Drymophila ferruginea (Ferruginous Antbird)
    SE Brazil to NE Argentina
Drymophila genei (Rufous-tailed Antbird)
    SE Brazil
Drymophila ochropyga (Ochre-rumped Antbird)
    SE Brazil
Drymophila devillei (Striated Antbird)
  D. d. devillei
    E Ecuador, E Peru, N Bolivia
  D. d. subochracea
    C Brazil
Drymophila caudata (Long-tailed Antbird)
  D. c. hellmayri
    NE Colombia
  D. c. klagesi
    N Venezuela
  D. c. caudata
    Colombia to N Bolivia
Drymophila malura (Dusky-tailed Antbird)
    SE Brazil, N Argentina
Drymophila squamata (Scaled Antbird)
    C & SE Brazil

TERENURA
Terenura maculata (Streak-capped Antwren)
    SE Brazil, NE Argentina
Terenura callinota (Rufous-rumped Antwren)
  T. c. callinota
    Panama to N Peru
  T. c. peruviana
    C Peru
  T. c. guianensis
    Guyana
Terenura humeralis (Chestnut-shouldered Antwren)
  T. h. humeralis
    E Ecuador, NE Peru, W Brazil
  T. h. transfluvialis
    C Brazil
Terenura sharpei (Yellow-rumped Antwren)
    SE Peru
Terenura spodioptila (Ash-winged Antwren)
  T. s. signata
    SE Colombia, NW Brazil

T. s. spodioptila
    S Venezuela, Guyana, NW Brazil
T. s. elaopteryx
    French Guiana, NE Brazil
T. s. meridionalis
    C Brazil

CERCOMACRA
Cercomacra cinerascens (Grey Antbird)
  C. c. cinerascens
    Upper Amazonia
  C. c. immaculata
    E Venezuela, the Guianas, N Brazil
  C. c. sclateri
    SW Amazonia
  C. c. iterata
    C Brazil
Cercomacra brasiliana (Rio de Janeiro Antbird)
    SE Brazil
Cercomacra tyrannina (Dusky Antbird)
  C. t. crepera
    S Mexico to W Panama
  C. t. rufiventris
    E Panama to W Ecuador
  C. t. tyrannina
    E Colombia, S Venezuela, NW Brazil
  C. t. vicina
    NE Colombia, W Venezuela
  C. t. saturatior
    E Venezuela, Guyana, Surinam
  C. t. laeta
    N & C Brazil
  C. t. sabinoi
    NE Brazil
Cercomacra nigrescens (Blackish Antbird)
  C. n. nigrescens
    Surinam, French Guiana
  C. n. aequatorialis
    E Ecuador, N Peru
  C. n. notata
    C Peru
  C. n. fuscicauda
    E Peru, W Brazil, N Bolivia
  C. n. approximans
    C Brazil
  C. n. ochrogyna
    C Brazil
Cercomacra serva (Black Antbird)
  C. s. serva
    E Ecuador, NE Peru
  C. s. hypomelaena
    E & SE Peru, N Bolivia, W Brazil
Cercomacra nigricans (Jet Antbird)
  C. n. nigricans
    E Panama to N Brazil
  C. n. atrata
    NW Colombia

Cercomacra carbonaria (Rio Branco
  Antbird)
    Rio Branco, Brazil
Cercomacra melanaria (Matto Grosso
  Antbird)
    N Bolivia, C & S Brazil
Cercomacra ferdinandi (Bananal Antbird)
    SE Brazil

SIPIA
Sipia berlepschi (Stub-tailed Antbird)
    W Colombia, NW Ecuador
Sipia rosenbergi (Esmeralda's Antbird)
    W Colombia, NW Ecuador

PYRIGLENA
**Pyriglena leuconota (White-backed Fire-
eye)**
    P. l. pacifica
      W Ecuador
    P. l. castanoptera
      E Ecuador, N Peru
    P. l. picea
      N & C Peru
    P. l. similis
      C Brazil
    P. l. marcapatensis
      SE Peru
    P. l. hellmayri
      W Bolivia
    P. l. maura
      SE Bolivia, SE Brazil
    P. l. interposita
      EC Brazil
    P. l. leuconota
      S Brazil
    P. l. pernambucensis
      E Brazil
Pyriglena atra (Swainson's Fire-eye)
    E Brazil
**Pyriglena leuconotera (White-shouldered
Fire-eye)**
    E Paraguay, SE Brazil

RHOPORNIS
Rhopornis ardesiaca (Slender Antbird)
    SE Brazil

MYRMOBORUS
**Myrmoborus leucophrys (White-browed
Antcreeper)**
    M. l. erythrophrys
      E Colombia
    M. l. leucophrys
      N & W Amazonia
    M. l. griseigula
      C Brazil, N Bolivia
    M. l. angustirostris
      N Amazonia

Myrmoborus lugubris (Ash-breasted
  Antcreeper)
    M. l. berlepschi
      NE Peru, W Brazil
    M. l. stictopterus
      C Brazil
    M. l. femininus
      C Brazil
    M. l. lugubris
      C Brazil
Myrmoborus myotherinus (Black-faced
  Antcreeper)
    M. m. elegans
      E Colombia, S Venezuela, NW Brazil
    M. m. napensis
      E Ecuador, NE Peru
    M. m. myotherinus
      S Peru, NE Bolivia, S & W Brazil
    M. m. incanus
      WC Brazil
    M. m. ardesiacus
      W Brazil
    M. m. proximus
      W Brazil
    M. m. ochrolaema
      C Brazil
    M. m. sororius
      C & S Brazil
Myrmoborus melanurus (Black-tailed
  Antcreeper)
    NE Peru

HYPOCNEMIS
Hypocnemis cantator (Warbling Antbird)
    H. c. flavescens
      S Venezuela, E Colombia, NW Brazil
    H. c. notaea
      SE Venezuela, Guyana, N Brazil
    H. c. cantator
      Surinam, French Guiana, N Brazil
    H. c. saturata
      SE Colombia, E Ecuador, NE Peru
    H. c. peruviana
      E Peru, W Brazil
    H. c. implicata
      C Brazil
    H. c. striata
      EC Brazil
    H. c. affinis
      EC Brazil
    H. c. subflava
      C Peru
    H. c. collinsi
      SE Peru, N Bolivia
    H. c. ochrogyna
      NE Bolivia, S Brazil

Hypocnemis hypoxantha (Yellow-browed Antbird)
H. h. hypoxantha
SE Colombia, E Ecuador, NE Peru
H. h. ochraceiventris
E Brazil
HYPOCNEMOIDES
Hypocnemoides melanopogon (Black-chinned Antcreeper)
H. m. occidentalis
E & S Colombia, Venezuela, NW Brazil
H. m. melanopogon
the Guianas, N Brazil
H. m. minor
C Brazil
Hypocnemoides maculicauda (Band-tailed Antcreeper)
H. m. maculicauda
Peru, N Bolivia, N Paraguay, W & S Brazil
H. m. orientalis
C & SE Brazil
MYRMOCHANES
Myrmochanes hemileucus (Black & White Antcatcher)
Peru, N Bolivia, W Brazil
GYMNOCICHLA
Gymnocichla nudiceps (Bare-crowned Antcatcher)
G. n. chiroleuca
E Guatemala to Costa Rica
G. n. erratilis
SW Costa Rica, W Panama
G. n. nudiceps
E Panama, NW Colombia
G. n. sanctaemartae
N Colombia
SCLATERIA
Sclateria naevia (Silvered Antcatcher)
S. n. naevia
NE Venezuela, the Guianas, N Brazil, Trinidad
S. n. diaphora
Venezuela
S. n. argentata
Upper Amazonia
S. n. toddi
C Brazil
PERCNOSTOLA
Percnostola rufifrons (Black-headed Antbird)
P. r. rufifrons
the Guianas, NE Brazil
P. r. subcristata
N Brazil
P. r. minor
NW Amazonia

Percnostola macrolopha (White-lined Antbird)
Peru
Percnostola schistacea (Slate-coloured Antbird)
SE Colombia, NE Peru, W Brazil
Percnostola leucostigma (Spot-winged Antbird)
P. l. subplumbea
E Colombia, E Ecuador, NE Peru
P. l. obscura
C Venezuela
P. l. saturata
SE Venezuela
P. l. leucostigma
S Venezuela, the Guianas, N Brazil
P. l. intensa
C Peru
P. l. brunneiceps
SE Peru
P. l. infuscata
S Venezuela, N & W Brazil
P. l. humaythae
C Brazil
P. l. rufifacies
C Brazil
Percnostola caurensis (Caura Antbird)
P. c. caurensis
C Venezuela
P. c. australis
S Venezuela, N Brazil
Percnostola lophotes (Rufous-crested Antbird)
Peru
MYRMECIZA
Myrmeciza longipes (Swainson's Antcatcher)
M. l. panamensis
E Panama, N Colombia
M. l. longipes
E Colombia, N Venezuela, Trinidad
M. l. boucardi
NC Colombia
M. l. griseipectus
SE Colombia, S Venezuela, Guyana, NE Brazil
Myrmeciza exsul (Chestnut-backed Antbird)
M. e. exsul
E Nicaragua to W Panama
M. e. occidentalis
W Costa Rica, S Panama
M. e. cassini
E Panama, N Colombia
M. e. niglarus
NW Colombia
M. e. maculifer
W Colombia, W Ecuador

Myrmeciza ferruginea (Ferruginous-backed Antbird)
  M. f. ferruginea
    the Guianas, N Brazil
  M. f. eluta
    C Brazil
Myrmeciza ruficauda (Rufous-tailed Antbird)
  M. r. soror
    NE Brazil
  M. r. ruficauda
    SE Brazil
Myrmeciza loricata (White-bibbed Antbird)
  SE Brazil
Myrmeciza squamosa (Squamate Antbird)
  SE Brazil
Myrmeciza laemosticta (Dull-mantled Antbird)
  M. l. laemosticta
    E Costa Rica
  M. l. palliata
    E Panama, NW Colombia
  M. l. bolivari
    C Colombia
  M. l. nigricauda
    SW Colombia, NW Ecuador
  M. l. venezuelae
    W Venezuela
Myrmeciza disjuncta (Yapacana Antbird)
  Venezuela
Myrmeciza pelzelni (Grey-bellied Antbird)
  E Colombia, Venezuela, N Brazil
Myrmeciza hemimelaena (Chestnut-tailed Antbird)
  M. h. hemimelaena
    W Amazonia
  M. h. pallens
    C Brazil
Myrmeciza hyperythra (Plumbeous Antbird)
  W Amazonia
Myrmeciza goeldii (Goeldi's Antbird)
  W Brazil
Myrmeciza melanoceps (White-shouldered Antbird)
  W Amazonia
Myrmeciza fortis (Sooty Antbird)
  M. f. fortis
    SE Colombia, Peru, W Brazil
  M. f. incanescens
    C Brazil
Myrmeciza immaculata (Immaculate Antbird)
  M. i. zeledoni
    E Costa Rica, W Panama
  M. i. berlepschi
    E Panama to W Ecuador

  M. i. immaculata
    E Colombia, W Venezuela
  M. i. brunnea
    NW Venezuela
Myrmeciza griseiceps (Grey-headed Antbird)
  SW Ecuador, NW Peru
Myrmeciza atrothorax (Black-throated Antbird)
  M. a. metae
    E Colombia
  M. a. atrothorax
    S Venezuela, the Guianas, N Brazil
  M. a. tenebrosa
    NE Peru, W Brazil
  M. a. maynana
    N Peru
  M. a. obscurata
    E Peru, W Brazil
  M. a. griseiventris
    W Bolivia
  M. a. melanura
    E Bolivia, SW Brazil
Myrmeciza stictothorax (Spot-breasted Antbird)
  C Brazil

PITHYS
Pithys albifrons (White-faced Antcatcher)
  P. a. albifrons
    S Venezuela, the Guianas, N Brazil
  P. a. brevibarba
    NW Amazonia
  P. a. peruviana
    N & E Peru
Pithys castanea (White-masked Antcatcher)
  W Ecuador

GYMNOPITHYS
Gymnopithys rufigula (Rufous-throated Antcatcher)
  G. r. pallida
    S Venezuela
  G. r. pallidigula
    S Venezuela
  G. r. rufigula
    E Venezuela, the Guianas, N Brazil
Gymnopithys salvini (White-throated Antcatcher)
  G. s. maculata
    E Peru, W Brazil
  G. s. salvini
    Bolivia, SW Brazil
Gymnopithys lunulata (Lunulated Antcatcher)
  E Peru

Gymnopithys leucaspis (Bicoloured Antcatcher)
  G. l. olivascens
    Honduras to W Panama
  G. l. bicolor
    E Panama, NW Colombia
  G. l. daguae
    W Colombia
  G. l. aequatorialis
    SW Colombia, W Ecuador
  G. l. ruficeps
    C Colombia
  G. l. leucaspis
    E Colombia
  G. l. castanea
    E Ecuador, NE Peru
  G. l. peruana
    N Peru
  G. l. lateralis
    W Brazil

RHEGMATORHINA
Rhegmatorhina gymnops (Bare-eyed Antcatcher)
  N Brazil
Rhegmatorhina berlepschi (Harlequin Antcatcher)
  N Brazil
Rhegmatorhina cristata (Chestnut-crested Antcatcher)
  NW Brazil
Rhegmatorhina hoffmannsi (White-breasted Antcatcher)
  W Brazil
Rhegmatorhina melanosticta (Hairy-crested Antcatcher)
  R. m. melanosticta
    E Ecuador
  R. m. brunneiceps
    N Peru
  R. m. purusiana
    E Peru, W Brazil
  R. m. badia
    SE Peru, N Bolivia, W Brazil

HYLOPHYLAX
Hylophylax naevioïdes (Spotted Antbird)
  H. n. capnitis
    E Nicaragua to W Panama
  H. n. naevioïdes
    E Panama to W Ecuador
  H. n. subsimilis
    WC Colombia
Hylophylax naevia (Spot-backed Antbird)
  H. n. theresae
    W Amazonia
  H. n. peruviana
    N Peru

  H. n. consobrina
    S Venezuela, NW Brazil
  H. n. naevia
    S Venezuela, the Guianas
  H. n. obscura
    N Brazil
  H. n. ochracea
    N Brazil
Hylophylax punctulata (Des Murs' Spotted Antbird)
  H. p. punctulata
    S & E Venezuela, NE Peru, Brazil
  H. p. subochracea
    C Brazil
Hylophylax poecilonota (Scale-backed Antbird)
  H. p. poecilonota
    SE Venezuela, the Guianas, N Brazil
  H. p. duidae
    E Colombia, S Venezuela, NW Brazil
  H. p. lepidonota
    SE Colombia, E Ecuador, NE Peru
  H. p. griseiventris
    SE Peru, N Bolivia, SW Brazil
  H. p. gutturalis
    W Brazil
  H. p. nigrigula
    C Brazil
  H. p. vidua
    EC Brazil

PHLEGOPSIS
Phlegopsis nigromaculata (Black-spotted Bare-eye)
  P. n. nigromaculata
    E Peru, N Bolivia, W & SW Brazil
  P. n. bowmani
    N Brazil
  P. n. confinis
    N Brazil
  P. n. paraensis
    N Brazil
Phlegopsis barringeri (Argus Bare-eye)
  Colombia
Phlegopsis erythroptera (Reddish-winged Bare-eye)
  P. e. erythroptera
    N & W Amazonia
  P. e. ustulata
    E Peru, W Brazil

SKUTCHIA
Skutchia borbae (Pale-faced Bare-eye)
  C Brazil

PHAENOSTICTUS
Phaenostictus mcleannani (Ocellated Antbird)
  P. m. saturatus
    SE Nicaragua to W Panama

P. m. mcleannani
EC Panama
P. m. chocoanus
E Panama, NW Colombia
P. m. pacificus
SW Colombia, NW Ecuador

FORMICARIUS
Formicarius colma (Rufous-capped Ant-thrush)
F. c. colma
E Colombia, S Venezuela, the Guianas, N Brazil
F. c. nigrifrons
E Ecuador, E Peru, NW Brazil
F. c. amazonicus
C Brazil
F. c. ruficeps
E & SE Brazil
Formicarius analis (Rufous-necked Ant-thrush)
F. a. moniliger
S Mexico, E Guatemala
F. a. pallidus
SE Mexico
F. a. intermedius
Belize, Honduras
F. a. umbrosus
E Nicaragua to W Panama
F. a. hoffmanni
S Costa Rica, SW Panama
F. a. panamensis
E Panama, NW Colombia
F. a. virescens
N Colombia
F. a. saturatus
NC Colombia, NW Venezuela, Trinidad
F. a. griseoventris
NE Colombia
F. a. connectens
E Colombia
F. a. zamorae
E Ecuador, NE Peru, W Brazil
F. a. olivaceus
N Peru
F. a. crissalis
SE Venezuela, the Guianas, N Brazil
F. a. analis
Peru, W Brazil, N & E Bolivia
Formicarius rufifrons (Rufous-fronted Ant-thrush)
E Peru
Formicarius nigricapillus (Black-headed Ant-thrush)
F. n. nigricapillus
E Costa Rica, W Panama
F. n. destructus
W Colombia, W Ecuador

Formicarius rufipectus (Rufous-breasted Ant-thrush)
F. r. rufipectus
E Costa Rica, Panama
F. r. carrikeri
W Colombia, W Ecuador
F. r. lasallei
NW Venezuela
F. r. thoracicus
E Ecuador, E Peru

CHAMAEZA
Chamaeza campanisona (Short-tailed Ant-thrush)
C. c. colombiana
E Colombia
C. c. punctigula
E Ecuador, N Peru
C. c. olivacea
C Peru
C. c. huachamacarii
C Peru
C. c. berlepschi
SE Peru
C. c. venezuelana
N Venezuela
C. c. yavii
SC Venezuela
C. c. obscura
E Venezuela
C. c. fulvescens
SE Venezuela, Guyana
C. c. boliviana
W Bolivia
C. c. campanisona
SE Brazil, E Paraguay
Chamaeza nobilis (Striated Ant-thrush)
C. n. rubida
SE Colombia, E Ecuador, NE Peru
C. n. nobilis
NE Peru, W Brazil
C. n. fulvipectus
C Brazil
Chamaeza ruficauda (Rufous-tailed Ant-thrush)
C. r. turdina
C Colombia
C. r. chionogaster
N Venezuela
C. r. ruficauda
SE Brazil
Chamaeza mollissima (Barred Ant-thrush)
C. m. mollissima
Colombia, Ecuador
C. m. yungae
N Brazil

Myrmornis torquata (Wing-banded Ant-thrush)
  M. t. stictoptera
    SE Nicaragua, Panama, NW Colombia
  M. t. torquata
    N & E Amazonia

PITTASOMA
Pittasoma michleri (Black-crowned Antpitta)
  P. m. zeledoni
    Costa Rica, W Panama
  P. m. michleri
    E Panama, NW Colombia
Pittasoma rufopileatum (Rufous-crowned Antpitta)
  P. r. rosenbergi
    W Colombia
  P. r. harterti
    SW Colombia
  P. r. rufopileatum
    NW Ecuador

GRALLARIA
Grallaria squamigera (Undulated Antpitta)
  G. s. squamigera
    Colombia, Venezuela, Ecuador
  G. s. canicauda
    Peru, NW Bolivia
Grallaria gigantea (Giant Antpitta)
  G. g. lehmanni
    C Colombia
  G. g. hylodroma
    W Ecuador
  G. g. gigantea
    E Ecuador
Grallaria excelsa (Great Antpitta)
  G. e. excelsa
    W Venezuela
  G. e. phelpsi
    N Venezuela
Grallaria varia (Variegated Antpitta)
  G. v. cinereiceps
    S Venezuela, NW Brazil
  G. v. varia
    the Guianas, NW Brazil
  G. v. distincta
    NC Brazil
  G. v. intercedens
    E Brazil
  G. v. imperator
    SE Brazil, Paraguay, NE Argentina
Grallaria alleni (Moustached Antpitta)
  C Colombia
Grallaria guatimalensis (Scaled Antpitta)
  G. g. ochraceiventris
    SW Mexico

  G. g. guatimalensis
    S Mexico to N Nicaragua
  G. g. princeps
    Costa Rica, W Panama
  G. g. chocoensis
    mountains of E Panama, NW Colombia
  G. g. regulus
    Ecuador, Peru
  G. g. carmelitae
    NE Colombia, NW Venezuela
  G. g. aripoensis
    N Trinidad
  G. g. roraimae
    S Venezuela, N Brazil
Grallaria chthonia (Tachira Antpitta)
  Venezuela
Grallaria haplonota (Plain-backed Antpitta)
  G. h. haplonota
    N Venezuela
  G. h. pariae
    NE Venezuela
  G. h. parambae
    NW Ecuador
Grallaria dignissima (Stripe-sided Antpitta)
  E Ecuador, NE Peru
Grallaria eludens (Elusive Antpitta)
  E Peru
Grallaria ruficapilla (Chestnut-crowned Antpitta)
  G. r. ruficapilla
    C Colombia, N Ecuador
  G. r. perijana
    NW Venezuela
  G. r. avilae
    N Venezuela
  G. r. nigrolineata
    W Venezuela
  G. r. connectens
    SW Ecuador
  G. r. albiloris
    S Ecuador, NW Peru
  G. r. interior
    N Peru
Grallaria watkinsi (Watkins' Antpitta)
  SW Ecuador, NW Peru
Grallaria bangsi (Santa Marta Antpitta)
  NE Colombia
Grallaria andicola (Stripe-headed Antpitta)
  C Peru
Grallaria punensis (Puno Antpitta)
  SE Peru
Grallaria rufocinerea (Bicoloured Antpitta)
  C Colombia
Grallaria nuchalis (Chestnut-naped Antpitta)
  G. n. ruficeps
    C Colombia

G. n. obsoleta
NW Ecuador

G. n. nuchalis
E Ecuador

Grallaria albigula (White-throated Antpitta)
SE Peru, E Bolivia

Grallaria erythroleuca (Chestnut-brown Antpitta)
SE Peru

Grallaria hypoleuca (Bay-backed Antpitta)

G. h. flavotincta
WC Colombia

G. h. castanea
C Colombia, E Ecuador

G. h. hypoleuca
W Colombia

Grallaria griseonucha (Grey-naped Antpitta)

G. g. tachirae
Venezuela

G. g. griseonucha
W Venezuela

Grallaria rufula (Rufous Antpitta)

G. r. spatiator
NE Colombia

G. r. saltuensis
NE Colombia

G. r. rufula
Colombia, W Venezuela, Ecuador

G. r. cajamarcae
N Peru

G. r. obscura
C Peru

G. r. occabambae
SE Peru

G. r. cochabambae
N Bolivia

Grallaria erythrotis (Rufous-faced Antpitta)
Yungas of N Bolivia

Grallaria quitensis (Tawny Antpitta)

G. q. quitensis
C Colombia, Ecuador

G. q. alticola
E Colombia

G. q. atuensis
N Peru

Grallaria milleri (Brown-banded Antpitta)
C Colombia

HYLOPEZUS

Hylopezus perspicillatus (Streak-chested Antpitta)

H. p. intermedius
Caribbean slope from E Costa Rica to W Panama

H. p. lizanoi
W Costa Rica, W Panama

H. p. perspicillatus
E Panama, NW Colombia

H. p. periophthalmicus
Pacific coast of W Colombia, W Ecuador

H. p. pallidior
C Colombia

Hylopezus macularius (Spotted Antpitta)

H. m. diversus
SE Colombia, NE Peru, S Venezuela

H. m. macularius
E Venezuela, the Guianas, N Brazil

H. m. paraensis
Brazil

H. m. auricularis
Bolivia

Hylopezus fulviventris (Fulvous-bellied Antpitta)

H. f. dives
Caribbean slope of Nicaragua, Costa Rica

H. f. flammulatus
Caribbean slope of W Panama

H. f. barbacoae
E Panama, W Colombia

H. f. caquetae
Colombia

H. f. fulviventris
E Ecuador

Hylopezus berlepschi (Amazonian Antpitta)

H. b. yessupi
Peru

H. b. berlepschi
N Bolivia, C & S Brazil

Hylopezus ochroleucus (Speckle-breasted Antpitta)

H. o. ochroleucus
E Brazil

H. o. nattereri
SE Brazil, E Paraguay, NE Argentina

MYRMOTHERA

Myrmothera campanisona (Thrush-like Antpitta)

M. c. modesta
SE Colombia

M. c. dissors
E Colombia, S Venezuela, NW Brazil

M. c. campanisona
SE Venezuela, the Guianas, N Brazil

M. c. signata
E Ecuador, NE Peru

M. c. minor
E Peru, W Brazil

M. c. subcanescens
N & NC Brazil

Myrmothera simplex (Brown-breasted
Antpitta)
  M. s. guaiquinimae
    SE Venezuela
  M. s. duidae
    S Venezuela
  M. s. simplex
    SE Venezuela

GRALLARICULA
Grallaricula flavirostris (Ochre-breasted
Antpitta)
  G. f. costaricensis
    Costa Rica, Panama
  G. f. brevis
    Mt Pirri (E Panama)
  G. f. ochraceiventris
    W Colombia
  G. f. mindoensis
    N Ecuador
  G. f. zarumae
    SW Ecuador
  G. f. flavirostris
    E Colombia, E Ecuador
  G. f. similis
    N Peru
  G. f. boliviana
    N Bolivia
Grallaricula ferrugineipectus (Rusty-
breasted Antpitta)
  G. f. rara
    E Colombia, NW Venezuela
  G. f. ferrugineipectus
    NE Colombia, N Venezuela
  G. f. leymebambae
    N Peru
Grallaricula nana (Slate-crowned
Antpitta)
  G. n. occidentalis
    W Colombia
  G. n. nana
    E Colombia, W Venezuela
  G. n. olivascens
    N Venezuela
  G. n. cumanensis
    N Venezuela
  G. n. pariae
    NE Venezuela
  G. n. kukenamensis
    SE Venezuela
Grallaricula loricata (Scallop-breasted
Antpitta)
  N Venezuela
Grallaricula peruviana (Peruvian
Antpitta)
  NW Peru
Grallaricula lineifrons (Crescent-faced
Antpitta)
  N Ecuador

Grallaricula cucullata (Hooded Antpitta)
  G. c. cucullata
    W Colombia
  G. c. venezuelana
    NW Venezuela

104 CONOPOPHAGIDAE (GNATEATERS)

CONOPOPHAGA
Conopophaga lineata (Silvery-tufted
Gnateater)
  C. l. lineata
    E & SE Brazil
  C. l. vulgaris
    SE Brazil, E Paraguay, NE Argentina
  C. l. cearae
    E Brazil
Conopophaga aurita (Chestnut-belted
Gnateater)
  C. a. inexpectata
    SE Colombia, NW Brazil
  C. a. aurita
    the Guianas, N Brazil
  C. a. occidentalis
    E Ecuador, NE Peru
  C. a. australis
    E Peru, W Brazil
  C. a. snethlageae
    C Brazil
  C. a. pallida
    Brazil
Conopophaga roberti (Hooded Gnateater)
  NE Brazil
Conopophaga peruviana (Ash-throated
Gnateater)
  E Ecuador, E Peru, W Brazil
Conopophaga ardesiaca (Slaty Gnateater)
  C. a. saturata
    SE Peru
  C. a. ardesiaca
    Bolivia
Conopophaga castaneiceps (Chestnut-
crowned Gnateater)
  C. c. chocoensis
    W Colombia
  C. c. castaneiceps
    E Colombia, NE Ecuador
  C. c. chapmani
    SE Ecuador, NE Peru
  C. c. brunneinucha
    C Peru
Conopophaga melanops (Black-cheeked
Gnateater)
  C. m. perspicillata
    E Brazil
  C. m. melanops
    SE Brazil

Conopophaga melanogaster (Black-bellied Gnateater)
  N Bolivia, Brazil

105 RHINOCRYPTIDAE (TAPACULOS)

PTEROPTOCHOS
Pteroptochos castaneus (Chestnut-breasted Huet-huet)
  C Chile
Pteroptochos tarnii (Huet-huet)
  S Chile, W Argentina
Pteroptochos megapodius (Moustached Turco)
  P. m. atacamae
    N Chile
  P. m. megapodius
    C Chile

SCELORCHILUS
Scelorchilus albicollis (White-throated Tapaculo)
  S. a. atacamae
    N Chile
  S. a. albicollis
    C Chile
Scelorchilus rubecula (Chucao Tapaculo)
  S. r. rubecula
    Chile, W Argentina
  S. r. mochae
    Mocha I

RHINOCRYPTA
Rhinocrypta lanceolata (Grey Gallito)
  R. l. saturata
    Paraguay
  R. l. lanceolata
    Argentina

TELEDROMAS
Teledromas fuscus (Sandy Gallito)
  Argentina

LIOSCELES
Liosceles thoracicus (Rusty-belted Tapaculo)
  L. t. dugandi
    SE Colombia, W Brazil
  L. t. erithacus
    E Ecuador, E Peru
  L. t. thoracicus
    SE Peru, C Brazil

MELANOPAREIA
Melanopareia torquata (Collared Crescentchest)
  M. t. torquata
    E Brazil
  M. t. rufescens
    C Brazil

Melanopareia maximiliani (Olive-crowned Crescentchest)
  M. m. maximiliani
    W Bolivia
  M. m. argentina
    W Bolivia, Paraguay, N Argentina
Melanopareia maranonica (Maranon Crescentchest)
  N Peru
Melanopareia elegans (Elegant Crescentchest)
  M. e. elegans
    W Ecuador
  M. e. paucalensis
    E Peru

PSILORHAMPHUS
Psilorhamphus guttatus (Spotted Bamboowren)
  SE Brazil, NE Argentina

MERULAXIS
Merulaxis ater (Slaty Bristlefront)
  SE Brazil
Merulaxis stresemanni (Stresemann's Bristlefront)
  Brazil

EUGRALLA
Eugralla paradoxa (Ochre-flanked Tapaculo)
  Chile, S Argentina

MYORNIS
Myornis senilis (Ash-coloured Tapaculo)
  C Colombia, N Ecuador

SCYTALOPUS
Scytalopus unicolor (Unicoloured Tapaculo)
  S. u. latrans
    Colombia, W Venezuela, E Ecuador, N Peru
  S. u. subcinereus
    SW Ecuador, W Peru
  S. u. intermedius
    N Peru
  S. u. unicolor
    N Peru
  S. u. parvirostris
    C & S Peru, N Bolivia
Scytalopus speluncae (Mouse-coloured Tapaculo)
  SE Brazil, NE Argentina
Scytalopus macropus (Large-footed Tapaculo)
  Peru
Scytalopus femoralis (Rufous-vented Tapaculo)
  S. f. sanctaemartae
    NE Colombia

S. f. atratus
E Colombia
S. f. confusus
C Colombia
S. f. micropterus
E Ecuador, N Peru
S. f. nigricans
NE Colombia
S. f. femoralis
C Peru
S. f. bolivianus
SE Peru, N Bolivia
Scytalopus argentifrons (Silvery-fronted Tapaculo)
S. a. argentifrons
Costa Rica, W Panama
S. a. chiriquensis
W Panama
Scytalopus panamensis (Pale-throated Tapaculo)
Mt Tacarcuna (Panama)
Scytalopus vicinior (Narino Tapaculo)
E Panama, W Colombia
Scytalopus latebricola (Brown-rumped Tapaculo)
S. l. latebricola
NE Colombia
S. l. meridanus
C & E Colombia, W Venezuela
S. l. caracae
N Venezuela
S. l. spillmanni
W Ecuador
Scytalopus novacapitalis (Brasilia Tapaculo)
SE Brazil
Scytalopus indigoticus (White-breasted Tapaculo)
SE Brazil
Scytalopus magellanicus (Andean Tapaculo)
S. m. griseicollis
E Colombia
S. m. fuscicauda
Venezuela
S. m. canus
W Colombia
S. m. opacus
E Ecuador
S. m. altirostris
N Peru
S. m. affinis
W Peru
S. m. acutirostris
C & SE Peru
S. m. urubambae
S Peru
S. m. simonsi
N Bolivia

S. m. zimmeri
C Bolivia
S. m. fuscus
N Chile, W Argentina
S. m. magellanicus
S Chile, S Argentina
Scytalopus superciliaris (White-browed Tapaculo)
NW Argentina

ACROPTERNIS
Acropternis orthonyx (Ocellated Tapaculo)
A. o. orthonyx
E Colombia, W Venezuela
A. o. infuscata
E Ecuador

106 COTINGIDAE (COTINGAS)

PHOENICERCUS
Phoenicercus carnifex (Guianian Red-Cotinga)
the Guianas, E Venezuela, Brazil
Phoenicercus nigricollis (Black-necked Red-Cotinga)
NW South America

LANIISOMA
Laniisoma elegans (Shrike-like Cotinga)
L. e. venezuelensis
NE Colombia, NW Venezuela
L. e. buckleyi
E Peru, E Ecuador
L. e. elegans
SE Brazil
L. e. cadwaladeri
Bolivia

PHIBALURA
Phibalura flavirostris (Swallow-tailed Cotinga)
P. f. flavirostris
Paraguay, SE Brazil, NW Bolivia,
NE Argentina
P. f. boliviana
NE Bolivia

TIJUCA
Tijuca atra (Black & Gold Cotinga)
SE Brazil
Tijuca condita (Grey-winged Cotinga)
SE Brazil

CARPORNIS
Carpornis cucullatus (Hooded Berryeater)
SE Brazil
Carpornis melanocephalus (Black-headed Berryeater)
SE Brazil

AMPELION
Ampelion rubrocristata (Red-crested Cotinga)
Venezuela, Colombia to NW Bolivia

Ampelion rufaxilla (Chestnut-crested Cotinga)
  A. r. antioquiae
    W Colombia
  A. r. rufaxilla
    Peru
Ampelion sclateri (Bay-vented Cotinga)
  C Peru
Ampelion stresemanni (White-cheeked Cotinga)
  W Peru

PIPREOLA
Pipreola riefferii (Green & Black Fruiteater)
  P. r. occidentalis
    W Colombia, W Ecuador
  P. r. riefferii
    E Colombia, E Ecuador
  P. r. melanolaema
    NW Venezuela
  P. r. confusa
    Peru, N Bolivia
  P. r. chachapoyas
    N Peru
  P. r. tallmanorum
    C Peru
Pipreola intermedia (Band-tailed Fruiteater)
  P. i. intermedia
    N & C Peru
  P. i. signata
    SE Peru, Bolivia
Pipreola arcuata (Barred Fruiteater)
  P. a. arcuata
    Colombia, W Venezuela
  P. a. viridicauda
    N Bolivia, C Peru
Pipreola aureopectus (Golden-breasted Fruiteater)
  P. a. decora
    N Colombia
  P. a. festiva
    N Venezuela
  P. a. aureopectus
    E Colombia, W Venezuela
Pipreola jucunda (Orange-breasted Fruiteater)
  W Colombia, W Ecuador
Pipreola lubomirskii (Black-chested Fruiteater)
  S Colombia, E Ecuador, E Peru
Pipreola pulchra (Masked Fruiteater)
  E Peru
Pipreola frontalis (Scarlet-breasted Fruiteater)
  P. f. squamipectus
    SE Ecuador, N Peru
  P. f. frontalis
    S Peru, Bolivia
Pipreola chlorolepidota (Fiery-throated Fruiteater)
  E Ecuador, E Peru

Pipreola formosa (Handsome Fruiteater)
  P. f. formosa
    N Venezuela
  P. f. rubidior
    NE Venezuela
  P. f. pariae
    NE Venezuela
Pipreola whitelyi (Red-banded Fruiteater)
  P. w. kathleenae
    SE Venezuela
  P. w. whiteleyei
    Guyana

AMPELIOIDES
Ampelioides tschudii (Scaled Fruiteater)
  NW Venezuela to N Peru

IODOPLEURA
Iodopleura fusca (Dusky Purpletuft)
  the Guianas, Venezuela
Iodopleura isabellae (White-browed Purpletuft)
  I. i. isabellae
    Colombia, E Ecuador, E Peru, N Brazil
  I. i. paraensis
    NE Brazil
Iodopleura pipra (Buff-throated Purpletuft)
  I. p. leucopygia
    Guyana
  I. p. pipra
    E Brazil

CALYPTURA
Calyptura cristata (Kinglet Calyptura)
  S Brazil

LIPAUGUS
Lipaugus subalaris (Grey-tailed Piha)
  E Ecuador, E Peru
Lipaugus cryptolophus (Olivaceus Piha)
  L. c. mindoensis
    W Ecuador, SW Colombia
  L. c. cryptolophus
    E Colombia, E Ecuador, E Peru
Lipaugus fuscocinereus (Dusky Piha)
  Colombia, E Ecuador
Lipaugus vociferans (Screaming Piha)
  the Guianas, N & W Amazonia
Lipaugus unirufus (Rufous Piha)
  L. u. unirufus
    SE Mexico to N Colombia
  L. u. castaneotinctus
    SW Colombia to NW Ecuador
Lipaugus lanioides (Cinnamon-vented Piha)
  SE Brazil
Lipaugus streptophorus (Rose-collared Piha)
  NW Guyana, Venezuela, N Brazil

CHIROCYLLA
Chirocylla uropygialis (Scimitar-winged Piha)
  N Bolivia

Xenopsaris albinucha (White-naped Xenopsaris)
X. a. albinucha
Brazil, Paraguay, Argentina
X. a. minor
Venezuela, the Guianas

PACHYRAMPHUS

Pachyramphus viridis (Green-backed Becard)
P. v. griseigularis
Guyana
P. v. xanthogenys
E Ecuador
P. v. peruanus
C Peru
P. v. viridis
E & S Brazil, Bolivia, Paraguay, N Argentina

Pachyramphus versicolor (Barred Becard)
P. v. costaricensis
Costa Rica
P. v. versicolor
W Venezuela, Colombia, Ecuador, Peru
P. v. meridionalis
Peru, N Bolivia

Pachyramphus spodiurus (Slaty Becard)
W Ecuador, NW Peru

Pachyramphus rufus (Cinereous Becard)
P. r. rufus
Panama, N South America
P. r. juruanus
E Peru, W Brazil

Pachyramphus castaneus (Chestnut-crowned Becard)
P. c. saturatus
SE Colombia, E Ecuador, N Peru, NW Brazil
P. c. intermedius
N Venezuela
P. c. parui
S Venezuela
P. c. amazonus
NE Brazil
P. c. castaneus
E Brazil, Paraguay, Argentina

Pachyramphus cinnamomeus (Cinnamon Becard)
P. c. cinnamomeus
E Panama, Colombia, Ecuador
P. c. fulvidior
SE Mexico to W Panama
P. c. magdalenae
N & E Colombia, W Venezuela
P. c. badius
W Venezuela

Pachyramphus polychopterus (White-winged Becard)
P. p. similis
Guatemala to Panama
P. p. cinereiventris
N Colombia
P. p. dorsalis
W Colombia, NW Ecuador
P. p. tenebrosus
S Colombia
P. p. tristis
N & NE South America
P. p. nigriventris
W Amazonia
P. p. polychopterus
E Brazil
P. p. spixii
S Brazil, E Bolivia to N Argentina

Pachyramphus marginatus (Black-capped Becard)
P. m. nanus
N South America
P. m. marginatus
E Brazil

Pachyramphus albogriseus (Black & White Becard)
P. a. ornatus
W Nicaragua to W Panama
P. a. coronatus
N Colombia, NW Venezuela
P. a. albogriseus
E Colombia, N Venezuela
P. a. guayaquilensis
E Ecuador
P. a. salvini
N Peru, E Ecuador

Pachyramphus major (Mexican Becard)
P. m. uropygialis
W Mexico
P. m. major
E Mexico
P. m. matudai
S Mexico, N Guatemala
P. m. itzensis
SE Mexico, Belize
P. m. australis
Guatemala to E Nicaragua

Pachyramphus surinamus (Glossy-backed Becard)
Surinam, E Brazil, French Guiana

Pachyramphus aglaiae (Rose-throated Becard)
P. a. albiventris
S Arizona, W Mexico
P. a. richmondi
NW Mexico
P. a. gravis
NE Mexico

P. a. yucatanensis
  E Mexico
P. a. insularis
  Tres Marias Is
P. a. aglaiae
  NE Mexico
P. a. sumichrasti
  SE Mexico to El Salvador
P. a. hypophaeus
  Honduras to NE Costa Rica
P. a. latirostris
  W Nicaragua, W Costa Rica
P. a. homochrous
  E Panama to NW Peru
P. a. quimarinus
  NW Colombia
P. a. canescens
  N Colombia, NW Venezuela
**Pachyramphus minor (Pink-throated
Becard)**
  N South America
Pachyramphus validus (Plain Becard)
P. v. audax
  S Peru, C Bolivia, NW Argentina
P. v. validus
  E Bolivia to C Brazil, N Argentina
Pachyramphus niger (Jamaicàn Becard)
  Jamaica

TITYRA
Tityra cayana (Black-tailed Tityra)
T. c. candida
  C & SW Colombia
T. c. cayana
  N South America, Trinidad
T. c. braziliensis
  E & S Brazil, Paraguay, NE Argentina
Tityra semifasciata (Masked Tityra)
T. s. hannumi
  NW Mexico
T. s. griseiceps
  W Mexico
T. s. deses
  Yucatan peninsula
T. s. personata
  E Mexico to El Salvador
T. s. costaricensis
  S Honduras to W Panama
T. s. columbiana
  E Panama, Colombia, W Venezuela
T. s. nigriceps
  SW Colombia, W Ecuador
T. s. semifasciata
  N & NW Amazonia
T. s. fortis
  C & SE Peru, N & E Bolivia, C Brazil
Tityra inquisitor (Black-crowned Tityra)
T. i. fraserii
  SE Mexico to W Panama

T. i. albitorques
  E Panama to Peru, N Brazil
T. i. buckleyi
  SE Colombia, E Ecuador
T. i. erythrogenys
  E Colombia, Venezuela, the Guianas
T. i. pelzelni
  E Bolivia, W Brazil
T. i. inquisitor
  E Brazil, Paraguay, N Argentina

PORPHYROLAEMA
**Porphyrolaema porphyrolaema (Purple-
throated Cotinga)**
  W Amazonia

COTINGA
Cotinga amabilis (Lovely Cotinga)
  SE Mexico to Costa Rica
Cotinga ridgwayi (Ridgway's Cotinga)
  SW Costa Rica, Panama
Cotinga nattererii (Blue Cotinga)
  NW Venezuela to N & E Peru
Cotinga maynana (Plum-throated Cotinga)
  W Amazonia
Cotinga cotinga (Purple-breasted Cotinga)
  E Colombia, to the Guianas, N Brazil
Cotinga maculata (Banded Cotinga)
  SE Brazil
Cotinga cayana (Spangled Cotinga)
  N & W South America

XIPHOLENA
Xipholena punicea (Pompadour Cotinga)
  N & NW Amazonia
**Xipholena lamellipennis (White-tailed
Cotinga)**
  E Brazil
**Xipholena atropurpurea (White-winged
Cotinga)**
  SE Brazil

CARPODECTES
Carpodectes hopkei (White Cotinga)
  E Panama to NW Ecuador
Carpodectes nitidus (Snowy Cotinga)
  E Honduras to E Panama
**Carpodectes antoniae (Yellow-billed
Cotinga)**
  W Costa Rica, W Panama

CONIOPTILON
**Conioptilon mcilhennyi (Black-faced
Cotinga)**
  SE Peru

GYMNODERUS
**Gymnoderus foetidus (Bare-necked
Fruitcrow)**
  N South America

HAEMATODERUS
Haematoderus militaris (Crimson Fruit-crow)
 the Guianas, Brazil
QUERULA
Querula purpurata (Purple-throated Fruitcrow)
 Costa Rica, Panama, N South America
PYRODERUS
Pyroderus scutatus (Red-ruffed Fruitcrow)
P. s. occidentalis
 W Colombia
P. s. granadensis
 E Colombia, W Venezuela
P. s. orenocensis
 N Venezuela, Guyana
P. s. masoni
 E Peru
P. s. scutatus
 SE Brazil, Paraguay, N Argentina
CEPHALOPTERUS
Cephalopterus glabricollis (Bare-necked Umbrellabird)
 Costa Rica, W Panama
Cephalopterus ornatus (Amazonian Umbrellabird)
 N & W South America
Cephalopterus penduliger (Long-wattled Umbrellabird)
 Colombia, Ecuador
PERISSOCEPHALUS
Perissocephalus tricolor (Capuchin Bird)
 the Guianas, Venezuela, N Brazil
PROCNIAS
Procnias tricarunculata (Three-wattled Bellbird)
 Nicaragua to Panama
Procnias alba (White Bellbird)
 Venezuela to Surinam, N Brazil
Procnias averano (Bearded Bellbird)
P. a. carnobarba
 N Venezuela, Trinidad, W Guyana
P. a. averano
 NE Brazil
Procnias nudicollis (Bare-throated Bellbird)
 S Brazil, Paraguay, NE Argentina
RUPICOLA
Rupicola rupicola (Guianan Cock of the Rock)
 E Colombia to the Guianas, N Brazil
Rupicola peruviana (Andean Cock of the Rock)
R. p. sanguinolenta
 W Colombia, W Ecuador

R. p. aequatorialis
 W Venezuela, Colombia, E Ecuador, N Peru
R. p. peruviana
 C Peru
R. p. saturata
 SE Peru, N Bolivia

107 PIPRIDAE (MANAKINS)

SCHIFFORNIS
Schiffornis major (Greater Manakin)
S. m. major
 N Brazil, E Peru
S. m. duidae
 SE Venezuela
Schiffornis virescens (Greenish Manakin)
 SE Brazil to NE Argentina
Schiffornis turdinus (Thrush-like Manakin)
S. t. veraepacis
 SE Mexico to W Panama
S. t. dumicola
 W & C Panama
S. t. panamensis
 E Panama, NW Colombia
S. t. acrolophites
 E Panama, NW Colombia
S. t. rosenbergi
 W Ecuador, W Colombia
S. t. stenorhynchus
 N Venezuela, E Colombia
S. t. aeneus
 E Ecuador, N Peru
S. t. amazonus
 S Venezuela to E Peru, W Brazil
S. t. olivaceus
 E Venezuela, Guyana
S. t. wallacei
 N Brazil, French Guiana, Surinam
S. t. steinbachi
 N Bolivia, SE Peru
S. t. intermedius
 E Brazil
S. t. turdinus
 E Brazil
SAPAYOA
Sapayoa aenigma (Broad-billed Manakin)
 E Panama to NW Ecuador
PIPRITES
Piprites griseiceps (Grey-hooded Manakin)
 Costa Rica, Nicaragua
Piprites chloris (Wing-barred Manakin)
P. c. antioquiae
 NC Colombia
P. c. perijanus
 N Colombia, W Venezuela
P. c. tschudii
 S Colombia to C Peru, NW Brazil

P. c. chlorion
the Guianas, N Brazil
P. c. grisescens
Para (Brazil)
P. c. bolivianus
N Bolivia, C Brazil
P. c. chloris
SE Brazil, Paraguay, NE Argentina
Piprites pileatus (Black-capped Manakin)
SE Brazil

NEOPIPO
Neopipo cinnamomea (Cinnamon Manakin)
N. c. helenae
Guyana, French Guiana, N Brazil
N. c. cinnamomea
E Ecuador, E Peru, W Brazil

CHLOROPIPO
Chloropipo flavicapilla (Yellow-headed Manakin)
Colombia
Chloropipo holochlora (Green Manakin)
C. h. suffusa
E Panama
C. h. litae
E Panama to NW Ecuador
C. h. holochlora
E Colombia, E Ecuador, N Peru
C. h. viridior
SE Peru
Chloropipo uniformis (Olive Manakin)
C. u. duidae
S Venezuela
C. u. uniformis
Guyana, N Brazil
Chloropipo unicolor (Jet Manakin)
Peru

XENOPIPO
Xenopipo atronitens (Black Manakin)
N & NW Amazonia

ANTILOPHIA
Antilophia galeata (Helmeted Manakin)
Brazil, Paraguay

TYRANNEUTES
Tyranneutes stolzmanni (Dwarf Tyrant Manakin)
N & W Amazonia
Tyranneutes virescens (Tiny Tyrant Manakin)
Venezuela to Surinam, N Brazil

NEOPELMA
Neopelma pallescens (Pale-bellied Tyrant Manakin)
WC Brazil

Neopelma chrysocephalum (Saffron-crested Tyrant Manakin)
the Guianas, N Brazil, S Venezuela, E Colombia
Neopelma sulphureiventer (Sulphur-bellied Tyrant Manakin)
E Peru, N Bolivia, W Brazil
Neopelma aurifrons (Wied's Tyrant Manakin)
N. a. aurifrons
SE Brazil
N. a. chrysolophum
E Brazil

HETEROCERCUS
Heterocercus aurantiivertex (Orange-crowned Manakin)
E Ecuador, NE Peru
Heterocercus flavivertex (Yellow-crowned Manakin)
E Colombia, Venezuela, N Brazil
Heterocercus linteatus (Flame-crowned Manakin)
NE Peru, WC Brazil

MACHAEROPTERUS
Machaeropterus deliciosus (Club-winged Manakin)
W Colombia, NW Ecuador
Machaeropterus regulus (Striped Manakin)
M. r. antioquiae
W & C Colombia
M. r. striolatus
E Colombia, E Ecuador, NE Peru
M. r. obscurostriatus
W Venezuela
M. r. zulianus
W Venezuela
M. r. aureopectus
SE Venezuela
M. r. regulus
SE Brazil
Machaeropterus pyrocephalus (Fiery-capped Manakin)
M. p. pallidiceps
E Venezuela
M. p. pyrocephalus
N Brazil, E Peru

MANACUS
Manacus candei (Cande's Manakin)
SE Mexico to Costa Rica
Manacus vitellinus (Golden-collared Manakin)
M. v. vitellinus
E Panama
M. v. milleri
N Colombia
M. v. viridiventris
W Colombia

***Manacus cerritus* (Almirante Manakin)**
NW Panama
***Manacus aurantiacus* (Salvin's Manakin)**
SW Costa Rica, W Panama
***Manacus manacus* (White-bearded Manakin)**
M. m. trinitatis
Trinidad, NE Venezuela
M. m. abditivus
N Colombia
M. m. flaveolus
E Colombia
M. m. bangsi
SW Colombia
M. m. interior
S Colombia, E Ecuador, N Peru,
NW Brazil
M. m. umbrosus
S Venezuela
M. m. manacus
the Guianas, N Brazil
M. m. leucochlamys
W Ecuador
M. m. gutturosus
SE Brazil, E Paraguay, NE Argentina
M. m. purus
N Brazil
M. m. subpurus
C Brazil

CORAPIPO
***Corapipo leucorrhoa* (White-ruffed
Manakin)**
C. l. altera
E Nicaragua, NW Costa Rica, Panama
C. l. heteroleuca
SW Costa Rica, W Panama
C. l. leucorrhoa
Colombia
***Corapipo gutturalis* (White-throated
Manakin)**
Guyana, Brazil, Venezuela

ILICURA
***Ilicura militaris* (Pin-tailed Manakin)**
SE Brazil

MASIUS
***Masius chrysopterus* (Golden-winged
Manakin)**
M. c. bellus
W Colombia
M. c. pax
SE Colombia
M. c. coronulatus
SW Colombia, W Ecuador
M. c. chrysopterus
E Colombia, NW Venezuela, E Ecuador
M. c. peruvianus
N Peru

CHIROXIPHIA
***Chiroxiphia caudata* (Swallow-tailed
Manakin)**
Brazil, Paraguay, N Argentina
***Chiroxiphia pareola* (Blue-backed Manakin)**
C. p. atlantica
Tobago I
C. p. pareola
the Guianas, N & E Brazil
C. p. regina
N Brazil
C. p. napensis
SE Colombia, E Ecuador, NE Peru
C. p. boliviana
SE Peru, Bolivia
***Chiroxiphia lanceolata* (Lance-tailed
Manakin)**
Panama to NW Venezuela
***Chiroxiphia linearis* (Long-tailed Manakin)**
S Mexico to Costa Rica

PIPRA
***Pipra filicauda* (Wire-tailed Manakin)**
Venezuela, Colombia, Peru, Brazil
***Pipra vilasboasi* (Golden-crowned Manakin)**
Brazil
***Pipra nattereri* (Snow-capped Manakin)**
Brazil
***Pipra iris* (Opal-crowned Manakin)**
P. i. iris
EC Brazil
P. i. eucephala
C Brazil
***Pipra serena* (White-fronted Manakin)**
P. s. suavissima
Guyana, SE Venezuela
P. s. serena
French Guiana, N Brazil
***Pipra coronata* (Blue-crowned Manakin)**
P. c. velutina
SW Costa Rica, W Panama
P. c. minuscula
E Panama to NW Ecuador
P. c. caquetae
C Colombia
P. c. carbonata
SE Colombia, NE Ecuador, NW Brazil
P. c. coronata
NW Brazil
P. c. caelestipileata
W Brazil, SE Peru
P. c. exquisita
C Peru
P. c. regalis
NC Bolivia

Pipra caeruleocapilla (Caerulean-capped Manakin)
C & SE Peru
Pipra isidorei (Blue-rumped Manakin)
P. i. isidorei
E Colombia, E Ecuador
P. i. leucopygia
N Peru
Pipra pipra (White-crowned Manakin)
P. p. anthracina
Costa Rica, W Panama
P. p. bolivari
NW Colombia
P. p. coracina
E Colombia, E Ecuador, NW Peru
P. p. discolor
NE Peru
P. p. minima
W Colombia
P. p. unica
NC Colombia
P. p. pipra
the Guianas, E Venezuela, N Brazil
P. p. occulta
NC Peru
P. p. pygmaea
NC Peru
P. p. microlopha
E Peru, W Brazil
P. p. comata
Peru
P. p. separabilis
EC Brazil
P. p. cephaleucos
E Brazil
Pipra cornuta (Scarlet-horned Manakin)
Guyana, Venezuela, Brazil
Pipra chloromeros (Round-tailed Manakin)
Peru, Bolivia
Pipra mentalis (Red-capped Manakin)
P. m. mentalis
SE Mexico to E Costa Rica
P. m. ignifera
W Costa Rica, W Panama
P. m. minor
E Panama to W Ecuador
Pipra rubrocapilla (Red-headed Manakin)
NE Peru, W Brazil
Pipra erythrocephala (Golden-headed Manakin)
P. e. erythrocephala
Panama, N South America
P. e. berlepschi
W Amazonia
P. e. flammiceps
E Colombia

Pipra fasciicauda (Band-tailed Manakin)
P. f. calamae
C & W Brazil
P. f. satura
N Peru
P. f. purusiana
W Brazil, E Peru
P. f. fasciicauda
E Bolivia, SE Peru
P. f. scarlatina
Paraguay, S Brazil
Pipra aureola (Crimson-hooded Manakin)
P. a. aureola
the Guianas, NE Venezuela, NE Brazil
P. a. aurantiicollis
N Brazil
P. a. flavicollis
N Brazil
P. a. borbae
C Brazil

108 TYRANNIDAE (TYRANT FLY-CATCHERS)

FLUVICOLINAE
AGRIORNIS
Agriornis livida (Great Shrike Tyrant)
A. l. livida
SC Chile
A. l. fortis
S Chile, S Argentina
Agriornis microptera (Grey-bellied Shrike Tyrant)
A. m. andecola
Bolivia, S Peru, N Chile, NW Argentina
A. m. microptera
Uruguay, Argentina
Agriornis montana (Black-billed Shrike Tyrant)
A. m. solitaria
Ecuador, Colombia
A. m. insolens
Peru
A. m. intermedia
W Bolivia, N Chile
A. m. montana
E Bolivia, NW Argentina
A. m. maritima
NC Chile
A. m. leucura
C Chile, C Argentina
Agriornis albicauda (White-tailed Shrike Tyrant)
Ecuador, Peru, W Bolivia, N Chile, N Argentina

NEOXOLMIS
Neoxolmis rufiventris (Chocolate-vented Tyrant)
Uruguay, Chile, Argentina

XOLMIS
Xolmis cinerea (Grey Monjita)
X. c. cinerea
S Brazil, Uruguay, N Argentina
X. c. pepoaza
E Bolivia, Paraguay, N Argentina
Xolmis velata (White-rumped Monjita)
E Bolivia, S Brazil, Paraguay
Xolmis dominicana (Black & White Monjita)
S Brazil, Uruguay, Paraguay, E Argentina
Xolmis coronata (Black-crowned Monjita)
E Bolivia, Uruguay, Paraguay, N Argentina
Xolmis irupero (White Monjita)
X. i. nivea
E Brazil
X. i. irupero
E Bolivia, S Brazil, Uruguay, Paraguay, N Argentina
Xolmis murina (Mouse-brown Monjita)
E Bolivia, Paraguay, N Argentina
Xolmis rubetra (Rusty-backed Monjita)
W Argentina
Xolmis rufipennis (Rufous-webbed Monjita)
Peru, Bolivia

PYROPE
Pyrope pyrope (Fire-eyed Diucon)
S Chile, S Argentina

MUSCISAXICOLA
Muscisaxicola rufivertex (Rufous-naped Ground-Tyrant)
M. r. occipitalis
Peru, NW Bolivia
M. r. pallidiceps
SW Bolivia, NW Argentina, N Chile
M. r. rufivertex
S Chile, SW Argentina
Muscisaxicola albilora (White-browed Ground-Tyrant)
Ecuador, Peru, Bolivia, Chile
Muscisaxicola juninensis (Puna Ground-Tyrant)
S Peru, N Chile, N Argentina
Muscisaxicola flavinucha (Ochre-naped Ground-Tyrant)
M. f. flavinucha
Peru, Bolivia, N Argentina, N Chile
M. f. brevirostris
S Argentina, S Chile
Muscisaxicola capistrata (Cinnamon-bellied Ground-Tyrant)
Bolivia, S Peru, Argentina, Chile

Muscisaxicola frontalis (Black-fronted Ground-Tyrant)
Bolivia, Peru, Argentina, Chile
Muscisaxicola albifrons (White-fronted Ground-Tyrant)
S Peru, W Bolivia, N Chile
Muscisaxicola alpina (Plain-capped Ground-Tyrant)
M. a. columbiana
WC Colombia
M. a. quesadae
C Colombia
M. a. alpina
N Ecuador
M. a. grisea
Peru, W Bolivia
M. a. argentina
NW Argentina
Muscisaxicola cinerea (Cinereous Ground-Tyrant)
N & C Chile
Muscisaxicola macloviana (Dark-faced Ground-Tyrant)
M. m. mentalis
Peru, Bolivia, Chile, Argentina
M. m. macloviana
Falkland Is
Muscisaxicola maculirostris (Spot-billed Ground-Tyrant)
M. m. niceforoi
C Colombia
M. m. rufescens
Ecuador
M. m. maculirostris
Peru, Bolivia, Chile, W Argentina
Muscisaxicola fluviatilis (Little Ground-Tyrant)
E Peru, N Bolivia, W Brazil, N Argentina

MUSCIGRALLA
Muscigralla brevicauda (Short-tailed Field-Tyrant)
SW Ecuador, W Peru, N Chile

LESSONIA
Lessonia rufa (Rufous-backed Negrito)
L. r. oreas
Peru, W Bolivia, N Chile, NW Argentina
L. r. rufa
S Brazil, Uruguay, E Chile, W Argentina

MYIOTHERETES
Myiotheretes striaticollis (Streak-throated Bush-Tyrant)
M. s. striaticollis
Venezuela, Colombia, Ecuador, Peru, W Bolivia
M. s. pallidus
NW Argentina, E Peru, Bolivia

Myiotheretes pernix (Santa Marta Bush-Tyrant)
NW Argentina, E Peru, Bolivia
Myiotheretes fumigatus (Smoky Bush-Tyrant)
M. f. olivaceus
N Colombia, W Venezuela
M. f. fumigatus
Colombia, Ecuador, Peru
M. f. lugubris
W Venezuela
M. f. cajamarcae
S Ecuador, N Peru
Myiotheretes fuscorufus (Rufous-bellied Bush-Tyrant)
Bolivia, SE Peru
Myiotheretes signatus (Jelski's Bush-Tyrant)
M. s. signatus
C Peru
M. s. cabanisi
SE Peru, NW Argentina
Miotheretes erythropygius (Red-rumped Bush-Tyrant)
M. e. orinomus
N Colombia
M. e. erythropygius
C Colombia to Ecuador, Peru, N Bolivia

OCHTHOECA
Ochthoeca oenanthoides (D'Orbigny's Chat-Tyrant)
O. o. polionota
Peru
O. o. oenanthoides
Bolivia, N Chile, NW Argentina
Ochthoeca fumicolor (Brown-backed Chat-Tyrant)
O. f. superciliosa
W Venezuela
O. f. ferruginea
C Colombia
O. f. fumicolor
E Colombia, W Venezuela
O. f. brunneifrons
Peru, Ecuador, W Colombia
O. f. berlepschi
SE Peru, W Bolivia
Ochthoeca leucophrys (White-browed Chat-Tyrant)
O. l. dissors
N Peru
O. l. interior
C Peru
O. l. urubambae
C & S Peru
O. l. leucometopa
W Peru, NW Chile
O. l. leucophrys
Bolivia

O. l. tucumana 315
W Argentina
Ochthoeca piurae (Piura Chat-Tyrant)
NW Peru
Ochthoeca rufipectoralis (Rufous-breasted Chat-Tyrant)
O. r. poliogastra
N Colombia
O. r. rubicundulus
NE Colombia, NW Venezuela
O. r. obfuscata
SW & W Colombia to Peru
O. r. rufopectus
C Colombia, Ecuador, NW Peru
O. r. centralis
N Peru
O. r. tectricialis
S Peru
O. r. rufipectoralis
Bolivia, SE Peru
Ochthoeca cinnamomeiventris (Slaty-backed Chat-Tyrant)
O. c. nigrita
W Venezuela
O. c. cinnamomeiventris
Colombia, E Ecuador
O. c. angustifasciata
N Peru
O. c. thoracica
Peru, Bolivia
Ochthoeca frontalis (Crowned Chat-Tyrant)
O. f. albidiadema
E Colombia
O. f. frontalis
W Ecuador, W Colombia
O. f. orientalis
E Ecuador, N Peru
O. f. boliviana
C & S Peru, E Bolivia
O. f. spodionota
C & SE Peru
Ochthoeca pulchella (Golden-browed Chat-Tyrant)
O. p. jelskii
NW Peru, SW Ecuador
O. p. similis
C Peru
O. p. pulchella
W Bolivia, SE Peru
Ochthoeca diadema (Yellow-bellied Chat-Tyrant)
O. d. rubellula
NE Colombia, NW Venezuela
O. d. jesupi
N Colombia
O. d. tovarensis
N Venezuela
O. d. diadema
Colombia, W Venezuela

O. d. meridana
NW Venezuela
O. d. gratiosa
NW Peru, W Ecuador, W Colombia

SAYORNIS

Sayornis phoebe (Eastern Phoebe)
C & SE Canada, E USA, E Mexico
Sayornis nigricans (Black Phoebe)
S. n. nigricans
SW USA, Mexico
S. n. salictaria
N Mexico
S. n. brunnescens
Baja California
S. n. semiatra
W Mexico, W USA
S. n. aquatica
Guatemala, Nicaragua
S. n. amnicola
Costa Rica, W Panama
S. n. angustirostris
C & N Colombia, E Panama, W Venezuela
to Peru
S. n. latirostris
Bolivia, NW Argentına
NW Argentina
Sayornis saya (Say's Phoebe)
S. s. yukonensis
SE Alaska, W Canada, California
S. s. saya
WC Canada, W USA, N Mexico
S. s. quiescens
NW Baja California

COLONIA

Colonia colonus (Long-tailed Tyrant)
C. c. leuconotus
S Honduras to Panama, W Colombia,
Ecuador
C. c. fuscicapillus
Colombia, E Ecuador, E Peru, W Brazil,
Bolivia
C. c. poecilonotus
the Guianas, SE Venezuela
C. c. niveiceps
S Peru, N Bolivia
C. c. colonus
S Brazil, Paraguay, N Argentina

GUBERNETES

**Gubernetes yetapa (Streamer-tailed
Tyrant)**
S Brazil, Paraguay, E Bolivia, N Argentina

ALECTRURUS

Alectrurus tricolor (Cock-tailed Tyrant)
S Brazil, Paraguay, E Bolivia, N Argentina

YETAPA

Yetapa risoria (Strange-tailed Tyrant)
S Brazil, Paraguay, Uruguay, N Argentina

KNIPOLEGUS

Knipolegus lophotes (Crested Black Tyrant)
S Brazil, Uruguay
**Knipolegus nigerrimus (Velvety Black
Tyrant)**
SE Brazil
**Knipolegus aterrimus (White-winged
Black Tyrant)**
K. a. heterogyna
N Peru
K. a. anthracinus
S Peru, W Bolivia
K. a. aterrimus
E Bolivia, W Argentina
K. a. franciscanus
CE Brazil
Knipolegus orenocensis (Riverside Tyrant)
K. o. orenocensis
Venezuela
K. o. xinguensis
N Brazil
K. o. sclateri
N Peru, C Brazil
**Knipolegus poecilurus (Rufous-tailed
Tyrant)**
K. p. poecilurus
Colombia
K. p. peruanus
Peru, Bolivia
K. p. venezuelanus
Trinidad, Venezuela, NW Brazil
K. p. salvini
Guyana
K. p. paraquensis
S Venezuela
**Knipolegus cyanirostris (Blue-billed
Black Tyrant)**
SE Brazil, Uruguay, Paraguay, E Argentina
**Knipolegus subflammulatus (Berlioz
Tyrant)**
Bolivia

PHAEOTRICCUS

**Phaeotriccus poecilocercus (Amazonian
Black Tyrant)**
Venezuela, Guyana, N Brazil, NE Peru
**Phaeotriccus hudsoni (Hudson's Black
Tyrant)**
S Brazil, E Bolivia, Argentina

ENTOTRICCUS

Entotriccus striaticeps (Cinereous Tyrant)
E Bolivia, SW Brazil, Paraguay,
N Argentina

Hymenops perspicillata (Spectacled Tyrant)
  H. p. perspicillata
    Argentina, Paraguay, Uruguay
  H. p. andina
    C Chile, NW Argentina, S Bolivia

MUSCIPIPRA
Muscipipra vetula (Shear-tailed Grey Tyrant)
  SE Brazil, Paraguay, Argentina

FLUVICOLA
Fluvicola pica (Pied Water-Tyrant)
  F. p. pica
    Trinidad, Venezuela, the Guianas,
    Colombia, N Brazil
  F. p. albiventer
    S Brazil, E Bolivia, Paraguay, N Argentina
Fluvicola nengeta (Masked Water-Tyrant)
  F. n. atripennis
    SW Ecuador, NW Peru
  F. n. nengeta
    E Brazil

ARUNDINICOLA
Arundinicola leucocephala (White-headed Marsh-Tyrant)
  NE South America

PYROCEPHALUS
Pyrocephalus rubinus (Vermilion Fly-catcher)
  P. r. mexicanus
    SW USA, Mexico
  P. r. flammeus
    N Mexico
  P. r. blatteus
    S Mexico to Honduras
  P. r. pinicola
    Nicaragua
  P. r. piurae
    W Colombia to NW Peru
  P. r. saturatus
    N Colombia to Surinam, N Brazil
  P. r. ardens
    NC Peru
  P. r. cocachacrae
    SW Peru, N Chile
  P. r. obscurus
    W Peru
  P. r. rubinus
    W & C Amazonia
  P. r. major
    SE Peru
  P. r. nanus
    Galapagos Is
  P. r. dubius
    Chatham I (Galapagos)

Ochthornis littoralis (Drab Water-Tyrant)
  Guyana, French Guiana, N Brazil,
  S Venezuela, Colombia, Ecuador, Peru

TUMBEZIA
Tumbezia salvini (Tumbes Tyrant)
  NW Peru

SATRAPA
Satrapa icterophrys (Yellow-browed Tyrant)
  Bolivia, Brazil, Paraguay, Uruguay,
  N Argentina

MACHETORNIS
Machetornis rixosus (Cattle Tyrant)
  M. r. flavigularis
    N Colombia, N Venezuela
  M. r. obscurodorsalis
    SW Venezuela, E Colombia
  M. r. rixosus
    E Bolivia, S Brazil, Paraguay, Uruguay,
    N Argentina

SIRYSTES
Sirystes sibilator (Sirystes)
  S. s. albogriseus
    E Panama, NW Colombia
  S. s. albocinereus
    S Colombia, E Ecuador, E Peru, W Brazil
  S. s. subcanescens
    NE Brazil, S Surinam
  S. s. sibilator
    E Brazil, Paraguay, NE Argentina
  S. s. atimastus
    SW Brazil

TYRANNINAE

MUSCIVORA
Muscivora forficata (Scissor-tailed Flycatcher)
  SC USA, Mexico, Central America
Muscivora tyrannus (Fork-tailed Flycatcher)
  M. t. tyrannus
    C & S South America
  M. t. sanctaemartae
    N Colombia, W Venezuela
  M. t. monachus
    S Mexico to C Brazil
  M. t. circumdatus
    EC Brazil

TYRANNUS
Tyrannus tyrannus (Eastern Kingbird)
  S Canada, C & E USA, Central America,
  N South America
Tyrannus cubensis (Giant Kingbird)
  Cuba, Gtr Antilles Is

Tyrannus melancholicus (Tropical Kingbird)
T. m. occidentalis
  W Mexico
T. m. chloronotus
  S Mexico to Panama, N Colombia
T. m. despotes
  N Venezuela, the Guianas, N Brazil,
  Trinidad
T. m. melancholicus
  S Colombia & S Venezuela to Paraguay
  & Argentina
Tyrannus couchii (Couch's Kingbird)
  S USA, E Mexico
Tyrannus dominicensis (Grey Kingbird)
T. d. fugax
  SE USA, Bahama Is
T. d. sequax
  Cuba, Cayman Is, S Bahama Is
T. d. dominicensis
  Gtr Antilles Is, N Lesser Antilles Is
T. d. tenax
  Margarita I, Curacao I, Bonaire I
T. d. vorax
  Trinidad, S Lesser Antilles Is
Tyrannus caudifasciatus (Loggerhead
Kingbird)
T. c. bahamensis
  Bahama Is
T. c. caudifasciatus
  Cuba
T. c. flavescens
  Isle of Pines, Gtr Antilles
T. c. caymanensis
  Cayman Is
T. c. jamaicensis
  Jamaica
T. c. taylori
  Puerto Rico
T. c. gabbii
  Haiti
Tyrannus verticalis (Western Kingbird)
  SW Canada, W USA, W Mexico,
  Guatemala
Tyrannus niveigularis (Snowy-throated
Kingbird)
  SW Colombia, Ecuador, NW Peru
Tyrannus albogularis (White-throated
Kingbird)
  Brazil, Venezuela to E Peru, N Bolivia
Tyrannus apolites (Heine's Kingbird)
  SE Brazil
Tyrannus vociferans (Cassin's Kingbird)
T. c. vociferans
  SW USA, W Mexico, Guatemala
T. c. xenopterus
  SW Mexico

Tyrannus crassirostris (Thick-billed
Kingbird)
T. c. sequestratus
  N Mexico
T. c. pompalis
  C Mexico
T. c. crassirostris
  S Mexico, W Guatemala

TYRANNOPSIS
Tyrannopsis sulphurea (Sulphury Flycatcher)
  Trinidad, the Guianas, Venezuela, Brazil,
  Peru, Ecuador
Tyrannopsis luteiventris (Dusky-chested
Flycatcher)
T. l. luteiventris
  Colombia, Ecuador, Peru, Brazil
T. l. septentrionalis
  Surinam

EMPIDONOMUS
Empidonomus varius (Variegated
Flycatcher)
E. v. varius
  E Bolivia, SE Brazil, Paraguay, N Argentina
E. v. rufinus
  N & E Brazil, E Peru, E Venezuela, Guyana,
  French Guiana
E. v. septentrionalis
  N Venezuela, E Colombia
Empidonomus aurantioatrocristatus
(Crowned Slaty Flycatcher)
E. a. aurantioatrocristatus
  E Peru, E Bolivia, S Brazil, Uruguay
  Paraguay, N Argentina
E. a. pallidiventris
  NE Brazil

LEGATUS
Legatus leucophaius (Piratic Flycatcher)
L. l. variegatus
  SE Mexico, Guatemala, Honduras
L. l. leucophaius
  Nicaragua to Panama, Trinidad,
  N & C South America

CONOPIAS
Conopias trivirgata (Three-striped
Flycatcher)
C. t. berlepschi
  N Brazil, SW Venezuela
C. t. trivirgata
  SE Brazil, Paraguay, NE Argentina
Conopias cinchoneti (Lemon-browed
Flycatcher)
C. c. icterophrys
  C Colombia, W Venezuela
C. c. cinchoneti
  E Ecuador, Peru

Conopias parva (White-ringed Flycatcher)
C. p. distincta
E Costa Rica
C. p. albovittata
E Panama, W Colombia, NW Ecuador
C. p. parva
Guyana, French Guiana, N Brazil

MEGARHYNCHUS
Megarhynchus pitangua (Boat-billed Flycatcher)
M. p. mexicanus
SE Mexico to NW Colombia
M. p. tardiusculus
NW Mexico
M. p. caniceps
W Mexico
M. p. deserticola
C Guatemala
M. p. pitangua
Trinidad, North & Central South America
M. p. chrysogaster
W Ecuador, NW Peru

MYIODYNASTES
Myiodynastes luteiventris (Sulphur-bellied Flycatcher)
M. l. swarthi
S USA, N Mexico
M. l. luteiventris
S Mexico to NW South America
Myiodynastes maculatus (Streaked Flycatcher)
M. m. insolens
SE Mexico to Honduras » N South America
M. m. nobilis
NE Colombia
M. m. difficilis
W Costa Rica to Venezuela
M. m. chapmani
SW Colombia to W Peru
M. m. maculatus
N Peru, Venezuela, the Guianas, N Brazil
M. m. tobagensis
Guyana, Trinidad, Tobago I
M. m. solitarius
S Peru to Uruguay, N Argentina
Myiodynastes bairdi (Baird's Flycatcher)
SW Ecuador, W Peru
Myiodynastes chrysocephalus (Golden-crowned Flycatcher)
M. c. cinerascens
NW Venezuela
M. c. intermedius
N Venezuela, N Colombia
M. c. minor
Colombia, Ecuador
M. c. chrysocephalus
Peru, Bolivia

Myiodynastes hemichrysus (Golden-bellied Flycatcher)
Costa Rica, W Panama

MYIOZETETES
Myiozetetes cayanensis (Rusty-margined Flycatcher)
M. c. harterti
E Panama
M. c. rufipennis
N Venezuela, E Colombia
M. c. hellmayri
Columbia, E Ecuador, NW Venezuela
M. c. cayanensis
the Guianas, N Brazil, E Bolivia,
S Venezuela
M. c. erythropterus
SE Brazil
Myiozetetes granadensis (Grey-capped Flycatcher)
M. g. granadensis
E Honduras to CE Panama
M. g. occidentalis
E Panama to NW Peru
M. g. obscurior
S Venezuela, S Colombia, E Ecuador,
W Brazil, SE Peru
Myiozetetes similis (Vermilion-crowned Flycatcher)
M. s. primulus
N Mexico
M. s. hesperis
W Mexico
M. s. texensis
S Mexico to N Costa Rica
M. s. colombianus
SW Costa Rica, Panama, N Colombia,
N Venezuela
M. s. connivens
Colombia, SE Peru, Venezuela, N Brazil
M. s. grandis
W Ecuador, NW Peru
M. s. pallidventris
E Brazil, E Paraguay, NE Argentina
M. s. similis
E Brazil, Paraguay, NE Argentina
Myiozetetes inornatus (White-bearded Flycatcher)
Venezuela

PITANGUS
Pitangus sulphuratus (Great Kiskadee)
P. s. derbianus
S Texas, C Mexico
P. s. palliatus
W Mexico
P. s. texanus
E Mexico, S Texas

P. s. guatimalensis
S Mexico, Guatemala to Pará
P. s. pallidus
Honduras to Costa Rica
P. s. trinitatis
C Colombia, Trinidad, Venezuela
P. s. caucensis
W Colombia
P. s. rufipennis
N Venezuela, Colombia
P. s. sulphuratus
S Colombia, the Guianas, N Brazil,
NE Peru, E Ecuador
P. s. maximiliani
E & C Brazil, E Bolivia
P. s. bolivianus
E Bolivia
P. s. argentinus
Paraguay, Bolivia, N Argentina
Pitangus lictor (Lesser Kiskadee)
P. l. panamensis
E Panama, N Colombia
P. l. lictor
Venezuela, the Guianas, N Brazil, E Peru,
E Ecuador, E Colombia

MYIARCHINAE

MYIARCHUS
Myiarchus semirufus (Rufous Flycatcher)
Peru
**Myiarchus validus (Rufous-tailed
Flycatcher)**
Jamaica
Myiarchus ferox (Short-crested Flycatcher)
M. f. brunnescens
Venezuela
M. f. ferox
S Colombia to E Peru, N Brazil, the Guianas
M. f. australis
E Bolivia to S Brazil, N Argentina
**Myiarchus venezuelensis (Venezuelan
Flycatcher)**
M. v. venezuelensis
NE Colombia, NW Venezuela
M. v. insulicola
Tobago I
Myiarchus panamensis (Panama Flycatcher)
M. p. actiosus
Costa Rica
M. p. panamensis
Panama, N Colombia, NW Venezuela
Myiarchus apicalis (Apical Flycatcher)
SW Colombia
**Myiarchus cephalotes (Pale-edged
Flycatcher)**
M. c. caucae
N Colombia

M. c. caribbaeus
Venezuela
M. c. cephalotes
Bolivia, Peru, Ecuador, W Colombia
**Myiarchus phaeocephalus (Sooty-crowned
Flycatcher)**
M. p. phaeocephalus
W Ecuador, NW Peru
M. p. interior
NW Peru
**Myiarchus tyrannulus (Brown Crested
Flycatcher)**
M. t. magister
SW USA, W Mexico, Tres Marias I
M. t. cooperi
SW USA, W Mexico to Honduras
M. t. tyrannulus
Trinidad, Venezuela, the Guianas, N Brazil,
N Colombia
M. t. brevipennis
North Venezuelan Islands
M. t. tobagensis
Tobago I
M. t. bahiae
N & E Brazil
M. t. chlorepiscius
S Brazil, Bolivia, Peru, Paraguay,
N Argentina
**Myiarchus nuttingi (Pale-throated
Flycatcher)**
M. n. inquietus
W & C Mexico
M. n. nuttingi
mountains of Central America
M. n. flavidior
Pacific coast of Central America
Myiarchus oberi (Wied's Crested Flycatcher)
M. o. oberi
Domenica I, Guadelupe I
M. o. sanctaeluciae
St Lucia I
M. o. berlepschii
Nevis I, St Kitts I
M. o. sclateri
Martinique I
Myiarchus nugator (Grenada Flycatcher)
Lesser Antilles Is
**Myiarchus yucatanensis (Yucatan
Flycatcher)**
M. y. yucatanensis
Yucatan peninsula, Guatemala, Belize
M. y. lanyoni
Cozumel I
Myiarchus stolidus (Stolid Flycatcher)
M. s. dominicensis
Hispaniola
M. s. stolidus
Jamaica

Myiarchus antillarum (Puerto Rican Flycatcher)
Puerto Rico
Myiarchus sagrae (La Sagra's Flycatcher)
M. s. sagrae
Cuba, Grand Cayman Is
M. s. lucaysiensis
Bahama Is
Myiarchus swainsoni (Swainson's Flycatcher)
M. s. swainsoni
E Paraguay, NE Argentina » E Colombia, N Venezuela
M. s. phaeonotus
S Guyana, S Venezuela
M. s. amazonus
NE Brazil
M. s. pelzelni
E Peru, SE Brazil, N Bolivia
M. s. ferocior
SE Bolivia, N Argentina » SE Colombia
Myiarchus crinitus (Great Crested Flycatcher)
E Canada, E USA » Mexico, Central America
Myiarchus cinerascens (Ash-throated Flycatcher)
M. c. cinerascens
W USA, W Mexico » Guatemala, NW Costa Rica
M. c. pertinax
Baja California
Myiarchus tuberculifer (Olivaceous Flycatcher)
M. t. olivascens
SW USA, W Mexico
M. t. tresmariae
Tres Marias Is
M. t. lawrencei
E & S Mexico
M. t. querulus
SW Mexico
M. t. platyrhynchus
SE Mexico
M. t. connectens
Guatemala to N Nicaragua
M. t. littoralis
Pacific coast from SE Honduras to Costa Rica
M. t. nigricapillus
SE Nicaragua, Costa Rica
M. t. bangsi
SW Costa Rica, W Panama
M. t. brunneiceps
E Panama, W Colombia
M. t. pallidus
N Colombia, W Venezuela

M. t. tuberculifer
Colombia and Surinam to Bolivia and S Brazil
M. t. tricolor
French Guiana, E Brazil
M. t. nigriceps
W Ecuador, W Colombia
M. t. atriceps
C Peru, C Bolivia, NW Argentina
Myiarchus barbirostris (Dusky-capped Flycatcher)
Jamaica
Myiarchus magnirostris (Galapagos Flycatcher)
Galapagos Is

ATTILA
Attila spadiceus (Bright-rumped Attila)
A. s. pacificus
NW Mexico
A. s. cozumelae
Cozumel I
A. s. gaumeri
SE Mexico
A. s. flammulatus
SE Mexico to El Salvador
A. s. citreopygus
Nicaragua to W Panama
A. s. sclateri
E Panama, NW Colombia
A. s. caniceps
N Colombia
A. s. parvirostris
NE Colombia, NW Venezuela
A. s. parambae
W Ecuador, W Colombia
A. s. spadiceus
the Guianas, Trinidad, N Venezuela N Brazil, NE Peru, N Bolivia
A. s. uropygiatus
SE Brazil
Attila bolivianus (Dull-capped Attila)
A. b. nattereri
N Brazil
A. b. bolivianus
SW Brazil, E Bolivia, E Peru
Attila rufus (Grey-hooded Attila)
SE Brazil
Attila citriniventris (Citron-bellied Attila)
Venezuela, Ecuador, N Peru, NW Brazil
Attila cinnamomeus (Cinnamon Attila)
South America
Attila torridus (Ochraceous Attila)
W Ecuador, SW Colombia

PSEUDATTILA
Pseudattila phoenicurus (Rufous-tailed Attila)
Venezuela, Brazil, Paraguay, N Argentina

RHYTIPTERNA
Rhytipterna simplex (Greyish Mourner)
R. s. frederici
N South America
R. s. simplex
SE Brazil
Rhytipterna immunda (Pale-bellied Mourner)
Surinam, French Guiana, SE Colombia, N Brazil
Rhytipterna holerythra (Rufous Mourner)
R. h. holerythra
Guatemala to Panama, N Colombia
R. h. rosenbergi
W Colombia, NW Ecuador

CASIORNIS
Casiornis rufa (Rufous Casiornis)
E Bolivia, C Brazil, Paraguay, N Argentina
Casiornis fusca (Ash-throated Casiornis)
NE Brazil

LANIOCERA
Laniocera hypopyrra (Cinereous Mourner)
the Guianas, Venezuela, Colombia, Bolivia, N & W Brazil
Laniocera rufescens (Speckled Mourner)
L. r. rufescens
Guatemala to Panama, W Colombia
L. r. tertia
NW Ecuador, SW Colombia
L. r. griseigula
NC Colombia

NESOTRICCUS
Nesotriccus ridgwayi (Cocos I Flycatcher)
Cocos I, Panama

DELTARHYNCHUS
Deltarhynchus flammulatus (Flammulated Flycatcher)
SW & S Mexico

NUTTALLORNIS
Nuttallornis borealis (Olive-sided Flycatcher)
W Canada, W USA, W Mexico, Central America, N South America

CONTOPUS
Contopus virens (Eastern Wood Pewee)
E Canada, E USA » Central America, N South America
Contopus sordidulus (Western Wood Pewee)
C. s. sordidulus
S Mexico » Colombia, Ecuador
C. s. siccicola
NW USA
C. s. veliei
W Mexico, SW USA » Panama

C. s. saturatus
W North America » N South America
C. s. peninsulae
S Baja California, SE Mexico
C. s. griscomi
Mexico
C. s. amplus
WC North America » N South America
Contopus cinereus (Tropical Pewee)
C. c. cinereus
SE Brazil, N Argentina, Paraguay
C. c. pallescens
S Brazil, N Paraguay
C. c. surinamensis
the Guianas, S Venezuela, N Brazil
C. c. bogotensis
Trinidad, N Venezuela, N Colombia
C. c. punensis
SW Ecuador, Peru
C. c. rhizophorus
W Costa Rica
C. c. brachytarsus
SE Mexico to Panama
C. c. aithalodes
Coiba I, Panama
Contopus albogularis (White-throated Pewee)
French Guiana, Surinam
Contopus nigrescens (Blackish Pewee)
C. n. nigrescens
E Ecuador
C. n. canescens
NE Peru
Contopus fumigatus (Smoke-coloured Pewee)
C. f. lugubris
Costa Rica, W Panama
C. f. cineraceus
N Venezuela
C. f. duidae
SE Venezuela
C. f. roraimae
SE Venezuela
C. f. ardosiacus
NE Peru, E Ecuador, Colombia, NW Venezuela
C. f. zarumae
W Ecuador, NW Peru
C. f. fumigatus
SE Peru, Bolivia
C. f. brachyrhynchus
NW Argentina
Contopus pertinax (Greater Pewee)
C. p. pertinax
C & S Mexico, Guatemala, Belize

C. p. pallidiventris
S Arizona, N Mexico » Guatemala
C. p. minor
Nicaragua, Honduras, Belize
Contopus caribaeus (Greater Antillean Pewee)
C. c. caribaeus
Cuba
C. c. morenoi
S Cuba
C. c. nerlyi
islands off SC Cuba
C. c. tacitus
Gonave I
C. c. bahamensis
Bahama Is
C. c. hispaniolensis
Hispaniola
C. c. pallidus
Jamaica
Contopus latirostris (Lesser Antillean Pewee)
C. l. latirostris
St Lucia I
C. l. brunneicapillus
Domenica I, Guadelupe I, Martinique I
C. l. blancoi
Puerto Rico
Contopus ochraceus (Ochraceous Pewee)
Costa Rica, W Panama

EMPIDONAX
Empidonax flaviventris (Yellow-bellied Flycatcher)
S Canada, N USA » S Mexico,
Central America
Empidonax virescens (Acadian Flycatcher)
E USA, E Mexico » Central America,
Colombia, W Ecuador
Empidonax traillii (Traill's Flycatcher)
Canada, USA » Mexico, Central America,
N South America
Empidonax alnorum (Alder Flycatcher)
E Canada, E USA » Central America
& South America
Empidonax minimus (Least Flycatcher)
E Canada, E USA » S Mexico,
Central America, NW South America
Empidonax hammondii (Hammond's Flycatcher)
W Canada, W USA » Mexico, Guatemala
Empidonax oberholseri (Wright's Flycatcher)
W USA, Mexico
Empidonax wrightii (Grey Flycatcher)
W USA, California » Mexico

Empidonax affinis (Pine Flycatcher)
E. a. pulverius
NW Mexico
E. a. trepidus
NE Mexico, Guatemala
E. a. affinis
C Mexico
E. a. bairdi
C & S Mexico
E. a. vigensis
E Mexico
Empidonax difficilis (Western Flycatcher)
E. d. difficilis
W Canada, W USA, NW Mexico
E. d. cineritus
Baja (California)
E. d. insulicola
Channel Is, S California
E. d. hellmayri
N Mexico
E. d. occidentalis
S & C Mexico
Empidonax flavescens (Yellowish Flycatcher)
E. f. dwighti
S Mexico
E. f. imperturbatus
S Mexico
E. f. salvini
SE Mexico to Nicaragua
E. f. flavescens
Costa Rica, W Panama
Empidonax euleri (Euler's Flycatcher)
E. a. euleri
N Peru, Brazil, Uruguay, Paraguay,
NE Argentina
E. e. argentinus
S Peru, W Paraguay, NW Argentina
E. e. bolivianus
NW & E Bolivia
Empidonax lawrencei (Lawrence's Flycatcher)
E. l. lawrencei
Trinidad, Venezuela, Surinam, N Brazil,
N Peru
E. l. johnstonei
Grenada I
Empidonax griseipectus (Grey-breasted Flycatcher)
SW Ecuador, NW Peru
Empidonax albigularis (White-throated Flycatcher)
E. a. timidus
NW Mexico
E. a. albigularis
C & S Mexico, Guatemala, Honduras

E. a. australis
Nicaragua to Panama
Empidonax atriceps (Black-capped Flycatcher)
Costa Rica, W Panama
Empidonax fulvifrons (Buff-breasted Flycatcher)
E. f. pygmaeus
SW USA, W Mexico
E. f. fulvifrons
NE Mexico
E. f. rubicundus
C & S Mexico
E. f. fusciceps
SE Mexico, Guatemala
E. f. brodkorbi
S Oaxaca
E. f. inexpectatus
SC Honduras

CNEMOTRICCUS
Cnemotriccus fuscatus (Fuscous Flycatcher)
C. f. cabanisi
Trinidad, Tobago I, Venezuela, Colombia,
C. f. fuscatior
SW Venezuela, N Brazil, E Peru
C. f. duidae
SE Venezuela
C. f. fumosus
the Guianas, N Brazil
C. f. bimaculatus
W & C Brazil, E Bolivia, Paraguay,
N Argentina
C. f. beniensis
N Bolivia
C. f. fuscatus
SE Brazil, N Argentina

MITREPHANES
Mitrephanes phaeocercus (Tufted Flycatcher)
M. p. tenuirostris
W Mexico
M. p. phaeocercus
S & E Mexico to Honduras
M. p. hidalgensis
C Mexico
M̃. p. burleighi
Guerrero, SW Oaxaca
M. p. nicaraguae
S Mexico to Nicaragua
M. p. aurantiiventris
Costa Rica, W Panama
M. p. vividus
C Panama

M. p. eminulus
E Panama, W Colombia
M. p. berlepschi
S Colombia, NW Ecuador
Mitrephanes olivacens (Olive Flycatcher)
E Peru, Bolivia

XENOTRICCUS
Xenotriccus callizonus (Belted Flycatcher)
Mexico

AECHMOLOPHUS
Aechmolophus mexicanus (Pileated Flycatcher)
S Mexico

TERENOTRICCUS
Terenotriccus erythrurus (Ruddy-tailed Flycatcher)
T. e. fulvigularis
Guatemala to Panama, Colombia,
Venezuela
T. e. signatus
C & S Colombia to NE Peru
T. e. venezuelensis
E Colombia, W Venezuela, NW Brazil
T. e. brunneifrons
SW Brail, E Peru, N Bolivia
T. e. erythrurus
the Guianas, S Venezuela, N Brazil
T. e. amazonus
C Brazil
T. e. hellmayri
N Brazil

APHANOTRICCUS
Aphanotriccus capitalis (Tawny-chested Flycatcher)
Nicaragua, Costa Rica
Aphanotriccus audax (Black-billed Flycatcher)
Panama, NW Colombia

MYIOBIUS
Myiobius villosus (Tawny-breasted Flycatcher)
M. v. villosus
E Panama, Colombia, W Ecuador
M. v. schaeferi
NW Venezuela, NE Colombia
M. v. clarus
E Ecuador
M. v. peruvianus
SE Peru, W Bolivia

Myiobius barbatus (Whiskered Flycatcher)
the Guianas, E Venezuela, SE Colombia,
E Ecuador, N Brazil

Myiobius sulphureipygius (Sulphur-rumped Flycatcher)
M. s. sulphureipygius
  S Mexico to Honduras
M. s. aureatus
  S Honduras to Panama, W Colombia,
    W Ecuador
M. s. amazonicus
  W Brazil, E Peru
M. s. insignis
  NE Brazil
M. s. mastacalis
  E Brazil
M. s. semiflavus
  E Colombia

Myiobius atricaudus (Black-tailed Flycatcher)
M. a. atricaudus
  SW Costa Rica, Panama, W Colombia
M. a. portovelae
  W Ecuador, N Peru
M. a. modestus
  E Venezuela
M. a. adjacens
  S Colombia, E Ecuador, E Peru, W Brazil
M. a. connectens
  NE Brazil
M. a. snethlagei
  NE Brazil
M. a. ridgwayi
  SE Brazil

MYIOTRICCUS
Myiotriccus ornatus (Ornate Flycatcher)
M. o. ornatus
  C Colombia
M. o. stellatus
  W Colombia, W Ecuador
M. o. phoenicurus
  SE Colombia, E Ecuador, N Peru
M. o. aureiventris
  S Peru

PYRRHOMYIAS
Pyrrhomyias cinnamomea (Cinnamon Flycatcher)
P. c. assimilis
  NW Colombia
P. c. pyrrhoptera
  Colombia, Venezuela, Ecuador, N Peru
P. c. vieillotioides
  Venezuela
P. c. spadix
  NE Venezuela
P.c. pariae
  NE Venezuela
P. c. cinnamomea
  Bolivia, Peru, NW Argentina

Myiophobus flavicans (Flavescent Flycatcher)
M. f. flavicans
  Colombia, Ecuador, N Peru
M. f. perijanus
  NW Venezuela
M. f. venezuelanus
  N Venezuela
M. f. caripensis
  NE Venezuela
M. f. superciliosus
  Peru

Myiophobus phoenicomitra (Orange-crested Flycatcher)
M. p. litae
  NW Ecuador, W Colombia
M. p. phoenicomitra
  E Ecuador, N Peru

Myiophobus cryptoxanthus (Olive-crested Flycatcher)
  E Ecuador, E Peru

Myiophobus inornatus (Unadorned Flycatcher)
  Peru, Bolivia

Myiophobus pulcher (Handsome Flycatcher)
M. p. pulcher
  W Colombia, W Ecuador
M. p. bellus
  E Colombia, E Ecuador
M. p. oblitus
  SE Peru

Myiophobus lintoni (Orange-banded Flycatcher)
  SE Ecuador

Myiophobus ochraceiventris (Ochraceous-breasted Flycatcher)
  C Peru, NW Bolivia

Myiophobus fasciatus (Bran-coloured Flycatcher)
M. f. furfurosus
  SW Costa Rica, Panama
M. f. fasciatus
  the Guianas, Trinidad, N Venezuela
    Colombia
M. f. crypterythrus
  S Colombia, W Ecuador, N Peru
M. f. saturatus
  E Peru
M. f. rufescens
  W Peru, N Chile
M. f. auriceps
  SE Peru, N & E Bolivia, N Argentina,
    W Paraguay
M. f. flammiceps
  Brazil, Bolivia, Uruguay, Paraguay,
    N Argentina

***Myiophobus roraimae* (Roraiman Flycatcher)**
Guyana

HIRUNDINEA
***Hirundinea ferruginea* (Cliff Flycatcher)**
H. f. ferruginea
Guyana, French Guiana, N Brazil
H. f. sclateri
E Colombia, Peru
H. f. bellicosa
S Brazil, Paraguay, NE Argentina
H. f. pallidior
Bolivia, NW Argentina

ONYCHORHYNCHUS
***Onychorhynchus coronatus* (Amazonian Royal Flycatcher)**
O. c. castelnaudi
Western Amazonia
O. c. coronatus
E Venezuela, the Guianas, N Brazil
O. c. occidentalis
W Ecuador
O. c. swainsoni
SE Brazil
***Onychorhynchus mexicanus* (Northern Royal Flycatcher)**
O. m. mexicanus
S Mexico to E Panama
O. m. fraterculus
N Colombia, W Venezuela

PLATYRINCHINAE

PLATYRINCHUS
***Platyrinchus platyrhynchos* (White crested Spadebill)**
P. p. platyrhynchos
S Venezuela, the Guianas, N Brazil
P. p. senex
E Ecuador, E Peru, NW Bolivia
P. p. nattereri
W Brazil
P. p. amazonicus
E Brazil
***Platyrinchus leucoryphus* (Russet-winged Spadebill)**
SE Brazil, E Paraguay
***Platyrinchus mystaceus* (White-throated Spadebill)**
P. m. neglectus
E Costa Rica to E Colombia
P. m. perijanus
NW Venezuela
P. m. insularis
Trinidad, N Venezuela
P. m. imatacae
E Venezuela

P. m. ventralis
S Venezuela
P. m. duidae
SE Venezuela, N Brazil
P. m. ptaritepui
SE Venezuela
P. m. albogularis
W Ecuador, W Colombia
P. m. zamorae
E Ecuador, N Peru
P. m. mystaceus
E Brazil, Paraguay, N Argentina
P. m. partridgei
C Bolivia
P. m. bifasciatus
SW Brazil
P. m. cancromus
E Brazil
P. m. niveigularis
NE Brazil
***Platyrinchus cancrominus* (Mexican Spadebill)**
P. c. cancrominus
S Mexico to E Nicaragua
P. c. timothei
SE Mexico to N Guatemala
P. c. dilutus
El Salvador to NW Costa Rica
***Platyrinchus coronatus* (Golden-crowned Spadebill)**
P. c. superciliaris
Nicaragua to W Ecuador
P. c. gumia
the Guianas, N Brazil
P. c. coronatus
W Amazonia
***Platyrinchus saturatus* (Cinnamon-crested Spadebill)**
P. s. saturatus
S Venezuela, the Guianas, N Brazil
P. s. pallidiventris
C Brazil
***Platyrinchus flavigularis* (Yellow-throated Spadebill)**
P. f. flavigularis
Colombia, Peru
P. f. vividus
W Venezuela

CNIPODECTES
***Cnipodectes subbrunneus* (Brownish Flycatcher)**
C. s. subbrunneus
W Ecuador, W Colombia
C. s. panamensis
E Panama, N Colombia

C. s. minor
  SE Colombia, E Peru, W Brazil

TOLMOMYIAS
Tolmomyias sulphurescens (Yellow-olive Flycatcher)
T. s. cinereiceps
  S Mexico to Costa Rica
T. s. flavoolivaceus
  Panama
T. s. berlepschi
  Trinidad
T. s. exortivus
  N Venezuela, N Colombia
T. s. asemus
  Colombia
T. s. confusus
  C Colombia, SW Venezuela, NE Ecuador
T. s. duidae
  SE Venezuela, NW Brazil
T. s. cherriei
  E Colombia to the Guianas, N Brazil
T. s. peruvianus
  SE Ecuador, N Peru
T. s. insignis
  NE Peru, W Brazil
T. s. mixtus
  NE Brazil
T. s. inornatus
  SE Peru
T. s. pallescens
  C Brazil to N Argentina
T. s. grisescens
  C Paraguay, N Argentina
T. s. sulphurescens
  S Brazil, N Argentina
Tolmomyias assimilis (Yellow-margined Flycatcher)
T. a. flavotectus
  Costa Rica to NW Ecuador
T. a. neglectus
  E Colombia, S Venezuela, NE Brazil
T. a. obscuriceps
  S Colombia to NE Peru
T. a. examinatus
  SE Venezuela, the Guianas, N Brazil
T. a. assimilis
  C Brazil
T. a. clarus
  C Peru
T. a. paraensis
  NE Brazil
T. a. calamae
  N Bolivia, SW Brazil
Tolmomyias poliocephalus (Grey-crowned Flycatcher)
T. p. poliocephalus
  W Amazonia

T. p. klagesi
  S Venezuela
T. p. sclateri
  the Guianas, N Brazil
Tolmomyias flaviventris (Yellow-breasted Flycatcher)
T. f. aurulentus
  N Colombia, N Venezuela
T. f. collingwoodi
  C & E Colombia to Guyana, N Brazil, Trinidad
T. f. dissors
  NE Brazil, SE Venezuela
T. f. viridiceps
  SE Colombia, E Ecuador, E Peru
T. f. borbae
  W Brazil
T. f. zimmeri
  NC Peru
T. f. subsimilis
  SE Peru, NW Bolivia, SW Brazil
T. f. flaviventris
  E Brazil

RHYNCHOCYCLUS
Rhynchocyclus olivaceus (Olivaceous Flatbill)
R. o. bardus
  E Panama, N Colombia
R. o. mirus
  NW Colombia
R. o. tamborensis
  Colombia
R. o. flavus
  NW Colombia, N Venezuela
R. o. aequinoctialis
  S Colombia, E Ecuador, E Peru, NC Bolivia
R. o. guianensis
  N & NW Amazonia
R. o. sordidus
  C Brazil
R. o. olivaceus
  SE Brazil
Rhynchocyclus brevirostris (Eye-ringed Flatbill)
R. b. brevirostris
  S Mexico to W Panama
R. b. pallidus
  S Mexico
R. b. hellmayri
  E Panama, N Colombia
R. b. pacificus
  NW Ecuador, W Colombia
Rhynchocyclus fulvipectus (Fulvous-breasted Flatbill)
  Colombia, E Ecuador, SE Peru

Ramphotrigon ruficauda (Rufous-tailed Flatbill)
N Amazonia

Ramphotrigon fuscicauda (Dusky-tailed Flatbill)
E Ecuador, S Colombia, E Peru

Ramphotrigon megacephala (Large-headed Flatbill)
R. m. pectoralis
S Colombia, S Venezuela
R. m. venezuelensis
W Venezuela
R. m. boliviana
SE Peru, W Brazil, N Bolivia
R. m. megacephala
SE Brazil, Paraguay, N Argentina

EUSCARTHMINAE

TODIROSTRUM

Todirostrum nigriceps (Black-headed Tody Flycatcher)
Costa Rica, Panama, N Colombia, W Ecuador

Todirostrum chrysocrotaphum (Yellow-browed Tody Flycatcher)
T. c. guttatum
SW Venezuela, Colombia, NW Brazil, N Peru
T. c. neglectum
E Peru, N Bolivia, SW Brazil
T. c. similis
NE Brazil
T. c. illigeri
NE Brazil
T. c. chrysocrotaphum
E Peru, N Bolivia, W Brazil

Todirostrum pictum (Painted Tody Flycatcher)
The Guianas, N Brazil

Todirostrum calopterum (Golden-winged Tody Flycatcher)
T. c. calopterum
S Colombia, E Ecuador
T. c. pulchellum
SE Peru

Todirostrum poliocephalum (Grey-headed Tody Flycatcher)
SE Brazil

Todirostrum cinereum (Common Tody Flycatcher)
T. c. virididorsale
SC Mexico
T. c. finitimum
S Mexico to Panama
T. c. wetmorei
C & E Costa Rica, Panama
T. c. sclateri
SW Colombia, W Ecuador, NW Peru

T. c. cinereum
the Guianas, N Brazil, S Venezuela, S Colombia
T. c. peruanum
E Ecuador, N & E Peru
T. c. coloreum
C Brazil, E Bolivia
T. c. cearae
E Brazil

Todirostrum viridanum (Short-tailed Tody Flycatcher)
NW Venezuela

Todirostrum maculatum (Spotted Tody Flycatcher)
T. m. amacurense
NE Venezuela, Guyana, Trinidad
T. m. maculatum
E Venezuela, the Guianas, N Brazil
T. m. signatum
E Ecuador, E Peru, W Brazil
T. m. diversum
WC Brazil
T. m. annectens
C Brazil

Todirostrum fumifons (Smoky-fronted Tody Flycatcher)
T. f. fumifrons
NE Brazil
T. f. penardi
French Guiana, Surinam

Todirostrum senex (Plumbeous-crowned Tody Flycatcher)
C Brazil

Todirostrum capitale (Black and White Tody Flycatcher)
SE Columbia, E Ecuador, NE Peru

Todirostrum tricolor (Tricoloured Tody Flycatcher)
C Brazil, SE Peru

Todirostrum russatum (Ruddy Tody Flycatcher)
SE Venezuela, NE Brazil

Todirostrum plumbeiceps (Ochre-faced Tody Flycatcher)
T. p. obscurum
SE Peru, N Bolivia
T. p. viridiceps
Bolivia, NW Argentina
T. p. plumbeiceps
SE Brazil, Paraguay, NE Argentina
T. p. cinereipectum
SC Brazil

Todirostrum latirostre (Rusty-fronted Tody Flycatcher)
T. l. mituense
Colombia
T. l. caniceps
SE Colombia, E Ecuador, E Peru

T. l. latirostre
C Brazil
T. l. mixtum
SE Peru
T. l. ochropterum
S Brazil, SE Bolivia
T. l. austroriparium
Santarem, Brazil
T. l. senectum
Lower Amazon, Brazil
Todirostrum sylvia (Slate-headed Tody Flycatcher)
T. s. schistaceiceps
S Mexico to Panama
T. s. superciliare
N Colombia
T. s. griseolum
N Venezuela
T. s. sylvia
Guyana, French Guiana, N Brazil
T. s. schulzi
NE Brazil

CERATOTRICCUS
Ceratotriccus furcatus (Fork-tailed Pygmy Tyrant)
SE Brazil

ONCOSTOMA
Oncostoma olivaceum (Southern Bentbill)
E Panama, N Colombia
Oncostoma cinereigulare (Northern Bentbill)
O. c. pacifica
W Mexico
O. c. cinereigulare
S Mexico to W Panama

IDIOPTILON
Idioptilon nidipendulum (Hangnest Tody Tyrant)
I. n. nidipendulum
E Brazil
I. n. paulistus
SE Brazil
Idioptilon rufigulare (Buff-throated Tody Tyrant)
C & SE Peru, NW Bolivia
Idioptilon striaticolle (Stripe-necked Tody Tyrant)
I. s. griseiceps
N Brazil
I. s. striaticolle
C & E Brazil, N Bolivia, N Peru, E Colombia
Idioptilon iohannis (Johanne's Pygmy Tyrant)
W Amazonia

Idioptilon spodiops (Yungas Tody Tyrant) 329
NE Brazil
Idioptilon aenigma (Zimmer's Tody Tyrant)
Brazil
Idioptilon inornatum (Pelzeln's Tody Tyrant)
NW Brazil
Idioptilon mirandae (Buff-breasted Tody Tyrant)
NE Brazil
Idioptilon kaempferi (Kaempfer's Tody Tyrant)
Santa Caterina (Brazil)
Idioptilon margaritaceiventer (Pearly-vented Tody Tyrant)
I. m. impiger
N Venezuela, N Colombia
I. m. septentrionalis
E Colombia, W Venezuela
I. m. duidae
SE Venezuela
I. m. breweri
Cerro Jaua (S Venezuela)
I. m. wuchereri
NE Brazil
I. m. margaritaceiventer
S Peru, E Bolivia, SW Brazil, Paraguay, N Argentina
I. m. auyantepui
SE Venezuela
Idioptilon granadense (Black-throated Tody Tyrant)
I. g. granadense
Colombia, NE Ecuador
I. g. intense
NW Venezuela
I. g. pyrrhops
S Ecuador, N Peru
I. g. andinum
E & C Colombia, W Venezuela
I. g. lehmanni
NW Colombia
I. g. federalis
N Venezuela
I. g. caesius
SE Peru
Idioptilon zosterops (White-eyed Tody Tyrant)
I. z. zosterops
NW Brazil, Venezuela, E Ecuador, SE Colombia
I. z. flaviviridis
N Peru
I. z. griseipectus
SE Peru, N Brazil
I. z. naumburgae
E Brazil

Idioptilon orbitatum (Olivaceous Tody Tyrant)
SE Brazil

MICROCOCHLEARIUS
Microcochlearius josephinae (Boat-billed Tody Tyrant)
Guyana, NE Brazil

SNETHLAGEA
Snethlagea minor (Snethlage's Tody Tyrant)
S. m. minor
N Brazil
S. m. pallens
W Brazil
S. m. minima
C Brazil

POECILOTRICCUS
Poecilotriccus ruficeps (Rufous-crowned Tody Tyrant)
P. r. melanomystax
C Colombia
P. r. ruficeps
E Ecuador, S Colombia, SW Venezeula
P. r. rufigenis
W Ecuador, W Colombia
P. r. peruvianus
NW Peru

TAENIOTRICCUS
Taeniotriccus andrei (Black-chested Tyrant)
T. a. andrei
SE Venezuela, N Brazil
T. a. klagesi
Rio Tapajoz (Brazil)

LOPHOTRICCUS
Lophotriccus pileatus (Scale-crested Pygmy Tyrant)
L. p. luteiventris
Costa Rica, W Panama
L. p. hesperius
W Andes of Colombia
L. p. sanctaeluciae
NE Colombia, N coast of Venezuela
L. p. squamaecrista
S & C Colombia, W Ecuador, W Venezuela
L. p. pileatus
Peru, E Ecuador
L. p. hypochlorus
SE Peru
Lophotriccus vitiosus (Double-banded Pygmy Tyrant)
L. v. affinis
SW Colombia to NE Peru, NW Brazil
L. v. guianensis
SC Colombia, the Guianas, NE Brazil

L. v. vitiosus
E Peru
L. v. congener
NW Brazil
Lophotriccus eulophotes (Long-crested Pygmy Tyrant)
W Brazil, Peru

COLOPTERYX
Colopteryx galeatus (Helmeted Pygmy Tyrant)
the Guianas, N Brazil, Venezuela

ATALOTRICCUS
Atalotriccus pilaris (Pale-eyed Pygmy Tyrant)
A. p. wilcoxi
W Panama
A. p. pilaris
W Venezuela, N & E Colombia
A. p. venezuelensis
N Venezuela
A. p. griseiceps
S Venezuela, W Guyana

MYIORNIS
Myiornis auricularis (Eared Pygmy Tyrant)
SE Brazil, N Argentina
Myiornis ecaudatus (Short-tailed Pygmy Tyrant)
M. e. miserabilis
C Colombia, Trinidad, Guyana, Venezuela, Surinam
M. e. ecaudatus
E Peru & Bolivia
M. e. atricapillus
E Costa Rica to NW Ecuador
Myiornis albiventris (White-breasted Pygmy Tyrant)
C Peru

PSEUDOTRICCUS
Pseudotriccus pelzelni (Bronze-olive Pygmy Tyrant)
P. p. berlepschi
E Panama
P. p. annectens
W Colombia, W Ecuador
P. p. pelzelni
E Colombia, E Ecuador
P. p. peruvianus
E Peru
Pseudotriccus simplex (Hazel-fronted Pygmy Tyrant)
Bolivia, SE Peru
Pseudotriccus ruficeps (Rufous-headed Pygmy Tyrant)
Colombia to NW Bolivia

Hemitriccus cinnamomeipectus
(Cinnamon-breasted Tody Tyrant)
  NC Peru
Hemitriccus diops (Drab-breasted Pygmy
Tyrant)
  SE Brazil, Paraguay
Hemitriccus obsoletus (Brown-breasted
Pygmy Tyrant)
  H. o. obsoletus
  SE Brazil
  H. o. zimmeri
  SE Brazil
Hemitriccus flammulatus (Flammulated
Pygmy Tyrant)
  H. f. flammulatus
  Peru, Bolivia, W Brazil
  H. f. olivascens
  E Bolivia

Pogonotriccus eximius (Southern
Bristle Tyrant)
  SE Brazil, Paraguay, N Argentina
Pogonotriccus ophthalmicus (Marble-
faced Bristle Tyrant)
  P. o. ophthalmicus
  NW Venezuela, Colombia, Ecuador, Peru
  P. o. ottonis
  SE Peru, W Bolivia
  P. o. purus
  coast of Venezuela
Pogonotriccus gualaquizae (Ecuadorean
Bristle Tyrant)
  E Ecuador, N Peru
Pogonotriccus poecilotis (Variegated
Bristle Tyrant)
  P. p. poecilotis
  N Colombia to Ecuador
  P. p. pifanoi
  NE Colombia, NW Venezuela
Pogonotriccus orbitalis (Spectacled
Bristle Tyrant)
  E Ecuador, Peru, S Colombia
Pogonotriccus venezuelanus (Venezuelan
Bristle Tyrant)
  NW Venezuela⁄
Pogonotriccus flaviventris (Yellow-bellied
Bristle Tyrant)
  NW Venezuela

Leptotriccus sylviolus (Bay-ringed
Tyrannulet)
  SE Brazil, Paraguay

Phylloscartes flavovirens (Yellow-green
Tyrannulet)
  Panama

Phylloscartes virescens (Olive-green   331
Tyrannulet)
  the Guianas
Phylloscartes ventralis (Mottle-cheeked
Tyrannulet)
  P. v. angustirostris
  Peru, Bolivia, NW Argentina
  P. v. tucumanus
  NW Argentina
  P. v. ventralis
  SE Brazil, Uruguay, Paraguay,
  NE Argentina
Phylloscartes chapmani (Chapman's
Tyrannulet)
  P. c. chapmani
  S Venezuela
  P. c. duidae
  SE Venezuela
Phylloscartes nigrifrons (Black-fronted
Tyrannulet)
  S Venezuela
Phylloscartes oustaleti (Oustalet's
Tyrannulet)
  SE Brazil, Uruguay, Paraguay,
  NE Argentina
Phylloscartes difficilis (Ihering's
Tyrannulet)
  SE Brazil
Phylloscartes paulistus (Sao Paulo
Tryrannulet)
  SE Brazil, Paraguay
Phylloscartes superciliaris (Rufous-
browed Tyrannulet)
  P. s. superciliaris
  Costa Rica to W Panama
  P. s. griseocapillus
  NW Venezuela
  P. s. palloris
  E Panama
Phylloscartes roquettei (Minas Geraes
Tyrannulet)
  Brazil

Capsiempis flaveola (Yellow Tyrannulet)
  C. f. semiflava
  Nicaragua to Panama
  C. f. cerula
  Venezuela, Colombia, Ecuador
  C. f. amazona
  French Guiana, N Brazil
  C. f. leucophrys
  Colombia, W Venezuela
  C. f. magnirostris
  SW Ecuador
  C. f. flaveola
  S Colombia, SE Brazil, E Bolivia, Paraguay

Euscarthmus meloryphus (Tawny-crowned Pygmy Tyrant)
E. m. padulus
Venezuela, Colombia
E. m. fulviceps
W Ecuador, W Peru
E. m. meloryphus
Brazil, E Bolivia, Paraguay, N Argentina
Euscarthmus rufomarginatus (Rufous-sided Pygmy Tyrant)
E. r. rufomarginatus
Brazil
E. r. savannophilus
Surinam

PSEUDOCOLOPTERYX
Pseudocolopteryx dinellianus (Dinelli's Doradito)
NW Argentina, SE Bolivia, W Paraguay
Pseudocolopteryx sclateri (Crested Doradito)
Trinidad, Guyana, Brazil, Paraguay, E Argentina
Pseudocolopteryx acutipennis (Subtropical Doradito)
Colombia, Ecuador, Peru, Bolivia, W Argentina
Pseudocolopteryx flaviventris (Warbling Doradito)
Uruguay, C Chile, N Argentina, S Brazil

POLYSTICTUS
Polystictus pectoralis (Bearded Tachuri)
P. p. bogotensis
Colombia
P. p. brevipennis
Guyana, S Venezuela, N Brazil
P. p. pectoralis
E Bolivia, SW Brazil, Uruguay, Paraguay, N Argentina
Polystictus superciliaris (Grey-backed Tachuri)
SE Brazil

CULICIVORA
Culicivora caudacuta (Sharp-tailed Tyrant)
S Brazil, E Bolivia, Paraguay, NE Argentina

SERPOPHAGINAE

TACHURIS
Tachuris rubigastra (Many-coloured Rush Tyrant)
T. r. libertatis
W Peru
T. r. alticola
Peru, W Bolivia, NW Argentina
T. r. rubigastra
SE Brazil, Paraguay, Uruguay, Chile, N Argentina

T. r. loaensis
N Chile

ANAIRETES
Anairetes parulus (Tufted Tit Tyrant)
A. p. aequatorialis
S Colombia, Ecuador, Peru, Bolivia, NW Argentina
A. p. patagonicus
C Argentina
A. p. parulus
SC Chile, W Argentina
A. p. lippus
S Chile
Anairetes fernandezianus (Juan Fernandez Tit Tyrant)
Masatierra I
Anairetes flavirostris (Yellow-billed Tit Tyrant)
A. f. huancabambae
NW Peru
A. f. arequipae
SW Peru, NW Chile
A. f. cuzcoensis
SE Peru
A. f. flavirostris
W Peru, Bolivia, N Chile, W Argentina
Anairetes reguloides (Pied-crested Tit Tyrant)
A. r. nigrocristatus
N Peru
A. r. albiventris
W Peru
A. r. reguloides
SW Peru, NW Chile
Anairetes alpinus (Ash-breasted Tit Tyrant)
Peru, NW Bolivia

UROMYIAS
Uromyias agilis (Agile Tit Tyrant)
Colombia, Ecuador
Uromyias agraphia (Unstreaked Tit Tyrant)
U. a. agraphia
SE Peru
U. a. plengei
C Peru
U. a. squamigera
E Peru

STIGMATURA
Stigmatura napensis (Lesser Wagtail Tyrant)
S. n. napensis
SE Colombia, NE Peru, W Brazil
S. n. bahiae
NE Brazil
Stigmatura budytoides (Greater Wagtail Tyrant)
S. b. budytoides
NC Bolivia

S. b. inzonata
SE Bolivia, N Argentina
S. b. flavocinerea
C Argentina
S. b. gracilis
Brazil

SERPOPHAGA
Serpophaga hypoleuca (River Tyrannulet)
S. h. venezuelana
N Venezuela
S. h. hypoleuca
SE Colombia, E Peru, Venezuela
S. h. pallida
EC Brazil
Serpophaga cinerea (Torrent Tyrannulet)
S. c. grisea
Costa Rica, W Panama
S. c. cana
Colombia, W Venezuela
S. c. cinerea
W Ecuador, W Peru, W Bolivia
Serpophaga subcristata (White-crested Tyrannulet)
S. s. straminea
SC Brazil, Uruguay
S. s. subcristata
Bolivia to E Brazil, Argentina
S. s. munda
E Bolivia, N Argentina
Serpophaga nigricans (Sooty Tyrannulet)
SE Brazil, Uruguay, Paraguay, N Argentina
Serpophaga araguayae (Bananal Tyrannulet)
Brazil

INEZIA
Inezia subflava (Pale-tipped Tyrannulet)
I. s. intermedia
NW Venezuela, N Colombia
I. s. caudata
the Guianas, Venezuela
I. s. subflava
EC N Brazil
I. s. saturatior
Maracaibo, Venezuela
I. s. obscura
NE Venezuela, NW Brazil
Inezia tenuirostris (Slender-billed Tyrannulet)
N Colombia, NW Venezuela
Inezia inornata (Plain Tyrannulet)
SW Brazil, E Bolivia, W Paraguay, S Peru

MECOCERCULUS
Mecocerculus leucophrys (White-throated Tyrannulet)
M. l. montensis
N Colombia

M. l. nigriceps
N Venezuela
M. l. notatus
W Colombia
M. l. setophagoides
E Colombia
M. l. palliditergum
coast of N Venezuela
M. l. gularis
W Venezuela
M. l. parui
S Venezuela
M. l. rufomarginatus
S Colombia, Ecuador, NW Peru
M. l. roraimae
C Venezuela
M. l. brunneomarginatus
C Peru
M. l. pallidor
W Peru
M. l. leucophrys
SE Peru, NW Argentina
Mecocerculus poecilocercus (White-tailed Tyrannulet)
Colombia, Ecuador, Peru
Mecocerculus hellmayri (Buff-banded Tyrannulet)
SE Peru, Bolivia, Argentina
Mecocerculus calopterus (Rufous-winged Tyrannulet)
W Ecuador, NW Peru
Mecocerculus minor (Sulphur-bellied Tyrannulet)
E Colombia, Venezuela, NW Peru
Mecocerculus stictopterus (White-banded Tyrannulet)
M. s. stictopterus
Colombia, Ecuador, N Peru
M. s. taeniopterus
SE Peru, W Bolivia
M. s. albocaudatus
NW Venezuela

COLORAMPHUS
Coloramphus parvirostris (Patagonian Tyrannulet)
C & S Chile

ELAENIINAE

ELAENIA
Elaenia flavogaster (Yellow-bellied Elaenia)
E. f. subpagana
Pacific coast of S Mexico to Panama
E. f. flavogaster
Trinidad, N South America
E. f. semipagana
W Ecuador, NW Peru

E. f. pallididorsalis
  Pearl Is (Panama)
Elaenia martinica (Caribbean Elaenia)
E. m. martinica
  Lesser Antilles Is
E. m. chinchorrensis
  Great Key I, E Mexico
E. m. barbadensis
  Barbados
E. m. riisii
  Virgin Is, Antigua I, Curaçao I
E. m. caymanensis
  Cayman Is
E. m. cinerescens
  St Andrew I, Old Providence I
E. m. remota
  Yucatan coast islands
Elaenia spectabilis (Large Elaenia)
E. s. spectabilis
  NE Peru, N & C Brazil, W Bolivia,
  N Argentina
E. s. ridleyana
  Fernando de Noronha I
Elaenia albiceps (White-crested Elaenia)
E. a. griseigularis
  Ecuador
E. a. diversa
  NC Peru
E. a. urubambae
  SE Peru
E. a. albiceps
  Bolivia, Brazil
E. a. modesta
  Peru, NW Chile
E. a. chilensis
  S Chile, SW Argentina
Elaenia parvirostris (Small-billed Elaenia)
  C & E South America
Elaenia mesoleuca (Olivaceous Elaenia)
  SE Brazil, Paraguay, NE Argentina
Elaenia strepera (Slaty Elaenia)
  Colombia, Venezuela, Peru, Bolivia,
  NW Argentina
Elaenia gigas (Mottle-backed Elaenia)
  C Colombia, E Ecuador, E Peru, NE Bolivia
Elaenia pelzelni (Brownish Elaenia)
  W Brazil, NE Peru, Bolivia
Elaenia cristata (Plain-crested Elaenia)
E. c. alticola
  S Venezuela, N Brazil
E. c. cristata
  French Guiana to E Peru, Venezuela
Elaenia chiriquensis (Lesser Elaenia)
E. c. chiriquensis
  SW Costa Rica, Panama
E. c. brachyptera
  SW Colombia, NW Ecuador

E. c. albivertex
  Trinidad, C & W Northern South America
Elaenia ruficeps (Rufous-crowned Elaenia)
  the Guianas, N Brazil, S Venezuela
Elaenia frantzii (Mountain Elaenia)
E. f. browni
  N Colombia, N Venezuela
E. f. pudica
  E Colombia, W Venezuela
E. f. ultima
  Guatemala to Nicaragua
E. f. frantzii
  Nicaragua to Panama
Elaenia obscura (Highland Elaenia)
E. o. sordida
  SE Brazil, E Paraguay, NE Argentina
E. o. obscura
  S Brazil, Peru, Bolivia, Paraguay,
  N Argentina
Elaenia dayi (Great Elaenia)
E. d. dayi
  Mt Roraima (S Venezuela)
E. d. auyantepui
  SE Venezuela
E. d. tyleri
  S Venezuela
Elaenia pallatangae (Sierran Elaenia)
E. p. pallatangae
  W Colombia, Ecuador
E. p. olivina
  S Guyana, S Venezuela
E. p. exsul
  Bolivian Andes
E. p. intensa
  Peru
Elaenia fallax (Greater Antillean Elaenia)
E. f. fallax
  Jamaica
E. f. cherriei
  Hispaniola

MYIOPAGIS
Myiopagis gaimardii (Forest Elaenia)
M. g. macilvainii
  E Panama, N Colombia
M. g. trinitatis
  Trinidad
M. g. bogotensis
  E Colombia, N Venezuela
M. g. guianensis
  the Guianas, N Brazil
M. g. gaimardii
  S Venezuela, Brazil, E Peru, N Bolivia
M. g. subcinereus
  EC Brazil
Myiopagis caniceps (Grey Elaenia)
M. c. parambae
  W Colombia, NW Ecuador

M. c. cinerea
S Venezuela, E Colombia, E Ecuador,
Peru, NW Brazil
M. c. caniceps
E & S Brazil, Paraguay, N Argentina
M. c. absita
Panama
Myiopagis subplacens (Pacific Elaenia)
SW Ecuador, NW Peru
Myiopagis flavivertex (Yellow-crowned Elaenia)
French Guiana, Surinam, S Venezuela,
N Peru, N Brazil
Myiopagis viridicata (Greenish Elaenia)
M. v. jaliscensis
SW Mexico
M. v. minima
Tres Marias Is
M. v. placens
S Mexico to Honduras
M. v. pacifica
SE Chiapas, Mexico
M. v. accola
Nicaragua to Panama, NW Colombia
M. v. pallens
NW Colombia, N Venezuela
M. v. restricta
N coast of Venezuela
M. v. zuliae
N Venezuela
M. v. implacens
S Colombia, W Ecuador
M. v. viridicata
SE Peru, E Bolivia, Brazil, Paraguay,
N Argentina
Myiopagis cotta (Yellow Elaenia)
Jamaica

SUIRIRI
Suiriri suiriri (Suiriri Flycatcher)
S. s. affinis
C Brazil, Surinam, NW Bolivia
S. s. bahiae
E Brazil
S. s. suiriri
E Bolivia, Brazil, Uruguay, Paraguay,
N Argentina

SUBLEGATUS
Sublegatus modestus (Short-billed Flycatcher)
S. m. atrirostris
Panama to NE Colombia
S. m. modestus
E Peru to E Brazil, N Argentina
Sublegatus obscurior (Dusky Flycatcher)
W Amazonia

Sublegatus arenarum (Scrub Flycatcher)
S. a. arenarum
SW Costa Rica
S. a. pallens
Arub I, Curaçao I, Bonaire I
S. a. tortugensis
Tortuga
S. a. orinocensis
C Venezuela
S. a. glaber
N Venezuela, Trinidad
PHAIOMYIAS
Phaiomyias murina (Mouse-coloured Tyrannulet)
P. m. incomta
Trinidad, the Guianas, Colombia
Venezuela, N Brazil
P. m. tumbezana
SW Ecuador, N Peru
P. m. inflava
W Peru
P. m. maranonica
NC Peru
P. m. wagae
E Peru, W Bolivia
P. m. ignobilis
S Bolivia, Paraguay, NW Argentina
P. m. murina
S Brazil
P. m. eremonoma
Panama
Phaiomyias leucospodia (Grey and White Tyrannulet)
P. l. cinereifrons
SW Ecuador
P. l. leucospodia
NW Peru

CAMPTOSTOMA
Camptostoma obsoletum (Southern Beardless Tyrannulet)
C. o. flaviventre
W Costa Rica, Panama
C. o. orphnum
Coiba I, Afuerita I
C. o. major
Pearl Is (Panama)
C. o. caucae
W Colombia
C. o. bogotensis
C Colombia
C. o. pusillum
N Colombia, NW Venezuela
C. o. napaeum
N Venezuela, the Guianas
N Brazil
C. o. venezuelae
N & C Venezuela, Trinidad

C. o. maranonicum
N Peru
C. o. olivaceum
S Colombia, E Ecuador, NE Peru, W Brazil
C. o. sclateri
W Ecuador, W Peru
C. o. griseum
W Peru
C. o. bolivianum
C Bolivia, NW Argentina
C. o. cinerascens
E Bolivia, E & C Brazil
C. o. obsoletum
SE Brazil, Uruguay, N Argentina
Camptostoma imberbe (Northern Beard-less Tyrannulet)
SW USA, Mexico to NW Costa Rica

XANTHOMYIAS
Xanthomyias virescens (Greenish Tyrannulet)
X. v. urichi
NE Venezuela
X. v. virescens
SE Brazil, Paraguay, NE Argentina
Xanthomyias reiseri (Reiser's Tyrannulet)
NE Brazil
Xanthomyias sclateri (Sclater's Tyrannulet)
X. s. subtropicalis
SE Peru
X. s. sclateri
Bolivia, NW Argentina

PHYLLOMYIAS
Phyllomyias fasciatus (Planalto Tyrannulet)
P. f. cearae
NE Brazil
P. f. virescens
C Brazil
P. f. fasciatus
E Brazil
P. f. brevirostris
S Brazil, Paraguay, NE Argentina
Phyllomyias griseiceps (Sooty-headed Tyrannulet)
P. g. cristatus
E Panama, N Colombia, N Venezuela
P. g. caucae
WC Colombia
P. g. griseiceps
Ecuador
P. g. pallidiceps
NE Brazil, Peru, SE Venezuela

TYRANNISCUS
Tyranniscus nigrocapillus (Black-capped Tyrannulet)
T. n. flavimentum
N Colombia

T. n. nigrocapillus
W Colombia, Ecuador, N Peru
T. n. aureus
W Venezuela
Tyranniscus uropygialis (Tawny-rumped Tyrannulet)
Colombia, Ecuador, Peru, W Bolivia, Venezuela
Tyranniscus cinereiceps (Ashy-headed Tyrannulet)
Colombia, Ecuador, Peru
Tyranniscus vilissimus (Paltry Tyrannulet)
T. v. vilissimus
S Mexico, Guatemala, Honduras
T. v. parvus
Nicaragua to Panama
T. v. tamae
N Colombia
T. v. improbus
N Colombia, W Venezuela
T. v. petersi
N Venezuela
Tyranniscus bolivianus (Bolivian Tyrannulet)
T. b. bolivianus
N Bolivia
T. b. viridissimus
SE Peru
Tyranniscus cinereicapillus (Red-billed Tyrannulet)
C Peru, NE Ecuador
Tyranniscus gracilipes (Slender-footed Tyrannulet)
T. g. acer
S Venezuela, the Guianas, N Brazil
T. g. gracilipes
S Venezuela, S Guyana, N Brazil, N Bolivia, E Peru
T. g. gilvus
W Brazil, NW Bolivia
Tyranniscus viridiflavus (Golden-faced Tyrannulet)
T. v. minimus
N Colombia
T. v. cumanensis
NE Venezuela
T. v. albigularis
W Ecuador, SW Colombia
T. v. flavidifrons
SW Ecuador
T. v. chrysops
N Peru, Ecuador, S Colombia, W Venezuela
T. v. viridiflavus
C Peru

OREOTRICCUS
Oreotriccus plumbeiceps (Plumbeous-crowned Tyrannulet)
Colombia, Ecuador, Peru
Oreotriccus griseocapillus (Grey-capped Tyrannulet)
SE Brazil

TYRANNULUS
Tyrannulus elatus (Yellow-crowned Tyrannulet)
T. e. panamensis
Panama, W Ecuador, Colombia, W Venezuela
T. e. elatus
E Venezuela, the Guianas, N Brazil, S Colombia, N Peru

ACROCHORDOPUS
Acrochordopus burmeisteri (Rough-legged Tyrannulet)
A. b. zeledoni
Costa Rica, W Panama
A. b. viridiceps
N Venezuela
A. b. wetmorei
NW Venezuela
A. b. bunites
SC Venezuela
A. b. leucogonys
Colombia, Ecuador, Peru
A. b. burmeisteri
SE Brazil, E Bolivia, Paraguay, N Argentina

ORNITHION
Ornithion inerme (White-lored Tyrannulet)
S Venezuela, the Guianas, Ecuador, N Brazil
Ornithion semiflavum (Yellow-bellied Tyrannulet)
S Mexico to Costa Rica
Ornithion brunneicapillum (Brown-capped Tyrannulet)
O. b. brunneicapillum
Costa Rica, Panama, W Colombia, NW Ecuador
O. b. dilutum
NW Venezuela, N Colombia

LEPTOPOGON
Leptopogon superciliaris (White-bellied Leptopogon)
L. s. superciliaris
SE Colombia, N Peru
L. s. poliocephalus
N & C Colombia
L. s. hellmayri
Costa Rica to W Panama
L. s. venezuelensis
N Venezuela, N Brazil

L. s. pariae
NE Venezuela, Trinidad
L. s. transandinus
SW Colombia, W Ecuador
L. s. albidiventer
Bolivia, SE Peru
Leptopogon amaurocephalus (Sepia-capped Leptopogon)
L. a. pileatus
S Mexico, Guatemala, Honduras
L. a. faustus
Costa Rica, Panama
L. a. idius
Coiba I
L. a. diversus
N Colombia
L. a. orinocensis
W & SW Venezuela
L. a. obscuritergum
S Venezuela
L. a. peruvianus
N & W Amazonia
L. a. amaurocephalus
SE Brazil, E Bolivia, N Argentina, Paraguay
Leptopogon rufipectus (Rufous-breasted Leptopogon)
L. r. rufipectus
E Ecuador, E Colombia, Peru
L. r. venezuelanus
NE Colombia, NW Venezuela
Leptopogon taczanowskii (Inca Leptopogon)
E Peru

MIONECTES
Mionectes striaticollis (Streak-necked Flycatcher)
M. s. colombianus
Colombia, E Ecuador
M. s. viridiceps
W Ecuador
M. s. palamblae
N Peru
M. s. poliocephalus
N & C Peru
M. s. striaticollis
Bolivia, SE Peru
M. s. selvae
WC Colombia
Mionectes olivaceus (Olive-striped Flycatcher)
M. o. olivaceus
Costa Rica, W Panama
M. o. hederaceus
E Panama, W Colombia, W Ecuador
M. o. galbinus
N Colombia

M. o. pallidus
E Colombia
M. o. venezuelanus
N Venezuela, Trinidad
M. o. fasciaticollis
E Ecuador, E Peru
M. o. meridae
NW Venezuela, NE Colombia

PIPROMORPHA
Pipromorpha oleaginea (Ochre-billed Flycatcher)
P. o. assimilis
S Mexico to Costa Rica
P. o. obscura
El Salvador
P. o. dyscola
W Costa Rica, W Panama
P. o. lutescens
W Panama
P. o. parca
E Panama, N Colombia, NW Venezuela
P. o. chloronota
W Amazonia
P. o. abdominalis
N Venezuela
P. o. pallidiventris
NE Venezuela, Trinidad
P. o. intensa
E Venezuela, Guyana
P. o. dorsalis
SE Venezuela
P. o. pacifica
W Colombia, W Ecuador
P. o. hauxwelli
E Ecuador, NE Peru
P. o. wallacei
N Brazil, the Guianas
P. o. maynana
E Peru
P. o. oleaginea
SE Brazil
Pipromorpha macconnelli (McConnell's Flycatcher)
P. m. macconnelli
Guyana, French Guiana, N Brazil, E Venezuela
P. m. roraimae
S Guyana, S Venezuela
P. m. peruana
C Peru
P. m. amazona
C Brazil, E Bolivia
Pipromorpha rufiventris (Grey-hooded Flycatcher)
SE Brazil, Paraguay, N Argentina

CORYTHOPIS
Corythopis delalandi (Delalande's Antpipit)
E Bolivia, S Brazil, E Paraguay, NE Argentina
Corythopis torquata (Ringed Antpipit)
C. t. sarayacuensis
SE Colombia, E Ecuador, NE Peru
C. t. torquata
C Peru, W Brazil
C. t. anthoides
S Venezuela, Guianas, N & E Brazil
C. t. subtorquata
NE Bolivia

109 OXYRUNCIDAE (SHARPBILL)

OXYRUNCUS
Oxyruncus cristatus (Sharpbill)
O. c. frater
Costa Rica, W Panama
O. c. brooksi
E Panama
O. c. hypoglaucus
Guyana, SE Venezuela
O. c. tocantinsi
C Brazil
O. c. cristatus
SE Brazil, Paraguay

110 PHYTOTOMIDAE (PLANTCUTTERS)

PHYTOTOMA
Phytotoma rara (Chilean Plantcutter)
S Chile, S Argentina, Falkland Is
Phytotoma rutila (Red-breasted Plant-cutter)
P. r. angustirostris
NW Argentina, Bolivia
P. r. rutila
N Argentina, Uruguay, Paraguay
Phytotoma raimondii (Peruvian Plantcutter)
NW Peru

111 PITTIDAE (PITTAS)

PITTA
Pitta phayrei (Phayre's Pitta)
P. p. phayrei
Burma, Thailand
P. p. obscura
N Indochina
Pitta nipalensis (Blue-naped Pitta)
P. n. nipalensis
Himalayas to Burma, S China
P. n. hendeei
N Vietnam
Pitta soror (Blue-backed Pitta)
P. s. soror
C Indochina

P. s. tonkinensis
C China to N Vietnam
P. s. douglasi
Hainan I
P. s. petersi
C Vietnam
Pitta oatesi (Fulvous Pitta)
P. o. oatesi
Burma, Thailand, NW Laos
P. o. castaneiceps
N Laos, N Vietnam
P. o. bolovenensis
S Laos
P. o. deborah
Malaysia
Pitta schneideri (Schneider's Pitta)
N Sumatra
Pitta caerulea (Giant Pitta)
P. c. caerulea
Malaysia, Sumatra, S Thailand
P. c. hosei
Borneo
Pitta kochi (Koch's Pitta)
N Luzon I
Pitta erythrogaster (Red-breasted Pitta)
P. e. erythrogaster
Philippine Is
P. e. thompsoni
Culion I
P. e. propinqua
Balabac I, Palawan I
P. e. inspeculata
Taulaut Is
P. e. caeruleitorques
Gr. Sanghir I
P. e. palliceps
Sanghir Is
P. e. cyanonota
Ternate I
P. e. rubrinucha
Buru I
P. e. celebensis
N Celebes
P. e. dohertyi
Sula Is
P. e. piroensis
Ceram I
P. e. rufiventris
Obi I to Morotai I, Damar I
P. e. novaehibernicae
New Ireland
P. e. gazellae
New Britain
P. e. extima
New Hanover
P. e. splendida
Tabar I

P. e. mackloti
W & S New Guinea, N Queensland
P. e. habenichti
N New Guinea
P. e. oblita
SE New Guinea
P. e. loriae
SE New Guinea
P. e. aruensis
Aru Is
P. e. finschii
D'Entrecasteaux Archipelago
P. e. meeki
Rossel I
P. e. kuehni
Kei Is
Pitta arcuata (Blue-banded Pitta)
Borneo
Pitta granatina (Garnet Pitta)
P. g. coccinea
Malaysia, E Sumatra
P. g. venusta
W Sumatra
P. g. ussheri
N Borneo
P. g. granatina
S Borneo
Pitta cyanea (Blue Pitta)
P. c. cyanea
Himalayas, Burma, N Thailand
P. c. aurantiaca
SE Thailand
P. c. willoughbyi
S Vietnam, S Laos
Pitta ellioti (Elliot's Pitta)
S Indochina
Pitta guajana (Blue-tailed Pitta)
P. g. irena
Malaysia, Sumatra
P. g. ripleyi
S Thailand
P. g bangkae
Bangka I
P. g. affinis
W Java
P. g. guajana
E Java, Bali
P. g. schwaneri
Borneo
Pitta gurneyi (Gurney's Pitta)
S Burma, S Thailand
Pitta baudi (Blue-headed Pitta)
Borneo
Pitta sordida (Hooded Pitta)
P. s. cucullata
Himalayas to Malaysia, Indochina

P. s. *mulleri*
Sumatra, Java, Borneo, S Thailand,
Malaysia
P. s. *abbotti*
Nicobar Is
P. s. *bangkana*
Bangka I, Billiton I
P. s. *novaeguineae*
New Guinea
P. s. *hebetior*
Dampier I
P. s. *sanghirana*
Sanghir Is
P. s. *forsteni*
Celebes
P. s. *goodfellowi*
Aru Is
P. s. *mafoorana*
Numfor I
P. s. *rosenbergii*
Biak I
P. s. *palawanensis*
Balabac I, Palawan I
P. s. *sordida*
Philippine Is
Pitta brachyura (Blue-winged Pitta)
P. b. *brachyura*
Himalayas, India
P. b. *nympha*
E China, NE Asia » Indochina, Borneo
Pitta angolensis (African Pitta)
P. a. *pulih*
Sierra Leone to S Cameroun
P. a. *angolensis*
Cameroun to N Angola
P. a. *longipennis*
Uganda, E Zaire to Transvaal
Pitta reichenowi (Green-breasted Pitta)
Cameroun to Uganda
Pitta superba (Superb Pitta)
Admiralty Is
Pitta maxima (Great Pitta)
P. m. *maxima*
Batjan I, Halmahera I
P. m. *morotaiensis*
Morotai I
Pitta steerei (Steere's Pitta)
P. s. *steerei*
Mindanao I
P. s. *coelstis*
Bohol I, Leyte I, Samar I
Pitta moluccensis (Moluccan Pitta)
P. m. *moluccensis*
S China, Burma » Borneo, Moluccas
P. m. *megarhyncha*
coast of Burma, Thailand, Malaysia,
Sumatra

Pitta versicolor (Noisy Pitta)
P. v. *virginalis*
Djampea I
P. v. *plesseni*
Kalao tua I
P. v. *kalaoensis*
Kalao I
P. v. *vigorsii*
Tukangbesi, Tenimber I
P. v. *hutzi*
S Nasa Penida I
P. v. *concinna*
Lombok I, Sumbawa I, Flores
P. v. *everetti*
Alor I
P. v. *maria*
Sumba I
P. v. *elegans*
Timor I, S Moluccas
P. v. *intermedia*
N Queensland
P. v. *simillima*
S New Guinea, N Queensland
P. v. *versicolor*
S Queensland, New South Wales
Pitta iris (Rainbow Pitta)
N Northern Territory
Pitta anerythra (Black-faced Pitta)
P. a. *anerythra*
Ysabel I
P. a. *pallida*
Bougainville I
P. a. *nigrifrons*
Choiseul I

112 XENICIDAE (NEW ZEALAND WRENS)

ACANTHISITTA
Acanthisitta chloris (Rifleman)
A. c. *granti*
North Island, New Zealand
A. c. *chloris*
South Island, New Zealand
A. c. *citrina*
SW South I, New Zealand

XENICUS
Xenicus longipes (Bush Wren)
X. l. *stokesi*
North Island, New Zealand **e?**
X. l. *longipes*
South Island, New Zealand
X. l. *variabilis*
SW of Stewart I, New Zealand
Xenicus gilviventris (Rock Wren)
South Island, New Zealand

113 PHILEPITTIDAE (ASITIES)

PHILEPITTA
Philepitta castanea (Velvet Asity)
E Madagascar
Philepitta schlegeli (Schlegel's Asity)
W Madagascar

NEODREPANIS
Neodrepanis coruscans (Wattled False Sunbird)
E Madagascar
Neodrepanis hypoxantha (Small-billed False Sunbird)
E Madagascar **e?**

114 MENURIDAE (LYREBIRDS)

MENURA
Menura superba (Superb Lyrebird)
  M. s. edwardi
    E Queensland
  M. s. superba
    New South Wales, Victoria
Menura alberti (Prince Albert's Lyrebird)
  E Queensland, New South Wales

115 ATRICHORNITHIDAE (SCRUBBIRDS)

ATRICHORNIS
Atrichornis clamosus (Western Scrubbird)
SW Australia
Atrichornis rufescens (Rufous Scrubbird)
SE Queensland, NE New South Wales

116 ALAUDIDAE (LARKS)

MIRAFRA
Mirafra javanica (Singing Bush Lark)
  M. j. marginata
    Somalia, Uganda, Kenya, Tanzania
  M. j. chadensis
    Senegal to Sudan
  M. j. simplex
    W Arabia
  M. j. cantillans
    N India
  M. j. williamsoni
    C Burma, Thailand, Indochina
  M. j. beaulieui
    S Vietnam
  M. j. philippinensis
    Luzon I, Mindoro I
  M. j. mindanensis
    Mindanao I
  M. j. javanica
    S Borneo, Java, Bali I
  M. j. parva
    Lombok I, Sumbawa I, Sumba I, Flores I

  M. j. timorensis
    Savu Is, Timor I
  M. j. sepikiana
    N New Guinea
  M. j. aliena
    NE New Guinea
  M. j. woodwardi
    WC Australia
  M. j. halli
    NW Australia
  M. j. subrufescens
    NW Australia
  M. j. soderbergi
    W Northern Territory
  M. j. melvillensis
    Melville I
  M. j. rufescens
    E Northern Territory, N Queensland
  M. j. horsfieldii
    C & S Queensland, New South Wales, Victoria
  M. j. secunda
    South Australia
Mirafra hova (Hova Lark)
  Madagascar
Mirafra cordofanica (Kordofan Bush Lark)
  Niger, Chad, W Sudan
Mirafra williamsi (Marsabit Lark)
  Kenya
Mirafra cheniana (Southern Singing Bush Lark)
  Rhodesia, Transvaal, Orange Free State, N & E Cape Province
Mirafra albicauda (Northern White-tailed Bush Lark)
  M. a. albicauda
    Chad to Ethiopia and Tanzania
  M. a. rukwensis
    S Tanzania
Mirafra passerina (White-tailed Bush Lark)
  Namibia, Botswana
Mirafra candida (Nyiro Bush Lark)
  Nyiro river, Kenya
Mirafra pulpa (Sagon Bush Lark)
  Sagon river, Ethiopia
Mirafra ashi (Ash's Lark)
  S Somalia
Mirafra hypermetra (Red-winged Bush Lark)
  M. h. kathangorensis
    Sudan
  M. h. kidepoensis
    S Sudan, N Uganda
  M. h. gallarum
    S Ethiopia
  M. h. hypermetra
    S Somalia, Kenya, N Tanzania

***Mirafra somalica* (Somali Long-billed Lark)**
M. s. somalica
N Somalia
M. s. rochei
S Somalia

***Mirafra africana* (Rufous-naped Bush Lark)**
M. a. henrici
Guinea, Liberia
M. a. batesi
Niger, N Nigeria
M. a. stresemanni
N Cameroun
M. a. bamendae
Cameroun
M. a. kurrae
E Chad
M. a. tropicalis
E Zaire, Uganda, Kenya, Tanzania
M. a. sharpii
Somalia
M. a. ruwenzoria
W Uganda
M. a. athi
Kenya
M. a. harterti
S Kenya
M. a. malbranti
SC Zaire
M. a. nyikae
E Zambia, N Malawi
M. a. chapini
SE Zaire, NW Zambia
M. a. occidentalis
Gabon, W & S Angola
M. a. irwini
Cuando, Angola
M. a. kabalii
NE Angola
M. a. anchietae
Huila, Angola
M. a. gomesi
E Angola
M. a. grisescens
W Zambia, Rhodesia
M. a. pallida
Namibia, Botswana
M. a. ghansiensis
SW Botswana
M. a. nigrescens
SW Tanzania
M. a. zuluensis
SW Tanzania, N Natal, Mozambique
M. a. transvaalensis
Transvaal, Natal, Rhodesia, Zambia, Malawi
M. a. africana
S Natal, E Cape Province

***Mirafra chuana* (Short-clawed Lark)**
W Transvaal, S Botswana

***Mirafra angolensis* (Angolan Lark)**
M. a. marungensis
SE Zaire
M. a. angolensis
W Angola
M. a. niethammeri
Cuando District (Angola)
M. a. antonii
E Angola
M. a. minyanyae
NW Zambia

***Mirafra rufocinnamomea* (Cinnamon Bush Lark)**
M. r. buckleyi
Gambia & Mali to Nigeria & Cameroun
M. r. serlei
E Nigeria
M. r. tigrina
NE Cameroun
M. r. furensis
W Sudan
M. r. sobatensis
E Sudan
M. r. rufocinnamomea
Ethiopia
M. r. omoensis
SW Ethiopia
M. r. kawirondensis
Uganda, Kenya, Tanzania
M. r. fischeri
SE Zaire & Zambia to Kenya & Mozambique
M. r. torrida
C Tanzania
M. r. pintoi
S Mozambique, NE Transvaal
M. r. mababiensis
SW Zambia, N Botswana

***Mirafra apiata* (Clapper Lark)**
M. a. reynoldsi
W Zambia
M. a. adendorffi
NW Cape Province
M. a. apiata
SW Cape Province
M. a. marjoriae
Cape Town
M. a. algoensis
SE Cape Province
M. a. jappi
W Barotseland

***Mirafra damarensis* (Damara Clapper Lark)**
M. d. damarensis
N Namibia
M. d. hewetti
NE Cape Province, Transvaal

M. d. deserti
C Namibia
M. d. kalaharica
SW Botswana
M. d. nata
E Botswana
Mirafra africanoides (Fawn-coloured Bush Lark)
M. a. intercedens
Ethiopia, Somalia, Kenya, NE Tanzania
M. a. alopex
S Somalia, Ethiopia
M. a. macdonaldi
S Ethiopia
M. a. longonotensis
E Uganda, W Kenya
M. a. omaruru
NW Namibia
M. a. trapnelli
W Zambia
M. a. harei
C Namibia
M. a. gobabisensis
E Namibia
M. a. rubidior
N Namibia
M. a. makarikari
S Zambia, NE Botswana
M. a. sarwensis
N Namibia, C Botswana, Mozambique
M. a. vincenti
Rhodesia, S Mozambique
M. a. austenrobertsi
SE Botswana, W Transvaal
M. a. africanoides
S Namibia, N Cape Province
Mirafra ruddi (Long-clawed Lark)
M. r. archeri
W Somalia
M. r. ruddi
SE Transvaal, N Orange Free State
Mirafra collaris (Collared Lark)
Somalia, N Kenya
Mirafra assamica (Rufous-winged Bush Lark)
M. a. assamica
N India, Nepal, Assam
M. a. affinis
S India, Sri Lanka
M. a. microptera
C Burma
M. a. subsessor
N Thailand
M. a. marionae
S Burma, S Thailand, S Indochina
Mirafra rufa (Rusty Bush Lark)
M. r. nigriticola
Mali

M. r. rufa
W Sudan
M. r. lynesi
C Sudan
Mirafra sidamoensis (Sidamo Bush Lark)
Ethiopia
Mirafra gilletti (Gillett's Bush Lark)
Ethiopia, Somalia
Mirafra poecilosterna (Pink-breasted Lark)
M. p. australoabyssinica
N Sudan, Ethiopia
M. p. poecilosterna
N & E Kenya
M. p. massaica
N Uganda, Kenya, Tanzania
Mirafra sabota (Sabota Lark)
M. s. sabotoides
W Botswana
M. s. veseyfitzgeraldi
NW Botswana
M. s. plebeja
SW Zaire
M. s. ansorgei
W Angola
M. s. sabota
S Mozambique, Transvaal, Natal, Cape Province
M. s. fradei
S Mozambique
Mirafra naevia (Large-billed Sabota Lark)
M. n. herero
SW Namibia
M. n. bradfieldi
E Cape Province
M. n. naevia
C Namibia
M. n. waibeli
N Namibia, NW Botswana
Mirafra erythroptera (Red-winged Bush Lark)
M. e. sindiana
NW India
M. e. furva
Kathiawar (NW India)
M. e. erythroptera
S & C India

PINAROCORYS
Pinarocorys nigricans (Dusky Bush Lark)
S Zaire & Angola to Natal & Mozambique
Pinarocorys erythropygia (Red-tailed Bush Lark)
Gambia to Sudan & Uganda

Certhilauda curvirostris (Long-billed Lark)
C. c. damarensis
　WC Namibia
C. c. bradshawi
　S Namibia, N Cape Province
C. c. subcoronata
　E Cape Province
C. c. curvirostris
　S & W Cape Province
C. c. semitorquata
　S Transvaal, Natal, E Cape Province
C. c. benguelensis
　W Angola
C. c. falcirostris
　NW Cape Province
C. c. kaokoensis
　W Namibia
C. c. algida
　E Cape Province

Certhilauda albescens (Karroo Lark)
C. a. erythrochlamys
　W Namibia
C. a. barlowi
　S Namibia
C. a. cavei
　S Namibia
C. a. patae
　NW Cape Province
C. a. saldanhae
　W Cape Province
C. a. albescens
　SW Cape Province
C. a. guttata
　C & W Cape Province

Certhilauda albofasciata (Spike-heeled Lark)
C. a. beesleyi
　N Tanzania
C. a. obscurata
　C Angola
C. a. longispina
　W Huila, Angola
C. a. erikssoni
　N Namibia
C. a. kalahariae
　S Botswana
C. a. boweni
　W Namibia
C. a. arenaria
　C Namibia
C. a. bathoeni
　SE Botswana
C. a. subpallida
　NE Transvaal
C. a. robertsi
　SC Transvaal

C. a. alticola
　N Orange Free State, S Transvaal
C. a. baddeleyi
　S Orange Free State, N Cape Province
C. a. albofasciata
　Natal, S Orange Free State, C & E Cape
　Province
C. a. meinertzhageni
　NW Cape Province
C. a. bradfieldi
　N Cape Province
C. a. garrula
　W Cape Province
C. a. macdonaldi
　S Karoo, Cape Province
C. a. latimerae
　Transkei

EREMOPTERIX
Eremopterix australis (Black-eared Finch Lark)
　S Namibia, Botswana, W Transvaal,
　N Cape Province
Eremopterix leucotis (Chestnut-backed Finch Lark)
E. l. melanocephala
　Senegal to Nile valley
E. l. leucotis
　Ethiopia
E. l. madaraszi
　Kenya, Tanzania, Mozambique
E. l. smithi
　S & SE Africa
Eremopterix signata (Chestnut-headed Finch Lark)
E. s. harrisoni
　SE Sudan, N Kenya
E. s. signata
　Ethiopia, Somalia, Kenya
Eremopterix verticalis (Grey-backed Finch Lark)
E. v. verticalis
　Botswana, W Rhodesia, Transvaal,
　W Cape Province
E. v. damarensis
　Angola, Namibia, NW Cape Province
E. v. khama
　NE Botswana
Eremopterix nigriceps (Black-crowned Finch Lark)
E. n. nigriceps
　Cape Verde Is
E. n. albifrons
　Mauretania to Nile valley
E. n. melanauchen
　Egypt, Ethiopia, Sudan, Socotra I,
　Arabia, Iraq
E. n. affinis
　Pakistan, NW India

Eremopterix grisea (Ashy-crowned Finch Lark)
Pakistan, India, Sri Lanka
Eremopterix leucopareia (Fischer's Finch Lark)
Uganda, Kenya, Malawi

AMMOMANES
Ammomanes cincturus (Bar-tailed Desert Lark)
A. c. cincturus
Cape Verde Is
A. c. pallens
Mali to Sudan
A. c. arenicolor
N Africa, Sinai, Arabia
A. c. zarudnyi
E Iran, Afghanistan, NW India
Ammomanes phoenicurus (Rufous-tailed Desert Lark)
A. p. phoenicurus
N India
A. p. testaceus
C India
Ammomanes deserti (Desert Lark)
A. d. payni
Morocco
A. d. algeriensis
Algeria, Tunisia
A. d. whitakeri
NW Libya
A. d. mya
S Algeria, Niger
A. d. janeti
S Algeria
A. d. geyri
S Algeria, Mauretania, N Nigeria
A. d. monodi
C Mauretania
A. d. mirei
Tibesti Mountains
A. d. kollmanspergeri
NE Chad
A. d. deserti
E Libya, Egypt
A. d. erythrochrous
Sudan
A. d. isabellinus
Egypt, Arabia, Israel, Syria
A. d. samharensis
E Sudan, S Arabia
A. d. taimuri
Oman
A. d. assabensis
Eritrea, N Somalia
A. d. akeleyi
Somalia
A. d. azizi
EC Arabia

A. d. saturatus
S Arabia
A. d. annae
Transjordan
A. d. insularis
Bahrain I
A. d. cheesmani
E Iraq, W Iran
A. d. parvirostris
Transcaspia
A. d. orientalis
N Afghanistan
A. d. iranicus
S Iran, S Afghanistan
A. d. phoenicuroides
NW India
Ammomanes dunni (Dunn's Lark)
A. d. dunni
S Sahara, W Sudan
A. d. eremodites
SW Arabia
Ammomanes grayi (Gray's Lark)
A. g. grayi
W & S Namibia
A. g. hoeschi
NW Namibia
Ammomanes burra (Ferruginous Lark)
S Namibia, W Cape Province

ALAEMON
Alaemon alaudipes (Hoopoe Lark)
A. a. boavistae
Cape Verde Is
A. a. alaudipes
N Africa, Sahara
A. a. doriae
E Arabia, Iraq to NW India
A. a. desertorum
Red Sea
Alaemon hamertoni (Lesser Hoopoe Lark)
A. h. altera
NE Somalia
A. h. tertia
EC Somalia
A. h. hamertoni
SE Somalia

RAMPHOCORIS
Ramphocoris clotbey (Thick-billed Lark)
N Africa, N Arabia, Syria

MELANOCORYPHA
Melanocorypha calandra (Calandra Lark)
M. c. calandra
S Europe, N Africa, Iran
M. c. psammochroa
Transcaspia, Iran, Afghanistan
M. c. gaza
Jordan

M. c. dathei
Turkey
Melanocorypha bimaculata (Bimaculated Lark)
M. b. bimaculata
SW Asia, Iran, NE Africa
M. b. torquata
E Iran, Afghanistan, NW India
M. b. rufescens
Asia Minor, Jordan, NE Africa
Melanocorypha mongolica (Mongolian Lark)
C Asia, Mongolia, Tsinghai
Melanocorypha maxima (Long-billed Calandra Lark)
M. m. maxima
Sikkim, S Tibet, W China
M. m. holdereri
NE Tibet, N Kashmir
Melanocorypha leucoptera (White-winged Lark)
S Russia, C Asia, Iran
Melanocorypha yeltoniensis (Black Lark)
S Russia, C Asia, Caucasus

CALANDRELLA
Calandrella razae (Raza Island Lark)
Raza I, Cape Verde Is
Calandrella cinerea (Short-toed Lark)
C. c. woltersi
Turkey
C. c. dukhunensis
N India, Burma, Mongolia, W China, Tibet
C. c. longipennis
C Asia, Afghanistan, N India
C. c. orientalis
C Asia, Mongolia, Manchuria
C. c. artemisiana
Caucasus, W Siberia, Asia Minor, Iran
C. c. brachydactyla
S Europe, Russia, N Africa
C. c. rubiginosa
S Morocco, S Algeria, S Tunisia
C. c. hermonensis
Lebanon, Israel, Red Sea
C. c. eremica
SW Arabia
C. c. erlangeri
Ethiopia
C. c. saturatior
Uganda to Botswana & Natal
C. c. williamsi
W Kenya
C. c. alluvia
S Mozambique
C. c. anderssoni
N Namibia
C. c. ongumaensis
N Namibia

C. c. witputzi
S Namibia
C. c. millardi
SW Kalahari
C. c. niveni
SW Transvaal, Orange Free State, Natal
C. c. spleniata
S Angola, W Namibia
C. c. cinerea
S Cape Province
Calandrella blanfordi (Blanford's Lark)
N Ethiopia, Somalia
Calandrella acutirostris (Hume's Short-toed Lark)
C. a. acutirostris
N Afghanistan, CS Asia, N & C India
C. a. tibetana
C Asia, S Tibet, N India
Calandrella raytal (Indian Sand Lark)
C. r. raytal
N India, N Burma
C. r. krishnarkumarsinhji
Kathiawar (NW India)
C. r. adamsi
NW India
Calandrella rufescens (Lesser Short-toed Lark)
C. r. rufescens
Tenerife I
C. r. polatzeki
Gran Canaria I, Lanzarote I
C. r. apetzii
S Spain
C. r. minor
N Sahara, Sinai
C. r. nicolli
N Egypt
C. r. aharonii
Asia Minor, Jordan
C. r. pseudobaetica
W Caspian Sea
C. r. persica
Iraq to Afghanistan
C. r. heinei
SE Russia, W Siberia
C. r. somalica
Somalia
C. r. vulpecula
Somalia
C. r. megaensis
S Ethiopia
C. r. athensis
S Kenya, NE Tanzania
Calandrella cheleënsis (Mongolian Short-toed Lark)
C. c. cheleënsis
N China, Manchuria

C. c. leucophaea
Turkestan
C. c. kukunoorensis
Kuku Nor
C. c. seebohmi
C Asia
C. c. biecki
N Kansu
C. c. tangutica
NE Tibet

SPIZOCORYS

Spizocorys conirostris (Pink-billed Lark)
S. c. damerensis
Namibia
S. c. crypta
NE Botswana
S. c. makawai
W Barotseland
S. c. griseovinacea
W Transvaal
S. c. conirostris
S Botswana, S Transvaal, N Cape Province
Spizocorys starki (Stark's Short-toed Lark)
Angola to W Transvaal
Spizocorys sclateri (Sclater's Short-toed Lark)
S. c. sclateri
Namibia, Cape Province
S. c. theresae
NW Cape Province
S. c. capensis
C & E Cape Province
Spizocorys obbiensis (Obbia Lark)
Somalia
Spizocorys personata (Masked Lark)
S. p. personata
E Ethiopia
S. p. yavelloensis
S Ethiopia
S. p. mechesneyi
N Kenya
S. p. intensa
C Kenya

BOTHA

Botha fringillaris (Botha's Lark)
S Transvaal, N Orange Free State

CHERSOPHILUS

Chersophilus duponti (DuPont's Lark)
C. d. duponti
S Spain, N Algeria, N Tunisia
C. d. margaritae
S Algeria, S Tunisia, Libya, NW Egypt

PSEUDALAEMON
Pseudalaemon fremantlii (Short-tailed Lark)
P. f. fremantlii
Somalia
P. f. megaensis
S Ethiopia
P. f. delamerei
SE Kenya, NE Tanzania

GALERIDA
Galerida cristata (Crested Lark)
G. c. pallida
Portugal, Spain
G. c. cristata
C Europe, Crimea, N Morocco
G. c. meridionalis
S Italy, SE Europe
G. c. subtaurica
C & S Asia Minor
G. c. caucasica
Caucasus, W Asia Minor, Cyprus, Crete
G. c. riggenbachi
W Morocco
G. c. macrorhyncha
S Algeria
G. c. randoni
C Algeria
G. c. carthaginis
N Algeria, N Tunisia
G. c. arenicola
SE Algeria, S Tunisia
G. c. balsaci
W Mauretania
G. c. festae
Libya
G. c. senegallensis
Senegal & Gambia to Sierra Leone & Mali
G. c. jordonsi
Aïr Mts (Niger)
G. c. alexanderi
N Cameroun, Mali, S Niger, Chad
G. c. zalingei
W Sudan
G. c. isabellina
N Chad C Sudan
G. c. somaliensis
Somalia
G. c. altirostris
Egypt, Arabia
G. s. maculata
C Egypt, SW Arabia
G. c. nigricans
N Egypt
G. c. cinnamomina
Lebanon

G. c. zion
Turkey, Syria
G. c. magna
C & S Asia, NW China, N India
G. c. leautungensis
Manchuria, N China
G. c. coreensis
Korea
G. c. lynesi
Kashmir
G. c. chendoola
N & NW India
Galerida theklae (Thekla Lark)
G. t. theklae
Portugal, Spain, Balearic Is
G. t. erlangeri
N Morocco
G. t. ruficolor
C Morocco, N Algeria, N Tunisia
G. t. superflua
E Morocco, C Algeria, S Tunisia,
Libya
G. t. deichleri
S Algeria, S Tunisia
G. t. harrarensis
Harar (Ethiopia)
G. t. huei
Bale (Ethiopia)
G. t. praetermissa
Ethiopia
G. t. ellioti
Somalia
G. t. mallablensis
S Somalia
G. t. huriensis
Kenya
**Galerida malabarica (Malabar Crested
Lark)**
W India
Galerida deva (Sykes' Crested Lark)
WC & SC India
Galerida modesta (Sun Lark)
G. m. giffardi
Ghana to Sudan
G. m. modesta
S Sudan
G. m. nigrita
Guinea, Sierra Leone
G. m. strümpelli
W Cameroun
G. m. bucolica
Central African Republic, N Zaire,
SW Sudan
CALENDULA
**Calendula magnirostris (Thick-billed
Lark)**
C. m. magnirostris
W & SW Cape Province

C. m. harei
SW Transvaal, Orange Free State, Cape
Province
C. m. montivaga
Lesotho
LULLULA
Lullula arborea (Wood Lark)
L. a. arborea
N & W Europe, N Africa
L. a. pallida
S Europe, N Africa, Caucasus, Iran
ALAUDA
Alauda arvensis (Sky Lark)
A. a. arvensis
N & W Europe
A. a. sierrae
N Portugal, Spain
A. a. harterti
W North Africa
A. a. cantarella
SE Europe, Iran, E North Africa
A. a. dulcivox
SE Russia, C Asia, N India
A. a. kiborti
EC Asia, Manchuria, E China
A. a. intermedia
NE Manchuria, E China
A. a. pekinensis
NC & NE Asia, Japan, N China
A. a. lönnbergi
Sakhalin I, Korea, NE China, Japan
A. a. japonica
Japan, Riukiu Is
Alauda gulgula (Oriental Skylark)
A. g. inconspicua
SW Asia, Afghanistan, NW India
A. g. lhamarum
W Himalayas
A. g. inopinata
SE Tibet, W China, N Burma, Nepal
A. g. sala
Hainan I
A. g. herberti
C & S Thailand, S Indochina
A. g. wattersi
Taiwan
A. g. wolfei
Philippine Is
A. g. vernayi
E Bhutan, SE Tibet, N Burma
A. g. weigoldi
C China
A. g. coelivox
SE China, N Vietnam
A. g. gulgula
S India, Sri Lanka, S Burma
A. g. australis
S India, Sri Lanka

Eremophila alpestris (Shore (Horned) Lark)
E. a. flava
  N Europe, N Asia
E. a. balcanica
  SE Europe
E. a. penicillata
  Asia Minor, W Iran
E. a. albigula
  N Iran, Afghanistan, C Asia
E. a. brandti
  EC Asia, N China
E. a. longirostris
  Baluchistan, NW Himalayas
E. a. teleschowi
  C Siking
E. a. przewalskii
  NW Tsinghai
E. a. argalea
  NW India
E. a. elwesi
  N India, Sikkim, Nepal, S Tibet
E. a. nigrifrons
  E Tsinghai, NW China
E. a. khamensis
  C Sikang
E. a. atlas
  C Morocco
E. a. bicornis
  S Asia Minor, Lebanon
E. a. arcticola
  N Alaska, W Canada, NW USA
E. a. alpina
  W Washington State
E. a. hoyti
  N Canada, N USA
E. a. alpestris
  NE Canada, NE USA
E. a. leucolaema
  S Canada, C & S USA, N Mexico
E. a. enthymia
  C Canada, C USA
E. a. praticola
  SE Canada, C & EC USA
E. a. strigata
  NW USA
E. a. merrilli
  W Canada, W USA
E. a. lamprochroma
  W & SW USA
E. a. utahensis
  WC USA
E. a. sierrae
  NE California
E. a. rubea
  C California
E. a. actia
  S California, N Baja California

E. a. insularis
  S California islands
E. a. ammophila
  SW USA, NE Baja California
  NW Mexico
E. a. leucansiptila
  SW USA, NE Baja California, NW Mexico
E. a. occidentalis
  S USA, N Mexico
E. a. adusta
  S USA
E. a. giraudi
  S Texas, NC Mexico
E. a. enertera
  WC Baja California
E. a. aphrasta
  NC Mexico
E. a. diaphora
  E Mexico
E. a. lactea
  Coahuila (Mexico)
E. a. chrysolaema
  SC Mexico
E. a. oaxacae
  S Mexico
E. a. peregrina
  Colombia
Eremophila bilopha (Temminck's Horned Lark)
  N Africa, N Arabia, Iraq

117 HIRUNDINIDAE (SWALLOWS, MARTINS)

PSEUDOCHELIDONINAE

PSEUDOCHELIDON
Pseudochelidon eurystomina (African River Martin)
  Zaire
Pseudochelidon sirintarae (White-eyed River Martin)
  C Thailand

HIRUNDININAE

TACHYCINETA
Tachycineta bicolor (Tree Swallow)
  W Canada, W USA, Central America, Cuba
Tachycineta albilinea (Mangrove Swallow)
  T. a. rhizophorae
    NW Mexico
  T. a. albilinea
    E & S Mexico, Central America
  T. a. stolzmanni
    W Peru

Tachycineta albiventer (White-winged Swallow)
NE South America, Trinidad
Tachycineta leucorrhoa (White-rumped Swallow)
SC South America
Tachycineta leucopyga (Chilean Swallow)
S South America
Tachycineta thalassina (Violet-green Swallow)
T. t. lepida
NW Canada, W & SW USA, NW Mexico,
Central America
T. t. brachyptera
C & S Baja California, NW Mexico
T. t. thalassina
C Mexico
Tachycineta cyaneoviridis (Bahama Swallow)
E Cuba, Bahama Is
Tachycineta euchrysea (Golden Swallow)
T. e. euchrysea
Jamaica
T. e. sclateri
Hispaniola

PHAEOPROGNE
Phaeoprogne tapera (Brown-chested Martin)
P. t. tapera
Colombia, Venezuela, the Guianas,
Ecuador, Peru, Brazil
P. t. fusca
Central South America

PROGNE
Progne subis (Purple Martin)
P. s. subis
S Canada, W USA, E Mexico to Panama,
N South America
P. s. hesperia
Arizona, Baja California, W Mexico to
Nicaragua
P. s. arboricola
Utah
Progne dominicensis (Caribbean Martin)
P. d. cryptoleuca
Cuba, Isle of Pines
P. d. dominicensis
Jamaica, Hispaniola, Lesser Antilles
P. d. sinaloae
NW Mexico
Progne chalybea (Grey-breasted Martin)
P. c. chalybea
S USA, Central America, N South America
P. c. macroramphus
C South America
Progne modesta (Southern Martin)
P. m. modesta
C & S Galapagos Is

P. m. elegans
Bolivia, Brazil, Argentina
P. m. murphyi
W Peru, N Chile

NOTIOCHELIDON
Notiochelidon murina (Brown-bellied Swallow)
N. m. murina
Colombia, Ecuador, Peru
N. m. meridensis
W Venezuela
N. m. cyanodorsalis
W Bolivia
Notiochelidon cyanoleuca (Blue and White Swallow)
N. c. cyanoleuca
Costa Rica, Panama, N & C South America
N. c. peruviana
W Peru
N. c. patagonica
S South America
Notiochelidon flavipes (Pale-footed Swallow)
Peru, Colombia
Notiochelidon pileata (Black-capped Swallow)
S Mexico, Guatemala

ATTICORA
Atticora fasciata (White-banded Swallow)
N & W Amazonia
Atticora melanoleuca (Black-collared Swallow)
N Amazonia

NEOCHELIDON
Neochelidon tibialis (White-thighed Swallow)
N. t. minimus
E Panama, Colombia, W Ecuador
N. t. griseiventris
S Colombia, SE Venezuela, E Ecuador,
E Peru, W Brazil
N. t. tibialis
SE Brazil

ALOPOCHELIDON
Alopochelidon fucata (Tawny-headed Swallow)
Venezuela to C Argentina

STELGIDOPTERYX
Stelgidopteryx serripennis (Northern Rough-winged Swallow)
S Canada, USA, Mexico, Central
America
Stelgidopteryx ruficollis (Southern Rough-winged Swallow)
S. r. psammochroa
SW USA, Baja California, S Mexico
S. r. fulvipennis
C & S Mexico to Costa Rica

S. r. ridgwayi
Yucatan
S. r. stuarti
SE Mexico, E Guatemala
S. r. decolor
W Costa Rica, W Panama
S. r. uropygialis
W Colombia, Ecuador, NW Peru
S. r. aequalis
N Colombia, W Venezuela, Trinidad
S. r. cacabata
E Venezuela, the Guianas
S. r. ruficollis
SE Colombia, E Ecuador, E Peru,
Bolivia, N Argentina

CHERAMOECA
Cheramoeca leucosterna (White-backed Swallow)
W, S & C Australia

RIPARIA
Riparia paludicola (African Sand Martin)
R. p. mauretanica
W Morocco
R. p. minor
Niger, Mali, Chad, Sudan, Ethiopia
R. p. newtoni
SE Nigeria
R. p. ducis
Uganda, E Zaire, Kenya, Tanzania
R. p. paludicola
Zambia, South Africa
R. p. cowani
Madagascar
R. p. chinensis
N India, South East Asia
R. p. tantilla
Luzon I
Riparia congica (Congo Sand Martin)
C Zaire
Riparia riparia (Sand Martin) (Bank Swallow)
R. r. riparia
North America, N South America, Europe,
Asia, N & E Africa
R. r. ijimae
NE Asia, Burma, Thailand, Philippine Is
R. r. tibetana
C Asia
R. r. diluta
NW India, Nepal
R. r. fokienensis
C & S China
R. r. indica
Afghanistan, NW India
R. r. shelleyi
Egypt, Sudan

Riparia cincta (Banded Sand Martin)   351
R. c. erlangeri
Ethiopia
R. c. suahelica
Uganda, Kenya, N Tanzania
R. c. parvula
S Zaire
R. c. cincta
W & S Africa
R. c. xerica
W Angola

PHEDINA
Phedina borbonica (Mascarene Martin)
P. b. borbonica
Mauritius I, Reunion I
P. b. madagascariensis
Malawi, Madagascar

PHEDINOPSIS
Phedinopsis brazzae (Brazza's Martin)
S Zaire, N Angola

HIRUNDO
Hirundo griseopyga (Grey-rumped Swallow)
H. g. liberiae
Liberia
H. g. gertrudis
NE Nigeria
H. g. melbina
Gabon
H. g. griseopyga
Ethiopia to Natal
Hirundo rupestris (Crag Martin)
H. r. rupestris
S Europe, C & SW Asia, NE Africa, India
H. r. theresae
S Morocco
Hirundo obsoleta (Pale Crag Martin)
H. o. spatzi
SC Algeria
H. o. presaharica
NC Algeria
H. o. buchanani
N Niger
H. o. obsoleta
Egypt, Sudan, Sinai, Iran
H. o. arabica
E Sudan, W Arabia, Somalia, Socotra I
H. o. perpallida
E Arabia
H. o. pallida
E Iran, Afghanistan, NW India
Hirundo fuligula (African Rock Martin)
H. f. pusilla
S Sudan, Ethiopia
H. f. rufigula
N Nigeria, Chad, S Sudan, Ethiopia,
Zaire, Uganda, N Tanzania

H. f. birwae
Sierra Leone, Guinea
H. f. bansoensis
SE Nigeria
H. f. fusciventris
S Tanzania, Malawi, N Mozambique
H. f. anderssoni
S Angola, Namibia, Botswana, W Cape
Province
H. f. fuligula
E Cape Province
H. f. pretoriae
E Transvaal, Natal
Hirundo concolor (Dusky Crag Martin)
H. c. concolor
India
H. c. sintaungensis
Burma, N Thailand, N Laos, N Vietnam
Hirundo rustica ((Barn) Swallow)
H. r. rustica
Europe, W Asia, Africa, India
H. r. transitiva
Asia Minor, Egypt, Kenya, Uganda
H. r. savignii
Egypt
H. r. gutteralis
NE Asia, India, S China, SE Asia, New
Guinea
H. r. tytleri
Bhutan, Siberia, W Mongolia, W China,
Burma
H. r. mandschurica
Manchuria, E China
H. r. saturata
E Siberia
H. r. erythrogaster
N & S America, West Indies
Hirundo lucida (Red-chested Swallow)
H. l. lucida
Senegal to Ghana
H. l. clara
Mali, Upper Volta
H. l. subalaris
E Zaire
H. l. rothschildi
Ethiopia
Hirundo angolensis (Angola Swallow)
H. a. arcticincta
Uganda, W Kenya, NW Tanzania
H. a. angolensis
SE Zaire, Tanzania, Angola, Malawi,
Zambia
Hirundo tahitica (Pacific Swallow)
H. t. domicola
S India, Sri Lanka
H. t. abbotti
Malaysia, Sumatra, Borneo, Philippine Is

H. t. nameyei
Riukiu Is
H. t. mallopega
Andaman Is, E Sumatra, Java
H. t. frontalis
Lesser Sunda Is, New Guinea, Celebes
Moluccas
H. t. ambiens
New Britain
H. t. subfusca
Polynesia, Melanesia, Fiji Is, Tonga I
H. t. tahitica
Society Is
H. t. carteri
W Australia
H. t. parsonsi
NE Queensland
H. t. neoxena
S Queensland, New South Wales,
Victoria, South Australia
**Hirundo albigularis (White-throated
Swallow)**
H. a. ambigua
N & E Angola, NW Zambia
H. a. albigularis
Southern Africa
Hirundo aethiopica (Ethiopian Swallow)
H. a. fulvipectus
Nigeria, Cameroun, Sudan
H. a. aethiopica
Ethiopia, Somalia, E Kenya, Tanzania
Hirundo smithii (Wire-tailed Swallow)
H. s. smithii
W, C, E & SE Africa
H. s. filifera
SW Asia, India, Burma, Thailand, Laos,
N Vietnam
Hirundo atrocaerulea (Blue Swallow)
Tanzania to Natal
**Hirundo nigrita (White-throated Blue
Swallow)**
W & C Africa
**Hirundo leucosoma (Pied-winged
Swallow)**
Senegal to Nigeria
**Hirundo megaensis (White-tailed
Swallow)**
S Ethiopia
**Hirundo nigrorufa (Black and Rufous
Swallow)**
Angola, S Zaire, Zambia
**Hirundo dimidiata (Pearl-breasted
Swallow)**
H. d. marwitzi
Angola, Zambia, SW Tanzania, Malawi
H. d. dimidiata
South Africa, Rhodesia

Hirundo cucullata (Greater Striped Swallow)
Southern Africa
Hirundo abyssinica (Lesser Striped Swallow)
H. a. puella
Sierra Leone to Nigeria
H. a. maxima
S Nigeria, Cameroun
H. a. bannermani
S Sudan
H. a. abyssinica
Ethiopia, Uganda, Kenya, Tanzania
H. a. unitatis
W Uganda, E Zaire, SE Africa
H. a. ampliformis
Caprivi Strip to NE Zambia
Hirundo semirufa (Red-breasted Swallow)
H. s. gordoni
W & C Africa
H. s. semirufa
SE Africa
Hirundo senegalensis (Mosque Swallow)
H. s. senegalensis
W & NC Africa
H. c. saturatior
C & E Africa
H. s. monteiri
SC Africa
Hirundo daurica (Red-rumped Swallow)
H. d. daurica
C Asia
H. d. japonica
E Asia, Japan, China, N India
H. d. gephyra
W China
H. d. nipalensis
Himalayas, India, N Burma
H. d. erythropygia
S India, Sri Lanka
H. d. hyperythra
Sri Lanka
H. d. rufula
S Europe, Iran, Afghanistan, NW India
H. d. domicella
NW Africa
H. d. disjuncta
Sierra Leone
H. d. kumboensis
Cameroun
H. d. emini
E Africa
H. d. melanocrissa
N Ethiopia

Hirundo striolata (Greater Striated Swallow)   353
H. s. striolata
Taiwan, Philippine Is, Borneo, Sumatra, Lesser Sunda Is
H. s. mayri
Assam, N Burma, NW Thailand
H. s. stanfordi
Burma, N Thailand, N Laos
H. s. vernayi
S Thailand
H. s. badia
C Malaysia

PETROCHELIDON
Petrochelidon rufigula (Red-throated Cliff Swallow)
Angola, S Zaire, Zambia
Petrochelidon preussi (Preuss' Cliff Swallow)
W Africa, N Zaire
Petrochelidon andecola (Andean Swallow)
P. a. oroyae
C Peru
P. a. andecola
S Peru, N Bolivia, N Chile
Petrochelidon nigricans (Tree Martin)
P. n. timoriensis
Timor I, Lesser Sunda Is
P. n. neglecta
W & N Australia
P. n. nigricans
E & S Australia, New Guinea, Solomon Is
Petrochelidon spilodera (South African Cliff Swallow)
Southern Africa
Petrochelidon pyrrhonota (American Cliff Swallow)
P. p. pyrrhonota
North America, Central America, N South America
P. p. tachina
SW USA, W Central America
P. p. minima
SW USA, N Mexico
P. p. melanogaster
S Mexico, S Brazil, N Argentina
Petrochelidon fulva (Cave Swallow)
P. f. pelodoma
S USA, Mexico, Guatemala
P. f. citata
SE Mexico
P. f. fulva
Puerto Rico, Cuba, Hispaniola, Jamaica
P. f. chapmani
SW Ecuador
P. f. rufocollaris
W Peru

Petrochelidon fluvicola (Indian Cliff
Swallow)
   Afghanistan, Himalayas, N India
Petrochelidon ariel (Fairy Martin)
   Australia, Tasmania
Petrochelidon fuliginosa (Dusky Cliff
Swallow)
   S Cameroun

DELICHON
Delichon urbica (House Martin)
   D. u. urbica
     Europe, C & W Asia, W & SE Africa
   D. u. meridionalis
     Mediterranean, N Africa, Iran, N India
   D. u. lagopoda
     E Asia, S China, Burma, Thailand
Delichon dasypus (Asian House Martin)
   D. d. cashmiriensis
     Himalayas, India, W China
   D. d. nigrimentalis
     S China, Taiwan
   D. d. dasypus
     NE Asia, N China, Malaysia, Borneo,
     Philippine Is
Delichon nipalensis (Nepal House Martin)
   D. n. nipalensis
     Himalayas, Assam
   D. n. cuttingi
     NE Burma

PSALIDOPROCNE
Psalidoprocne nitens (Square-tailed
Saw-wing)
   P. n. nitens
     W Africa, N Zaire
   P. n. centralis
     NE Zaire
Psalidoprocne fuliginosa (Cameroun
Saw-wing)
   Cameroun, Fernando Po I
Psalidoprocne albiceps (White-headed
Saw-wing)
   P. a. albiceps
     EC Africa
   P. a. suffusa
     Angola
Psalidoprocne pristoptera (African Blue
Saw-wing)
   P. p. pristoptera
     Somalia, N Ethiopia
   P. p. blanfordi
     S Ethiopia
   P. p. mangbettorum
     NE Zaire
Psalidoprocne oleaginea (Kaffa Saw-wing)
   SW Ethiopia
Psalidoprocne antinorii (Brown Saw-wing)
   S Ethiopia

Psalidoprocne petiti (Petit's Saw-wing)
   P. p. petiti
     Gabon, Cameroun, Central African
     Republic
   P. p. chalybea
     N Cameroun, NE Zaire
   P. p. reichenowi
     Angola, SW Zaire, Zambia
   P. p. orientalis
     Tanzania, Malawi, E Zambia, Mozambique
Psalidoprocne holomelaena (Black
Saw-wing)
   P. h. ruwenzori
     E Zaire, W Uganda
   P. h. massaica
     Kenya
   P. h. holomelaena
     Mozambique, Malawi, Transvaal, Natal,
     E Cape Province
Psalidoprocne obscura (Fantee Saw-wing)
   Port Guinea to Cameroun

118 MOTACILLIDAE (WAGTAILS, PIPITS)

DENDRONANTHUS
Dendronanthus indicus (Forest Wagtail)
   NE Asia, China, India, Thailand, Malaysia,
   Sumatra, Java, Borneo

MOTACILLA
Motacilla flava (Yellow Wagtail)
   M. f. flavissima
     NW Europe, Spain, N Africa
   M. f. flava
     N Europe, S Africa
   M. f. iberiae
     S France, Spain, NW Africa
   M. f. cinereocapilla
     Italy, Sardinia, Arabia, NE Africa
   M. f. pygmaea
     Egypt
   M. f. beema
     SE Russia, C Asia, India, NE Africa
   M. f. leucocephala
     Mongolia, C Asia, NW India
   M. f. lutea
     SE Russia, S Africa, India
   M. f. zaissanensis
     C Asia, India
   M. f. thunbergi
     NE Europe, C & S Africa
   M. f. plexa
     N Siberia, N Asia, India
   M. f. angarensis
     N & C Asia, E Mongolia, E China, Burma
   M. f. macronyx
     C Asia, E China, Burma, Malaysia,
     Sumatra
   M. f. simillima
     N Siberia, E China, Philippine Is

M. f. tschutschensis
NE Asia, Alaska, E China, Java
M. f. taivana
E Siberia, China, Philippine Is
M. f. feldegg
Balkans, Asia Minor, Iraq, Iran, E Africa
M. f. melanogrisea
SW Asia, NW & C India
Motacilla citreola (Citrine Wagtail)
M. c. citreola
Russia, C Asia, Manchuria, India, SE China
M. c. werae
Siberia, Iran, SW Asia, India
M. c. calcarata
E Iran, Himalayas, Tibet, Burma
Afghanistan
Motacilla cinerea (Grey Wagtail)
M. c. patriciae
Azores Is
M. c. schmitzi
Madeira I
M. c. canariensis
Canary Is
M. c. cinerea
Europe, N Africa, Iran, India, SE Asia
C & S Africa
M. c. robusta
NE Asia, Japan, E China, Philippine Is
Motacilla alba (Pied Wagtail)
M. a. yarrelli
British Isles, Spain, Morocco
M. a. alba
Europe, Russia, N & E Africa, Iran, Arabia
M. a. subpersonata
Morocco
M. a. dukhunensis
S Russia, SW Asia, Afghanistan, India
M. a. personata
Siberia, W Asia, Afghanistan, Iran, N India
M. a. persica
Iran
M. a. baicalensis
C Asia, Iran, India, Thailand, SW China
M. a. ocularis
E Siberia, E India, China, Thailand,
Philippine Is
M. a. lugens
NE Asia, NE China, Japan, Taiwan
M. a. leucopsis
E Asia, China, Thailand, Himalayas
M. a. alboides
S China, E Himalayas, Burma
Motacilla grandis (Japanese Pied Wagtail)
Japan, Korea, E China, Taiwan
**Motacilla maderaspatensis (Large Pied
Wagtail)**
Pakistan, India

Motacilla aguimp (African Pied Wagtail)
M. a. vidua
W, C & E Africa, S Africa
M. a. aguimp
Orange River, NW Cape Province
Motacilla clara (Mountain Wagtail)
M. c. chapini
Guinea to E Zaire
M. c. clara
Ethiopia
M. c. torrentium
Uganda and E Zaire, to W Angola and
Natal
Motacilla capensis (Cape Wagtail)
M. c. simplicissima
Angola, S Zaira, Zambia
M. c. capensis
Southern Africa
M. c. wellsi
E Zaire, Uganda, Kenya
**Motacilla flaviventris (Madagascar
Wagtail)**
Madagascar

TMETOTHYLACUS
Tmetothylacus tenellus (Golden Pipit)
Somalia, Kenya, Tanzania

MACRONYX
Macronyx capensis (Cape Longclaw)
M. c. capensis
W Cape Province
M. c. colletti
Botswana, Transvaal, C Cape Province,
Natal
M. c. stabilior
Rhodesia
**Macronyx croceus (Yellow-throated
Longclaw)**
W, E & Southern Africa
**Macronyx fuelleborni (Fülleborn's
Longclaw)**
M. f. fuelleborni
C Tanzania
M. f. ascensi
Angola, Zaire, Zambia, SW Tanzania
Macronyx sharpei (Sharpe's Longclaw)
Kenya
**Macronyx flavicollis (Abyssinian
Longclaw)**
Ethiopia
Macronyx aurantiigula (Pangani Longclaw)
Somalia, Kenya
**Macronyx ameliae (Rosy-breasted
Longclaw)**
Zaira, Kenya to Natal

***Macronyx grimwoodi* (Grimwood's Longclaw)**
M. g. grimwoodi
E Angola, NW Zambia
M. g. cuandocubangensis
Cuando, Angola

ANTHUS

***Anthus novaeseelandiae* (Richard's Pipit)**
A. n. cameroonensis
Cameroun
A. n. lynesi
E Cameroun, Sudan
A. n. cinnamomeus
Ethiopia, East Africa, Zambia
A. n. lacuum
E Africa
A. n. lwenarum
NW Zambia
A. n. bocagei
Angola, Namibia, Botswana
A. n. rufuloides
South Africa
A. n. editus
Lesotho, W Natal
A. n. richardi
C Asia, Pakistan, India, Thailand, Siberia, N Vietnam
A. n. dauricus
N Mongolia
A. n. centralasiae
C Asia
A. n. sinensis
E Siberia, E China, Malaysia, Sumatra
A. n. rufulus
Nepal, Burma, Thailand, Laos, Vietnam
A. n. waitei
Pakistan, NW India
A. n. malayensis
S India, Sri Lanka, Malaysia, Sumatra, Java Borneo
A. n. lugubris
Palawan, Philippine Is
A. n. albidus
Lesser Sunda Is
A. n. medius
Savu Is, Timor I
A. n. exiguus
C New Guinea
A. n. rogersi
N Australia
A. n. subaustralis
C & W Australia
A. n. bilbali
SW Australia
A. n. australis
SE Australia
A. n. bistriatus
Tasmania

A. n. reischeki
North I, New Zealand
A. n. novaeseelandiae
South I, New Zealand
A. n. chathamensis
Chatham I
A. n. aucklandicus
Auckland Is
A. n. steindachneri
Antipodes Is
***Anthus godlewskii* (Blyth's Pipit)**
EC Asia, Tibet, India, Burma, Sri Lanka
***Anthus campestris* (Tawny Pipit)**
A. c. campestris
Europe, N Africa, Iran, Arabia, SW Asia
A. c. griseus
C Asia, Afghanistan, W India
A. c. kastschenkoi
W Siberia, N India
***Anthus similis* (Long-billed Pipit)**
A. s. nicholsoni
Rhodesia, South Africa
A. s. leucocraspedon
Namibia
A. s. bannermani
Sierra Leone, Guinea
A. s. josensis
C Nigeria
A. s. asbenaicus
S Sahara
A. s. jebelmarrae
W Sudan
A. s. hararensis
Ethiopia, Kenya, N Tanzania
A. s. nivescens
NE Sudan, Red Sea
A. s. sokotrae
Socotra I
A. s. dewittei
C Zaire
A. s. hellae
E Zaire, W Uganda
A. s. nyassae
Angola, Zambia, Malawi, S Tanzania
A. s. moco
C Angola
A. s. petricola
Lesotho
A. s. schoutedeni
S Angola, S Zaire, Zambia, SW Tanzania
A. s. captus
Lebanon, Syria, Israel
A. s. arabicus
SW Arabia
A. s. decaptus
Afghanistan, Pakistan, NW India
A. s. jerdoni
E Afghanistan, Himalayas, Burma

A. s. yamethini
C Burma
A. s. similis
C & S India
A. s. travancoriensis
SW India
Anthus vaalensis (Sandy Plain-backed Pipit)
A. v. saphiroi
E Ethiopia, Somalia
A. v. goodsoni
Kenya
A. v. neumanni
Angola, S Zaire, Zambia
A. v. chobiensis
W Zambia, Botswana, Rhodesia
A. v. vaalensis
Namibia, W Rhodesia, Cape Province
A. v. daviesii
E Cape Province
Anthus leucophrys (Dark Plain-backed Pipit)
A. l. ansorgei
Senegal to N Nigeria
A. l. gouldii
Sierra Leone, Ivory Coast
A. l. zenkeri
S Nigeria to N Uganda & Kenya
A. l. omoensis
Ethiopia, Uganda, W Kenya
A. l. bohndorffi
Angola, S Zaire, Zambia, Malawi
A. l. leucophrys
S Angola, Botswana, South Africa
A. l. tephridorsus
NW Rhodesia
Anthus pallidiventris (Long-legged Pipit)
A. p. pallidiventris
Gabon, NW Angola
A. p. esobe
C Zaire
Anthus pratensis (Meadow Pipit)
A. p. theresae
W Ireland
A. p. pratensis
Greenland, Europe, N Africa, Asia Minor, Iran
Anthus trivialis (Tree Pipit)
A. t. trivialis
Europe, Asia, India, Africa
A. t. haringtoni
EC Asia, Himalayas, N India
Anthus hodgsoni (Indian Tree Pipit)
A. h. yunnanensis
N & E Asia, India, SE China, Borneo
A. h. hodgsoni
Himalayas, NW China, Japan, India

Anthus roseatus (Hodgson's Pipit)
C & E Asia, N India, Tibet, W China
Anthus cervinus (Red-throated Pipit)
E Europe, E Asia, W & E Africa, India
Anthus gustavi (Petchora Pipit)
A. g. gustavi
NE Asia, China, Philippine Is, Borneo Celebes
A. g. commanderensis
Commander Is
A. g. menzbieri
S Ussuriland
Anthus spinoletta (Rock Pipit)
A. s. rubescens
N & NE Asia, North America, Mexico, Guatemala
A. s. pacificus
W Canada, W USA, W Mexico
A. s. alticola
SW USA, NW Mexico
A. s. japonicus
E Asia, Japan, E China, N India, Burma
A. s. coutellii
C Asia, Tibet, China, N India, Iran
A. s. spinoletta
S & E Europe
A. s. kleinschmidti
Faroe Is
A. s. petrosus
British Isles
A. s. littoralis
NW Europe
Anthus nilghiriensis (Nilgiri Pipit)
S India
Anthus sylvanus (Upland Pipit)
Afghanistan, Himalayas, W China
Anthus berthelotii (Canarian Pipit)
A. b. berthelotii
Canary Is
A. b. madeirensis
Madeira I
Anthus lineiventris (Large-striped Pipit)
Angola, Tanzania to Natal
Anthus brachyurus (Short-tailed Pipit)
A. b. brachyurus
Natal
A. b. leggei
Angola, Zaire, Uganda, Tanzania, Zambia
Anthus caffer (Bushveld Pipit)
A. c. australoabyssinicus
S Ethiopia
A. c. blayneyi
S Kenya, Tanzania
A. c. mzimbaensis
Malawi
A. c. caffer
Botswana, Angola, Rhodesia, Mozambique, Transvaal, Natal

Anthus sokokensis (Sokoke Pipit)
SE Kenya, NE Tanzania
Anthus melindae (Malindi Pipit)
A. m. melindae
S Somalia, Kenya
A. m. pallidus
SC Somalia
Anthus chloris (Yellow-breasted Pipit)
S & E South Africa
Anthus crenatus (Large Yellow-tufted Pipit)
E Transvaal, Cape Province
Anthus gutturalis (New Guinea Pipit)
A. g. gutturalis
SE New Guinea
A. g. rhododendri
EC New Guinea
A. g. wollastoni
WC New Guinea
Anthus spragueii (Sprague's Pipit)
NC & S USA, S Mexico
Anthus furcatus (Short-billed Pipit)
A. f. brevirostris
Peru, Bolivia
A. f. furcatus
Brazil, Paraguay, Uruguay, Argentina
Anthus lutescens (Yellowish Pipit)
A. l. parvus
W Panama
A. l. peruvianus
Peru, N Chile
A. l. lutescens
Colombia, Venezula, the Guianas, Brazil, Argentina
Anthus chacoensis (Chaco Pipit)
Paraguay, Argentina
Anthus correndera (Correndera Pipit)
A. c. calcaratus
Peru
A. c. catamarcae
Bolivia, N Chile, NW Argentina
A. c. chilensis
S Chile, S Argentina
A. c. grayi
Fàlkland Is
A. c. correndera
S Brazil, Uruguay, Paraguay, N Argentina
Anthus antarcticus (South Georgia Pipit)
S Georgia I
Anthus nattereri (Ochre-breasted Pipit)
SE Brazil, Paraguay
Anthus hellmayri (Hellmayr's Pipit)
A. h. hellmayri
Peru, Bolivia, NW Argentina
A. h. dabbenei
Chile, W Argentina
A. h. brasilianus
SE Brazil, Uruguay, N Argentina

Anthus bogotensis (Paramo Pipit)
A. b. bogotensis
Colombia, Ecuador
A. b. immaculatus
Bolivia, Peru
A. b. shiptoni
Bolivia, NW Argentina
A. b. meridae
NW Venezuela

119 CAMPEPHAGIDAE (CUCKOO SHRIKES)

PTEROPODOCYS
Pteropodocys maxima (Ground Cuckoo Shrike)
P. m. pallida
N Australia
P. m. maxima
S Australia

CORACINA
Coracina novaehollandiae (Large Cuckoo Shrike)
C. n. macei
India
C. n. nipalensis
Assam, Himalayas
C. n. lushaiensis
S Assam
C. n. rexpineti
SE China, Taiwan, N Laos
C. n. layardi
Sri Lanka
C. n. andamani
Andaman Is
C. n. siamensis
Burma, Thailand, S Indochina
C. n. larutensis
N Malaysia
C. n. larvivorus
Hainan I
C. n. javensis
Java, Bali I
C. n. floris
Lesser Sunda Is, Sumbawa I
C. n. sumbensis
Sumba I
C. n. alfrediana
Lomblen I, Alor I
C. n. personata
Timor I, Wetar I
C. n. lettiensis
Sumba Is, Leti I, Moa I
C. n. subpallida
Kei Is, C Western Australia
C. n. didimus
N Australia, S Moluccas, W New Guinea
C. n. melanops
E New Guinea, Bismarck Archipelago, S & E Australia

C. n. novaehollandiae
Tasmania, Flinders I
Coracina fortis (Buru Is Cuckoo Shrike)
S Moluccas
Coracina atriceps (Moluccan Cuckoo Shrike)
C. a. magnirostris
N Moluccas
C. a. atriceps
S Moluccas
Coracina pollens (Kei Is Cuckoo Shrike)
C. p. pollens
Kei Is
C. p. unimoda
Tenimber Is
Coracina schistacea (Sula Is Cuckoo Shrike)
C. s. petersi
Peleng Is
C. s. schistacea
Sula Is
Coracina caledonica (Melanesian Greybird)
C. c. bougainvillei
Bougainville I
C. c. kulambangrae
Kulambangra I
C. c. welchmani
Ysabel I
C. c. amadonis
Guadalcanal I
C. c. thilenii
Espiritu Santo I, Malekula I
C. c. seiuncta
Erromango I
C. c. lifuensis
Lifu I, Loyalty Is
C. c. caledonica
New Caledonia I
Coracina caeruleogrisea (Stout-billed Greybird)
C. c. strenua
Japan, W & C New Guinea
C. c. caeruleogrisea
Aru Is, S New Guinea
C. c. adamsoni
SE New Guinea
Coracina temminckii (Temminck's Cuckoo Shrike)
C. c. temminckii
N Celebes
C. c. rileyi
C & SE Celebes
C. c. tonkeana
E Celebes
Coracina larvata (Black-faced Greybird)
C. l. melanocephala
Sumatra

C. l. larvata
Java
C. l. normani
Borneo
Coracina striata (Barred Cuckoo Shrike)
C. s. dobsoni
Andaman Is
C. s. sumatrensis
Thailand, Malaysia, Sumatra, Borneo
C. s. bungurensis
Anamba Is, Natuna Is
C. s. simalurensis
Simalur I, Sumatra
C. s. babiensis
Babi I, Sumatra
C. s. kannegieteri
Nias I
C. s. enganensis
Enggano I
C. s. vordermani
Kangean I
C. s. difficilis
Palawan I, Balabac I
C. s. striata
Luzon I, Lubang I
C. s. mindorensis
Mindoro I
C. s. panayensis
Masbate I, Panay I, Negros I
C. s. boholensis
Bohol I, Leyte I, Samar I
C. s. kochii
Mindanao I, Basilan I
C. s. guillemardi
Sulu Archipelago
Coracina bicolor (Muna Greybird)
Muna I, Celebes
Coracina lineata (Lineated Cuckoo Shrike)
C. l. axillaris
Waigeu I, C New Guinea
C. l. maforensis
Numfor I
C. l. sublineata
New Ireland, New Britain
C. l. nigrifrons
Bougainville I, Ysabel I
C. l. ombriosa
Kulambangra I, New Georgia I, Rendova I
C. l. pusilla
Guadalcanal I
C. l. malaitae
Malaita I
C. l. makirae
San Cristobal I
C. l. gracilis
Rennell I
C. l. lineata
E Queensland, E New South Wales

Coracina boyeri (White-lored Cuckoo Shrike)
  C. b. boyeri
    Japen I, W New Guinea
  C. b. subalaris
    S New Guinea
Coracina leucopygia (White-rumped Cuckoo Shrike)
  Muna I, Celebes
Coracina papuensis (Papuan Cuckoo Shrike)
  C. p. melanolora
    Misol I, Moluccas
  C. p. papuensis
    Japen I, W New Guinea
  C. p. intermedia
    S New Guinea
  C. p. oriomo
    SE New Guinea, N Queensland
  C. p. angustifrons
    SE New Guinea
  C. p. louisiadensis
    Louisiade Archipelago
  C. p. ingens
    Admiralty Is
  C. p. sclateri
    Bismarck Archipelago
  C. p. perpallida
    Bougainville I, Choiseul I, Ysabel I
  C. p. elegans
    New Georgia I, Rendova I, Guadalcanal I
  C. p. eyerdami
    Malaita I
  C. p. timorlaoensis
    Tenimber Is
  C. p. hypoleuca
    Aru Is, Melville I, N Australia
  C. p. stalkeri
    N & C Queensland
Coracina robusta (Little Cuckoo Shrike)
  E Australia
Coracina longicauda (Black-hooded Greybird)
  C. l. grisea
    WC New Guinea
  C. l. longicauda
    C & SE New Guinea
Coracina parvula (Halmahera Greybird)
  Halmahera I
Coracina abbotti (Celebes Mountain Greybird)
  C Celebes
Coracina analis (Caledonian Greybird)
  New Caledonia
Coracina caesia (African Grey Cuckoo Shrike)
  C. c. preussi
    E Nigeria, Fernando Po I

C. c. pura
  Ethiopia and Sudan to Malawi
C. c. caesia
  Rhodesia, South Africa
Coracina pectoralis (White-breasted Cuckoo Shrike)
  W, C, E & SC Africa
Coracina graueri (Grauer's Cuckoo Shrike)
  E Zaire
Coracina cinerea (Madagascar Cuckoo Shrike)
  C. c. cucullata
    Great Comoro I
  C. c. cinerea
    N & E Madagascar
  C. c. pallida
    C, W & SW Madagascar
Coracina azurea (African Blue Cuckoo Shrike)
  W & WC Africa
Coracina typica (Mauritius Greybird)
  Mauritius I
Coracina newtoni (Reunion Greybird)
  Réunion I
Coracina coerulescens (Philippine Black Greybird)
  C. c. coerulescens
    Luzon I
  C. c. deschauenseei
    Marinduque I
Coracina dohertyi (Black-barred Cuckoo Shrike)
  Sumba I
Coracina tenuirostris (Slender-billed Greybird)
  C. t. timoriensis
    Timor I, Lomblen I
  C. t. kalaotuae
    Kalaotua I
  C. t. emancipata
    Djampea I
  C. t. pererrata
    Tukangbesi I
  C. t. edithae
    S Celebes
  C. t. amboinensis
    Ambon I, Ceram I
  C. t. obiensis
    Obi I, Bisa I
  C. t. pelingi
    Peleng Is
  C. t. dispar
    Banda I, Kei Is
  C. t. tenuirostris
    Queensland, New South Wales, Victoria
  C. t. melvillensis
    N Queensland, Northern Territory, NW Australia

C. t. aruensis
  Aru Is, S New Guinea
C. t. muelleri
  Kofiau I, Misol I, New Guinea, D'Entre-
  casteaux Archipelago
C. t. nehrkorni
  Waigeu I
C. t. grayi
  N Moluccas
C. t. talautensis
  Talaut Is
C. t. salvadorii
  Sangir Is
C. t. numforana
  Numfor I
C. t. meyeri
  Biak I
C. t. tagulana
  Tagula I, Louisiade Archipelago
C. t. rostrata
  Rossel I
C. t. admiralitatis
  Admiralty Is
C. t. matthiae
  Storm I, St Matthias I
C. t. remota
  New Ireland, New Hanover
C. t. heinrothi
  New Britain
C. t. rooki
  Rook I
C. t. monacha
  Palau Is
C. t. nesiotis
  Yap I
C. t. saturatior
  N & C Solomon Is
C. t. nisoria
  Russell I
C. t. erythropygia
  Guadalcanal I, Malaita I
C. t. salomonis
  San Cristobal I
C. t. insperata
  Ponapé I
C. t. ultima
  Lihir Is, Tanga I
Coracina morio (Moluccan Greybird)
C. m. morio
  N & C Celebes
C. m. wiglesworthi
  S & SE Celebes
C. m. sula
  Sula Is
C. m. marginata
  Buru I
C. m. ceramensis
  Ceram I

C. m. hoogerwerfi
  Obi I
C. m. incerta
  Waigeu I, Japen I, New Guinea
C. m. everetti
  Sulu Is
C. m. mindanensis
  Mindanao I, Basilan I
C. m. elusa
  Mindoro I
C. m. lecroyae
  Luzon I
C. m. ripleyi
  Bohol I, Samar I, Leyte I
Coracina schisticeps (New Guinea Greybird)
C. s. schisticeps
  Misol I, NW New Guinea
C. s. reichenowi
  N New Guinea
C. s. poliopsa
  S New Guinea
C. s. vittata
  D'Entrecasteaux Archipelago
Coracina melaena (Black Greybird)
C. m. waigeuense
  Waigeu I
C. m. tommasonis
  Japen I
C. m. melaena
  W New Guinea
C. m. meeki
  E New Guinea
C. m. goodsoni
  Aru Is
C. m. batantae
  Batanta I
Coracina montana (Black-bellied Greybird)
C. m. montana
  New Guinea
C. m. bicinia
  Sepik district, New Guinea
Coracina holopolia (Black-bellied Cuckoo Shrike)
C. h. holopolia
  Bougainville I, Choiseul I, Guadalcanal I
C. h. pygmaea
  Kulambangra I, Vangunu I
C. h. tricolor
  Malaita I
Coracina mcgregori (Sharp-tailed Greybird)
  N Mindanao
Coracina panayensis (Philippines Greybird)
  Negros I, Panay I

Coracina polioptera (Indochinese Cuckoo Shrike)
C. p. jabouillei
N Vietnam
C. p. indochinensis
Burma, C Thailand, C Laos, S Vietnam
C. p. polioptera
S Burma, S Thailand, S Laos

Coracina melaschistos (Dark-grey Cuckoo Shrike)
C. m. melaschistos
N India, Himalayas
C. m. avensis
W China, Burma, N Thailand, N Vietnam
C. m. intermedia
C & S China, Burma, S Thailand, S Vietnam
C. m. saturata
N Vietnam, Hainan I

Coracina fimbriata (Lesser Cuckoo Shrike)
C. f. neglecta
S Burma, S Thailand
C. f. culminata
S Malaysia
C. f. schierbrandi
Sumatra, Borneo
C. f. compta
W Sumatran Islands
C. f. fimbriata
Java, Bali I

Coracina melanoptera (Black-headed Cuckoo Shrike)
C. m. melanoptera
N India
C. m. sykesi
S India, Sri Lanka

CAMPOCHAERA
Campochaera sloetii (Orange Cuckoo Shrike)
C. s. sloetii
NW New Guinea
C. s. flaviceps
SE New Guinea

CHLAMYDOCHAERA
Chlamydochaera jefferyi (Black-breasted Triller)
Borneo

LALAGE
Lalage melanoleuca (Black and White Triller)
L. m. melanoleuca
Luzon I, Mindoro I
L. m. minor
Samar I, Leyte I, Mindanao I

Lalage nigra (Pied Triller)
L. n. davisoni
Nicobar Is

L. n. nigra
Malaysia, Sumatra, Java
L. n. chilensis
Borneo, Philippine Is
L. n. leucopygialis
Sula Is, Celebes

Lalage sueurii (White-winged Triller)
L. s. sueurii
E Java, Lesser Sunda Is, S Celebes
L. s. tricolor
N & C Australia, SE New Guinea

Lalage aurea (Red-bellied Triller)
N Moluccas

Lalage atrovirens (Black-browed Triller)
L. a. moesta
Tenimber Is
L. a. atrovirens
Misol I, Waigeu I, N New Guinea
L. a. leucoptera
Biak I

Lalage leucomela (White-browed Triller)
L. l. keyensis
Kei Is
L. l. rufiventer
Melville I, Northern Territory
L. l. leucomela
E Queensland, NE New South Wales
L. l. yorki
N Queensland
L. l. polygrammica
Aru Is, E New Guinea
L. l. obscurior
D'Entrecasteaux Archipelago
L. l. trobriandi
Trobriand Is
L. l. pallescens
Louisiade Archipelago
L. l. falsa
New Britain, Rook I
L. l. karu
New Ireland
L. l. albidior
New Hanover
L. l. ottomeyeri
Lihir Is
L. l. tabarensis
Tabar I
L. l. conjuncta
St Matthias Is
L. l. sumunae
Dyaul I

Lalage maculosa (Spotted Triller)
L. m. ultima
Efate I
L. m. modesta
N & C New Hebrides
L. m. melanopygia
Santa Cruz I

L. m. vanikorensis
Vanikoro I
L. m. soror
Kandavu I
L. m. pumila
Viti Levu I
L. m. mixta
C & NW Fiji Is
L. m. woodi
Vanua Levu I
L. m. rotumae
Rotuma I
L. m. nesophila
Lau Archipelago
L. m. tabuensis
Tonga I
L. m. vauana
Vavau group, Fiji Is
L. m. keppeli
Keppel I, Boscawen I
L. m. futunae
Futuna I, Horne I
L. m. whitmeei
Niue I, Savage I
L. m. maculosa
Upolu I, Savaii I, Samoa Is
Lalage sharpei (Samoan Triller)
L. s. sharpei
Upolu I, Samoa Is
L. s. tenebrosa
Savaii I, Samoa Is
Lalage leucopyga (Long-tailed Triller)
L. l. affinis
San Cristobal I
L. l. deficiens
Torres I, Banks Is
L. l. albiloris
C & N New Hebrides
L. l. simillima
S New Hebrides, Loyalty Is
L. l. montrosieri
New Caledonia I
L. l. leucopyga
Norfolk I

CAMPEPHAGA

Campephega sulphurata (African Black Cuckoo Shrike)
Uganda, Somalia to Angola & South Africa
Campephega phoenicea (Red-shouldered Cuckoo Shrike)
Gambia to Ethiopia, N Zaire, Uganda
Campephaga petiti (Petit's Cuckoo Shrike)
S Cameroun to Kenya
Campephaga quiscalina (Purple-throated Cuckoo Shrike)
C. q. quiscalina
Sierra Leone to Cameroun & N Angola

C. q. martini
E Zaire, Uganda, Kenya
C. q. munzneri
Tanzania
Campephaga lobata (Wattled Cuckoo Shrike)
C. l. lobata
Liberia, Ghana
C. l. oriolina
S Cameroun, Gabon to E Zaire

PERICROCOTUS
Pericrocotus roseus (Rosy Minivet)
P. r. cantonensis
E China, Thailand, Laos
P. r. stanfordi
S China, S Thailand, S Laos
P. r. roseus
* SW China, Burma, Himalayas, N India
Pericrocotus divaricatus (Ashy Minivet)
P. d. divaricatus
NE Asia, Japan, E China, SE Asia, Philippine Is
P. d. tegimae
Riukiu Is
Pericrocotus cinnamomeus (Small Minivet)
P. c. malabaricus
W India
P. c. cinnamomeus
S India, Sri Lanka
P. c. pallidus
Pakistan
P. c. peregrinus
N India, Himalayas
P. c. vividus
Andaman Is
P. c. thai
Bhutan, Burma, N Thailand, Laos
P. c. sacerdos
Cambodia, S Vietnam
P. c. seperatus
S Burma, S Thailand
P. c. saturatus
Java, Bali I
P. c. igneus
Malaysia, Sumatra, Borneo, Palawan I
P. c. trophis
Simalur I
Pericrocotus lansbergei (Flores Minivet)
Sumbawa I, Flores I
Pericrocotus erythropygius (Jerdon's Minivet)
P. e. erythropygius
W Pakistan, C India
P. e. albifrons
C Burma

Pericrocotus solaris (Yellow-throated Minivet)
P. s. solaris
E Himalayas, NW Burma
P. s. rubrolimbatus
S Burma, N Thailand
P. s. montpellieri
SW China
P. s. griseogularis
SE China, Taiwan, N Indochina
P. s. deignani
S Vietnam
P. s. nassovicus
SE Thailand, Cambodia
P. s. montanus
Malaysia, W Sumatra
P. s. cinereigula
N Borneo
Pericrocotus ethologus (Flame-coloured Minivet)
P. e. favillaceus
Afghanistan, W Himalayas, W India
P. e. laetus
E Nepal, W Assam
P. e. ethologus
W China, N Thailand, N Indochina
P. e. yvettae
NE Burma
P. e. mariae
SE Assam, W Burma
P. e. ripponi
E Burma, NW Thailand
P. e. annamensis
S Vietnam
Pericrocotus brevirostris (Short-billed Minivet)
P. b. brevirostris
Himalayas, Nepal, W Assam
P. b. affinis
E Assam, NW Burma
P. b. neglectus
N Thailand, N Laos
P. b. anthoides
S China, N Vietnam
Pericrocotus miniatus (Sunda Minivet)
W Sumatra, Java
Pericrocotus flammeus (Scarlet Minivet)
P. f. flammeus
S India, Sri Lanka
P. f. siebersi
Java, Bali I
P. f. exul
Lombok I
P. f. andamanensis
Andaman Is
P. f. minythomelas
Simalur I

P. f. modiglianii
Enggano I
P. f. speciosus
Himalayas, N India
P. f. elegans
S Assam, N Burma, N Thailand, N Indochina
P. f. fohkiensis
Fukien
P. f. semiruber
E India, S Burma, Thailand
P. f. flammifer
S Thailand, N & C Malaysia
P. f. xanthogaster
S Malaysia, Sumatra
P. f. insulanus
Borneo
P. f. novus
Luzon I, Negros I
P. f. leytensis
Samar I, Leyte I
P. f. johnstoniae
Mt Apo (Mindanao I)
P. f. marchesae
Jolo I
P. f. gonzalesi
Mt Katanglad (Mindanao I)
P. f. nigroluteus
Mindanao I
P. f. fraterculus
Assam

HEMIPUS
Hemipus picatus (Bar-winged Flycatcher Shrike)
H. p. capitalis
Himalayas, N Burma, N Thailand, N Indochina
H. p. picatus
India, S Burma, S Thailand, S Indochina
H. p. intermedius
S Thailand, Malaysia, Sumatra, N Borneo
H. p. leggei
Sri Lanka
Hemipus hirundinaceus (Black-winged Flycatcher Shrike)
Malaysia, Sumatra, Java, Bali I, Borneo

TEPHRODORNIS
Tephrodornis gularis (Brown-tailed Wood Shrike)
T. g. sylvicola
W India
T. g. pelvica
E Himalayas, N Burma
T. g. jugans
S Burma, N Thailand
T. g. vernayi
SW Thailand

T. g. annectens
S Thailand, N Malaysia
T. g. fretensis
S Malaysia, Sumatra
T. g. gularis
SW Sumatra, Java
T. g. frenata
Borneo
T. g. mekongensis
E Thailand, Cambodia, S Indochina
T. g. hainana
N Indochina, Hainan I
T. g. latouchei
Fukien

Tephrodornis pondicerianus (Common Wood Shrike)
T. p. affinis
Sri Lanka
T. p. pondicerianus
E India, Burma, N Thailand, S Laos
T. p. pallidus
Pakistan, NW India
T. p. orientis
Cambodia, S Vietnam

120 PYCNONOTIDAE (BULBULS)

SPIZIXOS
Spizixos canifrons (Crested Finchbill)
S. c. canifrons
S Assam, W Burma
S. c. ingrami
E Burma to S China, N Indochina
Spizixos semitorques (Collared Finchbill)
S. s. semitorques
S China
S. s. cinereicapillus
Taiwan

PYCNONOTUS
Pycnonotus zeylanicus (Straw-crowned Bulbul)
Malaysia to Java, Borneo
Pycnonotus striatus (Striated Green Bulbul)
P. s. striatus
E Himalayas, W Burma
P. s. arctus
NE Assam
P. s. paulus
Burma to N Indochina, S China
Pycnonotus leucogrammicus (Striated Bulbul)
W Sumatra
Pycnonotus tympanistrigus (Olive-crowned Bulbul)
W Sumatra
Pycnonotus melanoleucos (Black & White Bulbul)
Malaysia, Sumatra, Borneo

Pycnonotus priocephalus (Grey-headed Bulbul)
SW India
Pycnonotus atriceps (Black-headed Bulbul)
P. a. fuscoflavescens
Andaman Is
P. a. atriceps
NE India to Bali I, Borneo, Palawan I
P. a. hyperemnus
W Sumatra Is
P. a. baweanus
Bawean I
P. a. hodiernus
Maratua I
Pycnonotus melanicterus (Black-crested Bulbul)
P. m. melanicterus
Sri Lanka
P. m. gularis
SW India
P. m. flaviventris
Himalayas, NE India, N Burma
P. m. vantynei
S Burma to N Indochina
P. m. xanthops
SE Burma, N Thailand
P. m. auratus
NE Thailand, W Laos
P. m. johnsoni
SE Thailand, S Indochina
P. m. elbeli
SE Thailand islands
P. m. negatus
SW Thailand
P. m. caecilii
N Malaysia
P. m. dispar
Sumatra, Java
P. m. montis
N Borneo
Pycnonotus squamatus (Scaly-breasted Bulbul)
P. s. weberi
Malaysia, Sumatra
P. s. squamatus
W & C Java
P. s. borneensis
Borneo
Pycnonotus cyaniventris (Grey-bellied Bulbul)
P. c. cyaniventris
Malaysia, Sumatra
P. c. paroticalis
Borneo
Pycnonotus jocusus (Red-whiskered Bulbul)
P. j. fuscicaudatus
W India

P. j. abuensis
N Bombay, SW Rajasthan
P. j. pyrrhotis
Nepal, N India
P. j. emeria
E India, Burma, SW Thailand
P. j. whistleri
Andaman Is
P. j. monticola
E Himalayas to SW China
P. j. pattani
Thailand, N Malaysia, S Indochina
P. j. hainanensis
N Vietnam, SE China
P. j. jocosus
S China

Pycnonotus xanthorrhous (Anderson's Bulbul)
P. x. xanthorrhous
NE Burma to N Vietnam
P. x. andersoni
S China

Pycnonotus sinensis (Chinese Bulbul)
P. s. hoyi
C China
P. s. sinensis
E China
P. s. hainanus
Hainan I, SE China, N Vietnam
P. s. formosae
Taiwan
P. s. orii
S Riukiu Is

Pycnonotus taivanus (Formosan Bulbul)
Taiwan

Pycnonotus leucogenys (White-cheeked Bulbul)
P. l. mesopotamiae
Iraq
P. l. dactylus
E Saudi Arabia
P. l. leucotis
S Iran to NW India
P. l. humii
NW Pakistan
P. l. leucogenys
Himalayas

Pycnonotus cafer (Red-vented Bulbul)
P. c. cafer
Sri Lanka
P. c. pusillus
S India
P. c. humayuni
Pakistan, NW India
P. c. wetmorei
NE India
P. c. intermedius
W Himalayas

P. c. bengalensis
E Himalayas, NE India
P. c. primrosei
S Assam
P. c. stanfordi
N Burma, W Yunnan
P. c. melanchimus
SC Burma

Pycnonotus aurigaster (White-eared Bulbul)
P. a. chrysorrhoides
S China
P. a. resurrectus
SE China, N Vietnam
P. a. dolichurus
C Vietnam
P. a. latouchei
Burma to SW China, N Vietnam
P. a. klossi
SE Burma, N Thailand
P. a. schauenseei
S Burma, SW Thailand
P. a. thais
S Thailand
P. a. germani
SE Thailand, S Indochina
P. a. aurigaster
Sumatra, Java

Pycnonotus xanthopygos (Black-capped Bulbul)
Syria to Aden

Pycnonotus nigricans (Red-eyed Bulbul)
P. n. nigricans
Namibia, S Botswana, N Cape Province
P. n. grisescentior
E & N Botswana, S Angola to Rhodesia
P. n. superior
NE Cape Province, S Transvaal

Pycnonotus capensis (Cape Bulbul)
S & SW Cape Province

Pycnonotus barbatus (Common Bulbul)
P. b. barbatus
North Africa
P. b. inornatus
Senegal to Ghana
P. b. goodi
S Sahara, N Cameroun
P. b. arsinoe
Nile valley, Sudan
P. b. schoanus
E Ethiopia
P. b. somaliensis
SE Ethiopia, Somalia
P. b. nigeriae
C & S Nigeria to Gabon
P. b. gabonensis
W Gabon

P. b. tricolor
N Namibia to S Uganda, S Tanzania
P. b. minor
N Zaire, S Sudan
P. b. spurius
S Ethiopia
P. b. fayi
Kenya, C Tanzania
P. b. ngamii
S Zambia, Botswana
P. b. layardi
SE Africa
P. b. tenebrior
E Cape Province, S Lesotho
P. b. micrus
SE Kenya, E Tanzania
P. b. peasei
S Ethiopia, E Kenya
P. b. dodsoni
N Kenya, S Somalia, E Ethiopia
Pycnonotus eutilotus (Puff-backed Bulbul)
Malaysia, Sumatra, Borneo
**Pycnonotus nieuwenhuisii (Blue-wattled
Bulbul)**
P. n. inexpectatus
Lesten (Sumatra)
P. n. nieuwenhuisii
Kayan river (Borneo)
**Pycnonotus urostictus (Yellow-wattled
Bulbul)**
P. u. ilokensis
N Luzon I
P. u. urostictus
C Luzon I
P. u. otricaudatus
Bohol I, Samar I, Leyte I
P. u. philippensis
Mindanao I
P. u. basilanicus
Basilan I
**Pycnonotus bimaculatus (Orange-spotted
Bulbul)**
P. b. snouckaerti
NW Sumatra
P. b. barat
SW Sumatra, W & C Java
P. b. bimaculatus
E Java, Bali I
**Pycnonotus finlaysoni (Stripe-throated
Bulbul)**
P. f. davisoni
S Burma
P. f. eous
Thailand, C & S Indochina
P. f. finlaysoni
Malaysia

**Pycnonotus xantholaemus (Yellow-
throated Bulbul)**
S India
**Pycnonotus penicillatus (Yellow-tufted
Bulbul)**
Sri Lanka
Pycnonotus flavescens (Flavescent Bulbul)
P. f. flavescens
S Assam, W Burma
P. f. vividus
Burma, Thailand, N Indochina
P. f. sordidus
S Indochina
P. f. leucops
N Borneo
**Pycnonotus goiavier (Yellow-vented
Bulbul)**
P. g. jambu
SE Thailand, S Indochina
P. g. personatus
Malaysia, Sumatra
P. g. analis
Java, Bali I, Lombok I
P. g. gourdini
Borneo
P. g. goiavier
N & C Philippine Is
P. g. suluensis
S Philippine Is
**Pycnonotus luteolus (White-browed
Bulbul)**
P. l. luteolus
C & S India
P. l. insulae
Sri Lanka
**Pycnonotus plumosus (Olive-brown
Bulbul)**
P. p. plumosus
Malaysia, E Sumatra, Java
P. p. porphyreus
W Sumatra and islands
P. p. billitonis
Billiton I, W & S Borneo
P. p. hutzi
N & E Borneo
P. p. chiroplethis
Anamba Is
P. p. hachisukae
N Borneo Is
P. p. cinereifrons
Palawan I
P. p. sibergi
Bawean I, Java Sea
**Pycnonotus blanfordi (Blanford's Olive
Bulbul)**
P. b. blanfordi
C & S Burma

P. b. conradi
Thailand, N Malaysia, S Indochina
P. b. robinsoni
C Malaysia
Pycnonotus simplex (White-eyed Brown Bulbul)
P. s. simplex
S Thailand, Malaysia, Sumatra
P. s. prillwitzi
Java
P. s. oblitus
Bangka I, Billiton I, S & W Borneo
P. s. halizonus
Anamba Is, N Natuna Is
P. s. perplexus
N & E Borneo
Pycnonotus brunneus (Red-eyed Brown Bulbul)
P. b. brunneus
Malaysia, Sumatra, Borneo
P. b. zapolius
Anamba Is
Pycnonotus erythrophthalmus (Lesser Brown Bulbul)
P. e. erythrophthalmus
Malaysia, Billiton I, Sumatra
P. e. salvadorii
Borneo
Pycnonotus masukuensis (Shelley's Greenbul)
P. m. kakamegae
E Zaire, W Kenya, W Tanzania
P. m. roehli
C Tanzania
P. m. masukuensis
SW Tanzania, N Malawi
Pycnonotus montanus (Mountain Little Greenbul)
Togo, Ghana, Cameroun
Pycnonotus virens (Little Greenbul)
P. v. erythropterus
Gambia to S Nigeria
P. v. virens
Gabon to Sudan, Uganda, Angola
P. v. holochlorus
W Uganda
P. v. zombensis
E Angola, SE Zaire to E Kenya,
Mozambique
P. v. marwitzi
SE Kenya
P. v. zanzibaricus
Zanzibar I
Pycnonotus hallae (Hall's Greenbul)
E Zaire
Pycnonotus gracilis (Little Grey Greenbul)
P. g. extremus
Sierra Leone to S Nigeria

P. g. gracilis
Cameroun to Uganda & N Angola
P. g. ugandae
E Zaire, Uganda
Pycnonotus ansorgei (Ansorge's Greenbul)
P. a. ansorgei
Sierra Leone to S Nigeria
P. a. muniensis
Cameroun, Gabon, N Zaire
P. a. kavirondensis
Kenya
Pycnonotus curvirostris (Cameroun Sombre Greenbul)
P. c. leoninus
Sierra Leone to Ghana
P. c. curvirostris
S Ghana to W Kenya, N Angola
Pycnonotus importunus (Zanzibar Sombre Greenbul)
P. i. fricki
WC Kenya
P. i. somaliensis
S Somalia
P. i. subalaris
S Kenya
P. i. insularis
E Tanzania, Zanzibar I
P. i. hypoxanthus
S Tanzania, Malawi, Mozambique
P. i. oleaginus
S Mozambique, N Natal
P. i. noomei
E Rhodesia to Natal, C Cape Province
P. i. importunus
S & E Cape Province
Pycnonotus latirostris (Yellow-whiskered Greenbul)
P. l. congener
Sierra Leone to S Nigeria
P. l. latirostris
SE Nigeria to W Zaire, N Angola
P. l. eugenius
S Sudan, E Zaire to NW Tanzania
P. l. saturatus
E Kenya, N Tanzania
P. l. australis
SW Tanzania
Pycnonotus gracilirostris (Slender-billed Greenbul)
P. g. gracilirostris
Senegal to Nigeria
P. g. congensis
S Cameroun to W Zaire, N Angola
P. g. chagwensis
N Zaire to W Kenya, NW Tanzania
P. g. percivali
C Kenya

Pycnonotus tephrolaemus (Olive-breasted Mountain Greenbul)
P. t. tephrolaemus
Cameroun Mt, Fernando Po I
P. t. bamendae
SE Nigeria, Cameroun
P. t. kikuyuensis
E Zaire to Uganda, W Kenya
P. t. kungwensis
W Tanzania
P. t. nigriceps
SW Kenya, N Tanzania
P. t. usambarae
NE Tanzania
P. t. neumanni
E Tanzania
P. t. fusciceps
SW Tanzania, Malawi, NW Mozambique
P. t. chlorigula
C Tanzania

Pycnonotus milanjensis (Stripe-cheeked Greenbul)
P. m. striifacies
SE Kenya, N Tanzania
P. m. olivaceiceps
SW Tanzania, N Malawi, N Mozambique
P. m. milanjensis
Malawi, Rhodesia, W Mozambique
P. m. disjuncta
E Rhodesia

Calyptocichla serina (Serine Greenbul)
Sierra Leone to N Zaire, Gabon

Baeopogon indicator (Honeyguide Greenbul)
B. i. leucurus
Sierra Leone, Liberia
B. i. togoensis
Ghana, Togo
B. i. indicator
Cameroun to N Angola, W Zaire
B. i. chlorosaturata
E Zaire to Sudan, Uganda

Baeopogon clamans (Sjostedt's Honeyguide Greenbul)
Cameroun to NE Zaire, Gabon

Ixonotus guttatus (Spotted Greenbul)
I. g. guttatus
Ghana, Gabon to C Zaire
I. g. bugoma
E Zaire, W Uganda

Chlorocichla falkensteini (Yellow-necked Greenbul)
C. f. viridescentior
River Ja, Cameroun
C. f. falkensteini
SW Zaire, N Angola

Chlorocichla simplex (Simple Greenbul)
Guinea to Zaire, N Angola

Chlorocichla flavicollis (Yellow-throated Leaf-Love)
C. f. flavicollis
Senegal to Cameroun
C. f. adamauae
N Cameroun
C. f. simplicicolor
E Cameroun
C. f. soror
Cameroun to Zaire, S Sudan
C. f. flavigula
Angola to NW Tanzania, Zambia
C. f. pallidigula
Uganda, W Kenya

Chlorocichla flaviventris (Yellow-bellied Greenbul)
C. f. centralis
Kenya, Tanzania, N Mozambique
C. f. occidentalis
N Namibia, S Angola to S Mozambique
C. f. flaviventris
Natal

Chlorocichla laetissima (Joyful Greenbul)
C. l. laetissima
E Zaire to S Sudan, W Kenya
C. l. schoutedeni
SE Zaire, SW Tanzania, NE Zambia

Chlorocichla prigoginei (Prigogine's Greenbul)
Lake Edward, E Zaire

Thescelocichla leucopleura (Swamp Bulbul)
Senegal to Gabon, W Uganda

Phyllastrephus scandens (Leaf-Love)
P. s. scandens
Senegal to Cameroun
P. s. acedis
S Cameroun, Gabon, SW Zaire
P. s. orientalis
Central African Republic to Sudan & Tanzania
P. s. upembae
S Zaire, W Tanzania

Phyllastrephus terrestris (Bristle-necked Brownbul)
P. t. bensoni
C Kenya
P. t. katangae
Katanga, Zaire
P. t. suahelicus
SE Kenya, E Tanzania, N Mozambique
P. t. intermedius
S Angola to Mozambique, N Natal
P. t. terrestris
Transvaal, S Natal, Cape Province
Phyllastrephus strepitans (Northern Brownbul)
S Sudan to E Tanzania
Phyllastrephus cerviniventris (Grey Olive Greenbul)
P. c. cerviniventris
C Kenya to Zambia & Mozambique
P. c. schoutedeni
Katanga, Zaire
Phyllastrephus fulviventris (Pale Olive Greenbul)
Central African Republic to Angola
Phyllastrephus poensis (Cameroun Olive Greenbul)
S Nigeria, Cameroun Mt
Phyllastrephus baumanni (Toro Olive Greenbul)
Sierra Leone to S Nigeria
Phyllastrephus poliocephalus (Grey-headed Greenbul)
SE Nigeria, Cameroun Mt
Phyllastrephus flavostriatus (Yellow-streaked Greenbul)
P. f. graueri
E Zaire
P. f. olivaceogriseus
E Zaire, SW Uganda
P. f. kungwensis
W Tanzania
P. f. uzungwensis
Morogoro, E Tanzania
P. f. tenuirostris
SE Kenya to NE Mozambique
P. f. alfredi
SW Tanzania, E Zambia, N Malawi
P. f. vincenti
S Malawi, W Mozambique
P. f. flavostriatus
E South Africa
Phyllastrephus debilis (Slender Greenbul)
P. d. rabai
E Kenya, E Tanzania
P. d. albigula
N Tanzania

P. d. debilis
S Tanzania, Mozambique
Phyllastrephus lorenzi (Sassi's Olive Greenbul)
E Zaire
Phyllastrephus albigularis (White-throated Greenbul)
P. a. albigularis
Sierra Leone to Sudan, Uganda
P. a. viridiceps
N Angola
Phyllastrephus fischeri (Fischer's Greenbul)
P. f. sucosus
S Sudan to E Zaire, W Tanzania
P. f. nandensis
N Nandi, Kenya
P. f. ngurumanensis
SW Kenya
P. f. fischeri
E Tanzania, Mozambique
Phyllastrephus cabanisi (Cabanis' Greenbul)
Angola, S Zaire, Zambia, W Tanzania
Phyllastrephus placidus (Olive Mountain Greenbul)
SE Kenya to Malawi, Mozambique
Phyllastrephus icterinus (Icterine Greenbul)
P. i. icterinus
Sierra Leone to Nigeria
P. i. tricolor
Cameroun to W Uganda, C Zaire
Phyllastrephus xavieri (Xavier's Greenbul)
P. x. serlei
Cameroun Mt
P. x. xavieri
Cameroun to S Central African Republic, N Zaire
P. x. sethsmithi
E Zaire, Uganda
Phyllastrephus madagascariensis (Madagascar Tetraka)
P. m. madagascariensis
E Madagascar
P. m. inceleber
N & W Madagascar
Phyllastrephus zosterops (Short-billed Tetraka)
P. z. fulvescens
N Madagascar
P. z. andapae
NE Madagascar
P. z. zosterops
E Madagascar
P. z. ankafanae
SE Madagascar

Phyllastrephus apperti (Appert's Tetraka)
SW Madagascar
Phyllastrephus tenebrosus (Dusky Tetraka)
E Madagascar

BLEDA
Bleda syndactyla (Common Bristle-Bill)
B. s. syndactyla
Senegal to S Nigeria
B. s. multicolor
S Nigeria to Zambia
B. s. woosnami
Sudan, Uganda, NW Kenya
B. s. nandensis
N Nandi, Kenya
Bleda eximia (Green-tailed Bristle-Bill)
B. e. eximia
Sierra Leone to Ghana
B. e. notata
S Nigeria to Central African Republic
B. e. ugandae
Sudan, Uganda, N Zaire
Bleda canicapilla (Grey-headed Bristle-Bill)
Gambia to S Nigeria

CRINIGER
Criniger barbatus (Bearded Greenbul)
C. b. barbatus
Sierra Leone to Togo
C. b. ansorgeanus
S Nigeria
C. b. chloronotus
Cameroun to Central African Republic
C. b. weileri
E Zaire
Criniger calurus (Red-tailed Greenbul)
C. c. verreauxi
Guinea to Nigeria
C. c. calurus
S Nigeria to Central African Republic
C. c. emini
Zaire, Uganda
Criniger ndussumensis (White-bearded Bulbul)
Cameroun to N Zaire
Criniger olivaceus (Yellow-throated Olive Bulbul)
Senegal to Ghana
Criniger finschii (Finsch's Bearded Bulbul)
Malaysia, Sumatra, Borneo
Criniger flaveolus (Ashy-fronted Bearded Bulbul)
C. f. flaveolus
Himalayas to NE Burma

C. f. burmanicus
SE Burma, W Thailand
Criniger pallidus (Olivaceus Bearded Bulbul)
C. p. griseiceps
S Burma
C. p. robinsoni
Tenasserim, S Burma
C. p. henrici
N Thailand, N Indochina
C. p. pallidus
Hainan I
C. p. isani
NE Thailand
C. p. annamensis
C Indochina
C. p. khmerensis
S Indochina
Criniger ochraceus (Ochraceous Bearded Bulbul)
C. o. hallae
S Vietnam
C. o. cambodianus
SE Thailand, SW Cambodia
C. o. ochraceus
S Burma, SW Thailand
C. o. sordidus
C Malaysia
C. o. sacculatus
S Malaysia
C. o. sumatranus
W Sumatra
C. o. fowleri
N Borneo
C. o. ruficrissus
NE Borneo
Criniger bres (Grey-cheeked Bearded Bulbul)
C. b. tephrogenys
Malaysia, E Sumatra
C. b. bres
W & C Java
C. b. balicus
E Java, Bali I
C. b. gutteralis
Borneo
C. b. frater
Palawan I
Criniger phaeocephalus (Grey-headed Bearded Bulbul)
C. p. phaeocephalus
Malaysia, Sumatra, Bangka I, Billiton I
C. p. connectens
NE Borneo
C. p. sulphuratus
C Borneo
C. p. diardi
W Borneo

Setornis criniger (Long-billed Bulbul)
E Sumatra, Bangka I, Borneo

HYPSIPETES

Hypsipetes viridescens (Blyth's Olive Bulbul)
H. v. cacharensis
S Assam
H. v. myitkyinensis
NE Burma
H. v. viridescens
S Burma, SW Thailand

Hypsipetes propinquus (Grey-eyed Bulbul)
H. p. aquilonis
N Vietnam
H. p. propinquus
E Burma, N Thailand, N Laos
H. p. simulator
SE Thailand, S Indochina
H. p. innectens
S Vietnam
H. p. lekhakuni
S Burma, SW Thailand
H. p. cinnamomeoventris
N Malaysia

Hypsipetes charlottae (Crested Olive Bulbul)
H. c. cryptus
Malaysia, Sumatra & islands
H. c. charlottae
S & W Borneo
H. c. perplexus
N & E Borneo

Hypsipetes palawanensis (Golden-eyed Bulbul)
Palawan I

Hypsipetes criniger (Hairy-backed Bulbul)
H. c. criniger
Malaysia, E Sumatra
H. c. sericeus
W Sumatra
H. c. viridis
Borneo

Hypsipetes philippinus (Rufous-breasted Bulbul)
H. p. philippinus
Luzon I, Samar I, Leyte I, Bohol I
H. p. guimarasensis
Masbate I, Panay I, Negros I
H. p. saturatior
E Mindanao I
H. p. mindorensis
Mindoro I
H. p. rufigularis
W Mindanao I, Basilan I

Hypsipetes siquijorensis (Slaty-crowned Bulbul)
H. s. cinereiceps
Tablas I, Romblon I
H. s. monticola
Cebu I
H. s. siquijorensis
Siquijor I

Hypsipetes everetti (Yellow-washed Bulbul)
H. e. everetti
Dinagat I, E & C Mindanao I
H. e. haynaldi
Sulu Archipelago
H. e. samarensis
Samar I, Leyte I
H. e. catarmanensis
Camiguin (South I)

Hypsipetes affinis (Golden Bulbul)
H. a. platenae
Sanghir Is
H. a. aureus
Togian I
H. a. harterti
Peleng Is, Banggai I
H. a. longirostris
Sula Is
H. a. chloris
Morotai I, Halmahera I, Batjan I
H. a. lucasi
Obi I
H. a. mystacalis
Buru I
H. a. affinis
Ceram I
H. a. flavicaudus
Ambon I

Hypsipetes indicus (Golden-browed Bulbul)
H. i. ictericus
W India
H. i. indicus
SW India, Sri Lanka
H. i. guglielmi
SW Sri Lanka

Hypsipetes mcclellandii (Mountain Streaked Bulbul)
H. m. mcclellandii
E Himalayas, Assam
H. m. ventralis
SW Burma
H. m. tickelli
E Burma, NW Thailand
H. m. similis
NE Burma to N Indochina
H. m. holtii
S China

H. m. loquax
N & E Thailand, S Laos
H. m. griseiventer
S Vietnam
H. m. canescens
SE Thailand
H. m. peracensis
S Thailand, N Malavsia
Hypsipetes malaccensis (Green-backed Bulbul)
S Vietnam, Malaysia, Sumatra, Borneo
Hypsipetes virescens (Sumatran Bulbul)
H. v. sumatranus
W Sumatra
H. v. virescens
Java
Hypsipetes flavalus (Ashy Bulbul)
H. f. flavalus
E Himalayas, NW Burma
H. f. cannipennis
S China, NE Vietnam
H. f. castanotus
Hainan I
H. f. bourdellei
E Thailand, N Laos
H. f. remotus
S Indochina
H. f. hildebrandi
S Burma, NW Thailand
H. f. davisoni
S Burma, SW Thailand
H. f. cinereus
Malaysia, Sumatra
H. f. connectens
N Borneo
Hypsipetes amaurotis (Chestnut-eared Bulbul)
H. a. hensoni
N Japan, S Korea, NE China
H. a. amaurotis
C Japan, Riukiu Is
H. a. matchiae
S Kyushu Is
H. a. squamiceps
Bonin Is
H. a. magnirostris
Volcano Is
H. a. borodinonis
Borodino Is
H. a. ogawae
N Riukiu Is
H. a. pryeri
C Riukiu Is
H. a. insignis
Miyakojima Is (S Riukiu Is)
H. a. stejnegeri
S Riukiu Is

H. a. nagamichii
S Taiwan
H. a. batanensis
Batjan I
H. a. fugensis
Calayan I, Fuga I
H. a. camiguinensis
Camiguin Is
Hypsipetes crassirostris (Thick-billed Bulbul)
Seychelles Is
Hypsipetes borbonicus (Reunion Bulbul)
H. b. borbonicus
Réunion I
H. b. olivaceus
Mauritius I
Hypsipetes madagascariensis (Black Bulbul)
H. m. madagascariensis
Madagascar
H. m. grotei
Glorioso I
H. m. parvirostris
Comoro Is
H. m. rostratus
Aldabra I
H. m. humii
Sri Lanka
H. m. ganeesa
SW India
H. m. psaroides
Himalayas
H. m. nigrescens
E Assam, W Burma
H. m. concolor
E Burma, SW China to S Vietnam
H. m. ambiens
NE Burma
H. m. sinensis
SW China, Thailand, Laos
H. m. stresemanni
SW China, Thailand, Laos
H. m. leucothorax
W China to N Vietnam
H. m. leucocephalus
SE China
H. m. nigerrimus
Taiwan
H. m. perniger
Hainan I
Hypsipetes nicobariensis (Nicobar Bulbul)
Nicobar Is
Hypsipetes thompsoni (Bingham's Bulbul)
S Burma, NW Thailand
NEOLESTES
Neolestes torquatus (Black-collared Bulbul)
Gabon, Zaire, Angola

Tylas eduardi (Kinkimavo)
  T. e. eduardi
    E Madagascar
  T. e. albigularis
    WC Madagascar

121 IRENIDAE (LEAFBIRDS, IORAS)

AEGITHINA
Aegithina tiphia (Common Iora)
  A. t. multicolor
    S India, Sri Lanka
  A. t. deignani
    SC India, N & C Burma
  A. t. humei
    C India
  A. t. tiphia
    NE India
  A. t. septentrionalis
    Pakistan, NW India
  A. t. philipi
    SW China, C Burma, N Thailand, Laos,
    N Vietnam
  A. t. cambodiana
    Cambodia, SE Thailand, S Vietnam
  A. t. horizoptera
    S Burma, S Thailand, Malaysia, Sumatra
  A. t. micromelaena
    N Malaysia
  A. t. singapurensis
    S Malaysia
  A. t. scapularis
    Java, Bali I
  A. t. viridus
    S Borneo
  A. t. aequanimis
    N Borneo, Palawan I
  A. t. trudiae
    Brunei Bay
Aegithina nigrolutea (Marshall's Iora)
    Pakistan, NC India
Aegithina viridissima (Green Iora)
  A. v. viridissima
    S Thailand, Malaysia, Sumatra, Borneo
  A. v. thapsina
    Anamba Is
Aegithina lafresnayei (Great Iora)
  A. l. lafresnayei
    S Thailand, Malaysia
  A. l. innotata
    S Burma, N Thailand, N Indochina
  A. l. xanthotis
    Cambodia, S Indochina

CHLOROPSIS
**Chloropsis flavipennis (Yellow-quilled
  Leafbird)**
    Cebu I, Mindanao I

**Chloropsis palawanensis (Palawan
  Leafbird)**
    Palawan I
**Chloropsis sonnerati (Greater Green
  Leafbird)**
  C. s. sonnerati
    Java
  C. s. zosterops
    S Thailand, Malaysia, Sumatra, Borneo
  C. s. parvirostris
    Nias I
**Chloropsis cyanopogon (Lesser Green
  Leafbird)**
  C. c. cyanopogon
    S Burma, Thailand, Malaysia, Sumatra,
    Borneo
  C. c. septentrionalis
    S Thailand
**Chloropsis cochinchinensis (Blue-winged
  Leafbird)**
  C. c. cochinchinensis
    Burma, SE Thailand, Cambodia,
    S Indochina
  C. c. kinneari
    E Thailand, N Indochina
  C. c. serithai
    S Thailand
  C. c. moluccensis
    S Thailand, Malaysia
  C. c. icterocephala
    S Malaysia, Sumatra
  C. c. natunensis
    Natuna Is
  C. c. billitonis
    Billiton I
  C. c. viridinucha
    Borneo
  C. c. nigricollis
    Java
  C. c. jerdoni
    S India, Sri Lanka
**Chloropsis aurifrons (Golden-fronted
  Leafbird)**
  C. a. aurifrons
    Himalayas, Burma, NE India
  C. a. frontalis
    C & S India
  C. a. insularis
    SW India, Sri Lanka
  C. a. pridii
    S Burma, N Thailand, N Laos
  C. a. inornata
    C & S Thailand, Cambodia, S Vietnam
  C. a. incompta
    SW Thailand, S Indochina
  C. a. media
    Sumatra

Chloropsis hardwickei (Orange-bellied Leafbird)
  C. h. hardwickei
    Burma, E Himalayas, N Thailand,
    N Vietnam
  C. h. malayana
    Malaysia
  C. h. melliana
    S China, N Vietnam
  C. h. lazulina
    Hainan I
Chloropsis venusta (Blue-masked Leafbird)
  Sumatra

IRENA
Irena puella (Blue-backed Fairy Bluebird)
  I. p. puella
    S India
  I. p. sikkimensis
    Sikkim, Assam, N India, Burma, Thailand
  I. p. malayensis
    Malaysia
  I. p. criniger
    Sumatra, Borneo
  I. p. turcosa
    Java
  I. p. tweeddalei
    Palawan I
Irena cyanogaster (Black-mantled Fairy Bluebird)
  I. c. cyanogaster
    Luzon I
  I. c. ellae
    Samar I, Leyte I
  I. c. melanochlamys
    Basilan I
  I. c. hoogstraali
    Mindanao I

122 LANIIDAE (SHRIKES)

PRIONOPINAE

EUROCEPHALUS
Eurocephalus rüppelli (Rüppells White-crowned Shrike)
  S Sudan to Tanzania
Eurocephalus anguitimens (White-crowned Shrike)
  E. a. anguitimens
    Namibia to E Transvaal
  E. a. niveus
    E Transvaal

PRIONOPS
Prionops plumata (Long-crested Helmet Shrike)
  P. p. plumata
    Senegal to Nigeria

  P. p. adamauae
    N Cameroun
  P. p. concinnata
    Cameroun to Sudan & Uganda
  P. p. cristata
    E & S Ethiopia, SE Sudan
  P. p. melanoptera
    Somalia, E Ethiopia
  P. p. vinaceigularis
    E & C Ethiopia, N & E Kenya
  P. p. angolica
    Namibia to E Zaire, S Kenya
  P. p. poliocephala
    E Tanzania to Transvaal, Natal
Prionops poliolopha (Grey-crested Helmet Shrike)
  SW Kenya, W Tanzania
Prionops caniceps (Red-billed Shrike)
  P. c. caniceps
    Sierra Leone to Togo
  P. c. harterti
    S Nigeria
  P. c. rufiventris
    Cameroun, Central African Republic,
    N Zaire
  P. c. mentalis
    E & S Zaire, W Uganda
Prionops alberti (Yellow-crested Helmet Shrike)
  E Zaire
Prionops retzii (Retz's Red-billed Helmet Shrike)
  P. r. neumanni
    S Somalia
  P. r. graculina
    E Kenya, NE Tanzania
  P. r. tricolor
    Tanzania, Zambia to Mozambique
  P. r. intermedia
    NW Tanzania
  P. r. nigricans
    W Tanzania, S Zaire to Angola
  P. r. retzii
    Namibia to NE Transvaal
Prionops gabela (Rand's Red-billed Helmet Shrike)
  Gabela (Angola)
Prionops scopifrons (Chestnut-fronted Helmet Shrike)
  P. s. keniensis
    C Kenya
  P. s. kirki
    E Kenya, NE Tanzania
  P. s. scopifrons
    SE Tanzania, Mozambique

LANIOTURDUS
Lanioturdus torquatus (Chat-Shrike)
  L. t. torquatus
    S Angola, Namibia
  L. t. mesicus
    Huila, Angola

NILAUS
Nilaus afer (Brubru Shrike)
  N. a. afer
    Senegal to Ethiopia
  N. a. camerunensis
    Cameroun, Central African Republic
  N. a. hilgerti
    C Ethiopia
  N. a. minor
    E Eritrea to E Kenya
  N. a. massaicus
    SW Kenya to Rwanda, E Zaire
  N. a. nigritemporalis
    SC Zaire to Tanzania & Natal
  N. a. brubru
    S Angola to N Cape Province
  N. a. solivagus
    Natal
  N. a. affinis
    N Angola
  N. a. miombensis
    Sul do Save, Mozambique

DRYOSCOPUS
Dryoscopus pringlii (Pringle's Puffback)
    Somalia to NE Tanzania
Dryoscopus gambensis (Puffback)
  D. g. gambensis
    Senegal to Cameroun & Chad
  D. g. congicus
    Gabon to SW Zaire
  D. g. malzacii
    Central African Republic to Sudan &
      Kenya
  D. g. erythreae
    E Sudan, Ethiopia
  D. g. erwini
    E Zaire to N Tanzania
Dryoscopus cubla (Black-backed Puffback)
  D. c. affinis
    E Kenya, Zanzibar
  D. c. nairobiensis
    S Kenya, N Tanzania
  D. c. hamatus
    S Kenya to Mozambique & Angola
  D. c. chapini
    S Mozambique to N Transvaal
  D. c. okavangensis
    N Botswana to S Angola, Namibia

  D. c. cubla
    Natal, Cape Province
Dryoscopus senegalensis (Red-eyed Puffback)
    S Nigeria to Uganda
Dryoscopus angolensis (Pink-footed Puffback)
  D. a. boydi
    Cameroun
  D. a. angolensis
    SW Zaire, N Angola
  D. a. nandensis
    E Zaire to Sudan & W Kenya
  D. a. kungwensis
    W Tanzania
Dryoscopus sabini (Sabine's Puffback)
  D. s. sabini
    Sierra Leone to S Nigeria
  D. s. melanoleucus
    Cameroun to C Zaire

TCHAGRA
Tchagra minuta (Lesser Bush Shrike)
  T. m. minuta
    Sierra Leone to Ethiopia & Kenya
  T. m. reichenowi
    E Kenya, NE Tanzania
  T. m. anchietae
    Angola to Tanzania, Malawi
  T. m. remota
    S Rhodesia
Tchagra senegala (Black-headed Bush Shrike)
  T. s. cucullata
    N Africa
  T. s. percivali
    S Arabia
  T. s. remigialis
    Sudan
  T. s. notha
    Mali to Chad
  T. s. senegala
    Senegal to Sierra Leone
  T. s. pallida
    Upper Volta, Ivory Coast to N Central
      African Republic
  T. s. camerunensis
    Cameroun to S Sudan, Uganda
  T. s. habessinica
    E Sudan to Somalia
  T. s. armena
    S Uganda to SE Zaire, Zambia
  T. s. orientalis
    S Somalia to E Tanzania
  T. s. confusa
    E Transvaal, Natal, E Cape Province
  T. s. kalahari
    Rhodesia to S Angola, Namibia

T. s. rufofusca
SW Zaire, N Angola

Tchagra tchagra (Levaillant's Bush Shrike)
T. t. tchagra
S Cape Province
T. t. natalensis
E Cape Province to Natal
T. t. caffrariae
E Cape Province

Tchagra australis (Brown-headed Bush Shrike)
T. a. ussheri
Sierra Leone to Nigeria
T. a. emini
E Zaire to S Sudan, W Kenya
T. a. frater
Nigeria to Gabon, W Zaire
T. a. minor
Kenya, NW Tanzania
T. a. littoralis
E Kenya to Rhodesia, Natal
T. a. congener
S Tanzania, Malawi, Zambia
T. a. ansorgei
W Angola
T. a. bocagei
Cuando, Angola
T. a. souzae
SE Zaire to Angola
T. a. australis
E Botswana, Transvaal, Rhodesia
T. a. damarensis
Namibia, W Botswana

Tchagra jamesi (Three-streaked Bush Shrike)
T. j. jamesi
Uganda to Somalia, N Kenya
T. j. mandana
E Kenya, Manda I, Lamu I

Tchagra cruenta (Rosy-patched Shrike)
T. c. cruenta
Sudan, N Ethiopia
T. c. hilgerti
Somalia, E Ethiopia, N Kenya
T. c. cathemagmena
S Kenya, E Tanzania

LANIARIUS
Laniarius ruficeps (Red-crowned Bush Shrike)
L. r. ruficeps
Somalia
L. r. rufinuchalis
Ethiopia to SE Kenya
L. r. kismayensis
S Somalia

Laniarius lühderi (Lühder's Bush Shrike)
L. l. lühderi
Cameroun to Sudan, Kenya

L. l. castaneiceps
S Uganda, W Kenya
L. l. brauni
NW Angola
L. l. amboimensis
W Angola

Laniarius turatii (Turati's Boubou)
Senegal to Sierra Leone

Laniarius aethiopicus (Tropical Boubou)
L. a. major
Sierra Leone to Sudan & Malawi
L. a. aethiopicus
Ethiopia, Somalia, N Kenya
L. a. ambiguus
Kenya, N Tanzania
L. a. erlangeri
S Somalia
L. a. sublacteus
E Kenya, Zanzibar I
L. a. mossambicus
S Zaire, E Zambia, Mozambique

Laniarius bicolor (Gabon Boubou)
L. b. bicolor
Cameroun, Gabon
L. b. guttatus
W Zaire, Angola
L. b. sticturus
S Angola, N Botswana, W Zambia

Laniarius ferrugineus (Southern Boubou)
L. f. limpopoensis
SE Rhodesia, N Transvaal
L. f. transvaalensis
S & E Transvaal
L. f. tongensis
S Mozambique, N Natal
L. f. natalensis
W Natal
L. f. pondoensis
E Cape Province
L. f. savensis
S Mozambique
L. f. ferrugineus
W Cape Province

Laniarius barbarus (Common Gonolek)
L. b. helenae
Sierra Leone
L. b. barbarus
Senegal to N Cameroun

Laniarius erythrogaster (Black-headed Gonolek)
N Cameroun to Tanzania

Laniarius mufumbiri (Mufumbiri Shrike)
Uganda, Rwanda

Laniarius atrococcineus (Burchell's Gonolek)
S Angola to Transvaal

Laniarius atroflavus (Yellow-breasted Boubou)
  L. a. atroflavus
    Cameroun Mt
  L. a. craterum
    highlands of Cameroun
Laniarius fülleborni (Fülleborn's Black Boubou)
  L. f. camerunensis
    W Cameroun
  L. f. poensis
    E Nigeria, Cameroun
  L. f. holomelas
    E Zaire, Uganda
  L. f. usambaricus
    W Tanzania
  L. f. ulugurensis
    Tanzania
  L. f. fulleborni
    SW Tanzania, N Malawi, E Zambia
Laniarius funebris (Slate-coloured Boubou)
  L. f. funebris
    S Sudan & Somalia to Tanzania
  L. f. degener
    S Ethiopia, S Somalia, E Kenya
Laniarius leucorhynchus (Sooty Boubou)
    Sierra Leone to Sudan, W Kenya

TELOPHORUS
Telophorus bocagei (Grey-green Bush Shrike)
  T. b. bocagei
    C Cameroun to N Angola
  T. b. jacksoni
    C Zaire, Uganda, W Kenya
  T. b. ansorgei
    SW Zaire, N Angola
Telophorus sulfureopectus (Sulphur-breasted Bush Shrike)
  T. s. sulfureopectus
    Senegal to NE Zaire
  T. s. similis
    Ethiopia to Angola & Cape Province
Telophorus olivaceus (Olive Bush Shrike)
  T. o. makawa
    C & S Malawi, E Rhodesia
  T. l. bertrandi
    S Malawi
  T. o. vitorum
    Sol do Save, Mozambique
  T. o. interfluvius
    Mozambique
  T. o. olivaceus
    S Mozambique, E Transvaal, E Cape Province

Telophorus nigrifrons (Black-fronted Bush Shrike)
  T. n. nigrifrons
    C Kenya, Tanzania, N Malawi
  T. n. manningi
    SE Zaire, N Namibia
  T. n. sandgroundi
    Mozambique, Rhodesia, NE Transvaal
Telophorus multicolor (Many-coloured Bush Shrike)
  T. m. multicolor
    Sierra Leone to Cameroun Mt
  T. m. batesi
    Cameroun to W Uganda, N Angola
  T. m. graueri
    E Zaire
Telophorus kupeensis (Serle's Bush Shrike)
    Kupé Mt (Cameroun)
Telophorus zeylonus (Bokmakierie Shrike)
  T. z. restrictus
    Rhodesia
  T. z. phanus
    S Angola, Namibia
  T. z. zeylonus
    Transvaal, Cape Province
Telophorus viridis (Perrin's Bush Shrike)
    S Zaire, N Angola, NW Zambia
Telophorus quadricolor (Four-coloured Bush Shrike)
  T. q. nigricauda
    SE Kenya, E Tanzania
  T. q. quadricolor
    Mozambique & S Malawi to Natal
Telophorus dohertyi (Doherty's Bush Shrike)
    W Kenya, W Uganda, E Zaire

MALACONOTUS
Malaconotus cruentus (Fiery-breasted Bush Shrike)
  M. c. cruentus
    Sierra Leone to Cameroun
  M. c. gabonensis
    Cameroun, Gabon
  M. c. adolfi-friederici
    E Zaire
Malaconotus lagdeni (Lagden's Bush Shrike)
  M. l. lagdeni
    Liberia to Ghana
  M. l. centralis
    E Zaire
Malaconotus gladiator (Green-breasted Bush Shrike)
    Cameroun Mt
Malaconotus blanchoti (Grey-headed Bush Shrike)
  M. b. blanchoti
    Senegal to N Cameroun

M. b. catharoxanthus
N Zaire to Ethiopia, W Kenya
M. b. approximans
S Ethiopia to N Tanzania
M. b. hypopyrrhus
Rwanda, Tanzania to Natal
M. b. extremus
E Cape Province
M. b. interpositus
SE Zaire, W Zambia
M. b. monteiri
Angola, S Zaire
M. b. citrinifuetus
SW Angola
**Malaconotus alius (Black-cap Bush
Shrike)**
Tanzania

NICATOR
Nicator chloris (Western Nicator)
Senegal to Sudan, Zaire, Uganda
Nicator gularis (Eastern Nicator)
Kenya & Zambia to Natal
Nicator vireo (Yellow-throated Nicator)
Cameroun to N Angola, Uganda

LANIINAE

CORVINELLA
**Corvinella corvina (Western Long-tailed
Shrike)**
C. c. corvina
Senegal & Gambia to Mali
C. c. affinis
Guinea to Uganda
C. c. chapini
NE Zaire, W Kenya
C. c. caliginosa
SW Sudan
**Corvinella melanoleuca (Eastern Long-
tailed Shrike)**
C. m. aequatorialis
S Kenya, Tanzania
C. m. melanoleuca
S Angola, Southern Africa

LANIUS
Lanius tigrinus (Tiger Shrike)
E Asia, Sumatra to Philippine Is
& Celebes
Lanius souzae (Souza's Shrike)
L. s. souzae
Zaire, Angola, Zambia
L. s. tacitus
E Zambia
L. s. burigi
SE Zaire to Tanzania, Mozambique
Lanius bucephalus (Bull-headed Shrike)
L. b. bucephalus
E Asia, Japan, China

L. b. sicarius
NW China
Lanius cristatus (Brown Shrike)
L. c. cristatus
E Asia, India, China
L. c. confusus
NE Asia » Thailand, Malaysia
L. c. superciliosus
Japan, E China » Sunda Is
L. c. lucionensis
China, Philippine Is, N Borneo
Lanius collurio (Red-backed Shrike)
L. c. juxtus
S Britain » W Europe
L. c. collurio
Europe, Siberia, W Asia, » S Africa
L. c. pallidifrons
W Siberia, WC Asia
L. c. kobylini
Iran, Arabia, E Africa
L. c. phoenicuroides
S Russia, NW India, NE Africa
L. c. speculigerus
Iran, C Asia
L. c. isabellinus
E Turkistan, NW India » NE Africa
L. c. tsaidamensis
W China
Lanius collurioides (Burmese Shrike)
L. c. collurioides
E India to N Vietnam
L. c. nigricapillus
S Vietnam
Lanius gubernator (Emin's Shrike)
Ghana to Sudan
Lanius vittatus (Bay-backed Shrike)
L. v. nargianus
Iran, Afghanistan, Pakistan
L. v. vittatus
N & C India
Lanius schach (Black-headed Shrike)
L. s. stresemanni
E New Guinea
L. s. bentet
Malaysia, Sumatra to Timor I
L. s. suluensis
Sulu Archipelago
L. s. nasutus
Philippine Is, N Borneo
L. s. schach
E & S China, N Vietnam
L. s. longicaudatus
C Thailand
L. s. tricolor
Himalayas, Burma, N Indochina
L. s. nigriceps
E India

L. s. caniceps
S & W India, Sri Lanka
L. s. erythronotus
C Asia, W India
L. s. lahulensis
NW India
L. s. tephronotus
Himalayas, S & W China
Lanius validirostris (Strong-billed Shrike)
L. v. validirostris
Luzon I
L. v. tertius
Mindoro I
L. v. hachisuka
SE Mindanao I
L. v. quartus
W Mindanao I
Lanius mackinnoni (Mackinnon's Shrike)
Cameroun to Angola and Tanzania
Lanius minor (Lesser Grey Shrike)
L. m. minor
S & E Europe » E & S Africa
L. m. turanicus
C Asia, Iran » E Africa
Lanius ludovicianus (Loggerhead Shrike)
L. l. gambeli
W North America » W Mexico
L. l. excubitorides
C Canada, C USA » E Mexico
L. l. migrans
E North America » NE Mexico
L. l. ludovicianus
SE USA
L. l. miamensis
S Florida
L. l. mexicanus
C Mexico
L. l. sonoriensis
SW USA, NW Mexico
L. l. grinnelli
N Baja California
L. l. nelsoni
S Baja California
L. l. anthonyi
Santa Barbara I
L. l. mearnsi
San Clemente I
Lanius excubitor (Great Grey Shrike)
L. e. borealis
E Canada, E USA
L. e. invictus
W Canada, W USA
L. e. sibiricus
E Siberia, NE Asia, Mongolia
L. e. excubitor
Europe, Asia Minor, W Siberia

L. e. bianchii
Sakhalin I, N Japan
L. e. mollis
C Asia
L. e. funereus
Chinese Turkistan
L. e. homeyeri
SE Europe, WC Asia
L. e. leucopterus
W Siberia, Russian Turkistan
L. e. meridionalis
S France, Iberia
L. e. koenigi
Canary Is
L. e. algeriensis
NW Africa
L. e. elegans
Sahara, S Egypt
L. e. leucopygus
S Sahara, Chad, W Sudan
L. e. aucheri
NE Africa, Arabia, S Iran
L. e. buryi
SW Arabia
L. e. uncinatus
Socotra I
L. e. lahtora
NW India
L. e. pallidirostris
SC Asia, Iraq, Arabia, NE Africa
Lanius excubitoroides (Grey-backed Fiscal)
L. e. excubitoroides
Sudan to E Zaire, W Kenya
L. e. intercedens
C Ethiopia, W Kenya
L. e. bohmi
Ethiopia to Tanzania
Lanius sphenocercus (Chinese Great Grey Shrike)
L. s. sphenocercus
NE Asia, Korea, N & E China
L. s. giganteus
NW China
Lanius cabanisi (Long-tailed Fiscal)
Somalia, Kenya, Tanzania
Lanius dorsalis (Taita Fiscal)
Ethiopia, E Uganda, NE Tanzania
Lanius somalicus (Somali Fiscal)
Somalia, E & S Ethiopia, N Kenya
Lanius collaris (Fiscal Shrike)
L. c. smithii
Sierra Leone to W Tanzania
L. c. humeralis
Ethiopia to Zambia, N Mozambique
L. c. marwitzi
SW Tanzania

L. c. capelli
W Uganda to Angola
L. c. pyrrhostictus
E Botswana to Rhodesia, Natal
L. c. collaris
Orange Free State, Cape Province
L. c. subcoronatus
SW Angola, Namibia, W Botswana
Lanius newtoni (Newton's Fiscal)
Sao Thomé I
Lanius senator (Woodchat Shrike)
L. s. senator
Europe, N Africa
L. s. badius
W Mediterranean Is, NW Africa
L. s. niloticus
Syria, Iran, NE Africa
Lanius nubicus (Masked Shrike)
SE Europe to Iraq, NE Africa

PITYRIASINAE

PITYRIASIS
Pityriasis gymnocephala (Bornean Bristlehead)
Borneo

123 VANGIDAE (VANGA SHRIKES)

CALICALICUS
Calicalicus madagascariensis (Red-tailed Vanga)
E Madagascar

SCHETBA
Schetba rufa (Rufous Vanga)
S. r. rufa
E Madagascar
S. r. occidentalis
WC Madagascar

VANGA
Vanga curvirostris (Hook-billed Vanga)
V. c. curvirostris
E & N Madagascar
V. c. cetera
SW Madagascar

XENOPIROSTRIS
Xenopirostris xenopirostris (Lafresnaye's Vanga)
SW Madagascar
Xenopirostris damii (Van Dam's Vanga)
NW Madagascar
Xenopirostris polleni (Pollen's Vanga)
NW & E Madagascar

FALCULEA
Falculea palliata (Sicklebill)
N & W Madagascar
ARTAMELLA
Artamella viridis (White-headed Vanga)
A. v. viridis

E Madagascar
A. v. annae
W Madagascar
LEPTOPTERUS
Leptopterus chabert (Chabert Vanga)
L. c. chabert
N & E Madagascar
L. c. schistocercus
SW Madagascar
Leptopterus madagascarinus (Blue Vanga)
L. m. madagascarinus
N & C Madagascar
L. m comorensis
Moheli I
L. m. bensoni
Grand Comoro I

ORIOLIA
Oriolia bernieri (Bernier's Vanga)
E Madagascar

EURYCEROS
Euryceros prevostii (Helmet Bird)
E Madagascar

HYPOSITTA
Hypositta corallirostris (Coral-billed Nuthatch)
Madagascar

124 BOMBYCILLIDAE (WAXWINGS)

BOMBYCILLINAE

BOMBYCILLA
Bombycilla garrulus (Bohemian Waxwing)
B. g. garrulus
N Europe
B. g. centralasiae
N, C & E Asia, China, Japan
B. g. pallidiceps
W Canada, N & W USA
Bombycilla japonica (Japanese Waxwing)
NE Asia, Japan
Bombycilla cedrorum (Cedar Waxwing)
Canada, USA, Mexico, Central America, Colombia, Venezuela

PTILOGONATINAE

PTILOGONYS
Ptilogonys cinereus (Grey Silky Flycatcher)
P. c. otofuscus
NW Mexico
P. c. cinereus
C & E Mexico
P. c. pallescens
SW Mexico
P. c. molybdophanes
S Mexico, W Guatemala

P. c. schistaceus
S Mexico
Ptilogonys caudatus (Long-tailed Silky Flycatcher)
Costa Rica, W Panama

PHAINOPEPLA
Phainopepla nitens (Phainopepla)
P. n. lepida
SW USA, NW Mexico
P. n. nitens
S Texas, NC Mexico

PHAINOPTILA
Phainoptila melanoxantha (Black & Yellow Silky Flycatcher)
Costa Rica, W Panama

HYPOCOLIINAE

HYPOCOLIUS
Hypocolius ampelinus (Grey Hypocolius)
Iraq, SW Arabia

125 DULIDAE (PALMCHAT)

DULUS
Dulus dominicus (Palm Chat)
Gonave I, Hispaniola

126 CINCLIDAE (DIPPERS)

CINCLUS
Cinclus cinclus (Dipper)
C. c. hibernicus
Ireland, W Scotland
C. c. gularis
Scotland, W & C England
C. c. cinclus
N Europe, Turkey, W Spain, Corsica
C. c. aquaticus
W Europe, Balkans
C. c. minor
NW Africa
C. c. caucasicus
Caucasus, Iraq, Iran
C. c. rufiventris
· W Syria
C. c. persicus
SW Iran
C. c. leucogaster
C Asia
C. c. cashmeriensis
Himalayas
C. c. przewalskii
S Tibet, W China
Cinclus pallasii (Brown Dipper)
C. p. tenuirostris
C Asia, Himalayas
C. p. dorjei
S Assam, N Burma, N Thailand

C. p. pallasii
NE Asia, Japan, W China, N Thailand, N Vietnam
C. p. marila
Khasia hills, India
Cinclus mexicanus (Mexican Dipper)
C.m. unicolor
W Canada, W USA
C. m. mexicanus
N & C Mexico
C. m. anthonyi
S Mexico, Guatemala
C. m. dickermani
S Mexico
C. m. ardesiacus
Costa Rica, W Panama
Cinclus leucocephalus (White-capped Dipper)
C. l. rivularis
N Colombia
C. l. leuconotus
W Venezuela, S Colombia, Ecuador
C. l. leucocephalus
Peru, Bolivia
Cinclus schulzi (Rufous-throated Dipper)
NW Argentina

127 TROGLODYTIDAE (WRENS)

CAMPYLORHYNCHUS
Campylorhynchus jocosus (Spotted Wren)
SC Mexico
Campylorhynchus gularis (Spotted Cactus-Wren)
NW & W Mexico
Campylorhynchus yucatanicus (Yucatan Cactus-Wren)
SE Mexico
Campylorhynchus brunneicapillus (Cactus Wren)
C. b. couesi
SW USA, N Baja California, NW Mexico
C. b. bryanti
W Baja California
C. b. purus
C Baja California
C. b. seri
Tiburon I
C. b. affinis
S Baja California
C. b. brunneicapillus
NW Mexico
C. b. guttatus
C Mexico
Campylorhynchus chiapensis (Giant Wren)
Chiapas

Campylorhynchus griseus (Bicoloured Wren)
C. g. albicilius
N Colombia, NW Venezuela
C. g. bicolor
Colombia
C. g. minor
E Colombia, N Venezuela
C. g. pallidus
S Venezuela
C. g. griseus
E Venezuela, Guyana, N Brazil
Campylorhynchus rufinucha (Rufous-naped Wren)
C. r. humilis
SW Mexico
C. r. rufinucha
E Mexico
C. r. nigricaudatus
S Mexico, W Guatemala
C. r. castaneus
Guatemala to Nicaragua
C. r. capistratus
El Salvador to NW Costa Rica
Campylorhynchus turdinus (Thrush-like Wren)
C. t. albobrunneus
C Panama
C. t. harterti
E Panama, W Colombia
C. t. aenigmaticus
SW Colombia
C. t. hypostictus
NW & W Amazonia
C. t. turdinus
EC Brazil
C. t. unicolor
E Bolivia, W Brazil
Campylorhynchus nuchalis (Stripe-backed Wren)
C. n. pardus
N Colombia
C. n. brevipennis
N Venezuela
C. n. nuchalis
C Venezuela
Campylorhynchus fasciatus (Fasciated Wren)
C. f. pallescens
SW Ecuador, NW Peru
C. f. fasciatus
W Peru
Campylorhynchus zonatus (Banded-backed Wren)
C. z. vanblockeri
Oaxaca (Mexico)
C. z. zonatus
EC Mexico

C. z. restrictus
S Mexico, Guatemala
C. z. vulcanius
S Mexico to Nicaragua
C. z. costaricensis
E Costa Rica, W Panama
C. z. curvirostris
N Colombia
C. z. brevirostris
N Colombia, NW Ecuador
Campylorhynchus megalopterus (Grey-barred Wren)
C. m. megalopterus
C Mexico
C. m. nelsoni
SC Mexico

ODONTORCHILUS
Odontorchilus cinereus (Tooth-billed Wren)
N Brazil
Odontorchilus branickii (Grey-mantled Wren)
O. b. branickii
Colombia, Ecuador, Peru
O. b. minor
N Ecuador

SALPINCTES
Salpinctes obsoletus (Rock Wren)
S. o. obsoletus
SW Canada, W USA, N & C Mexico
S. o. guadeloupensis
Guadeloupe I
S. o. tenuirostris
San Benito I
S. o. exsul
San Benedicto I
S. o. neglectus
SE Mexico to Honduras
S. o. guttatus
El Salvador to Costa Rica

CATHERPES
Catherpes mexicanus (Canyon Wren)
C. m. conspersus
W USA, NW Mexico
C. m. albifrons
SW USA, N Mexico
C. m. mexicanus
N, C & S Mexico
C. m. meliphonus
NW Mexico
C. m. cantator
S Mexico

HYLORCHILUS
Hylorchilus sumichrasti (Slender-billed Wren)
H. s. sumichrasti
Vera Cruz

H. s. navai
   Chiapas
CINNYCERTHIA
Cinnycerthia unirufa (Rufous Wren)
   C. u. unirufa
      NE Colombia
   C. u. chakei
      NW Venezuela
   C. u. unibrunnea
      S & C Colombia, Ecuador
Cinnycerthia peruana (Sepia-brown Wren)
   C. p. bogotensis
      W Colombia
   C. p. olivascens
      SW Colombia, W Ecuador
   C. p. peruana
      Peru
   C. p. fulva
      S Peru, N Bolivia

CISTOTHORUS
Cistothorus platensis (Short-billed Marsh Wren)
   C. p. stellaris
      E Canada, E USA, NE Mexico
   C. p. tinnulus
      W Mexico
   C. p. potosinus
      San Luis Potosi
   C. p. jalapensis
      Vera Cruz
   C. p. warneri
      W Chiapas
   C. p. russelli
      Belize
   C. p. graberi
      SE Honduras, NE Nicaragua
   C. p. elegans
      S Mexico, Guatemala
   C. p. lucidus
      S Costa Rica, W Panama
   C. p. alticola
      N Colombia, N Venezuela, N Guyana
   C. p. tamae
      Colombia, Venezuela
   C. p. tolimae
      C Colombia
   C. p. aequatorialis
      S Colombia, Ecuador, Peru
   C. p. graminicola
      C Peru
   C. p. minimus
      S Peru
   C. p. boliviae
      NW Bolivia
   C. p. polyglottus
      SE Brazil to NE Argentina

C. p. tucumanus
   NW Argentina
C. p. platensis
   C & E Argentina
C. p. hornensis
   S Chile, S Argentina
C. p. falklandicus
   Falkland Is
Cistothorus meridae (Paramo Wren)
   NW Venezuela
Cistothorus apolinari (Apolinar's Marsh Wren)
   C Colombia
Cistothorus palustris (Long-billed Marsh Wren)
   C. p. palustris
      E USA
   C. p. waynei
      CE USA
   C. p. griseus
      SE USA
   C. p. marianae
      SE USA
   C. p. thryophilus
      S USA
   C. p. iliacus
      C Canada, NC to SE USA
   C. p. laingi
      WC Canada, WC USA » N Mexico
   C. p. plesius
      SW Canada, W USA » NW Mexico
   C. p. paludicola
      W USA, N Baja California
   C. p. aestuarinus
      SW USA, NW Mexico
   C. p. tolucensis
      C Mexico

THRYOMANES
Thryomanes bewickii (Bewick's Wren)
   T. b. bewickii
      C & S USA
   T. b. altus
      EC & SC USA
   T. b. cryptus
      SC USA, NE Mexico
   T. b. eremophilus
      WC & SW USA, NW Mexico
   T. b. calophonus
      SW Canada, NW USA
   T. b. drymoecus
      W USA
   T. b. marinensis
      SW USA
   T. b. atrestus
      W USA
   T. b. spilurus
      SW USA

T. b. correctus
SW USA

T. b. nesophilus
Santa Cruz I (S California)

T. b. catalinae
Santa Catalina I, (California)

T. b. leucophrys
San Clemente I, (California)

T. b. charienturus
NW Baja California

T. b. cerroensis
WC Baja California

T. b. magdalenensis
SW Baja California

T. b. murinus
C Mexico

T. b. mexicanus
SC Mexico

Thryomanes sissonii (Revillagigedo Wren)
Socorro I, Revillagigedo Group

FERMINIA
Ferminia cerverai (Zapata Wren)
Cuba

THRYOTHORUS
Thryothorus atrogularis (Black-throated Wren)

T. a. atrogularis
Nicaragua, Costa Rica, W Panama

T. a. xerampelinus
E Panama

T. a. spadix
W Colombia

Thryothorus fasciatoventris (Black-bellied Wren)

T. f. melanogaster
SW Costa Rica, W Panama

T. f. albigularis
E Panama, W Colombia

T. f. fasciatoventris
N Colombia

Thryothorus euophrys (Plain-tailed Wren)

T. e. euophrys
Ecuador

T. e. longipes
Ecuador

T. e. atriceps
NW Peru

Thryothorus genibarbis (Moustached Wren)

T. g. macrurus
Colombia

T. g. amaurogaster
E Colombia

T. g. saltuensis
W Colombia

T. g. yananchae
SW Colombia

T. g. consobrinus
NW Venezuela

T. g. ruficaudatus
N Venezuela

T. g. tachirensis
NW Venezuela

T. g. mystacalis
Ecuador

T. g. genibarbis
NC Brazil

T. g. juruanus
W Brazil, NE Bolivia

T. g. intercedens
C Brazil

T. g. bolivianus
C Bolivia

Thryothorus coraya (Coraya Wren)

T. c. obscurus
E Venezuela

T. c. caurensis
E Colombia, S Venezuela, N Brazil

T. c. ridgwayi
E Venezuela, W Guyana

T. c. coraya
the Guianas, N Brazil

T. c. herberti
N Brazil

T. c. griseipectus
Colombia, Ecuador, W Brazil, N Peru

T. c. amazonicus
E Peru

T. c. albiventris
N Peru

T. c. cantator
C Peru

Thryothorus felix (Happy Wren)

T. f. sonorae
NW Mexico

T. f. pallidus
W Mexico

T. f. lawrencii
Maria Madre I, (Mexico)

T. f. magdalenae
Maria Magdalena I, (Mexico)

T. f. felix
C & S Mexico

T. f. grandis
C Mexico

Thryothorus maculipectus (Spot-breasted Wren)

T. m. microstictus
NE Mexico

T. m. maculipectus
E Mexico

T. m. umbrinus
Guatemala, Honduras, El Salvador,
E Nicaragua,S Mexico

T. m. canobrunneus
SE Mexico, Guatemala

Thryothorus rutilus (Rufous-breasted Wren)
T. r. hyperythrus
W Costa Rica, W Panama
T. r. tobagensis
Tobago I
T. r. rutilus
Trinidad, N Venezuela
T. r. intensus
NW Venezuela
T. r. laetus
NW Venezuela, N Colombia
T. r. interior
C Colombia
T. r. hypospodius
NC Colombia
T. r. columbianus
W Colombia
T. r. paucimaculatus
W Ecuador, NW Peru
T. r. sclateri
N Peru

Thryothorus nigricapillus (Bay Wren)
T. n. costaricensis
E Nicaragua, Costa Rica, NW Panama
T. n. semibadius
SW Costa Rica, SW Panama
T. n. castaneus
C Panama
T. n. schottii
E Panama, NW Colombia
T. n. reditus
NE Panama
T. n. connectens
SW Colombia
T. n. nigricapillus
W Ecuador

Thryothorus thoracicus (Stripe-throated Wren)
T. t. thoracicus
E Nicaragua, Costa Rica, W Panama
T. t. grisescens
E Panama
T. t. leucopogon
SE Panama, W Colombia, NW Ecuador

Thryothorus pleurostictus (Banded Wren)
T. p. nisorius
W & C Mexico
T. p. oaxacae
SW Mexico
T. p. acaciarum
S Mexico
T. p. oblitus
S Mexico, Guatemala, W El Salvador
T. p. pleurostictus
Guatemala

T. p. lateralis
El Salvador, W Honduras
T. p. ravus
Nicaragua, NW Costa Rica

Thryothorus ludovicianus (Carolina Wren)
T. l. ludovicianus
C, S, SE USA
T. l. miamensis
Florida
T. l. nesophilus
Florida
T. l. burleighi
Cat I
T. l. lomitensis
S USA, NE Mexico
T. l. berlandieri
NC & NE Mexico
T. l. tropicalis
NC Mexico
T. l. albinucha
SE Mexico, N Guatemala
T. l. subfulvus
Guatemala, Nicaragua

Thryothorus rufalbus (Rufous and White Wren)
T. r. transfinis
S Mexico
T. r. rufalbus
Guatemala, El Salvador
T. r. castanonotus
W Honduras to W Panama
T. r. cumanensis
N Colombia, N Venezuela
T. r. minlosi
EC Colombia, NW Venezuela

Thryothorus nicefori (Nicefero's Wren)
N Colombia

Thryothorus sinaloa (Bar-vented Wren)
T. s. cinereus
NW Mexico
T. s. sinaloa
WC Mexico
T. s. russeus
SW Mexico

Thryothorus modestus (Plain Wren)
T. m. modestus
S Mexico, Guatemala, Honduras, El Salvador, Nicaragua
T. m. zeledoni
E Nicaragua, E Costa Rica, NW Panama
T. m. elutus
W Panama

Thryothorus leucotis (Buff-breasted Wren)
T. l. galbraithii
E Panama, NW Colombia
T. l. conditus
Islas San Miguel, Panama

T. l. leucotis
N Colombia

T. l. collinus
NE Colombia

T. l. venezuelanus
NE Colombia, NW Venezuela

T. l. zuliensis
Colombia, Venezuela

T. l. hypoleucus
NC Venezuela

T. l. bogotensis
E Colombia, C Venezuela

T. l. albipectus
NE Venezuela, the Guianas, NE Brazil

T. l. peruanus
E Peru, W Brazil, SE Colombia,
   E Ecuador

T. l. rufiventris
C Brazil

Thryothorus superciliaris (Superciliated Wren)

T. s. superciliaris
Ecuador

T. s. baroni
S Ecuador, N Peru

Thryothorus guarayanus (Fawn-breasted Wren)
Bolivia, SW Brazil

Thryothorus longirostris (Long-billed Wren)

T. l. bahiae
NE Brazil

T. l. longirostris
C Brazil

Thryothorus griseus (Grey Wren)
W Brazil

TROGLODYTES

Troglodytes troglodytes ((Winter) Wren)

T. t. hiemalis
C & S Canada, C & E USA

T. t. pullus
SE USA

T. t. pacificus
W Canada, W USA

T. t. helleri
Kodiak I, Alaska

T. t. semidiensis
Semidi I, Alaska

T. t. kiskensis
Aleutian Is, Alaska

T. t. meligerus
Attu I, Agatta I, Aleutian Is

T. t. alascensis
Pribilof Is, Alaska

T. t. pallescens
Kamchatka, Commander Is

T. t. kurilensis
N Kurile Is

T. t. fumigatus
S Kurile Is, Japan, Izu Is

T. t. mosukei
Iku Is, Borodino Is

T. t. ogawae
Tanegashima I, Yakushima I

T. t. taivanus
Taiwan

T. t. dauricus
NE Asia, Korea

T. t. idius
N China

T. t. szetschuanus
W China

T. t. talifuensis
Sikang, NE Burma

T. t. subpallidus
Afghanistan

T. t. nipalensis
C & E Himalayas

T. t. neglectus
W Himalayas

T. t. magrathi
NW India

T. t. zagrossiensis
Iran

T. t. tianschanicus
NE Iran, C Asia

T. t. hyrcanus
Caucasus, NW Iran

T. t. cypriotes
Crete, Rhodes, Cyprus

T. t. juniperi
NW Libya

T. t. kabylorum
NW Africa, Balearic Is

T. t. koenigi
Corsica, Sardinia

T. t. troglodytes
Europe, Asia Minor

T. t. indigenus
Ireland, Scotland, England

T. t. hirtensis
St Kilda I, Scotland

T. t. hebridensis
Outer Hebrides, Scotland

T. t. fridariensis
Fair Isle, Scotland

T. t. zetlandicus
Shetland Is, Scotland

T. t. borealis
Faroe Is

T. t. islandicus
Iceland

Troglodytes aëdon (House Wren)

T. a. aëdon
SE Canada, E USA

T. a. parkmanii
SW Canada, C & W USA, N Mexico
T. a. cahooni
SW USA, NW Mexico
T. a. compositus
C & NE Mexico
T. a. brunneicollis
C & S Mexico
T. a. intermedius
S Mexico, Guatemala, Honduras, El
Salvador, Nicaragua, Costa Rica
T. a. tanneri
Isla Clarion, Revillagigedo
T. a. beani
Cozumel I, SE Mexico
T. a. inquietus
Panama
T. a. carychrous
Coiba I, Panama
T. a. rufescens
Dominica I
T. a. mesoleucus
St Lucia I
T. a. guadelupensis
Guadelupe I
T. a. musicus
St Vincent I
T. a. atopus
N Colombia
T. a. striatulus
Colombia, Venezuela
T. a. columbae
E Colombia
T. a. effutitus
NW & W Venezuela
T. a. albicans
Trinidad, Colombia, Venezuela
W Ecuador, N Peru, the Guianas, Brazil
T. a. tobagensis
Tobago I
T. a. audax
W Peru
T. a. puna
W Bolivia, Peru
T. a. carabayae
Peru
T. a. tecellatus
Peru, N Chile
T. a. rex
Bolivia, Paraguay, Argentina
T. a. atacamensis
N & C Chile
T. a. musculus
C & S Brazil, E Paraguay, N Argentina
T. a. bonariae
S Brazil, Uruguay, NE Argentina
T. a. chilensis
S Chile, S Argentina
T. a. cobbi
Falkland Is

***Troglodytes solstitialis* (Mountain Wren)**
T. s. chiapensis
S Mexico
T. s. rufociliatus
E Guatemala, N El Salvador
T. s. nannoides
W El Salvador
T. s. rehni
Honduras
T. s. ochraceus
Costa Rica
T. s. ligea
W Panama
T. s. festinus
E Panama
T. s. monticola
N Colombia
T. s. solitarius
Colombia, Venezuela
T. s. solstitialis
S Colombia, Ecuador, N Peru
T. s. macrourus
EC Peru
T. s. frater
SE Peru, Bolivia
T. s. auricularis
N Argentina
***Troglodytes rufulus* (Tepui Wren)**
T. r. rufulus
SE Venezuela
T. r. fulvigularis
SE Venezuela
T. r. yavii
S Venezuela
T. r. duidae
S Venezuela
T. r. wetmorei
S Venezuela
***Troglodytes browni* (Timberline Wren)**
T. b. ridgwayi
Costa Rica
T. b. basultoi
Costa Rica
T. b. browni
W Panama

UROPSILA
**Uropsila leucogastra* (White-bellied
Wren)**
U. l. leucogastra
EC & E Mexico
U. l. pacifica
SW Mexico
U. l. musica
S Mexico
U. l. brachyura
SE Mexico, Guatemala

**Henicorhina leucosticta (Lowland Wood
Wren)**
  H. l. prostheleuca
    S & E Mexico, Guatemala
  H. l. tropaea
    Guatemala, Honduras, Nicaragua, Costa
    Rica, NW Panama
  H. l. smithei
    Peten, Guatemala
  H. l. costaricensis
    Cartago, Costa Rica
  H. l. pittieri
    SW Costa Rica, W Panama
  H. l. dariensis
    E Panama, NW Colombia
  H. l. albilateralis
    C Colombia
  H. l. leucosticta
    S Venezuela, Guyana, Surinam, N Brazil
  H. l. eucharis
    Colombia
  H. l. inornata
    S Colombia, Ecuador
  H. l. hauxwelli
    S Colombia, E Ecuador, Peru
**Henicorhina leucophrys (Highland Wood
Wren)**
  H. l. mexicana
    E Mexico
  H. l. festiva
    W Mexico
  H. l. castanea
    Honduras, S Mexico, N Guatemala
  H. l. capitalis
    S Mexico, W Guatemala, El Slavador
  H. l. minuscula
    S Mexico
  H. l. collina
    Costa Rica, W Panama
  H. l. anachoreta
    N Colombia
  H. l. bangsi
    N Colombia
  H. l. manastarae
    NW Venezuela
  H. l. sanluisensis
    NW Venezuela
  H. l. venezuelensis
    N Venezuela
  H. l. meridana
    W Venezuela
  H. l. tamae
    E Colombia, NW Venezuela
  H. l. leucophrys
    W Colombia, Ecuador, Peru
  H. l. brunneiceps
    SW Colombia, N Ecuador

  H. l. hilaris
    SW Ecuador
  H. l. boliviana
    W Bolivia
**Henicorhina leucoptera (Bar-winged
Wood Wren)**
    NC Peru

**Microcerculus marginatus (Nightingale
Wren)**
  M. m. philomela
    S Mexico, Guatemala, Honduras, Costa
    Rica, Panama, NW Colombia
  M. m. taeniatus
    S Colombia, Ecuador
  M. m. corrasus
    N Colombia
  M. m. squamulatus
    NE Colombia, N Venezuela
  M. m. marginatus
    W Venezuela, E Colombia, E Ecuador,
    Peru, N Bolivia, W Brazil
Microcerculus ustulatus (Flutist Wren)
  M. u. duidae
    S Venezuela
  M. u. lunatipectus
    S Venezuela
  M. u. obscurus
    SE Venezuela
  M. u. ustulatus
    SE Venezuela, W Guyana
**Microcerculus bambla (Wing-banded
Wren)**
  M. b. albigularis
    E Ecuador, W Brazil
  M. b. caurensis
    S Venezuela
  M. b. bambla
    SE Venezuela, the Guianas, NE Brazil

**Cyphorinus thoracicus (Chestnut-
breasted Wren)**
  C. t. dichrous
    S Colombia, Ecuador, Peru
  C. t. thoracicus
    E Peru
Cyphorhinus aradus (Quadrille Wren)
  C. a. richardsoni
    Nicaragua, SE Honduras
  C. a. infuscatus
    Costa Rica, NW Panama
  C. a. laurencii
    Panama, NW Colombia
  C. a. propinquus
    N Colombia
  C. a. chocoanus
    W Colombia
  C. a. phaeocephalus
    SW Colombia, Ecuador

C. a. urbanoi
  S Venezuela
C. a. aradus
  S Venezuela, the Guianas, NE Brazil
C. a. faroensis
  N Brazil
C. a. griseolateralis
  N Brazil
C. a. interpositus
  S Brazil
C. a. transfluvialis
  N Brazil, SE Colombia
C. a. salvini
  SE Colombia, E Ecuador, NE Peru
C. a. modulator
  E Peru, W Brazil

128 MIMIDAE (MOCKING-BIRDS, THRASHERS)

DUMETELLA
Dumetella carolinensis (Catbird)
  S Canada, C, S & SE USA, Central
  America, West Indies

MELANOPTILA
Melanoptila glabrirostris (Black Catbird)
  SE Mexico, N Guatemala, N Honduras

MELANOTIS
Melanotis caerulescens (Blue Mockingbird)
  M. c. longirostris
    Tres Marias Is
  M. c. caerulescens
    C & S Mexico
Melanotis hypoleucus (Blue & White Mockingbird)
    SE Mexico, Guatemala, Honduras, El
    Salvador

MIMUS
Mimus polyglottos (Northern Mockingbird)
  M. p. polyglottos
    C, E & SE USA
  M. p. leucopterus
    SW USA, NW Mexico
  M. p. orpheus
    Bahama Is, Greater Antilles
Mimus gilvus (Tropical Mockingbird)
  M. g. gracilis
    S Mexico, Guatemala, Honduras, El
    Salvador
  M. g. leucophaeus
    SE Mexico, Belize
  M. g. antillarum
    Martinique I, Windward Is
  M. g. tobagensis
    Trinidad, Tobago I
  M. g. rostratus
    N Venezuela Is

M. g. magnirostris
  St Andrews I
M. g. tolimensis
  W & C Colombia
M. g. melanopterus
  N & E Colombia, Venezuela, Guyana,
  N Brazil
M. g. gilvus
  French Guiana, Surinam
M. g. antelius
  N & E Brazil
Mimus gundlachii (Bahama Mockingbird)
  M. g. gundlachii
    N Cuba, Inagua I, Caicos I
  M. g. hillii
    Jamaica
Mimus thenca (Chilean Mockingbird)
    C Chile
Mimus longicaudatus (Long-tailed Mockingbird)
  M. l. platensis
    La Plata I, W Ecuador
  M. l. albogriseus
    SW Ecuador, N Peru
  M. l. longicaudatus
    W Peru
  M. l. maranonicus
    NE Peru
Mimus saturninus (Chalk-browed Mockingbird)
  M. s. saturninus
    N Brazil
  M. s. arenaceus
    NE Brazil
  M. s. frater
    N Bolivia, SW Brazil
  M. s. modulator
    SE Bolivia, S Brazil, Uruguay, N Argentina
Mimus patagonicus (Patagonian Mockingbird)
    W & S Argentina, S Chile
Mimus triurus (White-banded Mockingbird)
    E Bolivia, S Brazil, Paraguay, Uruguay,
    Argentina
Mimus dorsalis (Brown-backed Mockingbird)
    Bolivia, NW Argentina

NESOMIMUS
Nesomimus trifasciatus (Galapagos Mockingbird)
  N. t. trifasciatus
    Gardner I, Champion I, Galapagos Is
  N. t. macdonaldi
    Hood I, Gardner I
  N. t. melanotis
    Chatham I

N. t. parvulus
  Narboro' I, Albemarle I, Daphne I,
    Seymour I, Indefatigable I
N. t. barringtoni
  Barrington I
N. t. personatus
  Abingdon I, Bindloe I, James I, Jervis I
N. t. wenmani
  Wenman I
N. t. hulli
  Culpeper I
N. t. bauri
  Tower I

MIMODES
Mimodes graysoni (Socorro Thrasher)
  Socorro I, Revillagigedo Is

OREOSCOPTES
Oreoscoptes montanus (Sage Thrasher)
  W & SW USA, Baja California

TOXOSTOMA
Toxostoma rufum (Brown Thrasher)
T. r. rufum
  SE Canada, NC, E & SE USA
T. r. longicauda
  SC Canada, C & S USA
Toxostoma longirostre (Long-billed Thrasher)
T. l. sennetti
  S Texas, NE Mexico
T. l. longirostre
  E Mexico
Toxostoma guttatum (Cozumel Thrasher)
  Cozumel I
Toxostoma cinereum (Grey Thrasher)
T. c. mearnsi
  W Baja California
T. c. cinereum
  S Baja California
Toxostoma bendirei (Bendire Thrasher)
T. b. bendirei
  SW USA, NW Mexico
T. b. candida
  CW Sonora, Mexico
T. b. rubricatum
  SE Sonora, Mexico
Toxostoma ocellatum (Ocellated Thrasher)
  SC Mexico
Toxostoma curvirostre (Curve-billed Thrasher)
T. c. palmeri
  S Arizona, N Sonora, Mexico
T. c. insularum
  San Esteban I, Tiburon I
T. c. maculatum
  NW Mexico
T. c. occidentale
  WC Mexico

T. c. celsum
  S USA, NC Mexico
T. c. curvirostre
  C & SC Mexico
T. c. oberholseri
  S Texas, NE Mexico
Toxostoma lecontei (Le Conte Thrasher)
T. l. lecontei
  SW USA, NW Mexico, N Baja California
T. l. macmillanorum
  S California
T. l. arenicola
  W Baja California
Toxostoma redivivum (California Thrasher)
T. r. sonomae
  N California
T. r. redivivum
  S California, NW Baja California
Toxostoma dorsale (Crissal Thrasher)
T. d. coloradense
  SW USA, NW Mexico, Baja California
T. d. dorsale
  SW USA, N Mexico
T. d. trinitatis
  N Baja California
T. d. dumosum
  NC Mexico

CINCLOCERTHIA
Cinclocerthia ruficauda (Brown Trembler)
C. r. pavida
  NW Leeward Is
C. r. tremula
  Guadeloupe I
C. r. ruficauda
  Dominica I
C. r. gutteralis
  Martinique I
C. r. macrorhyncha
  St Lucia I
C. r. tenebrosa
  St Vincent I

RAMPHOCINCLUS
Ramphocinclus brachyurus (White-breasted Trembler)
R. b. brachyurus
  Martinique I
R. b. sanctaeluciae
  St Lucia I

DONACOBIUS
Donacobius atricapillus (Black-capped Mockingthrush)
D. a. brachypterus
  E Panama, N Colombia
D. a. nigrodorsalis
  SE Colombia, E Ecuador, E Peru

D. a. atricapillus
Venezuela, the Guianas, Brazil, Paraguay'
NE Argentina
D. a. albovittatus
E Bolivia

ALLENIA
Allenia fusca (Scaly-breasted Thrasher)
Lesser Antilles

MARGAROPS
Margarops fuscatus (Pearly-eyed Thrasher)
M. f. fuscatus
S Bahama Is, Hispaniola, Puerto Rico,
N Leeward Is
M. f. densirostris
S Leeward Is
M. f. bonairensis
Bonaire I, Los Hermanos Is, N Venezuela

129 PRUNELLIDAE (ACCENTORS)
PRUNELLA
Prunella collaris (Alpine Accentor)
P. c. collaris
SW Europe, N Africa, W Mediterranean Is
P. c. subalpina
SE Europe, Crete, W Turkey
P. c. montana
Caucasus, S Iran, N Iraq
P. c. rufilata
Tadzhikistan, W Sinkiang, N Afghanistan
P. c. whymperi
NW India, W Himalayas
P. c. nipalensis
E Sinkiang, E Himalayas, SE Tibet,
SW China
P. c. tibetana
E Tibet, NW China
P. c. erythropygia
Altai, N China, Korea, Japan
P. c. fennelli
Taiwan
Prunella himalayana (Himalayan Accentor)
C Asia, Pakistan, N India, Himalayas
Prunella rubeculoides (Robin Accentor)
P. r. rubeculoides
N India, Pakistan, Himalayas, SE Tibet
P. r. fusca
E Tibet, W China
Prunella strophiata (Rufous-breasted Accentor)
P. s. jerdoni
NW Himalayas
P. s. strophiata
E Himalayas, N Burma, W China
Prunella montanella (Mountain Accentor)
Siberia, Mongolia, Korea
Prunella fulvescens (Brown Accentor)
P. f. fulvescens
Tien Shan, Afghanistan, Pakistan

P. f. dahurica
Altai, Mongolia
P. f. dresseri
SW Sinkiang, N Tibet
P. f. nanschanica
Nan Shan Mountains
P. f. khamensis
NE Tibet, W China
P. f. suinkini
S & SE Tibet
Prunella ocularis (Radde's Accentor)
P. o. ocularis
Iran, S Russia, NE Turkey
P. o. fagani
Yemen
Prunella atrogularis (Black-throated Accentor)
P. a. atrogularis
Ural Mts, Iran
P. a. huttoni
Altai, Sinkiang, Pakistan, W Himalayas
Prunella koslowi (Koslov's Accentor)
Mongolia, Ningsia
Prunella modularis (Dunnock)
P. m. hebridium
Ireland, W Scotland
P. m. occidentalis
E Scotland, England, W France
P. m. modularis
Scandinavia, E & C Europe, N Africa,
Turkey
P. m. mabbotti
Iberian peninsula, SW France
P. m. obscura
E Caucasus, N Iran, Lebanon
P. m. euxina
N Turkey, W Caucasus
Prunella rubida (Japanese Hedge Sparrow)
P. r. rubida
S Kurile Is, N Hokkaido I
P. r. fervida
Honshu I, Kyushu I, Japan
Prunella immaculata (Maroon-backed Accentor)
SE Tibet, N Burma, W China

Muscicapidae

130 TURDINAE (THRUSHES, CHATS)

BRACHYPTERYX
Brachypteryx stellata (Gould's Shortwing)
B. s. stellata
E Himalayas, SE Tibet, NE Burma
B. s. fusca
N Vietnam

Brachypteryx hyperythra (Rusty-bellied Shortwing)
E Himalayas, Assam
Brachypteryx major (White-bellied Shortwing)
B. m. major
Mysore, W Madras
B. m. albiventris
Kerala, SW Madras
Brachypteryx calligyna (Celebes Shortwing)
B. c. simplex
N Celebes
B. c. calligyna
SC Celebes
B. c. picta
SE Celebes
Brachypteryx leucophrys (Lesser Shortwing)
B. l. nipalensis
Himalayas, Burma, W Yunnan
B. l. carolinae
S China, N Thailand, N Indochina
B. l. langbianensis
S Indochina
B. l. wrayi
Malaysia
B. l. leucophrys
Sumatra, Java, Lesser Sunda Is, Timor I
Brachypteryx montana (Blue Shortwing)
B. m. cruralis
E Himalayas, N Burma, W China »
N Indochina
B. m. sinensis
NW Fukien
B. m. goodfellowi
Taiwan
B. m. sillimani
S Palawan I
B. m. poliogyna
Luzon I, Mindoro I
B. m. andersoni
Mt Isarog (S Luzon)
B. m. brunneiceps
Negros I
B. m. malindangensis
Mt Malindang (Mindanao I)
B. m. mindanensis
Mt Apo (Mindanao I)
B. m. erythrogyna
N Borneo
B. m. saturata
Sumatra
B. m. montana
Java
B. m. floris
Flores I

Erythropygia coryphaeus (Karroo Scrub Robin)
E. c. coryphaeus
Namibia, Botswana, W Cape Province
E. c. cinerea
SE Namibia, SW Cape Province
E. c. curina
Orange Free State
Erythropygia leucoptera (White-winged Scrub Robin)
S Sudan to Somalia, N Kenya, N Uganda
Erythropygia leucophrys (White-browed Scrub Robin)
E. l. eluta
S Somalia
E. l. brunneiceps
C Kenya, N Tanzania
E. l. vulpina
SC Kenya
E. l. zambesiana
E Kenya to S Mozambique, E Zambia
E. l. munda
N Angola, S Zaire, W Zambia
E. l. ovamboensis
S Angola, SW Zambia, N Namibia
E. l. makalaka
E Botswana, W Rhodesia
E. l. limpopoensis
NE Transvaal, SE Rhodesia,
S Mozambique
E. l. pectoralis
SW Rhodesia, Transvaal, Swaziland
E. l. leucophrys
Natal, S & E Cape Province
Erythropygia hartlaubi (Brown-backed Scrub Robin)
E. h. hartlaubi
Cameroun to W Kenya, N Angola
E. h. kenia
C Kenya
Erythropygia galactotes (Rufous Bushchat)
E. g. galactotes
W Mediterranean, N Africa » S Sahara
E. g. syriaca
E Mediterranean, Middle East » E Africa
E. g. familiaris
S Saudi Arabia, Iran to NW India
E. g. minor
Senegal to Sudan & Ethiopia
E. g. hamertoni
N Somalia
Erythropygia paena (Kalahari Sandy Scrub Robin)
E. p. benguellensis
S Angola

E. p. paena
Rhodesia, Botswana, W Transvaal,
N Cape Province
E. p. damarensis
Namibia
E. p. oriens
S Transvaal to N Cape Province
**Erythropygia leucosticta (Western
Bearded Scrub Robin)**
E. l. leucosticta
Sierra Leone to Ghana
E. l. collsi
NE Zaire
E. l. reichenowi
N Angola
**Erythropygia quadrivirgata (Eastern
Bearded Scrub Robin)**
E. q. erlangeri
Juba river, Somalia
E. q. quadrivirgata
E Kenya to Transvaal, C Mozambique
E. q. interna
SE Zambia, Rhodesia
E. q. wilsoni
SE Transvaal, Natal, S Mozambique
E. q. brunnea
NC Tanzania
E. q. greenwayi
Mafia I, Zanzibar
**Erythropygia barbata (Central Bearded
Scrub Robin)**
E. b. thamnodytes
NE Angola, S Zaire, N Zambia
E. b. barbata
Angola, NW Zambia
Erythropygia signata (Brown Scrub Robin)
E. s. oatleyi
N Transvaal
E. s. tongensis
N Natal
E. s. reclusa
W Natal
E. s. signata
E Cape Province, S Natal

NAMIBORNIS
Namibornis herero (Herero Chat)
Namibia

CERCOTRICHAS
Cercotrichas podobe (Black Bush Robin)
C. p. podobe
Senegal to N Scmalia
C. p. melanoptera
W Saudi Arabia, Yemen, Aden

PINARORNIS
Pinarornis plumosus (Boulder Chat)
E Zambia, Rhodesia, Mozambique

CHAETOPS
Chaetops frenatus (Rufous Rockjumper)
C. f. frenatus
W Cape Province

C. f. aurantius
Natal, E Cape Province

DRYMODES
**Drymodes brunneopygia (Southern Scrub
Robin)**
D. b. brunneopygia
Interior of New South Wales, Victoria,
E South Australia
D. b. pallidus
S & W South Australia
**Drymodes superciliaris (Northern Scrub
Robin)**
D. s. beccarii
NW New Guinea
D. s. nigriceps
WC New Guinea
D. s. brevirostris
Aru Is, S New Guinea
D. s. colcloughi
Northern Territory
D. s. superciliaris
N Queensland

POGONOCICHLA
Pogonocichla stellata (Starred Robin)
P. s. ruwenzorii
Kivu area, NE Zaire
P. s. elgonensis
Mt Elgon (Kenya)
P. s. keniensis
N Uganda
P. s. pallidiflava
S Sudan
P. s. friedmanni
Kigezi, Uganda
P. s. guttifer
S Sudan, Kenya, NE Tanzania
P. s. macarthuri
Chyulu Mts (SE Kenya)
P. s. orientalis
Malawi, Zambia, Tanzania, Mozambique
P. s. hygrica
SC Mozambique
P. s. transvaalensis
NE Transvaal, SW Mozambique
P. s. lebombo
Swaziland
P. s. margaritata
C Natal
P. s. stellata
S Natal, Cape Province
**Pogonocichla swynnertoni (Swynnerton's
Bush Robin)**
P. s. swynnertoni
E Rhodesia
P. s. rodgersi
Morogoro, E Tanzania
P. s. umbratica
W Mozambique

Erithacus gabela (Gabela Akelat)
Angola
Erithacus cyornithopsis (Common Akelat)
E. c. houghtoni
Sierra Leone, Liberia
E. c. cyornithopsis
S Cameroun
E. c. lopezi
NE Zaire, Uganda
E. c. pallidigularis
W Kenya
E. c. acholiensis
S Sudan
Erithacus aequatorialis (Jackson's Akelat)
E Zaire, S Uganda, W Kenya
Erithacus erythrothorax (Forest Robin)
E. e. erythrothorax
Sierra Leone to S Nigeria
E. e. gabonensis
Fernando Po I, W Gabon
E. e. xanthogaster
S Cameroun, N Zaire
E. e. mabirae
E Zaire, Uganda
Erithacus sharpei (Sharpe's Akelat)
E. s. usambarae
C Tanzania
E. s. sharpei
SW Tanzania, N Malawi
Erithacus gunningi (East Coast Akelat)
E. g. sokokensis
E Kenya, E Tanzania
E. g. bensoni
NW Malawi
E. g. gunningi
C Mozambique
Erithacus rubecula (European Robin)
E. r. melophilus
British Isles
E. r. rubecula
W Europe, NW Morocco » NE Africa
E. r. superbus
Teneriffe I, Gd Canary I
E. r. witherbyi
E Algeria, Tunisia
E. r. sardus
Corsica, Sardinia
E. r. balcanicus
Balkans, Turkey
E. r. hyrcanus
E Turkey, S Russia » Iran, Iraq
E. r. tataricus
W Siberia » Iran
Erithacus akahige (Japanese Robin)
E. a. akahige
Sakhalin I, N Japan » S China
E. a. rishirensis
Rishiri Is

E. a. tanensis
S Japan & Is
Erithacus komadori (Riukiu Robin)
E. k. komadori
Tanegashima I, N Riukiu Is
E. k. namiyei
Okinawa I
E. k. subrufus
S Riukiu Is
Erithacus sibilans (Swinhoe's Robin)
SE Siberia, N China » S China
Erithacus luscinia (Thrush Nightingale)
Europe, W Asia » SC Africa
Erithacus megarhynchos (Nightingale)
E. m. megarhynchos
W Europe, N Africa » W & C Africa
E. m. africanus
Syria, SW Iran » E Africa
E. m. hafizi
C Asia » E Africa
Erithacus calliope (Siberian Rubythroat)
Siberia » S China, India
Erithacus svecicus (Bluethroat)
E. s. svecicus
N Europe, N Asia » India, China
E. s. cyaneculus
C Europe » N Africa
E. s. volgae
SW Russia
E. s. luristanicus
Iran » Iraq, Sudan
E. s. pallidogularis
Turkistan, W Siberia » India
E. s. abbotti
Pakistan, NW India
E. s. saturatior
C Asia to E Tibet, Afghanistan
Erithacus pectoralis (Himalayan Rubythroat)
E. p. pectoralis
S Russia, W Himalayas » NW India
E. p. confusus
E Himalayas » NE India
E. p. tschebaiewi
Tibet, NW China » Assam, Burma
Erithacus ruficeps (Rufous-headed Robin)
SW Shensi
Erithacus obscurus (Black-throated Blue Robin)
SW Shensi, SE Kansu
Erithacus pectardens (David's Rubythroat)
SE Tibet, SW China
Erithacus brunneus (Indian Bluechat)
E. b. brunneus
Pakistan, N India, » S India
E. b. wickhami
Chin hills, Burma

Erithacus cyane **(Siberian Blue Robin)**
E. c. cyane
  C Siberia » SE Asia
E. c. bochaiensis
  E Siberia, Japan » Malaysia, Borneo
Erithacus cyanurus **(Red-flanked Bluetail)**
E. c. cyanurus
  N Russia, N Japan » S China
E. c. pallidior
  Pakistan, NW India
E. c. rufilatus
  Himalayas, W China » Burma, Indochina
Erithacus chrysaeus **(Golden Bush Robin)**
E. c. whistleri
  Pakistan, NW India
E. c. chrysaeus
  Nepal, NE India, W China » N Vietnam
Erithacus indicus **(White-browed Bush Robin)**
E. i. indicus
  E Himalayas, NE India
E. i. yunnanensis
  W China » N Burma, N Indochina
E. i. formosanus
  Taiwan
Erithacus hyperythrus **(Rufous-breasted Bush Robin)**
  Himalayas, N Burma, SE Tibet
Erithacus johnstoniae **(Collared Bush Robin)**
  Taiwan

COSSYPHA
Cossypha roberti **(White-bellied Robin Chat)**
C. r. roberti
  S Cameroun, Fernando Po I
C. r. rufescentior
  E Zaire
Cossypha natalensis **(Red-capped Robin Chat)**
C. n. intensa
  S Sudan & Ethiopia to Zambia & Mozambique
C. n. larischi
  N Angola
C. n. garguensis
  Mt Gargues (Kenya)
C. n. tennenti
  Mt Endau (Kenya)
C. n. natalensis
  Natal, Cape Province
C. n. egregior
  S Mozambique
C. n. hylophona
  Malawi
Cossypha dichroa **(Chorister Robin Chat)**
  E Transvaal, Natal, S Cape Province

Cossypha semirufa **(Black-tailed Robin Chat)**
C. s. semirufa
  S & W Ethiopia, SE Sudan, N Kenya
C. s. donaldsoni
  E & SE Ethiopia
C. s. intercedens
  C & S Kenya, N Tanzania
Cossypha heuglini **(White-browed Robin Chat)**
C. h. pallidior
  Chad
C. h. heuglini
  S Sudan, Ethiopia to Zambia, Malawi
C. h. subrufescens
  Gabon, W Zaire
C. h. intermedia
  E Somalia, E Kenya, E Tanzania
C. h. euronota
  N Natal, E Transvaal, Rhodesia, Mozambique
Cossypha cyanocampter **(Blue-shouldered Robin Chat)**
C. c. cyanocampter
  Sierra Leone to Cameroun, Gabon
C. c. bartteloti
  NE Zaire, Uganda, Kenya
C. c. pallidiventris
  N Nandi, Kenya
Cossypha caffra **(Cape Robin Chat)**
C. c. iolaema
  S Sudan to Zambia & Mozambique
C. c. kivuensis
  Kivu area (E Zaire)
C. c. drakensbergi
  E Transvaal
C. c. vespera
  E Rhodesia
C. c. namaquensis
  S Namibia, W Transvaal
C. c. caffra
  Natal, Swaziland, Cape Province
Cossypha humeralis **(White-throated Robin Chat)**
C. h. humeralis
  Rhodesia
C. h. crepuscula
  E Transvaal, Natal, S Mozambique
Cossypha ansorgei **(Ansorge's Robin Chat)**
  W Angola
Cossypha niveicapilla **(Snowy-headed Robin Chat)**
C. n. niveicapilla
  Senegal to Sudan & SW Ethiopia
C. n. melanonota
  NW Cameroun, Gabon, Zaire
Cossypha heinrichi **(Rand's Robin Chat)**
  N Angola, W Zaire

Cossypha albicapilla (White-crowned Robin Chat)
C. a. albicapilla
Senegal to Guinea
C. a. giffardi
Ghana to N Cameroun
C. a. omoensis
SE Sudan, SW Ethiopia

DRYOCICHLOIDES

Dryocichloides anomala (Olive-flanked Robin Chat)
D. a. mbuluensis
Mbulu dis (N Tanzania)
D. a. albigularis
S Tanzania
D. a. macclounii
N Malawi, SW Tanzania
D. a. anomala
Milanje, Malawi
D. a. gurue
N Mozambique

Dryocichloides bocagei (Rufous-cheeked Robin Chat)
D. b. insulana
Fernando Po I
D. b. granti
Mt Kupé (Cameroun)
D. b. kaboboensis
Kivu area (E Zaire)
D. b. kungwensis
W Tanzania
D. b. schoutedeni
E Zaire
D. b. chapini
NW Zambia
D. b. bocagei
SW Zaire, W Angola
D. b. hallae
SE Zaire

Dryocichloides polioptera (Grey-winged Robin Chat)
D. p. polioptera
S Sudan, Uganda, N Angola
D. p. nigriceps
Sierra Leone to W Cameroun
D. p. tessmanni
E Cameroun
D. p. grimwoodi
NW Zambia

Dryocichloides archeri (Archer's Robin Chat)
D. a. archeri
NE Zaire, W Uganda
D. a. albimentalis
Kivu area (E Zaire)
D. a. kimbutui
Mt Kabobo (SE Zaire)

Dryocichloides isabellae (Mountain Robin Chat)
D. i. batesi
E Nigeria

D. i. isabellae
Cameroun Mt

Dryocichloides montana (Usambara Robin Chat)
Usambara Mts, NE Tanzania

Dryocichloides lowei (Iringa Robin Chat)
S Tanzania, N Malawi

MODULATRIX

Modulatrix stictigula (Spot Throat)
M. s. stictigula
N Tanzania
M. s. pressa
N Malawi, SW Tanzania

Modulatrix orostruthus (Dappled Mountain Robin)
M. o. amani
N Tanzania
M. o. orostruthus
N Mozambique
M. o. sanjei
Morogoro, E Tanzania

CICHLADUSA

Cichladusa guttata (Spotted Morning Warbler)
C. g. guttata
S Sudan to SE Kenya, N Tanzania
C. g. rufipennis
SE Ethiopia, E Kenya, E Tanzania

Cichladusa arquata (Collared Morning Warbler)
SE Zaire, S Kenya to Zambia &
Mozambique

Cichladusa ruficauda (Red-tailed Morning Warbler)
Gabon to N Angola

ALETHE

Alethe diademata (White-tailed Alethe)
Guinea to Togo

Alethe castanea (Fire-crested Alethe)
A. c. castanea
Nigeria to Zaire
A. c. woosnami
E Zaire, Uganda

Alethe poliophrys (Red-throated Alethe)
A. p. poliophrys
NE Zaire
A. p. kaboboensis
E Zaire

Alethe fuelleborni (White-chested Alethe)
A. f. usambarae
E. Tanzania
A. f. fuelleborni
SW Tanzania, N Malawi
A. f. xuthera
S Mozambique

Alethe poliocephala (Brown-chested Alethe)
A. p. castanonota
Sierra Leone to Ghana
A. p. poliocephala
Fernando Po I, S Cameroun to N Angola

A. p. hallae
Gabela, Angola
A. p. giloensis
S Sudan
A. p. carruthersi
S Sudan, NE Zaire, Uganda
A. p. nandensis
W Kenya
A. p. akeleyae
C Kenya
A. p. kungwensis
W Tanzania
A. p. ufipae
SW Tanzania
Alethe choloensis (Cholo Mountain Alethe)
A. c. choloensis
E & S Malawi
A. c. namuli
Namuli Mt (Mozambique)

COPSYCHUS
Copsychus saularis (Magpie Robin)
C. s. saularis
Pakistan, N & W India
C. s. ceylonensis
SE India, Sri Lanka
C. s. erimelas
NE India to Thailand & Indochina
C. s. andamanensis
Andaman Is
C. s. prosthopellus
S & E China, Hainan I
C. s. musicus
S Thailand, Malaysia, Sumatra, Billiton I
C. s. nesiotes
Bangka I, SE Sumatra
C. s. zacnecus
Simalur I
C. s. nesiarchus
Nias I
C. s. masculus
Batu Is
C. s. pagiensis
Mentawei Is, Siberut I, Sipora I
C. s. javensis
W Java
C. s. amoenus
E Java, Bali I
C. s. problematicus
S & W Borneo
C. s. adamsi
N Borneo, Banguey I
C. s. pluto
Maratua I, E & SE Borneo
C. s. deuteronymus
Luzon I
C. s. mindanensis
S Philippine Is
Copsychus sechellarum (Seychelles Magpie Robin)
Seychelles Is

Copsychus albospecularis (Madagascar Magpie Robin)
C. a. albospecularis
N Madagascar
C. a. inexpectatus
E Madagascar
C. a. pica
W Madagascar
C. a. winterbottomi
SW Madagascar
Copsychus malabaricus (White-rumped Shama
C. m. malabaricus
S India
C. m. leggei
Sri Lanka
C. m. indicus
Nepal, Assam, NE India
C. m. albiventris
Andaman Is
C. m. interpositus
Burma, Thailand, Indochina
C. m. minor
Hainan I
C. m. mallopercnus
Malaysia
C. m. tricolor
Sumatra, W Java
C. m. mirabilis
Prinsen I
C. m. melanurus
N West Sumatra Is
C. m. opisthopelus
S West Sumatra Is
C. m. javanus
WC & C Java
C. m. omissus
E Java
C. m. ochroptilus
Anamba Is
C. m. abbotti
Bangka I, Billiton I
C. m. eumesus
Natuna Is
C. m. suavis
Borneo
C. m. nigricauda
Kangean I
Copsychus stricklandii (Strickland's Shama)
C. s. stricklandii
Banguey I, N Borneo
C. s. barbouri
Maratua I, E Borneo
Copsychus luzoniensis (White-browed Shama
C. l. luzoniensis
Cantaduanes I, Marinduque I, Luzon I
C. l. parvimaculatus
Polillo Is

C. l. superciliaris
Ticao I, Masbate I, Panay I, Negros I
Copsychus niger (Black Shama)
C. n. niger
Calamianes I, Balabac I, Palawan I
C. n. cebuensis
Cebu I
Copsychus pyrrhopygus (Orange-tailed Shama)
Malaysia, Sumatra, Borneo

IRANIA
Irania gutteralis (White-throated Robin)
Asia Minor, S Asia » E Africa

PHOENICURUS
**Phoenicurus alaschanicus (Przewalski's
Redstart)**
W China
**Phoenicurus erythronotus (Eversmann's
Redstart)**
C Asia » Iran, N India
**Phoenicurus caeruleocephalus (Blue-headed
Redstart)**
C Asia, Himalayas
Phoenicurus ochruros (Black Redstart)
P. o. gibraltariensis
Europe, N Africa » Israel, Egypt
P. o. ochruros
Asia Minor, N Iran » Israel, Iraq
P. o. semirufus
Syria, Lebanon » Israel
P. o. phoenicuroides
C Asia » NE Africa, N India
P. o. rufiventris
Himalayas, Tibet, NW China » India, N Burma
**Phoenicurus phoenicurus (Common
Redstart)**
P. p. phoenicurus
Europe, N Africa, C Asia » W & E Africa
P. p. samamisicus
Iran, S Russia » NE Africa
P. p. algeriensis
SW Iberian peninsula, NW Africa
Phoenicurus hodgsoni (Hodgson's Redstart)
W China » Burma, NE India
Phoenicurus frontalis (Blue-fronted Redstart)
N India, Tibet, W China » N Vietnam
**Phoenicurus fuliginosus (Plumbeous Water
Redstart)**
P. f. fuliginosus
Tibet, Himalayas to N Thailand, W China
P. f. affinis
Taiwan
**Phoenicurus leucocephalus (White-
capped Redstart)**
C Asia » India, E China, Indochina

**Phoenicurus schisticeps (White-throated
Redstart)**
Tibet, W China » Assam, N Burma
Phoenicurus auroreus (Daurian Redstart)
P. a. leucopterus
W China, Tibet » NE India, N Indochina
P. a. auroreus
Siberia, N China » Japan & S China
**Phoenicurus moussieri (Moussier's
Redstart)**
Tunisia, Algeria, Morocco
**Phoenicurus erythrogaster (Güldenstadt's
Redstart)**
P. e. erythrogaster
Caucasus, Iran
P. e. grandis
C Asia, Tibet, Pakistan, N India » NE China

RHYACORNIS
**Rhyacornis bicolor (Philippine Water
Redstart)**
N Luzon I

HODGSONIUS
**Hodgsonius phaenicuroides (White-
bellied Redstart)**
H. p. phaenicuroides
Himalayas, N India, Tibet, N Burma
H. p. ichangensis
W China » N Indochina

CINCLIDIUM
**Cinclidium leucurum (White-tailed Blue
Robin)**
C. l. leucurum
India, Indochina, Malaysia, Burma
C. l. cambodianum
Cambodia
Cinclidium diana (Sunda Blue Robin)
C. d. sumatranum
N & WC Sumatra
C. d. diana
Java
Cinclidium frontale (Blue-fronted Callene)
C. f. frontale
Nepal, Sikkim
C. f. orientale
N Indochina

GRANDALA
Grandala coelicolor (Hodgson's Grandala)
N India, Burma, W China

SIALIA
Sialia sialis (Eastern Bluebird)
S. s. sialis
E USA » N Mexico
S. s. grata
S Florida
S. s. fulva
Arizona, N Mexico » Guatemala

S. s. guatemalae
SE Mexico, Guatemala
S. s. meridionalis
El Salvador, Nicaragua
S. s. caribaea
Nicaragua
Sialia mexicana (Western Bluebird)
S. m. occidentalis
W Canada, W USA
S. m. bairdi
SW USA, NW Mexico
S. m. anabelae
N Baja California
S. m. amabilis
C Mexico
S. m. mexicana
NE Mexico
S. m. australis
SC Mexico
Sialia currucoides (Mountain Bluebird)
W Canada, W USA » SW USA, W Mexico

ENICURUS
Enicurus scouleri (Little Forktail)
E. s. scouleri
SE Russia, Himalayas, N India, W China
E. s. fortis
Taiwan
Enicurus velatus (Lesser Forktail)
E. v. sumatranus
Sumatra
E. v. velatus
Java
Enicurus ruficapillus (Chestnut-backed Forktail)
Malaysia, Borneo, Sumatra, S Thailand
Enicurus immaculatus (Black-backed Forktail)
Himalayas, Burma, Thailand
Enicurus schistaceus (Slaty-backed Forktail)
Himalayas, Burma, Thailand, Indochina
Enicurus leschenaulti (White-crowned Forktail)
E. l. indicus
NE India, Burma, Thailand, Indochina
E. l. sinensis
W & S China, Hainan I
E. l. frontalis
Malaysia, Sumatra, Nias I, Borneo
E. l. chaseni
Batu Is, W Sumatra
E. l. leschenaulti
Java, Bali I
E. l. borneensis
W Borneo
Enicurus maculatus (Spotted Forktail)
E. m. maculatus
W & C Himalayas

E. m. guttatus
E Himalayas, SW China
E. m. bacatus
S China, N Indochina
E. m. robinsoni
Dalat, S Vietnam

COCHOA
Cochoa purpurea (Purple Cochoa)
N India to N Vietnam
Cochoa viridis (Green Cochoa)
N India to S China, Indochina
Cochoa azurea (Malaysian Cochoa)
C. a. azurea
W & C Java
C. a. beccarii
W Sumatra

MYADESTES
Myadestes townsendi (Townsend's Solitaire)
M. t. townsendi
W Canada, W USA, W Mexico
M. t. calophonus
N Mexico
Myadestes obscurus (Brown-backed Solitaire)
M. o. obscurus
E Mexico
M. o. cinereus
C Mexico
M. o. occidentalis
N & W Mexico
M. o. insularis
Tres Marias Is
M. o. deignani
Oaxaca, S Chiapas
M. o. oberholseri
S Mexico, Guatemala, El Salvador
Myadestes elisabeth (Cuban Solitaire)
M. e. elisabeth
E & W Cuba
M. e. retrusus
Isle of Pines
Myadestes genibarbis (Rufous-throated Solitaire)
M. g. solitarius
Jamaica
M. g. montanus
Hispaniola
M. g. dominicanus
Dominica I
M. g. genibarbis
Martinique I
M. g. sanctaeluciae
St Lucia I
M. g. sibilans
St Vincent I

Myadestes ralloides (Andean Solitaire)
  M. r. melanops
    Costa Rica, W Panama
  M. r. coloratus
    E Panama
  M. r. plumbeiceps
    W Colombia, W Ecuador
  M. r. candelae
    NC Colombia
  M. r. venezuelensis
    N Venezuela, E Colombia to N Peru
  M. r. ralloides
    C & S Peru, W Bolivia
Myadestes unicolor (Slate-coloured Solitaire)
  M. u. unicolor
    S Mexico, Guatemala, N Honduras
  M. u. pallens
    Nicaragua
Myadestes leucogenys (Rufous-brown Solitaire)
  M. l. gularis
    Guyana
  M. l. chubbi
    W Ecuador
  M. l. peruvianus
    C Peru
  M. l. leucogenys
    SE Brazil

ENTOMODESTES
Entomodestes leucotis (White-eared Solitaire)
  Peru, Bolivia
Entomodestes coracinus (Black Solitaire)
  W Colombia, W Ecuador

STIZORHINA
Stizorhina fraseri (Rufous Broad-billed Ant-thrush)
  S. f. fraseri
    Fernando Po I
  S. f. rubicunda
    Cameroun to W Zaire & Angola
  S. f. vulpina
    N & E Zaire
Stizorhina finschii (Finsch's Broad-billed Ant-thrush)
  Sierra Leone to Nigeria

NEOCOSSYPHUS
Neocossyphus rufus (Red-tailed Ant-thrush)
  N. r. rufus
    Tanzania, N Kenya, Zanzibar
  N. r. gabunensis
    S Cameroun to Uganda
Neocossyphus poensis (White-tailed Ant-thrush)
  N. p. poensis
    Sierra Leone to Gabon, Fernando Po I

  N. p. praepectoralis
    N & E Zaire, W Uganda
  N. p. kakamegoes
    Kakamega, W Kenya
  N. p. nigridorsalis
    N Nandi, Kenya
  N. p. pallidigularis
    N Angola

CERCOMELA
Cercomela sinuata (Sicklewing Chat)
  C. s. hypernephela
    Lesotho
  C. s. ensifera
    E Transvaal, Orange Free State, N Cape Province
  C. s. sinuata
    S Cape Province
Cercomela familiaris (Familiar Chat)
  C. f. falkensteini
    Ghana to SW Sudan, N Ethiopia
  C. f. omoensis
    SE Sudan, SW Ethiopia
  C. f. modesta
    Uganda to Angola & Mozambique
  C. f. angolensis
    N Angola, N Namibia
  C. f. hoeschi
    NW Namibia
  C. f. galtoni
    E Namibia, W Botswana, N Cape Province
  C. f. hellmayri
    E Botswana, Rhodesia, Transvaal
  C. f. actuosa
    W Natal
  C. f. familiaris
    S Mozambique, Natal to S Cape Province
  C. f. richardi
    NW Cape Province
  C. f. dodsoni
    E Cape Province
Cercomela tractrac (Layard's Chat)
  C. t. hoeschi
    S Angola, N Namibia
  C. t. albicans
    N coastal Namibia
  C. t. barlowi
    Gt Namaqualand
  C. t. nebulosa
    S coastal Namibia
  C. t. tractrac
    Little Namaqualand
Cercomela schlegelii (Karroo Chat)
  C. s. benguellensis
    S Angola
  C. s. schlegelii
    coastal Namibia

C. s. namaquensis
Little Namaqualand
C. s. kobosensis
C Great Namaqualand
C. s. pollux
Orange Free State, Cape Province
Cercomela fusca (Brown Rockchat)
Pakistan, N & C India
Cercomela dubia (Sombre Rockchat)
Somalia, C Ethiopia
Cercomela melanura (Blackstart)
C. m. melanura
Israel to Saudi Arabia
C. m. neumanni
W Saudi Arabia, Yemen, Aden
C. m. lypura
W Red Sea coast
C. m. aussae
E Ethiopia
C. m. airensis
E Niger, Chad, Sudan
C. m. ultima
E Mali, W Niger
Cercomela scotocerca (Brown-tailed Rockchat)
C. s. furensis
W Sudan
C. m. scotocerca
Sudan coast
C. s. turkana
SW Ethiopia, NW Kenya
C. s. spectatrix
Somalia
C. s. validior
Run, Somalia
Cercomela sordida (Hill Chat)
C. s. sordida
Ethiopia
C. s. rudolfi
Mt Elgon (Kenya)
C. s. ernesti
Aberdare Mts, Mt Kenya
C. s. olimotiensis
N Tanzania
C. s. hypospodia
Mt Kilimanjaro (Tanzania)

SAXICOLA
Saxicola rubetra (Whinchat)
Europe, Asia, N Africa » W & C Africa
Saxicola macrorhyncha (Stoliczka's Bushchat)
S Afghanistan, N India
Saxicola insignis (Hodgson's Bushchat)
Russia, W China, Tibet » N India
Saxicola dacotiae (Canary Islands Chat)
S. d. dacotiae
Fuerteventura I

S. d. murielae
Allegranza I
Saxicola torquata (Stonechat)
S. t. hibernans
British Isles, W France
S. t. rubicola
W Europe, N Africa » Middle East
S. t. variegata
Asia Minor, NE Africa, Iraq
S. t. armenica
Iran, N Iraq, NE Africa, Saudi Arabia
S. t. maura
E Russia, C Asia » Iran, Iraq, N India
S. t. indica
Himalayas » C India
S. t. przewalskii
W China » Burma, N India
S. t. stejnergeri
E Siberia, Japan » S China, Burma, Indochina
S. t. felix
SW Saudi Arabia, Yemen
S. t. albofasciata
Ethiopia
S. t. jebelmarrae
W Sudan
S. t. moptana
S Mali
S. t. nebularum
Sierra Leone, Ivory Coast
S. t. adamauae
N & W Cameroun
S. t. pallidigula
Cameroun Mt, Fernando Po I
S. t. axillaris
E Zaire, Uganda, Kenya, N Tanzania
S. t. promiscua
C Tanzania
S. t. salax
Cameroun to N Angola & Rhodesia
S. t. stonei
Angola to Mozambique, N South Africa
S. t. clanceyi
W Namibia, NW Cape Province
S. t. torquata
SW Cape Province to Natal, Transvaal
S. t. oreobates
S Rhodesia, W Natal, Orange Free State
S. t. sibilla
Madagascar
S. t. voeltzkowi
Gt Comoro I
S. t. tectes
Réunion I
Saxicola leucura (White-tailed Stonechat)
Pakistan, N India

Saxicola caprata (Pied Stonechat)
S. c. rossorum
　SW Asia » Iran & Pakistan
S. c. bicolor
　Pakistan » N & C India
S. c. burmanica
　C India, Burma, N Thailand, Indochina
S. c. nilgiriensis
　S India
S. c. atrata
　Sri Lanka
S. c. caprata
　Luzon I, Mindoro I, Cebu I
S. c. randi
　Negros I, Bohol I, Siquijor I
S. c. anderseni
　C Mindanao I
S. c. fruticola
　Java I to Flores I & Alor I
S. c. pyrrhonota
　Kisser I, Wetar I, Savu Is, Timor I
S. c. francki
　Sumba I
S. c. albonotata
　Saleyer I, Celebes
S. c. cognata
　Babar I
S. c. aethiops
　New Britain, N New Guinea
S. c. belensis
　WC New Guinea
S. c. wahgiensis
　EC & E New Guinea
Saxicola jerdoni (Jerdon's Bushchat)
　E India, Burma, N Indochina
Saxicola ferrea (Grey Bushchat)
　Himalayas to S China »
　　S Indochina
Saxicola gutturalis (Timor Bushchat)
S. g. gutturalis
　Timor I
S. g. luctuosa
　Semau I

MYRMECOCICHLA
Myrmecocichla tholloni (Congo Moorchat)
　Gabon, N Angola
Myrmecocichla aethiops (Anteater Chat)
M. a. aethiops
　Senegal to Chad, N Nigeria, N Cameroun
M. a. sudanensis
　W Sudan
M. a. cryptoleuca
　C Kenya, N Tanzania
Myrmecocichla formicivora (Southern Anteater Chat)
M. f. formicivora
　E Botswana, Natal, C & E Cape Province

403

M. f. minor
　W Botswana, Namibia
Myrmecocichla nigra (Sooty Chat)
　Nigeria to Sudan, Angola, Tanzania
Myrmecocichla arnotti (White-headed Black Chat)
M. a. leucolaema
　SE Zaire, W Tanzania
M. a. harterti
　SW Zaire, Angola
M. a. arnotti
　E Angola & Namibia to Malawi,
　　N Transvaal
Myrmecocichla albifrons (White-fronted Black Chat)
M. a. frontalis
　Senegal to Nigeria & Chad
M. a. limbata
　N & E Cameroun, Central African Republic
M. a. albifrons
　N Ethiopia
M. a. pachyrhyncha
　SW Ethiopia
M. a. clericalis
　S Sudan, NE Zaire, N Uganda
Myrmecocichla melaena (Ruppells Chat)
　Ethiopia

THAMNOLAEA
Thamnolaea cinnamomeiventris (Cliffchat)
T. c. cavernicola
　Fiko, Mali
T. c. bambarae
　Kulikoro, Mali
T. c. albiscapulata
　E & S Ethiopia, E Sudan
T. c. subrufipennis
　Sudan & Ethiopia to Zambia & Malawi
T. c. odica
　E Botswana, Transvaal, Rhodesia,
　　Mozambique
T. c. cinnamomeiventris
　E Transvaal, Natal, E Cape Province
T. c. autochthones
　N Natal, S Mozambique
Thamnolaea coronata (White-crowned Cliffchat)
T. c. coronata
　Togo to N Cameroun, W Sudan
T. c. kordofanensis
　C Sudan
Thamnolaea semirufa (White-winged Cliffchat)
　Ethiopia

OENANTHE
Oenanthe bifasciata (Buff-streaked Chat)
　S Transvaal, Natal, Cape Province
Oenanthe isabellina (Isabelline Wheatear)
　E Europe, W China » India, C Africa

***Oenanthe bottae* (Red-breasted Wheatear)**
  O. b. bottae
    Yemen
  O. b. frenata
    Ethiopia
  O. b. heuglini
    Mali, Central African Republic, Sudan
***Oenanthe xanthoprymna* (Red-tailed Wheatear)**
  O. x. xanthoprymna
    SW Iran » NE Africa
  O. x. chrysopygia
    E Turkey, N Iran » Iraq, Saudi Arabia
  O. x. kingi
    Afghanistan » Pakistan, NW India
***Oenanthe oenanthe* (Common Wheatear)**
  O. o. leucorhoa
    Greenland, NE Canada » W Europe,
    W Africa
  O. o. oenanthe
    N & C Europe, N Asia » N & C Africa
  O. o. nivea
    Balearic Is, S Spain
  O. o. virago
    E Mediterranean Is » Israel, Egypt
  O. o. seebohmi
    Morocco, Algeria
  O. o. libanotica
    S Europe, NW Africa
  O. o. phillipsi
    Somalia
***Oenanthe deserti* (Desert Wheatear)**
  O. d. homochroa
    N Africa
  O. d. deserti
    W & C Asia » Pakistan, N India, NE Africa
  O. d. oreophila
    Tibet & Sinkiang » Pakistan, Saudi Arabia
***Oenanthe hispanica* (Black-eared Wheatear)**
  O. h. hispanica
    S Europe, N Africa » W Africa
  O. h. melanoleuca
    E Europe, Asia Minor » NE & W Africa
***Oenanthe finschii* (Finsch's Wheatear)**
  O. f. finschii
    Turkey, Saudi Arabia » Iran, Pakistan
  O. f. barnesi
    NE Iran, C Asia » S Iran, Pakistan
***Oenanthe picata* (Eastern Pied Wheatear)**
  Iran, Pakistan » N India
***Oenanthe lugens* (Mourning Wheatear)**
  O. l. halophila
    N Africa
  O. l. lugens
    N Egypt, Israel, Iraq

  O. l. persica
    S Egypt, S Israel, S Iran, N Sudan
  O. l. lugentoides
    SW Saudi Arabia, Yemen
  O. l. boscaweni
    S Saudi Arabia
  O. l. vauriei
    NE Somalia
  O. l. lugubris
    N & C Ethiopia
  O. l. schalowi
    S Kenya, NE Tanzania
***Oenanthe monacha* (Hooded Wheatear)**
  Egypt to Pakistan
***Oenanthe alboniger* (Hume's Wheatear)**
  S Iran, Afghanistan, Pakistan
***Oenanthe pleschanka* (Pied Wheatear)**
  O. p. pleschanka
    E Europe to W China » E Africa
  O. p. cypriaca
    Cyprus » E & N Africa
***Oenanthe leucopyga* (White-crowned Black Wheatear)**
  O. l. aegra
    Algeria, Tunisia
  O. l. ernesti
    Egypt, Saudi Arabia, Iraq
  O. l. leucopyga
    Mali to Ethiopia
***Oenanthe leucura* (Black Wheatear)**
  O. l. leucura
    W Mediterranean
  O. l. syenitica
    NW Africa
***Oenanthe monticola* (Mountain Chat)**
  O. m. albipileata
    Benguella, Angola
  O. m. nigricauda
    Huambo, Angola
  O. m. atmorii
    W Namibia
  O. m. monticola
    E Namibia, Cape Province
  O. m. griseiceps
    S Botswana, Natal, Transvaal
***Oenanthe moesta* (Red-rumped Wheatear)**
  O. m. moesta
    N Africa
  O. m. brooksbanki
    E Egypt, Jordan, Iraq
***Oenanthe pileata* (Capped Wheatear)**
  Angola to Kenya & Cape Province

SAXICOLOIDES
***Saxicoloides fulicata* (Black-backed Robin)**
  S. f. cambaiensis
    Pakistan, N & W India

S. f. erythrura
  NE India
S. f. intermedia
  C India
S. f. fulicata
  S India
S. f. leucoptera
  Sri Lanka

PSEUDOCOSSYPHUS
Pseudocossyphus imerinus (Madagascar Robin Chat)
P. i. erythronotus
  N Madagascar
P. i. sharpei
  C Madagascar
P. i. imerinus
  SE Madagascar
P. i. salomonseni
  E Madagascar
Pseudocossyphus bensoni (Farkas' Robin Chat)
  SW Madagascar

MONTICOLA
Monticola rupestris (Cape Rock Thrush)
  South Africa
Monticola explorator (Sentinel Rock Thrush)
M. e. explorator
  Transvaal, Natal, Cape Province
M. e. tenebriformis
  Lesotho » N Natal, S Mozambique
Monticola brevipes (Short-toed Rock Thrush)
M. b. niveiceps
  Huila, Angola
M. b. brevipes
  S Angola, Namibia, N Cape Province
M. b. leucocapilla
  S Botswana, W Transvaal, Orange Free State
Monticola rufocinereus (Little Rock Thrush)
M. r. rufocinereus
  Ethiopia, Sudan to NE Tanzania
M. r. sclateri
  W Saudi Arabia
Monticola angolensis (Miombo Rock Thrush)
M. a. angolensis
  S Zaire, Angola to Tanzania, Mozambique
M. a. hylophila
  NW Rhodesia
Monticola saxatilis (Rock Thrush)
M. s. saxatilis
  C & S Europe to W China » N India & E Africa

M. s. coloratus
  E Europe
Monticola cinclorhynchus (Blue-capped Rock Thrush)
  Himalayas » W Burma, S India
Monticola gularis (White-throated Rock Thrush)
  NE Asia » Burma, Thailand, Indochina
Monticola rufiventris (Chestnut-bellied Rock Thrush)
  Himalayas, W China » Indochina
Monticola solitarius (Blue Rock Thrush)
M. s. solitarius
  S Europe, Middle East » W & C Africa
M. s. longirostris
  N Iraq, Iran, Pakistan » N India & NE Africa
M. s. pandoo
  Himalayas, C Asia » India, SE Asia, Indonesia
M. s. philippensis
  NE Russia, China, Japan » Philippine Is, Indonesia
M. s. madoci
  Malaysia

MYIOPHONEUS
Myiophoneus blighi (Ceylon Whistling Thrush)
  Sri Lanka
Myiophoneus melanurus (Shiny Whistling Thrush)
  Sumatra
Myiophoneus glaucinus (Sunda Whistling Thrush)
M. g. glaucinus
  Java, Bali I
M. g. castaneus
  Sumatra
M. g. borneensis
  Borneo
Myiophoneus robinsoni (Malayan Whistling Thrush)
  Malaysia
Myiophoneus horsfieldii (Malabar Whistling Thrush)
  S India
Myiophoneus insularis (Formosan Whistling Thrush)
  Taiwan
Myiophoneus caeruleus (Himalayan Whistling Thrush)
M. c. temminckii
  C Asia, Pakistan, N India, Burma
M. c. eugenei
  S Burma, Thailand, W China, Indochina
M. c. caeruleus
  W China » C & S China, N Indochina

M. c. crassirostris
SE Thailand, N Malaysia
M. c. dichrorhynchus
C & S Malaysia, W Sumatra
M. c. flavirostris
Java

GEOMALIA
Geomalia heinrichi (Celebes Mountain Thrush)
G. h. heinrichi
SC Celebes
G. h. matinangensis
N & SE Celebes

ZOOTHERA
Zoothera schistacea (White-eared Ground Thrush)
Tenimber Is
Zoothera dumasi (Buru Ground Thrush)
Z. d. dumasi
Buru I
Z. d. joiceyi
Ceram I
Zoothera interpres (Kuhl's Ground Thrush)
Z. i. interpres
S Thailand, Sumatra to Flores I,
Borneo, Basilan I
Z. i. leucolaema
Enggano I
Zoothera erythronota (Celebes Ground Thrush)
Z. e. erythronota
Celebes
Z. e. dohertyi
Lombok I to Timor I
Z. e. mendeni
Peling Is
Zoothera wardii (Pied Ground Thrush)
N India» S India, Sri Lanka
Zoothera cinerea (Ashy Ground Thrush)
Mindoro I, N Luzon I
Zoothera peronii (Peroni's Ground Thrush)
Z. p. peronii
W Timor I
Z. p. audacis
N Timor I, Damar I
Zoothera citrina (Orange-headed Ground Thrush)
Z. c. citrina
Pakistan to N Burma » S India, Sri
Lanka
Z. c. cyanotus
S India
Z. c. innotata
Burma, S China, Indochina » Malaysia

Z. c. melli
SE China
Z. c. courtoisi
Anhwei
Z. c. aurimacula
S Vietnam, Hainan I
Z. c. andamanensis
Andaman Is
Z. c. albogularis
Nicobar Is
Z. c. gibsonhilli
S Burma, S Thailand
Z. c. aurata
N Borneo
Z. c. rubecula
W Java
Z. c. orientis
E Java, Bali I
Zoothera everetti (Everett's Ground Thrush)
N Borneo
Zoothera sibirica (Siberian Ground Thrush)
Z. s. sibirica
NE Asia » SE Asia, Java
Z. s. davisoni
Japan » S China, Thailand, Malaysia
Zoothera naevia (Varied Thrush)
Z. n. naevia
SE Alaska, W Canada, NW USA » SW USA
Z. n. meruloides
N Alaska, NW Canada » to WC USA
Zoothera pinicola (Aztec Thrush)
C Mexico
Zoothera piaggiae (Abyssinian Ground Thrush)
Z. p. piaggiae
Ethiopia, Sudan, E Zaire, N Kenya
Z. p. hadii
SE Sudan
Z. p. kilimensis
C & S Kenya, N Tanzania
Z. p. rowei
N Tanzania
Zoothera tanganjicae (Western Orange Ground Thrush)
SW Uganda
Zoothera oberlaenderi (Forest Ground Thrush)
NE Zaire, Uganda
Zoothera gurneyi (Orange Ground Thrush)
Z. g. chuka
Mt Kenya
Z. g. chyulu
SE Kenya
Z. g. otomitra
S Kenya to Angola, N Malawi

Z. g. gurneyi
Natal, E Cape Province
Z. g. disruptans
C & S Malawi, E Rhodesia, N Transvaa
Mozambique
Zoothera kibalensis (Prigogine's Golden Thrush)
W Uganda
Zoothera cameronensis (Black-eared Ground Thrush)
Z. c. cameronensis
Cameroun
Z. c. prigoginei
W Zaire
Zoothera princei (Grey Ground Thrush)
Z. p. princei
Sierra Leone to Ghana
Z. p. batesi
S Cameroun, N Zaire
Z. p. graueri
NE Zaire
Zoothera crossleyi (Crossley's Ground Thrush)
Z. c. crossleyi
Mt Kupé, Cameroun Mt
Z. c. pilettei
NE Zaire
Zoothera guttata (Spotted Ground Thrush)
Z. g. guttata
S Malawi, Natal, Cape Province
Z. g. fischeri
coast of Kenya & Tanzania
Z. g. belcheri
Thyolo Mt, Malawi
Z. g: maxis
S Sudan
Z. g. nataliens
Cape Prov, S Africa
Zoothera spiloptera (Spotted-winged Thrush)
Sri Lanka
Zoothera andromedae (Sunda Ground Thrush)
Sumatra to Timor I, Mindoro I, Mindanao I
Zoothera mollissima (Plain-backed Mountain Thrush)
Z. m. whiteheadi
N Pakistan, W Himalayas
Z. m. mollissima
E Himalayas, SE Tibet » Burma, Indochina
Z. m. griseiceps
SW China, N Vietnam
Zoothera dixoni (Long-tailed Mountain Thrush)
E Himalayas, Tibet » Burma, Thailand, N Vietnam
Zoothera dauma (White's Thrush)
Z. d. aurea
N & NE Asia » S China, Indochina
Z. d. dauma
Himalayas, Burma, China, Thailand » S India

Z. d. neilgherriensis
S India
Z. d. imbricata
Sri Lanka
Z. d. toratugumi
Manchuria, Japan » Taiwan
Z. d. major
N Riukiu Is
Z. d. hancii
S Ruikiu Is,;S Thailand,S Vietnam, Taiwan
Z. d. horsfieldi
Sumatra, Java, Lombok I
Z. d. machiki
Tenimber Is
Z. d. papuensis
SE New Guinea
Z. d. eichhorni
St Matthias Is
Z. d. choiseuli
Choiseul I
Z. d. cuneata
N Queensland
Z. d. heinei
S Queensland
Z. d. lunulata
New South Wales, Victoria, South Australia
Z. d. macrorhyncha
Tasmania
Zoothera talaseae (New Britain Ground Thrush)
New Britain
Zoothera margaretae (San Cristobal Ground Thrush)
Z. m. turipavae
Guadalcanal I
Z. m. margaretae
San Cristobal I
Zoothera monticola (Greater Long-billed Thrush)
Z. m. monticola
Himalayas, Assam, NE Burma
Z. m. atrata
N Vietnam
Zoothera marginata (Lesser Long-billed Thrush)
N India to Indochina

AMALOCICHLA
Amalocichla sclateriana (Greater New Guinea Thrush)
A. s. occidentalis
W New Guinea
A. s. sclateriana
SE New Guinea
Amalocichla incerta (Lesser New Guinea Thrush)
A. i. incerta
Arfak Mts (W New Guinea)
A. i. olivascentior
WC New Guinea

407

A. i. brevicauda
E & SE New Guinea

CATAPONERA
Cataponera turdoides (Cataponera Thrush)
C. t. abditiva
NC Celebes
C. t. tenebrosa
S Celebes
C. t. turdoides
SW Celebes
C. t. heinrichi
SE Celebes

NESOCICHLA
Nesocichla eremita (Tristan Thrush)
N. e. eremita
Tristan da Cunha I
N. e. gordoni
Inaccessible I
N. e. procax
Nightingale I

CICHLHERMINIA
Cichlherminia lherminieri (Forest Thrush)
C. l. lherminieri
Guadeloupe I
C. l. lawrencii
Montserrat I
C. l. dominicensis
Dominica I
C. l. sanctaelucae
St Lucia I

PHAEORNIS
Phaeornis obscurus (Hawaiian Thrush)
P. o. myadestinus
Kauai I
P. o. rutha
Molokai I **e?**
P. o. lanaiensis
Lanai I **e?**
P. o. obscurus
Hawaii I
Phaeornis palmeri (Small Kauai Thrush)
Kauai I

CATHARUS
Catharus gracilirostris (Slender-billed Nightingale Thrush)
C. g. gracilirostris
Costa Rica
C. g. accentor
W Panama
Catharus aurantiirostris (Orange-billed Nightingale Thrush)
C. a. aenopennis
NW Mexico
C. a. clarus
NC Mexico
C. a. melpomene
C Mexico to Costa Rica

C. a. russatus
SW Costa Rica, W Panama
C. a. griseiceps
W Panama
C. a. phaeoplurus
C Colombia
C. a. aurantiirostris
NE Colombia, NW Venezuela
C. a. birchalli
NE Venezuela, Trinidad
C. a. barbaritoi
C Venezuela
C. a. sierrae
Santa Marta Mts (Colombia)
C. a. inornatus
EC Colombia
C. a. insignis
N Colombia
Catharus fuscater (Slaty-backed Nightingale Thrush)
C. f. hellmayri
Costa Rica, W Panama
C. f. mirabilis
E Panama
C. f. sanctaemartae
N Colombia
C. f. fuscater
Ecuador, Colombia, W Venezuela
C. f. opertaneus
W Colombia
C. f. caniceps
N & C Peru
C. f. mentalis
SE Peru, N Bolivia
Catharus occidentalis (Russet Nightingale Thrush)
C. o. olivascens
N Mexico
C. o. durangensis
Durango
C. o. lambi
N Puebla
C. o. fulvescens
C Mexico
C. o. occidentalis
SE Mexico
Catharus frantzii (Frantzius' Nightingale Thrush)
C. f. chiapensis
C Chiapas
C. f. confusus
NE Puebla
C. f. nelsoni
E Oaxaca
C. f. waldroni
N Nicaragua
C. f. wetmorei
Chiriqui, Panama

C. f. juancitonis
S Mexico to Honduras
C. f. frantzii
Costa Rica, W Panama
Catharus mexicanus (Black-headed Nightingale Thrush)
C. m. mexicanus
EC Mexico
C. m. cantator
S Mexico, E Guatemala, Honduras
C. m. fumosus
Nicaragua, Costa Rica, W Panama
Catharus dryas (Spotted Nightingale Thrush)
C. d. harrisoni
Oaxaca
C. d. ovandensis
Chiapas
C. d. dryas
W Guatemala, Honduras, W Ecuador
C. d. maculatus
E Colombia, E Ecuador, Peru, Bolivia
C. d. ecuadoreanus
W Ecuador
C. d. blakei
Jujuy, Argentina
Catharus fuscescens (Veery)
C. f. fuscescens
E Canada, E USA » E Mexico, Panama
NE South America
C. f. fuliginosa
SE Canada » E USA
C. f. salicicola
W Canada, W USA » Mexico & N South America
C. f. subpallidus
NW USA » SW USA
Catharus minimus (Grey-cheeked Thrush)
C. m. minimus
E Siberia, Canada » E USA, N South America
C. m. aliciae
SE Canada » E USA, West Indies
Catharus ustulatus (Swainson's Thrush)
C. u. almae
S Alaska, W Canada » S USA
C. u. ustulatus
SE Alaska,W Canada » W USA, Mexico
C. u. oedicus
W USA » Mexico
C. u. swainsoni
C & E Canada, E USA » S Mexico, West Indies, E South America
Catharus guttatus (Hermit Thrush)
C. g. guttatus
Alaska, W Canada » W USA, N & C Mexico

C. g. nanus
SE Alaska, W Canada » W USA, Baja California
C. g. slevini
W USA » NW Mexico
C. g. sequoiensis
W USA » N Mexico
C. g. polionotus
W USA » S Mexico
C. g. auduboni
W & SW USA » Mexico, Guatemala
C. g. faxoni
Canada, E USA » SE USA
C. g. crymophilus
Newfoundland » SE USA

HYLOCICHLA
Hylocichla mustelina (Wood Thrush)
SE Canada, E USA » E Mexico, Cuba, Central America

PLATYCICHLA
Platycichla flavipes (Yellow-legged Thrush)
P. f. venezuelensis
Colombia, N & W Venezuela
P. f. melanopleura
NE Venezuela, Trinidad
P. f. xanthoscelus
Tobago I
P. f. polionota
S Venezuela, Guyana
P. f. flavipes
SE Brazil, Argentina, NE Paraguay
Platycichla leucops (Pale-eyed Thrush)
N South America

TURDUS
Turdus bewsheri (Comoro Thrush)
T. b. comorensis
Great Comoro I
T. b. moheliensis
Moheli I
T. b. bewsheri
Anjouan I
Turdus olivaceofuscus (Sao Thomé Thrush)
T. o. olivaceofuscus
Sao Thomé I
T. o. xanthorhynchus
Principé I
Turdus olivaceus (Olive Thrush)
T. o. chiguancoides
Senegal to W Ghana
T. o. saturatus
W Ghana to N Zaire
T. o. adamauae
N Cameroun
T. o. nigrilorum
Cameroun Mt

T. o. poensis
Fernando Po I
T. o. bocagei
S Zaire, N Angola, NW Tanzania
T. o. centralis
N Zaire, Uganda, Central African Republic
T. o. pelios
Sudan, Ethiopia
T. o. graueri
S Uganda, NW Tanzania
T. o. stormsi
SE Zaire, NE Angola, NW Zambia
T. o. williami
Zambia
T. o. swynnertoni
E Rhodesia
T. o. transvaalensis
N Transvaal
T. o. smithi
N Cape Province, Orange Free State,
Transvaal
T. o. olivaceus
SW Cape Province
T. o. pondoensis
Transkei, Natal, Swaziland
Turdus abyssinicus (Mountain Thrush)
(Northern Olive Thrush)
T. a. abyssinicus
Ethiopia, W Kenya, NE Tanzania
T. a. baraka
E Zaire, W & S Uganda
T. a. polius
N Kenya
T. a. mwaki
NW Kenya
T. a. porini
W Kenya
T. a. elgonensis
WC Kenya
T. a. deckeni
NE Tanzania
T. a. oldeani
NE Tanzania
T. a. bambusicola
· Ruanda, Kivu (E Zaire)
T. a. roehli
NE Tanzania
T. a. nyikae
C Tanzania, Malawi, NE Zambia
T. a. milanjensis
S Malawi, Mozambique
Turdus helleri (Taita Olive Thrush)
SE Kenya
Turdus libonyanus (Kurrichane Thrush)
T. l. verreauxi
S Zaire, Angola, N Namibia
T. l. chobiensis
E Namibia, Zambia, NW Rhodesia
T. l. libonyanus
E Botswana, Transvaal, N Natal
T. l. peripheris
C Natal

T. l. tropicalis
SE Zaire, Mozambique, Malawi, Tanzania
Turdus tephronotus (African Bare-eyed Thrush)
Ethiopia, Somalia, Kenya, E Tanzania
Turdus menachensis (Yemen Thrush)
S Saudi Arabia, Yemen
Turdus ludoviciae (Somali Blackbird)
N Somalia
Turdus litsipsirupa (Groundscraper Thrush)
T. l. simensis
Ethiopia
T. l. litsipsirupa
Botswana, Rhodesia, Zambia, S Africa
T. l. pauciguttatus
NW Botswana, Namibia
T. l. stierlingi
N Angola to W & S Tanzania
Turdus dissimilis (Black-breasted Thrush)
T. d. dissimilis
NE India to SW China, N Indochina
T. d. hortulorum
Siberia, Manchuria » SE China,
Vietnam
Turdus unicolor (Tickell's Thrush)
Pakistan, Nepal, N India
Turdus cardis (Japanese Grey Thrush)
Japan, China » Indochina
Turdus albocinctus (White-collared Blackbird)
Himalayas, SE Tibet, SW Sikang »
N Burma
Turdus torquatus (Ring Ousel)
T. t. torquatus
N Europe » S Europe, NW Africa
T. t. alpestris
S & E Europe » Asia Minor, N Africa
T. t. amicorum
Turkey, Caucasus, N Iran » S Iran
Turdus boulboul (Grey-winged Blackbird)
Himalayas, S China, N Indochina »
N Burma
Turdus merula (Blackbird)
T. m. merula
W Europe
T. m. azorensis
Azores Is
T. m. cabrerae
Madeira I, W Canary Is
T. m. mauretanicus
Morocco to Tunisia
T. m. aterrimus
SE Europe, Caucasus » Med Is
T. m. insularum
Crete, Rhodes, Mytilene I
T. m. syriacus
S Turkey, Middle East, Iran
T. m. intermedius
C Asia, Afghanistan » S Iraq
T. m. maximus
Pakistan, India, SE Tibet

T. m. sowerbyi
Szechwan

T. m. mandarinus
Kweichow

T. m. nigropileus
SC India

T. m. spencei
E India

T. m. simillimus
SE India

T. m. bourdilloni
S India

T. m. kinnisii
Sri Lanka

Turdus poliocephalus (Island Thrush)

T. p. erythropleurus
Christmas Is

T. p. loeseri
N Sumatra

T. p. indrapurae
C Sumatra

T. p. biesenbachi
Mt Papandajan (W Java)

T. p. fumidus
Mt Gedeh (W Java)

T. p. stresemanni
Mt Lawoe (C Java)

T. p. javanicus
C Java

T. p. whiteheadi
E Java

T. p. seebohmi
N Borneo

T. p. niveiceps
Taiwan

T. p. thomassoni
N Luzon I

T. p. mayonensis
S Luzon I

T. p. mindorensis
Mindoro I

T. p. nigrorum
Negros I

T. p. malindangensis
Mt Malindang (NW Mindanao I)

T. p. katanglad
Mt Katanglad (C Mindanao I)

T. p. kelleri
Mt Apo (SE Mindanao I)

T. p. hygroscopus
S Celebes

T. p. celebensis
SW Celebes

T. p. schlegelii
W Timor I

T. p. sterlingi
E Timor I

T. p. deningeri
Ceram I

T. p. versteegi
W New Guinea

T. p. carbonarius
Bismarck Mts, (New Guinea)

T. p. keysseri
Huon, SE New Guinea

T. p. papuensis
SE New Guinea

T. p. canescens
Goodenough I

T. p. heinrothi
St Matthias Is

T. p. bougainvillei
Bougainville I

T. p. kulambangrae
Kulambangra I

T. p. sladeni
Guadalcanal I

T. p. rennellianus
Rennell I

T.˙p. vanikorensis
Vanikoro I, Santa Cruz I, Espiritu
Santo I

T. p. placens
Ureparapara I, Vanue Lava I

T. p. whitneyi
Gaua I, Banks Is

T. p. malekulae
Pentecost I, Malekula I, Ambrim I

T. p. becki
Paema I, Lopevi I, Epi I, Mai I

T. p. efatensis
Efate I, Nguna I

T. p. albifrons
Erromanga I

T. p. pritzbueri
Tana I, Lifu I

T. p. mareensis
Maré I **e?**

T. p. xanthopus
New Caledonia I

T. p. poliocephalus
Norfolk I

T. p. layardi
Viti Levu I, Ovalau I, Yasawa I, Koro I

T. p. ruficeps
Kandavu I

T. p. vitiensis
Vanua Levu I

T. p. hades
Ngau I

T. p. tempesti
Taveuni I

T. p. samoensis
Savaii I, Upolu I

Turdus chrysolaus (Red-bellied Thrush)
T. c. orii
N & C Kurile Is » Japan, Riukiu Is
T. c. chrysolaus
N Japan » SE China, N Philippine Is
Turdus celaenops (Seven Islands Thrush)
Izu I, Yakushima I
Turdus rubrocanus (Grey-headed Thrush)
T. r. rubrocanus
Pakistan, Himalayas
T. r. gouldi
SE Tibet, W China
Turdus kessleri (Kessler's Thrush)
W China » E Tibet, SW Sikang
Turdus feae (Fea's Thrush)
N China » Burma, Assam
Turdus pallidus (Pale Thrush)
NE Siberia » China, Japan, Taiwan
Turdus obscurus (Eye-browed Thrush)
NE Asia » China, Indonesia
Turdus ruficollis (Black-throated Thrush)
T. r. atrogularis
W Siberia, C Asia » N India, China
T. r. ruficollis
E Siberia » W China, Burma, NE India
Turdus naumanni (Dusky Thrush)
T. n. eunomus
N Siberia » Japan, S China, Burma
T. n. naumanni
C Siberia, C Asia » N China
Turdus pilaris (Fieldfare)
N Europe, N Asia » S Europe, Caucasus
Turdus iliacus (Redwing)
T. i. coburni
Iceland, Faroe Is » NW Europe
T. i. iliacus
N Europe, C Asia » N Africa, Caucasus
Turdus philomelos (Song Thrush)
T. p. hebridensis
Outer Hebrides, Isle of Skye
T. p. clarkei
British Isles, W Europe
T. p. philomelos
C Asia, C & E Europe » N Africa, S Europe,
Iran
T. p. nataliae
C Asia, Iran
Turdus mupinensis (Mongolian Song Thrush)
W China
Turdus viscivorus (Mistle Thrush)
T. v. viscivorus
Europe, Asia Minor, S Russia
T. v. bonapartei
Siberia, C Asia, Himalayas » N India
Turdus aurantius (White-chinned Thrush)
Jamaica

Turdus ravidus (Grand Cayman Thrush)
Grand Cayman I
Turdus plumbeus (Red-legged Thrush)
T. p. plumbeus
N Bahama Is
T. p. schistaceus
E Cuba
T. p. rubripes
C & W Cuba, Isle of Pines
T. p. coryi
Cayman Brac I
T. p. ardosiaceus
Hispaniola, Puerto Rico, Gonave I
T. p. albiventris
Dominica I
Turdus chiguanco (Chiguanco Thrush)
T. c. chiguanco
coastal Peru, NW Bolivia
T. c. conradi
S Ecuador, C Peru
T. c. anthracinus
S Bolivia, NE Chile, W Argentina
Turdus nigrescens (Sooty Robin)
Costa Rica, W Panama
Turdus fuscater (Great Thrush)
T. f. opertaneus
NW Colombia
T. f. cacozelus
N Colombia
T. f. clarus
E Colombia, W Venezuela
T. f. quindio
S & W Colombia, N Ecuador
T. f. gigas
E Colombia, W Venezuela
T. f. gigantodes
S Ecuador, N Peru
T. f. ockendeni
SE Peru
T. f. fuscater
W Bolivia
Turdus serranus (Glossy-black Thrush)
T. s. infuscatus
SE Mexico, Guatemala, El Salvador,
Honduras
T. s. cumanensis
NE Venezuela
T. s. atrosericeus
NE Colombia, N Venezuela
T. s. fuscobrunneus
C & S Colombia, Ecuador
T. s. serranus
Peru, Bolivia
Turdus nigriceps (Slaty Thrush)
T. n. nigriceps
SE Ecuador, E Peru, E Bolivia, W Argentina
T. n. subalaris
S Brazil, Paraguay, N Argentina

Turdus reevei (Plumbeous-backed Thrush)
W Ecuador, NW Peru
Turdus olivater (Black-hooded Thrush)
T. o. sanctaemartae
N Colombia
T. o. olivater
E Colombia, Venezuela
T. o. paraquensis
S Venezuela
T. o. kemptoni
C Venezuela
T. o. duidae
Mt Duida (S Venezuela)
T. o. roraimae
S Venezuela, S Guyana
T. o. caucae
C Colombia
T. o. ptaritepui
SE Venezuela
Turdus maranonicus (Maranon Thrush)
N Peru
Turdus fulviventris (Chestnut-bellied Thrush)
E Colombia, Venezuela, E Ecuador
Turdus rufiventris (Rufous-bellied Thrush)
T. r. juensis
NE Brazil
T. r. rufiventris
S Brazil, Uruguay, Paraguay, N Argentina
Turdus falcklandii (Austral Thrush)
T. f. falcklandii
Falkland Is
T. f. magellanicus
S Chile, S Argentina
T. f. pembertoni
SC Argentina
Turdus leucomelas (Pale-breasted Thrush)
T. l. leucomelas
S Brazil, E Peru, Paraguay
T. l. albiventer
N Colombia, Venezuela, NE Brazil, the Guianas
T. l. cautor
N Colombia
Turdus amaurochalinus (Creamy-bellied Thrush)
Central South America
Turdus plebejus (Mountain Robin)
T. p. differens
SE Mexico, Guatemala
T. p. rafaelensis
Nicaragua, El Salvador
T. p. plebejus
Costa Rica, W Panama
Turdus ignobilis (Black-billed Thrush)
T. i. ignobilis
E Colombia

T. i. goodfellowi
W Colombia
T. i. debilis
SE Colombia, Venezuela, W Amazonia
T. i. murinus
SE Venezuela, Guyana
T. i. arthuri
SE Venezuela, Guyana, French Guiana
Turdus lawrencii (Lawrence's Thrush)
Upper Amazonia
Turdus fumigatus (Cocoa Thrush)
T. f. aquilonalis
NE Colombia, N Venezuela, Trinidad
T. f. orinocensis
E Colombia, W Venezuela
T. f. fumigatus
N & E Brazil, the Guianas
Turdus personus (Lesser Antillean Thrush)
T. p. bondi
St Vincent I
T. p. personus
Grenada I
Turdus obsoletus (Pale-vented Thrush)
T. o. obsoletus
Costa Rica, Panama, NW Colombia
T. o. parambanus
W Colombia, W Ecuador
T. o. colombianus
C Colombia
T. o. hauxwelli
Upper Amazonia
Turdus haplochrous (Unicoloured Thrush)
E Bolivia
Turdus grayi (Clay-coloured Thrush)
T. g. tamaulipensis
E Mexico
T. g. microrhynchus
San Luis Potosi
T. g. lanyoni
S Mexico, W Guatemala
T. g. linnaei
S Mexico
T. g. grayi
S Mexico to Guatemala
T. g. megas
W Guatemala to Nicaragua
T. g. casius
Costa Rica to NW Colombia
T. g. incomptus
N Colombia
Turdus nudigenis (Bare-eyed Thrush)
T. n. nudigenis
Lesser Antilles, Trinidad, NE South America
T. n. extimus
N Brazil
T. n. maculirostris
W Ecuador, NW Peru
Turdus jamaicensis (White-eyed Thrush)
Jamaica

Turdus albicollis (White-necked Thrush)
  T. a. calliphthongus
    NW Mexico
  T. a. lygrus
    C & S Mexico
  T. a. assimilis
    C Mexico
  T. a. renominatus
    SC Mexico
  T. a. oaxacae
    Oaxaca
  T. a. leucauchen
    S Mexico to Honduras
  T. a. rubicundus
    W Guatemala, El Salvador
  T. a. atrotinctus
    E Nicaragua
  T. a. oblitus
    Costa Rica
  T. a. cnephosus
    SW Costa Rica, W Panama
  T. a. coibensis
    Coiba I
  T. a. daguae
    E Panama to NW Ecuador
  T. a. minusculus
    NE Colombia
  T. a. phaeopygoides
    NE Colombia, N Venezuela, Trinidad
  T. a. phaeopygus
    E Colombia to the Guianas, N Brazil
  T. a. berlepschi
    C & S Colombia
  T. a. spodiolaemus
    E Ecuador to N Bolivia, W Brazil
  T. a. contemptus
    S Bolivia
  T. a. crotopezus
    E Brazil
  T. a. albicollis
    SE Brazil
  T. a. paraguayensis
    SW Brazil, Paraguay, N Argentina
Turdus rufopalliatus (Rufous-backed Robin)
  T. r. griseor
    NW Mexico
  T. r. rufopalliatus
    W Mexico
  T. r. graysoni
    Tres Marias Is
Turdus swalesi (La Selle Thrush)
  Haiti
Turdus rufitorques (Rufous-collared Robin)
  SE Mexico, Guatemala, El Salvador

Turdus migratorius (American Robin)
  T. m. migratorius
    Canada, C USA » E USA, E Mexico
  T. m. nigrideus
    E Canada, EC USA
  T. m. achrusterus
    S USA » SE Mexico
  T. m. caurinus
    SE Alaska, W Canada » SW USA
  T. m. propinquus
    W Canada, W USA, SW Mexico
    » Guatemala
  T. m. phillipsi
    C Mexico
  T. m. confinis
    S Baja California
  T. m. permixtus
    SW Mexico

MUSCICAPIDAE

131 ORTHONYCHINAE (LOGRUNNERS)

ORTHONYX
Orthonyx temminckii (Spine-tailed Logrunner)
  O. t. novaeguineae
    W New Guinea
  O. t. dorsalis
    W New Guinea
  O. t. victoriana
    SE New Guinea
  O. t. temminckii
    SE Queensland, E New South Wales
Orthonyx spaldingii (Spalding's Logrunner)
  N Queensland

ANDROPHOBUS
Androphobus viridis (Green-backed Babbler)
  W New Guinea

PSOPHODES
Psophodes olivaceus (Eastern Whipbird)
  P. o. lateralis
    N Queensland
  P. o. magnirostris
    C Queensland
  P. o. olivaceus
    S Queensland, E New South Wales, Victoria
Psophodes nigrogularis (Western Whipbird)
  P. n. leucogaster
    NW Victoria, SE South Australia
  P. n. nigrogularis
    SW Western Australia
  P. n. pondalowiensis
    S South Australia

SPHENOSTOMA
Sphenostoma cristatum (Wedgebill)
  C & W Australia

CINCLOSOMA
Cinclosoma punctatum (Spotted Quail Thrush)
  C. p. punctatum
    Eastern Australia
  C. p. dovei
    Tasmania
Cinclosoma castanotum (Chestnut Quail Thrush)
  C. c. castanotum
    SE Australia
  C. c. mayri
    New South Wales
  C. c. morgani
    South Australia
  C. c. clarum
    C Australia
  C. c. dundasi
    SW Western Australia
Cinclosoma alisteri (Nullarbor Quail Thrush)
  Nullarbor Plain
Cinclosoma cinnamomeum (Cinnamon Quail Thrush)
  C. c. castaneothorax
    S Queensland, N New South Wales
  C. c. cinnamomeum
    EC Australia
  C. c. samueli
    South Australia
  C. c. marginatum
    SW Australia
Cinclosoma ajax (Ajax Quail Thrush)
  C. a. ajax
    W New Guinea
  C. a. muscale
    S New Guinea
  C. a. alare
    SC New Guinea
  C. a. goldiei
    SE New Guinea

PTILORRHOA
Ptilorrhoa leucosticta (High Mountain Rail Babbler)
  P. l. leucosticta
    W New Guinea
  P. l. mayri
    W New Guinea
  P. l. centralis
    W New Guinea
  P. l. sibilans
    N New Guinea
  P. l. amabilis
    E New Guinea
  P. l. loriae
    SE New Guinea
  P. l. menawa
    N coast of New Guinea

Ptilorrhoa caerulescens (Lowland Rail Babbler)
  P. c. caerulescens
    W New Guinea
  P. c. neumanni
    N New Guinea
  P. c. nigricrissa
    S New Guinea
  P. c. geislerorum
    E New Guinea
Ptilorrhoa castanonota (Mid-mountain Rail Babbler)
  P. c. castanonota
    W New Guinea
  P. c. saturata
    W New Guinea
  P. c. uropygialis
    W New Guinea
  P. c. buergersi
    C New Guinea
  P. c. par
    E New Guinea
  P. c. pulcher
    SE New Guinea
  P. c. gilliardi
    Batanta I

EUPETES
Eupetes macrocerus (Malay Rail Babbler)
  E. m. macrocerus
    Malaysia, Thailand, Sumatra
  E. m. borneensis
    N Borneo

MELAMPITTA
Melampitta lugubris (Lesser Melampitta)
  M. l. lugubris
    W New Guinea
  M. l. rostrata
    W New Guinea
  M. l. longicauda
    NC & E New Guinea
Melampitta gigantea (Greater Melampitta)
  W New Guinea

IFRITA
Ifrita kowaldi (Blue-capped Babbler)
  I. k. kowaldi
    E & C New Guinea
  I. k. brunnea
    WC New Guinea

MUSCICAPIDAE

132 TIMALIINAE (BABBLERS)

PELLORNEUM
Pellorneum ruficeps (Spotted Babbler)
  P. r. olivaceum
    SW India

P. r. ruficeps
W & C India
P. r. punctatum
W Himalayas
P. r. mandellii
Sikkim, Bhutan, Nepal, NE India
P. r. chamelum
S Assam
P. r. pectorale
Mishmi Hills, NE Assam
P. r. ripleyi
Lakhimpur, NE Assam
P. r. vocale
C Manipur
P. r. stageri
NE Burma
P. r. shanense
SW Yunnan, C Burma
P. r. hilarum
C Burma
P. r. victoriae
Chin hills, N Burma
P. r. minus
S Burma
P. r. subochraceum
S Burma, SW Thailand
P. r. insularum
Mergui Archipelago
P. r. acrum
C Thailand, N Malaysia
P. r. chthonium
N Thailand
P. r. indistinctum
N Thailand
P. r. oreum
S China, N Indochina
P. r. vividum
N Vietnam
P. r. elbeli
E Thailand
P. r. ubonense
E Thailand, S Laos
P. r. deignani
S Vietnam
P. r. dilloni
S Indochina
P. r. euroum
W Cambodia, C & SE Thailand
P. r. smithi
coastal islands of SE Thailand &
Cambodia
**Pellorneum palustre (Marsh Spotted
Babbler)**
C & E Assam
**Pellorneum fuscocapillum (Brown-capped
Jungle Babbler)**
P. f. babaulti
N & E Sri Lanka

P. f. fuscocapillum
SW Sri Lanka
P. f. scortillum
SW Sri Lanka
**Pellorneum albiventre (Plain Brown
Babbler)**
P. a. ignotum
Mishmi hills, NE Assam
P. a. albiventre
Bhutan, Assam, W Burma
P. a. nagaense
Burma
P. a. cinnamomeum
C Burma, NW Thailand, S Indochina
P. a. pusillum
NW Vietnam, N Laos
**Pellorneum capistratum (Black-capped
Babbler)**
P. c. nigrocapitatum
Malaysia, N Natuna Is, Billiton I
P. c. nyctilampis
Sumatra, Bangka I
P. c. capistratoides
W & S Borneo
P. c. morrelli
Banggai I, N & E Borneo
P. c. capistratum
Java

TRICHASTOMA
**Trichastoma tickelli (Tickell's Jungle
Babbler)**
T. t. assamense
Assam, NW Burma
T. t. grisescens
Arakan Yoma, SW Burma
T. t. fulvum
SW Yunnan, NE Burma, N Thailand,
Indochina
T. t. annamense
S & C Vietnam, S Laos
T. t. tickelli
N Malaysia, E Burma, W Thailand
T. t. ochracea
S China
T. t. australis
N Malaysia
**Trichastoma pyrrogenys (Temminck's
Jungle Babbler)**
T. p. buettikoferi
Sumatra
T. p. pyrrogenys
W Java
T. p. besuki
E Java
T. p. erythrote
W Sarawak, N Borneo
T. p. longstaffi
Sarawak, N Borneo

T. p. canicapillum
N Borneo
Trichastoma malaccense (Short-tailed Jungle Babbler)
T. m. malaccense
N Natuna Is, Malaysia, Sumatra, Anamba Is
T. m. saturatum
Bangka I, Billiton I, W Borneo
T. m. poliogene
E Borneo
T. m. feriatum
Sarawak, N Borneo
Trichastoma cinereiceps (Ashy-headed Jungle Babbler)
Balabac I, Palawan I
Trichastoma rostratum (White-chested Jungle Babbler)
T. r. rostratum
Malaysia, Sumatra, Billiton I
T. r. macropterum
Banggai I, Borneo
Trichastoma bicolor (Ferruginous Jungle Babbler)
Malaysia, E Sumatra, Bangka I, Borneo
Trichastoma sepiarium (Horsfield's Jungle Babbler)
T. s. tardinatum
Malaysia
T. s. liberale
NW Sumatra
T. s. barussanum
SW Sumatra
T. s. sepiarium
W & C Java
T. s. minus
E Java, Bali I
T. s. rufiventre
W & S Borneo
T. s. harterti
N & E Borneo
Trichastoma celebense (Celebes Jungle Babbler)
T. c. celebense
N Celebes
T. c. connectens
NC Celebes
T. c. rufofuscum
C Celebes
T. c. finschi
SW Celebes
T. c. improbatum
Pulau Is, E & S Celebes
T. c. togianense
Togian I
Trichastoma abbotti (Abbott's Jungle Babbler)
T. a. abbotti
Himalayas, Burma, Thailand, NW Malaysia

T. a. williamsoni
E Thailand, NW Cambodia
T. a. obscurius
SE Thailand
T. a. rufescentior
Thailand
T. c. alterum
C Laos, C Vietnam
T. a. olivaceum
Thailand, Malaysia, E Sumatra
T. a. sirense
Pulau Mata Siri I, Billiton I
T. a. baweanum
Bawean I
T. a. finschi
Borneo
Trichastoma perspicillatum (Black-browed Jungle Babbler)
Borneo
Trichastoma vanderbilti (Vanderbilt's Jungle Babbler)
N Sumatra
Trichastoma pyrrhopterum (Mountain Thrush Babbler)
T. p. pyrrhopterum
East Africa, Malawi
T. p. kivuense
E Zaire, W Uganda, W Tanzania
Trichastoma cleaveri (Blackcap Thrush Babbler)
T. c. johnsoni
Sierra Leone, Liberia
T. c. cleaveri
Ghana
T. c. marchanti
S Nigeria
T. c. batesi
SE Nigeria, Gabon, Cameroun
T. c. poense
Fernando Po I
Trichastoma albipectus (Scaly-breasted Thrush Babbler)
T. a. barakae
N Zaire, Uganda, S Sudan, SW Kenya
T. a. albipectus
N Angola, W Zaire
Trichastoma rufescens (Rufous-winged Thrush Babbler)
Sierra Leone to Ghana
Trichastoma rufipenne (Pale-breasted Thrush Babbler)
T. r. bocagei
Fernando Po I
T. r. extremum
Sierra Leone to Ghana
T. r. rufipenne
S Nigeria to Uganda, Kenya

T. r. distans
NE Tanzania, Zanzibar I

Trichastoma fulvescens (Brown Thrush Babbler)

T. f. gulare
Sierra Leone to Ghana

T. f. moloneyanum
E Ghana, Togo

T. f. iboense
S Nigeria

T. f. fulvescens
Cameroun, W Zaire

T. f. ugandae
N Zaire, Uganda

T. f. dilutius
N Angola

Trichastoma puveli (Puvel's Thrush Babbler)

T. p. puveli
Guinea to Sierra Leone

T. p. strenuipes
S Nigeria to NE Zaire

KAKAMEGA

Kakamega poliothorax (Grey-chested Thrush Babbler)
S Cameroun, Fernando Po I, E Zaire, SW Kenya

LEONARDINA

Leonardina woodi (Bagobo Babbler)
Mindanao I

PTYRTICUS

Ptyrticus turdinus (African Thrush Babbler)

P. t. harterti
C Cameroun

P. t. turdinus
SW Sudan, NE Zaire

P. t. upembae
SE Zaire, N Zambia

MALACOPTERON

Malacopteron magnirostre (Moustached Tree Babbler)

M. m. magnirostre
S Burma, Thailand, Malaysia, Sumatra

M. m. cinereocapillum
Borneo

M. m. flavum
Anamba Is

Malacopteron affine (Sooty-capped Babbler)

M. a. affine
S Thailand, Malaysia, Sumatra

M. a. notatum
Banyak I

M. a. phoeniceum
Borneo

Malacopteron cinereum (Scaly-crowned Babbler)

M. c. indochinense
SE Thailand, S Indochina

M. c. rufifrons
Java

M. c. cinereum
Malaysia, Sumatra, Bangka I, Borneo

M. c. niasense
Nias I

M. c. bungurense
N Natuna Is

Malacopteron magnum (Rufous-crowned Tree Babbler)

M. m. magnum
S Burma, Malaysia, Sumatra, Borneo, Natuna Is

M. m. saba
NE Borneo

Malacopteron palawanense (Palawan Tree Babbler)
Balabac I, Palawan I

Malacopteron albogulare (Grey-breasted Babbler)

M. a. albogulare
Malaysia, NE Sumatra

M. a. moultoni
NW Borneo

POMATORHINUS

Pomatorhinus hypoleucos (Long-billed Scimitar Babbler)

P. h. hypoleucos
Assam, Bangladesh, W Burma

P. h. tickelli
Thailand, N Indochina

P. h. brevirostris
S Indochina

P. h. wrayi
Malaysia

P. h. hainanus
Hainan I

Pomatorhinus erythrogenys (Rusty-cheeked Scimitar Babbler)

P. e. erythrogenys
W Himalayas

P. e. ferrugilatus
W & C Nepal

P. e. haringtoni
W Himalayas

P. e. mcclellandi
S Assam, W Burma

P. e. imberbis
Karenni, Burma

P. e. celatus
C Burma, NW Thailand

P. e. odicus
NE Burma, N Laos, SW China

P. e. decarlei
S Szechwan, N Yunnan

P. e. dedekeni
  E & S Sikang, NW Yunnan
P. e. gravivox
  NW Szechwan, S Kansu
P. e. sowerbyi
  N Shensi
P. e. cowensae
  SW Hupeh, E Szechwan
P. e. swinhoei
  Anhwei, Kiangsi, Kwangsi, Hunan,
  Fukien
P. e. erythrocnemis
  Taiwan
**Pomatorhinus horsfieldii (Travencore
Scimitar Babbler)**
P. h. melanurus
  Sri Lanka
P. h. travancoreensis
  SW India
P. h. horsfieldii
  W India
P. h. obscurus
  NW India
P. h. maderaspatensis
  EC India
**Pomatorhinus schisticeps (Slaty-headed
Scimitar Babbler)**
P. s. leucogaster
  NW Himalayas
P. s. schisticeps
  E Himalayas, NE India, NW Burma
P. s. salimalii
  Mishmi hills, NE Assam
P. s. cryptanthus
  . Lakhimpur, NE Assam
P. s. mearsi
  W Burma
P. s. ripponi
  E Burma, N Thailand, N Laos
P. s. nuchalis
  E Burma
P. s. difficilis
  S Burma, SW Thailand
P. s. olivaceus
  S Burma, SW Thailand
P. s. fastidiosus
  Malaysia
P. s. humilis
  E Thailand, S Laos, C Vietnam
P. s. annamensis
  S Vietnam
P. s. klossi
  SE Thailand, SW Cambodia
**Pomatorhinus montanus (Chestnut-backed
Scimitar Babbler)**
P. m. occidentalis
  S Malaysia, Sumatra

P. m. montanus
  W & C Java
P. m. ottolanderi
  E Java, Bali I
P. m. bornensis
  Borneo
**Pomatorhinus ruficollis (Streak-breasted
Scimitar Babbler)**
P. r. ruficollis
  W & C Nepal
P. r. godwini
  E Himalyas, N Assam
P. r. bakeri
  SE Assam, W Burma
P. r. bhamoensis
  N Burma
P. r. similis
  NE Burma, NW Yunnan
P. r. albipectus
  SW Yunnan, N Laos
P. r. beaulieui
  N Laos
P. r. laurentei
  S Yunnan
P. r. reconditus
  SE Yunnan, N Vietnam
P. r. stridulus
  SE China
P. r. hunonensis
  C China
P. r. eidos
  S Szechwan
P. r. musicus
  Taiwan
P. r. nigrostellatus
  Hainan I
**Pomatorhinus ochraceiceps (Red-billed
Scimitar Babbler)**
P. o. stenorhynchus
  NE Assam, N Burma
P. o. austeni
  Manipur, E Assam
P. o. ochraceiceps
  Burma, N Thailand, N Indochina
P. o. alius
  E Thailand, S Indochina
**Pomatorhinus ferruginosus (Coral-billed
Scimitar Babbler)**
P. f. ferruginosus
  E Himalayas
P. f. formosus
  S Assam
P. f. phayrei
  Arakan Yoma, SW Burma
P. f. stanfordi
  NE Burma
P. f. mariae
  C Burma

P. f. albogularis
E Burma, NW Thailand
P. f. orientalis
N Indochina

GARRITORNIS
**Garritornis isidorei (Isidor's Rufous
Babbler)**
G. i. isidorei
C & S New Guinea, Misol I
G. i. calidus
N New Guinea

POMATOSTOMUS
**Pomatostomus temporalis (Grey-crowned
Babbler)**
P. t. tregellasi
SE South Australia, Victoria, SE New
South Wales
P. t. trivirgatus
E New South Wales, S Queensland
P. t. temporalis
coastal C Queensland
P. t. cornwalli
coastal N Queensland
P. t. strepitans
S New Guinea
P. t. intermedius
C Australia
P. t. mountfordae
N Northern Territory
P. t. browni
NW Northern Territory
P. t. rubeculus
C Northern Territory
P. t. bamba
Melville I
P. t. nigrescens
Western Australia
**Pomatostomus superciliosus (White-
browed Babbler)**
P. s. gilgandra
W New South Wales, Victoria, South
Australia
P. s. superciliosus
SE South Australia, Victoria
P. s. ashbyi
SW Western Australia
P. s. gwendolenae
Gascoyne valley, Western Australia
Pomatostomus halli (Hall Babbler)
SW Queensland
**Pomatostomus ruficeps (Chestnut-
crowned Babbler)**
SW Queensland, W New South Wales,
NW Victoria, NE South Australia

XIPHIRHYNCHUS
**Xiphirhynchus superciliaris (Slender-
billed Scimitar Babbler)**
X. s. superciliaris
E Himalayas
X. s. intextus
S Assam, W Burma
X. s. forresti
NE Burma, NW Yunnan
X. s. rothschildi
N Vietnam

JABOUILLEIA
Jabouilleia danjoui (Danjou's Babbler)
J. d. danjoui
C Vietnam
J. d. parvirostris
C Vietnam

RIMATOR
**Rimator malacoptilus (Long-billed Wren
Babbler)**
R. m. malacoptilus
E Himalayas, Assam, NE Burma
R. m. pasquieri
N Vietnam
R. m. albostriatus
W Sumatra

PTILOCICHLA
**Ptilocichla leucogrammica (Bornean
Wren Babbler)**
Borneo
**Ptilocichla mindanensis (Streaked Ground
Babbler)**
P. m. minuta
Leyte I, Samar I
P. m. fortichi
Bohol I
P. m. mindanensis
Mindanao I
P. m. basilanica
Basilan I
Ptilocichla falcata (Palawan Wren Babbler)
Balabac I, Palawan I

KENOPIA
Kenopia striata (Striped Wren Babbler)
Malaysia, E Sumatra, Borneo

NAPOTHERA
**Napothera rufipectus (Sumatran Wren
Babbler)**
W Sumatra
**Napothera atrigularis (Black-throated
Wren Babbler)**
Borneo
**Napothera macrodactyla (Large Wren
Babbler)**
N. m. macrodactyla
Malaysia

N. m. beauforti
NE Sumatra

N. m. lepidopleura
Java

Napothera marmorata (Marbled Wren Babbler)

N. m. grandior
C Malaysia

N. m. marmorata
W Sumatra

Napothera crispifrons (Limestone Wren Babbler)

N. c. annamensis
N Indochina

N. c. calcicola
NE Thailand

N. c. crispifrons
N Thailand, S Burma

Napothera brevicaudata (Streaked Wren Babbler)

N. b. striata
S Assam, SW Burma

N. b. venningi
W Yunnan, NE Burma

N. b. brevicaudata
N Thailand

N. b. stevensi
N Indochina

N. b. proxima
C Vietnam, S Laos

N. b. rufiventer
S Vietnam

N. b. griseigularis
SE Thailand, SW Cambodia

N. b. leucosticta
N Malaysia

Napothera crassa (Mountain Wren Babbler)
N Borneo

Napothera rabori (Luzon Wren Babbler)

N. r. rabori
Ilocos Norte, Luzon I

N. r. mesoluzonica
Laguna, Luzon I

N. r. sorsogonensis
Sorsogon, Luzon I

Napothera epilepidota (Lesser Wren Babbler)

N. e. guttaticollis
N Assam

N. e. roberti
S Assam, NW Burma

N. e. bakeri
C Burma

N. e. davisoni
N Thailand

N. e. amyae
N Indochina

N. e. delacouri
Kwangsi

N. e. hainana
Hainan I

N. e. clara
S Vietnam

N. e. granti
N Malaysia

N. e. lucilleae
N Sumatra

N. e. diluta
W Sumatra

N. e. mendeni
SW Sumatra

N. e. epilepidota
W & C Java

N. e. exsul
N Borneo

PNOEPYGA

Pnoepyga albiventer (Scaly-breasted Wren Babbler)

P. a. pallidior
N & C Himalayas

P. a. albiventer
E Himalayas, Assam, N Burma, S China

Pnoepyga pusilla (Pygmy Wren Babbler)

P. p. pusilla
Himalayas, Assam, N Burma, N Thailand, S China

P. p. formosana
Taiwan

P. p. annamensis
S Indochina

P. p. harterti
C Malaysia

P. p. lepida
W Sumatra

P. p. rufa
Java

P. p. everetti
Flores I

P. p. timorensis
Timor I

SPELAEORNIS

Spelaeornis caudatus (Short-tailed Wren Babbler)
Nepal, Sikkim, Bhutan

Spelaeornis badeigularis (Mishmi Wren Babbler)
Mishmi hills, NE Assam

Spelaeornis troglodytoides (Bar-winged Wren Babbler)

S. t. sherriffi
E Bhutan

S. t. souliei
NE Burma, NW Yunnan

S. t. rocki
NW Yunnan

S. t. troglodytoides
Sikang, NW Szechwan
S. t. halsueti
Shensi
Spelaeornis formosus (Spotted Wren Babbler)
E Himalayas, W Burma, S China
Spelaeornis chocolatinus (Godwin-Austin's Wren Babbler)
S. c. chocolatinus
S Assam, Manipur
S. c. oatesi
N Burma
S. c. reptatus
NE Burma, SW Yunnan
S. c kinneari
N Vietnam
Spelaeornis longicaudatus (Long-tailed Wren Babbler)
S Assam, Manipur

SPHENOCICLA
Sphenocicla humei (Wedge-billed Wren Babbler)
S. h. humei
Sikkim to N Assam
S. h. roberti
S Assam, NE Burma

NEOMIXIS
Neomixis tenella (Northern Jery)
N. t. tenella
N Madagascar
N. t. decaryi
W Madagascar
N. t. orientalis
C & S Madagascar
N. t. debilis
SW Madagascar
Neomixis viridis (Southern Green Jery)
N. v. delacouri
NE Madagascar
N. v. viridis
SE Madagascar
Neomixis striatigula (Stripe-throated Jery)
N. s. sclateri
NE Madagascar
N. s. striatigula
SE Madagascar
N. s. pallidior
SW Madagascar
Neomixis flavoviridis (Wedge-tailed Jery)
SE Madgascar

STACHYRIS
Stachyris rodolphei (Deignan's Babbler)
Thailand

Stachyris rufifrons (Red-fronted Tree Babbler)
S. r. pallescens
Arakan Yoma, SW Burma
S. r. rufifrons
SE Burma, W Thailand
S. r. obscura
S Thailand
S. r. poliogaster
W Malaysia, Sumatra
S. r. sarawacensis
Borneo
·Stachyris ambigua (Buff-chested Babbler)
S. a. ambigua
E Himalayas, Assam
S. a. planicola
NE Burma
S. a. adjuncta
N & E Thailand, N Indochina
S. a. insuspecta
S Laos
Stachyris ruficeps (Red-headed Tree Babbler)
S. r. ruficeps
E Himalayas, N Assam
S. r. rufipectus
NW Burma
S. r. bhamoensis
NE Burma, NW Yunnan
S. r. davidi
C & S China, N Indochina
S. r. praecognita
Taiwan
S. r. goodsoni
Hainan I
S. r. pagana
S Vietnam
Stachyris pyrrhops (Red-billed Tree Babbler)
Pakistan, W Himalayas
Stachyris chrysaea (Golden-headed Tree Babbler)
S. c. chrysaea
E Himalayas, Assam, N Burma
S. c. binghami
SE Assam, SW Burma
S. c. aurata
S Burma, N Indochina
S. c. assimilis
C Burma, NW Thailand
S. c. chrysops
C Malaysia
S. c. frigida
W Sumatra
Stachyris plateni (Pygmy Tree Babbler)
S. p. pygmaea
Samar I, Leyte I

S. p. plateni
Mindanao I

Stachyris capitalis (Rufous-crowned Tree Babbler)

S. c. dennistouni
NE Luzon I

S. c. affinis
S Luzon I

S. c. nigrocapitata
Samar I, N Leyte I

S. c. boholensis
Bohol I

S. c. capitalis
Dinagat I, Mindanao I

S. c. isabelae
Basilan I

Stachyris speciosa (Rough-templed Tree Babbler)
Negros I

Stachyris whiteheadi (Whitehead's Tree Babbler)
N Luzon I

Stachyris striata (Striped Tree Babbler)
N Luzon I

Stachyris nigrorum (Negros Tree Babbler)
Negros I

Stachyris hypogrammica (Palawan Tree Babbler)
Palawan I

Stachyris grammiceps (White-breasted Tree Babbler)
W Java

Stachyris herberti (Sooty Tree Babbler)
Laos

Stachyris nigriceps (Black-throated Tree Babbler)

S. n. nigriceps
E Himalayas

S. n. coei
Mishmi Hills, E Assam

S. n. coltarti
Naga Hills, E Assam, N Burma

S. n. spadix
S Assam, S Burma, NW Thailand

S. n. yunnanensis
N Thailand, E Burma, N Indochina,
SW Yunnan

S. n. rileyi
S Vietnam

S. n. dipora
N Malaysia

S. n. davisoni
C Malaysia

S. n. larvata
Lingga Archipelago, Sumatra

S. n. natunensis
N Natuna Is

S. n. tionis
Tioman I

S. n. hartleyi
W Sarawak

S. n. borneensis
Borneo

Stachyris poliocephala (Grey-headed Tree Babbler)

S. p. poliocephala
Malaysia, Sumatra, Borneo

S. p. pulla
NE Sumatra

Stachyris striolata (Spot-necked Tree Babbler)

S. s. swinhoei
Hainan I

S. s. tonkinensis
Kwansi, N Indochina

S. s. helenae
N Thailand, N Laos

S. s. guttata
W Thailand

S. s. nigrescentior
S Thailand

S. s. umbrosa
NE Sumatra

S. s. striolata
W Sumatra

Stachyris oglei (Austen's Spotted Tree Babbler)
E Assam

Stachyris maculata (Chestnut-rumped Tree Babbler)

S. m. pectoralis
C & S Malaysia

S. m. maculata
Sumatra, Borneo

S. m. banjakensis
Banyak I

S. m. hypopyrrha
Batu I

Stachyris leucotis (White-necked Tree Babbler)

S. l. leucotis
S Malaysia

S. l. sumatrensis
Sumatra

S. l. obscurata
Borneo

Stachyris nigricollis (Black-throated Tree Babbler)

S. n. erythronotus
N Malaysia

S. n. nigricollis
S Malaysia, E Sumatra, Borneo

424 ***Stachyris thoracica* (White-collared Tree Babbler)**
  S. t. thoracica
    S Sumatra, W & C Java
  S. t. orientalis
    E Java
***Stachyris erythroptera* (Chestnut-winged Tree Babbler)**
  S. e. erythroptera
    S Malaysia, N Natuna Is
  S. e. apega
    Bangka I, Billiton I
  S. e. pyrrhophaea
    Sumatra, Batu I
  S. e. fulviventris
    Banyak I
  S. e. bicolor
    Banggai I, N & E Borneo
  S. e. rufa
    SW Borneo
***Stachyris melanothorax* (Pearl-cheeked Tree Babbler)**
  S. m. melanothorax
    W Java
  S. m. albigula
    Java
  S. m. mendeni
    Java
  S. m. intermedia
    E Java
  S. m. baliensis
    Bali I

DUMETIA
***Dumetia hyperythra* (Rufous-bellied Babbler)**
  D. h. hyperythra
    SW Nepal, N & C India
  D. h. albogularis
    S India
  D. h. phillipsi
    Sri Lanka
  D. h. navarroi
    W India

RHOPOCICHLA
***Rhopocichla atriceps* (Black-headed Babbler)**
  R. a. atriceps
    C India
  R. a. bourdilloni
    SW India
  R. a. siccata
    N & E Sri Lanka
  R. a. nigrifrons
    SW Sri Lanka

MACRONOUS
***Macronous gularis* (Striped Tit-Babbler)**
  M. g. rubricapilla
    Nepal, NE India, Assam
  M. g. ticehursti
    W Burma
  M. g. sulphureus
    E Burma, N Thailand
  M. g. lutescens
    SE Yunnan, N & E Thailand, Laos, N Vietnam
  M. g. kinneari
    C Vietnam
  M. g. versuricola
    E Cambodia, S Vietnam
  M. g. saraburiensis
    E Thailand, W Cambodia
  M. g. connectens
    S Thailand
  M. g. inveteratus
    coastal islands of SE Thailand & Cambodia
  M. g. condorensis
    Pulau Kondor, S Vietnam
  M. g. archipelagicus
    Mergui Archipelago
  M. g. chersonesophilus
    N Malaysia
  M. g. gularis
    S Malaysia, Sumatra, Batu I
  M. g. zopherus
    Anamba Is
  M. g. zaperissus
    N Natuna Is
  M. g. everetti
    Bunguran I, N Natuna Is
  M. g. ruficoma
    Bangka I, Billiton I
  M. g. javanicus
    W & C Java
  M. g. flavicollis
    E Java
  M. g. prillwitzi
    Kangean I
  M. g. montanus
    NE Borneo
  M. g. bornensis
    Borneo
  M. g. cagayanensis
    Cagayan Sulu I
  M. g. argenteus
    N Borneo Islands
  M. g. woodi
    Palawan I
***Macronous kelleyi* (Grey-faced Tit-Babbler)**
  S Indochina
***Macronous striaticeps* (Brown Tit-Babbler)**
  M. s. mindanensis
    Samar I, Leyte I, Bohol I, Mindanao I

M. s. alcasidi
Dinagat I
M. s. striaticeps
Basilan I, Malamaui I
M. s. kettlewelli
Sulu Archipelago
Macronous ptilosus (Fluffy-backed Tit-Babbler)
M. p. ptilosus
Malaysia
M. p. trichorrhos
Sumatra, Batu Is
M. p. sordidus
Bangka I, Billiton I
M. p. reclusus
Borneo

MICROMACRONOUS
Micromacronous leytensis (Leyte Tit-Babbler)
M. l. leytensis
Leyte I
M. l. sordidus
Mindanao I

TIMALIA
Timalia pileata (Chestnut-capped Babbler)
T. p. bengalensis
E Himalayas, NW Burma
T. p. smithi
N Burma, S China, N Thailand, N Indochina
T. p. intermedia
C & S Burma, SW Thailand
T. p. patriciae
WC Thailand
T. p. dictator
S & E Thailand, S Indochina
T. p. pileata
Java

CHRYSOMMA
Chrysomma sinense (Oriental Yellow-eyed Babbler)
C. s. nasale
Sri Lanka
C. s. hypoleucum
Pakistan, India, Bangladesh, W Burma
C. s. sinense
S China, E Himalayas, Burma, Thailand, Indochina

MOUPINIA
Moupinia altirostris (Jerdon's Babbler)
M. a. scindica
Pakistan
M. a. griseigularis
N India, S Assam, NE Burma
M. a. altirostris
SC Burma

Moupinia poecilotis (Rufous-crowned Babbler)
W China

CHAMAEA
Chamaea fasciata (Wren-Tit)
C. f. phaea
coast of Oregon
C. f. rufula
coast of N California
C. f. intermedia
San Francisco area
C. f. fasciata
coast of C California
C. f. henshawi
SW Oregon, N & C California
C. f. canicauda
NW Baja California

TURDOIDES
Turdoides nipalensis (Spiny Babbler)
W & C Nepal
Turdoides altirostris (Iraq Babbler)
SE Iraq, SW Iran
Turdoides caudatus (Common Babbler)
T. c. salvadorii
SE Iraq, SW Iran
T. c. huttoni
Afghanistan, E Iran, S Pakistan
T. c. eclipes
N Pakistan
T. c. caudatus
SE Pakistan, India
Turdoides earlei (Striated Babbler)
T. e. sonivius
Pakistan, NW India
T. e. earlei
NE India, Assam, Burma
Turdoides gularis (White-throated Babbler)
C & S Burma
Turdoides longirostris (Slender-billed Babbler)
Nepal, Assam
Turdoides malcolmi (Large Grey Babbler)
C India
Turdoides squamiceps (Arabian Babbler)
T. s. squamiceps
coast of W & S Saudi Arabia
T. s. yemensis
S Yemen, Aden
T. s. muscatensis
coast of Oman
Turdoides fulvus (Fulvous Babbler)
T. f. maroccanus
SW Morocco
T. f. fulvus
N Algeria, Tunisia, NW Libya

T. f. buchanani
C Sahara
T. f. acaciae
S Egypt, N Sudan, NE Ethiopia
Turdoides aylmeri (Scaly Chatterer)
T. a. aylmeri
Somalia, SE Ethiopia
T. a. boranensis
SC Ethiopia
T. a. kenianus
C Kenya
T. a. loveridgei
SE Kenya, NE Tanzania
T. a. mentalis
NC Tanzania
Turdoides rubiginosus (Rufous Chatterer)
T. r. bowdleri
SE Ethiopia
T. r. rubiginosus
E Uganda, W Kenya, C & S Ethiopia,
S Sudan
T. r. heuglini
East African coast from Somalia to
Tanzania
T. r. schnitzeri
NW Tanzania
Turdoides subrufus (Rufous Babbler)
T. s. subrufus
SW India
T. s. hyperythrus
SW Madras
**Turdoides striatus (White-headed Jungle
Babbler)**
T. s. malabaricus
SW India
T. s. somervillei
W coast of India
T. s. sindianus
Pakistan, NW India
T. s. striatus
N India, E Assam
T. s. orientalis
C & S India
**Turdoides rufescens (Ceylon Jungle
Babbler)**
Sri Lanka
Turdoides affinis (White-headed Babbler)
T. a. affinis
S India
T. a. taprobanus
Sri Lanka
Turdoides melanops (Black-lored Babbler)
T. m. vepres
S Kenya
T. m. clamosus
C Kenya
T. m. sharpei
W Kenya, S Uganda, NW Tanzania

T. m. melanops
SW Angola, N Namibia, Botswana
T. m. angolensis
Huila, Angola
Turdoides tenebrosus (Dusky Babbler)
NE Zaire, S Sudan, SW Ethiopia
Turdoides reinwardtii (Blackcap Babbler)
T. r. reinwardtii
Senegal to Sierra Leone
T. r. stictilaemus
Ghana to N Zaire
T. r. houyi
N Cameroun, Central African Republic
Turdoides plebejus (Brown Babbler)
T. p. platycircus
Senegal to Sierra Leone, Togo, Niger
T. p. uamensis
E & C Cameroun.
T. p. plebejus
S Cameroun, Nigeria, Central African
Republic
T. p. leucocephalus
E Sudan, Ethiopia
T. p. cinereus
E Nigeria to Ethiopia, Sudan, W Kenya
T. p. gularis
W Cameroun, N Zaire
**Turdoides jardineii (Arrow-marked
Babbler)**
T. j. hypostictus
S Zaire, N Angola
T. j. tanganjicae
SE Zaire, N Zambia
T. j. emini
Uganda, Tanzania
T. j. kikuyuensis
SW Kenya, NW Tanzania
T. j. kirkii
coastal zone from Kenya to Mozambique
Malawi
T. j. tamalakanei
SW Zambia, N Botswana, S Angola
T. j. jardineii
Rhodesia, Mozambique, Transvaal, Natal
Turdoides squamulatus (Scaly Babbler)
T. s. jubaensis
S Somalia
T. s. carolinae
R Sheballi, S Somalia
T. s. squamulatus
coast of Kenya
**Turdoides leucopygius (White-rumped
Babbler)**
T. l. leucopygius
coast of E Ethiopia
T. l. limbatus
NW Ethiopia
T. l. smithii
W Somalia, SE Ethiopia

T. l. lacuum
SW Ethiopia

T. l. omoensis
SW Ethiopia, SE Sudan

T. l. ater
SE Zaire, NE Zambia, SW Tanzania

T. l. hartlaubii
W Zambia, S Angola, N Botswana

T. l. griseosquamatus
N Botswana

Turdoides hindei (Hinde's Pied Babbler)
E Kenya

Turdoides hypoleucus (Northern Pied Babbler)

T. h. hypoleucus
C Kenya

T. h. rufuensis
NE Tanzania

Turdoides bicolor (Pied Babbler)
Namibia, Botswana, W Transvaal

Turdoides gymnogenys (Bare-cheeked Babbler)

T. g. gymnogenys
SW Angola

T. g. kaokensis
N Namibia

BABAX

Babax lanceolatus (Chinese Babax)

B. l. lanceolatus
SW China, NE Burma

B. l. woodi
SE Assam, W Burma

B. l. latouchei
SE China

Babax waddelli (Giant Babax)

B. w. waddelli
SE Tibet

B. w. lumsdeni
NE Tibet

B. w. jomo
SE Tibet

Babax koslowi (Koslow's Babax)
N Sikang

GARRULAX

Garrulax cinereifrons (Ashy-headed Laughing Thrush)
SW Sri Lanka

Garrulax palliatus (Grey & Brown Laughing Thrush)

G. p. palliatus
W Sumatra

G. p. schistochlamys
N Borneo

Garrulax rufifrons (Red-fronted Laughing Thrush)

G. r. rufifrons
W Java

G. r. slamatensis
Java

Garrulax perspicillatus (Spectacled Laughing Thrush)
C & S China, N Vietnam

Garrulax albogularis (White-throated Laughing Thrush)

G. a. whistleri
Pakistan, W Himalayas, NW India

G. a. albogularis
E Himalayas, Bhutan

G. a. eous
SE Sikang, SW China, NW Vietnam

G. a. ruficeps
Taiwan

Garrulax leucolophus (White-crested Laughing Thrush)

G. l. leucolophus
Himalayas, N Assam

G. l. patkaicus
S Assam, W Burma

G. l. belangeri
S Burma, SW Thailand

G. l. diardi
SE Burma, Thailand, Yunnan, Indochina

G. l. bicolor
W Sumatra

Garrulax monileger (Lesser Necklaced Laughing Thrush)

G. m. monileger
E Himalayas, NE Burma

G. m. badius
Mishmi hills, NE Assam

G. m. stuarti
SE Burma, NW Thailand

G. m. fuscatus
SW Thailand

G. m. mouhoti
SE Thailand, S Indochina

G. m. pasquieri
C Vietnam

G. m. schauenseei
E Burma, NE Thailand, N Laos

G. m. tonkinensis
Kwangsi, N Vietnam

G. m. melli
Kwangtung to Anhwei, SE China

G. m. schmackeri
Hainan I

Garrulax pectoralis (Greater Necklaced Laughing Thrush)

G. p. pectoralis
Nepal

G. p. melanotis
E Himalayas, Assam, N Burma

G. p. subfusus
SE Burma, W Thailand, NW Laos

G. p. robini
NE Laos, N Vietnam

G. p. picticollis
Kwangtung to Anhwei, SE China

G. p. semitorquatus
Hainan I

Garrulax lugubris (Black Laughing Thrush)

G. l. lugubris
Malaysia, W Sumatra

G. l. calvus
NE Borneo

Garrulax striatus (Striated Laughing Thrush)

G. s. striatus
NW Himalayas

G. s. vibex
C Himalayas

G. s. sikkimensis
Sikkim, E Himalayas

G. s. cranbrooki
Bhutan, Assam, N & W Burma

Garrulax strepitans (Tickell's Laughing Thrush)

G. s. strepitans
E & S Burma, W Thailand, NW Laos

G. s. ferrarius
SE Thailand

Garrulax milleti (Black-hooded Laughing Thrush)
S Vietnam

Garrulax maesi (Maës' Laughing Thrush)

G. m. grahami
SE Sikang, SW China

G. m. maesi
Kwangsi, N Vietnam

G. m. varennei
NE & C Laos

G. m. castanotis
Hainan I

Garrulax nuchalis (Chestnut-backed Laughing Thrush)
NE Assam, N Burma

Garrulax chinensis (Black-throated Laughing Thrush)

G. c. lochmius
SW Yunnan, SE Burma, N Thailand, N Laos

G. c. propinquus
S Burma, SW Thailand

G. c. germaini
S Vietnam

G. c. chinensis
S China, NE Indochina

G. c. monachus
Hainan I

Garrulax vassali (White-cheeked Laughing Thrush)
S Indochina

Garrulax galbanus (Austen's Laughing Thrush)

G. g. galbanus
SE Assam, W Burma

G. g. courtoisi
NE Kiangsi

Garrulax delesserti (Rufous-vented Laughing Thrush)

G. d. delesserti
SW India

G. d. gularis
Bhutan, Assam, N Burma, N Laos

Garrulax variegatus (Variegated Laughing Thrush)

G. v. variegatus
W Himalayas

G. v. similis
Pakistan, NW India

Garrulax davidi (David's Laughing Thrush)

G. d. chinganicus
N Manchuria

G. d. davidi
N China, S Mongolia

G. d. experrectus
N Kansu

G. d. concolor
NW Szechwan

Garrulax sukatschewi (Black-fronted Laughing Thrush)
S Kansu

Garrulax cineraceus (Ashy Laughing Thrush)

G. c. cineraceus
S Assam, W Burma

G. c. strenuus
NE Burma, SW China

G. c. cinereiceps
C & SE China

Garrulax rufogularis (Rufous-chinned Laughing Thrush)

G. r. occidentalis
Pakistan, W Himalayas

G. r. grosvenori
W Nepal

G. r. rufogularis
E Himalayas, N Assam

G. r. assamensis
NE Assam

G. r. rufitinctus
S Assam

G. r. rufiberbis
N Burma

G. r. intensior
N Vietnam

Garrulax lunulatus (Bar-backed Laughing Thrush)
S Kansu, S Shensi

Garrulax bieti (Biet's Laughing Thrush)
SE Sikang, W Szechwan

Garrulax maximus (Giant Laughing Thrush)
W China, SE Tibet
Garrulax ocellatus (White-spotted Laughing Thrush)
G. o. griseicauda
W Himalayas
G. o. ocellatus
E Himalayas, S Tibet
G. o. maculipectus
NW Yunnan, NE Burma
G. o. artemisiae
SW Szechwan, E Sikang
Garrulax caerulatus (Grey-sided Laughing Thrush)
G. c. caerulatus
E Himalayas
G. c. subcaerulatus
S Assam
G. c. livingstoni
E Assam, NW Burma
G. c. kaurensis
N Burma
G. c. latifrons
W Yunnan, NE Burma
G. c. ricinus
S Yunnan
G. c. berthemyi
NW Fukien
Garrulax poecilorhynchus (Rufous Laughing Thrush)
Taiwan
Garrulax mitratus (Chestnut-capped Laughing Thrush)
G. m. mitratus
W Sumatra
G. m. major
C Malaysia
G. m. damnatus
E Sarawak
G. m. griswoldi
C Borneo
G. m. treacheri
N Borneo
Garrulax ruficollis (Rufous-necked Laughing Thrush)
E Himalayas, NE Burma
Garrulax merulinus (Spot-breasted Laughing Thrush)
G. m. merulinus
W Yunnan, N Burma, S Assam
G. m. obscurus
SE Yunnan, N Indochina
G. m. annamensis
S Vietnam
Garrulax canorus (Melodious Laughing Thrush (Hwamei))
G. c. canorus
S China, N Indochina

G. c. owstoni
Hainan I
G. c. taewanus
Taiwan
Garrulax sannio (White-browed Laughing Thrush)
G. s. albosuperciliaris
E Assam
G. s. comis
Yunnan, SE Sikang, NE Burma,
N Indochina
G. s. sannio
N Vietnam, S China
G. s. oblectans
WC China
Garrulax cachinnans (Nilgiri White-breasted Laughing Thrush)
Nilgiri Hills, W Madras
Garrulax jerdoni (White-breasted Laughing Thrush)
G. j. jerdoni
Coorg, W Mysore
G. j. fairbanki
Palni hills, S India
G. j. meridionalis
S Kerala, SW India
Garrulax lineatus (Himalayan Streaked Laughing Thrush)
G. l. bilkevitchi
Tadzhikistan, NW Pakistan
G. l. gilgit
NE Pakistan
G. l. lineatus
W Himalayas
G. l. setafer
Sikkim, Nepal, W Bengal
G. l. imbricatus
Bhutan, SE Tibet
Garrulax virgatus (Striped Laughing Thrush)
S Assam, SW Burma
Garrulax austeni (Brown-capped Laughing Thrush)
G. a. austeni
S Assam
G. a. victoriae
N Burma
Garrulax squamatus (Blue-winged Laughing Thrush)
E Himalayas, Burma, Assam, SW China
Garrulax subunicolor (Plain-coloured Laughing Thrush)
G. s. subunicolor
E Himalayas, E Assam
G. s. griseatus
NE Burma, NW Yunnan
G. s. fooksi
NW Vietnam

430　***Garrulax elliotii* (Elliot's Laughing Thrush)**
 G. e. prjevalskii
  Kansu, E Tsinghai
 G. e. elliotii
  C & SW China
***Garrulax henrici* (Prince Henry's Laughing Thrush)**
 G. h. henrici
  SE Tibet, SW Sikang
 G. h. gucenensis
  W China
***Garrulax affinis* (Black-faced Laughing Thrush)**
 G. a. affinis
  W & C Nepal
 G. a. bethelae
  E Himalayas
 G. a. oustaleti
  NE Assam, SW Sikang, N Burma, NW Yunnan
 G. a. muliensis
  NW Yunnan, SE Sikang
 G. a. blythii
  SW Szechwan, E Sikang
 G. a. saturatus
  N Vietnam
 G. a. morrisonianus
  Taiwan
***Garrulax erythrocephalus* (Red-headed Laughing Thrush)**
 G. e. erythrocephalus
  W Himalayas
 G. e. kali
  W & C Nepal
 G. e. nigrimentum
  Sikkim, Bhutan
 G. e. imprudens
  NE Assam
 G. e. chrysopterus
  S Assam
 G. e. godwini
  SE Assam
 G. e. erythrolaema
  E Manipur, SW Burma
 G. e. woodi
  NE Burma, SW Yunnan
 G. e. connectens
  N Indochina
 G. e. subconnectens
  NW Thailand
 G. e. schistaceus
  E Burma, NW Thailand
 G. e. melanostigma
  SE Burma, NW Thailand
 G. e. ramsayi
  S Burma
 G. e. peninsulae
  S Thailand, N Malaysia
***Garrulax yersini* (Yersin's Laughing Thrush)**
 S Vietnam

***Garrulax formosus* (Crimson-winged Laughing Thrush)**
 G. f. formosus
  SW Szechwan, NE Yunnan
 G. f. greenwayi
  NW Vietnam
***Garrulax milnei* (Red-tailed Laughing Thrush)**
 G. m. sharpei
  E Burma, Yunnan, NW Thailand, N Indochina
 G. m. vitryi
  S Laos
 G. m. sinianus
  Kwangsi
 G. m. milnei
  NW Fukien

LIOCICHLA
***Liocichla phoenicea* (Red-faced Liocichla)**
 L. p. phoenicea
  E Himalayas
 L. p. bakeri
  S Assam, NW Burma
 L. p. ripponi
  E & S Burma, NW Thailand
 L. p. wellsi
  S Yunnan, N Indochina
***Liocichla omeiensis* (Mount Omei Liocichla)**
 Mt Omei (Szechwan)
***Liocichla steerii* (Steere's Liocichla)**
 S Taiwan

LEIOTHRIX
***Leiothrix argentauris* (Silver-eared Mesia)**
 L. a. argentauris
  Himalayas, N Assam
 L. a. vernayi
  S Assam, Burma, W Yunnan
 L. a. galbana
  E Burma, N Thailand
 L. a. ricketti
  SE Yunnan, N Indochina
 L. a. cunhaci
  S Indochina
 L. a. tahanensis
  S Thailand, N Malaysia
 L. a. rookmakeri
  NW Sumatra
 L. a. laurinae
  W Sumatra
***Leiothrix lutea* (Pekin Robin)**
 L. l. kumaiensis
  W Himalayas
 L. l. calipyga
  E Himalayas
 L. l. luteola
  SW Burma, S Assam

L. l. yunnanensis
NE Burma, NW Yunnan, SE Sikang
L. l. kwangtungensis
S China, NE Vietnam
L. l. lutea
SE & C China

CUTIA
Cutia nipalensis (Nepal Cutia)
C. n. nipalensis
E Himalayas, Assam, W Burma
C. n. melanchima
E Burma, NW Thailand, N Indochina
C. n. cervinicrissa
N Malaysia
C. n. legalleni
S Vietnam

PTERUTHIUS
Pteruthius rufiventer (Rufous-bellied Shrike Babbler)
P. r. rufiventer
E Himalayas, Assam, N Burma, Yunnan
P. r. delacouri
NW Vietnam
Pteruthius flaviscapis (Red-winged Shrike Babbler)
P. f. validirostris
Himalayas, Assam, NW Burma
P. f. ricketti
NE Burma, S China, N Indochina
P. f. annamensis
S Vietnam
P. f. schauenseei
S Thailand, E Burma
P. f. cameranoi
Malaysia, W Sumatra
P. f. flaviscapis
Java
P. f. robinsoni
N Borneo
Pteruthius xanthochlorus (Green Shrike Babbler)
P. x. occidentalis
W Himalayas
P. x. xanthochlorus
E Himalayas
P. x. hybridus
Naga hills, Assam, W Burma
P. x. pallidus
NE Burma, SE Sikang, W & S China
Pteruthius melanotis (Black-eared Shrike Babbler)
P. m. melanotis
E Himalayas, Burma, N Thailand, N Indochina
P. m. tahanensis
C Malaysia

Pteruthius aenobarbus (Chestnut-fronted Shrike Babbler)
P. a. aenobarbulus
Garo hills, Assam
P. a. intermedius
E Burma, NW Thailand, N Indochina
P. a. yaoshanensis
Kwangsi
P. a. indochinensis
S Vietnam
P. a. aenobarbus
W Java

GAMPSORHYNCHUS
Gampsorhynchus rufulus (White-headed Shrike Babbler)
G. r. rufulus
Sikkim, Assam, Burma
G. r. torquatus
SE Burma, Thailand, S Laos, Vietnam
G. r. saturatior
C Malaysia

ACTINODURA
Actinodura egertoni (Rusty-fronted Barwing)
A. e. egertoni
Nepal, Sikkim, Bhutan, N Assam
A. e. lewisi
Mishmi hills, NE Assam
A. e. khasiana
S Assam
A. e. ripponi
E Assam, SW Burma
Actinodura ramsayi (Spectacled Barwing)
A. r. yunnanensis
SE Yunnan, N Vietnam
A. r. radcliffei
E Burma, N Laos
A. r. ramsayi
E Burma, NW Thailand
Actinodura nipalensis (Hoary Barwing)
A. n. nipalensis
W & C Nepal
A. n. vinctura
E Nepal, Sikkim, Bhutan
Actinodura waldeni (Austen's Barwing)
A. w. daflaensis
N Assam
A. w. waldeni
SE Assam, NW Burma
A. w. poliotis
Mt Victoria, N Burma
A. w. saturatior
NE Burma, NW Yunnan
Actinodura souliei (Streaked Barwing)
A. s. souliei
NW Yunnan
A. s. griseinucha
NW Vietnam

Actinodura morrisoniana (Formosan
Barwing)
Taiwan

MINLA
Minla cyanouroptera (Blue-winged Minla)
M. c. cyanouroptera
C & E Himalayas, E Assam
M. c. aglae
SE Assam, W Burma
M. c. sordida
E & S Burma, NW Thailand
M. c. wingatei
NE Burma, N Thailand, S China,
N Indochina
M. c. croizati
Szechwan
M. c. rufodorsalis
SE Thailand, SW Cambodia
M. c. orientalis
S Vietnam
M. c. sordidior
S Thailand, N Malaysia
Minla strigula (Chestnut-tailed Minla)
M. s. simlaensis
W Himalayas
M. s. strigula
E Himalayas, N Assam
M. s. cinereigenae
Mt Japvo (E Assam)
M. s. yunnanensis
E Assam, W Burma, N Indochina
M. s. castanicauda
S Burma, NW Thailand
M. s. malayana
C Malaysia
Minla ignotincta (Red-tailed Minla)
M. i. ignotincta
E Nepal, Burma, Assam, NW Yunnan
M. i. mariae
SE Yunnan, N Vietnam
M. i. sini
Kwangsi
M. i. jerdoni
SW Szechwan

ALCIPPE
**Alcippe chrysotis (Golden-breasted
Fulvetta)**
A. c. chrysotis
E Himalayas, E Assam
A. c. albilineata
S Assam
A. c. forresti
NE Burma, NW Yunnan
A. c. amoena
NW Vietnam
A. c. swinhoii
SE Sikang, S Szechwan

Alcippe variegaticeps (Variegated
Fulvetta)
Kwangsi
Alcippe cinerea (Yellow-throated Fulvetta)
E Himalayas, N Burma, N Laos
**Alcippe castaneceps (Chestnut-headed
Fulvetta)**
A. c. castaneceps
E Himalayas, Assam, Burma,
NW Thailand
A. c. exul
N Thailand, Laos, NW Vietnam
A. c. soror
C Malaysia
A. c. klossi
S Vietnam
Alcippe vinipectus (White-browed Fulvetta)
A. v. kangrae
W Himalayas
A. v. vinipectus
W & C Nepal
A. v. chumbiensis
E Nepal, SE Tibet, Sikkim, Bhutan
A. v. austeni
S Assam
A. v. ripponi
Chin hills, W Burma
A. v. perstriata
NE Burma
A. v. valentinae
N Vietnam
A. v. bieti
NW Yunnan, SE Sikang
**Alcippe striaticollis (Chinese Mountain
Fulvetta)**
NW China
Alcippe ruficapilla (Spectacled Fulvetta)
A. r. ruficapilla
S Shensi, Szechwan
A. r. sordidior
NW Yunnan
A. r. danisi
SE Yunnan, N Laos
**Alcippe cinereiceps (Streak-throated
Fulvetta)**
A. c. ludlowi
E Bhutan, SE Tibet
A. c. manipurensis
E Assam, N Burma, NW Yunnan
A. c. tonkinensis
NE Laos, NW Vietnam
A. c. guttaticollis
Fukien, N Kwangtung
A. c. formosana
Taiwan
A. c. fucata
Hupeh, Hunan

A. c. cinereiceps
W Hupeh, Szechwan, SE Sikang
A. c. fessa
SW Kansu
Alcippe rufogularis (Rufous-throated Fulvetta)
A. r. rufogularis
E Himalayas, N Assam
A. r. collaris
. E Assam, Bangladesh
A. r. major
E Burma, N & E Thailand, N Laos
A. r. stevensi
N Indochina
A. r. kelleyi
C Vietnam
A. r. khmerensis
SE Thailand, SW Cambodia
Alcippe brunnea (Gould's Fulvetta)
A. b. mandellii
S Assam, W Burma
A. b. intermedia
E Burma
A. b. dubia
S Burma
A. b. genestieri
SW China, N Indochina
A. b. superciliaris
E & SE China
A. b. brunnea
Taiwan
A. b. arguta
Hainan I
A. b. olivacea
W Hupeh, Szechwan
Alcippe brunneicauda (Brown Fulvetta)
A. b. brunneicauda
Malaysia, Sumatra, NW Borneo, N Natuna Is
A. b. eriphaea
Borneo
Alcippe poioicephala (Brown-cheeked Fulvetta)
A. p. poioicephala
S India
A. p. brucei
C & S India
A. p. fusca
S Assam, NW Burma
A. p. phayrei
SW Burma
A. p. haringtoniae
NE Burma, NW Thailand
A. p. alearis
N & E Thailand, N Indochina
A. p. karenni
SE Burma, SW Thailand
A. p. davisoni
S Thailand, Mergui Archipelago

Alcippe pyrrhoptera (Javanese Fulvetta) 433
W & C Java
Alcippe peracensis (Mountain Fulvetta)
A. p. grotei
N & C Vietnam, S Laos
A. p. annamensis
S Indochina
A. p. eremita
SE Thailand
A. p. peracensis
N & C Malaysia
Alcippe morrisonia (Grey-cheeked Fulvetta)
A. m. yunnanensis
SE Sikang, NW Yunnan, NE Burma
A. m. fraterculus
SW Yunnan, SE Burma, N Indochina
A. m. schaefferi
SE Yunnan, NW Vietnam
A. m. rufescentior
Hainan I
A. m. morrisonia
Taiwan
A. m. hueti
Kwangtung to Anhwei, SE China
A. m. davidi
W Hupeh, Szechwan
Alcippe nipalensis (Nepal Fulvetta)
A. n. nipalensis
E Himalayas
A. n. commoda
Bangladesh, Assam, N Burma
A. n. stanfordi
SW Burma
Alcippe abyssinica (African Hill Babbler)
A. a. monachus
Cameroun Mt
A. a. claudi
Fernando Po I
A. a. poliothorax
W Kenya
A. a. loima
NW Kenya
A. a. ansorgei
C & W Angola, SE Zaire, W Tanzania
A. a. stierlingi
S & C Tanzania, N Malawi
A. a. abyssinica
W Ethiopia, W Kenya, N Tanzania
A. a. atriceps
Cameroun, NE Zaire, W Uganda
A. a. hildegardae
SW Tanzania

LIOPTILUS
Lioptilus nigricapillus (Bush Blackcap)
E Cape Province, Natal, N Transvaal
Lioptilus gilberti (White-throated Mountain Babbler)
Mt Kupé (Cameroun)

Lioptilus rufocinctus (Red-collared Flycatcher Babbler)
E Zaire
Lioptilus chapini (Chapin's Flycatcher Babbler)
L. c. chapini
Ituri river, E Zaire
L. c. nyombensis
Mt Nyombe (E Zaire)
L. c. kalindei
E Zaire

PAROPHASMA
Parophasma galinieri (Abyssinian Catbird)
C & S Ethiopia

PHYLLANTHUS
Phyllanthus atripennis (Capuchin Babbler)
P. a. atripennis
Senegal to Liberia
P. a. rubiginosus
Ivory Coast to S Nigeria
P. a. bohndorffi
NE Zaire to W Uganda

CROCIAS
Crocias langbianis (Mt Langbian Sibia)
S Vietnam
Crocias albonotatus (Spotted Sibia)
W & C Java

HETEROPHASIA
Heterophasia annectens (Chestnut-backed Sibia)
H. a. annectens
E Himalayas, Assam, NW Burma
H. a. mixta
SE Burma, N Thailand, N Indochina
H. a. saturata
SE Burma, NW Thailand
H. a. eximia
Dalat, S Vietnam
Heterophasia capistrata (Black-capped Sibia)
H. c. capistrata
W Himalayas
H. c. nigriceps
C Himalayas
H. c. bayleyi
E Himalayas
Heterophasia gracilis (Grey Sibia)
S Assam, N Burma, W Yunnan
Heterophasia melanoleuca (Black-headed Sibia)
H. m. desgodinsi
NE Burma, W China
H. m. castanoptera
SE Burma
H. m. tonkinensis
N Vietnam

H. m. melanoleuca
E Burma, NW Thailand
H. m. engelbachi
S Laos
H. m. robinsoni
S Vietnam
Heterophasia auricularis (White-eared Sibia)
Taiwan
Heterophasia pulchella (Beautiful Sibia)
SE Tibet, Assam, NE Burma
Heterophasia picaoides (Long-tailed Sibia)
H. p. picaoides
E Himalayas, NE Burma
H. p. cana
E & S Burma, N Thailand, N Indochina
H. p. wrayi
C Malaysia
H. p. simillima
W Sumatra

YUHINA
Yuhina castaniceps (Striated Yuhina)
Y. c. rufigenis
W Benegal, Sikkim
Y. c. plumbeiceps
N Assam, N Burma
Y. c. castaniceps
S Assam, SW Burma
Y. c. striata
E Burma, NW Thailand
Y. c. torqueola
N Thailand, S China, N Indochina
Y. c. everetti
N Borneo
Yuhina bakeri (White-naped Yuhina)
E Himalayas, Assam
Yuhina flavicollis (Whiskered Yuhina)
Y. f. albicollis
W Himalayas
Y. f. flavicollis
E Himalayas
Y. f. rouxi
Assam, N Burma, SW China, N Indochina
Y. f. clarki
E Burma
Y. f. humilis
S Burma
Y. f. constantiae
N Laos
Y. f. rogersi
Thailand
Yuhina gularis (Striped-throated Yuhina)
Y. g. vivax
W Himalayas
Y. g. gularis
E Nepal, Burma, Assam, NW Vietnam
Y. g. omeiensis
SW China

Yuhina diademata (White-collared Yuhina)
NE Burma, N Vietnam, SW & S China
Yuhina occipitalis (Rufous-vented Yuhina)
Y. o. occipitalis
E Himalayas, SE Tibet, N Assam
Y. o. obscurior
NE Burma, NW Yunnan
Yuhina brunneiceps (Formosan Yuhina)
Taiwan
Yuhina nigrimenta (Black-chinned Yuhina)
Y. n. nigrimenta
Himalayas, Assam
Y. n. intermedia
NE Burma, SW China, N Indochina
Y. n. pallida
Fukien, SE China
Yuhina zantholeuca (White-bellied Yuhina)
Y. z. zantholeuca
E Himalayas, Burma, Thailand
Y. z. tyrannula
N Thailand, N Indochina, Hainan I
Y. z. griseiloris
Kwangtung, Fukien, Taiwan
Y. z. sordida
E Thailand, S Indochina
Y. z. canescens
SE Thailand, W Cambodia
Y. z. interposita
Malaysia
Y. z. saani
NW Sumatra
Y. z. brunnescens
Borneo

MALIA
Malia grata (Malia Babbler)
M. g. recondita
N Celebes
M. g. stresemanni
C & SE Celebes
M. g. grata
SW Celebes

MYZORNIS
Myzornis pyrrhoura (Fire-tailed Myzornis)
E Himalayas, SE Tibet, NE Burma

HORIZORHINUS
Horizorhinus dohrni (Dohrn's Thrush-Babbler)
Principé I

OXYLABES
Oxylabes cinereiceps (Grey-crowned Oxylabes)
E Madagascar
Oxylabes madagascariensis (White-throated Oxylabes)
E Madagascar

Oxylabes xanthophrys (Yellow-browed Oxylabes)
EC Madagascar

MYSTACORNIS
Mystacornis crossleyi (Crossley's Babbler)
Madagascar

MUSCICAPIDAE
133 PANURINAE (PARROTBILLS)
PANURUS
Panurus biarmicus (Bearded Reedling)
P. b. biarmicus
England, S & E Europe
P. b. occidentalis
Balkans
P. b. russicus
E Europe, Russia, Iran, Manchuria

CONOSTOMA
Conostoma oemodium (Great Parrotbill)
Himalayas, NE Burma, SE Tibet, SW China

PARADOXORNIS
Paradoxornis paradoxus (Three-toed Parrotbill)
P. p. paradoxus
NW China
P. p. taipaiensis
Shensi
Paradoxornis unicolor (Brown Parrotbill)
E Himalayas, N Burma, SE Tibet, SW China
Paradoxornis flavirostris (Gould's Parrotbill)
E Himalayas, W Burma
Paradoxornis guttaticollis (Spot-breasted Parrotbill)
Assam to N Indochina
Paradoxornis conspicillatus (Spectacled Parrotbill)
P. c. conspicillatus
WC China
P. c. rocki
Hupeh
Paradoxornis ricketti (Yunnan Parrotbill)
NW Yunnan
Paradoxornis webbianus (Vinous-throated Parrotbill)
P. w. mantschuricus
E Manchuria
P. w. suffusus
NW to SE China
P. w. fulvicauda
NE China, S Korea
P. w. webbianus
coast of S Kiangsu, N Chekiang
P. w. bulomachus
Taiwan

P. w. elisabethae
SE Yunnan
P. w. brunneus
NE Burma, NW Yunnan
Paradoxornis alphonsianus (Ashy-throated Parrotbill)
P. a. alphonsianus
WC China
P. a. yunnanensis
SE Yunnan, NW Vietnam
Paradoxornis zappeyi (Zappey's Parrotbill)
W Szechwan
Paradoxornis przewalskii (Grey-crowned Parrotbill)
S Kansu
Paradoxornis fulvifrons (Fulvous-fronted Parrotbill)
P. f. chayulensis
N Assam, SE Tibet
P. f. fulvifrons
Nepal, Sikkim, Bhutan
P. f. albifacies
NW Yunnan, SE Sikang
P. f. cyanophrys
NW Szechwan, SW Shensi
Paradoxornis nipalensis (Blyth's Parrotbill)
P. n. nipalensis
C Nepal
P. n. humii
E Nepal, Sikkim
P. n. crocotius
SE Tibet, E Bhutan
P. n. poliotis
Assam, NE Burma, NW Yunnan
P. n. patriciae
SE Assam
P. n. ripponi
Mt Victoria, N Burma
P. n. feae
SE Burma, NW Thailand
P. n. verreauxi
E Sikang, SW Szechwan
P. n. pallidus
NW Fukien
P. n. morrisonianus
Taiwan
P. n. beaulieu
N Laos
P. n. craddocki
NW Vietnam
Paradoxornis davidianus (David's Parrotbill)
P. d. davidianus
Fukien
P. d. tonkinensis
N Vietnam
P. d. thompsoni
E Burma, NW Laos, E Thailand

Paradoxornis atrosuperciliaris (Lesser Red-headed Parrotbill)
P. a. oatesi
W Bengal, Sikkim
P. a. atrosuperciliaris
Assam, N Burma, N Laos, W Yunnan
Paradoxornis ruficeps (Greater Red-headed Parrotbill)
P. r. ruficeps
E Himalayas
P. r. bakeri
Assam, N & E Burma
P. r. magnirostris
N Vietnam
Paradoxornis gularis (Grey-headed Parrotbill)
P. g. gularis
E Himalayas, N Assam
P. g. transfluvialis
S Assam, N & E Burma, NW Thailand
P. g. laotianus
E Burma, N Thailand, N Indochina
P. g. fokiensis
Fukien, Anhwei
P. g. hainanus
Hainan I
P. g. rasus
Chin hills, W Burma
P. g. margaritae
S Vietnam
Paradoxornis heudei (Heude's Parrotbill)
P. h. heudei
Kiangsu, C China
P. h. polivanovi
Lake Khanka, USSR

MUSCICAPIDAE

134 PICATHARTINAE (ROCKFOWL)

PICATHARTES
Picathartes gymnocephalus (White-necked Bald Crow)
Sierra Leone to Ghana
Picathartes oreas (Grey-necked Bald Crow)
Cameroun

MUSCICAPIDAE

135 POLIOPTILINAE (GNATWRENS)

MICROBATES
Microbates collaris (Collared Gnatwren)
M. c. paraguensis
Venezuela
M. c. collaris
SE Colombia to French Guiana
M. c. perlatus
N Brazil

Microbates cinereiventris (Half-collared Gnatwren)
M. c. semitorquatus
S Nicaragua to W Panama
M. c. magdalenae
E Panama, N Colombia
M. c. cinereiventris
W Colombia, SW Ecuador
M. c. peruvianus
Colombia, E Ecuador, Peru

RAMPHOCAENUS
Ramphocaenus melanurus (Long-billed Gnatwren)
R. m. rufiventris
SE Mexico, Central America to E Ecuador
R. m. ardeleo
Yucatan, N Guatemala
R. m. sanctaemarthae
N Colombia, NW Venezuela
R. m. griseodorsalis
W Colombia
R. m. pallidus
NE Colombia, N Venezuela
R. m. trinitatis
E Colombia to Trinidad
R. m. duidae
S Venezuela to NE Ecuador
R. m. badius
NE Peru, SE Ecuador
R. m. obscurus
Peru
R. m. amazonum
E Peru, NW Brazil
R. m. sticturus
NW Brazil
R. m. albiventris
E Venezuela, the Guianas, NE Brazil
R. m. austerus
Brazil
R. m. melanurus
N & E Brazil

POLIOPTILA
Polioptila caerula (Blue-grey Gnatcatcher)
P. c. caerula
C & E USA, E Mexico, West Indies
P. c. amoenissima
SW USA, NW Mexico, N Baja California
P. c. obscura
S Baja California
P. c. gracilis
SE Sonora (Mexico)
P. c. mexicana
SE Mexico
P. c. nelsoni
SW & S Mexico
P. c. deppei
Yucatan

P. c. cozumelae
Cozumel I
Polioptila melanura (Black-tailed Gnatcatcher)
P. m. californica
SW California, NW Baja California
P. m. lucida
SW USA, N Mexico, NE Baja California
P. m. melanura
S USA
P. m. pontilis
C Baja California
P. m. margaritae
S Baja California, Santa Margarita I
P. m. curtata
Tiburon I
Polioptila lembeyei (Cuban Gnatcatcher)
E Cuba
Polioptila albiloris (White-lored Gnatcatcher)
P. a. vanrossemi
S & W Mexico
P. a. albiventris
N Yucatan
P. a. albiloris
Guatemala to Costa Rica
Polioptila nigriceps (Black-capped Gnatcatcher)
P. n. restricta
Sonora (Mexico)
P. n. nigriceps
N Sinaloa (Mexico)
Polioptila plumbea (Tropical Gnatcatcher)
P. p. brodkorbi
SE Mexico to Nicaragua
P. p. superciliaris
SE Mexico to Panama
P. p. cinericia
Coiba I (Panama)
P. p. bilineata
Colombia to W Peru
P. p. plumbiceps
N Colombia, N Venezuela
P. p. anteocularis
Colombia
P. p. daguae
Colombia
P. p. innotata
E Colombia, S Venezuela, N Brazil
P. p. plumbea
the Guianas, NE Brazil
P. p. maior
N Peru
P. p. parvirostris
E Peru
P. p. atricapilla
NE Brazil

Polioptila lactea (Cream-bellied Gnatcatcher)
SE Brazil to Argentina

Polioptila guianensis (Guianan Gnat-catcher)
P. g. facilis
Venezuela, NE Brazil
P. g. guianensis
the Guianas
P. g. paraensis
Brazil

Polioptila schistaceigula (Slate-throated Gnatcatcher)
E Panama to W Ecuador

Polioptila dumicola (Masked Gnatcatcher)
P. d. berlepschi
Brazil, E Bolivia
P. d. dumicola
Bolivia to Uruguay, Argentina
P. d. saturata
Bolivia

MUSCICAPIDAE

136 SYLVINAE (OLD WORLD WARBLERS)

TESIA
Tesia castaneocoronata (Chestnut-headed Ground Warbler)
T. c. castaneocoronata
Himalayas, Burma, Thailand, S China
T. c. abadiei
N Vietnam
T. c. ripleyi
SW China

Tesia cyaniventer (Grey-bellied Ground Warbler)
Himalayas, Burma, Thailand, Laos, S China

Tesia olivea (Slaty-bellied Ground Warbler)
Burma, Thailand, Laos, SW China, N Vietnam

Tesia superciliaris (Java Ground Warbler)
Java

PSAMATHIA
Psamathia annae (Palau Bush Warbler)
Palau Is

CETTIA
Cettia subulata (Timor Bush Warbler)
Timor I

Cettia whiteheadi (Bornean Short-tailed Bush Warbler)
Borneo

Cettia squameiceps (Short-tailed Bush Warbler)
E Siberia, Japan, S China

Cettia pallidipes (Pale-footed Bush Warbler)
C. p. pallidipes
Sikkim

C. p. laurentei
W China
C. p. osmastoni
S Andaman Is

Cettia diphone (Japanese Bush Warbler)
C. d. borealis
Manchuria, Korea, S China
C. d. canturians
N China
C. d. sakhalinensis
Sakhalin I, N Japan
C. d. cantans
C & S Japan
C. d. takahashii
Quelpart I
C. d. ijimae
Tanegashima I
C. d. panafidinica
Panafidin I
C. d. riukiuensis
Riukiu Is
C. d. restricta
Borodino I
C. d. diphone
Bonin Is
C. d. iwootoensis
Iwo Jima I
C. d. seebohmi
N Luzon

Cettia fortipes (Strong-footed Bush Warbler)
C. f. pallida
Pakistan, NW India
C. f. fortipes
Nepal
C. f. davidiana
WS China
C. f. sinensis
SE China

Cettia vulcania (Müller's Bush Warbler)
C. v. oreophila
NE Borneo
C. v. banksi
Borneo
C. v. sepiaria
N Sumatra
C. v. sumatrana
C Sumatra
C. v. vulcania
E Sumatra, Java, Bali I, Lombok I
C. v. everetti
Timor I
C. v. palawanae
Palawan I

Cettia major (Large Bush Warbler)
C. m. major
Nepal, Burma, W China
C. m. vafer
Assam

***Cettia flavolivacea* (Aberrant Bush Warbler)**
  C. f. flavolivacea
    Nepal, S Tibet
  C. f. intricata
    S China
  C. f. weberi
    Chin hills, Burma
  C. f. alexanderi
    Burma
  C. f. oblita
    W China, N Vietnam
  C. f. stresemanni
    Assam
***Cettia acanthizoides* (Verreaux's Bush Warbler)**
  C. a. brunnescens
    SE Assam, Nepal, SE Tibet
  C. a. acanthizoides
    E Burma, W China
  C. a. robustipes
    S China, Taiwan
***Cettia brunnifrons* (Rufous-capped Bush Warbler)**
  C. b. whistleri
    NW Himalayas
  C. b. brunnifrons
    E Himalayas, Nepal
  C. b. muroides
    Assam
  C. b. umbratica
    Burma
***Cettia cetti* (Cetti's Warbler)**
  C. c. cetti
    S Europe, Asia Minor, N Africa
  C. c. orientalis
    Middle East, N Iran
  C. c. cettioides
    WC Asia, SE Iran, Turkistan
  C. c. interpositus
    Iran
  C. c. albiventris
    W Pakistan

BRADYPTERUS
***Bradypterus baboecala* (African Sedge Warbler)**
  B. b. centralis
    S Nigeria, Cameroun to E Zaire
  B. b. chadensis
    Lake Chad
  B. b. elgonensis
    E Chad, Uganda, N Kenya
  B. b. tongensis
    Sudan
  B. b. sudanensis
    S Sudan
  B. b. abyssinicus
    Ethiopia
  B. b. moreaui
    SE Kenya, Tanzania, Malawi, Mozambique

  B. b. msiri
    Angola, S Zaire, Botswana
  B. b. benguellensis
    S Angola
  B. b. baboecalus
    Rhodesia, Transvaal, Natal, Cape Province
***Bradypterus graueri* (Grauer's Warbler)**
  E Zaire
***Bradypterus grandis* (Ja River Warbler)**
  Cameroun, Gabon
***Bradypterus carpalis* (White-winged Warbler)**
  NE Zaire, Uganda
***Bradypterus cinnamomeus* (Cinnamon Bracken Warbler)**
  B. c. bangwaensis
    E Nigeria, Cameroun
  B. c. cavei
    S Sudan
  B. c. macdonaldi
    W Ethiopia
  B. c. cinnamomeus
    S Ethiopia, Kenya, NE Zaire
  B. c. mildbreadi
    E Zaire
  B. c. rufoflavidus
    SE Kenya, N Tanzania
  B. c. nyassae
    E Tanzania, Malawi
***Bradypterus victorini* (Victorin's Scrub Warbler)**
  S Cape Province
***Bradypterus barratti* (Scrub Warbler)**
  B. b. boultoni
    C Angola
  B. b. priesti
    Zimbabwe
  B. b. barratti
    E Transvaal, Natal
  B. b. godfreyi
    Lesotho, E Cape Province
***Bradypterus mariae* (Evergreen Forest Warbler)**
  B. m. mariae
    SE Kenya, NE Tanzania
  B. m. usambarae
    S Kenya, W Tanzania, E Zambia, N Malawi
  B. m. ufipae
    S Tanzania, Zambia
  B. m. granti
    W & S Malawi
***Bradypterus lopezi* (Lopez' Warbler)**
  B. l. lopezi
    Fernando Po I
  B. l. camerunensis
    Cameroun Mt
  B. l. manengubae
    Manenguba Mt (Cameroun)
  B. l. barakae
    E Zaire, W Uganda

Bradypterus sylvaticus (Knysna Scrub
Warbler)
S Natal, SE Cape Province
Bradypterus alfredi (Bamboo Warbler)
B. a. kungwensis
N Zambia, SW Tanzania
B. a. alfredi
E Zaire
B. a. albicrissalis
W Uganda
Bradypterus thoracicus (Spotted Bush
Warbler)
B. t. davidi
NE Asia, S China
B. t. suschkini
C Asia, N Vietnam
B. t. przewalskii
W Himalayas, S & W China
B. t. thoracicus
Bangladesh, E Himalayas, Nepal
B. t. shanensis
Burma
Bradypterus major (Large-billed Bush
Warbler)
B. b. major
W Himalayas, Turkistan, Sinkiang
B. b. netrix
W China
Bradypterus tacsanowskius (Chinese Bush
Warbler)
B. t. tacsanowskius
SE Siberia, N China, Burma, N Indochina
B. t. chui
S China
Bradypterus luteoventris (Brown Bush
Warbler)
B. l. luteoventris
Assam, Nepal, SE Tibet
B. l. ticehursti
Burma
Bradypterus seebohmi (Mountain Scrub
Warbler)
B. s. idoneus
Taiwan, N Thailand, S Indochina
B. s. melanorhynchus
NW Fukien
B. s. seebohmi
N Luzon I
B. s. montis
E Java
B. s. timorensis
Timor I
Bradypterus caudatus (Long-tailed Ground
Warbler)
B. c. caudatus
N Luzon I

B. c. unicolor
Mindanao I
B. c. malindangensis
S Mindanao I
Bradypterus accentor (Kinabalu Scrub
Warbler)
Borneo
Bradypterus castaneus (East Indies Bush
Warbler)
B. c. disturbans
Buru I
B. c. musculus
Ceram I
B. c. castaneus
C Moluccas
Bradypterus palliseri (Palliser's Warbler)
Sri Lanka

LOCUSTELLA
Locustella fasciolata (Gray's Grasshopper
Warbler)
NE Asia, Sakhalin, Japan » Philippine Is,
Celebes, New Guinea
Locustella amnicola (Stepanyan's
Grasshopper Warbler)
Sakhalin I, Kurile Is
Locustella luscinioides (Savi's Warbler)
L. l. luscinioides
C & E Europe, Iberia, N Africa
L. l. sarmatica
S Russia
L. l. fusca
WC Asia
Locustella fluviatilis (River Warbler)
NE Europe, NW Asia, » SE Africa
Locustella certhiola (Pallas's Grasshopper
Warbler)
L. c. certhiola
NC Asia » NW India
L. c. centralasiae
C Asia, Himalayas » Burma
L. c. rubescens
E Siberia » C & S India, Sri Lanka
L. c. minor
E China, Indochina
Locustella ochotensis (Middendorff's
Grasshopper Warbler)
NE Asia, Kurile I, Sakhalin I » Philippine Is,
Borneo
Locustella pleskei (Styan's Grasshopper
Warbler)
Japan, Korea » SE China & Sunda Is
Locustella naevia (Grasshopper Warbler)
L. n. naevia
Europe, N Africa, Russia
L. n. obscurior
Caucasus
L. n. straminea
Iran, N India, W Siberia, C Asia

L. n. mongolica
Afghanistan, W Mongolia

***Locustella lanceolata* (Lanceolated Warbler)**
NC & NE Asia, Sakhalin I » Philippine Is, SE Asia

ACROCEPHALUS

***Acrocephalus paludicola* (Aquatic Warbler)**
CS & E Europe, W Russia, Asia Minor, Egypt

***Acrocephalus schoenobaenus* (Sedge Warbler)**
Europe & W & C Asia » EC & SE Africa

***Acrocephalus agricola* (Paddyfield Warbler)**
A. a. agricola
WC Asia, N India
A. a. brevipennis
S Turkistan, Pakistan, N & C China
A. a. tangorum
Manchuria

***Acrocephalus concinens* (Blunt-winged Paddyfield Warbler)**
A. c. harringtoni
Afghanistan, NW India, Pakistan
A. c. stevensi
Bangladesh, Assam, Burma
A. c. concinens
N & C China » S Burma, S Thailand

***Acrocephalus bistrigiceps* (Schrenk's Reed Warbler)**
NE Asia » Burma, S China, N Vietnam

***Acrocephalus sorghophilus* (Speckled Reed Warbler)**
N & E China » Philippine Is

***Acrocephalus orinus* (Large-billed Reed Warbler)**
N India

***Acrocephalus baeticatus* (African Reed Warbler)**
A. b. hopsoni
Lake Chad
A. b. cinnamomeus
S Sudan, S & E Zaire, Uganda, Angola
A. b. suahelicus
Kenya, Tanzania, Malawi
A. b. hallae
Namibia
A. b. baeticatus
Rhodesia, South Africa
A. b. dumetorum
E Europe, W & C Asia, N Iran, Himalayas, India, Burma

***Acrocephalus scirpaceus* (Reed Warbler)**
A. s. scirpaceus
Europe, W Russia » WC & E Africa
A. s. fuscus
Asia Minor, C Asia » E Africa

***Acrocephalus palustris* (Marsh Warbler)**
N Europe, Russia » NW & SE Africa

***Acrocephalus melanopogon* (Moustached Warbler)**
A. m. melanopogon
Europe, N Africa
A. m. mimica
C Asia, S Russia, Iraq, Iran, Afghanistan
A. m. albiventris
Krasnodor (USSR)

***Acrocephalus arundinaceus* (Great Reed Warbler)**
A. a. arundinaceus
Europe, Asia Minor » NW, W & SC Africa
A. a. zarudnyi
S Russia C Asia » C Africa
A. a. griseldis
S Iran » E Africa

***Acrocephalus orientalis* (Oriental Great Reed Warbler)**
SE Siberia, N China, » Philippine Is

***Acrocephalus stentoreus* (Clamorous Reed Warbler)**
A. s. stentoreus
Egypt, Sinai
A. s. brunnescens
Iran, Afghanistan, NW India
A. s. amyae
N India, Thailand, Indochina
A. s. meridionalis
Sri Lanka
A. s. siebirsi
W Java
A. s. lentecaptus
Lombok I, Sumbawa I
A. s. sumbae
Moluccas, Sumba I
A. s. celebensis
Celebes
A. s. toxopei
Buru I
A. s. harterti
Philippine Is
A. s. meyeri
Bismarck Archipelago, Solomon Is
A. s. cervinus
N Queensland, New Guinea
A. s. gouldi
Western Australia
A. s. australis
SE Australia, Tasmania

***Acrocephalus luscinia* (Nightingale Reed Warbler)**
A. l. luscinia
Guam I, Saipan I, Almagan I
A. l. syrinx
Caroline Is

A. l. yamashinae
Pagan I
A. l. nijoi
Agiguan I
A. l. astrolabii
Mariana Is

**Acrocephalus aedon (Thick-billed Reed
Warbler)**
A. a. aedon
NC Asia, Burma, Thailand, Indonesia
A. a. rufescens
NE Asia, Korea, Japan, Malaysia

**Acrocephalus rehsei (Finsch's Reed
Warbler)**
Gilbert Is

**Acrocephalus kingii (Hawaiian Reed
Warbler)**
Nihoa (Hawaii)

**Acrocephalus aequinoctialis (Polynesian
Reed Warbler)**
A. a. aequinoctialis
Christmas I
A. a. pistor
Fanning I

**Acrocephalus caffra (Long-billed Reed
Warbler)**
A. c. caffra
Tahiti I, Society Is
A. c. longirostris
Moorea I
A. c. garretti
Tahiti I

Acrocephalus atypha (Tuamotu Warbler)
A. a. atypha
NW Tuamotu Is
A. a. rava
SE Tuamotu Is
A. a. palmarum
Anaa I
A. a. niauensis
Niau I
A. a. erema
Makatea I
A. a. flavida
Napuka I

**Acrocephalus mendanae (Marquesas
Warbler)**
A. m. mendanae
Takuata I
A. m. percernis
Nukuhiva I
A. m. consobrina
Motane I
A. m. fatuhivae
Fatuhiva I
A. m. idae
Ua Huka I

A. m. dido
Ua Pou I
A. m. aquilonis
Eiao I
A. m. postrema
Hatutu I

Acrocephalus vaughanii (Pitcairn Warbler)
A. v. vaughanii
Pitcairn I
A. v. rimitarae
Rimitara I
A. v. taiti
Henderson I
A. v. kerearako
Mangaia I (Cook Is)
A. v. kaoko
Mitiaro I (Cook Is)

**Acrocephalus gracilirostris (Swamp
Warbler)**
A. g. neglecta
Lake Chad
A. g. tsanae
N Ethiopia
A. g. nilotica
Sudan, Uganda, W Kenya, E Zaire,
N Zambia
A. g. jacksoni
NE Zaire, Uganda, S Sudan
A. g. parva
S Kenya
A. g. leptorhyncha
Tanzania, S Zaire, Angola to Mozambique
A. g. winterbottomi
E Angola, W Zambia
A. g. cunenensis
S Angola
A. g. gracilirostris
Namibia, Botswana, South Africa

**Acrocephalus rufescens (Rufous Swamp
Warbler)**
A. r. rufescens
W & WC Africa
A. r. chadensis
Chad
A. r. nilotica
S Sudan to Zambia
A. r. foxi
E Zaire, SW Uganda
A. r. ansorgei
N Angola

**Acrocephalus brevipennis (Cape Verde
Swamp Warbler)**
Cape Verde Is

**Acrocephalus newtoni (Madagascar
Swamp Warbler)**
Madagascar

BEBRORNIS
Bebrornis rodericanus (Rodriguez Brush Warbler)
Rodriguez I
Bebrornis sechellensis (Seychelles Brush Warbler)
Cousin I

NESILLAS
Nesillas typica (Tsikirity Warbler)
N. t. ellisii
NW Madagascar
N. t. typica
C & E Madagascar
N. t. lentzii
S & W Madagascar
N. t. longicaudata
Anjouan I
N. t. brevicaudata
Great Comoro I
Nesillas mariae (Comoro Warbler)
Moheli I (Comores)
Nesillas aldabranus (Aldabra Warbler)
Aldabra I

THAMNORNIS
Thamnornis chloropetoides (Kiritika)
S Madagascar

CHLOROPETA
Chloropeta natalensis (Yellow Warbler)
C. n. batesi
E Nigeria, Cameroun, Gabon, E Zaire
C. n. massaica
Zaire to Ethiopia & Tanzania
C. n. major
Angola, S Zaire, Zambia
C. n. natalensis
S Tanzania, Malawi, Rhodesia, N South Africa
Chloropeta similis (Mountain Yellow Warbler)
Zaire to Sudan, Malawi, Tanzania
Chloropeta gracilirostris (Yellow Swamp Warbler)
C. g. gracilirostris
E Zaire, W Uganda
C. g. bensoni
Lake Mweru, NE Zambia

HIPPOLAIS
Hippolais icterina (Icterine Warbler)
H. i. icterina
C & E Europe, W Siberia » South Africa
H. i. alaria
Asia Minor, Iran
Hippolais polyglotta (Melodious Warbler)
SW Europe » NW & W Africa
Hippolais olivetorum (Olive-tree Warbler)
SE Europe, Asia Minor, N Africa

Hippolais languida (Upcher's Warbler)
Egypt, Syria to Afghanistan
Hippolais pallida (Olivaceous Warbler)
H. p. opaca
S Spain, NW Africa
H. p. elaeica
SE Europe, Iran, SE Asia » Ethiopia
H. p. reiseri
S Algeria, S Tunisia
H. p. pallida
Egypt, Sudan
H. p. laeneni
Lake Chad
Hippolais caligata (Booted Warbler)
H. c. caligata
C & E Russia » S & W India
H. c. annectens
Altai, NW Mongolia » N India
H. c. rama
E Iran to Pakistan

SYLVIA
Sylvia nisoria (Barred Warbler)
S. n. nisoria
C & E Europe, W Russia, E Africa
S. n. merzbacheri
N Iran, Afghanistan, C Asia
Sylvia hortensis (Orphean Warbler)
S. h. hortensis
S Europe, N & W Africa
S. h. crassirostris
Asia Minor, Iran, Afghanistan, Arabia
S. h. jerdoni
Pakistan, N India
S. h. balchanica
Iraq, W Iran
Sylvia leucomelaena (Red Sea Warbler)
S. l. leucomelaena
Saudi Arabia
S. l. blanfordi
Eritrea
S. l. somaliensis
NE Somalia
Sylvia borin (Garden Warbler)
S. b. borin
Europe, W Russia » WC Africa
S. b. pallida
C Asia, W Siberia » E Africa
S. b. woodwardi
N Iran
Sylvia atricapilla (Blackcap)
S. a. atricapilla
W Europe, W Russia » N & E Africa
S. a. dammholzi
Caucasus, Asia Minor, W Iran » E Africa
S. a. heineken
Madeira I
S. a. riphaea
W Siberia

S. a. pauluccii
Sardinia, Balearic Is
Sylvia communis (Whitethroat)
S. c. communis
Europe, N Africa, Russia » C & S Africa
S. c. icterops
Iran, Asia Minor » NW India
S. c. volgensis
Altai, W Siberia
Sylvia curruca (Lesser Whitethroat)
S. c. curruca
Europe, W Russia » N & C Africa
S. c. blythi
Siberia » Pakistan, India
S. c. telengitica
SW Altai, C Asia » N India
S. c. halimodendri
Kazakhstan, SC Asia » N India
S. c. minula
W Mongolia, Tibet, Pakistan, NW India
S. c. caucasica
Caucasus, Iran
S. c. margelanica
NE Tsinghai, Gobi, NW China
S. c. althaea
Transcaspia, Iran
S. c. monticola
S Russia, Turkistan
S. c. zagrossiensis
Iraqi, SW Iran
Sylvia nana (Desert Whitethroat)
S. n. nana
Iran, Afghanistan, Tibet, N India
S. n. deserti
N & NE Africa
S. n. theresae
NW India
Sylvia rüppelli (Rüppell's Warbler)
SE Europe, NE Africa
Sylvia melanocephala (Sardinian Warbler)
S. m. melanocephala
S Europe, N Africa
S. m. muricolor
Portugal
S. m. carmichael-lowi
SE Italy
S. m. leucogastra
Canary Is
S. m. pasiphaë
Rhodes, Crete
S. m. norrisae
Egypt
S. m. momus
Syria, Israel, Sinai
Sylvia melanothorax (Cyprus Warbler)
Cyprus

Sylvia mystacea (Ménétries' Warbler)
NE Africa, Iran, Afghanistan
Sylvia cantillans (Subalpine Warbler)
S. c. cantillans
SW Europe, NW Africa
S. c. albistriata
SE Europe, Asia Minor, NE Africa
S. c. inornata
N Africa
Sylvia conspicillata (Spectacled Warbler)
S. c. conspicillata
S Europe, N Africa
S. c. orbitalis
Canary Is, Cape Verde Is
Sylvia deserticola (Tristram's Warbler)
S. d. deserticola
Algeria, Tunisia
S. d. maroccana
W Morocco
Sylvia ticehursti (Meinertzhagen's Warbler)
Morocco
Sylvia undata (Dartford Warbler)
S. u. dartfordiensis
S England
S. u. tingitana
Morocco
S. u. undata
SW Europe
S. u. toni
Portugal, S Spain, N Africa
S. u. corsa
Corsica, Sardinia
Sylvia sarda (Marmora's Warbler)
S. s. balearica
Balearic Is
S. s. sarda
Corsica, Sardinia, S France, N Africa

PHYLLOSCOPUS
Phylloscopus trochilus (Willow Warbler)
P. t. trochilus
Britain, W Europe » W & WC Africa
P. t. acredula
Scandinavia, C & E Europe, W Siberia »
C Africa
P. t. yakutensis
N & NE Asia » E Africa
Phylloscopus collybitus (Chiff-chaff)
P. c. abietinus
N & E Europe » Asia Minor, Arabia,
Somalia
P. c. collybitus
W & S Europe » N Africa
P. c. canariensis
Canary Is

P. c. exsul
  Lanzarote I
P. c. lorenzii
  Caucasus
P. c. ibericus
  Iberia, Algeria
P. c. tristis
  C Asia, N India, Bangladesh
P. c. sindianus
  Pamir, W Himalayas
Phylloscopus neglectus (Plain Willow Warbler)
  NE Iran, N Afghanistan
Phylloscopus bonelli (Bonelli's Warbler)
P. b. bonelli
  S Europe, N Africa
P. b. orientalis
  Balkans, Asia Minor
Phylloscopus tytleri (Tytler's Willow Warbler)
  Pakistan, India
Phylloscopus sibilatrix (Wood Warbler)
  WC & NE Europe » C Africa
Phylloscopus affinis (Tickell's Willow Warbler)
  S Tibet, India, Burma, W China
Phylloscopus subaffinis (Grant's Leaf Warbler)
P. s. arcanus
  W Nepal
P. s. subaffinis
  W China, N Burma, N Indochina
Phylloscopus griseolus (Jerdon's Willow Warbler)
  C Asia, W Himalayas » N India
Phylloscopus fuligiventer (Smoky Warbler)
P. f. fuligiventer
  Bhutan, Sikkim, Himalayas
P. f. tibetanus
  SE Tibet, SW Sikiang
Phylloscopus fuscatus (Dusky Warbler)
P. f. fuscatus
  C & NE Asia » India, China, Burma, Thailand
P. f. weigoldi
  S Tibet, E Himalayas, W China
Phylloscopus armandii (Milne-Edwards' Willow Warbler)
P. a. armandii
  Mongolia, E China
P. a. perplexus
  Sikiang, W China
Phylloscopus schwarzi (Radde's Bush Warbler)
  NC & NE Asia » Burma, Thailand, Indochina

Phylloscopus pulcher (Orange-barred Willow Warbler)
P. p. kangrae
  NW Himalayas
P. p. pulcher
  N Burma, E Nepal, S Tibet
Phylloscopus inornatus (Yellow-browed Warbler)
P. i. inornatus
  N India, Assam, Bangladesh
P. i. humei
  C Asia, Himalayas, Altai
P. i. mandellii
  Burma, Sikkim, S Tibet, W China
Phylloscopus subviridis (Brooks's Willow Warbler)
  Afghanistan, Pakistan, N India
Phylloscopus proregulus (Pallas's Leaf Warbler)
P. p. proregulus
  NE & C Asia, Sakhalin I, N China
P. p. simlaensis
  Afghanistan, NW India, W Himalayas
P. p. chloronotus
  E Himalayas, W China » Thailand, Malaysia
P. p. kansuensis
  NW China
Phylloscopus maculipennis (Grey-faced Willow Warbler)
P. m. virens
  NW Himalayas
P. m. centralis
  W & C Nepal
P. m. maculipennis
  E Himalayas, SW China, N Burma, N Indochina
P. m. debilis
  SW China
Phylloscopus borealis (Arctic Warbler)
P. b. borealis
  NE Europe, N & NE Asia » SE China, Philippine Is
P. b. hylebata
  C Asia, Mongolia, Sakhalin I » Indochina
P. b. xanthodryas
  Kamchatka, N Kurile Is » Philippine Is, Indochina
P. b. examinandus
  S Kurile Is, Japan » Borneo, Sumatra
P. b. kennikotti
  Alaska
P. b. talovka
  N Russia, N Siberia, NW Mongolia
P. b. transbaicalicus
  E Siberia, N Mongolia

***Phylloscopus magnirostris* (Large-billed Willow Warbler)**
Himalayas, India, W China, E Tibet

***Phylloscopus trochiloides* (Greenish Warbler)**
P. t. viridanus
NE Europe, W & C Asia » Pakistan, W India
P. t. trochiloides
Himalayas, Tibet, W China, Burma
P. t. ludlowi
Ladakh, NW Himalayas
P. t. obscuratus
NW China
P. t. plumbeitarsus
E Asia, Manchuria » Thailand, Indochina

***Phylloscopus nitidus* (Green Willow Warbler)**
Caucasus, Iran, W India

***Phylloscopus tenellipes* (Pale-legged Willow Warbler)**
P. t. tenellipes
E Manchuria, Korea, Sakhalin I » Burma, Indochina
P. t. borealoides
Japan » N Vietnam

***Phylloscopus occipitalis* (Large Crowned Willow Warbler)**
C Asia, Afghanistan » W India

***Phylloscopus coronatus* (Temminck's Crowned Willow Warbler)**
NE Asia, Korea, Japan. » Indochina, Malaysia

***Phylloscopus ijimae* (Ijima's Willow Warbler)**
Izu Is

***Phylloscopus reguloides* (Blyth's Crowned Willow Warbler)**
P. r. kashmirensis
NW India
P. r. reguloides
NE India, Nepal, Bangladesh
P. r. assamensis
Assam, N Burma, SE Tibet
P. r. claudiae
W China
P. r. fokiensis
S China
P. r. ticehursti
S Vietnam

***Phylloscopus davisoni* (White-tailed Willow Warbler)**
P. d. davisoni
E & S Sikang » Burma, N Indochina
P. d. disturbans
SW China
P. d. ogilviegranti
SE China, N Vietnam

P. d. klossi
S Indochina

***Phylloscopus presbytes* (Timor Leaf Warbler)**
P. p. presbytes
Timor I
P. p. floris
Flores I

***Phylloscopus cantator* (Yellow-faced Leaf Warbler)**
N India

***Phylloscopus ricketti* (Rickett's Willow Warbler)**
P. r. ricketti
S China, N Vietnam
P. r. goodsoni
S Hainan I

***Phylloscopus trivirgatus* (Island Leaf Warbler)**
P. t. parvirostris
Malaysia
P. t. trivirgatus
Sumatra, Java, Bali I, NW Borneo
P. t. kinabaluensis
NE Borneo
P. t. sarawacensis
W Borneo
P. t. nesophilus
SC Celebes
P. t. sarasinorum
S Celebes
P. t. capitalis
SE Celebes
P. t. waterstradti
Moluccas
P. t. everetti
Buru I
P. t. matthiae
St Matthias Is
P. t. avicola
Great Kei Is
P. t. ceramensis
Ceram I
P. t. maforensis
Numfor I
P. t. misoriensis
Biak I
P. t. poliocephala
NW New Guinea
P. t. albigularis
WC New Guinea
P. t. paniaiae
W New Guinea
P. t. cyclopum
N New Guinea
P. t. henrietta
N Halmahera I

P. t. giulianettii
C & SE New Guinea
P. t. hamlini
Goodenough I
P. t. becki
Gualdalcanal I, Malaita I
P. t. bougainvillei
Bougainville I
P. t. pallescens
Kulambangra I
P. t. makirensis
San Cristobal I
P. t. crookshanki
D'Entrecasteaux Archipelago
P. t. nigrorum
Luzon I, Negros I, Mindoro I
P. t. diuttae
NE Mindanao I
P. t. mindanensis
Mindanao I
P. t. malindangensis
Mt Malindang (Mindanao I)
P. t. flavostriatus
Mindanao I
P. t. petersoni
Palawan I
P. t. moorhousei
New Britain
P. t. leletensis
New Ireland
Phylloscopus amoenus (Kulambangra Warbler)
Kulambangra I
Phylloscopus olivaceus (Philippine Leaf Warbler)
Philippine Is
Phylloscopus cebuensis (Dubois' Leaf Warbler)
P. c. cebuensis
Cebu I, Negros I
P. c. luzonensis
N Luzon I
P. c. sorsogonensis
S Luzon I
Phylloscopus ruficapilla (Yellow-throated Woodland Warbler)
P. r. ochrogularis
W Tanzania
P. r. minullus
SE Kenya, E Tanzania
P. r. johnstonei
SW Tanzania, Malawi, Rhodesia
P. r. quelimanensis
N Mozambique
P. r. alacris
Manica e Sofala (Mozambique)
P. r. ruficapilla
E Transvaal, Natal, S Cape Province

Phylloscopus laurae (Mrs Boulton's Woodland Warbler)
P. l. eustacei
SE Zaire, NE Zambia
P. l. laurae
Angola, W Zambia
Phylloscopus laetus (Red-faced Woodland Warbler)
P. l. schoutedeni
E Zaire
P. l. laetus
Rwanda, W Uganda
Phylloscopus budongoensis (Uganda Woodland Warbler)
E Zaire, Uganda, W Kenya
Phylloscopus herberti (Black-capped Woodland Warbler)
P. h. herberti
Fernando Po I
P. h. camerunensis
S Nigeria, Cameroun Mt
Phylloscopus umbrovirens (Brown Woodland Warbler)
P. u. umbrovirens
N & C Ethiopia, Somalia
P. u. mackenzianus
S Sudan, Uganda, Kenya
P. u. omoensis
W & S Ethiopia
P. u. wilhelmi
E Zaire
P. u. alpinus
W Uganda
P. u. dorchadichrous
NE Tanzania
P. u. fugglescouchmani
E Tanzania

SEICERCUS
Seicercus burkii (Yellow-eyed Flycatcher Warbler)
S. b. whistleri
Himalayas
S. b. burkii
Assam, SE Tibet, Nepal
S. b. tephrocephala
N Thailand, Burma
S. b. distincta
NW Thailand, W China
S. b. latouchei
SW China
S. b. valentini
S China
S. b. intermedia
S China, Indochina
S. b. cognita
NW Fukien

Seicercus poliogenys (Grey-cheeked
Flycatcher Warbler)
N India, N Burma
Seicercus affinis (Allied Flycatcher
Warbler)
Himalayas, S China, Burma, Indonesia
Seicercus montis (Yellow-breasted
Flycatcher Warbler)
S. m. davisoni
Malaysia
S. m. montis
Borneo
S. m. xanthopygius
Palawan I
S. m. floris
S Flores I
S. m. paulinae
Timor I
S. m. neglecta
Waigeu I, Misol I
Seicercus castaneiceps (Chestnut
Flycatcher Warbler)
S. c. castaneiceps
Assam, Nepal
S. c. collinsi
N Thailand
S. c. butleri
Malaysia
S. c. muelleri
Sumatra
S. c. stresemanni
S Laos
S. c. sinensis
N Indochina, S & W China
S. c. joungi
S Thailand
S. c. annamensis
S Vietnam
Seicercus xanthoschista (Grey-headed
Flycatcher Warbler)
S. x. albosuperciliaris
Pakistan, NW India
S. x. xanthoschista
Sikkim, Bhutan, Nepal
S. x. tephrodiras
E Assam, Burma
S. x. flavogularis
Assam, Burma
Seicercus grammiceps (Sunda Flycatcher
Warbler)
S. g. sumatrana
Sumatra
S. g. grammiceps
Java, Bali I

ABROSCOPUS
Abroscopus hodgsoni (Broad-billed
Flycatcher Warbler)
A. h. hodgsoni
Himalayas, Burma
A. h. tonkinensis
N Vietnam
Abroscopus albogularis (White-throated
Flycatcher Warbler)
A. a. albogularis
Assam, Nepal
A. a. hugonis
N Thailand
A. a. fulvifacies
S China
Abroscopus superciliaris (Yellow-bellied
Flycatcher Warbler
A. s. albigularis
E Himalayas
A. s. superciliaris
N India, Burma, W Thailand
A. s. drasticus
N India, SW Thailand
A. s. smythiesi
Burma
A. s. sakaiorum
Malaysia, Sumatra
A. s. schwaneri
Borneo
A. s. vordermani
Java
A. s. bambusarum
S Thailand
Abroscopus schisticeps (Black-faced
Flycatcher Warbler)
A. s. schisticeps
Nepal
A. s. flavimentalis
SE Tibet, Burma
A. s. ripponi
W China

REGULUS
Regulus calendula (Ruby-crowned Kinglet)
R. c. calendula
N & E Canada, E USA » Central America
R. c. arizonensis
Arizona
R. c. cineraceus
SW USA, W Mexico
R. c. obscurus
Guadelupe I (Mexico)
Regulus regulus (Goldcrest)
R. r. anglorum
British Isles
R. r. regulus
Europe, Asia Minor, Russia, WC Asia
R. r. azoricus
San Miguel (Azores)

R. r. sanctaemariae
Santa Maria (Azores)
R. r. inermis
Azores Is
R. r. interni
Corsica, Sardinia
R. r. buturlini
Crimea, Caucasus
R. r. hyrcanus
N Iran
R. r. coatsi
W Siberia, Altai
R. r. tristis
C Asia
R. r. himalayensis
W Himalayas
R. r. sikkimensis
Nepal, E Himalayas, NW China
R. r. japonensis
NE Asia, Japan, N China, Manchuria
R. r. yunnanensis
SE Tibet, SW China
Regulus ignicapillus (Firecrest)
R. i. ignicapillus
C & S Europe, Asia Minor
R. i. madeirensis
Madeira I
R. i. balearicus
Balearic Is, N Africa
R. i. teneriffae
Canary Is
Regulus goodfellowi (Taiwan Firecrest)
Taiwan
Regulus satrapa (Golden-crowned Kinglet)
R. s. amoensis
W Canada, W USA » W Mexico,
Guatemala
R. s. satrapa
SE Canada, E USA » NE Mexico
R. s. clarus
S Mexico, Central America

LEPTOPOECILE

**Leptopoecile sophiae (Severtzov's Tit
Warbler)**
L. s. sophiae
Pakistan, NW India, C Asia
L. s. stoliczkae
SC Asia, W Gobi Desert
L. s. major
E Tien Shan
L. s. obscura
NW China, Tibet, E Himalayas
Leptopoecile elegans (Crested Tit Warbler)
L. e. meissneri
SE Tibet
L. e. elegans
S China

SCOTOCERCA
**Scotocerca inquieta (Streaked Scrub
Warbler)**
S. i. theresae
S Morocco
S. i. saharae
SE Morocco, Algeria
S. i. harterti
Cyrenaica
S. i. grisea
W Arabia
S. i. buryi
S Arabia
S. i. inquieta
E Egypt, N Arabia
S. i. platyura
Transcaspia, Afghanistan
S. i. striata
Iran, Baluchistan, Pakistan, NW India
S. i. montana
Turgak, USSR

RHOPOPHILUS
**Rhopophilus pekinensis (White-browed
Chinese Warbler)**
R. p. albosuperciliaris
Tarim Basin to Lop Nor
R. p. leptorhynchus
Kansu, NE Tsinghai
R. p. pekinensis
S Manchuria, Korea, Shansi, Ningsia

CISTICOLA
Cisticola textrix (Tink-tink Cisticola)
C. t. bulubulu
W & C Angola, W Zambia
C. t. anselli
E Angola, NW Zambia
C. t. major
Transvaal, E Cape Province
C. t. marleyi
N Natal
C. t. textrix
SW Cape Province
**Cisticola brunnescens (Pectoral-patch
Cisticola)**
C. b. mbangensis
Cameroun
C. b. lynesi
Cameroun
C. b. wambera
W Ethiopia
C. b. brunnescens
E Ethiopia, Somalia
C. b. midcongo
W Zaire
C. b. cinnamomea
E Zaire, Tanzania, Zambia, Rhodesia

C. b. hindii
W Kenya, N Tanzania
C. b. nakuruensis
Kenya, Tanzania
C. b. egregia
S Rhodesia, E Transvaal, Natal
Cisticola ayresii (Wing-snapping Cisticola)
C. a. gabun
Gabon
C. a. imatong
S Sudan
C. a. entebbe
E Zaire, Uganda, NW Tanzania
C. a. itombwensis
E Zaire
C. a. mauensis
Kenya
C. a. ayresii
C, E & SE Africa
Cisticola eximia (Black-necked Cisticola)
C. e. occidens
Guinea to Nigeria
C. e. winneba
S Ghana
C. e. eximia
NE Zaire to Sudan, Ethiopia
Cisticola dambo (Cloud-scraping Cisticola)
C. d. kasai
C Zaire
C. d. dambo
Angola, S Zaire, Zambia
Cisticola exilis (Gold-capped Cisticola)
C. e. tytleri
Bangladesh, Assam, Nepal, N India, China
C. e. erythrocaphala
S India
C. e. equicaudata
Thailand
C. e. lineocapilla
Java, Bali I, Northern Territory (Australia)
C. e. rustica
Celebes, Moluccas, Philippine Is
C. e. exilis
Australia
C. e. diminuta
Solomon Is, N Queensland, New Guinea
C. e. alexandrae
NW Australia, W Queensland
C. e. mixta
S Queensland
C. e. volitans
Taiwan, SW China
C. e. courtoisi
Kiangsi, Fukien
C. e. semirufa
Philippine Is
C. e. polionota
Bismarck Archipelago

Cisticola juncidis (Zitting Cisticola)
(Fan-tailed Warbler)
C. j. juncidis
S Europe, Asia Minor, Egypt
C. j. intermedia
Balearic Is
C. j. cisticola
Iberian peninsula, NW Africa
C. j. annae
Cyprus
C. j. neurotica
Syria, Iraq
C. j. uropygialis
W & NC Africa
C. j. perennia
E Africa
C. j. terrestris
S Africa
C. j. cursitans
Pakistan, India, Sri Lanka
C. j. salimalii
SW India
C. j. omalura
Sri Lanka
C. j. malaya
Malaysia
C. j. brunneiceps
Japan, Batjan I
C. j. tinnabulans
E China, Philippine Is
C. j. nigrostriatus
Palawan I
C. j. fuscicapilla
Lesser Sunda Is, Moluccas, Celebes
C. j. leanyeri
Northern Territory (Australia)
C. j. normani
W Queensland
Cisticola haesitata (Socotra Cisticola)
Socotra I
Cisticola cherina (Madagascar Cisticola)
Madagascar
Cisticola aridula (Desert Cisticola)
C. a. aridula
Niger, Chad, Sudan
C. a. lavendulae
Ethiopia, Somalia
C. a. tanganyika
Kenya, Tanzania
C. a. lobito
S Angola
C. a. perplexa
E Angola, S Zambia
C. a. kalahari
Namibia
C. a. traylori
NE Angola, W Zambia

Cisticola natalensis (Croaking Cisticola)
C. n. strangei
 Senegal to W & C Zaire
C. n. inexpectata
 Ethiopia
C. n. argentea
 S Ethiopia, N Kenya
C. n. tonga
 Sudan
C. n. valida
 E Zaire, W Sudan, NW Kenya,
 NW Tanzania
C. n. kapitensis
 C Kenya
C. n. littoralis
 E Kenya, E Tanzania
C. n. katanga
 NE Angola, S Zaire, Zambia
C. n. huambo
 N & C Angola
C. n. natalensis
 SE Africa
C. n. willi
 W Angola
C. n. holubi
 NE Botswana, SW Rhodesia
Cisticola robusta (Stout Cisticola)
C. r. schraderi
 S Eritrea
C. r. robusta
 Ethiopia
C. r. omo
 SW Ethiopia
C. r. santae
 Cameroun
C. r. nuchalis
 NE Zaire, S Sudan, N Kenya, NW Tanzania
C. r. ambigua
 C & S Kenya, NE Tanzania
C. r. angolensis
 N & C Angola, NW Zambia
C. r. awemba
 SW Tanzania, NE Zambia
Cisticola aberdare (Aberdare Mountain Cisticola)
 C Kenya
Cisticola subruficapilla (Red-headed Cisticola)
C. s. newtoni
 Mossamedes, Angola
C. s. karaensis
 Namibia
C. s. namaqua
 NW Cape Province
C. s. subruficapilla
 SW Cape Province
C. s. jamesi
 E Cape Province

Cisticola lais (Wailing Cisticola)
C. l. distincta
 E Uganda, N Kenya
C. l. mashona
 E Rhodesia, N Transvaal
C. l. namba
 C Angola
C. l. semifasciata
 S Tanzania, Malawi, N Mozambique
C. l. lais
 SE Southern Africa
C. l. monticola
 S Transvaal
C. l. maculata
 SW & S Cape Province
C. l. oreobates
 Mozambique
Cisticola rufilata (Grey Cisticola)
C. r. ansorgei
 Angola to Malawi
C. r. rufilata
 N Namibia to W Transvaal
C. r. vicinior
 Rhodesia
Cisticola cinereola (Ashy Cisticola)
C. c. cinerola
 E & S Ethiopia
C. c. schillingsi
 N & E Kenya
Cisticola restricta (Tana River Cisticola)
 Tana river, Kenya
Cisticola chiniana (Rattling Cisticola)
C. c. simplex
 S Sudan, N Kenya
C. c. victoria
 W Kenya, N Tanzania
C. c. fricki
 Ethiopia, N Kenya
C. c. humilis
 C Kenya
C. c. fischeri
 E Zaire, Tanzania
C. c. ukamba
 SW Kenya, Tanzania
C. c. heterophrys
 E Kenya, E Tanzania
C. c. fortis
 S Zaire, Angola, N Zambia
C. c. emendata
 S Tanzania, N Malawi, N Mozambique
C. c. procera
 C Malawi, C Mozambique
C. c. frater
 Namibia, N Botswana, W Zambia,
 S Angola

C. c. huilensis
Huila, Angola
C. c. smithers
NE Botswana, S Zambia
C. c. campestris
S Mozambique, Natal
C. c. chiniana
E Botswana, Rhodesia, Transvaal
Cisticola bodessa (Boran Cisticola)
C. b. bodessa
E Sudan, S Ethiopia, N Kenya
C. b. kaffensis
Kaffa (S Ethiopia)
Cisticola njombe (Churring Cisticola)
C. n. njombe
S Tanzania
C. n. mariae
W Malawi
Cisticola ruficeps (Red-pate Cisticola)
C. r. guinea
Gambia to N Nigeria
C. r. ruficeps
Central African Republic to Sudan
C. r. scotoptera
E Sudan, N Ethiopia
C. r. mongalla
S Sudan, N Uganda
Cisticola nana (Tiny Cisticola)
S Ethiopia, E Kenya, N Tanzania
Cisticola brachyptera (Siffling Cisticola)
C. b. brachyptera
Senegal to Sudan, Uganda
C. b. zedlitzi
Ethiopia
C. b. hypoxantha
SE Sudan, N Uganda
C. b. reichenowi
N Kenya
C. b. ankole
SW Uganda, NW Tanzania
C. b. kericho
C & S Kenya
C. b. katonae
S Kenya, N Tanzania
C. b. loanda
C Angola, S Zaire, Zambia
C. b. isabellina
S Tanzania, Malawi, Rhodesia,
Mozambique
Cisticola rufa (Rufous Cisticola)
Gambia to N Cameroun
Cisticola troglodytes (Foxy Cisticola)
C. t. troglodytes
Niger to Sudan, Kenya
C. t. ferruginea
E Sudan, W Ethiopia

Cisticola fulvicapilla (Piping Cisticola)
C. f. dispar
Angola
C. f. muelleri
Zambia to Mozambique
C. f. hallae
S Angola, NE Namibia, NW Botswana
C. f. nigricapilla
N Namibia, N Botswana, Rhodesia,
Transvaal
C. f. lebombo
N Natal
C. f. fulvicapilla
S Natal, Cape Province
C. f. silberbaueri
SW Cape Province
C. f. dexter
Botswana, S Zambia
Cisticola angusticauda (Tabora Cisticola)
SW Kenya to Zambia
Cisticola aberrans (Lazy Cisticola)
C. a. petrophila
N Nigeria to Sudan & NE Zaire
C. a. admiralis
Mali & Sierra Leone to Ghana
C. a. emini
E Zaire, NW Tanzania
C. a. nyika
NE Zambia, Botswana to Mozambique
C. a. aberrans
Transvaal, Natal
C. a. minor
E Cape Province, S Natal
Cisticola lateralis (Whistling Cisticola)
C. l. lateralis
Gambia to Cameroun
C. l. modesta
N Angola to Gabon, W Zaire
C. l. antinorii
NE Zaire, Sudan, Uganda
C. l. vincenti
Angola, S Zaire
Cisticola woosnami (Trilling Cisticola)
C. w. woosnami
E Zaire, Uganda to N Malawi
C. w. lufira
SE Zaire, Zambia, W Tanzania
C. w. schusteri
N & E Tanzania
Cisticola anonyma (Chattering Cisticola)
Ghana to Zaire, Angola
Cisticola bulliens (Bubbling Cisticola)
N & C Angola
Cisticola erythrops (Red-faced Cisticola)
C. e. erythrops
Gambia to Zaire
C. e. pyrrhomitra
Ethiopia, S Sudan

C. e. nilotica
SW Sudan
C. e. sylvia
E Zaire, Sudan to Tanzania
C. e. lepe
N & S Angola
C. e. arcana
Zambia
C. e. elusa
Zimbabwe
C. e. nyasa
SE Africa

Cisticola cantans (Singing Cisticola)
C. c. swanzii
Gambia to S Nigeria
C. c. concolor
Niger to Sudan
C. c. adamauae
Cameroun, NW Zaire
C. c. cantans
N Ethiopia
C. c. belli
E Zaire & S Sudan to Tanzania
C. c. pictipennis
Kenya, N Tanzania
C. c. munzneri
Zambia to Mozambique

Cisticola hunteri (Hunter's Cisticola)
C. h. masaba
NW Kenya
C. h. prinioides
N Kenya
C. h. hunteri
C Kenya
C. h. hypernephala
NE Tanzania

Cisticola chubbi (Chubb's Cisticola)
C. c. discolor
Cameroun Mt
C. c. adametzi
highlands of Cameroun
C. c. chubbi
NE Zaire, Kenya, Tanzania
C. c. marungensis
Marungu highland (E Zaire)
C. c. nigriloris
S Tanzania, Malawi

Cisticola galactotes (Winding Cisticola)
C. g. amphilecta
Senegal to Cameroun, N Zaire
C. g. zalingei
N Cameroun to W Sudan
C. g. grisea
Gabon
C. g. lugubris
Ethiopia
C. g. marginata
S Sudan, N Uganda
C. g. haematocephala
S Somalia, E Kenya, E Tanzania

C. g. nyansae
S Uganda, Kenya, NW Tanzania
C. g. suahelica
E Zaire, Zambia
C. g. schoutedeni
NW Zambia
C. g. luapula
Angola, Namibia to Mozambique
C. g. galactotes
Malawi, Rhodesia, Natal
C. g. stagnans
N Botswana

Cisticola carruthersi (Carruthers' Cisticola)
NE Zaire, Kenya

Cisticola pipiens (Chirping Cisticola)
C. p. congo
E Angola, S Zaire, Zambia, N Botswana
C. p. pipiens
S Angola

Cisticola tinniens (Levaillant's Cisticola)
C. t. dyleffi
E Zaire
C. t. oreophila
C Kenya
C. t. shiwae
NE Zambia, SE Zaire
C. t. perpulla
Angola
C. t. tinniens
SE Africa

PRINIA
Prinia subflava (Tawny-flanked Prinia)
P. s. subflava
Senegal to Ethiopia
P. s. melanorhyncha
Sierra Leone to Gabon
P. s. pallescens
Mali, Niger, Sudan
P. s. tenella
C Uganda, Kenya, Tanzania
P. s. affinis
SE Zaire, Zambia to Mozambique
P. s. kasokae
N Angola
P. s. graueri
C Angola, S Zaire, W Zambia
P. s. bechuanae
N Botswana, S Angola, N Namibia
P. s. pondoensis
E Cape Province, Natal
P. s. terricolor
Pakistan, N India
P. s. inornata
SE & C India
P. s. franklinii
SW India
P. s. insularis
Sri Lanka
P. s. fusca
Nepal, Assam, Bangladesh

P. s. blanfordi
Burma
P. s. blythi
Java
P. s. herberti
S Thailand, C Indochina
P. s. extensicauda
W & S China, N Indochina
P. s. formosa
Taiwan
Prinia flavicans (Black-chested Prinia)
P. f. bihe
E Angola, W Zambia
P. f. ansorgei
S Angola
P. f. flavicans
Namibia, Botswana
P. f. ortleppi
N Cape Province, Transvaal, Rhodesia
Prinia maculosa (Karroo Prinia)
P. m. maculosa
Namibia, Botswana, W Cape Province
P. m. hypoxantha
E Cape Province, Natal, E Transvaal
Prinia somalica (Pale Prinia)
P. s. somalica
N Somalia
P. s. erlangeri
S Ethiopia, S Somalia, SE Sudan, N Kenya
Prinia leucopogon (White-chinned Prina)
P. l. leucopogon
Gabon to Zambia
P. l. reichenowi
NE Zaire, S Sudan, Kenya, Tanzania
Prinia leontica (Sierra Leone Prinia)
Sierra Leone to Ghana
Prinia robertsi (Roberts' Prinia)
E Rhodesia
Prinia substriata (White-breasted Prinia)
W & C Cape Province
Prinia molleri (Sao Thomé Prinia)
Sao Thomé I
Prinia bairdii (Banded Prinia)
P. b. bairdii
Cameroun, Gabon
P. b. melanops
E Zaire, W Kenya
P. b. obscura
Kivu, Ruwenzori
P. b. heinrichi
N Angola
Prinia pectoralis (Rufous-eared Prinia)
P. p. ocularia
N Namibia, Botswana, N Cape Province
P. p. pectoralis
S Namibia, Cape Province, W Transvaal

Prinia gracilis (Graceful Prinia)
P. g. carlo
NE Sudan, Somalia
P. g. gracilis
Nile valley
P. g. deltae
Nile delta
P. g. natronensis
lower Egypt
P. g. palestinae
Suez to Syria
P. g. irakensis
Iraq to SW Iran
P. g. lepida
S Iran to NW India
P. g. hufufae
Bahrein I, Hasa, E Arabia
P. g. yemensis
S Arabia
P. g. carpenteri
Oman
Prinia socialis (Ashy Prinia)
P. s. stewarti
Pakistan, N India
P. s. inglisi
NE India, Nepal, Bhutan, Assam,
Bangladesh
P. s. socialis
S India
P. s. brevicauda
Sri Lanka
Prinia rufescens (Lesser Brown Prinia)
P. r. rufescens
Bhutan, Nepal to Burma
P. r. extrema
Malaysia
P. r. peninsularis
S Thailand
P. r. objurgans
S China, N Vietnam
P. r. dalatensis
S Vietnam
Prinia hodgsoni (Franklin's Prinia)
P. h. rufula
Pakistan, Himalayas to Burma
P. h. albogularis
SW India
P. h. pectoralis
Sri Lanka
P. h. hodgsoni
N & C India, S Bangladesh, Burma
P. h. stevensi
NE India
P. h. confusa
N Bangladesh, Assam
P. h. erro
Thailand

Prinia flaviventris **(Yellow-bellied Prinia)**
  P. f. sindiana
    NW India, Pakistan
  P. f. flaviventris
    Bhutan, Himalayas, Bangladesh
  P. f. delacouri
    Thailand
  P. f. sonitans
    SE China, Taiwan, Hainan I
  P. f. rafflesi
    Malaysia, Sumatra, Java
  P. f. halistona
    Nias I
  P. f. chaseni
    Borneo
Prinia familiaris **(Bar-winged Prinia)**
  P. f. olivacea
    Sumatra, W Java
  P. f. familiaris
    E Java, Bali I
Prinia polychroa **(Brown Hill Prinia)**
  P. p. cooki
    S Burma
  P. p. catharia
    W China
  P. p. striata
    C China
  P. p. parumstriata
    SE China
  P. p. polychroa
    Java
Prinia criniger **(Hill Prinia)**
  P. c. striatula
    W Pakistan
  P. c. criniger
    Himalayas, Assam
  P. c. yunnanensis
    N Burma, SW China
Prinia sylvatica **(Jungle Prinia)**
  P. s. gangetica
    Nepal, N India, Bangladesh
  P. s. mahendrae
    Orissa
  P. s. sylvatica
    S India
  P. s. valida
    Sri Lanka
Prinia atrogularis **(White-browed Prinia)**
  P. a. atrogularis
    Nepal, N India, SE Tibet
  P. a. khasiana
    Assam, Burma
  P. a. erythropleura
    Burma
  P. a. superciliaris
    SE China, Burma
  P. a. waterstradti
    Malaysia

  P. a. albogularis
    Sumatra
  P. a. klossi
    N Indochina
Prinia burnesi **(Long-tailed Grass Warbler)**
    Pakistan, N India
Prinia cinerascens **(Assam Prinia)**
    Assam, Bangladesh
Prinia buchanani **(Rufous-fronted Prinia)**
    Pakistan, India
Prinia cinereocapilla **(Hodgson's
    Long-tailed Warbler)**
    N India
APALIS
Apalis flavida **(Yellow-chested Apalis)**
  A. f. caniceps
    Cameroun to Sudan, NW Kenya
  A. f. viridiceps
    NE Ethiopia
  A. f. abyssinica
    Illubabor, Ethiopia
  A. f. malensis
    SW Ethiopia, E Uganda, N Kenya
  A. f. flavocincta
    SW Uganda, Kenya
  A. f. pugnax
    Mt Kenya
  A. f. tenerrima
    E Kenya, Tanzania
  A. f. golzi
    SE Kenya, N Tanzania
  A. f. neglecta
    Angola to Mozambique
  A. f. flavida
    S Angola, Namibia, Botswana
  A. f. florisuga
    E Cape Province, Natal
  A. f. renata
    Sol do Save, Mozambique
Apalis binotata **(Masked Apalis)**
  A. b. binotata
    Cameroun to W Uganda
  A. b. personata
    SW Uganda, E Zaire
  A. b. marungensis
    SE Zaire
Apalis ruddi **(Rudd's Apalis)**
  A. r. ruddi
    S Mozambique, N Natal
  A. r. caniviridis
    S Malawi
Apalis jacksoni **(Black-throated Apalis)**
  A. j. bambuluensis
    N Cameroun
  A. j. minor
    S Cameroun, Central African Republic
  A. j. jacksoni
    SE Sudan, Uganda, Kenya, Angola

Apalis chariessa (White-winged Apalis)
A. c. chariessa
Tana R, Kenya
A. c. macphersoni
E Tanzania
Apalis nigriceps (Black-capped Apalis)
A. n. nigriceps
Sierra Leone to Cameroun
A. n. collaris
NE Zaire, W Uganda
Apalis thoracica (Bar-throated Apalis)
A. t. fuscigularis
SE Kenya
A. t. griseiceps
SE Kenya, NE Tanzania
A. t. uluguru
E Tanzania
A. t. lynesi
N Mozambique
A. t. quarta
Mozambique
A. t. pareensis
NE Tanzania
A. t. iringae
S Tanzania
A. t. youngi
SW Tanzania, N Malawi
A. t. murina
NE Zambia, N Malawi
A. t. whitei
Zambia, Tanzania, Malawi
A. t. flavigularis
Malawi
A. t. rhodesiae
W Rhodesia
A. t. arnoldi
E Rhodesia
A. t. drakensbergensis
E Transvaal, N Natal
A. t. flaviventris
W & C Transvaal
A. t. spelonkensis
E Transvaal
A. t. lebomboensis
NE Natal
A. t. capensis
W Cape Province
A. t. venusta
E Cape Province, Natal
A. t. thoracica
S Cape Province
Apalis cinerea (Grey Apalis)
A. c. cinerea
Cameroun to N Tanzania
A. c. sclateri
Fernando Po I
A. c. grandis
Angola
Apalis alticola (Brown-headed Apalis)
A. a. marungensis
NE Zaire

A. a. alticola
S Tanzania, NE Zambia
A. a. brunneiceps
S Tanzania, Zambia, Malawi
Apalis karamojae (Karamoja Apalis)
E Uganda
Apalis rufogularis (Buff-throated Apalis)
A. r. rufogularis
Fernando Po I, S Nigeria to Gabon
A. r. sanderi
SW Nigeria
A. r. nigrescens
S Sudan to Zambia
A. r. angolensis
N Angola
A. r. brauni
C & S Angola
Apalis argentea (Kungwe Apalis)
A. a. argentea
W Tanzania
A. a. eidos
Idjwi Is, Kivu Lake
Apalis porphyrolaema (Chestnut-throated Apalis)
A. p. porphyrolaema
Uganda, Kenya, NE Tanzania
A. p. kaboboensis
E Zaire
Apalis sharpii (Sharpe's Apalis)
A. s. sharpii
Sierra Leone, Ivory Coast
A. s. bamendae
Cameroun
A. s. goslingi
Cameroun to N Zaire
A. s. strausae
SW Tanzania, Zambia, Malawi
A. s. chapini
SE Tanzania
Apalis melanocephala (Black-headed Apalis)
A. m. ellinorae
C Kenya
A. m. nigrodorsalis
C Kenya
A. m. moschi
SE Kenya, NE Tanzania
A. m. muhuluensis
S Tanzania
A. m. melanocephala
E Tanzania
A. m. lightoni
Malawi, Mozambique
A. m. fuliginosa
S Malawi
A. m. tenebricosa
Mozambique

A. m. adjacens
N Mozambique
A. m. addenda
Sol do Save, Mozambique
Apalis chirindensis (Chirinda Apalis)
E Rhodesia
Apalis pulchra (Black-collared Apalis)
A. p. pulchra
Cameroun to S Sudan, Kenya
A. p. murpheyi
SE Zaire
Apalis ruwenzori (Collared Apalis)
A. r. catiodes
SW Lake Kivu (E Zaire)
A. r. ruwenzori
NW Lake Kivu
Apalis moreaui (Long-billed Apalis)
A. m. moreaui
NE Tanzania
A. m. sousae
N Mozambique
Apalis melanura (Angolan Slender-tailed Apalis)
Angola, S Zaire

GRAMINICOLA
Graminicola bengalensis (Large Grass Warbler)
G. b. bengalensis
Himalayas, N India, Bangladesh
G. b. sinica
S China
G. b. striata
N Vietnam

SPHENOEACUS
Sphenoeacus mentalis (Moustached Grass Warbler)
S. m. mentalis
Guinea to Central African Republic &
C Zaire
S. m. granviki
W Ethiopia
S. m. amauroura
S Sudan to N Zambia
S. m. orientalis
Tanzania
S. m. grandis
Angola to N Mozambique
S. m. luangwae
S Zambia
Sphenoeacus afer (Cape Grassbird)
S. a. transvaalensis
E Rhodesia, NE Transvaal
S. a. excisus
Rhodesia
S. a. natalensis
Transvaal, Natal
S. a. intermedius
E Cape Province

S. a. afer
S Cape Province
Sphenoeacus pycnopygius (Damaraland Rock Jumper)
S. p. pycnopygius
S Angola, N Namibia
S. p. spadix
Huila, Angola

DROMAEOCERCUS
Dromaeocercus brunneus (Brown Feather-tailed Warbler)
EC Madagascar
Dromaeocercus seebohmi (Seebohm's Feather-tailed Warbler)
SC Madagascar

INCANA
Incana incana (Socotra Grass Warbler)
Socotra I

SPILOPTILA
Spiloptila clamans (Cricket Warbler)
Mali to N Ethiopia
Spiloptila rufifrons (Red-faced Warbler)
S. r. rufifrons
Sudan, Ethiopia, Somalia
S. r. smithi
SE Ethiopia to N Tanzania
S. r. rufidorsalis
SE Kenya

UROLAIS
Urolais epichlora (Green Longtail)
U. e. epichlora
N Cameroun
U. e. mariae
Fernando Po I
U. e. cinderella
W Cameroun

HELIOLAIS
Heliolais erythroptera (Red-winged Warbler)
H. e. erythroptera
Guinea to Nigeria
H. e. jodoptera
Cameroun to Sudan
H. e. major
Ethiopia
H. e. rhodoptera
W Kenya, Zambia to Mozambique

PHYLLOLAIS
Phyllolais pulchella (Buff-bellied Warbler)
Chad, Ethiopia to Tanzania

DRYMOCICHLA
Drymocichla incana (Red-winged Grey Warbler)
Cameroun to Uganda

Poliolais lopezi (White-tailed Warbler)
P. l. lopezi
Fernando Po I
P. l. alexanderi
Cameroun Mt
P. l. manengubae
Manenguba, Kupé Mt (Cameroun)

ORTHOTOMUS

Orthotomus sutorius (Long-tailed Tailor Bird)
O. s. guzuratus
NW Himalayas, N India
O. s. patia
Nepal, NE India, Burma
O. s. sutorius
Sri Lanka
O. s. fernandonis
Sri Lanka
O. s. luteus
NE Assam, N Burma
O. s. inexpectatus
W China
O. s. longicauda
S China
O. s. maculicollis
Malaysia
O. s. edela
Java

Orthotomus atrogularis (Black-necked Tailor Bird)
O. a. nitidus
Assam, Burma
O. a. atrogularis
Borneo, Malaysia, Sumatra
O. a. humphreysi
N Borneo
O. a. major
Anamba Is
O. a. davao
SE Mindanao I
O. a. mearnsi
Basilan I
O. a. rabori
Negros I
O. a. chloronotus
N Luzon I
O. a. castaneiceps
Masbate I, Panay I, Ticao I
O. a. frontalis
Bohol I, Leyte I, Mindanao I, Samar I

Orthotomus derbianus (Luzon Tailor Bird)
S Catanduanes I, C Luzon I

Orthotomus ruficeps (Ashy Tailor Bird)
O. r. ruficeps
Sumatra, Malaysia, Java

O. r. sepium
Java
O. r. borneonensis
Borneo
O. r. palliolatus
Karimon Is
O. r. concinnus
Siberut I, Sipora I
O. r. cagayanensis
Cagayan Sulu I

Orthotomus sericeus (Red-headed Tailor Bird)
O. s. hesperius
Burma, Malaysia, Sumatra
O. s. sericeus
Borneo, Palawan I
O. s. rubicundulus
Sirhassen I, Natuna Is
O. s. nuntius
Balabac I, Cagayan Sulu I

Orthotomus cucullatus (Mountain Tailor Bird)
O. c. coronatus
E Himalayas, Assam
O. c. malayensis
Malaysia
O. c. cucullatus
Sumatra, Java, Bali I
O. c. riedeli
Celebes
O. c. cinereicollis
Borneo
O. c. thais
Thailand
O. c. everetti
Flores I
O. c. dumasi
Buru I
O. c. batjanensis
Batjan I
O. c. viridicollis
Palawan I
O. c. philippinus
Luzon I
O. c. heterolaemus
Mindanao I

Orthotomus cinereiceps (White-eared Tailor Bird)
Basilan I, Mindanao I

Orthotomus samarensis (Samar Tailor Bird)
Samar I, Bohol I, Leyte I

Orthotomus nigriceps (Black-headed Tailor Bird)
Mindanao I

Orthotomus metopias (Red-capped Forest Warbler)
Tanzania, N Mozambique

BATHMOCERCUS
Bathmocercus cerviniventris (Black-capped Rufous Warbler)
  Sierra Leone, Ghana
Bathmocercus rufus (Black-faced Rufous Warbler)
  B. r. rufus
    Cameroun, Gabon
  B. r. vulpinus
    E Cameroun to Sudan, N Kenya

SCEPOMYCTER
Scepomycter winifredae (Mrs Moreau's Warbler)
  E Tanzania

CAMAROPTERA
Camaroptera brachyura (Green-backed Camaroptera)
  C. b. bororensis
    SE Zaire to Mozambique
  C. b. pileata
    E Kenya, E Tanzania, Zanzibar
  C. b. fugglescouchmani
    S Tanzania, N Malawi
  C. b. transitiva
    Sabi river, Rhodesia
  C. b. constans
    S Mozambique, E Transvaal, N Natal
  C. b. brachyura
    SE Transvaal, S Cape Province, Natal
Camaroptera brevicaudata (Grey-backed Camaroptera)
  C. b. brevicaudata
    Senegal to Ethiopia
  C. b tincta
    Sierra Leone to Tanzania, S Zaire
  C. b. abessinica
    NE Sudan to Kenya
  C. b. erlangeri
    E Somalia, E Kenya, E Tanzania
  C. b. griseigula
    S Kenya, N Tanzania
  C. b. aschani
    E Zaire
  C. b. harterti
    W Angola
  C. b. intercalata
    S Zaire, Angola, S Zambia
  C. b. sharpei
    Southern Africa
Camaroptera fasciolata (Barred Camaroptera)
  C. f. pallidior
    S Angola
  C. f. fasciolata
    SW Africa
  C. f. aurophila
    W Transvaal

Camaroptera stierlingi (Stierling's Wren Warbler)
  C. s. buttoni
    N Malawi, NW Zambia
  C. s. stierlingi
    S Malawi, Tanzania, Mozambique
  C. s. irwini
    W Malawi, Zambia, S Rhodesia
  C. s. pintoi
    S Mozambique, E Transvaal
  C. s. olivascens
    Mozambique
Camaroptera simplex (Grey Wren Warbler)
  C. s. simplex
    Ethiopia, Somalia, N Kenya
  C. s. undosus
    S Kenya, Tanzania, Zambia
  C. s. cinerea
    S Zaire, N Angola
  G. s. katangae
    SE Zaire, W Zambia
  C. s. huilae
    S Angola
Camaroptera superciliaris (Yellow-browed Camaroptera)
  C. s. willoughbyi
    Sierra Leone to Ghana
  C. s. flavigularis
    S Nigeria to C Zaire
  C. s. superciliaris
    Fernando Po I
  C. s. pulchra
    N Angola, S Zaire
  C. s. ugandae
    E Zaire, Uganda
Camaroptera chloronota (Olive-green Camaroptera)
  C. c. kelsalli
    Senegal to Ghana
  C. c. chloronota
    Togo to Cameroun, W Zaire
  C. c. kamitugaensis
    E Zaire
  C. c. toroensis
    S Uganda, E Zaire

EURYPTILA
Euryptila subcinnamomea (Kopje Warbler)
  W Namibia, NW Cape Province

HYPERGERUS
Hypergerus atriceps (Oriole Warbler)
  Senegal to Central African Republic
Hypergerus lepida (Grey-capped Warbler)
  Uganda, Kenya, Tanzania

Eremomela icteropygialis (Yellow-bellied Eremomela)

E. i. alexanderi
Niger, Chad, Sudan

E. i. griseoflava
Somalia, Ethiopia, N Kenya

E. i. abdominalis
C Tanzania

E. i. belli
SE Tanzania

E. i. polioxantha
E Angola to Mozambique

E. i. luandae
N Angola

E. i. puellula
S Angola

E. i. icteropygialis
Namibia, NW Cape Province

E. i. perimacha
NW Cape Province to W Transvaal

E. i. viriditincta
Lesotho

E. i. saturatior
C & E Cape Province

Eremomela salvadorii (Salvadori Eremomela)
Angola, S Zaire, W Zambia

Eremomela flavocrissalis Yellow-vented Eremomela)
Somalia, NE Kenya

Eremomela scotops (Green-cap Eremomela)

E. s. congensis
W & C Zaire

E. s. mentalis
E Zaire

E. s. citriniceps
E Zaire, Uganda, Tanzania

E. s. occipitalis
E Kenya, E Tanzania

E. s. angolensis
N Angola

E. s. pulchra
E Angola to Malawi

E. s. scotops
Botswana to Tanzania, Mozambique

E. s. chlorochlamys
Rhodesia

Eremomela canescens (Green-backed Eremomela)

E. c. elegans
Cameroun, Chad, W Sudan

E. c. abyssinica
Ethiopia, E Sudan

E. c. canescens
S Sudan, Uganda, W Kenya

Eremomela pusilla (Smaller Green-backed Eremomela)
Senegal to N Cameroun

Eremomela gregalis (Yellow-rumped Eremomela)

E. g. damarensis
N & C Namibia

E. g. gregalis
S Namibia, NW Cape Province

Eremomela badiceps (Brown-crowned Eremomela)

E. b. fantiensis
Sierra Leone to Ghana

E. b. badiceps
Fernando Po I, Cameroun to N Angola

E. b. latukae
S Sudan

Eremomela turneri (Turner's Eremomela)

E. t. kalindei
E & C Zaire

E. t. turneri
Uganda, W Kenya

Eremomela atricollis (Black-necked Eremomela)

E. a. venustula
NW Zambia, SW Zaire

E. a. atricollis
W Angola, SE Zaire, Zambia

Eremomela usticollis (Burnt-neck Eremomela)

E. u. usticollis
C Southern Africa

E. u. rensi
Mozambique, Malawi

SYLVIETTA

Sylvietta ruficapilla (Red-capped Crombec)

S. r. schoutedeni
W Tanzania

S. r. rufigenis
W & S Zaire

S. r. chubbi
E Zaire to Mozambique

S. r. mackayi
N Angola

S. r. ruficapilla
S Angola, W Zambia

S. r. gephyra
SE Zaire, SW Zambia

Sylvietta leucophrys (White-browed Crombec)

S. l. leucophrys
Uganda, N Kenya

S. l. chloronata
E Zaire, SW Uganda, W Tanzania

S. l. chapini
E Zaire

Sylvietta virens (Green Crombec)
S. v. flaviventris
  Sierra Leone to Ghana
S. v. nigeriae
  S Nigeria
S. v. virens
  SE Nigeria to W Zaire
S. v. baraka
  S Sudan, Uganda
S. v. tando
  W Angola
S. v. meridionalis
  C Angola
Sylvietta denti (Lemon-bellied Crombec)
S. d. hardyi
  Sierra Leone to Ghana
S. d. denti
  S Cameroun
Sylvietta whytii (Red-faced Crombec)
S. w. abayensis
  SE Sudan, S Ethiopia, NW Kenya
S. w. jacksoni
  S & E Uganda, Kenya, Tanzania
S. w. minima
  E Kenya, E Tanzania
S. w. whytii
  S Malawi, Rhodesia, Mozambique
Sylvietta brachyura (Northern Crombec)
S. b. brachyura
  Senegal to Ethiopia
S. b. carnapi
  N Cameroun, Central African Republic
S. b. leucopsis
  Ethiopia, Sudan to N Tanzania
S. b. dilutior
  SE Sudan, Uganda, W Kenya
Sylvietta philippae (Somali Short-billed Crombec)
  Somalia
Sylvietta rufescens (Long-billed Crombec)
S. r. flecki
  N Angola
S. r. adelphe
  E & SE Zaire
S. r. ansorgei
  S Angola
S. r. pallida
  Zambia, Botswana to Mozambique
S. r. transvaalensis
  Rhodesia, E Botswana, Transvaal
S. r. mossamedes
  S Angola
S. r. rufescens
  Namibia, S Botswana, W Cape Province
S. r. diverga
  E Cape Province

S. r. resurga
  Natal
Sylvietta isabellina (Somali Long-billed Crombec)
  Ethiopia, Somalia, N Kenya

HEMITESIA
Hemitesia neumanni (Neumann's Short-tailed Warbler)
  E Zaire

GRAUERIA
Graueria vittata (Grauer's Warbler)
  E Zaire

PARISOMA
Parisoma subcaeruleum (Southern Tit Warbler)
P. s. ansorgei
  S Angola
P. s. cinerascens
  Namibia to W Rhodesia
P. s. orpheanum
  C Natal
P. s. subcaeruleum
  Transvaal, S Natal, E Cape Province
Parisoma layardi (Layard's Tit Warbler)
P. l. aridicola
  Namibia, S Botswana, N & C Cape Province
P. l. barnesi
  Lesotho
P. l. layardi
  SW Cape Province
Parisoma lugens (Brown Tit Warbler)
P. l. lugens
  N Ethiopia
P. l. griseiventris
  C Ethiopia
P. l. jacksoni
  E Zaire, Tanzania, Zambia, Malawi
P. l. prigoginei
  SE Zaire
Parisoma bohmi (Banded Tit Warbler)
P. b. somalicum
  Ethiopia, N Somalia
P. b. marsabit
  N Kenya
P. b. bohmi
  E & S Kenya, N Tanzania
Parisoma buryi (Yemen Tit Warbler)
  S Arabia

MACROSPHENUS
Macrosphenus concolor (Grey Longbill)
M. c. concolor
  Sierra Leone to Uganda
M. c. griscens
  Kamituga, Zaire
Macrosphenus pulitzeri (Pulitzer's Longbill)
  Angola

Macrosphenus kretschmeri (Kretschmer's Longbill)
Tanzania, Mozambique

Macrosphenus flavicans (Yellow Longbill)
M. f. flavicans
Cameroun, Gabon
M. f. leoninus
Fernando Po I
M. f. hypochondriacus
E Zaire, W Uganda
M. f. angolensis
N Angola

Macrosphenus kempi (Kemp's Longbill)
M. k. kempi
Sierra Leone
M. k. flammeus
S Nigeria

RANDIA
Randia pseudozosterops (Marvantsetra Warbler)
Madagascar

AMAUROCICHLA
Amaurocichla bocagei (Bocage's Longbill)
Sao Thomé I

CHAETORNIS
Chaetornis striatus (Bristled Grass Warbler)
Pakistan, N India

SCHOENICOLA
Schoenicola platyura (Broad-tailed Warbler)
S. p. alexinae
Sierra Leone to Angola, Tanzania
S. p. brevirostris
Southern Africa
S. p. platyura
SW India, Sri Lanka

MEGALURUS
Megalurus pryeri (Japanese Marsh Warbler)
M. p. sinensis
China
M. p. pryeri
Japan

Megalurus timoriensis (Tawny Marshbird)
M. t. timoriensis
Timor I
M. t. stresemanni
NW New Guinea
M. t. mayri
N New Guinea
M. t. wahgiensis
C New Guinea
M. t. montanus
C New Guinea

M. t. macrurus
C & S E New Guinea
M. t. harterti
E New Guinea
M. t. alpinus
SE New Guinea
M. t. muscalis
S New Guinea
M. t. celebensis
Celebes
M. t. amboinensis
Ambon I
M. t. interscapularis
New Britain
M. t. alisteri
N Western Australia, Northern Territory, N Queensland
M. t. oweni
S Queensland, New South Wales
M. t. tweeddalei
Luzon I, Panay I, Tablas I
M. t. mindorensis
Mindoro I
M. t. alopex
Bohol I, Cebu I, Leyte I
M. t. crex
Mindanao I

Megalurus albolimbatus (Fly River Grass Warbler)
SE New Guinea

Megalurus palustris (Striated Canegrass Warbler)
M. p. toklao
NE India to Indochina, S China
M. p. palustris
Java
M. p. forbesi
Luzon I Mindanao I

Megalurus gramineus (Little Marshbird)
M. g. papuensis
New Guinea
M. g. milligani
WC Australia
M. g. goulburni
New South Wales
M. g. thomasi
S Western Australia
M. g. wilsoni
South Australia, Victoria
M. g. halmaturinus
Kangaroo I
M. g. flindersi
Flinders I
M. g. gramineus
Tasmania

BOWDLERIA
Bowdleria punctata (Fernbird)
  B. p. vealeae
    North I (New Zealand)
  B. p. punctata
    South I (New Zealand)
  B. p. stewartiana
    Stewart I
  B. p. caudata
    Snares I
  B. p. wilsoni
    Codfish I

CINCLORHAMPHUS
Cinclorhamphus mathewsi (Rufous Songlark)
  Australia
Cinclorhamphus cruralis (Brown Songlark)
  Australia

EREMIORNIS
Eremiornis carteri (Spinifex Bird)
  E. c. rogersi
    N Western Australia
  E. c. carteri
    WC Australia, Barrow I
  E. c. queenslandicus
    W Queensland

MEGALURULUS
Megalurulus mariei (New Caledonian Grass Warbler)
  New Caledonia

CICHLORNIS
Cichlornis whitneyi (Thicket Warbler)
  C. w. whitneyi
    Espiritu Santo I
  C. w. turipavae
    Guadalcanal I
Cichlornis grosvenori (Whiteman Mountains Warbler)
  New Britain
Cichlornis llaneae (Bougainville Thicket Warbler)
  Bougainville I

ORTYGOCICHLA
Ortygocichla rubiginosa (Rufous-faced Thicket Warbler)
  New Britain

TRICHOCICHLA
Trichocichla rufa (Long legged Warbler)
  T. r. rufa
    Viti Levu I, Fiji Is
  T. r. cluniei
    Vanua Levu I

BUETTIKOFERELLA
Buettikoferella bivittata (Buettikofer's Warbler)
  Timor I

VITIA
Vitia ruficapilla (Fiji Warbler)
  V. r. ruficapilla
    Kandavu I
  V. r. badiceps
    Viti Levu I
  V. r. castaneoptera
    Vanua Levu I
  V. r. funebris
    Taviuni I
Vitia parens (Shade Warbler)
  San Cristobal I

STENOSTIRA
Stenostira scita (Fairy Flycatcher)
  S Transvaal, Natal, Cape Province

HYLIOTA
Hyliota flavigaster (Yellow-bellied Flycatcher)
  H. f. flavigaster
    Senegal to Ethiopia, Kenya
  H. f. barbozae
    Angola to Tanzania, Mozambique
Hyliota australis (Southern Yellow-bellied Flycatcher)
  H. a. australis
    W Uganda, W Kenya
  H. a. usambarae
    E Tanzania
  H. a. inornata
    Angola to Mozambique
  H. a. slatini
    E Zaire to Zambia, Malawi
  H. a. pallidipectus
    W Zambia, E Angola
Hyliota violacea (Violet-backed Flycatcher)
  H. v. nehrkorni
    Liberia to Ghana
  H. v. violacea
    Togo to S Cameroun, W Zaire

HYLIA
Hylia prasina (Green Hylia)
  H. p. prasina
    Cameroun, Angola to W Kenya
  H. p. superciliaris
    Guinea to S Nigeria
  H. p. poensis
    Fernando Po I

MUSCICAPIDAE

137 MALURINAE (AUSTRALIAN WRENS)
MALURINI

CLYTOMIAS
Clytomias insignis (Rufous Wren Warbler)
  C. i. insignis
    NW New Guinea

C. i. oorti
C and SE New Guinea

Chenorhamphus grayi (Broad-billed Wren Warbler)
C. g. grayi
NW New Guinea
C. g. pileatus
N New Guinea

Todopsis wallacei (Wallace's Wren Warbler)
T. w. wallacei
Misol I
T. w. coronata
Aru Is
Todopsis cyanocephala (Blue Wren Warbler)
T. c. cyanocephala
W New Guinea
T. c. dohertyi
N New Guinea
T. c. bonapartii
S New Guinea, Aru Is
T. c. mysorensis
Biak I

Malurus coronatus (Purple-crowned Wren)
M. c. rogersiana
NW Australia
M. c. coronatus
Northern Territory
M. c. caeruleus
NW Queensland
Malurus cyaneus (Blue Wren)
M. c. cyanochlamys
S Queensland, NE New South Wales
M. c. australis
New South Wales. Victoria
M. c. ashbyi
Kangaroo I
M. c. elizabethae
King I
M. c. cyaneus
Tasmania
Malurus splendens (Banded Wren)
M. s. perthi
SW Western Australia
M. s. splendens
S Western Australia
M. s. aridus
EC Western Australia
M. s. riordani
E Western Australia
M. s. callainus
S Northern Territory, N South Australia

M. s. whitei
S Queensland
M. s. musgravi
W New South Wales
M. s. melanotus
SE South Australia, NW Victoria
Malurus lamberti (Variegated Wren)
M. l. dulcis
NW Western Australia, Northern Territory
M. l. bernieri
Bernier I
M. l. mastersi
Western & C Australia, Northern Territory
M. l. assimilis
SW Queensland, W New South Wales, South Australia, NW Victoria
M. l. amabilis
N Queensland
M. l. lamberti
E Queensland, E New South Wales
Malurus pulcherrimus (Blue-breasted Wren)
Western & South Australia
Malurus elegans (Red-winged Wren)
SW Western Australia
Malurus leucopterus (White-winged Wren)
M. l. leucopterus
Barrow I, Dirk Hartog I
M. l. leuconotus
S W, S & EC Australia
Malurus melanocephalus (Red-backed Wren)
M. m. boweri
N Western Australia
M. m. cruentatus
N Northern Territory
M. m. pyrrhonotus
N Queensland
M. m. melanocephalus
S Queensland, N New South Wales
Malurus alboscapulatus (Black & White Wren)
M. a. alboscapulatus
NW New Guinea
M. a. aida
NW New Guinea
M. a. tappenbecki
NE New Guinea
M. a. randi
W New Guinea
M. a. balim
WC New Guinea
M. a. lorentzi
SW New Guinea
M. a. dogwa
S New Guinea

M. a. mortoni
SE New Guinea
M. a. naimii
SE New Guinea
M. a. mafulu
SE New Guinea
M. a. kutubu
S New Guinea

AMYTORNIS

Amytornis textilis (Thick-billed Grass Wren)
A. t. textilis
Western Australia, W South Australia
A. t. macrourus
S Western Australia
A. t. myalli
Eyre Peninsula
A. t. everardi
C South Australia
A. t. modestus
W New South Wales
A. t. inexpectatus
NE South Australia

Amytornis goyderi (Eyrean Grass Wren)
South Australia

Amytornis striatus (Striped Grass Wren)
A. s. whitei
NW Western Australia, S Northern Territory
A. s. merrotsyi
N South Australia
A. s. striatus
NW New South Wales
A. s. owensi
NW Victoria

Amytornis barbatus (Grey Grass Wren)
New South Wales

Amytornis dorotheae (Red-winged Grass Wren)
Northern Territory

Amytornis woodwardi (White-throated Grass Wren)
Northern Territory

Amytornis housei (Black Grass Wren)
N Western Australia

Amytornis purnelli (Dusky Grass Wren)
A. p. purnelli
Northern Territory
A. p. ballarae
NW Queensland

STIPITURUS

Stipiturus malachurus (Southern Emu Wren)
S. m. hartogi
Dirk Hartog I

S. m. westernensis
S Western Australia
S. m. malachurus
SE South Australia, E New South Wales, Victoria
S. m. tregellasi
S Victoria
S. m. littleri
Tasmania

Stipiturus ruficeps (Rufous-crowned Emu Wren)
S. r. ruficeps
Western & C Australia
S. r. mallee
SE South Australia, NW Victoria

ACANTHIZINI

DASYORNIS

Dasyornis brachypterus (Eastern Bristlebird)
D. b. brachypterus
E New South Wales
D. b. victoriae
NE Victoria

Dasyornis longirostris (Western Bristlebird)
SW Western Australia

Dasyornis broadbenti (Rufous Bristlebird)
D. b. litoralis
SW Western Australia
D. b. broadbenti
South Australia, Victoria
D. b. whitei
South Australia

GERYGONE

Gerygone olivacea (White-throated Flyeater)
G. o. cinerascens
SE New Guinea
G. o. rogersi
NW Australia
G. o. flavigaster
NW Queensland
G. o. olivacea
S Queensland, New South Wales, Victoria

Gerygone hypoxantha (Biak Flyeater)
Biak I

Gerygone mouki (Brown Flyeater)
G. m. mouki
N Queensland
G. m. amalia
S Queensland
G. m. richmondi
N New South Wales

Gerygone palpebrosa (Black-headed Flyeater)
G. p. palpebrosa
Aru Is, NW New Guinea

G. p. wahnesi
Japen I, NW New Guinea
G. p. inconspicua
SE New Guinea
G. p. tarara
S New Guinea
G. p. personata
N Queensland
G. p. johnstoni
NE Queensland
Gerygone flavida (Fairy Flyeater)
N Queensland
Gerygone magnirostris (Large-billed Flyeater)
G. m. mimikae
S & SE New Guinea
G. m. conspicillata
NW New Guinea
G. m. affinis
Japen I, Dampier I, N New Guinea
G. m. brunneipectus
Aru Is
G. m. cobana
Waigeu I, Batanta I
G. m. occasa
Kofiau I
G. m. proxima
D'Entrecasteaux Archipelago
G. m. onerosa
Misima I
G. m. tagulana
Tagula I
G. m. rosseliana
Sudest I
G. m. magnirostris
N Queensland
Gerygone tenebrosa (Dusky Flyeater)
coast of N Western Australia
Gerygone chloronota (Green-backed Flyeater)
G. c. cinereiceps
New Guinea
G. c. aruensis
Waigau I, Aru Is
G. c. chloronota
N Western Australia, N Northern Territory
Gerygone levigaster (Mangrove Flyeater)
G. l. broomei
N Western Australia
G. l. levigaster
Northern Territory
G. l. mastersi
N Queensland
G. l. cantator
E Queensland

Gerygone fusca (White-tailed Flyeater)
G. f. simplex
Philippine Is
G. f. pallida
S New Guinea
G. f. dendyi
N Western Australia
G. f. wayensis
WC Australia
G. f. fusca
S Western Australia
G. f. musgravei
C Australia
G. f. exsul
S Queensland to Victoria
G. f. keyensis
Kei Is
Gerygone cinerea (Grey Flyeater)
New Guinea
Gerygone chrysogaster (Yellow-bellied Flyeater)
G. c. leucothorax
NW New Guinea
G. c. notata
NW New Guinea, Misol I, Batanta I
G. c. neglecta
Waigeu I
G. c. dohertyi
SW New Guinea
G. c. chrysogaster
S & E New Guinea, Japen I, Aru Is
Gerygone ruficollis (Treefern Flyeater)
G. r. ruficollis
NW New Guinea
G. r. insperata
C & SE New Guinea
Gerygone flavolateralis (Fan-tailed Flyeater)
G. f. flavolateralis
New Caledonia
G. f. lifuensis
Loyalty Is
G. f. correiae
Banks Is
G. f. citrina
Rennell I
Gerygone igata (New Zealand Grey Flyeater)
G. i. flaviventris
North I (New Zealand)
G. i. macleani
North I (New Zealand)
G. i. igata
South I (New Żealand)
G. i. sylvestris
South I (New Zealand)

Gerygone albofrontata (Chatham Is Flyeater)
Chatham I
Gerygone inornata (Plain Flyeater)
G. i. inornata
Timor I
G. i. everetti
Savu I
G. i. keyensis
Kei Is
G. i. kuhni
Dammer I
Gerygone sulphurea (Yellow-breasted Flyeater)
Malaysia

SMICRORNIS
Smicrornis brevirostris (Weebill)
S. b. cairns
NE Queensland
S. b. flavescens
W Northern Territory
S. b. pallescens
C Queensland
S. b. stirlingi
S Western Australia
S. b. mathewsi
South Australia
S. b. brevirostris
New South Wales
S. b. mallee
Victoria

APHELOCEPHALA
Aphelocephala leucopsis (Southern White-face)
A. l. castaneiventris
Western Australia
A. l. whitei
C Australia
A. l. leucopsis
South Australia, New South Wales, Victoria
Aphelocephala pectoralis (Chestnut-breasted Whiteface)
C South Australia
Aphelocephala nigricincta (Banded Whiteface)
A. n. tanami
C Northern Territory
A. n. nigricincta
C South Australia

ACANTHIZA
Acanthiza nana (Little Thornbill)
A. n. flava
N Queensland
A. n. modesta
C Queensland

A. n. nana
S Queensland, New South Wales
A. n. burtoni
SE Queensland
A. n. mathewsi
South Australia, Victoria
A. n. laetior
Mt Lofty Range
Acanthiza lineata (Striated Thornbill)
A. l. alberti
S Queensland
A. l. lineata
New South Wales
A. l. clelandi
South Australia
A. l. chandleri
Victoria
Acanthiza pusilla (Brown Thornbill)
A. p. bunya
S Queensland
A. p. pusilla
S Queensland, E New South Wales
A. p. maculata
Victoria
A. p. zietzi
Kangaroo I
A. p. diemenensis
Tasmania
Acanthiza apicalis (Broad-tailed Thornbill)
A. a. whitlocki
S Northern Territory, N Western Australia
A. a. apicalis
S Western Australia
A. a. leeuwinensis
S Western Australia
A. a. tanami
C Australia
A. a. albiventris
SW New South Wales
Acanthiza katharina (Mountain Thornbill)
Queensland
Acanthiza murina (De Vis' Tree Warbler)
C & SE New Guinea
Acanthiza ewingi (Tasmanian Thornbill)
Tasmania
Acanthiza robustirostris (Robust Thornbill)
A. r. robustirostris
Western Australia
A. r. marianae
C Australia
Acanthiza inornata (Western Thornbill)
A. i. mastersi
SW Western Australia
A. i. inornata
SC Western Australia

Acanthiza iredalei (Samphire Thornbill)
A. i. iredalei
Western Australia
A. i. hedleyi
South Australia
A. i. rosinae
S South Australia
Acanthiza reguloides (Buff-tailed Thornbill)
A. r. squamata
Queensland
A. r. reguloides
New South Wales
A. r. australis
South Australia
A. r. nesa
N New South Wales
Acanthiza chrysorrhoa (Yellow-tailed Thornbill)
A. c. multi
S Western Australia
A. c. alexanderi
W C Australia
A. c. ferdinandi
C Australia
A. c. addenda
E C Australia
A. c. normantoni
N Queensland
A. c. chrysorrhoa
S Queensland, New South Wales
A. c. sandlandi
South Australia, Victoria, Tasmania
Acanthiza uropygialis (Chestnut-tailed Thornbill)
A. u. augusta
W C Australia, W New South Wales
A. u. uropygialis
C & South Australia

SERICORNIS
Sericornis magnus (Scrub Tit)
Tasmania
Sericornis spilodera (Pale-billed Sericornis)
S. s. spilodera
Japen I, NW New Guinea
S. s. granti
WC New Guinea
S. s. wuroi
S New Guinea
S. s. guttatus
SE New Guinea
S. s. ferrugineus
Waigeu I
S. s. aruensis
Aru Is
S. s. intermedia
Batanta I

Sericornis virgatus (Perplexing Sericornis)
S. v. cantans
NW New Guinea
S. v. imitator
NW New Guinea
S. v. jobiensis
Japen I
S. v. boreonesioticus
coast of N New Guinea
S. v. idenburgi
Snowy Mountains
S. v. pontifex
NC New Guinea
Sericornis beccarii (Little Sericornis)
S. b. wondiwoi
NW New Guinea
S. b. cyclopum
coast of N New Guinea
S. b. weylandi
Weyland mountains
S. b. randi
S New Guinea
S. b. beccarii
Aru Is
S. b. minimus
Cape York
S. b. dubius
N Queensland
Sericornis nouhuysi (Large Mountain Sericornis)
S. n. nouhuysi
Weyland & Snowy mountains
S. n. stresemanni
Schrader Mountains
S. n. oorti
Huon peninsula
S. n. monticola
SE New Guinea
Sericornis frontalis (White-browed Sericornis)
S. f. geraldtoni
W Western Australia
S. f. maculatus
S Western Australia
S. f. mellori
W South Australia
S. f. balstoni
W New South Wales, W Victoria
S. f. laevigaster
NW Queensland
S. f. herbertoni
NE Queensland
S. f. frontalis
S Queensland, New South Wales
S. f. rosinae
NE South Australia

S. f. harterti
Victoria
S. f. archboldi
N Tasmania
S. f. humilis
Tasmania
S. f. gularis
Kent I
S. f. insularis
Forsyth I
S. f. flindersi
Flinders I
S. f. tregellasi
King I
Sericornis perspicillatus (Buff-faced Sericornis)
C & SE New Guinea
Sericornis magnirostris (Large-billed Sericornis)
S. m. viridior
Queensland
S. m. magnirostris
New South Wales, Victoria
Sericornis rufescens (Arfak Buff-faced Sericornis)
NW New Guinea
Sericornis nigroviridis (Morobe Sericornis)
Morobe district, New Guinea
Sericornis papuensis (Papuan Sericornis)
S. p. meeki
W New Guinea
S. p. burgersi
C New Guinea
S. p. papuensis
SE New Guinea
Sericornis arfakianus (Grey-green Sericornis)
S. a. arfakianus
NW New Guinea
S. a. olivaceus
C & E New Guinea
Sericornis citreogularis (Yellow-throated Sericornis)
S. c. cairnsi
N Queensland
S. c. citreogularis
NE Australia
Sericornis keri (Atherton Sericornis)
NE Queensland
Sericornis fuliginosus (Striated Field Wren)
S. f. hartogi
Dirk Hartog I
S. f. dorrie
Dorrie I
S. f. perone
Western Australia

S. f. rubiginosus
Western Australia
S. f. campestris
SW Western Australia
S. f. montanellus
S Western Australia
S. f. carteri
S Western Australia
S. f. wayensis
WC Australia
S. f. isabellinus
C Australia
S. f. macgillivrayi
N South Australia, W New South Wales
S. f. ethelae
South Australia
S. f. obscurior
E New South Wales
S. f. albiloris
Victoria
S. f. howei
S Victoria
S. f. fuliginosus
Tasmania
Sericornis pyrrhopygia (Chestnut-rumped Heath Wren)
S. p. pyrrhopygia
New South Wales
S. p. belcheri
South Australia, Victoria
Sericornis cautus (Shy Heath Wren)
S. c. whitlocki
S Western Australia
S. c. cautus
South Australia, Victoria
Sericornis brunneus (Redthroat)
Western C & South Australia
Sericornis sagittata (Little Field Wren)
S. s. sagittata
Queensland, New South Wales
S. s. inexpectata
South Australia, Victoria

CRATEROSCELIS

Crateroscelis gutturalis (Fern Wren)
NE Queensland
Crateroscelis murina (Lowland Mouse Warbler)
C. m. murina
Japen I, New Guinea
C. m. monacha
Aru Is
C. m. pallida
SE New Guinea
C. m. capitalis
Waigeu I
C. m. fumosa
Misol I

Crateroscelis nigrorufa (Mid-mountain
Mouse Warbler)
  C. n. blissi
    N New Guinea
  C. n. nigrorufa
    SE New Guinea
Crateroscelis robusta (Mountain Mouse
Warbler)
  C. r. peninsularis
    NW New Guinea
  C. r. ripleyi
    NW New Guinea
  C. r. bastille
    coast of N New Guinea
  C. r. deficiens
    N New Guinea
  C. r. sanfordi
    C New Guinea
  C. r. robusta
    SE New Guinea

ORIGMA
Origma solitaria (Rock Warbler)
  New South Wales

PYCNOPTILUS
Pycnoptilus floccosus (Pilot Bird)
  P. f. floccosus
    New South Wales
  P. f. sandlandi
    Victoria

MOHOUINI

MOHOUA
Mohoua albicilla (Whitehead)
  North I (New Zealand)
Mohoua ochrocephala (Yellowhead)
  South I (New Zealand)

FINSCHIA
Finschia novaeseelandiae (New Zealand
Creeper)
  South I (New Zealand)

EPHTHIANURINI

EPHTHIANURA
Ephthianura albifrons (White-faced
Chat)
  E. a. albifrons
    S Western to Victoria, New South
    Wales
  E. a. tasmanica
    Tasmania
Ephthianura tricolor (Crimson Chat)
  C & E Australia
Ephthianura aurifrons (Orange Chat)
  all Australia except SW
Ephthianura crocea (Yellow Chat)
  E. c. boweri
    Fitzroy river (NW Australia)

  E. c. tunneyi
    Aligator river (Northern Territory)
  E. c. crocea
    Norman river (W Queensland)
  E. c. macgregori
    Fitzroy river (Queensland)

ASHBYIA
Ashbyia lovensis (Desert Chat)
  N South Australia

LAMPROLIA
Lamprolia victoriae (Silktail)
  L. v. victoriae
    Taviuni I
  L. v. kleinschmidti
    Vanua Levu I

MUSCICAPIDAE

138 MUSCICAPINAE (OLD WORLD
    FLYCATCHERS)

BRADORNIS
Bradornis microrhynchus (Grey Flycatcher)
  B. m. microrhynchus
    Ethiopia, Somalia to Tanzania
  B. m. pumilis
    S Sudan, Uganda, W Kenya
  B. m. burae
    Tana river (Kenya)
Bradornis mariquensis (Mariqua
Flycatcher)
  B. m. acaciae
    SW Angola, Namibia, NW Cape Province
  B. m. mariquensis
    SW Zambia, S Botswana, NE Cape
    Province
Bradornis pallidus (Pale Flycatcher)
  B. p. nigeriae
    Gambia to N Central African Republic
  B. p. modestus
    Guinea to Cameroun
  B. p. murinus
    Gabon to Angola & Natal
  B. p. bowdleri
    NE Ethiopia
  B. p. duyerali
    NE Ethiopia
  B. p. neumanni
    S Ethiopia
  B. p. pallidus
    Sudan, NW Uganda
  B. p. griseus
    NE Zaire to Kenya, Tanzania
  B. p. bafirawari
    E Kenya
  B. p. subalaris
    Zambia to Cape Province
  B. p. sibilans
    E Natal

Bradornis infuscatus (African Brown Flycatcher)
  B. i. benguellensis
    S Angola
  B. i. namaquensis
    Namibia, W Botswana
  B. i. seimundi
    S Botswana, W Transvaal, N Cape Province
  B. i. infuscatus
    W Cape Province

EMPIDORNIS
Empidornis semipartitus (Silver Bird)
  E. s. semipartitus
    N Ethiopia
  E. s. orleansi
    S Sudan, W Ethiopia
  E. s. kavirondensis
    SE Sudan to N Tanzania

MELAENORNIS
Melaenornis chocolatina (Abyssinian Slaty Flycatcher)
  M. c. chocolatina
    N Ethiopia
  M. c. reichenowi
    W Ethiopia
Melaenornis ardesiaca (Berlioz' Black Flycatcher)
  E Zaire
Melaenornis annamarulae (Liberian Black Flycatcher)
  Liberia
Melaenornis edolioides (Black Flycatcher)
  M. e. edolioides
    Senegal to Cameroun
  M. e. lugubris
    Ethiopia, Sudan to N Tanzania
  M. e. schistacea
    E Ethiopia, N Kenya
Melaenornis pammelaina (South African Black Flycatcher)
  M. p. tropicalis
    Kenya, Tanzania
  M. p. pammalaina
    Angola to Mozambique & Natal
Melaenornis silens (Fiscal Flycatcher)
  SE South Africa

DIOPTRORNIS
Dioptrornis fischeri (White-eyed Slaty Flycatcher)
  D. f. toruensis
    E Zaire, W Uganda
  D. f. semicinctus
    E Zaire
  D. f. nyikensis
    N Tanzania, N Malawi

  D. f. fischeri
    Tanzania
Dioptrornis brunneus (Angolan Flycatcher)
  D. b. brunneus
    N Angola
  D. b. bailundensis
    S Angola

FRASERIA
Fraseria ocreata (Forest Flycatcher)
  F. o. kelsalli
    Sierra Leone
  F. o. prosphora
    Liberia to Ghana
  F. o. ocreata
    Cameroun to Zaire, Uganda
Fraseria cinerascens (White-browed Forest Flycatcher)
  F. c. guineae
    Guinea to Ivory Coast
  F. c. cinerascens
    Liberia to Gabon, N Zaire

RHINOMYIAS
Rhinomyias addita (Buru Jungle Flycatcher)
  Buru I
Rhinomyias oscillans (Flores Jungle Flycatcher)
  Flores I
Rhinomyias olivacea (Olive-backed Jungle Flycatcher)
  R. o. olivacea
    Malaysia, Burma
  R. o. nicobarica
    Nicobar Is
  R. o. perolivacea
    Banguey I
Rhinomyias brunneata (White-gorgetted Jungle Flycatcher)
  S China
Rhinomyias umbratilis (White-throated Jungle Flycatcher)
  Malaysia
Rhinomyias ruficauda (Rufous-tailed Jungle Flycatcher)
  R. r. isola
    Sarawak
  R. r. ruficrissa
    Kinabalu
  R. r. ocularis
    Sulu Is, Pangamican I, Tawitawi Is
  R. r. ruficauda
    Basilan I
  R. r. zamboanga
    W Mindanao I
  R. r. boholensis
    Bohol I
  R. r. samarensis
    Leyte I, Samar I, E Mindanao I

Rhinomyias colonus (Sula Jungle Flycatcher)
Sula I
Rhinomyias gularis (White-browed Jungle Flycatcher)
R. g. gularis
Borneo
R. g. albigularis
Negros I
R. g. insignis
N Luzon I
R. g. goodfellowi
Mindanao I

FICEDULA
Ficedula hypoleuca (Pied Flycatcher)
F. h. hypoleuca
N Europe, W Siberia » NC Africa
F. h. iberiae
Spain, Portugal
F. h. speculigera
N Africa
F. h. semitorquata
Asia Minor, Syria, Iraq
F. h. tomensis
SW Asia » C Africa
Ficedula albicollis (Collared Flycatcher)
C & E Europe » SC Africa
Ficedula zanthopygia (Yellow-rumped Flycatcher)
NE Asia » Malaysia
Ficedula narcissina (Narcissus Flycatcher)
F. n. narcissina
Sakhalin, Japan » Philippine Is,
N Borneo
F. n. jakuschimae
Yakushima I
F. n. shonis
N Riukiu Is
F. n. owstoni
S Riukiu Is
Ficedula mugimaki (Mugimaki Flycatcher)
C & E Asia » Philippine Is
Ficedula parva (Red-breasted Flycatcher)
F. p. parva
C & E Europe, W Himalayas » N India
F. p. albicilla
C & NE Asia » Burma, S China
F. p. subrubra
NW Himalayas » Sri Lanka
Ficedula strophiata (Orange-gorgetted Flycatcher)
F. s. strophiata
Himalayas to N Thailand, S China
F. s. fuscogularis
Vietnam

Ficedula monileger (White-gorgetted Flycatcher)
F. m. moniléger
C Nepal
F. m. submoniléger
Burma
F. m. arakanensis
Burma
F. m. leucops
NE India to NW Thailand
F. m. malayana
Malaysia
Ficedula solitaria (Rufous-browed Flycatcher)
Malaysia, Indochina, Sumatra
Ficedula hyperythra (Thicket Flycatcher)
F. h. hyperythra
Himalayas, Burma, Thailand
F. h. annamensis
C Vietnam
F. h. sumatrana
Malaysia, Sumatra, Borneo
F. h. mjobergi
W Borneo
F. h. vulcani
Java, Bali I
F. h. trinitatis
Luzon I, Mindoro I
F. h. calayensis
Calayan I
F. h. nigrorum
Negros I
F. h. montigena
Mindanao I
F. h. daggayana
N Mindanao I
F. h. malindangensis
SE Mindanao I
F. h. jugosae
Celebes
F. h. negroides
Ceram I
F. h. pallidipectus
Batjan I, Buru I
F. h. alifurus
Buru I
F. h. luzoniensis
Luzon I, Mindoro I
Ficedula rufigula (White-vented Flycatcher)
Celebes
Ficedula dumetoria (Orange-breasted Flycatcher)
F. d. muelleri
Malaysia, Sumatra, Borneo
F. d. dumetoria
Java, Lombok I

F. d. riedeli
Tenimber Is
**Ficedula basilanica (Little Slaty
Flycatcher)**
F. b. basilanica
Basilan I, Mindanao I
F. b. samarensis
Leyte I, Samar I
Ficedula buruensis (Buru Flycatcher)
F. b. buruensis
Buru I
F. b. ceramensis
Ceram I
F. b. siebersi
Kei Is
Ficedula henrici (Damar Flycatcher)
Damar I
**Ficedula hodgsonii (Rusty-breasted
Blue Flycatcher)**
Nepal to W China
Ficedula platenae (Palawan Flycatcher)
Palawan I
Ficedula crypta (Vaurie's Flycatcher)
F. c. crypta
Mindanao I
F. c. disposita
Luzon I
Ficedula bonthaina (Mountain Flycatcher)
Celebes
Ficedula harterti (Hartert's Flycatcher)
Sumba I
**Ficedula nigrorufa (Black and Orange
Flycatcher)**
SW India
**Ficedula timorensis (White-throated
Flycatcher)**
Timor I
**Ficedula westermanni (Little Pied
Flycatcher)**
F. w. collini
Himalayas
F. w. australorientis
S China, Indochina, Indonesia
F. w. langbianus
S Vietnam
F. w. hasselti
Sumatra, Java, Bali I
F. w. palawanensis
Palawan I
F. w. westermanni
Luzon I, Negros I, Mindanao I
F. w. rabori
Culion I
**Ficedula superciliaris (White-browed
Blue Flycatcher)**
F. s. superciliaris
W Himalayas, C India

F. s. aestigma
E Himalayas, Tibet, W China
**Ficedula tricolor (Slaty Blue
Flycatcher)**
F. t. tricolor
W Himalayas
F. t. minuta
E Himalayas, SE Tibet, S China
F. t. cerviniventris
Assam, Burma
F. t. notata
NE India, Nepal
**Ficedula sapphira (Sapphire-headed
Flycatcher)**
F. s. sapphira
E Himalayas, N Laos, S China
F. s. laotiana
S Laos

CYANOPTILA
**Cyanoptila cyanomelaena (Blue and
White Flycatcher)**
C. c. intermedia
N Asia
C. c. cumatilis
NE Asia » S Burma, S Thailand
C. c. cyanomelaena
Japan » Philippine Is, Borneo

NILTAVA
Niltava grandis (Large Niltava)
N. g. grandis
E Himalayas to Malaysia, Vietnam
N. g. decipiens
Sumatra
Niltava macgregoriae (Small Niltava)
N. m. macgregoriae
W & C Himalayas
N. m. signata
E Himalayas, Assam
Niltava davidi (Fukien Niltava)
S China
**Niltava sundara (Rufous-bellied
Niltava)**
N. s. whistleri
W Himalayas
N. s. sundara
E Himalayas, SW China, N Laos
N. s. denotata
S China, Thailand
Niltava sumatrana (Sumatran Niltava)
Malaysia, Sumatra
Niltava vivida (Vivid Niltava)
N. v. oatesi
NE India to N Vietnam
N. v. vivida
Taiwan
**Niltava hyacinthina (Blue-backed
Niltava)**

N. h. hyacinthina
Timor I
N. h. kuhni
Wetar I
Niltava hoevelli (Celebes Niltava)
C Celebes
Niltava sanfordi (Sanford's Niltava)
N Celebes
Niltava concreta (White-tailed Niltava)
N. c. cyanea
NE India, Burma
N. c. leucoprocta
Burma
N. c. concreta
Malaysia, Sumatra
N. c. everetti
Borneo
Niltava ruecki (Rueck's Niltava)
Malaysia
Niltava herioti (Blue-breasted Niltava)
N. b. herioti
N & C Luzon I
N. h. comorinensis
S Luzon I
Niltava hainana (Grant's Niltava)
S China
Niltava pallipes (White-bellied Niltava)
SW India
Niltava poliogenys (Brooks' Niltava)
N. p. poliogenys
C Himalayas, NE India
N. p. vernayi
EC India
N. p. cachariensis
E Himalayas, NW Burma
Niltava unicolor (Pale Niltava)
N. u. unicolour
Himalayas, Burma, N Laos
N. u. infuscata
Malaysia, Sumatra, Java
N. u. harterti
Borneo
Niltava rubeculoides (Blue-throated Niltava)
N. r. rubeculoides
Himalayas, Burma, India
N. r. dialilaema
Burma
N. r. rogersi
Burma
N. r. glaucicomans
S Thailand, S & C China
N. r. klossi
S Vietnam
Niltava banyumas (Hill Blue Niltava)
N. b. magnirostris
E Himalayas, Assam, Burma
N. b. whitei
Burma

N. b. caerulifrons
Thailand, Malaysia
N. b. deignani
C Thailand
N. b. cantatrix
W Java
N. b. banyumas
C & E Java
N. b. montana
Borneo
N. b. lemprieri
Palawan I, Balabac I
Niltava superba (Bornean Niltava)
Borneo
Niltava caerulata (Large-billed Niltava)
N. c. albiventer
Sumatra
N. c. rufifrons
W Borneo
N. c. caerulata
Borneo
Niltava turcosa (Malaysian Niltava)
N. t. rupatensis
Malaysia, Sumatra, W Borneo
N. t. turcosa
C & E Borneo
Niltava tickelliae (Tickell's Niltava)
N. t. tickelliae
NE, C & S India
N. t. jerdoni
Sri Lanka
N. t. sumatrensis
Malaysia, Sumatra
N. t. indochina
Indochina
Niltava rufigastra (Mangrove Niltava)
N. r. rufigastra
Malaysia, Sumatra, Borneo
N. r. indochina
S Vietnam
N. r. sumatrensis
NE Sumatra
N. r. rhizophorae
W Java
N. r. lampra
Anamba Is
N. r. longipennis
Karimon-Java I
N. r. karimatensis
Karimata I
N. r. omissa
Celebes
N. r. simplex
Luzon I
N. r. marinduquensis
Marinduque I
N. r. mindorensis
Mindoro I

N. r. litoralis
Palawan I
N. r. philippinensis
Philippine Is

MUSCICAPELLA
Muscicapella hodgsoni (Pygmy Blue Flycatcher)
M. h. hodgsoni
C Himalayas to Thailand, SW China
M. h. sondaica
Malaysia, Sumatra, Borneo

MUSCICAPA
Muscicapa striata (Spotted Flycatcher)
M. s. striata
Europe, Asia Minor » S Africa
M. s. neumanni
W & S Asia » E Africa
M. s. tyrrhenica
Corsica, Sardinia
M. s. balearicae
Balearic Is » W & S Africa
M. s. sarudnyi
N Iran, Caucasus, Afghanistan
Muscicapa sibirica (Siberian Flycatcher)
M. s. sibirica
E Asia, Japan
M. s. gulmergi
Pakistan, W Himalayas
M. s. cacabata
E Himalayas, Tibet
M. s. rothschildi
SW China
Muscicapa griseisticta (Spot-breasted Flycatcher)
NE Asia » New Guinea, Philippine Is
Muscicapa latirostris (Brown Flycatcher)
M. l. daurica
NE Asia, Japan
M. l. poonensis
E India, Burma, SW China
M. l. siamensis
N Thailand
M. l. randi
Philippine Is
M. l. umbrosa
NE Borneo
M. l. latirostris
Sumatra
M. l. williamsoni
Burma, Thailand, Malaysia, Sumatra
M. l. segregata
Sumba I
Muscicapa muttui (Brown-breasted Flycatcher)
NE & SW India
Muscicapa ruficauda (Rufous-tailed Flycatcher)
W Himalayas, W India

Muscicapa ferruginea (Ferruginous Flycatcher)
Mindoro I, Palawan I
Muscicapa gambagae (Gambaga Spotted Flycatcher)
Ghana to Somalia, Arabia
Muscicapa adusta (Dusky Flycatcher)
M. a. albiventris
Cameroun
M. a. sjostedti
Cameroun Mt, Fernando Po I
M. a. grotei
Central African Republic
M. a. pumilis
NE Zaire, S Sudan, Uganda
M. a. minima
NE Ethiopia
M. a. interposita
S Sudan, N Kenya
M. a. subtilis
E Zaire
M. a. subadusta
S Zaire to Rhodesia,Mozambique
M. a. angolensis
Angola, SW Zaire
M. a. marsabit
N Kenya
M. a. murina
SE Kenya
M. a. chyulu
NE Tanzania
M. a. fuelleborni
Tanzania
M. a. roehli
E Tanzania
M. a. adusta
S E Africa
Muscicapa aquatica (Swamp Flycatcher)
M. a. aquatica
Senegal to Sudan
M. a. infulatus
S Sudan, NE Zaire, W Kenya
M. a. ruandae
Rwanda, S Uganda
M. a. lualabae
SE Zaire
M. a. grimwoodi
C Zambia
Muscicapa olivascens (Olivaceous Flycatcher)
M. o. olivascens
Liberia to Gabon, E Zaire
M. o. itombwensis
Itombwe (E Zaire)
Muscicapa lendu (Chapin's Flycatcher)
Lake Albert (NE Zaire)

Muscicapa cassini (Cassin's Grey
Flycatcher)
 Sierra Leone to Uganda, Zambia
Muscicapa epulata (Little Grey Flycatcher)
 Liberia to Gabon, E Zaire
Muscicapa sethsmithi (Yellow-footed
Flycatcher)
 Cameroun, Gabon to Uganda
Muscicapa coerulescens (Ashy Flycatcher)
 M. c. nigrorum
 Guinea to Togo
 M. c. brevicauda
 S Nigeria to Gabon, Sudan
 M. c. cinereolus
 S Angola to Kenya, Mozambique
 M. c. impavida
 N Namibia to N Mozambique
 M. c. coerulescens
 E Transvaal, Natal, E Cape Province
Muscicapa comitata (Dusky Blue
Flycatcher)
 M. c. aximensis
 Sierra Leone to S Nigeria
 M. c. camerunensis
 Cameroun
 M. c. comitata
 Gabon to Uganda, Angola
Muscicapa tessmanni (Tessman's
Flycatcher)
 Ivory Coast to N Zaire
Muscicapa infuscata (African Sooty
Flycatcher)
 M. i. chapini
 S Nigeria
 M. i. in fuscata
 Cameroun to Angola
 M. i. minuscula
 NE Zaire to Sudan, Uganda
Muscicapa ussheri (Ussher's Dusky
Flycatcher)
 Sierra Leone to Ghana

MYIOPORNIS

Myiopornis böhmi (Böhm's Flycatcher)
 M. b. sharpei
 Angola, Zambia
 M. b. bohmi
 SE Zambia, Tanzania, Malawi

EUMYIAS

Eumyias sordida (Sri Lanka Dusky Blue
Flycatcher)
 Sri Lanka
Eumyias thalassina (Indian Verditer
Flycatcher)
 E. t. thalassina
 Himalayas to N Laos
 E. t. thalassoides
 Malaysia, Sumatra, Borneo

Eumyias panayensis (Philippine
Verditer Flycatcher)
 E. p. septentrionalis
 N Celebes
 E. p. meridionalis
 S Celebes
 E. p. obiensis
 Obi I, Moluccas
 E. p. harterti
 Ceram I
 E. p. panayensis
 Negros I, Panay I
 E. p. nigrimentalis
 Luzon I, Mindoro I
 E. p. nigriloris
 Mindanao I
Eumyias albicaudata (Nilgiri Verditer
Flycatcher)
 SW India
Eumyias indigo (Indigo Flycatcher)
 E. i. ruficrissa
 Sumatra
 E. i. indigo
 Java
 E. i. cerviniventris
 Borneo

MYIOPARUS

Myioparus plumbeus (Grey Tit Flycatcher)
 M. p. plumbeus
 Senegal to Ethiopia, Uganda
 M. p. orientalis
 Kenya to Angola, Natal
 M. p. grandior
 C Tanzania to Natal
Myioparus griseigularis (Grey-throated
Flycatcher)
 M. g. parelii
 Ivory Coast
 M. g. holospodius
 E Nigeria to Gabon
 M. g. griseigularis
 E Zaire, Uganda

HUMBLOTIA

Humblotia flavirostris (Humblot's
Flycatcher)
 Comoro Is

NEWTONIA

Newtonia amphichroa (Tulear Newtonia)
 NE Madagascar
Newtonia brunneicauda (Common
Newtonia)
 N. b. brunñeicauda
 Madagascar
 N. b. monticola
 Mt Ankarata
Newtonia archboldi (Tabity Newtonia)
 SW Madagascar

Newtonia fanovanae (Fanovana Newtonia)
  E Madagascar

MICROECA
Microeca leucophaea (Australian Brown Flycatcher)
  M. l. zimmeri
    New Guinea
  M. l. pallida
    Northern Territory, N Queensland
  M. l. leucophaea
    S Queensland, New South Wales
  M. l. barcoo
    C Australia
  M. l. assimilis
    S Western Australia
Microeca tormenti (Brown-tailed Flycatcher)
  N Western Australia
Microeca flavigaster (Lemon-breasted Flycatcher)
  M. f. tarara
    New Guinea
  M. f. laeta
    New Guinea
  M. f. terraereginae
    N Queensland
  M. f. flavigaster
    Northern Territory
Microeca hemixantha (Tenimber Microeca Flycatcher)
  Tenimber Is
Microeca griseoceps (Yellow-footed Flycatcher)
  M. g. occidentalis
    NW New Guinea
  M. g. poliocephala
    NE New Guinea
  M. g. bartoni
    S New Guinea
  M. g. griseoceps
    SE New Guinea, S Queensland
Microeca flavovirescens (Olive Microeca Flycatcher)
  M. f. flavovirescens
    Aru Is, New Guinea
  M. f. cuicui
    New Guinea
Microeca papuana (Papuan Microeca Flycatcher)
  M. p. papuana
    NW New Guinea
  M. p. punctata
    Arfak mountains, New Guinea

CULICICAPA
Culicicapa ceylonensis (Grey-headed Canary Flycatcher)
  C. c. calochrysea
    N India, Burma

C. c. ceylonensis
  S India, Sri Lanka
C. c. antioxantha
  Thailand
C. c. percnocara
  Malaysia
C. c. connectens
  Celebes
C. c. sejuncta
  Flores I
Culicicapa helianthea (Citrine Canary Flycatcher)
  C. h. helianthea
    Banggai I, Celebes
  C. h. panayensis
    Leyte I, Mindanao I, Palawan I
  C. h. mayri
    Bongao I, Tawitawi Is
  C. h. septentrionalis
    NW Luzon I
  C. h. zimmeri
    C & S Luzon I

PELTOPS
Peltops blainvillii (Lowland Peltops Flycatcher)
  New Guinea
Peltops montanus (Mountain Peltops Flycatcher)
  New Guinea

MONACHELLA
Monachella muelleriana (River Flycatcher)
  M. m. saxicolina
    NW New Guinea
  M. m. muelleriana
    SW New Guinea
  M. m. albofrontata
    SE New Guinea
  M. m. coultasi
    New Britain

EUGERYGONE
Eugerygone rubra (Red-backed Warbler)
  E. r. rubra
    NW New Guinea
  E. r. saturatior
    C New Guinea

PETROICA
Petroica multicolor (Scarlet Robin)
  P. m. kleinschmidti
    Fiji Is
  P. m. pusilla
    Samoa Is
  P. m. feminina
    Efate I, Mai I
  P. m. soror
    Vanua Levu I
  P. m. similis
    Tanna I

P. m. ambrynensis
  New Hebrides, Banks Is
P. m. cognata
  Erromanga I
P. m. becki
  Kandavu I
P. m. polymorpha
  San Cristobal I
P. m. septentrionalis
  Bougainville I
P. m. kulambangrae
  Kulambangra I
P. m. campbelli
  S Western Australia
P. m. boodang
  E Australia, Tasmania
P. m. multicolor
  Norfolk I
P. m. dennisi
  Guadalcanal I
Petroica goodenovii (Red-capped Robin)
  W, C & E Australia
Petroica phoenicea (Flame Robin)
  New South Wales, SE Australia
  Tasmania
Petroica archboldi (Rock Robin)
  C New Guinea
Petroica rodinogaster (Pink Robin)
  SE Australia, Tasmania
Petroica rosea (Rose Robin)
  coastal S Queensland to Victoria
Petroica bivittata (Forest Robin)
P. b. caudata
  C New Guinea
P. b. bivittata
  SE New Guinea
Petroica cucullata (Hooded Robin)
P. c. picata
  Western Australia
P. c. cucullata
  S Queensland, New South Wales, Victoria
Petroica macrocephala (New Zealand Tit)
P. m. toitoi
  North I (New Zealand)
P. m. macrocephala
  South I (New Zealand)
P. m. marrineri
  Auckland Is
P. m. chathamensis
  Chatham I
P. m. dannefaerdi
  Snares I
Petroica vittata (Dusky Robin)
P. v. kingi
  King I
P. v. vittata
  Tasmania

Petroica australis (New Zealand Robin)
P. a. longipes
  North I (New Zealand)
P. a. australis
  South I (New Zealand)
P. a. rakiura
  Stewart I
Petroica traversi (Chatham I Robin)
  Chatham I

TREGELLASIA
Tregellasia leucops (White-faced Robin)
T. l. leucops
  NW New Guinea
T. l. mayri
  WC New Guinea
T. l. nigroorbitalis
  NC New Guinea
T. l. heurni
  C New Guinea
T. l. nigriceps
  EC New Guinea
T. l. melanogenys
  N New Guinea
T. l. wahgiensis
  C & E New Guinea
T. l. albifacies
  SE New Guinea
T. l. auricularis
  S New Guinea
T. l. albigularis
  N Queensland
Tregellasia capito (Pale Yellow Robin)
T. c. nana
  N Queensland
T. c. capito
  S Queensland, New South Wales

EOPSALTRIA
Eopsaltria australis (Eastern Yellow Robin)
E. a. magnirostris
  N Queensland
E. a. chrysorrhoa
  C Queensland
E. a. coomooboolaroo
  EC Queensland
E. a. australis
  S Queensland, New South Wales
E. a. austina
  C & N New South Wales
E. a. viridior
  Victoria
Eopsaltria griseogularis (Western Yellow Robin)
E. g. griseogularis
  S Western Australia
E. g. rosinae
  South Australia

Eopsaltria georgiana (White-breasted Robin)
  coastal S Western Australia
Eopsaltria flaviventris (Yellow-bellied Robin)
  New Caledonia

PENEOENANTHE
Peneoenanthe pulverulenta (Mangrove Robin)
  P. p. pulverulenta
    S New Guinea
  P. p. leucura
    Aru Is, N Queensland
  P. p. cinereiceps
    N Western Australia
  P. p. alligator
    NC Australia

PHILENTOMA
Philentoma pyrrhoptera (Chestnut-winged Monarch Flycatcher)
  P. p. pyrrhoptera
    S Vietnam, Malaysia, Sumatra, Borneo
  P. p. dubia
    Natuna Is
Philentoma velata (Maroon-breasted Monarch Flycatcher)
  P. v. caesia
    Malaysia, Borneo, Sumatra
  P. v. velata
    Java

POECILODRYAS
Poecilodryas brachyura (White-breasted Robin)
  P. b. brachyura
    NW New Guinea
  P. b. albotaeniata
    Japen I, New Guinea
  P. b. dumasi
    N New Guinea
Poecilodryas hypoleuca (Black and White Robin)
  P. h. hypoleuca
    NW New Guinea
  P. h. steini
    Misol I, W New Guinea
  P. h. hermani
    N New Guinea
Poecilodryas superciliosa (White-browed Robin)
  P. s. superciliosa
    N Queensland
  P. s. cerviniventris
    N Western Australia, Northern Territory
Poecilodryas placens (Olive-yellow Robin)
  SE New Guinea

Poecilodryas albonotata (Black-throated Robin)   479
  P. a. albonotata
    NW New Guinea
  P.a. griseiventris
    SW New Guinea
  P. a. correcta
    SE New Guinea

PENEOTHELLO
Peneothello sigillatus (White-winged Thicket Flycatcher)
  P. s. saruwagedi
    NE New Guinea
  P. s. quadrimaculatus
    W New Guinea
  P. s. hagenensis
    EC New Guinea
  P. s. sigillatus
    SE New Guinea
Peneothello cryptoleucus (Grey Thicket Flycatcher)
  P. c. cryptoleucus
    NW New Guinea
  P. c. albidior
    WC New Guinea
Peneothello cyanus (Slaty Thicket Flycatcher)
  P. c. cyanus
    NW New Guinea
  P. c. atricapillus
    NE New Guinea
  P. c. subcyanus
    SE & C New Guinea
Peneothello bimaculatus (White rumped Thicket Flycatcher)
  P. b. bimaculatus
    NW New Guinea
  P. b. vicarius
    SE New Guinea

HETEROMYIAS
Heteromyias albispecularis (Ground Thicket Robin)
  H. a. albispecularis
    NW New Guinea
  H. a. atricapillus
    NW New Guinea
  H. a. rothschildi
    WC New Guinea
  H. a. centralis
    C New Guinea
  H. a. armiti
    SE New Guinea
Heteromyias cinereifrons (Grey-headed Thicket Robin)
  N Queensland

Pachycephalopsis hattamensis (Green Thicket Flycatcher)
P. h. hattamensis
NW New Guinea
P. h. ernesti
NW New Guinea
P. h. axillaris
WC New Guinea

Pachycephalopsis poliosoma (White-throated Thicket Flycatcher)
P. p. idenburgi
N New Guinea
P. p. hypopolia
NE New Guinea
P. p. albigularis
WC New Guinea
P. p. balim
WC New Guinea
P. p. approximans
C New Guinea
P. p. hunsteini
EC New Guinea
P. p. poliosoma
SE New Guinea

MUSCICAPIDAE

139 PLATYSTEIRINAE (PUFFBACK & WATTLED FLYCATCHERS)

MEGABYAS
Megabyas flammulatus (African Shrike Flycatcher)
M. f. flammulatus
Sierra Leone to Gabon, Fernando Po I
M. f. carolathi
N Angola
M. f. aequatorialis
NE Angola to S Sudan, Uganda

BIAS
Bias musicus (Black & White Flycatcher)
B. m. musicus
Sierra Leone to C Zaire
B. m. femininus
C Zaire to SW Sudan, Uganda
B. m. pallidiventris
N Angola, S Zaire
B. m. changamwensis
E Kenya to Rhodesia, Mozambique
B. m. clarens
S Mozambique

PSEUDOBIAS
Pseudobias wardi (Ward's Flycatcher)
Madagascar

Batis capensis (Cape Puff-back Flycatcher)
B. c. dimorpha
Zambia, S Malawi, Mozambique
B. c. reichenowi
SE Tanzania
B. c. kennedyi
W Rhodesia
B. c. capensis
E Rhodesia, South Africa
B. c. erythrophthalma
S Rhodesia, W Mozambique

Batis mixta (Short-tailed Puff-back Flycatcher)
SE Kenya, Tanzania, N Malawi

Batis margaritae (Boulton's Puff-back Flycatcher)
B. m. margaritae
S Angola
B. m. kathleenae
NW Zambia

Batis diops (Ruwenzori Puff-back Flycatcher)
E Zaire, S Uganda

Batis fratrum (Zululand Puff-back Flycatcher)
B. f. ultima
SE Kenya
B. f. fratrum
Mozambique, N Natal

Batis molitor (Chin Spot Puff-back Flycatcher)
B. m. molitor
Sudan & Kenya to S Africa
B. m. pintoi
Angola

Batis soror (Paler Chin-spot Puff-back Flycatcher)
E Kenya to Mozambique

Batis pirit (Pirit Puff-back Flycatcher)
S Angola to Cape Province

Batis senegalensis (Senegal Puff-back Flycatcher)
Senegal to Nigeria

Batis orientalis (Grey-headed Puff-back Flycatcher)
B. o. chadensis
Niger to W Sudan
B. o. lynesi
N Sudan
B. o. orientalis
Ethiopia, E Sudan, N Kenya

Batis perkeo (Pygmy Puff-back Flycatcher)
S Ethiopia, Kenya, Somalia

Batis minor (Black-headed Puff-back Flycatcher)
B. m. batesi
Cameroun
B. m. erlangeri
Cameroun & Angola to Somalia
B. m. minor
Somalia
B. m. suahelica
E Kenya, E Tanzania
Batis minulla (Angola Puff-back Flycatcher)
Cameroun to Angola
Batis minima (Verreaux's Puff-back Flycatcher)
B. m. minima
Gabon
B. m. ituriensis
NE Zaire
Batis poensis (Fernando Po Puff-back Flycatcher)
Liberia to Cameroun

PLATYSTEIRA
Platysteira cyanea (Brown-throated Wattle-eye)
P. c. cyanea
Senegal to Gabon, Central African Republic
P. c. nyanzae
N Zaire, Uganda, S Sudan, Kenya
P. c. aethiopica
E Ethiopia
Platysteira albifrons (White-fronted Wattle-eye)
N Angola, SW Zaire
Platysteira peltata (Black-throated Wattle-eye)
P. p. laticincta
Cameroun
P. p. mentalis
Angola to Zambia & Uganda
P. p. peltata
S E Africa
Platysteira concreta (Yellow-bellied Wattle-eye)
P. c. concreta
Sierra Leone to Ghana
P. c. harterti
Cameroun, Gabon
P. c. kumbaensis
SW Cameroun
P. c. ansorgei
Angola
P. c. graueri
E Zaire, Uganda
P. c. silvae
W Kenya

P. c. kungwensis
W Tanzania
Platysteira blissetti (Red-cheeked Wattle-eye)
P. b. blissetti
Sierra Leone to Cameroun
P. b. chalybea
Cameroun to N Angola
P. b. jamesoni
C Zaire to S Sudan & N Kenya
Platysteira castanea (Chestnut Wattle-eye)
P. c. castanea
Sierra Leone to Togo
P. c. hormophora
S Nigeria to Angola & W Kenya
Platysteira tonsa (White-spotted Wattle-eye)
S Nigeria to N Zaire

MUSCICAPIDAE

140 MONARCHINAE (MONARCH FLYCATCHERS)

ERYTHROCERCUS
Erythrocercus holochlorus (Little Yellow Flycatcher)
Kenya, Tanzania
Erythrocercus mccallii (Chestnut-capped Flycatcher)
E. m. nigeriae
Guinea to Nigeria
E. m. mccallii
Cameroun, Gabon
E. m. congicus
E Zaire, Uganda
Erythrocercus livingstonei (Livingstone's Flycatcher)
E. l. thomsoni
S Tanzania, N Mozambique
E. l. livingstonei
S Zambia, S Malawi, C Mozambique
E. l. francisci
N Malawi

ERANNORNIS
Erannornis longicauda (Blue Flycatcher)
E. l. longicauda
Sierra Leone to Central African Republic
E. l. teresita
Cameroun to S Sudan & Kenya
E. l. loandae
N & C Angola
Erannornis albicauda (White-tailed Blue Flycatcher)
Angola to Tanzania

TROCHOCERCUS

Trochocercus albonotatus (White-tailed Crested Flycatcher)
T. a. albonotatus
Uganda to Tanzania & Malawi
T. a. swynnertoni
E Rhodesia
T. a. subcaeruleus
N Tanzania, NE Zambia, N Mozambique

Trochocercus albiventris (White-bellied Crested Flycatcher)
T. a. albiventris
Cameroun, Fernando Po I
T. a. toroensis
NE Zaire, Uganda

Trochocercus nigromitratus (Dusky Crested Flycatcher)
Liberia to Uganda

Trochocercus cyanomelas (Cape Crested Flycatcher)
T. c. vivax
Uganda to S Zaire, Zambia
T. c. kikuyuensis
C Kenya
T. c. bivittatus
E Kenya to Mozambique, Malawi
T. c. cyanomelas
E South Africa

Trochocercus nitens (Blue-headed Crested Flycatcher)
T. n. reichenowi
Sierra Leone to Togo
T. n. nitens
Nigeria to E Zaire & Angola

TERPSIPHONE

Terpsiphone viridis (African Paradise Flycatcher)
T. v. viridis
Senegal to N Nigeria & Central African Republic
T. v. speciosa
S Ivory Coast to Gabon & W Sudan
T. v. violacea
Cameroun to Botswana & Kenya
T. v. ferretti
Ethiopia to Tanzania
T. v. restricta
N Kenya
T. v. ruwenzoriae
E Zaire, W Uganda, NW Tanzania
T. v. kivuensis
Rwanda, Kivu, NW Tanzania
T. v. suahelica
E Tanzania
T. v. ungujaensis
E Tanzania, Zambia
T. v. plumbeiceps
Angola, W Zaire, Namibia

T. v. granti
E South Africa

Terpsiphone rufocinerea (Rufous-vented Paradise Flycatcher)
T. r. bates
Cameroun to C Zaire
T. r. rufocinerea
Gabon to N Angola
T. r. bannermani
N Angola

Terpsiphone atrochalybea (Sao Thomé Paradise Flycatcher)
Sao Thomé I

Terpsiphone mutata (Madagascar Paradise Flycatcher)
Madagascar

Terpsiphone corvina (Seychelles Paradise Flycatcher)
Seychelles

Terpsiphone bourbonnensis (Mascarene Paradise Flycatcher)
Mauritius I

Terpsiphone paradisi (Asiatic Paradise Flycatcher)
T. p. harterti
Arabia
T. p. turkestanica
Turkistan
T. p. leucogaster
Afghanistan, Pakistan, W India
T. p. paradisi
C & S India, Sri Lanka
T. p. ceylonensis
Sri Lanka
T. p. incei
China, Manchuria, Korea
T. p. saturatior
E Himalayas, Assam, Bangladesh
T. p. burmae
Burma
T. p. affinis
S Burma, Thailand, Laos, Malaysia
T. p. nicobarica
Nicobar Is, Andaman Is
T. p. indochinensis
S Thailand, Cambodia
T. p. borneensis
Borneo
T. p. matzoedi
N Sumatra
T. p. australis
Java, S Sumatra
T. p. procera
Simalur I
T. p. insularis
Nias I
T. p. sumbaensis
Sumba I

T. p. floris
Sumbawa I, Alor I, Flores I
Terpsiphone atrocaudata (Black Paradise Flycatcher)
T. a. atrocaudata
Japan, SE Asia
T. a. illex
S Japan, Riukiu Is
T. a. periophthalmica
Mindoro I, Botel Tobago I
Terpsiphone rufiventer (Red-bellied Paradise Flycatcher)
T. r. rufiventer
Senegal to Guinea
T. r. nigriceps
Guinea to Togo
T. r. fagani
S Nigeria
T. r. tricolor
Fernando Po I
T. r. smithii
Annobon I
T. r. neumanni
Cameroun, Gabon
T. r. schubotzi
Central African Republic
T. r. bedfordi
N Zaire
T. r. mayombe
W Zaire
T. r. somereni
W Uganda
T. r. emini
SW Uganda, NW Tanzania
T. r. ignea
S Zaire, N Angola, Zambia
Terpsiphone unirufa (Luzon Paradise Flycatcher)
Luzon I, Mindoro I, Negros I
Terpsiphone cinnamomea (Rufous Paradise Flycatcher)
T. c. cinnamomea
Mindanao I, Basilan I, Sulu Archipelago
T. c. talautensis
Talaut I
Terpsiphone cyanescens (Blue Paradise Flycatcher)
Palawan I

EUTRICHOMYIAS
Eutrichomyias rowleyi (Rowley's Flycatcher)
Gt Sangai I, Peleng I, Banggai I

HYPOTHYMIS
Hypothymis helenae (Short-crested Blue Monarch)
H. h. helenae
Luzon I, Samar I

483

H. h. agusanae
NE Mindanao I
H. h. personata
Camiguin I, (North)
Hypothymis coelestis (Celestial Blue Monarch)
H. c. coelestis
Luzon I, Mindanao I, Basilan I, Samar I
H. c. rabori
Negros I
Hypothymis azurea (Black-naped Blue Monarch)
H. a. styani
India to S China & Vietnam
H. a. forrestia
Burma
H. a. ceylonensis
Sri Lanka
H. a. prophata
Malaysia, Sumatra, Borneo
H. a. tytleri
Andaman Is, Cocos Is
H. a. idiochroa
Car Nicobar I
H. a. nicobarica
S Nicobar Is
H. a. javana
Java
H. a. karimatensis
Karimata I
H. a. opisthocyanea
Anamba Is
H. a. gigantoptera
Bunguran I, Natuna Is
H. a. aeria
Maratua I
H. a. consobrina
Simalur I
H. a. leucophila
Siberut I
H. a. richmondi
Enggano I
H. a. abbotti
Babi I, Masia I
H. a. symmixta
Lesser Sunda Is
H. a. azurea
Philippine Is
H. a. catarmanensis
Camiguin I (South)
Hypothymis puella (Small Monarch)
H. p. puella
Celebes
H. p. blasii
Sula Is

Seisura inquieta (Restless Flycatcher)
S. i. nana
N Western Australia, Northern Territory
S. i. westralensis
S Western Australia
S. i. inquieta
E Australia

MACHAERIRHYNCHUS
Machaerirhynchus flaviventer (Yellow-breasted Flatbill Flycatcher)
M. f. albifrons
Waigeu I, Misol I, N New Guinea
M. f. albigula
NW New Guinea
M. f. novus
NE New Guinea
M. f. xanthogenys
S New Guinea, Aru Is
M. f. secundus
N Queensland
M. f. flaviventer
Queensland
Machaerirhynchus nigripectus (Black-breasted Flatbill Flycatcher)
M. n. nigripectus
NW New Guinea
M. n. saturatus
C New Guinea
M. n. harterti
SE New Guinea

CHASIEMPIS
Chasiempis sandwichensis (Elepaio)
C. s. sandwichensis
Hawaii I
C. s. bryani
Mauna Kea I
C. s. sclateri
Kauai I
C. s. gayi
Oahu I

POMAREA
Pomarea dimidiata (Raratonga Flycatcher)
Raratonga I
Pomarea nigra (Society Is Flycatcher)
Tahiti Is
Pomarea mendozae (Marquesas Flycatcher)
P. m. mendozae
Tahuata I, Hivaoa I
P. m. motanensis
Motane I
P. m. mira
Huapu I
P. m. nukuhivae
Nukuhiva I

Pomarea iphis (Allied Flycatcher)
P. i. iphis
Huahuna I
P. i. fluxa
Eioa I
Pomarea whitneyi (Large Flycatcher)
Fatuhiva I

MAYRORNIS
Mayrornis schistaceus (Small Slaty Flycatcher)
Vanikoro I
Mayrornis versicolor (Versicolored Flycatcher)
Ongea Levu I
Mayrornis lessoni (Slaty Flycatcher)
M. l. lessoni
NW Fiji Is
M. l. orientalis
S Fiji Is

NEOLALAGE
Neolalage banksiana (Buff-bellied Flycatcher)
Banks Is, New Hebrides

CLYTORHYNCHUS
Clytorhynchus pachycephaloides (Southern Shrikebill)
C. p. pachycephaloides
New Caledonia
C. p. grisescens
Banks Is, New Hebrides
Clytorhynchus vitiensis (Fiji Shrikebill)
C. v. powelli
Manua I
C. v. compressirostris
Kandavu I
C. v. vitiensis
Viti Levu I, Ovalau I
C. v. buensis
Vanua Levu I
C. v. layardi
Taviuni I
C. v. pontifex
Ngambia I, Rambi I
C. v. vatuana
N Lau Archipelago
C. v. heinei
Tonga I
C. v. wiglesworthi
Rotuma I
C. v. nesiotes
S Lau Archipelago
C. v. fotunae
Fotuna I, Alofa I
C. v. keppeli
Keppel I, Boscawen I

Clytorhynchus nigrogularis (Black-
throated Shrikebill)
　C. n. nigrogularis
　　Fiji Is
　C. n. sanctaecrucis
　　Santa Cruz I
Cytorhynchus hamlini (Rennell
Shrikebill)
　Rennell I

Metabolus rugiensis (Truk Monarch)
　Truk I

Monarcha axillaris (Black Monarch)
　M. a. axillaris
　　NW New Guinea
　M. a. fallax
　　EC New Guinea
　M. a. reichenowi
　　N New Guinea
Monarcha rubiensis (Rufous Monarch)
　M. r. rubiensis
　　Rubi I, NW New Guinea
　M. r. rufum
　　NE New Guinea
Monarcha alecto (Shining Monarch)
　M. a. alecto
　　Ternate I, Moluccas
　M. a. chalybeocephalus
　　New Ireland
　M. a. lucidus
　　Woodlark I
　M. a. manumudari
　　Vulcan I
　M. a. rufolateralis
　　Aru Is
　M. a. longirostris
　　Timor I
　M. a. nitens
　　Batjan I
　M. a. novaeguineensis
　　W New Guinea
　M. a. tormenti
　　N Western Australia
　M. a. nitida
　　Northern Territory
　M. a. wardelli
　　N Queensland
Monarcha hebetior (Dull Monarch)
　M. h. hebetior
　　St Matthias Is
　M. h. eichhorni
　　New Hanover
　M. h. cervinicolor
　　Dyaul I
Monarcha sericeus (New Hebrides Monarch)
　New Hebrides

Monarcha pileatus (Moluccan Monarch)　485
　M. p. pileatus
　　Halmahera I
　M. p. buruensis
　　Buru I
　M. p. castus
　　Tenimber Is
Monarcha cinerascens (Island Grey-
headed Monarch)
　M. c. cinerascens
　　Gt Banda I, Sulu Is, Timor I
　M. c. disjuncta
　　Kalao I, Djampea I
　M. c. perpallidus
　　St Matthias Is, Emirau I, New Hanover
　M. c. inornatus
　　NW New Guinea
　M. c. steini
　　New Guinea
　M. c. geelvinkianus
　　Misol I, Japen I
　M. c. fuscescens
　　Jamna I
　M. c. nigrirostris
　　New Guinea
　M. c. rosselianus
　　Rossel I
　M. c. impediens
　　Lihir Is, Feni I
　M. c. fulviventris
　　Ninigo I, Echiquier I
　M. c. kisserensis
　　Kei Is, Kisser I, Tenimber Is
　M. c. commutator
　　Sangi Is
　M. c. harterti
　　Halmahera I, Ternate I, Buru I
　M. c. tenchi
　　Tench I (St Matthias)
　M. c. intercedens
　　Tukangbesi I
Monarcha melanopsis (Pearly-winged
Monarch)
　M. m. melanopsis
　　S New Guinea, Queensland,New South
　　Wales
　M. m. pallida
　　N Queensland
Monarcha frater (Black-winged Monarch)
　M. f. everetti
　　Djampea I
　M. f. frater
　　NW New Guinea
　M. f. kunupi
　　C New Guinea
　M. f. periophthalmicus
　　SE New Guinea

M. f. canescens
N Queensland

Monarcha erythrosticta (Bougainville Monarch)
Bougainville I

Monarcha castaneiventris (Chestnut-bellied Monarch)
M. c. castaneiventris
Guadalcanal I, Malaita I, Choiseul I
M. c. obscurior
Rossel I
M. c. megarhyncha
San Cristobal I
M. c. ugiensis
Ugi Is
M. c. florenciae
Rubiana I

Monarcha richardsii (Richards' Monarch)
C Solomon Is

Monarcha leucotis (White-eared Monarch)
Queensland

Monarcha guttula (Spot-winged Monarch)
E New Guinea, Aru Is

Monarcha julienae (Kofiau Monarch)
Kofiau I

Monarcha mundus (Tenimber Monarch)
Tenimber Is

Monarcha trivirgatus (Spectacled Monarch)
M. t. trivirgatus
Timor I, Flores I, Alor I
M. t. bernsteini
NW New Guinea
M. t. melanopterus
Louisiade Archipelago
M. t. diadematus
Obi I
M. t. wellsi
Goram I
M. t. bimaculatus
Halmahera I, Batjan I
M. t. morotensis
Morotai I
M. t. nigrimentum
Ceram I, Ambon I
M. t. albiventris
N Queensland
M. t. gouldi
S Queensland, New South Wales
M. t. boanensis
Boano I
M. t. loricata
Buru I

Monarcha sacerdotum (Mees' Monarch)
Flores I

Monarcha leucurus (Kei Monarch)
Kei Is

Monarcha barbatus (Pied Monarch)
M. b. barbatus
Bougainville I, Guadalcanal I
M. b. floridanus
Florida I
M. b. squamulatus
Ugi I
M. b. meeki
Rendova I
M. b. malaitae
Malaita I

Monarcha infelix (Unhappy Monarch)
M. i. infelix
Manus I
M. i. coultasi
Rambutyo I

Monarcha menckei (St Matthias Monarch)
St Matthias Is

Monarcha viduus (San Cristobal Monarch)
San Cristobal I

Monarcha browni (Kulambangra Monarch)
M. b. browni
Kulambangra I
M. b. ganongae
Ganonga I
M. b. nigrotectus
Vella Lavella I

Monarcha verticalis (New Britain Pied Monarch)
Bismarck Archipelago

Monarcha ateralba (Bismarck Monarch)
Dyaul I

Monarcha godeffroyi (Yap Monarch)
Yap I

Monarcha brehmii (Biak Monarch)
Biak I, Misol I

Monarcha manadensis (Black & White Monarch)
New Guinea

Monarcha chrysomela (Black & Yellow Monarch)
M. c. chrysomela
New Hanover, New Ireland
M. c. kordensis
Biak I, Misol I
M. c. melanonotus
New Guinea
M. c. aurantiacus
NE New Guinea
M. c. praerepta
D'Entrecasteaux Archipelago, New Guinea
M. c. aruensis
Aru Is, S New Guinea
M. c. pulcherrima
Dyaul I

M. c. whitneyorum
  Lihir Is
M. c. tabarensis
  Tabar I
Monarcha takatsukasae (Tinian Monarch)
  Tinian I

ARSES
Arses kaupi (Pied Flycatcher)
  N Queensland
**Arses telescophthalmus (Frilled
  Flycatcher)**
  A. t. telescophthalmus
    Misol I, NW New Guinea
  A. t. insularis
    Japen I, N New Guinea
  A. t. batantae
    Batanta I, Waigeu I
  A. t. aruensis
    Aru Is
  A. t. lauterbachi
    NE New Guinea
  A. t. harterti
    SW & S New Guinea
  A. t. henkei
    SE New Guinea
  A. t. orientalis
    SE New Guinea
  A. t. lorealis
    N Queensland

MYIAGRA
**Myiagra pluto (Ponapé Myiagra
  Flycatcher)**
  Ponapé I
**Myiagra oceanica (Truk Myiagra
  Flycatcher)**
  Truk I
**Myiagra freycineti (Guam Myiagra
  Flycatcher)**
  Guam I
**Myiagra erythrops (Palau Myiagra
  Flycatcher)**
  Palau Is
Myiagra galeata (Helmet Flycatcher)
  M. g. galeata
    Batjan I
  M. g. goramensis
    Goram I
  M. g. seranensis
    Ceram I
  M. g. buruensis
    Buru I
Myiagra rubecula (Leaden Flycatcher)
  M. r. papuana
    New Guinea
  M. r. sciurorum
    Louisiade Archipelago

M. r. concinna
  N Western Australia, Northern Territory,
    N Queensland
M. r. yorki
  NE Queensland
M. r. rubecula
  S Queensland to South Australia &
    Victoria
Myiagra atra (Black Myiagra Flycatcher)
  Misol Is
**Myiagra ferrocyanea (Steel-blue
  Flycatcher)**
  M. f. ferrocyanea
    Ysabel I, Choiseul I, Guadalcanal I
  M. f. feminina
    Kulambangra I
  M. f. pallida
    Vella Lavella I
  M. f. cinerea
    Bougainville I
  M. f. malaitae
    Malaita I
  M. f. cervinicauda
    Ugi I, San Cristobal I
**Myiagra caledonica (New Caledonian
  Myiagra Flycatcher)**
  M. c. caledonica
    New Caledonia
  M. c. melanura
    Tanna I, Erromanga I, Maré I
  M. c. marina
    N & C New Hebrides
  M. c. perspicillata
    Nu I (New Caledonia)
  M. c. viridinitens
    Lifu I, Urea I
  M. c. occidentalis
    Rennell I
**Myiagra vanikorensis (Red-bellied
  Flycatcher)**
  M. v. vanikorensis
    Santa Cruz I, Vanikoro I
  M. v. castaneiventris
    Samoa Is
  M. v. rufiventris
    Navigator I, NW Fiji Is
  M. v. townsendi
    S Lau Is
  M. v. kandavensis
    Kandavu I
  M. v. dorsalis
    SC Fiji Is, N Lau Is
**Myiagra albiventris (White-vented
  Flycatcher)**
  Samoa Is
Myiagra cyanoleuca (Satin Flycatcher)
  M. c. novaepomeraniae
    New Britain

M. c. nupta
Louisiade Archipelago
M. c. robinsoni
N Queensland
M. c. cyanoleuca
E Australia, Tasmania
Myiagra ruficollis (Broad-billed Flycatcher)
M. r. ruficollis
Alor I, Timor I
M. r. rufigula
Timor I
M. r. mimikae
New Guinea, N Queensland
M. r. fulviventris
Tenimber Is
M. r. colonus
Kalao I, Djampea I
Myiagra azureocapilla (Blue-headed Flycatcher)
M. a. azureocapilla
Taviuni I
M. a. castaneigularis
Vanua Levu I, Kambara I
M. a. whitneyi
Viti Levu I

MUSCICAPIDAE

141 RHIPIDURINAE (FANTAIL FLY-
CATCHERS)

RHIPIDURA
Rhipidura hypoxantha (Yellow-bellied Fantail)
Himalayas, S China
Rhipidura threnothorax (Sooty Thicket Fantail)
R. t. threnothorax
E New Guinea
R. t. novaeguineensis
New Guinea
R. t. fumosa
Japen I
R. t. rosenbergi
Aru Is
Rhipidura maculipectus (Black Thicket Fantail)
R. m. maculipectus
Ambon I, Aru Is
R. m. mimika
New Guinea
R. m. saturata
Salawati I (New Guinea)
Rhipidura clamosa (Karimui Thicket Fantail)
E Highlands, New Guinea

Rhipidura leucothorax (White-breasted Fantail)
R. l. leucothorax
NW New Guinea
R. l. episcopalis
SE New Guinea
Rhipidura superciliaris (Blue Fantail)
R. s. superciliaris
Basilan I, N Mindanao
R. s. apo
SE Mindanao
R. s. samarensis
Bohol I, Samar I, Leyte I
Rhipidura cyaniceps (Blue-headed Fantail)
R. c. cyaniceps
Luzon I
R. c. pinicola
NW Luzon I
R. c. albiventris
Masbate I, Negros I, Panay I
R. c. sauli
Tablas I
Rhipidura phoenicura (Red-tailed Fantail)
Java
Rhipidura nigrocinnamomea (Black and Cinnamon Fantail)
R. n. hutchinsoni
N Mindanao I
R. n. nigrocinnamomea
SE Mindanao I
Rhipidura opistherythra (Tenimber Rufous Fantail)
Tenimber Is
Rhipidura lepida (Palau Fantail)
Palau Is
Rhipidura dedemi (Ceram Rufous Fantail)
Ceram I
Rhipidura superflua (Moluccan Fantail)
Buru I
Rhipidura sulaensis (Sula Fantail)
Sula Is
Rhipidura teijsmanni (Celebes Rufous Fantail)
R. t. teijsmanni
S & C Celebes
R. t. toradja
mountains of Celebes
Rhipidura rufifrons (Rufous Fantail)
R. r. uraniae
Mariana Is, Guam I
R. r. saipanensis
Saipan I, Tinian I
R. r. mariae
Rota I

R. r. kubaryi
Ponapé I
R. r. versicolor
Yap I
R. r. griseicauda
Waigeu I
R. r. torrida
Halmahera I, Ternate I
R. r. semicollaris
Timor I
R. r. sumbensis
Sumba I
R. r. agilis
Santa Cruz I
R. r. melaenolaema
Vanikoro I
R. r. utupuae
Utupua I
R. r. commoda
Bougainville I
R. r. rufofronta
Guadalcanal I
R. r. granti
Rendova I
R. r. russata
San Cristobal I
R. r. semirubra
Admiralty Is
R. r. hamadryas
Tenimber Is
R. r. astrolabi
Santa Cruz I
R. r. brunnea
Malaita I
R. r. kuperi
Santa Anna I
R. r. ugiensis
Ugi I
R. r. streptophora
SW New Guinea
R. r. mimosae
Kalao I
R. r. celebensis
Djampea I
R. r. elegantula
Roma I, Leti I, Moa I, Damar I
R. r. reichenowi
Babar I
R. r. squamata
Banda I
R. r. henrici
Ceram I, Kei Is
R. r. louisiadensis
Louisiade Archipelago
R. r. dryas
N Western Australia, Northern Territory
R. r. rufifrons
Queensland to Victoria

Rhipidura dahli (Island Rufous Fantail)
R. d. dahli
New Britain
R. d. antonii
New Ireland
Rhipidura matthiae (St Matthias Rufous Fantail)
St Matthias Is
Rhipidura personata (Kandavu Fantail)
Kandavu I (Fiji Is)
Rhipidura rufidorsa (Grey-breasted Rufous Fantail)
R. r. rufidorsa
Misol I, Japen I, NW New Guinea
R. r. kumusi
SE New Guinea
R. r. kubuna
S New Guinea
R. r. nova
E New Guinea
R. r. montana
SE New Guinea
Rhipidura brachyrhyncha (Dimorphic Rufous Fantail)
R. b. brachyrhyncha
NW New Guinea
R. b. devisi
SE New Guinea
Rhipidura spilodera (Spotted Fantail)
R. s. sancta
New Hebrides
R. s. spilodera
N & C New Hebrides, Banks Is
R. s. layardi
Ovalau I, Viti Levu I
R. s. erythronota
Yanganga I, Vanua Levu I
R. s. rufilateralis
Taviuni I
R. s. verreauxi
Lifu I, Meré I, New Caledonia
Rhipidura rennelliana (Rennell Fantail)
Rennell I
Rhipidura drownei (Mountain Fantail)
R. d. drownei
Bougainville I
R. d. ocularis
Guadalcanal I
Rhipidura tenebrosa (Dusky Fantail)
San Cristobal I
Rhipidura fuliginosa (Collared Grey Fantail)
R. f. bulgeri
Lifu I, New Caledonia
R. f. erromangae
Erromanga I

R. f. phasiana
New Guinea
R. f. brenchleyi
New Hebrides, Banks Is
R. f. preissi
S Western Australia
R. f. subphasiana
N Western Australia
R. f. buchanani
Melville I, Northern Territory
R. f. albicauda
C Australia
R. f. harterti
N Queensland
R. f. frerei
C Queensland
R. f. alisteri
S Queensland to Victoria
R. f. albiscapa
King I, Tasmania
R. f. placabilis
North I (New Zealand)
R. f. fuliginosa
South I (New Zealand)
R. f. penitus
Chatham I
R. f. pelzelni
Norfolk I
R. f. cervina
Lord Howe I
Rhipidura nebulosa (Samoan Fantail)
R. n. nebulosa
Upolu I
R. n. altera
Savaii I
**Rhipidura malaitae (Malaita Rufous
Fantail)**
Malaita I
Rhipidura atra (Black Fantail)
R. a. atra
NW New Guinea
R. a. vulpes
N New Guinea
**Rhipidura hyperythra (Chestnut-bellied
Fantail)**
R. h. hyperythra
Aru Is
R. h. mulleri
SW New Guinea
R. h. castaneothorax
SE New Guinea
R. h. manayoensis
SE New Guinea
Rhipidura euryura (White-bellied Fantail)
Java
Rhipidura albolimbata (Friendly Fantail)
R. a. albolimbata
NW New Guinea

R. a. lorentzi
SW New Guinea
R. a. auricularis
SE New Guinea
**Rhipidura albicollis (White-throated
Fantail)**
R. a. canescens
W Himalayas
R. a. albicollis
N India, Nepal
R. a. orissae
NE India
R. a. stanleyi
E Himalayas, Assam, Burma
R. a. robinsoni
Malaysia
R. a. atrata
Sumatra
R. a. sarawacensis
N Borneo
R. a. kinabalu
Borneo
R. a. cinerescens
S Indochina
**Rhipidura albogularis (White-spotted
Fantail)**
R. a. albogularis
SW India
R. a. vernayi
SE India
Rhipidura aureola (White-browed Fantail)
R. a. aureola
N India
R. a. compressirostris
S India, Sri Lanka
R. a. burmanica
Assam, Burma
Rhipidura javanica (Pied Fantail)
R. j. longicauda
Sumatra
R. j. javanica
Java
R. j. nigritorquis
Philippine Is
**Rhipidura rufiventris (Red-vented
Fantail)**
R. r. rufiventris
Timor I
R. r. perneglecta
Tiandu I
R. r. finitima
Watubela I
R. r. assimilis
Kei Is
R. r. buruensis
Buru I
R. r. obiensis
Obi I

R. r. pallidiceps
  Wetar I
R. r. gigantea
  Lihir Is, Tabar I
R. r. tangensis
  Boang I, Tanga I
R. r. cinerea
  Ceram I
R. r. lenzi
  Ambon I
R. r. buttikoferi
  Damar I
R. r. hoedti
  Leti I
R. r. diluta
  Flores I
R. r. sumbawensis
  Sumbawa I
R. r. tenkatei
  Rotti I
R. r. niveiventris
  Admiralty Is
R. r. mussaui
  St Matthias Is
R. r. setosa
  New Ireland
R. r. finschii
  New Britain
R. r. vidua
  New Guinea
R. r. gularis
  Waigeu I, Japen I
R. r. nigromentalis
  Sudest I
R. r. kordensis
  Misol I
R. r. superciliosa
  N Australia
R. r. isura
  coast of N Western Australia
Rhipidura perlata (Pearlated Fantail)
  Malaysia
Rhipidura cockerelli (Cockerell's Fantail)
R. c. cockerelli
  Guadalcanal I
R. c. coultasi
  N Solomon Is
R. c. septentrionalis
  Bougainville I
R. c. interposita
  Ysabel I
R. c. floridana
  Florida I, Tulagi I
R. c. lavellae
  Vella Lavella I
R. c. albina
  Kulambangra I, Rendova I

Rhipidura leucophrys (Black & White 491
Fantail) (Willie Wagtail)
R. l. amboinensis
  Ambon I, Ceram I, Buru I
R. l. melanoleuca
  Solomon Is, New Guinea
R. l. atripennis
  Aru Is, SW New Guinea
R. l. picata
  N Western Australia, Northern Territory
R. l. leucophrys
  S Australia
R. l. melaleuca
  Bismarck Archipelago

MUSCICAPIDAE

142 PACHYCEPHALINAE (WHISTLERS)

EULACESTOMA
Eulacestoma nigropectus (Wattled Shrike
Tit)
E. n. clara
  C New Guinea
E. n. nigropectus
  SE New Guinea

FALCUNCULUS
Falcunculus frontatus (Crested Shrike Tit)
F. f. leucogaster
  S Western Australia
F. f. whitei
  Northern Territory, NW Western Australia
F. f. frontatus
  E Australia

OREOICA
Oreoica gutturalis (Crested Bellbird)
O. g. pallescens
  N Western Australia
O. g. gutturalis
  WC & E Australia

PACHYCARE
Pachycare flavogrisea (Golden-faced
Pachycare)
P. f. flavogrisea
  W New Guinea
P. f. subaurantia
  C New Guinea
P. f. randi
  N New Guinea
P. f. subpallida
  SE New Guinea

RHAGOLOGUS
Rhagologus leucostigma (Mottled
Whistler)
R. l. leucostigma
  NW New Guinea
R. l. novus
  N New Guinea

R. l. obscurus
C & SE New Guinea

HYLOCITREA
Hylocitrea bonensis (Buff-throated Thickhead)
H. b. bonensis
NC & SE Celebes
H. b. bonthaina
S Celebes

PACHYCEPHALA
Pachycephala raveni (Raven's Whistler)
C & SE Celebes
Pachycephala rufinucha (Rufous-naped Whistler)
P. r. rufinucha
NW New Guinea
P. r. niveifrons
C New Guinea
P. r. lochmia
E New Guinea
P. r. gamblei
SE New Guinea
P. r. prasinonota
SE New Guinea
Pachycephala tenebrosa (Sooty Whistler)
P. t. atra
N New Guinea
P. t. tenebrosa
S New Guinea
Pachycephala olivacea (Olive Whistler)
P. o. macphersoniana
New South Wales, S Queensland
P. o. olivacea
S Victoria, SE South Australia, Tasmania
Pachycephala rufogularis (Red-lored Whistler)
NW Victoria, E South Australia
Pachycephala inornata (Gilbert Whistler)
P. i. gilbertii
S Western Australia
P. i. inornata
SE Australia
Pachycephala hypoxantha (Bornean Mountain Whistler)
P. h. hypoxantha
N Borneo
P. h. sarawacensis
Poi mountains, NW Borneo
Pachycephala cinerea (Mangrove Whistler)
P. c. cinerea
W Malaysia, Bangladesh, Burma, Thailand, Mergui Archipelago
P. c. vandepolli
E Malaysia, S Indochina
P. c. butaloides
Bangka I, Billiton I, S Borneo, Java, Bali I, Lombok I

P. c. secedens
N Borneo, Natuna Is
P. c. homeyeri
Sulu Is
P. c. plateni
Palawan I
P. c. winchelli
C Philippine Is
P. c. mindorensis
Mindoro I
P. c. crissalis
SC Luzon I
P. c. albiventris
N Luzon I
Pachycephala phaionota (Island Whistler)
P. p. phaionota
Aru Is, N Moluccas, NW New Guinea islands
P. p. stresemanni
Majau I (N Moluccas)
Pachycephala hyperythra (Rufous-breasted Whistler)
P. h. hyperythra
W New Guinea
P. h. sepikiana
C New Guinea
P. h. reichenowi
NE New Guinea
P. h. salvadorii
SE New Guinea
Pachycephala modesta (Brown-backed Whistler)
P. m. modesta
SE New Guinea
P. m. hypoleuca
NE New Guinea
P. m. telefolminensis
C New Guinea
Pachycephala philippinensis (Yellow-bellied Whistler)
P. p. fallax
Calayan I
P. p. illex
Camiguin I (North)
P. p. philippinensis
Luzon I
P. p. siquijorensis
Siquijor I
P. p. apoensis
Samar I, Leyte I, Mindanao I
P. p. basilanica
Basilan I
P. p. boholensis
Bohol I
Pachycephala sulfuriventer (Yellow-vented Whistler)
P. s. sulfuriventer
N, C & SE Celebes

P. s. meridionalis
S Celebes
Pachycephala meyeri (Vogelkop Whistler)
NW New Guinea
Pachycephala soror (Sclater's Whistler)
P. s. soror
W New Guinea
P. s. klossi
C & E New Guinea
P. s. bartoni
SE New Guinea & Goodenough I
Pachycephala simplex (Brown Whistler)
P. s. simplex
Northern Territory, Melville I
P. s. rufipennis
Kei Is
P. s. gagiensis
Gagi I
P. s. waigeunensis
Waigeu I
P. s. griseiceps
Aru Is, NE New Guinea
P. s. miosnomensis
Meos Num I
P. s. jobiensis
Japen I, N New Guinea
P. s. perneglecta
S New Guinea
P. s. peninsulae
N Queensland
P. s. dubia
SE New Guinea, D'Entrecasteaux
   Archipelago
P. s. sudestensis
Tagula I, Louisiade Archipelago
Pachycephala orpheus (Timor Whistler)
P. o. orpheus
Timor I
P. o. wetterensis
Wetar I
Pachycephala pectoralis (Golden Whistler)
P. p. teysmanni
Saleyer I
P. p. everetti
Djampea I, Kalao Tua I, Madu I
P. p. javana
E Java, Bali I
P. p. fulvotincta
Sumbawa I, Flores I
P. p. jubilarii
Lomblen I, Pantar I, Alor I
P. p. fulviventris
Sumba I
P. p. calliope
Timor I, Semau I
P. p. arthuri
Wetar I

P. p. sharpei
Babar I
P. p. dammeriana
Damar I
P. p. par
Roma I
P. p. compar
Leti I, Moa I
P. p. fuscoflava
Larat I (Tenimber Is)
P. p. macrorhynchus
Ambon I
P. p. alfurorum
Ceram I
P. p. buruensis
Buru I
P. p. clio
Sula Is
P. p. pelengensis
Banggai I, Peleng I
P. p. obiensis
Obi I
P. p. tidorensis
Tidore I, Ternate I
P. p. mentalis
Batjan I, Halmahera I, Morotai I
P. p. occidentalis
S Western Australia
P. p. fuliginosa
South Australia, W Victoria
P. p. glaucura
Tasmania, King I
P. p. youngi
E Victoria
P. p. pectoralis
New South Wales
P. p. ashbyi
N New South Wales, S Queensland
P. p. queenslandica
N Queensland
P. p. contempta
Lord Howe I
P. p. xanthoprocta
Norfolk I
P. p. collaris
Louisiade Archipelago
P. p. rosseliana
Rossel I
P. p. fergussonis
Fergusson I
P. p. misimae
Misima I
P. p. citreogaster
New Hanover, New Britain, New Ireland
P. p. sexuvaria
St Matthias Is
P. p. goodsoni
Admiralty Is

P. p. tabarensis
Tabar I
P. p. ottomeyeri
Lihir I
P. p. whitneyi
Whitney I
P. p. bougainvillei
Buka I, Bougainville I
P. p. orioloides
Choiseul I, Ysabel I, Florida I
P. p. cinnamomea
Beagle I, Guadalcanal I
P. p. sanfordi
Malaita I
P. p. pavuvu
Pavuvu Is
P. p. centralis
E New Georgia Is
P. p. feminina
Rennell I
P. p. melanoptera
S New Georgia Is
P. p. melanonota
Ganonga I, Vella Lavella I
P. p. christophori
Santa Ana I, San Cristobal I
P. p. littayei
Loyalty Is
P. p. cucullata
Aneiteum I
P. p. chlorura
Erromango I
P. p. intacta
Banks Is, N & C New Hebrides
P. p. vanikorensis
Vanikoro I, Santa Cruz I
P. p. utupuae
Utupua I
P. p. ornata
N Santa Cruz I
P. p. kandavensis
Kandavu Is
P. p. lauana
S Lau Archipelago
P. p. vitiensis
Ngau I
P. p. bella
Vatu Vara I
P. p. koroana
Karo I
P. p. torquata
Taviuni I
P. p. ambigua
Rambi I, Kio I
P. p. optata
Ovalau I, SE Viti Levu I
P. p. graeffii
Waia I, Viti Levu I

P. p. aurantiiventris
Yanganga I, Vanua Levu I
Pachycephala melanops (Tonga Whistler)
Vavau I, Tonga I
Pachycephala melanura (Mangrove Golden Whistler)
P. m. balim
N New Guinea
P. m. dahli
islands off S New Guinea
P. m. bynoei
Western Australia
P. m. hilli
N Western Australia
P. m. melanura
N Western Australia
P. m. violatae
Northern Territory, Melville I
P. m. spinicauda
N Queensland, Torres Straits islands
Pachycephala flavifrons (Yellow-fronted Whistler)
Samoa Is
Pachycephala caledonica (New Caledonian Whistler)
New Caledonia
Pachycephala implicata (Mountain Whistler)
P. i. implicata
Guadalcanal I
P. i. richardsi
Bougainville I
Pachycephala lorentzi (Lorentz's Whistler)
C & E New Guinea
Pachycephala nudigula (Bare-throated Whistler)
P. n. nudigula
Sumbawa I
P. n. ilsa
Flores I
Pachycephala schlegelii (Schlegel's Whistler)
P. s. schlegelii
W New Guinea
P. s. obscurior
C & E New Guinea
P. s. cyclopum
WC New Guinea
Pachycephala aurea (Yellow-backed Whistler)
SE New Guinea
Pachycephala rufiventris (Rufous Whistler)
P. r. kebirensis
Moa I, Roma I, Damar I, Wetar I
P. r. arctitorquis
Tenimber Is
P. r. tianduana
Tiandou I, (W Kei Is)

P. r. falcata
Melville I, Northern Territory
P. r. colletti
N Western Australia
P. r. pallida
NW Queensland
P. r. dulcior
N Queensland
P. r. rufiventris
South Australia
P. r. maudeae
C Australia
P. r. xanthetraea
New Caledonia
P. r. cinerascens
N Moluccas, Ternate I
P. r. johni
Obi Major I
P. r. lineolata
Sula Is
P. r. examinata
Buru I
P. r. griseonota
Ceram I
P. r. kuehni
Kei Is
P. r. monarcha
Aru Is
P. r. dorsalis
C & E New Guinea
P. r. leucogaster
SE New Guinea
P. r. meeki
Rossel I

Pachycephala lanioides (White-bellied Whistler)
P. l. carnarvoni
Shark Bay (Western Australia)
P. l. bulleri
coast of Western Australia
P. l. lanioides
N Western Australia
P. l. fretorum
Northern Territory, NW Queensland

COLLURICINCLA
Colluricincla megarhyncha (Rufous Shrike Thrush)
C. m. sanghirensis
Sanghir Is
C. m. affinis
Waigeu I
C. m. batantae
Batanta I
C. m. misoliensis
Misol I
C. m. megarhyncha
W New Guinea

C. m. ferruginea
NW New Guinea
C. m. aruensis
Aru Is
C. m. goodsoni
S New Guinea
C. m. wuroi
S New Guinea
C. m. palmeri
S New Guinea
C. m. despecta
SE New Guinea
C. m. superflua
SE New Guinea
C. m. nea
E New Guinea
C. m. madaraszi
E New Guinea
C. m. tappenbecki
NE New Guinea
C. m. maeandrina
NE New Guinea
C. m. idenburgi
N New Guinea
C. m. hybrida
N New Guinea
C. m. obscura
Japen I
C. m. melanorhyncha
Biak I
C. m. fortis
D'Entrecasteaux Archipelago
C. m. trobriandi
Trobriand Is
C. m. discolor
Tagula I
C. m. parvula
Northern Territory, Melville I
C. m. conigravi
N Western Australia
C. m. griseata
Cape York islands
C. m. normani
N Queensland
C. m. parvissima
N Queensland
C. m. gouldii
C & S Queensland
C. m. rufogaster
N New South Wales
Colluricincla boweri (Stripe-breasted Shrike-Thrush)
N Queensland
Colluricincla harmonica (Grey Shrike-Thrush)
C. h. roebucki
Roebuck Bay, N Western Australia

C. h. parryi
Kimberley, Western Australia
C. h. julietae
N Western Australia
C. h. brunnea
Northern Territory, Melville I
C. h. superciliosa
N Queensland
C. h. tachycrypta
SE New Guinea
C. h. pallescens
NC Queensland
C. h. harmonica
S Queensland to E Victoria
C. h. strigata
Tasmania, Bass Strait islands
C. h. halmaturina
SW New South Wales, NW Victoria,
SE South Australia
C. h. anda
NE South Australia
C. h. whitei
C South Australia
C. h. rufiventris
W & C Australia

Colluricincla woodwardi (Sandstone Shrike-Thrush)
C. w. woodwardi
Northern Territory
C. w. assimilis
N Western Australia

PITOHUI
Pitohui kirhocephalus (Variable Pitohui)
P. k. kirhocephalus
NW New Guinea
P. k. salvadorii
NW New Guinea
P. k. dohertyi
NW New Guinea
P. k. rubiensis
NW New Guinea
P. k. stramineipectus
SW New Guinea
P. k. decipiens
SW New Guinea
P. k. adiensis
Adi I
P. k. carolinae
SW New Guinea
P. k. brunneivertex
W New Guinea
P. k. jobiensis
Kurudu I, Japen I
P. k. meyeri
N New Guinea
P. k. senex
N New Guinea

P. k. brunneicaudus
N New Guinea
P. k. meridionalis
SE New Guinea
P. k. brunneiceps
S New Guinea
P. k. nigripectus
S New Guinea
P. k. aruensis
Aru Is
P. k. uropygialis
Salawati I, Misol I
P. k. tibialis
NW New Guinea
P. k. pallidus
Sagewin I, Batanta I
P. k. cerviniventris
Waigeu I
Pitohui dichrous (Black-headed Pitohui)
P. d. dichrous
N New Guinea
P. d. monticola
C New Guinea
Pitohui incertus (Mottle breasted Pitohui)
S New Guinea
Pitohui ferrugineus (Rusty Pitohui)
P. f. leucorhynchus
Waigeu I
P. f. fuscus
Batanta I
P. f. brevipennis
Aru Is
P. f. ferrugineus
Misol I, NW New Guinea
P. f. holerythrus
Japen I, N New Guinea
P. f. clarus
SE New Guinea
Pitohui cristatus (Crested Pitohui)
P. c. cristatus
W New Guinea
P. c. arthuri
N & S New Guinea
P. c. kodonophonos
SE New Guinea
Pitohui nigrescens (Black Pitohui)
P. n. nigrescens
NW New Guinea
P. n. wandamensis
N New Guinea
P. n. meeki
C New Guinea
P. n. burgersi
N & C New Guinea
P. n. schistaceus
SE New Guinea
P. n. harterti
E New Guinea

Pitohui tenebrosus (Morning Bird)
  Palau Is

TURNAGRA
Turnagra capensis (New Zealand Thrush)
  T. c. turnagra
    North I,(New Zealand)
  T. c. capensis
    South I,(New Zealand)

143 AEGITHALIDAE (LONG-TAILED TITS)

AEGITHALOS
Aegithalos caudatus (Long-tailed Tit)
  A. c. caudatus
    N Europe, N Asia, N Korea
  A. c. rosaceus
    British Isles
  A. c. europaeus
    C Europe
  A. c. aremoricus
    NW & C France
  A. c. taiti
    N Iberia, S France
  A. c. irbii
    S Iberia, Corsica
  A. c. italiae
    Italy
  A. c. siculus
    Sicily
  A. c. macedonicus
    Albania, Greece
  A. c. tauricus
    S Russia
  A. c. major
    Caucasus
  A. c. tephronotus
    Asia Minor
  A. c. alpinus
    N Iran
  A. c. passekii
    SW Iran
  A. c. vinaceus
    N & W China
  A. c. glaucogularis
    C China
  A. c. trivirgatus
    Honshu I
  A. c. kiusiuensis
    S Japan
  A. c. magnus
    S Korea
Aegithalos leucogenys (White-cheeked Tit)
  Afghanistan to NW India
Aegithalos concinnus (Red-headed Tit)
  A. c. iredalei
    Pakistan, W Himalayas
  A. c. rubricapillus
    E Himalayas, Assam

  A. c. manipurensis
    S Assam, NE India, W Burma
  A. c. talifuensis
    NE Burma, W China, N Vietnam
  A. c. pulchellus
    E Burma
  A. c. concinnus
    C & E China, Taiwan
  A. c. annamensis
    S Indochina
Aegithalos iouschistos (Blyth's Long-tailed Tit)
  A. i. niveogularis
    Pakistan, W Himalayas
  A. i. iouschistos
    E Himalayas, SE Tibet
  A. i. bonvaloti
    NE Burma, SW China
  A. i. obscuratus
    W Szechwan
  A. i. sharpei
    E Burma
Aegithalos fuliginosus (Sooty Long-tailed Tit)
    W & C China

PSALTRIA
Psaltria exilis (Pygmy Tit)
    W & C Java

PSALTRIPARUS
Psaltriparus minimus (Common Bushtit)
  P. m. minimus
    W USA
  P. m. californicus
    S Oregon, California
  P. m. sociabilis
    S California
  P. m. melanurus
    NW Baja California
  P. m. grindae
    S Baja California
  P. m. plumbeus
    WC & S USA, N Mexico
  P. m. providentialis
    SE California, S Nevada
  P. m. cecaumenorum
    NW Mexico
Psaltriparus melanotis (Black-eared Bushtit)
  P. m. lloydi
    S USA, N Mexico
  P. m. dimorphicus
    N Mexico
  P. m. iulus
    W & C Mexico
  P. m. melanotis
    S Mexico, Guatemala

144 REMIZIDAE (PENDULINE TITS)

REMIZ
Remiz pendulinus (Penduline Tit)
R. p. pendulinus
S & E Europe, Asia Minor, W Siberia
R. p. caspius
N & W Caspian Sea
R. p. coronatus
C Asia, NW India
R. p. macronyx
WC Asia, N Iran
R. p. nigricans
E Iran
R. p. stoliczkae
N Mongolia
R. p. consobrinus
Manchuria, N China, Korea

ANTHOSCOPUS
Anthoscopus punctifrons (Sennar Kapok Tit)
S Sahara
Anthoscopus parvulus (Yellow Penduline Tit)
Senegal to Sudan
Anthoscopus musculus (Mouse-coloured Tit)
NE & E Africa
Anthoscopus flavifrons (Yellow-fronted Tit)
A. f. waldroni
Ghana
A. f. flavifrons
Gabon, Cameroun, N Zaire
A. f. ruthae
E Zaire
Anthoscopus caroli (African Penduline Tit)
A. c. roccattii
S Uganda
A. c. taruensis
S Kenya, N Tanzania
A. c. pallescens
Tanzania
A. c. ansorgei
Angola, Zaire
A. c. rhodesiae
SE Zaire, NE Zambia, S Tanzania
A. c. robertsi
NE Zambia to Mozambique
A. c. caroli
Namibia to S Mozambique
A. c. winterbottomi
NW Zambia
A. c. rankinei
Zambia

Anthoscopus sylviella (Rungwe Penduline Tit)
S Kenya, Tanzania
Anthoscopus minutus (Southern Kapok Tit)
A. m. damarensis
Namibia, Rhodesia, W Transvaal
A. m. minutus
W Cape Province

AURIPARUS
Auriparus flaviceps (Verdin)
A. f. flaviceps
Baja California, NW Mexico
A. f. acaciarum
SW USA, NW Mexico
A. f. ornatus
SW USA, N Mexico
A. f. fraterculus
N Mexico

CEPHALOPYRUS
Cephalopyrus flammiceps (Fire-capped Tit Warbler)
C. f. flammiceps
Pakistan, W Himalayas, N India
C. f. olivaceus
E Himalayas, W China

145 PARIDAE (TITS, CHICKADEES)

PARUS
Parus palustris (Marsh Tit)
P. p. palustris
Italy, NW Europe
P. p. brandtii
N Caucasus
P. p. brevirostris
C Asia, Manchuria, N China
P. p. hensoni
S Kurile Is, N Japan
P. p. hellmayri
S Korea, China
P. p. hypermelaena
W China, E Burma
Parus lugubris (Sombre Tit)
P. l. lugubris
Hungary, N Greece
P. l. lugens
C & S Greece
P. l. anatoliae
Asia Minor
Parus hyrcanus (Iranian Sombre Tit)
P. h. hyrcanus
N Iran
P. h. dubius
W Iran
P. h. kirmanensis
SE Iran
P. h. talischensis
Azerbaidjan (USSR)

Parus montanus (Willow Tit)
P. m. loennbergi
  Lapland, N Russia
P. m. borealis
  NE & EC Europe, Siberia
P. m. montanus
  SE Europe
P. m. salicarius
  NW Europe
P. m. kamtschatkensis
  N Kurile Is, Kamchatka
P. m. sachalinensis
  S Kurile Is, Sakhalin I
P. m. restrictus
  N Japan
P. m. songarus
  C Asia
P. m. affinis
  NW China
P. m. stoetzneri
  N China, SW Manchuria
P. m. weigoldicus
  W China

Parus atricapillus (Black-capped Chickadee)
P. a. turneri
  NW Canada
P. a. occidentalis
  W Canada, W USA
P. a. septentrionalis
  WC Canada, C USA
P. a. nevadensis
  WC USA
P. a. atricapillus
  E Canada, NE USA
P. a. bartletti
  Newfoundland
P. a. practicus
  NE USA

Parus carolinensis (Carolina Chickadee)
P. c. atricapilloides
  SC USA
P. c. agilis
  S USA
P. c. carolinensis
  SE USA
P. c. extimus
  E USA
P. c. impiger
  Florida

Parus sclateri (Mexican Chickadee)
P. s. eidos
  S USA, N Mexico
P. s. sclateri
  SC Mexico
P. s. rayi
  S Mexico

Parus gambeli (Mountain Chickadee)
P. g. abbreviatus
  W Canada, NW USA
P. g. inyoensis
  W USA
P. g. gambeli
  SW USA
P. g. baileyae
  SW California
P. g. atratus
  N Baja California

Parus superciliosus (White-browed Tit)
  W China

Parus davidi (Père David's Tit)
  W China

Parus cinctus (Siberian Tit)
P. c. lapponicus
  Lapland
P. c. cinctus
  Siberia
P. c. sayanus
  C Asia
P. c. lathami
  NW Alaska

Parus hudsonicus (Boreal Chickadee)
P. h. columbianus
  W Canada
P. h. cascadensis
  NW USA
P. h. hudsonicus
  Canada
P. h. littoralis
  SE Canada, NE USA

Parus rufescens (Chestnut-backed Chickadee)
P. r. rufescens
  W Canada, W USA
P. r. neglectus
  California
P. r. barlowi
  S California

Parus wollweberi (Bridled Titmouse)
P. w. phillipsi
  SW USA, NW Mexico
P. w. wollweberi
  C & S Mexico
P. w. caliginosus
  SW Mexico

Parus rubidiventris (Black-crested Tit)
P. r. rubidiventris
  C Himalayas
P. r. beavani
  E Himalayas, W China, NE Burma
P. r. saramatii
  NW Burma

Parus rufonuchalis (Rufous-naped Tit)
  W & C Asia, N India

***Parus melanolophus* (Vigors Crested Tit)**
Pakistan, W Himalayas
***Parus ater* (Coal Tit)**
P. a. ater
Europe, Siberia
P. a. britannicus
Great Britain
P. a. hibernicus
Ireland
P. a. vieirae
Spain, Portugal
P. a. sardus
Corsica, Sardinia
P. a. atlas
N Morocco
P. a. ledouci
N Africa
P. a. cypriotes
Cyprus
P. a. moltchanovi
S Russia
P. a. michaelowskii
Caucasus
P. a. derjugini
N Armenia
P. a. gaddi
Iran
P. a. chorassanicus
NE Iran
P. a. phaeonotus
SW Iran
P. a. rufipectus
C Asia
P. a. aemodius
E Himalayas, W China, N Burma
P. a. pekinensis
N China
P. a. insularis
Japan
P. a. kuatunensis
SE China
P. a. ptilosus
Taiwan
***Parus venustulus* (Yellow-bellied Tit)**
S & W China
***Parus elegans* (Elegant Tit)**
P. e. edithae
Babuyan I
P. e. montigenus
N Luzon I
P. e. gilliardi
Batjan I (Luzon)
P. e. elegans
S Luzon I, Panay I, Mindoro I
P. e. visayanus
Cebu I
P. e. albescens
Guimares I, Masbate I, Negros I

P. e. mindanensis
Mindanao I
P. e. suluensis
Tawitawi Is, Sulu I
P. e. bongaoensis
Bongao I
***Parus amabilis* (Palawan Tit)**
Balabac I, Palawan I
***Parus cristatus* (Crested Tit)**
P. c. cristatus
N & E Europe, Alps
P. c. scoticus
NC Scotland
P. c. abadiei
NW France
P. c. weigoldi
S & W Iberia
P. c. mitratus
C & W Europe
P. c. baschkirikus
C Russia
***Parus dichrous* (Brown Crested Tit)**
P. d. kangrae
Pakistan, NW Himalayas
P. d. dichrous
C & E Himalayas
P. d. dichroides
NW China
P. d. wellsi
SW China, NE Burma
***Parus afer* (Acacia Grey Tit)**
P. a. thruppi
Ethiopia, Somalia
P. a. barakae
Uganda, Kenya, Tanzania
P. a. benguelae
SW Angola
P. a. cinerascens
Namibia, Rhodesia, South Africa
P. a. afer
W Cape Province
***Parus griseiventris* (Miombo Grey Tit)**
Zambia, Rhodesia, Tanzania
***Parus niger* (Southern Black Tit)**
P. n. ravidus
S Rhodesia, Transvaal, E Zambia
P. n. niger
Southern Africa
P. n. xanthostomus
S Zambia
***Parus leucomelas* (White-winged Black Tit)**
P. l. guineensis
W & WC Africa
P. l. leucomelas
Ethiopia
P. l. insignis
C & SC Africa

P. l. carpi
  S Angola, N Namibia
Parus albiventris (White-breasted Tit)
  Nigeria to Sudan, Tanzania
Parus leuconotus (White-backed Black Tit)
  Ethiopia
Parus funereus (Dusky Tit)
  P. f. funereus
    Cameroun to Kenya
  P. f. gabela
    Angola
Parus fasciiventer (Stripe-breasted Tit)
  P. f. fasciiventer
    Rwanda (E Zaire)
  P. f. tanganjicae
    S Kivu (E Zaire)
  P. f. kaboboensis
    Mt Kabobo (SE Zaire)
Parus fringillinus (Red-throated Tit)
  S Kenya, N & C Tanzania
Parus rufiventris (Rufous-bellied Tit)
  P. r. rufiventris
    WC Africa
  P. r. masukuensis
    Zambia, Malawi
  P. r. pallidiventris
    Tanzania, Malawi, Mozambique
    Rhodesia
Parus major (Great Tit)
  P. m. newtoni
    British Isles
  P. m. major
    Europe, Asia Minor, C Asia
  P. m. excelsus
    NW Africa
  P. m. corsus
    Corsica, Sardinia
  P. m. aphrodite
    S Greece, Mediterranean islands
  P. m. terraesanctae
    Lebanon, Israel, Jordan, Syria
  P. m. blanfordi
    Iran
  P. m. karelini
    NW Iran
  P. m. intermedius
    W Iran
  P. m. kapustini
    C Asia
  P. m. caschmirensis
    NW India, Pakistan
  P. m. decolorans
    E Afghanistan
  P. m. ziaratensis
    N Baluchistan, S Afghanistan
  P. m. mahrattarum
    S India, Sri Lanka

P. m. stupae
  C & W India
P. m. nipalensis
  Nepal, N India, W Burma
P. m. vauriei
  E Assam
P. m. templorum
  W Thailand, S Indochina
P. m. cinereus
  Java, Lesser Sunda Is
P. m. ambiguus
  SE Burma, Malaysia, Sumatra
P. m. sarawacensis
  W Sarawak
P. m. hainanus
  Hainan I
P. m. nigriloris
  S Riukiu Is
P. m. commixtus
  S China, N Vietnam
P. m. okinawae
  C Riukiu Is
P. m. amamiensis
  N Riukiu Is
P. m. kagoshimae
  S Kyushu I, Goto I
P. m. dageletensis
  Dagelet I (Japan)
P. m. minor
  Japan, E Asia, N China, E Tibet
P. m. tibetanus
  Tibet, SW China, N Burma
P. m. nubicolus
  E Burma, N Thailand, W Indochina
Parus bokharensis (Turkestan Tit)
  P. b. bokharensis
    Russia, C Asia
  P. b. turkestanicus
    W Mongolia
Parus monticolus (Green-backed Tit)
  P. m. monticolus
    W Himalayas
  P. m. yunnanensis
    E Himalayas, Burma, W China
  P. m. legendrei
    S Vietnam
  P. m. insperatus
    Taiwan
Parus nuchalis (White-naped Tit)
  NW India
Parus xanthogenys (Black-spotted Yellow Tit)
  P. x. xanthogenys
    W Himalayas
  P. x. aplonotus
    C India
  P. x. travancoreensis
    S India

502 **Parus spilonotus (Chinese Yellow Tit)**
  P. s. spilonotus
    E Himalayas
  P. s. subviridis
    Burma, Thailand, Assam
  P. s. rex
    S China, N Vietnam
  P. s. basileus
    · S Indochina
Parus holsti (Formosan Yellow Tit)
  Taiwan
Parus caeruleus (Blue Tit)
  P. c. obscurus
    British Isles
  P. c. caeruleus
    N & E Europe
  P. c. ogliastrae
    S Iberia, Corsica, Sardinia
  P. c. balearicus
    Majorca I
  P. c. orientalis
    E & C Russia
  P. c. satunini
    Caucasus, NW Iran
  P. c. raddei
    N Iran
  P. c. persicus
    SW Iran
  P. c. ultramarinus
    NW Africa
  P. c. cyrenaicae
    Libya
  P. c. ombriosus
    Hierro I (Canary Is)
  P. c. palmensis
    Palma I
  P. c. teneriffae
    Grand Canary I, Tenerife I
  P. c. degener
    Fuerteventura I, Lanzarote I
Parus cyanus (Azure Tit)
  P. c. cyanus
    W Russia, WC Asia
  P. c. yenisseensis
    C Asia
  P. c. tianschanicus
    C & E Asia, Manchuria
  P. c. kotkalensis
    S Russia
  P. c. flavipectus
    WC Asia
  P. c. carruthersi
    N Iran
  P. c. berezowskii
    NW China
Parus varius (Varied Tit)
  P. v. varius
    Japan, Korea

  P. v. sunsunpi
    S Japanese Is
  P. v. amamii
    Amami I
  P. v. orii
    C Riukiu Is
  P. v. olivaceus
    S Riukiu Is
  P. v. castaneoventris
    Taiwan
  P. v. namiyei
    N Izu Is
  P. v. owstoni
    S Izu Is
Parus semilarvatus (White-fronted Tit)
  P. s. snowi
    N Luzon I
  P. s. semilarvatus
    C & S Luzon I, Negros I
  P. s. nehrkorni
    Mindanao I
Parus inornatus (Plain Titmouse)
  P. i. sequestratus
    SW Oregon, NW California
  P. i. zaleptus
    SE Oregon, E California, W Nevada
  P. i. inornatus
    WC California
  P. i. kernensis
    SC California
  P. i. mohavensis
    SE California
  P. i. transpositus
    SW California
  P. i. affabilis
    N Baja California
  P. i. cineraceus
    S Baja California
  P. i. ridgwayi
    WC USA
  P. i. plumbescens
    SW New Mexico, SW Arizona
Parus bicolor (Tufted Titmouse)
  P. b. bicolor
    E, C & SE USA
  P. b. sennetti
    C & S Texas
  P. b. paloduro
    N Texas
  P. b. dysleptus
    W Texas, N Mexico
  P. b. atricristatus
    S Texas, NE Mexico
MELANOCHLORA
Melanochlora sultanea (Sultan Tit)
  M. s. sultanea
    E Himalayas, Assam, Burma, N Thailand

M. s. flavocristata
S Burma, Malaysia, Sumatra
M. s. seorsa
S China, Hainan I, N Indochina
M. s. gayeti
C Vietnam

SYLVIPARUS
Sylviparus modestus (Yellow-browed Tit)
S. m. simlaensis
NW Himalayas
S. m. modestus
C & E Himalayas, N Burma, SW China,
N Laos
S. m. klossi
S Vietnam

146 SITTIDAE (NUTHATCHES)

SITTINAE

SITTA
Sitta europaea (European Nuthatch)
S. e. europaea
NW Europe
S. e. asiatica
Russia, N Asia, N Japan
S. e. seorsa
W Sinkiang
S. e. amurensis
Manchuria, Korea, C Japan
S. e. arctica
N Siberia
S. e. albifrons
Kamchatka
S. e. roseilia
S Japan
S. e. bedfordi
Quelpart I
S. e. caesia
WC Europe, N Mediterranean
S. e. hispaniensis
Spain, NW Africa
S. e. levantina
Israel, Lebanon, Turkey
S. e. persica
W Iran
S. e. caucasica
Caucasus
S. e. rubiginosa
N Iran, SE Russia
S. e. sinensis
W & S China, Taiwan
S. e. montium
SE Tibet
S. e. nagaensis
N India, Assam, N Burma, N Thailand,
SW China
S. e. griseiventris
S Burma, S Vietnam

S. e. nebulosa
C China
S. e. whistleri
S Thailand
Sitta castanea (Chestnut-bellied Nuthatch)
S. c. cashmirensis
Pakistan, NW India
S. c. almorae
W Himalayas
S. c. cinnamoventris
E Himalayas, Bangladesh
S. c. koelzi
E Assam, N Burma
S. c. neglecta
Burma, S Thailand, S Laos, S Vietnam
S. c. castanea
C India
S. c. prateri
EC India
S. c. tonkinensis
N Thailand, N Laos, N Vietnam
Sitta himalayensis (White-tailed Nuthutch)
S. h. himalayensis
Himalayas, Assam, Nepal
S. h. australis
S Assam, Burma, N Vietnam
Sitta victoriae (White-browed Nuthatch)
W Burma
Sitta pygmaea (Pygmy Nuthatch)
S. p. pygmaea
W California
S. p. melanotis
SW Canada, W USA, NW Mexico
S. p. canescens
Nevada
S. p. leuconucha
S California, Baja California
S. p. chihuahuae
NW Mexico
S. p. brunnescens
W Mexico
S. p. flavinucha
E Mexico
Sitta pusilla (Brown-headed Nuthatch)
S. p. pusilla
S USA
S. p. caniceps
Florida
S. p. insularis
Gd Bahama I
Sitta whiteheadi (Corsican Nuthatch)
Corsica
Sitta yunnanensis (Yunnan Nuthatch)
W China
Sitta canadensis (Red-breasted Nuthatch)
Canada, USA

Sitta villosa **(Chinese Nuthatch)**
  S. v. bangsi
    W China
  S. v. villosa
    NE China
Sitta leucopsis **(White-cheeked Nuthatch)**
  S. l. leucopsis
    Pakistan, W Himalayas
  S. l. przewalskii
    SE Tibet, NW China
Sitta carolinensis **(White-breasted Nuthatch)**
  S. c. aculeata
    W USA
  S. c. tenuissima
    SW Canada, NW & W USA
  S. c. atkinsi
    Florida
  S. c. lagunae
    S Baja California
  S. c. nelsoni
    C & S USA, N Mexico
  S. c. alexandrae
    N Mexico
  S. c. umbrosa
    N Mexico
  S. c. mexicana
    C Mexico
  S. c. oberholseri
    C Mexico
  S. c. kinneari
    SW Mexico
  S. c. carolinensis
    E Canada, E USA
Sitta krüperi **(Kruper's Nuthatch)**
  Turkey, Caucasus
Sitta ledanti **(Kabylie Nuthatch)**
  N Algeria
Sitta neumayer **(Rock Nuthatch)**
  S. n. neumayer
    SE Europe
  S. n. syriaca
    Turkey, N Israel
  S. n. rupicola
    Caucasus, Iran
  S. n. tschitscherini
    Iraq, Iran
  S. n. plumbea
    SE Iran
Sitta tephronota **(Eastern Rock Nuthatch)**
  S. t. tephronota
    C Asia, N Iran, Afghanistan, Pakistan
  S. t. obscura
    N & E Iran
  S. t. dresseri
    SW Asia

Sitta frontalis **(Velvet-fronted Nuthatch)**
  S. f. frontalis
    India, Burma, N Thailand, N Vietnam,
    S Sumatra, Java
  S. f. saturatior
    Malaysia, N Sumatra
  S. f. corallipes
    Borneo
  S. f. palawana
    Palawan I
  S. f. isarog
    NE, E & S Luzon I
  S. f. mesoleuca
    N Luzon I
  S. f. oenochlamys
    Cebu I, Panay I, Negros I
  S. f. lilacea
    Samar I, Leyte I
  S. f. apo
    SE Mindanao I
  S. f. zamboanga
    Mindanao I, Basilan I
Sitta solangiae **(Lilac Nuthatch)**
  S. s. solangiae
    N Vietnam
  S. s. fortior
    C & S Vietnam
Sitta azurea **(Azure Nuthatch)**
  S. a. expectata
    Malaysia, Sumatra
  S. a. nigriventer
    W Java
  S. a. azurea
    E Java
Sitta magna **(Giant Nuthatch)**
  S. m. ligea
    SW China
  S. m. magna
    C Burma, N Thailand
Sitta formosa **(Beautiful Nuthatch)**
  E Himalayas to N Laos

TICHODROMADINAE

TICHODROMA
Tichodroma muraria **(Wallcreeper)**
  T. m. muraria
    S & E Europe, Turkey, NW Iran
  T. m. nepalensis
    C Asia, Pakistan, Himalayas, China

DAPHOENOSITTINAE

NEOSITTA
Neositta chrysoptera **(Varied Sitella)**
  N. c. pileata
    C Australia
  N. c. lathami
    E Victoria

N. c. chrysoptera
  E New South Wales
N. c. leucocephala
  C & SE Queensland
N. c. lumholzi
  E Queensland
N. c. albata
  Bowen, E Queensland
N. c. magnirostris
  NE Queensland
N. c. rothschildi
  N Queensland
N. c. striata
  N & NW Queensland
N. c. leucoptera
  Northern Territory, NC Australia
Neositta papuensis (Papuan Sitella)
N. p. toxopeusi
  NW New Guinea
N. p. intermedia
  NW New Guinea
N. p. wahgiensis
  W New Guinea
N. p. papuensis
  W New Guinea
N. p. alba
  C New Guinea
N. p. albifrons
  SE New Guinea

DAPHOENOSITTA
Daphoenositta miranda (Pink-faced Nuthatch)
D. m. miranda
  SE New Guinea
D. m. kuboriensis
  NE New Guinea
D. m. frontalis
  NW New Guinea

147 CERTHIIDAE (TREECREEPERS)

CERTHIINAE

CERTHIA
Certhia familiaris (Treecreeper)
C. f. britannica
  Britain, Ireland
C. f. macrodactyla
  C & S Europe
C. f. pyrenaica
  Pyrenees
C. f. familiaris
  N & E Europe, W Siberia
C. f. corsa
  Corsica
C. f. persica
  Caucasus, N Iran
C. f. tianschanica
  Russian & Chinese Turkistan

C. f. hodgsoni
  Pakistan, W Himalayas
C. f. mandellii
  E Himalayas
C. f. bianchii
  W China
C. f. khamensis
  SE Tibet, SW China, N Burma
C. f. daurica
  E Siberia, N Mongolia, N Korea, N Japan
C. f. montana
  W Canada, W USA
C. f. occidentalis
  NW Canada, W USA
C. f. zelotes
  S California
C. f. leucosticta
  S Nevada, Utah
C. f. albescens
  SW USA, NW Mexico
C. f. molinensis
  C Mexico
C. f. jaliscensis
  SW Mexico
C. f. guerrerensis
  SW Mexico
C. f. alticola
  SE Mexico
C. f. pernigra
  S Mexico, Guatemala
C. f. extima
  Nicaragua
C. f. americana
  C & E Canada, CE & SE USA
C. f. nigrescens
  EC USA
Certhia brachydactyla (Short-toed Treecreeper)
  C & E Europe, Caucasus
Certhia himalayana (Himalayan Treecreeper)
C. h. taeniura
  SW Asia, Afghanistan
C. h. himalayana
  N Pakistan, W Himalayas
C. h. limes
  Pakistan, NW India
C. h. infima
  W Nepal
C. h. yunnanensis
  W China
C. h. ripponi
  N Burma
Certhia nipalensis (Stoliczka's Treecreeper)
  SE Tibet, C Nepal, NE Burma

***Certhia discolor* (Brown-throated Tree-creeper)**
C. d. discolor
E Himalayas, Nepal, Assam
C. d. manipurensis
E Assam, W Burma
C. d. shanensis
N Burma, N Thailand
C. d. laotiana
Laos
C. d. meridionalis
S Vietnam

SALPORNITHINAE

SALPORNIS
***Salpornis spilonotus* (Spotted Grey Creeper)**
S. s. emini
Portuguese Guinea to Sudan, Uganda
S. s. erlangeri
SW Ethiopia
S. s. salvadori
Angola to Tanzania & Mozambique
S. s. rajputanae
NW India
S. s. spilonotus
N & C India
S. s. xylodromus
E Rhodesia, W Mozambique

148 RHABDORNITHIDAE (PHILIPPINE CREEPERS)

RHABDORNIS
***Rhabdornis mystacalis* (Stripe-headed Creeper)**
R. m. mystacalis
Luzon I, Masbate I, Negros I, Panay I
R. m. minor
Samay I, Leyte I, Mindanao I
***Rhabdornis inornatus* (Plain-headed Creeper)**
R. i. grandis
N Luzon I
R. i. inornatus
Samar I
R. i. rabori
Negros I
R. i. alaris
Mindanao I
R. i. zamboanga
Mt Malindang (Mindanao I)
R. i. leytensis
Leyte I

149 CLIMACTERIDAE (AUSTRALIAN CREEPERS)

CLIMACTERIS
***Climacteris erythrops* (Red-browed Treecreeper)**
C. e. erythrops
E New South Wales, E & S Victoria
C. e. olinda
S Victoria
***Climacteris affinis* (White-browed Treecreeper)**
C. a. superciliosus
WC Australia
C. a. affinis
C Australia
***Climacteris picumnus* (Brown Treecreeper)**
C. p. melanota
N Queensland
C. p. picumnus
S & E Australia
***Climacteris rufa* (Rufous Treecreeper)**
SW Western Australia
***Climacteris melanura* (Black-tailed Treecreeper)**
C. m. melanura
N Western Australia, Northern Territory, NW Queensland
C. m. wellsi
NW Western Australia
***Climacteris leucophaea* (White-throated Treecreeper)**
C. l. minor
N Queensland
C. l. leucophaea
E Australia
C. l. grisescens
S South Australia
***Climacteris placens* (Papuan Treecreeper)**
C. p. placens
NW New Guinea
C. p. steini
W New Guinea
C. p. inexpectata
N New Guinea
C. p. meridionalis
SE New Guinea

150 DICAEIDAE (FLOWERPECKERS)

MELANOCHARIS
***Melanocharis arfakiana* (Obscure Berrypecker)**
New Guinea
***Melanocharis nigra* (Black Berrypecker)**
M. n. pallida
Waigeu I
M. n. nigra
Misol I, W New Guinea

M. n. unicolor
    Japen I, N & E New Guinea
M. n. chloroptera
    Aru Is, S New Guinea
Melanocharis longicauda (Mid-mountain Berrypecker)
M. l. longicauda
    NW New Guinea
M. l. chloris
    NW New Guinea
M. l. umbrosa
    NW New Guinea
M. l. captata
    C & E New Guinea
M. l. orientalis
    SE New Guinea
Melanocharis versteri (Fan-tailed Berrypecker)
M. v. versteri
    NW New Guinea
M. v. meeki
    NW New Guinea
M. v. virago
    N & NE New Guinea
M. v. maculiceps
    SE New Guinea
Melanocharis striativentris (Streaked Berrypecker)
M. s. axillaris
    NW New Guinea
M. s. striativentris
    C & SE New Guinea
M. s. prasina
    SE New Guinea
M. s. chrysocome
    E New Guinea

RHAMPHOCHARIS
Rhamphocharis crassirostris (Spotted Berrypecker)
R. c. crassirostris
    NW & C New Guinea
R. c. piperata
    SE New Guinea
R. c. viridescens
    SE New Guinea

PRIONOCHILUS
Prionochilus olivaceus (Olive-backed Flowerpecker)
P. o. parsonsi
    NE Luzon I
P. o. olivaceus
    Basilan I, Mindanao I, Bohol I
P. o. samarensis
    Samar I, Leyte I
Prionochilus maculatus (Yellow-throated Flowerpecker)
P. m. septentrionalis
    S Burma, S Thailand

P. m. oblitus
    Malaysia
P. m. maculatus
    Sumatra, Billiton I, Nias I, Borneo
P. m. natunensis
    Great Natuna I
Prionochilus percussus (Crimson-breasted Flowerpecker)
P. p. ignicapilla
    S Burma to Sumatra & Borneo
P. p. regulus
    Batu I
P. p. percussus
    Java
Prionochilus plateni (Palawan Yellow-rumped Flowerpecker)
    Palawan I, Culion I
Prionochilus xanthopygius (Borneo Yellow-rumped Flowerpecker)
    Borneo
Prionochilus thoracicus (Scarlet-breasted Flowerpecker)
    Malaysia, Billiton I, Borneo

DICAEUM
Dicaeum annae (Sunda Flowerpecker)
D. a. sumbavense
    Sumbawa I
D. a. annae
    Flores I
Dicaeum agile (Thick-billed Flowerpecker)
D. a. agile
    N India
D. a. zeylonicum
    Sri Lanka
D. a. deignani
    Assam, N Burma
D. a. modestum
    Bangladesh, S Burma, Thailand, N Vietnam
D. a. remotum
    S Burma, S Thailand, Malaysia
D. a. atjehense
    N Sumatra
D. a. finschi
    W Java
D. a. tinctum
    Sumba I, Flores I, Alor I
D. a. obsoletum
    Timor I
Dicaeum everetti (Everett's Flowerpecker)
D. e. sordidum
    Bintan I, Malaysia
D. e. everetti
    Labuan I, Borneo
D. e. bungurense
    Great Natuna I

Dicaeum aeruginosum **(Striped Flowerpecker)**
  D. a. striatissimum
    Sibuyan I, Luzon I
  D. a. aeruginosum
    Cebu I, Negros I, Mindoro I, Mindanao I
  D. a. affine
    Palawan I
Dicaeum proprium **(Grey-breasted Flowerpecker)**
  Mt Mayo (Mindanao)
Dicaeum chrysorrheum **(Yellow-vented Flowerpecker)**
  D. c. chrysoclore
    E Himalayas to SW China, Indochina
  D. c. chrysorrheum
    S Thailand to Sumatra, Borneo, Java
Dicaeum melanoxanthum **(Yellow-bellied Flowerpecker)**
  E Himalayas to SW China
Dicaeum vincens **(Legge's Flowerpecker)**
  Sri Lanka
Diceaum aureolimbatum **(Celebean Flowerpecker)**
  D. a. aureolimbatum
    Muna I, Buton I, Celebes
  D. a. laterale
    Great Sanghir I
Dicaeum nigrilore **(Olive-capped Flowerpecker)**
  Mindanao I
Dicaeum anthonyi **(Yellow-crowned Flowerpecker)**
  D. a. anthonyi
    Cagayan I, Luzon I,
  D. a. masawan
    NW Mindanao I
  D. a. kampalili I
    SE Mindanao I
Dicaeum bicolor **(Bicoloured Flowerpecker)**
  D. b. inexpectatum
    Luzon I, Mindanao I, Leyte I, Samar I
  D. b. bicolor
    Mindanao I
  D. b. viridissimum
    Negros I
Dicaeum australe **(Philippine Flowerpecker)**
  D. a. australe
    Philippine Is
  D. a. haematostictum
    Panay I, Negros I
Diceaum retrocinctum **(Mindoro Flowerpecker)**
  Mindoro I

Diceaum trigonostigma **(Orange-bellied Flowerpecker)**
  D. t. rubropygium
    Assam, S Burma, S Thailand
  D. t. trigonostigma
    S Thailand
  D. t. melanostigma
    Bangka I, Billiton I, Malaysia, Sumatra
  D. t. antioproctum
    Simalur I
  D. t. megastoma
    Great Natuna I
  D. t. flaviclunis
    Java, Bali I
  D. t. dayakanum
    Borneo, N Borneo islands
  D. t. sibutuense
    Sibutu I
  D. t. assimile
    Tawitawi Is, Jolo I, Siasi I
  D. t. cinereigulare
    Mindanao I, Samar I, Leyte I, Bohol I
  D. t. besti
    Siquijor I
  D. t. dorsale
    Masbate I, Panay I, Negros I
  D. t. intermedium
    Romblon I, Tablas I
  D. t. sibuyanicum
    Sibuyan I
  D. t. isidroi
    Camiguin I (South)
  D. t. xanthopygium
    Marinduque I, Mindoro I, Luzon I
Dicaeum hypoleucum **(White-bellied Flowerpecker)**
  D. h. lagunae
    N & C Luzon I
  D. h. pontifex
    Bohol I, Samar I, Leyte I, Mindanao I
  D. h. hypoleucum
    W Mindanao I, Basilan I, Sulu Is
  D. h. cagayanensis
    NE Luzon I
Dicaeum erythrorhynchos **(Tickell's Flowerpecker)**
  D. e. erythrorhynchos
    W Burma, Bangladesh, India
  D. e. ceylonense
    Sri Lanka
Dicaeum concolor **(Plain Flowerpecker)**
  D. c. olivaceum
    Himalayas to S China, N Indochina
  D. c. concolor
    SW India
  D. c. virescens
    S Andaman Is

D. c. minullum
Hainan I

D. c. uchidai
Taiwan

D. c. borneanum
Malaysia, Sumatra, Borneo

D. c. sollicitans
Java, Bali I

**Dicaeum pygmaeum (Palawan Flower-
pecker)**

D. p. salomonseni
N Luzon I

D. p. pygmaeum
S Luzon I, Mindoro I, Negros I, Leyte I,
Cebu I

D. p. davao
Mindanao I

D. p. palawanorum
Balabac I, Palawan I

**Dicaeum nehrkorni (Red-headed Flower-
pecker)**
Celebes

**Dicaeum vulneratum (Ashy-fronted
Flowerpecker)**
S Moluccas

**Dicaeum erythrothorax (White-throated
Flowerpecker)**

D. e. schistaceiceps
Halmahera I

D. e. erythrothorax
Buru I

**Dicaeum pectorale (Olive-crowned
Flowerpecker)**

D. p. ignotum
Gebe I

D. p. pectorale
Misol I, Waigeu I, NW New Guinea

**Dicaeum geelvinkianum (Red-capped
Flowerpecker)**

D. g. maforense
Numfor I

D. g. misoriense
Biak I

D. g. geelvinkianum
Japen I

D. g. obscurifrons
W New Guinea

D. g. setekwa
SW New Guinea

D. g. diversum
N New Guinea

D. g. centrale
C New Guinea

D. g. albopunctatum
SC New Guinea

D. g. rubrigulare
S New Guinea

D. g. rubrocoronatum
SE New Guinea

D. g. violaceum
D'Entrecasteaux Archipelago

Dicaeum nitidum (Louisiade Flowerpecker)

D. n. nitidum
Tagula I, Misima I

D. n. rosseli
Rossel I

**Dicaeum eximium (New Ireland Flower-
pecker)**

D. e. layardorum
New Britain

D. e. eximium
New Ireland, New Hanover

D. e. phaeopygium
Dyaul I

**Dicaeum aeneum (Solomon Is Flower-
pecker)**

D. a. aeneum
N Solomon Is

D. a. becki
Guadalcanal I

D. a. malaitae
Malaita I

**Dicaeum tristrami (San Cristobal Flower-
pecker)**
San Cristobal I

**Dicaeum igniferum (Black-banded
Flowerpecker)**

D. i. igniferum
Sumbawa I, Flores I

D. i. cretum
Pantar I, Alor I

**Dicaeum maugei (Blue-cheeked Flower-
pecker)**

D. m. maugei
Semau I, Timor I, Sawu I

D. m. romae
Roma I, Damar I

D. m. salvadorii
Babar I, Moa I

D. m. splendidum
Saleyer I, Djampea I

D. m. neglectum
Lombok I

**Dicaeum hirundinaceum (Mistletoe
Flowerpecker)**

D. h. hirundinaceum
Australia

D. h. ignicolle
Aru Is

D. h. keiense
Kei Is

D. h. fulgidum
Tenimber Is

Dicaeum celebicum (Black-sided Flower-
pecker)
 D. c. kuehni
  Tukangbesi I
 D. c. sulaense
  Sula Is, Banguey I
 D. c. celebicum
  Muna I, Buton I, Celebes
 D. c. sanghirense
  Sanghir Is
 D. c. talautense
  Talaut I
Dicaeum monticolum (Bornean Fire-
breasted Flowerpecker)
 Borneo
Dicaeum ignipectus (Green-backed
Flowerpecker)
 D. i. ignipectus
  Himalayas to S China, Indochina
 D. i. dolichorhynchum
  S Thailand, Malaysia
 D. i. cambodianum
  Cambodia, SE Thailand
 D. i. formosum
  Taiwan
 D. i. luzoniense
  N Luzon I
 D. i. apo
  Negros I, Mindanao I
 D. i. bonga
  Samar I
 D. i. beccarii
  N Sumatra
 D. i. sanguinolentum
  Java, Bali I
 D. i. rhodopygiale
  Flores I
 D. i. wilhelminae
  Sumba I
 D. i. hanieli
  Timor I
Dicaeum cruentatum (Scarlet-backed
Flowerpecker)
 D. c. cruentatum
  NE India to S China, Indochina
 D. c. siamense
  E Thailand
 D. c. ignitum
  Malaysia
 D. c. sumatranum
  Sumatra
 D. c. batuense
  Mentawai Is
 D. c. simalurense
  Simalur I
 D. c. nigrimentum
  Borneo

D. c. niasense
 Nias I
Dicaeum trochileum (Scarlet-headed
Flowerpecker)
 D. t. trochileum
  Java, Bali I, SE Borneo, Kangean Is
 D. t. stresemanni
  Lombok I

OREOCHARIS
Oreocharis arfaki (Tit Berrypecker)
 New Guinea

PARAMYTHIA
Paramythia montium (Crested Berrypecker)
 P. m. olivaceum
  C New Guinea
 P. m. montium
  C & SE New Guinea
 P. m. brevicauda
  SE New Guinea

PARDALOTUS
Pardalotus quadragintus (Forty-spotted
Pardalote)
 Tasmania
Pardalotus punctatus (Spotted Pardalote)
 W Western Australia, E Australia, Tasmania
Pardalotus xanthopygus (Yellow-tailed
Pardalote)
 Western Australia to NW Victoria
Pardalotus rubricatus (Red-browed
Pardalote)
 P. r. parryi
  N Australia
 P. r. rubricatus
  C Australia
 P. r. carpenteriae
  NW Queensland
 P. r. yorki
  NE Queensland
Pardalotus striatus (Yellow-tipped
Pardalote)
 E Australia, Tasmania
Pardalotus ornatus (Red-tipped Pardalote)
 S Queensland to S Victoria
Pardalotus substriatus (Striated Pardalote)
 Southern Australia
Pardalotus melanocephalus (Black-headed
Pardalote)
 P. m. uropygialis
  N Western Australia to NW Queensland
 P. m. melvillensis
  Melville I
 P. m. restrictus
  N Queensland
 P. m. barroni
  NC Queensland
 P. m. bowensis
  E Queensland

P. m. melanocephalus
SE Queensland, NE New South Wales

151 NECTARINIIDAE (SUNBIRDS)

ANTHREPTES
Anthreptes gabonicus (Brown Sunbird)
Gambia to Gabon
Anthreptes fraseri (Scarlet-tufted Sunbird)
A. f. cameroonensis
S Nigeria, Cameroun, Central African
Republic, N Angola
A. f. idius
Sierra Leone to Ghana
A. f. fraseri
Fernando Po I
A. f. axillaris
NE Zaire, Uganda
**Anthreptes reichenowi (Plain-backed
Sunbird)**
A. r. yokanae
S Kenya, NE Tanzania
A. r. reichenowi
SE Rhodesia, Mozambique
Anthreptes anchietae (Anchieta's Sunbird)
Angola, N Zambia, SW Tanzania, Malawi,
W Mozambique
**Anthreptes simplex (Plain-coloured
Sunbird)**
S Burma, S Thailand, Malaysia, Sumatra,
Borneo
**Anthreptes malacensis (Plain-throated
Sunbird)**
A. m. malacensis
S Burma to Indochina, Sumatra, S Borneo
A. m. mjobergi
Maratua Is
A. m. borneensis
N Borneo
A. m. birgitae
Luzon I
A. m. chlorigaster
WC Philippine Is, SW Mindanao I
A. m. griseigularis
Samar I, Leyte I, NE Mindanao I
A. m. heliolusius
W Mindanao I, Basilan I
A. m. cagayanensis
Cagayan I
A. m. paraguae
Palawan I
A. m. wiglesworthi
Sulu Archipelago (except Sibutu)
A. m. iris
Sibutu I
A. m. heliocalus
Sangi Is
A. m. celebensis
S & C Celebes

A. m. citrinus
SE Celebes
A. m. extremus
Sula Is
A. m. convergens
Lesser Sunda Is
A. m. rubrigena
Sumba I
**Anthreptes rhodolaema (Shelley's
Sunbird)**
S Burma, S Thailand, Malaysia, Sumatra,
Borneo
**Anthreptes singalensis (Ruby-cheeked
Sunbird)**
A. s. assamensis
E Nepal, Bangladesh, N Burma, N Thailand
A. s. internotus
S Burma, S Thailand
A. s. koratensis
E Thailand, Laos, Vietnam
A. s. interpositus
S Thailand
A. s. singalensis
Malaysia
A. s. panopsius
W Sumatra Is, Nias I
A. s. sumatranus
Sumatra, Billiton I
A. s. pallidus
N Natuna Is
A. s. borneanus
Banguey I, Borneo
A. s. phoenicotis
E & C Java
A. s. bantenensis
W Java
**Anthreptes longuemarei (Violet-backed
Sunbird)**
A. l. longuemarei
Senegal to Guinea
A. l. haussarum
Liberia to Cameroun, N Zaire, Sudan,
Uganda
A. l. angolensis
S Zaire, Angola, Zambia, Malawi,
W Tanzania
A. l. nyassae
SE Tanzania, N Mozambique, E Rhodesia
**Anthreptes orientalis (Kenya Violet-backed
Sunbird)**
A. o. orientalis
S Sudan, Ethiopia, N Uganda, Kenya,
E Tanzania
A. o. neumanni
NE Kenya, Somalia
**Anthreptes neglectus (Uluguru Violet-
backed Sunbird)**
SE Kenya, NE Tanzania, N Mozambique

Anthreptes aurantium (Violet-tailed Sunbird)
S Nigeria, Gabon, Central African Republic, NE Angola
Anthreptes pallidigaster (Amani Sunbird)
E Kenya, NE Tanzania
Anthreptes rectirostris (Green Sunbird)
A. r. rectirostris
Sierra Leone to Ghana
A. r. tephrolaema
Fernando Po I, S Nigeria to Angola & Uganda
Anthreptes rubritorques (Banded Green Sunbird)
NE Tanzania
Anthreptes collaris (Collared Sunbird)
A. c. subcollaris
Guinea to Nigeria
A. c. hypodilus
Fernando Po I
A. c. somereni
SE Nigeria, N & W Zaire, N Angola, SW Sudan
A. c. jubaensis
S Ethiopia, Somalia, N Kenya
A. c. djamdjamensis
SW Ethiopia
A. c. garguensis
C & E Zaire, Uganda
A. c. elachior
E Kenya, NE Tanzania, Zanzibar I
A. c. philipsi
E Angola, SE Zaire, N Zambia
A. c. zambesianus
S Tanzania, SE Zambia, Botswana
A. c. patersonae
E Rhodesia, W Mozambique
A. c. zuluensis
Rhodesia, N Natal, Mozambique, Transvaal
A. c. collaris
E Cape Province, S Natal, Swaziland
Anthreptes platurus (Pygmy Sunbird)
A. p. platurus
Senegal to NW Kenya
A. p. metallicus
NE Africa, SW Arabia

HYPOGRAMMA
Hypogramma hypogrammicum (Blue-naped Sunbird)
H. h. lisettae
N Burma, N Thailand, N & C Indochina
H. h. mariae
Cambodia, S Indochina
H. h. nuchale
S Burma, S Thailand, Malaysia
H. h. hypogrammicum
Sumatra, Borneo

H. h. natunense
N Natuna Is

NECTARINIA
Nectarinia seimundi (Little Green Sunbird)
N. s. kruensis
Sierra Leone to Ghana
N. s. seimundi
Fernando Po I
N. s. traylori
Nigeria to Zaire, Uganda, N Angola
Nectarinia batesi (Bates's Olive Sunbird)
Fernando Po I, S Nigeria to Zaire, Zambia
Nectarinia olivacea (Olive Sunbird)
N. o. guineensis
Guinea to W Ghana
N. o. cephaëlis
E Ghana to Zaire, N Angola
N. o. obscura
Principé I, Fernando Po I
N. o. vincenti
S Sudan, NW Kenya, Uganda
N. o. ragazzii
Sudan, Ethiopia to N Zambia, N Malawi
N. o. neglecta
C Kenya, N Tanzania
N. o. changamwensis
E Kenya, E Tanzania
N. o. granti
Pemba I, Zanzibar I
N. o. lowei
W Tanzania, N Zambia
N. o. alfredi
S Tanzania, Malawi, Zambia
N. o. sclateri
E Rhodesia
N. o. olivacina
E Mozambique, N Natal
N. o. olivacea
C Natal
Nectarinia ursulae (Fernando Po Sunbird)
Fernando Po I, Cameroun Mt
Nectarinia veroxii (Mouse-coloured Sunbird)
N. v. fischeri
Somalia, E Kenya, E Tanzania, Mozambique, E Natal
N. v. zanzibarica
Zanzibar I
N. v. veroxii
E Natal, E Cape Province
Nectarinia balfouri (Socotra Sunbird)
Socotra I
Nectarinia reichenbachii (Reichenbach's Sunbird)
Ghana to N Zaire
Nectarinia hartlaubii (Principé Sunbird)
Principé I

Nectarinia newtonii (Newton's Yellow-breasted Sunbird)
Sao Thomé I
Nectarinia thomensis (Sao Thomé Giant Sunbird)
Sao Thomé I
Nectarinia oritis (Cameroun Blue-headed Sunbird)
N. o. poensis
mountains of Fernando Po I
N. o. oritis
Cameroun Mt
N. o. bansoensis
W Cameroun
Nectarinia alinae (Blue-headed Sunbird)
N. a. alinae
E Zaire, SW Uganda
N. a. tanganjicae
SE Zaire
Nectarinia bannermani (Bannerman's Sunbird)
Angola, S Zaire, NW Zambia
Nectarinia verticalis (Green-headed Sunbird)
N. v. verticalis
Senegal to Nigeria
N. v. bohndorffi
Cameroun to Zaire, Angola
N. v. cyanocephala
W Gabon
N. v. viridisplendens
S Sudan, E Zaire, W Kenya to NE Zambia
Nectarinia cyanolaema (Blue-throated Brown Sunbird)
N. c. magnirostrata
Sierra Leone to Ghana
N. c. cyanolaema
Fernando Po I
N. c. octaviae
Ghana to Uganda & N Angola
Nectarinia fuliginosa (Carmelite Sunbird)
N. f. aurea
Liberia to Gabon
N. f. fuliginosa
Zaire, Angola
Nectarinia rubescens (Green-throated Sunbird)
N. r. stangerii
Fernando Po I
N. r. crossensis
Cameroun
N. r. rubescens
Cameroun to Sudan, Angola, Zambia, Kenya
Nectarinia amethystina (Amethyst Sunbird)
N. a. kalckreuthi
Somalia, E Kenya, NE Tanzania

N. a. doggetti
W Kenya, Uganda, NW Tanzania
N. a. kirkii
SW Tanzania, SE Zaire, Rhodesia, E Zambia
N. a. deminuta
S Zaire, W Zambia, Angola, W Botswana
N. a. adjuncta
E Transvaal, N Natal, S Mozambique
N. a. amethystina
S Natal, S Transvaal, Cape Province
Nectarinia senegalensis (Scarlet-chested Sunbird)
N. s. senegalensis
Senegal to N Nigeria
N. s. adamauae
NE Cameroun
N. s. acik
Cameroun to S Sudan, Uganda
N. s. cruentata
SE Sudan, Ethiopia
N. s. lamperti
E Zaire, Kenya, Tanzania
N. s. saturatior
Angola, W Zambia, Namibia
N. s. gutteralis
SE Africa
Nectarinia hunteri (Hunter's Sunbird)
Somalia, Kenya, Tanzania
Nectarinia adelberti (Buff-throated Sunbird)
N. a. adelberti
Sierra Leone to Ghana
N. a. eboensis
Togo to SE Nigeria
Nectarinia zeylonica (Purple-rumped Sunbird)
N. z. flaviventris
Bangladesh, India
N. z. sola
S India
N. z. zeylonica
Sri Lanka
Nectarinia minima (Small Sunbird)
W & S India
Nectarinia sperata (Van Hasselt's Sunbird)
N. s. phayrei
Burma
N. s. brasiliana
Assam, Bangladesh, Thailand, Malaysia, Borneo, Java, Sumatra
N. s. emmae
Cambodia, S Laos, S Vietnam
N. s. mecynorhyncha
Simalur I
N. s. eumecis
Anamba Is

N. s. axantha
Natuna Is
N. s. henkei
N Luzon I
N. s. theresae
C Luzon I
N. s. davoensis
SE Mindanao I
N. s. juliae
W & S Mindanao I, Basilan I
N. s. marinduquensis
Marinduque I
N. s. sperata
Maratua Is, Palawan I, C Philippine Is
Nectarinia sericea (Black Sunbird)
N. s. talautensis
Talaut I
N. s. sangirensis
Sanghir Is
N. s. grayi
N Celebes
N. s. porphyrolaema
C & S Celebes
N. s. auriceps
Peleng I, N Moluccas
N. s. auricapilla
Kajoa I (W Moluccas)
N. s. proserpina
Buru I
N. s. aspasioides
S Moluccas
N. s. chlorolaema
Kei Is
N. s. sericea
New Guinea, except SE
N. s. vicina
SE New Guinea
N. s. mariae
Kofiau I
N. s. cochrani
Misol I, Waigeu I
N. s. maforensis
Numfor I
N. s. salvadorii
W Japen I
N. s. chlorocephala
Aru Is
N. s. nigriscapularis
Meos Num I, Rani I
N. s. mysorensis
Biak I
N. s. veronica
Liki I
N. s. cornelia
Tarawai I
N. s. christianae
D'Entrecasteaux & Louisiade Archipelagos

N. s. caeruleogula
New Britain, Rook I
N. s. corinna
Bismarck Archipelago
N. s. eichhorni
Feni I (Bismarck Archipelago)
Nectarinia calcostetha (Macklot's Sunbird)
Burma to Malaysia, Indochina, Sumatra,
Borneo, Java, Philippine Is
Nectarinia dussumieri (Seychelles Sunbird)
Seychelles Is
Nectarinia lotenia (Loten's Sunbird)
N. l. hindustanica
S India
N. l. lotenia
Sri Lanka
Nectarinia jugularis (Yellow-bellied Sunbird)
N. j. andamanica
Andaman Is
N. j. klossi
N Nicobar Is
N. j. proselia
Car Nicobar I
N. j. flammaxillaris
Burma, Thailand, Cambodia, N Malaysia
N. j. pectoralis
C Malaysia
N. j. microleuca
S Malaysia, Singapore
N. j. rhizophorae
N Vietnam, Hainan I
N. j. ornata
Sumatra, Java, Borneo, Lesser Sunda Is
N. j. polyclysta
Enggano
N. j. obscurior
N Luzon I
N. j. jugularis
S Luzon I & C & S Philippine Is
N. j. aurora
Palawan I
N. j. woodi
Sulu Archipelago
N. j. meyeri
N & SE Celebes
N. j. plateni
S Celebes
N. j. saleyerensis
Saleyer I
N. j. infrenata
Tukangbesi I
N. j. robustirostris
Sula Is
N. j. teijsmanni
Djampea I, Kalao I
N. j. buruensis
Buru I

N. j. clementiae
  S Moluccas
N. j. keiensis
  Kei Is
N. j. idenburgi
  N New Guinea
N. j. frenata
  N Moluccas, Aru Is, New Guinea,
  N Queensland
N. j. flavigaster
  Solomon Is, Bismarck Archipelago
Nectarinia buettikoferi (Sumba I Sunbird)
  Sumba I
**Nectarinia solaris (Timor
  Sunbird)**
N. s. degener
  Sumbawa I, Flores I, Lomblen I, Alor I
N. s. solaris
  Timor I, Samau I
N. s. exquisita
  Wetar I
Nectarinia asiatica (Purple Sunbird)
N. a. brevirostris
  SE Arabia, SE Iran, Afghanistan, Pakistan,
  N India
N. a. asiatica
  S India, Sri Lanka
N. a. intermedia
  Bangladesh, Assam, Burma, Thailand,
  N Vietnam
**Nectarinia souimanga (Souimanga
  Sunbird)**
N. s. souimanga
  Glorioso I, Madagascar
N. s. apolis
  SW Madagascar
N. s. aldabrensis
  Aldabra I
N. s. abbotti
  Assumption I (Aldabra)
N. s. buchenorum
  Cosmoledo I (Aldabra)
Nectarinia humbloti (Humblot's Sunbird)
N. h. humbloti
  Great Comoro I
N. h. mohelica
  Moheli I (Comoro Is)
Nectarinia comorensis (Anjouan Sunbird)
  Anjouan I (Comoro Is)
Nectarinia coquerellii (Mayotte Sunbird)
  Mayotte I (Comoro Is)
Nectarinia venusta (Variable Sunbird)
N. v. venusta
  Senegal to Cameroun
N. v. falkensteini
  Gabon, Angola, Zaire, Zambia, Rhodesia,
  Tanzania

N. v. igneiventris
  Uganda, E Zaire
N. v. fazoqlensis
  Sudan, Ethiopia
N. v. albiventris
  Somalia, E Ethiopia, N Kenya
N. v. blicki
  S Ethiopia, S Sudan, NW Kenya
**Nectarinia talatala (Southern White-
  bellied Sunbird)**
  Angola, Namibia, Zambia, Tanzania,
  Mozambique, Natal
**Nectarinia oustaleti (Oustalet's White-
  bellied Sunbird)**
N. o. oustaleti
  C Angola
N. o. rhodesiae
  N Zambia
Nectarinia fusca (Dusky Sunbird)
N. f. fusca
  S Angola to W Cape Province
N. f. indusa
  Mossamedes, Angola
**Nectarinia chalybea (Lesser Double-
  collared Sunbird)**
N. c. pintoi
  Angola, S Zaire, W Zambia
N. c. gertrudis
  Tanzania, Malawi
N. c. manoensis
  SW Tanzania, S Malawi, S Zambia,
  Rhodesia
N. c. subalaris
  Transvaal, Natal, E Cape Province
N. c. chalybea
  S Cape Province
N. c. albilateralis
  W Cape Province
**Nectarinia afra (Greater Double-collared
  Sunbird)**
N. a. stuhlmanni
  W Uganda
N. a. graueri
  Rwanda, SW Uganda
N. a. chapini
  E Zaire, S Burundi
N. a. prigoginei
  SE Zaire
N. a. whytei
  Zambia, Malawi
N. a. afra
  South Africa
N. a. amicorum
  S Mozambique
**Nectarinia preussi (Northern Double-
  collared Sunbird)**
N. p. preussi
  Fernando Po I, Cameroun Mt

N. p. eriksoni
S Sudan, Uganda, W Kenya, NE Zaire
N. p. ludovicensis
Angola
Nectarinia mediocris (Eastern Double-collared Sunbird)
N. m. mediocris
Kenya, Zambia
N. m. usambarica
SE Kenya, NE Tanzania
N. m. fuelleborni
Tanzania, N Malawi, NE Zambia
N. m. bensoni
Malawi, Zambia, Mozambique
Nectarinia neergaardi (Neergaard's Sunbird)
S Mozambique, N Natal
Nectarinia chloropygia (Olive-bellied Sunbird)
N. c. kempi
Sierra Leone to Ivory Coast
N. c. chloropygia
Ghana to Nigeria
N. c. insularis
Fernando Po I
N. c. luhderi
Cameroun, Zaire, Angola
N. c. bineschensis
SW Ethiopia
N. c. orphogaster
NE Angola, E Zaire, S Sudan, Uganda,
W Tanzania
Nectarinia minulla (Tiny Sunbird)
N. m. amadoni
Fernando Po I
N. m. minulla
Ghana to W Uganda
Nectarinia regia (Regal Sunbird)
N. r. regia
Uganda
N. r. kivuensis
E Zaire, SW Uganda
N. r. anderseni
W Tanzania
Nectarinia loveridgei (Loveridge's Sunbird)
E Tanzania
Nectarinia moreaui (Moreau's Sunbird)
NE Tanzania
Nectarinia rockefelleri (Rockefeller's Sunbird)
E Zaire
Nectarinia violacea (Orange-breasted Sunbird)
Cape Province
Nectarinia habessinica (Shining Sunbird)
N. h. kinneari
W Saudi Arabia

N. h. hellmayri
S Arabia
N. h. habessinica
NE Sudan, W Ethiopia
N. h. altera
E Ethiopia, N Somalia
N. h. turkanae
S Ethiopia, S Sudan, S Somalia, N Kenya,
Uganda
Nectarinia bouvieri (Orange-tufted Sunbird)
Cameroun to W Kenya & N Angola
Nectarinia osea (Palestine Sunbird)
N. o. osea
Syria, Israel, Arabia
N. o. decorsei
Mali to S Sudan
Nectarinia cuprea (Coppery Sunbird)
N. c. cuprea
Senegal to Zaire, Uganda, Tanzania
N. c. chalcea
Malawi, Rhodesia, Angola, W Zambia
Nectarinia tacazze (Tacazze Sunbird)
N. t. tacazze
Ethiopia
N. t. jacksoni
S Sudan, Uganda, W Kenya, N Tanzania
Nectarinia bocagii (Bocage's Sunbird)
Angola, Zaire
Nectarinia purpureiventris (Purple-breasted Sunbird)
Uganda, E Zaire
Nectarinia shelleyi (Shelley's Sunbird)
N. s. hofmanni
E Tanzania
N. s. shelleyi
SE Zaire, E Zambia to N Mozambique
Nectarinia mariquensis (Mariqua Sunbird)
N. m. osiris
Ethiopia, S Sudan, N Kenya, N Uganda
N. m. suahelica
S Uganda, E Zaire to NE Zambia
N. m. mariquensis
S Angola to Rhodesia
N. m. lucens
E Rhodesia, S Mozambique, Natal
Nectarinia pembae (Violet-breasted Sunbird)
N. p. chalcomelas
Somalia, E Kenya
N. p. pembae
Pemba I
Nectarinia bifasciata (Purple-banded Sunbird)
N. b. bifasciata
Gabon to C Angola

N. b. microrhyncha
Uganda to Angola, N Malawi,
Mozambique
N. b. tsavoensis
E Kenya, NE Tanzania
N. b. strophium
SE Zambia, S Mozambique, N Natal
**Nectarinia coccinigastra (Splendid
Sunbird)**
Senegal to NE Zaire
**Nectarinia erythrocerca (Red-chested
Sunbird)**
Sudan, Uganda, NW Tanzania
**Nectarinia congensis (Congo Black-
bellied Sunbird)**
Zaire
Nectarinia pulchella (Beautiful Sunbird)
N. p. pulchella
Senegal, Mali, Niger, W Sudan
N. p. aegra
S Niger, Aïr Massif
N. p. lucidipectus
S Sudan, Ethiopia, NE Zaire, Uganda,
NW Kenya
N. p. melanogastra
S Kenya, Tanzania
**Nectarinia nectarinioides (Smaller
Black-bellied Sunbird)**
N. n. erlangeri
S Somalia
N. n. nectarinioides
E Kenya, NE Tanzania
**Nectarinia famosa (Yellow-tufted
Malachite Sunbird)**
N. f. cupreonitens
Ethiopia, SE Sudan
N. f. aeneigularis
Kenya, Uganda, E Zaire, N Malawi
N. f. famosa
Rhodesia, South Africa
**Nectarinia johnstoni (Red-tufted
Malachite Sunbird)**
N. j. johnstoni
W Kenya, N Tanzania
N. j. dartmouthi
E Zaire, W Uganda
N. j. nyikensis
S Tanzania, Zambia, Malawi
Nectarinia notata (Noted Sunbird)
N. n. notata
Madagascar
N. n. moebii
Gt Comoro I
N. n. voeltzkowi
Moheli I (Comoro)

**Nectarinia johannae (Madame Verreaux's
Sunbird)**
N. j. fasciata
Sierra Leone to Benin
N. j. johannae
Cameroun, Zaire
Nectarinia superba (Superb Sunbird)
N. s. ashantiensis
Sierra Leone to Ghana
N. s. nigeriae
S Nigeria
N. s. superba
S Cameroun, W Zaire, Angola
N. s. buvuma
E Zaire, Uganda
Nectarinia kilimensis (Bronze Sunbird)
N. k. kilimensis
E Zaire, Uganda, W Kenya, Tanzania
N. k. arturi
S Tanzania, Malawi, NE Zambia,
E Rhodesia
N. k. gadowi
C Angola
**Nectarinia reichenowi (Golden-winged
Sunbird)**
N. r. shelleyae
E Zaire
N. r. lathburyi
N Kenya
N. r. reichenowi
C & S Kenya, NE Tanzania, Mozambique
AETHOPYGA
**Aethopyga primigenius (Hachisuka's
Sunbird)**
A. p. diuatae
NE Mindanao
A. p. primigenius
C & E Mindanao
Aethopyga boltoni (Apo Sunbird)
A. b. malindangensis
C & W Mindanao
A. b. boltoni
E Mindanao
Aethopyga flagrans (Flaming Sunbird)
A. f. decolor
NE Luzon I
A. f. flagrans
W & S Luzon I
A. f. guimarasensis
Panay I, Guimaras I
A. f. daphoenonota
Negros I
**Aethopyga pulcherrima (Mountain
Sunbird)**
A. p. jeffreyi
Luzon I
A. p. pulcherrima
Basilan I, Samar I, Leyte I, Mindanao I

A. p. decorosa
Bohol I

Aethopyga duyvenbodei (Sanghir Yellow-backed Sunbird)
Sanghir Is

Aethopyga shelleyi (Palawan Sunbird)
A. s. flavipectus
Luzon I, Mindoro I
A. s. rubrinota
Lubang Is
A. s. bella
Samar I, Leyte I, Mindanao I
A. s. bonita
Ticao I, Masbate I, Panay I, Negros I, Cebu I
A. s. arolasi
Sulu Archipelago
A. s. shelleyi
Balabac I, Palawan I

Aethopyga gouldiae (Mrs Gould's Sunbird)
A. g. gouldiae
N Assam, Himalayas, SE Tibet
A. g. isolata
S Assam, Bangladesh, Burma
A. g. dabryii
E Sikang, SW China, N Vietnam
A. g. annamensis
S Laos, S Vietnam

Aethopyga nipalensis (Green-tailed Sunbird)
A. n. horsfieldii
W Himalayas
A. n. nipalensis
C Nepal, Sikkim
A. n. koelzi
E Himalayas, NE Burma, S Assam, N Vietnam
A. n. victoriae
W Burma
A. n. karenensis
SE Burma
A. n. angkanensis
N Thailand
A. n. australis
S Thailand
A. n. blanci
Laos
A. n. ezrai
S Vietnam

Aethopyga eximia (Kuhl's Sunbird)
Java

Aethopyga christinae (Fork-tailed Sunbird)
A. c. latouchii
SE China, N Vietnam
A. c. christinae
Hainan I

Aethopyga saturata (Black-throated Sunbird)
A. s. saturata
W Himalayas
A. s. assamensis
Bangladesh, Assam, N Burma, W China
A. s. galenae
NW Thailand
A. s. petersi
E Burma, Laos, N Vietnam, SE Yunnan
A. s. sanguinipectus
SE Burma
A. s. anomala
S Thailand
A. s. wrayi
Malaysia
A. s. ochra
S Laos, C Vietnam
A. s. cambodiana
SW Cambodia
A. s. johnsi
S Vietnam

Aethopyga siparaja (Yellow-backed Sunbird)
A. s. vigorsii
N India
A. s. seheriae
Nepal, Assam, Bangladesh, NE India, Burma, N Thailand
A. s. labecula
NE India, S Bangladesh
A. s. owstoni
Nauchow I (Hainan)
A. s. tonkinensis
NE Vietnam
A. s. mangini
SE Thailand, C & S Indochina
A. s. insularis
Phuquoc I (Cambodia)
A. s. cara
S Burma, Thailand
A. s. trangensis
S Thailand
A. s. siparaja
Malaysia, Sumatra, Borneo
A. s. nicobarica
Nicobar Is
A. s. heliogona
Java
A. s. natunae
N Natuna Is
A. s. magnifica
WC Philippine Is
A. s. flavostriata
N Celebes
A. s. beccarii
S Celebes

Aethopyga mystacalis (Scarlet Sunbird)
A. m. temminckii
Malaysia, Sumatra, Borneo
A. m. mystacalis
Java
Aethopyga ignicauda (Fire-tailed Sunbird)
A. i. ignicauda
Himalayas, Sikang, N Burma, Yunnan
A. i. flavescens
NW Burma

ARACHNOTHERA
Arachnothera longirostra (Little Spider-hunter)
A. l. longirostra
SW India, Nepal, Assam, Burma,
W Thailand
A. l. sordida
S Yunnan, NE Thailand, N Indochina
A. l. pallida
SE Thailand, C Indochina
A. l. cinereicollis
S Thailand, Malaysia, Sumatra
A. l. niasensis
Nias I
A. l. prillwitzi
Java
A. l. buettikoferi
Borneo
A. l. atita
S Natuna Is
A. l. rothschildi
N Natuna Is
A. l. dilutior
Palawan
A. l. flammifera
Samar I, Leyte I, Bohol I, Mindanao I
A. l. randi
Basilan I
Arachnothera crassirostris (Thick-billed Spiderhunter)
S Thailand, Malaysia, Sumatra, Borneo
Arachnothera robusta (Long-billed Spiderhunter)
A. r. robusta
Malaysia, Sumatra, Borneo
A. r. armata
Java
Arachnothera flavigaster (Greater Yellow-eared Spiderhunter)
S Thailand, Malaysia, Sumatra, Borneo
Arachnothera chrysogenys (Lesser Yellow-eared Spiderhunter)
A. c. chrysogenys
S Burma, S Thailand, Malaysia, Sumatra,
Java, W Borneo
A. c. harrissoni
E Borneo

Arachnothera clarae (Naked-faced Spiderhunter)
A. c. philippinensis
Samar I, Leyte I
A. c. clarae
E Mindanao I
A. c. malindangensis
C & W Mindanao I
A. c. luzonensis
C Luzon I, Laguna I
Arachnothera affinis (Grey-breasted Spiderhunter)
A. a. caena
S Burma, Thailand
A. a. modesta
S Thailand, Malaysia, W Borneo
A. a. pars
E Borneo
A. a. affinis
Java, Bali I
A. a. concolor
Sumatra
Arachnothera magna (Streaked Spider-hunter)
A. m. magna
Himalayas, N Burma, Yunnan
A. m. aurata
EC Burma
A. m. musarum
SE Burma, N Thailand, N Laos
A. m. pagodarum
S Burma, SW Thailand
A. m. remota
S Vietnam
Arachnothera everetti (Everett's Spiderhunter)
N & C Borneo
Arachnothera juliae (Whitehead's Spiderhunter)
N Borneo

152 ZOSTEROPIDAE (WHITE EYES)

ZOSTEROPS
Zosterops erythropleura (Chestnut-flanked White eye)
Manchuria, Amur, N Korea, China
Zosterops japonica (Japanese White eye)
Z. j. yesoensis
Hokkaido I
Z. j. japonica
Honshu I, S Japan
Z. j. stejnegeri
Bonin Is, Izu Is
Z. j. alani
Iwo Jima I
Z. j. insularis
Tanegashima I, Yakushima I

Z. j. loochooensis
Riukiu Is
Z. j. daitoensis
Borodino Is
Z. j. simplex
Sikang, China, Burma, N Vietnam, Taiwan
Z. j. hainana
Hainan I

Zosterops meyeni (Philippine White eye)
Z. m. batanis
Botel Tobago I, Kashoto I, Batan I
Z. m. meyeni
Luzon I, Calayan I, Lubang I

Zosterops palpebrosa (Oriental White eye)
Z. p. occidentis
NW India
Z. p. palpebrosa
C India, Sri Lanka, Bangladesh, W Assam, Nepal, Bhutan
Z. p. nilgiriensis
SW India
Z. p. salimalii
SE India
Z. p. siamensis
SE Tibet, Burma, N Thailand, SW China, Indochina
Z. p. nicobarica
Andaman Is, Nicobar Is
Z. p. williamsoni
S Thailand, Malaysia
Z. p. joannae
W China
Z. p. auriventer
S Burma, Malaysia, Bangka I, W Borneo
Z. p. sumatrana
W Sumatra
Z. p. buxtoni
E Sumatra, W Java
Z. p. melanura
E & C Java, Bali I
Z. p. unica
Sumbawa I, Flores I

Zosterops ceylonensis (Large Sri Lanka White eye)
Sri Lanka

Zosterops conspicillata (Bridled White eye)
Z. c. saypani
Tinian I, Saipan I
Z. c. conspicillata
Guam I
Z. c. rotensis
Rota I
Z. c. semperi
Palau Is
Z. c. owstoni
Truk I

Z. c. takatsukasai
Ponapé I
Z. c. hypolais
Yap I

Zosterops salvadorii (Enggano White eye)
Enggano I

Zosterops atricapilla (Black-capped White eye)
Z. a. viridicata
N Sumatra
Z. a. atricapilla
C & S Sumatra, N Borneo

Zosterops everetti (Everett's White eye)
Z. e. everetti
Cebu I
Z. e. basilanica
Samar I, Leyte I, Mindanao I, Basilan I
Z. e. boholensis
Bohol I
Z. e. siquijorensis
Siquijor I
Z. e. mandibularis
Sulu Archipelago
Z. e. babelo
Talaut I
Z. e. tahanensis
N Borneo, Malaysia, S Thailand
Z. e. wetmorei
S Thailand

Zosterops nigrorum (Philippine Yellow White eye)
Z. n. meyleri
Camiguin Is
Z. n. aureiloris
N Luzon I
Z. n. sierramadrensis
Cagayan Province, Luzon I
Z. n. luzonica
SE Luzon I
Z. n. nigrorum
Masbate I, Negros I, Panay I
Z. n. richmondi
Cagayancillo I (Sulu Sea)
Z. n. mindorensis
Mindoro I
Z. n. catarmanensis
Camiguin I (South)

Zosterops montana (Mountain White eye)
Z. m. ternatana
Ternate I
Z. m. obstinata
Batjan I
Z. m. seranensis
Ceram I
Z. m. whiteheadi
N Luzon I

Z. m. halconensis
Mindoro I
Z. m. gilli
Marinduque I
Z. m. parkesi
Palawan I
Z. m. diuatae
N Mindanao
Z. m. vulcani
Mt Apo & Mt Katanglad (Mindanao)
Z. m. pectoralis
N Negros I
Z. m. steini
Timor I
Z. m. montana
Sumatra, Java, Bali I, Lesser Sunda Is,
Celebes, Buru I
Z. m. difficilis
S Sumatra
Zosterops wallacei (Wallace's White eye)
Sumbawa I, Sumba I, Flores I
Zosterops flava (Javan White eye)
NW Java, S Borneo
Zosterops chloris (Moluccan White eye)
Z. c. maxi
Lombok I
Z. c. intermedia
Sumbawa I, Flores I, SW Celebes
Z. c. mentoris
NC Celebes
Z. c. flavissima
Tukangbesi I
Z. c. solombensis
Solombo Besar I
Z. c. zachlora
Kalambau I
Z. c. chloris
Aru Is, Kei Is, Ceram I, Misol I, Halmahera I
Z. c. albiventris
S Moluccan Is, Tenimber Is, Torres Straits Is
Z. c. citrinella
Timor I, Sumba I
Z. c. harterti
Alor I
Zosterops consobrinorum (Peninsular White eye)
SE Celebes
Zosterops grayi (Gt Kei I White eye)
Gt Kei I
Zosterops uropygialis (Little Kei I White eye)
Little Kei I
Zosterops anomala (Celebean White eye)
S Celebes
Zosterops atriceps (Batjan White eye)
Z. a. dehaani
Morotai I

Z. a. fuscifrons
Halmahera I
Z. a. atriceps
Batjan I
Zosterops atrifrons (Moluccan Black-fronted White eye)
Z. a. nehrkorni
Gt Sanghir Is, Celebes
Z. a. atrifrons
Banggai I, N Celebes
Z. a. surda
NC Celebes
Z. a. sulaensis
Sula Is
Z. a. stalkeri
Ceram I
Zosterops minor (New Guinea Black-fronted White eye)
Z. m. minor
Japen I, New Guinea
Z. m. chrysolaema
NW New Guinea
Z. m. rothschildi
C New Guinea
Z. m. gregaria
E New Guinea
Z. m. tenuifrons
SE New Guinea
Z. m. delicatula
SE New Guinea
Z. m. pallidogularis
Fergusson I, Goodenough I
Zosterops meeki (White throated White eye)
Z. m. meeki
Tagula I, Louisiade Archipelago
Z. m. hypoxantha
New Britain
Z. m. ultima
New Hanover, New Ireland
Z. m. admiralitatus
Manus I (Admiralty Is)
Zosterops mysorensis (Biak White eye)
Biak I, New Guinea
Zosterops fuscicapilla (Yellow-bellied Mountain White eye)
Z. f. fuscicapilla
C & W New Guinea
Z. f. crookshanki
Goodenough I
Zosterops buruensis (Buru I White eye)
Buru I
Zosterops kuehni (Ambon white eye)
Ambon I
Zosterops novaeguineae (New Guinea Mountain White eye)
Z. n. novaeguineae
NW New Guinea

Z. n. aruensis
Aru Is
Z. n. wuroi
S New Guinea
Z. n. wahgiensis
C New Guinea
Z. n. crissalis
SE New Guinea
Z. n. oreophila
E New Guinea
Z. n. magnirostris
NW New Guinea
Zosterops metcalfii (Yellow-throated White eye)
Z. m. exigua
Buka I, Bougainville I, Choiseul I
Z. m. metcalfii
Ysabel I, St George I
Z. m. floridana
Florida I
Zosterops natalis (Christmas Island White eye)
Christmas I
Zosterops lutea (Yellow Silver eye)
Z. l. balstoni
NW Western Australia
Z. l. lutea
Nothern Territory, N Queensland
Zosterops griseotincta (Louisiades White eye)
Z. g. pallidipes
Rossel I (Louisiade Archipelago)
Z. g. aignani
Louisiade Archipelago
Z. g. griseotincta
Louisiade Archipelago
Z. g. longirostris
Bonvouloir I (Louisiade Archipelago)
Z. g. eichhorni
Nauna I, Nissan I, Long I (New Britain)
Zosterops rennelliana (Rennell Is White eye)
Rennell I
Zosterops rendovae (Solomon Is White eye)
Z. r. vellalavella
Bagga I, Vella Lavella I
Z. r. luteirostris
Gizo I
Z. r. splendida
Ganonga I
Z. r. kulambangrae
Kulambangra I, Vangunu I, New Georgia I
Z. r. rendovae
Rendova I
Z. r. tetiparia
Tetipari I

Zosterops murphyi (Kulambangra Mountain White eye)
Kulambangra I
Zosterops ugiensis (Grey-throated White eye)
Z. u. ugiensis
San Cristobal I
Z. u. oblita
Guadalcanal I
Z. u. hamlini
Bougainville I
Zosterops stresemanni (Malaita White eye)
Malaita I
Zosterops sanctaecrucis (Santa Cruz White eye)
Santa Cruz I
Zosterops samoensis (Savaii White eye)
Savaii I (Samoa Is)
Zosterops explorator (Layard's White eye)
Fiji Is
Zosterops flavifrons (Yellow-fronted White eye)
Z. f. gauensis
Gaua I (Banks Is)
Z. f. perplexa
N New Hebrides, Vanua Levu I
Z. f. brevicauda
Malo I, Espiritu Santo I
Z. f. macgillivrayi
Malekula I
Z. f. efatensis
Nguna I, Efate I, Erromanga I
Z. f. flavifrons
Tanna I
Z. f. majuscula
Aneitum I
Zosterops minuta (Small Lifu White eye)
Lifu I, Loyalty Is
Zosterops xanthochroa (New Caledonia White eye)
New Caledonia
Zosterops gouldi (Western Silvereye)
S Western Australia
Zosterops lateralis (Grey-backed White eye)
Z. l. halmaturina
Tasmania, W Victoria, SE South Australia
Z. l. lateralis
Victoria, E New South Wales,
SE Queensland, New Zealand
Z. l. familiaris
E New South Wales
Z. l. ramsayi
E Queensland
Z. l. tephropleura
Lord Howe I **e?**

Z. l. chlorocephala
Capricorn I
Z. l. griseonota
New Caledonia
Z. l. nigrescens
Maré I, Uvea I (Loyalty Is)
Z. l. melanops
Lifu I (Loyalty Is)
Z. l. macmillani
Tanna I, Aniwa I (New Hebrides)
Z. l. tropica
Espiritu Santo I
Z. l. vatensis
N New Hebrides, Banks Is, Torres Is
Z. l. valuensis
Valua I (Banks Is)
Z. l. flaviceps
Fiji Archipelago
Zosterops tenuirostris (Slender-billed White eye)
Norfolk I
Zosterops albogularis (White-chested White eye)
Norfolk I
Zosterops inornata (Large Lifu White eye)
Lifu I
Zosterops cinerea (Grey-brown White eye)
Z. c. finschii
Palau Is
Z. c. ponapensis
Ponapé I
Z. c. cinerea
Kusaie I
Zosterops abyssinica (White-breasted White eye)
Z. a. abyssinica
E Ethiopia, SE Sudan
Z. a. socotrana
Socotra I, N Somalia
Z. a. arabs
Yemen, Aden
Z. a. omoensis
SW Ethiopia
Z. a. jubaensis
SE Ethiopia, Somalia, N Kenya
Z. a. flavilateralis
E Kenya, E Tanzania
Zosterops pallida (Pale White eye)
Z. p. pallida
Namibia, SW Transvaal, NW Cape Province
Z. p. sundevalli
N Cape Province
Z. p. caniviridis
W Transvaal, E Botswana

Zosterops senegalensis (African Yellow White eye) 523
Z. s. senegalensis
Senegal to Ethiopia, Uganda
Z. s. demeryi
Sierra Leone, Liberia, Ivory Coast
Z. s. stenocricota
Fernando Po I, SE Nigeria to Gabon
Z. s. stuhlmanni
E Zaire, Uganda
Z. s. reichenowi
E Zaire
Z. s. toroensis
NE Zaire
Z. s. jacksoni
W Kenya, N Tanzania
Z. s. kasaica
SW Zaire, NE Angola
Z. s. heinrichi
N Angola
Z. s. quanzae
C Angola
Z. s. anderssoni
S Angola to Mozambique, Natal
Z. s. stierlingi
S Tanzania, Zambia, Malawi
Z. s. kirki
Gt Comoro I
Z. s. poliogastra
C Ethiopia
Z. s. kaffensis
W Ethiopia
Z. s. kulalensis
N Kenya
Z. s. kikuyuensis
W Kenya
Z. s. silvana
SE Kenya
Z. s. eurycricota
N Tanzania
Z. s. mbuluensis
N Tanzania
Z. s. winifredae
NE Tanzania
Zosterops virens (Green White eye)
Z. v. capensis
W Cape Province
Z. v. virens
S Mozambique to C & E Cape Province
Z. v. atmorii
W Natal, Lesotho
Zosterops borbonica (Bourbon White eye)
Z. b. mauritiana
Mauritius I
Z. b. borbonica
Reunion I
Z. b. alopekion
Cilaos I, Reunion I

Z. b. xerophila
  Etang les Bains, Reunion I
Zosterops ficedulina (Principé White eye)
Z. f. ficedulina
  Principé I
Z. f. feae
  Sao Thomé I
Zosterops griseovirescens (Annobon White eye)
  Annobon I
Zosterops hovarum (Hova Grey-backed White eye)
  Madagascar
Zosterops maderaspatana (Madagascar White eye)
Z. m. aldabransis
  Aldabra I
Z. m. maderaspatana
  Madagascar, Glorioso I
Z. m. anjouanensis
  Anjouan I
Z. m. comorensis
  Moheli I
Z. m. voeltzkowi
  Europa I
Z. m. menaiensis
  Cosmoledo Atoll
Zosterops mayottensis (Chestnut-sided White eye)
  Mayotte I
Zosterops modesta (Seychelles Brown White eye)
  Mahé I
Zosterops mouroniensis (Grand Comoro White eye)
  Gt Comoro I
Zosterops olivacea (Olive White eye)
  Reunion I
Zosterops chloronothos (Mauritius Olive White eye)
  Mauritius I
Zosterops vaughani (Pemba White eye)
  Pemba I

WOODFORDIA
Woodfordia superciliosa (Woodford's White eye)
  Rennell I
Woodfordia lacertosa (Sanford's White eye)
  Santa Cruz I

RUKIA
Rukia palauensis (Palau White eye)
  Palau Is
Rukia oleaginea (Yap White eye)
  Yap I
Rukia ruki (Truk White eye)
  Truk I

Rukia longirostra (Ponapé White eye)
  Ponapé I

TEPHROZOSTEROPS
Tephrozosterops stalkeri (Ceram White eye)
  Ceram I

MADANGA
Madanga ruficollis (Madanga White eye)
  NW Buru I

LOPHOZOSTEROPS
Lophozosterops pinaiae (Brown-breasted White eye)
  C Ceram I
Lophozosterops goodfellowi (Goodfellow's White eye)
L. g. goodfellowi
  Mt Apo (Mindano I)
L. g. malindangensis
  Mt Malindang (NW Mindanao I)
L. g. gracilis
  NE Mindanao I
L. s. stresemanni
  N Celebes
L. s. heinrichi
  N Celebes
L. s. striaticeps
  NC Celebes
L. s. stachyrina
  SC Celebes
L. s. squamiceps
  S Celebes
L. s. analoga
  SE Celebes
Lophozosterops javanica (Javan Grey-throated White eye)
L. j. frontalis
  W Java
L. j. javanica
  C & E Java
L. j. elongata
  E Java, Bali I
Lophozosterops superciliaris (White-browed White eye)
L. s. hartertiana
  W Sumbawa I
L. s. superciliaris
  Flores I
Lophozosterops dohertyi (Crested White eye)
L. d. dohertyi
  Sumbawa I
L. d. subcristata
  Flores I

Oculocincta squamifrons (Pygmy White eye)
N & W Borneo

HELEIA
Heleia muelleri (Timor White eye)
W Timor I
Heleia crassirostris (Stripe-headed White eye)
H. c. crassirostris
Flores I
H. c. junior
Sumbawa I

CHLOROCHARIS
Chlorocharis emiliae (Olive Black eye)
C. e. emiliae
Mt Kinabalu (N Borneo)
C. e. trinitae
Mt Trus Madi (N Borneo)
C. e. fusciceps
NE Sarawak
C. e. moultoni
Sarawak

HYPOCRYPTADIUS
Hypocryptadius cinnamomeus (Cinnamon White eye)
Mindanao I

SPEIROPS
Speirops brunnea (Fernando Po Speirops)
Fernando Po I
Speirops leucophaea (Prince's I Speirops)
Principé I
Speirops lugubris (Black-capped Speirops)
S. l. melanocephala
Mt Cameroun
S. l. lugubris
Sao Thomé I

153 MELIPHAGIDAE (HONEY EATERS)

TIMELIOPSIS
Timeliopsis fulvigula (Mountain Straight-billed Honeyeater)
T. f. fulvigula
NW New Guinea
T. f. meyeri
C & SE New Guinea
T. f. fuscicapilla
E New Guinea
Timeliopsis griseigula (Lowland Straight-billed Honeyeater)
T. g. griseigula
W New Guinea
T. g. fulviventris
SE New Guinea

Melilestes megarhynchus (Long-billed Honeyeater)
M. m. vagans
Batana I, Waigeu I
M. m. brunneus
NW New Guinea
M. m. megarhynchus
Aru Is, S & SE New Guinea
M. m. stresemanni
N New Guinea, Japen I
Melilestes bougainvillei (Bougainville Honeyeater)
Bougainville I

TOXORHAMPHUS
Toxorhamphus novaeguineae (Yellow-bellied Longbill)
T. n. novaeguineae
W New Guinea & islands
T. n. flaviventris
Aru Is, S New Guinea
Toxorhamphus poliopterus (Slaty-chinned Longbill)
T. p. maximus
NC New Guinea
T. p. poliopterus
C & SE New Guinea

OEDISTOMA
Oedistoma iliolophum (Grey-bellied Honeyeater)
O. i. cinerascens
Waigeu I
O. i. affine
NW New Guinea
O. i. iliolophum
Japen I, N New Guinea
O. i. flavum
S & SE New Guinea
O. i. fergussonis
D'Entrecasteaux Archipelago
Oedistoma pygmaeum (Pygmy Honeyeater)
O. p. waigeuense
Waigeu I
O. p. pygmaeum
Misol I, W New Guinea
O. p. flavipectus
S New Guinea
O. p. olivascens
SE New Guinea
O. p. meeki
D'Entrecasteaux Archipelago

GLYCICHAERA
Glycichaera fallax (White-eyed Honeyeater)
G. f. pallida
Batanta I, Waigeu I
G. f. poliocephala
Misol I, Aru Is, NW New Guinea

G. f. fallax
Japen I, E & S New Guinea
G. f. sylvia
N New Guinea
G. f. claudi
N Queensland

LICHMERA
Lichmera lombokia (Lombok Honeyeater)
L. l. lombokia
Lombok I
L. l. fumidigula
Flores I, Sumbawa I
Lichmera argentauris (Plain Olive Honeyeater)
L. a. argentauris
Waigeu I, W New Guinea islands
L. a. chloris
Halmahera I
L. a. patasiwa
Lusaolate I (Ceram)
Lichmera indistincta (Brown Honeyeater)
L. i. limbata
Bali I, Lombok I, Timor I, Lesser Sunda Is
L. i. indistincta
Western Australia, Northern Territory
L. i. ocularis
NE Australia, S New Guinea
L. i. melvillensis
Melville I
L. i. nupta
Aru Is
Lichmera incana (Silver-eared Honeyeater)
L. i. incana
New Caledonia
L. i. poliotis
Loyalty Is
L. i. mareensis
Maré Is (Loyalty Is)
L. i. griseoviridis
C New Hebrides
L. i. flavotincta
Erromanga I (New Hebrides)
Lichmera alboauricularis (White-eared Honeyeater)
L. a. alboauricularis
SE New Guinea
L. a. olivacea
N New Guinea
Lichmera squamata (Tenimber Honeyeater)
L. s. squamata
Kei Is
L. s. salvadorii
Tenimber Is
L. s. kebirensis
S Banda Sea Islands

Lichmera deningeri (Buru Honeyeater)
Buru I
Lichmera monticola (Ceram Honeyeater)
Ceram I
Lichmera flavicans (Timor Honeyeater)
Timor I
Lichmera notabilis (Wetar Honeyeater)
Wetar I
Lichmera cockerelli (White-streaked Honeyeater)
N Queensland

MYZOMELA
Myzomela blasii (Ambon Honeyeater)
Ceram I, Ambon I
Myzomela albigula (White-chinned Honeyeater)
M. a. albigula
Rossel I
M. a. pallidior
W Louisiade Archipelago
Myzomela cineracea (Sclater's Honeyeater)
M. c. cineracea
New Britain
M. c. rooki
Umboi I (Bismarck Archipelago)
Myzomela eques (Red-spot Honeyeater)
M. e. eques
NW New Guinea & islands
M. e. primitiva
N New Guinea
M. e. nymani
S & E New Guinea
M. e. karimuiensis
E New Guinea
Myzomela obscura (Dusky Honeyeater)
M. o. harterti
E Queensland
M. o. munna
N Queensland, Torres Strait
M. o. obscura
Northern Territory, Melville I
M. o. fumata
S New Guinea
M. o. aruensis
Aru Is
M. o. simplex
Damar I, Ternate I, Batjan I, Halmahera I
M. o. rubrotincta
Obi Is
M. o. mortyana
Morotai I
M. o. rubrobrunnea
Biak I
Myzomela cruentata (Red Honeyeater
M. c. cruentata
Japen I, New Guinea
M. c. coccinea
New Britain, Duke of York Is

M. c. erythrina
New Ireland
M. c. lavongai
New Hanover
M. c. cantans
Tabar I (Bismarck Archipelago)
M. c. vinacea
Dyaul I (Bismarck Archipelago)
Myzomela nigrita (Black Honeyeater)
M. n. steini
Waigeu I
M. n. nigrita
Aru Is, S New Guinea
M. n. meyeri
Japen I, N New Guinea
M. n. pluto
Meos Num I
M. n. forbesi
D'Entrecasteaux Archipelago
M. n. louisiadensis
Louisiade Archipelago
M. n. hades
St Matthias Is (Bismarck Archipelago)
M. n. ramsayi
Tingwon I (Bismarck Archipelago)
M. n. pammelaena
Admiralty Is
M. n. ernstmayri
Manus I, Admiralty Is
M. n. nigerrima
Long I (NE New Guinea)
Myzomela pulchella (New Ireland Honey-eater)
New Ireland
Myzomela kuehni (Wetar Honeyeater)
Wetar I
Myzomela erythrocephala (Mangrove Red-headed Honeyeater)
M. e. erythrocephala
coast of N Western Australia
M. e. infuscata
NE Australia, Aru Is, S New Guinea
M. e. dammermanni
Sumba I
Myzomela adolphinae (Mountain Red-headed Honeyeater)
New Guinea
Myzomela sanguinolenta (Scarlet Honeyeater)
M. s. chloroptera
N Celebes
M. s. charlottae
C & SE Celebes
M. s. juga
SW Celebes
M. s. eva
Djampea I, Saleyer I (Flores Sea)

M. s. batjanensis
Batjan I
M. s. elisabethae
Ceram I
M. s. wakoloensis
Buru I
M. s. annabellae
Babar I, Tenimber Is
M. s. boiei
Banda I
M. s. caledonica
New Caledonia
M. s. sanguinolenta
coast of E Queensland, New South Wales
Myzomela cardinalis (Cardinal Honeyeater)
M. c. lifuensis
Loyalty Is
M. c. cardinalis
S New Hebrides
M. c. tenuis
N New Hebrides
M. c. tucopiae
Tikopia I
M. c. nigriventris
Samoa Is
M. c. sanctaecrucis
Torres Is, Santa Cruz I
M. c. sanfordi
Rennell I
M. c. pulcherrima
San Cristobal I, Ugi I
M. c. kobayashii
Palau Is
M. c. kurodai
Yap I
M. c. saffordi
S Marianas Is
M. c. asuncionis
N Marianas Is
M. c. major
Truk I
M. c. dichromata
Ponapé I
M. c. rubratra
Kusaie I (Caroline Is)
M. c. chermesina
Rotuma Is
Myzomela sclateri (Sclater's Honeyeater)
N New Guinea islands & New Britain
Myzomela lafargei (Small Bougainville Honeyeater)
Bougainville Group, Solomon Is
Myzomela melanocephala (Black-headed Honeyeater)
Guadalcanal Group, Solomon Is

Myzomela eichhorni (Yellow-vented Honeyeater)
M. e. eichhorni
  Solomon Is
M. e. ganongae
  Ganonga I
M. e. atrata
  Vella Lavella I, Baga I
Myzomela malaitae (Malaita Honeyeater)
  Malaita I
Myzomela tristrami (Tristram's Honey-eater)
  San Cristobal I, Santa Ana I
Myzomela jugularis (Orange-breasted Honeyeater)
  Fiji Is
Myzomela erythromelas (Black-bellied Honeyeater)
  New Britain
Myzomela vulnerata (Sunda Honeyeater)
  Timor I
Myzomela rosenbergii (Black & Red Honeyeater)
M. r. rosenbergii
  NW New Guinea
M. r. longirostris
  Goodenough I (D' Entrecasteaux Archipelago)
M. r. wahgiensis
  W & C New Guinea

CERTHIONYX
Certhionyx niger (Black Honey-eater)
  C Australia
Certhionyx variegatus (Pied Honeyeater)
  C Australia

MELIPHAGA
Meliphaga mimikae (Large Spot-breasted Honeyeater)
M. m. rara
  N New Guinea
M. m. mimikae
  C New Guinea
M. m. bastille
  E New Guinea
M. m. granti
  SE New Guinea
Meliphaga auga (Southern White-eared Mountain Honeyeater)
M. a. gretae
  SC New Guinea
M. a. setekwa
  SC New Guinea
M. a. auga
  SE New Guinea

Meliphaga montana (White-eared Mountain Honeyeater)
M. m. montana
  NW New Guinea
M. m. margaretae
  Batanta I
M. m. sepik
  C New Guinea
M. m. steini
  Japen I
M. m. germanorum
  N New Guinea
M. m. huonensis
  NE New Guinea
M. m. aicora
  SE New Guinea
Meliphaga orientalis (Small Spot-breasted Honeyeater)
M. o. facialis
  E, N & E New Guinea, Waigeu I,
M. o. becki
  NE New Guinea
M. o. orientalis
  SE New Guinea
M. o. citreola
  N New Guinea
Meliphaga albonotata (White-marked Honeyeater)
  New Guinea
Meliphaga aruensis (Puff-backed Honey-eater)
M. a. sharpei
  W, N & E New Guinea, Waigeu I,
  D'Entrecasteaux Archipelago
M. a. aruensis
  S New Guinea, Aru Is
Meliphaga analoga (Mimic Meliphaga)
M. a. papuae
  S New Guinea
M. a. analoga
  S New Guinea, W Papuan islands
M. a. longirostris
  Aru Is
M. a. flavida
  N New Guinea, Japen I
M. a. connectens
  N New Guinea
Meliphaga vicina (Louisiades Honey-eater)
  Tagula I
Meliphaga gracilis (Graceful Honeyeater)
M. g. stevensi
  SE New Guinea
M. g. cinereifrons
  SE New Guinea
M. g. gracilis
  S New Guinea, Aru Is, N Queensland
M. g. imitatrix
  NE Queensland

Meliphaga notata (Lesser Lewin Honey-eater)
　M. n. notata
　　Torres Strait (N Queensland)
　M. n. mixta
　　NE Queensland
Meliphaga flavirictus (Yellow-gaped Honeyeater)
　M. f. flavirictus
　　SE New Guinea
　M. f. crockettorum
　　N & W New Guinea
Meliphaga lewinii (Lewin Honeyeater)
　M. l. lewinii
　　E Queensland, E New South Wales
　M. l. nea
　　E Victoria
Meliphaga flava (Yellow Honeyeater)
　E Queensland
Meliphaga albilineata (White-striped Honeyeater)
　Northern Territory
Meliphaga virescens (Singing Honeyeater)
　M. v. virescens
　　SC, S & Western Australia,
　　S & W Australia islands
　M. v. insularis
　　Rottnest I (Western Australia)
　M. v. westwoodia
　　S Queensland
　M. v. forresti
　　NW & C Australia
　M. v. cooperi
　　N Northern Territory, Melville I
Meliphaga versicolor (Varied Honeyeater)
　M. v. sonoroides
　　W Papuan Is, NW New Guinea
　M. v. vulgaris
　　Japen I, N New Guinea, Fergusson I
　M. v. intermedia
　　Samarai I (E New Guinea)
　M. v. versicolor
　　S New Guinea, Torres Strait,
　　NE Queensland
Meliphaga fasciogularis (Mangrove Honeyeater)
　E Queensland, N New South Wales
Meliphaga inexpectata (Guadalcanal Honeyeater)
　Guadalcanal I
Meliphaga fusca (Fuscous Honeyeater)
　M. f. fusca
　　SE South Australia, Victoria, E New
　　South Wales
　M. f. dawsoni
　　SE Queensland
　M. f. subgermana
　　E Queensland

　M. f. zanda
　　NW Queensland, E Northern Territory
　M. f. flavescens
　　N Western Australia, N Northern Territory
　M. f. deserticola
　　N Western Australia
　M. f. melvillensis
　　Melville I
　M. f. germana
　　SE New Guinea
Meliphaga plumula (Yellow-fronted Honeyeater)
　M. p. planasi
　　N Western Australia
　M. p. plumula
　　C Australia
　M. p. ethelae
　　E South Australia, NW Victoria, W New
　　South Wales
Meliphaga chrysops (Yellow-faced Honeyeater)
　M. c. samueli
　　SE South Australia
　M. c. chrysops
　　E Victoria, E New South Wales,
　　E Queensland
Meliphaga cratitia (Purple-gaped Honeyeater)
　M. c. cratitia
　　W Victoria, SE South Australia,
　　SW Western Australia
　M. c. halmaturina
　　Kangaroo I
Meliphaga keartlandi (Grey-headed Honeyeater)
　C Australia
Meliphaga penicillata (White-plumed Honeyeater)
　M. p. carteri
　　NW Western Australia
　M. p. geraldtonensis
　　W Western Australia
　M. p. ladasi
　　C Western Australia
　M. p. centralia
　　C Australia
　M. p. leilavalensis
　　W Queensland, NE South Australia
　M. p. interioris
　　NW New South Wales, SC Queensland
　M. p. penicillata
　　E & N Victoria, E South Australia,
　　W New South Wales, SE Queensland
　M. p. mellori
　　SW Victoria, SE South Australia
Meliphaga ornata (Mallee Honeyeater)
　S & Western Australia

***Meliphaga reticulata* (Reticulated Honeyeater)**
Timor I
***Meliphaga leucotis* (White-eared Honeyeater)**
M. l. novaenorciae
S Western Australia
M. l. leucotis
SE South Australia, Victoria, New South Wales, Kangaroo I
***Meliphaga flavicollis* (Yellow-throated Honeyeater)**
Tasmania, King I
***Meliphaga melanops* (Yellow-tufted Honeyeater)**
M. m. melanops
E New South Wales, E & C Victoria, SE Queensland
M. m. cassidix
S Victoria
***Meliphaga unicolor* (White-gaped Honeyeater)**
Northern Australia
***Meliphaga flaviventer* (Tawny-breasted Honeyeater)**
M. f. fusciventris
Waigeu I, Batanta I
M. f. flaviventer
W Papuan Is, NW New Guinea
M. f. rubiensis
WC New Guinea
M. f. saturatior
Aru Is, S New Guinea
M. f. tararae
S New Guinea
M. f. giulianettii
SE New Guinea
M. f. visi
SE New Guinea
M. f. kumusii
SE New Guinea
M. f. madaraszi
NE New Guinea
M. f. philemon
N New Guinea
M. f. meyeri
Japen I
M. f. spilogaster
Trobriand Is (D'Entrecasteaux Archipelago)
M. f. filigera
N Queensland
***Meliphaga polygramma* (Spotted Honeyeater)**
M. p. polygramma
Waigeu I
M. p. kuehni
Misol I
M. p. poikilosternos
Salawati I, NW & C New Guinea

M. p. septentrionalis
N New Guinea
M. p. lophotis
SE New Guinea
M. p. candidior
S New Guinea
***Meliphaga macleayana* (Yellow-streaked Honeyeater)**
NE Queensland
***Meliphaga frenata* (Bridled Honeyeater)**
NE Queensland
***Meliphaga subfrenata* (Black-throated Honeyeater)**
M. s. subfrenata
NW New Guinea
M. s. melanolaema
C New Guinea
M. s. utakwensis
SC New Guinea
M. s. salvadorii
SE New Guinea
***Meliphaga obscura* (Obscure Honeyeater)**
M. o. viridifrons
NW New Guinea
M. o. obscura
C & SE New Guinea

OREORNIS
***Oreornis chrysogenys* (Orange-cheeked Honeyeater)**
C New Guinea

FOULEHAIO
***Foulehaio carunculata* (Carunculated Honeyeater)**
F. c. carunculata
Samoan Islands, Tonga, E Fiji Is
F. c. taviunensis
Taveuni I, Vanua Levu I
F. c. procerior
W Fiji Is
***Foulehaio provocator* (Yellow-faced Honeyeater)**
Kandavu I

CLEPTORNIS
***Cleptornis marchei* (Golden Honeyeater)**
Saipan I (Mariana Is)

APALOPTERON
***Apalopteron familiare* (Bonin Island Honeyeater)**
A. f. familiare
N Bonin Is
A. f. hahasima
S Bonin Is

MELITHREPTUS
Melithreptus brevirostris (Brown-headed Honeyeater)
M. b. augustus
S Western Australia, S South Australia, NW Victoria
M. b. brevirostris
SE Queensland, E New South Wales, Victoria
M. b. magnirostris
Kangaroo I
Melithreptus lunatus (White-naped Honeyeater)
M. l. lunatus
E Queensland, SE New South Wales, SE South Australia
M. l. chloropsis
SW Western Australia
Melithreptus albogularis (White-throated Honeyeater)
M. a. subalbogularis
N Western Australia
M. a. albogularis
Northern Territory, N Queensland, NE New South Wales, S New Guinea
Melithreptus affinis (Black-headed Honeyeater)
M. a. alisteri
King I, Furneaux Group
M. a. affinis
Tasmania
Melithreptus gularis (Black-chinned Honeyeater)
SE Queensland, New South Wales, Victoria, SE South Australia
Melithreptus laetior (Golden-backed Honeyeater)
M. l. normantoniensis
N Queensland
M. l. carpentarianus
C Queensland
M. l. laetior
N Western Australia, S Northern Territory, NW South Australia
M. l. parus
WC Western Australia
Melithreptus validirostris (Strong-billed Honeyeater)
M. v. kingi
King I, Furneaux Group
M. v. validirostris
Tasmania

ENTOMYZON
Entomyzon cyanotis (Blue-faced Honeyeater)
E. c. albipennis
N Western Australia, Northern Territory
E. c. apsleyi
Melville I

E. c. cyanotis
E South Australia, Victoria, New South Wales, E & C Queensland
E. c. harterti
S New Guinea, N Queensland

NOTIOMYSTIS
Notiomystis cincta (Stitch-bird)
N. c. hautura
Little Barrier I (New Zealand)
(N. c. cincta — extinct)

PYCNOPYGIUS
Pycnopygius ixoides (New Guinea Brown Honeyeater)
P. i. simplex
N New Guinea
P. i. proximus
N New Guinea
P. i. unicus
NE New Guinea
P. i. ixoides
NW New Guinea
P. i. cinereifrons
S New Guinea
P. i. finschi
SE New Guinea
Pycnopygius cinereus (Grey-fronted Honeyeater)
P. c. cinereus
NW New Guinea
P. c. dorsalis
WC New Guinea
P. c. marmoratus
SE New Guinea
Pycnopygius stictocephalus (Streak-capped Honeyeater)
Aru Is, New Guinea

PHILEMON
Philemon meyeri (Meyer's Friarbird)
E New Guinea
Philemon brassi (Brass's Friarbird)
NW New Guinea
Philemon citreogularis (Little Friarbird)
P. c. papuanus
S New Guinea
P. c. kisserensis
S Banda Sea islands
P. c. occidentalis
N Western Australia
P. c. breda
Melville I
P. c. sordidus
N Northern Territory
P. c. carpentariae
NW Queensland
P. c. johnstoni
NE Queensland

P. c. citreogularis
SE South Australia, Victoria, New South Wales, E & C Queensland
Philemon inornatus (Plain Friarbird)
P. i. inornatus
W Timor I
P. i. robustus
E Timor I
Philemon gilolensis (Striated Friarbird)
N Moluccas
Philemon fuscicapillus (Morotai I Friarbird)
N Moluccas
Philemon subcorniculatus (Ceram Friarbird)
Ceram I
Philemon moluccensis (Moluccas Friarbird)
P. m. moluccensis
Buru I
P. m. timorlaoensis
Tenimber Is
P. m. plumigenis
Kei Is
Philemon buceroides (Timor Helmeted Friarbird)
P. b. neglectus
Lombok I, Sumbawa I, Flores I
P. b. sumbanus
Sumba I
P. b. plesseni
Lomblen I, Pantar I, Alor I
P. b. pallidiceps
Wetar I
P. b. buceroides
N Western Australia, Timor I, Savu Is
Philemon gordoni (Melville I Friarbird)
Melville I, N Northern Territory
Philemon novaeguineae (New Guinea Friarbird)
P. n. novaeguineae
NW & S New Guinea, West Papuan islands
P. n. aruensis
Aru Is
P. n. jobiensis
Japen I, N New Guinea
P. n. brevipennis
S New Guinea
P. n. trivialis
SE New Guinea
P. n. subtuberosus
Trobriand Is (D'Entrecasteaux Archipelago)
P. n. tagulanus
Tagula I
P. n. yorki
Torres Strait, N Queensland
P. n. confusus
NE Queensland

Philemon cockerelli (New Britain Friarbird)
P. c. umboi
Rook I
P. c. cockerelli
New Britain
Philemon eichhorni (New Ireland Friarbird)
New Ireland
Philemon albitorques (White-naped Friarbird)
Manus I
Philemon argenticeps (Silver-crowned Friarbird)
P. a. argenticeps
N Western Australia
P. a. melvillensis
Melville I
P. a. alexis
N Northern Territory
P. a. kempi
N Queensland
Philemon corniculatus (Noisy Friarbird)
P. c. ellioti
S New Guinea, NE Queensland
P. c. clamans
SE Queensland
P. c. corniculatus
NE Victoria, E New South Wales
Philemon diemenensis (New Caledonian Friarbird)
Loyalty Is, New Caledonia
PTILOPRORA
Ptiloprora plumbea (Leaden Honeyeater)
P. p. granti
C New Guinea
P. p. plumbea
SE New Guinea
Ptiloprora meekiana (Meek's Streaked Honeyeater)
P. m. occidentalis
C New Guinea
P. m. meekiana
SE New Guinea
Ptiloprora erythropleura (Red-sided Streaked Honeyeater)
P. e. erythropleura
NW New Guinea
P. e. dammermani
C New Guinea
Ptiloprora guisei (Red-backed Honeyeater)
P. g. acrophila
N coast of New Guinea
P. g. umbrosa
N New Guinea
P. g. mayri
N New Guinea
P. g. guisei
SE New Guinea

Ptiloprora perstriata (Black-backed Streaked Honeyeater)
P. p. praedicta
NW New Guinea
P. p. incerta
WC New Guinea
P. p. perstriata
C & E New Guinea

MELIDECTES
Melidectes fuscus (Sooty Honeyeater)
M. f. occidentalis
C New Guinea
M. f. gilliardi
E New Guinea
M. f. fuscus
E & SE New Guinea
Melidectes whitemanensis (Gilliard's Honeyeater)
New Britain
Melidectes princeps (Long-bearded Honeyeater)
EC New Guinea
Melidectes nouhuysi (Short-bearded Honeyeater)
WC New Guinea
Melidectes ochromelas (Mid-mountain Honeyeater)
M. o. ochromelas
W New Guinea
M. o. batesi
C & SE New Guinea
M. o. lucifer
NE New Guinea
Melidectes leucostephes (White-fronted Melidectes)
NW New Guinea
Melidectes belfordi (Belford's Melidectes)
M. b. brassi
NW New Guinea
M. b. joiceyi
W New Guinea
M. b. kinneari
S New Guinea
M. b. belfordi
SE New Guinea
M. b. schraderensis
Schrader mountains, New Guinea
Melidectes rufocrissalis (Reichenow's Melidectes)
M. r. rufocrissalis
C New Guinea
M. r. thomasi
E New Guinea
M. r. gilliardi
EC New Guinea
Melidectes foersteri (Foerster's Melidectes)
NE New Guinea

Melidectes torquatus (Cinnamon-breasted Wattle Bird) 533
M. t. torquatus
NW New Guinea
M. t. nuchalis
C New Guinea
M. t. mixtus
C New Guinea
M. t. cahni
NE New Guinea
M. t. polyphonus
NE New Guinea
M. t. emilii
SE New Guinea

MELIPOTES
Melipotes gymnops (Arfak Melipotes)
NW New Guinea
Melipotes ater (Huon Melipotes)
NE New Guinea
Melipotes fumigatus (Common Melipotes)
M. f. goliathi
C New Guinea
M. f. fumigatus
SE New Guinea

MYZA
Myza celebensis (Brown Honeysucker)
M. c. celebensis
N & C Celebes
M. c. parvirostris
SE Celebes
M. c. meridionalis
S Celebes
Myza sarasinorum (Spot-headed Honey-Sucker)
M. s. sarasinorum
N Celebes
M. s. chionogenys
SC Celebes
M. s. pholidota
SE Celebes

MELIARCHUS
Meliarchus sclateri (San Cristobal Honeyeater)
San Cristobal I

GYMNOMYZA
Gymnomyza viridis (Green Honeyeater)
G. v. viridis
Taveuni I, Vanua Levu I
G. v. brunneirostris
Viti Levu I
Gymnomyza samoensis (Black-breasted Honeyeater)
Samoa Is
Gymnomyza aubryana (Red-faced Honeyeater)
New Caledonia

Moho braccatus (Kauai O-o)
Kauai I (Hawaii)

PHYLIDONYRIS
Phylidonyris pyrrhoptera (Crescent Honeyeater)
P. p. pyrrhoptera
E New South Wales, S Victoria
P. p. indistincta
SE South Australia
P. p. halmaturina
Kangaroo I
P. p. rex
King I, Furneaux Group
P. p. inornata
Tasmania
Phylidonyris novaehollandiae (Yellow-winged Honeyeater)
P. n. longirostris
SW Western Australia
P. n. novaehollandiae
SE Australian coast, S Queensland
to South Australia
P. n. campbelli
Kangaroo I
P. n. caudata
King I, Furneaux Group
P. n. canescens
Tasmania
Phylidonyris nigra (White-cheeked Honeyeater)
P. n. nigra
E Queensland, E New South Wales
P. n. gouldii
SW Western Australia
Phylidonyris albifrons (White-fronted Honeyeater)
C Australia
Phylidonyris melanops (Tawny-crowned Honeyeater)
P. m. melanops
New South Wales, Victoria, South
Australia, SW Western Australia
P. m. braba
Kangaroo I
P. m. crassirostris
King I (Tasmania)
Phylidonyris undulata (Barred Honeyeater)
New Caledonia
Phylidonyris notabilis (White-bellied Honeyeater)
P. n. notabilis
Banks Is, NW New Hebrides
P. n. superciliaris
N New Hebrides

RAMSAYORNIS
Ramsayornis fasciatus (Bar-breasted Honeyeater)
R. f. fasciatus
N Northern Territory, N Queensland
R. f. apsleyi
Melville I
R. f. broomei
N Western Australia
Ramsayornis modestus (Brown-backed Honeyeater)
New Guinea, N Queensland

PLECTORHYNCHA
Plectorhyncha lanceolata (Striped Honeyeater)
E Queensland, New South Wales,
Victoria, SE South Australia

CONOPOPHILA
Conopophila whitei (Grey Honeyeater)
C Western Australia, S Northern Territory
Conopophila albogularis (Rufous-banded Honeyeater)
C. a. mimikae
NW & S New Guinea, Aru Is
C. a. albogularis
N Queensland, N Northern Territory
Conopophila rufogularis (Red-throated Honeyeater)
C. r. rufogularis
N Western Australia, N Northern Territory
C. r. queenslandica
N Queensland
Conopophila picta (Painted Honeyeater)
E Australia

XANTHOMYZA
Xanthomyza phrygia (Regent Honeyeater)
S Queensland, New South Wales,
Victoria, SE South Australia

CISSOMELA
Cissomela pectoralis (Banded Honeyeater)
N Australia

ACANTHORHYNCHUS
Acanthorhynchus tenuirostris (Eastern Spinebill)
A. t. cairnsensis
E Queensland
A. t. trochiloides
SE Queensland
A. t. tenuirostris
E New South Wales, E & S Victoria,
SE South Australia
A. t. loftyi
S South Australia
A. t. halmaturinus
Kangaroo I

A. t. regius
King I, Furneaux Group
A. t. dubius
Tasmania
Acanthorhynchus superciliosus (Western Spinebill)
SW Western Australia

MANORINA
Manorina melanophrys (Bell Miner)
SE Australia
Manorina melanocephala (Noisy Miner)
M. m. melanocephala
New South Wales, Victoria, Tasmania
M. m. crassirostris
E Queensland
Manorina obscura (Dusky Miner)
M. o. obscura
S Western Australia
M. o. clelandi
SW Western Australia
Manorina flavigula (Yellow-throated Miner)
M. f. casuarina
N Western Australia
M. f. lutea
C Western Australia
M. f. alligator
Northern Territory
M. f. melvillensis
Melville I
M. f. pallida
C Australia
M. f. flavigula
W Queensland, New South Wales, Victoria, E & S South Australia, SE Western Australia
Manorina melanotis (Black-eared Miner)
NW Victoria, E South Australia

ANTHORNIS
Anthornis melanura (New Zealand Bell Bird)
A. m. obscura
Three Kings I
A. m. dumerilii
North I (New Zealand)
A. m. melanura
South I (New Zealand) Stewart I
A. m. incoronata
Auckland Is

ACANTHAGENYS
Acanthagenys rufogularis (Spiny-cheeked Honeyeater)
A. r. rufogularis
C Australia
A. r. parker
Friday I, Torres Str

ANTHOCHAERA
Anthochaera chrysoptera (Little Wattle Bird)
A. c. chrysoptera

S Queensland, New South Wales, Victoria, SE South Australia
A. c. halmaturina
Kangaroo I
A. c. tasmanica
Tasmania
A. c. lunulata
SW Western Australia
Anthochaera carunculata (Red Wattle Bird)
A. c. carunculata
S & SE coast of Australia
A. c. woodwardi
SW Western Australia
Anthochaera paradoxa (Yellow Wattle Bird)
Tasmania, King I

PROSTHEMADURA
Prosthemadura novaeseelandiae (Parson Bird) (Tui)
P. n. novaeseelandiae
New Zealand, Auckland Is, Stewart I
P. n. kermadecensis
Kermadec Is
P. n. chathamensis
Chatham I

PROMEROPS
Promerops cafer (Cape Sugarbird)
Cape Province, South Africa
Promerops gurneyi (Gurney's Sugarbird)
P. g. gurneyi
Cape Province, Natal, E Transvaal
P. g. ardens
E Rhodesia

EMBERIZIDAE

154 EMBERIZINAE (BUNTINGS)

MELOPHUS
Melophus lathami (Crested Bunting)
Pakistan to S China, Indochina
LATOUCHEORNIS
Latoucheornis siemsseni (Fokien Blue Bunting)
C China
EMBERIZA
Emberiza calandra (Corn Bunting)
Europe to Sinkiang » S Iran
Emberiza citrinella (Yellow Hammer)
E. c. caliginosa
N & W British Isles
E. c. citrinella
NW Europe, C Russia » N Africa
E. c. erythrogenys
E Europe to Siberia » Mongolia & Iraq
Emberiza leucocephala (Pine Bunting)
E. l. leucocephala
Tibet, Siberia » Iraq, India, China

E. l. fronto
NE China
Emberiza cia (Rock Bunting)
E. c. cia
S Europe, Asia Minor
A. c. africana
N Africa
E. c. prageri
Caucasus, NW Iran
E. c. par
C Asia, Pakistan, N India
E. c. stracheyi
W Himalayas
E. c. decolorata
Sinkiang
E. c. godlewskii
Mongolia, NW China
E. c. khamensis
NE Tibet, W China
E. c. yunnanensis
SE Tibet, SW China
E. c. omissa
NE China
E. c. flemingorum
Nepal
Emberiza cioides (Siberian Meadow Bunting)
E. c. tarbagataica
C Asia » N Mongolia
E. c. cioides
NC Asia
E. c. weigoldi
NE Asia » Shensi, C Korea
E. c. castaneiceps
S Korea, E China
E. c. ciopsis
N Japan » S Japan
Emberiza jankowskii (Jankowski's Bunting)
NE Manchuria
Emberiza buchanani (Grey-necked Bunting)
E. b. cerrutii
E Turkey, SW Russia, Iran
E. b. buchanani
Afghanistan, W Pakistan » SE India
E. b. neobscura
C Asia, W Mongolia
Emberiza stewarti (White-capped Bunting)
S Russia, Afghanistan » Pakistan, NW India
Emberiza cineracea (Cinereous Bunting)
E. c. cineracea
SW Turkey » Eritrea
E. c. semenowi
Yemen, SW Iran » NE Africa

Emberiza hortulana (Ortolan Bunting)
Europe, N Africa, C Asia » Senegal, Sudan, Iran
Emberiza caesia (Cretzschmar's Bunting)
E Europe, NE Africa » Iran, Sudan
Emberiza cirlus (Cirl Bunting)
E. c. cirlus
S British Isles, S Europe, N Africa
E. c. nigrostriata
Corsica, Sardinia
Emberiza striolata (Striped Bunting)
E. s. sahari
NW Africa
E. s. sanghae
S Mali
E. s. saturatior
W Sudan, Ethiopia, NW Kenya
E. s. jebelmarrae
Darfur, Kordofan
E. s. striolata
NE Africa, Iran, Pakistan, N & C India
Emberiza impetuani (Larklike Bunting)
E. s. impetuani
Angola, Namibia, Botswana, W Cape Province
E. s. sloggetti
C Cape Province
Emberiza tahapisi (Cinnamon-breasted Rock Bunting)
E. t. arabica
S Arabia
E. t. insularis
Socotra I
E. t. septemstriata
E Sudan, NW Ethiopia
E. t. tahapisi
Gabon, Zaire, E & S Africa
E. t. goslingi
Sierra Leone to Sudan, N Zaire
Emberiza socotrana (Socotra Mountain Bunting)
Socotra I
Emberiza capensis (Cape Bunting)
E. c. vincenti
C Malawi, E Zambia
E. c. smithersii
E Rhodesia, Mozambique
E. c. plowesi
Rhodesia, NE Botswana
E. c. reidi
S Transvaal, Natal, Orange, Free State, N Lesotho
E. c. limpopoensis
C & SW Transvaal
E. c. basutoensis
Lesotho, W Natal
E. c. vinacea
N Cape Province

E. c. media
S Transvaal, C Cape Province
E. c. capensis
S Namibia, W Cape Province
E. c. nebularum
SW Angola
E. c. bradfieldi
N Namibia
**Emberiza yessoensis (Japanese Reed
Bunting)**
E. y. yessoensis
N Japan » S Japan
E. y. continentalis
E Manchuria » S Korea, E China
Emberiza tristrami (Tristam's Bunting)
Ussuri region » SW China, Burma
Emberiza fucata (Grey-hooded Bunting)
E. f. arcuata
Pakistan, W Himalayas » N Burma, S China
E. f. fucata
E Asia, N Japan, SE China » Indochina
E. f. kuatunensis
S China
Emberiza pusilla (Little Bunting)
N Asia » N India, Burma, S China
**Emberiza chrysophrys (Yellow-browed
Bunting)**
Siberia, NE Asia » SE China
Emberiza rustica (Rustic Bunting)
E. r. rustica
N Europe, N Asia » E China, Japan
E. r. latifascia
NE Siberia » E China & Japan
Emberiza elegans (Yellow-headed Bunting)
E. e. elegans
Manchuria » S Japan, E China
E. e. ticehursti
E Amur » S Manchuria
E. e. elegantula
SW China
**Emberiza aureola (Yellow-breasted
Bunting)**
E. a. aureola
N Asia » India, Malaysia, Indochina
E. a. ornata
NE Asia
**Emberiza poliopleura (Somali Golden-
breasted Bunting)**
EC Africa
**Emberiza flaviventris (Golden-breasted
Bunting)**
E. f. flavigaster
Mali to Ethiopia
E. f. flaviventris
C,E & Southern Africa
E. f. carychroa
Nairobi, Kenya

E. f. princeps
S Angola, N Namibia
Emberiza affinis (Brown-rumped Bunting)
E. a. affinis
S Sudan, SW Ethiopia, N Uganda,
NE Zaire
E. a. vulpecula
Cameroun, Central African Republic
E. a. nigeriae
Gambia to W Cameroun
**Emberiza cabanisi (Cabanis's Yellow
Bunting)**
E. c. cabanisi
W & NC Africa
E. c. cognominata
SW Zaire, N Angola
E. c. orientalis
Zambia, Tanzania, Rhodesia, Mozambique
Emberiza rutila (Chestnut Bunting)
NE Asia » SE China, Burma, Indochina
Emberiza koslowi (Koslow's Bunting)
Tibet, Tsinghai
**Emberiza melanocephala (Black-headed
Bunting)**
SE Europe, Iran, Caucasus » N & C India
Emberiza bruniceps (Red-headed Bunting)
C Asia, Altai » S India
**Emberiza sulphurata (Japanese Yellow
Bunting)**
C Japan » S Japan, SE China, N Philippine Is
**Emberiza spodocephala (Black-faced
Bunting)**
E. s. spodocephala
C & E Asia » E China, Taiwan
E. s. personata
Sakhalin I, N Japan » S Japan
E. s. sordida
W China » E India, N Burma
**Emberiza variabilis (Japanese Grey
Bunting)**
Sakhalin I, N Japan
Emberiza pallasi (Pallas' Reed Bunting)
E. p. pallasi
C & E Asia » Sinkiang & Mongolia
E. p. polaris
NE Asia » Manchuria & E China
E. p. lydiae
C Mongolia
Emberiza schoeniclus (Reed Bunting)
E. s. schoeniclus
NW Europe, C Russia » Turkey, N Africa
E. s. passerina
NW Siberia » Mongolia, N Iran
E. s. parvirostris
C Siberia » Mongolia
E. s. pyrrhulina
NE Asia » Japan

E. s. minor
SE Siberia, Manchuria
E. s. pallidior
SW Siberia » NW India, Mongolia
E. s. ukrainae
S Russia » N Caucasus
E. s. incognita
C Russia » Sinkiang
E. s. pyrrhuloides
W & C Asia, W Mongolia, Sinkiang
E. s. zaidamensis
N Tsinghai
E. s. witherbyi
W Spain, Sardinia, Balearic Is
E. s. canetti
SE Europe, N Turkey
E. s. reiseri
S Yugoslavia, N Greece
E. s. caspia
E Caucasus, W & S Iran
E. s. korejewi
E Iran

CALCARIUS
Calcarius mccownii (McCown's Longspur)
SC Canada, WC USA » S USA, N Mexico
Calcarius lapponicus (Lapland Bunting)
C. l. lapponicus
N Canada, S Greenland » N Europe,
E USA, N Asia
C. l. coloratus
E Siberia » N China
C. l. alascensis
Alaska, W Canada » W USA
Calcarius pictus (Smith's Longspur)
N Canada » SC USA
Calcarius ornatus (Chestnut-coloured Longspur)
S Canada » S USA, N Mexico

PLECTROPHENAX
Plectrophenax nivalis (Snow Bunting)
P. n. nivalis
N North America, N Europe » S USA,
S Europe
P. n. insulae
Iceland » N Scotland
P. n. vlasowae
NE Asia » C Asia, Manchuria
P. n. townsendi
W Aleutian Is, Commander Is
Plectrophenax hyperboreus (McKay's Bunting)
Bering Sea Is » W Alaska

CALAMOSPIZA
Calamospiza melanocorys (Lark Bunting)
S Canada » C & S USA, N Mexico

PASSERELLA
Passerella iliaca (Fox Sparrow)
P. i. iliaca
E Canada » E USA
P. i. zaboria
W Canada » C & S USA
P. i. altivagans
SW Canada » California
P. i. unalaschensis
Aleutian Is » S California
P. i. ridgwayi
Alaska » S California
P. i. sinuosa
Alaska » S Califorina
P. i. annectens
Alaska » S California
P. i. townsendi
SE Alaska » C California
P. i. fuliginosa
W Canada » S California
P. i. olivacea
SW Canada » NW Mexico
P. i. schistacea
NW USA » SW USA
P. i. swarthi
NW Utah, SE Idaho
P. i. fulva
C Oregon, California » NW Mexico
P. i. megarhyncha
SW Oregon » NW Mexico
P. i. brevicauda
N California » S California
P. i. monoensis
C California » S California
P. i. canescens
E California, Nevada » S California
P. i. stephensi
S California

MELOSPIZA
Melospiza melodia (Song Sparrow)
M. m. melodia
S Canada » SE USA
M. m. atlantica
NE USA » E USA
M. m. euphonia
NC USA » S USA
M. m. juddi
WC Canada » WC USA
M. m. montana
WC USA » SW USA, N Mexico
M. m. fallax
SE Nevada, SW Utah, Arizona,
New Mexico
M. m. saltonis
S Nevada, SE California
M. m. inexpectata
SE Alaska » S Oregon

M. m. rufina
SE Alaska » W Washington
M. m. merrilli
SW Canada » S California
M. m. morphna
SW Canada » N California
M. m. fisherella
Oregon » S California, W Nevada
M. m. maxima
Aleutian Is
M. m. sanaka
Seguam I, Sanak I, Unimak I
M. m. amaka
Amak I
M. m. insignis
Kodiak I
M. m. kenaiensis
S Alaska
M. m. caurina
SE Alaska » N California
M. m. cleonensis
NW California
M. m. gouldii
WC California
M. m. mailliardi
C California
M. m. samuelis
NW California
M. m. maxillaris
NW California
M. m. pusillula
NW California
M. m. heermani
C California
M. m. cooperi
SW California, N Baja California
M. m. micronyx
San Miguel I
M. m. clementae
Santa Roza I, Santa Cruz I
M. m. coronatorum
Coronados I
M. m. rivularis
SC Baja California
M. m. goldmani
WC Mexico
M. m. niceae
EC Mexico
M. m. mexicana
SC Mexico
M. m. azteca
SC Mexico
M. m. villai
W Mexico
M. m. yuriria
C Mexico

M. m. adusta
SW Mexico
M. m. zacapu
W Mexico
Melospiza lincolnii (Lincoln's Sparrow)
M. l. lincolnii
Canada » SW USA, S Mexico, Guatemala
M. l. gracilis
S Alaska, W Canada » California
M. l. alticola
NW USA » Mexico, Guatemala
Melospiza georgiana (Swamp Sparrow)
M. g. ericrypta
W & C Canada » SW USA, NW Mexico
M. g. georgiana
NE USA » SE USA

ZONOTRICHIA
Zonotrichia capensis (Rufous-collared Sparrow)
Z. c. septentrionalis
S Mexico, Guatemala, El Salvador, Honduras
Z. c. antillarum
Dominica I
Z. c. costraricensis
Costa Rica, Panama, Venezuela, Colombia
Z. c. orestera
W Panama
Z. c. insularis
Curaçao I, Aruba I
Z. c. venezuelae
N Venezuela
Z. c. inaccessibilis
C Venezuela
Z. c. roraimae
S Colombia, E Venezuela, Guyana, N Brazil
Z. c. macconelli
Venezuela
Z. c. capensis
French Guiana
Z. c. tocantinsi
E Brazil
Z. c. matutina
NE Brazil, E Bolivia
Z. c. subtorquata
E & C Brazil, Paraguay, Uruguay
Z. c. mellea
C Paraguay, N Argentina
Z. c. hypoleuca
E & S Bolivia, NE Argentina
Z. c. choraules
W Argentina
Z. c. australis
S Chile, S Argentina » N Bolivia
Z. c. chilensis
Chile, S Argentina

Z. c. sanborni
Chile, W Argentina
Z. c. antofagastae
Chile
Z. c. pulacayensis
Peru, W Bolivia, N Argentina
Z. c. peruviensis
W Peru
Z. c. carabayae
Peru, Bolivia
Z. c. huancabambae
N Peru
Z. c. illescasensis
N Peru
Zonotrichia querula (Harris' Sparrow)
W Canada » W USA
Zonotrichia leucophrys (White-crowned Sparrow)
Z. l. leucophrys
C & E Canada » SE USA, Cuba
Z. l. gambelii
NW & W Canada » W USA, N Mexico
Z. l. oriantha
SW Canada » WC USA, N Mexico
Z. l. pugetensis
SW Canada » SW California
Z. l. nuttalli
WC California
Zonotrichia albicollis (White-throated Sparrow)
Canada, N & E USA » S USA, E Mexico
Zonotrichia atricapilla (Golden-crowned Sparrow)
Alaska, W Canada » W USA, NW Mexico

JUNCO
Junco vulcani (Volcano Junco)
Costa Rica, W Panama
Junco hyemalis (Slate-coloured Junco)
J. h. hyemalis
N Canada, NC USA » S USA, N Mexico
J. h. carolinensis
EC USA
J. h. aikeni
WC USA » S USA
J. h. oreganus
S Alaska, W Canada » C California
J. h. cismontanus
W Canada » W USA
J. h. shufeldti
NW USA » S California
J. h. montanus
W Canada, W USA » NW Mexico
J. h. mearnsi
SW Canada » WC USA, NW Mexico
J. h. thurberi
S Oregon » California, N Baja California
J. h. pinosus
C & S California

J. h. pontilus
N Baja California
J. h. townsendi
N Baja California
J. h. insularis
Guadeloupe I
Junco caniceps (Grey-headed Junco)
J. c. caniceps
C & SC USA » S USA & N Mexico
J. c. dorsalis
New Mexico, N Arizona
J. c. mutabilis
S Nevada, SE California
Junco phaeonotus (Mexican Junco)
J. p. palliatus
SW USA, N Mexico
J. p. phaeonotus
C & S Mexico
J. p. bairdi
S Baja California
J. p. fulvescens
S Mexico
J. p. alticola
S Mexico, W Guatemala

PASSERCULUS
Passerculus sandwichensis (Savannah Sparrow)
P. s. labradorius
E Canada » SE USA
P. s. savanna
SE Canada » SE USA, SE Mexico
P. s. princeps
Sable I » SE USA
P. s. mediogriseus
SE Canada, NE USA » SE USA
P. s. oblitus
C Canada, C USA, NE Mexico
P. s. nevadensis
SW Canada, WC USA » SC USA, N Mexico
P. s. brooksi
SW Canada » California, Baja California
P. s. athinus
Alaska, W Canada, W USA » SW USA, W Mexico
P. s. sandwichensis
Alaska » W USA
P. s. crassus
Aleutian Is, W Alaska » C California
P. s. alaudinus
N & C California
P. s. beldingi
S California, N Baja California
P. s. anulus
WC Baja California
P. s. sanctorum
San Benito I, Baja California

P. s. guttatus
W & S Baja California
P. s. magdalenae
S Baja California
P. s. rostratus
S California, Baja California, W Mexico
P. s. rufofuscus
Arizona, New Mexico, N Mexico
P. s. atratus
NW Mexico
P. s. brunnescens
NC Mexico
P. s. wetmorei
SW Guatemala

AMMODRAMUS

Ammodramus maritimus (Seaside Sparrow)
A. m. maritimus
NE USA » SE USA
A. m. macgillivrayi
SE USA
A. m. pelonota
SE USA
A. m. mirabilis
SE USA
A. m. peninsulae
SE USA
A. m. junicola
SE USA
A. m. nigrescens
E Florida
A. m. fisheri
SW & S USA
A. m. sennetti
S USA

Ammodramus caudacutus (Sharp-tailed Sparrow)
A. c. nelsoni
WC Canada » SE USA
A. c. alterus
E Canada » SE USA
A. c. subvirgatus
E Canada » SE USA
A. c. caudacutus
NE USA » SE USA
A. c. diversus
NE USA » SE USA

Ammodramus leconteii (Le Conte's Sparrow)
WC Canada » C & SE USA

Ammodramus bairdii (Baird's Sparrow)
WC Canada, W USA » N Mexico

Ammodramus henslowii (Henslow's Sparrow)
A. h. susurrans
NE » SE USA
A. h. henslowii
C USA » SE USA

Ammodramus savannarum (Grasshopper Sparrow) 541
A. s. pratensis
S Canada, E USA » SE Mexico, West Indies
A. s. floridanus
Florida
A. s. perpallidus
SW Canada, C & SW USA » Mexico, Guatemala
A. s. ammolegus
S Arizona, NW Mexico » Guatemala
A. s. bimaculatus
S Mexico, Honduras, Nicaragua, NW Costa Rica, W Panama
A. s. cracens
Guatemala, E Honduras, NE Nicaragua
A. s. caucae
Colombia
A. s. savannarum
Jamaica
A. s. intricatus
Hispaniola
A. s. borinquensis
Puerto Rico
A. s. caribaeus
Bonaire I, Curaçao I

XENOSPIZA

Xenospiza baileyi (Sierra Madre Sparrow)
N & C Mexico

MYOSPIZA

Myospiza humeralis (Grassland Sparrow)
M. h. humeralis
Colombia, Venezuela, Guyana, French Guiana, Brazil
M. h. pallidulus
Colombia, Venezuela
M. h. xanthornus
Bolivia, Brazil, Paraguay, Uruguay, Argentina
M. h. tarijensis
E Bolivia

Myospiza aurifrons (Yellow-browed Sparrow)
M. a. apurensis
NE Colombia, W Venezuela
M. a. cherriei
E Colombia
M. a. tenebrosus
Venezuela, Colombia
M. a. aurifrons
SE Colombia, E Ecuador, Peru, Bolivia, Brazil

SPIZELLA

Spizella arborea (Tree Sparrow)
S. a. arborea
N Canada, N USA » C USA

S. a. ochracae
NW & W Canada » W USA
Spizella passerina (Chipping Sparrow)
S. p. passerina
SE Canada, C USA » S USA
S. p. arizonae
W Canada » SW USA, W Mexico
S. p. atremaeus
NC Mexico
S. p. mexicana
C & S Mexico, Guatemala
S. p. repetens
Guerrero, Oaxaca
S. p. comparanda
Nayarit to Vera Cruz
S. p. pinetorum
S Guatemala to NE Nicaragua
Spizella pusilla (Field Sparrow)
S. p. pusilla
SE Canada » C & SE USA
S. p. arenacea
C USA » SE USA, NE Mexico
S. p. wortheni
NE & E Mexico
Spizella atrogularis (Black-chinned Sparrow)
S. a. evura
SW USA » NW Mexico
S. a. caurina
C California
S. a. cana
SW California » S Baja California
S. a. atrogularis
NC Mexico
Spizella pallida (Clay-coloured Sparrow)
SC Canada, C & SC USA » W Mexico
Spizella breweri (Brewer's Sparrow)
S. b. taverneri
SW Canada » SW USA
S. b. breweri
SW Canada, W & SW USA » NW Mexico

POOECETES
Pooecetes gramineus (Vesper Sparrow)
P. g. gramineus
SE Canada, E USA » S Mexico
P. g. confinis
SW Canada, WC USA » SW USA,
W Mexico
P. g. affinis
W USA » NW Baja California

CHONDESTES
Chondestes grammacus (Lark Sparrow)
C. g. grammacus
N & C USA » SE USA, E & S Mexico
C. g. strigatus
SW Canada, W USA » Mexico, Guatemala

AMPHISPIZA
Amphispiza bilineata (Black-throated Sparrow)
A. b. bilineata
NC Texas, NE Mexico
A. b. opuntia
SC USA, N Mexico
A. b. deserticola
WC USA » NW Mexico, Baja California
A. b. bangsi
S Baja California
A. b. tortugae
Tortuga I
A. b. belvederei
Cerralvo I
A. b. pacifica
NW Mexico
A. b. cana
San Esteban I
A. b. grisea
C Mexico
Amphispiza belli (Sage Sparrow)
A. b. nevadensis
W USA » SW USA, N Baja California,
NW Mexico
A. b. canescens
SW California, W Nevada, NE Baja
California
A. b. belli
S California, NW Baja California
A. b. clementeae
San Clemente I
A. b. cinerea
C Baja California

AIMOPHILA
Aimophila mystacalis (Bridled Sparrow)
SC Mexico
Aimophila humeralis (Black-chested Sparrow)
WC Mexico
Aimophila ruficauda (Stripe-headed Sparrow)
A. r. acuminata
WC Mexico
A. r. lawrencii
S Mexico
A. r. connectens
E Guatemala
A. r. ruficauda
SE Guatemala, El Salvador, Honduras,
Nicaragua
Aimophila sumichrasti (Cinnamon-tailed Sparrow)
S Mexico
Aimophila strigiceps (Stripe-capped Sparrow)
A. s. strigiceps
E Argentina

A. s. dabbenei
NW Argentina
Aimophila aestivalis (Bachman's Sparrow)
A. a. bachmani
SC USA » SE USA
A. a. illinoensis
NC USA » S USA
A. a. aestivalis
S California, Georgia, Florida
Aimophila botterii (Botteri's Sparrow)
A. b. arizonae
SE Arizona, NW Mexico
A. b. texana
S Texas, NE Mexico
A. b. mexicana
NC Mexico
A. b. goldmani
W Mexico
A. b. botterii
SC & S Mexico
A. b. petenica
SE Mexico, Guatemala, Honduras
A. b. tabascensis
E coast of Mexico
A. b. spadiconigrescens
N Honduras, NE Nicaragua
A. b. vantynei
C Guatemala
A. b. vulcanica
Nicaragua, N Costa Rica
Aimophila cassinii (Cassin's Sparrow)
SC USA » C Mexico
Aimophila quinquestriata (Five-striped Sparrow)
A. q. septentrionalis
NW Mexico
A. q. quinquestriata
W Mexico
Aimophila carpalis (Rufous-winged Sparrow)
A. c. carpalis
SC Arizona, NW Mexico
A. c. distinguenda
NW Mexico
A. c. cohaerens
NW Mexico
Aimophila ruficeps (Rufous-crowned Sparrow)
A. r. eremoeca
SC USA » E Mexico
A. r. scottii
Arizona, New Mexico
A. r. ruficeps
C California
A. r. canescens
SW California, NE Baja California
A. r. pallidissima
S Nuevo Leon

A. r. extima
S Oaxaca
A. r. obscura
Santa Catalina I
A. r. sanctorum
Todos Santos I
A. r. soraria
S Baja California
A. r. rupicola
SW Arizona
A. r. simulans
NW Mexico
A. r. fusca
W Mexico
A. r. boucardi
E Mexico
A. r. australis
S Mexico
Aimophila notosticta (Oaxaca Sparrow)
S Mexico
Aimophila rufescens (Rusty Sparrow)
A. r. antonensis
NW Mexico
A. r. mcleodii
NW Mexico
A. r. disjuncta
Guerrero
A. r. rufescens
W & SW Mexico
A. r. pyrgitoides
Guatemala, Honduras, El Salvador,
E & SE Mexico
A. r. discolor
N Honduras, NE Nicaragua
A. r. pectoralis
SE Mexico, Guatemala, El Salvador
A. r. hypaethrus
NW Costa Rica
A. r. brodkorbi
SW Chiapas
A. r. newmani
NE Puebla

RHYNCHOSPIZA
Rhynchospiza stolzmanni (Tumbes Sparrow)
SW Ecuador, N Peru

TORREORNIS
Torreornis inexpectata (Zapata Sparrow)
T. i. inexpectata
SW Cuba
T. i. sigmani
S Cuba

ORITURUS
Oriturus superciliosus (Striped Sparrow)
O. s. palliatus
NW & W Mexico

O. s. superciliosus
C & SW Mexico

PHRYGILUS
Phrygilus atriceps (Black-hooded Sierra Finch)
P. a. chloronotus
Peru
P. a. punensis
Peru, Bolivia
P. a. atriceps
Peru, Bolivia, Chile, Argentina
Phrygilus gayi (Grey-hooded Sierra Finch)
P. g. gayi
N Chile
P. g. minor
C Chile
P. g. caniceps
S Chile, Argentina
Phrygilus patagonicus (Patagonian Sierra Finch)
Chile, Argentina
Phrygilus fruticeti (Mourning Sierra Finch)
P. f. peruvianus
Peru, Bolivia
P. f. fruticeti
SW Bolivia, Chile, Argentina
Phrygilus unicolor (Plumbeous Sierra Finch)
P. u. nivarius
N Colombia, NW Venezuela
P. u. geospizopsis
S Colombia, Ecuador
P. u. inca
Peru, Bolivia
P. u. unicolor
SW Peru, Chile, W Argentina
P. u. tucumanus
Bolivia, NW Argentina
P. u. ultimus
Argentina
Phrygilus dorsalis (Red-backed Sierra Finch)
Bolivia, Chile, Argentina
Phrygilus erythronotus (White-throated Sierra Finch)
Peru, Bolivia, Chile
Phrygilus plebejus (Ash-breasted Sierra Finch)
P. p. ocularis
Ecuador, N Peru
P. p. plebejus
Peru, Chile, Bolivia, Argentina
Phrygilus carbonarius (Carbonated Sierra Finch)
C Argentina

Phrygilus alaudinus (Band-tailed Sierra Finch)
P. a. bipartitus
W Ecuador, Peru
P. a. humboldti
S Ecuador, N Peru
P. a. excelsus
S Peru, Bolivia
P. a. alaudinus
C Chile
P. a. venturii
Argentina

MELANODERA
Melanodera melanodera (Black-throated Finch)
M. m. princetoniana
Chile, Argentina
M. m. melanodera
Falkland Islands
Melanodera xanthogramma (Yellow-bridled Finch)
M. x. barrosi
Chile, W Argentina
M. x. xanthogramma
S Argentina

HAPLOSPIZA
Haplospiza rustica (Slaty Finch)
H. r. uniformis
S Mexico
H. r. barrilesensis
Honduras, Costa Rica, W Panama
H. r. arcana
Venezuela
H. r. rustica
N Venezuela, Colombia, Ecuador, Peru, Bolivia
Haplospiza unicolor (Uniform Finch)
SE Brazil, E Paraguay, NE Argentina

ACANTHIDOPS
Acanthidops bairdii (Peg-billed Sparrow)
Costa Rica

LOPHOSPINGUS
Lophospingus pusillus (Black-crested Finch)
S Bolivia, Paraguay, Argentina
Lophospingus griseocristatus (Grey-crested Finch)
Bolivia, N Argentina

DONACOSPIZA
Donacospiza albifrons (Long-tailed Reed Finch)
Brazil, Paraguay, Uruguay, Argentina

ROWETTIA
Rowettia goughensis (Gough I Finch)
Gough I

NESOSPIZA
Nesospiza acunhae (Nightingale Finch)
  N. a. acunhae
    Inaccessible I
  N. a. questi
    Nightingale I, Tristan de Cunha I
Nesospiza wilkinsi (Wilkins's Finch)
  N. w. wilkinsi
    Nightingale I, Tristan de Cunha I
  N. w. dunnei
    Inaccessible I

DIUCA
Diuca speculifera (White-winged Diuca Finch)
  D. s. magnirostris
    Peru
  D. s. speculifera
    SE Peru, N Chile, N Bolivia
Diuca diuca (Common Diuca Finch)
  D. d. crassirostris
    N Chile, Argentina
  D. d. diuca
    NC Chile, Argentina
  D. d. chiloensis
    SC Chile
  D. d. minor
    Argentina

IDIOPSAR
Idiopsar brachyurus (Short-tailed Finch)
  Peru, Bolivia, Argentina

PIEZORHINA
Piezorhina cinerea (Cinereous Finch)
  NW Peru

XENOSPINGUS
Xenospingus concolor (Slender-billed Finch)
  S Peru, N Chile

INCASPIZA
Incaspiza pulchra (Great Inca Finch)
  Peru
Incaspiza personata (Rufous-backed Inca Finch)
  Peru
Incaspiza ortizi (Grey-winged Inca Finch)
  Peru
Incaspiza laeta (Buff-bridled Inca Finch)
  Peru
Incaspiza watkinsi (Little Inca Finch)
  Peru

POOSPIZA
Poospiza thoracica (Bay-chested Warbling Finch)
  SE Brazil
Poospiza boliviana (Bolivian Warbling Finch)
  C Bolivia

Poospiza alticola (Plain-tailed Warbling Finch)
  N Peru
Poospiza hypochondria (Rufous-sided Warbling Finch)
  P. h. hypochondria
    Bolivia
  P. h. affinis
    Argentina
Poospiza erythrophrys (Rusty-browed Warbling Finch)
  P. e. cochabambae
    Bolivia
  P. e. erythrophrys
    Bolivia, NW Argentina
Poospiza ornata (Cinnamon Warbling Finch)
  NW Argentina
Poospiza nigrorufa (Black & Rufous Warbling Finch)
  P. n. nigrorufa
    S Brazil, Uruguay, Paraguay
  P. n. whitii
    Bolivia, NW Argentina
  P. n. wagneri
    Bolivia
Poospiza lateralis (Red-rumped Warbling Finch)
  P. l. lateralis
    SE Brazil
  P. l. cabanisi
    SE Brazil, Uruguay, Paraguay, NE Argentina
Poospiza rubecula (Rufous-breasted Warbling Finch)
  N Peru
Poospiza caesar (Chestnut-breasted Mountain Finch)
  SE Peru
Poospiza hispaniolensis (Collared Warbling Finch)
  SW Ecuador, Peru
Poospiza torquata (Ringed Warbling Finch)
  P. t. torquata
    Bolivia
  P. t. pectoralis
    SE Bolivia, W Paraguay, N & C Argentina
Poospiza cinerea (Grey & White Warbling Finch)
  P. c. cinerea
    C Brazil
  P. c. melanoleuca
    Bolivia, Paraguay, Uruguay, SW Brazil
    N Argentina

SICALIS
Sicalis citrina (Stripe-tailed Yellow Finch)
  S. c. browni
    Colombia, Venezuela, Guyana, NE Brazil

. *S. c. citrina*
E Brazil
S. c. occidentalis
Peru
Sicalis lutea (Puna Yellow Finch)
Peru, Bolivia, Argentina
Sicalis uropygialis (Bright-rumped Yellow Finch)
S. u. sharpei
N Peru
S. u. connectens
Peru
S. u. uropygialis
S Peru, Bolivia, N Chile, NW Argentina
Sicalis luteocephala (Citron-headed Yellow Finch)
C Bolivia
Sicalis auriventris (Greater Yellow Finch)
Chile, Argentina
Sicalis olivascens (Greenish Yellow Finch)
S. o. salvini
N Peru
S. o. chloris
C Peru, N Chile
S. o. olivascens
SE Peru, W Bolivia, NW Argentina
S. o. mendozae
W Argentina
Sicalis lebruni (Patagonian Yellow Finch)
S Argentina, S Chile
Sicalis colombiana (Orange-fronted Yellow Finch)
S. c. colombiana
Venezuela, E Colombia
S. c. leopoldinae
E Brazil
S. c. goeldii
E Peru, E Brazil
Sicalis flaveola (Saffron Finch)
S. f. flaveola
Colombia, Venezuela, the Guianas, Trinidad
S. f. valida
Ecuador, NW Peru
S. f. brasiliensis
NE Brazil
S. f. pelzelni
SE Brazil, E Bolivia, Paraguay, Uruguay, N Argentina
Sicalis luteola (Grassland Yellow Finch)
S. l. chrysops
S Mexico, Guatemala, E Honduras, Nicaragua
S. l. mexicana
S Mexico
S. l. eisenmanni
Panama

S. l. bogotensis
Colombia, Ecuador, Peru, Venezuela
S. l. luteola
Colombia, Venezuela, Guyana, Brazil
S. l. flavissima
N Brazilian islands
S. l. chapmani
NE Brazil
S. l. luteiventris
C & SC South America
Sicalis raimondii (Raimondi's Yellow Finch)
Peru
Sicalis taczanowskii (Sulphur-breasted Finch)
SW Ecuador, N Peru

COMPOSPIZA
Compospiza garleppi (Cochabamba Mountain Finch)
Bolivia
Compospiza baeri (Tucuman Mountain Finch)
NW Argentina

EMBERIZOIDES
Emberizoides herbicola (Wedge-tailed Grass Finch)
E. h. lucaris
SW Costa Rica
E. h. hypochondriacus
W & C Panama
E. h. floresae
Panama
E. h. apurensis
E Colombia, W Venezuela
E. h. sphenurus
N Colombia to the Guianas, N Brazil
E. h. herbicola
E & S Brazil, E Bolivia, NE Argentina
Emberizoides ypiranganus (Lesser Grass Finch)
S Venezuela
Emberizoides duidae (Mt Duida Grass Finch)
SE Venezuela

EMBERNAGRA
Embernagra platensis (Great Pampa Finch)
E. p. platensis
SE Brazil, Paraguay, Uruguay, E Argentina
E. p. olivascens
SE Bolivia, W Paraguay, NW Argentina
Embernagra longicauda (Buff-throated Pampa Finch)
Brazil

VOLATINIA
Volatinia jacarina (Blue-black Grassquit)
V. j. splendens
Central America, N South America, Trinidad

V. j. jacarina
  E & C Brazil, SE Peru, E Bolivia,
    N Argentina
V. j. peruviensis
  Ecuador, Peru, N Chile

SPOROPHILA
**Sporophila frontalis (Buffy-throated
Seedeater)**
  SE Brazil, Paraguay, N Argentina
**Sporophila falcirostris (Temminck's
Seedeater)**
  SE Brazil
**Sporophila schistacea (Slate-coloured
Seedeater)**
S. s. subconcolor
  S Mexico
S. s. schistacea
  Costa Rica, Panama, N Colombia
S. s. incerta
  W Colombia, Ecuador
S. s. longipennis
  Venezuela, E Colombia, N Brazil
Sporophila intermedia (Grey Seedeater)
S. i. intermedia
  Colombia, N Venezuela, Guyana, Trinidad
S. i. bogotensis
  W Colombia
S. i. agustini
  N Colombia
S. i. anchicayae
  Colombia
**Sporophila plumbea (Plumbeous
Seedeater)**
S. p. colombiana
  N Colombia
S. p. whiteleyana
  E Colombia, S Venezuela, the Guianas,
    N Brazil
S. p. plumbea
  C & S Brazil, Paraguay, NW Bolivia,
    N Argentina
Sporophila aurita (Variable Seedeater)
S. a. corvina
  Central America from E Mexico to Panama
S. a. aurita
  Costa Rica, Panama
S. a. chocoana
  Panama, W Colombia
**Sporophila americana (Wing-barred
Seedeater)**
S. a. ophthalmica
  SW Colombia, Ecuador, Peru
S. a. murallae
  SE Colombia
S. a. americana
  NE Venezuela, the Guianas, Brazil,
    Tobago I

S. a. dispar
  Brazil
**Sporophila torqueola (White-collared
Seedeater)**
S. t. sharpei
  S Texas, NE Mexico
S. t. torqueola
  C & SW Mexico
S. t. morelleti
  Atlantic slopes of Central America,
    S Mexico to Panama
S. t. mutanda
  Pacific slopes from SW Mexico to
    El Salvador
**Sporophila collaris (Rusty-collared
Seedeater)**
S. c. ochrascens
  N Bolivia, W Brazil
S. c. collaris
  È Brazil
S. c. melanocephala
  Brazil, Paraguay, N Argentina
Sporophila lineola (Lined Seedeater)
S. l. bouvronides
  Trinidad, Tobago I
S. l. restricta
  Colombia
S. l. lineola
  NW and C South America to Argentina
**Sporophila luctuosa (Black & White
Seedeater)**
  NW South America
**Sporophila nigricollis (Yellow-bellied
Seedeater)**
S. n. nigricollis
  Costa Rica, Panama & N South America
    to Bolivia
S. n. vivida
  SW Colombia, W Ecuador
S. n. inconspicua
  W Peru
Sporophila ardesiaca (Dubois' Seedeater)
  Brazil
Sporophila melanops (Hooded Seedeater)
  Brazil
**Sporophila obscura (Dull-coloured
Seedeater)**
S. o. haplochroma
  N Colombia, NW Venezuela
S. o. pauper
  S Colombia, Ecuador, NW Peru
S. o. obscura
  C Peru, Bolivia, Argentina
S. o. pacifica
  W Peru

***Sporophila caerulescens* (Double-collared Seedeater)**
S. c. caerulescens
Brazil, Bolivia, Paraguay, Uruguay, Argentina
S. c. hellmayri
Brazil
S. c. yungae
N Bolivia

***Sporophila albogularis* (White-throated Seedeater)**
NE Brazil

***Sporophila leucoptera* (White-bellied Seedeater)**
S. l. mexianae
Mexiana I, Brazil
S. l. cinereola
E Brazil
S. l. leucoptera
C & SW Brazil, Paraguay, N Argentina
S. l. bicolor
E Bolivia

***Sporophila peruviana* (Parrot-billed Seedeater)**
S. p. devronis
C Ecuador, N Peru
S. p. peruviana
Peru

***Sporophila simplex* (Drab Seedeater)**
Peru

***Sporophila nigrorufa* (Black & Tawny Seedeater)**
Brazil, E Bolivia

***Sporophila bouvreuil* (Capped Seedeater)**
S. b. bouvreuil
E Brazil
S. b. crypta
Rio de Janeiro, Brazil
S. b. pileata
S Brazil, Paraguay, N Argentina
S. b. saturata
Brazil

***Sporophila insulata* (Tumaco Seedeater)**
SW Colombia

***Sporophila minuta* (Ruddy-breasted Seedeater)**
S. m. parva
Central America from SW Mexico to Nicaragua
S. m. centralis
SW Costa Rica, W Panama
S. m. minuta
Trinidad and N South America to S Brazil

***Sporophila hypoxantha* (Tawny-bellied Seedeater)**
Paraguay, E & C Brazil, Uruguay

***Sporophila hypochroma* (Rufous-naped Seedeater)**
E Bolivia

***Sporophila ruficollis* (Dark-throated Seedeater)**
S Brazil, Bolivia, Uruguay, Argentina

***Sporophila palustris* (Marsh Seedeater)**
SE Brazil, Paraguay, Uruguay, N Argentina

***Sporophila castaneiventris* (Chestnut-bellied Seedeater)**
N South America

***Sporophila cinnamomea* (Chestnut Seedeater)**
Brazil, E Paraguay

***Sporophila melanogaster* (Black-bellied Seedeater)**
SE Brazil

***Sporophila telasco* (Chestnut-throated Seedeater)**
W Ecuador, Peru, N Chile

ORYZOBORUS
***Oryzoborus crassirostris* (Large-billed Seed Finch)**
O. c. nuttingi
Nicaragua, N Costa Rica, Panama
O. c. crassirostris
Colombia, Venezuela, the Guianas, N Brazil
O. c. magnirostris
Trinidad, E Venezuela
O. c. maximiliani
Brazil
O. c. occidentalis
Colombia, NW Ecuador
O. c. atrirostris
N Peru
O. c. gigantirostris
N Bolivia

***Oryzoborus angolensis* (Lesser Seed Finch)**
O. a. funereus
S Mexico, Central America, Colombia, Ecuador
O. a. torridus
Trinidad, Peru, Ecuador, S Colombia, Venezuela, the Guianas, Brazil
O. a. angolensis
S Brazil, Bolivia, Paraguay, N Argentina

AMAUROSPIZA
***Amaurospiza concolor* (Blue Seedeater)**
A. c. relicta
S Mexico
A. c. concolor
Honduras, Nicaragua, Costa Rica, Panama
A. c. aequatorialis
SW Colombia, Ecuador

Amaurospiza moesta (Blackish-blue Seedeater)
E Brazil, N Argentina

MELOPYRRHA
Melopyrrha nigra (Cuban Bullfinch)
M. n. nigra
Cuba, Isle of Pines
M. n. taylori
Grand Cayman I

DOLOSPINGUS
Dolospingus fringilloides (White-naped Seedeater)
Venezuela, Brazil

CATAMENIA
Catamenia analis (Band-tailed Seedeater)
C. a. alpica
N Colombia
C. a. schistaceifrons
C Colombia
C. a. soederstromi
N Ecuador
C. a. insignis
Peru
C. a. analoides
W Peru
C. a. griseiventris
SE Peru
C. a. analis
N Chile, Bolivia, NW Argentina
Catamenia inornata (Plain-coloured Seedeater)
C. i. mucuchiesi
Venezuela
C. i. minor
W Venezuela, Colombia, Ecuador, Peru
C. i. inornata
SE Peru, Bolivia, NW Argentina
Catamenia homochroa (Paramo Seedeater)
C. h. homochroa
W Venezuela, Colombia, Ecuador, Peru, Bolivia
C. h. duncani
Venezuela, NE Brazil
Catamenia oreophila (Colombian Seedeater)
N Colombia

TIARIS
Tiaris canora (Cuban Grassquit)
Cuba
Tiaris olivacea (Yellow-faced Grassquit)
T. o. pusilla
E Mexico, Central America, Colombia, Venezuela
T. o. intermedia
Cozumel I, Holbox I, E Mexico
T. o. ravida
Panama

T. o. olivacea
Cuba, Jamaica, Cayman Is
T. o. bryanti
Puerto Rico
Tiaris bicolor (Black-faced Grassquit)
T. b. bicolor
Bahama Is, Cuba
T. b. marchii
Jamaica, Hispaniola
T. b. omissa
Puerto Rico, Tobago I, Colombia, Venezuela
T. b. huilae
Colombia
T. b. grandior
Old Providence I, St Andrew I
T. b. johnstonei
La Blanquilla I
T. b. sharpei
Aruba I, Curaçao I
T. b. tortugensis
La Tortuga I
Tiaris fuliginosa (Sooty Grassquit)
T. f. fumosa
Trinidad, Venezuela
T. f. zuliae
Venezuela
T. f. fuliginosa
NE & C Brazil

LOXIPASSER
Loxipasser anoxanthus (Yellow-shouldered Grassquit)
Jamaica

LOXIGILLA
Loxigilla portoricensis (Puerto Rican Bullfinch)
Puerto Rico
Loxigilla violacea (Greater Antillean Bullfinch)
L. v. violacea
Bahama Is
L. v. maurella
Tortue I, Gonave I, Saona I
L. v. affinis
Hispaniola
L. v. parishi
Ile-à-vache, Beata I
L. v. ruficollis
Jamaica
Loxigilla noctis (Lesser Antillean Bullfinch)
L. n. coryi
St Kitts I, Monserrat I
L. n. ridgwayi
Anguilla I, Antigua I, Barbuda I
L. n. desiradensis
Desirade I

L. n. dominicana
Guadeloupe I, Dominica I
L. n. noctis
Martinique I
L. n. sclateri
St Lucia I
L. n. crissalis
St Vincent I
L. n. grenadensis
Grenada I
L. n. barbadensis
Barbados I

MELANOSPIZA
Melanospiza richardsoni (St Lucia Black Finch)
St Lucia I

GEOSPIZA
Geospiza magnirostris (Large Ground Finch)
Galapagos Is
Geospiza fortis (Medium Ground Finch)
Galapagos Is
Geospiza fuliginosa (Small Ground Finch)
Galapagos Is
Geospiza difficilis (Sharp-beaked Ground Finch)
G. d. difficilis
Tower I, Abingdon I
G. d. debilirostris
James I, Albemarle I, Narborough I
G. d. septentrionalis
Culpepper I, Wenman I
Geospiza scandens (Cactus Ground Finch)
G. s. scandens
James I, Jervis I
G. s. intermedia
Barrington I, Charles I, Duncan I,
Indefatigable I, Albemarle I
G. s. abingdoni
Abingdon I
G. s. rothschildi
Bindloe I
Geospiza conirostris (Large Cactus Ground Finch)
G. c. conirostris
Hood I
G. c. propinqua
Tower I
G. c. darwini
Culpepper I

CAMARHYNCHUS
Camarhynchus crassirostris (Vegetarian Tree Finch)
Galapagos Is

Camarhynchus psittacula (Large Insectivorous Tree Finch)
C. p. habeli
Abingdon I, Bindloe I
C. p. affinis
Albemarle I, Narborough I
C. p. psittacula
Seymour I, Barrington I, Indefatigable I,
Charles I, Duncan I, Jervis I, James I
Camarhynchus pauper (Charles Insectivorous Tree Finch)
Charles I
Camarhynchus parvulus (Small Insectivorous Tree Finch)
C. p. parvulus
James I, Jervis I, Indefatigable I,
Seymour I, Barrington I, Albemarle I,
Duncan I, Charles I, Narborough I
C. p. salvini
Chatham I
Camarhynchus pallidus (Woodpecker Finch)
C. p. pallidus
James I, Jervis I, Seymour I, Duncan I,
Indefatigable I, Charles I
C. p. productus
Albemarle I, Narborough I
C. p. striatipectus
Chatham I
Camarhynchus heliobates (Mangrove Finch)
Albemarle I, Narborough I

CERTHIDEA
Certhidea olivacea (Warbler Finch)
C. o. becki
Culpepper I, Wenman I
C. o. mentalis
Tower I
C. o. fusca
Abingdon I, Bindloe I
C. o. olivacea
James I, Jervis I, Seymour I, Duncan I,
Albemarle I, Narborough I
C. o. bifasciata
Barrington I
C. o. luteola
Chatham I
C. o. cinerascens
Hood I
C. o. ridgwayi
Charles I

PINAROLOXIAS
Pinaroloxias inornata (Cocos Finch)
Cocos Is

Pipilo ocai (Collared Towhee)
 P. o. alticola
  W Mexico
 P. o. nigrescens
  W Mexico
 P. o. guerrerensis
  SW Mexico
 P. o. brunnescens
  S Mexico
 P. o. ocai
  EC Mexico
Pipilo erythrophthalmus (Rufous-sided Towhee)
 P. e. erythrophthalmus
  S Canada, E USA » S USA
 P. e. rileyi
  SE USA
 P. e. alleni
  Florida
 P. e. canaster
  SC USA » SE USA
 P. e. arcticus
  S Canada, NC, C & SC USA » N Mexico
 P. e. montanus
  SW USA » N Mexico
 P. e. gaigei
  Texas
 P. e. curtatus
  SW Canada, W USA » SE California
 P. e. oregonus
  W USA » S California
 P. e. falcinellus
  W USA
 P. e. falcifer
  SW USA
 P. e. megalonyx
  SW USA, NW Baja California
 P. e. clementae
  San Clemente I
 P. e. umbraticola
  NW Baja California
 P. e. magnirostris
  S Baja California
 P. e. griseipygius
  W Mexico
 P. e. orientalis
  EC Mexico
 P. e. maculatus
  E Mexico
 P. e. macronyx
  SC Mexico
 P. e. vulcanorum
  SC Mexico
 P. e. oaxacae
  S Mexico
 P. e. repetens
  S Mexico, W Guatemala

 P. e. chiapensis
  S Mexico
 P. e. socorroensis
  Socorro I, Revillagigedo Group
 P. e. sympatricus
  Vera Cruz
Pipilo fuscus (Brown Towhee)
 P. f. bullatus
  SW Oregon, NC California
 P. f. carolae
  SC California
 P. f. petulans
  NC California
 P. f. crissalis
  WC California
 P. f. eremophilus
  EC California
 P. f. senicula
  S California, NW Baja California
 P. f. aripolius
  C Baja California
 P. f. albigula
  S Baja California
 P. f. mesoleucus
  SW USA, N Mexico
 P. f. intermedius
  N Mexico
 P. f. jamesi
  Tiburon I
 P. f. mesatus
  SW USA
 P. f. texanus
  W & C Texas, N Mexico
 P. f. perpallidus
  N & C Mexico
 P. f. fuscus
  E & C Mexico
 P. f. potosinus
  N & C Mexico
 P. f. campoi
  EC Mexico
 P. f. toroi
  SC Mexico
Pipilo aberti (Abert's Towhee)
 P. a. aberti
  SW USA
 P. a. vorhiesi
  Arizona
 P. a. dumeticolus
  NE Baja California, NW Mexico
Pipilo albicollis (White-throated Towhee)
 P. a. albicollis
  SC Mexico
 P. a. marshalli
  Puebla, Mexico
Chlorurus chlorurus (Green-tailed Towhee)
  W USA » C Mexico

Melozone kieneri (Rusty-crowned Ground Sparrow)
M. k. grisior
NW Mexico
M. k. kieneri
W Mexico
M. k. rubricatum
C & SW Mexico
M. k. obscurior
SW Oaxaca
Melozone biarcuatum (Prévost's Ground Sparrow)
M. b. biarcuatum
S Mexico to W Honduras
M. b. cabanisi
C Costa Rica
Melozone leucotis (White-eared Ground Sparrow)
M. l. occipitalis
S Mexico, Guatemala, El Salvador
M. l. nigrior
Nicaragua
M. l. leucotis
Costa Rica

ARREMON
Arremon taciturnus (Pectoral Sparrow)
A. t. axillaris
Colombia, W Venezuela
A. t. taciturnus
SE Venezuela, the Guianas, Brazil, Bolivia
A. t. semitorquatus
EC Brazil
A. t. nigrirostris
SE Peru, N Bolivia
Arremon flavirostris (Saffron-billed Sparrow)
A. f. flavirostris
EC Brazil
A. f. dorbignii
E Bolivia, NW Argentina
A. f. devillii
Brazil, E Bolivia
A. f. polionotus
Brazil, Paraguay, Argentina
Arremon aurantiirostris (Orange-billed Sparrow)
A. a. saturatus
SE Mexico, Guatemala, Belize
A. a. rufidorsalis
Honduras, Nicaragua, Costa Rica
A. a. aurantiirostris
W Costa Rica, Panama
A. a. strictocollaris
E Panama, NW Colombia
A. a. occidentalis
W Colombia, NW Ecuador

A. a. erythrorhynchus
N Colombia
A. a. spectabilis
SE Colombia, E Ecuador, Peru
A. a. santarosae
SW Ecuador
Arremon schlegeli (Golden-winged Sparrow)
A. s. fratruelis
N Colombia
A. s. canidorsum
Colombia
A. s. schegeli
E Colombia, Venezuela
Arremon abeillei (Black-capped Sparrow)
A. a. abeillei
NW Peru, SW Ecuador
A. a. nigriceps
NW Peru

ARREMONOPS
Arremonops rufivirgatus (Olive Sparrow)
A. r. rufivirgatus
S Texas, NE Mexico
A. r. ridgwayi
E Mexico
A. r. crassirostris
SE Mexico
A. r. verticalis
SE Mexico, Guatemala, Belize
A. r. sinaloae
W Mexico
A. r. sumichrasti
SW Mexico
A. r. rhyptothorax
Yucatan, Mexico
A. r. chiapensis
S Mexico
A. r. superciliosus
W Costa Rica
Arremonops tocuyensis (Tocuyo Sparrow)
NE Colombia, NW Venezuela
Arremonops chloronotus (Green-backed Sparrow)
A. c. chloronotus
SE Mexico, Guatemala, NW Honduras
A. c. twomeyi
NC Honduras
Arremonops conirostris (Black-striped Sparrow)
A. c. richmondi
E Honduras, Nicaragua, Costa Rica, Panama
A. c. striaticeps
C & E Panama, Colombia, W Ecuador
A. c. inexpectatus
Colombia
A. c. conirostris
E Colombia, N Venezuela, N Brazil

A. c. umbrinus
 E Colombia, W Venezuela

Atlapetes albinucha (White-naped Brush Finch)
 A. a. albinucha
 E Mexico
 A. a. griseipectus
 S Mexico, W Guatemala, El Salvador
 A. a. fuscipygius
 Honduras, El Salvador, NW Nicaragua
 A. a. parvirostris
 Costa Rica
 A. a. brunnescens
 Panama
 A. a. coloratus
 Panama
 A. a. azuerensis
 S Panama
 A. a. gutturalis
 N Colombia
Atlapetes pallidinucha (Pale-naped Brush Finch)
 A. p. pallidinucha
 E Colombia, SW Venezuela
 A. p. papallactae
 Colombia, Ecuador
Atlapetes rufinucha (Rufous-naped Brush Finch)
 A. r. phelpsi
 Venezuela, Colombia
 A. r. elaeoprorus
 Colombia
 A. r. simplex
 Colombia
 A. r. caucae
 Colombia
 A. r. spodionotus
 S Colombia, N Ecuador
 A. r. comptus
 SW Ecuador, Peru
 A. r. latinuchus
 SE Ecuador, NE Peru
 A. r. chugurensis
 NW Peru
 A. r. baroni
 N Peru
 A. r. melanolaemus
 SE Peru
 A. r. rufinucha
 Bolivia
 A. r. carrikeri
 E Bolivia
Atlapetes leucopis (White-rimmed Brush Finch)
 S Colombia, N Ecuador

 N Colombia
Atlapetes pileatus (Rufous-capped Brush Finch)
 A. p. dilutus
 N & C Mexico
 A. p. pileatus
 S Mexico
Atlapetes flaviceps (Olive-headed Brush Finch)
 Colombia
Atlapetes fuscoolivaceus (Dusky-headed Brush Finch)
 Colombia
Atlapetes tricolor (Tricoloured Brush Finch)
 A. t. crassus
 Colombia, Ecuador
 A. t. tricolor
 C Peru
Atlapetes albofrenatus (Moustached Brush Finch)
 A. a. meridae
 Venezuela
 A. a. albofrenatus
 Colombia
Atlapetes schistaceus (Slaty Brush Finch)
 A. s. castaneifrons
 Venezuela
 A. s. tamae
 Venezuela, Colombia
 A. s. fumidus
 Venezuela, Colombia
 A. s. schistaceus
 Colombia, Ecuador
 A. s. taczanowskii
 C Peru
 A. s. canigenis
 EC Peru
Atlapetes nationi (Rusty-bellied Brush Finch)
 A. n. celicae
 S Ecuador
 A. n. nationi
 W Peru
 A. n. brunneiceps
 SW Peru
 A. n. simonsi
 S Ecuador
 A. n. seebohmi
 NW Peru

Atlapetes leucopterus **(White-winged Brush Finch)**
  A. l. leucopterus
    Ecuador
  A. l. dresseri
    SW Ecuador, NW Peru
Atlapetes albiceps **(White-headed Brush Finch)**
  SE Ecuador, NW Peru
Atlapetes pallidiceps **(Pale-headed Brush Finch)**
  S Ecuador
Atlapetes rufigenis **(Rufous-eared Brush Finch)**
  A. r. rufigenis
    NW Peru
  A. r. forbesi
    SC Peru
Atlapetes semirufus **(Ochre-breasted Brush Finch)**
  A. s. denisei
    Venezuela
  A. s. benedettii
    Venezuela
  A. s. albigula
    Venezuela
  A. s. zimmeri
    Venezuela, NE Colombia
  A. s. majusculus
    Colombia
  A. s. semirufus
    Colombia
Atlapetes personatus **(Tepui Brush Finch)**
  A. p. personatus
    Venezuela
  A. p. collaris
    Venezuela
  A. p. duidae
    Venezuela
  A. p. parui
    Venezuela
  A. p. paraquensis
    Venezuela
  A. p. jugularis
    Venezuela, N Brazil
Atlapetes fulviceps **(Fulvous-headed Brush Finch)**
  Bolivia, NW Argentina
Atlapetes citrinellus **(Yellow-striped Brush Finch)**
  Argentina
Atlapetes apertus **(Plain-breasted Brush Finch)**
  E Mexico
Atlapetes brunneinucha **(Chestnut-capped Brush Finch)**
  A. b. brunneinucha
    E Mexico

  A. b. suttoni
    S Mexico
  A. b. nigrilatera
    Oaxaca (Mexico)
  A. b. parkesi
    S Vera Cruz
  A. b. macrourus
    S Mexico, SW Guatemala
  A. b. alleni
    El Salvador, Honduras, W Nicaragua
  A. b. elsae
    Costa Rica, W & C Panama
  A. b. frontalis
    E Panama, Colombia Venezuela, Ecuador, Peru
  A. b. allinornatus
    NW Venezuela
  A. b. inornatus
    WC Ecuador
Atlapetes torquatus **(Stripe-headed Brush Finch)**
  A. t. colimae
    W Mexico
  A. t. verecundus
    NW Mexico
  A. t. virenticeps
    C Mexico
  A. t. basilicus
    N Colombia
  A. t. perijanus
    E Colombia, W Venezuela
  A. t. larensis
    Venezuela
  A. t. phaeopleurus
    N Venezuela
  A. t. phygas
    NE Venezuela
  A. t. assimilis
    Venezuela, Ecuador, Colombia, Peru
  A. t. nigrifrons
    SW Ecuador, NW Peru
  A. t. poliophrys
    C & SE Peru
  A. t. torquatus
    NW Bolivia
  A. t. fimbriatus
    Bolivia
  A. t. borelli
    Bolivia, Argentina
Atlapetes atricapillus **(Black-headed Brush Finch)**
  A. a. atricapillus
    N Colombia
  A. a. costaricensis
    SW Costa Rica, W Panama
  A. a. tacarcunae
    E Panama

Pezopetes capitalis (Big-footed Sparrow)
Costa Rica, W Panama

OREOTHRAUPIS
Oreothraupis arremonops (Tanager Finch)
SW Colombia, NW Ecuador

PSELLIOPHORUS
Pselliophorus tibialis (Yellow-thighed Sparrow)
Costa Rica, W Panama
Pselliophorus luteoviridis (Yellow-green Sparrow)
E Panama

LYSURUS
Lysurus castaneiceps (Olive Finch)
L. c. crassirostris
Costa Rica, Panama
L. c. castaneiceps
Colombia, Ecuador, SE Peru

UROTHRAUPIS
Urothraupis stolzmanni (Black-backed Bush Tanager)
C Colombia to C Ecuador

CHARITOSPIZA
Charitospiza eucosma (Coal-crested Finch)
C & E Brazil, NE Argentina

SALTATRICULA
Saltatricula multicolor (Many-coloured Chaco Finch)
Bolivia, Paraguay, Uruguay, N Argentina

CORYPHASPIZA
Coryphaspiza melanotis (Black-masked Finch)
C. m. marajoara
Marajoara I, Brazil
C. m. melanotis
Brazil, Bolivia, Paraguay, NE Argentina

CORYPHOSPINGUS
Coryphospingus pileatus (Pileated Finch)
C. p. rostratus
Colombia
C. p. brevicaudus
N Colombia, N Venezuela
C. p. pileatus
EC Brazil
Coryphospingus cucullatus (Red-crested Finch)
C. c. cucullatus
the Guianas, Brazil
C. c. rubescens
S Brazil, E Paraguay, Uruguay, Argentina
C. c. fargoi
Peru, Bolivia, N Argentina, W Paraguay

Rhodospingus cruentus (Crimson Finch)
Ecuador, Peru

EMBERIZIDAE

155 CATAMBLYRHYNCHINAE (PLUSH-CAPPED FINCH)

CATAMBLYRHYNCHUS
Catamblyrhynchus diadema (Plush-capped Finch)
C. d. federalis
N Venezuela
C. d. diadema
NW Venezuela, Colombia, Ecuador
C. d. citrinifrons
Peru, Bolivia, NW Argentina

EMBERIZIDAE

156 CARDINALINAE (CARDINAL-GROSBEAKS)

GUBERNATRIX
Gubernatrix cristata (Yellow Cardinal)
Uruguay, N & E Argentina

PAROARIA
Paroaria coronata (Red-crested Cardinal)
Bolivia, Paraguay, Uruguay, Argentina
Paroaria dominicana (Red-cowled Cardinal)
NE Brazil
Paroaria gularis (Red-capped Cardinal)
P. g. nigrogenis
Trinidad, E Colombia, Venezuela
P. g. gularis
Colombia, Venezuela, the Guianas, Ecuador, Peru, W Brazil
P. g. cervicalis
E Bolivia, Brazil
Paroaria baeri (Crimson-fronted Cardinal)
P. b. baeri
Brazil
P. b. xinguensis
Brazil
Paroaria capitata (Yellow-billed Cardinal)
P. c. capitata
Brazil, Paraguay, N Argentina
P. c. fuscipes
SE Bolivia

SPIZA
Spiza americana (Dickcissel)
E North America » Central America, Trinidad, Colombia, Venezuela

PHEUCTICUS
Pheucticus chrysopeplus (Yellow Grosbreak)
P. c. dilutus
NW Mexico

P. c. chrysopeplus
 W Mexico
P. c. rarissimus
 SC Mexico
P. c. aurantiacus
 S Mexico, Guatemala
P. c. laubmanni
 N Colombia, N Venezuela
Pheucticus tibialis (Black-thighed Grosbeak)
 C Costa Rica, W Panama
Pheucticus chrysogaster (Yellow-bellied Grosbeak)
 SW Colombia, Ecuador, Peru
Pheucticus aureoventris (Black-backed Grosbeak)
P. a. meridensis
 Venezuela
P. a. uropygialis
 Colombia
P. a. crissalis
 SW Colombia, Ecuador
P. a. terminalis
 Peru
P. a. aureoventris
 S Peru, Bolivia, Brazil, Paraguay, NW Argentina
Pheucticus ludovicianus (Rose-breasted Grosbeak)
 S Canada, C & SE USA » Mexico, Central America, N South America
Pheucticus melanocephalus (Black-headed Grosbeak)
P. m. melanocephalus
 S Canada, WC USA, Mexico
P. m. maculatus
 SW Canada, W USA, Mexico, Baja California

CARDINALIS
Cardinalis cardinalis (Common Cardinal)
C. c. cardinalis
 E USA
C. c. floridanus
 SE Georgia, Florida
C. c. magnirostris
 SE Texas, Louisiana
C. c. canicaudus
 SC USA, C & E Mexico
C. c. coccineus
 E Mexico
C. c. littoralis
 E Mexico
C. c. yucatanicus
 SE Mexico
C. c. flammigerus
 SE Mexico, Guatemala, Belize
C. c. sinaloensis
 W Mexico

C. c. saturatus
 Cozumel I, SE Mexico
C. c. superbus
 SW USA, NW Mexico
C. c. townsendi
 Tiburon I, NW Mexico
C. c. affinis
 WC Mexico
C. c. mariae
 Tres Marias Is
C. c. carneus
 W & S Mexico
C. c. seftoni
 C Baja California
C. c. igneus
 S Baja California
C. c. dintoni
 Cerralvo I

PYRRHULOXIA
Pyrrhuloxia phoeniceus (Vermilion Cardinal)
 Colombia, Venezuela
Pyrrhuloxia sinuatus (Pyrrhuloxia)
P. s. sinuatus
 S USA, N & C Mexico
P. s. fulvescens
 S Arizona, NW Mexico
P. s. peninsulae
 Baja California

CARYOTHRAUSTES
Caryothraustes canadensis (Yellow-green Grosbeak)
C. c. canadensis
 Colombia, Venezuela, the Guianas, Brazil
C. c. frontalis
 NE Brazil
C. c. brasiliensis
 EC Brazil
Caryothraustes poliogaster (Black-faced Grosbeak)
C. p. poliogaster
 SE Mexico, Guatemala, Honduras
C. p. scapularis
 Nicaragua, Costa Rica, W Panama
C. p. simulans
 E Panama
Caryothraustes humeralis (Yellow-shouldered Grosbeak)
 Colombia, Ecuador, Brazil

RHODOTHRAUPIS
Rhodothraupis celaeno (Crimson-collared Grosbeak)
 NE Mexico

PERIPORPHYRUS
Periporphyrus erythromelas (Red & Black Grosbeak)
Venezuela, Guyana, French Guiana, Brazil

PITYLUS
Pitylus grossus (Slate-coloured Grosbeak)
P. g. saturatus
Nicaragua to Ecuador
P. g. grossus
Venezuela, Guyana, Brazil, W Colombia, W Ecuador, Peru, Bolivia
Pitylus fuliginosus (Black-throated Grosbeak)
Brazil, Paraguay, N Argentina

SALTATOR
Saltator atriceps (Black-headed Saltator)
S. a. atriceps
E Mexico, Guatemala, Honduras, Costa Rica
S. a. suffuscus
SE Vera Cruz, Mexico
S. a. flavicrissus
Guerrero, Mexico
S. a. peeti
S Mexico
S. a. raptor
SE Mexico
S. a. lacertosus
W Costa Rica, Panama
Saltator maximus (Buff-throated Saltator)
S. m. gigantodes
E & S Mexico
S. m. magnoides
S Mexico to Panama
S. m. intermedius
SW Costa Rica, NW Panama
S. m. iungens
E Panama, NW Colombia
S. m. maximus
Colombia, Venezuela, the Guianas, Ecuador, Peru, Bolivia, Paraguay
Saltator atripennis (Black-winged Saltator)
S. a. atripennis
Colombia, NW Ecuador
S. a. caniceps
Colombia, W Ecuador
Saltator similis (Green-winged Saltator)
S. s. similis
Brazil, Bolivia, Paraguay, Uruguay, Argentina
S. s. ochraceiventris
SE Brazil
Saltator coerulescens (Greyish Saltator)
S. c. vigorsii
NW Mexico

S. c. richardsoni
WC Mexico
S. c. grandis
E Mexico, Guatemala, Honduras Nicaragua, Costa Rica
S. c. yucatanensis
SE Mexico
S. c. hesperis
Guatemala, El Salvador, Honduras, Nicaragua
S. c. brevicaudus
W Costa Rica
S. c. plumbeus
N Colombia
S. c. brewsteri
NE Colombia, Venezuela, Trinidad
S. c. olivascens
Venezuela, the Guianas, N Brazil
S. c. azarae
E Colombia, Ecuador, E Peru, Bolivia, Brazil
S. c. mutus
N Brazil
S. c. superciliaris
NE Brazil
S. c. coerulescens
E Bolivia, SW Brazil, Paraguay, N Argentina
Saltator orenocensis (Orinocan Saltator)
S. o. rufescens
NE Colombia, NW Venezuela
S. o. orenocensis
Venezuela
Saltator maxillosus (Thick-billed Saltator)
SE Brazil, Paraguay, N Argentina
Saltator aurantiirostris (Golden-billed Saltator)
S. a. iteratus
N Peru
S. a. albociliaris
Peru, N Chile
S. a. hellmayri
Bolivia
S. a. aurantiirostris
Bolivia, N Argentina, Paraguay, Uruguay, S Brazil
S. a. nasica
W Argentina
Saltator cinctus (Masked Saltator)
E Ecuador
Saltator atricollis (Black-throated) Saltator)
E Bolivia, Paraguay, S Brazil
Saltator rufiventris (Rufous-bellied Saltator)
Bolivia,

558　**Saltator albicollis (Streaked Saltator)**
　　S. a. albicollis
　　　Martinique I, St Lucia I
　　S. a. guadelupensis
　　　Guadeloupe I, Dominica I
　　S. a. furax
　　　SW Costa Rica, Panama
　　S. a. isthmicus
　　　W Panama
　　S. a. scotinus
　　　Coiba I (Panama)
　　S. a. melicus
　　　Taboga I (Panama)
　　S. a. speratus
　　　Pearl I (Panama)
　　S. a. striatipectus
　　　E Panama, W Colombia
　　S. a. perstriatus
　　　NE Colombia, Venezuela, Trinidad
　　S. a. flavidicollis
　　　SW Colombia, Ecuador, NW Peru
　　S. a. immaculatus
　　　W Peru
　　S. a. peruvianus
　　　N Peru

CYANOLOXIA
Cyanoloxia glaucocaerulea (Indigo Grosbeak)
　　S Brazil, Uruguay, N Argentina

CYANOCOMPSA
Cyanocompsa cyanoides (Blue-black Grosbeak)
　　C. c. concreta
　　　SE Mexico, Guatemala, Honduras
　　C. c. toddi
　　　Nicaragua, Costa Rica, W Panama
　　C. c. cyanoides
　　　E Panama, Colombia, W Venezuela, Ecuador
　　C. c. rothschildii
　　　Upper Amazonia, W Brazil
Cyanocompsa brissonii (Ultramarine Grosbeak)
　　C. b. caucae
　　　W Colombia
　　C. b. minor
　　　N Venezuela
　　C. b. brissonii
　　　NE Brazil
　　C. b. sterea
　　　E & S Brazil, NE Argentina, W Paraguay
　　C. b. argentina
　　　W Brazil, E Bolivia, Paraguay, N Argentina
Cyanocompsa parellina (Blue Bunting)
　　C. p. beneplacita
　　　NE Mexico

　　C. p. indigotica
　　　W & SW Mexico
　　C. p. lucida
　　　NE Mexico
　　C. p. parellina
　　　E & S Mexico to Nicaragua

GUIRACA
Guiraca caerulea (Blue Grosbeak)
　　G. c. caerulea
　　　SE USA » E Mexico & Central America
　　G. c. interfusa
　　　SW USA » W Mexico, Guatemala, Honduras
　　G. c. salicaria
　　　SW USA » W Mexico, Baja California
　　G. c. eurhyncha
　　　C & S Mexico
　　G. c. chiapensis
　　　S Mexico
　　G. c. deltarhyncha
　　　W coast of Mexico
　　G. c. lazula
　　　Honduras, Nicaragua, Costa Rica

PASSERINA
Passerina cyanea (Indigo Bunting)
　　S Canada, E USA » Central America, Cuba, Jamaica, Colombia, Venezuela
Passerina amoena (Lazuli Bunting)
　　W USA » W Mexico, Baja California
Passerina versicolor (Varied Bunting)
　　P. v. versicolor
　　　S USA, C & S Mexico
　　P. v. dickeyae
　　　S Arizona, W Mexico
　　P. v. pulchra
　　　S Baja California, NW Mexico
　　P. v. purpurascens
　　　S Mexico, Guatemala
Passerina ciris (Painted Bunting)
　　P. c. ciris
　　　SE USA » SE Mexico, Bahama Is
　　P. c. pallidior
　　　S USA » Mexico, Central America
Passerina rositae (Rose-bellied Bunting)
　　S Mexico
Passerina leclancherii (Orange-breasted Bunting)
　　P. l. grandior
　　　Oaxaca (Mexico)
　　P. l. leclancherii
　　　SW Mexico

PORPHYROSPIZA
Porphyrospiza caerulescens (Blue Finch)
　　Brazil, SE Bolivia

EMBERIZIDAE
157 THRAUPINAE (TANAGERS)

ORCHESTICUS
Orchesticus abeillei (Brown Tanager)
SE Brazil

SCHISTOCLAMYS
Schistoclamys ruficapillus (Cinnamon Tanager)
S. r. capistrata
NE Brazil
S. r. sicki
E Mato Grosso (Brazil)
S. r. ruficapillus
SE Brazil
Schistoclamys melanopis (Black-faced Tanager)
S. m. aterrima
NE Colombia, Venezuela, W Guyana
S. m. melanopis
the Guianas, NE Brazil
S. m. grisea
EC Peru
S. m. olivina
E Bolivia, SC Brazil
S. m. amazonica
SE Brazil

NEOTHRAUPIS
Neothraupis fasciata (White-banded Tanager)
E & S Brazil, E Bolivia, NE Paraguay

CYPSNAGRA
Cypsnagra hirundinacea (White-rumped Tanager)
C. h. pallidigula
C Brazil, NE Bolivia
C. h. hirundinacea
S Brazil, E Bolivia, NE Paraguay

CONOTHRAUPIS
Conothraupis speculigera (Black & White Tanager)
S Ecuador, N & E Peru
Conothraupis mesoleuca (Cone-billed Tanager)
Mato Grosso (Brazil)

LAMPROSPIZA
Lamprospiza melanoleuca (Red-billed Pied Tanager)
the Guianas, N Brazil, SE Peru, N Bolivia

CISSOPIS
Cissopis leveriana (MagpieTanager)
C. l. leveriana
Upper Amazonia
C. l. major
Paraguay, SE Brazil, N Argentina

CHLORORNIS 559
Chlorornis riefferii (Grass-green Tanager)
C. r. riefferii
Colombia, Ecuador
C. r. diluta
N Peru
C. r. elegans
C Peru
C. r. celata
SE Peru
C. r. boliviana
W Bolivia

COMPSOTHRAUPIS
Compsothraupis loricata (Scarlet-throated Tanager)
E Brazil

SERICOSSYPHA
Sericossypha albocristata (White-capped Tanager)
SW Venezuela, Colombia, Ecuador, E Peru

NESOSPINGUS
Nesospingus speculiferus (Puerto Rican Tanager)
Puerto Rica

CHLOROSPINGUS
Chlorospingus ophthalmicus (Common Bush Tanager)
C. o. albifrons
SW Mexico
C. o. wetmorei
E Mexico
C. o. persimilis
S Oaxaca
C. o. ophthalmicus
SE Mexico
C. o. dwighti
S Mexico, E Guatemala
C. o. postocularis
S Mexico, W Guatemala
C. o. honduratius
El Salvador, Honduras
C. o. regionalis
Nicaragua, E Costa Rica
C. o. novicius
SW Costa Rica, W Panama
C. o. jaqueti
NE Colombia, N Venezuela
C. o. falconensis
NW Venezuela
C. o. venezuelanus
SW Venezuela
C. o. ponsi
W Venezuela
C. o. eminens
NE Colombia

C. o. flavopectus
C Colombia
C. o. macarenae
E Colombia
C. o. nigriceps
C Colombia
C. o. phaeocephalus
Ecuador
C. o. cinereocephalus
C Peru
C. o. hiaticolus
C Peru
C. o. peruvianus
S Peru
C. o. bolivianus
WC Bolivia
C. o. fulvigularis
C Bolivia
C. o. argentinus
C Bolivia, N Argentina
Chlorospingus tacarcunae (Tacarcuna Bush Tanager)
E Panama
Chlorospingus inornatus (Pirre Bush Tanager)
E Panama
Chlorospingus punctulatus (Dotted Bush Tanager)
W Panama
Chlorospingus semifuscus (Dusky-bellied Bush Tanager)
C. s. livingstoni
W Colombia
C. s. semifuscus
SW Colombia, W Ecuador
Chlorospingus zeledoni (Zeledon's Bush Tanager)
Costa Rica
Chlorospingus pileatus (Pileated Bush Tanager)
C. p. pileatus
Costa Rica, W Panama
C. p. diversus
W Panama
Chlorospingus parvirostris (Short-billed Bush Tanager)
C. p. huallagae
S Colombia, Peru
C. p. medianus
EC Peru
C. p. parvirostris
SE Peru, W Bolivia
Chlorospingus flavigularis (Yellow-throated Bush Tanager)
C. f. hypophaeus
W Panama
C. f. marginatus
SW Colombia, W Ecuador
C. f. flavigularis
S Colombia, E Ecuador, E Peru

Chlorospingus flavovirens (Yellow-green Bush Tanager)
W Ecuador
Chlorospingus canigularis (Ash-throated Bush Tanager)
C. c. olivaceiceps
W Costa Rica
C. c. canigularis
C Colombia, SW Venezuela
C. c. conspicillatus
W Colombia
C. c. paulus
SW Ecuador
C. c. signatus
E Ecuador, NW Peru

CNEMOSCOPUS
Cnemoscopus rubrirostris (Grey-hooded Bush Tanager)
C. r. rubrirostris
SW Venezuela, Colombia, E Ecuador
C. r. chrysogaster
N & C Peru

HEMISPINGUS
Hemispingus atropileus (Black-capped Hemispingus)
H. a. atropileus
SW Venezuela, Colombia, Ecuador
H. a. auricularis
E Peru
Hemispingus calophrys (Yungas Hemispingus)
W Bolivia
Hemispingus parodii (Parodi's Tanager)
Cuzco, Peru
Hemispingus superciliaris (Superciliaried Hemispingus)
H. s. chrysophrys
SW Venezuela
H. s. superciliaris
C Colombia
H. s. nigrifrons
Colombia, Ecuador
H. s. maculifrons
SW Ecuador, NW Peru
H. s. insignis
N Peru
H. s. leucogaster
C Peru
H. s. urubambae
S Peru, W Bolivia
Hemispingus reyi (Grey-capped Hemispingus)
SW Venezuela
Hemispingus frontalis (Oleaginous Hemispingus)
H. f. frontalis
Colombia, E Ecuador, E Peru

H. f. ignobilis
  W Venezuela
H. f. flavidorsalis
  W Venezuela
H. f. hanieli
  N Venezuela
H. f. iteratus
  NE Venezuela
Hemispingus melanotis (Black-eared Hemispingus)
H. m. melanotis
  SW Venezuela, C & E Colombia,
  E Ecuador
H. m. ochraceus
  SW Colombia, W Ecuador
H. m. piurae
  NW Peru
H. m. macrophrys
  W Peru
H. m. berlepschi
  C Peru
H. m. castaneicollis
  SE Peru, W Bolivia
Hemispingus goeringi (Slaty-backed Hemispingus)
  SW Venezuela
Hemispingus rufosuperciliaris (Rufous-browed Hemispingus)
  C Peru
Hemispingus verticalis (Black-headed Hemispingus)
  S & C Colombia, E Ecuador
Hemispingus xanthophthalmus (Drab Hemispingus)
  C Peru
Hemispingus trifasciatus (Three-striped Hemispingus)
  SE Peru, W Bolivia

PYRRHOCOMA
Pyrrhocoma ruficeps (Chestnut-headed Tanager)
  SE Brazil, E Paraguay, N Argentina

THLYPOPSIS
Thlypopsis fulviceps (Fulvous-headed Tanager)
T. f. fulviceps
  NE Colombia, NW Venezuela
T. f. obscuriceps
  W Venezuela
T. f. meridensis
  W Venezuela
T. f. intensa
  NE Colombia
Thlypopsis ornata (Rufous-chested Tanager)
T. o. ornata
  SW Colombia, W Ecuador

T. o. media
  S Ecuador, N & C Peru
T. o. macropteryx
  C & S Peru
Thlypopsis pectoralis (Brown-flanked Tanager)
  C Peru
Thlypopsis sordida (Orange-headed Tanager)
T. s. orinocensis
  EC Venezuela
T. s. chrysopis
  E Ecuador, E Peru, W Brazil
T. s. sordida
  E & S Brazil, E Bolivia, Paraguay,
  N Argentina
Thlypopsis inornata (Buff-bellied Tanager)
  N Peru
Thlypopsis ruficeps (Rust and Yellow Tanager)
  SE Peru, NW Argentina

HEMITHRAUPIS
Hemithraupis guira (Guira Tanager)
H. g. nigrigula
  NC Colombia to NE Brazil
H. g. roraimae
  SE Venezuela, Guyana
H. g. guirina
  W Colombia to NW Peru
H. g. huambina
  SE Colombia to NE Peru, W Brazil
H. g. boliviana
  NE Bolivia, NW Argentina
H. g. amazonica
  C Brazil
H. g. guira
  E Brazil
H. g. fosteri
  SE Brazil, Paraguay, NE Argentina
Hemithraupis ruficapilla (Rufous-headed Tanager)
H. r. ruficapilla
  SE Brazil
H. r. bahiae
  E Brazil
Hemithraupis flavicollis (Yellow-backed Tanager)
H. f. ornata
  E Panama, NW Colombia
H. f. albigularis
  Colombia
H. f. peruana
  SC Colombia to NE Peru
H. f. sororia
  N Peru
H. f. centralis
  SE Peru, N Bolivia, C Brazil

H. f. aurigularis
SE Colombia, S Venezuela,N Brazil
H. f. hellmayri
SE Venezuela, W Guyana
H. f. flavicollis
Surinam, French Guiana,NE Brazil
H. f. obidensis
N Brazil
H. f. melanoxantha
E Brazil
H. f. insignis
SE Brazil

CHRYSOTHLYPIS
Chrysothlypis chrysomelas (Black & Yellow Tanager)
C. c. chrysomelas
E Costa Rica, W Panama
C. c. ocularis
E Panama
Chrysothlypis salmoni (Scarlet & White Tanager)
W Colombia, NW Ecuador

NEMOSIA
Nemosia pileata (Hooded Tanager)
N. p. hypoleuca
N Colombia, N Venezuela
N. p. surinamensis
Guyana, Surinam
N. p. pileata
French Guiana, Brazil, N Bolivia
N. p. interna
N Brazil
N. p. nana
NE Peru, W Brazil
N. p. caerulea
S & E Brazil, E Bolivia, Paraguay,
N Argentina
Nemosia rourei (Cherry-throated Tanager)
SE Brazil

PHAENICOPHILUS
Phaenicophilus palmarum (Black-crowned Palm Tanager)
Hispaniola, Saona I
Phaenicophilus poliocephalus (Grey-crowned Palm Tanager)
P. p. poliocephalus
S Haiti
P. p. coryi
Gonave I

CALYPTOPHILUS
Calyptophilus frugivorus (Chat-Tanager)
C. f. frugivorus
Dominica I
C. f. tertius
S Haiti

C. f. abbotti
Gonave I

RHODINOCICHLA
Rhodinocichla rosea (Rose-breasted Thrush Tanager)
R. r. schistacea
W Mexico
R. r. eximia
SW Costa Rica, W Panama
R. r. harterti
C Colombia
R. r. beebei
NE Colombia, NW Venezuela
R. r. rosea
NW Venezuela

MITROSPINGUS
Mitrospingus cassinii (Dusky-faced Tanager)
M. c. costaricensis
E Costa Rica, W Panama
M. c. cassinii
E Panama, W Colombia, W Ecuador
Mitrospingus oleagineus (Olive-backed Tanager)
M. o. obscuripectus
SE Venezuela, N Brazil
M. o. oleagineus
SE Venezuela, Guyana

CHLOROTHRAUPIS
Chlorothraupis carmioli (Carmiol's Tanager)
C. c. carmioli
Nicaragua to NW Panama
C. c. magnirostris
W Panama
C. c. lutescens
E Panama, NW Colombia
C. c. frenata
S Colombia, SE Peru
Chlorothraupis olivacea (Lemon-browed Tanager)
E Panama to NW Ecuador
Chlorothraupis stolzmanni (Ochre-breasted Tanager)
C. s. dugandi
SW Colombia
C. s. stolzmanni
W Ecuador

ORTHOGONYS
Orthogonys chloricterus (Olive-green Tanager)
SE Brazil

EUCOMETIS
Eucometis penicillata (Grey-headed Tanager)
E. p. pallida
SE Mexico to E Guatemala

E. p. spodocephala
  Nicaragua, W Costa Rica
E. p. stictothorax
  SW Costa Rica, W Panama
E. p. cristata
  E Panama to W Venezuela
E. p. affinis
  N Venezuela
E. p. penicillata
  SE Colombia, E Ecuador, E Peru, the
  Guianas, N Brazil
E. p. albicollis
  E Bolivia, SC Brazil, N Paraguay

LANIO
Lanio fulvus (Fulvous Shrike-Tanager)
L. f. peruvianus
  S Colombia to NE Peru
L. f. fulvus
  S Venezuela, the Guianas, N Brazil
Lanio versicolor (White-winged Shrike-Tanager)
L. v. versicolor
  E Peru, N Bolivia, W Brazil
L. v. parvus
  S Brazil
Lanio aurantius (Black-throated Shrike-Tanager)
  SE Mexico to Honduras
Lanio leucothorax (White-throated Shrike-Tanager)
L. l. leucothorax
  E Honduras to E Costa Rica
L. l. reversus
  NW Costa Rica
L. l. melanopygius
  SW Costa Rica, W Panama
L. l. ictus
  NW Panama

CREURGOPS
Creurgops verticalis (Rufous-crested Tanager)
  SW Venezuela to Peru
Creurgops dentata (Slaty Tanager)
  SE Peru, N Bolivia

HETEROSPINGUS
Heterospingus xanthopygius (Scarlet-browed Tanager)
H. x. rubrifrons
  E Costa Rica, Panama
H. x. xanthopygius
  E Panama, N Colombia
H. x. berliozi
  W Colombia, NW Ecuador

Tachyphonus cristatus (Flame-crested Tanager)
T. c. cristatus
  French Guiana, NE Brazil
T. c. intercedens
  E Venezuela, Guyana, Surinam
T. c. orinocensis
  E Colombia, S Venezuela
T. c. cristatellus
  S Venezuela to N Peru
T. c. fallax
  S Colombia to NE Peru
T. c. huarandosae
  N Peru
T. c. madeirae
  C Brazil
T. c. pallidigula
  NE Brazil
T. c. brunneus
  E Brazil
T. c. nattereri
  SW Brazil
Tachyphonus rufiventer (Yellow-crested Tanager)
  E Peru, N Bolivia, W Brazil
Tachyphonus surinamus (Fulvous-crested Tanager)
T. s. surinamus
  E & S Venezuela, the Guianas, N Brazil
T. s. brevipes
  S Venezuela to NE Peru
T. s. napensis
  E Peru, NW Brazil
T. s. insignis
  N Brazil
Tachyphonus luctuosus (White-shouldered Tanager)
T. l. axillaris
  E Honduras to W Panama
T. l. nitidissimus
  SW Costa Rica, W Panama
T. l. panamensis
  E Panama to W Ecuador, W Venezuela
T. l. luctuosus
  tropical South America
T. l. flaviventris
  NE Venezuela, Trinidad
Tachyphonus delatrii (Tawny-crested Tanager)
  Nicaragua to W Ecuador
Tachyphonus coronatus (Ruby-crowned Tanager)
  SE Brazil to NW Argentina
Tachyphonus rufus (White-lined Tanager)
  Costa Rica, Panama, N South America

Tachyphonus phoenicius (Red-shouldered Tanager)
N South America

TRICHOTHRAUPIS
Trichothraupis melanops (Black-goggled Tanager)
SW Amazonia

HABIA
Habia rubica (Red-crowned Ant-Tanager)
H. r. holobrunnea
E Mexico
H. r. rosea
SW Mexico
H. r. affinis
S Mexico
H. r. nelsoni
SE Mexico
H. r. rubicoides
S Mexico to El Salvador
H. r. vinacea
W Costa Rica, W Panama
H. r. alfaroana
NW Costa Rica
H. r. rubra
Trinidad
H. r. crissalis
NE Venezuela
H. r. mesopotamia
E Bolivar (Venezuela)
H. r. perijana
NE Colombia, NW Venezuela
H. r. coccinea
NC Colombia, W Venezuela
H. r. rhodinolaema
SE Colombia to NE Peru, NW Brazil
H. r. peruviana
E Peru, NC Bolivia
H. r. hesterna
C Brazil
H. r. bahiae
E Brazil
H. r. rubica
SE Brazil, Paraguay, N Argentina
Habia fuscicauda (Red-throated Ant-Tanager)
H. f. salvini
SE Mexico to El Salvador
H. f. insularis
SE Mexico, N Guatemala
H. f. discolor
Nicaragua
H. f. fuscicauda
S Nicaragua to W Panama
H. f. willisi
C Panama
H. f. erythrolaema
N Colombia

Habia atrimaxillaris (Black-cheeked Ant-Tanager)
SW Costa Rica
Habia gutturalis (Sooty Ant-Tanager)
NW Colombia
Habia cristata (Crested Ant-Tanager)
W Colombia

PIRANGA
Piranga bidentata (Flame-coloured Tanager)
P. b. bidentata
W Mexico
P. b. alvarezi
S Mexico
P. b. flammea
Tres Marias Is
P. b. sanguinolenta
E Mexico to El Salvador
P. b. citrea
Costa Rica, W Panama
Piranga flava (Hepatic Tanager)
P. f. hepatica
SW USA, W Mexico
P. f. intensa
SW Oaxaca
P. f. dextra
SW USA, E Mexico » W Guatemala
P. f. figlina
E Guatemala, Belize
P. f. savannarum
Honduras, NE Nicaragua
P. f. albifacies
W Guatemala to N Nicaragua
P. f. testacea
Costa Rica, Panama
P. f. desidiosa
SW Colombia
P. f. lutea
W Ecuador to NW Bolivia
P. f. haemalea
S Venezuela, W Guyana, N Brazil
P. f. faceta
N Colombia, N Venezuela, Trinidad
P. f. toddi
Magdelena (Colombia)
P. f. macconnelli
S Guyana, N Brazil
P. f. saira
E Brazil
P. f. rosacea
E Bolivia
P. f. flava
S Bolivia to Uruguay, N Argentina
Piranga rubra (Summer Tanager)
P. r. cooperi
SW USA » C Mexico
P. r. rubra
SE USA » Central & South America

P. r. ochracea
  Arizona & W Mexico
Piranga roseogularis (Rose-throated Tanager)
P. r. roseogularis
  SE Mexico
P. r. tincta
  SE Mexico, N Guatemala
P. r. cozumelae
  Cozumel I
Piranga olivacea (Scarlet Tanager)
  SE Canada, NE USA » NW South America
Piranga ludoviciana (Western Tanager)
  W North America » W Mexico, W Central America
Piranga leucoptera (White-winged Tanager)
P. l. leucoptera
  E Mexico to Nicaragua
P. l. latifasciata
  Costa Rica, W Panama
P. l. venezuelae
  Colombia, Venezuela, N Brazil
P. l. ardens
  SW Colombia to Bolivia
Piranga erythrocephala (Red-headed Tanager)
P. e. candida
  NW Mexico
P. e. erythrocephala
  SC & S Mexico
Piranga rubriceps (Red-hooded Tanager)
  W Colombia to N Peru

CALOCHAETES
Calochaetes coccineus (Vermilion Tanager)
  S Colombia to E Peru

RAMPHOCELUS
Ramphocelus sanguinolentus (Crimson-collared Tanager)
R. s. sanguinolentus
  SE Mexico to Honduras
R. s. apricus
  E Honduras to NW Panama
Ramphocelus nigrogularis (Masked Crimson Tanager)
  SE Colombia to E Peru, N Brazil
Ramphocelus dimidiatus (Crimson-backed Tanager)
R. d. isthmicus
  W & C Panama
R. d. arestus
  Coiba I
R. d. limatus
  Pearl Archipelago
R. d. dimidiatus
  E Panama, N Colombia, W Venezuela

R. d. molochinus
  N Colombia
Ramphocelus melanogaster (Black-bellied Tanager)
R. m. melanogaster
  N Peru
R. m. transitus
  EC Peru
Ramphocelus carbo (Silver-beaked Tanager)
R. c. unicolor
  E Colombia
R. c. capitalis
  NE Venezuela
R. c. magnirostris
  Trinidad
R. c. carbo
  E Peru to Surinam
R. c. venezuelensis
  E Colombia, W Venezuela
R. c. connectens
  SE Peru, NW Bolivia
R. c. atrosericeus
  N & E Bolivia
R. c. centralis
  EC Brazil, N Paraguay
Ramphocelus bresilius (Brazilian Tanager)
R. b. bresilius
  NE Brazil
R. b. dorsalis
  SE Brazil
Ramphocelus passerinii (Scarlet-rumped Tanager)
R. p. passerinii
  SE Mexico to W Panama
R. p. costaricensis
  W Costa Rica
Ramphocelus flammigerus (Flame-rumped Tanager)
R. f. icteronotus
  Panama to W Ecuador
R. f. flammigerus
  W Colombia

SPINDALIS
Spindalis zena (Stripe-headed Tanager)
S. z. townsendi
  N Bahama Is
S. z. zena
  C Bahama Is
S. z. pretrei
  Cuba, Isle of Pines
S. z. salvini
  Grand Cayman I
S. z. benedicti
  Cozumel I
S. z. dominicensis
  Hispaniola

S. z. portoricensis
Puerto Rico
S. z. nigricephala
Jamaica

THRAUPIS
Thraupis episcopus (Blue-grey Tanager)
T. e. cana
SE Mexico to N Venezuela
T. e. caesitia
W Panama
T. e. cumatilis
Coiba I
T. e. nesophilus
E Colombia to Trinidad
T. e. berlepschi
Tobago I
T. e. mediana
SE Colombia, NW Brazil, N Bolivia
T. e. episcopus
the Guianas, N Brazil
T. e. leucoptera
C Colombia
T. e. quaesita
SW Colombia, W Ecuador, NW Peru
T. e. caerulea
SE Ecuador, N Peru
T. e. major
C Peru
T. e. urubambae
SE Peru
T. e. coelestis
SE Colombia to C Peru, W Brazil
Thraupis sayaca (Sayaca Tanager)
T. s. boliviana
NW Bolivia
T. s. obscura
C & S Bolivia, W Argentina
T. s. sayaca
E & S Brazil, Paraguay to Uruguay
T. s. glaucocolpa
N Colombia, Venezuela
Thraupis cyanoptera (Azure-shouldered Tanager)
E Paraguay, SE Brazil
Thraupis ornata (Golden-chevroned Tanager)
SE Brazil
Thraupis abbas (Yellow-winged Tanager)
E Mexico to Nicaragua
Thraupis palmarum (Palm Tanager)
T. p. atripennis
E Nicaragua to NW Venezuela
T. p. violilavata
SW Colombia, W Ecuador
T. p. melanoptera
Amazonia, Trinidad
T. p. palmarum
E Bolivia, Paraguay, E & S Brazil

Thraupis cyanocephala (Blue-capped Tanager)
T. c. cyanocephala
W Ecuador to N Bolivia
T. c. annectens
C Colombia
T. c. auricrissa
NC Colombia, W Venezuela
T. c. margaritae
N Colombia
T. c. hypophaea
NW Venezuela
T. c. olivicynanea
N Venezuela
T. c. subcinerea
NE Venezuela
T. c. buesingi
NE Venezuela, Trinidad
Thraupis bonariensis (Blue & Yellow Tanager)
T. b. darwinii
Ecuador to N Chile
T. b. composita
E & C Bolivia
T. b. schulzei
Paraguay, NW Argentina
T. b. bonariensis
S Brazil to EC Argentina

CYANICTERUS
Cyanicterus cyanicterus (Blue-backed Tanager)
E Venezuela, the Guianas

BUTHRAUPIS
Buthraupis arcaei (Arce's Tanager)
B. a. caeruleigularis
E Costa Rica
B. a. arcaei
W Panama
Buthraupis melanochlamys (Black & Gold Tanager)
W Colombia
Buthraupis rothschildi (Golden-chested Tanager)
SW Colombia, NW Ecuador
Buthraupis edwardsi (Moss-backed Tanager)
SW Colombia, NW Ecuador
Buthraupis aureocincta (Gold-ringed Tanager)
W Colombia
Buthraupis montana (Hooded Mountain Tanager)
B. m. gigas
NC Colombia, Venezuela
B. m. cucullata
W Colombia, Ecuador

B. m. cyanonota
N & C Peru
B. m. saturata
SE Peru
B. m. montana
N Bolivia
Buthraupis eximia (Black-chested Mountain Tanager)
B. e. eximia
NC Colombia, SW Venezuela
B. e. zimmeri
WC Colombia
B. e. chloronota
SE Colombia, NW Ecuador
B. e. cyanocalyptra
SC Ecuador
Buthraupis aureodorsalis (Golden-backed Mountain Tanager)
C Peru
Buthraupis wetmorei (Masked Mountain Tanager)
SW Colombia, SC Ecuador

WETMORETHRAUPIS
Wetmorethraupis sterrhopteron (Orange-throated Tanager)
N Peru

ANISOGNATHUS
Anisognathus lacrymosus (Lacrimose Mountain Tanager)
A. l. melanogenys
N Colombia
A. l. pallididorsalis
E Colombia, Venezuela
A. l. melanops
W Venezuela
A. l. tamae
NC Colombia, SW Venezuela
A. l. intensus
SW Colombia
A. l. olivaceiceps
W Colombia
A. l. palpebrosus
SW Colombia, E Ecuador
A. l. caerulescens
S Ecuador, N Peru
A. l. lacrymosus
C Peru
Anisognathus igniventris (Scarlet-bellied Mountain Tanager)
A. i. lunulatus
NC Colombia, W Venezuela
A. i. erythrotus
S Colombia, Ecuador
A. i. ignicrissus
NC Peru
A. i. igniventris
SE Peru, Bolivia

Anisognathus flavinuchus (Blue-winged   567
Mountain Tanager)
A. f. venezuelanus
N Venezuela
A. f. virididorsalis
Venezuela
A. f. antioquiae
Colombia
A. f. victorini
C Colombia, SW Venezuela
A. f. cyanopterus
SW Colombia, W Ecuador
A. f. baezae
S Colombia, E Ecuador
A. f. alamoris
SW Ecuador
A. f. somptuosus
SE Ecuador, E Peru
A. f. flavinuchus
SE Peru, Bolivia
Anisognathus notabilis (Black-chinned Mountain Tanager)
SW Colombia, NW Ecuador

STEPHANOPHORUS
Stephanophorus diadematus (Diademed Tanager)
SE Brazil, N Argentina

IRIDOSORNIS
Iridosornis porphyrocephala (Purplish-mantled Tanager)
W Colombia, W Ecuador
Iridosornis analis (Yellow-throated Tanager)
E Ecuador, E Peru
Iridosornis jelskii (Golden-collared Tanager)
I. j. jelskii
Peru
I. j. bolivianus
SE Peru, W Bolivia
Iridosornis rufivertex (Golden-crowned Tanager)
I. r. rufivertex
W Venezuela to E Ecuador
I. r. caeruleoventris
NW Colombia
I. r. ignicapillus
SW Colombia
I. r. subsimilis
W Ecuador
Iridosornis reinhardti (Yellow-scarfed Tanager)
E Peru

Dubusia taeniata (Buff-breasted
Mountain Tanager)
D. t. carrikeri
N Colombia
D. t. taeniata
W Venezuela to Ecuador
D. t. stictocephala
SE Peru

DELOTHRAUPIS
Delothraupis castaneoventris (Chestnut-
bellied Mountain Tanager)
D. c. peruviana
E Peru
D. c. castaneoventris
W Bolivia

PIPRAEIDEA
Pipraeidea melanonota (Fawn-breasted
Tanager)
P. m. venezuelensis
Venezuela to W Bolivia, N Argentina
P. m. melanonota
Paraguay, SE Brazil to NE Argentina

EUPHONIA
Euphonia jamaica (Jamaican Euphonia)
Jamaica
Euphonia plumbea (Plumbeous Euphonia)
S Venezuela to Surinam, N Brazil
Euphonia affinis (Scrub Euphonia)
E. a. godmani
W Mexico
E. a. affinis
E Mexico to Costa Rica
Euphonia luteicapilla (Yellow-crowned
Euphonia)
E Nicaragua to Panama
Euphonia chlorotica (Purple-throated
Euphonia)
E. c. cynophora
E Colombia, S Venezuela, N Brazil
E. c. chlorotica
the Guianas, N & NE Brazil
E. c. serrirostris
SE Bolivia to Uruguay, S Brazil
E. c. taczanowskii
E Peru, N Bolivia
E. c. amazonica
C Brazil
Euphonia trinitatis (Trinidad Euphonia)
N Colombia to Trinidad
Euphonia concinna (Velvet-fronted
Euphonia)
C Colombia
Euphonia saturata (Orange-crowned
Euphonia)
W Colombia to NW Peru

Euphonia finschi (Finsch's Euphonia)
E Venezuela, the Guianas
Euphonia violacea (Violaceous Euphonia)
E. v. rodwayi
E Venezuela, Trinidad
E. v. violacea
the Guianas, N Brazil
E. v. aurantiicollis
SE Brazil, Paraguay
Euphonia laniirostris (Thick-billed
Euphonia)
E. l. crassirostris
Costa Rica to N Venezuela
E. l. melanura
Colombia to N Peru, W Brazil
E. l. hypoxantha
E Ecuador, NW Peru
E. l. zopholega
EC Peru
E. l. laniirostris
E Bolivia, SW Brazil
Euphonia hirundinacea (Yellow-throated
Euphonia)
E. h. suttoni
E Mexico
E. h. russelli
SE Mexico
E. h. caribbaea
SE Mexico
E. h. hirundinacea
E Mexico to E Nicaragua
E. h. gnatho
NW Nicaragua to W Panama
Euphonia chalybea (Green-throated
Euphonia)
SE Brazil, Paraguay
Euphonia musica (Blue-hooded Euphonia)
E. m. rileyi
NW Mexico
E. m. elegantissima
C & S Mexico to Honduras
E. m. vincens
SE Guatemala to Panama
E. m. pelzelni
S Colombia, W Ecuador
E. m. insignis
S Ecuador
E. m. aureata
N South America
E. m. musica
Hispaniola
E. m. sclateri
Puerto Rico
E. m. flavifrons
Lesser Antilles

Euphonia fulvicrissa (Fulvous-vented Euphonia)
  E. f. fulvicrissa
    Panama, NW Colombia
  E. f. omissa
    C Colombia
  E. f. purpurascens
    SW Colombia, NW Ecuador
Euphonia imitans (Tawny-billed Euphonia)
  W Costa Rica, W Panama
Euphonia gouldi (Olive-backed Euphonia)
  E. g. loetscheri
    E Mexico
  E. g. gouldi
    SE Mexico to Honduras
  E. g. praetermissa
    E Honduras to Panama
Euphonia chrysopasta (Golden-bellied Euphonia)
  E. c. chrysopasta
    Western Amazonia
  E. c. nitida
    E Colombia to French Guiana, N Brazil
Euphonia mesochrysa (Bronze-green Euphonia)
  E. m. mesochrysa
    C Colombia, E Ecuador
  E. m. media
    N Peru
  E. m. tavarae
    SE Peru, C Bolivia
Euphonia minuta (White-vented Euphonia)
  E. m. humilis
    S Mexico to W Ecuador
  E. m. minuta
    the Guianas to C Bolivia, W Brazil
Euphonia anneae (Tawny-capped Euphonia)
  E. a. anneae
    W Costa Rica, W Panama
  E. a. rufivertex
    W Panama, NW Colombia
Euphonia xanthogaster (Orange-bellied Euphonia)
  E. x. chocoensis
    E Panama to NW Ecuador
  E. x. quitensis
    W Ecuador
  E. x. dilutior
    S Colombia, NE Peru
  E. x. cyanonota
    W Brazil
  E. x. brunneifrons
    SE Peru
  E. x. ruficeps
    W Bolivia
  E. x. brevirostris
    N & W Amazonia

  E. x. exsul
    NE Colombia, N Venezuela
  E. x. xanthogaster
    S & E Brazil
Euphonia rufiventris (Rufous-bellied Euphonia)
  Western Amazonia
Euphonia pectoralis (Chestnut-bellied Euphonia)
  SE Brazil, Paraguay
Euphonia cayennensis (Golden-sided Euphonia)
  SE Venezuela, the Guianas, N Brazil

CHLOROPHONIA
Chlorophonia flavirostris (Yellow-collared Chlorophonia)
  C. f. minima
    SW Colombia
  C. f. flavirostris
    Ecuador
Chlorophonia cyanea (Blue-naped Chlorophonia)
  C. c. psittacina
    N Colombia
  C. c. frontalis
    N Venezuela
  C. c. minuscula
    NE Venezuela
  C. c. roraimae
    S Venezuela, Guyana
  C. c. intensa
    W Colombia
  C. c. longipennis
    W Venezuela to W Bolivia
  C. c. cyanea
    SE Brazil, Paraguay, NE Argentina
Chlorophonia pyrrhophrys (Chestnut-breasted Chlorophonia)
  W Venezuela to E Ecuador
Chlorophonia occipitalis (Blue-crowned Chlorophonia)
  C. o. occipitalis
    SE Mexico to Nicaragua
  C. o. callophrys
    Costa Rica, W Panama

CHLOROCHRYSA
Chlorochrysa phoenicotis (Glistening-green Tanager)
  W Colombia, W Ecuador
Chlorochrysa calliparaea (Orange-eared Tanager)
  C. c. bourcierci
    Colombia to NE Peru
  C. c. calliparaea
    EC Peru
  C. c. fulgentissima
    SE Peru, N Bolivia

***Chlorochrysa nitidissima* (Multicoloured Tanager)**
  W Colombia

TANGARA
***Tangara inornata* (Plain-coloured Tanager)**
  T. i. rava
    Costa Rica, W Panama
  T. i. languens
    Panama, NW Colombia
  T. i. inornata
    N Colombia
***Tangara cabanisi* (Azure rumped Tanager)**
  S Mexico, SW Guatemala
***Tangara palmeri* (Grey and Gold Tanager)**
  E Panama to W Ecuador
***Tangara mexicana* (Turquoise Tanager)**
  T. m. vieilloti
    Trinidad
  T. m. media
    S & E Venezuela, NW Brazil
  T. m. mexicana
    the Guianas
  T. m. boliviana
    Western Amazonia
  T. m. brasiliensis
    SE Brazil
***Tangara chilensis* (Paradise Tanager)**
  T. c. paradisea
    the Guianas, N Brazil
  T. c. coelicolor
    E Colombia, S Venezuela
    NW Brazil
  T. c. chlorocorys
    NC Peru
  T. c. chilensis
    Western Amazonia
***Tangara fastuosa* (Seven-coloured Tanager)**
  E Brazil
***Tangara seledon* (Green-headed Tanager)**
  SE Brazil, Paraguay, N Argentina
***Tangara cyanocephala* (Red-necked Tanager)**
  T. c. cearensis
    NE Brazil
  T. c. corallina
    E Brazil
  T. c. cyanocephala
    SE Brazil, E Paraguay, N Argentina
***Tangara desmaresti* (Brassy-breasted Tanager)**
  SE Brazil
***Tangara cyanoventris* (Gilt-edged Tanager)**
  SE Brazil
***Tangara johannae* (Blue-whiskered Tanager)**
  W Colombia, NW Ecuador

***Tangara schrankii* (Green and Gold Tanager)**
  T. s. venezuelana
    S Venezuela
  T. s. anchicayae
    W Colombia
  T. s. schrankii
    Upper Amazonia
***Tangara florida* (Emerald Tanager)**
  T. f. florida
    Costa Rica, W Panama
  T. f. auriceps
    W Colombia, E Panama
***Tangara arthus* (Golden Tanager)**
  T. a. arthus
    N & E Venezuela
  T. a. palmitae
    Magdalena (E Colombia)
  T. a. sclateri
    E Colombia
  T. a. aurulenta
    C Colombia, NW Venezuela
  T. a. occidentalis
    W Colombia
  T. a. goodsoni
    W Ecuador
  T. a. aequatorialis
    E Ecuador, N Peru
  T. a. pulchra
    C Peru
  T. a. sophiae
    SE Peru, W Bolivia
***Tangara icterocephala* (Silver-throated Tanager)**
  T. i. frantzii
    Costa Rica, W Panama
  T. i. oresbia
    WC Panama
  T. i. icterocephala
    E Panama, W Colombia, W Ecuador
***Tangara xanthocephala* (Saffron-crowned Tanager)**
  T. x. venusta
    W Venezuela to N & C Peru
  T. x. xanthocephala
    C Peru
  T. x. lamprotis
    SE Peru
***Tangara chrysotis* (Golden-eared Tanager)**
  S Colombia to N Bolivia
***Tangara parzudakii* (Flame-faced Tanager)**
  T. p. parzudakii
    SW Venezuela to Peru
  T. p. urubambae
    S Peru
  T. p. lunigera
    W Colombia, W Ecuador

Tangara xanthogastra **(Yellow-bellied Tanager)**
T. x. xanthogastra
S Venezuela to N Bolivia
T. x. phelpsi
S Venezuela, N Brazil
Tangara punctata **(Spotted Tanager)**
T. p. punctata
S Venezuela, the Guianas, N Brazil
T. p. zamorae
E Ecuador, N Peru
T. p. perenensis
E Peru
T. p. annectens
SE Peru
T. p. punctulata
N Bolivia
Tangara guttata **(Speckled Tanager)**
T. g. eusticta
Costa Rica, W Panama
T. g. tolimae
Tolima (Colombia)
T. g. bogotensis
E Colombia, W Venezuela
T. g. chrysophrys
Venezuela, NW Brazil
T. g. guttata
SE Venezuela, N Brazil
T. g. trinitatis
N Trinidad
Tangara varia **(Dotted Tanager)**
S Venezuela, the Guianas, N Brazil
Tangara rufigula **(Rufous-throated Tanager)**
W Colombia, NW Ecuador
Tangara gyrola **(Bay-headed Tanager)**
T. g. bangsi
Costa Rica, W Panama
T. g. deleticia
E Panama, W Colombia
T. g. nupera
SW Colombia, W Ecuador
T. g. toddi
N Colombia, NW Venezuela
T. g. viridissima
Trinidad, NE Venezuela
T. g. catharinae
E Colombia, to C Bolivia
T. g. parva
S Venezuela to NE Peru, NW Brazil
T. g. gyrola
S Venezuela, the Guianas, N Brazil
T. g. albertinae
C Brazil
Tangara lavinia **(Rufous-winged Tanager)**
T. l. cara
E Guatemala to Costa Rica

T. l. dalmasi
W Panama
T. l. lavinia
E Panama to NW Ecuador
Tangara cayana **(Burnished Buff Tanager)**
T. c. fulvescens
C Colombia
T. c. cayana
the Guianas to E Peru, N Brazil
T. c. huberi
NE Brazil
T. c. flava
NE Brazil
T. c. sincipitalis
C Brazil
T. c. chloroptera
SE Brazil, Paraguay
T. c. margaritae
C Brazil
Tangara cucullata **(Hooded Tanager)**
T. c. versicolor
St Vincent I
T. c. cucullata
Grenada I
Tangara peruviana **(Black-backed Tanager)**
SE Brazil
Tangara preciosa **(Chestnut-backed Tanager)**
Paraguay to Uruguay, SE Brazil
Tangara vitriolina **(Scrub Tanager)**
W Colombia, NW Ecuador
Tangara rufigenis **(Rufous-cheeked Tanager)**
N Venezuela
Tangara ruficervix **(Golden-naped Tanager)**
T. r. ruficervix
Colombia
T. r. leucotis
W Ecuador
T. r. taylori
SE Colombia, E Ecuador
T. r. amabilis
N Peru
T. r. inca
S Peru
T. r. fulvicervix
N Bolivia
Tangara labradorides **(Metallic-green Tanager)**
T. l. labradorides
W Colombia, W Ecuador
T. l. chaupensis
NW Peru
Tangara cyanotis **(Blue-browed Tanager)**
T. c. lutleyi
S Colombia, Ecuador, E Peru
T. c. cyanotis
NW Bolivia

Tangara cyanicollis (Blue-necked Tanager)
  T. c. granadensis
    W Colombia
  T. c. caeruleocephala
    C Colombia to N Peru
  T. c. cyanicollis
    E Peru, E Bolivia
  T. c. cyanopygia
    W Ecuador
  T. c. hannahiae
    E Colombia, W Venezuela
  T. c. melanogaster
    C Brazil
  T. c. albotibialis
    Goias (Brazil)
Tangara larvata (Golden-masked Tanager)
  T. l. larvata
    S Mexico to N Costa Rica
  T. l. centralis
    E Costa Rica, W Panama
  T. l. franciscae
    W Costa Rica, W Panama
  T. l. fanny
    E Panama to NW Ecuador
Tangara nigrocincta (Masked Tanager)
  N & W Amazonia
Tangara dowii (Dow Tanager)
  T. d. dowii
    Costa Rica, W Panama
  T. d. fucosa
    E Panama
Tangara nigroviridis (Beryl-spangled Tanager)
  T. n. cyanescens
    NW Venezuela to W Ecuador
  T. n. consobrina
    C Colombia
  T. n. nigroviridis
    E Colombia, E Ecuador
  T. n. berlepschi
    E Peru, Bolivia
Tangara vassorii (Blue and Black Tanager)
  T. v. vassorii
    NW Venezuela to NW Peru
  T. v. branickii
    N Peru
  T. v. atrocoerulea
    S Peru, Bolivia
Tangara heinei (Black-capped Tanager)
  NW Venezuela to E Ecuador
Tangara viridicollis (Silvery Tanager)
  T. v. fulvigula
    S Ecuador, N Peru
  T. v. viridicollis
    C & S Peru

Tangara argyrofenges (Green-throated Tanager)
  T. a. caeruleigularis
    N Peru
  T. a. argyrofenges
    WC Bolivia
Tangara cyanoptera (Black-headed Tanager)
  T. c. whitelyi
    S Venezuela, Guyana
  T. c. cyanoptera
    N Colombia, N & W Venezuela
Tangara pulcherrima (Yellow-collared Tanager)
  T. p. pulcherrima
    Colombia to E Peru
  T. p. aureinucha
    W Ecuador
Tangara velia (Opal-rumped Tanager)
  T. v. velia
    the Guianas, N Brazil
  T. v. iridina
    NW Amazonia
  T. v. signata
    NE Brazil
  T. v. cyanomelaena
    SE Brazil
Tangara callophrys (Opal-crowned Tanager)
  SE Colombia to E Peru, W Brazil
DACNIS
Dacnis albiventris (White-bellied Dacnis)
  S Venezuela to NE Peru
Dacnis lineata (Black-faced Dacnis)
  D. l. egregia
    C Colombia
  D. l. aequatorialis
    W Ecuador
  D. l. lineata
    N & W Amazonia
Dacnis flaviventer (Yellow-bellied Dacnis)
  N & W Amazonia
Dacnis hartlaubi (Turquoise Dacnis)
  W Colombia
Dacnis nigripes (Black-legged Dacnis)
  SE Brazil
Dacnis venusta (Scarlet-thighed Dacnis)
  D. v. venusta
    Costa Rica, W Panama
  D. v. fuliginata
    E Panama to NW Ecuador
Dacnis cayana (Blue Dacnis)
  D. c. callaina
    W Costa Rica, W Panama
  D. c. ultramarina
    E Nicaragua to NW Colombia

D. c. napaea
N Colombia
D. c. baudoana
SW Colombia, W Ecuador
D. c. coerebicolor
C Colombia
D. c. cayana
E Colombia to French Guiana, N & C Brazil
D. c. glaucogularis
S Colombia to N & E Bolivia
D. c. paraguayensis
S & E Brazil, Paraguay, NE Argentina
Dacnis viguieri (Viridian Dacnis)
E Panama, NW Colombia
Dacnis berlepschi (Scarlet-breasted Dacnis)
SW Colombia, NW Ecuador

CHLOROPHANES
Chlorophanes spiza (Green Honeycreeper)
C. s. guatemalensis
S Mexico to Honduras
C. s. arguta
E Honduras to NW Colombia
C. s. exsul
SW Colombia, W Ecuador
C. s. subtropicalis
Colombia, W Venezuela
C. s. spiza
Venezuela, Trinidad, the Guianas, N Brazil
C. s. caerulescens
SE Colombia to Bolivia
C. s. axillaris
E Brazil

CYANERPES
Cyanerpes nitidus (Short-billed Honey-creeper)
C. n. nitidus
NW Amazonia
C. n. caquetae
SW Colombia
Cyanerpes lucidus (Shining Honeycreeper)
C. l. lucidus
S Mexico to N Nicaragua
C. l. isthmicus
Costa Rica to NW Colombia
Cyanerpes caeruleus (Purple Honey-creeper)
C. c. chocoanus
W Colombia, W Ecuador
C. c. caeruleus
Colombia to the Guianas, NE Brazil
C. c. hellmayri
Guyana
C. c. longirostris
Trinidad
C. c. microrhynchus
W & C Amazonia

Cyanerpes cyaneus (Red-legged Honey-creeper)   573
C. c. carneipes
E & S Mexico to N Colombia
C. c. striatipectus
W Chiapas (Mexico)
C. c. gemmeus
N Colombia
C. c. eximius
N Colombia, N Venezuela
C. c. tobagensis
Tobago I
C. c. cyaneus
SE Venezuela, Trinidad, the Guianas, N Brazil
C. c. brevipes
C Brazil
C. c. dispar
S Venezuela to NE Peru, W Brazil
C. c. holti
E Brazil
C. c. violaceus
C Bolivia, W Brazil
C. c. pacificus
W Colombia, W Ecuador
C. c. gigas
Gorgona I (W Colombia)

XENODACNIS
Xenodacnis parina (Tit-like Dacnis)
X. p. bella
N Peru
X. p. petersi
WC Peru
X. p. parina
SC Peru

OREOMANES
Oreomanes fraseri (Giant Conebill)
O. f. fraseri
SW Colombia, Ecuador
O. f. binghami
Peru
O. f. sturninus
W Bolivia

DIGLOSSA
Diglossa baritula (Slaty Flower-piercer)
D. b. baritula
C Mexico
D. b. montana
S Mexico to El Salvador
D. b. parva
E Guatemala, Honduras
D. b. plumbea
Costa Rica, W Panama
D. b. veraguensis
W Panama
D. b. hyperythra
NE Colombia, N Venezuela

D. b. mandeli
NE-Venezuela
D. b. coelestis
W Venezuela
D. b. dorbignyi
E Colombia, W Venezuela
D. b. decorata
Ecuador, Peru
D. b. sittoides
Bolivia, NW Argentina
Diglossa lafresnayii (Glossy Flower-piercer)
D. l. gloriosissima
W Colombia
D. l. lafresnayii
W Venezuela to Ecuador, N Peru
D. l. unicincta
N Peru
D. l. pectoralis
C Peru
D. l. albilinea
SE Peru
D. l. mystacalis
W Bolivia
Diglossa carbonaria Coal-black Flower-piercer)
D. c. gloriosa
W Venezuela
D. c. nocticolor
N Colombia, W Venezuela
D. c. humeralis
C Colombia, SW Venezuela
D. c. aterrima
W Colombia, Ecuador, NW Peru
D. c. vuilleumieri
NW Colombia, Ecuador
D. c. brunneiventris
NW Colombia to N Chile
D. c. carbonaria
Bolivia
Diglossa venezuelensis (Venezuelan Flowerpiercer)
NE Venezuela
Diglossa albilatera (White-sided Flower-piercer)
D. a. federalis
N Venezuela
D. a. albilatera
W Venezuela to Ecuador
D. a. schistacea
SW Ecuador to NW Peru
D. a. affinis
NC Peru
Diglossa duidae (Scaled Flowerpiercer)
D. d. hitchcocki
S Venezuela
D. d. duidae
S Venezuela, N Brazil

Diglossa major (Greater Flowerpiercer)
D. m. gilliardi
SE Venezuela
D. m. disjuncta
SE Venezuela
D. m. chimantae
SE Venezuela
D. m. major
SE Venezuela, N Brazil
Diglossa indigotica (Indigo Flower-piercer)
SW Colombia, W Ecuador
Diglossa glauca (Deep-blue Flower-piercer)
D. g. tyrianthina
S Colombia, E Ecuador
D. g. glauca
SE Peru, NW Bolivia
Diglossa caerulescens (Bluish Flower-piercer)
D. c. caerulescens
N Venezuela
D. c. ginesi
NW Venezuela
D. c. saturata
SW Venezuela, Colombia
D. c. media
S Ecuador, NW Peru
D. c. pallida
C Peru
D. c. mentalis
SE Peru, NW Bolivia
Diglossa cyanea (Masked Flowerpiercer)
D. c. tovarensis
N Venezuela
D. c. obscura
NW Venezuela
D. c. cyanea
W Venezuela, to Ecuador
D. c. dispar
SW Ecuador, NW Peru
D. c. melanopis
Peru, NW Bolivia

EUNEORNIS
Euneornis campestris (Orangequit)
Jamaica

EMBERIZIDAE

158 TERSININAE (SWALLOW TANAGER)

TERSINA
Tersina viridis (Swallow Tanager)
T. v. grisescens
N Colombia

T. v. occidentalis
E Panama, Colombia, Venezuela,
the Guianas, Ecuador, NE Peru,
N Bolivia, N Brazil
T. v. viridis
E & S Brazil, E Bolivia, Paraguay,
NE Argentina

159 PARULIDAE (NEW WORLD WARBLERS)

MNIOTILTA
Mniotilta varia (Black & White Warbler)
NW, C & SE Canada, C & E USA » Central
America, West Indies, Venezuela,
Colombia

VERMIVORA
Vermivora bachmanii (Bachman's Warbler)
C & SE USA » Cuba
Vermivora chrysoptera (Golden-winged Warbler)
E USA » Central America, Colombia,
Venezuela
Vermivora pinus (Blue-winged Warbler)
E USA » E Mexico, Central America
Vermivora peregrina (Tennessee Warbler)
NW, C & SE Canada, E USA » S Mexico,
Colombia, Venezuela
Vermivora celata (Orange-crowned Warbler)
V. c. celata
N & NW Canada, S USA » Mexico,
Guatemala
V. c. lutescens
W Canada, W USA » W Mexico
V. c. orestera
WC Canada, WC USA » C Mexico
V. c. sordida
S California, N Baja California and islands
Vermivora ruficapilla (Nashville Warbler)
V. r. ridgwayi
W USA » W Mexico, Guatemala
V. r. ruficapilla
S Canada, C & E, USA » Mexico,
Guatemala
Vermivora virginiae (Virginia's Warbler)
SW USA » W Mexico
Vermivora crissalis (Colima Warbler)
S USA » EC Mexico
Vermivora luciae (Lucy's Warbler)
SW USA » W Mexico
Vermivora gutteralis (Irazu Warbler)
Costa Rica, W Panama
Vermivora superciliosa (Crescent-chested Warbler)
V. s. sodalis
NC Mexico

V. s. mexicana
E Mexico
V. s. palliata
SW Mexico
V. s. superciliosa
S Mexico, Guatemala, W Honduras
V. s. parva
E Honduras, Nicaragua

PARULA
Parula americana (Parula Warbler)
SE Canada, E USA, E Mexico » Central
America, West Indies
Parula pitiayumi (Olive-backed Warbler) (Tropical Parula)
P. p. graysoni
Socorro I, Revillagigedo Is
P. p. insularis
Tres Marias Is
P. p. pulchra
NW Mexico
P. p. nigrilora
S Texas, NE Mexico
P. p. inornata
S Mexico, E Guatemala, N Honduras
P. p. speciosa
S Honduras, Nicaragua, Costa Rica,
W Panama
P. p. cirrha
Coiba I (Panama)
P. p. nana
E Panama, NW Colombia
P. p. elegans
Colombia, N Venezuela, N Brazil, Trinidad
P. p. roraimae
S Venezuela, N Brazil
P. p. alarum
E Ecuador, N Peru
P. p. pacifica
SW Colombia, W Ecuador, NW Peru
P. p. melanogenys
S Peru, W Bolivia
P. p. pitiayumi
E Bolivia, C & S Brazil, Uruguay, Paraguay,
N Argentina

DENDROICA
Dendroica petechia (Yellow Warbler)
D. p. amnicola
Canada » Mexico, Central America,
N South America
D. p. rubiginosa
W Canada » Mexico, Central America
D. p. aestiva
S Canada, C USA » Central America,
N South America
D. p. morcomi
W USA » Central America, N South
America

D. p. sonorana
SW USA » Central America, Colombia,
Ecuador
D. p. brewsteri
Baja California
D. p. hueyi
C Baja, California
D. p. inedita
NE Mexico
D. p. dugesi
C Mexico
D. p. rufivertex
Cozumel I
D. p. flavida
St Andrew I
D. p. armouri
Old Providence I
D. p. eoa
Jamaica, Cayman Is
D. p. gundlachi
Cuba, Bahama Is
D. p. albicollis
Hispaniola
D. p. cruciana
Puerto Rica, Virgin Is
D. p. bartholemica
N Lesser Antilles
D. p. melanoptera
C Lesser Antilles
D. p. ruficapilla
Martinique I
D. p. babad
St Lucia I
D. p. petechia
Barbados I
D. p. alsiosa
Grenadine Is
D. p. rufopileata
Curaçao I, Bonaire I
D. p. obscura
Los Roques I
D. p. chrysendeta
NE Colombia, NW Venezuela
D. p. paraguanae
NW Venezuela
D. p. cienagae
NC Venezuela
D. p. aurifrons
NC Venezuela and islands
D. p. castaneiceps
S Baja California
D. p. rhizophorae
NW Mexico
D. p. oraria
E Mexico
D. p. bryanti
Caribbean, SE Mexico to Costa Rica

D. p. xanthotera
Pacific, W Guatemala to Costa Rica
D. p. aureola
Cocos Is, Galapagos Is
D. p. aequatorialis
Pearl Archipelago (Panama)
D. p. erithachorides
E Panama, N Colombia
D. p. peruviana
SW Colombia, W Ecuador, N Peru
***Dendroica pensylvanica* (Chestnut-sided Warbler)**
S Canada, E USA » Central America
***Dendroica cerulea* (Cerulean Warbler)**
Venezuela, Ecuador, Peru, Bolivia
E USA » Colombia
***Dendroica caerulescens* (Black-throated Blue Warbler)**
D. c. caerulescens
SE Canada, NE USA » Bahama Is,
Gtr Antilles
D. c. cairnsi
EC USA » Gtr Antilles
***Dendroica plumbea* (Plumbeous Warbler)**
Dominica I, Guadeloupe I
***Dendroica pharetra* (Arrow-headed Warbler)**
Jamaica
***Dendroica angelae* (Puerto Rico Warbler)**
Puerto Rico
***Dendroica pinus* (Pine Warbler)**
D. p. pinus
SE Canada » SE USA
D. p. florida
S Florida
D. p. achrustera
Bahama Is
D. p. chrysoleuca
Hispaniola
***Dendroica graciae* (Grace's Warbler)**
D. g. graciae
SW USA » W Mexico
D. g. yaegeri
W Mexico
D. g. remota
S Mexico, Guatemala, El Salvador,
W Honduras
D. g. decora
Belize, E Honduras, Nicaragua
***Dendroica adelaidae* (Adelaide's Warbler)**
D. a. adelaidae
Puerto Rico
D. a. subita
Barbuda I
D. a. delicata
St Lucia I

Dendroica pityophila (Olive-capped Warbler)
Cuba, Bahama Is
Dendroica dominica (Yellow-throated Warbler)
D. d. albilora
EC & SE USA » E Mexico, Central America, Cuba, Jamaica
D. d. dominica
E & SE USA » Gtr Antilles
D. d. stoddardi
SE USA
D. d. flavescens
Bahama Is
Dendroica nigrescens (Black-throated Grey Warbler)
D. n. nigrescens
SW Canada, W USA » N Mexico, Guatemala
D. n. halseii
SW USA, NW Mexico, N Baja California
Dendroica townsendi (Townsend's Warbler)
W Canada, W USA » Mexico, Guatemala, Honduras, Nicaragua
Dendroica occidentalis (Hermit Warbler)
SW USA » W Mexico, Guatemala, Honduras, Nicaragua
Dendroica chrysopareia (Golden-cheeked Warbler)
S USA » Mexico, Guatemala, Honduras, Nicaragua
Dendroica virens (Black-throated Green Warbler)
C & SE Canada, E USA » Mexico, Central America, West Indies
Dendroica discolor (Prairie Warbler)
D. d. discolor
E USA, West Indies
D. d. paludicola
SE USA » Gtr Antilles
Dendroica vitellina (Vitelline Warbler)
D. v. crawfordi
Little Cayman I
D. v. vitellina
Grand Cayman I
D. v. nelsoni
Swan I
Dendroica tigrina (Cape May Warbler)
C & SE Canada, NC & E USA » West Indies, E Central America
Dendroica fusca (Blackburnian Warbler)
SE Canada, E USA » Central America, Venezuela, Colombia, Ecuador, Peru
Dendroica magnolia (Magnolia Warbler)
S Canada, E USA » Mexico, Central America, Gtr Antilles

Dendroica coronata (Yellow-rumped Warbler)
D. c. coronata
Canada, C & E USA » Central America, West Indies
D. c. auduboni
SW Canada, W USA » Mexico, Guatemala, W Honduras
D. c. nigrifrons
NC Mexico
D. c. goldmani
W Guatemala
D. c. hooveri
SW USA, NW Mexico
Dendroica palmarum (Palm Warbler)
D. p. palmarum
C & E Canada, E USA » Gtr Antilles, Central America
D. p. hypochrysea
SE Canada, NE USA » SE USA
Dendroica kirtlandii (Kirtland's Warbler)
C Michigan » Bahama Is
Dendroica striata (Blackpoll Warbler)
Canada, C & E USA » West Indies, N & C South America
Dendroica castanea (Bay-breasted Warbler)
C & SE Canada, E USA » Central America, Colombia, Venezuela

CATHAROPEZA
Catharopeza bishopi (Whistling Warbler)
St Vincent I

SETOPHAGA
Setophaga ruticilla (American Redstart)
S Canada, C & E USA » Mexico, Central America, West Indies, N South America

SEIURUS
Seiurus aurocapillus (Ovenbird)
S. a. aurocapillus
C & SE Canada, E USA » W Indies, Mexico to Colombia and Venezuela
S. a. cinereus
WC USA » S Mexico, El Salvador, Honduras, Costa Rica
S. a. furvior
Newfoundland » Bahamas, Cuba, E Central America
Seiurus noveboracensis (Northern Water-thrush)
S. n. noveboracensis
Canada, E USA » West Indies, Central America, N South America
S. n. limnaeus
W USA, NW Mexico
S. n. notabilis
SW USA, W Mexico

***Seiurus motacilla* (Louisiana Water-thrush)**
E USA » Mexico, West Indies, Central
America, Colombia, Venezuela

LIMNOTHLYPIS
***Limnothlypis swainsonii* (Swainson's Warbler)**
SE USA » E Mexico, West Indies

HELMITHEROS
***Helmitheros vermivorus* (Worm-eating Warbler)**
E USA » E Central America, West Indies

PROTONOTARIA
***Protonotaria citrea* (Prothonotary Warbler)**
E USA » Central America, West Indies,
N South America

GEOTHLYPIS
***Geothlypis trichas* (Yellowthroat)**
G. t. trichas
SE Canada, EC USA » Mexico, West
Indies, Central America, Colombia,
Venezuela
G. t. typhicola
SC USA, NE Mexico
G. t. ignota
SE USA
G. t. insperata
S Texas
G. t. campicola
W Canada, NW USA, SW USA » N Mexico
G. t. arizela
W Canada, W USA & NW Mexico
G. t. occidentalis
WC USA » Mexico to Honduras
G. t. sinuosa
N California
G. t. scirpicola
S California, N Baja California
G. t. chryseola
W Texas, NW Mexico
G. t. modesta
W Sonora, Mexico
G. t. melanops
C Mexico
G. t. chapalensis
Jalisco
G. t. riparia
S Sonora
G. t. brachydactyla
E USA, E & S Mexico
***Geothlypis beldingi* (Peninsular Yellow-throat)**
G. b. goldmani
C Baja California
G. b. beldingi
S Baja California

***Geothlypis flavovelata* (Yellow-crowned Yellowthroat)**
E Mexico
***Geothlypis rostrata* (Bahama Yellowthroat)**
G. r. tanneri
N Bahama Is
G. r. rostrata
W Bahama Is
G. r. coryi
Eleuthera I, Cat I
***Geothlypis semiflava* (Olive-crowned Yellowthroat)**
G. s. bairdi
S Honduras, Nicaragua, Costa Rica,
NW Panama
G. s. semiflava
W Colombia, W Ecuador
***Geothlypis speciosa* (Black-polled Yellowthroat)**
G. s. speciosa
C Mexico
G. s. limnatis
Guanajuata (Mexico)
***Geothlypis nelsoni* (Hooded Yellowthroat)**
G. n. nelsoni
E Mexico
G. n. karlenae
SW Mexico
***Geothlypis chiriquensis* (Chiriqui Yellowthroat)**
W Panama
***Geothlypis aequinoctialis* (Masked Yellowthroat)**
G. a. aequinoctialis
NE Colombia, Venezuela, the Guianas,
Surinam, N Brazil
G. a. auricularis
W Ecuador, W Peru
G. a. peruviana
N Peru
G. a. velata
S Peru, Bolivia, Brazil, Paraguay, Uruguay,
N Argentina
***Geothlypis poliocephala* (Grey-crowned Yellowthroat)**
G. p. poliocephala
N & W Mexico
G. p. ralphi
NE Mexico
G. p. palpebralis
E & S Mexico, Guatemala, Honduras,
Nicaragua, Costa Rica
G. p. caninucha
SW Mexico, W Guatemala, S Honduras,
El Salvador
G. p. icterotis
W Nicaragua, W Costa Rica

G. p. pontilis
W Mexico

G. p. ridgwayi
SW Costa Rica, W Panama

Geothlypis formosa (Kentucky Warbler)
SE USA » E Mexico, Central America,
Colombia, Venezuela

Geothlypis agilis (Connecticut Warbler)
EC Canada, NC USA » Venezuela,
NE Brazil, Colombia

**Geothlypis philadelphia (Mourning
Warbler)**
C & E Canada, NE USA » Nicaragua, Costa
Rica, Colombia, Venezuela

Geothlypis tolmei (MacGillivray's Warbler)
SW Canada, W USA » Central America

MICROLIGEA
**Microligea palustris (Green-tailed Ground
Warbler)**
M. p. palustris
Hispaniola
M. p. vasta
SW Dominica I

XENOLIGEA
**Xenoligea montana (White-winged Ground
Warbler)**
Hispaniola

TERETISTRIS
**Teretistris fernandinae (Yellow-headed
Warbler)**
W Cuba

Teretistris fornsi (Oriente Warbler)
E Cuba

LEUCOPEZA
Leucopeza semperi (Semper's Warbler)
St Lucia I

WILSONIA
Wilsonia citrina (Hooded Warbler)
E USA » E Mexico, Central America

Wilsonia pusilla (Wilson's Warbler)
W. p. pileolata
W Canada, WC USA » C Mexico,
Central America
W. p. chryseola
SW USA » W & S Mexico, Guatemala,
W. p. pusilla
S & E Canada, NE USA » E Mexico,
Central America

Wilsonia canadensis (Canada Warbler)
SE Canada, NE USA » Central America,
N South America

CARDELLINA
Cardellina rubifrons (Red-faced Warbler)
SW USA » W & S Mexico, Guatemala,
W Honduras

ERGATICUS   579
Ergaticus ruber (Red Warbler)
E. r. melanauris
NW Mexico
E. r. ruber
W & S Mexico
E. r. rowleyi
Oaxaca (Mexico)

**Ergaticus versicolor (Pink-headed
Warbler)**
S Mexico, W Guatemala

MYIOBORUS
Myioborus pictus (Painted Redstart)
M. p. pictus
SW USA, N Mexico
M. p. guatemalae
S Mexico to N Nicaragua

**Myioborus miniatus (Slate-throated
Redstart)**
M. m. miniatus
W & SW Mexico
M. m. molochinus
E Mexico
M. m. intermedius
·S Mexico, E Guatemala
M. m. hellmayri
W Guatemala, El Salvador
M. m. connectens
El Salvador, Honduras
M. m. comptus
W Costa Rica
M. m. aurantiacus
E Costa Rica, W Panama
M. m. ballux
E Panama, Colombia, W Venezuela,
NW Ecuador
M. m. sanctaemartae
N Colombia
M. m. pallidiventris
N Venezuela
M. m. subsimilis
SW Ecuador, NW Peru
M. m. verticalis
SE Ecuador, Peru, Bolivia,
SE Venezuela, Guyana, NW Brazil

**Myioborus brunniceps (Brown-capped
Redstart)**
M. b. castaneocapillus
SE Venezuela, W Guyana, N Brazil
M. b. duidae
SE Venezuela
M. b. maguirei
SE Venezuela
M. b. brunniceps
Bolivia, N Argentina

**Myioborus pariae (Yellow-faced
Redstart)**
NE Venezuela

Myioborus cardonai **(Saffron-breasted Redstart)**
SE Venezuela
Myioborus torquatus **(Collared Redstart)**
Costa Rica, W Panama
Myioborus ornatus **(Golden-fronted Redstart)**
M. o. ornatus
E Colombia, SW Venezuela
M. o. chrysops
W Colombia
Myioborus melanocephalus **(Spectacled Redstart)**
M. m. ruficoronatus
SW Colombia, S Ecuador
M. m. griseonuchus
NW Peru
M. m. malaris
N Peru
M. m. melanocephalus
E Peru
M. m. bolivianus
S Peru, W Bolivia
Myioborus albifrons **(White-fronted Redstart)**
W Venezuela
Myioborus flavivertex **(Yellow-crowned Redstart)**
N Colombia
Myioborus albifacies **(White-faced Redstart)**
S Venezuela

EUTHLYPIS
Euthlypis lachrymosa **(Fan-tailed Warbler)**
E. l. tephra
W Mexico
E. l. schistacea
W Chiapas
E. l. lachrymosa
S Mexico to N Nicaragua

BASILEUTERUS
Basileuterus fraseri **(Grey & Gold Warbler)**
B. f. ochraceicrista
W Ecuador
B. f. fraseri
C Ecuador, NW Peru
Basileuterus bivittatus **(Two-banded Warbler)**
B. b. roraimae
Guyana, SE Venezuela, N Brazil
B. b. bivittatus
SE Peru, W Bolivia
B. b. argentinae
SE Bolivia, NW Argentina

Basileuterus chrysogaster **(Golden-bellied Warbler)**
B. c. chlorophrys
SW Colombia, NW Ecuador
B. c. chrysogaster
E Peru
Basileuterus flaveolus **(Flavescent Warbler)**
Colombia, Venezuela, Brazil, Peru, Bolivia
Basileuterus luteoviridis **(Citrine Warbler)**
E. l. luteoviridis
SW Venezuela, E Colombia, E Ecuador
B. l. quindianus
C Colombia
B. l. richardsoni
W Colombia
B. l. striaticeps
N Peru
B. l. euophrys
SW Peru, W Bolivia
Basileuterus signatus **(Pale-legged Warbler)**
B. s. signatus
C Peru
B. s. flavovirens
SE Peru, W Bolivia, NW Argentina
Basileuterus nigrocristatus **(Black-crested Warbler)**
Venezuela, Colombia, Ecuador
Basileuterus griseiceps **(Grey-headed Warbler)**
NE Venezuela
Basileuterus basilicus **(Santa Marta Warbler)**
NE Colombia
Basileuterus cinereicollis **(Grey-throated Warbler)**
B. c. pallidulus
W Venezuela, NE Colombia
B. c. cinereicollis
E Colombia
Basileuterus coronatus **(Russet-crowned Warbler)**
B. c. conspicillatus
N Colombia
B. c. regulus
Venezuela, Colombia
B. c. elatus
SW Colombia, W Ecuador
B. c. orientalis
E Ecuador
B. c. castaneiceps
SW Ecuador, NW Peru
B. c. chapmani
NW Peru
B. c. inaequalis
N Peru
B. c. coronatus
SE Peru, W Bolivia

B. c. notius
C Bolivia

Basileuterus culicivorus (Golden-crowned Warbler)

B. c. flavescens
W Mexico

B. c. brasherii
E Mexico

B. c. culicivorus
S Mexico to Costa Rica

B. c. godmani
S Costa Rica, W Panama

B. c. occultus
W Colombia

B. c. austerus
C Colombia

B. c. indignus
N Colombia

B. c. cabanisi
NW Venezuela, NE Colombia

B. c. olivascens
Venezuela, Colombia, Trinidad

B. c. segrex
SE Venezuela, W Guyana, N Brazil

B. c. auricapillus
C Brazil

B. c. azarae
S Brazil, Paraguay, Uruguay, NE Argentina

B. c. viridescens
E Bolivia

Basileuterus rufifrons (Rufous-capped Warbler)

B. r. caudatus
NW Mexico

B. r. dugesi
W & C Mexico

B. r. jouyi
E Mexico

B. r. rufifrons
S Mexico, N Guatemala

B. r. salvini
SW Mexico, N Guatemala

B. r. delattrii
W Guatemala to N Costa Rica

B. r. mesochrysus
S Costa Rica, Panama, N Colombia,
W Venezuela

B. r. actuosus
Coiba I (Panama)

Basileuterus belli (Golden-browed Warbler)

B. b. bateli
W Mexico

B. b. belli
C & E Mexico

B. b. clarus
SW Mexico

B. b. scitulus
SE Mexico, Guatemala, W Honduras

B. b. subobscurus
C Honduras

Basileuterus melanogenys (Black-cheeked Warbler)

B. m. melanogenys
Costa Rica

B. m. eximus
Panama

B. m. bensoni
Panama

B. m. ignotus
Panama

Basileuterus tristriatus (Three-striped Warbler)

B. t. chitrensis
W Panama

B. t. tacarcunae
E Panama, NW Colombia

B. t. daedalus
W Colombia, W Ecuador

B. t. auricularis
E Colombia, SW Venezuela

B. t. meridanus
W Venezuela

B. t. bessereri
N Venezuela

B. t. pariae
NE Venezuela

B. t. baezae
E Ecuador

B. t. tristriatus
SE Ecuador, C Peru

B. t. inconspicuus
SE Peru, NW Bolivia

B. t. punctipectus
C Bolivia

B. t. canens
E Bolivia

Basileuterus trifasciatus (Three-banded Warbler)

B. t. nitidior
SW Ecuador, NW Peru

B. t. trifasciatus
NW Peru

Basileuterus hypoleucus (White-bellied Warbler)
C Brazil, E Paraguay

Basileuterus leucoblepharus (White-browed Warbler)

B. l. leucoblepharus
S Brazil to NE Argentina

B. l. lemurum
Uruguay

Basileuterus leucophrys (White-striped Warbler)
SC Brazil

Basileuterus rivularis (River Warbler)
　　B. r. leucopygia
　　　Honduras to W Panama
　　B. r. veraguensis
　　　SW Costa Rica, C Panama
　　B. r. semicervina
　　　E Panama to NW Peru
　　B. r. motacilla
　　　N Colombia
　　B. r. fulvicauda
　　　E Colombia, E Ecuador, NE Peru, W Brazil
　　B. r. significans
　　　SE Peru
　　B. r. mesoleuca
　　　E Venezuela, the Guianas, N Brazil
　　B. r. rivularis
　　　SE Brazil, E Paraguay, NE Argentina
　　B. r. boliviana
　　　E Bolivia

NEPHELORNIS
Nephelornis oneilli (Pardusco)
　　C Peru

ZELEDONIA
Zeledonia coronata (Wren-Thrush)
　　Costa Rica, W Panama

PEUCEDRAMUS
Peucedramus taeniatus (Olive Warbler)
　　P. t. arizonae
　　　SW USA, N Mexico
　　P. t. jaliscensis
　　　NW Mexico
　　P. t. giraudi
　　　C Mexico
　　P. t. aurantiacus
　　　Chiapas (S Mexico)
　　P. t. taeniatus
　　　S Mexico, W Guatemala
　　P. t. micrus
　　　El Salvador, Honduras, N Nicaragua

GRANATELLUS
Granatellus venustus (Red-breasted Chat)
　　G. v. francescae
　　　Tres Marias Is
　　G. v. venustus
　　　W & SW Mexico
　　G. v. melanotis
　　　W coast of Mexico
Granatellus sallaei (Grey-throated Chat)
　　G. s. sallaei
　　　E Mexico
　　G. s. boucardi
　　　SE Mexico, E Guatemala, Belize
Granatellus pelzelni (Rose-breasted Chat)
　　G. p. pelzelni
　　　SE Venezuela, Guyana, Surinam,
　　　　NW Brazil
　　G. p. paraensis
　　　N Brazil

ICTERIA
Icteria virens (Yellow-breasted Chat)
　　I. v. auricollis
　　　SW Canada, W USA » W Mexico,
　　　　Guatemala
　　I. v. virens
　　　E USA » E Mexico, Central America
　　I. v. tropicalis
　　　S Sonora (Mexico)

CONIROSTRUM
Conirostrum speciosum (Chestnut-vented Conebill)
　　C. s. guaricola
　　　C Venezuela
　　C. s. amazonum
　　　the Guianas to Ecuador » N Peru
　　C. s. speciosum
　　　SE Peru & Bolivia to N Argentina
Conirostrum leucogenys (White-eared Conebill)
　　C. l. panamense
　　　E Panama, NW Colombia
　　C. l. leucogenys
　　　N Colombia, NE Venezuela
　　C. l. cyanochrous
　　　W Venezuela
Conirostrum bicolor (Bicoloured Conebill)
　　C. b. bicolor
　　　N Colombia to the Guianas, N Brazil
　　C. b. minor
　　　W Brazil, E Ecuador, E Peru
Conirostrum margaritae (Pearly-breasted Conebill)
　　N Brazil, NE Peru
Conirostrum cinereum (Cinereous Conebill)
　　C. c. fraseri
　　　SW Colombia, E Ecuador
　　C. c. littorale
　　　W Peru, N Chile
　　C. c. cinereum
　　　SE Peru, W Bolivia
Conirostrum tamarugensis (Tamarugo Conebill)
　　SC Peru, N Bolivia
Conirostrum ferrugineiventre (White-browed Conebill)
　　S Peru, W Bolivia
Conirostrum rufum (Rufous-browed Conebill)
　　N Colombia
Conirostrum sitticolor (Blue-backed Conebill)
　　C. s. intermedium
　　　W Venezuela
　　C. s. sitticolor
　　　S Colombia, Ecuador, NW Peru

C. s. cyaneum
Peru, W Bolivia
Conirostrum albifrons (Capped Conebill)
C. a. cyanonotum
N Venezuela
C. a. albifrons
W Venezuela, E Colombia
C. a. centralandium
C Colombia
C. a. atrocyaneum
SW Colombia, Ecuador, N Peru
C. a. sordidum
S Peru, W Bolivia
C. a. lugens
E Bolivia

COEREBA
Coereba flaveola (Bananaquit)
C. f. mexicana
SE Mexico, Central America
C. f. cerinoclunis
Pearl Archipelago (Panama)
C. f. columbiana
E Panama, C Colombia, SC Venezuela
C. f. gorgonae
Gorgona I, W Colombia
C. f. caucae
W Colombia
C. f. intermedia
SW Venezuela to Ecuador, W Brazil
C. f. magnirostris
N Peru
C. f. pacifica
NW Peru
C. f. dispar
SE Peru, NW Bolivia
C. f. caboti
Cozumel I, Holbox I
C. f. tricolor
Old Providence I
C. f. oblita
St Andrew I
C. f. sharpei
Cayman Is
C. f. bahamensis
Bahama Is
C. f. flaveola
Jamaica
C. f. bananivora
Hispaniola
C. f. nectarea
Tortue I, Haiti
C. f. portoricensis
Puerto Rico
C. f. sanctithomae
Virgin Is
C. f. newtoni
St Croix I

C. f. bartholemica
N Lesser Antilles
C. f. martinicana
Martinique I, St Lucia I
C. f. barbadensis
Barbados I
C. f. atrata
St Vincent I
C. f. aterrima
Grenada I
C. f. uropygialis
Aruba I, Curaçao I
C. f. bonairensis
Bonaire I
C. f. melanornis
Cayo Sal I
C. f. lowii
Los Roques I
C. f. ferryi
La Tortuga I
C. f. frailensis
Los Frailes I, Los Hermanos I
C. f. laurae
Los Testigos I
C. f. luteola
N Colombia to Trinidad & Tobago I
C. f. obscura
NE Colombia, W Venezuela
C. f. montana
W Venezuela
C. f. bolivari
E Venezuela
C. f. guianensis
E Venezuela, Guyana
C. f. roraimae
SE Venezuela, NW Brazil, SW Guyana
C. f. minima
N Brazil, French Guiana, Surinam
C. f. chloropyga
S Peru, Bolivia to NE Argentina
C. f. alleni
C Brazil, E Bolivia

160 DREPANIDIDAE (HAWAIIAN HONEY-CREEPERS)

PSITTIROSTRINAE

LOXOPS
Loxops virens (Amakihi)
L. v. stejnegeri
Kauai I
L. v. chloris
Oahu I
L. v. wilsoni
Maui I, Molokai I
L. v. virens
Hawaii I

Loxops parva (Lesser Amakihi)
Kauai I
Loxops maculata (Hawaiian Creeper)
L. m. bairdi
Kauai I
L. m. maculata
Oahu I
L. m. flammea
Molokai I **e?**
L. m. montana
Lanai I **e?**
L. m. newtoni
Maui I
L. m. mana
Hawaii I
Loxops coccinea (Akepa)
L. c. coccinea
Hawaii I
L. c. caerulirostris
Kauai I
L. c. ochracea
Maui I

MELAMPROSOPS
Melamprosops phaeosoma (Po'o uli)
Maui I

HEMIGNATHUS
Hemignathus obscurus (Akialoa) e?
Hawaii I
Hemignathus procerus (Kauai Akialoa)
Kauai I
Hemignathus lucidus (Nukupuu) e?
H. l. affinis
Maui I
H. l. hanepepe
Kauai I
Hemignathus wilsoni (Akiapolaau)
Hawaii I

PSEUDONESTOR
Pseudonestor xanthoprys (Maui Parrotbill)
Maui I

PSITTIROSTRA
Psittirostra psittacea (Ou)
Maui I, Hawaii I
Psittirostra cantans (Yellow Laysan Finch)
P. c. cantans
Laysan I
P. c. ultima
Nihoa I
Psittirostra bailleui (Palila)
Hawaii I

DREPANIDINAE

HIMATIONE
Himatione sanguinea (Apapane)
All main Hawaiian Is

PALMERIA
Palmeria dolei (Crested Honeycreeper)
Maui I

VESTIARIA
Vestiaria coccinea (Iiwi)
Molokai I, Oahu I, Kauai I, Maui I, Hawaii I

161 VIREONIDAE (VIREOS)

CYCLARHINAE

CYCLARHIS
Cyclarhis gujanensis (Rufous-browed Pepper Shrike)
C. g. flaviventris
C Mexico, E Guatemala, N Honduras
C. g. yucatanensis
SE Mexico
C. g. insularis
Cozumel I
C. g. nicaraguae
S Mexico, Guatemala, El Salvador, Honduras, Nicaragua
C. g. subflavescens
Costa Rica, W Panama
C. g. perrygoi
WC Panama
C. g. flavens
E Panama
C. g. coibae
Coiba I (Panama)
C. g. canticus
N & E Colombia
C. g. flavipectus
NE Venezuela, Trinidad
C. g. parvus
E Colombia, N Venezuela
C. g. gujanensis
E Colombia, S Venezuela, the Guianas Brazil, E Peru, NW Bolivia
C. g. cearensis
E Brazil
C. g. ochrocephala
SE Brazil, Paraguay, Uruguay, NE Argentina
C. g. viridis
Paraguay, N Argentina
C. g. virenticeps
Ecuador, NW Peru
C. g. contrerasi
N Peru
C. g. saturatus
C Peru
C. g. pax
EC Bolivia
C. g. dorsalis
C Bolivia
C. g. tarijae
SE Bolivia, NW Argentina

***Cyclarhis nigrirostris* (Black-billed Pepper Shrike)**
  C. n. nigrirostris
    C Colombia, E Ecuador
  C. n. atrirostris
    SW Colombia, W Ecuador

VIREOLANIINAE

VIREOLANIUS
***Vireolanius melitophrys* (Chestnut-sided Shrike Vireo)**
  V. m. goldmani
    SC Mexico
  V. m. melitophrys
    S Mexico, W Guatemala
***Vireolanius pulchellus* (Green Shrike Vireo)**
  V. p. pulchellus
    SE Mexico to Honduras
  V. p. verticalis
    Nicaragua, Costa Rica
  V. p. viridiceps
    W Costa Rica, W Panama
  V. p. mutabilis
    E Panama, NW Colombia
  V. p. eximius
    N Colombia, NW Venezuela
***Vireolanius leucotis* (Slaty-capped Shrike Vireo)**
  V. l. mikettae
    W Colombia, NW Ecuador
  V. l. leucotis
    N & W Amazonia
  V. l. simplex
    N Brazil, S Peru
  V. l. bolivianus
    SE Peru, N Bolivia

VIREONINAE

VIREO
***Vireo brevipennis* (Slaty Vireo)**
  V. b. browni
    Guerrero
  V. b. brevipennis
    S Mexico
***Vireo huttoni* (Hutton's Vireo)**
  V. h. insularis
    Vancouver I
  V. h. huttoni
    SW Canada, W USA, N Baja California
  V. h. cognatus
    S Baja California
  V. h. stephensi
    SW USA, NW Mexico
  V. h. carolinae
    S USA, NE Mexico
  V. h. pacificus
    W & SW Mexico

V. h. mexicanus
    C & S Mexico
V. h. vulcani
    S Mexico, W Guatemala
***Vireo atricapillus* (Black-capped Vireo)**
    C & S USA » N & W Mexico
***Vireo griseus* (White-eyed Vireo)**
  V. g. noveboracensis
    C & E USA » E Mexico, Guatemala, Cuba
  V. g. griseus
    SE USA » E Mexico, N Honduras, W Cuba
  V. g. maynardi
    S Florida
  V. g. bermudianus
    Bermuda I
  V. g. micrus
    S Texas, E Mexico
  V. g. perquisitor
    EC Mexico
***Vireo pallens* (Pale Vireo)**
  V. p. paluster
    NW Mexico
  V. p. ochraceus
    W Guatemala, W El Salvador
  V. p. pallens
    W Honduras, W Nicaragua, W Costa Rica
  V. p. semiflavus
    E Mexico, E Guatemala, E Honduras, Nicaragua
***Vireo caribaeus* (St Andrew Vireo)**
    St Andrew I
***Vireo bairdi* (Cozumel Vireo)**
    Cozumel I
***Vireo gundlachii* (Cuban Vireo)**
  V. g. magnus
    W Cuba
  V. g. sanfelipensis
    W Cuba
  V. g. gundlachii
    C & E Cuba
***Vireo crassirostris* (Thick-billed Vireo)**
  V. c. crassirostris
    Bahama Is
  V. c. tortugae
    Tortue I, Haiti
  V. c. approximans
    Old Providence I, St Catalina I
***Vireo vicinior* (Grey Vireo)**
    SW USA » NW Mexico
***Vireo bellii* (Bell's Vireo)**
  V. b. pusillus
    S California » S Baja California
  V. b. arizonae
    SW USA » NW Mexico
  V. b. medius
    S USA » NC Mexico

V. b. bellii
  C & S USA » Mexico, Guatemala,
  El Salvador, Honduras, N Nicaragua
Vireo nelsoni (Dwarf Vireo)
  S Mexico
Vireo hypochryseus (Golden Vireo)
V. h. nitidus
  S Sonora, Mexico
V. h. hypochryseus
  W & SW Mexico
V. h. sordidus
  Tres Marias Is
Vireo modestus (Jamaican White-eyed
Vireo)
  Jamaica
Vireo nanus (Flat-billed Vireo)
  Hispaniola
Vireo latimeri (Puerto Rican Vireo)
  W Puerto Rico
Vireo osburni (Blue Mountain Vireo)
  Jamaica
Vireo carmioli (Carmiol's Vireo)
  Costa Rica, W Panama
Vireo solitarius (Solitary Vireo)
V. s. solitarius
  Canada, NC & E USA » E Mexico, Central
  America, W Cuba
V. s. alticola
  EC USA » SE USA
V. s. plumbeus
  WC USA » NW Mexico
V. s. cassinii
  W USA » Mexico, Guatemala
V. s. lucasanus
  S Baja California
V. s. pinicolus
  N Mexico
V. s. repetens
  C Mexico
V. s. notius
  Belize
V. s. montanus
  S Mexico, Guatemala, Honduras,
  El Salvador
Vireo flavifrons (Yellow-throated Vireo)
  S Canada, E & C USA » Colombia,
  Venezuela, Central America
Vireo philadelphicus (Philadelphia Vireo)
  W Canada, N USA » Mexico, Central
  America, Colombia
Vireo olivaceus (Red-eyed Vireo)
V. o. olivaceus
  Canada, WC & E USA » Cuba, C South
  America
V. o. forreri
  Tres Marias Is, N Mexico » Upper
  Amazonia

V. o. hypoleucus
  NW Mexico
V. o. flavoviridis
  S Mexico, Central America » Upper
  Amazonia
V. o. insulanus
  Pearl Is (Panama)
V. o. caucae
  W Colombia
V. o. griseobarbatus
  W Ecuador, NW Peru
V. o. pectoralis
  N Peru
V. o. solimoensis
  E Ecuador, NE Peru
V. o. vividior
  Colombia, Venezuela, the Guianas,
  N Brazil, Trinidad
V. o. tobagensis
  Tobago I
V. o. agilis
  NE Brazil
V. o. gracilirostris
  Fernando de Noronha I
V. o. diversus
  SE Brazil, E Paraguay
V. o. chivi
  W & SW Amazonia
Vireo magister (Yucatan Vireo)
V.m. magister
  SE Mexico, Belize
V. m. caymanensis
  Grand Cayman I
Vireo altiloquus (Black-whiskered Vireo)
V. a. barbatulus
  S Florida, Cuba, Haiti » Colombia,
  Venezuela, Brazil, Peru
V. a. altiloquus
  Gtr Antilles » N South America
V. a. barbadensis
  St Croix I, Barbados I
V. a. bonairensis
  Aruba I, Curaçao I, Bonaire I
V. a. grandior
  Old Providence I, St Catalina I
V. a. canescens
  St Andrew I
Vireo gilvus (Warbling Vireo)
V. g. swainsonii
  W Canada, W USA » W Mexico,
  Guatemala, Honduras, Nicaragua
V. g. victoriae
  S Baja California
V. g. leucopolius
  WC USA » N Mexico
V. g. gilvus
  SW Canada, C, S & NE USA » S Mexico,
  El Salvador

V. g. brewsteri
NW Mexico
V. g. eleanorae
NE Mexico
V. g. bulli
Oaxaca
V. g. amauronotus
EC Mexico
V. g. connectens
SC Mexico
V. g. strenuus
S Mexico, Guatemala, Honduras
V. g. chiriquensis
Costa Rica, W Panama
V. g. disjunctus
NC Colombia
V. g. mirandae
N Colombia, NW Venezuela
V. g. leucophrys
C Colombia, Ecuador, N Peru
V. g. dissors
W Colombia
V. g. josephae
SW Colombia, W Ecuador
V. g. maranonicus
N Peru
V. g. laetissimus
SE Peru, N Bolivia

HYLOPHILUS
Hylophilus poicilotis (Rufous-crowned Greenlet)
H. p. amaurocephalus
E Brazil
H. p. poicilotis
SE Brazil, Paraguay, NE Argentina
Hylophilus thoracicus (Lemon-chested Greenlet)
H. t. aemulus
Colombia, Ecuador, Peru,
N Bolivia
H. t. griseiventris
E Venezuela, the Guianas, N Brazil
H. t. thoracicus
SE Brazil
Hylophilus semicinereus (Grey-chested Greenlet)
H. s. viridiceps
S Venezuela, the Guianas, N Brazil
H. s. semicinereus
N Brazil
H. s. juruanus
NW Brazil
Hylophilus pectoralis (Ashy-headed Greenlet)
the Guianas, N Brazil
Hylophilus sclateri (Tepui Greenlet)
S Venezuela, Guyana, NC Brazil

Hylophilus muscicapinus (Buff-chested Greenlet)
H. m. muscicapinus
S Venezuela, the Guianas, N Brazil
H. m. griseifrons
N Brazil
Hylophilus brunneiceps (Brown-headed Greenlet)
H. b. brunneiceps
E Colombia, S Venezuela, NW Brazil
H. b. inornatus
N Brazil
Hylophilus semibrunneus (Rufous-naped Greenlet)
N Colombia, NW Venezuela, E Ecuador
Hylophilus aurantiifrons (Golden-fronted Greenlet)
H. a. aurantiifrons
E Panama, N Colombia
H. a. helvinus
NW Venezuela
H. a. saturatus
E Colombia, N Venezuela, Trinidad
Hylophilus hypoxanthus (Dusky-capped Greenlet)
H. h. hypoxanthus
SE Colombia
H. h. fuscicapillus
E Ecuador, N Peru
H. h. flaviventris
C Peru
H. h. ictericus
W Brazil, NE Peru, N Bolivia
H. h. albigula
N Brazil
Hylophilus flavipes (Scrub Greenlet)
H. f. viridiflavus
SW Costa Rica, W Panama
H. f. xuthus
Coiba I (Panama)
H. f. flavipes
C & N Colombia
H. f. melleus
N Colombia
H. f. galbanus
NE Colombia, NW Venezuela
H. f. acuticauda
N Venezuela
H. f. insularis
Tobago I
H. f. olivaceus
E Ecuador, N Peru
Hylophilus ochraceiceps (Tawny-crowned Greenlet)
H. o. ochraceiceps
S Mexico, Guatemala

H. o. pallidipectus
Honduras, El Salvador, Nicaragua,
Costa Rica
H. o. nelsoni
E Panama
H. o. bulunensis
E Panama, W Colombia, W Ecuador
H. o. ferrugineifrons
SE Colombia, S Venezuela, Guyana,
Ecuador, Peru, NW Brazil
H. o. viridior
S Peru, N Bolivia
H. o. luteifrons
E Venezuela, the Guianas, N Brazil
H. o. lutescens
N Brazil
H. o. rubrifrons
NE Brazil
**Hylophilus decurtatus (Grey-headed
Greenlet)**
H. d. decurtatus
E Mexico, Central America
H. d. darienensis
E Panama, N Colombia
H. d. minor
SW Colombia, W Ecuador

**162 ICTERIDAE (NEW WORLD
BLACKBIRDS)**

ICTERINAE

PSAROCOLIUS
Psarocolius oseryi (Casqued Oropendola)
E Ecuador, E Peru
**Psarocolius latirostris (Band-tailed
Oropendola)**
E Ecuador, N Peru, W Brazil
**Psarocolius decumanus (Crested
Oropendola)**
P. d. melanterus
Panama, N Colombia
P. d. insularis
Trinidad, Tobago l
P. d. decumanus
N South America
P. d. maculosus
E Peru to Paraguay, N Argentina
Psarocolius viridis (Green Oropendola)
N Amazonia
**Psarocolius atrovirens (Dusky-green
Oropendola)**
SE Peru, E Bolivia
**Psarocolius angustifrons (Russet-backed
Oropendola)**
P. a. salmoni
C Colombia

P. a. atrocastaneus
W Ecuador
P. a. sincipitalis
NC Colombia
P. a. neglectus
E Colombia, NW Venezuela
P. a. oleagineus
NC Venezuela
P. a. angustifrons
W Amazonia
P. a. alfredi
SE Ecuador, E Peru, E Bolivia
**Psarocolius wagleri (Chestnut-headed
Oropendola)**
P. w. wagleri
SE Mexico to NE Nicaragua
P. w. ridgwayi
S Nicaragua to Panama, W Ecuador
**Psarocolius montezuma (Montezuma
Oropendola)**
S Mexico to Panama
**Psarocolius cassini (Chestnut-mantled
Oropendola)**
NW Colombia
Psarocolius bifasciatus (Para Oropendola)
N Brazil
**Psarocolius guatimozinus (Black
Oropendola)**
E Panama, NW Colombia
Psarocolius yuracares (Olive Oropendola)
P. y. yuracares
W Amazonia
P. y. neivae
N Brazil

CACICUS
Cacicus cela (Yellow-rumped Cacique)
C. c. vitellinus
Panama, N Colombia
C. c. flavicrissus
W Ecuador, NW Peru
C. c. cela
N South America, Trinidad
**Cacicus haemorrhous (Red-rumped
Cacique)**
C. h. haemorrhous
SE Colombia, E Ecuador, N Brazil
C. h. affinis
E & S Brazil, Paraguay, NE Argentina
**Cacicus uropygialis (Scarlet-rumped
Cacique)**
C. u. microrhynchus
S Honduras to Panama
C. u. pacificus
E Panama, Colombia, E Ecuador
C. u. uropygialis
S Venezuela to N Peru

Cacicus chrysopterus (Golden-winged Cacique)
E Bolivia to Uruguay
Cacicus koepckeae (Selva Cacique)
Peru
Cacicus leucoramphus (Mountain Cacique)
C. l. leucoramphus
NW Venzuela to E Ecuador
C. l. peruvianus
N Peru
C. l. chrysonotus
S Peru, Bolivia
Cacicus sclateri (Ecuadorian Black Cacique)
E Ecuador, N Peru
Cacicus solitarius (Solitary Cacique)
Central & Northern South America
Cacicus melanicterus (Yellow-winged Cacique)
W & SW Mexico
Cacicus holosericeus (Yellow-billed Cacique)
C. h. holosericeus
SE Mexico to Colombia
C. h. flavirostris
W Colombia to NW Peru
C. h. australis
Western Amazonia

ICTERUS
Icterus cayanensis (Epaulet Oriole)
I. c. cayanensis
Surinam, French Guiana
I. c. chrysocephalus
N Peru to S Surinam
I. c. tibialis
E Brazil
I. c. valenciobuenoi
SE Brazil
I. c. periporphyrus
NE Bolivia, W Brazil
I. c. pyrrhopterus
SE Bolivia to Uruguay
Icterus chrysater (Yellow-backed Oriole)
I. c. chrysater
S Mexico to Nicaragua
I. c. mayensis
SE Mexico
I. c. hondae
Panama, N Colombia
I. c. giraudii
C Colombia, N Venezuela
Icterus nigrogularis (Yellow Oriole)
I. n. nigrogularis
NE South America
I. n. curasoensis
Aruba, Curaçao I, Bonaire I
I. n. helioeides
Margarita I

I. n. trinitatis
NE Venezuela, Trinidad
Icterus leucopteryx (Jamaican Oriole)
I. l. bairdi
Grand Cayman I
I. l. leucopteryx
Jamaica
I. l. lawrencii
St Andrew I
Icterus auratus (Orange Oriole)
SE Mexico
Icterus mesomelas (Yellow-tailed Oriole)
I. m. mesomelas
SE Mexico to Honduras
I. m. salvinii
Nicaragua to Panama
I. m. carrikeri
N & W Colombia, NW Venezuela
I. m. taczanowskii
W Ecuador, NW Peru
Icterus auricapillus (Orange-crowned Oriole)
E Panama to N Venezuela
Icterus graceannae (White-edged Oriole)
SW Ecuador, NW Peru
Icterus xantholaemus (Yellow-throated Oriole)
Ecuador
Icterus pectoralis (Spotted-breasted Oriole)
I. p. pectoralis
S Mexico to N Nicaragua
I. p. espinachi
S Nicaragua to NW Costa Rica
Icterus gularis (Lichtenstein's Oriole)
I. g. tamaulipensis
S Texas, E Mexico
I. g. yucatanensis
SE Mexico
I. g. flavescens
SW Mexico
I. g. gularis
S Mexico
I. g. troglodytes
S Mexico, W Guatemala
I. g. gigas
S Guatemala, Honduras
Icterus pustulatus (Streak-backed Oriole)
I. p. microstictus
W Mexico
I. p. graysonii
Tres Marias Is
I. p. pustulatus
SW & C Mexico
I. p. formosus
S Mexico, NW Guatemala

I. p. alticola
. Guatemala, E Honduras
I. p. sclateri
El Salvador to NW Costa Rica
Icterus cucullatus (Hooded Oriole)
I. c. nelsoni
SW USA, NW Mexico
I. c. sennetti
S Texas, E Mexico
I. c. cucullatus
SW Texas, NC & C Mexico
I. c. californicus
N Baja California
I. c. trochiloides
S Baja California
I. c. restrictus
S Sonora
I. c. igneus
SE Mexico, Belize
I. c. cozumelae
Cozumel I
I. c. duplexus
Mujeres I, Holbox I
I. c. masoni
SE Quintana Roo
Icterus icterus (Troupial)
I. i. ridgwayi
N Colombia, NW Venezuela, Aruba I,
Curaçao I
I. i. icterus
E Colombia, NW Venezuela
I. i. metae
SW Venezuela
I. i. croconotus
SW Guyana, N Brazil, E Ecuador, E Peru
I. i. jamaicaii
E Brazil
I. i. strictifrons
N & E Bolivia, SW Brazil
Icterus galbula (Northern Oriole)
I. g. galbula
Canada, E USA » Colombia
I. g. bullockii
SW Canada, W USA » W Mexico to
Nicaragua
I. g. parvus
SW USA » NW Mexico
I. g. abeillei
SC Mexico
Icterus spurius (Orchard Oriole)
I. s. spurius
C Canada, E USA » Colombia, Cuba
I. s. phillipsi
C Mexico
I. s. fuertesi
E Mexico

**Icterus dominicensis (Black-cowled
Oriole)**
I. d. prosthemelas
SE Mexico to Nicaragua
I. d. praecox
E Costa Rica, W Panama
I. d. northropi
Andros I (Bahamas)
I. d. melanopsis
Cuba
I. d. dominicensis
Hispaniola
I. d. portoricensis
Puerto Rico
Icterus wagleri (Black-vented Oriole)
. *I. w. castaneopectus*
NW Mexico
I. w. wagleri
W & S Mexico to Nicaragua
Icterus laudabilis (St Lucia Oriole)
St Lucia I
Icterus bonana (Martinique Oriole)
Martinique I
Icterus oberi (Monserrat Oriole)
Monserrat I
Icterus graduacauda (Black-headed Oriole)
I. g. audubonii
N Mexico
I. g. nayaritensis
WC Mexico
I. g. richardsoni
Oaxaca
I. g. dickeyae
Guerrero
I. g. graduacauda
C & S Mexico
Icterus maculialatus (Bar-winged Oriole)
S Mexico to El Salvador
Icterus parisorum (Scott's Oriole)
SC USA, C & W Mexico

NESOPSAR
Nesopsar nigerrimus (Jamaican Blackbird)
Jamaica

XANTHOPSAR
**Xanthopsar flavus (Saffron-cowled
Blackbird)**
Paraguay, NE Argentina

GYMNOMYSTAX
**Gymnomystax mexicanus (Oriole
Blackbird)**
N South America

XANTHOCEPHALUS
**Xanthocephalus xanthocephalus (Yellow-
headed Blackbird)**
SW Canada, W USA, W Mexico

Agelaius xanthophthalmus (Yellow-eyed Blackbird)
Peru
Agelaius thilius (Yellow-winged Blackbird)
A. t. alticola
SE Peru, NW Bolivia
A. t. thilius
S Chile, SW Argentina
A. t. petersii
SE Brazil, Uruguay, N Argentina
Agelaius phoeniceus (Red-winged Blackbird)
A. p. arctolegus
Canada, E USA » SC USA
A. p. fortis
WC USA
A. p. nevadensis
SW Canada, SW USA
A. p. caurinus
W USA
A. p. mailliardorum
WC California
A. p. californicus
C California
A. p. aciculatus
SC California
A. p. neutralis
S California, NW Baja California
A. p. sonoriensis
SW USA, NW Mexico
A. p. nyaritensis
SW Mexico
A. p. gubernator
NC Mexico
A. p. pallidulus
N Yucatan
A. p. nelsoni
SC Mexico
A. p. arthuralleni
N Guatemala
A. p. grinnelli
W Guatemala to NW Costa Rica
A. p. phoeniceus
SE Canada, E & S USA
A. p. littoralis
SE USA
A. p. mearnsi
SE USA
A. p. floridanus
S Florida
A. p. megapotamus
S Texas, NE Mexico
A. p. richmondi
S & SE Mexico, N Guatemala
A. p. matudae
SE Mexico

A. p. brevirostris
E Honduras, SE Nicaragua
A. p. bryanti
NW Bahama Is
A. p. assimilis
W Cuba
A. p. subniger
Isle of Pines
Agelaius tricolor (Tricoloured Blackbird)
W USA
Agelaius icterocephalus (Yellow-hooded Blackbird)
A. i. bogotensis
E Colombia
A. i. icterocephalus
Surinam to NE Peru
Agelaius humeralis (Tawny-shouldered Blackbird)
A. h. humaralis
Hispaniola
A. h. scopulus
Cuba
Agelaius xanthomus (Yellow-shouldered Blackbird)
A. x. xanthomus
Puerto Rico
A. x. monensis
Mona I (Puerto Rico)
Agelaius cyanopus (Unicoloured Blackbird)
A. c. xenicus
NE Brazil
A. c. atroolivaceus
E Brazil
A. c. beniensis
N Bolivia
A. c. cyanopus
E Bolivia, Paraguay, N Argentina
Agelaius ruficapillus (Chestnut-capped Blackbird)
A. r. frontalis
French Guiana, E Brazil
A. r. ruficapillus
SE Bolivia to Uruguay, N Argentina

Sturnella superciliaris (Bonaparte's Blackbird)
S Peru to Uruguay
Sturnella militaris (Red-breasted Blackbird)
South America
Sturnella bellicosa (Peruvian Red-breasted Meadowlark)
S. b. bellicosa
Ecuador, N Peru
S. b. albipes
SW Peru, N Chile
S. b. catamarcanus
NW Argentina

***Sturnella defilippi* (Lesser Red-breasted Meadowlark)**
SE Brazil, Uruguay, NE Argentina

***Sturnella loyca* (Long-tailed Meadowlark)**
S. l. loyca
S Chile, S Argentina
S. l. falklandicus
Falkland Is

***Sturnella magna* (Eastern Meadowlark)**
S. m. magna
SE Canada, C & E USA
S. m. argutula
SC & SE USA
S. m. hippocrepis
Cuba
S. m. hoopesi
S Texas, NE Mexico
S. m. lilianae
SW USA, NW Mexico
S. m. auropectoralis
C & SW Mexico
S. m. saundersi
Oaxaca, Mexico
S. m. alticola
S Mexico to Nicaragua
S. m. mexicana
SE Mexico
S. m. griscomi
SE Mexico
S. m. inexpectata
E Guatemala, Honduras
S. m. subulata
W Panama
S. m. meridionalis
N Colombia, NW Venezuela
S. m. paralios
N Colombia, W Venezuela
S. m. praticola
Northern Amazonia

***Sturnella neglecta* (Western Meadowlark)**
SW Canada, W USA » NW Mexico

PSEUDOLEISTES

***Pseudoleistes guirahuro* (Yellow-rumped Marshbird)**
SE Brazil, N Argentina, Paraguay, Uruguay

***Pseudoleistes virescens* (Brown-yellow Marshbird)**
SE Brazil, Uruguay, NE Argentina

AMBLYRAMPHUS

***Amblyramphus holosericeus* (Scarlet-headed Blackbird)**
Bolivia, Brazil, Paraguay, Uruguay, Argentina

HYPOPYRRHUS

***Hypopyrrhus pyrohypogaster* (Red-bellied Grackle)**
Colombia

CURAEUS

***Curaeus curaeus* (Austral Blackbird)**
C. c. curaeus
S Argentina, Chile
C. c. recurvirostris
Magellanes, Chile
C. c. reynoldsi
Tierra del Fuego

***Curaeus forbesi* (Forbes's Blackbird)**
E Brazil

GNORIMOPSAR

***Gnorimopsar chopi* (Chopi Blackbird)**
G. c. sulcirostris
E Bolivia, NW Argentina, E Brazil
G. c. chopi
SE Bolivia to Uruguay
N Argentina

OREOPSAR

***Oreopsar bolivianus* (Bolivian Blackbird) -**
Bolivia

LAMPROPSAR

***Lampropsar tanagrinus* (Velvet-fronted Grackle)**
L. t. guianensis
NE Venezuela, NW Guyana
L. t. tanagrinus
Ecuador, N Peru, W Brazil
L. t. macropterus
W Brazil
L. t. boliviensis
N Bolivia
L. t. violaceus
W Brazil

MACROAGELAIUS

***Macroagelaius subalaris* (Mountain Grackle)**
M. s. subalaris
C Colombia
M. s. imthurni
S Venezuela, N Brazil, W Guyana

DIVES

***Dives atroviolacea* (Cuban Blackbird)**
Cuba

***Dives dives* (Melodious Blackbird)**
D. d. dives
E Mexico to Nicaragua
D. d. warszewiczi
SW Ecuador, NW Peru
D. d. kalinowskii
W Peru

Quiscalus mexicanus (Great-tailed Grackle)
Q. m. nelsoni
SW USA, NW Mexico
Q. m. graysoni
NW Mexico
Q. m. obscurus
W Mexico
Q. m. monsoni
S USA, C Mexico
Q. m. prosopidicola
S USA, NE Mexico
Q. m. mexicanus
C & S Mexico to N Nicaragua
Q. m. loweryi
Belize
Q. m. peruvianus
Costa Rica to Peru, Venezuela
Quiscalus major (Boat-tailed Grackle)
Q. m. torreyi
E USA
Q. m. major
SE USA
Quiscalus nicaraguensis (Nicaraguan Grackle)
Nicaragua
Quiscalus quiscula (Common Grackle)
Q. q. versicolor
C & SE Canada, NE & C USA » S USA
Q. q. stonei
NC USA » SE USA
Q. q. quiscula
SE USA
Quiscalus niger (Antillean Grackle)
Q. n. caribaeus
W Cuba
Q. n. gundlachii
C & E Cuba
Q. n. caymanensis
Grand Cayman I
Q. n. bangsi
Little Cayman I
Q. n. crassirostris
Jamaica
Q. n. niger
Hispaniola
Q. n. brachypterus
Puerto Rico
Quiscalus lugubris (Carib Grackle)
Q. l. guadeloupensis
Monserrat I, Guadeloupe I, Martinique I
Q. l. inflexirostris
St Lucia I
Q. l. contusus
St Vincent I
Q. l. luminosus
Grenada I

Q. l. fortirostris
Barbados I, Antigua I
Q. l. orquillensis
Los Hermanos I (Venezuela)
Q. l. insularis
Margarita I
Q. l. lugubris
Trinidad, N Venezuela, the Guianas,
NE Brazil
EUPHAGUS
Euphagus carolinus (Rusty Blackbird)
E. c. carolinus
Canada, NE & C USA » SE USA
E. c. nigrans
Newfoundland » SE USA
Euphagus cyanocephalus (Brewer's Blackbird)
SW Canada, W USA » Mexico
MOLOTHRUS
Molothrus badius (Bay-winged Cowbird)
M. b. fringillarius
NE Brazil
M. b. badius
Bolivia to Uruguay, N Argentina
M. b. bolivianus
S Bolivia
Molothrus rufoaxillaris (Screaming Cowbird)
S Bolivia to Uruguay
Molothrus bonariensis (Common Cowbird)
M. b. cabanisii
E Panama, Colombia
M. b. aequatorialis
SW Colombia, W Ecuador
M. b. occidentalis
SW Ecuador, W Peru
M. b. venezuelensis
E Colombia, N Venezuela
M. b. minimus
S Lesser Antilles, the Guianas,
N Brazil
M. b. riparius
E Peru
M. b. bonariensis
Central South America
Molothus aeneus (Bronzed Cowbird)
M. a. loyei
SW USA, NW Mexico
M. a. assimilis
S & SW Mexico
M. a. aeneus
S Texas, E Mexico to Panama
M. a. armenti
N Colombia
Molothus ater (Brown-headed Cowbird)
M. a. artemisiae
W Canada, W USA » C Mexico

M. a. obscurus
SW USA » S Mexico
M. a. ater
C & S USA » SE USA
M. a. californicus
SW USA, Los Coronados Is

SCAPHIDURA
Scaphidura oryzivora (Giant Cowbird)
S. o. impacifa
S Mexico to W Panama
S. o. oryzivora
E Panama, Trinidad, N South America

DOLICHONYCHINAE

DOLICHONYX
Dolichonyx oryzivorus (Bobolink)
S Canada » N South America, West Indies

163 FRINGILLIDAE (FINCHES)

FRINGILLINAE

FRINGILLA
Fringilla coelebs (Chaffinch)
F. c. moreletti
Azores Is
F. c. maderensis
Madeira I
F. c. canariensis
Gran Canaria I, Tenerife I
F. c. ombriosa
Hierro I
F. c. palmae
Las Palmas I
F. c. africana
NW Africa
F. c. spodiogenys
Tunisia
F. c. coelebs
continent Europe, Siberia, C Asia, N Africa
F. c. gengleri
British Isles
F. c. sarda
Sardinia
F. c. schiebeli
Crete
F. c. solomkoi
Crimea
F. c. alexsandrovi
N Iran
F. c. transcaspica
S Transcaspia
Fringilla teydea (Blue Chaffinch)
F. t. teydea
Tenerife I

F. t. polatzeki
Gran Canaria I
Fringilla montifringilla (Brambling)
Europe to Japan » N Africa, N India, China

CARDUELINAE

SERINUS
Serinus pusillus (Red-fronted Serin)
Asia Minor to Tibet » Israel
Serinus serinus (Serin)
W & C Europe, Asia Minor, N Africa
Serinus syriacus (Syrian Serin)
Lebanon, Syria » Iraq, Egypt
Serinus canaria (Canary)
Canary Is, Azores Is, Madeira I
Serinus citrinella (Citril Finch)
S. c. citrinella
S Europe
S. c. corsicana
Corsica, Sardinia
Serinus thibetanus (Tibetan Siskin)
Nepal, SE Tibet » NE Burma & W China
Serinus canicollis (Yellow-crowned Canary)
S. c. flavivertex
Ethiopia to N Tanzania
S. c. sassii
S Zaire to N Malawi
S. c. huillensis
C Angola
S. c. griseitergum
E Rhodesia
S. c. thompsonae
Transvaal, N Cape Province
S. c. canicollis
Cape Province
Serinus nigriceps (Black-headed Siskin)
N Ethiopia
Serinus citrinelloides (African Citril Finch)
S. c. citrinelloides
Ethiopia, SE Sudan
S. c. kikuyensis
W Kenya
S. c. brittoni
Kapenguria, Kenya
S. c. frontalis
W Uganda, E Zaire, NW Tanzania
S. c. hypostictus
S Kenya, E Zambia to Mozambique
S. c. martinsi
Mexico, Angola
Serinus capistratus (Black-faced Canary)
S. c. capistratus
Gabon to N Angola, Zambia
S. c. hildegardae
S Angola
Serinus koliensis (Van Someren's Canary)
Uganda, W Kenya, Rwanda

Serinus scotops (Forest Canary)
S. s. transvaalensis
  N & E Transvaal
S. s. umbrosus
  SE Transvaal, Natal, S Cape Province
S. s. scotops
  S Natal, E Cape Province
**Serinus leucopygius (White-rumped
Seedeater)**
S. l. riggenbachi
  Senegal to Chad, Central African Republic
S. l. pallens
  Air to N Nigeria
S. l. leucopygius
  E Sudan, N Ethiopia
**Serinus atrogularis (Yellow-rumped
Seedeater)**
S. a. rothschildi
  E Arabia
S. a. xanthopygius
  N Ethiopia
S. a. reichenowi
  S Sudan to NE Tanzania
S. a. somereni
  E Zaire, W Uganda, W Kenya
S. a. lwenarum
  S Zaire, Angola, Zambia
S. a. atrogularis
  Rhodesia, W Transvaal
S. a. impiger
  SE Transvaal, W Natal, N Cape Province
S. a. semideserti
  S Angola, N Namibia, S Zambia
S. a. deserti
  SW Angola, NW Namibia
**Serinus citrinipectus (Lemon-breasted
Seedeater)**
  S Malawi, SE Rhodesia, S Mozambique
**Serinus mozambicus (Yellow-fronted
Canary)**
S. m. caniceps
  Senegal to N Cameroun
S. m. punctigula
  Cameroun
S. m. barbatus
  N Zaire, Sudan to Kenya
S. m. santhome
  Sao Thomé I
S. m. tando
  SW Zaire, N Angola
S. m. samaliyae
  SE Zaire, Zambia
S. m. vansoni
  SE Angola, Namibia, SW Zambia
S. m. mozambicus
  Kenya to Zambia, Mozambique
S. m. granti
  S Mozambique, South Africa

S. m. grotei
  E Sudan, W Ethiopia
S. m. gommaensis
  W Ethiopia
Serinus donaldsoni (Grosbeak Canary)
S. d. donaldsoni
  Ethiopia, N Kenya
S. d. buchanani
  S Kenya, N Tanzania
Serinus flaviventris (Yellow Canary)
S. f. maculicollis
  S Ethiopia, Kenya, Somalia
S. f. dorsostriatus
  N Tanzania
S. f. damarensis
  Namibia, Botswana
S. f. flaviventris
  W Cape Province
S. f. quintoni
  S & C Cape Province
S. f. marshalli
  NW Cape Province, Transvaal
S. f. guillarmodi
  Lesotho
Serinus sulphuratus (Brimstone Canary)
S. s. sharpii
  Angola to Kenya, Mozambique
S. s. wilsoni
  S Mozambique, South Africa
S. s. sulphuratus
  S Cape Province
**Serinus albogularis (White-throated
Seedeater)**
S. a. crocopygius
  SW Angola, N Namibia
S. a. sordahlae
  S Namibia, NW Cape Province
S. a. albogularis
  W Cape Province
S. a. hewitti
  C Cape Province
S. a. orangensis
  Orange Free State
**Serinus gularis (Streaky-headed
Seedeater)**
S. g. canicapilla
  Senegal to N Cameroun
S. g. montanorum
  Cameroun
S. g. uamensis
  W Central African Republic
S. g. elgonensis
  N Zaire, S Sudan, W Kenya
S. g. striatipectus
  S Sudan, S Ethiopia, N Kenya
S. g. reichardi
  S Zaire, Zambia to Tanzania

S. g. benguellensis
C Angola, W Zambia
S. g. mendosus
NE Botswana, NW Transvaal
S. g. gularis
Rhodesia to N Cape Province
S. g. endemion
S Mozambique, E South Africa
S. g. humilis
SW Cape Province
Serinus mennelli (Black-eared Seedeater)
E Angola to Mozambique
Serinus tristriatus (Brown-rumped Seedeater)
E Ethiopia
Serinus ankoberensis (Ankober Serin)
C Ethiopia
Serinus menachensis (Menacha Seedeater)
Saudi Arabia
Serinus striolatus (Streaky Seedeater)
S. s. striolatus
Ethiopia, N Kenya
S. s. affinis
Kenya, N Tanzania
S. s. graueri
Uganda, W Kenya, W Tanzania
S. s. whytii
S Tanzania, N Malawi
Serinus burtoni (Thick-billed Seedeater)
S. b. burtoni
Cameroun
S. b. tanganjicae
E Zaire, W Uganda
S. b. kilimensis
N Kenya, N Tanzania
S. b. albifrons
E Kenya
S. b. melanochrous
S Tanzania
Serinus rufobrunneus (Principé Seedeater)
S. r. rufobrunneus
Principé I
S. r. thomensis
Sao Thomé I
Serinus leucopterus (White-winged Seedeater)
SW Cape Province
Serinus totta (Cape Siskin)
S. t. totta
S Cape Province
S. t. symonsi
E Cape Province, W Natal, Lesotho
Serinus alario (Black-headed Canary)
S. a. leucolaema
Namibia, Botswana, W Cape Province
S. a. alario
N & C Cape Province

Serinus estherae (Malay Goldfinch)
S. e. vanderbilti
N Sumatra
S. e. estherae
W Java
S. e. orientalis
E Java
S. e. renatae
Celebes
S. e. mindanensis
Mindanao I

NEOSPIZA
Neospiza concolor (Grosbeak-Weaver)
Sao Thomé I **e?**

LINURGUS
Linurgus olivaceus (Oriole-Finch)
L. o. olivaceus
SE Nigeria, Cameroun, Fernando Po I
L. o. prigoginei
E Zaire
L. o. elgonensis
SE Sudan, N Kenya
L. o. kilimensis
Tanzania, N Malawi

RHYNCHOSTRUTHUS
Rhynchostruthus socotranus (Golden-winged Grosbeak)
R. s. louisae
N Somalia
R. s. percivali
SW Arabia
R. s. socotranus
Socotra I

CARDUELIS
Carduelis chloris (Greenfinch)
C. c. chloris
N Europe » S Europe
C. c. aurantiiventris
S Europe, N Africa
C. c. chlorotica
Syria, Lebanon » Egypt
C. c. turkestanica
Caucasas » Iran, Afghanistan & Iraq
Carduelis sinica (Oriental Greenfinch)
C. s. sinica
E & C China
C. s. chabarovi
Manchuria, Mongolia
C. s. ussuriensis
E Manchuria
C. s. kawarahiba
Sakhalin I, NE Asia » Japan
C. s. minor
S Japan
C. s. kittlitzi
Bonin Is

Carduelis spinoides (Black-headed Green-finch)
C. s. spinoides
Pakistan, N India, E Himalayas
C. s. heinrichi
S Assam, W Burma
C. s. monguilloti
S Vietnam
Carduelis ambigua (Yunnan Greenfinch)
C. a. taylori
SE Tibet, Sikang
C. a. ambigua
SW China, N Burma
Carduelis spinus (Siskin)
N Asia, N Europe » Japan, N Africa & China
Carduelis pinus (Pine Siskin)
C. p. pinus
Canada, USA » C Mexico
C. p. macroptera
N Baja California, NW & C Mexico
C. p. perplexa
S Mexico, W Guatemala
Carduelis atriceps (Black-capped Siskin)
S Mexico, W Guatemala
Carduelis spinescens (Andean Siskin)
C. s. spinescens
Colombia, W Venezuela
C. s. capitanea
N Colombia
C. s. nigricauda
N Colombia
Carduelis yarrellii (Yellow-faced Siskin)
N Venezuela, N Brazil
Carduelis cucullata (Red Siskin)
NE Colombia, N Venezuela
Carduelis crassirostris (Thick-billed Siskin)
C. c. amadoni
SE Peru
C. c. crassirostris
S Bolivia, C Chile, W Argentina
Carduelis magellanica (Hooded Siskin)
C. m. capitàlis
S Colombia, Ecuador, NW Peru
C. m. paula
S Ecuador, W Peru
C. m. peruana
C Peru
C. m. urubambensis
S Peru, N Chile
C. m. boliviana
S Bolivia
C. m. tucumana
NW Argentina
C. m. santaecrucis
EC Bolivia
C. m. alleni
SE Bolivia, Paraguay, NE Argentina

C. m. icterica
SE Brazil, E & S Paraguay
C. m. magellanica
Uruguay, E Argentina
C. m. longirostris
SE Venezuela, Guyana, N Brazil
Carduelis dominicensis (Antillean Siskin)
Hispaniola
Carduelis siemiradzkii (Saffron Siskin)
SW Ecuador
Carduelis olivacea (Olivaceous Siskin)
SE Ecuador, Peru, Bolivia
Carduelis notata (Black-headed Siskin)
C. n. notata
E & C Mexico, N Guatemala
C. n. forreri
W Mexico
C. n. oleacea
Belize to N Nicaragua
Carduelis xanthogastra (Yellow-bellied Siskin)
C. x. xanthogastra
Costa Rica to Colombia, Venezuela
C. x. stejnegeri
C Bolivia
Carduelis atrata (Black Siskin)
S Peru to N Chile, W Argentina
Carduelis uropygialis (Yellow-rumped Siskin)
S Peru to Chile, W Argentina
Carduelis barbata (Black-chinned Siskin)
S Chile, W Argentina
Carduelis tristis (American Goldfinch)
C. t. tristis
C USA » SE USA, E Mexico
C. t. pallida
W Canada. WC USA » N Mexico
C. t. jewetti
SW Canada, NW USA
C. t. salicamans
SW USA, N Baja California
Carduelis psaltria (Dark-backed Green-finch)
C. p. hesperophila
W USA, NW Mexico
C. p. witti
Tres Marias Is
C. p. psaltria
SC USA, N Mexico
C. p. jouyi
SE Mexico
C. p. colombiana
S Mexico to Peru, Venezuela
Carduelis lawrencei (Lawrence's Goldfinch)
SW USA » NW Mexico

Carduelis carduelis (Goldfinch)
   C. c. carduelis
      W & C Europe
   C. c. britannica
      British Isles, Netherlands
   C. c. parva
      W Mediterranean, Azores Is, Canary Is
   C. c. tschusii
      Corsica, Sardinia, Sicily
   C. c. balcanica
      E Mediterranean
   C. c. niediecki
      Cyprus, Asia Minor, Iraq, Iran, Egypt
   C. c. major
      SW Siberia
   C. c. brevirostris
      Caucasus
   C. c. loudoni
      N Iran
   C. c. paropanisi
      Central Asia » S Iran
   C. c. subulata
      NC Asia » Turkistan
   C. c. caniceps
      Pakistan, W Himalayas, Nepal

ACANTHIS
Acanthis flammea (Redpoll)
   A. f. flammea
      N Europe, Asia, North America » S Europe
      & N China
   A. f. rostrata
      NE Canada » NE USA, NW Europe
   A. f. islandica
      Iceland
   A. f. cabaret
      British Is, Switzerland
Acanthis hornemanni (Arctic Redpoll)
   A. h. exilipes
      N Eurasia, N North America » C Europe
   A. h. hornemanni
      Greenland, C & E Canada » British Isles &
      S Canada
Acanthis flavirostris (Twite)
   A. f. flavirostris
      NE & C Europe » S Europe
   A. f. pipilans
      N British Isles, Ireland
   A. f. brevirostris
      Caucasus, NW Iran
   A. f. korejevi
      C Asia
   A. f. altaica
      EC Asia
   A. f. montanella
      N Pakistan, Altai, W Sinkiang
   A. f. miniakensis
      E Sinkiang, NW China

   A. f. rufostrigata
      Pakistan, Tibet, Himalayas, N India
Acanthis cannabina (Linnet)
   A. c. cannabina
      Europe, NW Asia » N Africa
   A. c. autochthona
      Scotland
   A. c. nana
      Madeira I
   A. c. meadewaldoi
      W Canary Is
   A. c. harterti
      E Canary Is
   A. c. bella
      Asia Minor, SW Asia » Egypt, N India
Acanthis yemensis (Yemeni Linnet)
   SW Arabia
Acanthis johannis (Warsangli Linnet)
   NE Somalia

LEUCOSTICTE
**Leucosticte nemoricola (Hodgson's Rosy
Finch)**
   L. n. altaica
      W Pakistan, W Sinkiang, Altai
   L. n. nemoricola
      Himalayas, W China » N Burma
Leucosticte brandti (Brandt's Rosy Finch)
   L. b. margaritacea
      W Mongolia, SE Altai
   L. b. brandti
      W Tien Shan, W Sinkiang
   L. b. pamirensis
      W Tien Shan, NE Afghanistan
   L. b. haematopygia
      N Pakistan, Himalayas, Tibet
   L. b. pallidior
      SW Sinkiang, NE Tsinghai
Leucosticte arctoa (Rosy Finch)
   L. a. arctoa
      Altai
   L. a. cognata
      Tannu Tuva
   L. a. sushkini
      N Mongolia
   L. a. gigliolii
      Transbaicalia
   L. a. brunneonucha
      E Siberia, Kurile Is
   L. a. griseonucha
      Aleutian Is, Kodiak I, Alaska
   L. a. umbrina
      St Matthew I, Pribilof Is
   L. a. irvingi
      N Alaska
   L. a. littoralis
      E Alaska, W Canada » SW USA
   L. a. tephrocotis
      WC Canada » WC USA

L. a. dawsoni
 E California
L. a. wallowa
 NE Oregon » W Nevada
L. a. atrata
 WC USA » SC USA
L. a. australis
 SW USA

CALLACANTHIS
Callacanthis burtoni (Red-browed Rose Finch)
 W Pakistan, Himalayas

RHODOPECHYS
Rhodopechys sanguinea (Crimson-winged Finch)
 R. s. aliena
  Morocco
 R. s. sanguinea
  Caucasus, Iran, SC Asia
Rhodopechys githaginea (Trumpeter Finch)
 R. g. amantum
  Canary Is
 R. g. zedlitzi
  N Africa
 R. g. githaginea
  S Egypt, N Sudan
 R. g. crassirostris
  Arabia, Iran » NW India
Rhodopechys mongolica (Mongolian Trumpeter Finch)
 E Asia, India » E China
Rhodopechys obsoleta (Lichenstein's Desert Finch)
 Asia Minor » N Pakistan

URAGUS
Uragus sibiricus (Long-tailed Rose Finch)
 U. s. sibiricus
  S Siberia, N Manchuria » Turkistan
 U. s. ussuriensis
  C Manchuria, Korea » NE China
 U. s. sanguinolentus
  Sakhalin I, S Kurile Is » S Japan
 U. s. lepidus
  NW China
 U. s. henrici
  Sikang

UROCYNCHRAMUS
Urocynchramus pylzowi (Przewalski's Rosefinch)
 W China

CARPODACUS
Carpodacus rubescens (Blanford's Rosefinch)
 Himalayas, W China

Carpodacus nipalensis (Dark Rosefinch) 599
 C. n. kangrae
  W Himalayas
 C. n. nipalensis
  C Himalayas, N Assam
 C. n. intensicolor
  Sikang, W China » N Burma
Carpodacus erythrinus (Common Rosefinch)
 C. e. erythrinus
  E Europe, W Asia » India, Indochina
 C. e. grebnitskii
  E Siberia, Manchuria » SE China
 C. e. kubanensis
  Caucasus, Iran, W India
 C. e. ferghanensis
  C Asia » NW India
 C. e. roseatus
  Himalayas, Tibet, China » S India, Indochina
Carpodacus purpureus (Purple Finch)
 C. p. purpureus
  Canada, NE USA » SE USA
 C. p. californicus
  SW Canada » SW USA, Baja California
Carpodacus cassinii (Cassin's Finch)
 SW Canada, W USA » N Mexico
Carpodacus mexicanus (House Finch)
 C. m. frontalis
  SW Canada, W USA, NW Mexico
 C. m. clementis
  San Clemente I, Los Coronados Is
 C. m. mcgregori
  San Benito I
 C. m. amplus
  Guadeloupe I
 C. m. ruberrimus
  S Baja California, NW Mexico
 C. m. rhodopnus
  C Sinaloa
 C. m. coccineus
  SW Mexico
 C. m. potosinus
  NC Mexico
 C. m. centralis
  C Mexico
 C. m. mexicanus
  SC Mexico
 C. m. griscomi
  Guerrero
Carpodacus pulcherrimus (Beautiful Rosefinch)
 C. p. pulcherrimus
  Himalayas
 C. p. waltoni
  SE Tibet, SW Sikang
 C. p. argyrophrys
  E Tsinghai, W China

C. p. davidianus
C Mongolia
***Carpodacus eos* (Stresemann's Rosefinch)**
W China, E Sikang
***Carpodacus rhodochrous* (Pink-browed Rosefinch)**
Himalayas
***Carpodacus vinaceus* (Vinaceous Rosefinch)**
C. v. vinaceus
W China, E Sikang
C. v. formosanus
Taiwan
***Carpodacus edwardsii* (Large Rosefinch)**
C. e. edwardsii
W China, E Sikang
C. e. rubicunda
Himalayas, SE Tibet » N Burma
***Carpodacus synoicus* (Sinai Rosefinch)**
C. s. synoicus
Sinai
C. s. salimalii
NE Afghanistan
C. s. stoliczkae
SW Sinkiang
C. s. beicki
NE Tsinghai, NW China
***Carpodacus roseus* (Pallas's Rosefinch)**
Altai, E Asia » N China, C Japan
***Carpodacus trifasciatus* (Three-banded Rosefinch)**
W China » SE Tibet
***Carpodacus rhodopeplus* (Spot-winged Rosefinch)**
C. r. rhodopeplus
Himalayas
C. r. verreauxii
W China » N Burma
***Carpodacus thura* (White-browed Rosefinch)**
C. t. blythi
NE Afghanistan, Pakistan, W Himalayas
C. t. thura
C Himalayas
C. t. femininus
SE Tibet, W China
C. t. dubius
SE Tsinghai, NW China
C. t. deserticolor
NE Tsinghai
***Carpodacus rhodochlamys* (Red-mantled Rosefinch)**
C. r. rhodochlamys
C Asia
C. r. kotschubeii
SC Asia
C. r. grandis
Pakistan, W Himalayas

***Carpodacus rubicilloides* (Eastern Great Rosefinch)**
C. r. lucifer
Ladakh, Himalayas
C. r. rubicilloides
E Sikang, E Tsinghai » SW China
***Carpodacus rubicilla* (Caucasian Great Rosefinch)**
C. r. rubicilla
Caucasus
C. r. diabolica
NE Afghanistan
C. r. kobdensis
Altai, W Mongolia
C. r. severtzovi
Pakistan to W China
***Carpodacus puniceus* (Rose-breasted Rosefinch)**
C. p. kilianensis
SC Asia
C. p. humii
Pakistan, N India, W Himalayas
C. p. puniceus
C Himalayas, SW Sikang, SE Tibet
C. p. sikangensis
Sikang
C. p. longirostris
E Tsinghai, W China
***Carpodacus roborowskii* (Tibet Rosefinch)**
Tsinghai

PINICOLA
***Pinicola enucleator* (Pine Grosbeak)**
P. e. enucleator
Scandinavia, Russia
P. e. pacatus
Siberia, Altai, Manchuria
P. e. kamschatkensis
NE Asia, Kamchatka
P. e. sakhalinensis
Sakhalin I, Kurile Is
P. e. alascensis
Alaska, W Canada, NW USA
P. e. flammulus
W Canada » NW USA
P. e. carlottae
Queen Charlotte Is, Vancouver I
P. e. montanus
SW Canada, WC USA
P. e. californicus
E California
P. e. leucurus
C & E Canada » NE USA
P. e. eschatosus
SE Canada » NE USA
***Pinicola subhimachalus* (Red-headed Finch)**
Himalayas, S Sikang

Haematospiza sipahi (Scarlet Finch)
Himalayas to N Vietnam

LOXIA
Loxia pytyopsittacus (Parrot Crossbill)
NE Europe, W Siberia
Loxia scotica (Scottish Crossbill)
Scotland
Loxia curvirostra (Red Crossbill)
L. c. curvirostra
N Europe, N & NE Asia
L. c. corsicana
Corsica
L. c. balearica
Balearic Is
L. c. poliogyna
Algeria, Tunisia
L. c. guillemardi
Cyprus
L. c. mariae
SW Crimea
L. c. altaiensis
Altai
L. c. tianschanica
Sinkiang
L. c. himalayensis
Himalayas, W China » N Burma
L. c. meridionalis
S Vietnam
L. c. japonica
NE Asia » EC China, S Japan
L. c. luzoniensis
N Luzon I
L. c. pusilla
Newfoundland » NE USA
L. c. minor
SE Canada, NE USA » SE USA
L. c. benti
WC USA » S USA
L. c. bendirei
SW Canada, W USA » S USA
L. c. sitkensis
Canada, W & C USA » E USA
L. c. grinnelli
SW USA
L. c. stricklandi
S USA, Mexico
L. c. mesamericana
Guatemala to N Nicaragua
Loxia leucoptera (White-winged Crossbill)
L. l. bifasciata
E Europe, N Asia, Japan
L. l. leucoptera
Canada, N USA
L. l. megaplaga
Hispaniola

Pyrrhula nipalensis (Brown Bullfinch)
P. n. nipalensis
Pakistan, N India
P. n. ricketti
Tibet to N Vietnam
P. n. victoriae
Burma
P. n. waterstradti
Malaysia
P. n. uchidai
Taiwan
Pyrrhula leucogenys (Philippine Bullfinch)
P. l. leucogenys
N Luzon I
P. l. steerei
W Mindanao I
P. l. coriaria
C Mindanao I
P. l. apo
SE Mindanao I
Pyrrhula aurantiaca (Orange Bullfinch)
Pakistan, NW Himalayas
Pyrrhula erythrocephala (Red-headed Bullfinch)
Himalayas, SE Tibet
Pyrrhula erythaca (Beavan's Bullfinch)
P. e. erythaca
Himalayas to W China
P. e. wilderi
NE China
P. e. owstoni
Taiwan
Pyrrhula pyrrhula (Bullfinch)
P. p. pyrrhula
N Europe to W Mongolia » S Europe, Iran
P. p. pileata
British Isles
P. p. europoea
NW Europe
P. p. iberiae
Azores Is, N Iberia
P. p. murina
San Miguel I (Azores)
P. p. rossikowi
Caucasus, W Turkey
P. p. caspica
NE & N Iran
P. p. cineracea
N Altai » Amur, Manchuria
P. p. cassinii
Kamchatka » Japan, N China
P. p. griseiventris
Ussuri, Sakhalin I to Korea, S Japan

Coccothraustes coccothraustes (Hawfinch)
C.ˉc. coccothraustes
N Europe, W Asia » N Africa
C. c. burryi
NW Africa
C. c. nigricans
Ukraine, N Iran » S Iran
C. c. humii
C Russia » NW India
C. c. japonicus
Sakhalin I, Japan » E China & Bonin I
Coccothraustes migratorius (Black-tailed Hawfinch)
C. m. migratorius
S Ussuri » N Korea & E China
C. m. sowerbyi
E China
Coccothraustes personatus (Masked Hawfinch)
C. p. personatus
N Japan » S Japan, E China
C. p. magnirostris
NE Asia
Coccothraustes icterioides (Black and Yellow Grosbeak)
Afghanistan to N India
Coccothraustes affinis (Allied Grosbeak)
Pakistan to W China, N Burma
Coccothraustes melanozanthos (Spotted-wing Grosbeak)
Pakistan to W China, Thailand
Coccothraustes carnipes (White-winged Grosbeak)
C. c. speculigerus
NE Iran to Pakistan
C. c. carnipes
Pakistan to W China
Coccothraustes vespertinus (Evening Grosbeak)
C. v. vespertinus
C & E Canada » NE USA
C. v. brooksi
W Canada » SW USA
C. v. montanus
W & SW Mexico
Coccothraustes abeillei (Hooded Grosbeak)
C. a. pallidus
NW Mexico
C. a. saturatus
W Mexico
C. a. abeillei
C & S Mexico
C. a. cobanensis
S Mexico, Guatemala

Pyrrhoplectes epauletta (Gold-headed Finch)
Himalayas, SE Tibet » N Burma

164 ESTRILDIDAE (WAXBILLS)

PARMOPTILA
Parmoptila woodhousei (Flowerpecker Weaver Finch)
P. w. woodhousei
SE Nigeria, Cameroun, W Zaire
P. w. ansorgei
N Angola
Parmoptila jamesoni (Red-fronted Flowerpecker Weaver Finch)
P. j. rubrifrons
Ghana
P. j. jamesoni
E Zaire, W Uganda

NIGRITA
Nigrita fusconota (White-breasted Negro Finch)
N. f. uropygialis
Guinea to S Nigeria
N. f. fusconota
Fernando Po I, Gabon, Cameroun Mt to Angola, Uganda, Kenya
Nigrita bicolor (Chestnut-breasted Negro Finch)
N. b. bicolor
Guinea to Ghana
N. b. brunnescens
S Nigeria to W Uganda & N Angola
Nigrita luteifrons (Pale-fronted Negro Finch)
N. l. luteifrons
S Nigeria to N Zaire & Gabon
N. l. alexanderi
Fernando Po I
Nigrita canicapilla (Grey-crowned Negro Finch)
N. c. emilae
Guinea to Ghana
N. c. canicapilla
S Nigeria to W Zaire & Uganda
N. c. angolensis
SW Zaire, NW Angola
N. c. sparsimguttata
S Sudan, E Zaire, Uganda, NW Tanzania
N. c. schistacea
SE Sudan, Kenya, N Tanzania
N. c. diabolica
C Kenya
N. c. candida
W Tanzania

Nesocharis shelleyi (Fernando Po Olive-back)
N. s. shelleyi
Fernando Po I, Cameroun Mt
N. s. bansoensis
SE Nigeria, Cameroun
Nesocharis ansorgei (White-collared Olive-back)
E Zaire, W Uganda
Nesocharis capistrata (Grey-headed Olive-back)
Gambia to Sudan, Uganda

Pytilia phoenicoptera (Crimson-winged Pytilia) (Aurora Finch)
P. p. phoenicoptera
Senegal to Cameroun
P. p. emini
Cameroun to Uganda & S Sudan
P. p. lineata
N Ethiopia
Pytilia hypogrammica (Red-faced Pytilia)
Sierra Leone to Cameroun
Pytilia afra (Orange-winged Pytilia)
Sudan to Angola, Zambia
Pytilia melba (Green-winged Pytilia)
P. m. citerior
Senegal to Sudan
P. m. soudanensis
E Sudan, Ethiopia, Kenya
P. m. jessei
E Ethiopia
P. m. percivali
SW Kenya, N Tanzania
P. m. belli
Uganda, E Zaire to Malawi
P. m. grotei
NE Tanzania to Mozambique
P. m. melba
Zaire & Tanzania to Namibia & Transvaal
P. m. hygrophila
N Zambia, N Malawi
P. m. thermophila
E Mozambique, E Natal

Mandingoa nitidula (Green-backed Twin-spot)
M. n. schlegeli
Sierra Leone to Zaire, Angola
M. n. virginiae
Fernando Po I
M. n. chubbi
S Ethiopia, S Sudan, Kenya, Tanzania, Zanzibar I
M. n. nitidula
Mozambique & Zambia to E Cape Province

Cryptospiza reichenovii (Red-faced Crimson-wing)
C. r. reichenovii
Cameroun to Uganda, N Angola
C. r. australis
S Uganda, Tanzania, Malawi, Rhodesia, Mozambique
C. r. homogenes
E Rhodesia
Cryptospiza salvadorii (Ethiopian Crimson-wing)
C. s. salvadorii
S Ethiopia, N Kenya
C. s. ruwenzori
E Zaire, W Uganda
C. s. kilimensis
SE Sudan, Kenya, N Tanzania
Cryptospiza jacksoni (Dusky Crimson-wing)
E Zaire, W Uganda
Cryptospiza shelleyi (Shelley's Crimson-wing)
E Zaire, W Uganda

Pyrenestes sanguineus (Crimson Seed-cracker)
P. s. sanguineus
Senegal to Ivory Coast
P. s. coccineus
Sierra Leone to Gabon
Pyrenestes ostrinus (Black-bellied Seedcracker)
P. o. ostrinus
Ghana to Togo
P. o. frommi
C Togo to Cameroun, N Zaire
P. o. rothschildi
Ghana to Zaire, Angola
Pyrenestes minor (Lesser Seedcracker)
Tanzania, Malawi, Rhodesia

Spermophaga poliogenys (Grant's Bluebill)
E Zaire, W Uganda
Spermophaga haematina (Western Bluebill)
S. h. haematina
Gambia to Ghana
S. h. togoensis
Togo to SW Nigeria
S. h. pustulata
S Nigeria, Cameroun to N Zaire, N Angola
Spermophaga ruficapilla (Red-headed Bluebill)
S. r. ruficapilla
Angola to E Zaire, Uganda,S Sudan, W Kenya
S. r. kilgoris
SW Kenya
S. r. cana
Tanzania

Clytospiza monteiri (Brown Twin-spot)
Cameroun to Sudan, Uganda

Hypargos margaritatus (Rosy Twin-spot)
N Natal, Mozambique
Hypargos niveoguttatus (Peters's Twin-spot)
H. n. macrospilotus
E Zaire, Kenya, Tanzania, Malawi
H. n. idius
Zambia
H. n. interior
Rhodesia
H. n. niveoguttatus
Mozambique
H. n. baddeleyi
Nacola, Mozambique

EUSCHISTOSPIZA
Euschistospiza dybowskii (Dybowski's Dusky Twin-spot)
Sierra Leone to Sudan
Euschistospiza cinereovinacea (Dusky Twin-spot)
E. c. cinereovinacea
W Angola
E. c. graueri
E Zaire, W Tanzania

LAGONOSTICTA
Lagonosticta rara (Black-bellied Fire Finch)
L. r. forbesi
Sierra Leone to Nigeria
L. r. rara
N Cameroun to S Sudan, Uganda, Kenya
Lagonosticta rufopicta (Bar-breasted Fire Finch)
L. r. rufopicta
Senegal to N Cameroun, Central African Republic
L. r. lateritia
Sudan, NE Zaire, W Uganda
Lagonosticta nitidula (Brown Fire Finch)
L. n. nitidula
E Angola, S Zaire, N Zambia
L. n. plumbaria
S Zambia, Botswana
Lagonosticta senegala (Red-billed Fire Finch)
L. s. senegala
Senegal to Nigeria
L. s. guineensis
coast of Guinea & Sierra Leone
L. s. rhodopsis
Chad to SW Sudan
L. s. brunneiceps
Ethiopia
L. s. somaliensis
Somalia, Kenya, Tanzania

L. s. kikuyuensis
C Kenya, N Tanzania
L. s. ruberrima
Uganda, SE Zaire, Zambia, W Tanzania
L. s. rendalli
SE Zaire, S Tanzania, South Africa
L. s. pallidicrissa
S Angola, N Namibia
Lagonosticta virata (Kuli Koro Fire Finch)
Mali
Lagonosticta rubricata (African Fire Finch)
L. r. polionota
Guinea to Nigeria
L. r. ugandae
Cameroun to N Tanzania
L. r. congica
Gabon to S Zaire, NW Zambia
L. r. haematocephala
S Tanzania, Mozambique
L. r. rubricata
S Mozambique to Cape Province
Lagonosticta landanae (Pale-billed Fire Finch)
Cabinda, W Angola
Lagonosticta rhodopareia (Jameson's Fire Finch)
L. r. bruneli
S Chad
L. r. rhodopareia
Ethiopia, N Kenya
L. r. jamesoni
S Kenya to Transvaal, Natal
L. r. ansorgei
Cabinda, W Angola
Lagonosticta larvata (Masked Fire Finch)
W Ethiopia, Sudan
Lagonosticta vinacea (Vinaceous Fire Finch)
L. v. vinacea
Senegal to Guinea
L. v. togoensis
Ghana, Togo to N Cameroun, W. Sudan
L. v. nigricollis
Central African Republic to Sudan & Uganda

URAEGINTHUS
Uraeginthus angolensis (Cordon-bleu)
U. a. angolensis
SW Zaire, N Angola, NW Zambia
U. a. cyanopleurus
Rhodesia, N Botswana, W Transvaal
U. a. niassensis
E Tanzania, SE Zaire, to Rhodesia, Transvaal
U. a. damarensis
Botswana, N Namibia

Uraeginthus bengalus (Red-cheeked Cordon-bleu)
U. b. bengalus
  W, NC & E Africa
U. b. brunneigularis
  Kenya
U. b. littoralis
  E Kenya, Tanzania
U. b. ugogoensis
  N & W Tanzania
U. b. katangae
  S Zaire, Zambia
Uraeginthus cyanocephala (Blue-capped Cordon-bleu)
  Ethiopia to Tanzania
Uraeginthus granatina (Common Grenadier)
U. g. granatina
  S Angola to Natal
U. g. siccata
  W Angola to N Cape Province
U. g. retusa
  Mozambique
Uraeginthus ianthinogaster (Purple Grenadier)
U. i. ianthinogaster
  Somalia, N Kenya, N Uganda
U. i. hawkeri
  SE Sudan, Uganda, N Kenya
U. i. roosevelti
  Kenya
U. i. rothschildi
  Kenya

ESTRILDA
Estrilda caerulescens (Lavender Waxbill)
  Senegal to Central African Republic
Estrilda perreini (Black-tailed Waxbill)
E. p. perreini
  Gabon to N Angola & Tanzania
E. p. poliogastra
  S Tanzania to Rhodesia, Mozambique
E. p. torrida
  Sufala, Mozambique
E. p. incana
  Natal

Estrilda thomensis (Cinderella Waxbill)
  Sao Thomé I
Estrilda melanotis (Swee Waxbill)
E. m. quartinia
  Ethiopia, SE Sudan
E. m. kilimensis
  E Zaire, Uganda to Zambia, Rhodesia
E. m. bocagei
  W Angola
E. m. stuartirwini
  S Mozambique

E. m. melanotis
  South Africa
Estrilda poliopareia (Anambra Waxbill)
  S Nigeria
Estrilda paludicola (Fawn-breasted Waxbill)
E. p. paludicola
  N Zaire, N Uganda, S Sudan
E. p. ochrogaster
  Ethiopia, SE Sudan
E. p. roseicrissa
  S Uganda, NW Tanzania
E. p. marwitzi
  W Tanzania
E. p. benguellensis
  Angola, N Zambia
E. p. ruthae
  C Zaire
Estrilda melpoda (Orange-cheeked Waxbill)
E. m. melpoda
  Gambia to N Zaire, N Angola, Zambia
E. m. tschadensis
  Cameroun, Chad
Estrilda rhodopyga (Crimson-rumped Waxbill)
E. r. rhodopyga
  Sudan, Ethiopia, N Somalia
E. r. centralis
  S Ethiopia, SE Sudan, Uganda to Tanzania, Malawi
Estrilda rufibarba (Arabian Waxbill)
  SW Arabia
Estrilda troglodytes (Black-rumped Waxbill)
  Senegal to Ethiopia
Estrilda astrild (Common Waxbill)
E. a. kempi
  Sierra Leone, Liberia
E. a. occidentalis
  Fernando Po I, Cameroun to N Zaire
E. a. sousae
  Sao Thomé I
E. a. peasei
  Ethiopia
E. a. macmillani
  Sudan
E. a. adesma
  Uganda, NW Tanzania
E. a. massaica
  Kenya, N Tanzania
E. a. minor
  E Kenya, NE Tanzania, Zanzibar
E. a. cavendeshi
  S Tanzania to Zambia, Transvaal, Mozambique
E. a. schoutedeni
  S Zaire

E. a. ngamiensis
E Angola, Zambia, Rhodesia
E. a. angolensis
S Zaire, W Angola
E. a. jagoensis
W Angola, Cape Verde Is
E. a. rubriventris
Gabon
E. a. damarensis
Namibia
E. a. astrild
S Botswana, W Transvaal, Orange
Free State, W Cape Province
E. a. tenebridorsa
E Cape Province, SE Transvaal, Natal
Estrilda nigriloris (Black-faced Waxbill)
Zaire
Estrilda nonnula (Black-crowned Waxbill)
E. n. elizae
Fernando Po I
E. n. eisentrauti
Cameroun Mt
E. n. nonnula
E Cameroun to Sudan, Kenya, Tanzania
Estrilda atricapilla (Black-headed Waxbill)
E. a. atricapilla
S Cameroun to NE Zaire
E. a. marungensis
Marungu
E. a. avakubi
E Zaire, NE Angola
E. a. kandti
SE Zaire, Uganda, Kenya
Estrilda erythronotos (Black-cheeked Waxbill)
E. e. delamerei
Uganda, Kenya, Tanzania
E. e. soligena
Angola, Namibia to N Transvaal,
N Rhodesia
E. e. erythronotos
S Rhodesia, Transvaal, N Cape Province
Estrilda charmosyna (Red-rumped Waxbill)
E. c. charmosyna
Somalia, S Ethiopia, S Sudan, Uganda,
N Kenya
E. c. pallidior
C Kenya
E. c. kiwanukae
S Kenya, N Tanzania
AMANDAVA
Amandava amandava (Red Munia)
A. a. amandava
Pakistan, India

A. a. flavidiventris
SW China, Burma, Lesser Sunda Is
A. a. punicea
Indochina, Java, Bali I
Amandava formosa (Green Munia)
C India
Amandava subflava (Zebra Waxbill)
A. s. subflava
Senegal to Ethiopia, Uganda
A. s. clarkei
Angola to Mozambique, South Africa
ORTYGOSPIZA
Ortygospiza atricollis (African Quail-finch)
O. a. atricollis
Senegal to Chad, N Zaire
O. a. ansorgei
Guinea to Ivory Coast
O. a. ugandae
S Sudan, Uganda, W Kenya
O. a. fuscocrissa
Ethiopia
O. a. muelleri
S Kenya, Tanzania, Malawi
O. a. smithersi
NE Zambia
O. a. pallida
Botswana, Rhodesia
O. a. bradfieldi
N Namibia
Ortygospiza gabonensis (Red-billed Quailfinch)
O. g. gabonensis
Gabon to C Zaire
O. g. fuscata
Angola, S Zaire, Zambia
O. g. dorsostriata
E Zaire, Uganda
Ortygospiza locustella (Locust Finch)
O. l. uelensis
N Zaire
O. l. locustella
S Zaire, Zambia, Malawi, Mozambique,
Rhodesia
O. l. rendalli
Southern Africa

AEGINTHA
Aegintha temporalis (Red-browed Waxbill)
A. t. loftyi
S Australia
A. t. temporalis
Eastern Australia
A. t. minor
N Queensland

Emblema picta (Painted Finch)
C Australia
Emblema bella (Beautiful Firetail Finch)
SE Australia, Tasmania
Emblema oculata (Red-eared Firetail Finch)
SW Western Australia
Emblema guttata (Diamond Firetail Finch)
WC & SC Australia

OREOSTRUTHUS
Oreostruthus fuliginosus (Crimson-sided Mountain Finch)
O. f. fuliginosus
SE New Guinea
O. f. pallidus
W New Guinea
O. f. hagenensis
C New Guinea

NEOCHMIA
Neochmia phaeton (Crimson Finch)
N. p. evangelinae
S New Guinea
N. p. albiventer
N Queensland
N. p. phaeton
N Western Australia, Northern Territory
Neochmia ruficauda (Star Finch)
N. r. ruficauda
C Queensland
N. r. clarescens
N Queensland, Northern Territory, N Western Australia

POEPHILA
Poephila guttata (Spotted-sided Finch)
P. g. guttata
Lesser Sunda Is
P. g. castanotis
Australia
Poephila bichenovii (Double-barred Finch)
P. b. annulosa
Northern Territory, N Western Australia
P. b. bichenovii
E Northern Territory, Queensland, N New South Wales
Poephila personata (Masked Finch)
P. p. personata
Northern Territory, W Queensland
P. p. leucotis
N Queensland
Poephila acuticauda (Long-tailed Finch)
P. a. acuticauda
Northern Australia
P. a. hecki
N Western Australia

Poephila cincta (Black-throated Finch) 607
P. c. nigrotecta
N Queensland
P. c. atropygialis
C Queensland
P. c. cincta
S Queensland, N New South Wales

ERYTHRURA
Erythrura hyperythra (Bamboo Parrot Finch)
E. h. brunneiventris
N Luzon I, Mindoro I
E. h. borneensis
Borneo
E. h. malayana
N Malaysia
E. h. hyperythra
W Java
E. h. intermedia
Lombok I
E. h. obscura
Lesser Sunda Is
E. h. microrhyncha
Celebes
E. h. ernstmayri
S Celebes
Erythrura prasina (Pin-tailed Parrot Finch)
E. p. prasina
S Burma, S Thailand, Malaysia, Java, Sumatra
E. p. coelica
Borneo
Erythrura viridifacies (Green-faced Parrot Finch)
Luzon I
Erythrura tricolor (Three-coloured Parrot Finch)
Timor I, Wetar I
Erythrura coloria (Mount Katanglad Parrot Finch)
Mindanao I
Erythrura trichroa (Blue-faced Parrot Finch)
E. t. sanfordi
SC Celebes
E. t. modesta
N Moluccas
E. t. pinaiae
S Moluccas
E. t. sigillifera
NE Australia, New Guinea, New Britain, New Ireland
E. t. eichhorni
St Matthias Is, Bismarck Archipelago
E. t. pelewensis
Palau Is
E. t. clara
Truk I, Ponapé I

E. t. trichroa
Kusaie I, Caroline Is
E. t. woodfordi
Guadalcanal I
E. t. cyanofrons
New Hebrides, Loyalty Is
Erythrura papuana (Papuan Parrot Finch)
New Guinea
**Erythrura psittacea (Red-throated
Parrot Finch)**
New Caledonia
Erythrura pealii (Fiji Parrot Finch)
Fiji Is
**Erythrura cyaneovirens (Red-headed
Parrot Finch)**
E. c. cyaneovirens
Samoa Is
E. c. regia
N New Hebrides
E. c. serena
S New Hebrides
E. c. efatensis
Efate I
E. c. gaughrani
Savaii I
**Erythrura kleinschmidti (Pink-billed
Parrot Finch)**
Viti Levu I

CHLOEBIA
Chloebia gouldiae (Gouldian Finch)
Northern Australia

AIDEMOSYNE
Aidemosyne modesta (Plum-headed Finch)
W Queensland, W New South Wales

LEPIDOPYGIA
Lepidopygia nana (Bib-Finch)
Madagascar
LONCHURA
Lonchura cantans (African Silverbill)
L. c. cantans
Senegal to W Sudan
L. c. orientalis
Somalia, Ethiopia to Tanzania, S Yemen
Lonchura malabarica (Indian Silverbill)
Saudi Arabia to N India, Sri Lanka
**Lonchura griseicapilla (Grey-headed
Silverbill)**
S Ethiopia to Tanzania
Lonchura cucullata (Bronze Mannikin)
L. c. cucullata
Senegal to Sudan, Uganda
L. c. scutata
Ethiopia to Angola & Cape Province
**Lonchura bicolor (Black & White
Mannikin)**
L. b. bicolor
Guinea to Cameroun

L. b. poensis
Cameroun to Angola, Ethiopia, Kenya
L. b. stigmatophora
SW Ethiopia, Uganda
L. b. nigriceps
East Africa to Natal
L. b. minor
S Somalia
L. b. woltersi
SE Zaire, NW Zambia
Lonchura fringilloides (Magpie Mannikin)
Senegal to Somalia & Natal
Lonchura striata (White-backed Munia)
L. s. acuticauda
N India, Bangladesh, Nepal, Burma
L. s. striata
S India, Sri Lanka
L. s. fumigata
Andaman Is
L. s. semistriata
Nicobar Is
L. s. subsquamicollis
S Thailand, Malaysia, Sumatra, Indochina
L. s. swinhoei
S China, Taiwan
**Lonchura leucogastroides (Javanese
Mannikin)**
S Sumatra, Java, Bali I, Lombok I
Lonchura fuscans (Dusky Mannikin)
Borneo
Lonchura molucca (Moluccan Mannikin)
L. m. molucca
N Celebes
L. m. vagans
S Celebes
L. m. propinqua
Lesser Sunda Is
Lonchura punctulata (Nutmeg Mannikin)
L. p. punctulata
India, S Nepal
L. p. subundulata
Bhutan, Bangladesh, Assam
W Burma
L. p. yunnanensis
SW China, NE Burma
L. p. topela
S China, Thailand, Indochina
L. p. cabanisi
Luzon I, Mindoro I
L. p. fretensis
Malaysia, Sumatra
L. p. nisoria
Java, Bali I
L. p. fortior
Lombok I, Sumbawa I
L. p. sumbae
Sumba Is

L. p. blasii
Flores I, Timor I, Lesser Sunda Is
L. p. particeps
Celebes
Lonchura kelaarti (Rufous-bellied Mannikin)
L. k. vernayi
E India
L. k. jerdoni
SW India
L. k. kelaarti
Sri Lanka
Lonchura leucogastra (White-headed Munia)
L. l. leucogastra
S Thailand, Malaysia, Sumatra
L. l. everetti
Luzon I, Mindoro I,
L. l. manueli
C & S Philippine Is
L. l. palawana
Palawan I, N & E Borneo
L. l. smythiesi
SW Sarawak
L. l. castanonota
S Borneo
Lonchura tristissima (Streak-headed Mannikin)
L. t. tristissima
NW New Guinea
L. t. hypomelaena
C New Guinea
L. t. calaminoros
S New Guinea
Lonchura leucosticta (White-spotted Mannikin)
S New Guinea
Lonchura quinticolor (Coloured Finch)
Timor I, Lesser Sunda Is
Lonchura malacca (Chestnut Mannikin)
L. m. rubroniger
N India, E Napal
L. m. malacca
S India, Sri Lanka
L. m. atricapilla
NE India, Bangladesh, Assam, Burma
L. m. deignani
N Thailand, Indochina
L. m. sinensis
S Thailand, Malaysia, Sumatra
L. m. bakatana
N Sumatra
L. m. formosana
N Luzon I, Taiwan
L. m. jagori
Philippine Is, Palawan I, Borneo, N Celebes

L. m. brunneiceps
S Celebes
L. m. ferruginosa
Java
Lonchura maja (Pale-headed Mannikin)
S Thailand, Malaysia, Sumatra, Java, Bali I
Lonchura pallida (Pallid Finch)
L. p. pallida
Lombok I, Lesser Sunda Is
L. p. subcastanea
W Celebes
Lonchura grandis (Great-billed Mannikin)
L. g. grandis
SE New Guinea
L. g. ernesti
N New Guinea
L. g. destructa
N New Guinea
L. g. heurni
N New Guinea
Lonchura vana (Arfak Mannikin)
NW New Guinea
Lonchura caniceps (Grey-headed Mannikin)
L. c. caniceps
SE New Guinea
L. c. scratchleyana
SE New Guinea
L. c. kumusii
SE New Guinea
Lonchura nevermanni (White-crowned Mannikin)
S New Guinea
Lonchura spectabilis (New Britain Mannikin)
L. s. wahgiensis
E New Guinea
L. s. gajduseki
C New Guinea
L. s. mayri
N New Guinea
L. s. spectabilis
New Britain
Lonchura forbesi (New Ireland Finch)
New Ireland
Lonchura hunsteini (White-headed Finch)
L. h. hunsteini
N New Ireland
L. h. nigerrima
New Hanover
L. h. minor
Ponapé I
Lonchura flaviprymna (Yellow-tailed Mannikin)
N Australia

Lonchura castaneothorax (Chestnut-breasted Mannikin)
L. c. uropygialis
  NW New Guinea
L. c. sharpii
  N New Guinea
L. c. boschmai
  C New Guinea
L. c. ramsayi
  SE New Guinea
L. c. assimilis
  Northern Territory
L. c. castaneothorax
  E Queensland, E New South Wales
Lonchura stygia (Black Mannikin)
  S New Guinea
Lonchura teerinki (Grand Valley Mannikin)
L. t. teerinki
  NC New Guinea
L. t. mariae
  W New Guinea
Lonchura monticola (Alpine Mannikin)
  SE New Guinea
Lonchura montana (Snow Mountain Mannikin)
  C New Guinea
Lonchura melaena (New Britain Finch)
  New Britain
Lonchura pectoralis (Pictorella Finch)
  Northern Australia

PADDA
Padda fuscata (Timor Dusky Sparrow)
  Timor I
Padda oryzivora (Java Sparrow)
  Java, Bali I

AMADINA
Amadina erythrocephala (Paradise Sparrow)
A. e. erythrocephala
  Angola, Rhodesia, Southern Africa
A. e. dissita
  E Cape Province, S Natal
Amadina fasciata (Cut-throat Weaver)
A. f. fasciata
  Senegal & N Nigeria to Sudan, Uganda
A. f. alexanderi
  Ethiopia, Somalia, Kenya, Tanzania
A. f. meridionalis
  Malawi, Zambia, Rhodesia, Transvaal, Mozambique

PHOLIDORNIS
Pholidornis rushiae (Tit-Hylia)
P. r. ussheri
  Sierra Leone to Ghana
P. r. rushiae
  S Nigeria to Angola

P. r. bedfordi
  Fernando Po I
P. r. denti
  E Zaire, Uganda

165 PLOCEIDAE (WEAVERS, SPARROWS)

VIDUINAE

VIDUA
Vidua chalybeata (Village Indigobird)
V. c. chalybeata
  Senegal to Sierra Leone
V. c. neumanni
  Mali to Sudan
V. c. ultramarina
  Ethiopia
V. c. centralis
  Kenya, Uganda, W Tanzania
V. c. amauropteryx
  Somalia to Zambia, Mozambique
V. c. okavangoensis
  W Zambia, Botswana, Angola
Vidua purpurascens (Dusky Indigobird)
  Kenya to Angola, Transvaal
Vidua funerea (Variable Indigobird)
V. f. nigerrima
  Angola, Zambia, Tanzania
V. f. codringtoni
  S Zambia, Malawi, W Rhodesia
V. f. lusituensis
  E Rhodesia
V. f. funerea
  C & E South Africa
Vidua wilsoni (Pale-winged Indigobird)
  "V. f. wilsoni"
  N Nigeria to W Sudan
  "V. f. camerunensis"
  Gambia to Ethiopia
  "V. f. nigeriae"
  S Nigeria, Cameroun, S Sudan
(These constitute groups rather than true sub-species)
Vidua hypocherina (Steel-blue Whydah)
  Ethiopia & Somalia to Tanzania
Vidua fischeri (Fischer's Whydah)
  Somalia to Uganda & N Tanzania
Vidua regia (Shaft-tailed Whydah)
  S Angola to S Mozambique
Vidua macroura (Pin-tailed Whydah)
  Senegal to Ethiopia & Cape Province
Vidua paradisaea (Paradise Whydah)
  E Sudan to S Angola & Natal
Vidua orientalis (Broad-tailed Paradise Whydah)
V. o. acupum
  Senegal to N Nigeria
V. o. togoensis
  Sierra Leone to Togo

V. o. orientalis
Chad to Ethiopia
V. o. interjecta
N Cameroun to S Sudan
V. o. obtusa
Angola to Kenya & Mozambique

BUBALORNITHINAE

BUBALORNIS
Bubalornis albirostris (White-billed Buffalo Weaver)
B. a. albirostris
Senegal to Ethiopia, N Uganda, Kenya
B. a. intermedius
S Ethiopia, Somalia, Kenya
S Tanzania
B. a. niger
S Angola to Mozambique, Transvaal

DINEMELLIA
Dinemellia dinemelli (White-headed Buffalo Weaver)
D. d. dinemelli
S Sudan, S Ethiopia, Somalia
N Kenya
D. d. boehmi
SE Zaire, Tanzania

PASSERINAE

PLOCEPASSER
Plocepasser mahali (White-browed Sparrow Weaver)
P. m. melanorhynchus
S Sudan, S Ethiopia, Uganda, Kenya
P. m. propinquatus
S Somalia
P. m. pectoralis
Zambia, N Botswana to S Tanzania, Mozambique
P. m. ansorgei
S Angola, N Namibia
P. m. stentor
Namibia, W Cape Province, S Botswana, Transvaal
P. m. mahali
W Orange Free State, N Cape Province
Plocepasser superciliosus (Chestnut-crowned Sparrow Weaver)
P. s. superciliosus
Senegal to Sudan
P. s. brunnescens
Central African Republic to SW Sudan, Uganda
Plocepasser donaldsoni (Donaldson-Smith's Sparrow Weaver)
N Kenya

Plocepasser rufoscapulatus (Chestnut-mantled Sparrow Weaver)
S Angola, SE Zaire to Malawi
HISTURGOPS
Histurgops ruficauda (Rufous-tailed Weaver)
Tanzania

PSEUDONIGRITA
Pseudonigrita arnaudi (Grey-headed Social Weaver)
P. a. arnaudi
SW Sudan, Kenya, Uganda, N Tanzania
P. a. australoabyssinicus
S Ethiopia
P. a. dorsalis
C Tanzania
Pseudonigrita cabanisi (Black-capped Social Weaver)
S Ethiopia, E Kenya, NE Tanzania

PHILETAIRUS
Philetairus socius (Sociable Weaver)
P. s. geminus
N & C Namibia
P. s. socius
S Namibia
P. s. lepidus
S Botswana, W Transvaal, N Cape Province
P. s. eremnus
N Cape Province

PASSER
Passer ammodendri (Saxaul Sparrow)
P. a. korejewi
Transcaspia, Iran
P. a. ammodendri
Russian Turkistan
P. a. stoliczkae
W China
P. a. timidus
S Mongolia
Passer domesticus (House Sparrow)
P. d. domesticus
Europe, N Asia, Americas, South Africa, Australia
P. d. italiae
SE France, Italy, Crete
P. d. tingitanus
NW Africa
P. d. biblicus
Asia Minor, S Arabia, Caucasus, Iran
P. d. hufufae
E Arabia
P. d. niloticus
NE Africa
P. d. rufidorsalis
Sudan

P. d. indicus
S Afghanistan, Pakistan, India,
Bangladesh, Burma
P. d. hyrcanus
Transcaspia, N Iran
P. d. bactrianus
SC Asia
P. d. parkini
Himalayas
Passer hispaniolensis (Spanish Sparrow)
P. h. hispaniolensis
SW Europe, North Africa, Asia Minor
P. h. transcaspicus
Caucasus, Tien Shan » S Iran, N India
Passer pyrrhonotus (Sind Jungle Sparrow)
SE Iran, Pakistan, NW India
Passer castanopterus (Somali Sparrow)
P. c. fulgens
Ethiopia, N Kenya
P. c. castanopterus
Somalia
Passer rutilans (Cinnamon Sparrow)
P. r. cinnamomeus
NE Afghanistan, Himalayas
SE Tibet
P. r. intensior
Assam, N Burma, Laos, S China
N Vietnam
P. r. rutilans
China, Taiwan, Korea, N Japan
Passer flaveolus (Pegu House Sparrow)
N Burma, Thailand, Laos, S Vietnam
Passer moabiticus (Dead Sea Sparrow)
P. m. moabiticus
Jordan, Iraq, SW Iran
P. m. yatii
E Iran, W Afghanistan
Passer motitensis (Great Sparrow)
P. m. iagoensis
Cape Verde Is
P. m. cordofanicus
NW Sudan
P. m. shelleyi
S Sudan, N Uganda
P. m. hemileucus
Abd el Kuri I
P. m. motitensis
Botswana, Transvaal
P. m. benguellensis
SW Africa, S Angola
Passer melanurus (Cape Sparrow)
P. m. damarensis
SW Angola, Namibia, Botswana
P. m. melanurus
South Africa
Passer insularis (Socotra Sparrow)
Socotra I

Passer rufocinctus (Kenya Rufous Sparrow)
Kenya, N Tanzania
Passer griseus (Grey-headed Sparrow)
P. g. griseus
Niger, Chad, Senegal to Ghana
P. g. ugandae
Ghana to Somalia, N Zaire
P. g. laeneni
E Chad
P. g. luangwae
Zambia
P. g. mosambicus
E Tanzania, Malawi, Mozambique
P. g. diffusus
Angola, N Namibia, Botswana to Natal
P. g. stygiceps
S Natal, E Cape Province
Passer swainsonii (Swainson's Sparrow)
Somalia, E & S Ethiopia
Passer gongonensis (Parrot-billed Sparrow)
Kenya, SE Tanzania
Passer suahelicus (Swahili Sparrow)
Kenya, C Tanzania
Passer simplex (Desert Sparrow)
P. s. zarudnyi
E Iran
P. s. simplex
S Sahara
P. s. saharae
W Sahara
Passer montanus (Tree Sparrow)
P. m. montanus
Europe, W, N & NE Asia, Asia Minor
P. m. transcaucasicus
Transcaucasia, N Iran
P. m. zaissanensis
C Asia, NE Mongolia
P. m. kansuensis
NE Tsinghai, Kansu
P. m. iubilaeus
N, C & E China
P. m. dilutus
NE Iran, Pakistan, Sinkiang, Manchuria,
W China
P. m. tibetanus
N Himalayas, Tibet, NW China
P. m. saturatus
Sakhalin I, S Korea, Japan, Taiwan
P. m. hepaticus
NE Assam, NW Burma
P. m. malaccensis
S Himalayas, Burma, Thailand,
Indochina, Malaysia, Sumatra, Java

AURIPASSER
Auripasser luteus (Sudan Golden Sparrow)
 N Nigeria, Chad, Sudan, N Ethiopia
Auripasser euchlorus (Arabian Golden Sparrow)
 SW Arabia, Somalia

SORELLA
Sorella eminibey (Chestnut Sparrow)
 Sudan to N Tanzania

PETRONIA
Petronia brachydactyla (Pale Rock Sparrow)
 Syria, Iran » NE Africa
Petronia xanthosterna (Yellow-spotted Petronia)
 P. x. pallida
  Senegal, Mauretania to S Sudan
 P. x. pyrgita
  Ethiopia, Somalia to NE Tanzania
 P. x. transfuga
  S Iraq, Iran, Afghanistan, Pakistan, NW India
 P. x. xanthosterna
  India
Petronia petronia (Rock Sparrow)
 P. p. petronia
  S Europe, Morocco, W Asia Minor
 P. p. barbara
  N Africa
 P. p. puteicola
  S Syria, Israel
 P. p. exigua
  Caucasus, Iraq, Iran
 P. p. intermedia
  Transcaspia, N Iran, C Asia
  Pakistan
 P. p. brevirostris
  E Siberia, Mongolia, N China
Petronia superciliaris (South African Rock Sparrow)
 Angola to Tanzania, South Africa
Petronia dentata (Lesser Rock Sparrow)
 P. d. dentata
  Senegal to Ethiopia, SW Arabia
 P. d. buchanani
  S Niger

MONTIFRINGILLA
Montifringilla nivalis (Snow Finch)
 M. n. nivalis
  SW Europe
 M. n. alpicola
  Transcaucasus, Iran, C Asia
 M. n. kwenlunensis
  S Sinkiang, W China
 M. n. henrici
  Tibet, W China

Montifringilla adamsi (Adams' Snow Finch)
 M. a. xerophila
  NW China
 M. a. adamsi
  Tibet, N Himalayas, Nepal
Montifringilla taczanowskii (Mandelli's Snow Finch)
 Tibet, N Sikang, Tsinghai
Montifringilla davidiana (Père David's Snow Finch)
 M. d. potanini
  Altai, N Mongolia
 M. d. davidiana
  S Mongolia, NW China
Montifringilla ruficollis (Red-necked Snow Finch)
 M. r. isabellina
  NW China, N Tsinghai
 M. r. ruficollis
  Tibet, W China
Montifringilla blanfordi (Blanford's Snow Finch)
 M. b. barbara
  N China
 M. b. ventorum
  NW China, Sinkiang
 M. b. blanfordi
  N Himalayas, Tibet, W China
Montifringilla theresae (Meinertzhagen's Snow Finch)
 Afghanistan

SPOROPIPES
Sporopipes squamifrons (Scaly Weaver)
 S. s. pallidus
  Mossamedes, Angola
 S. s. squamifrons
  SW Angola to Transvaal, Cape Province
Sporopipes frontalis (Speckle-fronted Weaver)
 S. f. frontalis
  Senegal to E Ethiopia
 S. f. pallidior
  S Sahara
 S. f. emini
  S Sudan, NE Uganda, Kenya, N Tanzania

PLOCEINAE

AMBLYOSPIZA
Amblyospiza albifrons (Grosbeak Weaver)
 A. a. capitalba
  Sierra Leone to Nigeria
 A. a. saturata
  Cameroun to N Zaire
 A. a. melanota
  NE Zaire, Ethiopia, Uganda, NW Kenya

A. a. montana
S Kenya, Zambia, Tanzania, Rhodesia
Malawi
A. a. unicolor
E Kenya, E Tanzania
A. a. tandae
N Angola
A. a. kasaica
S Zaire
A. a. maxima
N Botswana
A. a. woltersi
S Mozambique
A. a. albifrons
South Africa

PLOCEUS
Ploceus baglafecht (Baglafecht Weaver)
P. b. baglafecht
Ethiopia, S Sudan
P. b. reichenowi
Kenya, N Tanzania
P. b. stuhlmanni
E Zaire, S Uganda; W Tanzania
P. b. sharpii
SW Tanzania
P. b. nyikae
Zambia, Malawi
P. b. neumanni
Cameroun
P. b. eremobius
NE Zaire, SE Sudan
P. b. emini
S Sudan, N Uganda
Ploceus bannermani (Bannerman's Weaver)
Cameroun
Ploceus batesi (Bates's Weaver)
Cameroun
Ploceus nigrimentum (Black-chinned Weaver)
W Angola, S Zaire
Ploceus bertrandi (Bertrand's Weaver)
Tanzania, Malawi, Mozambique
Ploceus pelzelni (Slender-billed Weaver)
P. p. pelzelni
Uganda, Kenya, Tanzania, E Zaire
P. p. tuta
SE Zaire
P. p. monachus
Ghana to Gabon & N Angola
Ploceus subpersonatus (Loanga Slender-billed Weaver)
S Gabon
Ploceus luteolus (Little Masked Weaver)
P. l. luteolus
Senegal to Ethiopia

P. l. kavirondensis
Uganda, W Kenya, NW Tanzania
Ploceus ocularis (Spectacled Weaver)
P. o. crocatus
Cameroun to Ethiopia » Tanzania & Angola
P. o. suahelicus
E Kenya, E Tanzania, E Zambia,
Mozambique
P. o. ocularis
Transvaal, Natal, Cape Province
Ploceus nigricollis (Black-necked Weaver)
P. n. brachypterus
Senegal to Nigeria
P. n. nigricollis
Cameroun to Sudan, Zaire, Angola,
W Kenya
P. n. po
Fernando Po I
P. n. melanoxanthus
S Ethiopia, Somalia, E Kenya,
NE Tanzania
Ploceus alienus (Strange Weaver)
E Zaire, W Uganda
Ploceus melanogaster (Black-billed Weaver)
P. m. melanogaster
E Nigeria, W Cameroun, Fernando Po I
P. m. stephanophorus
S Sudan, E Zaire, SW Uganda, NW Kenya
Ploceus capensis (Cape Weaver)
P. c. olivaceus
E Cape Province, Transvaal, Natal
P. c. capensis
W Cape Province
Ploceus temporalis (Bocage's Weaver)
S Angola, W Zambia
Ploceus subaureus (Golden Weaver)
P. s. aureoflavus
E Kenya, E Tanzania, Malawi,
Mozambique
P. s. tongensis
S Mozambique
P. s. subaureus
Natal, E Cape Province
Ploceus xanthops (Holub's Golden Weaver)
Zaire & Angola to Kenya & Mozambique
Ploceus aurantius (Orange Weaver)
P. a. aurantius
Senegal to Cameroun, Gabon, Zaire
P. a. rex
Uganda, NW Tanzania
Ploceus heuglini (Heuglin's Masked Weaver)
Senegal to NW Kenya
Ploceus bojeri (Golden Palm Weaver)
S Somalia, Kenya

Ploceus castaneiceps (Taveta Golden Weaver)
SE Kenya, NE Tanzania
Ploceus princeps (Principé Golden Weaver)
Principé I
Ploceus xanthopterus (Brown-throated Golden Weaver)
P. x. castaneigula
N Botswana, SW Zambia
P. x. marleyi
Natal
P. x. xanthopterus
Transvaal, Natal, S Rhodesia, Malawi, Mozambique
Ploceus castanops (Northern Brown-throated Weaver)
E Zaire, Uganda
Ploceus galbula (Rüppell's Weaver)
E Sudan, N Ethiopia, SW Arabia
Ploceus taeniopterus (Northern Masked Weaver)
P. t. furensis
W Sudan
P. t. taeniopterus
SE Sudan, N Uganda
Ploceus intermedius (Lesser Masked Weaver)
P. i. intermedius
Sudan, Ethiopia, Somalia to E Zaire, Tanzania
P. i. cabanisii
SE Zaire to Botswana & Transvaal
P. i. beattyi
W Angola
Ploceus velatus (African Masked Weaver)
P. v. uluensis
Sudan & Somalia to Tanzania
P. v. velatus
N Cape Province, SW Transvaal
P. v. tahatali
E Transvaal, Natal
P. v. caurinus
S Angola, N Namibia, Botswana
P. v. shelleyi
Malawi, Mozambique, N Natal
P. v. finschi
coast of SW Angola
P. v. nigrifrons
E Cape Province
Ploceus ruweti (Lufira Masked Weaver)
S Zaire
Ploceus katangae (Katanga Masked Weaver)
P. k. upembae
SE Zaire
P. k. katangae
NW Zambia, SE Zaire

Ploceus reichardi (Tanzanian Masked Weaver)
SW Tanzania
Ploceus vitellinus (Vitelline Masked Weaver)
P. v. vitellinus
Senegal to Chad, W Sudan
P. v. peixotoi
Sao Thomé I
Ploceus spekei (Speke's Weaver)
S Ethiopia, Somalia, Kenya, N Tanzania
Ploceus spekeoides (Fox's Weaver)
Uganda
Ploceus cucullatus (Village Weaver)
P. c. cucullatus
Senegal to Cameroun, Chad, Fernando Po I
P. c. collaris
Gabon, Zaire, N Angola
P. c. bohndorffi
N Zaire, Uganda, Sudan, NW Tanzania
P. c. abyssinicus
Ethiopia
P. c. frobenii
S Zaire
P. c. graueri
E Zaire, W Tanzania
P. c. spilonotus
S Mozambique, Natal, Transvaal, E Cape Province
Ploceus nigriceps (Layard's Blackheaded Weaver)
Somalia, East Africa, N Mozambique
Ploceus grandis (Giant Weaver)
Sao Thomé I
Ploceus nigerrimus (Vieillot's Black Weaver)
P. n. castaneofuscus
Sierra Leone to W Nigeria
P. n. nigerrimus
E Nigeria, Cameroun to W Kenya
Ploceus weynsi (Weyns's Weaver)
N Zaire, S Uganda, NW Tanzania
Ploceus golandi (Clarke's Weaver)
E Kenya
Ploceus dicrocephalus (Salvadori's Weaver)
S Ethiopia, Somalia, N Kenya
Ploceus melanocephalus (Black-headed Weaver)
P. m. melanocephalus
Senegal to Benin, Niger, Chad
P. m. capitalis
Nigeria, S Chad, Central African Republic
P. m. duboisi
Zaire, N Zambia
P. m. dimidiatus
NE Sudan

P. m. fischeri
Uganda, Kenya, Tanzania
Ploceus jacksoni (Golden-backed Weaver)
S Sudan, Kenya, Uganda
Ploceus badius (Cinnamon Weaver)
P. b. badius
E Sudan
P. b. axillaris
S Sudan
Ploceus rubiginosus (Chestnut Weaver)
P. r. rubiginosus
Ethiopia, Somalia, Uganda, Kenya,
N Tanzania
P. r. trothae
SW Angola, N Namibia
Ploceus aureonucha (Gold-naped Weaver)
NE Zaire
Ploceus tricolor (Yellow-mantled Weaver)
P. t. tricolor
Guinea to Cameroun, Gabon, Angola
P. t. interscapularis
Zaire, W Uganda
Ploceus albinucha (Maxwell's Black Weaver)
P. a. albinucha
Sierra Leone to Ghana
P. a. maxwelli
Fernando Po I
P. a. holomelas
E Nigeria to Gabon, Central African
Republic, N Zaire
Ploceus nelicourvi (Nelicourvi Weaver)
N & E Madagascar
Ploceus hypoxanthus (Asian Golden Weaver)
P. h. hymenaicus
S Burma, Thailand, S Indochina
P. h. hypoxanthus
Sumatra, Java
Ploceus superciliosus (Compact Weaver)
Sierra Leone to Ethiopia, Uganda, Kenya
& Angola
Ploceus benghalensis (Bengal Weaver)
Pakistan, N India, Nepal, Bangladesh
Ploceus manyar (Streaked Weaver)
P. m. flaviceps
Pakistan, W India, Sri Lanka
P. m. peguensis
NE India, Bangladesh, Burma
P. m. williamsoni
Thailand, Vietnam
P. m. manyar
Java, Bali I
Ploceus philippinus (Baya Weaver)
P. p. philippinus
Pakistan, India, Sri Lanka

P. p. travencoreensis
SW India
P. p. burmanicus
NE India, Bangladesh, Burma
P. p. infortunatus
S Vietnam, Malaysia, Sumatra
P. p. angelorum
C Thailand
Ploceus megarhynchus (Finn's Weaver)
P. m. megarhynchus
S Himalayas
P. m. salimalii
NE India
Ploceus bicolor (Forest Weaver)
P. b. tephronotus
E Nigeria, Cameroun, Fernando Po I
P. b. analogus
S Cameroun
P. b. amaurocephalus
N Angola
P. b. mentalis
S Sudan, NE Zaire, Uganda, W Kenya
P. b. kigomaensis
S Zaire, Zambia, W Tanzania
P. b. kersteni
Somalia, E Kenya, E Tanzania
P. b. stictifrons
E Rhodesia, SE Tanzania, Mozambique,
Malawi
P. b. bicolor
S Mozambique, South Africa
Ploceus preussi (Golden-backed Weaver)
Sierra Leone to Cameroun, Central
African Republic
Ploceus dorsomaculatus (Yellow Capped Weaver)
Cameroun, Central African Republic,
Congo, Zaire
Ploceus olivaceiceps (Olive-headed Golden Weaver)
S Tanzania, Malawi, Mozambique
Ploceus nicolli (Usambara Weaver)
Tanzania
Ploceus insignis (Brown-capped Weaver)
P. i. insignis
Cameroun to Sudan, Angola, Zaire,
Kenya, Tanzania
P. i. unicus
Fernando Po I
Ploceus angolensis (Bar-winged Weaver)
Angola, N Namibia, S Zaire, Zambia
Ploceus sanctaethomae (Sao Thomé Weaver)
Sao Thomé I

MALIMBUS
Malimbus flavipes (Yellow-legged Malimbe)
NE Zaire
Malimbus coronatus (Red-crowned Malimbe)
Cameroun

Malimbus cassini (Black-throated Malimbe)
  S Cameroun, Gabon, Congo
Malimbus racheliae (Rachel's Malimbe)
  E Nigeria to Gabon
Malimbus ballmani (Tai Malimbe)
  Tai, Ivory Coast
Malimbus scutatus (Red-vented Malimbe)
  M. s. scutatus
    Sierra Leone to Ghana
  M. s. scutopartitus
    S Nigeria, W Cameroun
Malimbus ibadanensis (Ibadan Malimbe)
  E Nigeria
Malimbus nitens (Gray's Malimbe)
  M. n. nitens
    Guinea to S Nigeria
  M. n. moreaui
    Cameroun, Gabon, NW Zaire
  M. n. microrhynchus
    NE Zaire, W Uganda
Malimbus rubricollis (Red-headed Malimbe)
  M. r. bartletti
    Sierra Leone to Ghana
  M. r. nigeriae
    Benin, W Nigeria
  M. r. rubricollis
    E Nigeria to Sudan, Chad, Central
      African Republic
  M. r. rufovelatus
    Fernando Po I
  M. r. praedi
    N Angola
Malimbus erythrogaster (Red-bellied Malimbe)
  E Nigeria to E Zaire
Malimbus malimbicus (Crested Malimbe)
  M. m. nigrifrons
    Sierra Leone to Nigeria
  M. m. malimbicus
    Cameroun to Uganda, S Zaire, N Angola

ANAPLECTES
Anaplectes melanotis (Red-headed Weaver)
  A. m. melanotis
    Senegal to Ethiopia, Uganda, W Kenya
  A. m. jubaensis
    S Somalia, NE Kenya
  A. m. rubriceps
    S Angola to Tanzania, Mozambique
  A. m. gurneyi
    N Namibia

QUELEA
Quelea cardinalis (Cardinal Quelea)
  Q. c. cardinalis
    S Sudan, S Ethiopia, Uganda, Kenya,
      NW Tanzania
  Q. c. rhodesiae
    Tanzania, Zambia
Quelea erythrops (Red-headed Quelea)
  Senegal to Ethiopia, Natal &
    Cape Province

Quelea quelea (Red-billed Quelea)
  Q. q. quelea
    Senegal to Chad, Central African
      Republic
  Q. q. aethiopica
    Sudan, Somalia to E Zaire, N Tanzania
  Q. q. lathamii
    Angola, S Zaire, Zambia, Southern
      Africa

FOUDIA
Foudia madagascariensis (Madagascan Red
  Fody)
    Madagascar, Mauritius I, Reunion I
Foudia eminentissima (Mascarene Fody)
  F. e. aldabrana
    Aldabra I
  F. e. consobrina
    Great Comoro I
  F. e. anjuanensis
    Anjouan I
  F. e. eminentissima
    Moheli I
  F. e. algondae
    Mayotte I
Foudia omissa (Red Forest Fody)
  E Madagascar
Foudia rubra (Mauritius Fody)
  Mauritius I
Foudia sechellarum (Seychelles Fody)
  Seychelles Is
Foudia flavicans (Rodriguez Fody)
  Rodriguez I
Foudia sakalava (Sakalava Fody)
  F. s. sakalava
    N & NE Madagascar
  F. s. minor
    W & SW Madagascar

BRACHYCOPE
Brachycope anomala (Bob-tailed
  Weaver)
    SE Cameroun, Congo

EUPLECTES
Euplectes afer (Golden Bishop)
  E. a. afer
    Senegal to Chad, Central African
      Republic
  E. a. ladoensis
    S Sudan, Uganda, N Kenya, N Tanzania
  E. a. strictus
    Ethiopia
  E. a. taha
    Southern Africa
Euplectes diademata (Fire-fronted Bishop)
  E Kenya, NE Tanzania
Euplectes gierowii (Gierow's Bishop)
  E. g. ansorgei
    S Sudan, S Ethiopia, E Zaire, Uganda

E. g. friederichseni
  SW Kenya, N Tanzania
E. g. gierowii
  N Angola, SW Zaire
Euplectes nigroventris (Zanzibar Red Bishop)
  E Kenya, E Tanzania, E Mozambique,
    Zanzibar I
Euplectes hordeacea (Red-crowned Bishop)
E. h. hordeacea
  Senegal to W Sudan, Angola, Rhodesia
E. h. craspedoptera
  S Sudan, SW Ethiopia, Uganda,
    NW Kenya
Euplectes orix (Red Bishop)
E. o. franciscana
  Senegal to Ethiopia, Uganda, Kenya
E. o. pusilla
  SE Ethiopia, Somalia
E. o. nigrifrons
  E Zaire, S Kenya, Tanzania,
    Mozambique, Malawi
E. o. orix
  N Angola to S Mozambique and
    Southern Africa
Euplectes aurea (Golden-backed Bishop)
  Sao Thomé I, W Angola
Euplectes capensis (Yellow-rumped Bishop)
E. c. phoenicomera
  SE Nigeria, Cameroun, Fernando Po I
E. c. xanthomelas
  Sudan, Ethiopia, East Africa, Angola
    to Transvaal
E. c. approximans
  E Transvaal, Natal, E Cape Province
E. c. capensis
  W & S Cape Province
E. c. macrorhynchus
  NW Cape Province
Euplectes axillaris (Fan-tailed Whydah)
E. a. bocagei
  Niger, Cameroun, Angola, S Zaire,
    Zambia
E. a. quanzae
  C Angola
E. a. traversii
  N Ethiopia
E. a. phoeniceus
  S Ethiopia, Sudan, Uganda, W Kenya,
    W Tanzania
E. a. batesi
  Upper Volta to Upper Niger
E. a. zanzibaricus
  Somalia, E Kenya, E Tanzania
E. a. axillaris
  Zambia to Mozambique & E South Africa
**Euplectes macrourus (Yellow-mantled
Whydah)**
E. m. macrocercus
  Uganda, W Kenya

E. m. macrourus
  West Africa to Sudan, Zaire, Angola
    to Mozambique
E. m. conradsi
  NW Tanzania
E. m. intermedius
  W Tanzania
Euplectes hartlaubi (Marsh Whydah)
E. h. humeralis
  Cameroun to Uganda, W Kenya
E. h. hartlaubi
  Angola, S Zaire, Zambia
E. h. psammocromius
  SW Tanzania, Malawi
Euplectes albonotatus (White-winged Whydah)
E. a. eques
  Sudan to Tanzania
E. a. sassii
  E Zaire
E. a. asymmetrurus
  Gabon to N Namibia
E. a. albonotatus
  SE Zaire and Zambia to Tanzania, Natal
Euplectes ardens (Red-collared Whydah)
E. a. concolor
  Senegal to S Sudan, Uganda, Chad
E. a. laticauda
  SE Sudan, Ethiopia
E. a. suahelicus
  Kenya, NE Tanzania
E. a. ardens
  EC Southern Africa
Euplectes progne (Long-tailed Whydah)
E. p. delamerei
  E Kenya
E. p. ansorgei
  E Angola, W Zambia
E. p. progne
  E Zambia, S Africa
E. p. definita
  W Zambia
Euplectes jacksoni (Jackson's Whydah)
  Kenya, N Tanzania

ANOMALOSPIZA
Anomalospiza imberbis (Parasitic Weaver)
  Sierra Leone to Ethiopia & Transvaal

166 STURNIDAE (STARLINGS)

STURNINAE

APLONIS
Aplonis zelandica (New Hebrides Starling)
A. z. rufipennis
  C & N New Hebrides, Banks Is
A. z. maxwellii
  Santa Cruz I
A. z. zelandica
  Vanikoro I

***Aplonis santovestris* (Mountain Starling)**
Espiritu Santo I
***Aplonis pelzelni* (Ponapé Starling)**
Ponapé I
***Aplonis atrifusca* (Samoan Starling)**
Samoan Is
***Aplonis cinerascens* (Raratonga Starling)**
Cook I
***Aplonis tabuensis* (Striped Starling)**
A. t. pachyramphus
Santa Cruz I
A. t. tucopiae
Tucopia I
A. t. rotumae
Rotuma I
A. t. vitiensis
Fiji Is
A. t. manuae
Manuan I
A. t. tabuensis
Tonga I
A. t. fortunae
Fotuna I, Alofa I, Uea I
A. t. tenebrosa
Keppel I, Boscawen I
A. t. nesiotes
Niuafou I
A. t. brunnescens
Niué I
A. t. tutuilae
Tutuila I
A. t. brevirostris
Upolu I, Savaii I
***Aplonis striata* (Striated Starling)**
A. s. striata
New Caledonia
A. s. atronitens
Loyalty Is
***Aplonis fusca* (Norfolk I Starling)**
Norfolk I
***Aplonis opaca* (Micronesian Starling)**
A. o. aeneus
Takatsukasa I
A. o. guami
Guam I
A. o. orii
Palau Is
A. o. kurodai
Yap I
A. o. ponapensis
Ponapé I
A. o. opaca
Kusaie I
A. o. angus
Truk I
***Aplonis cantoroides* (Singing Starling)**
New Guinea, Bismarck Archipelago

***Aplonis crassa* (Tenimber Starling)**   619
Tenimber Is
***Aplonis feadensis* (Fead Is Starling)**
A. f. feadensis
Solomon Is
A. f. heureka
Bismarck Archipelago
***Aplonis insularis* (Rennell I Starling)**
Rennell I
***Aplonis dichroa* (San Cristobal Starling)**
San Cristobal I
***Aplonis grandis* (Large Glossy Starling)**
A. g. malaitae
Malaita I
A. g. macrura
Guadalcanal I
A. g. grandis
Bougainville I, Choiseul I, Ysabel I
***Aplonis mysolensis* (Moluccan Starling)**
A. m. mysolensis
W New Guinea Is
A. m. forsteni
Moluccas
A. m. sulaensis
Sula Is
A. m. persimilis
Banggai I
***Aplonis magna* (Long-tailed Starling)**
A. m. magna
Biak I
A. m. brevicauda
Numfor I
***Aplonis minor* (Lesser Glossy Starling)**
A. m. minor
Lesser Sunda Is
A. m. montosa
Celebes
A. m. todayensis
Mindanao I
***Aplonis panayensis* (Philippine Glossy Starling)**
A. p. affinis
Assam, W Burma, S Vietnam
A. p. strigata
S Thailand, Malaysia, Sumatra, Java
W Borneo
A. p. eustathis
E Borneo
A. p. heterochlora
Anamba Is, Natuna Is
A. p. tytleri
Andaman Is, Nicobar Is
A. p. altirostris
W Sumatran Is
A. p. leptorrhyncha
W Sumatran Is
A. p. pachistorhina
W Sumatran Is

A. p. enganensis
Enggano I
A. p. gusti
Bali I
A. p. alipodis
Maratua I, E Borneo
A. p. sanghirensis
Sanghir Is, Talaut I
A. p. panayensis
Celebes, Philippine Is
Aplonis metallica (Shining Starling)
A. m. circumscripta
Tenimber Is, Damar I
A. m. metallica
Moluccas, New Guinea, NE Queensland
A. m. nitida
Solomon Is, Bismarck Archipelago
A. m. purpureiceps
Admiralty Is
A. m. inornata
Biak I, Numfor I
Aplonis mystacea (Grant's Starling)
W & S New Guinea
Aplonis brunneicapilla (White-eyed Starling)
Bougainville I, Rendova I

POEOPTERA
Poeoptera kenricki (Kenrick's Starling)
P. k. bensoni
Kenya
P. k. kenricki
S Kenya, N Tanzania
Poeoptera stuhlmanni (Stuhlmann's Starling)
SW Ethiopia, W Kenya, Uganda, E Zaire
Poeoptera lugubris (Narrow-tailed Starling)
P. l. lugubris
Sierra Leone to W Uganda, N Angola
P. l. webbi
Kigezi, Uganda

GRAFISIA
Grafisia torquata (White-collared Starling)
Cameroun, N Zaire, Central African
Republic

ONYCHOGNATHUS
Onychognathus walleri (Waller's Red-winged Starling)
O. w. preussi
Cameroun, Fernando Po I
O. w. elgonensis
S Sudan, Uganda, E Zaire, W Kenya
O. w. walleri
S Kenya, Tanzania, N Malawi

Onychognathus nabouroup (Pale-winged Starling)
O. n. benguellensis
E Angola, N Namibia
O. n. nabouroup
S Namibia, Botswana, N Cape Province
Onychognathus morio (African Red-winged Starling)
O. m. modicus
Senegal, Mali, W Niger
O. m. neumanni
N Nigeria to Central African Republic
& W Sudan
O. m. rüppellii
Ethiopia & Sudan to Tanzania
O. m. morio
Rhodesia, S Malawi, S Mozambique,
Southern Africa
Onychognathus blythii (Somali Chestnut-winged Starling)
Somalia, Socotra I
Onychognathus frater (Socotra Chestnut-winged Starling)
Socotra I
Onychognathus tristramii (Tristram's Grackle)
Israel, Arabia
Onychognathus fulgidus (Chestnut-winged Starling)
O. f. fulgidus
Sao Thomé I
O. f. hartlaubii
Guinea to W Uganda & Angola
Onychognathus tenuirostris (Slender-billed Red-winged Starling)
O. t. tenuirostris
Ethiopia, N Kenya
O. t. theresae
E Zaire to Uganda, Kenya, Tanzania,
Malawi
Onychognathus albirostris (White-billed Starling)
Ethiopia
Onychognathus salvadorii (Bristle-crowned Starling)
Somalia, S Ethiopia, N Kenya

LAMPROTORNIS
Lamprotornis iris (Iris Glossy Starling)
Guinea to Ivory Coast
Lamprotornis cupreocauda (Copper-tailed Glossy Starling)
Sierra Leone to Ghana
Lamprotornis purpureiceps (Purple-headed Glossy Starling)
S Nigeria to Gabon & Uganda

Lamprotornis corruscus (Black-bellied Glossy Starling)
  L. c. corruscus
    E & SE Africa
  L. c. vaughani
    Pemba I
Lamprotornis purpureus (Purple Glossy Starling)
  L. p. purpureus
    Senegal to Nigeria, Mali
  L. p. amethystinus
    Nigeria & Chad to Sudan & N Kenya
Lamprotornis nitens (Red-shouldered Glossy Starling)
  L. n. nitens
    Gabon to Angola
  L. n. phoenicopterus
    SW & SC Africa
  L. n. culminator
    Cape Province, S Natal
Lamprotornis chalcurus (Bronze-tailed Glossy Starling)
  L. c. chalcurus
    Senegal to Ghana
  L. c. emini
    Togo to Central African Republic, NE Zaire, Uganda, Kenya
Lamprotornis chalybaeus (Greater Blue-eared Glossy Starling)
  L. c. chalybaeus
    Senegal to Somalia, Kenya
  L. c. cyaniventris
    Ethiopia, W Kenya, Uganda, E Zaire
  L. c. sycobius
    Tanzania, Zambia, Malawi, Mozambique
  L. c. nordmanni
    S Angola, Zambia, Botswana, Transvaal
Lamprotornis chloropterus (Lesser Blue-eared Glossy Starling)
  L. c. chloropterus
    Senegal to Ethiopia, Uganda, Kenya
  L. c. cyanogenys
    SE Sudan, Ethiopia, N Uganda
  L. c. elisabeth
    S Uganda, S Kenya, Tanzania, Zambia, Mozambique
Lamprotornis acuticaudus (Sharp-tailed Glossy Starling)
    Angola, Zambia, S Zaire
Lamprotornis splendidus (Splendid Glossy Starling)
  L. s. chrysonotis
    Senegal to Sierra Leone
  L. s. splendidus
    Nigeria & Ethiopia to Angola, W Tanzania
  L. s. lessoni
    Fernando Po I

L. s. bailundensis
    S Angola, S Zaire, Zambia, S Tanzania
Lamprotornis ornatus (Principé Glossy Starling)
    Principé I
Lamprotornis australis (Burchell's Starling)
  L. a. australis
    E Angola to Rhodesia
  L. a. degener
    NW Transvaal to S Mozambique
Lamprotornis mevesii (Long-tailed Purple Starling)
  L. m. chalceus
    C Angola
  L. m. mevesii
    S Angola to S Malawi
  L. m. violacior
    NW Namibia, SW Angola
  L. m. benguelensis
    SW & W Angola
Lamprotornis purpuropterus (Rüppell's Long-tailed Glossy Starling)
  L. p. aeneocephalus
    E Sudan, N Ethiopia
  L. p. purpuropterus
    S Ethiopia, S Sudan, Uganda, Kenya, W Tanzania
Lamprotornis caudatus (Long-tailed Purple Starling)
    Senegal to Sudan

CINNYRICINCLUS
Cinnyricinclus femoralis (Abbott's Starling)
    S Kenya, N Tanzania
Cinnyricinclus sharpii (Sharpe's Starling)
    E Zaire to Ethiopia & Tanzania
Cinnyricinclus leucogaster (Violet Starling)
  C. l. leucogaster
    Senegal to Uganda, Kenya, Tanzania
  C. l. arabicus
    SW Arabia, NE Sudan, Somalia, N Ethiopia
  C. l. friedmanni
    S Ethiopia
  C. l. verreauxi
    Angola to Kenya & Cape Province

SPECULIPASTOR
Speculipastor bicolor (Magpie Starling)
    S Ethiopia, N Kenya

NEOCICHLA
Neocichla gutturalis (White-winged Starling)
  N. g. gutturalis
    S Angola, W Zambia
  N. g. angusta
    E Zambia, Tanzania, Malawi

SPREO
Spreo fischeri (Fischer's Starling)
S Somalia, Kenya, N Tanzania
Spreo bicolor (Pied Starling)
Ethiopia, E & South Africa
Spreo albicapillus (White-crowned Starling)
S Ethiopia, Somalia
Spreo superbus (Superb Starling)
SE Sudan to Somalia & Tanzania
Spreo pulcher (Chestnut-bellied Starling)
S. p. pulcher
Senegal to S Sudan
S. p. rufiventris
Chad, Sudan, Ethiopia
Spreo hildebrandti (Hildebrandt's Starling)
S Kenya, N Tanzania
Spreo shelleyi (Shelley's Starling)
S Ethiopia, S Somalia, Kenya

COSMOPSARUS
Cosmopsarus regius (Golden-breasted Starling)
C. r. regius
S Ethiopia, S Somalia, Kenya
C. r. magnificus
E Kenya
Cosmopsarus unicolor (Ashy Starling)
S Kenya, Tanzania

SAROGLOSSA
Saroglossa aurata (Madagascar Starling)
Madagascar
Saroglossa spiloptera (Spot-winged Starling)
Himalayas, Burma, Thailand

CREATOPHORA
Creatophora cinerea (Wattled Starling)
Ethiopia to Angola & Cape Province

STURNUS
Sturnus senex (Ceylon White-headed Starling)
SW Sri Lanka
Sturnus malabaricus (Ashy-headed Starling)
S. m. blythii
SW India
S. m. malabaricus
C & E India, Assam
S. m. nemoricola
E India, Burma, Thailand, SW China, Indochina
Sturnus erythropygius (White-headed Starling)
S. e. erythropygius
Andaman Is
S. e. andamanensis
Car Nicobar I

S. e. katchalensis
Katchal I
Sturnus pagodarum (Black-headed Starling)
Afghanistan, India, Sri Lanka
Sturnus sericeus (Silky Starling)
S China
Sturnus philippensis (Violet-backed Starling)
Japan, Borneo, Philippine Is
Sturnus sturninus (Daurian Starling)
E & SE Asia
Sturnus roseus (Rose-coloured Starling)
E Europe, W & C Asia » India
Sturnus vulgaris (Common Starling)
S. v. faroensis
Faroe Is
S. v. zetlandicus
Outer Hebrides, Shetland Is
S. v. vulgaris
N & C Europe, N Africa, N America
S. v. tauricus
SE Europe » Iraq, W Iran
S. v. caucasicus
N Iran
S. v. purpurascens
S Russia » Iraq, Egypt
S. v. nobilior
Transcaspia, NE Iran » N India
S. v. poltaratskyi
C Siberia » E Iran & E India
S. v. porphyronotus
Turkistan » Nepal & N India
S. v. humii
W Himalayas » N India
S. v. minor
Sind
Sturnus unicolor (Spotless Starling)
S Europe, N Africa
Sturnus cineraceus (Grey Starling)
C Asia to Japan » S China
Sturnus contra (Asian Pied Starling)
S. c. contra
N & C India
S. c. sordidus
N Assam
S. c. superciliaris
E Assam, Burma
S. c. floweri
S Burma, Thailand, Laos
S. c. jalla
Sumatra, Java, Bali I
Sturnus nigricollis (Black-collared Starling)
S China, Burma, Thailand, Malaysia, Indochina

Sturnus burmannicus (Jerdon's Starling)
  S. b. burmannicus
   Burma
  S. b. leucocephalus
   S Thailand, Cambodia, S Indochina
Sturnus melanopterus (Black-winged Starling)
  S. m. melanopterus
   W Java
  S. m. tricolor
   E Java
  S. m. tertius
   Bali I, Lombok I
Sturnus sinensis (Chinese Starling)
   S China, N Indochina » Malaysia

Leucopsar rothschildi (Rothschild's Mynah)
   Bali I

Acridotheres tristis (Common Mynah)
  A. t. tristis
   Afghanistan, India, SE Asia
  A. t. melanosturnus
   Sri Lanka
  A. t. tristoides
   C & N Burma, Nepal & South Africa (intro.)
Acridotheres ginginianus (Bank Mynah)
   Pakistan, N India
Acridotheres fuscus (Indian Jungle Mynah)
  A. f. mahrattensis
   W & S India
  A. f. fuscus
   N India, Burma
  A. f. fumidus
   NE Assam
  A. f. torquatus
   N & C Malaysia
  A. f. javanicus
   Java
  A. f. cinereus
   S Celebes
Acridotheres grandis (Great Mynah)
   Assam, Burma, Indochina
Acridotheres albocinctus (White-collared Mynah)
   E India to NW Yunnan
Acridotheres cristatellus (Chinese Jungle Mynah)
  A. c. cristatellus
   C & S China, E Burma
  A. c. formosanus
   Taiwan
  A. c. brevipennis
   Hainan I, Indochina

Ampeliceps coronatus (Gold-crested Mynah)
   Assam, Burma, Thailand, Laos

Mino anais (Golden-breasted Mynah)
  M. a. anais
   NW New Guinea
  M. a. orientalis
   N New Guinea
  M. a. robertsoni
   S New Guinea
Mino dumontii (Yellow-faced Mynah)
  M. d. dumontii
   New Guinea, Aru Is
  M. d. kreffti
   Bismarck Archipelago
  M. d. sanfordi
   Guadalcanal I, Malaita I

Basilornis celebensis (Celebes King Starling)
   Celebes
Basilornis galeatus (Greater King Starling)
   Banggai I, Sula Is
Basilornis corythaix (Ceram King Starling)
   Ceram I
Basilornis miranda (Mount Apo King Starling)
   Mindanao I

Streptocitta albicollis (Celebes Magpie)
  S. a. torquata
   N & E Celebes
  S. a. albicollis
   S & SE Celebes
Streptocitta albertinae (Sula Magpie)
   Sula Is

Sarcops calvus (Bald Starling)
  S. c. calvus
   N Philippine Is
  S. c. melanotus
   C & SE Philippine Is
  S. c. lowii
   Sulu Is

Gracula ptilogenys (Ceylon Grackle)
   Sri Lanka
Gracula religiosa (Southern Grackle) (Hill Myna)
  G. r. indica
   SW India, Sri Lanka
  G. r. peninsularis
   NE India

G. r. intermedia
  N India, Burma, Thailand, Indochina
G. r. andamanensis
  Andaman Is, Nicobar Is
G. r. religiosa
  Malaysia, Sumatra, Java, Bali I, Borneo,
  Bangka I
G. r. batuensis
  W Sumatran Is
G. r. robusta
  Babi I, Nias I
G. r. palawanensis
  Palawan I
G. r. venerata
  Sumbawa I
G. r. mertensi
  Flores I, Pantar I, Alor I

ENODES
**Enodes erythrophris (Celebes Enodes
Starling)**
E. e. erythrophris
  N Celebes
E. e. centralis
  NC & SE Celebes
E. e. leptorhynchus
  SC Celebes

SCISSIROSTRUM
Scissirostrum dubium (Grosbeak Starling)
S. d. dubium
  Celebes
S. d. pelingense
  Togian I, Peling I

BUPHAGINAE

BUPHAGUS
**Buphagus africanus (Yellow-billed
Oxpecker)**
B. a. africanus
  Senegal & SW Ethiopia to Namibia and
  Natal
B. a. langi
  Gabon, W Congo
**Buphagus erythrorhynchus (Red-billed
Oxpecker)**
B. e. erythrorhynchus
  Ethiopia, Sudan
B. e. caffer
  Botswana, W Rhodesia, W Transvaal
B. e. angolensis
  S Angola to W Zambia
B. e. scotinus
  S Kenya to S Mozambique

167 ORIOLIDAE (ORIOLES)

ORIOLUS
Oriolus szalayi (Brown Oriole)
  New Guinea

Oriolus phaeochromus (Moluccan Oriole)
  Halmahera I
Oriolus forsteni (Ceram Oriole)
  Ceram I
Oriolus bouroensis (Buru Oriole)
O. b. bouroensis
  Buru I
O. b. decipiens
  Tenimber Is
Oriolus viridifuscus (Timor Oriole)
O. v. finschi
  Wetar I
O. v. viridifuscus
  Timor I
**Oriolus sagittatus (Olive-backed
Oriole)**
O. s. magnirostris
  S New Guinea, N Queensland
O. s. affinis
  N Western Australia
O. s. sagittatus
  E & SE Australia
Oriolus flavocinctus (Yellow Oriole)
O. f. flavocinctus
  N Northern Territory, N Queensland
O. f. mülleri
  Aru Is, S New Guinea
**Oriolus xanthonotus (Dark-throated
Oriole)**
O. x. xanthonotus
  Malaysia, Sumatra, Java, SW Borneo
O. x. consobrinus
  N, C & E Borneo
O. x. mentawi
  W Sumatran Is, Siberut I
O. x. cinereogenys
  Sulu Is
O. x. persuasus
  Palawan I
O. x. basilanicus
  Basilan I, W Mindanao I
O. x. samarensis
  E Mindanao I, Samar I, Leyte I
O. x. steerii
  Masbate I, Negros I
O. x. assimilis
  Cebu I
**Oriolus albiloris (White-lored
Oriole)**
  Bataan I, Luzon I
Oriolus isabellae (Isabella Oriole)
  Bataan I, Luzon I
Oriolus oriolus (Golden Oriole)
O. o. oriolus
  Europe, W & WC Asia » E & S Africa,
  NW India
O. o. kundoo
  C Asia, N India

Oriolus auratus **(African Golden Oriole)**
O. a. auratus
W & NC Africa
O. a. notatus
Eastern & Southern Africa
Oriolus chinensis **(Black-naped Oriole)**
O. c. tenuirostris
E Nepal, C Burma » S Burma, Thailand
O. c. invisus
S Vietnam
O. c. diffusus
E Asia » India, Malaysia, Indochina
O. c. andamanensis
Andaman Is
O. c. macrourus
Nicobar Is
O. c. chinensis
Philippine Is
O. c. suluensis
Sulu Is
O. c. melanisticus
Talaut I
O. c. sanghirensis
Sanghir Archipelago
O. c. formosus
Siau I
O. c. frontalis
Sula Is, Peling I
O. c. saani
Moluccas
O. c. mundus
Simalur I
O. c. sipora
Sipora I
O. c. richmondi
Siberut I, Pagi I
O. c. insularis
Kangean I
O. c. broderipii
Flores I, Lombok I, Sumba I, Sumbawa I
O. c. lamprochryseus
Solombo Besar I
O. c. oscillans
Tukangbesi I
O. c. boneratensis
Flores Sea Is
O. c. maculatus
Sumatra, Java, Borneo, Bali I, Nias I
O. c. celebensis
N Celebes
O. c. macassariensis
S Celebes
Oriolus chlorocephalus **(Green-headed Oriole)**
O. c. amani
Tanzania
O. c. chlorocephalus
Malawi, Mozambique

O. c. speculifer   625
S Mozambique
Oriolus crassirostris **(Sao Thomé Oriole)**
Sao Thomé I
Oriolus brachyrhynchus **(Western Black-headed Oriole)**
O. b. brachyrhynchus
W Africa
O. b. laetior
WC & C Africa
Oriolus monacha **(Dark-Headed Oriole)**
O. m. monacha
N Ethiopia
O. m. meneliki
S Ethiopia
Oriolus larvatus **(African Black-headed Oriole)**
O. l. percivali
Zaire, Kenya
O. l. rolleti
Angola, Namibia to Tanzania, Natal
O. l. larvatus
South Africa
Oriolus nigripennis **(Black-winged Oriole)**
O. n. alleni
W Africa
O. n. nigripennis
WC & C Africa
Oriolus xanthornus **(Asian Black-headed Oriole)**
O. x. xanthornus
N India, Thailand, Indochina
O. x. maderaspatanus
S India, Andaman Is
O. x. ceylonensis
Sri Lanka
O. x. tanakae
NE Borneo
O. x. thaiocous
S Thailand, N Malaysia
O. x. andamanensis
S Andaman Is
Oriolus hosii **(Black Oriole)**
Borneo
Oriolus cruentus **(Crimson-breasted Oriole)**
O. c. cruentus
Java
O. c. malayanus
C Malaysia
O. c. consanguineus
Sumatra
O. c. vulneratus
N Borneo
Oriolus traillii **(Maroon Oriole)**
O. t. traillii
Himalayas, Burma, Thailand

O. t. robinsoni
S Indochina
O. t. nigellicauda
N Vietnam, Hainan I
O. t. ardens
Taiwan
Oriolus mellianus (Stresemann's Maroon Oriole)
W China

SPHECOTHERES
Sphecotheres viridis (Figbird)
S. v. viridis
Timor I
S. v. hypoleucus
Wetar I
S. v. vieilloti
NE Australia
S. v. salvadorii
NE Queensland, S New Guinea
S. v. flaviventris
N & NE Australia
S. v. cucullatus
Kei Is, Arafura Sea

168 DICRURIDAE (DRONGOS)

CHAETORHYNCHUS
Chaetorhynchus papuensis (Papuan Mountair Drongo)
New Guinea

DICRURUS
Dicrurus ludwigii (Square-tailed Drongo)
D. l. sharpei
W, WC & C Africa
D. l. saturnus
Angola
D. l. ludwigii
Eastern & Southern Africa
D. l. tephrogaster
Mozambique, E Rhodesia, S Malawi
Dicrurus atripennis (Shining Drongo)
W Africa
Dicrurus adsimilis (Fork-tailed Drongo)
D. a. adsimilis
EC & Southern Africa
D. a. divaricatus
W Africa, Chad, Sudan, Ethiopia
D. a. coracinus
WC & C Africa
D. a. atactus
Upper Guinea, Nigeria
D. a. modestus
Principé I
D. a. apivorus
Namibia
Dicrurus fuscipennis (Comoro Drongo)
Great Comoro I
Dicrurus aldabranus (Aldabra Drongo)
Aldabra I

Dicrurus forficatus (Crested Drongo)
D. f. forficatus
Madagascar
D. f. potior
Anjouan I
Dicrurus waldenii (Mayotte Drongo)
Mayotte I
Dicrurus macrocercus (Black Drongo)
D. m. albirictus
SE Iran, Afghanistan, N India
D. m. macrocercus
S India
D. m. minor
Sri Lanka
D. m. cathoecus
China, N Burma, N Thailand, Laos
N Vietnam, Malaysia
D. m. thai
S Burma, S Thailand, S Vietnam
D. m. harterti
Taiwan
D. m. javanus
Java, Bali I
Dicrurus leucophaeus (Pale Ashy Drongo)
D. l. longicaudatus
E Afghanistan » S India, Sri Lanka
D. l. hopwoodi
Sikkim, Bhutan, Assam, Burma, S China,
» S Indochina
D. l. mouhoti
S Burma, N Thailand » S Vietnam,
Indochina
D. l. bondi
S Thailand, Cambodia
D. l. nigrescens
S Thailand, Malaysia
D. l. leucogenis
Manchuria, E China » S Indochina
D. l. salangensis
SE China, S Thailand » Hainan I,
Malaysia
D. l. innexus
Hainan I
D. l. stigmatops
N Borneo
D. l. phaedrus
S Sumatra
D. l. batakensis
N Sumatra
D. l. periophthalmicus
Sipora I, Mentawei Group
D. l. siberu
Siberut I
D. l. leucophaeus
Java, Bali I, Lombok I, Palawan I

Dicrurus caerulescens (White-bellied Drongo)
D. c. caerulescens
Peninsular India
D. c. insularis
N Sri Lanka
D. c. leucopygialis
S Sri Lanka
Dicrurus annectans (Crow-billed Drongo)
Himalayas, Burma, Thailand, Malaysia, India
Dicrurus aeneus (Bronzed Drongo)
D. a. aeneus
India, Burma, S China, Thailand, Indochina
D. a. malayensis
S Malaysia, Sumatra, Borneo
D. a. braunianus
Taiwan
Dicrurus remifer (Lesser Racquet-tailed Drongo)
D. r. tectirostris
Himalayas, Burma, S China, Thailand, Indochina
D. r. remifer
Java, Sumatra
D. r. peracensis
W Laos, S Thailand, Malaysia
D. r. lefoli
S Cambodia
Dicrurus balicassius (Balicassio Drongo)
D. b. balicassius
Lubang, C & S Luzon I, Mindoro I
D. b. abraensis
N Luzon I
D. b. mirabilis
Panay I, Cebu I, Negros I, Masbate I
Dicrurus hottentottus (Spangled Drongo)
D. h. samarensis
Samar I, Leyte I, Bohol I
D. h. striatus
Mindanao I, Basilan I
D. h. morotensis
Morotai I
D. h. atrocaeruleus
Kofiau I, Halmahera I
D. h. carbonarius
New Guinea, D'Entrecasteaux Archipelago
D. h. bracteatus
N & E Australia » S New Guinea
D. h. laemostictus
New Britain
D. h. meeki
Guadalcanal I
D. h. longirostris
San Cristobal I

D. h. amboinensis
S Moluccas
D. h. buruensis
Buru I
D. h. densus
Timor I
D. h. kühni
Tenimber Is
D. h. megalornis
Kei Is
D. h. sumbae
Sumba I
D. h. bimaënsis
Lombok I, Flores I, Alor I
D. h. renschi
Sumbawa I
D. h. sumatranus
Sumatra
D. h. guillemardi
Obi Is
D. h. pectoralis
Sula Is
D. h. banggaiensis
Banggai Is
D. h. leucops
Celebes
D. h. jentincki
Bali I, Kangean I
D. h. viridinitens
Mentawei Is
D. h. borneensis
N Borneo
D. h. suluensis
Sibutu I, Sulu Archipelago
D. h. hottentottus
India, Burma, Thailand, S Indochina
D. h. brevirostris
China, N Burma, N Laos, N Vietnam
D. h. palawanensis
Cagayan I, Sulu Is, Palawan I
D. h. cuyensis
Cuyo I, Semirara I, Philippine Is
D. h. menagei
Tablas I
Dicrurus megarhynchus (New Ireland Drongo)
New Ireland
Dicrurus montanus (Celebes Mountain Drongo)
Celebes
Dicrurus andamanensis (Andaman Drongo)
D. a. andamanensis
S Andaman Is
D. a. dicruriformis
Gt Cocos I, Table I

Dicrurus paradiseus (Greater Racquet-tailed Drongo)
 D. p. brachyphorus
  Borneo
 D. p. banguey
  N Borneo Is
 D. p. microlophus
  Tioman I, Anamba Is, N Natuna Is
 D. p. platurus
  S Malaysia, Sumatra, NW Sumatra Is
 D. p. formosus
  Java
 D. p. malayensis
  N Malaysia
 D. p. paradiseus
  S India, S Thailand, Indochina
 D. p. rangoonensis
  S Burma, W Thailand, C Laos
 D. p. grandis
  N India, N Burma, N Vietnam
 D. p. johni
  Hainan I
 D. p. ceylonicus
  Sri Lanka
 D. p. lophorinus
  W Sri Lanka
 D. p. otiosus
  Andaman Is
 D. p. nicobariensis
  Nicobar Is

169 CALLAEIDAE (WATTLEBIRDS)

CALLAEAS
Callaeas cinerea (Kokako)
 C. c. wilsoni
  North I (New Zealand)
 C. c. cinerea
  South I (New Zealand) Stewart I

CREADION
Creadion carunculatus (Saddleback)
 C. c. rufusater
  North Island (New Zealand)
 C. c. carunculatus
  Stewart I

170 GRALLINIDAE (MAGPIE LARKS)

GRALLININAE

GRALLINA
Grallina cyanoleuca (Magpie Lark)
 Australia
Grallina bruijni (Torrent Lark)
 New Guinea

CORCORACINAE
CORCORAX
Corcorax melanorhamphos (White-winged Chough)
 E & SE Australia

STRUTHIDEA
Struthidea cinerea (Apostle Bird)
 S. c. cinerea
  Eastern Australia
 S. c. dalyi
  Northern Territory

171 ARTAMIDAE (WOOD SWALLOWS)

ARTAMUS
Artamus fuscus (Ashy Wood Swallow)
 India to S China, Indochina
Artamus leucorhynchus (White-breasted Wood Swallow)
 A. l. pelewensis
  Palau Is
 A. l. leucorhynchus
  Philippine Is, Palawan I, Borneo
 A. l. amydrus
  Sumatra, Bangka I, Java, Bali I
 A. l. humei
  Andaman Is, Cocos Is
 A. l. celebensis
  Celebes, Lombok I, Sumbawa I, Flores I
 A. l. albiventer
  Alor I, Wetar I, Timor I
 A. l. musschenbroeki
  Tenimber Is
 A. l. leucopygialis
  Moluccas, Aru Is, New Guinea, N Australia
 A. l. melaleucus
  New Caledonia, Loyalty Is
 A. l. tenuis
  New Hebrides
 A. l. mentalis
  N Fiji Is
Artamus monachus (White-backed Wood Swallow)
 A. m. monachus
  Celebes
 A. m. sulaensis
  Sula Is
Artamus maximus (Papuan Wood Swallow)
 New Guinea
Artamus insignis (Bismarck Wood Swallow)
 New Britain, New Ireland
Artamus personatus (Masked Wood Swallow)
 Australia

Artamus superciliosus (White-browed
 Wood Swallow)
  SE Australia
Artamus cinereus (Black-faced Wood
 Swallow)
  A. c. perspicillatus
   Timor I
  A. c. cinereus
   W, C & SE Australia
  A. c. hypoleucos
   S New Guinea, N Queensland
  A. c. normani
   N Queensland
  A. c. inkermani
   C Queensland
Artamus cyanopterus (Dusky Wood
 Swallow)
  A. c. cyanopterus
   E & SE Australia, Tasmania
  A. c. perthi
   S Western Australia
Artamus minor (Little Wood Swallow)
  N & C Australia

172 CRACTICIDAE (BUTCHER BIRDS)

CRACTICUS
Cracticus mentalis (Black-backed
 Butcher Bird)
  C. m. mentalis
   SE New Guinea
  C. m. kempi
   N Queensland
Cracticus torquatus (Grey Butcher Bird)
  C. t. argenteus
   Northern Territory, NW Western Australia
  C. t. leucopterus
   Central Australia
  C. t. torquatus
   E Australia
  C. t. cinereus
   Tasmania
Cracticus nigrogularis (Black-throated
 Butcher Bird)
  C. n. picatus
   Northern Territory, NW Western Australia
  C. n. kalgoorli
   Central Australia, Western Australia
  C. n. nigrogularis
   E & SE Australia
Cracticus cassicus (Black-headed
 Butcher Bird)
  C. c. cassicus
   New Guinea
  C. c. hercules
   Trobriand Is, D'Entrecasteaux
    Archipelago

Cracticus louisiadensis (White-rumped
 Butcher Bird)
  Tagula I
Cracticus quoyi (Black Butcher Bird)
  C. q. quoyi
   New Guinea
  C. q. spaldingi
   Aru Is, Northern Territory, N Queensland
  C. q. rufescens
   NC Queensland

GYMNORHINA
Gymnorhina tibicen (Black-backed
 Magpie)
  G. t. papuana
   S New Guinea
  G. t. eylandtensis
   Northern Territory
  G. t. longirostris
   Western Australia
  G. t. finki
   Central Australia
  G. t. terraereginae
   N Northern Territory, C Queensland
  G. t. tibicen
   New South Wales, Victoria, South
    Australia
  G. t. leuconota
   SE South Australia, W Victoria
  G. t. dorsalis
   S Western Australia
  G. t. hypoleuca
   E Victoria, Tasmania

STREPERA
Strepera graculina (Pied Currawong)
  S. g. robinsoni
   Queensland
  S. g. graculina
   New South Wales
  S. g. ashbyi
   Victoria
  S. g. crissalis
   Lord Howe I
Strepera fuliginosa (Black Currawong)
  Tasmania
Strepera versicolor (Grey Currawong)
  S. v. versicolor
   New South Wales, E Victoria
  S. v. centralia
   N South Australia
  S. v. plumbea
   S Western Australia
  S. v. howei
   NW Victoria, E South Australia
  S. v. melanoptera
   SE South Australia, Kangaroo I
  S. v. intermedia
   S South Australia

S. v. arguta
Tasmania

173 PTILONORHYNCHIDAE (BOWERBIRDS)

AILUROEDUS
Ailuroedus buccoides (White-eared Catbird)
A. b. cinnamomeus
S New Guinea
A. b. buccoides
W Papuan Is, NW New Guinea
A. b. stonii
SE New Guinea
A. b. geislerorum
Japen I, N New Guinea
Ailuroedus crassirostris (Green Catbird)
SE Queensland to N Victoria
Ailuroedus melanotis (Spotted Catbird)
A. m. maculosus
N Queensland
A. m. melanotis
Aru Is, S New Guinea
A. m. melanocephalus
SE New Guinea
A. m. facialis
WC New Guinea
A. m. guttaticollis
N New Guinea
A. m. astigmaticus
E New Guinea
A. m. jobiensis
WC New Guinea
A. m. arfakianus
NW New Guinea
A. m. misoliensis
Misol I

SCENOPOEETES
Scenopoeetes dentirostris (Tooth-billed Catbird)
NE Queensland

ARCHBOLDIA
Archboldia papuensis (Archbold's Bowerbird)
A. p. papuensis
WC New Guinea
A. p. sanfordi
EC New Guinea

AMBLYORNIS
Amblyornis inornatus (Vogelkop Gardener Bowerbird)
NW New Guinea
Amblyornis macgregoriae (Macgregor's Gardener Bowerbird)
A. m. mayri
WC New Guinea

A. m. macgregoriae
EC New Guinea
A. m. germanus
E New Guinea
A. m. kombok
EC New Guinea
A. m. nubicola
SE New Guinea
Amblyornis subularis (Striped Gardener Bowerbird)
SE New Guinea
Amblyornis flavifrons (Yellow-fronted Gardener Bowerbird)
W New Guinea?

PRIONODURA
Prionodura newtoniana (Newton's Golden Bowerbird)
NE Queensland

SERICULUS
Sericulus aureus (Flamed Bowerbird)
S. a. aureus
N & W New Guinea
S. a. ardens
S New Guinea
Sericulus bakeri (Adelbert Bowerbird)
NE New Guinea
Sericulus chrysocephalus (Regent Bowerbird)
S. c. chrysocephalus
NE New South Wales
S. c. rothschildi
C & S Queensland

PTILONORHYNCHUS
Ptilonorhynchus violaceus (Satin Bowerbird)
P. v. violaceus
SE Queensland to Victoria
P. v. minor
NE Queensland

CHLAMYDERA
Chlamydera maculata (Spotted Bowerbird)
C. m. maculata
EC Australia
C. m. guttata
WC Australia
Chlamydera nuchalis (Great Grey Bowerbird)
C. n. oweni
N Western Australia
C. n. nuchalis
N Western Australia to NW Queensland
C. n. yorki
N Queensland
C. n. orientalis
NW Queensland

Chlamydera lauterbachi (Lauterbach's Bowerbird)
  C. l. lauterbachi
    NC New Guinea
  C. l. uniformis
    C New Guinea
Chlamydera cerviniventris (Fawn-breasted Bowerbird)
    E New Guinea, N Queensland

174 PARADISAEIDAE (BIRDS OF PARADISE)

CNEMOPHILINAE

LORIA
Loria loriae (Loria's Bird of Paradise)
  L. l. inexpectata
    WC New Guinea
  L. l. loriae
    SE New Guinea
  L. l. amethystina
    EC New Guinea

LOBOPARADISEA
Loboparadisea sericea (Wattle-billed Bird of Paradise)
  L. s. sericea
    C New Guinea
  L. s. aurora
    E New Guinea

CNEMOPHILUS
Cnemophilus macgregorii (Sickle Crested Bird of Paradise)
  C. m. sanguineus
    EC New Guinea
  C. m. macgregorii
    SE New Guinea

PARADISAEINAE
MACGREGORIA
Macgregoria pulchra (Macgregor's Bird of Paradise)
  M. p. pulchra
    SE New Guinea
  M. p. carolinae
    WC New Guinea

LYCOCORAX
Lycocorax pyrrhopterus (Paradise Crow)
  L. p. obiensis
    Obi Is
  L. p. pyrrhopterus
    Batjan I, Halmahera I
  L. p. morotensis
    Morotai I, Rau I

MANUCODIA
Manucodia ater (Glossy-mantled Manucode)
  M. a. ater
    C & W New Guinea
  M. a. subalter
    Aru Is, SE New Guinea
  M. a. alter
    Tagula I
Manucodia jobiensis (Jobi Manucode)
  M. j. jobiensis
    Japen I
  M. j. rubiensis
    N & W New Guinea
Manucodia chalybatus (Crinkle-collared Manucode)
    Misol I, all New Guinea except mountains
Manucodia comrii (Curl-crested Manucode)
  M. c. comrii
    Ferguson I, Goodenough I, Normanby I
  M. c. trobriandi
    Trobriand Is

PHONYGAMMUS
Phonygammus keraudrenii (Trumpet Bird)
  P. k. keraudrenii
    NW New Guinea
  P. k. adelberti
    N New Guinea
  P. k. neumanni
    NC New Guinea
  P. k. mayri
    NE New Guinea
  P. k. jamesii
    Aru Is, S New Guinea
  P. k. purpureoviolaceus
    SE New Guinea
  P. k. hunsteini
    D'Entrecasteaux Archipelago
  P. k. gouldii
    N Queensland

PTILORIS
Ptiloris paradiseus (Paradise Riflebird)
    SE Queensland, NE New South Wales
Ptiloris victoriae (Queen Victoria Riflebird)
    NE Queensland
Ptiloris magnificus (Magnificent Riflebird)
  P. m. intercedens
    E New Guinea
  P. m. magnificus
    S & W New Guinea
  P. m. alberti
    N Queensland

632 *SEMIOPTERA*

Semioptera wallacei (Wallace's Standardwing)
S. w. halmaherae
Halmahera I
S. w. wallacei
Batjan I

SELEUCIDIS
Seleucidis melanoleuca (Twelve-wired Bird of Paradise)
S. m. melanoleuca
Salawati I, coast of New Guinea
S. m. auripennis
N New Guinea

PARADIGALLA
Paradigalla carunculata (Long-tailed Paradigalla)
P. c. carunculata
Arfak mountains, New Guinea
P. c. intermedia
WC New Guinea
Paradigalla brevicauda (Short-tailed Paradigalla)
C New Guinea

DREPANORNIS
Drepanornis albertisii (Black-billed Sicklebill)
D. a. albertisii
NW New Guinea
D. a. cervinicauda
C New Guinea
D. a. geisleri
E New Guinea
Drepanornis bruijnii (Pale-billed Sicklebill)
NW New Guinea

EPIMACHUS
Epimachus fastosus (Black Sicklebill)
E. f. fastosus
NW New Guinea
E. f. atratus
WC New Guinea
E. f. ultimus
Mt Menawa (N New Guinea)
E. f. stresemanni
EC New Guinea
Epimachus meyeri (Brown Sicklebill)
E. m. megarhynchus
Weyland mountains, New Guinea
E. m. albicans
C New Guinea
E. m. bloodi
EC New Guinea
E. m. meyeri
SE New Guinea

ASTRAPIA
Astrapia nigra (Arfak Bird of Paradise)
Arfak mountains, New Guinea
Astrapia splendidissima (Splendid Bird of Paradise)
A. s. helios
NW New Guinea
A. s. splendidissima
Weyland mountains, New Guinea
A. s. elliottsmithi
WC New Guinea
Astrapia mayeri (Ribbon-tailed Bird of Paradise)
EC New Guinea
Astrapia stephaniae (Princess Stephanie's Bird of Paradise)
A. s. feminina
EC New Guinea
A. s. ducalis
E New Guinea
A. s. stephaniae
SE New Guinea
Astrapia rothschildi (Huon Bird of Paradise)
E New Guinea

LOPHORINA
Lophorina superba (Superb Bird of Paradise)
L. s. superba
Arfak mountains, NW New Guinea
L. s. niedda
Mt Wondiwoi (W New Guinea)
L. s. feminina
WC New Guinea
L. s. pseudoparotia
EC New Guinea
L. s. latipennis
E New Guinea
L. s. connectens
E New Guinea
L. s. minor
SE New Guinea
L. s. sphinx
SE New Guinea

PAROTIA
Parotia sefilata (Arfak Parotia)
Arfak mountains, New Guinea
Parotia carolae (Queen Carola's Parotia)
P. c. clelandiae
Victor Emmanuel mountains, N New Guinea
P. c. meeki
Nassau, Oranje mountains, W New Guinea
P. c. carolae
Weyland mountains, C New Guinea

P. c. chalcothorax
    Idenburg river, C New Guinea
P. c. berlepschi
    Van Rees mountains, C New Guinea?
P. c. chrysenia
    Bismarck mountains, C New Guinea
Parotia lawesii (Lawes' Parotia)
    C & SE New Guinea
Parotia helenae (Eastern Parotia)
    SE New Guinea
Parotia wahnesi (Wahnes' Parotia)
    E New Guinea

PTERIDOPHORA
Pteridophora alberti (King of Saxony Bird of Paradise)
    P. a. alberti
        C New Guinea
    P. a. hallstromi
        EC New Guinea
    P. a. bürgersi
        EC New Guinea

CICINNURUS
Cicinnurus regius (King Bird of Paradise)
    C. r. regius
        Aru Is
    C. r. rex
        W New Guinea Is, New Guinea
    C. r. coccineifrons
        Japen I
    C. r. similis
        N New Guinea
    C. r. cryptorhynchus
        NW New Guinea
    C. r. gymnorhynchus
        NE New Guinea

DIPHYLLODES
Diphyllodes magnificus (Magnificent Bird of Paradise)
    D. m. magnificus
        NW New Guinea, Salawati I
    D. m. intermedius
        Weyland mountains, C New Guinea
    D. m. chrysopterus
        Japen I, N New Guinea
    D. m. hunsteini
        E New Guinea
Diphyllodes respublica (Wilson's Bird of Paradise)
    Waigeu I, Batanta I

PARADISAEA
Paradisaea apoda (Greater Bird of Paradise)
    P. a. apoda
        Aru Is, Lt Tobago I, West Indies (intro)
    P. a. novaeguineae
        S New Guinea

Paradisaea raggiana (Raggiana Bird of Paradise)
    P. r. augustaevictoriae
        NE New Guinea
    P. r. intermedia
        E New Guinea
    P. r. granti
        E New Guinea
    P. r. salvadorii
        S New Guinea
    P. r. raggiana
        SE New Guinea
Paradisaea minor (Lesser Bird of Paradise)
    P. m. minor
        NW & W New Guinea
    P. m. finschi
        NC New Guinea
    P. m. jobiensis
        Japen I
    P. m. pulchra
        Misol I
Paradisaea decora (Goldie's Bird of Paradise)
    Fergusson I, Normanby I
Paradisaea rubra (Red Bird of Paradise)
    Batanta I, Waigeu I, Saonek I
Paradisaea guilielmi (Emperor of Germany Bird of Paradise)
    E New Guinea
Paradisaea rudolphi (Blue Bird of Paradise)
    P. r. ampla
        Hertzog mountains, W New Guinea
    P. r. margaritae
        WC New Guinea
    P. r. rudolphi
        E New Guinea

175 CORVIDAE (CROWS, JAYS)

PLATYLOPHUS
Platylophus galericulatus (Crested Shrike-Jay)
    P. g. ardesiacus
        S Thailand, Malaysia
    P. g. coronatus
        Borneo, Sumatra
    P. g. galericulatus
        Java

PLATYSMURUS
Platysmurus leucopterus (White-winged Magpie)
    P. l. leucopterus
        Malaysia, Sumatra
    P. l. aterrimus
        Borneo

GYMNORHINUS
Gymnorhinus cyanocephala (Pinyon Jay)
W USA, NW Mexico

CYANOCITTA
Cyanocitta cristata (Blue Jay)
  C. c. bromia
    S Canada, C USA » SE USA
  C. c. cristata
    EC & SE USA
  C. c. semplei
    S Florida
  C. c. cyanotephra
    SC USA
Cyanocitta stelleri (Steller's Jay)
  C. s. stelleri
    W Canada, NW USA
  C. s. carlottae
    Queen Charlotte Is
  C. s. annectens
    W Canada, WC USA
  C. s. frontalis
    W USA
  C. s. carbonacea
    W California
  C. s. macrolopha
    C & S USA, N Mexico
  C. s. diademata
    NC Mexico
  C. s. coronata
    SC Mexico
  C. s. purpurea
    SW Mexico
  C. s. azteca
    C Mexico
  C. s. teotepecencis
    S Mexico
  C. s. ridgwayi
    S Mexico to El Salvador
  C. s. suavis
    Honduras, Nicaragua

APHELOCOMA
Aphelocoma coerulescens (Scrub Jay)
  A. c. immanis
    W Oregon
  A. c. caurina
    W USA
  A. c. oocleptica
    W USA
  A. c. californica
    W California
  A. c. cana
    California
  A. c. obscura
    N Baja California
  A. c. cactophila
    C Baja California

  A. c. hypoleuca
    C & S Baja California
  A. c. insularis
    Santa Cruz I
  A. c. nevadae
    WC USA, N Mexico
  A. c. woodhouseii
    WC & SC USA
  A. c. texana
    WC Texas
  A. c. grisea
    NW Mexico
  A. c. cyanotis
    EC Mexico
  A. c. sumichrasti
    SC Mexico
  A. c. remota
    SW Mexico
  A. c. coerulescens
    S Florida
Aphelocoma ultramarina (Mexican Jay)
  A. u. arizonae
    SW USA, NW Mexico
  A. u. wollweberi
    W Mexico
  A. u. gracilis
    WC Mexico
  A. u. couchii
    S Texas, NE Mexico
  A. u. potosina
    EC Mexico
  A. u. ultramarina
    SC Mexico
  A. u. colimae
    SW Mexico
Aphelocoma unicolor (Unicoloured Jay)
  A. u. guerrerensis
    C Mexico
  A. u. oaxacae
    S Mexico
  A. u. concolor
    SE Mexico
  A. u. unicolor
    SE Mexico
  A. u. griscomi
    El Salvador, W Honduras

CYANOLYCA
Cyanolyca viridicyana (White-collared Jay)
  C. v. joylaea
    NC Peru
  C. v. cyanolaema
    SE Peru
  C. v. viridicyana
    W Bolivia

Cyanolyca armillata (Collard Jay)
C. a. meridana
NW Venezuela
C. a. armillata
E Colombia, W Venezuela
C. a. quindiuna
S Colombia, N Ecuador
Cyanolyca turcosa (Turquoise Jay)
S Colombia, N Peru
Cyanolyca pulchra (Beautiful Jay)
SW Colombia, W Ecuador
Cyanolyca cucullata (Azure-hooded Jay)
C. c. mitrata
E & S Mexico, Guatemala
C. c. guatemalae
Chiapas, SE Mexico
C. c. hondurensis
W Honduras
C. c. cucullata
Costa Rica, W Panama
Cyanolyca pumilo (Black-throated Jay)
S Mexico to Honduras
Cyanolyca nana (Dwarf Jay)
S Mexico
Cyanolyca mirabilis (White-throated Jay)
SW Mexico
Cyanolyca argentigula (Silvery-throated Jay)
C. a. albior
Costa Rica
C. a. argentigula
S Costa Rica

CISSILOPHA
Cissilopha melanocyanea (Bushy-crested Jay)
C. m. melanocyanea
Guatemala to Honduras
C. m. chavezi
S Honduras, N Nicaragua
Cissilopha sanblasiana (San Blas Jay)
C. s. nelsoni
SW Mexico
C. s. sanblasiana
SW Mexico
Cissilopha yucatanica (Yucatan Jay)
C. y. yucatanica
SE Mexico, Guatemala
C. y. rivularis
SE Mexico
Cissilopha beecheii (Purplish-backed Jay)
NW Mexico

CYANOCORAX
Cyanocorax caeruleus (Azure Jay)
SE Brazil to N Argentina
Cyanocorax cyanomelas (Purplish Jay)
SE Peru to N Argentina

Cyanocorax violaceus (Violaceous Jay) 635
C. v. pallidus
N Venezuela
C. v. violaceus
N South America
Cyanocorax cristatellus (Curl-crested Jay)
C & E Brazil
Cyanocorax heilprini (Azure-naped Jay)
S Venezuela, NW Brazil
Cyanocorax cayanus (Cayenne Jay)
SE Venezuela, the Guianas, N Brazil
Cyanocorax affinis (Black-chested Jay)
C. a. zeledoni
S Costa Rica, Panama
C. a. affinis
N Colombia, NW Venezuela
Cyanocorax chrysops (Plush-crested Jay)
C. c. diesingii
N Brazil
C. c. chrysops
E Bolivia to SE Brazil
C. c. tucumanus
NW Argentina
Cyanocorax cyanopogon (White-naped Jay)
E Brazil
Cyanocorax mystacalis (White-tailed Jay)
SW Ecuador, NW Peru
Cyanocorax dickeyi (Tufted Jay)
W Mexico
Cyanocorax yncas (Green Jay)
C. y. glaucescens
NE Mexico
C. y. speciosus
W Mexico
C. y. vividus
SW Mexico
C. y. luxuosus
E Mexico
C. y. centralis
SE Mexico, Guatemala, Honduras
C. y. maya
SE Mexico
C. y. cozumelae
Cozumel I
C. y. galeatus
C Colombia
C. y. cyanodorsalis
E Colombia
C. y. andicolus
NW Venezuela
C. y. guatimalensis
N Venezuela
C. y. yncas
SW Colombia, Ecuador, Peru, N Boliviá

C. y. *longirostris*
  N Peru

PSILORHINUS
Psilorhinus morio (Brown Jay)
  P. m. *palliatus*
    NE & C Mexico
  P. m. *morio*
    SE Mexico
  P. m. *cyanogenys*
    SE Mexico, Central America
  P. m. *mexicanus*
    E Mexico
  P. m. *vociferus*
    SE Mexico

CALOCITTA
Calocitta formosa (White-throated Magpie-Jay)
  C. f. *formosa*
    SW Mexico
  C. f. *azurea*
    SE Mexico, Guatemala
  C. f. *pompata*
    S Mexico to Costa Rica
Calocitta colliei (Collie's Magpie-Jay)
  W Mexico

GARRULUS
Garrulus glandarius (Jay)
  G. g. *rufitergum*
    S Scotland, England, N France
  G. g. *hibernicus*
    N Scotland, Ireland
  G. g. *glandarius*
    N & C Europe
  G. g. *fasciatus*
    Iberia
  G. g. *ichnusae*
    Sardinia
  G. g. *corsicanus*
    Corsica
  G. g. *albipectus*
    Italy
  G. g. *cretorum*
    Greece, Crete
  G. g. *glaszneri*
    Cyprus
  G. g. *hansguentheri*
    Istanbul
  G. g. *cervicalis*
    E Algeria, Tunisia
  G. g. *whitakeri*
    N Morocco, W Algeria
  G. g. *minor*
    NW Africa
  G. g. *atricapillus*
    Iraq, W Iran
  G. g. *rhodius*
    Rhodes

G. g. *krynicki*
  Turkey, Caucasus
G. g. *iphigenia*
  Crimea
G. g. *hyrcanus*
  N Iran
G. g. *suianae*
  Kurdistan, NE Iran
G. g. *severzowii*
  Scandinavia, S Russia
G. g. *brandtii*
  NE Russia, C & NE Asia
G. g. *kansuensis*
  W China
G. g. *pekingensis*
  N China, NW Manchuria
G. g. *sinensis*
  SW China, NE Burma
G. g. *taivanus*
  Taiwan
G. g. *leucotis*
  E Burma, Thailand, Indochina
G. g. *oatesi*
  C Burma
G. g. *haringtoni*
  SC Burma
G. g. *interstinctus*
  E Himalayas, SE Tibet
G. g. *persaturatus*
  Assam
G. g. *bispecularis*
  W Himalayas
G. g. *japonicus*
  N Japan
G. g. *tokugawae*
  Sado I
G. g. *hiugaensis*
  S Japan
G. g. *orii*
  Yakushima Is
G. g. *namiyei*
  Tsushima I
Garrulus lanceolatus (Lanceolated Jay)
  W Himalayas, N India
Garrulus lidthi (Purple Jay)
  N Riukiu Is

PERISOREUS
Perisoreus canadensis (Grey Jay)
  P. c. *pacificus*
    NW Alaska
  P. c. *canadensis*
    C Canada, N USA
  P. c. *nigricapillus*
    NE Canada
  P. c. *arcus*
    SW Canada
  P. c. *albescens*
    W Canada, NW USA

P. c. bicolor
SW Canada, NW USA
P. c. capitalis
WC & SC USA
P. c. griseus
SW Canada, NW USA
P. c. obscurus
NW USA
Perisoreus infaustus (Siberian Jay)
P. i. infaustus
Lapland
P. i. ostjakorum
NW Siberia
P. i. yakutensis
N & NE Asia
P. i. ruthenus
C Russia, C Scandinavia
P. i. opicus
NC Asia
P. i. rogosowi
C Siberia
P. i. sibericus
Outer Mongolia
P. i. varnak
N Manchuria
P. i. sakhalinensis
N Sakhalin I
P. i. maritimus
Lower Amur river
Perisoreus internigrans (Szechwan Grey Jay)
W China

Urocissa ornata (Ceylon Blue Magpie)
Sri Lanka
Urocissa caerulea (Formosan Blue Magpie)
Taiwan
Urocissa flavirostris (Yellow-billed Blue Magpie)
U. f. cucullata
W Himalayas
U. f. flavirostris
E Himalayas, N Burma
U. f. schaferi
W Burma
U. f. robini
N Vietnam
Urocissa erythrorhyncha (Red-billed Blue Magpie)
U. e. brevivexilla
N China
U. e. erythrorhyncha
C & S China, N Vietnam
U. e. alticola
SW China, NE Burma
U. e. occipitalis
Himalayas

U. e. magnirostris
Assam to Indochina
Urocissa whiteheadi (White-winged Magpie)
U. w. whiteheadi
Hainan I
U. w. xanthomelana
C Laos, N Vietnam

Cissa chinensis (Green Magpie)
C. c. chinensis
Himalayas, N Indochina
C. c. robinsoni
Malaysia
C. c. klossi
C Indochina
C. c. margaritae
S Vietnam
C. c. minor
Sumatra, NW Borneo
Cissa hypoleuca (Eastern Green Magpie)
C. h. jini
SE China
C. h. concolor
N Vietnam
C. h. chauleti
C Vietnam
C. h. hypoleuca
E Thailand, S Indochina
C. h. katsumatae
Hainan I
Cissa thalassina (Short-tailed Green Magpie)
C. t. thalassina
Java
C. t. jeffreyi
NW Borneo

Cyanopica cyana (Azure-winged Magpie)
C. c. cooki
W Spain, Portugal
C. c. cyana
C & EC Asia
C. c. pallescens
NE Asia
C. c. koreensis
Korea
C. c. stegmanni
Manchuria
C. c. swinhoei
E China
C. c. interposita
N China
C. c. kansuensis
W China
C. c. japonica
Japan

DENDROCITTA

Dendrocitta vagabunda (Indian Tree Pie)
D. v. pallida
W Himalayas, NW India
D. v. vagabunda
E Himalayas, NE India
D. v. parvula
SW India
D. v. vernayi
SE India
D. v. sclateri
W Burma
D. v. kinneari
S Burma, NW Thailand
D. v. saturatior
S Thailand
D. v. sakeratensis
E Thailand, Indochina
Dendrocitta occipitalis (Malaysian Tree Pie)
D. o. occipitalis
Sumatra
D. o. cinerascens
Borneo
Dendrocitta formosae (Himalayan Tree Pie)
D. f. occidentalis
W Himalayas
D. f. himalayensis
E Himalayas, Burma, N Laos
D. f. sarkari
E India
D. f. assimilis
S Burma, Thailand, Andaman Is
D. f. sinica
E & S China, N Vietnam
D. f. sapiens
W China
D. f. formosae
Taiwan
D. f. insulae
Hainan I
Dendrocitta leucogastra (Southern Tree Pie)
S India
Dendrocitta frontalis (Black-browed Tree Pie)
Himalayas to N Vietnam
Dendrocitta bayleyi (Andaman Tree Pie)
Andaman Is

CRYPSIRINA
Crypsirina temia (Black Racquet-tailed Tree Pie)
S Burma to Indochina & Java
Crypsirina cucullata (Hooded Racquet-tailed Tree Pie)
N & C Burma

TEMNURUS
Temnurus temnurus (Notch-tailed Tree Pie)
N Vietnam, Hainan I

PICA
Pica pica (Magpie)
P. p. fennorum
N Scandinavia, W Russia
P. p. pica
British Isles, C & E Europe
P. p. galliae
W Europe
P. p. melanotos
Spain, Portugal
P. p. mauretanica
NW Africa
P. p. asirensis
SW Arabia
P. p. bactriana
C Russia, to N India
P. p. hemileucoptera
W & S Siberia, WC Asia
P. p. leucoptera
EC Asia
P. p. camtschatika
NE Asia
P. p. sericea
S China, Burma, Indochina
P. p. bottanensis
N Himalayas, Tibet
P. p. hudsonia
W Canada, W USA
Pica nuttalli (Yellow-billed Magpie)
W California

ZAVATTARIORNIS
Zavattariornis stresemanni (Stresemann's Bush Crow)
S Ethiopia

PODOCES
Podoces hendersoni (Henderson's Ground Jay)
C Asia, W China
Podoces biddulphi (Biddulph's Ground Jay)
W Sinkiang
Podoces panderi (Pander's Ground Jay)
S Russia
Podoces pleskei (Pleske's Ground Jay)
E Iran

PSEUDOPODOCES
Pseudopodoces humilis (Hume's Ground Chough)
Tsinghai, W China

NUCIFRAGA
Nucifraga columbiana (Clark's Nutcracker)
SW Canada, W USA
Nucifraga caryocatactes (Nutcracker)
N. c. caryocatactes
N & E Europe » S Russia
N. c. macrorhynchos
N & NE Asia » N Iran & N China
N. c. rothschildi
Russia, Turkistan
N. c. japonica
N Japan
N. c. owstoni
Taiwan
N. c. interdicta
N China
N. c. multipunctata
Pakistan, NW India
N. c. hemispila
W Himalayas
N. c. macella
E Himalayas, Burma, W China
N. c. yunnanensis
SW China

PYRRHOCORAX
Pyrrhocorax pyrrhocorax (Chough)
P. p. pyrrhocorax
England, Ireland
P. p. erythrorhamphus
W Europe
P. p. barbarus
Canary Is, NW Africa
P. p. baileyi
N Ethiopia
P. p. docilis
E Europe to Arabia, Iran
P. p. centralis
C Asia, Pakistan, NW India
P. p. himalayanus
N India, Himalayas, W China
P. p. brachypus
N China, NE Asia
Pyrrhocorax graculus (Alpine Chough)
P. g. graculus
Europe, N Africa, Caucasus
P. g. digitatus
Iran, C Asia, Himalayas

PTILOSTOMUS
Ptilostomus afer (Piapiac)
Senegal to Ethiopia, Uganda

CORVUS
Corvus monedula (Jackdaw)
C. m. monedula
Scandinavia
C. m. spermologus
W & C Europe

C. m. soemmerringii
E Europe, N & C Asia » Iran, W India
C. m. cirtensis
N Africa
Corvus dauuricus (Daurian Jackdaw)
C & NE Asia » SE China & Japan
Corvus splendens (House Crow)
C. s. zugmayeri
Baluchistan, NW India
C. s. splendens
India
C. s. protegatus
Sri Lanka, Malaysia
C. s. maledivicus
Laccadive Is, Maldive Is
C. s. insolens
S Burma SW Thailand, W Yunnan
Corvus moneduloides (New Caledonian Crow)
New Caledonia, Loyalty Is
Corvus enca (Slender-billed Crow)
C. e. compilator
Malaysia, Sumatra, Borneo
C. e. enca
Java, Bali I, Montawi Is
C. e. celebensis
Celebes
C. e. unicolor
Banggai I
C. e. mangoli
Sula Archipelago
C. e. violaceus
Ceram I
C. e. pusillus
Balabac I, Palawan I, Mindoro I
C. e. sierramadrensis
NE Luzon I
C. e. samarensis
Samar I, Mindanao I
Corvus typicus (Celebean Crow)
C & S Celebes
Corvus florensis (Flores Crow)
Flores I
Corvus kubaryi (Marianas Crow)
Guam I, Rota I
Corvus validus (Moluccan Crow)
N Moluccas
Corvus woodfordi (White-billed Crow)
C. w. meeki
Bougainville I
C. w. woodfordi
Guadalcanal I
C. w. vegetus
Choiseul I, Ysabel I

Corvus fuscicapillus (Brown-headed Crow)
  C. f. fuscicapillus
    Aru Is, New Guinea
  C. f. megarhynchus
    Waigeu I, Geimen I
Corvus tristis (Grey Crow)
    New Guinea, D'Entrecasteaux
    Archipelago
Corvus capensis (Black Crow)
    Eastern & Southern Africa
Corvus frugilegus (Rook)
  C. f. frugilegus
    Europe, W & C Asia » N Africa &
    NW India
  C. f. pastinator
    E Asia » Japan & SE China
Corvus brachyrhynchos (Common American Crow)
  C. b. hesperis
    W Canada, W USA
  C. b. brachyrhynchos
    C & E Canada, C & NE USA » E USA
  C. b. paulus
    E & SE USA
  C. b. pascuus
    S Florida
Corvus caurinus (Northwestern Crow)
    W Canada, NW USA
Corvus imparatus (Tamaulipas Crow)
    N Mexico
Corvus sinaloae (Sinaloa Crow)
    NW Mexico
Corvus ossifragus (Fish Crow)
    E USA
Corvus palmarum (Palm Crow)
  C. p. minutus
    Cuba
  C. p. palmarum
    Hispaniola
Corvus jamaicensis (Jamaican Crow)
    Jamaica
Corvus nasicus (Cuban Crow)
    Cuba, Grand Caicos I
Corvus leucognaphalus (White-necked Crow)
    Hispaniola, Puerto Rico
Corvus corone (Carrion Crow)
  C. c. corone
    W Europe » N Africa
  C. c. cornix
    N & E Europe
  C. c. sardonius
    S & SE Europe, Asia Minor
  C. c. sharpii
    Siberia, Iraq, Iran to Turkistan,
    NW India

C. c. capellanus
    S Iraq, SW Iran
C. c. orientalis
    E Asia, Japan » NW India, S China
Corvus macrorhynchos (Jungle Crow)
  C. m. japonensis
    Sakhalin I, Japan
  C. m. connectens
    C & S Riukiu Is
  C. m. osai
    S Riukiu Is
  C. m. mandschuricus
    NE Asia
  C. m. colonorum
    China, N Indochina
  C. m. hainanus
    Hainan I
  C. m. mengtszensis
    SW China
  C. m. tibetosinensis
    E Himalayas, N Burma, W China
  C. m. intermedius
    W Himalayas, NW India
  C. m. culminatus
    S India, Sri Lanka
  C. m. levaillantii
    NE India, Burma, Thailand
  C. m. macrorhynchos
    Malaysia, S Indochina, Sunda Is
  C. m. philippinus
    Philippine Is
  C. m. timoriensis
    Alor I, Timor I
Corvus orru (Australian Crow)
  C. o. orru
    Moluccas, New Guinea
  C. o. insularis
    New Britain, New Ireland, New Hanover
  C. o. latirostris
    Tenimber Is
  C. o. ceciliae
    Australia
Corvus bennetti (Little Crow)
    W & C Australia
Corvus coronoides (Australian Raven)
  C. c. coronoides
    E, S & SW Australia
  C. c. boreus
    New South Wales, Victoria
Corvus tasmanicus (Forest Raven)
  C. t. novaanglica
    NE New South Wales
  C. t. tasmanicus
    Tasmania, Wilson's Promontory
Corvus mellori (Little Raven)
    SE Australia
Corvus torquatus (Collared Crow)
    E & C China, N Vietnam

Corvus albus **(Pied Crow)**
W, C, E & Southern Africa, Madagascar
Corvus tropicus **(Hawaiian Crow)**
Hawaii Is
Corvus cryptoleucus
(White-necked Raven)
SW USA, N Mexico
Corvus ruficollis **(Brown-necked Raven)**
C. r. ruficollis
N Africa to Pakistan
C. r. edithae
Somalia
Corvus corax **(Raven)**
C. c. principalis
Alaska, Canada, N USA
C. c. sinuatus
WC USA, Central America
C. c. varius
Iceland, Faroe Is
C. c. corax
Europe, W Asia
C. c. subcorax
SE Europe, Asia Minor to Pakistan
C. c. tingitanus
N Africa
C. c. tibetanus
C Asia, Himalayas
C. c. kamtschaticus
NE Asia, N Japan
Corvus rhipidurus **(Fan-tailed Raven)**
NE Africa to Syria, Arabia
Corvus albicollis **(African White-necked Raven)**
E & S Africa
Corvus crassirostris **(Thick-billed Raven)**
Ethiopia, E Sudan

Index

653

667

673

Index of English Names

715

Chestnut-mantled 588, Crested 588, Dusky
Green 588, Green 588, Montezuma 588, Olive
588, Para 588, Russet-backed 588
Osprey 75
Ostrich 49
Ou 584
Ovenbird 577. See also under Hornero
Owl See also under Scops Owl, Screech Owl,
Eagle Owl, Pygmy Owl, Hawk Owl, Wood Owl.
Abyssinian Long-eared 192, African Marsh 192,
Band-bellied 186, Bare-legged 189, Barking
188, Barn 180, Barred 191, Bay 181, Black and
White 190, Black-banded 190, Blakiston's Fish
186, Boobook 188, Brown 189, Brown Fish
186, Buff-fronted 192, Burrowing 189, Celebes
Barn 181, Crested 184, Cuckoo 187, Eastern
Grass 181, Elf 188, Fearful 192, Flammulated
182, Forest Little 189, Grass 181, Great Grey
191, Great Horned 184, Hume's Tawny 190,
Jamaican 192, Little 189, Long-eared 191,
Madagascar Grass 180, Madagascar
Long-eared 192, Malay Fish 185, Masked 181,
Minahassa Barn 181, Mottled 190, New Britain
Barn 181, Pel's Fishing 186, Philippine Horned
186, Powerful 188, Rufous 188, Rufous-banded
190, Rufous Fishing 186, Rufous-legged 191,
Rusty-barred 191, Saw-whet 192, Short-eared
192, Snowy 186, Sooty 181, Spectacled 186,
Spotted 191, Striped 191, Stygian 191, Sula Is
Barn 181, Tanzanian Bay 181, Tawny 191,
Tawny-browed 186, Tawny Fish 186,
Tengmalm's 192, Unspotted Saw-whet 192,
Ural 191, Vermiculated Fishing 186, Whiskered
183, White-browed 188, White-faced 189
Owlet Barred 187, Forest Spotted 189, Jungle
187, Long-whiskered 188, Pearl-spotted 187,
Red-chested 187, Sjostedt's Barred 187
Owlet-Nightjar 193, Barred 194, Eastern
Mountain 194, Halmahera 193, Large 193,
Mountain 194, New Caledonian 194, Wallace's
194
Oxpecker Red-billed 624, Yellow-billed 624
Oxylabes Grey-crowned 435, White-throated
435, Yellow-browed 435
Oystercatcher 121, African Black 121,
American Black 121, Blackish 121, Magellanic
121, New Zealand Sooty 121, Sooty 121

Pachycare Golden-faced 491
Painted Snipe 121, South American 121
Palila 584
Palmcreeper Point-tailed 285
Pampa Finch Buff-throated 546, Great 546
Paradigalla Long-tailed 632, Short-tailed 632
Paradise Flycatcher African 482, Asiatic 482,
Black 483, Black-bellied 483, Blue 483, Luzon
483, Madagascar 482, Mascarene 482, Rufous
483, Rufous-vented 482, Sao Thomé 482,
Seychelles 482
Paradise Kingfisher Aru 231, Biak 232,
Brown-backed 232, Common 231, Kofiau 232,
Numfor 232, Pink-breasted 232
Parakeet Alexandrine 164, Andean 167,
Antipodes Green 161, Barred 167,
Blossom-headed 164, Blyth's 164,
Brown-backed 169, Canary-winged 168,
Cobalt-winged 168, Derbyan 164,
Emerald-collared 164, Golden-tailed 169,
Golden-winged 168, Grey-cheeked 168, Horned

162, Long-tailed 164, Malabar 164, Mauritius
164, Monk 167, Mountain 167, Moustached
164, Orange-chinned 168, Orange-fronted 162,
Plain 168, Plum-headed 164, Red-fronted 161,
Red-winged 168, Rose-ringed 164,
Rufous-fronted 167, Sapphire-rumped 168,
Scarlet-shouldered 168, Seven-coloured 168,
Sierra 167, Slaty-headed 164, Spot-winged 169,
Tepui 167, Tui 168, Yellow-fronted 161
Pardalote Black-headed 510, Forty-spotted
510, Red-browed 510, Red-tipped 510, Spotted
510, Striated 510, Yellow-tailed 510,
Yellow-tipped 510
Pardusco 582
Parotia Arfak 632, Eastern 633, Lawes 633,
Queen Carola's 632, Wahnes' 633
Parrot See also under Fig Parrot, Hanging
Parrot, Pygmy Parrot. Amboina King 160,
Australian King 160, Barraband's 169, Black
162, Black-lored 160, Black-winged 169,
Blue-collared 159, Blue-crowned Raquet-tailed
159, Blue-headed 169, Blue-naped 159,
Blue-rumped 158, Blue-winged 162, Bourke's
162, Brehm's 158, Bronze-winged 169,
Brown-headed 162, Brown-hooded 169, Buru
Raquet-tailed 159, Caica 169, Cape 162, Dusky
170, Eclectus 160, Elegant 162,
Golden-mantled Raquet-tailed 159,
Golden-shouldered 161, Great-billed 159, Green
Raquet-tailed 159, Green-winged King 160,
Grey 162, Ground 162, Hawk-headed 171,
Intermediate 164, Jardine's 162, Maderasz'
158, Mallee Ringneck 161, Masked Shining
160, Meyer's 162, Modest 158, Mountain
Raquet-tailed 159, Mulga 161, Müller's 159,
Niam-Niam 162, Night 162, Orange-bellied 162,
Painted 158, Paradise 161, Pesquet's 160,
Pileated 169, Plum-crowned 169, Port Lincoln
161, Princess 160, Purple-bellied 171,
Red-billed 169, Red-bellied 162, Red-capped
160, Red-cheeked 158, Red-rumped 161, Red
Shining 160, Red-spotted Raquet-tailed 159,
Red-winged 160, Regent 160, Rock 162,
Rose-faced 169, Rufous-tailed 160, Ruppell's
163, Rusty-faced 169, Saffron-headed 169,
Scaly-headed 169, Scarlet-chested 162, Senegal
162, Short-tailed 169, Singing 159, Superb 160,
Swift 162, Thick-billed 166, Timor Red-winged
160, Turquoise 162, Vasa 162, Vulturine 169,
White-capped 169, White-headed 169,
Yellow-faced 163
Parrotbill Ashy-throated 436, Blyth's 436,
Brown 435, David's 436, Fulvous-fronted 436,
Gould's 435, Great 435, Greater Red-headed
436, Grey-crowned 436, Grey-headed 436,
Heude's 436, Lesser Red-headed 436, Maui
584, Spectacled 435, Spot-breasted 435,
Three-toed 435, Vinous-throated 435, Yunnan
435, Zappey's 436
Parrot Finch Bamboo 607, Blue-faced 607, Fiji
608, Green-faced 607, Mount Katanglad 607,
Papuan 608, Pink-billed 608, Pin-tailed 607,
Red-headed 608, Red-throated 608,
Three-coloured 607
Parrotlet Blue-winged 168, Green-rumped 168,
Mexican 168, Pacific 168, Sclater's 168,
Spectacled 168, Yellow-faced 168
Parson Bird 535
Partridge See also under Hill Partridge, Rock

Notes

Notes

Notes

Notes

Notes

Notes

Notes

Notes

Notes

Notes

Notes

Notes